Travaux
d'Humanisme et Renaissance

N° DLVI

ELSIE ANNE MCKEE

THE PASTORAL MINISTRY
AND WORSHIP
IN
CALVIN'S GENEVA

LIBRAIRIE DROZ S.A.
11, rue Massot
GENÈVE
2016

Avec le soutien de
la République et Canton de Genève

REPUBLIQUE
ET CANTON
DE GENEVE

POST TENEBRAS LUX

www.droz.org

Distribué en France par de Boccard :
www.deboccard.com

ISBN : 978-2-600-01962-0
ISSN : 0082-6081

In honor of all pastoral leaders of the Church of Christ in Congo

and in memory of

George Ntalaja McKee and Elsie Tshimunyi McKee
Kasai, 1911-1941

Charles Ngulumingi McKee (1923-41) and Anne Ngolela McKee
Kasai, 1949-1975

mu njila muimpe

ACKNOWLEDGEMENTS
AND THANKS

It is a sincere pleasure to express my gratitude to the institutions and people who have so generously helped during the writing of this book.

Fundamental to all research is access to the sources, archival and printed. Special thanks to the Archives d'Etat de Genève for the *Registres du Conseil*, both the meticulous new critical editions and more recently for the online manuscripts, and for various other materials such as the Procès Criminels. Very special thanks to Prof. Robert Kingdon and his colleagues, and the H. Henry Meeter Center for Calvin Studies for the *Registres du Consistoire*, both the critical editions and the transcriptions, which have so enriched our knowledge of daily life in Geneva. Many thanks to the Archives d'Etat de Genève and the Church of Jesus Christ of the Latter Day Saints for the films of the baptismal and marriage records of St. Pierre, St. Gervais, and La Magdeleine, which brought these amazing files to me in North America. Particular thanks to the Bibliothèque de Genève for access to its precious manuscripts of Calvin's sermons, and to this library, the Zentral Bibliothek in Zürich, and the new e-rara.ch collection for hundreds of hours of happy digging in rare books. The Musée and Institut de la Réformation resources have been a favorite hunting ground since graduate student days; being able to go directly to the shelves full of sixteenth-century Bibles, Psalters, Calvin texts, and many other rare books is a never-ending delight as well as enormous help, especially for comparing editions. My life-time debt to them can only be recognized and passed forward. In each of these repositories of early modern treasures the archivists and guardians have been most gracious.

The fine libraries of Princeton Theological Seminary and Princeton University have provided many resources old and new, and the librarians have been very generous with their time and help over the course of years of locating this text or buying or borrowing that one. May all those who have shared in enabling me to find the wide range of fascinating materials which have contributed to this book know that I never take for granted their assistance and kindness, and that I am deeply grateful for being able to revel in such marvelous "sixteenth-century dust."

There are other individuals whom I want also to thank, for encouragement and for practical assistance in bringing this research to publication. Members of various scholarly groups who heard some of the earlier versions of these ideas have been happily encouraging. Teaching Calvin and preparing a volume of his *Writings on Pastoral Piety* (2001) for the Classics of Western Spirituality series launched the project. A final presentation at the International Congress for Calvin Research in August 2014 formed a kind of "book-end" to some fifteen or sixteen years of investigation into questions about Calvin the pastor of Geneva. Conferences around the world in the great "Calvin Year 2009" added a wonderful range of attentive listeners. Here I would like to express my particular thanks for permission from colleagues at International Christian University (Tokyo), Vandenhoeck & Ruprecht (Göttingen), and ATF Theology (Adelaide) to (re)print material previously used in the following articles: "Places, Times, and People in Worship in Calvin's Geneva," pp. 101-20 in *Humanities. Christianity and Culture* 41 (journal of the Institute for the Study of Christianity and Culture, ICU Tokyo, March 2010). "Calvin's Day of Prayer: Origins, Nature, and Significance," pp. 315-32 in *Calvin und Calvinismus – Europäische Perspektiven*, ed. Irene Dingel & Herman Selderhuis (Göttingen: Vandenhoeck & Ruprecht, 2011). "A Week in the Life of John Calvin," pp. 61-77 in *Calvin: the Man and the Legacy*, ed. Murray Rae, Peter Matheson, & Brett Knowles (Adelaide: ATF Theology, 2014). To all, my warm thanks.

Throughout the long journey of research and writing my husband, Dr. John McGlaughlin, has been the most interested and supportive partner a scholar could have! He has been not only patient but also genuinely curious, not only understanding about this obsession with digging in dusty old tomes – and the footnotes and more footnotes which seem to result – but also eager to know more about the fruits of the request. Most special thanks, John!

No project can be done without technical assistance. I want to thank several of my students and associates for this. Mr. Charles Johnson proofread some of the appendices; Mr. Lawrence Anglin made the graphs and compiled the indices, and I am very grateful. The IT staff at Princeton Seminary have kept the computers and printers functioning (always a necessity for a technologically-challenged person) and answered questions with cheerful grace. Mr. Gordon Govens, JD, friend, student, and budding Calvin scholar, has generously proofread the manuscript. Thank you so much!

It is a particular pleasure to thank Dr. Max Engammare for welcoming this third volume on Calvin's ecclesiology into Droz's highly respected series Travaux d'Humanisme et Renaissance: finally the pastors join the deacons and elders![1] Dr. Engammare has also been very helpful in the research over the years, both in

---

[1] *John Calvin on the Diaconate and Liturgical Almsgiving* (Genève: Droz, 1984), and *Elders and the Plural Ministry: The Role of Exegetical History in Illuminating John Calvin's Theology* (Genève, Droz, 1988).

his own studies of Reformed preaching and especially with regard to Calvin's sermons. His editions of Genesis and Isaiah have been a wonderful resource, and he has also generously provided transcriptions of prayer incipits from the manuscript sermons on Ezekiel.

This book is dedicated to my parents and grandparents and all the other pastoral ministers of the Church of Christ in Congo, past, present, and future.

Elsie Anne McKee
Tshimunyi wa Ngulumingi ne Ngolela

INTRODUCTION

Religious life is both spiritual and embodied, and this is particularly true of public corporate worship. Protestant reformers were pastors, active leaders in the day to day business of preaching, teaching, and counseling, celebrating the Lord's Supper, baptisms, and weddings, visiting the sick and dying and comforting the bereaved. In the midst of all this, they also wrote commentaries and treatises, argued doctrine, and advised princes and magistrates. Although the theology and politics have received much attention from contemporaries and later scholars, the pastoral work has often been neglected. More recently, social historians have done a great deal to fill out the picture of popular religion and how ordinary folk made reforming movements their own. There remain, however, lacunae or fissures in the landscape. The whole story can never be recovered but it is possible to build some bridges between the "high theology" and the "popular piety."

The present study intends to be such a bridge for the city of Geneva during the ministry of John Calvin (1536-1564). The focus is the meeting point between teaching and practice, as those were made visible and tangible in the corporate worship life of this small city-state which became a model for many Reformed churches. There is naturally a fair amount of theology, although not enough to satisfy a theologian. There is also a fair amount of attention to popular (community-wide) religious practices, although not enough to please a social historian. The object, however, is to bring to the fore what pastors and people were saying and doing together as they re-formed the religious life of their little world. To do so calls for digging into neglected corners and then drawing the scattered pieces together so that they illuminate each other and cast new light on the whole.

Before delving into the practice of worship and ministry in Geneva, however, it is helpful to sketch the larger theological context in which the concrete activities of preaching, sacraments, and pastoral care were situated. In a word, what was the church, according to Calvin? The answer includes two parts: a summary of the issues in the sixteenth-century debates, and an overview of Calvin's doctrine of the church. This will conclude with an outline of the book: the practical exploration of pastoral ministry and worship.

I: The Nature of the Church

For all early modern European participants in the discussion about the church, the fundamental point of departure was Cyprian's famous dictum: "Outside the church there is no salvation." The problem was that there was no consensus on how to define, or – more to the point – how to find the true church.[1] The two questions were intertwined. "What makes the church be the church? Who is in and who is not?" Another way to approach the issue can be phrased as "How is the true church visible to human beings?" and "How is the membership of the visible church related to the true church as God sees it?"

An over-simplified paradigm may provide a useful grid to illustrate the kinds of answers which were available to these questions in the sixteenth century. This is only a heuristic device; however, the three positions described here under the names: "Rome," "Anabaptist," and "Protestant," can clarify the various approaches. Each position is identified by its claim for truth or the evidence offered for authenticity: "What makes the true church visible?" and by the way it defines the visible boundaries of the church: "Who is in and who is out?" The response to the second question is focused only on the members living on earth, as all agreed that the true church included also those who had already died in the faith. Rome believed that people on earth could influence the fate of the dead in purgatory and that conviction played an important role in the devotions of the living. Protestants and Anabaptists rejected this view and the change affected their re-defined piety. For purposes of church membership, however, this distinction is secondary.

For Rome, the structure of the visible church was defined by the sacraments administered through clergy properly ordained in apostolic succession, and this formed the bounds of the true church on earth. Not all individuals within those boundaries were elect, but in principle there were no elect outside the visible Roman Church.[2] Apostolic succession served as the assurance of truth and the church's sacraments were the guaranteed means of grace but also the limits of salvation. Individual uncertainty remained for those in the Roman communion since only a special revelation could assure any specific person of his or her

---

[1]   For a good overview of the ecclesiological situation, particularly the theological definitions of Church and how to identify it, see Schreiner, "Church," pp. 323-27. Calvin quotes the phrase although at first without naming Cyprian; see *Institutes*, OS I, p. 92.

[2]   To this clear theological position there had been added over time the conviction that baptism conferred salvation if the one baptized died immediately (i.e., with no further sins which would require penance). However, baptized people who left the visible church and thus denied their baptism were of course outside its bounds.

election. "Anabaptists" are here understood as those Radicals who formed communities; some were based on the Old Testament but the more common and enduring pattern was communities shaped by the New Testament. Anabaptist ways of defining the church tended to have in common a literal approach to scripture. Where the events and practices of Acts are replicated, with believer's baptism, fraternal admonition, shunning the world, persecution, and other marks, there is the true church. Those who choose and fulfill these commitments are the elect and those who do not are the reprobate. The true church for Anabaptists was therefore the earthly visible part of the total number of the elect, a one-to-one correspondence of the visible with the invisible. For Anabaptists, apostolic restoration was the assurance of truth; the winnowing took place before one could be admitted to the fellowship, so all who entered were elect – as long as they were members. Here, as with Rome, excommunication was equivalent to reprobation; outside the true visible church there is no salvation. In effect, both Roman and Anabaptist models could and did provide clear answers to where to find the true church and how to determine its outer bounds, even though they did not agree about whether all within those bounds were elect.

The position of Protestants was somewhat more complex or even fuzzy. Their first reaction in breaking with tradition was to deny the identification of Rome with the true church because for Protestants the means of continuity with the Biblical church was apostolic teaching. Structure (apostolic succession) is of no importance if the essence has been lost. Protestants defined the true church as all the elect, but following medieval theologians like Wycliffe and Hus, they maintained that the boundaries of this church are not humanly visible. That is, unlike Anabaptists, Protestants insisted that human beings cannot with certainty distinguish the elect from the reprobate. The church can be found where there is apostolic teaching and thus has a concrete presence on earth. However, its visible boundaries are not the limits of election, and excommunication from the visible church is not equivalent to reprobation; there are wheat and tares in the visible church and wheat and tares outside. With this conclusion, Protestants practically redefined how the "invisible church" (the sum of the elect, known only to God) is related to the "visible church" ("church" as it can be identified by those living on earth and in which the living can participate). Unlike Rome, for Protestants there are multiple parts of the visible church. The apostolic teaching identifies where the church becomes visible, and even minor confessional differences of scattered parts of the Christian community do not in fact divide the church (at least in theory).

The Protestant definition raises two questions. One of these was explicitly addressed by the first generation: How should apostolic teaching be defined for the purpose of identifying the church on earth? One common answer was to focus on the "marks of the church," or basic Biblical doctrine and the early church creedal statements, along with the two sacraments of baptism and Eucharist.[3] The other question of physical dimensions was answered implicitly by identifying existing parishes of worshipers as the embodied extent of the church.[4] This was a functional solution within Christendom, in the territorially established Protestant churches. The pastors preached and administered sacraments to all the inhabitants, who were members of the church because they were baptized as infants and participated in the parish's life. The boundaries and enforcement of discipline, such as making people learn the creed or attend church (if they needed incentives) and regulating their behavior according to church law, could or should be left to the Christian princes or magistrates. The latter naturally applied this parish-based definition of church membership to the whole territory they ruled. In Zwingli's theology, such governance was the duty of the Christian ruler, the successor to the Davidic kings (like Jehosephat in 2 Chron. 19:6).[5] Luther adopted the practice but felt no need to provide particular Biblical grounds for giving princes temporary "episcopal" powers. The conclusion that the existing parish structures were sufficient to define the limits of the visible church fitted perfectly into the political perspectives of their societies. Christian rulers were only too happy to find themselves assigned the role of discipline, moral oversight, and control of excommunication.

The appearance of the word discipline in this practical solution to the doctrine of the church raises a question which had been present from the beginning but only became critical over the course of time. The moral laxity of the late medieval church was a significant problem commonly recognized by all reformers, those within Rome as well as those who broke with Rome. Anabaptists essentially rejected Christendom and made the exercise of discipline a necessary mark of the church. For Protestants, a solution to this question was slightly delayed, and development of the content of apostolic teaching came in two stages. The earliest

---

3   Cf. Schreiner, "Church," pp. 324-25.

4   Schreiner's article does not address this point (which is discussed in a different article). Most Protestants assumed that the church continued where the newly defined teaching was preached in the traditional parishes, but specific attention to this physical boundary was not necessary as long as the tradition of Christendom was maintained.

5   Ulrich Zwingli, commentary on Rom. 12:8 gives 2 Chron. 19:6 as a cross reference to signify that "those who preside" are civil rulers; cf. *Huldrici Zwinglii Opera, Completa editio prima* [Zurich: F. Schulthess, 1828-42], vol. 6, part 2 *In Epistolam ad Romanos Annotationes*, p. 121. The Bucer-Calvin Reformed tradition clearly regards Rom. 12:8 as referring to elders of the church; cf. McKee, *Elders and the Plural Ministry*, pp. 50-55.

focus was Biblical teaching, and the "marks of the church" were usually preaching and the sacraments of baptism and the Lord's Supper. These were the tasks of pastors. The practical, moral reform of the church was very important but it was not typically identified as a mark of the true church; it was assigned to the Christian ruler. However, before long the problem of unreformed behavior became a critical issue to some theologians; Martin Bucer and others observed that princes did not exercise what they regarded as adequate or appropriate discipline. The church must correspond to the holiness of Christ. Although they did not go as far as Anabaptists in demanding perfect moral purity, Protestants like Bucer, Philip Melanchthon, and others, believed that reformed behavior was a necessary manifestation of apostolic teaching. Logically, they concluded that discipline should be counted as one of the marks of the church.[6] They did not, however, resolve the theoretical consequences of making discipline a mark.

II: Calvin's Teaching on the Church

The doctrine of the church is arguably Calvin's most creative contribution to historical theology. That gift is particularly evident in the way he identified and addressed the theoretical challenges in the Protestant teaching on the visible church. As early as 1536, Calvin provided the basic categories of his response to the question of how to relate the church's visibility on earth to the true church known (only) to God. Over the years, his exposition developed more clarity and fullness, as the theologian had to implement a practical church order. The terms in which the doctrine of the church was posed in the sixteenth century focused on the character of the apostolic teaching and the role of discipline, so the implications of Calvin's subtle yet ingenious solution to the visible-invisible conundrum have been obscured.

The first part of this explanation will be an examination of the 1536 *Institutes of the Christian Religion* and some later clarifications. That is followed by a schematic picture of how this teaching is worked out in three "levels" of Calvin's doctrine of the church. The purpose is to provide an overview of his ways of relating the various levels in order to illuminate the context for the practice of worship and the pastoral ministry that serve to make the church visible.

---

6   Cf. Amy Nelson Burnett, *The Yoke of Christ: Martin Bucer and Christian Discipline* (Kirksville, MO: Sixteen Century Journal, 1994). For Melanchthon, this developed over the years in different language, expressed particularly as "obedience to the ministry" (e.g., CR 12:433). Discipline as a mark of the church is also found in various Reformed confessions: e.g., Belgic, Scots.

Calvin's Teaching

The 1536 *Institutes of the Christian Religion*

The nugget containing Calvin's creative teaching on the church is present already in the first edition of the *Institutes*. The three key points are the true church (invisible), the church as it is known on earth (visible), and the relationship between divine law and church law or the powers of the church. The first two of these are explained in the context of the larger discussion of the church in his exposition of the Apostles' Creed (chapter two), the third under the powers of the church (chapter six).

The discussion of the church in the Creed begins with the question of membership and distinguishes two definitions of election. First is the church as "the whole number of the elect" throughout time and space; "whether angels or men... dead or still living... in whatever lands... [They] are one church, and one people of God, of which Christ, our Lord, is Leader and Ruler."[7] Then Calvin explains that scripture also describes election in an accommodated way to mean those who are manifested as elect by visible calling and justification. This includes some who have experienced God's working but are not actually elect and it excludes the elect who have not yet received their call to faith. The purpose of this use of "election" is not to identify God's choice but to serve the earthly need for a way to describe those who are moved by the Spirit. This brief overview introduces the church as known to God and the membership of the church as known on earth.

Calvin organizes his presentation with a pastoral purpose in mind. He is sensitive to the problem of a community reeling from having been told that the church in which they had grown up was no church, so he affirms clearly that because of God's mercy the church has never ceased to exist on earth. He then immediately assures the faithful of their own personal inclusion in that church, secure in God's promise to recognize as children "those who have received his only-begotten Son." He explains:

> For since Christ our Lord is he in whom the Father from eternity has chosen those he has willed to be his own and to be brought into the flock of his church, we have a clear enough testimony that we are among God's elect and of the church, if we partake in Christ... Otherwise if each one of us did not believe himself to be a member of it, we would vainly and fruitlessly believe there to be a church catholic.[8]

---

[7]   *Institution 1536*, p. 78, slightly modified. OS I, p. 86.

[8]   *Institution 1536*, p. 81. OS I, p. 88.

Here the personal faith relationship is the believer's assurance of her or his own election and membership in the church. Calvin makes explicit the *pro me* aspect: for practical purposes it would be fruitless for the individual to believe that the church existed if she or he did not believe himself or herself to be a part of it. Obviously the reformer is concerned with the application, not simply the truth of the doctrine.

Intertwined with this pastoral reassurance, Calvin states clearly that human beings cannot know the exact boundaries of the church. Only God can distinguish elect from reprobate; believers know their own faith relationship with Christ but not the election of other people. In these circumstances, and since he is speaking to church members, Calvin continues to address the very concrete questions they have about boundaries. Here the precocious young theologian proceeds to express his unique contribution to the issue of the visibility of the church: his distinction between the marks of the church and the marks of Christians ("the faithful"). First he expounds at considerable length what we can know about the membership of other people in the visible church.

> The elect cannot be recognized by us with assurance of faith, yet Scripture describes certain sure marks to us,... by which we may distinguish the elect and the children of God from the reprobate and the alien, insofar as He wills us so to recognize them. By a certain charitable judgment all those should be accounted as elect and members of the church who by confession of faith and example of life and participation in the sacraments, confess with us the same God and Christ.[9]

The operative terms here are the contrast between certainty of faith [*fidei certitudine*] which one has only for oneself and the charitable judgment [*caritatis iudicio*] which applies to other people. The second point combines the criteria with their limits. The "certain sure marks" [*certas quasdam notas*] for the judgment of love are given by God but they are accommodated, not absolute; they provide the extent of human knowledge of God's will [*quatenus a nobis vult agnosci*] that is necessary for the church visible to do its job. The church "accounts as elect" those who show the specific visible marks. Individuals have assurance of their own faith-election but the visible community needs only to assess with charity these three tangible criteria that God has seen to be useful. It is notable that the formulation indicates that "confessing the same God and Christ" is the act or fruit of all three marks: knowledge and profession of faith, appropriate behavior, and sharing in the

---

9   OS I, p. 88. See *Institution 1536*, p. 82, which is a little confusing, as punctuation suggests that the phrase "confess the same God and Christ" applies only to the first point of confession of faith.

distinctive corporate worship liturgies. Moral perfection is not required, as long as people are not content with their sinfulness and one can hope for better for them. [10]

Then Calvin provides the opposite face of the charitable judgment, that is, the general signs of those who do not belong.

> But those who either do not agree with us on the same faith, or, even though they have confession on their lips, still deny by their actions the God whom they confess with their mouth (as those whom we see wicked and lost throughout life, drunk with the love of sinning, and quite unconcerned over their own wickedness) – all of this sort show themselves by their traits that they are not members at present of the church. [11]

Here it is evident that the profession of faith listed in the criteria of charitable judgment is intended as a verbal, conscious act of affirming knowledge, which can be contradicted by sinful behavior and particularly by obstinate refusal to repent. Again, however, the careful teacher insists that these marks must not be taken as eternal judgments: the persons in question are not members of the church *at present*. This is the reverse of the "accounting" of church members by visible marks, and serves as a reminder that human beings can only judge external signs, good or bad. Christians are not allowed to despair of these people; the only one who can determine their status is God. It is true that God has pronounced against those "who, with set purpose and with resolute evil intent, should attack the truth, oppress the gospel, snuff out God's name, and resist the Holy Spirit.... the sin against the Holy Spirit." However, even though we may see these signs, the cautious reformer hastens to add that a true correlation between the behavior and the status "can only rarely be sensed by us (if it is ever possible), so it would be a more discreet plan to await the day of revelation." [12] In other words: Do not rush to judgment.

However, there are two things the church should do: discipline and prayer. These depend in part on proximity to the ones who are manifesting behavior which denies God verbally or by actions. Within the church those who are "accounted" as members must be taught and corrected, that is, disciplined. Calvin

---

[10]   OS I, p. 89: "etiamsi aliquid imperfectionis in eorum moribus resideat (ut nullus hic perfectus conspicitur), modo in suis vitiis non sibi nimium placeant et blandiantur, ac de iis bene sperandum." For the way that this affects the practice of baptism, see quotations from Calvin's sermons on 1 Corinthians and Genesis, in chap. 5 nn.158, 170.

[11]   *Institution 1536*, p. 83. OS I, p. 89. For Calvin's homiletical treatment of this, see sermons quoted in chap. 5 nn.158, 170.

[12]   *Institution 1536*, p. 83. OS I, p. 90.

names the three purposes of this oversight, i.e., maintaining the honor of God who will be defamed by public wickedness, protecting the purity of the rest of the community, and calling the sinner to repentance. [13] (It is noteworthy that he does not identify the agents of this action; that development will come later.) For those outside the church, that is, who are not "at present" reckoned as members, Christians are told to pray for their salvation.

> Nevertheless let us commit them to God's hand, commend them to his goodness, hoping for better things from them than we now see. ... Let us not sentence the person himself (who is in the hand and judgment of God) to death; but let us only weigh the works of each according to God's law, the rule of good and evil. [14]

The concern to pray for those who are not at present visibly in the church is a frequent theme for Calvin. It is repeated in his exposition of the Lord's Prayer and later put into practice in the Genevan liturgy, where it stands as a constant parallel to the Genevan church's organization of discipline. [15] Clearly, the visible church has two tasks with regard to those who do not manifest the marks of Christians: one is to pray for them (wherever they may be) and the other is to preach and act to re-form their confession and behavior (if they are in reach).

After this extensive discussion of how the boundaries of the church are visible to humans, Calvin turns to a very short statement about what makes the church be the church, or what makes the true church visible.

> Where we see the word of God soundly [*sincere*] preached and heard, where the sacraments are administered according to Christ's institution, there without any doubt for the time [*aliquam*] the church of God exists, for His promise cannot fail, "where two or three are gathered in my name, there I am in the midst of them." There can be no other more certain marks of God's church on earth. [16]

Note that Calvin ties the church's existence to the presence of the word and sacraments in an absolute fashion. This is both positive and negative. The marks

---

[13] OS I, pp. 89-90.

[14] *Institution 1536*, p. 84. OS I, p. 90. In fact, Calvin himself demonstrates this restraint in refusing to approve the action of his colleague in identifying the Duc de Guise as reprobate; cf. his letter to Duchess Renée of Ferrara on Jan. 24, 1564; #4074, OC 20:246.

[15] OS I, p. 107. In fact, Calvin's letter to the Duchess indicates that he has prayed for the Duc, mostly in regard to changing the Duc's behavior towards French Protestants, but the latter would be in some sort a sign of the Duc's repentance or conversion.

[16] OS I, p. 91. *Institution 1536*, p. 85, appears to skip the word *aliquam*.

can and must be trusted while they bear fruit. However, when those marks are
lost, the church no longer exists visibly in that place. There is not a once-for-all
determination of a body as church; that designation is dependent on the continuation of the necessary marks of apostolic teaching. Calvin's description of the
marks of the church is both distinctive and similar to those named by others. For
example, the Augsburg Confession, which set the standard of Lutheran ortho-
doxy, names the word purely preached and the sacraments rightly administered.
Calvin adds to this "the word heard": for him, response is a vital aspect of the
mark.

   The gospel proclaimed in spoken and visible word is central. Calvin insists that
the Biblical passage about binding and loosing (Matt.16:19) does not mean
humans can distinguish between elect and reprobate. That verse is not a criterion
for determining who is in and who is out; it is rather a proclamation of the gospel
of salvation in Christ.

> [T]hey who shall hear and receive in faith the gospel promise by which
> Christ is offered upon earth as redemption and liberation, that is pro-
> claimed in this life by man to himself [*ab homine sibi*] –... they, I say, are truly
> loosed and freed in heaven, that is, before God [*coram Deo*] and His
> judgment; but those who will reject and hold it in contempt, to them [it
> is] the testimony that, in heaven and before God [*coram Deo*], they remain
> in their chains and so in their condemnation. [17]

Receiving the promise in Christ means freedom from God's judgment, rejecting it
the opposite; both actions manifest the crucial importance of preaching and
hearing the word. In addition, Calvin wants to make the point that the proclamation of the gospel in the visible church is the means by which God has chosen
to implement election in Christ. The reformer explicitly indicates that this proclamation is offered by one human to another; it does not descend from the sky as
an oracle but is given through the instrument of human beings as well as human
words.

   The marks of the church and of Christians are God-given, but the visible
church is also a human institution. Chapter six of the 1536 *Institutes* deals with the
powers of the church and Christian freedom. Calvin's key focus of polemic is
Rome's clerical abuse of power. It has usurped God's prerogative of determining
what is necessary for salvation and made its own rules to bind people's consciences. It is in this context that the reformer identifies the proper role of pastors,
which connects this passage with the earlier references to the marks of the church.

---

[17]   *Institution 1536*, p. 82; slightly modified. OS I, p. 89.

"[T]heir whole task is limited to the ministry of God's Word; their whole wisdom to the knowledge of his Word; their whole eloquence, to its proclamation."[18] Ministers are just that: they (ad)minister what God has given in God's word, and add nothing of their own to the essential message. In effect, Calvin briefly identifies the heart of the pastoral *function* as preaching but does not set out any theory of *office*. He cites Eph. 4:11, his primary Biblical text for the office of pastors, pointing to God's provision of special gifts for those who build up the church, but it is clear that this is not yet a full picture of the ministry.[19]

The second point here is the aspect of Christian liberty which encompasses church order at the level of practical organization, things like times and places of worship. These *adiaphora*, indifferent things, are necessary for human society but do not bind the conscience. This might be called the third part of Calvin's discussion of the church, i.e., the space-time embodiment of the marks in the visible church. Preaching and sacraments take place in specific buildings at particular hours on designated days. None of these practical details are sacrosanct; they are intended to maintain good order and peace.

> The days themselves, the hours, the structure of the places of worship, what psalms are to be sung on what day, are matters of no importance. But it is fitting to have definite days and stated hours, and a place suitable to receive all, if there is any concern for the preservation of peace.[20]

Calvin was quite clear that all human organizations need polity. So for the sake of the Christian community's life together, the word and sacraments, which are the means of the proclamation of the gospel, need to be enacted in orderly fashion. The visible marks must be arranged in space and time in ways that the members of the church in that place may gather, profess, and participate.

Later Developments

Calvin's teaching on the marks of the church and the marks of Christians is virtually complete in 1536. In later editions of the *Institutes*, however, the exposition

---

[18] *Institution 1536*, pp. 262, 268 (quotation). OS I, pp. 240, 245. See also p. 258 which presents a rhetorically full picture of what this proclamation is: "they may boldly dare to do all things by God's Word, whose ministers and stewards they have been appointed; may compel all worldly power, glory, loftiness to yield and obey [God's] majesty; may build up Christ's household and cast down Satan's kingdom; may feed the sheep and kill the wolves; may exhort and instruct the teachable; may accuse, rebuke, and subdue the rebellious and stubborn; may bind and loose; and finally may launch lightnings and thunderbolts: but do all things in God's Word." OS I, p. 237.

[19] *Institution 1536*, p. 265, OS I, p. 243.

[20] *Institution 1536*, p. 283. OS I, p. 257.

is ordered more logically rather than primarily pastorally, and fitted into a considerably expanded discussion of the visible church. In 1539/41 Calvin first adds an important transitional statement in the exposition of the Creed to locate the efficacy of the church in relation to the work of the three Persons of the trinity.

> For the one who understands God's power and paternal goodness, Christ's righteousness and the efficaciousness of the Holy Spirit, has the cause of his salvation. But he does not yet see how salvation is accomplished in people unless he comes down to the church, the forgiveness of sins, and life eternal. [21]

The triune God alone saves; God does this through the church. Calvin expands and clarifies the description of the church by adding the image of the mother of all the faithful, "to which our Lord has committed all the treasures of His grace in order that it may be their guardian and distribute them by its ministry." [22] The fullness of this church is recognized by faith, not by sight, and faith is our assurance of being part of it.

> [I]n order to keep in the unity of that church it is not necessary that we see one church with our eyes or be able to touch it with our hands. Rather, since we must "believe the church," by that is meant that we must recognize it not less when it is invisible than if we clearly see it. And our faith is no worse when it recognizes the church that our understanding cannot grasp, since here we are not commanded to distinguish the elect from the reprobate (that belongs to God alone and not to us), but to have this certainty in our hearts: that all those, who by the mercy of God the Father and the power of the Holy Spirit have come to participation in Christ, are set apart as the proper inheritance of God; and since we are among their number, we are heirs of such a grace. [23]

Christians affirm the church as it is known to God, even though they cannot see or touch it. There is no practical need to be able to define the membership of the church of the elect; all that is necessary is to believe its character and recognize its reality, and know by one's own faith that one is in that elect group.

After setting out what is sure but not seen, Calvin turns to discuss "the visible church which we can grasp with our senses." [24] Much of the 1536 text is simply

---

[21] *Institutes 1541*, p. 242; cf. *Inst.* 4.1.1.

[22] *Institutes 1541*, p. 242; cf. *Inst.* 4.1.1

[23] *Institutes 1541*, p. 245; cf. *Inst.* 4.1.3.

[24] *Institutes 1541*, p. 245; cf. *Inst.* 4.1.4.

reordered; for example, there is relatively little change in the discussion of the marks of Christians. There are some important clarifications of other significant issues, however. One is the relationship of the earthly church universal to local churches.

> The church universal is all the multitude which accepts God's truth and the teaching of His word, of whatever nation they may be or whatever place, since it is united by the tie of religion. Under this universal church are comprised the churches which are distributed in each city and village in such a way that each one has the title and authority of church.[25]

This statement about all the visible churches and each individual instance might seem redundant. However, the implications of unity in diversity become evident a little later when Calvin discusses what is included under the "tie of religion," and makes it clear that unity does not require uniformity in every detail of teaching, much less of polity. In effect, here he is recognizing the validity of the claim of all the scattered communities which share the apostolic teaching to be understood as parts of the visible church, whether or not they share visible structural connections.

A second point which is expanded in 1539 is the earlier very short statement about word and sacraments; Calvin now explains more adequately how to recognize the existence of the church in practice. First, the marks "cannot be without fruit," something he goes on to define more clearly. Where "the gospel is reverently heard and the sacraments are not neglected, there one cannot doubt that a sure form of the church appears for the time."[26] Reverence for the word (active hearing) and faithful participation in the sacraments are evidence of gospel fruit. However, every congregation which claims to be the church must be tested. The phrase "appears *for the time*" signifies that it is a true church only as long as the marks are evident and fruitful. Calvin also gives more specificity to the brief 1536 reference to the content of the gospel, noting what is essential and what (limited) differences in teaching may be tolerated within the "tie of religion."

> For all the articles of God's teaching are not of the same kind. There are some which are so necessary to know that no one should doubt them any more than they doubt the principles of Christianity. As, for example, that there is one God, that Jesus Christ is God and Son of God, that our salvation rests firmly on His mercy alone, and other such teachings. There

---

25 *Institutes 1541*, pp. 246; cf. pp. 245-47.
26 *Institutes 1541*, p. 247; cf. *Inst.* 4.1.9, 10.

> are others which are disputed among the churches and nevertheless do
> not break their unity. To give an example: if it happens that one church
> holds that when souls are separated from the body they are transferred to
> heaven at once and another, without daring to name the place, thinks
> simply that they live in God, and such a difference exists without quarre-
> ling or obstinacy, why should they separate from each other? [27]

Some points are fundamental, and emphasis on *solus Christus* gives this statement a
Protestant inflexion. However, Calvin wishes to make it plain that precise doctrinal uniformity is not essential as long as minor differences do not lead to
quarrels.

Having dealt with the permissible variations in teaching, Calvin turns to the
issue of morals. Here the standard is less strict because human failings cannot
destroy the church even though the lack of an honorable witness in word and
deed is a very serious fault. For present purposes, discussing the details about
what severity in discipline is appropriate is less important than how the question
of behavior factors into the recognition of the church. Given the imperfect
holiness of church members, is the truth of the church threatened? Or the
unity of the body broken? Does the corrupt behavior of members invalidate
the word and sacraments at any point?

> For since our Lord wanted the communion of His church to be preserved
> by us through maintaining public assemblies where we have His word and
> sacraments, whoever separates from such a society because of hatred for
> the wicked enters into a path by which it is very easy to separate from the
> communion of the saints. [28]

For Calvin, as long as the gospel is fruitfully proclaimed in word and sacraments, it
is the church. The issue of morality is important but not on the same level. God
highly values the unity of the visible church embodied in assemblies gathered for
worship, so abandoning that fellowship is a very serious matter. Leaving a body
which has the word and sacraments because there are wicked members is not
equivalent to abandoning the church, but it is a very large step in that direction. As
Calvin goes on to insist, such an action also expresses disrespectful doubt about
God's saving power in the marks of the church and their ordained function in
identifying the church.

---

[27]   *Institutes 1541*, p. 248; cf. *Inst.* 4.1.12.

[28]   *Institutes 1541*, p. 250; cf. *Inst.* 4.1.16.

> Let [such people] consider that the word of God and His holy sacraments have more power and importance for preserving a church than the vices of some rotten members have for breaking it apart. Lastly let them consider that God's judgment should have more authority for determining where there is a church and where there is not, than human opinion. [29]

This firm statement emphasizes the power of the "marks which our Lord considered sufficient to point out His church." [30] Whatever people may think about the behavior of other members, they must remember that God has determined that the word and sacraments have greater power to make the church present than human immorality has to destroy it. As long as the word and sacraments are bearing fruit, by God's grace, the church continues to exist and the individual believer should not leave it.

This does not mean, however, that the church as such, as the corporate body, can take questions of behavior lightly. Calvin goes on to deal with the issue of discipline as he had done in 1536: its accommodated character and its three purposes. He refines the point by adding the suggestion that there is a temporal connection between discipline and the marks of the church.

> Those who think that the churches can exist over a long time without being tied and joined together by this discipline greatly deceive themselves, since there is no doubt that we cannot do without a remedy which the Lord foresaw to be necessary for us. [31]

Discipline cannot be a mark of the church because if it were, the individual communities where the gospel is proclaimed and is bearing fruit, but which lack discipline, would not be churches at all. However, a long-term lack of discipline (which sums up the enforcement of the marks of Christians) threatens even the word and sacraments. Perhaps another way to describe what Calvin means is to say that neglect of discipline dishonors God because it pays no attention to a gift which God specifically gave to the church for its *bene esse*. Such neglect demonstrates a disregard for the church's "maternal" task of correcting and training its children. [32] It is a form of unfaithfulness which (if unchecked) contradicts the gospel it proclaims, not because discipline is necessary

---

[29]   *Institutes 1541*, p. 250-51; cf. *Inst.* 4.1.16.

[30]   *Institutes 1541*, p. 247; cf. *Inst.* 4.1.11.

[31]   *Institutes 1541*, p. 251; punctuation altered.

[32]   Calvin adds a polemical section clarifying how Rome fits into the larger picture of the marks of the church, concluding with a curiously balanced "yes and no." *Institutes 1541*, p. 256; cf. *Inst.* 4.2.

for the church to exist but because long-term neglect is evidence that the word is not bearing fruit.

Summary of Calvin's Teaching on Marks of the Church and Marks of Christians

For Calvin, the marks of the church: the word purely preached and heard and sacraments rightly administered, together express the apostolic teaching. Both are forms of the same gospel, the good news which is the means of salvation. These marks are the way Christians identify the church. They are in a sense constitutive of the visibility of the church. Where these marks are, the church can be found, in fellowship with these marks one can be sure of being in the church. Alongside the marks of the church Calvin places the marks of Christians, the faithful. This is his creative insight, honoring the importance of discipline without making it a constitutive mark of the church. Christians hear and answer the proclamation of the word by attesting that they understand and affirm the basic content of the gospel, by manifesting this affirmation in their lives, and by sharing in the gathered worship of the body of Christ visible on earth. Overseeing the marks of Christians is the domain of discipline. The purpose of discipline is educational: to insure that believers know and act on their faith, and constructive: to see that those who do not meet these standards can be properly (re)taught and (re)formed for the sake of God's honor, for the wellbeing of the rest of the church, and for their own salvation.

Two important factors in the discussion of the marks of Christians are the phrase "loving or charitable judgment" and the reason Calvin believes God gave these marks. This completes the circle to show the relationship between the church as it is visible to God and the church as it is known on earth. Calvin, like other Protestants, affirmed clearly that the church as the full number of the elect is known only to God, although each individual knows her or his own election by the experience of faith. Where the word and sacraments are in their proper form, there is a community which is part of the true church known to God. The teaching says that there are reprobate inside as well as outside the visible church, but there are no practical implications of this. Why? Because, according to Calvin, God does not consider it necessary for humans to know how to separate sheep and goats, but only how to administer the earthly church properly. For that it is necessary to have some way "to reckon" the bounds of the church as it is visible on earth. For Calvin, affirming the parish limits of an established geographic church structure and its civil oversight is not sufficient, and it certainly cannot be necessary because there were no such structures or leaders in the model church of the New Testament. However, God gave the earthly church an accommodated way to handle the matter of delineating boundaries, insofar as that is needed. By a charitable or loving assessment of what is humanly visible, ministers and members of the earthly church can define who should be recognized as faithful members of the visible church and who (at present) should not. That is all. But that is enough for them to do their job.

The Ministers of the Marks

The marks of the church and the marks of Christians are both carried out by visible human ministers. In the 1536 *Institutes,* Calvin emphasizes the necessary functions of the marks without particular attention to the agents. Over time he developed his understanding of the latter, working out the relationship of tasks and gifts and ecclesiastical offices. The next stage is found in 1539, primarily in the course of explaining Biblical texts like Eph. 4:11, 1 Cor. 12:28, and Rom. 12:8, because Calvin, like the rest of the Reformed tradition, believed that scripture provides a pattern for the right ordering of the visible church's practice, specifically its worship and ministries. This is not a blueprint but serves as guidelines, and the practice of the early church (up to Gregory I) plays a role in how Calvin fleshes out the Biblical patterns. [33] The complete outline of the ministers appears in the 1541 *Ecclesiastical Ordinances,* where Calvin identifies four: pastors, teachers (or doctors), elders, and deacons (of whom there are two kinds). This is more fully worked out in the next edition of the *Institutes* in 1543. [34] The pastors are the ministers of the marks of the church, the pastors and elders together as the consistory are the ministers of the marks of Christians.

The doctors and deacons have vital roles in the visibility of the church, also, although in less direct fashion than pastors and elders. At the highest level, the doctors are the colleagues and nursery of pastors, who keep the church faithful to the full apostolic teaching. One might say that they are the ones who write books of theology, while the pastors are more focused on making sure that everyone knows, understands, and follows the basic teaching. The distinction is evident in the preface to Calvin's Latin translation of the Geneva Catechism where he explains the different kinds of religious texts. He contrasts "the specific points which should be common and familiar to all Christians," i.e., the catechism which

---

[33] Full exegetical dimensions in McKee, *Elders and the Plural Ministry,* chap. 6-8. See Irena Backus, "These holy men: Calvin's Patristic Models for Establishing the Company of Pastors," *Calvin and the Company of Pastors,* ed. David Foxgrover (Grand Rapids: CRC for the Calvin Studies Society, 2004), pp. 25-51, for emphasis that Calvin based his practical church order on the church fathers. Note the "Response," by Anthony N. S. Lane, pp. 53-55, with the reminder that Calvin used the fathers in various ways.

[34] *Ordinances,* OS II, pp. 329-43. *Institutes 1559,* OS V, esp. 4:3.

everyone should know at least in essence, with "other kinds of writings [which] show what are our views in all matters of religion."[35] Calvin himself wore both hats, of course, with the *Institutes* detailing the theology and the daily preaching conveying the fundamental Biblical teaching to the people in the pew. If the doctors have a connection with the marks of the church, the deacons' role is related to a corporate expression of the marks of Christians. The main task of deacons is care of the poor, sick, and otherwise afflicted. At the individual level, love of neighbor is part of responding to the word and living in right relationship with God. The diaconate embodies the conviction that such love is a corporate as well as an individual task. According to Calvin's reading of such texts as Acts 6:1-6, 1 Tim. 3:8-13, and others, the deacons' ministry is Biblically necessary for the church to be the church. In recognition of this, and following the early church practice, Calvin considered it appropriate that (male) deacons should also participate in the Lord's Supper by offering the cup.[36]

Scholars have explored the reformer's thought on church ministries rather fully, and some questions will be considered briefly elsewhere. However, the primary focus of this project is the public work of pastors. So, for present purposes a summary of the 1559 additions about the importance of preaching and corporate worship will round out this discussion of the primary agents of the gospel. Calvin explains that while God could instantly bring people to salvation, God has instead chosen to use human beings and ordained preaching for this purpose.

> God breathes faith into us only by the instrument of his gospel, as Paul points out that "faith comes from hearing" [Rom. 10:17]. Likewise, the power to save rests with God [Rom. 1:16]; but (as Paul again testifies) He displays and unfolds it in the preaching of the gospel [ibid.]. By this plan He willed of old that holy assemblies be held at the sanctuary in order that the doctrine taught by the mouth of the priest might foster agreement in faith. .... [S]o also today it is his will to teach us through human means.[37]

The Old Testament people of God had both law and priests, so the church-people now have the Bible and should attend to knowing it, but they should also

---

[35] Geneva Catechism, *Calvin: Theological Treatises*, p. 90; OS II, p. 73.

[36] See McKee, *John Calvin on the Diaconate*, chap. 5-9, esp. pp. 129-30, 154 (offering cup in Supper). This definition of deacon was a change from the traditional medieval usage; for discussion, see chap. 2 at nn.10ff. The role of deacons in the Lord's Supper has been disputed; see chap. 3 at nn.37ff.

[37] *Institutes 1559*, p. 1017. *Inst.* 4.1.5; OS V, p. 8.

have teachers to help. Calvin insists on the divinely ordained role of human preaching; God's power is not bound to external means but humans must use those means which God has provided. What is perhaps the preacher's highest praise for his vocation is the description of what happens in worship as presenting "God's living image" [*viva Dei imago*]. Calvin cites Paul and various Old Testament figures as the authorities for the necessity of gathering for preaching and other acts of worship.

> [T]he church is built up solely by outward preaching, and... the saints are held together by one bond only: that with common accord, through learning and advancement, they keep the church order established by God [cf. Eph. 4:12]. It was especially to this end that I have said, in ancient times [*olim*] under the law all believers were commanded to assemble at the sanctuary....[Exod. 20:24, Ps. 84:2-3]...Surely this is because believers have no greater help [*adminiculo*] than public worship, for by it God raises his own folk upward step by step.[38]

The centrality of corporate worship for the edification of God's people had never been in doubt for Protestants, but it is clear that as he grew older and considered how to make his teaching on the church complete, Calvin believed that the point needed to be stressed. The people of God *must* gather regularly, frequently, to hear the word and share the sacraments so as to bear fruit as the body of Christ.

The Three Levels of the Church

Calvin's exposition of the marks of the church, the marks of Christians, and the power of the earthly church to implement both, can be explained as a three-level teaching on the doctrine of the church. The following summary reformulates the more abstract theological discussion above to illustrate its practical application in the Genevan situation.

The Affirmation of the True Church

Genevans were taught that the church as it is known to God is all the elect. It is "invisible" because no one on earth can see its exact boundaries, but that does not mean that the truth of the church is invisible. The consequence on the practical level, e.g., in sixteenth-century Geneva, was that all Christians were called upon to affirm the reality of this church with absolute conviction, that is, to confess its

---

[38] *Institutes 1559*, p. 1019: note that Battles substitutes "public worship" for pronouns "hoc adminiculo" and "ce moyen" of the French of 1560. *Inst.* 4.1.5; OS V, p. 10. Other references: Ps. 105:4, 27:8, 100:2, 1 Chron. 16:11, 2 Chron. 7:14.

truth. They were also expected to experience it individually or personally by faith. They were not supposed to be able to define its exact boundaries with regard to other members but were to pray for the salvation of all the living who did not appear to be in the visible church. [39]

Belonging to the True Church as it is Visible

The main focus for Genevans was the church as it is visible to human beings. They were taught that this is the true church (part of the church visible to God) as long as it has the marks of the word purely preached and heard and the sacraments rightly administered, because where these marks are visible, the true church is visible. This church is God's chosen instrument for the gospel to be offered to human beings, so anyone who departs from that proclamation is leaving the means which God ordained for salvation. Calvin does not claim that the preaching and sacraments effect faith in people; that is the work of the Holy Spirit. What he does say is that because God established the word and sacraments in the church as the instruments of salvation, human beings are bound to those means and that body. If the gospel were no longer there, then it would no longer be the church. Thus, the Genevans should be diligent in attendance and strong in supporting the pastors' struggle to insure faithful teaching and pure sacraments.

What would Genevans need to know about the content of the all-important apostolic teaching in order to do their part in keeping the church pure and fruitful? The first step was to believe that what God's word teaches is the only absolute: *sola scriptura*. The second was to distinguish between necessary knowledge of the faith and what that requires of each person for salvation, and the accommodated ways that these are implemented in church life. Given the sole authority of the Bible, is everything in scripture on the same level? Protestant teachers had to explain to their people that there can be differences within the Bible in terms of what is essential, and what is significant but not a matter of life and death. One consequence is that there can be some diversity among the communities who make up the visible church in various places. The practical implication of this for ordinary Genevans was the distinction between catechism and theology, as was noted above in the quotations from preface to the Genevan Catechism. The first level of religious knowledge is found in the catechism, or "the rudiments with which both the learned and the unlearned among us were from youth constantly instructed, all the faithful holding them as the solemn symbol of Christian communion." This is supposed to be universal, maintained by "all the faithful."

---

[39]   In addition to requiring everyone to learn the Apostles' Creed, it was probably used at every catechism as well as sung on Supper Sundays, chap. 3 at nn.138, 154-55. It was recited in daily worship and household devotions, chap. 4 at n.5; chap. 7 at n.40.

The second level of knowledge is contained in the books of theology about "all the matters of our religion." [40] The latter texts, like the *Institutes*, Genevans were required to respect because defaming their chief theologian was seen as an attack on the gospel he preached. However, they did not need to trouble themselves with the details, as long as they knew the catechism.

Besides learning the fundamental teachings for the sake of their own salvation, Genevans needed these in order to live as responsible members of the visible church. That is, they must use them to learn to recognize as members of the earthly church those who shared these catechetical basics ("the solemn symbol of Christian communion"), even when there was not identity in every detail of teaching, much less liturgy. For example, when the special day of prayer services were held in November 1545 Calvin apparently had to emphasize to his congregation that the Lutherans for whom they were praying were fellow members of the church. He does not mention the catechism specifically but his argument implies that his congregation should know and acknowledge those distant German-speaking people of another confession as their brothers and sisters in the faith. [41]

Besides knowing the fundamental Biblical teaching and recognizing all who shared it as fellow members of the visible church, Genevans were expected to learn how to embody their knowledge in their lives. They experienced the reality of living in the visible church through how the marks of word and sacraments were implemented in forming and reforming them to look like the church. (This is external, not internal conformity; the latter is the job of the Holy Spirit. Calvin is very clear that the church must distinguish its job from God's job, and do what it is supposed to do with all its energy and leave alone what belongs to God.) Discipline or formation of Christians, in knowledge, in behavior, in active participation in worship: these are the tasks of the church. The most obvious point was no doubt the effort Genevans had to make to attend worship, learn the catechism, and follow it as well as they could. The fruit of such formation was the affirmation that, insofar as human knowledge extends, both they and those around them were members of the true church because they were members in good standing of the visible church where they lived. On the other hand, excommunication does not mean a judgment of reprobation but a statement that the person is not a member of the visible church at present, and is not manifesting evidence of faith or faithfulness. A neighbor suspended from the sacraments (not really excommunication), or even one who apostacized, should be taught or corrected and reconciled, not condemned as reprobate.

---

[40] Geneva Catechism, *Calvin: Theological Treatises*, pp. 88, 90; OS II, p. 73.

[41] For the day of prayer service, see chap. 4 at n.157.

Most Genevans, like the wider tradition, understood the purposes of discipline as maintaining the purity and health of the church, and bringing sinners to repentance and reconciliation. The proper honor of the community was important to many, as was evident in the ways they participated in calling each other to account when one saw another publicly at fault. Individually they were certainly very aware of the problem of conflict and discord, because they were extremely sensitive to the dangers of participating in the Lord's Supper (and sometimes even the Lord's Prayer) if they were involved in a quarrel or felt bitterness toward someone about a wrong. [42] Calvin's third purpose for discipline, which he puts in first place and which seems to be his distinctive contribution to the topic, is the glory of God. Ignorance of the gospel and disgraceful conduct and defiance of the church (e.g., rejecting the sacraments) are ways members of the visible church bring dishonor on the God whom they profess to worship. For Genevans, learning this aspect of the visible church's role in their lives took more time. However, before Calvin's death the church in Geneva had developed a liturgical enactment for reconciling members who had "apostacized" by participating in the Mass or other forms of papal worship, which were widely regarded as among the most notorious ways to dishonor God and deny the true church. [43]

Practical Church Order

What might be called a third level of church in Calvin's theology is the nuts and bolts or implementation of practice. This would have been one of the most obvious expressions of church for the Genevans. In the strict sense this level is made up of *adiaphora*, indifferent things, i.e., the arrangement of times and places and all the minutiae of embodying the church's visibility somewhere – in this case, the sixteenth-century city state beside Lac Leman. The church (like every human society) needs laws to organize its life. These are in no way salvific, whether they set the hours of worship services or liturgical words spoken, whether they define catechetical procedures or household devotions. The point is that the marks of the church and marks of Christians must be given concrete form in a particular time and place. Calvin explains this to his congregation in a sermon on 1 Cor. 11:2-3, preached in 1556. He starts by naming the two levels: doctrine and "polity" (*adiaphora*). First he outlines the essentials, that is, the doctrine, which he divides into parts roughly corresponding to faith and life. Both are part of the basic Christian teaching which is found in God's word.

---

42   For examples, see chap. 3 at n.230, chap. 7 at n.6.

43   See chap. 3 at n.177.

> [Doctrine] contains two things. The first is what we must believe about
> God, the other, how we all ought to behave toward Him. Thus the
> teaching shows us in the first place where we ought to place the trust
> for our salvation; how we can call upon God and be certain of being heard
> by Him. This is what has to do with our faith; and the sacraments are aids
> to this, so that we may know why we are baptized in the name of our Lord
> Jesus Christ and why we receive the Supper. Then there is the second part
> of the teaching, i.e., how we ought to serve God and what we must do,
> what is our duty to Him. Now the content of both of these points of
> doctrine must be reserved to God alone: for it belongs to God to show us
> from where our salvation comes and how we should rule ourselves in this
> life. [44]

Only God in God's word may define what Christians must believe and how they
should live. This is the basic requirement for all the church. (In speaking to his
congregation Calvin does not distinguish between the various levels within doctrine, i.e., catechetical and matters about which different church bodies may
disagree, probably because in this context he would normally be focused only
on the necessary essentials. Matters of theological nuance would be out of place in
preaching to laity unless such fine points were currently being debated and needed
to be publicly addressed.)

Having identified what the church receives without question, the teacher turns
to the level of polity, the domain in which the church implements God's teaching
"freely" and determines its practical organization. These are matters of *adiaphora*
(although he does not use that word in the sermon).

> There is also polity, and this polity is freely left to us. As for example, now
> we are assembled at eight o'clock; it could well have been at seven o'clock,
> or the form could be changed in some way. And in fact, we often see that
> one church does not have a form exactly like the other. When we celebrate
> the Supper, the tables are not set out as they are in another place; baptism
> is not administered in the same place as in other churches, and does that
> mean we have a different Christianity? Not at all. For things having to do
> with the external order and polity, as I have said, are left to human liberty.
> It is true that we must proceed with soberness and modesty, and must
> always consider what is appropriate for the edification of His church. [45]

It is notable that the examples the preacher uses are precisely the times of worship
and physical arrangements of the celebration of the sacraments. He obviously

---

[44]   Sermon 11 on 1 Cor. 2, 3; OC 49:710-711.

[45]   Sermon 11 on 1 Cor. 2, 3; OC 49:711.

knows that these are matters which his hearers will have remarked for themselves. They also have seen that other churches with whom they are in communion have different liturgical practices. Perhaps in the back of Calvin's mind was the long conflict with Bern over exactly these kinds of issues; the use of baptisteries had probably been discontinued relatively recently, and his hearers would remember that. Naming such visible examples, the preacher can be confident that the point he is making will be clear, so he can also emphasize that this diversity in no way serves to divide Christians from each other. The reference to "8 o'clock" not only illustrates what Calvin means but also gives theological grounding for the flexibility which Genevans experienced in their seasonal changes of worship schedule.[46] Regulations can be changed as the community's needs require. On the other hand, when an ordinance is in effect, the whole church operates according to those agreements. Calvin's positive emphasis on edification implicitly serves to justify the need for matters of indifference to be regulated in a "decent and orderly" way, so that all of the church may be built up together.

What specifics were Genevans told about how to do their common worship? Prominent among the early instances of Calvin's instructions about gathering for worship is the 1542 preface to the Psalter. This formed part of the Calvinist devotional and liturgical "service book" and so continued to shape the tradition in fundamental ways long after the reformer's death.[47] Calvin begins with the necessity of regular corporate worship and then draws some conclusions.

> As it is a thing rightly required by Christianity, and one of the most necessary, that each of the faithful observe and maintain the communion of the church in his neighborhood, attending the assemblies which are held on Sundays as well as the other days to honor and serve God, so it is also expedient and reasonable that everyone know and understand what is said and done in the temple in order to receive benefit and edification from it. For our Lord did not institute the order which we are bound to observe when we gather together merely to amuse the world by a spectacle, but rather desired that from it profit would come to all His people.[48]

---

[46] For second removal of baptisteries see chap. 5 at n.185; for seasonal time changes, see chap. 1 at nn.54, 145 *et passim*.

[47] This little essay was first printed with the liturgy and Psalms together and, although subsequently fixed at the front of the book of metrical Psalms, was reunited with the liturgy when these two texts plus the catechism were published as the Calvinist Reformed "service book" usually called simply the Psalter. See chap. 3 at n.58.

[48] *Pastoral Piety*, p. 91; OS II, p. 12.

At the beginning of this essay introducing the Reformed prayer and liturgy book, Calvin seems to assume that his readers know that they should gather for worship in their local community and do so frequently. He names the central focus of the Lord's Day but also includes other days, and affirms that the community should gather where it is, i.e., not go seeking especially holy places (as in the tradition of pilgrimages). Probably the appropriateness of the parish system is in the reformer's mind, but the real point is that the church means the people, and in any given location they should be united; the building does not matter. The conclusion Calvin draws is that since God wants the church-people to benefit from their assembly, they must understand "what is said and done." This demand for an intelligible liturgy is of course one of the consistent Protestant innovations in corporate worship.

The reference to "what God instituted" is the content of the service: the word and sacraments. Calvin then goes on to name various aspects of how these are manifested: preaching and prayer and sacraments. At this point (1542) he affirms that preaching "is not in question" so he concentrates on the other two and the fact that it is essential for them to be understood.

> [W]e have the express commandment of the Holy Spirit that prayers be made in the common language and understood by the people.... As for the sacraments... if these are visible words, as Saint Augustine calls them, they must not be merely an exterior spectacle, but doctrine must be joined to them to give them understanding. [49]

Previously Calvin indicated that God wants worship to edify the people; "prayers" here is taken in the larger sense for the whole liturgy, as is evident in the title *La forme des prières*. Here Calvin shows explicitly that the authority is the Holy Spirit in God's word. The next point is the sacraments, which Protestants insisted are not magical actions but must be accompanied by the teaching of the gospel; therefore preaching is essential – another fundamental demand in the reform of worship. For Calvin, the Lord's Supper and baptism cannot be held without the proclamation of the Biblical promises. After a brief discussion of the Supper, Calvin turns to the "public prayers" (here speaking of prayers in the narrower sense) which, he says, take two forms, spoken and sung. This is a third key Protestant contribution to worship: vocal congregational participation through song. Since this innovation was more surprising than the claim for preaching, Calvin cites Biblical grounds such as Col. 3:16. He then expands this reference to the scriptural authorization for singing by advocating Biblical texts as the actual

---

[49]   *Pastoral Piety*, pp. 92, 93; OS II, pp. 13,14; cf. quotation in chap. 3 n.55.

substance of the sung prayers. The "psalms of David which the Holy Spirit made and spoke through him" are the best and right way to praise God. [50]

What Calvin is treating in this essay are the divinely established aspects of the marks of the church. He also has to explain how what God has ordained is brought into human practice.

> But it is certainly right, if we are disciples of Jesus Christ, that we prefer His institution to our practice. ... [F]or the use of our church, it seemed well advised to us to have a formulary of prayers and the sacraments published, in order that everyone might know what he should say and do in the Christian assembly. [51]

Calvin clearly affirms that his worship service follows what Christ instituted instead of traditional human practices, and then in the next breath he says in essence that "we" (he drew on the work of other reformers) have prepared a form or liturgy! The audacity of it! Whether the people gasped or applauded, Calvin was putting into practice the claim for scripture as the source and the human minister as the voice of the gospel. The substance must remain Christ's and the Holy Spirit's, but the role of the pastor is to transmit God's ordained teaching in a form which the church can actually use. As a consequence, the individual words of the liturgy and prayers are not holy in themselves, as was the Mass; after all, even the Biblical ones are translations and the Psalms are in metrical form. The details can be changed, but whatever liturgies Christians use must always be measured by the standard of God's word.

The Psalter preface shows how Calvin understood his task of maintaining the doctrine (what came from God) while doing what was necessary to make a practicable form for the visible church in Geneva to use when they gathered for corporate worship. In fact, the experience of being the church-people was primarily manifested and embodied in such acts. This book is an exploration of that story, giving both Calvin's explanation of the grounds in God's word and the practical working out which he and his colleagues achieved in the city of Geneva.

---

[50] *Pastoral Piety*, pp. 94, 96; OS II, pp. 15, 17. In claiming congregational singing for Protestants, it is important to note that they were not the first to practice congregational singing; in the Latin west that honor goes to the Bohemian Brethren. However the spread and influence of congregational song is usually attributed to Protestants.

[51] *Pastoral Piety*, p. 94; OS II, p. 15.

III: An Outline of Pastoral Ministry and Worship

The story of pastoral ministry and worship in early modern Geneva is organized into four parts, of which the second and third build on the first in different ways. Part One attends to the nitty-gritty matters of the lowest, practical level of Calvin's teaching on the church: when and where, who and how. Parts Two and Three examine the second level, the marks which make the church visible, that is, the what and why of word and sacraments as these were enacted. Part Four explores the ways that corporate worship was extended into the practices of daily life.

Part One gives particular attention to the nuts and bolts, or perhaps more appropriately, the pulpits and pews, of Geneva. The first chapter addresses the issue of places of worship and the somewhat debated matter of the times and schedules of public services, in order to provide a physical frame for the rest of the story. The program of sermons is laid out: four on Sundays in at least two parishes, two on all weekdays and three on Mondays, Wednesdays, and Fridays. This may seem very unlikely, but parishioners appearing before the consistory in 1542-44 mention attendance on every day and at every time. Chapter two carries the picture further by exploring the shape of collegial ministry in Geneva – the practical business of who was preaching where and when. It thus uncovers the dynamic symbiosis of the corps of ministers and how, in spite of illness and other challenges, they managed the very ambitious and strenuous schedule described in the previous chapter.

Part Two examines the teaching and practice of liturgies in space and time. First the understanding and practice of the Lord's Day is described, with attention to Calvin's teaching, the various texts of the "service books" (liturgy, Psalter, catechism), the order of worship for Sunday morning and Sunday afternoon, and the practice of the Lord's Supper. This includes the role of corporate discipline in preparation for the sacrament and the special "rituals of the Supper" which developed as a kind of annual liturgical rhythm. Chapter four complements the discussion of Sunday with a study of how Geneva dealt with the traditional liturgical year. It gives particular attention to the remarkably creative development of the weekly day of prayer that expresses the characteristic Calvinist Reformed understanding of providence. Chapter five rounds out the picture of forms of public worship with an exploration of the two special liturgies, baptism and marriage, which were practiced on an individual schedule. One a sacrament and the other no longer so, these two religious high points in the life of a family were now necessarily celebrated in the context of a regular preaching service in the presence of the whole parish. This congregational locus provided a very impor-

tant bridge between the Christian's personal and communal religious lives. It thus
embodied in the "private" liturgies of worship a significant characteristic of
Reformed piety, the emphasis on continuity between the corporate and the
individual, the unity of the members in the body of Christ.

Part Three turns from the detailed discussion of liturgical patterns focused
particularly on the sacraments, to the other key, and indeed most prominent and
pervasive part of public worship, the preaching of the word. Since, regrettably,
there is very little extant to show for the preaching of most of his colleagues, this
section concentrates on Calvin. Part Three is one long chapter six – which did not
lend itself easily to being divided into several chapters and is sufficiently distinctive not to be included in Part Two. The first short section of this chapter sets the
context of preaching generally, and in Geneva. That is followed by an overview
of the pulpits Calvin filled and what he was doing there. This includes known
sermons and a hypothetical investigation of his preaching before his sermons
were recorded (a forgotten lacuna in his work), and concludes with an example of
how he would expound the Catechism. The next section studies the sermons as
objects: recording, preservation (!) and dating. The last section examines what can
be learned about Calvin's audiences from the sermons: both what can be inferred
about the preacher's view of his hearers, and what the publication of these
extempore texts reveals about how (at least some of) his congregation perceived
and appreciated them.

Part Four recognizes that not all worship is conducted in the parish church,
and both pastors and people in Geneva were expected to live their faith in the
daily round of ordinary life. Chapter seven explores, from several angles, "private"
aspects of "liturgical" worship. This is not the personal prayer lives of individuals,
but worship based in the home which was planned by and involved communal
guidance and/or participation. One part is the practice of household devotions,
for which the Catechism and sometimes the liturgy provided models and instructions. A second is ministry to the sick and dying, which was a vital pastoral
responsibility and of great importance to parishioners. Because Geneva's reform
of the rites of death was more radical than elsewhere, here particular attention is
given to positive aspects of that process which have often been obscured. The
third part of this chapter on the "daily round" follows Calvin the pastor through a
period just over one month, cataloguing his activities, in order to give an idea of
the typical day-to-day life of Geneva's senior minister.

The conclusion serves essentially as reflection, drawing on the foregoing
detailed analysis to offer an overview of what this study contributes to understanding Calvin's theology and Geneva's practice. One particular fruit is a new,

coherent picture of the Calvinist Reformed reshaping of liturgical time. In particular it shows how the practice of corporate worship makes visible a significant characteristic of Reformed piety. For Calvin and those who followed him, believers live every day *coram Deo*, before God, in the providential awareness that in all of life it is with God that we have to do, *negotium cum Deo*. Believers also know that they never stand alone, but are always before God in the context of the rest of the church-people. This is particularly evident in the way their personal lives are shaped by gathered worship: frequent, regular, corporate, attending to God's word and sacraments together. If the conclusion is for the theologians, the appendices should make the social historians happy: dozens of pages of statistics from baptismal and marriage records, and Calvin's sermons, and old prayers: fascinating details found in digging through sixteenth-century sources… you are invited to share the fruits of a treasure hunt.

PART ONE

The Structures: Time, Space, and People

The reformation in Geneva involved a number of concrete changes in the practice of corporate worship. The replacement of the daily parish Mass with regular preaching as the central and most frequent act of the liturgy was much more than a theological change. It required reorganizing time and space in often radical ways, and replacing traditional priests with pastors whose education and duties had significant differences from earlier clergy. In Protestant Geneva for many years the villages usually had preaching only on Sundays and the day of prayer, but in the city itself there were daily sermons. In either case, the new shape of public worship entailed a considerable change in the spatial organization of the buildings and temporal schedules of the people. It also involved recruiting new leaders and re-organizing how they functioned in Calvin's ambitious program of preaching services and sacramental liturgies.

It is appropriate to identify the various kinds of sources which are available for investigating the question of days, times, frequency, and personnel of public worship. Some materials are prescriptive, others descriptive. The short 1538 treatise by Antoine Saunier on the Genevan schools, and 1541 *Ecclesiastical Ordinances* give outlines, descriptive and prescriptive respectively. The *Registres du Conseil* and *Registres du Consistoire* and *Registres de la Compagnie des Pasteurs* provide "incidental" references to implementation or practice. Baptismal and marriage records also play a role in identifying who was leading worship where, and when those liturgies were held. Other materials, such as civil ordinances or court cases, letters or sermons, chronicles like those of Jeanne de Jussie and Michel Roset which contribute eye-witness accounts, add occasional details.

CHAPTER ONE

PLACES AND TIMES OF WORSHIP

The time and space of corporate worship in Calvin's Geneva can be clearly defined by 1550, when the reformer's recorded sermons and the regularly-kept registers of baptisms and marriages begin to provide fuller details about dates and places. Usually descriptions of the city's worship life have concentrated on this period, although scholars frequently refer to the early years of Protestantism or give a brief sketch of the general arrangements. Most often evidence is drawn from such prescriptive texts as the *Ecclesiastical Ordinances* of 1541, but recently social historians have explored other avenues and have called into question the reliability of the *Ordinances* as a guide to actual practice before 1550.

The purpose of the present chapter is to re-examine where and when Genevans worshipped from the beginning of the Protestant reform to the end of Calvin's life. Particular attention is given to the early period, especially 1536-1550, since that is the least clear and thus the most controversial. The project is divided into two main parts. First is a shorter discussion of the physical locations of worship, from the Rive before Calvin's arrival until the full urban parish system was functioning. Brief notes about accommodations for the worship of refugee communities are included. Part two addresses the times of worship. In this longer section the historiographical arguments are outlined, the evidence for the types and frequency of services is examined, and the development of the organization over time is traced.

I: The Places of Worship

Where did Protestant Geneva worship? This seems like a simple question, and the answer is straightforward for most of Calvin's ministry. The common names for the locations of worship are the three parishes established by the 1541 *Ecclesiastical Ordinances*: St. Pierre, St. Gervais, and La Magdeleine.[1] That is not the whole story, however, and there has been some controversy recently, so it is worthwhile to outline the rather confused situation prior to the 1541 *Ordinances*, before turning to the developments over the course of the rest of Calvin's service in Geneva.

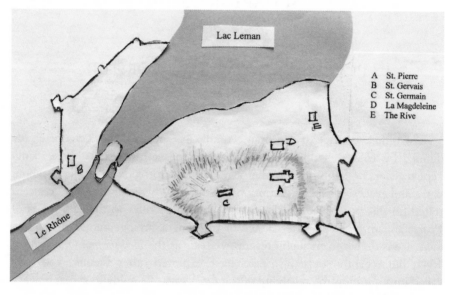

Chap. 1, Fig. 1. Map of the City of Geneva's geographic regions and main churches. Left is the parish of St. Gervais and its church (B), right is Greater Geneva. The oval in the lower middle of Greater Geneva is the Haute Ville, with St. Pierre (A) and St. Germain (C). Surrounding the Haute Ville is the Bas Ville, with La Magdeleine (D) and the Rive (E). Map by John McGlaughlin, based on a 1837 drawing in Doumergue, Tome III, *La Ville, La Maison*, p. 111.

First, however, it is helpful to sketch an overview of the geographic and parochial shape of early modern Geneva. The map in Figure 1 outlines the topography, which to some extent also provides a basic guide to the parishes.[2] The

---

1   *Ordinances*, OC 10:20-21; RCP II, p. 5; OS II, p. 337.

2   The main source for the following description of the city of Geneva is Binz, *Vie religieuse*, pp. 263-69. The basic outline of the map comes from Doumergue, *Tome III: La Ville, La Maison*, p. 111,

smaller part of the city, on the "right bank" of the Rhone descending from the lake (which is actually on the left side of the map), had a single parish, St. Gervais. This was originally a separate village (*vicus*) with its own church, probably dating from the ninth or tenth century. St. Gervais had only been enclosed in the Genevan city fortifications within the last generation; it was sometimes identified as Geneva Minor/"Lesser Geneva" in contrast to the original, larger part of the city east of the Rhone, Geneva Major/"Greater Geneva."[3]

Greater Geneva was made up of two geographic regions. Historically the first to be settled was the section of higher elevation which came to be called the "Haute Ville." This had been enclosed in walls about the sixth century. Here the cathedral of St. Pierre dominated the view; within it was situated the altar of St. Croix which was the focal point of the first parish of Geneva. Not far away was the parish of St. Germain, probably dating before the eleventh century and thus the second one on this side of the river. About that time Geneva began to expand beyond the old walls and into the lower land leading down to Lac Leman to form the "Bas Ville," a kind of half-circle to the north and east of the "Haute Ville." The main parish church of the "Bas Ville" was La Magdeleine, established around the end of the eleventh century and so the third in Greater Geneva. As the crow flies La Magdeleine is quite near St. Pierre, but considerably lower; steep steps built into the retaining wall lead down from the cathedral to the "Bas Ville." The Franciscan house of the Rive was also on this level, closer to the fourteenth-century city walls than La Magdeleine; this was where the first public Protestant preaching took place. The fourth and fifth parishes of St. Victor and St. Leger were established about the same time as La Magdeleine but outside the late medieval fortifications. Along with other extra-mural suburbs, St. Victor and St. Leger were razed in 1531 for the city's defense. About 1250 the tiny parish of Notre Dame la Neuve, in the chapel next to St. Pierre, was carved out as a sixth separate entity, completing the number of parishes in Greater Geneva and its immediate environs.

---

although several maps by Louis Blondel have also been consulted; see Blondel, *Développement urbain de Genève à travers les siècles* (Genève: Cahiers de préhistoire et d'archéologie, 1946), pp. 39, 49. Doumergue's map was drawn by General Dufour in 1837, based on his own observations of the three levels of city fortifications: the Burgundian @500, the episcopal between 1364 and 1378 , and the early modern for which building started in the parish of St. Gervais in 1475 although progress was slow and the walls were not begun until 1490. See Doumergue, pp. 91, 98, 112 et passim. The present map was drawn by Dr. John McGlaughlin, using Dufour's outlines.

3   The terms "Geneva Major/ Geneva Minor" come from the map of Geneva by Rudolf-Manuel Deutsch, published in Sebastian Münster's *Cosmographia Universalis*, 1550. RC IV, p. 467 n.27 identifies this as the first realist view of Geneva.

The seven parishes of late medieval Geneva were served by perhaps as many as twenty parish ministers. The latter carried out the sacramental liturgies, both in the churches and in the homes of their parishioners; respect for parish boundaries was a significant concern, and priests were liable to judicial procedures if they operated outside their own jurisdictions. For example, there were disputes about pastoral care for members of St. Gervais who happened to live across the Rhone in Greater Geneva. If someone was dying at night and the priest could not come because the bridge was closed, the person might die without the final rites because a neighboring priest from outside the parish would not come and risk the repercussions of infringing on someone else's territory.[4] On the other hand, the people were much less concerned about such niceties. Although they were supposed to participate regularly in their home parishes, Genevans often attended Mass in other communities, such as their confraternities. There were probably about four hundred clergy in the city; since each priest had to celebrate one Mass each day, and the houses of the friars were popular, there were considerably more options than dutifully going to one's own parish.[5]

The physical structures are only one part of the equation; the other is the character of the religious services which take place in those structures. While the main liturgical work of a parish priest was administering the sacraments, Protestant worship gave pride of place to preaching, which required a rather different set of skills and much more education than practically any Genevan priest could claim. This point will be considered more in the next chapter. For present purposes, the issue is the effect on worship of this emphasis on preaching. Simply put, when the Protestant services began, there were very few qualified preachers, so the number of places where worship could be held was much more limited than before the reform. Even providing services for all the parishes was out of the question. When Geneva voted "to follow the gospel," where would the new preaching be established? For St. Gervais, there was no question. However, determining a suitable place or places in Greater Geneva was not a foregone conclusion. Besides the fact that preachers were limited, one reason may have been that for years the city government apparently resisted reorganizing (and consolidating) the parishes. This was finally accomplished when Calvin returned in 1541. Then the people of the five small parishes in Greater Geneva – all except those of La Magdeleine – would be combined into one parish of St. Pierre, which

---

4   Burnett suggests that pre-Reformation Geneva "had at least nine, and perhaps as many as twenty parish clergy," "A Tale of Three Cities," p. 110. Binz describes the pastoral problems of St. Gervais, *Vie religieuse*, pp. 267-69.

5   See Lambert, *Preaching, Praying and Policing*, pp. 199-203, 113-19.

would cover essentially the "Haute Ville," since the residents of St. Victor and St. Leger had to move within the city walls when their communities were razed. The result would be the three known parishes of Calvin's day: St. Gervais on one side of the Rhone, and St. Pierre and La Magdeleine on the other.[6]

Buildings formed the concrete topography of Geneva, but the religious landscape also included the bells which called people to worship on either side of the city. The traditional liturgical and devotional life of medieval Geneva was woven through with the sound of bells. These rang not only for the Mass and holy day celebrations of the community, for processions and to drive away plague from the city, but also for the monastic hours of the monks and nuns in their chapels, for deaths and particular moments in personal life (such as a woman in childbed or the miracle of a still-born child "resurrected" to be baptized at Notre Dame de Grace). Church buildings of all kinds, not just parishes, had bells. The cathedral possessed an impressive series; the largest bell, called "Clemence," was inscribed with the words: "I praise God, I call the people, I gather the clergy together, I weep for the dead, I drive away the plague, I provide decoration for the feasts. My voice is the terror of all the demons."[7]

One of the acts of Protestants which markedly changed the daily religious ambiance of Geneva was the silencing of most of the bells, most of the time. Beginning even before the reform had gained official acceptance, the magistrates took over control of the bells. After May 1536, "bells were rung only to indicate the hours, to call the faithful to worship and the citizens to meetings of the [various larger] councils." The Senate also determined to dismantle most of the bells and melt them down to make the cannons which Geneva so much needed to defend itself against Savoy.[8] In principle, one set of bells for each part of the city was sufficient, those of St. Pierre for Greater Geneva and those of St. Gervais for that side of the Rhone.

---

6   *Ordinances*, OS II, p. 337. Lambert, *Preaching, Praying and Policing*, pp. 205-07. Calvin's complaint to Bullinger in 1538 about the parishes and installing preachers indicates the reluctance to reorganize the parishes; see chap. 2 at n.7. Burnett points out that even when it was reorganized, the city parish system in Geneva was weaker than that in Basel or Strasbourg, see "A Tale of Three Cities," pp.109-10. It is noteworthy that Doumergue does not provide a map of the parishes, despite all his detailed exploration of each feature and building of the city in Tome III, *La Ville, La Maison*. Evidently the parochial structure was not graven into the city's new topography as it had been earlier.

7   Grosse, *Les rituels de la Cène*, pp. 59-61; *"Laudo Deum, plebem voco, cungrego clerum, defunctes ploro, pestem fugo, festa decoro. Vox mea cunctorum sit terror daemoniorum,"* p. 59.

8   Grosse, *Les rituels de la Cène*, pp. 64-68, quotation p. 67.

Places of Worship 1536-1541

A reasonably reliable picture of places of worship in the period 1536 to 1541/42 can be pieced together from various sources, producing the picture of three main places where services were held. The first was the auditorium at the Franciscan monastery of the Rive, the other two were the church buildings of St. Gervais and St. Pierre. The development of this organization and the evidence for it can be set out in several stages, from the informal to the official, with special attention to which buildings were associated with what days and times. Since St. Gervais was essentially self-contained, the question about places is principally concerned with Greater Geneva.

Sundays

When the small group of Protestants grew too large to gather in a private house, the Rive became the first "public" location of Protestant preaching in the early 1530s,[9] and it seems to have retained the role of a favored worship site in Greater Geneva until at least late in 1540. After the city-state voted "to follow the gospel" in May 1536, the cathedral came into Protestant control, but it appears to have functioned chiefly for Sundays, perhaps in part because it was too large for ordinary gatherings. What may be the first explicit order about the new worship practices antedates the actual confessional change; on Feb. 22, 1536, the council established a sermon service at dawn in St. Pierre for servants.[10] The *Articles*, the church order enacted at the beginning of 1537, gives some information about actual practice when it plans that the Lord's Supper will be held once each month in "one of the three places where preaching is now being held, that is St. Pierre, the Rive, and St. Gervais."[11] The rotating monthly sacrament (one month at St. Pierre, the next at the Rive, the next at St. Gervais and then the cycle repeated) which Calvin proposed was rejected by the government; however, for present

---

9   See Antoine Froment, *Les actes et gestes merveilleux de la cité de Genève...*, ed. G. Revilliod (Genève: Fick, 1854), p. 82. Farel also preached in St. Pierre even before Protestants received control; Grosse, *Les rituels de la Cène*, p.57.

10 On Feb. 3, 1538, the General Council gathered for the election of the syndics in the cloister of St. Pierre, not the church, because the acoustics were better in the smaller place; see RC III, p. 62: "pour ce que l'audience y est melleur que en ce grand tabernacle dict l'esglise, auquel, à cause de sa grandeur et aulteur, si fort retonné..." Feb. 22, 1536, RC 29 f22v: "pour l'instruction des serviteurs et des chambrieres aux afferes de leurs maistres occupés sera presche à sainct Pierre les dimanches matin au son de la cloche," archives@etat.ge.ch accessed Aug. 1, 2013. For the meaning of "matin" as a designation of time, see below.

11 *Articles*, OS 1, p. 371. In fact, the monthly communion rotating among the three worship places was not enacted, but the statement indicates that the three places were indeed in use.

purposes the point is that there was preaching in all three locations. It is almost certain that this meant Sunday services held during the morning but not simultaneously. Evidently there was still either some confusion or more likely foot-dragging, and particular individuals (e.g., servants) did not come to worship; so on March 30, 1537, the government ordered that everyone must attend Sunday worship (no churches specified), and specifically repeated the instruction for servants to come to the [dawn] "morning" service in St. Pierre. [12]

Notes from council records contribute to the pieces of the puzzle, and knowledge of later practice can suggest ways to interpret the scanty evidence. In another instruction, also dated March 30, 1537, the Senate told all its members and the city officers to come for the Lord's Supper and sermon together in the chapel of St. Ambrose in the Rive. [13] Since the sacrament was held only on Sundays and only in the mornings, this evidently meant the upcoming Easter communion. Perhaps the point of ordering all the magistrates to the Rive was to be able to verify their presence in the smaller venue. It is almost certain the dawn service at St. Pierre was a celebration of the Lord's Supper because it was necessary for all Genevans, including the servants who typically attended the early sermon, to have the opportunity to share in the sacrament. The rotation of Supper services which Calvin proposed in the 1537 *Articles* would make sense only if the service at St. Pierre included the sacrament. Regulations about bells provide some further information; on Saturday April 28, 1537, an order is given to pay two men to ring the "bishop's" bell on Sunday "[early] morning." Here it is apparently the dawn service at St. Pierre which is intended; the largest bell was used only for the main Sunday and day of prayer services. [14]

The following year, St. Pierre, St. Gervais, and the Rive are in fact the three places where the Senate anticipated having the Lord's Supper celebrated when on Thursday, April 18, 1538, they appointed three of their number who would

---

[12] *Sources du Droit de Genève* II, pp. 336-37, for March 30, 1537: "Que toutes manieres de gens soyent tenus et doebjent venir le dimenche ouyr la parolle de Dieu, icelle devotement escouter et selon icelle se regir ... Les serviteurs et chambrieres doenjent venir au sermon le matin le dimenche en l'esglise nommee Sainct Pierre," as quoted in Lambert, *Preaching, Praying and Policing*, p. 183 n.66.

[13] RC II, p. 126: "Icy est arresté que l'on doege faire venir tous les conseilliers et officiers de la ville au sermon et à la Cene de Nostre-Seigneur, et doegent estre ensemble en la chappelle Sainct-Ambroye, à Riva."

[14] April 28, 1537 (RC II, p. 156): "L'on a laché le curtil de Nostre-Dame-la Nove à Dolen et à mestre Jhoan Coctaid pour la poenne de se qu'il sonne la cloche de l'Esvesque le dym[en]che matin." For identifying "dimenche matin" as dawn, see below, at nn.75ff. See May 31, Sept. 17, Dec. 19, 1539, paying for ringing largest bell (for Sunday); RC IV, pp. 246, 434, 568. Nov. 26, 1541, OC 21:285 (RC 35 f370) ringing largest bell for day of prayer.

arrange for the Easter communion the next Sunday.[15] Before that day the conflict
with ministers Farel, Calvin, and Corauld came to a head; after they were exiled,
for a time the city had only two preachers, Henri de la Mare and Jacques Bernard.
On Friday April 26, 1538, the Easter Lord's Supper was rescheduled for the
following Sunday, to be held in only two of the regular places, St. Gervais and the
Rive, owing to the lack of sufficient preachers for the three usual places. The same
situation continued for the next Supper service in June.[16] Apparently in the early
years, when the Senate was forced to choose between the cathedral and the Rive,
the latter was preferred. (It is possible that this meant the temporary omission
of the servants' dawn service at St. Pierre. Since there was such an effort to get
them in the habit of attending at dawn, it is possible that the reduction of services
primarily had to do with the complex preparations for the Supper and some
preaching services continued.)

Weekdays

Although there is very little information about the location of weekday
worship, it is most likely that St. Gervais and the Rive were the usual locations.
St. Gervais was the only preaching place in that part of Geneva and this served
for daily as well as Sunday services. For Greater Geneva, the earliest official
location for the daily sermon was probably St. Germain, according to a Senate
decision on Sept. 8, 1536.[17] However, within a few months (February 1537),
this building was requested by the butchers for commercial use and by
March 29 the Council of Two Hundred had granted it to them,[18] so it was
obviously no longer a worship place. This timing coincides perfectly with the
decision by the Senate on March 30, cited above, to order its members to attend
sermon and Supper in the chapel of St. Ambrose at the Rive. While the order
refers to Easter Sunday, the Senate seems to be signaling a change from
previous practice, so this is probably the instruction to supersede the order
about daily worship at St. Germain. In fact the actual displacement of the
services almost certainly took place sooner, since the January 1537 *Articles* do
not mention St. Germain in their list of the "three places where preaching is

---

[15]   RC III, p. 225: "Son esté helyeuz pour mectre ordre de fere laz Cennaz dymenche prochaien, az
       Sainct-Pierre: le seygneur [Anthoenne] Ciquand, az Sainct-Gervays: Fransoys Lullin et az Rivaz:
       le seygneur Gerardin de laz Rivaz, et fere pourvysion du paien et du vin etc." It is not perfectly
       clear what the three men will do besides provide the elements, but it appears that each one is
       charged to participate in a specific location.

[16]   April 26, 1538, RC III, p. 239; Fri. June 7, 1538, for following Sunday; RC III, p. 306.

[17]   RC I, p. 134.

[18]   Feb. 27 & March 29, 1537, RC II, pp. 91, 123.

now being held,"[19] and the March instruction to the Senate members and city officials may be a belated and official recognition of this.

No further explicit references to the place of daily worship in Greater Geneva seem to be available until October 1540. On Oct. 20 that year a request to build a bath next to the Rive is rejected because "there is preaching at the Rive." However, there was apparently some further reflection about when there would be services at the Rive. A few days later, on Oct. 28, it was decided to remain in the customary place at the Rive "established for preaching on Sunday" but to hold the weekday sermons in the choir of St. Pierre on days when the Senate met.[20] The implication is that the Rive was established for Sunday worship and will continue so, but the daily preaching which had been held there would be moved to the cathedral. However, it is quite possible that the daily service did not actually change location for some months, because on June 27, 1541, the Senate again ordered that St. Pierre be repaired for use on weekdays when the council met (so apparently weekday worship was still located at the Rive).[21] To summarize, therefore: for most of the early years of Protestant preaching there were weekday sermons in two of the three regularly used places: the Rive and St. Gervais.

Repairs and Changes

Another index of which buildings were used for worship is the ways the latter were being equipped or repaired, and this could also indicate changes in the location of services. On the one hand, the newly universal emphasis on hearing sermons brought with it the need for benches to seat the congregation, so regular "pews" for all the people were a typical Protestant innovation in churches. As Christian Grosse points out, benches were not invented by Protestants and had in fact been introduced in St. Pierre in the thirteenth and fourteenth centuries when preaching began to be more important; nonetheless episcopal authorities had resisted the generalizing of this practice and most churches had no regular seating.[22] Some churches also lacked pulpits, or if they had such things these were not always well suited to projecting voices and needed improvements, such as a sounding board overhead. On the other hand, the traditional equipment of

---

[19] *Articles*, OS I, p. 371.

[20] Oct. 20 & 28, 1540, RC V, p. 588 proposed; p. 609 : "que l'on demore en laz place mesme az Rivaz accoustumé, establye pour prescher les dymenches, et aut cueur de Sainct-Pierre pour prescher les jours ordinayres du Conseyl. "

[21] OC 21:280 (RC 35 f245); cf. Lambert, *Preaching, Praying and Policing*, p. 206 n.117.

[22] Grosse indicates that while some medieval churches had seating, and benches were introduced in the cathedral in the 13th and 14th centuries when preaching began to be more important, church authorities resisted the generalizing of this practice; *Les rituels de la Cène*, p. 268.

churches included baptisteries and altars, all of which were removed in the first
Protestant reforms of Geneva in 1536.[23] The Supper was celebrated only three or
at most four times a year in the city, and tables could be set up more easily.
Baptisms, however were naturally much more frequent so the decisions about
furnishings for this liturgy became fairly urgent when the city again changed its
mind about ceremonies in 1538.

Senate notes about benches and pulpits and baptisteries provide glimpses of
the buildings Genevans used for worship. In May 1538, in accordance with the
decision to follow Bernese ceremonial practice, the Senate issued an order to set
up baptisteries again in three places: St. Pierre, St. Gervais, and La Magdeleine.
Evidently, however, this was not immediately implemented. In December of
1538, the preachers asked for repairs at the Rive so that snow would not fall
through the roof onto the communion table; they also repeated their request for
baptisteries, and further asked that one be placed at the Rive.[24] This request
supports the idea that the Rive was functioning as a regular worship place on
weekdays as well as Sundays. As a monastic chapel it would not originally have
been used for baptisms on any regular basis and probably never had a baptistery,
but now that piece of furniture was needed. The following March the ministers
came to the Senate again about lack of proper equipment and poor conditions "in
places where there is preaching"; benches are explicitly named and must have
been the most serious lacuna in proper furnishings. The council responded
positively and in July 1539 payment was ordered for the boatman who trans-
ported wood for the benches.[25]

The order for re-installing baptisteries had included the church of La Magdeleine. However, there is no evidence of preaching being held in this building until
1541, although La Magdeleine had been "the most populous parish in the city" (as
well as the wealthiest) before the Reformation.[26] In August 1539 a Senate note
approved moving ammunition from the chapel of the Molard to La Magdeleine, so
apparently the building was being used for storage. However, a few months later,
on Dec. 6, 1539, La Magdeleine was identified as a suitable place for preaching.[27]

---

[23] Roset, *Les chroniques de Genève*, pp. 249, 255.

[24] Thurs. May 16, Tues. Dec. 3, 10 and 20, RC III, pp. 267, 507-08, 515, 527.

[25] RC IV, pp. 120, 121, 301.

[26] See Lambert, *Praying, Preaching and Policing*, p. 35.

[27] Aug. 29 & Dec. 6, 1539; RC IV, pp. 396, 540. These dates and all but one of those in the next note
     (which is an order for payment for wood for La Magdeleine) are Saturdays, not regular council
     days, which suggests that concerns about churches were less vital matters to the Senate than some
     other business, but that they were willing to meet even on a Saturday to get the work done.

Over the course of the next year the floors and windows (decorated with the city coat of arms) were repaired, work was done on the pulpit to add a sounding board (and "painting"!), and the church was furnished with benches.[28]

Places of Worship 1541-1564

The church of St. Gervais remained the fixed locus of worship in its parish, but the years 1541-42 were a time of transition with regard to the location of worship services on the other side of the Rhone in Greater Geneva. At the beginning of this period, the two buildings in use were the cathedral and the Rive; by the middle of 1542, La Magdeleine had replaced the Rive. As noted above, the repairs on St. Pierre seem to have been undertaken rather more slowly than the Senate intended, and it is not clear precisely when the cathedral came into use for daily worship (as well as on Sundays).

When the 1541 *Ordinances* were being written, although Sunday dawn services were to be held at St. Pierre (as had been the practice since 1536), the location for the main Sunday morning service was first marked as "the Rive (St. Pierre)" and then the Rive was struck from the text in favor of St. Pierre.[29] (All) the Sunday services would be held at St. Pierre. Apparently the Rive was still on the roster but its state of disrepair was so great that on May 19, 1542, the Senate decreed that "for the present it is ordered that the sermon be done every day at St. Pierre."[30] Whether this reference to the daily use of the cathedral was put into practice or not is unclear because other arrangements had apparently already been made for weekday worship – probably by April. Daily worship at the "ordinary" hour had begun at La Magdeleine at least by the end of that month; for example, on April 27, 1542, the consistory decided that Claudaz, wife of Michel Julliard, and Jehan de La Pierre were to be reconciled next "Monday after the sermon at La Magdeleine."[31] Preaching assignments from this same period make no

---

28 Jan. 10 & 16, Feb. 7, April 2, 1540; RC V, pp. 28-29, 51, 102, 219. On Jan. 10 the carpenter is paid "pour le tabernacle et accoustrement de laz chiere du temple de laz Magdalene..." (p. 29). The "tabernacle" is the sounding board. The "pictures" on the pulpit are somewhat of a puzzle; Feb. 7, RC V, p. 102: "Fayct mandement aut tressorier de lyvrer az maystre Jacques de L'Arpaz, pinctre, pour les pictures* qu'il az fayct à laz chiere du temple de laz Magdalene, 12 ff." There is no further explanation for these "pictures" – from the word for painting, not necessarily meaning an image or scene; perhaps he was painting over some inappropriate art, or perhaps putting the city coat of arms on the pulpit?

29 *Ordinances*, OS 1, p. 337.

30 OC 21:296 (RC 36 f18); archives@etat.ge.ch accessed July 24, 2014.

31 *Consist.* I, p. 48.

mention of the Rive.[32] Despite the complicated route to reach that point, it is clear that by mid-1542 regular worship was being held on Sundays and weekdays in the three parishes defined by the 1541 *Ordinances*: St. Pierre, St. Gervais, and La Magdeleine. Which specific services, on which days, were done in which parish building, however, will be examined later in this chapter.

Worship in these three parishes remained the basic organization[33] during Calvin's ministry, with some additions in the 1550s when the influx of refugees into Geneva led to a need for more spaces. Accommodating the small Italian congregation in 1551 did not require another building; they were allowed to hold their weekday services at La Magdeleine after the regular French sermon there.[34] However, by 1555 there were not only more refugees but also more language groups. First the Rive (which was used during the weekdays for the main city school) was made available on Sunday for the catechism lessons of the Italian church.[35] Then in November Notre Dame la Neuve, next door to the cathedral, was refurbished with pulpit and benches for use by the Italian and English language congregations; each would have certain days for their weekday services.[36] In 1557 St. Germain was re-opened as a French-speaking parish, with its

---

[32] See chap. 2, at nn.36, 43. There certainly were not two sets of sermons at the "ordinary" time in Greater Geneva, so if there was daily worship at La Magdeleine there would not have been at St. Pierre except for the Mon.-Wed.-Fri. dawn services.

[33] On occasion, practical circumstances might influence a temporary dislocation, e.g., when the fabric of La Magdeleine needed repairs, the service was temporarily moved to St. Pierre. On Feb. 5, 1545: "Le temple de La Magdeleine. Lequelt l'on doubte qu'il ne tombe en ruyne. Ordonné qu'il soyt raccoustré et cependant soyt presché aut temple Saint-Pierre"; RC 39 f124; quoted in Lambert, *Preaching, Praying, and Policing*, p. 213 n.141. Another factor was the weather: a particularly hot or cold season, especially in later years when there were crowds of people, might lead to moving services from one place to another. See examples in 1559 cited below at nn.145f.

[34] Nov. 26, 1551, OC 21:493 (RC 45 f102): "Sus ce qu'il a proposé que plusieurs ytaliens que sont icy qu'il desireroit que la doctrine de Dieu leur fusse annuncee en leur langue... leur soit donne place au temple de la Magdalenne et l'heure asçavoir incontinent apres le sermon ordinaire que se y faict."

[35] May 30, 1555 (RC 49 f93): Calvin explains that the Italians "n'ont lieu commode pour faire leur catechisme. Qu'il plaise à Messieurs leur permettre en la sale de Rive faire ledict catechisme. ... Quant à ladicte sale pour le catechisme qu'on le concede ainsin qu'est requys.

[36] June 10, 1555, OC 21:608 (RC 49 f102): "Des anglois. ledict Spectable Calvin a proposé que aucuns anglois seroient en desir de retirer icy pour la parolle de Dieu et qu'il plaise à messieurs leur auctroyer eglise pour pouvoir prescher et ministrer les sacremens." Oct. 24, 1555, OC 21:617 (RC 50 f17v): Nothing has been done; "qu'il pleut de recevoir des Anglois qui debvoient venir icy pour l'evangile et de leur conceder ung temple pour administrer la parolle et sacremens, dont luy fut allors respondu que on leur provoistroit ou à Saint Germain ou à nostre dame la nove: parquoy attendu qu'il y en a desja partie qui sont venuz requiert continuer le bon vouloir: car autrefoys lesdictz Anglois ont receu les autres nations et leur ont donné eglise: mais

own ministers and parish book for baptisms and marriages. The following year the small group of Spanish refugees was also given space to worship there.[37] With the continuing advent of refugees, more services were begun in St. Pierre and La Magdeleine, buildings already in regular use, but no more locations were added.

By 1560 French and English refugees were returning home and ministers were being called to serve in France, either in parishes or (temporarily) in the religious colloquies, so some of the additional services (the dawn sermons at La Magdeleine, and weekday ones at St. Germain) were suspended in September,[38] and in October 1561 the parish of St. Germain was closed.[39] Now the city of Geneva functioned again with its three parishes of St. Pierre, St. Gervais, and La Magde-

---

maintenant il a pleu à Dieu de les affliger: parquoy requiert leur proveoir." Nov. 14, 1555, OC 21:619 (RC 50 f35v): "qu'on leur concede le temple de Marie la nove et qu'ilz y facent leurs commoditez requises. " Nov. 25, 1555, OC 21:620-621 (RC 50 f46): "Calvin. en premier a proposé suyvant l'ordonnace faictes pour les sermons des Italliens et Angloys et que ont establie chascungs deulx troys jours asavoir les Italliens le jeudy le vendredy et sambedy et precheront à l'heure qui hont acoustumé et lesdictz Angloys hont establié le lundy mardy et mescredi et precheront à neufz heures requerant que leurs soit proveu d'une cloche etc. Et pareillementz que presenteront ledit ministre pour le examine[r] et accepter. Arresté qu'il leurs soit baillier pour sonne[r] la cloche de la temousaz (?) et que Messieurs facent faire la chiere et les bamps à nostre dame la novez ainsi appellé."

37 July 12, 1557, OC 21:668-69 (RC 53 f234): electing ministers "pour nostres eglise de Saint Germain nouvellement preparee pour l'abondance du peuple par la grace de Dieu en ceste cité ce qui a esté faict par la grace de Dieu…." Oct. 10, 1558, OC 21:706 (RC 54 f302): "Eglise des Hispanolz. Ledit Sr. Calvin a aussi proposé que les Hespagnolz luy ont donné charge de requerir Messieurs de leur donner place au temple S. Germain pour y ouir la parolle de Dieu en leur langue veu qu'il y a ung homme ancien de bonne conversation qui leur preschera. Arresté qu'on accorde qu'ilz preschent à S. Germain à l'heure qui leur sera la plus commode."

38 Sept. 6, 1560, OC 21:735 (RC 56 f76v): "Ministres Sermons. Les spectables Calvin et Viret ministres ont proposé comme ilz sont fort chargés à cause de l'absence de deux de leurs compagnons et des malades et mortz tellement qu'ilz sont contrainctz d'envoyer aux villages. Mais quand il plaira à Messieurs qu'à cause des malades l'on se pourra bien passer de prescher de matin à la Magdeleine et à S. Germain les jours ovriers. A esté sus ce arresté qu'on face comme ilz auront cognu et cognoistront estre à faire et qu'on s'en remet à leur discretion et prudence." The dawn services at La Magdeleine were those on Sundays and Wednesdays begun in late 1559 for about a year.

39 Oct. 13, 1561, OC 21:763 (RC 56 f248v): "Ici a esté parlé que les Srs. ministres sont fort chargés de faire tant de sermons et d'aultant qu'il y en a plusieurs absens pour le colloque que se tient en France aussi que le peuple n'est si grand comme il souloit par cy devant: arresté qu'on advise d'admoindrir qu'on ne presche en tant de lieux et cela servira aussi que là ou l'on preschera sera mieux furni de gens et y aura plus grande audience." Oct. 14, 1561, OC 21:763 (RC 56 249v): "Sermons. Suivant l'advis de M. Calvin d'aultant que beaucoup de gens s'en sont allés aussi que aucuns des ministres sont absens: arresté qu'on ne [presche] plus à S. Germain jusques à plus grande opportunité." It would be reopened in 1569 ; cf. chap. 2 at n.100.

leine, although with an expanded number of services, and this organization was given post-facto recognition in the revised *Ordinances* in 1561.[40]

II: Times of Worship

The question of times and frequency of worship in Geneva's early years as a Protestant city is more elusive and complicated than the choice of buildings. This is true not only because of the limited amount of evidence before 1550, but also because of the more uneven nature of that documentation and the many more variables involved. Use of three to five buildings can be traced, but the organization of dozens of sermons at different times is rather more complicated. The first short section surveys the earliest Protestant period before Calvin's return in 1541. These years usually receive only a few sentences; given the paucity of sources, scholars normally focus on the church order as established by the *Ecclesiastical Ordinances*.[41] Here that is also the case, but an effort has been made to provide a fuller overview of the initial schedule of public worship (1534)1536-1541. Then the second part of this investigation turns to an analysis of the historiographical arguments about the number and organization of services as defined by the *Ordinances* in 1541, especially recent scholars' challenges to the value of that text as a reliable index of actual practice. The third section examines evidence which can illuminate what was in fact done, i.e., how many and when services were held both on Sundays and on weekdays.

Times of Worship 1536-1541

There are several sources for the number and times of worship services for the period 1534 to 1541, and various eye witness accounts name both Sundays and weekday sermons. Daily Protestant preaching appears to have begun already even

---

[40] *Ordinances* 1561, OC 10:99-100. "Les jours ouvriers qu'il y ait presche tous les jours es trois parroisses, sainct Pierre, la Magdalene et sainct Gervais à une mesme heure: assavoir, d'esté depuis Pasques jusques au premier d'octobre, des six heures jusques à sept; et d'hyver, des sept heures jusques à huict. Mais que les prières soyent faites specialement le jour de Mercredi, sinon que ci apres fust establi autre jour selon l'opportunité du temps. Outre lesdites predications, qu'on presche trois fois la sepmaine de matin à sainct Pierre: assavoir le Lundi, Mercredi et Vendredi: et à sainct Gervais le Mercredi, avant les susdits sermons ordinaires." The dawn services at St. Gervais on Wednesdays had not been foreseen in 1541; the weekday services at St. Pierre at the regular hour had not been planned.

[41] Lambert's discussion of the 1530s explains the establishment of the reform and briefly cites Saunier as evidence for "five sermons on Sundays and two on each of the other days," *Preaching, Praying, Policing*, p. 285. From this he moves directly to the organization of preaching after Calvin's return in 1541.

before 1534. Antoine Froment, one of the preachers in the circle around Farel, describes daily sermons preached in homes during the transitional conflict.[42] Jeanne de Jussie, the chronicler of the St. Clare convent, complains that in Lent 1534 the "heretics" began to preach at the Rive and "from then on never failed any day, and twice on all the feasts and Sundays."[43] Another hostile source, the preacher Cutellier, adds some details, complaining that bells were rung to call people to the sermon when Farel preached every afternoon in Lent 1534.[44] Evidently before the city declared itself Protestant, the times of preaching were not fixed; some were in the morning and some (particularly when competing with the traditional Lenten series) were in the afternoon – but still publicly announced by the ringing of bells. The vote by which Geneva declared itself for the reform on May 21, 1536, speaks of daily sermons since the abolition of the Mass.[45]

The organization became somewhat more orderly when the new preachers were in charge. Antoine Saunier, another who served with Farel as a preacher in the early years of the reform and who then became head of the school until he left Geneva at the end of 1538, is a significant witness for the period 1536-38. The information Saunier provides is more helpful for the number and days of services than for specific times or places. In 1538 he summarizes the worship practice.

> [E]very Sunday there are five sermons of the pure and simple Word of God, but on each of the other days there are only two. The hours are set so that one can easily attend all the aforesaid sermons, one after the other.[46]

[42] Antoine Froment, *Les actes et gestes merveilleux de la cité de Geneve* (Genève : Jules Guillaume Fick, 1854), chap. 15, pp. 91-92 : "Lesquelz preschoint tous les jours en publicque, et d'heure en heure ça et là par les maysons au grand aduancement de la parolle de Dieu."

[43] Jeanne de Jussie, *Le levain du Calvinisme*, p. 86: "Et l'an 1534, preschant le Caresme le Venerable Pere Gardien des grands Cordeliers de sainct François de Chambery. Le premier Dimanche, qui estoit le premier jour de Mars, apres le sermon dudit Reverend Pere, les Lutheriens estoient assemblez au Conuent de Rive, ils se pendent à la cloche, & sonnent environ une heure, & puis veulent ou non les Chrestiens, prindrent la possession de prescher, & depuis n'y faillirent nuls jours, & toutes les festes & Dimanches deux fois, dont les Chrestiens estoient bien marris."

[44] Grosse, *Les rituels de la Cène*, p. 63.

[45] May 21, 1536 ; OC 21:201-02 (RC 29 f112): the people are asked if they want to live "selon l'evangille et la parole de Dieu ainsy que dempuis l'abolition des messes nous est esté preschee et se presche tous les jours..."

[46] Saunier, *L'ordre et maniere d'enseigner*, p. 12 of non-paginated text : "En la mesme ville tous les dimenches y a cinq sermons de la pure & simple parolle de Dieu, mais chacun des autres jours y en a seulement deux : & sont les heures distribuées de telle sorte qu'on peult facilement assister à tous les dessusdicts sermons l'vng après l'autre." (Since the punctuation of Saunier's reference to sequential times of the service is modern, it is unclear whether it refers to Sundays, weekdays, or both. The grammar implies Sundays are included, the later Genevan practice suggests that it refers to weekdays.)

(Precisely what is meant by the sequencing of the different service times will be examined below; the instruction seems to have been a popular one in Geneva, as the council added this to Calvin's draft *Ordinances* in 1541.[47])

Sunday worship was regularly held at St. Pierre, St. Gervais, and the Rive, according to the statement in the 1537 *Articles*, so at least one of Saunier's five services must have been held at each location. As noted above, on Feb. 22, 1536, a service specifically for servants was established, to be held at dawn on Sunday at St. Pierre; the point was explicitly to accommodate members of the community who would normally be busy with their masters' affairs. It also served members of smaller households who had to attend worship in relays.[48] The order to the servants was repeated on March 30, 1537. Then on Feb. 16, 1540, it is noted that they are (still) not obeying so the language this time implies that masters should be sending their servants.[49] Obviously the services were happening but the participation was not what was hoped. This would then be one of Saunier's Sunday services. There must have been one at mid-morning in St. Gervais because all the residents of that part of the city could not be expected to cross the river every week; this would be another of Saunier's five. There was then either a second at St. Pierre at mid-morning, or at the Rive, or possibly both; this may have changed over time. On May 12, 1536, the Roman priests who had broken the prohibition against saying Mass were ordered brought to the Rive on the next Sunday "at the sermon" to confess their fault before the people and be forgiven.[50] Although it is not stated that this is a morning service, everything points to that, since the object was the most public possible occasion for repentance and reconciliation. It is

---

[47] See below at nn.131ff.

[48] See n.8 above. Examples of families attending in relays : cf. *Consist.* I, on Oct. 19, 1542, p. 132, Pierre Dolen: "il vaz aux sermons quand il peult aller et qu'il fault que se garde la mayson quand saz femme vaz au sermon." On Nov. 9, 1542, p. 137, Jana, wife of Jaques Symond, says she cannot go to sermons [on weekdays] because her husband scarcely stays at home and she has to keep house. On Sundays she goes willingly and her husband goes on Wednesdays while she keeps the shop. On May 15, 1544, p. 369, Jaquemaz, wife of Jehan Papilliez, says he goes to sermons and makes her stay home to keep house, though she would like to go. On Nov. 9, 1542, p. 135, La Donne Jaqueline goes on Sunday but other days she orders her servant to go. On Sept. 11, 1550, servants confess fornicating while their master and mistress were at the afternoon service, *Consist.* V, p. 209.

[49] *Sources du Droit de Genève* II, pp. 336-37 for March 30, 1537, orders everyone to attend worship on Sundays and instructs servants to come "au sermon le matin le dimanche en l'esglise nommee Sainct Pierre" as quoted in Lambert, *Preaching, Praying and Policing*, p. 183 n.66. Feb. 16, 1540, RC V, p. 118: "De fere allez les serviteurs et serventes aut sermons les dymenches matin."

[50] May 12, 1536; OC 21:200 (RC 29 f105v): "arresté et resolu que il soyent menez à Riva au sermon dimanche prochain à confesser devant chescung leur meffaict et par telz moyen leur sera pardonné."

possible that later, as the Protestant organization became more firmly established, the main Sunday morning service for Greater Geneva was moved to St. Pierre. This fits with what is known about the major preachers' activities by the time Calvin came, i.e., Farel usually preached at St. Gervais and Calvin at St. Pierre. A single service in Greater Geneva at mid-morning would make (along with the St. Pierre dawn and the St. Gervais main service) the third of Saunier's five. If the fourth service was a morning one, it would be at the Rive, perhaps at a different hour from the one at St. Pierre. Saunier's fifth was almost certainly an afternoon service, although its location is not certain; as will be seen below, it is likely to have been the Rive. If there was not a fourth morning service, then there would have been two Sunday afternoon services, perhaps at the Rive and St. Gervais?

This is where the sequencing of services may have been crucial; the two mid-morning sermons in Greater Geneva might have followed each other, St. Pierre first and then the Rive? If this were the case, it would give a span of three different times on Sunday mornings in that part of the city: dawn, mid-morning, later morning. There would have been a fourth time in Greater Geneva because there is also evidence for a Sunday afternoon service at the Rive at latest by early 1538. On Easter morning, April 21, 1538, Farel was in the pulpit at St. Gervais and Calvin at St. Pierre (despite the Senate's prohibition), and in the afternoon Calvin was at the Rive.[51] It would seem that four of the five sermons: at dawn and mid-morning at St. Pierre, and during the morning and afternoon at the Rive, were in Greater Geneva, leaving only one Sunday service at St. Gervais. In the lead up to the Easter conflict, the Senate ordered Henri de la Mare to preach and celebrate the Supper at St. Gervais. At first he refused to obey the council, on the grounds that Farel and Calvin would not like it, but once the latter were exiled, he conformed.[52] This somewhat odd act on the part of the Senate raises a question which may explain their actions after the troublesome ministers were gone. The question: was the council more doubtful that Farel could be persuaded to conform to the Bernese instructions than Calvin, or was there some other reason they told de La Mare to replace Farel at St. Gervais but do not seem to have prepared someone to step in for Calvin? As was

---

[51] April 21, 1538; RC III, p. 232: "Ay esté proposé coment Faret et Calvin, oultre les deffenses az leur faycte de non poient precher az cause de ce qu'il ne veullent pas optemperer az laz missive envoyé de Berne, lesqueulx, oultre ladt deffence, en mesprisant laz justice, sont aller precher, Calvin à Sainct-Pierre et Faret az Sainct-Gervays." Roset describes the events, *Les Chroniques de Genève*, p. 252 : "& le jour de Pasque preschans devant & après disné, remonstroient au peuple pourquoy ils ne devoient, à leur escient, polluer le Sainct-Sacrament. Le matin fut suscité trouble contre Farel au temple S. Gervais, le soir à Rive contre Calvin."

[52] April 19 & 26, 1538, RC III, pp. 228-41, 239; on April 30 (p. 240) he asks to be settled at St. Gervais.

noted above, after Farel, Calvin, and Corauld were gone the Senate decreed that the Easter communion would be held at the Rive and St. Gervais the following Sunday; there was no mention of St. Pierre. Perhaps the council had already decided that if they could not control Farel and Calvin, they would simply reduce the number of places where services were held and the largest building would be temporarily dropped. For the next several months, as the city struggled with a shortage of preachers, there were probably one or several fewer than five Sunday sermons.

The precise details about the two daily weekday sermons which Saunier mentions are equally difficult to pin down. There is some incidental evidence for there being two sermons on (at least some) weekdays. On Monday June 7, 1540, after a riot on June 6, the preachers ask the authorities for special prayers for "good order," and the Council of Two Hundred orders this to be done the next day "at the two sermons."[53] The language: "the two sermons" implies that everyone knows what is meant, so these are regular occurrences and they are both on the same day; in fact, as will be seen later, this same phrase is used in the *Ordinances*. Logic suggests that "the two sermons" took place in the two parts of the city, St. Gervais and Greater Geneva, since the norm was to provide for the residents on both sides of the river. The services may well have been scheduled at the same time unless this is what Saunier means by the sequencing,[54] and that hour would be set by the traditional times of the daily Mass.

The challenge is verifying that the services were in fact held every weekday, as Saunier says. For this period before the 1541 *Ordinances*, information about the daily sermons is often linked with the governing authorities' devotions. In late medieval Geneva it was the practice for the Senate to attend Mass together before starting their regular meetings which, at least since 1513, had been held at 7 a.m. from Easter until St. Michael's and then at 8 a.m. for the rest of the year. Thus the daily Mass would begin at 6 a.m. in summer and 7 a.m. in winter. This "ordinary" schedule would become the time for the weekday sermon, according to Senate notes from September 1536 and July 1541.[55] The question is how often did the

---

[53]   RC V, p. 341: "aux deux sermons." See below at nn.63f.

[54]   If the number of preachers was so limited that the same ones were doing all the sermons, the two daily sermons could have been sequential. However, it is not likely that the people on the less favored side, St. Gervais, would have tolerated waiting for the preachers to come from Greater Geneva after they had done the service there.

[55]   Sept. 8, 1536, RC I, p. 134: "M. Guil. Farellus [speaks]... Super quod fuit arrestatum quod habeatur sermo matutinus statim post sextam horam de mane in ecclesia S. Germani, in quo consilium teneatur venire ut possent septima intrare consilium." Lambert, *Preaching, Praying, and Policing*, p. 291 n.24 quotes July 18, 1541: "Affin que personne ne perde le sermon, az esté ordonné que le sermon ce doybje sonné az cinq heures et demy du matin et parachevé devant sept" (RC 35 f267v).

Senate meet and were these the only times when services were held? In 1485, regular meetings of this council were scheduled on Tuesdays and Fridays, but on May 30, 1539, Monday meetings were added as well.[56] (These were the required meetings for which councilors were paid a small sum; there were in fact other meetings on almost every day of the week, including sometimes Sundays![57] Meeting time was normally the morning hours, but there are many occasions when at least some of the Senate gathered several times during one day, often after the mid-day dinner at 11 a.m., but occasionally also in the evening or early morning.[58]) The Senate worship obligations only cover two or, after May 1539, three work days: Mondays, Tuesdays, and Fridays. Saunier's text was published in 1538, which means that if there were sermons only on council days (two at that time), then either he was greatly exaggerating the number of weekday sermons, or there was preaching on days when the Senate was not regularly scheduled to meet. The latter seems to have been the case. That preaching services were held on other weekdays can be corroborated by other council notes – usually criticizing some aspect of a sermon. Besides references to Mondays and Tuesdays, Saturdays are also mentioned (April 20, 1538, and Dec. 25, 1540).[59] The latter Saturday was Christmas, which according to the Bernese ceremonies would naturally have a sermon, so it cannot be counted as an ordinary service.

---

56 See the introduction to RC IV: p. xxxii n. 99, cites regulation of 1513, p. xxxii n. 102, adds the meeting on Mondays; cf. also entry for May 30, 1539, RC IV, p. 241.

57 RC I, (for the period May 22 to July 11, 1536), pp. 18, 34, 50, 57 (Mondays), pp. 5, 13, 19, 27, 34, 39, 52, 58, 67 (Tuesdays), pp. 14, 19, 41, 61-62 (Wednesdays), pp. 30, 36, 43, 62 (Thursdays), pp. 7, 15, 23, 30, 36, 46, 54, 64 (Fridays), pp. 4, 26, 38, 49, 55, 66 (Saturdays), pp. 10, 39, 56 (Sundays), etc.

58 Some examples: beginning on Wed. June 21, 1536, until Fri. June 30, there were meetings twice a day except Sunday and Tuesday; once it was the Two Hundred in the morning and Senate "post prandium"; the rest of the times the Senate met both in morning and "post prandium" or later "eodem die"; on Sat. July 1, 1536, it was morning and "post cenam" (RC I, pp. 41-56), and in fact this rhythm is not unusual. "Post prandium" is the most common but "post cenam" also appears fairly regularly (sometimes in the form "après diner," p. 212). The "eodem die" is so frequent as not to be worth citing; "post prandium" also continues regularly in the following years (e.g., RC II, pp. 32, 50, 52, 62, 66, 77, 78, 80, 85, 88, 92, 105, 112, 122, 131, *et passim.*); "apres diner" (RC II, pp. 135, 140, 144, 200). Also "paulo post" (RC II, pp. 192, 196). Later, e.g., 1539, all is French but the sense is the same: "ledict jour" and/or "après diner" (RC IV, pp. 56, 99, 104, 123, 152, 163,184, 205, 215, 220, *et passim.*). Infrequent emergency meetings might be held at other times, as in the emergency of mid-1540; on Sun. June 6, the Senate met at 9 p.m. and ordered a meeting of the Two Hundred the next morning at 5 a.m.; on Sat. June 12, they met at 9 p.m.; on Mon. July 5, they met "de soyer" (RC V, pp. 334, 336, 354, 387).

59 Monday, Sept. 27, 1540; RC V, p. 549. Tuesday, May 7, 1538; RC III, p. 249. Tuesday, May 6, 1539, RC IV, p. 205. Saturdays, April 20, 1538, RC III, p. 230; Dec. 25, 1540, RC V, p. 714.

However, the reference to Corauld's sermon on April 20, 1538, when put in context, gives more weight to Saunier's statement about weekday services on every day. Corauld's appearance in the Senate minutes in April 1538 suggests that he was preaching regularly during the week. On Friday April 19 he is prohibited from any further preaching, with a general reference to "his sermons" criticizing the magistracy. The next morning he preached anyway, for which the council promptly put him in prison.[60] Usually a rebuke comes immediately after a troublesome sermon, either the same day or the following one.[61] The fact that this order comes late in the week yet without reference to "today" or "yesterday," which are common identifiers of particular sermons, seems to imply that what is in view is not a specific sermon but the continuing tenor of his preaching. Earlier notes make it clear that for some time Corauld had been annoying the council with his sermons, and this week – perhaps repeatedly – he had gone too far. Although it is possible that there was special preaching for this period because this was Holy Week and the larger time frame was the traditional Lent, that is extremely improbable. In 1536 Geneva had abolished all special feasts, the Bernese ceremonies did not include such observances, and Geneva did not (re)introduce attention to Passion Week sermons until 1544.[62] Thus it is reasonable to posit that when he was prohibited from preaching and then defied the council by returning to his pulpit on Saturday after their explicit order on Friday, Corauld was in the pulpit daily. Even if this rebuke only had reference to his disobedience on Saturday, it is evidence for a service that day because he would hardly have been preaching if the people where not accustomed to coming on that day, since a congregation or audience was essential for the exercise to make sense. Further, a note on Nov. 18, 1541 (before the *Ordinances* went into effect) appears to indicate regular services, with particular reference to Thursday.[63]

These incidental references to services on Thursdays and Saturdays, added to the Mondays, Tuesdays, and Fridays of the Senate meetings, cover practically the

---

[60] RC III, pp. 227, 229.

[61] For example, on Monday April 8, just a few weeks earlier, Corauld was reprimanded for his preaching, presumably the previous day; RC III, p. 212. See also the Senate's immediate response to Farel and Calvin on Easter day itself, and Monday, Sept. 27, 1540; Tuesday May 7, 1538; Tuesday May 6, 1539; Saturday, Dec. 25, 1540; as well as Saturday April 20, and Sunday April 21, 1538. Calvin's sermon referred to on Tuesday March 12, 1538, RC III, pp. 174-75, is not identified by specific date but is likely to have been that same day.

[62] Passion Week preaching was ordered only in 1544 (Fri. April 21; OC 21:332; cf. chap. 4, nn.67ff).

[63] "Me. Champereaulx az hier dire en luy faysant commandement de alle[r] presche[r] az S. Gervex…" Friday Nov. 18, 1541; OC 21:286 (RC 35 f404).

whole week. It is unlikely that there would have been Saturday or Thursday services and none on Wednesdays. The fact that specific references to sermons on every weekday are not available to corroborate Saunier's generalization about "other days" must not be read as an argument from silence that there were none. For example, no disputes at Friday sermons left traces of those regularly scheduled sermons in the council records but it is accepted that the services were held. So it is reasonable to affirm (unless or until further evidence is found) that Saunier was correct in affirming that there were weekday services, Monday through Saturday, in Geneva before Calvin's *Ordinances* in 1541.

That being the case, it would seem logical to expect some indication of a change in practice if the *Ordinances* did not provide such frequent daily preaching; at the least, one would anticipate expostulations from Calvin. Nothing of the kind is recorded, however; those scholars who maintain that the *Ordinances* were not fully implemented cite Saunier as evidence for preaching in 1538 yet do not explain why the reduction in numbers of services from the period before Calvin's return would be accepted without any comment or protest. It is reasonable then to consider the possibility – or probability – that there was in fact no diminution of the number of weekday services in 1541. Assuming that Saunier was correct, multiple services on Sundays in several places, and two on every weekday (also in different places), were the norm before 1541 and, as will be seen, these continued after Calvin's return.

Scholars' Debates on Schedules of Preaching, 1541-1549/51

The schedule of worship in Calvin's Geneva, especially under the *Ecclesiastical Ordinances'* regulations, has for some time been variously understood. This has been particularly though not exclusively true in the English-speaking world, which has been the locus of most of the interest in actual practice. The issue of how often Calvin preached, or what the schedule of services in Geneva was, has been treated as a subordinate aspect of some other topic. Until now, however, it has not been the subject of a focused investigation. In view of the value of the topic for understanding both Calvin's ministry, and the shape of reform in the city which would become a model for many other churches, it is worth unraveling the somewhat confused story.

Sources

There are multiple potential sources of evidence about the preaching in Protestant Geneva. For many years, scholars were focused on Calvin himself and his sermons; in the last generation attention has shifted in significant degree to the practice in Geneva, for which Calvin is still the primary representative but no longer the chief concern. In keeping with their differing interests, each generation has drawn on the sources which it deemed most appropriate. Older works use texts that Calvin or his friends and colleagues or editors wrote: the reformer's sermons and letters and *Ecclesiastical Ordinances*, his biographers' accounts, and the remarkable assemblage of notes in the Annales volume of the *Opera Calvini*. More recently, scholars have privileged those social historical materials that uncover the Genevan world in which Calvin lived and worked: the *Registres du Conseil, Registres du Consistoire, Registres de la Compagnie des Pasteurs,* and other archival collections (as well as the *Ordinances* and sometimes Calvin's sermons). Besides drawing on different sources, scholars have not always read their common texts in the same way; this is particularly true of the use of the *Ecclesiastical Ordinances*. For some, the meaning of the *Ordinances* has apparently been unclear, while for others this edict has been considered an inaccurate guide to what was actually practiced. Here the key paragraphs of the text of the *Ordinances*, plus the description of Calvin's practice in the biography by Nicolas Colladon, are quoted to provide the primary sources at the basis of many of the arguments.

The most important prescriptive text is naturally Geneva's church order, the *Ecclesiastical Ordinances*, voted into law in November 1541. One section is entitled: "Of the number, place and time of preaching." The form quoted here is from the *Opera Calvini*, giving the draft version.

> On Sunday there is a sermon at the break of day at St. Pierre and St. Gervais and at the customary hour at the said St. Pierre and St. Gervais. At noon there is catechism, that is, instruction for the young children in all three churches, that is La Magdeleine, St. Pierre and St. Gervais. At three o'clock in St. Pierre and St. Gervais the second sermon. [...] On work days besides the two sermons which are done, three times a week they preach at St. Pierre, i.e., Monday, Tuesday, and Friday, one hour before they begin in the other places. [64]

In the received version there are a number of changes from the draft, here marked by italics.

---

[64]   *Ordinances*, CO 10:20-21: "Le dymanche qu'il y ait sermon au poinct du jour à sainct pierre et sainct gervais et à l'heure accoustumee auditz sainct pierre (g) et sainct gervais. A mydy qu'il y ait cathechisme, cest à dire instruction de petis enfans en toutes les troys esglises, assavoir la magdelene (h), sainct pierre et sainct gervais. A troys heures en (i) sainct pierre et sainct gervais le second sermon. [instructions about catechism & sacraments] Es jours ouvriers oultre les deux predications qui se font, que troys fois la sepmaine on presche à sainct pierre, assavoir le lundy, mardy (a) et vendredy une (b) heure, devant qu'on commence aux aultres lieux (1)."

On Sunday there is a sermon at the break of day at St. Pierre and St. Gervais and at the customary hour at the said St. Pierre, *at La Magde-leine*, and St. Gervais. At noon there is catechism, that is, instruction for the young children, in all three churches, that is St. Pierre, La Magdeleine and St. Gervais. At three o'clock as well in all *three* parishes. [...] On work days besides the two sermons which are done, three times a week they preach at St. Pierre, i.e., Monday, Wednesday, and Friday, *and let these sermons be rung and done one after the other at such an hour that they can be finished before they begin somewhere else.* [65]

La Magdeleine is added to the Sunday morning and Sunday afternoon services, and the instructions about sequencing are modified in a very confusing way. Most scholars seem to have worked from the received text of the *Ordinances*, although using various forms of the final instruction about the bell ringing.

The other text which is cited, though less frequently, is the brief description by Calvin's biographer Nicolas Colladon of the reformer's regular practices. The sentence about preaching is part of a larger summary of Calvin's pastoral work in Geneva and beyond.

Calvin for his part never spared himself, working much more than his strength and regard for his health allowed. For ordinarily, of every two weeks he preached all the days of one; he taught in theology three times each week; he was in the consistory on the appointed day...; every Friday in the ... Congregation ....; he never failed in visiting the sick... he had a great concern for the faithful in France... Nevertheless that did not hinder him at all from working in his own study and composing several beautiful and very useful books; as I will now touch on some which he made in these first years... So then in the year 1543, because of the Sorbonne in Paris ... he composed a book... [66]

Colladon then continues with a fairly detailed (though not perfect[67]) list of the reformer's writings. The most obvious mistake in this summary is claiming that

---

[65] *Ordinances*, CO 10:20-21, with changes drawn from notes "(g) à la Magdeleine"; "(h) S. Pierre, la magdelene, et S. Gervais": "(i) à troys heures aussi bien touttes les parroisses. " On 10:20 and notes "(a) mercredi"; and "(1) *Les derniers mots* : une heure devant etc. *sont rayés et l'autre main les a remplacé par ceux-ci* : Et que les sermons soyent sonnés et faict l'un appres l'aultre." On OC 10:21 "(b): *La rédaction définitive de la fin de cet article est ainsi conçue* : Et que ces sermons soyent sonnez l'un apres l'autre à telle heure qu'ilz puissent estre finitz devant qu'on commence ailleurs." Here note (l) is omitted in favor of (b). For discussion see below at nn.119ff.

[66] Colladon, CO 21:66.

[67] For example, he gives the date of *La forme des prières* as 1543 (OC 21:67), no doubt because that is the year named on the preface when Calvin added a further section to the undated 1542 preface, OS II, pp. 15, 18.

the Biblical lectures happened every week, instead of alternate ones. It should be noted that this description is not precisely dated but intended to cover Calvin's life generally so it cannot be read as an exact picture of his earliest ministry, especially since neither of his biographers, Colladon and Theodore Beza, had any personal memories of Geneva before the late 1540s. It does claim to point to some of the "first writings" which would naturally be better documented than the details of practice in those same years. However, the purpose of Colladon's description is a summary of Calvin's usual life-long activities and not a detailed schedule of a specific period.

Questions

There are a number of points of disagreement about how these sources should be interpreted with regard to the actual practice of worship "on the ground." One has to do with Sunday services: How many were ordered and at what times? Of those ordered, how many were actually practiced, and in which churches (St. Pierre, La Magdeleine, and St. Gervais)? A second and more common focus of disagreement has to do with the number and times of weekday sermons. Were these held only three times a week before October 1549 or were there sermons every day, Monday through Saturday, before 1549? If services were held on the weekdays, when were they scheduled? At dawn or at another time? If there was another time, what was it and how often were there services? How should the specific details about the sequencing of sermons be understood, that is, were the bells actually rung and the sermons held at staggered times? A third relatively minor issue regards how to interpret changes to the preaching schedules which are recorded in the *Registres du Conseil* notes printed in the <u>Annales</u> section of the *Opera Calvini*. In the following overview of the historiography, the scholars, their sources, and their writings are briefly introduced. Then the discussion is organized topically, and within each topic, chronologically.

Scholars, Sources, Writings

In the first half of the twentieth century scholars were content to cite the information found in the recently completed *Opera Calvini*: recorded sermons, the biographical writings of Theodore Beza and Nicolas Colladon, and the <u>Annales</u> material assembled by the editors of the *Opera*. Most leading scholars of Calvin's preaching, especially Erwin Mülhaupt and T. H. L. Parker, have also been involved in editing the reformer's manuscript sermons for the critical edition in the *Supplementa Calviniana* series. Here primary attention is given to their monographs, although any other comments about the times and frequency of sermons in Geneva will be noted. Several other very influential sermon editors, notably Rodolphe Peter, whose discussions have been primarily focused in their prefaces, are also included here or later.

The first outstanding voice among the twentieth-century interpreters of Calvin's preaching was Erwin Mülhaupt, with his study *Die Predigt Calvins, ihre Geschichte, ihre Form und ihre religiösen Grundgedanken* (1931). Besides a translation of some sermons (1934), Mülhaupt also wrote an extensive introduction to his edition of the sermons on Psalms and feast days (1981), where he adds some remarks about schedule. [68] Also well known is Richard Stauffer, although his most extensive treatment of Calvin's sermons is his earliest book, the 1953 thesis *L'homilétique de Calvin*, which does not discuss the reformer's preaching schedule at all. Stauffer offers some comments in later texts: "Les sermons inédits de Calvin sur le livre de la Genèse" (1965) and *Dieu, la création, et la Providence dans la prédication de Calvin* (1978). [69] The author of the most widely read English-language expositions of Calvin's preaching is T. H. L. Parker. Like Mülhaupt and Stauffer, Parker focuses exclusively on Calvin himself, and thus considers Geneva only through Calvin's eyes. Unlike his continental colleagues and fellow sermon editors, Parker has produced not one but two monographs on Calvin's preaching, separated in time by forty-five years: *The Oracles of God* (1947) and *Calvin's Preaching* (1992). Since he does not simply copy the information from one book into the next, both monographs need to be examined. The fine French Calvin scholar Rodolphe Peter provides a discussion of Calvin's preaching in his introduction to the sermons on Jeremiah and Lamentations (1971). [70]

In the second half of the twentieth century interest in Calvin's preaching was overtaken by interest in Geneva's worship schedules as part of its practical reform movement. The sources of evidence here have expanded from the prescriptive to the more "down-to-earth" descriptive or reported: *Registres du Consistoire, Registres du Conseil, Registres de la Companie des Pasteurs,* [71] baptismal and marriage records,

---

68   Mülhaupt, *Die Predigt Calvins*. See *Johannes Calvin Diener am Wort Gottes*, ed. E. Mülhaupt (Göttingen: Vandenhoeck & Ruprecht, 1934). Idem, "Einführung," p. xlv (cf. n.99 below).

69   Stauffer, *L'homilétique de Calvin*. Idem, "Les sermons inédits"; Idem, *Dieu, la création et la providence dans la prédication de Calvin* (Bern/ Frankfurt/ Las Vegas, 1978).

70   Peter, "Introduction," *Sermons sur les Livres de Jérémie et des Lamentations* (1971).

71   To date (2014) *Registres du Conseil* in five volumes covering 1536-40 (2003-2011); printed volumes are cited as RC I-V, manuscript as RC vol. folio (e.g., RC 35 f290v). *Registres du Consistoire* in seven volumes covering 1542-53 (1996-2013); printed volumes are cited as Consist. I-VII, manuscript as Consistory vol. folio (e.g., Consistory IX:1, IX, 48). *Compagnie des Pasteurs*, two volumes for Calvin's lifetime (1962, 1964) although this series continues. Some RC manuscript citations are marked archives@etat.ge.ch ; others are derived through the OC *Annales* volume 21 although in any case of doubt these have been checked against the archives. The Consistory manuscripts are cited from the transcription of Prof. Kingdon and his colleagues which was generously deposited in the Princeton Theological Seminary Library (as also at the H. H. Meeter Center of Calvin College).

other legal materials. One voice is William Naphy, who devotes part of a chapter to Calvin's sermons in his helpful (and lively!) study, *John Calvin and the Consolidation of the Genevan Reformation* (1992, 1994). His object is to use the sermons as one way to understand the political, social, and ecclesiastical organization of the Reformation "on the ground." Since when Calvin was preaching is incidental to what his sermons reveal about Genevans' reactions, Naphy does not add fresh insight into the schedule.

Attention to preaching in Calvin's Geneva moved to a whole different level with the work of Thomas A. Lambert, who applied a social historical approach to this "liturgical" aspect of early modern Geneva in his fine pioneering work, *Preaching, Praying, and Policing the Reform in Sixteenth-Century Geneva* (1998). [72] Lambert has also been one of the major editors of the *Registres du Consistoire*, which has put scholars of Geneva much in his debt. In his monograph Lambert attends to prescriptive sources but gives primary attention to the more "factual" material in the consistory, Senate, and baptismal and marriage records to create his presentation of Genevan practice. The fruit of Lambert's pioneering work in the city archives has been widely influential, and there are at least two significant books on Geneva's practice which rely on his discoveries. The first is Max Engammare's innovative study, *On Time, Punctuality, and Discipline in Early Modern Calvinism* (French 2004, English 2010). Engammare describes Lambert as "the first to examine the varied sources in order to give an account of church service times in Reformation Geneva." [73] The second is Christian Grosse's massive and detailed book, *Les rituels de la Cène: Le culte eucharistique réformé à Genève (XVIe-XVIIe siècles)*, (2008). [74] These constitute the major voices in research on matters of the preaching schedules of Geneva in Calvin's day.

It is a privilege to build on the work of other scholars, especially the creative work of Lambert. As with all pioneering studies, further refinements and corrections are left to be made by later research. One important basis of the present study includes the fruit of my more systematic examination of the early years of the reform, thanks to the edited volumes of the *Registres du Conseil* (now 1536-40) and the growing number of *Registres du Consistoire* (1542-51, which have

---

[72]   Lambert, *Preaching, Praying, and Policing*, sets Calvin's Geneva in the larger context of the late medieval heritage of liturgy and piety, providing rich excerpts from the various *Registres* as well as provocative theses and helpful appendices.

[73]   Engammare, *L'ordre du temps*. Quotation, *L'ordre du temps*, p.49-50 n. 13: Lambert "c'est lui le premier qui a dériché le terrain des sources multiples." cf. *On Time, Punctuality, and Discipline*, p. 42 n. 15.

[74]   Grosse, *Les rituels de la Cène*, pp. 177-78, 182, 293.

appeared since Dr. Lambert's work was completed), and of my tabulating many more years of the baptismal and marriage records of Geneva than he was able to do. The years in Lambert's sample are December 1550 – December 1551. My own research covers the years 1550-51, 1553, 1555, 1557, 1559, 1562, 1564 of both baptisms and marriages for St. Pierre, St. Gervais, and La Magdeleine, as well as adding the 1552 and 1554 baptisms for La Magdeleine and its complete marriage register 1550-64 (because this parish has the most irregular schedule).[75]

Note on Language

Part of the confusion in reading some of these Genevan texts is owed to the variety of words used to designate sermons, something which has usually been overlooked. The terms are especially related to the multiple services on Sundays, but distinguishing the ways Genevans described different services can also illuminate daily worship practice. One traditional term, "ordinary" or "customary" hour, needs to be recognized before the Protestant nomenclature is discussed. In effect, "ordinary" designated continuity with the traditional hours of Mass: as noted above, on weekdays this was 6 a.m. in summer, 7 a.m. in winter; the "customary" time on Sundays was probably mid-morning, i.e., 8 a.m. or 9 a.m. References to these synonyms have been passed over quickly but they functioned as a kind of technical term.

When Protestants began multiple preaching services – two on weekdays and as many as four on Sundays – the nomenclature had to develop more precision, even though it remained fairly flexible. The most important distinction is between the dawn sermon and another one during the morning. The former is variously called "sermon du/ de matin" or "premier sermon/ premier presche," or described as "au poinct du jour" or "devant le jour," or occasionally "a l'aube du jour" or more rarely "le matin."[76] (This language was used not only for

---

75   See Lambert, *Preaching, Praying and Policing*, pp. 291-96. For my research, see Appendices One and Two.

76   *Consist.* I, Jan. 25, 1543, p. 173, Tevena Glectire, a servant, "fust dymenche au sermon à Saint Gervays et de matin." March 8, 1543, p. 237, Magdeleyne, wife of Giard Le Mugnier, says that last Sun. she was "au premier presche à Saintz Gervays et aprit le Pater." March 29, 1543, p. 210, Jehan Mouri from Jussier, was "au premier presche de Saint Pierre... et receupt la Cene au grand presche." Nov. 29, 1543, p. 278, Tevene, widow of Marquet Peronet, "fust dymenche au premier sermon à Sainct Pierre." May 8, 1544, p. 367, Pernon, wife of Anthoyne Valloz, says she received the [Easter] Supper at St. Pierre with the servant of M. Velluti "au premier sermon" and "fust dymenche au premier sermon." *Ordinances*: OC 10:20, 99f: "au poinct du jour," "de matin... avant les... sermons ordinaires." Below at n.114 for "devant le jour" in RCP. Sept. 22, 1558, moving from summer to winter schedule, OC 21:704 (RC 54 f292): "Des Sermons. Icy est arresté que dimenche on sonne le sermon du matin à cinq heures et celuy de lundy à sept et

sermons but also for other gatherings at dawn; when either of the councils meets in emergency session, the time is written in similar fashion, e.g., "az cinq heures de matin."[77]) When the mid-morning Sunday service is to be distinguished from others it may be called "grande presche/ gros presche" or "devant dyne" or "de huict heures" or sometimes "second sermon." Usually "dymenche az/au matin" without another modifier is the mid-morning service; this must be distinguished from the dawn service, which is "de/ du matin," although the language is not absolutely fixed. In fact, "grand sermon" can also be used for the second service on Wednesday, the day of prayer, as a way to distinguish it from the dawn service on that same day.[78]

The noon catechism might seem to need no further designation, and in fact it is usually called that, but it may also be named "sermon de mydi" and at least once "sermon de l'examen." In the early years a parishioner appearing before the consistory seems once to have called it "apres dyné" but this may simply have been a mistake. Technically the noon catechism was after dinner/ the mid-day meal at 11 a.m., and the parishioner was probably simply identifying the actual time. Since the custom of an afternoon service was new, the language had not yet become

---

ainsin tous les jours." The baptismal and marriage records regularly say "de 4/5 heures du matin," or sometimes just "du matin," and occasionally "l'aube du jour." (These descriptions are used primarily for dawn services on Sundays, but become common for any dawn service when there are two services on a single day, especially Wednesdays.) For "le matin" see OC 21:301; Aug. 18, 1542 (RC 36 f98) "maystre Henry & monsieur de Geneston auroyent à fere les sermons à St. Pierre le matin."

[77] Meeting of the Two Hundred is called for this hour after the June 6 riot (RC V, p. 336). Senate meeting on "Mescredy 21 de Septembre 1558 de matin à cinq heures" (RC 54 f290v).

[78] *Consist.* I. March 23, 1542, p. 19, Pernete, widow of Pierre Puvel, "fust dimenche passé à Saintz Pierre à matin et à vespres." Oct. 19, 1542, p. 132, Michiaz, widow of Tyvent de Jussiez, says she went the other week to the sermon "à heure de vespres aux enseignes qu'il espouse la fillie de Glaude Marchiand et fust dymenche passé au sermon de mydi au cathesesme et n'y fust pas au matin ny au soir." [not mid-morning or 3 p.m.] April 6, 1542, p. 35, "le premier... le second" (reference to two Sunday morning services of Supper on Easter the following Sun. at 4 a.m. and 7:30 a.m.: "Et entrer en chayre à 4 heures pour le premier et pour le second à VII heures et dymi"). May 11, 1542, p. 63, Jana, daughter of Jehan Bovier, was "au grand sermon" at St. Pierre [and apparently another occasion "au sermon à matin"]. April 5, 1543, p. 213, Noble Pernete Du Payn: was "devant dyné" at St. Gervais. April 26, 1543, p. 232, Tybaudaz, daughter of Claude Le Guex, went to sermon at St. Pierre "du gros presche," and names Calvin [as preacher]. Other examples are found in the baptismal records. E.g., "grand sermon" at St. Pierre in the informal beginning of records is used for two of Poupin's sons, once for the second service on Wed. the day of prayer, once for the main Sun. service; see n.150 below. Also regularly "de huict heures" in St. Pierre and St. Gervais, and at La Magdeleine after 1555 (before that it was apparently assumed that anything not marked catechism was morning). The exceptions: "le matin" for dawn, Aug. 18, 1542 (chap. 2 at n.43); "de matin" for mid-morning/ 8 a.m., Oct. 28, 1549 (cf. at n.115).

fixed.[79] "After dinner" is usually reserved for the Sunday afternoon service: "apres dyné" or "vespres" or "[du] soir" or "a trois heures" or after 1549 "a deux heures" in deep winter when the afternoon service temporarily moved an hour earlier.[80]

Sunday Services

Scholars have identified the number of services and times of worship on Sundays in different ways. Their lists range from two to four, depending on various factors, including both interpretation of language and choice of sources. Mülhaupt speaks of only two sermons on Sundays, identified as times when Calvin was preaching. (Presumably he also knew of the catechism hour but did not consider it a "sermon" since he was detailing Calvin's sermons and there are no records of Calvin doing the catechism regularly, even in the early years.) Reckoning on only one Sunday morning service, Mülhaupt struggles to deal with a single fixed time which is mentioned: "daybreak."

> As for the times of preaching, it appears that the afternoon sermon was fixed at 3 p.m. We do not hear of anything else. For the "early sermon" the Ordinances give only the general time: "at day break"; perhaps an hour later than the weekday sermons. These [weekday sermons] were also fitted to the seasonal change and were held from Easter to St. Michael's (Oct. 1) early at 6 a.m., otherwise at 7 a.m.[81]

---

[79] OC 10:20. Baptismal records commonly say "au catechisme" though very rarely Fabri will write "au sermon de mydy" (cf. St. Pierre record for April 13, 1550) and at least once Macar says "sermon de l'examen" (cf. St. Gervais record for March 19, 1559). *Consist.* I. Nov. 9, 1542, p. 135 La Donne Jaqueline "ne peult vaquer aler au sermon et n'y peult aller sinon les dymenches... fust dymenche passé apres dyné a Saintz Pierre et au cathasesme." Dec. 7, 1542, La Pernon Veyrona says she went to sermon Sunday [morning] at St, Pierre and "apres dyné at La Magdeleine" and does not know what Calvin said (see *Consist.* I, p. 146); see April 3, 1544 in chap. 2 n.134.The language might have meant a Sunday afternoon service, but there is no other evidence for such a sermon at La Magdeleine before 1555, so it could perhaps be a reference to catechism, if not simply a mistake. The reference to Calvin is probably to the morning service at St. Pierre.

[80] *Consist.* I. March 23, 1542, p. 19, Pernete, widow of Pierre Puvel, was "à Sainctz Pierre à matin et à vespres." July 20, 1542, p. 89, Maister Pierre Calabri, says he goes "les dymenches apres dyné." Oct. 26, 1542, p. 133, Claude Vaurin, says he was at worship "dymenche passé ... fust dymenche à Sainctz Gervays apres dyné. " (For "soir" see quotation for Oct. 19, 1542 in n.77.) OC 10:20, 99 ("trois heures"). Baptismal but especially marriage records regularly say "à trois heures"/ "à deux heures"/ "apres midy"/ "apres disne"/ "du soir"/ "vespres"; for examples of most of these, see appendices three and four, Calvin's marriage and baptismal records. For change of time, see below at n.145ff.

[81] Mülhaupt, *Die Predigt Calvins*, p. 16: "Was die Predigtzeiten angeht, so liegt, wie es scheint, die Nachmittagspredigt auf 3 Uhr fest, man hört nie anders; für die Frühpredigt gibt die Kirchenordnung nur die allgemeine Zeitangabe „bei Tagesanbruck"; viellicht eine Stunde später als die Wochentagpredigten. Auch diese sind nämlich den Jahreszeiten angepasst gewesen und lagen von Ostern bis Michaelis (1. Oktober) früh 6 Uhr, sonst 7 Uhr."

In a footnote Mülhaupt explains why he calculates the time of the Sunday morning service as he does. He quotes one of Calvin's sermons dated "probably at latest at the end of September 1556" in which Calvin says "you are now gathered at 8 o'clock." Mülhaupt continues:

> Even if the winter time is already stated [that is, Calvin is speaking in Sept., before the seasonal change of schedule], it is still an hour later than the weekday sermon; I trust this witness of Calvin more than the statement in CR 49, 704 [=OC 21:704], according to which the Sunday early sermon – and even still during the winter time – came at 5 a.m. [82]

For Mülhaupt, there is one morning service on Sunday. Thus, when Calvin affirms that he is preaching at 8 a.m., and the note in the *Registres du Conseil* (cited in the <u>Annales</u>) for Sept. 22, 1558, about seasonal alternation says that the dawn service is at 5 a.m., Mülhaupt feels obliged to choose one over the other. His effort to combine sources leads to several mistakes with regard to the times of services. One, the idea that the sermon at which Calvin was preaching changed seasonally, is minor. The main issue is that Mülhaupt appears not to realize that there are two morning services, and that the "daybreak" times (and seasonal alternation) refer to the earlier one. One reason for Mülhaupt's confusion may be that his source is Calvin's sermons, and Calvin never preached at the dawn services so all of his Sunday morning sermons would be at the later hour. It may be noted that Mülhaupt does not explicitly draw on the *Ecclesiastical Ordinances* at all, but his interpretation of the preaching schedule in Geneva influenced other writers who claimed that source.

The works of Parker offer the widest span of options with regard to the number of Sunday services, from four to two (or possibly three). In *The Oracles of God*, published in 1947, Parker gives the following description of the worship practice in the first years after Calvin's return to Geneva.

> Sunday began with a sermon (that is, a service in which the sermon had the principal place) at daybreak in the first two churches [St. Peter's, St. Gervais], of which Calvin and Viret were the chief pastors. There were further sermons in all three churches at nine o'clock, and again at three, and in the meanwhile, at noon, the children were catechized. [83]

---

[82] Mülhaupt, *Die Predigt Calvins*, p. 16 n. 3: "CR 77,711 sagt Calvin in einer Sonntagpredigt, wohl spätestens Ende September 1556, sie seien jetzt „à huit heure" versammelt; selbst wenn damit schon die Winterzeit angegeben ist, ist es noch eine Sunde später als die Werktagpredigt; ich traue diesem Zeugnis Calvins mehr als der Angabe CR 49,704, wonach die Sonntag-frühpredigt – und gar noch in der Winterzeit – auf 5 Uhr fiele."

[83] Parker, *The Oracles of God*, p. 33.

Parker apparently reads "customary" hour in the *Ordinances* as 9 a.m., which is a logical interpretation. He indicates that there were there were three sermons plus catechism on Sundays. Although he seems to associate Calvin and Viret with the dawn services by implication, this is not explicit or necessarily intentional. Parker names the *Ecclesiastical Ordinances* as his source (which would be appropriate for naming four worship times) although he explicitly cites only the 1561 edition to explain the seasonal alternation. [84]

The outline of the frequency of Sunday worship is slightly but significantly revised in Parker's second book on the subject, *Calvin's Preaching*, published in 1992, and here the influence of Mülhaupt's work in narrowing the number and times of worship appears to be a factor.

> The pattern of services was that there was to be a *sermon...* 'at daybreak in S. Pierre and S. Gervais, and at the customary hour' (that is, in the afternoon) in all three churches (*Registres* I.5). [85]

In this later work Parker indicates only two services on Sundays (although he probably still includes catechism, he does not mention it). He provides a reference to the version of the *Ordinances* found in the *Registres de la Compagnie des Pasteurs*, but in fact with regard to the Sunday services, Parker seems here to follow Mülhaupt's idea of one morning service. (Although he does not provide a footnote to this effect, he does include Mülhaupt's book in his bibliography, and what he says fits Mülhaupt's interpretation better than it does the *Ordinances*.) In effect Parker changes from four services (daybreak, 9 a.m., and 3 p.m., as well as catechism at noon) in 1947 to two (daybreak and afternoon) in 1992, reading "customary" as 3 p.m. (!). He names several church buildings, joining these with references to Calvin and Viret in his first book though not in the second.

Parker incidentally adds one further detail of confusion. When drawing on the *Registres du Conseil* from the <u>Annales</u> he introduces a point which is intended to contribute to the fuller picture of the reformer's burden of preaching. After citing Calvin's letter to Farel in July 1542 in which Calvin speaks of needing "to preach more frequently" because of his new and less experienced colleagues, Parker refers to a note from the *Registres du Conseil* to explain a reduction in Calvin's sermons.

> This [extra preaching] seems to have laid a heavier burden on him than he could sustain, for on September 11 the Council noted that 'Sr. Calvin ought to be exempt from preaching except once on Sundays'

---

[84] Parker, *Oracles of God*, p. 33.

[85] Parker, *Calvin's Preaching*, p. 59.

(CO 21.302.25-30). It is not clear whether this means only one Sunday
sermon as well as the three in the week or only one sermon at all.[86]

In fact, this change in Calvin's schedule was temporary, because the city had put
him (their highly trained lawyer) on a small committee to revise the civil laws;[87] the
limiting of his preaching is not connected to the comment to Farel in particular.
That is, Calvin was not relieved of sermons because the load was too great in itself;
he was temporarily relieved of a part of his preaching duties to spend his time on
another job for the city. Parker's intent to include all the details which he knows
results in adding confusion, because he does not have a larger framework in which
to place the individual notes.[88]

Nothing is added to the picture of Geneva's services by Naphy, who draws
upon Parker's writings and the *Ordinances* to describe Calvin's preaching schedule.
"Three sermons were preached every Sunday in Geneva, at dawn, 9 a.m. and
3 p.m. ... Catechism lessons were held every Sunday at noon."[89] Without going
into the larger issue of why Calvin was relieved of some of his preaching in
September 1542, Naphy refers to notes from the *Registres du Conseil* to show that
this was a temporary change in the reformer's Sunday schedule from two sermons
to one (and then back again).[90]

---

[86]   Parker, *Calvin's Preaching*, p. 60.

[87]   Sept. 11, 1542, OC 21:302 (RC 36 f117v): "Affin que ung chascun aye moyeant de vivre en
       bonne amitié: Resoluz que l'on suyve à fere des esdyct et la charge à icyeulx donné à M. Calvin et
       aut Sr. Sindique Claude Rosset et que ledit Sr. Calvin doybge estre exempt de prescher synon
       une foys les dymenches."

[88]   The introduction to the Isaiah sermons edited by Parker, Francis Higman, and Lewis Thorpe
       (S. III, 1995), does not discuss Calvin's schedule, but it does indicate the need for the present
       kind of clarification of the latter. The authors say that the sermon on Monday, Sept. 6, 1557, was
       preached on a day when Calvin did a wedding at St. Pierre and baptized a baby at La Magdeleine
       ("Introduction," p. ix). The footnote refers generally to the weddings and baptisms for five
       months of sermons, as recorded in OC 21:671-81. However, careful reading of OC 21:674 for
       Sept. 6 indicates that both the wedding and the baptism were at La Magdeleine. Calvin did not
       preach twice on a weekday; he would not have performed either a baptism or a wedding without
       a full preaching service. Thus it is clear that there was only one sermon, one service, and any
       other liturgies: baptism or wedding, must be part of the same worship service and thus in the
       same parish/ building.

[89]   Naphy, *Calvin and the Consolidation*, n.81 on pp.164-65; for this note, he cites "T. H. L. Parker,
       Supplementa Calviniana (London: 1962), p. 8, and *The Oracles of God* (London: 1947), pp. 33-9." On
       p. 154 Naphy introduces the sermons which will be the subject of the "remainder of this
       chapter."

[90]   Naphy, *Calvin and the Consolidation*, n.93 on p.165: "T. H. L. Parker, *Calvin's Preaching* (Edinburgh:
       1992), pp. 59-62. Prior to October 1549 sermons had been delivered on only three weekdays.
       For a brief period Calvin preached only on Sundays before renewing the early pattern."

Lambert discusses preaching practice more thoroughly than any previous writer and his work has been extremely influential.[91] He affirms that "eight services" were planned for Sundays; these were "'au point du jour' at Saint-Pierre and Saint-Gervais, and a sermon 'à l'heure accoustumee' at all three temples. Similarly there was to be a catechism and a three o'clock service at all three temples."[92] When he counts the "eight services on Sunday" which the *Ordinances* mandated, Lambert does not include catechism; the eight are two dawn services at St. Pierre and St. Gervais, and morning and afternoon services in all three parishes. (The omission of catechism may be because he does not consider it a service; he comments on the oddity of Genevans calling it the "sermon de midi."[93]) Note that this discussion refers to the prescriptive text of the received *Ordinances*, not to what actually happened.

It appears that Lambert believes only the services at St. Pierre and St. Gervais were implemented, and he adds that even the dawn service at St. Gervais was delayed until August of 1542.[94] He goes on to say that "the services at Madeleine were slowly added and the full schedule was not attained until after 1551 ..."[95] Before 1551 "[a]t Madeleine there was only one service each day, plus catechism on Sunday."[96] (Lambert does not carry his investigation far enough forward to see the addition of the Sunday afternoon service in 1555.)[97]

Clearly, while earlier writers who focused on Calvin did not agree on the number of Sunday services or the times, later authors interested in Genevan practice per se affirm that three sermons plus catechism were present as the regular schedule for St. Pierre and St. Gervais. The key difference for scholars like Lambert is found in the actual implementation of the Sunday regulations for the parish of La Magdeleine in

---

[91]   Engammare, *L'ordre du temps*, p.49-50 n. 13 : Lambert "c'est lui le premier qui a dériché le terrain des sources multiples." *On Time, Punctuality, and Discipline*, p. 42 n. 15. Grosse, *Les rituels de la Cène*, pp.177-78, 293, follows Lambert in challenging the implementation of the *Ordinances*.

[92]   Lambert, *Praying, Preaching and Policing*, pp. 285-90, esp. n.12; see full quotation in n.111 below.

[93]   Lambert, *Praying, Preaching and Policing*, p. 289: "Odd though it may seem, the catechism quite frequently went by the name "noon sermon" (sermon de midi). Calvin himself treated it much like any other service (except for the fact that he himself rarely if ever actually taught catechism). Some Genevans who were unable to go to the regular sermons substituted catechism instead."

[94]   Lambert, *Praying, Preaching and Policing*, pp. 285-90, esp. n.12; see full quotation in n.111 below.

[95]   Lambert, *Praying, Preaching and Policing*, pp. 285-90, esp. n.12; see full quotation in n.111 below.

[96]   Lambert, *Praying, Preaching and Policing*, pp. 288-90. Grosse also follows Lambert in giving the time of the Sunday morning service at La Magdeleine as 6 a.m. in summer, 7 a.m. or 8 a.m. in winter, *Les rituels de la Cène*, p. 293.

[97]   Because he is describing the schedule in 1551 Lambert does not note the addition of the afternoon service in 1555; for that, see below at n.152.

particular. He cites notes about the delay in completing the full program at St. Gervais. He concludes that when it was held, the morning service at La Magdeleine occurred at a different time than in the other parishes.

Weekday Services

Confusion about the number and times of Sunday worship is more than matched by debates about the days and times of weekday services. Here the oldest source seems to be the clearest. Mülhaupt cites Colladon for Calvin's schedule.

> His normal preaching load was …. once on Weekdays, with the limitation that he only had to preach every second week. The sermons on Deuteronomy show this, and Colladon speaks of that already in 1543, and indeed in a tone as if this were self-evident. [98]

Mülhaupt affirms daily worship on all weekdays, although there is some confusion here because he refers to the Deuteronomy series preached in 1555-56, and then appears to believe that Colladon's reference to the year 1543 is evidence for this having been the case for many years. (In fact when Colladon named the date he referred to publications, but since this phrase appears shortly after the summary sentence about Calvin's practice of preaching Mülhaupt read these together. [99]) Nevertheless, despite this mistake Mülhaupt may be counted as affirming worship on all weekdays. He also goes a step further, however, to state that there were daily sermons in all three parishes, [100] although this was not in fact the case until 1559.

Most of the rest of the scholars examined on this subject think that worship was only on selected weekdays. [101] Parker's explanation of the reformer's weekday

---

[98] Mülhaupt, *Die Predigt Calvins*, p. 16: "Sein normales Predigtmass also Sunntags zwei, Werktags eine Predigt, mit der Einschränkung, dass er nur jede zweite Woche zu predigen hatte. Dies letztere zeigen die Deuteron-predigten in CR 53-57, Colladon redet schon 1543 davon, und zwar im Ton der Selbstverständlichkeit." The citation of Colladon is the one quoted above at n.65 which does not join the date and the preaching as Mülhaupt interprets it. On pp. 7-10 Mülhaupt refers to the "spärlich und zufällig" information before 1549, drawn essentially from CO records; on pp. 12-16 he gives tables for 1549-64.

[99] Colladon, OC 21:66.

[100] Mülhaupt, "Einführung," p. xlcv: "Wir erfahren ferner, dass auch werktages täglich in allen Kirchen Genfs gepredigt wurde." This is Mülhaupt's interpretation of the *Ordinances*, which he cites (p. xlv n.59) from the German edition edited by Niesel, which is in fact the 1561 revision, not 1541; see *Bekenntnisschriften und Kirchenordnungen*, 2nd. ed. (Zürich: EVZ, 1938), p. 48.

[101] Stauffer, "Les sermons inédits," p. 26 : "En plus des deux homélies qu'il prononçait chaque dimanche, … monta quotidiennement en chaire toutes les deux semaines dès 1549." Based on n. 4 : "cf. les 'Annales' à la date du 24 octobre 1549, in *I.C. opera… omnia*, vol. XXI, p. 457. Avant cette date, il n'y avait que trois cultes par semaine, les lundi, mardi et vendredi (cf. *J. C. opera selecta*, vol. II, p. 337)."

preaching identifies three times. In *Oracles of God* in 1547 he writes "During the week sermons were held on Monday, Wednesday, and Friday"; these services increased "from once every other day to once a day" in October 1549 by order of the Senate, a statement which he bases on a quotation from the *Registres du Conseil* in the Annales. Parker goes on to explain, on the basis of Colladon's biography, that Calvin preached in alternate weeks, and this is the pattern which he treats in editing Calvin's sermons on Isaiah from 1557-58.[102]

In *Calvin's Preaching* in 1992 Parker repeats the three days but adds the reference to "staggering the times so that the service in the one church should be ended before the next church began,"[103] with the change marked in 1549, from "three during the week to one every day."[104] Naphy follows Parker although there is some ambiguity in his description.

> [Calvin preached] every weekday service on alternating weeks (CO, vol. 21, col. 302). ... Weekday sermons, originally on Mondays, Wednesdays, and Fridays, were increased to every day in October 1549.[105]

Presumably what Naphy means is that Calvin preached in alternate weeks on every weekday that there were services, which he follows Parker and others in identifying as Monday, Wednesday, and Friday until 1549.

In the introduction to the sermons on Jeremiah and Lamentations which he edited, Peter provides a variant reading of the organization of weekday worship in Geneva both before and after 1549. He understands the 1541 *Ordinances* as mandating a morning service in all three parishes on Mondays, Wednesdays, and Fridays, and affirms that there was already preaching three days a week at La Magdeleine and St. Gervais so this signified the extension of the practice to St. Pierre.[106] When he

---

[102] Parker, *The Oracles of God*, p. 39: "In October 1549 the sermons in Geneva were increased from once every other day to once a day by order of the Council: 'Ordered that the preachers ought to preach every morning.' This did not mean, however, that Calvin himself preached every day, for Colladon tells us that 'he ordinarily preached every day every other week.'" Here Parker cites OC 21:457, and OC 21:66.

[103] Parker, *Calvin's Preaching*, p. 59.

[104] Parker, *Calvin's Preaching*, p. 62.

[105] Naphy, *Calvin and the Consolidation*, as cited above in nn.88f. (Naphy's discussion treats all the schedule together. Since I have divided the discussion between Sundays and weekdays, the notes apply to both.)

[106] Peter, "Introduction," p. xxv : "dans chacune des trois Eglises, Saint-Pierre, la Madeleine et Saint-Gervais, un culte matinal les lundis, mercredis et vendredis." n.2 : "On prêchait déjà trois fois par semaine à la Madeleine et à Saint-Gervais, les Ordonnances ajoutent Saint-Pierre comme troisième lieu de culte."

turns to the Old Testament sermons in question here, Peter says: these "show that in 1549 they preached every day at St. Pierre,...; it is however probable that this was the same in the other two parishes of the city." Attributing the need for more sermons to the influx of refugees, Peter cites the Senate note of Jan. 18, 1549, as the first mention of "daily preaching." [107] He then adds a reference to the Senate's Oct. 24, 1549, order about "an additional daily service [which] would precede the morning service at St. Pierre," but which Calvin did not accept. [108]

Somewhat surprisingly, the application of a social historical approach to the question of weekday services in Geneva does not in fact change the picture. Lambert has devoted the most extensive study to this issue and he comes to the conclusion that the *Ordinances'* provisions for sermons were not implemented in 1541: "No historian that I know of agrees with the schedule." [109] While this is a general statement, [110] it seems to be Sunday at La Magdeleine and the weekday services to which it particularly applies. The debate here involves several distinct issues: first is the question of specific weekdays and the number of days as mandated in 1541. A second aspect is the point at which the Genevan schedule of weekday services came to cover all six days, an issue which also involves the times of services.

Lambert begins with listing the days on which sermons were held. He affirms that there was preaching in most of Geneva only on the days when the Senate met, i.e., Mondays, Tuesdays, and Fridays, and there was no sermon on Thursday or Saturday.

> The draft of the Ordinances originally called for services at Saint-Pierre on Monday, Tuesday, and Friday, but the Tuesday sermon was replaced with a Wednesday sermon. This, however, only held for Saint-Pierre. When the Ordinances referred to the 'deux predications que se font que trois fois la

---

[107] Peter, "Introduction," pp. xxvi-xxvii : "Notre suite de sermons montre qu'en 1549 on prêchait tous les jours à Saint-Pierre, le mercredi étant régulièrement réservé au culte d'intercession et de repentance ; il est d'ailleurs vraisemblable qu'il en fut de même dans les deux autres paroisses de la ville. L'afflux des réfugiés rendeait la mesure nécessaire et la plus ancienne mention d'un culte journalier se trouve dans la proclamation du Conseil du 18 janvier 1549." p. xxvii in n. 2 cites CO XIII, c. 159 : "la parolle de Dieu, la quelle leur est journellement preschée."

[108] Peter, "Introduction," p. xxvii: "Le Magistrat décréta en effet de son propre chef le 24 octobre 1549 qu'un service journalier supplémentaire précéderait le culte matinal à Saint-Pierre."

[109] Lambert, *Praying, Preaching and Policing*, p. 285 n.12; see full quotation in n.111 below.

[110] Lambert, *Praying, Preaching and Policing*, p. 285: "The Ecclesiastical ordinances of 1541 called for eight sermons on Sundays and sermons on Monday, Tuesday, Wednesday and Friday, though it took years before the full schedule was implemented." Lambert's fullest picture of the complete schedule is quoted in n.123 below.

sepmaine,' they referred to the sermons at Saint-Gervais and somewhere else (either the Rive or Madeleine?) on Monday, Tuesday and Friday. These were the traditional sermons in Geneva on Council days that had replaced the obligatory pre-Council Mass at the altar of Saint-Michel in the cathedral (the Small Council met only Monday, Tuesday and Friday unless called for extraordinary sessions). [111]

Like Parker and Naphy, Lambert reads this as three weekdays when there were services. Unlike the others, Lambert specifies the places as well as the days: Mondays, Tuesdays, and Fridays at St. Gervais and another temple (possibly Rive or Magdeleine); and Mondays, Wednesdays, and Fridays at St. Pierre. This would make nine sermons total; the times are not clearly stated, although the reference to the pre-council Mass sets the sermons at St. Gervais and in Greater Geneva at 6 a.m./7 a.m. [112]

---

[111] Lambert, *Praying, Preaching and Policing*, pp. 285-86 n.12. At the risk of repetition, the footnote is given here in continuous form, though excerpts are used in several places. "No historian that I know of agrees with the schedule and the Ecclesiastical Ordinances of 1541 (RCP 1, p. 5) do not specifically mention the Tuesday sermons, but is it implied, as I shall explain. The Sunday schedule in the Ordinances called for services 'au point du jour' at Saint-Pierre and Saint-Gervais, and a sermon 'à l'heure accoustumee' at all three temples. Similarly there was to be a catechism and a three o'clock service at all three temples. On weekdays, 'oultre des deux predications que se font que trois fois la sepmaine, on presche à Saint-Pierre, asscavoir le lundy, mecredi et vendredy.' The draft of the Ordinances originally called for services at Saint-Pierre on Monday, Tuesday, and Friday, but the Tuesday sermon was replaced with a Wednesday sermon. This, however, only held for Saint-Pierre. When the Ordinances referred to the 'deux predications que se font que trois fois la sepmaine,' they referred to the sermons at Saint-Gervais and somewhere else (either Rive or Madeleine?) on Monday, Tuesday and Friday. These were the traditional sermons in Geneva on Council days that had replaced the obligatory pre-Council Mass at the altar of Saint-Michel in the cathedral (the Small Council met only Monday, Tuesday and Friday unless called for extraordinary sessions. See SDG II, p. 421). However, the services at Madeleine were slowly added and the full schedule was not attained until after 1551, as we will eventually see. Even the services at Saint-Gervais were not imme-diately in keeping with the Ordinances. See for example, RC 36, f. 91 (8 August 1542): 'Ordonne que les dymenches matin l'on doybge presché aut temple Saint Gervex.' Thus it would seem that at least one of the two Sunday morning sermons at Saint-Gervais was lacking until that time. The Tuesday morning sermon was, however, still offered. [examples from consistory] The Ordinances were written under the assumption that all Genevans knew when the 'deux predications que se font que trois fois la sepmaine' were. In general, the schedule provided by the Ecclesiastical Ordinances must be considered purely theoretical, a schedule that Calvin and the city fathers hoped to enact as resources became available."

[112] Engammare, *On Time, Punctuality, and Discipline*, pp. 44-45: "Clearly, therefore, Sunday services took place at three different times, namely at dawn, at 'the accustomed hour,' and at three o'clock, though specific times for the first two services are lacking. In 1541, plans were for services on Mondays, Wednesdays, and Fridays at Saint Pierre alone, prior to the 1549 statement that services would take place there daily at dawn, and expanded to all three churches by 1551."

A second part of Lambert's argument on weekday sermons is the point at which sermons on every day of the week were instituted. He cites the same Senate order as Parker and Naphy, although he adds more of the discussion in the *Registres du Conseil* and other sources. Here Lambert summarizes the whole picture.

> In 1549, the Council unilaterally ordered the ministers to offer at least one sermon every day. Calvin declared that he *would rather be dead* than accede to the demand and offered instead an additional sermon at Madeleine. By 1551 at the latest, though, the Genevan pastors were preaching every day in all three temples in the city. [113]

Lambert seems to be saying that there was no place in the city where sermons were being preached every day, Monday through Saturday, until 1551, and then there were sermons all six days in three churches.

Here it is helpful first to address the reason why Lambert identifies 1549 as the date when daily sermons began to be held. The evidence which he presents for this dispute between the Senate and the ministers about "daily sermons" is a rather complex and confusing set of entries in the *Registres du Conseil* from October and November 1549. On Oct. 24, 1549, Calvin appeared before the Senate to protest in no uncertain terms against the order to preach "tous les jours de mattin," but the council insists that this will be done. [114] As Lambert points out on the basis of the discussion of this argument in the *Registres de la Compagnie des Pasteurs*, the sermons which the council demanded and the ministers refused were dawn services. [115] Four days later on Oct. 28 the ministers offer to preach at La Magdeleine on Sunday mornings "before dinner" but refuse (again) to do the daily dawn services. [116]

---

[113] Lambert, *Praying, Preaching and Policing*, p. 286.

[114] Oct. 24, 1549, OC 21:457 (RC 44 f247v) "Sur ce qui az proposer avoir advis en ce que l'on leur donne charge de prescher tous les jours de mattin de quoy il se sentz grandement charge… Arresté que les prescheurs doibgent prescher tout les matins…"

[115] Lambert, *Praying, Preaching and Policing*, p. 286 n.13. RCP I, p. 63, for Oct. 28, 1549: The ministers object to the Senate order "que doresnavant il y auroit predication à S. Pierre tous les jours du matin devant le jour, d'autant que ceste charge ne seroit proffitable à l'eglise et qu'on n'y pourroit fournir et n'en se ensuyvroit que trouble et scandale. Mais fut bien offert de fere un sermon tous les dimenches à la Magdalene à l'heure de huict, d'autant qu'il y avoit si grand peuple à S. Pierre que tous ne pouvoient pas ouyr, dont mesd. Seigneurs peuvent cognoistre qu'ilz ne se vouloient pas espargner où ilz voyoient l'edification de l'eglise."

[116] Oct. 28, 1549, OC 21:457 (RC 44 f250): "Ministres. Sur ce qui leurs avoit esté donné charge de prescher tous les jours de mattin pour myeulx instruyre le peuple/ jouxte les resolution

There are several difficulties with Lambert's conclusions. One appears to be that he does not factor into his discussion the difference between sermons at the "ordinary" hour and those at dawn. For another, he does not bring together all the evidence available; e.g., he does not explain how Calvin could be preaching daily if there were not daily weekday services even without the addition of the dawn ones the council demanded. In fact, the extant Jeremiah sermons begin on June 14, 1549, and there are full weeks for June 24, 25, 26, 27, 28, 29, and July 8, 9, 10, 11, 12, 13, and July 22, 24, 25, 26, 27, and Aug. 5, 7, 8, 9, 10 (the last two weeks are missing Tuesdays from the regular set of six sermons). Clearly there were daily sermons before the arguments in October1549. Further, when in 1559 Geneva did have daily services in all three original parishes, these were not at dawn but at the "ordinary" hour of 6 a.m. or 7 a.m.

The Senate's request for a daily dawn sermon was apparently dropped. As a result of this argument, however, a service at 8 a.m. (the usual time for the main sermon) was begun on Sunday mornings at La Magdeleine. In effect, this dispute was not about having sermons every weekday (that was already in place), but about the addition of dawn services on every weekday (that is, adding three more to the Monday-Wednesday-Friday dawn sermons at St. Pierre and Wednesday at St. Gervais). The ministers do not consider the extra dawn services to be useful at this point, and Calvin voices their refusal to have the Senate or General Council dictate church affairs without consulting the pastors (one hears echoes of April 1538). As a compromise, however, the ministers agree to extend themselves to add one of the Sunday sermons which had been planned in the *Ordinances* (not in Calvin's draft but added by the council and missing until this point). It should be noted that Calvin's exclamation that he "would rather be dead" refers to the Senate's exerting its power without consulting the pastors, not whether there would be daily sermons; the phrase is repeated with regard to the Senate's order about multiple recitations of the

---

d[u] conseilz et sur ce hont faict leurs excuses disant mesme que l'on ne debvoit faire cella ny conclure sans les appelle[r] & debattre la matiere avec eulx touteffois qui seroit bon de prescher de mattin avant digne (*dîner*) en la Magdeleine les dimenche si plaict à Messieurs." Archives@etat.ge.ch accessed July 31, 2013. Lambert, *Praying, Preaching and Policing*, p. 290 n.23 for Nov. 11, 1549. See Engammare, *On Time, Punctuality, and Discipline*, p. 46. *L'ordre du temps*, pp. 53-54: "We should also note that the Small Council's decision in October 1549 to order that a morning service be held in all three churches only included the daily dawn service and not the service 'at the usual time.' The Council's decision still led Calvin to exclaim dramatically 'that he would rather die' than accede to the Council's demand. Indeed, Calvin was already preaching daily prior to the Council's decision. The oldest surviving sermons transcribed by the notetaker Denis Ragunier date from June through August 1549."

Lord's Prayer. Both of these issues were matters of principle for Calvin, but the number of services was not. [117]

Bells and Staggered Times for Services

One further aspect of the preaching schedule in Geneva which has been touched upon briefly but which requires more attention is the issue of the times of worship, especially the staggered ringing of the bells and sequencing of the sermons. Lambert deals with this the most fully, though not always with complete clarity. His general summary is that "[t]he schedule of sermons was never the same from year to year," and one example which he provides is La Magdeleine in 1551. "At Madeleine, on Sundays as during the week, there was apparently still only a single sermon at 6:00 a.m. in the summer (mid-April to early September), at 7:00 a.m. most of the rest of the year except in the dead of winter when sermons began at 8:00 a.m." [118] The accompanying footnote offers a collection of individual minutes from the *Registres du Conseil* about the hours of worship at different churches, and it does appear that there is considerable change. [119] However, there is more regularity than a casual glance at an assemblage of discrete Senate orders would suggest; part of Lambert's confusion is owed to the fact that the council minutes which he cites are not fitted into their larger context.

The other part of the timing debate is the issue of staggered times for sermons. Saunier affirmed that this was the practice for "all the sermons." He might have meant both Sunday and weekday sermons, although this is not entirely clear because Geneva later mandated this practice only for weekdays. [120] (Given the limited number of preachers available, especially after Farel, Calvin, and Corauld departed, Saunier may have meant that Sunday services in Greater Geneva were staggered: dawn and 8 a.m. at St. Pierre, and then an hour or so later at the Rive.)

---

[117] Lambert, *Praying, Preaching and Policing*, p. 286, n.13. Lambert quotes several Senate orders; the one for Oct. 28, 1549 (RC 44, f268c) does use the term "rather be dead" but the point is that the ministers object to being unilaterally ordered to do something without being consulted. In the order quoted in OC 21:457 (RC 44 f250) the reference is to a magical recitation of the Lord's Prayer. I have read both of these at archives@etat.ge.ch accessed July 31, 2013.

[118] Lambert, *Praying, Preaching and Policing*, p. 290.

[119] Lambert, *Praying, Preaching and Policing*, p. 290 n. 23. Lambert affirms that this "is but the smallest sample of such resolutions and decrees" ordered by the Senate; March 30, 1543; Feb. 4, 1544; Sept. 23, 1544; Nov. 11, 1549; Feb. 6, 1550; June 10 & 24, 1555. All of these individual examples except Sept. 23, 1544 (which is simply the marker of seasonal change) are discussed elsewhere in this book, see present chap. nn.145, 150, 166, 35; chap. 2, at n.36. Engammare follows Lambert's organization of the worship schedule. Engammare, *On Time, Punctuality, and Discipline*, pp. 44-45; *L'ordre du temps*, pp. 51-52.

[120] See above at n.15.

In *Calvin's Preaching*, Parker affirms that weekday sermons were staggered but does not discuss the matter further.[121] Lambert cites Saunier and says that this "was the practice during Calvin's first stay in Geneva." However, he goes on to say that "[a]s with the number of sermons offered, however, it is not clear that the Ordinances were ever followed and that the weekday sermons were ever staggered after Calvin's return."[122] Immediately following this Lambert gives a full – and simplified – schedule in 1551, based on baptismal and marriage records.[123] Note that Lambert does not appear to question the accuracy of Saunier's statement, but indicates his doubts that the *Ordinances'* regulation for weekday sequencing was ever implemented. The interpretation of this point is related to the multiple revisions of the *Ordinances* and will be treated below in that context. The full picture based on an extended examination of the baptismal and marriage records will also complete that picture.

Examining the Text of the 1541 *Ecclesiastical Ordinances*

The provisions for services made by the 1541 *Ecclesiastical Ordinances* seem clear but have been disputed. Part of the reason may be that there are a number of different versions of the *Ordinances*. Of these, the distinction between Calvin's "draft" version and the Senate's "received" ones is known and these variants are found in the *Opera Calvini* (*Corpus Reformatorum*), although the *Compagnie des Pasteurs* text gives only the received version.[124] There are, however, some further differences in the text as found in the *Opera Selecta*, which seems to record an earlier version of the "draft." For clarity this will be called "draft 1" and the

---

[121] See above at n.102.

[122] Lambert, *Praying, Preaching and Policing*, p. 288; he refers to Saunier in n.17.

[123] Lambert, *Praying, Preaching and Policing*, pp. 288-90. "At any rate, by the time the Etat Civil provide us with a complete schedule of services, the system used in practice was much simpler. Sermons took place at the same time at Saint-Gervais and Saint-Pierre. Since there was only one morning service at Magdeleine, it was generally, though not always offered at a compromise time between the early and late sermons at the other temples. In Saint-Gervais and Saint-Pierre, the early sermon was at 4:00 when the days were longer (essentially April through September) and at 5:00 the rest of the year. The main service was at 8:00 year-round. Catechism, being at noon, required no change with the seasons. ... Finally, there was an afternoon service at 3:00 p.m. on Sunday. By November, however, it was no longer possible for people to see each other, so the afternoon service had to be pushed back to 2:00 p.m. until February. At Madeleine, on Sundays as during the week, there was apparently still only a single sermon at 6:00 a.m. in the summer (mid-April to early September), at 7:00 a.m. most of the rest of the year except in the dead of winter when sermons began at 8:00 a.m. The schedule of sermons was never the same from year to year, but this schedule gives a rough idea of the daily weekly rhythm in Geneva."

[124] *Ordinances*, OC 10:15-30; RCP I, pp. 1-13; OS 2, pp. 328-45.

version of the draft in the *Opera Calvini* will be called "draft 2." The *Opera Calvini* printing also records several stages of revisions, particularly in dealing with the sequencing of the bells for weekday worship. Again, for the sake of clarity the different days and issues are divided: first the Sunday schedule, then the weekday sermons, and finally the sequencing of the bells.

Sundays: French Text

The discussion of Sunday includes questions in the original text and then a minor but influential mistake in the English translations. The text of the *Ecclesiastical Ordinances* went through various stages, beginning with Calvin's or the committee's draft 1 in the *Opera Selecta*.

> On Sunday there is to be a sermon at the break of day at St. Pierre and St. Gervais, and at the customary hour at the Rive/(the said St. Pierre) and St. Gervais. At noon there is to be catechism.... at all three places, i.e., La Magdeleine, St. Pierre, and St. Gervais. At three o'clock at the Rive/(in St. Pierre) and St. Gervais the second sermon. [125]

The reference to the Rive found here in the *Opera Selecta* appears to represent the earliest known stage of the *Ordinances*, i.e., draft 1. It may reflect the practice of regular mid-morning and afternoon services at the Rive, along with the question about moving these to St. Pierre. The next version, published in the *Opera Calvini* and here called draft 2, does not mention the Rive at all.

> On Sunday there is to be a sermon at the break of day at St. Pierre and St. Gervais, and at the customary hour at the said St. Pierre and at St. Gervais. At noon there is to be catechism.... at all three churches, i.e., La Magdeleine, St. Pierre, and St. Gervais. At three o'clock in St. Pierre and St. Gervais the second sermon. [126]

The received text (found also in the *Opera Selecta* and *Opera Calvini*) is the only one printed in the *Registres de la Compagnie des Pasteurs* (there are no variants). Note that St. Pierre has definitively superseded the Rive for Sunday services. This received

---

[125] OS II, p. 337: "Le dymanche qu'il y ait sermon au poinct du jour à sainct pierre et sainct gervais et à l'heure accoustumee à Rive (auditz sainct pierre) et sainct gervais. A mydy qu'il y ait catechisme, c'est à dire instruction de petiz enfans en touttes les troys esglises, assavoir la magdelene, sainct pierre et sainct gervais. A troys heures à Rive (en sainct pierre) et sainct gervais le second sermon."

[126] OC 10:20: "Le dymanche qu'il y ait sermon au poinct du jour à sainct pierre et sainct gervais et à l'heure accoustumee auditz sainct pierre et sainct gervais. A mydy quil y ait cathechisme,... en touttes les troys esglises, assavoir la magdelene, sainct pierre et sainct gervais. A troys heures en sainct pierre et sainct gervais le second sermon."

text in the *Compagnie des Pasteurs* version adds "La Magdeleine" to the list of Sunday morning services "at the customary hour" and alters the last point about the afternoon services to include La Magdeleine there also.

> Sundays there is to be a sermon at the break of day at St. Pierre and St. Gervais, and at the customary hour at the said St. Pierre, La Magdeleine, and St. Gervais. At noon there is to be catechism… in all the three churches, i.e., St. Pierre, La Magdeleine, and St. Gervais. At three o'clock as well in all three parishes. [127]

It should be noted that the received version adds two services at La Magdeleine, on Sunday morning and Sunday afternoon, which were not present in the earlier drafts. It may be no accident that these were precisely the two Sunday services which were missing for many years. One might hypothesize that Calvin and the drafters of the *Ordinances* knew how many sermons they could manage and where they did not need to spread themselves so thin, but the Senate decided to fill out the planned Sunday schedule as they conceived it… with the result that their additions were not – could not be – immediately implemented.

Sundays: English Translations

The various stages of development contribute to confusion in the modern punctuation of the *Ordinances* in one of the most commonly used English translations and its derivative(s). The Library of Christian Classics [LCC] volume *Calvin: Theological Treatises,* prints draft 2 but gives the received text in notes. However, it makes a mistake in locating a footnote; here the text is given with the footnote inserted in brackets. "Each Sunday, there is to be a sermon at St. Peter [LCC editor adds: the Magdalene], and St. Gervais at break of day, and at the usual hour at the said St. Peter and St. Gervais." [128] In fact, as seen above, "La Magdeleine" should be added in the second part of the sentence: "and at the usual hour at the said St. Peter, La Magdeleine, and St. Gervais." By putting the reference to the La Magdeleine in the wrong place it appears that this parish was to have a dawn service on Sundays but not a mid-morning one, which constitutes an exact reversal of the French. [129]

---

[127] RCP I, p. 5. "Le dimanche qu'il y ayt sermon au point du jour à Sainct Pierre et Sainct Gervais, et à l'heure accoustumee audit Sainct Pierre, à la Magdeleine et Sainct Gervais. A mydy qu'il y ayt cathechisme … en toutes les trois esglises, assavoir Sainct Pierre, la Magdeleine et Sainct Gervais. A trois heures aussi bien en toutes les trois paroisses."

[128] "Draft Ecclesiastical Ordinances," *Calvin: Theological Treatises,* p. 62.

[129] The error is perpetuated in another commonly used anthology, *John Calvin: Selections from His Writings,* edited with an introduction by John Dillenberger (Missoula: Scholars Press, 1975), p. 233.

Weekdays: Days of Sermons

The instructions in the 1541 *Ordinances* about the weekdays when worship would be held were not revised from the original draft, but the interpretation of this part of the edict has been confused by modern punctuation of a text which originally had nothing fixed and the failure to place this ordinance in continuity with prior Genevan practice. In fact, two different modern editors of the *Ordinances* change the sense by the places where they choose to put a comma. The words are: "Es jours ouvriers oultre les deux predications que se font que trois fois la sepmaine on presche à Sainct Pierre asscavoir le lundy mecredi et vendredy..." The *Compagnie des Pasteurs* puts the comma between "sepmaine," and "on presche à Sainct Pierre" which is followed by Parker and Lambert and others; it explains why they say that sermons are held three times per week. "On weekdays besides the two sermons which are done three times a week, there is preaching at St. Peter's on Mondays, Wednesdays, and Fridays." [130]

However, the *Opera Calvini* editors placed the comma between "se font" and "que trois fois la sepmaine" which makes the three sermons refer to St. Pierre and not to the daily worship at the ordinary time. "On weekdays besides the two sermons, there is preaching three times a week at St. Peter's, that is, on Mondays, Wednesdays, and Fridays." [131] The language "the two sermons" in fact echoes the earlier Genevan reference to daily worship and the definite article emphasizes that this is a known practice. Reading the order this way fits the rest of the evidence better, because it is clear from other sources that there were in fact two sermons every weekday at the customary time, one in St. Gervais and one at La Magdeleine, plus an early service on three days at St. Pierre.

Weekdays: Sequence of Sermons

The one part of the 1541 *Ordinances'* instructions about weekdays which changes in the various French versions is the phrase about staggering/ sequencing the sermons. In drafts 1 and 2 the text reads: "On work days besides the two preachings which are done, three times a week they preach at St. Pierre, i.e., Monday, Tuesday, and Friday, one hour before they begin in the other places." [132] This means a dawn service at St. Pierre earlier than the "ordinary" hour at La Magdeleine and St. Gervais. The first Senate revision changes Tuesday to Wednesday and replaces "one hour before they begin in the other places" with "And

---

[130] RCP I, p. 5. Lambert, *Praying, Preaching and Policing*, p. 285 n.12.

[131] OC 10:21.

[132] OS II, p. 337, and CO 10:20.

let the sermons be rung and done one after the other."[133] The second revision/ received version reads: "On work days besides the two preachings which are done, three times a week they preach at St. Pierre, i.e., Monday, Wednesday, and Friday, and these sermons are rung one after the other at such an hour that they may be finished before they begin elsewhere."[134]

Here again, as with the development of the Sunday program, one can see a move from a simple form to a more complex one and the addition of confusion along the way. The drafts plan for the three (dawn) services at St. Pierre to be "an hour before the other places." Although the time would change from one to two hours, this is indeed what was done: dawn services three times/ week at St. Pierre were at 4 a.m./5 a.m. and the weekday services in the other two parishes were at 6 a.m./7a.m. The revised versions of the *Ordinances* complicated the language, but they may not actually have changed what was intended. It can be deduced that the intent is to distinguish between the dawn sermons and those at the ordinary time. Given the fact that the bells were often rung half-an-hour before a weekday sermon (and longer before the main Sunday services),[135] it would be very important to have the different worship hours clearly marked off. Thus, if the bell was rung at 3:30 a.m. for the 4 a.m. service, and at 5:30 a.m. for the 6:00 a.m. service, there would be a noticeable break between the periods of ringing. The bell for the dawn service would ring at 3:30 & 4:00 a.m., then silence for about an hour and a half, and then the bell would ring again at 5:30 & 6:00 a.m. for the 6:00 a.m. daily sermon. The same proportion of time would hold when the winter schedule went into effect: 4:30 & 5:00 a.m. bell for the 5:00 a.m. dawn service, then 6:30 & 7:00 a.m. the bell for the 7:00 a.m. daily sermon. The only time there would be a significant difference would be on Wednesdays for the day of prayer services: 3:30 & 4:00 a.m. for the dawn service in summer, 6:30 & 7:00 a.m. for the main service, and then in winter 4:30 & 5:00 a.m. for the dawn service and 7:30 & 8:00 a.m. for

---

[133] CO 10:20: "(1) *Les derniers mots*: une heure devant etc. *sont rayés et l'autre main les a remplacé par ceux-ci*: Et que les sermons soyent sonnés et faict l'un appres l'aultre."

[134] OC 10:21: "(b): *La rédaction définitive de la fin de cet article est ainsi conçue*: Et que ces sermons soyent sonnez l'un apres l'autre à telle heure qu'ilz puissent estre finitz devant qu'on commence ailleurs." OS II, p. 337 note e explains this as added by the received text.

[135] July 18, 1541 (RC 35 f267v) the Senate decreed "Affin que personne ne perde le sermon, az esté ordonné que le sermon ce doybje sonné az cinq heures et demy du matin et parachevé devant sept" (quoted in Lambert, *Preaching, Praying, and Policing*, p. 291 n.24). Apparently on Sundays the bells might be rung starting an hour before the sermon: on Feb. 21, 1549 (RC 44 f25v) "Sonnement de sermon. Resoluz que les dymenches le sermon du soyer soyt commencé à troy[r]s heures appres midy et sonner à deux heures" (also quoted in Lambert, p. 291 n.24). Often, however, the note about ringing the bell refers to the time the sermon was supposed to begin, rather than when the bell ringing began.

the main sermon. This is an interpretation of the *Ordinances*, but it fits all the various pieces of evidence into a coherent pattern which aligns with the rest of the schedule.

The Practice of the 1541 *Ecclesiastical Ordinances*

Taking a leaf from Lambert's approach and drawing on other sources such as the Consistory minutes and baptismal and marriage records, and drawing on a fuller range of these, it is possible to unravel the confusions about the practice of the 1541 *Ordinances*. The most commonly debated issue is the daily worship schedule. On how many workdays did Geneva have sermons from 1541 to 1549? Related to this is the question of the times and places of these services.

The Days of the Week and Places of Services

It has been argued above that the prescriptive texts required daily worship in two places on all six weekdays, as well as three dawn services in St. Pierre. The clearest evidence for practices consistent with the *Ordinances* in the early years is found in the consistory records, as people who were called before that newly established body answered questions about their attendance at worship. In 1542 and 1543 parishioners respond to this question by naming all the different days of the week: Mondays, Tuesdays, Wednesdays, Thursdays, Fridays, and Saturdays, as well as Sundays of course. For St. Gervais there are explicit references to Monday, Wednesday, Thursday, Friday, and Saturday.[136] For La Magdeleine there are references to Monday, Tuesday, Thursday, and Friday.[137] For St. Pierre there

---

[136] *Consist*. I. On Tues. May 2, 1542, p. 53, Jana wife of Cortagiez, said she "fust dymenche au sermon et lundi à Saintz Gervays..." (Monday). On Thurs. April 6, 1542, p. 30, La gueyniere: "Qu'elle se trouve demain au sermon avec son mari..." (i.e., Friday). On Fri. May 26, 1542, p. 74, Francoys Dupra and wife & her family to be reconciled "demain apres le sermon à Sainctz Gervays" (Saturday). On Thurs. Aug. 10, 1542, p. 100, Françoyse, widow of Claude Loup, says she goes "au sermon à Sainct Gervays"... every three days and "fut mecredi hier passé" (Wednesday). On Thurs. Sept. 7, 1542, p. 111, Gonyn Floutet "esté ajourd'huy et hyer au sermon à Sainctz Gervays" (Wednesday and Thursday). On Tues. Aug. 28, 1543, p. 251, Jane Lulliemon "fust dymenche au sermon az Saint Gervays apres dyné et quelque foys les mecredi" (Wednesday).

[137] *Consist*. I: On Thurs. April 27, 1542, pp. 46, 48, Claudaz, wife of Maystre Michel Julliard and husband to be reconciled with nephew Mermet and servant Jehan de La Pierre, "lundi à la Madeleine apres le sermon" (Monday). On Thurs. Aug. 10, 1542, p. 98, Noble Pernete and three children to be reconciled "demain... à la Magdelene apres le sermon" (Friday); on Thurs. Sept. 7, 1542, p. 110, reconciling Noble Jehan Gringallet with C. Savoex, "demain à la Magdaleine apres le sermon" (Friday). On Thurs. Oct. 25, 1543, p. 264, Françoyse, widow of Tyvent Tissot, and son should be reconciled "à la fin de quelque sermon... [specifies] apres le sermon à demain à la La Magdeleine" [Friday]; on Friday Oct. 26, 1543, p. 266, "apres le

are only references to Monday and Wednesday.[138] Some other parishioners, who do not identify the parish, refer to services on Monday, Tuesday, Wednesday, Thursday, and Saturday.[139] In addition to confirming that there was preaching daily on weekdays, this list reveals that most of these services were held at St. Gervais and La Magdeleine ("the two sermons" decreed by the *Ordinances*), and that the only two days when St. Pierre is mentioned by parishioners are two of the three which were so designated by the *Ordinances*.

Another source of evidence for daily sermons on weekdays is the 1543 ordinance about the work of civic officials. Here the instructions about the first syndic's job make it clear that there were services even when the Senate did not meet, as well as when it did.

---

sermon" at La Magdeleine reconciled Tissot family (Friday). On Thurs. Aug. 10, 1542, p. 99, Guygonaz says "az esté aujourd'huys en la Magdalene" (Thursday); and on Thurs. 15 March 1543, p. 195, Anthoyne de Crouz says "az esté aujourd'huy au sermon à la Magdaleine et a presché le Sr. Calvin et de Joseph az partie" (Thursday). Tuesday 27 May 1544, p. 371, Michiel Cochet says that his baby "fust bastisé à la Magdalene il i a VII jour" (which, if it can be taken exactly, would mean the previous Tuesday).

138 *Consist.* I: On Thurs. Aug. 3, 1542, p. 94, Michiel Cochet, "ne fust pas au sermon et qu'il n'y fut dempuis huyctz jors à Saint Pierre" (apparently Wednesday). On Thurs. Dec. 21, 1542, p. 151, La Donne Jane Begaz, "fust lundi au sermon et à la priere à Saint Pierre" (Monday).

139 *Consist.* I: On Thurs. Sept. 21, 1542, p. 121, Tybauldaz, wife of Glaude Martin, says "vaz aux sermons les dymenches et les lundi" (Monday). On Thurs. Aug. 17, 1542, p. 104, Mama Buctin & his wife Claudaz: "saz femme respond qu'elle fust mardi au sermon et n'a rien retenu" (Tuesday). On Tues. Dec. 19, 1542, p. 150, Françoise, wife of Jehan Bornant, "az esté aujourd'uy au sermon et n'a rien retenu" (Tuesday). On Thurs. March 22, 1543, p. 204, Loys Piaget, "fust mardi au sermon" (Tuesday). On Thurs. 10 Aug. 1542, p. 98, Aymoz, son of Egrege Nycod de Prato, "n'y peult aller bonnement sinon la dymenche et le mecredi" (Wednesday). On Thurs. Nov. 9, 1542, Jana, wife of Jaques Symond, "fust au sermon hier" (Wednesday). On Thurs. April 6, 1542, p. 32 Venturinayz, wife of Sollier: "qu'elle vaz quand elle peult et y a esté aujourd'huys et az presché Mayster Viret" (i.e., Thursday). On Thurs. Dec. 28, 1542, p. 159, the wife of Jehan Corajod "elle viendra tous les samedis et dymenches et mecredis pour venir aux sermons et cathequesme" (Wednesday and Saturday). Examples from *Registres du Conseil*, May 1 & June 2, 1542, OC 21: 312, 313 (RC 37 f80 f112), refer to "demaien appres le sermon," meaning Wednesday and Saturday.
There are multiple references to "tous les jours"; sometimes it is instruction by the consistory, sometimes an excuse from the accused. On Thurs. March 30, 1542, p. 22 Jaques Emyn is told "qu'il vienne tous les jours ou plus souvent à la predication"; on Wed. May 17, 1542, p. 65, Jaques Emyn is ordered to go to catechism "toutes les dymenches" & "tous les jours aux sermons." On Thurs. July 20, 1542, p. 88, Aymoz Cortagier says he goes to sermons but "pas tous les jours"; p. 90, Andri Arnod says he cannot go "tous les jours." On Nov. 23, 1542, p. 142, the mother of M. Hugoz says she goes to the sermon "tous les jours" and makes her apprentices go. In addition, the reconciliation of the Tissot family (above) speaks of doing this "à quelque sermon" as if these were regular occasions.

> Every day that there is no Council meeting let him come at some time in the morning to the city hall, that is at the end of the sermon, to see whether any orders of the Council remain to be executed or to hear those who come there. On Council days, immediately after the time of the sermon, let him be at the city hall to write [the names of] those who request a hearing. [140]

Obviously the reference to the sermon had already become a regular marker of time each day. If the first syndic was ordered to come to city hall after the sermon every day, ordinary folk who had something to ask the Senate would also know when they could find him. Thus it is clear that after Calvin's return from exile Geneva had worship services every day, Monday through Saturday, held in the parishes of St. Gervais and La Magdeleine, with three (earlier) services, Mondays, Wednesdays, and Fridays at St. Pierre, as the *Ordinances* planned. [141]

Although later explicit references to days become fewer, there are still instances which indicate where and when services are being held on weekdays which confirm that this practice continued. The main places are St. Gervais and La Magdeleine. For example, on Thursday Jan. 21, 1546, a woman is instructed by the consistory to come to St. Gervais to the sermon next morning (Friday) for a disciplinary action. A few months later, on Thursday, May 6, a man being questioned says he was at the sermon at La Magdeleine "this morning" but he does not identify the minister correctly and the consistory secretary corrects him. [142] In October 1549 the Senate deals with vendors who cry their baked wares in front of La Magdeleine one Monday morning during the sermon. On a Thursday in 1550 bakers' assistants are called before the consistory for disturbing the services at both La Magdeleine and St. Gervais by hawking their goods around the churches during worship; the days of their infraction are not named but it was very likely they had been hawking both that same morning and probably every day. [143]

The Times of Weekday Services

What was the schedule of services? If the *Ordinances'* regulations are correct about the days and places of daily worship, do they also give an accurate picture of

---

[140] Witte & Kingdon, *Courtship, Engagement, and Marriage*, pp. 83-84.

[141] Lambert's affirmation that by 1551 daily sermons were being given "in all three temples" (above at n.112) is not the case, as a full examination of the baptismal and marriage records demonstrates; see Appendices One and Two.

[142] *Consist.* II, Thurs. Jan. 21, 1546, p. 124; Thurs. May 6, 1546, p. 218.

[143] RC for Monday, Oct. 21, 1549, edited in *Consist.* IV, p. 235. *Consist.* V, Thurs. Oct. 2, 1550, p. 220.

the rest of the practice? Lambert claims that "the schedule of services was never the same from year to year"[144] but there is in fact much more regularity than his pioneering investigations revealed.

Senate notes regarding the organization of preaching in the city indicate that the early morning services at St. Pierre were distinguished from the other daily services because these were often – although not always – the only ones identified by time. On Aug. 18, 1542, a notice indicates where each of the ministers was assigned to preach during the week, and the sermons at St. Pierre are marked as "morning." (This certainly meant dawn, since all the daily services were held in the morning and specific language would be needed only for the services not at the "ordinary" hour to which people had long been accustomed if they were devout enough to have attended daily Mass).[145] On March 30, 1543, the Senate set the times for the services in relation to their own scheduled meetings.

> It is ordered that from Easter until next St. Michael's Day [Sept. 29] the bell for the morning sermon ("sermon de matin") should be rung before four o'clock and the service should begin at four [a.m.]. The "ordinary" sermon should begin at six o'clock and the Wednesday sermon at seven. And the council meeting should begin at seven o'clock. From St. Michael's Day until Easter the council will begin at eight o'clock.[146]

Here the specific times of daily worship are identified. There is a dawn service which begins at 4 a.m. (this is three days/ week at St. Pierre) and there are regular daily services at the "ordinary" time of 6 a.m. (at St. Gervais and La Magdeleine). The reference to Wednesday has to do with the day of prayer service which was a particularly important time of worship, second only to Sunday and thus given more significance by being set at a later hour. For the present it is sufficient to note this anomaly in the weekday schedule, postponing full examination to a later

---

[144] Lambert, *Praying, Preaching and Policing*, p. 290: "The schedule of sermons was never the same from year to year, but this schedule [pp. 285-90] gives a rough idea of the daily weekly rhythm in Geneva."

[145] Aug. 18, 1542, OC 21:301 (RC 36 f98), quoted chap. 2 at n.43.

[146] March 30, 1543 (RC 37 45v): "Ordonné que dempuys Pasques jusques à la St. Michel prochain, le sermon de matin ce doybge sonner devant quattre heures et commencé à quattre heures. L'ordinayre sermon ce doybge commencé à six heures et le sermon de mecredy à sept heures. Et que l'on doybge entré en conseyl à sept heures et dempuys la St. Michel jusque à Pasques à huyct heures." Lambert, *Praying, Preaching and Policing*, p. 290 n.23; however, he writes "L'ordinayre sermon ce doybge commencé a IX heures." In fact, in the manuscript the scribe wrote "sept" and began the word "heures" but realized his mistake and crossed out the "sept heu" and substitued "six," though the "s" is not easily visible. This explains why Lambert read "ix" instead of "six." See Appendix One: Baptismal Records.

point.[147] There is some further information which can be drawn from this quotation. As had been the practice for many years for the Mass, the hour for each service changes twice each year, alternating between a winter time and a summer one. Here the rotation is named only for the ordinary sermon but in fact it applied to the dawn services also, as incidental notes (e.g., March 1547; see below) demonstrate, even before the practice comes into full view in the baptismal records. It was 4 a.m. or 5 a.m. for the dawn services, and 6 a.m. or 7 a.m. for the ordinary ones.[148] The dawn hour might seem impossible to modern sensibilities, but in fact it was considered the normal beginning of the day in early modern Geneva. Already on Feb. 22, 1536, in the course of making various arrangements for the city's safety, e.g., closing the gates before sunset, the Senate had ordered one of the small bells at St. Pierre to be rung every day at 4 a.m. to awaken the people.[149]

The picture of Geneva's weekday services is fully visible in the baptismal and marriage records which began on a regular basis for the city churches in 1550. These demonstrate that St. Gervais had daily services, Monday through Saturday, 6 a.m. or 7 a.m., with the exception of Wednesday when there were two sermons at different hours, dawn and 7 a.m. or 8 a.m. (This day of prayer service at dawn was not planned in the *Ordinances*, but it is evident at least by 1550 and was almost certainly in practice considerably earlier.[150]) La Magdeleine had a very similar schedule, with services Monday-Tuesday, Thursday-Saturday at 6 a.m. or 7 a.m. The only differences were on Wednesday, when there was no dawn service or day of prayer service in La Magdeleine, but a (second) service at St. Pierre at the later hour of 7 a.m. or 8 a.m. St. Pierre itself had the three dawn services planned in the 1541 *Ordinances*, on Mondays, Wednesdays, and Fridays at 4 a.m. or 5 a.m, but on Wednesdays it also hosted the day of prayer service which would otherwise have been at La Magdeleine.

---

[147] See chap. 4, pp. ___, esp. at n.52.

[148] In some cases the announcement of the time change appears to be a simple statement, as on April 13, 1540; in this case it came two weeks after Easter, which was early that year; see RC V, p. 238: "Retardé l'estee ordinairement d'ung heure." See n.145 above and Appendices One and Two.

[149] Feb. 22, 1536, RC 29 f22v: "Item le matin ladicte cloche [une des petites cloches de sainct Pierre] sera sonnees à quattres heures pour reveiller les gens." archives@etat.ge.ch accessed Aug. 1, 2013.

[150] Dawn baptisms on Wed. are recorded in the St. Gervais registers from the beginning of those records in 1550. As yet I have not seen concrete evidence for the exact date of institution of these dawn day of prayer services in a second location (besides St. Pierre). It seems probable that it was in place by 1545, see chap. 4 at n.79. Given the intense concern about keeping the whole city on one schedule, it is probable that St. Gervais had two services on special weekdays like the day of prayer.

There is some confusion about the place of the day of prayer liturgy. It was assigned to St. Pierre from its inception in Nov. 1541, even though the only service planned for this church in the *Ordinances* was at dawn and that would not have been an appropriate hour for the kind of public intercession for neighboring cities suffering from plague which Calvin and the Senate had in mind. In addition, there is evidence for the actual practice of worship at 7 a.m./8 a.m. at St. Pierre from the 1540s and 1550s, while there was still no Wednesday service at La Magdeleine until 1555. For example, the baptism of Poupin's second son was held at St. Pierre "au grand sermon" on Wednesday, Aug. 17, 1546. In the give-and-take between the Senate and the ministers in the October-November 1549 debates over "dawn sermons every day," the "Wednesday and day of prayer" sermon was added to the issues under discussion; on Nov. 11, 1549, it is ordered that the sermon be returned to the "said location" and the bell rung at 7 a.m. [151] What this cryptic phrase means is not immediately obvious. It appears, however, that the Senate wanted the day of prayer service to be held at La Magdeleine (which is where the *Ordinances* had established a morning sermon not at the dawn hour) but conceded that it should be returned to the place where it had been, i.e., St. Pierre. In any event, when the baptismal records begin shortly thereafter, there are effectively no baptisms listed for La Magdeleine on Wednesdays, while there are quite a significant number of baptisms at St. Pierre at 7 a.m. or 8 a.m. as well as the mandated dawn hour. [152]

---

[151] For the directives locating the day of prayer services at St. Pierre, see chap. 4 at n.61. Lambert, *Praying, Preaching and Policing*, p. 290 n.23 for Nov. 11, 1549: "Le sermon de mescredi. Sur ec [ce] qui hont prier avoir advis sur ce que mescredi et jour de la priere et la dimenche, que il seroit bon de faire ung sermont à l'eglisse de la Magdeleine de mattin. Arresté que ilz puissent faire les sermons la dimenche mattin à l'eglisse de la Magdeleine et que le sermont soit renvier aud. lieu et sonné à sept heures comme dessus." At the beginning of the baptismal books for La Magdeleine and St. Pierre, Poupin recorded the baptisms of his three sons. On Thursday April 10, 1544, Benjamin was baptized at La Magdeleine by de Geneston; his godfather was his mother's brother, Cybouz (?) Grifferat. On Wednesday Aug. 17, 1546, Joseph was baptized at St. Pierre by Des Gallars "mecredi au grand sermon"; his godfather was Jehan Druzet, a brother-in-law. On Sunday, June 3, 1548, Samuel was baptized at St. Pierre by Des Gallars "au grand sermon"; his godfather was Francoys Vunilland (?).

[152] A few examples from the baptismal records: At St. Pierre for 1550: among the 38 baptisms for 46 babies performed on Wednesdays, there are a number of examples of two liturgies on the same day at different times, e.g., on Jan. "21" = 22 Bourgoing did services at 5 and 8 a.m.; on July 23 he did services at 4 and 7 a.m. On Sept. 3 Cop did one 4 a.m. and Bourgoing at 7 a.m. In 1551: there are 43 (45) baptisms of 54 (56) babies performed on Wednesdays, again with notice of sermons at two times: Cop gives the dawn time every baptism, Bourgoing gives the dawn time about half the days. Fabri and Chauvet both do baptisms at 7 a.m. or 8 a.m. on a number of days. By contrast Wednesdays at La Magdeleine have virtually no baptisms; the only entry in 1550 is by Poupin (almost certainly a mistake either of day or parish) and there are none at all in 1551. For more examples, see chap. 5, pp. 431 ff.

The expanding population of Geneva in the 1550s, especially the latter part of the decade, meant not only that new church buildings needed to be opened but also that the number of services provided in the three original parishes had to be increased. In mid-1555 the ministers offered to provide a service on Wednesday at La Magdeleine, and this was begun then, as the baptismal records demonstrate. In effect, this service has an anomalous place with regard to the *Ordinances*; the latter had established a sermon on every weekday, including Wednesdays, but the Wednesday day of prayer service had been displaced to St. Pierre to allow for a larger crowd on that special day. [153] Now that lacuna was being filled so Magdeleine would henceforth have a Wednesday service even while there continued to be two at St. Pierre. When the church of St. Germain was refurbished for regular use in 1557, daily services at the ordinary hour were planned. To this point, the schedule at the original three parishes had not been altered since it achieved its full complement of planned services: i.e., daily (at "the ordinary time" except on Wednesdays) at St. Gervais and La Magdeleine, and three at St. Pierre. To these had been added a dawn service on Wednesday at St. Gervais (sometime in the 1540s) and the extra Wednesday service at La Magdeleine (1555).

However, in mid-1559 another set of daily services at the ordinary time (6 a.m. or 7 a.m.) was begun at St. Pierre (in addition to the three dawn services on Monday, Wednesday, and Friday which had been in practice since the beginning). The reason given when the decision was made on June 19 was the enormous crowds which caused the summer heat to be unbearable in the smaller church buildings so the weekday sermon at St. Germain was moved to St. Pierre. The move was put into effect immediately, as is evident from the baptismal records of the parish of St. Pierre – within three days the St. Pierre register begins recording baptisms on Tuesdays, Thursdays, and Saturdays, days which had not previously

---

[153] June 10, 1555, OC 21:609 (RC 49 f102): "Et daventage qu'on leur dise [to ministers] qu'ilz facent encores ung presche apres diner la dimenche à la Magdelene et aussi ung le mescredy et s'ilz ne peulvent satisfaire à cela qu'on advisera de les soulager d'ung compagnon ou deux ainsin qu'il sera besoing." June 24, 1555, 21:609 (RC 49 f114): "M. Calvin. Sur ce qu'il a proposé que suyvant ce que ca devant Messieurs ont dressé, qu'il y aye encor ung sermon à la Magdelene le dimenche au matin et le mecredy qu'il seroit requys d'avoir encore ung prescheur à cause de beaucoub de charges... et semblablement que le temple de la Magdelene maintenant qu'il faict chaut est fort estoffé et qu'il est dangereux que la senteur ne cause quelque infection parquoy seroit bon de faire ouvrir les fenstres et y mettre des treillis de fil archant pour peur des arondelles. Arresté qu'on face encore ung prescheur." The record appears to be confused here, since there was already a Sunday morning service at La Magdeleine; logic says that what is meant is an afternoon Sunday service, because that is what the ministers offer, and that is what the baptismal and marriage records indicate was begun.

had services. [154] The continuation of baptisms on all weekdays demonstrates that this expanded version of the daily schedule was accepted as the regular practice even before it was confirmed by the 1561 revision of the *Ecclesiastical Ordinances*. [155] Now the weekday services at the "ordinary" time were held in all three of the original parishes. According to long-standing practice there were dawn services on three days each week and Sundays at St. Pierre and on Sundays and Wednesdays at St. Gervais. In late 1559 La Magdeleine was also provided with a dawn service on Sundays and Wednesdays, for a brief time. Again, the weather seems to have played a role; in winter the unheated cathedral was extremely cold, so in November it was decided to move the weekday dawn services from St. Pierre to La Magdeleine and St. Germain. [156] In effect this doubled the number of early morning sermons on the Greater Geneva side of the river, since there is no record that St. Germain had had dawn services before this. La Magdeleine records its first Wednesday dawn service wedding on Nov. 28 and first dawn baptism on Dec. 20, 1559. [157] In addition, the timing of the second Wednesday service at La Magdeleine was now at 7 a.m./8 a.m., which made its schedule identical to that of St. Gervais (services at the ordinary time Mon.-Tues. and Thurs.-Sat., and two on Wednesdays at dawn and 7 a.m./8 a.m.). [158]

Even after the short-lived parish of St. Germain was closed again in 1561, this organization of the three original parishes remained, with only one minor alte-

---

154 Aug. 7, 1559, OC 21:719-20 (RC 55 78v). "M. Jeh. Calvin – temples. Sur ce a proposé que à cause de la multitude du peuple il soit requys de trover moyen qu'on ayt encor ung temple ou prescher/ mesme s'il estoit possible que Rive fut restauré veu que une grande partie du peuple qui entre à Saint Pierre ne peult entendre/ et cela au moins mal qu'il seroit possible... Arresté que quant es temples pour le present on presche à Nostre Dame la nefve..."

155 June 19, 1559, OC 21:718 (RC 55 f59) : "Sermons. Pour ce qu'il fait si grande chaleur qu'on ne peult durer à la Magdelaine à cause de la multitude qui sy trouve pour ouir Monsieur Calvin et Monsieur Pierre Viret. A este arresté que doresnavant pendant qu'il fera chault on presche à Saint Pierre la sepmaine au lieu de Saint Germain." The move must have been made immediately because baptisms are recorded for the days of the week which had never been used for daily worship [since 1542?]. For weekday services at St. Pierre at the "ordinary" time of 6 a.m./ 7 a.m., six days/ week, see evidence of baptismal records; the earliest date for a Thursday baptism is June 22, 1559; for a Tuesday baptism is July 11, 1559; for a Saturday baptism is July 29, 1559. See Appendix One.

156 Nov. 7, 1559, OC 21:724 (RC 55 f141) : "Sermons. Sur ce que maistre Calvin a proposé que au lieu du sermon qu'on fait le matin à Saint Pierre à cause du grand froid il seroit bon de prescher à la Magdelenne et Saint Germain. Esté arresté qu'on declaire audict Sr. Calvin qu'il advise comme la chose sera mieux et que ainsin soit fait."

157 For La Magdeleine dawn baptisms, see baptismal record for Wednesday dawn service Dec. 20, 1559; Appendix One.

158 For evidence of these changes, see the baptismal records.

ration when La Magdeleine dropped back to one service on Wednesday, which was probably held at the ordinary time rather than an hour later as had been the case in 1559-61. This practice of weekday sermons in the three parishes St. Pierre, La Magdeleine, and St. Gervais, which included some significant additions not planned in 1541, was formally legislated in the revised *Ordinances* in 1561. [159]

Practice of the 1541 *Ordinances* on Sundays

The schedule of Sunday services in 1541 is not so complicated as that for the weekdays but it offers certain challenges of its own because for Sunday the *Ordinances* cannot be taken at face value, at least at the beginning. The reason is that there was a lack of sufficient trained clergy and therefore the need to limit the number of places that services were held. Theoretically there should have been eleven sermons (counting catechism as a service): four each at St. Pierre and St. Gervais, and three at La Magdeleine (although it may be noted from the draft ordinances that Calvin did not plan a either a morning or afternoon service at La Magdeleine; those were added by the Senate's wish). St. Pierre and St. Gervais had services at dawn, mid-morning, catechism at noon, and in the afternoon at 3 p.m. These eight services were organized immediately on the basis of what were probably two existing morning sermons at St. Pierre, one at St. Gervais, and one at the Rive, plus one afternoon one at the Rive, although it took a few months to get the dawn service at St. Gervais functioning. [160] Thus worship was held at four times throughout the day, beginning at 4 a.m. and concluding at 4 p.m., in two parishes.

Even before the baptismal and marriage records confirm that these services were in fact taking place at St. Pierre and St. Gervais as scheduled, there is evidence from consistory records. A Senate instruction about details of the Lord's Supper for Easter 1542 indicates "first" and "second" morning services. This must have been at St. Pierre since the dawn service at St. Gervais was not begun until August that year. By 1543 there are specific instances of people

---

[159] *Ordinances* 1561, OC 10:99-100. "Les jours ouvriers qu'il y ait presche tous les iours es trois parroisses, sainct Pierre, la Magdalene et sainct Gervais à une mesme heure: assavoir, d'esté depuis Pasques iusques au premier d'octobre, des six heures iusques à sept; et d'hyver, des sept heures iusques à huict. Mais que les prières soyent faites specialement le jour de Mercredi, sinon que ci apres fust establi autre jour selon l'opportunité du temps. Outre lesdites predications, qu'on presche trois fois la sepmaine de matin à sainct Pierre: assavoir le Lundi, Mercredi et Vendredi: et à sainct Gervais le Mercredi, avant les susdits sermons ordinaires."

[160] Aug. 8, 1542, OC 21:300 (RC 36 f91). "Sermon à St. Gervex. Ordonné que les dymenches matin l'on doybge prescher aut temple St. Gervex."

affirming that they had attended dawn services: "au premier sermon à Sainct Pierre," "au premier presche à Saintz Gervays."[161] Others speak of going to St. Pierre or to St. Gervais on Sunday mornings and/or afternoons.[162] Only attendance at catechism is not identified with specific place names; this is probably because people were supposed to go to their own parish for that service and felt no need to name the place. This was the one service which was absolutely required in every parish even if no other was held (as was the case at La Magdeleine for some years), and the records of disputes over baptismal names, although they come from several years later, make it clear that catechism was being maintained in all the parishes.[163]

The times for the four services were set effectively from the beginning, although the seasonal variations can make following the scattered and incomplete references confusing if the patterns of alternation are not explicitly recognized. The dawn services were held at 4 a.m. from Easter to St. Michael's in September, 5 a.m. the rest of the year. Incidental references in the consistory records not only witness to the practice but also indicate that naming the time was the usual way to identify these sermons. In 1547 a man says he was at the 5 a.m. service at St. Pierre but does not know who preached, or any ministers' names. The following year on March 8 a married woman is found with a young man at a very early hour on Sunday morning and claims she was going to the 4 a.m. (!) service. When witnesses are called, the man who apprehended her identifies himself as the guard for the 5 a.m. Sunday sermon.[164] Here the woman confused the actual time (the date was before Easter so the winter schedule would still be in effect), while the guard gave the correct one.

The time for the main morning service was usually 8 a.m. – mid-morning by the early modern clock. Although in the early years this sermon may have been held at 9 a.m. (in 1542 and 1543 some parishioners speak of attending the

---

161 See the examples in n.75 which name both churches in reference to attendance at the dawn service.

162 Morning and afternoon at St. Pierre, *Consist.* I: March 23, 1542, p. Pernete, widow of Pierre Puvel, was "à Sainctz Pierre à matin et à vespres." Morning and afternoon at St. Gervais, *Consist.* I: April 5, 1543, p. 213 Noble Pernete Du Payn: was "devant dyné" at St. Gervais. Tues. Aug. 28, 1543, p. 251, Jane Lulliemon "fust dymenche au sermon az Saint Gervays apres dyné et quelque foys les mecredi."

163 For some examples, see n.78; for further discussion see chap. 5 at nn.204ff.

164 *Consist.* II, Thurs. March 31, 1547, p. 59: Tivent Papa says he went to sermon "le matin à Sainct-Pierre de cinq heures." *Consist.* III, Thurs., March 8 & 22, 1548, pp. 13, 22: La Jeanne, wife of Antoyne Du Villars, was caught with her boyfriend pretending "aller au presche à 4 heures." Two weeks later the man who caught her "se prinst garde à cinq heures du matin que l'on va au presche le dimenche."

service at that hour),[165] within a few years the time was fixed at 8 a.m. year-round. In 1549 when the ministers offer to do the morning service at La Magdeleine they speak of it as "l'heure de huict" and that numerical designation is common in the baptismal records (including the very occasional notes before 1550).[166]

The catechism was held at mid-day ("midi") and also seems not to have experienced the seasonal change, or at least there is no evidence of this. The afternoon service was affected by its own form of seasonal variation, with a change of time in deep winter. Normally the Sunday afternoon service was set for 3 p.m., but at least by 1549 it was decided that in the depth of winter the days were too short; it was completely dark when people left the service at 4 p.m. The solution was to advance the hour of the Sunday afternoon sermon to 2 p.m. from early November until the beginning of February ("Candlemas").[167]

The story of Sundays at La Magdeleine is different, however. There the only regular Sunday service for many years was the noon catechism, although a mid-morning service was held on the four days per year when the Lord's Supper was celebrated in the city. On other Sundays the people of La Magdeleine parish

---

[165] *Consist.* I, Dec. 28, 1542, p. 157, La Maurisaz Tallucheta says she "az receup la Cene lundi passé [= Dec. 25, Christmas day]... comme les aultres à neufz heures." April 12, 1543, p. 221, Pierre Guilliermet du Villard, says he goes twice on Sundays and "prescha Messieurs Calvin au matin à IX heures." The first of these instances comes from the winter schedule, the second from the summer schedule, so possibly the main Sunday or holy day service was at 9 a.m. year-round in this earliest period, or perhaps these parishioners were confused? Certainly by 1550, when the baptismal records become available, there is no question of any other time than 8 a.m. year-round, and this had probably been the case for some years.

[166] See nn.77, 114 and Appendices One and Two.

[167] Nov. 11, 1549 the council decreed: (RC 44, f261) "Sermont establir. Sur ce que les Srs. ministres hont acoustumee de prescher les dimenches à trois heures et finissent à 4 heures et que allors il n'est possible de voir les ungs les aultres/ dont seroit requis de suyvre à la forme des esdictz. Arresté que ledict sermont soyt commencé à deux heures jusques à la Chandelleuse" (quoted in Lambert, *Preaching, Praying, and Policing*, pp. 289-90 n. 22). An entry for Feb. 6, 1550 marks the end of the period when the sermon was at 2 p.m. (RC 44 f316v) "Du sermon. Icy est proposé et arresté que le sermon soit retorné aux heures par avant devant l'yvert accoustumees" (quoted in Lambert, p. 290 n.23). It is not perfectly clear whether this practice of temporarily changing the time of the afternoon service in mid winter had been in place before or not. On the one hand, the November entry explains the reason in a way which suggests this is the initial proposal. On the other hand, there is a reference earlier in 1549 to a February afternoon sermon at 3 p.m. which may have to do only with the length of the bell ringing but might also indicate a return to the regular time of 3 p.m. from 2 p.m. On Feb. 21, 1549 (RC 44 f25v) "Sonnement de sermon. Resoluz que les dymenches le sermon de soyer soyt commencé à troyr troys heures appres midy et sonner à deux heures" (also quoted in Lambert, p. 291 n.24). This may have been an experiment which was deemed successful and so led to the regulation in November. There is clear evidence in the baptismal and marriage records, which begin, of course, in 1550.

probably attended worship at St. Pierre.[168] Although they were actually free to choose any service, attending the other morning one which was held at St. Gervais would have meant walking some distance. As a result of the arguments with the Senate in October 1549, the ministers offered to provide a main Sunday morning service at La Magdeleine (on a regular basis), and this is visible in the baptismal records which begin the following year.[169] By mid-1555 the afternoon service was added so that all three Sunday services called for in the *Ordinances* were finally in practice at La Magdeleine, as the marriage records plainly demonstrate.[170]

---

[168] The existence of a service on Supper Sundays is witnessed by the fact that elders are assigned to serve the cup, beginning with first Supper recorded in Consistory records, at the meeting on April 6, 1542, for Easter Sunday April 10; at the meeting on March 22, 1543 for Easter March 25 and Aug. 30, 1543, for the September Supper (*Consist.* I, pp. 34-35, 207, 254) and references by parishioners to having taken communion there, e.g., Colleta, daughter of Andrier Berthier, Sept. 14, 1542 (*Consist.* I, p. 116) who says that she took the Lord's Supper at La Magdeleine, and goes to the [daily] sermons at the La Magdeleine and to St. Pierre on Sundays [evidently except when the Supper is celebrated]. For the regulations and further discussion of the practice, see chap. 3 at nn.190ff.

[169] See quotations in nn.114f. See baptismal and marriage records in Appendices One and Two.

[170] June 10 & 24, 1555, OC 21:608-09 quoted above in n.152; Appendices One and Two.

Chap. 1, Fig. 2. A Table of Worship Services, 1542-1564

Sunday Schedule – 4 services, most alternate summer-winter times
    D = Dawn = 4 a.m. summer, 5 a.m. winter
    M = (Main) Morning = 8 a.m. (usually year-round; a few years: 9 a.m. year round)
    C = Catechism = noon (year-round)
    A = Afternoon = 3 p.m. usually, after 1549 change to 2 p.m. November-February

Weekday Schedule – 1-3 services/ day, all alternate summer-winter times
    D = Dawn = 4 a.m. summer, 5 a.m. winter
    O = "Ordinary" = 6 a.m. summer, 7 a.m. winter
    P = Day of Prayer on Wednesday = 7 a.m. summer, 8 a.m. winter

1542-1549	Sun.	Mon.	Tues.	Wed.	Thurs.	Fri.	Sat.
St. Pierre	4: dmca	1: d		[2][171] dp		1: d	
Magdeleine	1: c	1: o	1: o	[0]	1: o	1: o	1: o
St. Gervais	4: dmca	1: o	1: o	[2][172] dp	1: o	1: o	1: o

1550-1555	Sun.	Mon.	Tues.	Wed.	Thurs.	Fri.	Sat.
St. Pierre	4: dmca	1: d		2: dp		1: d	
Madeleine	2: mc	1: o	1: o	[0]	1: o	1: o	1: o
St. Gervais	4: dmca	1: o	1: o	2: dp	1: o	1: o	1: o

1555-1559	Sun.	Mon.	Tues.	Wed.	Thurs.	Fri.	Sat.
St. Pierre	4: dmca	1: d		2: dp		1: d	
Madeleine	3: mca	1: o	1: o	1: o	1: o	1: o	1: o
St. Gervais	4: dmca	1: o	1: o	2: dp	1: o	1: o	1: o

---

[171] A day of prayer was supposed to be at La Magdeleine, but probably from the beginning it was moved to St. Pierre; see quotation of Nov. 11, 1541, chap. 4 at n.61.

[172] At some point in the 1540s – probably by 1545 – a Wed. dawn service was added at St. Gervais and the second service was later, as at St. Pierre.

1559-1564	Sun.	Mon.	Tues.	Wed.	Thurs.	Fri.	Sat.
St. Pierre	4: dmca	2: do	1: o	2: do	1: o	2: do	1: o
Madeleine	3 [173] mca	1: o	1: o	1 [174]	1: o	1: o	1: o
St. Gervais	4: dmca	1: o	1: o	2: dp	1: o	1: o	1: o

III: Conclusion

So what can be concluded? It is clear that the 1541 *Ecclesiastical Ordinances* as received provide an accurate basic guide to the worship life in Calvin's Geneva. The parishes of St. Pierre and St. Gervais followed the decree exactly, although over the years they also added a number of services (not found in the draft or received versions). The most significant change came in 1559 when worship began to be held at the "ordinary time" on all six weekdays at St. Pierre, in addition to the original three dawn sermons. The services at La Magdeleine were the one place where the plans of 1541 *Ordinances* were not followed precisely; on weekdays the practice was quite close, with only the Wednesday day of prayer service missing (because it was moved to St. Pierre, until a sermon on this day was specifically added in 1555). On Sundays for many years La Magdeleine lacked two of the three services stipulated by the received text (though it followed the draft versions). It had only the catechism regularly, but there was a morning service on the days when the Lord's Supper was celebrated. Then in 1549 a regular morning sermon was added and in 1555 the mandated afternoon one was begun. In 1559 a dawn service on Sundays and Wednesdays was temporarily added at La Magdeleine, only to be dropped about a year later. The additions in all three parishes that went beyond the 1541 *Ordinances*, which included summer time-winter time alternations as well as more services, were essentially codified in the 1561 revised *Ordinances*.

---

[173] For about a year, 1559-60, there were dawn services on Sun. and Wed. but these are not listed here.

[174] The day of prayer service probably changed times, being at 7 a.m./ 8 a.m. for a time but then most likely back to 6 a.m./7 a.m. ("ordinary").

CHAPTER TWO

PREACHERS AND PEOPLE IN CHURCH

Daily worship in sixteenth-century Protestant Geneva gathered preachers and parishioners at various times and in several places; it was regular and predictable but far from static. The buildings and schedules were established with a considerable degree of orderliness by the 1541 *Ecclesiastical Ordinances*, while the persons in the pulpits or pews were much more mobile. The main subject of this chapter is the preaching patterns of the ministers, in historical context. A shorter final part observes some aspects of the presence of the people in the pews.

I: The Preachers of Geneva

The pastors of Calvin's Geneva have been studied from various angles, but not as a functioning collegial body in the practice of daily preaching and worship leadership. Tracing that corporate pastoral organization, especially as regards preaching, is the main purpose here. Before investigating the "men at work," however, it is necessary to clarify some terms and contexts.

Historical Context: Continuities and Discontinuities in Definitions

It is well known that there were significant differences between what was expected of Roman priests and of Protestant pastors in worship. There was also continuity of various kinds as well as some confusion because terminology might remain in use even though the task to which it referred had changed.

Some of the continuity is found in the activities of ministers. Medieval clergy and Protestant pastors both recognized and practiced the leadership of liturgy (public services), the administration of the sacraments, and the work of preaching. However, they divided the responsibilities differently and gave greater weight to different parts. One difference was a function of (re)distributing clerical tasks. Medieval clergy had a number of different ranks and groups, and the specific duties required of each were usually not the same. Parish priests were obligated to celebrate the sacraments, especially the daily Mass, but preaching was not required of them. It was desirable, but not essential to their role. Technically, preaching was required of bishops, but bishops had many other duties, including especially administration and discipline, so that regular preaching was often compromised (sometimes quite seriously). In practice it was usually the regular clergy, namely the friars, who were the main preachers of the late medieval world because they were normally much better educated than the secular priests and more numerous than the bishops.

The frequency of sermons available to ordinary laity is impossible to determine exactly, although preaching was much more widespread than Protestants have usually claimed. Citizens of great cities like Strasbourg and Basel established endowed pulpits so that their people might have ready access to good preaching, and their parish clergy might also have more education than was generally the case.[1] Small rural villages rarely heard sermons unless an itinerant friar happened to pass through the region. Most communities of any size tried to arrange special sermons for important church seasons, particularly Lent and often Advent. Jeanne de Jussie, a leader of Geneva's St. Clare convent, gives a picture of preaching in that city in the years just before and during the conflict with the new "heretics." There were regular sermons in the religious houses, and at least sometimes in the cathedral on Sundays and feast days.[2] The most important

---

[1] Geiler von Kaysersberg was famous for his sermons and reforming spirit ; see Jane D. Douglass, *Justification in Late Medieval Preaching: A Study of John Geiler of Keisersberg* (Leiden: Brill, 1966). For Basel, see Burnett, "A Tale of Three Cities," pp. 97-98.

[2] Jeanne de Jussie, *Le Levain du Calvinisme*, p. 64: "Le Lundy de Pasques le Beau-pere prescheur print congé, & se retira… Depuis l'on ne preschoit point, chose qui estoit bien estrange: car de coustume tous les Dimanches, & festes solennelles on preschoit infailliblement aux Couvents." cf. p. 93 et *passim*. For specific days when preaching occurred in what appear to be public places: p. 79 ("le jour de l'An"), p. 82 (the Sunday of Septuagesima, the preacher set out to cover "tous les principaux points qu'il avoit presché durant l'Advent," but after he made the sign of the cross and said the Ave Maria, he was interrupted and dragged out of the pulpit by a heretic), p. 95 (Pentecost 1534, after the sermon, Jacques Bernard made public his conversion), p. 99 (the last Sunday in July 1534; after the bell for the sermon the monk took off his robe and began to preach a "Lutheran"/ heretical sermon).

events were the special holy seasons, when notable preachers were invited to serve the whole city and usually gave their sermons in the open, in front of the cathedral or the church of a religious order. For example, Geneva engaged the learned Dominican Guy Furbity to preach during Advent in 1533 and a prominent Franciscan for Lent 1534.[3] Sermons were not a necessary part of worship, however, and most parish priests did not preach often, much less regularly. Amy Nelson Burnett has compared preaching and pastoral care in pre-reform Geneva with those in Basel and Strasbourg. She concludes that in Geneva these seem to have been weaker than in the other cities, probably because a good number of the benefices were controlled by distant patrons and non-resident rectors.[4]

The Protestant understanding of ministerial responsibility, as is well known, gave primary attention to preaching as the main task of clergy. The importance of the sacraments varied among those who broke with Rome, or rather, the way sacraments were important was different for different reformers and their followers. It was clear, however, that regular preaching was now an (or even sometimes *the*) essential part of every Protestant parish minister's responsibilities. Many Protestants saw pastors as the rightful counterparts of bishops in this regard: preaching was a requirement of the office. The episcopal function of exercising discipline might also be part of the pastoral role, although most Protestants allocated this task, as well as others like the care of the poor, to the Christian prince or a combination of magistrates and pastors under civil control. (As is well known, only the Calvinist Reformed insisted that ecclesiastical oversight and other functions were necessary to the church as church and not subject to civil rulers or even in essence a shared task.[5]) One might say that when Protestants

---

3   Jeanne de Jussie, *Le Levain du Calvinisme*, pp. 62-63 (Palm Sunday 1534, a Dominican from Auxerre was preaching at the OP convent "& pour la multitude du people preschoit en la grande place devant l'Eglise" but there heretics came and he feared being killed so he fell out of the pulpit, people left and the sermon was not finished); pp. 74 & 86 (Furbity in Advent and a Franciscan in Lent); p. 90 (Lent 1534, quoted in chap. 6 n.6); p. 103 (Advent 1534, "De tout l'Advent ne fut faict sermon à Geneve que des chetifs [heretics], ce qui n'auoit esté de vie d'homme, & estoit bien estrange aux Chrestiens."); p. 63 (Good Friday 1534 there was much tumult and people were armed and priests did not dare to go out in the streets without weapons. "Et pour le moins le peuple se communia, & fut determiné par Messieurs du Chapitre que la Passion se prescheroit le Vendredy sainct dedans l'Eglise Sainct Pierre, ce que de vie d'homme n'avoit esté faict.") Lambert interprets this last note to mean that preaching was rare (*Preaching, Praying, Policing*, p. 159, p. 207 n.117) but in fact the point is that the service was held indoors [*dedans*] rather than in the open square in front of the cathedral.

4   Burnett, "A Tale of Three Cities," p. 110-11.

5   For more on this aspect of pastoral ministry, see chap. 3 at nn.199f, 227ff; chap. 7 at nn.180, 188, 191, 194, 198f, 204, 209f.

rejected the monastic orders, they incorporated into their parish pastors' obligations the ministerial roles that the friars had often filled.

The tasks of administering the sacraments and leading the parish liturgy (however altered those might be from their medieval counterparts) remained an important part of the Protestant pastoral vocation. Thus there was continuity as well as significant change. Not surprisingly the changes contributed to a (sometimes considerable) degree of confusion, not least with regard to terminology for the ministerial offices.

Developing Terminology and an Identity for Ministers in Protestant Geneva

Part of the reform of the ministry in Geneva was the development of a coherent language and identity for the several offices which came to distinguish the Calvinist Reformed tradition. First was the struggle to differentiate between Catholic and Protestant clergy, both in terms of titles and authority. When Farel and his friends were accepted by the Genevan authorities as the religious leaders of the city in 1535-36, they were called and understood as "preachers," in contrast to the Roman "priests."[6] The new church leaders were taking on the "cure of souls," i.e., pastoral work, but legally they were viewed in the same category as friars, not parish priests established in a fixed office. For years the disorganization and its significant limitations plagued the reformers, perhaps particularly Calvin, who was protesting the issue in a letter to Heinrich Bullinger just two months before he and Farel and Corauld were exiled.

> We have not yet been able to obtain… that the city, which in proportion to its extent is very populous, may be distributed into parishes, as is rendered necessary by the complicated administration of the church. The generality of men are more ready to acknowledge us as preachers than as pastors.[7]

The common impression that they were "hired for the sermon" and did not have the status of parish priests is also one reason it was so easy for the Protestant preachers to be forced out of the city.

---

[6]   Examples: *predicant* or *prescheur* used for Protestants and *prestre* for Roman, April 28 & May 10 & 12, 1536, OC 21:200, 213, 221 (RC 29 f 92v, 103v, 105v). *predicant* or *prescheur* or *magister/maistre* for Protestants: Sept. 8, 1536; March 30, July 28 & 29, 1537; Jan. 3 & 25, April 19, 1538; RC I, p. 134; RC II, pp. 126, 272f; RC III, pp. 4, 45, 226f. See July 3, 1537 quoted in n.11.

[7]   *Letters of John Calvin*, vol. 1, p. 66. Letter 93, Feb. 21, 1538, OC 10:154: "Nondum extorquere potuimus… Ut urbs quae est pro amplitudinis suae modo populosissima in paroecias distribueretur. Quemadmodum enim fert confusanea haec administratio, vulgus hominum concionatores nos magis agnoscit quam pastores."

Following the departure of Farel, Calvin and Corauld, the Genevan authorities apparently decided to put the remaining and newly hired clergy on a regular salary, and began to refer to them – at least occasionally – as "ministres evangeliques."[8] This was not a full establishment as parish pastors in the traditional sense, since the old parish structure was not revised until Calvin made that part of his re-entry plan. With the 1541 *Ecclesiastical Ordinances* the city was re-organized into a legal system of three parishes, and the formal process for official recognition as regularly installed pastors was defined. Calvin was named as minister of St. Pierre and Viret as minister of St. Gervais,[9] even though in the new church order the way pastors were acknowledged to be "established" and how they functioned were no longer tied to a particular parish... intriguing developments with very interesting consequences which will be explored below. For present purposes, the words "pastor" and "minister" are used interchangeably for ministers of word and sacrament, i.e., the men who replaced the parish priests.

A second aspect of the new Calvinist Reformed formation of ministerial identity and calling was the development of the office of pastors in the context of other ministries. On the one hand, Calvin wanted to re-shape both language and function according to his understanding of New Testament teaching. On the other, he needed to accommodate his organization to the Genevans' fears as well as to educate them. The most common source of confusion in naming ministers was the use of the word "deacon"; one of the most objectionable terms was "bishop." Examining Calvin's use of these words in his concrete pastoral situation illustrates how he and the Genevans worked out what ecclesiastical leadership would replace the Roman priests.

The name "deacon" is one of the most ambiguous terms among sixteenth-century Protestant church offices. For centuries, "deacons" had been clergy on the way to the priesthood; in the Roman orders of ministry they held the third rank after bishops and priests. Deacons functioned as assistants to the higher clergy until they were elevated to that sacramental office themselves. For many Protestants, particularly in German-speaking areas, the name "deacon" continued to be used at least occasionally for an assistant minister. In Geneva the same

---

8   Naphy, *Calvin and the Consolidation*, p. 34. On May 19, 1536 (OC 21:201, RC 29 f 111v) the whole phrase "ministres de la parole de Dieu" is used; on Sept. 13, 1541, Calvin is called "ministre evangelique" (OC 21:282, RC 35:324). However, most of the time the clergy are still identified as "predicant."

9   Nov. 7, 1541, OC 21:285 (RC 35 f383): "Pource que Geneve est reduyse en 3 parroches assavoyer S. Pierre laz Magdalene et S. Gervex advisé que les Srs. Predicans Calvin et Viret doybjent servyr az S. Pierre et S. Gervex." Despite the word "predicans" they were recognized as established pastors.

language was common at first, but over the course of Calvin's ministry this changed. According to Calvinist Reformed theology, the function of deacons is to care for the poor, the sick, the afflicted; that is, it is a ministry of social welfare. Calvin understood this to be the true Biblical vocation of deacons, although he readily agreed that it was appropriate for them to assist pastors in the administration of the cup in the Lord's Supper, as a sign that their vocation to serve the poor was indeed a religious calling.[10]

For present purposes, it is important to note that "deacon" in Geneva was used for two significantly different sets of people and different kinds of tasks. At the beginning the traditional meaning of deacon was prevalent, and may even have been used by Farel – and perhaps Calvin? The Senate records in 1537 that when the two came to ask for more colleagues, they said that "it would be good to have four preachers and two deacons"[11] for a total of six ministers. (The choice of language here may be that of the Senate secretary, but it may well have been Farel's, also.) A few years later, Jean Morand and Antoine Marcourt, the men who led the Genevan church after Farel and Calvin were exiled, returned to ask again (unsuccessfully) for deacons to help them.

> Besides, it would be quite allowable to have two deacons in this city to baptize, celebrate marriages, visit the sick, and help administer the Supper, as they have in all the other parts of evangelical countries.[12]

The description of what these deacons were to do makes it clear that they were to be pastoral assistants. Probably they were not adequately educated to serve as preachers, but Morand and Marcourt felt the need of help with the more traditional priestly functions even if they did not expect to have men capable of sharing the preaching. It is noteworthy that, although the term is effectively a continuation of Roman usage, the pastors appeal to the "universal" practice of

---

[10] See McKee, *John Calvin on the Diaconate*, e.g., pp. 149-58, 182-84. For one example of the distinction of functions combined with the use of "deacon" for both assistant pastor and minister of social welfare, see Poullain, *Liturgia Sacra*. The French text describes deacons of the poor and their election, then a single deacon chosen by the pastor to be his assistant, p. 231; the Latin text adds somewhat more specific details, pp. 230 & 238. For example of German use of "deacon" for assistant minister, see chap. 4 n.90.

[11] July 3, 1537; RC II, p. 243: "Sur ce que maistre Guillaume Farel et Cauvin, prescheurs, hont proposé, est arresté que l'on veult bien avoir quattres prescheurs et deux dyacres ... " It is unclear whether this is the ministers' term or that of the Senate or whether both used it.

[12] March 18, 1539; RC IV, p. 120: "Oultre plus, qu'il seroy bien licite d'avoyer deux diacres en ceste ville pour baptizer, fere les espousement, visiter les malades et se ayder az donnez laz Cennez, comme en toutes aultres part des contrees evangeliques az."

other Protestants to support their request. In German-speaking churches it was "deacons" who assisted the preaching ministers. [13]

However, in 1541 some theological revisions were introduced into the language used for the ministry, in good part because of Calvin's ways of defining and thus distinguishing ministers. The reformer had not previously formulated his teaching of a plurality of offices necessary for the ordinary functioning of the church visible on earth, but now in the *Ecclesiastical Ordinances* he sketched out the complete pattern of four distinct offices: pastors, teachers, elders, and deacons (of whom there were two kinds).

> The fourth order of ecclesiastical government, that is, the deacons. There were always two kinds in the early church, those delegated to receive, dispense, and take care of the goods for the poor, daily alms as well as property, rents, and pensions. The others were to care for and tend the sick and administer the daily portion of the poor. We have this custom still to the present, for we have procurators and hospitaliers. [14]

The "procurators and hospitaliers" are office titles often used by contemporaries for the agents of the social welfare reform which began to spread across Europe in the early 1520s. Procurators managed the money and accounts, while the person (s) who administered the hands-on poor relief were named hospitalers; the latter were the only agents whose office was a full-time job. Genevans began to use these terms when the city centralized the organization of welfare in the General Hospital in 1535; what these men did, however, was what Calvin called the task of "deacons." [15] In this case, the reformer was re-purposing a traditional religious term for a very different kind of task and hoping to alter the old habits of usage.

The key office in view here, however, is the pastor, and Calvin also wanted to modify both the concept and the language for these men, the human beings who administered the marks of the church. His draft description of this ministry in the *Ecclesiastical Ordinances* employs what he considered Biblically correct terms for the office and identifies their tasks clearly.

> As for the pastors, whom scripture also sometimes calls "bishops," elders and ministers, their office is to proclaim the word of God, to teach,

---

13 See McKee, *John Calvin on the Diaconate*, pp. 129-30.

14 *Calvin: Theological Treatises*, p. 64. OS II, pp. 340-41. In 1561 "we have this custom still to the present" is replaced by "A quoy c'est bien raison que toutes villes Chrestiennes se conforment, comme nous y avons tasché et voulons encore continuer à l'advenir."

15 See summary in McKee, *John Calvin on the Diaconate*, chap. 4, esp. pp.106-08.

admonish, exhort, and rebuke both in public and individually, to administer the sacraments and to make fraternal corrections with the elders.[16]

To Genevan ears "bishop" was a term with negative connotations; the received
text of the *Ordinances* eliminated the word and replaced it with "overseers"
(*surveillans*). Calvin, however, still maintained the concept that pastors are also
bishops, in part at least because their primary task is to preach. At the end of the
section which details the work and discipline of pastors, that episcopal identification is echoed in the language he uses to replace the traditional title "deacon."
"To support these tasks and others which pertain to the ministry there must
be five ministers and three coadjutors who are also ministers, to help and assist
as necessary."[17] It is certainly not an accident that Calvin appropriates the term
"coadjuteur," a name associated with a bishop's assistant, for the lower rank
of pastor. The Genevans do not seem to have challenged the term, perhaps
because it was not really an office. There was apparently not any real difference
in function between "ministers" and "coadjutors" because in practice every
minister had to be able to preach; the distinction was a matter of status or
experience. When Viret was preparing to return to Lausanne in July 1542, Calvin
asked for four new colleagues, two "predicans" and two "coadjuteurs." After the
men were appointed they were all assigned regular responsibility for sermons and
attendance at consistory, although at first the city records still speak of them as
"ministers" and "deacons."[18] Evidently Genevans did not immediately grasp
Calvin's altered language. Probably more onerous for the chief pastor than the
issue of language, however, was the fact that for several years the city had to
manage with a total of six men; it did not achieve the full mandated eight until the
mid-1550s.

Who were these men? Though few in number, the Genevan pastoral corps
was a remarkable body. It has long been recognized that the reform in this city
state was a very significant break with the past; Robert Kingdon calls it a
"revolution,"[19] and it has been frequently remarked that in Geneva the new
Protestant ministry was just that: virtually completely new personnel. William
Naphy, *Calvin and the Consolidation of the Genevan Reformation* (1992), and Scott

---

[16] *Ordinances*, OS II, p. 328.

[17] *Ordinances*, OS II, p. 338: "Pour soubstenir ces charges et aultres qui sont du ministere il sera
besoin d'avoir cinq ministres et troys coadiuteurs qui seront aussi ministres pour aider et
soubvenir selon que la necessité le requerra." For numbers of ministers actually in service,
see below at nn.36ff.

[18] Quoted below in n.38.

[19] Kingdon, "Was the Genevan Reformation a Revolution?" pp. 60 *et passim*.

Manetsch, *Calvin's Company of Pastors* (2012), have examined the development of the corps of ministers under Calvin's leadership. Only one native Genevan, Jaques Bernard, remained as an active pastor in the new church; all the rest of the preachers were foreigners from France. In fact, unlike other Reformed city-states such as Basel and Zurich, where a number of Roman priests converted and where by mid-century more than half of the new ministers came from the community (often from clerical families), in Geneva the development of a home-grown corps of ministers came much later, around the end of the century. In addition, not only were the early pastors foreigners, but in the first generation a number were aristocrats and others of high social rank, which gave them a certain easy-to-resent status in Geneva. (On the other hand, these Frenchmen came from urban contexts more than rural ones, which probably contributed to a better understanding of their parishioners in a developing commercial center.) Both Manetsch and Naphy recognize the problematic character of many of the early recruits; and the latter gives this particular emphasis. However, they agree that by the mid-1540s the Company of Pastors was a strong, qualified, and unified body. A few more ministers would be deposed for scandal later, but 1546 marked a turning point in the character of the city pastors.[20] Building on these fine studies, the purpose here is to show how that pastoral corps carried out its primary task of preaching.

Qualifications of Genevan Pastors and the Development of a Company of Pastors

Education

The first point to note is what special qualifications ministers in Calvin's Geneva must possess in order to do their job. All ministers were, of course, expected to be convinced converts to the "gospel" and to behave in accordance with that commitment. This requirement, however, applied to all leaders in the Genevan church, lay or clerical, although only for pastors and "doctors" (the highest ranks of teachers) were there legal standards of behavior.[21] The key qualification which applied only to ministers (again, both pastors and teachers) was advanced education, preferably some time at a university or one of the new humanist colleges. Ministers in Calvin's Geneva must be learned, even if for the

---

[20] Naphy, *Calvin and the Consolidation*, chap. 2, esp. pp. 53-54, 57-72. Manetsch, *Calvin's Company of Pastors*, chap. 1, esp. pp. 39-51; for comparison with Basel and Zurich, pp. 43-44.

[21] *Ordinances*, OS II, pp. 338, 339: "Que touz ceulx qui seront là soient subiectz à la discipline ecclesiastique comme les ministres."

first generation that often meant men who had not formally studied theology. Competence in languages and the humanist disciplines was the basis on which further Biblical and theological knowledge would be built. Naturally, then, the earliest reformers did not distinguish sharply between preachers and teachers, since the main qualification was the same. Antoine Saunier is remembered as the head of the school in the 1530s, but he actually began as a preacher alongside Farel, and city authorities continued to expect him to preach even when he was "just" a teacher.[22]

In fact, Saunier's story illustrates very well the close ties between teachers and preachers. Especially after the exile of Calvin and Farel, the city government assumed that the school master and his junior colleagues were available to preach. Saunier and the other teachers, however, were very much on the side of the deposed preachers and they dragged their feet – or worse – when the Senate asked them to fill in during the shortage of ministers. Saunier stopped preaching and his salary was cut in half (July 10, 1538).[23] The conflict between the Senate and the city's teaching staff was growing through the fall of 1538, and came to a head with the Christmas celebration of the Lord's Supper. Saunier and his colleagues had not participated in the previous communion, which was already a mark against them. They were asked to help administer the communion at Christmas and read the passion story, and said they would do so if their consciences allowed. When they failed to come to the service, the Senate decided it had had enough and effectively dismissed Saunier. The latter had asked leave to go and help the refugees from France who had fled from religious persecution, but the council was sure that he was departing because he disagreed with them on the Supper (and other Bernese ceremonies).[24]

Although not all had Saunier's degree of loyalty to Calvin's theology, the teaching staff in Geneva continued to be the key source of future pastoral personnel. To become a preacher was clearly regarded as an advance both socially and economically, so it was also very attractive to teachers. In the better-organized church after Calvin's return, a more formal distinction between pastors and teachers began to develop. The fact remained, though, that the specialized background which a preacher required was a university-level education. On April 7, 1542, Sebastian Castellion, newly accepted as head of the school, offered to

---

[22]   May 19, 1536; RC I, p. 8. The Waldensian refugee pastor Jean Girard, remembered in Geneva as a printer, was also considered as a preacher for a village church during these early years. Aug. 21, 1537, RC II, p. 295.

[23]   July 9 & 10, 1539; RC III, pp. 336, 337.

[24]   Dec. 17 & 20 & 23 & 26 & 27, 1539; RC III, pp. 522-23, 528, 530, 534, 536-38.

preach at the village of Vandoeuvres in addition to his teaching, with the expectation of receiving a higher salary for the whole. The Senate voted to give him some wheat,[25] which does not seem to have met his demands, but the fact that he proposed to combine school and preaching was apparently no problem. With the exception of Viret, of course, who was in Geneva on loan from his church in Lausanne until July 1542, the ministers with whom Calvin worked in the early 1540s were educated men but not of the committed caliber he wanted, and whom he began to attract in the next several years.

A Collegial Company of Pastors

By 1546 Calvin had gathered a group of colleagues who were both highly educated and clearly dedicated to the ministry. In 1544 Nicolas Des Gallars was added; in 1545 three more outstanding Frenchmen joined the Company of Pastors: Raymond Chauvet, François Bourgoing, and Michel Cop. Des Gallars and Bourgoing were aristocrats, Cop and Chauvet were already well-known leaders when they came to Geneva, and all four were sufficiently well educated to write and publish.[26] As more highly qualified ministers were added to the Company of Pastors, others who had been preaching in the city were moved to the intellectually less demanding village churches. Several ministers also died in service. A few of the ministers from the earlier years left or were deposed for scandal (such as questionable sexual behavior, or suspicion of usury). In the 1550s the number of pastors increased, as more people and more services were added. The largest expansion came in 1557 with the addition of a complete new parish, St. Germain, although this development was short-term and by 1561 Geneva had lost enough ministers to the new mission in France that it was back to a smaller corps, preaching again in the original three parishes.

The coming and going of pastors in Geneva is not the whole story, though; in fact it is the context for a more subtle but intriguing collegial creation on Calvin's part: ministerial deployment in a regular "pulpit exchange." Virtually as soon as he returned to Geneva and set up the parish system, Calvin began an organized pattern of moving preachers around the city. The principle was that all the city pastors were established as salaried parish ministers of the city as such. This might seem a contradiction in terms, since traditionally a parish priest would have authority only in his own parish. In fact, Burnett points out that this organization constituted a significant difference from late medieval "parish-

---

25 April 5 & 7, 1542; OC 21:294 (RC 35 f550, f543v).

26 Naphy, *Calvin and the Consolidation*, pp. 72-75. Manetsch, *Calvin's Company of Pastors*, chap. 2, pp. 51-59, describes some of the outstanding French ministers, though the only one from this first period whom he discusses is Michel Cop. For more on this, see chap. 6 at nn.30ff.

based churches" and "more closely resembled the city-wide churches of the apostolic and patristic period."[27] It illustrates yet another way that the reform in Geneva was distinctive, if not revolutionary, by comparison with the more traditional changes in other Reformed cities.

In Geneva, "parish pastors" functioned as ministers in the city as a whole, although they were usually designated as pastors of specific parishes. As evidence of this, at first they were presented to the whole people gathered at a General Council meeting, as happened on July 16, 1542, with the four new ministers approved by the Senate and the Council of Two Hundred.[28] Later, when the system was well in place, there would be a formal presentation of each newly elected minister to the people on both sides of the city during worship as a visible manifestation of this city-wide responsibility. For example, on Sunday, May 10, 1556, Jean Macar and Louis Enoch were presented at St. Pierre at the 8 a.m. service and at St. Gervais at the 3 p.m. service. On July 18, 1557, Calvin presented three new city ministers at St. Pierre and St. Gervais, although in fact two of the men would be serving the new parish of St. Germain, i.e., neither would be at St. Pierre or St. Gervais.[29] Evidently making someone known in these two locations served as an introduction to the whole city. Sometimes particular geographic assignments were made for residence; it became customary for the two ministers who had the main responsibility for St. Gervais to live there, although the rest

---

[27] Burnett, "A Tale of Three Cities," p.120. She notes that this "weak parish structure also changed each pastor's relationship with his colleagues," p. 112. Whereas in Basel or Strasbourg, each one was assigned to a particular post and named by that position, "entrance into Geneva's ministry was closer to matriculation in a corporation such as university faculty or guild than it was to the reception of the legal rights and responsibilities of an ecclesiastical benefice," p. 114. There was also no sharp distinction between city and rural clergy, as there was in Basel or Strasbourg, p. 109. "Geneva's rural churches were thus closer to the 'suburban' churches of Basel and Strasbourg than they were to the genuinely rural parishes of the two cities," p. 110.

[28] OC 21:299; see n.38 below. Each minister was also "presented" to the people in his new parish by one of the other pastors; when Jacques Bernard moved from the city to the village of Satigny at the end of July 1542, Calvin made the presentation; July 24, 1542; OC 21:300 (RC 36 f76v).

[29] RCP II, p. 67 : "Dimanche 10 de may 1556, M. Jean Macart, ministre de Ressin et de Dardainiés, estant appellé pour prescher en ville, fut presenté, ensemble ledit M. Lois Enoch, au peuple, assavoir en la predicacion du matin 8 heures à Sainct Pierre, et à .3. heures aprés midi à St. Gervais." p. 77 : "Le dimanche 18 de julliet, Monsieur Calvin presenta au peuple, tant au temple de Sainct Pierre qu'à Sainct Gervais, maistre Nicolas Colladon, maistre François de Morel, dict de Coulonge, et maistre Claude Du Pont, pour estre pasteurs en l'Eglise de Geneve." Then Colladon and Morel were assigned to St. Germain and Du Pont to St. Gervais, pp. 77-78.

were probably housed across the river in the other two parishes. Wherever a man lived, however, he might and often did preach in at least two and often all three parishes.

The objective of the "pulpit exchange" was partly pedagogical and theological: to have a variety of preachers in each parish, and to prevent a personality cult; people should come to worship to hear the word of God, not a particular minister. [30] While Calvin does not write about the "rotation" directly, what the reformer thought about how the instruments of God's word should exercise their calling was certainly known to his parishioners as well as his colleagues. It was expressed in many sermons, of which those on the epistles to Timothy and Titus are only the most prominent, and the reformer's teaching on the pastoral ministry has been the subject of books. [31] The object here is to explore the activity of the ministers rather than what Calvin taught about it; thus it is sufficient to glance at what the reformer had to say about one Biblical example of conflict and coope-ration to illumine the exegetical grounds for collegial work.

In expounding 1 Cor. 3:4-9 about the factional fighting in Corinth and Paul's reminder that all must work together even if some plant and some water, Calvin addresses both the difficulties of pastors serving together and the importance of such a common vocation. The major part of the instruction is directed to his fellow ministers. There are different gifts but that should not divide God's servants; all share the special honor of being called to build up God's spiritual temple. [32]

> God has yoked us together with a sacred tie to serve His glory and advance the kingdom of His Son, and yet we regress instead of advancing, we only dispute with each other, each has his own separate business, we do not pay attention to unite so that each may help his companion: and is that serving God? So then now we see St. Paul's intent. He says that the one who

---

30 See McKee, "Calvin and His Colleagues as Pastors," pp. 9-42.

31 The sermons on the Pastoral Epistles were among the first full series to be published, and were soon translated into English as well, evidence of their importance to Calvin's contemporaries; cf. chap. 6 at n.273 and Appendix Nine. For a modern example, see Louis Goumaz, *Timothée, ou le ministère évangélique, d'après Calvin et ses commentaires sur le Nouveau Testament* (Lausanne: La Concorde, 1948).

32 Sermon #18, 1 Cor. 3:8-10, ms. fr. 26, f145a: "Combien que les graces de Dieu ne soient point eslargies toutes en mesure egale, que l'ung soit plus excellent que l'aultre, que l'ung ayt receu ung don divers de ses freres, qu'il ne fault point que cela nous divise. Que nous regardions: puis qu'ainsi est que Dieu s'est monstré si liberal envers nous, puis qu'il nous a faict cest honneur que nous le servions en ouvrage si digne et si sacré comme d'edifier son temple spirituel, que nous nous y employons de tant meilleur courage."

> plants and the one who waters are only one [vocation]; by that he indicates
> that we ought to serve the edification of the church.[33]

The preacher uses the homely image of horses or oxen yoked together (a very apt description of the pairing of pastors in collegial rotation!). Calvin understands this text to be directed to the whole community, people as well as preachers. The congregation also has a responsibility to contribute to maintaining cooperation among their leaders; they must not feed any rivalry or ambition, and they must make use of their ministers in such a way that they help to keep them in agreement.[34] It should be noted that what unites pastors with each other and with the people is not "mutual liking" but a common vocation; collegiality means all the members of the body working together in the service of God, and not (necessarily) any personal attachment.

At first the organization of rotating preachers was probably a way to offset the disadvantages of less competent ones, but since the practice continued long after all those pastors had been replaced, it is clear that Calvin considered this rotation a valuable thing in itself. It was one manifestation of the collegiality which took institutional form in the Company of Pastors; in fact, the structured exchange of pulpits may well have contributed to building other kinds of cooperation neces-sary for establishing a new church order. The story of *Calvin's Company of Pastors* (2012) has been richly developed in Scott Manetsch's new book, which spans a much longer time than is in view here. The present purpose is also somewhat

---

[33] Sermon #18, 1 Cor. 3:8-10, ms. fr. 26, f144b-145a: "Or voicy Dieu qui nous accouple d'ung lyen sacré pour servir à sa gloire et pour advancer le regne de son filz, et ce pendant nous reculons au lieu d'advancer, nous ne ferons que rechiner l'ung l'aultre, chacun a son cas separé, nous ne regardons point à nous unir afin qu'ung checun ayde son compagnon: est ce servir à Dieu? Ainsi donc maintenant nous voyons l'intention de S[ainct] Paul. Il dict que celuy qui plante et celuy qui arouse ne sont qu'ung, par cela il signifie que nous debvons servir à l'edification de l'eglise."

[34] Sermon #18, I Cor. 3:8-10, ms. fr. 26, 145a-b: "Et au reste notons que S[ainct] Paul n'a point seulement parlé à ceulx qui avoient la charge d'enseigner en l'eglise mais en general à tous fidelles, car le vice aussi n'est pas seulement à ceulx qui par leur ambition se veullent advancer mais à ceulx qui les nourrissent, comme quoy? Si quelcun qui doibt travailler pour l'edification de l'eglise cerche à se faire valloir, il sera inutile quand à Dieu, il ne fera que gaster tout en l'eglise, car il fault que la doctrine de verité soit desguisee et qu'elle soit corrompue, quand les hommes si veullent ainsi acquerir credict et faveur, or ce pendant si on ne les nourrist en ce mal là ilz auront homte, mais s'ilz trouvent gens à leur poste, voila qui est cause qu'il n'y a plus d'edification, que la doctrine de l'evangile perist et qu'elle s'escoule au lieu que nous en debvrions sentir la vertu à nostre salut, que tout s'en va à neant et c'est pource que le peuple ne regarde point comme il se doibt servir des ministres de la parolle." cf. f145b: "Voila donc comme tous fidelles sont admonestez en ce passage de tellement se servir des ministres de la parolle de Dieu, qu'ilz leur aydent à les entretenir en concorde."

different from Manetsch's; this work focuses on the collegiality of the pastors specifically in their activity as ministers of word and sacraments in the pulpits of Geneva.

II: Ministers' Rotation: Collegial Preaching Patterns

What was the "collegial rotation" of the pastoral corps which Calvin developed in Geneva and how did it function? The following overview first sketches its introduction and early development. It then lays out the picture in much fuller detail as the rotation is concretely revealed in the faded and sometimes almost illegible records in which the baptisms and weddings of each parish were preserved. Specific examples are also drawn from other sources, such as the *Registres de la Compagnie des Pasteurs, du Conseil* and *du Consistoire*.

There were two main aspects to the practice of "collegial rotation." The first and most consistent was the regular assignment of two preachers to alternate weeks in the daily services. By extension, two ministers were often paired for other specific services, e.g., catechism in alternate weeks. The second part of the rotation involved the movement of preachers from one parish to another, also frequently though not always on the basis of paired responsibilities. One of the significant and long-neglected facts which this rotation brings to light is the symbiotic relationship between St. Pierre and La Magdeleine, the two parishes in Greater Geneva during most of Calvin's life. Another is the discovery that for many years Calvin regularly preached in all three parishes. Pulpit assignments were usually arranged by the Company of Pastors, although occasionally the Senate would decide that it wanted something different, so the collegial rotation also reveals how the men organized their common vocation as a whole.

The Historical Development of Ministerial Rotations

The Origin of the Practice

What may be the first evidence for collegial rotation is found in several minutes of the Senate. The first is an order on Dec. 2, 1541, that Aimé Champereau and Henri de La Mare should preach at St. Pierre.[35] Since it is certain that Calvin was preaching at the main Sunday service, this assignment must refer to some other time, and in view of the next information available, it is probable that Champereau and de La Mare were to do the dawn services at the cathedral which

---

[35]   OC 21:288 (RC f418): "Champereaulx et De la Mare. Ordonné que par ordre il doybjent fere les sermons aut temple S. Pierre."

had been established by the *Ecclesiastical Ordinances*. The Sunday dawn had been in practice since 1536, but weekday services were new in 1541.

Within a few months, another directive fills out the picture. This is an undated sheet which must, by internal evidence, have been written no later than April 1542.

> The sermon St. Pierre at six a.m. Champereau must preach at St. Pierre. Calvin [and] Viret at La Magdeleine except for Sundays at St. Pierre. Henry [de La Mare] and [Jaques] Bernard at St. Gervais. [36]

First it is important to establish the approximate date of this text, which must be before the departures of Bernard and Viret. The note assumes five ministers, who were in fact the regular participants at Consistory meetings during the first half of 1542. In April Bernard moved to the village of Satigny, and July 13 is marked as Viret's last day on the consistory before he returned to his regular post in Lausanne. [37] On July 10 Calvin requested new colleagues, two "preachers" and two "coadjutors" or "deacons" (Genevans' language), [38] and within the next week four new ministers, Philip de Ecclesia and Pierre Blanchet, Matthew de Geneston and Louis Treppereau, joined the corps of ministers. The first two began attendance at consistory meetings immediately on July 20, and the other two on Nov. 23. [39]

From the quotation above it can be determined that by early 1542 the ministers in Geneva were distributed through the three parishes for preaching. The primary focus may have been the organization of weekday services. Henry de La Mare and Bernard would alternate at St. Gervais, and Aimé Champereau was assigned the early morning services at St. Pierre (Sunday and three weekdays).

---

[36] "Le sermon St. Pierre az six heures de matin. Champereaux doybje presche à St. Pierre. Calvin, Vyret à laz Madelaine reservé les dymenches à St. Pierre. Henry et Bernard à St. Gervex." Now found in RC 38 f55, this was originally a separate sheet; it bears no date and is not part of a specific council meeting. The present location of the sheet has led later scholars to date it as Feb. 4, 1544, but this does not fit with other evidence of 1544 and it is consonant with early 1542.

[37] Bernard moved to Satigny in April 1542; *Consist.* I, p. 2 n. 6. Viret left in July 1542, though he was back for a visit in June 1544; see *Consist.* I, p. 84 n. 389, p. 378 n.332.

[38] With the departure of Viret "le nombre des predicans restant ne pourroyent satisfayre aut ministere parquoy est necessité d'en havoyer encore deux predicans et deux coadjuteus" and four men are presented: Philip Osias, Pierre Blanchet; Matthieu Geneston & Louis Treppereau. On Friday July 14 the Two Hundred votes to accept the ministers, and on Sunday the 16th they are presented to the people at the Conseil Général and take their oaths: "Le mode de serment faictz par les predicans et dyacres presentés par devant tout le peuple..." July 10 & 14 &16, 1542; OC 21:298-299 (RC 36 f65v, f70v, f72).

[39] *Consist.* I, p. 87 n. 404 (July 20), p. 141 n. 586 (Nov. 23).

Given the scarcity of ministers, one preacher was enough for the dawn services at St. Pierre because there were half as many weekday sermons as in the other two churches.[40] The only time Sunday worship is mentioned is in reference to Calvin and Viret, the outstanding ministers. They were instructed to alternate for weekday sermons at La Magdeleine, but it is clearly stated that Sundays were excepted, when Calvin would preach at St. Pierre. The fact that Viret was assigned as pastor of St. Gervais, when Calvin was designated pastor of St. Pierre in Nov. 1541, suggests that Viret may well have preached in his own parish on Sundays, at least some of the time. (The evidence is not conclusive, but this would also replicate the assignment of pulpits in Calvin's first Geneva sojourn, when Farel was at St. Gervais.)[41]

Whatever its other ambiguities, this short instruction by the Senate directing the location of each preacher points to several kinds of movement of Geneva's ministers spatially and temporally: they could serve in several parishes simultaneously, and also share a single pulpit on the same schedule but in different weeks. The alternation between St. Pierre and La Magdeleine explicitly expresses the symbiotic relationship between these two parishes: it provides preaching at La Magdeleine on weekdays when a smaller number would attend the service and the cathedral was not needed, but at St. Pierre on Sundays for the same people of the two joint parishes when "everyone" was expected to attend.[42] This fits with the sermon schedule as practiced at this time, according to which St. Pierre did not have services on every weekday but only three days at dawn (plus the day of prayer), and La Magdeleine did not have services on Sunday morning or afternoon. The note also indicates an alternation between ministers, as well as the general Genevan determination to supply Greater Geneva with the "best" ministers. (Wherever he was on Sundays, Viret was wanted for weekdays at La Magdeleine in order to have the best preachers for the largest concentration of people.) In fact the rotation might have been introduced in part because Calvin was the pastor of the parish of St. Pierre and would of course preach there on

---

[40]   The note about time: "at 6 a.m." may be a reference to the schedule for the ordinary sermons (narrowing the date for this instruction to after Easter, which was April 9 in 1542), or it may be simply an error, because other evidence places the sermons at St. Pierre at dawn. In fact, however, the other weekday sermons listed in the note were at 6 a.m.

[41]   According to the council, Calvin and Viret were assigned to St. Pierre and St. Gervais, respectively, Nov. 7, 1541 (OC 21:285 RC f383). See above, at nn.6ff for 1536-38.

[42]   Later the weekday service at La Magdeleine was moved to St. Pierre on Wednesday precisely because more people were expected to attend on the day of prayer, but that may well not have been the case at this point. See chap. 1 at n.150; Appendix One for baptismal records of St. Pierre and La Magdeleine for Wednesdays.

Sundays, but restricting him to preach only in his parish would mean wasting his gifts on the relatively few dawn services originally planned for servants. Given the symbiosis of St. Pierre and La Magdeleine, it was logical for Calvin to go back and forth between the places, just as he also alternated weeks with Viret for the daily sermons at La Magdeleine for the limited time that the latter was available in Geneva.

Another Senate order several months later, on Aug. 18, 1542, after the departure of Viret and relocation of Bernard, marks the redistribution of the (now six) city ministers to conduct weekday worship.

> Master Calvin explained that it would be very suitable to have a change of ministers from time to time so that the people may be so much the better edified. [The ministers having consulted] among themselves have proposed that he [Calvin] and Champereau would do their duty at La Magdeleine, Master Henry [de La Mare] and M. De Geneston would do the [early] morning sermons at St. Pierre, and de Ecclesia and Master Pierre [Blanchet] at St. Gervais. [43]

Here it is seen that two men worked in each of the two main preaching stations for weekday sermons, one for each side of the city, i.e. St. Gervais and La Magdeleine. The two assigned to St. Pierre for "the morning service" (the only one which is given a specific temporal description) were responsible for the dawn services; the change from the previous assignment is that now there are alternates for the dawn services as well as those at the "ordinary" hour of 6 a.m. or 7 a.m. Although preaching days are not named, it is clear that the basic intent is weekday sermons because, as was made explicit in the earlier instructions, Calvin was certainly preaching at St. Pierre at least on Sunday morning, [44] and probably both morning and afternoon. In fact, his assignment has not changed: La Magdeleine on weekdays and St. Pierre on Sundays, although all the other preachers appear to be set in new places and Calvin's alternate has changed.

---

[43] Aug. 18, 1542, OC 21:301 (RC 36 f98): "[Monsieur Calvin predicant]. Lequelt a exposé qu'il seroyt bien convenable par ung temps fere changement de ministres affin que le peuple soyt tant meulx ediffié & entre eulx hont advisé que luy & Champereaulx feroyent leur debvoyer à la Magdelene, maystre Henry & monsieur de Geneston auroyent à fere les sermons à St. Pierre le matin et de Eglesia & maystre Pierre à St. Gervex, ce que luy a esté accordé."

[44] See quotation, n.36 above; *Consist.* II, Thurs. Nov. 19, 1545, p. 77, woman being questioned about swearing/ blasphemy is asked if she was at sermon last Sun. She says yes, that Calvin preached; the consistory secretary says that this is false because Calvin preached at St. Pierre. According to the consistory editors, p. 77 n. 240, the woman was probably from St. Gervais.

This redistribution of the preachers in August 1542 may be the formal establishment of the rotation practice since it offers an explanation for the exchange of pulpits, or it may simply be the regularizing of the practice by explaining it to the Senate to receive official authorization. The reassignment of personnel was necessitated by the departures of Bernard and Viret. It is worthwhile to note that the most experienced ministers were given responsibility for the daily sermons in Greater Geneva, while the new men went across the river to St. Gervais. In addition, the new men were paired as preacher-and-coadjutor/deacon, preacher-and-coadjutor/deacon, which underlines the supposition that the distinction between preacher and coadjuteur was experience.

Development of the Theory and Practice of Ministerial Exchanges in the 1540s

Through the rest of the 1540s it is more difficult to trace the rotation of ministers, either as pairs working in one assignment or in their movements among the parishes. However, the records from the Company of Pastors, consistory, and Senate deliberations afford limited indications of how the concept itself matured through practice. It is perhaps not surprising that some of the development was shaped by the situation in St. Gervais, the smallest city preaching unit. In 1543 the council ordered "one of the preachers" of St. Gervais to substitute for a country minister,[45] implying that there were at least two men preaching in that parish. It appears that this did not mean two resident ministers, however, although the exact relationship between a preaching assignment and a minister's house in Geneva was perhaps not yet clear.

What is plain is that in 1545 a problem at St. Gervais led to more interchange between the two parts of Geneva and thus contributed to the development of the system of mutual support among the distinct parishes. At this time Pierre Ninault was the minister of St. Gervais. Although he was sufficiently learned for his task, he was not popular with his hearers: when they saw him heading to the church, his parishioners turned away. (Evidently at least some people of St. Gervais did not have the ministerial rotation fixed in their minds, and so they started toward the church until they realized who would be in the pulpit and then changed their minds.) The problem may have come to a head because the other preacher in St. Gervais, De Geneston, had recently died of the plague and Ninault was apparently alone. Thus, on Aug. 24, 1545, the Senate decided that there should be pulpit exchanges across the river: ministers from "the city" should go to preach at St. Gervais and those working at St. Gervais should

---

[45]   March 2, 1543, OC 21:308 (RC 37 f25).

come to "the city."[46] (This may well have been the origin of Calvin's assignment to include St. Gervais in his preaching schedule.) Just a few weeks before the crisis with Ninault, the talented French refugee Raymond Chauvet had arrived,[47] so a highly qualified replacement for the late De Geneston was at hand: indeed, one who was more fit than Ninault. By the end of August, Chauvet had been elected to the pastoral corps and assigned to St. Gervais and Ninault had been sent to a village church. The Company of Pastors said that Ninault was better suited to the city than the country, but the Senate had evidently decided that he was a problem and should be assigned to a rural parish, although they continued his salary at the previous level.[48]

It is interesting to observe what the language reveals about the relative prominence of Greater Geneva and St. Gervais. When the Senate secretary needed to distinguish between them, he spoke of "the city" and St. Gervais; the parish across the Rhone was traditionally regarded as a suburb of secondary status. More important, however, was the idea that there should be regular interchanges among otherwise self-sufficient parishes. From the Senate's side this may have been intended to ease tensions by giving St. Gervais a chance at the best preachers. It also probably led the pastors to realize that it was not enough simply to assign a pair of men to alternate in a set of duties, or even to move them from one assignment to another; there should be exchanges among the parishes even when there was no emergency, and even if St. Gervais was considered a second rank assignment.

These events may well have contributed – or at least given new urgency – to another development in the concept and practice of ministerial rotation: articulation of the principle that pairing ministers provided a certain level of mutual support and should be mandated. The need for this at the highest level had been tacitly recognized earlier in the year when Viret came back from Lausanne in May

---

[46] Aug. 24, 1545, OC 21:360 (RC 39 f222): "Combien que Me Pierre (Ninaulx) minister de S. Gervaix soyt bien scavant ceulx de S. Gervaix ne le hont pas agriable et que quant il va à S. Gervaix les gens le voyant s'ent retornentz. Ordonné que iceulx de la ville et ceulx de S. Gervaix les ungs les aultres viegnent prescher en la ville et ceulx de la ville à S. Gervaix ainsi que myeulx commodement se pourra faire." Calvin was apparently preaching regularly at St. Gervais on Sunday afternoons for a number of years between 1546 and 1552; see chap. 6 at nn.49ff.

[47] Aug. 11 & 17, 1545, OC 21:359 (RC 39 f212, 216v).

[48] Aug. 31, 1545, OC 21:361 (RC 39 f227v): "Me. Abel ministre a exposé qui hont advisé en leur congregation que Me. Pierre seroy plus propre pour aller prescher à S. Gervex et en la ville que sus les champs toutesffois qui layssent cella à la discretion de la Seigneurie. Ordonné que ledit Me. Pierre allé servyr sus les champs soub le mesme gage qu'il ast et ledit Me. Raymon doybge servyr en la ville."

1545 to cover for Calvin while the latter was traveling on diplomatic business for the church.[49] The Senate was apparently prepared to make some financial compensation for the benefit of having a first-rate preacher during Calvin's scheduled absence,[50] i.e., not simply leave the pastoral leadership of the city to his alternate or one of the other less qualified men. Then came the problem with Ninault at St. Gervais in August, which highlighted the difficulty of having one (perhaps unpopular) preacher in charge of a parish, to which the Senate responded by ordering exchanges of ministers between the two sides of Geneva. Then in the following year, May 1546, Calvin proposed that St. Gervais should have two (resident) ministers, and the council accepted this as an interpretation of its order for pulpit exchange.

> M. Calvin … [said] that it would be good to provide for two preachers at St. Gervais so that they can relieve each other… as for the said two preachers, it is allowed anyway that those [ministers] from the city may come here and those from the city who are elected may go there.[51]

When Calvin made this request there were already two men called "minister of St. Gervais"; Jean Ferron was working there along with Chauvet in December 1545.[52] Ferron may even have been residing in St. Gervais since the Senate note on Dec. 15, 1545, refers to the rent for his house (though it is not stated that the house is in the parish where he is preaching). It is possible that Calvin's presentation to the Senate in 1546 was in the nature of a request for official status for an arrangement already in place. The Senate's response seems to be an acceptance of the idea that the ministers may determine who preaches where: "those… who are elected [by the pastors] may go…" From the Senate's viewpoint this assignment is

---

49   He was working to gain the support of German-speaking Protestants for the Waldensians being persecuted in Provence.

50   May 22, 1545, OC 21:353-54 (RC 40 f124v): "Me Pierre Viret predicant de Lausanne. Lequelt causant l'absence de M. Calvin ministre qu'est aux Allemagnyes pour la persequucion des fideles de Provence est venuz servyr l'eglise de Geneve. Ordonné que il luy soyt donné quelque accoustrement pour son retour."

51   May 11, 1546, OC 21:380 (RC 40 f89): "M. Calvin [asks for church repairs] et qui seroyt bon de pourvoystre de deux preschers à S. Gervaix pour se soullaigé l'ung l'aultre. …[repairs] et quant es ditz deux preschers que soyt permis touttesffois que ceulx de la ville viegne icy et ceulx de la ville qui seront esleu allent là." The name "city" is apparently used for both sides of the river. Was this a possible increase in status for St. Gervais or simply a way for the Senate to emphasize that all the ministers belonged to the whole city and they should work out plans for mutual assistance among themselves?

52   The name identifies the man ("le minstre de S. Gervex Ferron") because the Senate needs to pay the rent for his house; Dec. 15, 1545, OC 21:366 (RC 39 f327).

one possible form of implementing their prior order for an exchange of ministers between St. Gervais and Greater Geneva. Whether Ferron was given a new status at St. Gervais as a result of this request is not clear, but the fact that Calvin spoke signals a move toward what became the "custom" of having two officially designated pastors in this parish,[53] and affirms the right of the Company of Pastors to assign their members where needed.

More significant for understanding the system of ministerial rotation is the fact that here Calvin clearly stated his principle of the mutual assistance made possible by a recognized and well-ordered system of established alternates. A pair of ministers assigned to one parish (or, by extension, one set of responsibilities) could thus be expected to support each other in a reliable way when there were unexpected absences. Although probably it was not a new idea, Calvin's words on this occasion serve as a public statement to the leaders of Geneva which complemented the earlier argument that preachers should be moved from one preaching station to another around the city for the sake of the congregations.[54] That exchange of pulpits gave the people a wider range of sermons, while pairing colleagues gave a regular way to guarantee that the pulpits would be filled. Ministers would be in the habit of helping each other according to an orderly plan and thus could more easily fill in when something happened to interrupt the normal order. This was critically important for preachers as well as people because it meant that pastors could allow themselves the luxury of some flexibility, such as going to bed when they were ill.

To maintain the regularity of preaching in the face of sickness and other circumstances which would interrupt a minister's work, Calvin developed the argument for a certain level – it can hardly be called redundancy – of pastoral personnel. To put the issue in perspective, it is helpful to see the ratio of ministers in service to those on paper. The *Ecclesiastical Ordinances* called for eight men: five ministers and three coadjutors; there were only five preachers at first, and then six by the middle of 1542. The original schedule of services planned in the *Ordinances* as Calvin drafted them had been marginally feasible for six men to carry out; but in the received text the Senate added two more Sunday services. It also did not in fact complete the stated number of pastors. By 1544 a seventh minister was added, which made the work more manageable, although the two extra services were not provided. In September 1549, Jean Ferron was deposed for sexual scandal, and the city was reduced to functioning with six

---

[53]   See reference to this custom in 1564, RCP II, p. 109, quoted in n.81.

[54]   See above Aug. 18, 1542, at n.43.

preachers.[55] When Calvin requested a replacement for Ferron, the Senate refused; there were complaints about having too many preachers, and the council said they could not afford a seventh minister.[56] The Company of Pastors continued their argument for another colleague. Finally on Oct. 14 the Senate changed its mind, agreeing to hire a seventh minister,[57] but ten days later they told the ministers to expand the number of dawn services on weekdays from three to six. Calvin said that the preachers "felt greatly burdened." The next week the ministers offered instead to put into practice the Sunday morning service at La Magdeleine which the council had added to the draft *Ordinances* in 1541, and this was accepted.[58]

This record looks like part of an on-going negotiation. In 1541 the Senate had not completed the number of ministers and the ministers in turn did not carry out the "extra" services which the council had added to the *Ordinances*: a kind of compromise. In 1549 when they lost Ferron the Company of Pastors was still below the originally mandated eight ministers, so at this point they demand a replacement and negotiations begin again. A seventh preacher is restored, and then the ministers are told to add at least three weekday dawn sermons (in addition to the three already in practice at St. Pierre). Through Calvin they protest to the Senate and another compromise is reached: the preachers will do no (additional) dawn services but they will do a regular 8 a.m. one on Sundays at La Magdeleine, one of the "extra" ones mandated by the council in 1541 which had not been in practice.

A similar negotiation is seen some years later in 1555, when the Senate was more amenable to the preachers' views. The issue was prompted by the council's

---

55 For addition of seventh, see chart in Naphy, *Calvin and the Consolidation*, p. 58. For Sept. 13, 1549, RCP I, pp. 61-62: "Le vendredi 13e jour …esleurent Me Jehan Fabri… Depuis fut entendu par les frères que Messieurs ne vouloient point qu'on esleust autre ministre au lieu dud. Ferron, et que l'eglise pourroit bien estre servye de six, et que ce nombre suffiroit…"

56 Sept. 16, 1549, OC 21:456 (RC 43 f215v): "Le minstre S. Calvin: sur ce que il a aulcungs qui mourmurentz à cause de ce qui az tropt de prescheurs en ceste ville et que combien qui en aye beaucopt cella le merite bien veulx que ceste ville en az plus grand besoings que piece d'aultre causant la difficulté etc. par plusieurs raisons requerant il mectre ordre et pourvoistre d'ung au lieu de M. Ferron affin de myeulx servir et rendre leurs office et debvoir devant Dieu etc. Ordonné et resolut que il soit faictes bonnes remonstrances audit S. Calvin qui luy plaise le prendre à la bonne partz si l'on ne peult acepter sa requeste causant ce que la ville est tant chargé et qui semble bien qui ny aye sinon six prescheurs pour le presentz."

57 Oct. 14, 1549: Calvin and the other ministers say that they cannot do their work without the additional colleague who was promised to them, and complain that the Senate acted without consulting them [when it decided not to add another minister] which one would not do with a stable-hand [!]; the Senate agrees to hire another minister and will set his salary (RC 44 f239v). Archives@etat.ge.ch accessed Aug. 2, 2013.

58 See discussion and quotations in chap. 1 at nn.113ff.

decision to implement the Sunday afternoon service at La Magdeleine (which they had added to the 1541 *Ordinances*) plus one on Wednesday – perhaps because there were more refugees flowing into Geneva. Calvin explained to the Senate the need for some flexibility in personnel and on June 24 he presented the ministers' counter proposal.

> About the proposal, following what the council previously ordered: that there be another sermon at La Magdeleine on Sunday morning, and on Wednesday. It is necessary to have another preacher because there are many tasks and in order to be able to administer God's word in a more holy and diligent way, seeing that sometimes they fall sick, sometimes they are absent because of circumstances, etc. ... Ordered that there be another preacher.[59]

No doubt the ministers were glad to agree with the Senate's plan since this time they were accorded another colleague without dispute. From Calvin's viewpoint, these negotiations had their basis in a realistic understanding of the circumstances which could interrupt regular preaching and the critical imperative of a "holy and diligent" proclamation of the gospel. The key strategy for insuring regular services by qualified men was to pair the ministers.

However, especially when the press of increasing numbers of refugees meant that all the pastors were stretched even more, the Company of Pastors sometimes tried other ways to insure that back-up personnel were available. One plan for this was to identify dual roles for someone who was not actually named as a minister. In January 1557, when they elected a teacher for the General Hospital, the pastors explained that they wanted a single man (not burdened with wife and children) "who would also be able to serve to do some sermons when needed, because of illness or some other [absence] of the ministers."[60] At this time it appears that two preachers were handling St. Gervais essentially without the help of their usual part-time third colleague and there must have times when they needed to call on the Hospital teacher for help.[61]

---

[59] June 24, 1555, OC 21:609 (RC 49 f114): "...seroit requys d'avoir encore ung prescheur à cause de beaucoub de charges et pour pouvoir d'autant plus sainctement et diligemment administrer la parolle de Dieu: veu que quelquefoys on tombe en maladie quelquefoys on est absent à cause des occurrens etc. ... Arresté qu'on face encore ung prescheur..." cf. chap. 1 n.152.

[60] RCP II, p. 70: "... homme n'aiant charge de femme ny d'enfans, qui aussi pourroit servir de faire quelzques sermons en deffault et necessité, par maladie ou autrement des ministres."

[61] See below after n.75.

The Developed Form of Ministerial Leadership and Rotation in Geneva

By the mid-1540s Calvin had not only gathered a strong and talented corps of ministers as his colleagues, but there was also a much greater stability in the pastoral organization, including the orderly movement and rotation of preachers in the urban churches. Among these men, there were three in particular who anchored the pulpit ministry in the city: Calvin, Chauvet, and Cop. Calvin was naturally settled at St. Pierre, even though he preached daily at La Magdeleine and also regularly at St. Gervais beginning early in 1546. Chauvet was settled at St. Gervais; at least once the consistory records explicitly refer to him as "minister of St. Gervais."[62] He would be the mainstay of that parish until he eventually moved to La Magdeleine in the early 1560s, probably in part for health reasons as a form of semi-retirement or reward for his long service at St. Gervais. However, even while he was at St. Gervais, Chauvet was frequently found visiting in the other parishes. The third preacher was Cop. Evidence from various sources demonstrates that he was perhaps the single most stable element in the services at St. Pierre, and he was certainly the mainstay of the Sunday and weekday dawn services there. Cop was also regularly engaged in teaching catechism. In 1548 (when he was a pivotal figure in the arguments over baptismal names), he was teaching catechism at St. Pierre,[63] but a few years later this assignment was changed to catechism at La Magdeleine. While Cop's ministry was centered at St. Pierre, the baptismal and marriage records reveal that he was among the most flexible ministers, the most likely to fill in for any absentee, in any parish and at practically any time.[64]

The practice of preachers moving about among the three main parishes of Geneva, as well as general patterns of pairs of ministers alternating in specific assignments, becomes much more visible after 1550 when baptisms and marriages began to be regularly recorded. For each liturgy, the minister had to record the date and the names of all the participants: baby, parents, godfather, and pastor, or groom, bride, and pastor. This identifies where a given minister was active on a specific day. Since people had to receive the sacraments in their home parish, they would probably come to the minister on duty on the day when they wanted their baby baptized. There was no official regulation about weddings but these were usually performed in the parish where the bride and groom, or at least one of them, regularly worshiped (although for many years the residents of Greater Geneva were an exception[65]).

---

[62] *Consist.* III, p. 274; Aug. 12, 1546.

[63] For Cop's work, see Appendix Three: Ministers' Rotations. For catechism, see *Consist.* IV, pp. 73, 75, May 31, 1548. For baptismal controversy, see Naphy, *Calvin and the Consolidation*, pp. 148-49.

[64] See Appendix Three: Ministers' Rotations.

[65] See chap. 5 at p. 388.

Thus baptismal and marriage records indicate with a considerable degree of accuracy where a particular minister was, particularly when the same man celebrated a wedding at the start of a service and a baptism at the end of the same service. When these statistical records are combined with the occasional instructions found in the *Registres de la Compagnie des Pasteurs* or the *Registres du Conseil*, plus the dates of Calvin's preaching, which begin to be concretely visible in 1549, it is possible to establish a fairly detailed picture of ministerial rotation in Geneva.[66]

Before examining the concrete manifestation of the ministers' movements in specific parishes, it may be useful to sketch general outlines of the system. As is obvious in the early instructions about distributing preachers throughout the city, perhaps the most challenging requirement of Geneva's ecclesiastical order with regard to worship was the insistence on having daily weekday preaching in at least two places, Monday through Saturday, plus three days each week in a different place at an earlier time. Thus, pairs of alternates were usually identified by their weekday responsibilities. Two men were paired for the daily services; each preached for a week in turn, one week on and one week off. If there were only six ministers there were barely enough for three sets of daily sermons, even though one set was half the number of days, because there were also at least nine services on Sundays and sometime in the 1540s (probably before 1545), another dawn service at St. Gervais was added to the mix.

The organization of the Sunday services might take several forms. At St. Gervais, one common practice was for the two resident ministers to alternate for the main Sunday morning service (8 a.m.); they might take Sunday of the week when they were doing the daily sermons but apparently it was left to the two men to decide exactly how they wanted to divide the Sunday services. At St. Pierre, Calvin always preached on Sunday morning and his alternate would thus be available to do catechism until 1549, when La Magdeleine's regular Sunday morning service began. Usually dawn services and catechism were also grouped together. If there was only one weekday dawn service (Wednesday, as at St. Gervais), one man usually did this and the Sunday dawn service – perhaps every week, plus catechism in one of the parishes, not necessarily St. Gervais. Where there were multiple weekday dawn services (as at St. Pierre: Monday-Wednesday-Friday) plus Sunday, this assignment was considered more demanding and two men would alternate for the four dawn services and for catechism – although again, not necessarily at St. Pierre. The Sunday afternoon service seems to have been somewhat more loosely tied to any of the patterns. One of the two ministers in charge of the parish might do it,

---

[66] The main source for the following, unless otherwise noted, is Appendix Three: Ministers Rotations.

in the week when he was not preaching in the morning and during the week; or another minister either from the same parish or a different one might take Sunday afternoon at a particular church. Within this framework, the minimum was two ministers to a parish and six for three churches, but it is obvious that having a seventh man was extremely important, to cover the St. Gervais dawn and take catechism regularly, probably in Greater Geneva. He would also fill in for colleagues, because the system sketched out here does not allow for any minister to miss any scheduled service, something that was virtually impossible to assure.

Even for St. Gervais, the most self-contained parish, the organization of preaching was never interpreted in isolation from the other parishes, however, and there was usually at least one inter-parish exchange in the regular order, and often several. In addition, assignments for all except the two or three most senior ministers could be and were changed around fairly often; this meant both that pairs of men were not fixed, and that almost every preacher had a role in the other parishes, sooner or later. Calvin was naturally established at St. Pierre, although he regularly preached elsewhere as well; until 1559 he did almost as many sermons in other churches as at St. Pierre. In fact, he is the only one of the three ministers permanently anchored in one place who had a scheduled rotation serving in all three parishes at once. Chauvet was settled at St. Gervais until very late in his life and during that time served in other parishes only on an ad hoc basis. Although no formal appointment appears to have been made, Cop was based at St. Pierre throughout his ministry, even though the baptismal and marriage records attest to his activity in the other parishes.

For purposes of visualizing the probable organization it is helpful to sketch the distribution of sermons from 1542 until 1556 for the three parishes. The beginning date of 1542 is chosen because by mid-year Geneva achieved the number of six ministers and implemented the St. Gervais Sunday dawn service, the later date covers when the Sunday and Wednesday services at La Magdeleine were added (1549, 1555). After that point, with the addition of a new parish in 1557 and other factors, the coordination of numbers of men and services becomes less easy to trace.[67] Since the cycle functioned essentially in two week increments, it is

---

[67] In 1557 the new parish of St. Germain and three new ministers were added, along with at least nine more services per week, but that cannot be factored into the picture here. In 1559 six more daily sermons were added at St. Pierre, plus two temporary dawn times at La Magdeleine, and several more ministers were available. The 1561 revision of the *Ordinances* fixed the number of sermons at 11 on Sundays and 22 on weekdays (OC 10:99-100). Meanwhile, the pastoral situation in these years was in considerable flux not only because of deaths and the brain-drain to France but also because senior men like Beza who were technically still working in Geneva were in actuality absent for more-or-less extended periods.

convenient to list each man's schedule for four weeks, multiply by twelve, and then add one more four week period to approximate a year. One thing which this visualization reveals is that Calvin always regularly preached more often than any other single colleague: an average of twenty times every four weeks! Calvin was responsible for Sunday morning and afternoon every week, plus six weekdays in alternate weeks. That comes to ten sermons every two weeks and 260 over the course of thirteen four-week periods. This did not change until in his last years when for health reasons he probably no longer did Sunday afternoons.

In 1542, there were 100 sermons preached in each four week period in Geneva, and probably before 1545 one more was added, making the total 101. Since other colleagues' schedules were never as tightly fixed as Calvin's, the following outline is representative, not exact. For example, at St. Gervais the two resident pastors did not necessarily alternate precisely for Sunday services. Sometimes they may have taken more than the average number of sermons calculated below, simply because they were in charge, and those with less services in their assigned schedule might have been expected to compensate for fewer obligatory sermons by increased flexibility filling in during illness or absence. Often the Sunday afternoon service was not a fixed place assignment; for a number of years (1546-52) Calvin was preaching regularly at St. Gervais on Sunday afternoon, which meant that the men in that parish could do something not ordinarily in their rotation (e.g., dawn or catechism), while one of the St. Pierre dawn service pair would be needed on Sunday afternoon in that church. For simplicity in aligning typical assignments with numbers of services here, the blocks of preaching and personnel are outlined according to averages.

Calvin's alternate did at least twelve weekday sermons, and probably four catechisms,[68] making sixteen total; for the year that would come to 208. The two men at St. Gervais each did twelve weekday sermons and four Sundays (since each one would have either morning or afternoon), making sixteen each; again 208 each for the year. The two men at St. Pierre for dawn each did eight dawn and two catechisms, making ten each; this would be 130 each for the year. If there were only six men total, then someone – probably one of the St. Pierre pair – would have to pick up the Sunday and Wednesday dawn services at St. Gervais plus the third parish's catechism, which would add a total of twelve more sermons

---

[68]   Here catechism is not identifed with any specific person, because a minister from Greater Geneva was likely to be in St. Gervais and those assigned to St. Pierre at dawn might be at La Magdeleine at noon. Calvin's alternate could have done the catechism at St. Gervais or St. Pierre, while the two men at St. Pierre split the other two between them. Before the baptismal and marriage records identify locations, it is very difficult to tell.

in four weeks and another 156 for the year. If everything was averaged out exactly, Calvin would do 260 and every other man 208 sermons per year... assuming no one got sick or had to be absent for any reason! When a seventh minister was added in 1544, this schedule was somewhat more manageable. In 1549 one more Sunday morning service was added at La Magdeleine (but not the three additional dawn ones the Senate wanted). Even with pairs able to fill in for each other for a limited time, this was difficult. Add to the mix the fact that from January 1553 until a new minister was added in mid-1555, one of the seven men in service was the chronically ill Poupin, and it is clear that trying to cover 102 services must have been like having only six ministers again. In June 1555 two more services were added at La Magdeleine: Sunday afternoon and Wednesday and in this case the council agreed to hiring an eighth minister – although until Poupin died and was replaced about a year later, there were effectively still only seven preachers to cover 112 services every four weeks. Since there were many other tasks which pastors had to do, the Company of Pastors was not being unreasonable to think that they were over-burdened!

Even with the rotation system working perfectly, the moment anyone was unable to fill his assigned pulpit, there was going to be stress on the whole corps. If there had not been an ordered pattern of rotation, it would have been far more difficult to determine quickly who could substitute where. Calvin's determination to provide the city with such an ample menu of sermons was matched by his practical skills in imagining and organizing a structured plan to make this humanly feasible. It is one measure of his leadership ability that he made it work – by persuasion, by insistence, and by example: after all, he did take the heaviest load himself.

The Rotation System in Practice: The Example of St. Gervais, 1550-1564

The parish of St. Gervais was somewhat different from the more complicated symbiosis between St. Pierre and La Magdeleine, which makes it useful to begin the examination of the rotation of ministers in this more self-contained parish. Normally there were two resident ministers in St. Gervais who had the primary responsibility for all the services in that church, although usually they also had a third part-time associate part. (He worked full time but some of his preaching was in Greater Geneva.)

The key factor in the rotation of the two main preachers was the alternating responsibility for the daily sermon on weekdays. The ways that the Sunday morning and afternoon services were fitted into the rotation might vary, especially depending on the role of the third associate – or, for at least a number of years,

Calvin himself. In the early 1550s, it appears that Des Gallars was Chauvet's opposite for the weekdays at St. Gervais (6 a.m./ 7 a.m. except on Wednesday when the service was later). Jean Fabri was their third colleague, and his regular task was the two dawn services, Sunday and Wednesday, and partial responsibility for catechism. Chauvet and Des Gallars alternated for the Sunday morning (8 a.m.) services. Chauvet and Fabri did the catechism. However, Des Gallars and Fabri were also alternating teaching catechism at St. Pierre, across the city, while Calvin was probably doing much of the Sunday afternoon preaching at St. Gervais. Thus, although worship was mostly in the hands of three men assigned to the parish, St. Gervais was not entirely self-contained, and its ministers also participated in work elsewhere in Geneva.

By 1553 there were a number of changes at St. Gervais, primarily owed to the health of Poupin, whose normal place of work had been La Magdeleine. This was not a temporary illness but a chronic impediment, a "broken voice"; the minutes of the Company of Pastors indicate that the Senate had requested the pastors to find a solution.

> Friday the 6th of the said month [January] it was decided by the brothers that from now on M. Jean Fabri and Des Gallars would do M. Abel [Poupin's] week at La Magdeleine, and they would divide the two weeks at St. Gervais and La Magdeleine between them. This is because the council members have asked that someone be put in the place of M. Abel because he cannot be heard [when he preaches]. As for the day of prayers, M. Calvin is asked to do the sermon in the said [Poupin's] week, always at his convenience and not as if required, and in place of the said Wednesday sermon, M. Jean Fabri would preach on Saturday at La Magdeleine for the said M. Calvin. And this until something better can be arranged.[69]

A fuller picture of the way this difficulty was handled will be found below in the section on how sickness or absence was managed in the ministerial rotations. For a description of services at St. Gervais, it is sufficient to indicate that, while Chauvet remained the anchor, and Des Gallars and Fabri continued to work with him, adjustments had become necessary. In effect, Fabri could no longer do all the dawn and catechism at St. Gervais if he was needed as part of the "pair" responsible for half of the weekdays at La Magdeleine.

The Senate version of this order regarding the ministers' assignments gives a slightly different picture.

---

[69]   RCP I, p.150.

> Calvin has proposed that the ministers have arranged among themselves to organize because of M. Abel [Poupin's] illness. From now on Des Gallars will preach at La Magdeleine and M. de St. André and M. Raymond [Chauvet] at St. Gervais. M. Fabri in the mornings. Ordered that it be done as the said ministers advise.[70]

Jean de St. André, who had been working in Greater Geneva for some months,[71] was apparently assigned to be Chauvet's alternate at St. Gervais, while Des Gallars became Calvin's for weekdays at La Magdeleine. This instruction is slightly but significantly different from that which the Company of Pastors set out on January 6, a few days before they went to the Senate. Perhaps they had revised their plans because now St. André was included, or perhaps they simply presented the matter in the simplest way. In fact, the evidence from the baptismal and marriage records suggests that what happened was a combination of the two proposals. In some ways it was closer to the original form, but with the addition of St. André; he seems to have taken on the dawn services at St. Gervais,[72] the "mornings" the Senate had assigned to Fabri, plus catechism at St. Pierre.

Des Gallars and Fabri together took responsibility for half of the weekday services at St. Gervais and half at La Magdeleine, on a rotating schedule. That is, both men shared the weeks opposite Chauvet at St. Gervais, and also the weeks opposite Calvin at La Magdeleine. One week Fabri and Des Gallars would divide the preaching at St. Gervais while Chauvet was off, and the next week they would divide the preaching at La Magdeleine while Calvin was off. Actually, Fabri and Des Gallars were usually not responsible for the entire week at La Magdeleine, since the record of Calvin's sermons indicates that he was preaching almost every Wednesday (as the Company had requested), with Fabri to do the service on the Saturday of Calvin's week. In mid-year Des Gallars was moved to the country church of Jussy (to the dismay of the Company of Pastors because they had not been consulted), and Bourgoing was brought back to the city and fitted into the place of Des Gallars,[73] dividing his time between St. Gervais and La Magdeleine. Meanwhile, since Des Gallars never had a week off, his alternate Chauvet was

---

[70] Jan. 11, 1553, OC 21:616 (RC 47 f8).

[71] *Consist.* II, p. 311 n.1181; *Consist.* VI, p. 61 n. 370. St. André moved to the city in 1552 because his preaching in the village of Jussy jointly ruled with Bern had led to his imprisonment; cf. RCP I, p. 132.

[72] Occasionally Chauvet or Fabri did a dawn baptism; since they were long-time pastors, particular individuals might have requested them, and it is probable that St. André was doing the preaching at least the great majority of the time. St. André also did dawn at St. Pierre sometimes.

[73] RCP I, pp. 160-61; RCP II, pp. 1-2.

taking the greater part of the Sunday preaching at St. Gervais, at least the 8 a.m. service and catechism, with some help from Des Gallars and Fabri for catechism. Calvin was no longer preaching at St. Gervais on Sunday afternoons but Cop filled in for some of those services and occasionally others did also. By the end of 1553 the ministers were questioning whether Fabri should preach at La Magdeleine because his voice was as hard to hear as Poupin's,[74] but he may well have continued to do some services, especially the Saturdays of Calvin's week.

Over the course of 1554 Poupin's "broken voice" had improved and by 1555 he was doing at least some preaching at St. Gervais,[75] possibly a full role as Chauvet's opposite for the weekday sermons. Fabri was back to covering dawn, both Sunday and Wednesday, and sharing catechism with Chauvet. Bourgoing seems to have taken most of the Sunday afternoons, although he was primarily preaching in the other part of the city. In mid-August 1555, however, Poupin's health failed completely and so there was again a crunch, as efforts were made to cover the services in this parish. Various ministers came to help Chauvet with the weekday preaching. Some were from village churches: Pierre D'Airebaudouze, Jean Macar, Mathieu Matisien, Jean Perrier; some from other parts of the city: Nicolas Colladon, Des Gallars, and – naturally – Cop. (Des Gallars had returned to the city in mid-1555 but had been assigned to La Magdeleine, not St. Gervais.) Fabri's schedule of dawn and catechism did not really change, but he also occasionally assisted on weekdays.

Early in 1556, Geneva lost two of its city ministers, with major consequences for the work at St. Gervais. Poupin died on March 5 and a few days later Fabri was deposed for misconduct. On April 24 Louis Enoch was elected to replace Poupin and was assigned as the second minister for St. Gervais. Thus, in 1557 Chauvet and Enoch were alternating for the weekday services, doing not only the usual six services Monday through Saturday but also the Wednesday dawn service (since there was apparently no one else to help). On Sundays Chauvet did the morning and most afternoon services, and Enoch did some afternoons, plus dawn and catechism with occasional help from colleagues in the city. In July a new minister,

---

[74] Tuesday Dec. 26, 1553, OC 21:565 (RC 47 f200): "Calvin. Sus ce qu'il a proposé l'enrochement et la basse voix tant de Me. I. Fabri que de M. Abel [Poupin] respectivement que n'est propre à l'audience qui vient à la Magdeleine pource que plus aulte voix y seroit requyse supplie y adviser." Consultation with elders was ordered, but the baptismal records for La Magdeleine in 1554 indicate that Fabri did a considerable number of Friday and Saturday baptisms. The Fridays he may have been baptizing when Calvin preached, but the Saturdays he might have preached.

[75] June 10, 1555, he tells the Senate that he is well and petitions to return to La Magdeleine, but the council refuses to make a change simply on the basis of a personal wish. OC 21:608 (RC 49 f102).

Claude DuPont, was elected and assigned "Sunday and Wednesday at St. Gervais at 4 a.m., with the catechism,"[76] thus taking over part of Enoch's work so the latter could return to a more normal schedule (e.g., share Sunday morning with Chauvet). For a significant part of 1557, then, responsibility for worship at St. Gervais was almost entirely in the hands of two men, Chauvet and Enoch, until in late summer DuPont arrived to be the third.

Changes came to St. Gervais again in 1559. DuPont died in February, and after some months Theodore Beza was installed to be one of the parish's resident ministers.[77] Between the loss of DuPont and the coming of Beza, Chauvet and Enoch continued alternating the daily services and again took on dawn and catechism. Both did Sunday mornings and afternoons, although Chauvet apparently had the majority of these and Enoch may have had more of the dawn services. In early summer Beza began preaching on weekdays, opposite Chauvet most of the time. Although occasionally Enoch still took a week at St. Gervais and continued to do catechism, he was now spending more time preaching in the other part of the city because more weekday services had been added there.

By 1562 the leadership of St. Gervais had experienced further changes. The most remarkable one was the departure of Chauvet, who was now working at La Magdeleine. (No reason is given, but it might have been a form of semi-retirement; the Company may have decided he had earned a chance to live in the central part of Geneva, after at least fifteen years at St. Gervais.) Enoch had become the senior minister at St. Gervais; Beza was no longer available since he was in France, occupied with international religious diplomacy.[78] It is not clear who was Enoch's alternate, or even whether he had a regular alternate in the first part of 1562, since so many men had been sent off to France in response to the continual stream of demands for pastors for the new churches there. Probably Enoch was doing almost all the services himself, with occasional help for Sundays (dawn, catechism, some afternoons) from Chauvet, Cop, Colladon, D'Airebaudouze, Jean-Reymond Merlin, and various village pastors: Jean Boulier, Corneille, Pierre Le Duc, Jean Du Perril, Giles of Vandoeuvres, Jean Pinault.[79] By mid-1559 Jean Le Gaigneux had been elected to join the ministerial corps and, contrary to common practice, he was not sent first to a village church but directly to St. Gervais to be Enoch's alternate.[80]

---

76 RCP II, p. 78; for quotation see below at n.94.

77 RCP II, p. 85.

78 RCP II, pp. 95, 97.

79 See Appendix Three: Ministers' Rotation, under Enoch 1562.

80 RCP II, p. 98-99.

The organization of worship leadership at St. Gervais apparently remained stable for the next several years, until September 1564. Enoch and Gaigneux alternated for weekdays and also covered the Sundays; on the day one of them did the 8 a.m. service, he also did the catechism and the daily sermons that week, and on the other Sunday he did the dawn and afternoon services and was off during the week. In late summer two new ministers, Jaques Des Bordes and Jean Trembley, came to take over St. Gervais; they began some Sunday services in August and September, and then were fully involved in the weekday work by October. On Aug. 21, 1564, the new organization for St. Gervais was established.

> M. de Beze reported the same day that the council members want there to be two ministers residing at St. Gervais, according to custom, and that these should be M. [Des] Bordes and Trembley, and that M. Enoch (because of his age), should come and reside here. [81]

Thus Enoch, like Chauvet before him, moved to the central part of Geneva for the final days of his ministry, leaving two young men, Des Bordes and Trembley, in charge of St. Gervais.

The Practice of Ministerial Rotation in the Parishes of St. Pierre and La Magdeleine, 1550-1564

In the central and larger part of Geneva, the practice of ministerial rotation was considerably more complicated than in St. Gervais. At least at first glance, the two parishes of St. Pierre and La Magdeleine seem rather different from St. Gervais with its two or three preachers working in (mostly) orderly alternation.

In fact, however, in the 1540s and indeed, most of the 1550s, St. Pierre and La Magdeleine functioned more like one large parish, with certain exceptions. The exceptions were catechism and, on specific occasions, Sunday mornings. The regular noon catechism class was held in both church buildings, because according to the *Ecclesiastical Ordinances* everyone was supposed to attend that service in her or his own parish. Until 1549, La Magdeleine did not have any other Sunday services, except on the four days each year when the Lord's Supper was celebrated, because the *Ordinances* also required Genevans to participate in the sacraments in their home parish and so a Supper service had to be available in every parish. [82] Thus, except for four Sunday mornings per year and weekly catechism, there was only one place to go for Sunday worship in Greater Geneva, and that was St. Pierre. On

---

[81]   RCP II, pp. 101, 109.

[82]   *Ordinances*, OS II, p. 337.

the other hand, daily worship at St. Pierre was limited to three dawn services on Mondays, Wednesdays, and Fridays, plus the special day of prayer service at 7 a.m. or 8 a.m. on Wednesdays. For weekdays, La Magdeleine was the place for regular preaching; on all days except Wednesdays there was a service at 6 a.m. or 7 a.m. Thus, in the 1540s, all the people of Greater Geneva had a common schedule except for catechism and four Sunday mornings. If you wanted to go to worship at dawn, St. Pierre was the place, Sundays, Mondays, Wednesdays, and Fridays. For Sunday morning at 8 a.m. or afternoon at 3 p.m., or the Wednesday day of prayer service, St. Pierre was again the place. On the other hand, if you wanted to attend a weekday sermon at the "ordinary" time of 6 a.m. or 7 a.m., that was available only at La Magdeleine, Mondays through Saturdays (except Wednesdays).

By 1549, a Sunday morning service had been established at La Magdeleine, so there was regularly a choice for that hour. By 1555, a service on Sunday afternoon and another on Wednesday were also in place. (This completed the requirements of the *Ordinances* for Sundays and added a further Wednesday service, so that there was now the special day of prayer service in both St. Pierre and La Magdeleine at 7 a.m. or 8 a.m. on that day.) Thus, in the 1550s, it was possible to attend Sunday worship at La Magdeleine or St. Pierre in the mornings, but only St. Pierre in the afternoon until 1555, when the 3 p.m. or 2 p.m. service was established at La Magdeleine. Until mid-1559, most daily worship was held at La Magdeleine, but in June of that year a service at the "ordinary" time of 6 a.m. or 7 a.m. was added at St. Pierre. This had not been planned in the 1541 *Ordinances*. It was a response to the great crowds of people filling Geneva at this highpoint of the influx of refugees, and would be confirmed as a permanent part of the schedule in the 1561 revision of the *Ordinances*.

Simply put, for most of Calvin's ministry, the worship life of Greater Geneva, although defined as two parishes, functioned as a kind of large parish worshiping in two locations. In 1559, the two became much more distinct, since for the first time it was possible for a parishioner to find almost the full range of services in either place. Here the exception was the dawn services, which were almost exclusively the domain of St. Pierre. (Briefly, from late 1559 until September 1560, La Magdeleine had a dawn service on Sundays and Wednesdays, making its schedule almost identical to that of St. Gervais across the river, but otherwise anyone in Greater Geneva who needed to attend worship early – and that was the duty of servants, so that they could be home while the rest of the household went to church – had to go to St. Pierre.)

Discussing ministerial rotation in Greater Geneva, therefore, means taking into account a larger number of moving pieces than at St. Gervais, although the principles of the practice were the same. The following gives an overview of the main features of this process, grouped by years, as that is visible in the baptismal and marriage records and the infrequent instructions of the Company of Pastors or the Senate. Because Greater Geneva had two rather different sets of weekday services, unlike the one set at St. Gervais, two clarifications are needed. One is simple: there had to be two pairs of ministers for the weekday sermons. The second clarification regards the differences between the two series of daily services in Greater Geneva; it is necessary to distinguish between "dawn" and "ordinary" times, even though these usually correspond to the practices in St. Pierre and La Magdeleine respectively. Each set of weekday services may be identified by time or by place: "dawn" or St. Pierre for the one, and "ordinary" or La Magdeleine for the other. The dawn services were three days per week, and "ordinary" ones every day except Wednesday, the day of prayer. That day of prayer service at 7 a.m. or 8 a.m. was a special case; it was held only at St. Pierre, until in mid-1555 a comparable service was added at La Magdeleine, probably at first at the same hour.[83] For practical purposes, the following overview of Greater Geneva (1550-1564) is organized by pairs of ministers. Usually it first identifies the pair of ministers assigned to the dawn services, and explains all their tasks; then it discusses the pair who did the "ordinary" time and Wednesday day of prayer, and adds the arrangements for Sundays. (For 1552 and 1554, only the records of La Magdeleine have been examined, so the information is more limited.)

Before beginning and just for perspective, it is worth recounting a little story which illustrates the way that symbiosis could be manifested in one preacher's schedule.[84] On Wednesday May 19, 1557, Pastor Macar managed to conduct three baptismal liturgies in the same morning, in two parishes! At St. Pierre at dawn, which was his usual assignment, he baptized one baby; he then went next door to La Magdeleine, which was not his normal place to preach, and baptized two more babies. Then he hurried back up the hill to St. Pierre, where he baptized yet another infant at a third service. How was this physically possible!? See the map in chap. 1, Figure 1. Fortunately the two church buildings were very close to each other as the crow flies, although St. Pierre was much higher in elevation, on a hill from which a steep outdoor stairway led down to La Magdeleine. As far as the time goes, probably the service at La Magdeleine was being held at the "ordinary" hour of 6 a.m. and the second one at St. Pierre was at 7 a.m. (May 19 was the

---

[83]   There is a reference to a baptism by St. André at 8 a.m. on Nov. 6, but that is the only time listed, and in later years this may have varied; see example of Macar in following note.

[84]   See baptismal records for St. Pierre and Magdeleine for Wed., May 19, 1557.

summer schedule.) It is virtually certain that Macar preached at the first service; it is possible (although not very unlikely) that he next filled in for a colleague at La Magdeleine and then perhaps for Calvin at the second service at St. Pierre. This was Calvin's week to preach, but the record of his sermons on Isaiah inexplicably skips from May 18 to May 20. [85] It looks as if Macar was called upon to be Super-Pastor on this day... running back and forth between the two parishes of Greater Geneva and celebrating three baptismal liturgies, and preaching at least once and probably two or even three times. This was very unusual but it evidently was possible. The need to spread the few ministers over too many services may help to account for the fact that the day of prayer service at La Magdeleine must have been moved from the later hour (7 a.m. or 8 a.m. practiced at St. Pierre and St. Gervais and initially at La Magdeleine) to the "ordinary" time of 6 a.m. or 7 a.m. Normally the life of a pastor in Greater Geneva was not quite so exciting... So back to a "regular schedule"!

In 1550-51, Cop and Bourgoing did the dawn service (4 a.m. or 5 a.m.) at St. Pierre in alternate weeks and the catechism at La Magdeleine in the same rhythm. Cop would have dawn at St. Pierre one week and the catechism at La Magdeleine that same day; the next week Bourgoing would have the St. Pierre dawn service and catechism at La Magdeleine. When one man was ill the other had to fill in for these absences. In the first half of 1550 the one who did the Sunday dawn at St. Pierre and catechism at La Magdeleine did not do the weekday dawn services at St. Pierre. However, about the end of July the two evidently switched weeks, so the one who did Sunday dawn also did the weekday dawn services, leaving his alternate free of this responsibility for that week. (Free of preaching did not mean skipping worship; ministers usually attended services even when they were not in charge.) The catechism services at St. Pierre in these years were being done by colleagues from St. Gervais; as noted above, Des Gallars and Fabri came across the river to alternate for this catechism while Cop and Bourgoing took turns at La Magdeleine. This is further evidence for the conscious distribution of ministers through several parishes. Cop and Bourgoing could have been assigned to their "home" parish of St. Pierre, and Des Gallars and Fabri (coming across the city) could just as easily have done catechism at La Magdeleine. However, to maintain the commitment to vary the preaching, Cop and Bourgoing went next door to La Magdeleine, and Des Gallars and Fabri did catechism at St. Pierre. In addition, Cop and Bourgoing had responsibility for the Sunday afternoon service at St. Pierre, in opposite weeks from when they did the St. Pierre dawn and La Magdeleine catechism.

---

[85]   See Appendix Seven and/or Appendix Eight: Part One, under Isaiah, May 1557.

Calvin and Poupin were paired for ordinary weekdays and the special day of prayer service in the years 1550-51. On Monday and Tuesday, the one "on duty" that week would preach at La Magdeleine at 6 a.m. or 7 a.m., then go to St. Pierre on Wednesday at 7 a.m. or 8 a.m. for the day of prayer, then return to La Magdeleine for the rest of the week: Thursday, Friday, Saturday at 6 a.m. or 7 a.m. The next week the alternate would follow the same pattern. On Sunday mornings Calvin would preach at St. Pierre, and on Sunday afternoons most of the time at St. Gervais. Poupin would do the Sunday morning services at La Magdeleine. It should be noted that Calvin rarely performed baptisms, but his colleagues often came to hear him preach and did the baptisms on those days. Thus sometimes it appears from the baptismal records that different ministers alternate with Poupin on weekdays at La Magdeleine, but in fact these are colleagues stepping in at the end of Calvin's sermons to help him. (This matter will be examined more fully later. [86])

To summarize: Greater Geneva had several pairs of alternates, consonant with the fact that it had two sets of weekday services and two places of worship on Sunday mornings, and all the ministers served regularly in both St. Pierre and La Magdeleine. One pair of ministers, Cop and Bourgoing, did the dawn services (St. Pierre), the catechism at La Magdeleine, and the Sunday afternoon services at St. Pierre, alternating with each other in both cases. One pair of ministers, Calvin and Poupin, followed a similar rotation for weekdays (at La Magdeleine except on Wednesdays, when they moved to St. Pierre), Calvin one week and Poupin the next, but on Sunday mornings Calvin was always at St. Pierre, Poupin at La Magdeleine, and in the afternoon Calvin was at St. Gervais. To fill out the picture, a pair of colleagues from St. Gervais: Fabri and Des Gallars, came to do the St. Pierre catechism.

The baptismal and marriage records for La Magdeleine in 1552 indicate that the system just described was probably unchanged in Greater Geneva, with one exception. On weekdays Calvin and Poupin continued to alternate at La Magdeleine, except for the Wednesday day of prayer service at St. Pierre. Certainly Calvin was at St. Pierre on Sunday mornings and, beginning in mid-April, also on Sunday afternoons; Poupin was at La Magdeleine for Sunday mornings (there was no afternoon service there yet). Cop and Bourgoing continued to do the catechism at La Magdeleine in alternate weeks, until mid-year, when Bourgoing was moved to a village and Des Gallars took his place. (Presumably Cop and Bourgoing or Des Gallars also continued to do the St. Pierre dawn services.) The one change was

---

[86] See chap. 6 at nn.174ff, and Appendix Three: Ministerial Rotations, under Calvin.

that by Easter time Calvin was now regularly preaching at St. Pierre instead of St. Gervais on Sunday afternoons.[87]

The year 1553 brought changes to the ministerial rotation in Greater Geneva in parallel to the effects on St. Gervais. Poupin was still on the roll of preachers (so he could not be replaced) but he was unable to serve in La Magdeleine or even St. Gervais (much less St. Pierre) because he could not be heard. His illness affected both sets of weekday services in Greater Geneva. The more obvious problem was the "ordinary" daily schedule at La Magdeleine, and the solution was to borrow someone from St. Gervais. As noted above, on Jan. 6, 1553, the decision was made to send Des Gallars and Fabri to La Magdeleine for the services at 6 a.m. or 7 a.m., in alternate weeks when they were not on duty at St. Gervais. The baptismal and marriage records indicate that these were the weeks beginning Monday January 9 and 23, February 6 and 20, and so forth; they also show that the two men chose to divide the weeks, so that Fabri had the first half and Des Gallars the second. When Des Gallars was moved to a country church in mid-year and Bourgoing replaced him at St. Gervais, Bourgoing became Fabri's co-preacher for the week at La Magdeleine. In this case, however, after dividing the weeks for a while, Fabri and Bourgoing evidently decided between them that Fabri would do the full week at La Magdeleine and Bourgoing at St. Gervais.[88] As long as both pulpits were covered, the two men seem to have been free to arrange it as they wanted.

Meanwhile Cop probably did most of the dawn services (weekdays and Sundays) at St. Pierre, with occasional help from St. André or Bourgoing.[89] The ministers from St. Gervais also led the Sunday morning service at La Magdeleine, which Poupin had done, while Calvin was naturally at St. Pierre on

---

[87] What duties Cop and his alternate now had in place of preaching on Sun. afternoon at St. Pierre cannot be identified without examination of the records of the other parishes, but it is probable that they did have another task, given the limited number of ministers. They may have helped Chauvet at St. Gervais, since that was where Calvin had been the previous years.

[88] At least, that appears to be what the baptismal and marriage records indicate. First they divide the weeks; at La Magdeleine Fabri does a baptism on Tues. Aug. 8 and Bourgoing on Fri. and Sat. Aug. 11 and 12; at St. Gervais Bourgoing does baptisms on Mon. and Tues. Sept. 4 and 5, and Fabri on Thurs. and Sat. Sept. 7 and 9). Then they divide the parishes and each take a full week. At La Magdeleine Fabri is the only one baptizing for several weeks of their schedule: Mon. and Tues. Sept. 18 and 19; Mon., Thurs., and Sat. Oct. 2 and 5 and 7. At St. Gervais Bourgoing works opposite Chauvet, having the week of Mon. Oct. 9 and Mon. Oct. 23.

[89] Poupin did some baptisms late in the year, but it is not clear whether he would be preaching, even if the group gathered for the dawn service was rather small and might have been close enough to him to hear. It is probable that those who came to dawn services at St. Pierre would gather around the pulpit.

Sundays. Cop and Fabri appear to have had primary responsibility for catechism at La Magdeleine, although Des Gallars and Bourgoing also helped sometimes, or at least performed baptisms. St. André seems to have had the main responsibility for catechism at St. Pierre, but again with occasional help.[90] It was common to link dawn and catechism services as an assignment, and new ministers often began that way. What was unusual about this was that St. André did dawn on one side of the river and catechism on the other. Calvin remained the single constant at La Magdeleine on weekdays, as Cop did at St. Pierre for the dawn weekday services.

For 1554 only La Magdeleine has been examined, but again it suggests the picture for Greater Geneva. It appears that St. André became the primary anchor of worship at La Magdeleine this year; he seems to have had responsibility for "ordinary" weekdays opposite Calvin. The latter continued to do almost every Wednesday day of prayer service at St. Pierre as part of his weekday duty at La Magdeleine. (There are rare occasions when he misses a Wednesday in his off-week.) To balance Calvin's extra day of prayer sermon, Fabri continued to do the Saturdays in Calvin's week, and a number of Calvin's colleagues came to hear him preach and performed baptisms for those requesting the sacrament that day. Naturally, Calvin was also preaching at St. Pierre on Sunday mornings and afternoons. St. André did the parallel Sunday morning at La Magdeleine and also took a share of the catechism, along with various colleagues from around the city: Cop and Bourgoing (from St. Pierre) and Fabri and Poupin (from St. Gervais). All the evidence points to Cop as the anchor of the dawn services at St. Pierre, probably alternating with Bourgoing, and Cop may also have been the key for catechism at St. Pierre.

The worship life of Greater Geneva in 1555 began as a continuation of the previous year, but partway through there were several important changes which demonstrate the influence of the burgeoning population. It is appropriate to identify the continuities first. As usual Cop anchored the dawn services (at St. Pierre) and, as had been the case in 1550-51, he was paired with Bourgoing for both that duty and for catechism, this time at St. Pierre instead of La Magdeleine. (Although Cop did far more baptismal services at both Sunday dawn and catechism, and Bourgoing did more on the weekday dawn services, they were probably alternating week-by-week.) Fabri continued to cross the river from his home parish in St. Gervais to be the mainstay of catechism at La Magdeleine, with some help from St. André. As usual, Calvin was preaching on

---

[90] Cop and Bourgoing also do baptisms at the catechism at St. Pierre on occasion, perhaps because they were long-standing pastors and particular individuals may have requested them to perform the sacrament for their babies. They may also have been helping St. André.

weekdays at La Magdeleine, except for Wednesdays at St. Pierre. For the first part of the year St. André continued his 1554 role as Calvin's alternate at La Magdeleine for Monday-Tuesday and Thursday-Saturday – while Calvin normally did all the Wednesdays. St. André was apparently doing all the Sunday morning services at La Magdeleine while Calvin was at St. Pierre for both morning and afternoon.

However, on June 10, 1555, the Senate asked the ministers to provide two more services at La Magdeleine. One would be the Sunday afternoon service planned in the *Ecclesiastical Ordinances*, and the other would be a Wednesday service which would in effect be an unforeseen addition. (The one planned for La Magdeleine had been customarily held at St. Pierre because larger crowds were expected on the day of prayer; this will be examined in detail in a later chapter.) To the ministers' great relief, the Senate also promised them another colleague, so in the course of June Pierre D'Airebaudouze was elected and sent to Jussy, the country church which Des Gallars had served since 1553, and the latter was called back to the city. The two additional services meant changes in the schedule of La Magdeleine and also resulted in changes in the personnel. Des Gallars appears to have taken the role at La Magdeleine which St. André had filled, as Calvin's alternate for the weekday services. The baptismal records suggest that Des Gallars and Bourgoing became the alternates for the Sunday morning service, with Bourgoing probably (at least partially) responsible for the newly established Sunday afternoon service. In effect, Des Gallars now had a nearly "normal" pattern of work at La Magdeleine: half of the weeks plus half of the Sunday mornings. Calvin also had a nearly "normal" pattern, divided between La Magdeleine and St. Pierre: half the weeks at La Magdeleine except for nearly all the Wednesdays at St. Pierre, and Sunday morning and afternoon at St. Pierre. Bourgoing, Cop's alternate for the St. Pierre dawn and catechism, did some of the extra services at La Magdeleine. Fabri and others still did some of the Saturdays in Calvin's week, but Calvin too did a number of Saturdays even though he was also preaching the extra Wednesday service most weeks.

In 1556 there were a number of changes. As noted above in discussing St. Gervais, early in March Poupin died and a few days later Fabri was deposed for misconduct. In April one of the Greek teachers, Claude Baduel, was elected as minister, but despite his considerable learning his voice was considered too soft to be heard in a city church, so he could not replace Poupin. Thus Baduel was sent to the village of Russin where Jean Macar had been, and the latter was called to the city, presented in church on Sunday, May 10, 1556,[91] and assigned to St. Pierre to help Cop.

---

[91]   RCP II, pp. 66-67.

Continuity and discontinuity are still visible in the shape of the preaching staff in Greater Geneva in 1557. Cop and Macar served as alternates for the dawn services, both Sundays and weekdays (St. Pierre). Des Gallars was Calvin's alternate for the weekday services ("ordinary time") held at La Magdeleine, except for Wednesdays when they moved to St. Pierre and Bourgoing had the service at La Magdeleine. Bourgoing was doing the Sunday 8 a.m. at La Magdeleine when Calvin was at St. Pierre, and he may have been doing La Magdeleine's catechism. Des Gallars was probably doing La Magdeleine's Sunday afternoon service while Calvin was preaching at St. Pierre.

Part way through the year the Company of Pastors was busy with a number of changes in personnel. They needed to replace St. André, who had died in the spring; to settle a French pastor François de Morel who had been working in Paris but had become dangerously well-known to the Roman church authorities and thus needed to leave France; and to prepare to open a fourth parish in the church of St. Germain because of the huge influx of refugees.[92] On Friday June 4 the Company of Pastors began the process and by July 18 the newly elected city pastors Morel and Claude DuPont were presented to the people at the morning service at St. Pierre and in the afternoon at St. Gervais.[93] Then assignments were discussed.

> On Friday July 23, it was resolved among the brothers that Messieurs Calvin and Des Gallars would be the weekly preachers at La Magdeleine. Messieurs Morel and Colladon would be at St. Germain, Messieurs Chauvet and Enoch at St. Gervais, Messieurs Cop and Macar the morning [dawn] at St. Pierre, and Monsieur Bourgoing would preach on Sundays at 8 a.m. at La Magdeleine and on Wednesday, and also do the catechism. Monsieur DuPont: Sunday and Wednesday at 4 a.m. at St. Gervais, with the catechism.[94]

Rarely was the preaching program in Geneva set out in such detail, and in effect what was decided at this point was mostly a continuation of the schedules for St. Pierre, St. Gervais, and La Magdeleine. That is, Calvin and Des Gallars were alternates for the daily weekday services at La Magdeleine, Cop and Macar for the dawn services at St. Pierre, Chauvet and Enoch for the regular Sunday and weekday services at St. Gervais, and Bourgoing for most of the remaining services

---

[92] This constituted a third parish in Greater Geneva. Its baptismal and marriage records have not been examined.

[93] RCP II, pp. 73, 75-77.

[94] RCP II, pp. 77-78.

at La Magdeleine. (Calvin was of course at St. Pierre on Sunday mornings and afternoons.) What was new was adding Dupont to the St. Gervais staff to do the dawn and catechism services (which until then had apparently been covered by Chauvet or Enoch or anyone who could help). The major change was the addition of the new parish of St. Germain, which involved electing three new pastors; one for the country so that Nicolas Colladon could be recalled to the city, and two others to complete the staffing needs for what was now a four-parish system, even though on weekdays St. Pierre and La Magdeleine still functioned in symbiosis.

All seemed well in place, with the parishes once again fully supplied with preachers, but less than a month after this disposition of personnel, Des Gallars left for France on Aug. 16, 1557, to minister in Paris.[95] The baptismal and marriage records indicate that Bourgoing then became Calvin's alternate in place of Des Gallars.

Changes for the rotation of ministers in Greater Geneva continued in 1558. In January Macar was sent to Paris in place of Des Gallars, who returned to Geneva, but by the end of the year Macar had been recalled and Morel sent to Paris in his stead. While Macar was gone, Farel wrote to invite Calvin to his wedding. When the latter answered in September he explained that (in addition to his objections to Farel's plans) it was simply not possible to leave Geneva at this time because two of his colleagues were sick in bed and the "rest of us can scarcely meet the additional burden imposed on us. Certainly I cannot be absent without causing interruption to our meetings for public worship."[96] In fact, within the next month Calvin himself became seriously ill (his last dated sermon was on Saturday Oct. 8, although he might have been in the pulpit on Sunday for another week), and for many months he was unable to preach. It is not clear exactly how his absence was covered, but it is probable that the colleagues who had been his alternates for the daily preaching, i.e., Des Gallars and Bourgoing, took over his weeks, with help from Macar when he got back from Paris late in the year. Together with Cop and others they must have covered Sunday mornings and afternoons at St. Pierre.

The organization of leadership for worship in Greater Geneva in 1559 was both complex and expanding. Cop continued to be the mainstay for dawn and catechism at St. Pierre, with Colladon now as his alternate. On the day that Cop or Colladon did the Sunday dawn service he did only that service; in the alternate week whichever one was on duty did the catechism and the three weekday dawn

---

95   RCP II, p. 78.

96   For Macar and Morel, see RCP II, pp. 80, 82, 84. For Calvin's letter to Farel, Bonnet #516, OC 17:335-36, as quoted in Witte & Kingdon, *Courtship, Engagement, and Marriage*, p. 305.

services. Des Gallars and Macar alternated for the daily services at La Magdeleine, with some help from other colleagues (Cop, Colladon, Bourgoing) on occasion, mostly for the Wednesday service when Des Gallars or Bourgoing would be at St. Pierre. In January 1559 a call was sent to Viret in Lausanne and by early March he was actively serving at St. Pierre in Calvin's place on Sunday mornings and afternoons. He was also probably preaching (on Isaiah) on at least some weekdays in alternate weeks. Sermons for Sunday and Wednesday are recorded for March 5, 8, 12, and 15; probably these were held in St. Pierre since that was the location for the day of prayer as well as Sunday. By early June Calvin was ready to take up daily preaching again. On Monday, June 12, 1559, he resumed his sermons on Isaiah where he had left off on Oct. 8, 1558.[97]

Almost as soon as Calvin was back in the pulpit, and paired with Viret, there was a significant surge in attendance. By June 19 the ministers requested to move the daily sermon in Greater Geneva from La Magdeleine to St. Pierre because of the crowded conditions at the smaller church which they thought would endanger the health of the congregation. Within a few days the move had been accomplished and by the beginning of July 1559 there were services at the "ordinary" hour of 6 a.m. or 7 a.m. at St. Pierre on every weekday except Wednesday when the day of prayer service was later. However, daily services also continued at La Magdeleine, which meant that by the middle of 1559 the two parishes of Greater Geneva were finally functioning as two separate – or at least distinct – entities. St. Pierre now had nine weekday services: the original three at dawn on Mondays, Wednesdays, and Fridays; plus one on each of the weekdays, Monday through Saturday, at the ordinary hour (or, in the case of Wednesday, a little later). These six services had not been foreseen in the 1541 *Ordinances* but they would be confirmed in the 1561 revision. Cop and Colladon continued to carry the dawn services, but now Calvin and Viret were at St. Pierre all week for the daily sermons. La Magdeleine continued to have six weekday services at the ordinary time; Macar remained the stable figure for these services, with Bourgoing as his regular alternate now that Calvin was permanently at St. Pierre for daily worship.

The reorganization of Greater Geneva into two parishes meant that the ministerial rotation for St. Pierre was essentially based in that building, and the same was true for La Magdeleine. On Sunday mornings Calvin preached at St. Pierre and on Sunday afternoons Viret had the pulpit; on weekdays they alternated for the ordinary services, while Cop and Colladon continued the dawn sermons. At La Magdeleine, Des Gallars had the main responsibility for

---

[97]   It is notable that Viret and Calvin were both preaching from Isaiah, though in fact their series were independent; see chap. 6 at n.37.

Sunday morning 8 a.m. and catechism, with some help from Cop and Bourgoing for catechism, while Cop seems to have taken Sunday afternoon, with help from Morel late in the year when the latter returned from Paris. In fact, by November 1559, La Magdeleine's schedule was extended in an unexpected way: a dawn service on Sundays and Wednesdays was added and weddings and baptisms at dawn began on Nov. 28.[98] This made the schedule at La Magdeleine almost identical with that at St. Gervais.

By 1560, the population in Geneva was beginning to decline; not only were refugees returning home, to France and England and Scotland, but also the "brain drain" of ministers was reaching new heights. Des Gallars went to serve the French church in London in 1560, and Macar died that September. On Sept. 6, 1560, Calvin requested that the weekday sermons in French at St. Germain (opened in 1557) and the dawn services at La Magdeleine (begun just the previous year) be discontinued, and this was done.[99] The changes continued the following year. In October, there was a second retrenchment; the French-language parish at St. Germain was closed, including the Sunday services which had remained (although when refugees again flowed back to the city in 1569 it was reopened). Viret had already left for France at the end of Sept. 1561, and Bourgoing followed early in November. Beza was also in France most of this time, although Merlin returned to Geneva in Oct. 1561.[100] After Viret's departure, on Dec. 23 the Senate decided to ask Calvin if D'Airebaudouze could be chosen as his alternate.[101] D'Airebaudouze had been working at La Magdeleine, and appears to have continued there in 1562, so evidently this request did not bear the fruit the Senate had hoped.

---

[98] There are weddings at Sun. dawn Nov. 28, Dec. 17 & 31 by Morel; a baptism on Wed. Dec. 20 by Colladon.

[99] For Des Gallars and Macar, see RCP II, pp. 91-92. Dropping services, note for Sept. 6, 1560, quoted in chap. 1 n.37. Dawn weddings at La Magdeleine are no longer recorded after summer of 1560; the last one identified by time is July 21, 1560, by Morel, although there might have been several later at services when Morel did not note the times.

[100] See RC notes for Oct. 13 & 14, 1561, quoted in chap. 1, n.38. For Viret and Bourgoing, see Sept. 29 and Nov. 6, 1561 (OC 21:762, 765). For Merlin, see Oct. 23 & 27, 1561 (OC 21:764). St. Germain continued to be used for worship by the Italian congregation, until with another influx of French refugees in 1569, the French-language parish was re-established.

[101] Dec. 23, 1561 OC 21:769 (RC 56 f282): "A esté baille charge au S. Chasteauneufz de parler à M. Calvin si on pourroit avoir M. D'Anduse (en marge: Pierre D'Arebaudose) à S. Pierre l'aultre sepmaine que M. Calvin ne presche pas." Perhaps they were not entirely pleased to have Merlin as Calvin's alternate? He was rather critical of the magistracy and was dismissed after a particular sermon on Oct. 18, 1564; cf. RCP II, p. 110.

By 1562, the organization of worship services in Greater Geneva had been fixed in two distinct parishes, St. Pierre and La Magdeleine. The plan followed the pattern defined in the 1541 *Ecclesiastical Ordinances*, with a few changes and additions which had been worked out over the intervening years and regularized in the 1561 revision of the *Ordinances*: i.e., essentially the second set of daily worship services at St. Pierre was completely new since 1541. Cop and Colladon were still responsible for the dawn services at St. Pierre, both Sundays and weekdays; they also did catechism. Merlin was now Calvin's alternate for the "ordinary" time weekday services at St. Pierre; Calvin was preaching on Sunday mornings but it is probable that Merlin took the afternoon service to spare Calvin's fragile health. At La Magdeleine, Chauvet was the main figure, alternating with D'Airebaudouze for weekday services and also for Sunday mornings and afternoons, as well as catechism. Along with Cop, several village ministers assisted at La Magdeleine; Charles Maubué, and Pinault and DuPerrill appear in the baptismal and marriage records from time to time.

The pastoral scene continued to change significantly. By the beginning of 1563 it was clear that Viret would not return to Geneva. Beza and Morel were still in France, so Bourgoing (who was now back in Geneva) was employed for a time. In February Merlin was sent to the court of Jeanne d'Albret. Beza returned to Geneva in May.[102] In 1564 Cop and Colladon continued as the alternates for the dawn services at St. Pierre and for the catechism. The baptismal and marriage records show that, as Calvin could no longer preach after February, Beza took over Calvin's place in St. Pierre. Beza's alternate for the daily "ordinary" sermons at St. Pierre was to be Merlin, but the latter was still retained in Navarre so country pastor Maubué was called to take on Colladon's work and the latter temporarily became Beza's alternate until Merlin's return to Geneva in August.[103] At that point, Colladon moved to La Magdeleine to replace Des Bordes. Chauvet was the mainstay at La Magdeleine, working with Des Bordes until Colladon came in mid-

---

[102] Bourgoing back in Geneva; to be employed for a time, Oct. 2, 1562, Feb. 16, 1563, until his departure in early Sept. 1563 (OC 21:790, 797, 808). Viret remaining in Lyon, Jan. 12 & May 13, 1562 (OC 21:795, 801). Beza and Morel in France, Feb. 16, 1562 (OC 21:797). Merlin to Queen of Navarre and retained there, Feb. 24 & Aug. 16, 1563 (OC 21:797). Beza back in Geneva, May 5, 1563 (OC 21:800).

[103] RCP II, pp. 101-02: "Un peu auparavant [death of Calvin], pource que M. Merlin ne venoit, combine qu'il luy eust esté declairé que l'eglise avoit affaire de sa presence, fut advisé par ledit M. Calvin et la compaignie que M. Charles Maubué, minister de Moins, veindroyt comme par emprunt et pour ung temps prescher en la ville la sepmaine à 4. heures du matin, et que M. Gabriel Ragaue ordonné pour l'eglise de Tours, iroit les dimanches prescher à Moins et Jento pour ledit Maubué, et que M. Colladon prescheroit la sepmaine à six heures à S. Pierre jusques au retour dudit Merlin."

summer. The pattern of distinct organization for the parishes of St. Pierre and La Magdeleine, which had come into practice in mid-1559, had become the norm.

The principle and main features of the rotation system remained but the flexibility had considerably diminished. Two ministers continued to alternate in specific roles. However, one (or occasionally both) could be reassigned to a different parish or schedule, in which case each was paired with a different colleague. There was still a need to borrow preachers from the village on occasion. There was still movement of individual pastors according to general criteria, such as younger and newer men in St. Gervais, senior preachers or elderly ones in the more prominent or pleasanter posts in Greater Geneva. Almost anyone could be called upon for one or several brief replacements. The one major change was that, unlike the first eighteen years of the system (1541-59), the symbiosis between the parishes of Greater Geneva had been reduced to a limited sharing of pastors on Sunday mornings. With a more stable population, however, the three parishes were mostly self-contained for the regular practice of weekday worship services.

Adjustments to the Rotation System

The organization of preaching in the city of Geneva was both complex and flexible. Its first stated purpose was to provide the people with a broader range of Biblical education. However, it also served to insure that the schedule was reliable despite human and circumstantial accidents which would prevent a single man from preaching on every occasion when he should. Village churches did suffer from absences from time to time, but the corps of ministers and its organized rotations also helped to minimize these problems. To grasp the full workings of Geneva's "pulpit exchanges" it is illuminating to see how the system handled routine or more severe adjustments to the schedule of preaching.

Managing Illnesses

One of the most obvious challenges to the provision of regular sermons was, naturally, the illness or absence of a minister. In the case of a temporary condition, e.g., one of a pair of preachers falling sick for a short time, it is probable that the man's alternate simply took over. That was one of the beauties of having two men assigned to the same responsibilities in alternate weeks, and was no doubt one of the reasons which had prompted Calvin's request for two ministers at St. Gervais (as noted above). An illness might well account for occasions when one of the pair did baptisms and marriages in two consecutive weeks; in 1550 at St. Pierre Cop took the Sunday dawn service for Bourgoing on May 4 as well as his own assigned May 11, and Bourgoing took Cop's turn on June 22 as well as his own on June 15 and 29. Sometimes a minister might preach for two consecutive weeks; this broke the pattern of one week on, one week off. The effect of one minister being off for two weeks was that each one would take on his alternate's schedule. At St. Gervais in 1550, Chauvet and Des Gallars were paired for the daily service; in early April they changed weeks, and then again in early October, so that apparently one did two weeks in a row and the schedule thereafter was the opposite of what it had been. [104] Whether the causes for these changes were illness or other circumstances, the flexibility of the organization demonstrates the way the system of alternates allowed one to substitute for the other at need without requiring further administrative effort on the part of the Company of Pastors.

When an illness or absence was extended, however, the rotation system had to compensate in other ways. This was most often the case for country churches, where there was only one minister. The baptismal records note that on May 31, 1562, a man from Tonne brought his son to be baptized in the city (at La Magdeleine) because there had not been a minister in his village for three weeks, but this was probably an exceptional case. Although it was undesirable to leave any pulpit vacant on a Sunday, occasionally that was inevitable. If such a situation lasted more than a week or two, city ministers were assigned to go to that village for the Sunday service. Usually a problem in filling a country church pulpit was dealt with on an ad hoc basis, but sometimes a minister would anticipate a need and write to request assistance, as Des Gallars did in 1554. He describes an eight-day illness in some detail, saying that he fears he will not be able to preach on Sunday and hopes that one of his colleagues might come to substitute for him. [105] There was probably no immediate response, since Des Gallars seemed able still to do his work, or at least his illness was likely to be brief.... and the Company of Pastors was simply spread too thin to re-organize its work until the situation was more desperate.

The circumstance of Abel Poupin's "broken voice" was one of these long-term, if not actually desperate, cases. As noted above, the city magistrates made

---

[104] In 1564 at St. Pierre when Beza was preaching on weekdays, his alternate Colladon (and/or another colleague) took two weeks in mid-March, so that when Beza did his next week (the last of March) he and Colladon each had the other's original schedule. Sometimes such a change was owed to integrating a new colleague. Chauvet and Enoch were alternating at St. Gervais in 1559 until the end of May, but Chauvet also took the first week of June, before Beza began; thus Chauvet's schedule changed to give him the weeks which had been his alternate's.

[105] Letter from Des Gallars to Calvin on Jan. 5, 1554, #1892, OC 15:2-3: "Sic mihi hisce octo diebus epiphora molesta fuit, neque solum oculos, sed totum caput ita conturbavit, ut neque pedes neque manus satis officio suo fungi possint. Nunc vero malas et fauces occupat, ut verear ne non habendae concioni die dominico idoneus sim futurus. Hoc enim biduo me plus solito cruciat et vocem prope ademit. Spero tamen eam paulatim defluxuram esse. Interea fratres rogandos putavi, ut aliquem meo loco substituant. Quod ut meo nomine facias vehementer a te peto."

the request (demand?) of the Company of Pastors at the beginning of January 1553. Poupin was Calvin's alternate and thus one of the most visible ministers in Greater Geneva, preaching in alternate weeks at La Magdeleine where most of the city and certainly the majority of the Senate members regularly worshiped on weekdays. Probably Poupin's voice had been failing for a while, because the ministers acceded to the request immediately and within a few days the preaching schedules had been re-organized.... quite extensively, as far as the ministers themselves were concerned, in order to maintain the established rhythm of services. The second and third members of the pastoral team at St. Gervais, Des Gallars and Fabri, were called upon to take on Poupin's weekday preaching at La Magdeleine, in addition to their own work at St. Gervais. Certain adjustments were made in St. Gervais, however; Chauvet took on somewhat more, adding part of the responsibility for catechism to his other duties of weekday preaching and Sunday morning. St. André was assisting in several city parishes after he was forced out of his village charge by complaints from Bern; he was charged with Sunday dawn at St. Gervais and catechism at St. Pierre, which had been part of Fabri's assignment. Fabri himself was asked to help Calvin in his regular preaching, taking the Saturday of Calvin's weekly sermons so that Calvin could do every Wednesday. Thus in effect Poupin was replaced by three colleagues: Des Gallars and Fabri for the La Magdeleine services on weekdays, and Calvin for the St. Pierre service on Wednesday. Des Gallars, Fabri, and Chauvet all took on extra preaching, St. André was officially added to the corps of city ministers, and another junior colleague was sent to fill his village post. Meanwhile Poupin apparently continued some pastoral work, especially tasks that did not require a strong speaking voice, such as baptisms or, no doubt, visiting the sick.

As noted above in the discussion of ministerial rotation in Greater Geneva, Calvin's illness in late 1558 introduced a significant problem for preaching at both La Magdeleine and St. Pierre. At first his colleagues no doubt tried to cover, but when it became evident that he would not soon be well, Viret was called to Geneva in the beginning of 1559 to take Calvin's place until the latter could resume work. (Calvin's preaching schedule will be examined in more detail in a later chapter.) Here again, as in 1545, the Genevan authorities reached outside their own usual pastoral corps when it was necessary to replace their most prominent preacher. In fact this time Viret was facing more troubles at home and would soon have to leave Lausanne permanently[106] so the invitation was timely for him.

---

[106] See Dec. 25, 1559, OC 21:725 (RC55 f163) Viret and other ministers are made bourgeois and Viret continues to work with Calvin until he leaves for France in 1561.

Other Various Absences and Moves Affecting Pastoral Rotation

In addition to illnesses there were also a variety of absences by ministers which complicated the preaching system. Most often in the early years, when the village parishes were the most seriously understaffed, ministers from the city would be assigned to fill in on a temporary basis. In March 1543 "one of the preachers at St. Gervais" is ordered to preach on Sundays at Genthod and Dardagny, and country pastor Bernard is told to preach at Dardagny (evidently when the city pastor is not there) and is promised financial support so that he can have a horse. Managing a two-point charge was a physical challenge, and the logistics of getting to and from a preaching place had to be considered.[107] Two observations may be made here: St. Gervais had more than one minister (even if he was not yet officially appointed there), and it was assumed that the one who did not go to the country church would cover the Sunday services at St. Gervais. Later that same year, on Sept. 28, 1543, a "minister from the city" is told to go to Celigny on Sundays to preach because the pastor assigned to the village is "not fit" (and the latter is forbidden to continue his work). As an inducement the city preacher is promised the loan of a horse from the hospital and "something for his pains."[108] Nothing is said about how the minister is to be chosen, or whether it must always be the same person, but it is probable that the Company of Pastors made the decision and likely that one man was designated, since Calvin regarded it as unsettling to the congregation to have too much change in the village parishes.[109] Whoever was sent to Celigny left his regular preaching to his alternate. The process of borrowing a city minister for a country pulpit continued in later years, although then it was more often scheduled, as in August 1553 when Des Gallars, who had just been assigned to the village of Jussy, asked for a month's leave to attend to business in France before going to his new parish.[110] Someone else from the city would have had the task of filling that post for the intervening weeks.

When a city minister was asked to cover for a rural one, the assignment was intended to be short-term, but occasionally things happened... In 1554 pastor

---

[107] Mar. 2, 1543, OC 21:308 (RC 37 f25): "Ordonné que l'on des predicans de S. Gervex aye à aller les dymenche prescher à Gento et semblablement à Dardagnyez. Ordonné que M. Jq. Bernard predicant de Satignyez aye à allé prescher à Dardagnyez et qu'il luy soyt donner quelque chose pour entretenyr ung cheval." For question of St. Gervais having two ministers, see above at nn.45ff.

[108] OC 21:321 (RC 37 f231): "M. Jaques Baud minister de Cilligny n'est capable à desservyr aut ministere: il luy est fayct deffence de non plus s'en mesler et soyt envoyer les dymenches ung predicant de la ville auquelt soyt ballie ung cheval de l'hospital et quelquechose pour sa poienne."

[109] RCP II, pp. 98-99.

[110] July 25 & 31, 1553, OC 21:547 (RC 47 f118, 120).

Ninault left his church at Draillans without permission, and Chauvet was sent to preach there on several Sundays, May 27 and June 3, while another minister was sought as Ninault's permanent replacement. On the second occasion he preached, Chauvet was arrested after his sermon because of theological conflicts between Geneva and Bern, which shared jurisdiction of the village, and he spent the better part of two months in prison. Finally he was released on July 25. Meanwhile, a new minister had been chosen for Draillans... and less than three weeks after his return to Geneva Chauvet was back in Draillans to present its new minister on Aug. 12, 1554.[111] What had begun as a short replacement for a village post had turned into an extended absence for the chief minister of St. Gervais... which probably meant his alternate and anyone else available had to cover while Chauvet was away.

Complications in a village church could sometimes lead to a fairly large-scale re-organization of ministers. In early February 1552 St. André, the pastor of Jussy and Foncenex, was preaching at the second of these village churches when he was imprisoned because the content of his sermon touched on the sacramental diffe-rences between Bern and Geneva. Bernese authorities were upset, and St. André was arrested, imprisoned, and banished from Bernese territory. A new minister acceptable to Bern had to be found for the parish of Jussy and Foncenex. At first the plan was to move some of the village preachers around, but Philip Ecclesia refused to change parishes, although Fabri agreed to replace Ecclesia in his village church. The Genevan Senate intervened and ended up sending Bourgoing to Jussy, which in turn led to a vocational crisis; Bourgoing believed that his calling to the ministry was brought into question if he was ordered to a church by the civil authority but not by his fellow ministers. The Company of Pastors reassured Bourgoing about his vocation and finally agreed to accept the magistrates' deci-sion, but explicitly under protest because the civil authorities had acted in church matters without even consulting the pastors.[112] Bourgoing's departure meant that his responsibilities at St. Pierre and La Magdeleine had to be assigned to someone else, and St. André seems to have taken that place "temporarily."[113]

---

[111] RCP II, pp. 55, 56; while Chauvet was in prison his keeper offered to free him for a large sum of money, but Chauvet refused, seeing that as an admission of guilt and being sure that he was innocent, p. 55.

[112] RCP I, pp. 132-33.

[113] See St. André's presence in the baptismal records of La Magdeleine for 1552, Appendix One. This whole story was in fact replayed the next year, when Bourgoing claimed that he was having problems at Foncenex because of a sermon he preached, and asked the Senate to bring him back to the city. They did this, without consulting the Company of Pastors, and Des Gallars found himself moved to the country to replace Bourgoing. See RCP II, pp. 1-2.

Helping country parishes was one but certainly not the only reason for Geneva's city pastors to be away from their preaching assignments. Ecclesiastical politics might cause short or extended absences (in more controlled circumstances than when the preachers were under arrest!), and short-term mutual assistance would be arranged to fill the gaps. For example, over the course of several years the Company of Pastors sent delegations to Bern to complain about theological attacks on Calvin's teaching. In October 1554 Fabri made a trip, and in early 1555 a series of missions were undertaken. Chauvet's effort in February 1555 did not resolve matters, so he came home, and on March 6 he and Calvin and some members of the Genevan Senate left for Bern again. This was a short stay leading to plans for a formal conference the last Sunday of the month.[114] The Genevans returned home, and Calvin and Chauvet both did some of their regular duties for a short space of time: Calvin preached several sermons, and baptized a baby at La Magdeleine on March 25; at St. Gervais Chauvet was preaching and celebrated a baptism at the 8 a.m. service on Sunday March 24 and another the next day.[115] By March 28 Calvin, Chauvet, and Senate representatives were again on their way to Bern, where agreement was reached that Calvin and his teaching were approved, and on April 5 the Genevans started home.[116] On Sunday May 26 Chauvet and Macar were sent to Bern about moral problems in jurisdictions shared by Geneva and Bern; Chauvet left Macar to continue the efforts, and the latter did not return home until June 6.[117]

How were these absences in 1555 covered? No complete answer is possible, but the baptismal and marriage records offer some clues. It is helpful to deal with each minister separately. Calvin[118] was away for the Sunday of March 10; at 8 a.m. Bourgoing did a baptism at St. Pierre (and presumably preached); Cop did a wedding at 3 p.m. (and presumably preached). Calvin's weekday alternate at La Magdeleine was St. André, who seems to have covered some of Calvin's absences. However, for this week, Fabri baptized a baby on Monday, Cop on Thursday, and St. André on Friday, and presumably they also preached. (Perhaps each took two days? Fabri on Monday-Tuesday, Cop on Wednesday-Thursday, and St. André on Friday-Saturday?) For Calvin's second absence at the end of March, probably

---

[114] RCP II, pp. 58, 59-61.

[115] See Appendix Three: Ministers' Rotations for 1553. Also Appendix Four: Calvin's Baptisms and Appendix Seven for sermons of this year.

[116] RCP II, pp. 61-62.

[117] RCP II, pp. 63, 64..

[118] See Appendix Three: Ministers' Rotations, for 1555; also Appendix Seven for sermons in this year.

Bourgoing did the Sunday afternoon service on March 31 in addition to his regular alternation at the dawn service (he does baptisms at both times). It is possible that Cop did the morning service in addition to his regular turn at catechism. The week that the party left for Bern on March 28 was Calvin's time to preach, and it appears that Fabri and Cop filled out the rest of his services at La Magdeleine (baptisms on Thursday the 28th and Friday the 29th).

For Chauvet's three journeys, several people also covered his work at St. Gervais.[119] Poupin did a baptism on the afternoon of March 10 (and presumably preached); Fabri probably did the morning service in addition to his regular dawn sermon, while St. André took the catechism which would have been Fabri's. Poupin and Macar seem to have filled in for Chauvet during the week; there is a baptism by Poupin on Wednesday March 12, and baptisms by Macar on Thursday and Friday, March 13 & 14. For the second trip to Bern when the party left on March 28, it is unclear who completed Chauvet's week at St. Gervais. However, it is probable that Poupin did the Sunday morning service on March 31 and Fabri the Sunday afternoon, because baptisms are recorded for them at those hours. For Chauvet's May visit to Bern, it is not stated whether he and Macar left early in the morning or after worship on Sunday the 26th. Assuming that the latter, this trip might not have interfered too much with Chauvet's schedule, since the week of his absence he was not scheduled to do the daily service, and he was back by the beginning of the following week, as a baptism on Monday June 3 attests. Such full details are not available for every absence, but these examples provide at least some idea of how a short-term, planned absence might be covered.

Absences for church business might involve any minister, but it was most often the senior men who were called upon to do the negotiations. While Chauvet took a major role in the discussions with Bern, it was usually Calvin who needed to be away from his pulpit for theological or pastoral purposes. Some of the ways his absences were covered have been illustrated above: importing Viret in 1545 and 1559 to cover extensive travel or long-term illness, organizing the colleagues to pick up pieces of the work in 1555 during the negotiations with Bern. In the last instance all Calvin's services could not be entirely covered by his alternate because this was the period when Poupin was ill and the ministers were more than usually over-extended. Although the amount of evidence is more limited, there is a similar example from the first part of April the previous year (1554) when Calvin made a trip to Strasbourg and was absent from consistory on April 5 and 12. The latter date would have been part of his regular week to preach; Chauvet does a

---

119 See Appendix Three: Ministers' Rotations, for 1555.

baptism at La Magdeleine on Tuesday April 10, so he was one of those filling in
for Calvin. [120]

Ministers' Movements Beyond the Rotation System

Responsibility for preaching shaped most Genevan pastors' public worship
life, but they were also present at and involved in services in various different
parishes when they were not in the pulpit. One reason for a minister to be in a
church when he was not assigned to preach there was to carry out a baptism or a
wedding. Most of the time, when one of the city ministers recorded either of these
rites, he was probably preaching as well. Parishioners brought their babies to the
pastor on duty at their parish church when they wanted a baby baptized, or came
to the service at which they wanted to be married. [121]

There were exceptions to this rule, however. It is not clear how often someone
like Cop, who was based in Greater Geneva and especially in St. Pierre, would
preach in another parish such as St. Gervais. He seems to have celebrated
baptisms outside of his usual rotations (for dawn at St. Pierre and catechism at
either St. Pierre or La Magdeleine) on a more flexible basis than most of the other
preachers. Even reckoning only the years for which complete records have been
examined, the range of services and times and places where Cop baptized babies is
quite extensive. Examples beyond his regular assignments include baptisms at
La Magdeleine on weekdays (he was probably not preaching) and on Sunday
mornings (8 a.m.) and afternoons (when he probably was preaching). The baptisms at St. Gervais are the more surprising: there are weekdays in every year, as
well as various times on Sundays (dawn, 8 a.m., catechism and afternoon). Many
of these were probably times when he filled in for a colleague on an ad hoc basis
and not as a regular replacement, but it does suggest that he was very flexible. [122]
When the marriage records are added to the baptisms, the numbers of Cop's
"extra" services increase; he was at La Magdeleine fairly often on Sunday afternoons, and at St. Gervais at Sunday dawn and especially Sunday afternoons. [123]

---

[120] April 5 & 12, 1554 (OC 21:571, 572); Appendix Three: Ministerial Rotations.

[121] See chap. 5 after n.215.

[122] Years: 1550-51, 1553, 1555, 1557, 1559, 1562, 1564. La Magdeleine baptisms: Thurs. 1550.
Mon. 1551. Sun. 8 a.m. & every weekday 1555. Wed. 1557. Sun. 8 a.m. & p.m., Tues-Wed-
Thurs. 1559; Sun. p.m. 1562. Sun. p.m. 1564. St. Gervais baptisms: Mon. 1551. Sun. 8 a.m.
1553. Tues. & Wed. 1553. Tues. & Wed. 1555. Sun. dawn & 8 a.m. & every weekday except
Wed. 1557. catechism & Mon. 1559. Sun. 8 a.m.& catechism 1562. Sun. dawn & 8 a.m. & p.m.
& Mon.-Wed.-Thurs. 1564.

[123] La Magdeleine weddings: Mon. 1555. 4 Sun. p.m. 1559. Sun. p.m. 1562. St. Gervais weddings:
Sun. dawn & 5 Sun. afternoons 1553. 4 Sun. afternoons 1555. Sun. dawn 1557. Sun. dawn &
p.m. 1562. Sun. dawn 1564.

It is probable that a number of these baptisms were celebrated at services where Cop was filling in for an absent colleague. This is practically certain for the dates when he did a wedding as well as a baptism, but it is very likely that he also preached at other baptisms, especially in the years like 1553-56 when Poupin's illness put the whole system under a strain. It is also very possible, if not probable, that sometimes a family specifically asked Cop to baptize their baby, and thus he would go to their home parish for the sacrament. This would be natural if the family had particular ties with a pastor. However, probably it was not uncommon when a new minister came to a parish that some members of the congregation would invite their former pastor back, even if he had been reassigned to another parish. When the family wanted their baby baptized by someone other than the minister on duty in their parish, it would be necessary to discuss the day and time of the service with both the chosen man (here Cop) and the parish minister. Normally parents may have notified their pastor only shortly before the service, so that he would know to prepare for the baptismal liturgy at the end of the sermon. (Presumably the ministers assigned to a parish knew when women in their community expected babies and were not surprised to have a child presented with little forewarning.)

A second and more individual or informal cause for preachers to move among the three city parishes was the desire to attend worship themselves outside their customarily assigned places. Certainly Calvin insisted that all pastors must continue hearing and learning God's word,[124] so ministers were expected to attend services when they were not on duty. This privilege was, naturally, not available for village preachers except when they were able to come into Geneva on a weekday (when they were usually not preaching), but in the city it was apparently a frequent if not daily practice for ministers to attend worship. It is impossible to trace in general how much this happened, and the particular case of those who came to hear Calvin cannot be taken as typical of how often pastors heard other colleagues. It does, however, serve as evidence for their regular presence in worship when they were not in the pulpit. In fact, it appears that most of the Company of Pastors chose to attend Calvin's sermons on a semi-regular basis, if they were free to do so.

The evidence for the presence of other ministers at Calvin's services is found in the number of occasions when a colleague celebrated a baptism at a time and place when Calvin was definitely preaching. (Weddings were a slightly different case; these will be examined later.[125]) When the dates of Calvin's extant sermons are

---

124 For one example, see sermon #17 on 1 Cor. 3:2b-7, ms. fr. 26, f138b.

125 See chap. 6 at nn.172f; Appendix Five: Calvin's Weddings.

correlated with the baptisms celebrated by other members of the city Company of Pastors in the parish where he was preaching, it becomes clear that his colleagues often performed the sacrament when he was in the pulpit. Two conclusions may be drawn from this. One is that there was no rule which mandated that a baptism had to be celebrated by the preacher or, to put it another way, preaching and the sacrament of baptism (or the rite of marriage) could be done by different men, so long as the sacrament was never held without the word. The second conclusion is that ministers who did baptisms or weddings were attending the service at which the rites were celebrated, because the people involved (the baptismal party or the couple being married) had to be present for the whole service. It is virtually impossible to imagine Calvin allowing a minister to appear only for the marriage or baptismal liturgy! Obviously his colleagues could visit Calvin's sermons only when they were not preaching elsewhere themselves, a fact supported by an examination of the occasions when Chauvet, the main minister at St. Gervais and thus the one least likely to be free to go across the river, is registered as doing baptisms at La Magdeleine or St. Pierre when Calvin was preaching. (Chauvet's regular rotation at St. Gervais is documented in opposite weeks from the baptisms he recorded on Calvin's side of the city.) [126]

A Concluding Comment

Geneva's city ministers were both organized in stable patterns of preaching, in pairs, and also flexible in their movements, whether these were necessitated by illnesses or absences of colleagues or chosen by themselves when they were "off duty." The system of ministerial rotation for preaching, combined with changes of assignments (different parishes, even different sides of the city), made for a stable yet varied provision of sermons. From the preachers' own point of view, it allowed for flexibility for necessary absences from the pulpit (e.g., illnesses) along with the possibility of attending worship themselves on a reasonably frequent basis. The preachers were only one part of the equation, however; the people in the pew were the other very significant and equally necessary part of the whole.

III: The People in the Pews

Where were the people of Geneva in corporate worship, and what were they doing? The experience of worship in Protestant Geneva had both similarities to and differences from the medieval practice. It is appropriate first to consider briefly pre-reformation Geneva.

---

[126] See Appendix Three: Ministers' Rotations, under both Calvin and Chauvet.

By medieval church law, each person was required to confess to his or her parish priest and receive communion at least once a year, and the intent was that members of a parish would regularly attend Mass in their home church on Sundays and holy days. By the fifteenth century, Genevans often attended Mass in different sanctuaries all over the city; the friars' churches (Franciscan, Dominican) and confraternity altars were particularly popular. The major occasions for preaching would normally be services offered to the whole city at specific seasons such as Lent or Advent, and these would be held at the cathedral or sometimes at the church of the religious order which sponsored the sermon.[127] On the other hand, when baptisms and weddings were celebrated as liturgies they were usually held in the family's parish church with the godparents and other invited guests. However, neither sacrament was bound to any specific location; emergency baptisms and common law marriages were not infrequent, and these were held in homes or other private places.

As is well known, when they came to church for the regular services of the Mass on Sundays or holy days, most people would expect to stand and observe the priest, paying special attention to the elevation of the bread and wine which marked their transubstantiation into the body and blood of Christ. There were some places to sit, but these were usually reserved for the elderly and sick or very important people; there were sometimes benches but the clergy resisted the introduction of general seating.[128] Depending on their level of education, the devout might well spend most of their time repeating their (Latin) prayers, reading a book of hours, or gazing meditatively at the paintings and statues of saints on the walls and set around the side altars of larger churches.[129] Truly engaged laity were encouraged to participate in the Mass in various ways complementary to the actions of the priest, as if they were attending the court of a feudal lord,[130] but it is

---

[127] Lambert, *Preaching, Praying, and Policing*, provides one summary of late medieval devotion and liturgical worship, chap. 4-6; for Genevans' fondness for going to Mass elsewhere than their parishes, pp.113-15.

[128] Grosse, *Les rituels de la Cène*, p. 268.

[129] The Ménagier de Paris gives a charming example of proper behavior in the advice he provides for his young wife; cf. *The Goodman of Paris: A treatise on moral and domestic economy by a citizen of Paris, @1393*, trans. Eileen Powers (Woodbridge, UK; Rochester, NY: Boydell, 2006), pp. 52ff.

[130] Virginia Reinburg, "Liturgy and the Laity," *Sixteenth Century Journal* (1992), pp. 529-30: "What we find in the [late medieval French] laity's prayer books, as distinct from the clergy's missal, is a notion of lay participation in the mass quite different from that on which the Protestant and Catholic reformers later insisted. Before the Reformation, the laity's participation was supposed to be less concerned with intellectual grasp of eucharistic doctrine or scriptural teachings, than with assuming a proper role in the drama of the mass. ... the clerical celebrant had a sacramentally necessary role in the liturgy... the laity's role [was] equally necessary in a social sense." p. 530 n.6.

doubtful that this form of worship was widely practiced. In effect, there were often two or more parallel forms of worship happening at the same time: the priest at the altar (with his back to the people at least part of the time), the laity in various places around the nave of the church, praying or watching or sometimes doing less devout things.

The reform of the Genevan parish system in 1541 re-organized the movements and experience of worship in ways both like and unlike the past. According to the *Ecclesiastical Ordinances*, every person was to receive the sacraments in her or his home parish. In this sense there was some continuity of regulation (the role of a person's home parish) and some discontinuity with regard to specifics (which sacraments). Penance as a sacrament no longer existed, of course, but both baptism and the Lord's Supper were now bound to the parish. (The Reformed teaching and practice of the sacraments and the rite of marriage will be examined in later chapters. The point here is to sketch the ways people in Protestant Geneva experienced the places of worship and moved about the city as they did so.) Also according to the *Ordinances*, catechism was linked to one's home parish; children, or any others who needed to be instructed, were to be sent or brought to the weekly catechetical service in their own parish. Such religious education by the parish clergy on a fixed and frequent basis was something new. The regulations mandated both corporate teaching by the parish pastors and regular compliance by all households, which resulted in a structured plan for the time and place of weekly worship at least for children.[131]

Also with regard to the places of preaching in Geneva, the reform brought continuity as well as discontinuity.[132] For attendance at sermons Genevans were left free to choose where they wanted to worship, and at least some people certainly moved between the two parts of the city, while parishioners of St. Pierre and La Magdeleine constantly went back and forth between church buildings or parishes (at least until 1559).[133] New, however, was the requirement

---

[131] *Ordinances*, OS II, p.337; cf. chap. 3 at nn.129ff.

[132] Manetsch, *Calvin's Company of Pastors*, p. 20, reads Calvin's complaint in 1538 about Protestants being regarded as only preachers and not settled pastors as an objection to people moving about the city to different services. The two are different issues; see above at n.7 for Calvin's letter to Bullinger in 1538. Calvin was in favor of people being free to move about, even for the sacraments; it was essentially the Senate which insisted on their being bound to the parishes; see chap. 3 at nn.202ff.

[133] The consistory records provide examples of people attending two different churches. *Consist.* I: April 20, 1542, p. 44, a man goes to sermons "ici à Sainctz Pierre et à La Magdeleine." April 27, 1542, p. 48, a woman was at St. Pierre last Sunday; she is told to go to sermon and catechism at St. Gervais every Sunday which means she was from St. Gervais. Sept. 14, 1542, p. 116: a woman goes to sermons at La Magdeleine [evidently weekdays] and on Sundays to St. Pierre

that one must attend worship somewhere at least once a week; or rather the requirement was not new but the pressure and expectations were considerably increased. Certainly the access to daily worship was different: no longer could one go to any one of a dozen or more locations where a priest might be saying Mass. Now there were a limited number of places to hear sermons, distributed in a coherently organized fashion between the two sides of the city, and more abundant in Greater Geneva where the majority of the population lived.

That Genevans did move about the city for worship is evident in the comments of people who came before the consistory, especially in the early years when the elders most often asked almost every parishioner they interviewed about her or his attendance at sermons. Sometimes the respondents name the parish or the preacher, as if they needed to identify the place where they worshiped; if they had been expected to attend their home parish they could have mentioned their place of residence. [134] That the people took advantage of the liberty to move about is also seen in the cases when they get the preacher's identity wrong and the consistory secretary corrects them. [135] Sometimes no doubt they simply were not paying attention. Sometimes, however, they may have thought that their own parish minister would catch them if they claimed (falsely) to have been at church when

---

and receives the Supper at La Magdeleine [obviously her own parish]. Dec. 7, 1542, p. 146: a woman was at St. Pierre on Sun. and after dinner at La Magdeleine [catechism, her parish]. Feb 22, 1543, p. 84: a woman sometimes goes to St. Gervais and St. Pierre to sermons; p. 186: another woman always goes to St. Gervais or La Magdeleine when she can. April 3, 1544, p. 348: man says he was at sermon twice on Sun., once at St. Pierre and the other at St. Gervais.

[134] *Consist.* I. March 16, 1542, p. 16: a man heard Farel at St. Pierre. April 27, 1542, p. 48: a woman was at St. Pierre last Sunday and Champereau preached [probably dawn; cf. above at nn.35-36]. Jan. 11, 1543, p. 168: a man received the Supper at St. Gervais along with others, and Trippereau preached. March 15, 1543, p. 195: a man says he was at sermon at La Magdeleine today and Calvin preached and it was about Joseph's departure (see chap. 6 at n.102). April 3, 1544, p. 345: a woman says on Sunday she was at La Magdeleine "après dyne" and it was Calvin (probably wrong; see chap. 1 n.78, unless Calvin was filling in for a colleague at catechism, which is possible but unlikely). April 26, 1543, p. 233: a man says he goes to sermons and last Sun. he was there twice and Calvin preached.

[135] *Consist.* I. Sept. 7, 1542, p. 111: a man was at St. Gervais today and yesterday and Master Henri [de la Mare] preached; the secretary says: that is lie, because he has not preached for ten days. March 1, 1543, p. 187: a woman says she was at St. Pierre on Sun. and Henri [de la Mare] preached; the consistory secretary says "it was Genesto." April 3, 1544, p. 345: p. 348: a man was at St. Gervais "devant dyné et apres dyné" and does not know who preached; he then seems to change his mind and guess that it was Champereau. The secretary writes "this is lie; it was not Champereau." [Exactly who said what is not entirely clear from the syntax, but this makes better sense than the alternative which would have the secretary stating that it was Champereau and the man disputing this.] This continues in later years, though perhaps not as frequently; cf. Nov. 19, 1545; April 1 & 8, 1546, May 6, 1546, *Consist.* II, p. 77, 185-86, 195, 218.

he was preaching, so it was better to name "Calvin" and trust that the crowd in St. Pierre on Sunday morning was too large for anyone to be counting heads. In any case, it is certain that at least a portion of the inhabitants of Geneva moved about to attend services in different parishes, even before the influx of refugees who were eager to crowd into the church whenever Calvin or Viret preached.[136]

When they came to church the place and the experience of worship itself were significantly changed from their pre-reform lives. Not only were there fewer buildings where services were held, but these looked rather different inside. The statues and most of the religious art had been removed in the first icono-clastic days; progressively the rest of the medieval devotional material was dis-mantled, although it took some years to complete the process.[137] There is some question about whether anything visual was substituted; in later Reformed communities panels on which the Decalogue had been written were placed on the walls, but some scholars deny that this was the case in Geneva.[138]

There is some evidence to the contrary, although the interpretation is not clear. In August 1540 the Senate ordered old religious paintings ("tablaux") to be covered over with the ten commandments.[139] Some years later in 1549 Calvin brought to the attention of the Senate that the division of the commandments into two tables was not accurate and he was told to correct them.[140] The

---

[136] June 19 & Aug. 7, 1559, OC 21:718, 719-20 (RC 55 f59, 78v). See Pierre Poyent from La Magdeleine who followed Calvin across the city to hear him preach at St. Gervais; chap. 6 at n.214.

[137] Grosse, *Les rituels de la Cène*, pp. 256-61 provides the most recent summary outline of the process.

[138] Grosse, *Les rituels de la Cène*, p. 261 n.85. Grosse cites Guichardin for the French churches and Grendjean for the Pays de Vaud. "A partir d'une date inconnue, celui de Jussy porte un verset du psaume 119 ainsi que le décalogue. Débattant de la proposition d'inscrire les dix commandements dans tous les temples, la Compagnie des pasteurs juge en 1639 'qu'il n'estoit besoin d'introduire ceste nouveauté,' tout en laissant aux pasteurs de la campagne la possibilité d'adopter cet usage," citing Charles Bonnet, "L'Eglise de Jussy," in *Genava*, nouvelle série, 25 (1977), p. 87.

[139] On Aug. 9, 1540, the Senate records: "(*Tablaux*)- Ledtz Claude Humbert az exposé coment ledtz Matellin az charge de demandé s'il y az quelque ymages aut tablaux az vendre. Resoluz, si en parle, de luy fere respondre qu'il il n'en n'y az poient, et du tablaux qu'est resté, que l'on fasse escripre les comandement de Dieu," RC V, p. 449. There would be no point to writing the Decalogue on the paintings if they were not going to be returned to a church or other public setting. It is possible this order was not carried out, but assuming this was done it would offer an explanation for the problem in 1549.

[140] Oct. 24, 1549: "Pareillementz d'avoir advis aussi sus les commandementz que icy separe en deux tables etc. et mesme il az de l'erreur : aussi qui plaise à Messieurs il mecte ordre. Ordonné que ledit Calvin ayent à couraigé (corriger ?) lesditz mandementz." OC 21:457 (RC 43 f247v). (This was the last of the items named to the Senate for change; the first, the issue of adding more dawn services, has received the most attention; cf. chap. 1 at nn.113ff.)

problem may well have been that the commandments were divided five and five between the commandment to honor parents and the one forbidding murder; this was the organization found in the first vernacular Protestant catechism published in Geneva in 1537. Although other texts refer to "two tables," this 1537 ABC is the only French-language one that indicated which commandments belonged in each table, until the *Institutes* in 1541 and Geneva Catechism of 1542.[141] By that time, Genevans already had an image of the printed decalogue as five and five (contrary to Calvin's four and six numbering which placed the division between the Sabbath commandment and the one about honoring parents). Logically the only context in which the requested 1549 correction of the mistake in the Decalogue would be needed would be if the placard were posted in a public place. In 1536 and 1537, the Senate had already affixed copies of the Ten Commandments to the walls of the Molard and Hôtel de Ville.[142] Perhaps the instructions in August 1540 about covering the old religious paintings with the Decalogue were an extension of this. Yet it seems possible that these "tablaux" with the commandments could have been hanging in the churches – unless it is too difficult to believe that Calvin would have tolerated the mistaken division of the two tables for so many years! There do not seem to be further records discussing this point, but it is probable that, wherever they were hung, the text of the Decalogue was corrected and replaced on the walls. If printed texts of the Ten Commandments were present in the Genevan churches in Calvin's day, at some later point they must have been removed. In 1639 the idea of putting such hangings on the walls of all the Genevan churches was considered a novelty and rejected, although it was practiced in at least some rural parishes.[143]

The most notable change of behavior for the majority of people who came to worship in Protestant Geneva was that now they were expected to sit down and listen for the whole service. Benches and other seats were installed for all those in attendance. At least some Catholic critics regarded this arrangement as turning the event into a school lesson; the critics also claimed that people sat

---

[141] For the catechism, see chap. 3 at nn.120ff. Farel's *La maniere et fasson* recites the Decalogue in the baptismal service but does not divide it at all; p. B2v-B4r (*Early French Reform*, pp. 201-02). In the 1536 *Institutes* Calvin identifies the two tables with four and six laws respectively, OS I, p. 41; however, the 1537 catechism written for the Genevans speaks of two tables but does not say which commandments belong in each, OS I, pp. 383-88. The 1541 French *Institutes* and 1542 Geneva Catechism (Q.185) might have been the first vernacular instruction available to Genevans about where to divide the two tables.

[142] Grosse, *Les rituels de la Cène*, p. 248.

[143] Grosse, *Les rituels de la Cène*, n.138 above.

anywhere, without heed to social status. (There was a distinction of places but it was less marked than before the Reformation – or in later Genevan practice.)[144] At least in the cathedral, and probably in other churches, the pulpit was moved to or set up in a prominent place. In St. Pierre it was relocated to a pillar of the transept crossing and the seating was arranged around it on four sides, with women and children closest to the pulpit and the men behind. The Senate and other city officials were provided with the better accommodations, usually the old choir stalls from the various church structures (especially those no longer in use); these came to be grouped prominently near the preacher.[145] It was clear that every member of the faithful was expected to sit still and pay attention to one and the same liturgy for the entire service. Indeed, they might be – and were – reprimanded for walking about or murmuring their individual prayers.[146]

All those present at once were hearing the same liturgy, but in the city of Geneva neither people nor ministers were fixed in any one place, so the preaching (which was the central feature of most services) could offer more diversity than might appear at first glance. Someone living in Geneva could expect to be exposed to a wide range of voices and breadth of scripture. In theory, the Reformed practice of *lectio continua* could be extremely monotonous if not painfully boring, but in actuality anyone who wished to vary the sermon diet usually only had to go to a different parish or attend worship at a different hour at the church nearest home. While it is not known what Biblical books most Genevan pastors were expounding, except in specific cases (Calvin, Cop), it seems improbable that more than two or three were explaining the same book at any given time or Calvin would not have been so insistent on moving them around.[147] So a parishioner moving from pew to pew could hear a broad range of

---

[144] See Cathelan, *Passevent Parisien*, pp. 26-27: "C'est tout un comme dedens un collége ou escolle, tout y est plain de bancz, et une chaire au milieu pour le prêcheur, et au devant d'icelle les bancz plus bas pour les femmes et petits enfans: et tout autour les plus haultz pour assoyr les hommes, sans différence des personnes." Florimond de Raemond, *L'histoire de la naissance, progrez et decadence de l'heresie*, Rouen, 1623, Book 8, chap. 10, p. 1005. See Grosse, *Les rituels de la Cène*, pp. 272-77, 579-84 for later conflict over seating.

[145] Grosse, *Les rituels de la Cène*, pp. 262-77, for description.

[146] See especially complaints about people leaving before the baptismal liturgy at the end of a service, see chap. 5 at nn.202f, or "muttering" their (old Latin) prayers: Nov. 9, 1542, *Consist.* I, p. 136. Cf. Lambert, *Preaching, Praying, and Policing*, pp. 352-57.

[147] For contents of Calvin's preaching, see chap. 6, pp. 467 ff. In his fine new book on the congregations, *The Genevan School of the Prophets* (2012), Erik de Boer suggests that these study sessions may have resulted in series of sermons on whichever book the congregation meetings were expounding, and implies the same book would therefore be preached in

texts; for example, from St. Pierre at Sunday dawn to La Magdeleine at 8 a.m. or St. Gervais at 3 p.m. there would be at least two and possibly three New Testament books or Psalms; from St. Pierre Wednesday at dawn to Wednesday at 7 a.m.: two Old Testament books; from St. Gervais at catechism to Monday at 6 a.m. in any parish: catechism and a variety of Old Testament books depending on where one went and whose turn it was to preach... This might sound like a recipe for confusion, but it would hardly be boring. Very few people attended daily services regularly, so they rarely heard an Old Testament book in full; however, following a sequence on a New Testament book would be reasonably easy simply by regularly attending one parish church on Sundays. In fact, quite a significant number of Genevans did attend sermons on Sundays and even on Wednesdays, the day of prayer, as they were supposed to do.[148] Not a few also were present on at least one or several weekdays – although they might not be

---

various pulpits; p. 51: "The exposition of biblical books in lectio continua may have resulted in series of sermons on the book which was being expounded in the Bible studies. Since no record of preaching by other ministers was kept, this suggestion remains a hypothesis." P. 149: "During the Sunday morning services he had preached on Hebrews already in 1549, ending the series in mid-August. The commentary on Hebrews thus appeared before the series of sermons was finished. Could it be that the same letter was expounded on Sundays by Geneva's other ministers following their preparation in the *congrégations*, and that they looked forward to the publication of Calvin's commentary?" While the diversity of books may well not have been as great as I am suggesting was possible if all the ministers were preaching on different books, it is very unlikely that all the Sunday sermons in Geneva were on a single book. For one thing, Calvin would understandably think that there was no point in people moving around the city to hear different ministers, if they were all preaching (more-or-less poor) imitations of his own exegesis. Furthermore, it is obvious from Cop's published sermons on Proverbs that some preachers took on books which Calvin and the *congrégations* never touched. If that might be considered an exceptional occurrence because Cop was so talented, the same would go for Chauvet and Des Gallars and Bourgoing and later others who were also independent thinkers. It is clear that the *congrégations* helped form preachers and the participants would use what they had learned when they entered the pulpit, but it seems extremely improbable that there was anything like a cohort of sermons on whichever book the Bible studies were expounding.

148 *Consist.* I, Aug. 10, 1542, p. 98: a man says he cannot go to sermon except Sun. & Wed. Sept. 21, 1542, p. 121: woman goes on Sun. & Wed. and cannot on other days. Oct. 19, 1542, p. 132: a woman was at the "sermon de catechism" last Sun. and not at morning or afternoon. Nov. 9, 1542, p. 135: a woman can only go on Sun, but orders servants to go other days; last Sun. she was at St. Pierre after dinner and at catechism. March 1, 1543, p. 187: a man goes on Sun. and cannot other days; another man says he was at St. Gervais last Sun. May 8, 1543, p. 237: a man says he was at church Sun. at vespers and not morning because he was not well. Aug. 28, 1543, p. 251: a woman was at St. Gervais on Sun. after dinner and sometimes goes on Wed. Nov. 22, 1543, p. 277: a man says he goes to sermons every Sun. morning at S. Pierre. July 3, 1544, p. 386: woman was at sermon Sun. morning and vespres. See also examples in chap. 1 nn.75ff, 161, 163.

able to remember much about what they heard[149] – and practically everyone attended the Supper services[150].

Besides sermons and prayers and singing Psalms and sharing in the corporate sacrament of the Lord's Supper, the worship services were also important to the people as the places where aspects of their personal lives were celebrated or sometimes their most serious religious failings were brought to communal notice. Parish services were where the banns for couples planning to marry were announced, and all baptisms and marriages were performed at preaching services. The members of the baptismal or wedding party were required to be present for the entire sermon as well as their personal liturgy, and the members of the congregation were expected to pay attention to both sermon and special liturgy also.[151] People who had been in conflict were often told to present themselves at the end of the service for reconciliation. (This was not a liturgical act, but it was associated with worship in both time and place.)[152] There were more communal aspects of the Sunday services, such as the presentation of new city ministers or the reading of religious regulations.[153] As the organization of Geneva's church life continued to be shaped by Calvin and his supporters in the later 1550's, these liturgically-situated occasions either increased or became more prominent. The main Sunday morning service was where the public reconciliation was carried out for those who had committed the most terrible sins such as apostasy from the faith, and it was the time when there were special exhortations for the annual elections of elders.[154]

---

[149] *Consist.* I, Aug. 10, 1542, p. 99: woman was at La Magdeleine today and has been three times this week. Sept. 7, 1542, p. 111: a man was at St. Gervais today and yesterday. Dec. 21, 1542, p. 151: a woman was at sermon on Mon. and at prayer [day of prayer] at St. Pierre. May 8, 1543, p. 237: a man says he was at sermon last Thurs.

[150] *Consist.* I, Sept. 7, 1542, p. 112: a woman says she goes to sermons when she can "et à la saincte Cene" [as if this were a matter of course]. Chap. 3 at n.208.

[151] See chap. 5 at nn.92ff, 192f.

[152] Many examples in the Consistory records, e.g., May 26, 1542, Sept. 7, 1542; sometimes a full text of the reconciliation is given, e.g., Friday Aug. 31, 1543. *Consist.* I, p. 74, 110, 255. Jan. 21, 1546, *Consist.* II, p. 124. *et passim.*

[153] See above at nn.27ff for presentation of ministers; also chap. 7 at n.214. For religious announcements, there is an example in RCP I, p. 45: "S'ensuyt la coppie des letters qui ont esté publiees aux sermons et aux catechismes le dimenche 18e jour de janvier par le commandement de Messieurs." [correction says Jan. 20, 1549]. See chap. 3 at nn.171ff.

[154] Calvin's sermons on the Gospel Harmony provide examples of both instances; Sermon #29 (probably Feb. 11, 1560) includes an exhortation about electing elders; Sermon #33 (probably March 10, 1560) including reconciling penitents; see OC 46:361-62, 412. There were also special seats for those who needed correction, either because of their ignorance (so they were told to sit near the pulpit) or as a form of public shaming. The latter meant sitting in a

Attending worship in Geneva changed in significant ways when the Protestant reforms were implemented, but there were also still continuities. The importance of the parish was one continuity, but the precise reasons it was central were not quite the same. Now participation in such things as the sacraments and formal religious education, which had either not been restricted to the parish or not been mandated as corporate actions, were bound to a person's parish. The expectation that all parishioners would regularly attend worship services was another continuity, but the number of places such worship took place, the character of the setting, and the content of the services, had undergone significant change. There were fewer churches, which looked unfamiliarly bare and where one was expected to behave rather differently: sitting for an hour, paying attention to an expository Biblical sermon and prayers in the vernacular, and joining in the communal singing. The church was still the center of communication for the whole community; announcements such as marriage banns were still heard from the pulpit. It was becoming both more and less the social center of the people's lives: less, because socializing opportunities like the churching of women, or casual almsgiving to beggars, were no longer allowed; more, because all the people's most important personal family rites, such as baptisms and marriages, were held in the midst of the gathered parish. The next chapters examine in detail what the experience of worship was like in Calvin's Geneva.

---

prominent place, although the actual benches for the purpose appear to have been an occasional thing until 1569; see Grosse, *Les rituels de la Cène*, pp. 277-81. See several examples in the consistory records of those ordered to make amends before the whole church at the main Sunday service at St. Pierre "ce dimanche prochain au temple de S. Pierre au grand presche devant toute l'eglise" (21:767). June 5,1561, the case of a man who had left Geneva to join some Anabaptists and be rebaptized and is now repentant. Nov. 20, 1561, a man banished for rejecting Calvin's teaching on predestination has been forgiven by the Senate and readmitted. OC 21:750-51,767.

PART TWO

Worship Services, Sacraments, and Other Liturgies
in Time and Space

The regular worship life of Protestant Geneva was set on a weekly rhythm which gave central place to the Lord's Day. The organization of times of sermons and the distribution of preachers were based on a theology which privileged a weekly liturgical cycle in place of the annual one which had previously been dominant. This does not imply that the essential Christological observances were abandoned, or ritual disappeared. Not at all. It does mean that the temporal shape of liturgical time was significantly reconceived. The common legend says that Calvin did away with the liturgical year, particularly eliminating Christmas, and rejected all ritual. Recent scholarship has demonstrated that this kind of sweeping dismissal of the Genevan reformer and his practice is, if not wrong, at the least considerably exaggerated.

On the contrary, Geneva established a new kind of annual rhythm which found its high points in the four seasons of preparation for and participation in the Lord's Supper. It also pioneered a new conception of the context of the sacrament of baptism and the rite of marriage in the corporate calendar of community worship. What is often obscured or missing, however, is an appreciation for the relationship between Calvin's own theological sense of liturgical time and the rhythm and character of worship as it was practiced in Geneva, the model for many other Reformed churches.

This subject is wide-ranging and somewhat more complex than appears at first glance, so it will be divided into three chapters. The first examines Calvin's teaching on "holy time," the centrality of the Lord's Day, and the way that Geneva developed a new annual calendar shaped by the Lord's Supper. The next chapter examines the question of special religious observance of other days (i.e., weekdays), particularly the distinctive Calvinist weekly day of prayer. The third chapter explores the rhythms of the public liturgies of baptism and marriage which formed the personal counter-point within the corporate flow of worship in Calvin's Geneva.

CHAPTER THREE

WORSHIP CENTERED ON THE LORD'S DAY

The chapters of Part One have demonstrated the practical ways that ecclesiastical and civil authorities in Geneva re-formed the places and times of worship and the movements of the preachers and people. The present purpose is to identify the convictions about the theological grounds for changes in liturgical time, and the religious content of the key liturgical practices which replaced the worship of the medieval Roman church. First is a summary of Calvin's teaching on "Sabbath" time and how this influenced the redefining of all liturgical time. The second part outlines Calvin's application of Biblical authority to worship and the ministers who lead it. This is followed by an overview of the texts: *La forme des prieres*, Psalter, and catechism, which contained the public and published material of the new worship services. The fourth part surveys the shape of the Sunday liturgies. The final segment treats the development of the pattern of "sacramental seasons" which became characteristic of many Calvinist Reformed churches.

I: Calvin, "Holy" Time, and the Practice of Worship

It is well known that Protestants challenged and changed the traditional understanding of the holy. In principle, the teaching of justification by faith alone, grace alone, carried with it a re-definition of the sacred. The most popularly acclaimed implication of this is the doctrine of the priesthood of believers, the idea that all believers are equally acceptable before God by the faith God has freely given them, and thus all are qualified to pray directly to God. Alhough it is less frequently made explicit, the revised teaching on the holy had very important consequences for liturgical time and space: no longer were any particular places or days more holy than any others – at least in theory. A family home or common field could be holy when dedicated to God, just as a church building could be "profane" when it was treated as an idol, i.e., salvific in itself. Market day or harvest season could be holy when the believer lived that time as under God's eye (*coram Deo*) and in relationship to God's immediate lordship (*negotium cum Deo*).[1]

Calvin's First Exposition of the Sabbath/ Fourth Commandment

The implications of this new perspective on holiness were frequently demonstrated in the context of explaining how the fourth/ Sabbath commandment of the Decalogue applied to Christians. One issue was how the law is superceded and the significance of this for religious time. From the beginning, in the *Institutes of the Christian Religion* in 1536, Calvin emphasized several points. First of all, in Christ, the legal force of the commandment has been abolished;[2] Christians have been freed from the condemnation justly deserved by those who do not keep the law perfectly, that is, all people. Related to this was the meaning of "hallowing" the day, or what constitutes the kind of "rest" which fulfills the law. This is expressed in part as an attack on medieval sabbatarianism; Calvin says that the "sophists" have simply changed the day from the Sabbath to Sunday "to spite the Jews," but they have continued the legalistic force of the commandment.[3]

Secondly, Calvin explains his positive interpretation of the law, i.e., how it is still authoritative for Christians. This has two main parts: a kind of spiritualizing of the idea of rest, and a "Christian" reason for maintaining a serious practice of a/the day. The purpose of the fourth commandment was to represent the "spiritual worship of God." For Christians (like the Jews before them) "the truth [is to learn] to fear and love God, ... to seek [their] rest in him."[4] This entails ceasing "from all works ... which are not of God's spirit, whatever appearance of human wisdom they may put forth."[5] The perfection signified by the "seventh day" begins in this life but it is not complete until the end of all things. "For we have now through faith begun our rest in God, in which we are also daily making progress so that at least it may be completed when that saying

---

1   *Inst.* 3.7.2 et passim; cf. n.30 below.

2   *Institution 1536*, p. 31, OS I, p. 47. cf. 2.8.28, 31.

3   *Institution 1536*, p. 32, OS I, p. 48. cf. 2.8.34.

4   *Institution 1536*, p. 31, OS I, p: 47; cf. 2.8.28.

5   *Institution 1536*, p. 31, OS I, p. 47. [cf. 2.8.31]

of Isaiah will be fulfilled, in which Sabbath upon Sabbath is promised to God's church [Is. 66:23]."[6] Although human sinfulness continues throughout this life, Christians should grow continually in resting-from-sin, and that spiritual obedience to the fourth commandment has no temporal (or spatial) limits. Obviously, therefore, keeping the Sabbath is not a one-day-per-week observance; if the heart of the commandment is to worship God spiritually by turning away from sin, then obedience is a daily vocation.

Having set out his fundamental understanding of holiness as the relationship with God which shapes everything else in the Christian life, Calvin goes on to explain how this spiritual worship is related to the practice of Sunday and in the process indicates the specific elements of the liturgy.

> [The Lord's Day] was not established for us to hallow it before all others, that is to count it more holy. For this is the prerogative of God alone, who has honored all days equally [Rom. 14:5]. But it was established for the church to gather for prayers and praises of God, for hearing the word, for the use of the sacraments [Gal. 4:8-11; Col. 3:16]. The better to devote all our effort, singlemindedly to these tasks, we are to stop all mechanical and manual labor, and all pursuits which have to do with the conduct of this life.[7]

The main point here is the accommodated nature of the Christian day of rest; it is not holy in itself but is meant for the practical purpose of worshiping God. That is the reason for ceasing from ordinary work (and not because work is profane). The specific aspects of the church gathering listed here: prayer, preaching, and sacraments, correspond to the three most clearly identified elements in Acts 2:42, the Calvinist Reformed paradigm for a properly complete pattern of worship.[8] Calvin goes on in the first *Institutes* to summarize the observance of the Lord's Day.

> [I]t is not by religion that we distinguish one day from another, but for the sake of the common polity. For we have certain prescribed days not simply to celebrate, as if by our stopping labor God is honored and pleased, but because it is needful for the church to meet together on a certain day. Moreover it is important for there to be a set time and

---

6   *Institution 1536*, pp. 31-32, OS I, p. 47. cf. 2.8.30. See chap. 7 at nn.156ff on continuity through death.

7   *Institution 1536*, p. 32; OS I, pp. 47-48. cf. 2.8.30.

8   The fourth element, *koinonia* or fellowship, is often neglected but may be represented by almsgiving or the kiss of peace. See below at nn.32ff. McKee, *John Calvin on the Diaconate*, chap. 3.

appointed day, that all things may be done according to order and without disturbance [1 Cor. 14:40].[9]

Here Calvin distinguishes between "religion" (what God commands, in this case the idea that no day is intrinsically more holy than another) and "polity" or organization which is necessary for human society but actually an *adiaphoron* and intrinsically indifferent. In this case, that is the choice of a specific day for corporate worship. Worship is necessary; its corporate time and place are accommodated to the reality that human beings are finite and social creatures.

Although that is not his primary point in this place, Calvin's discussion identifies what things should be included in the observance of the day which is chosen for worship. To the list of liturgical acts named above he adds another point, in order to explain the remainder of what is commanded in the law about the Sabbath. This is the instruction that servants and animals are to be given a day of physical rest. Calvin believes that this applies to Christians as well as Jews; again, he insists that this does not have to do with "religion" but is for "the preservation of equity" or love.[10] By that he means that providing rest for servants is not intrinsically a part of the worship of God because it is directed to one's neighbors. Worship of God means fulfilling the first table of the law or the great commandment, while love of neighbors is the second table or the second great commandment, and God takes precedence over other people. As Calvin will explain more fully later, however, external worship is only truly holy when it is the expression of inward adoration, so if the external (liturgy) becomes hypocritical, the real (inward) worship of God is more reliably evident in love for neighbors. Thus in a way the latter is also an aspect of corporate worship, which can be embodied in almsgiving or the kiss of peace[11] – the fourth element of Acts 2:42, *koinonia* or fellowship, which was missing in the first list but is included in a later chapter.[12] The essence of spiritual worship does not require a particular day for assemblies for preaching, sacraments, prayer and almsgiving, or a holiday for servants and animals, but polity (human community) and love make setting apart a specific day an appropriate means to embody right spiritual worship.

There is one further point in the 1536 *Institutes* about special occasions for worship which is worth noting. After he describes the practice of the Lord's Day, Calvin goes on to say something about other "holy days."

---

[9]   *Institution 1536*, p. 32, OS I, p. 48. cf. 2.8.33.

[10] *Institution 1536*, p. 33, OS I, p. 48.

[11] McKee, *John Calvin on the Diaconate*, chap. 10, esp. pp. 258-59.

[12] *Institution 1536*, p. 153, OS I, p. 149.

> Of the same sort [as the Lord's Day, when the church gathers for prayer, preaching, and sacraments, and people cease their daily work] are other solemn days, wherein the mysteries of our salvation are called to mind. [13]

This short phrase clearly refers to the observance of such special occasions as Christmas. It is probably intended to cover all of the Christological "holy days" which Protestants – or, more likely, Reformed communities like Basel, where Calvin was living when he completed the 1536 *Institutes* – did observe. [14] Note that there is no pejorative connotation, and apparently implicit acceptance, since he uses the plural first person pronoun. This sentence would completely and permanently disappear in the next edition.

Between the first and second editions of the *Institutes* Calvin prepared the Catechism of 1537 for use in Geneva. Here the main features of his thought were presented succinctly, with much nuance omitted but one practical detail (why only one day?) clarified. First he lists the purposes for which God gave the law to the Jews, providing an orderly summary.

> The Lord wanted, under the rest of the seventh day, to give the people of Israel a figure of the spiritual rest by which the faithful ought to cease from their own works in order to allow the Lord to work in them. Secondly He wanted there to be a certain day on which they might assemble to hear His law and do His ceremonies. Thirdly He wanted there to be a day for rest allowed to servants and those who live under the authority of others, in order that they might have some ease from their labor, although this is more something added on than a principal reason. [15]

As Calvin explains to the Genevans, the first purpose has been superseded for Christians because in Christ the truth has come and the figures have passed away. However, the second and third purposes were not "shadows, but pertain equally to all ages ... that we come together on certain days to hear the word of God, for the breaking of the bread of the Supper, and for public prayers," and to give relief

---

[13] *Institution 1536*, p. 32, OS I, p. 48: "Eiusdem rationis sunt et solemnes alii dies, quibus mysteria salutis nostrae memoria repetuntur."

[14] See Burnett, *Teaching the Reformation*, pp. 57-60, and nn.43ff.; she notes also that one of Basel's early catechisms (1538) included prayers "for special days in the church year," p. 53.

[15] *Inst.* OS I, p. 385. Elsewhere, in his exposition of the commandment in the commentary, Calvin explains why rest for servants is not a principal reason here; i.e., care for the neighbor is really a part of the second table of the law, and thus not directly related to the worship ordained in the first table; cf. comments on Exod. 20:8, 23:10 & 12 (OC 24:579, 582-83, 585-86) et passim.; discussion in McKee, *John Calvin on the Diaconate*, p. 237.

to servants and workers. [16] Then Calvin adds a practical note on the choice of one day: "In view of our weakness such assemblies cannot be done every day." He also summarizes: the reason for changing the day was "to do away with superstition" while another day was chosen "to keep and maintain order and peace in the church." [17]

Development in the *Institutes*

Calvin's teaching on the fourth commandment in the 1536 edition was considerably developed in 1539. Thereafter very little changed: a short insert appears in 1543, a few additional phrases come from 1545, and one concluding sentence from 1559. In 1539 the material was greatly expanded from 1536, but was essentially developed in the same trajectory, with fuller discussion of spiritual rest, the "seventh day," the practice of the Lord's Day, and what it means to keep one day. Some additions, however, changed the picture slightly and demonstrate a certain influence from Calvin's experience as a pastor.

In 1539 the earlier criticism of the traditional (Roman) sabbatarian teaching was now balanced by a response to the "Anabaptist" argument against continuing to set apart any day. Calvin defends this as a practical matter for the purpose of church order; it is not any kind of "superstitious observance of days." [18] The reference in 1536 to "the other solemn days wherein the mysteries of our salvation are recalled" is dropped and the focus becomes even more concentrated on the Lord's Day. Calvin does not categorically reject the idea of observing other days besides Sunday, and in fact he allows that other churches may do so, as long as they do not consider these necessary or divinely required.

> And I shall not condemn churches that have other solemn days for their meetings, provided that there be no superstition. This will be so if they have regard solely to the maintenance of discipline. [19]

---

[16] *Inst.* OS I, pp. 385-86.

[17] *Inst.* OS I, p. 386: "Car selon qu'est nostre infirmité cela ne se peult obtenir que telles assemblees se facent tous les jours. Pour laquelle chose le jour observé par le Juifz à esté osté (ce qui estoit expedient pour abolir la superstition), et un aultre jour a esté destiné à cest usage, ce qui estoit necessaire pour retenir et conserver ordre et paix en l'Eglise."

[18] *Institutes* McNeill-Battles, p. 397. From 1539 = 2.8.31, OS III, p. 373.

[19] *Institutes* McNeill-Battles, p. 400. *Institutio 1539*, Wevers, p. 67 (3.16.47-49) "Nec [neque sic tamen] septenarium numerum moror, ut eius servituti Ecclesiam astringam. Neque enim ecclesias damnavero, quae alios convenitibus suis solemnes dies habeant, modo a superstitione absint. Quod erit, si ad solam observationem disciplinae [et ordinis bene composite] referantur." = 2.8.34; OS III, p. 375: 1559 adds the words in brackets.

Later the phrase "and good order" is added at the end. Here it is clear that by 1539 Calvin had effectively changed his mind regarding "holy days" other than Sundays. In 1536, when he was responding primarily to the Roman church and speaking as a scholar, he implicitly accepted "other solemn days." By the time he had spent several years as a pastor, including personal arguments with Anabaptists (the other front against which Protestants argued), Calvin had decided against these celebrations for himself and his church, without condemning the liturgies of other (Protestant) communities.

In effect, Calvin affirms that all days are equally holy and yet maintains that Christians should meet one day a week for reasons of polity, which leads to the need to explain the reason for this specific limiting of their meetings. As he clearly says, it would be right for believers to gather every day for worship, and in the 1539 *Institutes* he expands his brief note in the 1537 catechism.

> Why do we not assemble daily, you ask, so as to remove all distinction of days? If only this had been given us! Spiritual wisdom truly deserved to have some portion of time set apart for it each day. But if the weakness of many makes it impossible for daily meetings to be held, and the rule of love does not allow more to be required of them, why should we not obey the order we see laid upon us by God's will? [20]

Here Calvin expresses a fundamental desire and reason for daily corporate worship, while also recognizing that by God's generosity only one day in seven must be observed as a day of rest. The brief addition to the *Institutes* made in 1543 explains why Sunday was chosen to be that day; it was not fixed by some essential value of the day itself, but was chosen by the church fathers as an appropriate way to honor Christ's resurrection on that day.

> [T]he ancients did not substitute the Lord's Day (as we call it) for the Sabbath without careful discrimination. The purpose and fulfillment of that true rest, represented by the ancient Sabbath, lies in the Lord's resurrection. Hence, by the very day that brought the shadows to an end, Christians are warned not to cling to the shadow rite. [21]

---

[20] *Institutes* McNeill-Battles, p. 398. *Institutio 1539*, Wevers, p. 67 (3.16.18-23): "Cur non quotidie, inquies, potius conveniamus, ut ita tollatur dierum discretio? Utinam illud quidem daretur : et sane digna erat spiritualis sapientia, cui quotidie decideretur particula aliqua temporis. Sed si a multorum infirmitate obtineri non potest: ut quotidiani conventus agantur, et charitatis ratio plus ab illis exigere non permittit, cur non pareamus rationi, quam nobis videmus Dei voluntate impositam?" = 2.8.32; OS III, p. 374, slightly modified.

[21] *Institutes* McNeill-Battles, pp. 399-400. 2.8.34, OS III, p. 375.

For Calvin, there is no absolute requirement that the day of worship be a specific day, but he thinks it is right to follow the early church in making the Lord's Day the one-day-in-seven appointed by God for rest because it is a fitting way to recognize that the old law has been fulfilled and superceded in Christ.

In the process of expanding and recasting this passage on the fourth commandment in the 1539 *Institutes*, Calvin reorganized the presentation, much as he had done in the catechism. Particularly this is evident in the more succinct and orderly summary of the purposes for the practice of the Lord's Day, where again as in the 1537 catechism he repeats this in two slightly different forms. The first instance is at the beginning of the exposition of the commandment, giving the law for the Jews.[22] The second version of this summary is found at the end of the exposition, reshaped slightly to be applied to Christians.

> First, we are to meditate throughout life upon an everlasting Sabbath rest from all our works, that the Lord may work in us through his Spirit. Then we should all observe together the lawful order set by the church for the hearing of the Word, the administration of the sacraments, and for public prayers. In the third place, we should not inhumanly oppress those subject to us.[23]

In 1545, when the *Institutes* was only slightly revised, a phrase was inserted in each of these summaries. In the second point regarding corporate worship, Calvin added a kind of personal dimension of piety which each person should maintain, although the shape of this differed in the two cases. In the first instance, he was speaking of the Jews.

> [1539] Then, [God] willed there to be a stated day on which they would assemble to hear the law and perform the rites, [1545] or at least that they should give themselves particularly to meditation upon His works, in order by this remembrance they might exercise themselves in piety.[24]

---

[22] *Institutio 1539*, Wevers, p. 65 (3.15.13-18); cf. 2.8.28, OS III, p. 371.

[23] *Institutes* McNeill-Battles, p. 400 (slightly altered: phrase added in 1545 is omitted between "Spirit." And "Then"). *Institutio 1539*, Wevers, p. 67 (3.16.50-55): "Summa sit: ut sub figura iudaeis tradebatur veritas, ita nobis sine umbris commendatur. Primum ut perpetuum tota vita sabbathismum meditemur a nostris operibus, quo Dominus in nobis per suum spiritum operetur. Deinde ut legitimum ecclesiae ordinem, ad verbum audiendum, ad sacramentorum administrationem, ad publicas orationes constitutum, observemus. Tertio, ne nobis subditos inhumaniter premamus." cf. 2.8.34, OS III, pp. 375-76.

[24] *Institutes* McNeill-Battles, p. 395. 2.8.28, OS III, p. 371: "vel saltem quem operum suorum meditationi peculiariter darent: ut hac recordatione ad pietatem exercerentur."

Here Calvin's alteration is evidence of attending now more closely to the wording of the text, since the commandment itself speaks of rest but not of corporate worship. In the second summary, for Christians, the new and personal exhortation is added at the beginning of the one about corporate worship (which is included in the necessary practice).

> [1545] Let each one privately exercise himself diligently in devout reflection on God's works as often as he has free time; [1539] then also let us all keep together the right order of the church established for hearing the word, administering the sacraments, and public prayers. [25]

The young pastor had been focused on corporate worship as part of his the conviction that the practice of the medieval Mass was not corporate, while the maturing leader realized the need to balance this with more weight on personal and frequent devotion. This new emphasis in 1545 exhorts the faithful to conscious acts of religious meditation which are not bound to specific times, a reminder that for Christians the observance of the fourth commandment should pervade their whole lives.

There were no further changes in the exposition of the fourth commandment in the *Institutes*, although in the final edition Calvin added one sentence of exhortation, urging the faithful to attend corporate worship. "[I]n order to prevent religion from either perishing or declining among us, we should diligently frequent the sacred meetings, and make use of those external aids which can promote the worship of God." [26] Evidently the aging pastor felt the need to emphasize the importance of more attentive engagement in corporate worship as a complement to or expression of the inward devotion of the heart.

Preaching on the Commandment: The Holy and Daily Work

The exposition in the *Institutes* covered the main points of Calvin's thought about the fourth commandment, but some further aspects were more fully expressed in his exegetical work. The picture of Sabbath observance which came to the people in the pew in Geneva is found in the context of the reformer's daily sermons on the book of Deuteronomy in 1555. In the course of applying the

---

25 *Institutes* McNeill-Battles, p. 400. 2.8.34, OS III, p. 376: "Deinde ut pia operum Dei recognitione privatim se quisque, quoties vacat, diligenter exerceat: tum etiam, ut omnes simul legitimum Ecclesiae ordinem, ad verbum audiendum, ad sacramentorum administrationem, ad publicas orationes constitutum, observemus."

26 *Institutes* McNeill-Battles, p. 401. 2.8.34, OS III, p. 376.

Sabbath commandment in Deut. 5:13-15 to his congregation, Calvin treats the question of labor, i.e., the opposite of physical rest. He explains clearly that the command to work is not a result of sin, although sin has now made the work a punishment.

> [W]e know that God does not intend for us to be lazy living in this world, for He has given people hands and feet; He has given them industry. … [B]efore sin had come into the world and we were condemned by God to painful and forced work, people were already required to engage in some [type of] labor. And why? Because it is contrary to our nature to be like a block of useless wood. Therefore it is certain that we must apply ourselves to some [form of] labor all the days of our life. [27]

Daily labor is a part of the Christian's vocation; it is not profane, it is not a contradiction of spiritual worship. Another implication of justification by faith and grace alone (besides denying an essential holiness for particular days or times) was a changed value for ordinary work in the world. Believers are supposed to engage in resting from sin continuously throughout their lives, while at the same time serving God and neighbor in their "mundane" activities.

The Protestant hallowing of ordinary life could supply an argument for neglecting worship, however. If work does not profane the day, and Christians are being obedient in their spiritual rest (in God, from sin), why is it necessary to stop the common business of daily life to go to church? Calvin's sermons reveal that, besides Biblical exegesis, [28] his pastoral experience was a further influence on his elaboration of his teaching on the practice of the Sabbath. Genevans had apparently taken the preachers at their word and decided that attending worship was not essential… Preaching on the fourth commandment, Calvin speaks directly to this problem with a vigorous defense of the rightness of giving God one day out of seven.

> It is as if [God] were saying: "Is it asking too much of you to choose one day that can be fully reserved for my service in order that you might do nothing else in it but read and practice my law, or at least hear the doctrine that will be preached to you, or come to the temple in order that you might be confirmed there by the sacrifices which are offered in it, or call upon my name and confess that you belong to the company of my people? Is it

---

[27] Sermon #2 on 4th commandment, June 21, 1555; *Writings on Pastoral Piety*, p. 251.

[28] For exegetical completeness, Calvin also mentions the other Jewish special "holy days" (essentially the three pilgrimage feasts), but he sets them aside as not being concerned with rest. Sermon #2 on 4th commandment, June 21, 1555; *Writings on Pastoral Piety*, p. 251.

not fitting that you should do that, seeing that you have six entire free days for taking care of your needs and business affairs? Therefore, when I act with such humanity toward you, asking not for seven but only for one day, does it not amount to unacceptable ingratitude when you complain about that time as if it were badly employed, or behave parsimoniously toward me over the seventh part of time? [29]

Calvin believed that God had, for good reason, determined that believers should keep one day of rest for corporate worship and personal meditation. Such observance did not hallow the day in an essential way but it was required for the good of the church itself, and in gratitude to God for limiting the corporate expression of God's rightful claim on every moment of every day. [30]

Re-forming the people's understanding of holiness was a major task for Calvin, particularly because the concept of unending spiritual worship seemed to undercut the importance of assembling for actual acts of corporate worship. His explanation of the purposes of liturgical gatherings, however, coheres with their role in the reconceived location of the holy. Assembling for worship is not intended to mark off a day or a time as more holy than any other. Rather, it is to provide for the people the regular occasion to join together in prayer and praise to God, in hearing God's word and growing in the knowledge of God, in sharing in the sacraments and fellowship (*koinonia*) with the rest of the Christian community. These are what he calls "external aids" to the right worship. Specific times and places for these acts of corporate worship should never be considered holy in themselves but fixing days and hours serves the practical necessity of enabling the worship to be corporate. To put this another way, the fact that no time or place is intrinsically holy must be balanced by the absolute need for the marks of the church: the word purely preached and heard, the sacraments rightly administered – and these are things which are done in the gathered body of the Christian people who are the church. For that reason, the earthly church organizes specific times and places for corporate worship, so that the church may become visible and its members may be nourished.

---

[29] Sermon #2 on 4th commandment, June 21, 1555; *Writings on Pastoral Piety*, pp. 251-52.

[30] In the long chapter on Christian life which he added to the *Institutes* in 1539, Calvin emphasizes that it is with God that we have to do (*negotium cum Deo*) in every moment of every day. Cf. 3.7.2 et *passim*. (for repetition of the idea in other places in later editions).

II: Biblical Authority and *Adiaphora* in Reformed Worship

As is well-known, and is evident from their attention focused on understanding and practicing the Sabbath commandment, the basic rule for Reformed worship was that it must embody Biblical teaching. No human additions were permitted. Like all Protestants, Calvin insisted that the fundamental worship of God must be spiritual, but like most other reformers except some Radicals, he also affirmed that the corporate expression of worship must have a visible form. This factor introduced the question of how scripture shapes practice, and it was a significant point of the reaction against the medieval church. The basic outline has been noted elsewhere, but a brief summary may be useful.

For Protestants generally there was a clear distinction between what is necessary for salvation and what is not. Usually this argument on the difference between *esse* (what is necessary or essential) and *adiaphora* (indifferent things), and the need to distinguish the two, was directed against the medieval tendency to make everything either required or prohibited. When debating with each other, however, Protestants (e.g., Lutherans and Reformed) tended to divide *adiaphora* into two categories: those things about which scripture gives some instruction and those completely free. For the Reformed, the texts identified as ordering the right service of God (*bene esse*) included theological aspects of church polity and worship. These are not essential but because the Bible provides instruction in these matters, that guidance should be honored and applied appropriately in the church's contemporary place and time. The object was not a one-to-one correspondence between a text and its practice, but the purpose was always an intensely serious effort to live out the intent of the text as closely as possible, consonant with wise application.

Wise application: at least two aspects of this wisdom may be identified. One is exegetical or theological, in which the substance of the teaching should be followed but the details should not be considered a blueprint. For instance, in the Lord's Supper not only bread but also wine must be offered to every communicant, but whether the wine is red or white is a matter of indifference. This example does not make having both elements necessary for salvation but it demonstrates that a practice scripture ordains should be the human rule of faithful Christians. Likewise, the celebration of the Supper must follow the words and intent of Christ's institution, but it does not have to be celebrated in the evening or sitting around a table even though that was the case for the Last Supper.[31] So the liturgy should follow one of the Biblical accounts but various translations and orders of

---

[31]   The form of receiving the Supper did come to be interpreted more literally in some Reformed communities, e.g., Scottish and some puritan churches did practice sitting at table.

administration are acceptable; differences should not endanger fellowship among Christian churches, although for reasons of edification each church should be consistent with itself. On the other hand, the hour and format are expressions of the second kind of *adiaphora*, i.e., matters which the church can decide for itself because (in Calvin's view) these were not intended to be copied. This second example points to a pastoral dimension of wise application. A new minister entering a church should not disrupt the community over a matter of relative indifference, such as using leavened or unleavened bread, so long as this practice is not required as necessary. On the other hand a liturgy may appropriately be changed when a different church adopts it. Calvin practiced both of these; he followed the liturgical practice of Farel in Geneva and Bucer in Strasbourg, and when he became the senior leader he adapted his Strasbourg liturgy for Geneva.

The following sections sketch two points which illustrate how the authority of scripture for ecclesiastical practice was manifested. The first examines briefly the Biblical guide(s) for the elements – not the order – of a complete service of worship, something particularly useful before laying out Calvin's liturgy for the Lord's Day. The second point resolves some confusion about the ministers who might appropriately participate in that service when the Lord's Supper was celebrated.

Biblical Authority for the Elements of Worship

For most of the Calvinist Reformed tradition, Acts 2:42 was the single most important paradigm for the embodiment of corporate worship. As Calvin wrote in the first *Institutes* in 1536, this verse described the "practice of the apostolic church" which had "the unvarying rule that no meeting of the church take place without the Word, prayers, partaking of the Supper, and almsgiving."[32] The fourfold character of this definition represents an example of the new Biblical scholarship affecting Reformed worship practice. The Vulgate reading of the text had three elements: word, prayers, and "the fellowship of the breaking of bread (*communicatione fractionis panis*)" but Erasmus' patristic research had recovered the more accurate Greek: "fellowship (*te koinonia*), and the breaking of bread (*te klasei tou artou*)."[33] Reformed exegetical and theological application of this verse therefore had to include fellowship and its practical expression in almsgiving.

---

[32] *Institution 1536*, p. 153; OS I, p. 149: "Talem fuisse ecclesiae apostolicae usum Lucas in Actis commemorat (Act. 2), cum fideles ait perseverantes fuisse in doctrina apostolorum, communicatione, fractione panis et orationibus. Sic agendum omnino erat, ut nullus ecclesiae conventus fieret sine verbo, orationibus, participatione coenae, et eleemosynis." cf. 4.17.44 ; OS V, p. 410.

[33] See McKee, *John Calvin on the Diaconate*, chap. 3, quotations p. 79.

Calvin discusses the first three points of the definition fairly fully in various places, but the *koinonia* aspect receives little elaboration in the *Institutes*. Thus it is appropriate to include here Calvin's teaching, as it is found in the essay on the Lord's Supper which appears in both Strasbourg editions of the liturgy. The context is another listing of the elements of Acts 2:42 which takes the Supper as the central point.

> So that we may be made more ardent and desirous of receiving this holy meat and drink of eternal life [the Supper, breaking bread], we appropriately add, along with Psalms and hymns of praise [prayers], the reading of the gospel, the confession of the faith [both aspects of the apostles' teaching], and the holy sacrifices and offerings [koinonia]. [34]

Then Calvin goes on to explain the last point more fully.

> And it is not without reason that we have added the sacrifices to what we have previously said. For when, aroused and moved by the reading and explanation of the gospel, and the confession of our faith which followed it, that Jesus Christ is given to us by the infinite goodness of the heavenly Father, and with Him all things… by good and just cause we offer and submit ourselves wholly to God the Father and to our Lord Jesus Christ in recognition of so many and such great gifts. And we testify this by offerings and holy gifts (as Christian charity/love requires), which are administered to Jesus Christ in His least ones, i.e., the one who is hungry, who is thirsty, who is naked, who is a stranger, who is sick, who is imprisoned. For all who live in Christ and have Him living in them freely do what the law commands, which is that one should not appear before God empty-handed. [35]

The allusions to the parable of the sheep and the goats in Matt. 25:31-46 is obvious; the Old Testament reference to the law is Deut. 16:16 (and parallels, Exod. 23:15 & 34:20, as well as Ecclesiasticus 35:6, although Calvin would not have included this last). [36] Although Acts 2:42 remained the chief liturgical guide for Calvin the theologian, Calvin the pastor did not expect every service to include all four of the elements of this paradigm. Almsgiving was frequently omitted in his

---

[34] *La forme des prières*, OS II, p. 41: "…que nous soyons rendus plus ardans et convoyteux à recepvoir ceste saincte viande et breuvaige de vie eternelle, nous adjoustons tresbien/ avecques pseaulmes et hymmes laudatoires, la lecture de l'evangile/ la confession de la Foy / et les sainctes oblations et offrandes."

[35] *La forme des prières*, OS II, p. 42.

[36] See McKee, *John Calvin on the Diaconate*, p. 53-57.

general references to worship and often in early Genevan practice, and the celebration of the Supper was also much less frequent than services of prayer and preaching. The Biblical paradigm set the ideal to guide right order, but the circumstances of a given community might well influence details of application. In this as in other ways, Calvin distinguished between what was essential and what could be accommodated to the historical situation.

Biblical Authority for Ministers in Worship

The offices of ministry were another and more contentious focus of the application of scripture to church practice. As previously noted, the Calvinist Reformed pattern of ministry included four offices which were paradigmatically outlined in the 1541 *Ecclesiastical Ordinances* and explained more fully in the *Institutes*. In developing this model, Calvin followed Bucer, first distinguishing two main offices of ministry, presbyters and deacons, but then defining the resulting polity more precisely. The presbyters were of three kinds: pastors, teachers, and elders; the deacons of two kinds: men and women (or administrators and nurses).[37] The practical implementation of these ministries in Geneva took time, and some aspects were honored in word (Calvin's preaching on women deacons) but not in fact (no deaconesses in the poor relief system).[38] For purposes of the study of worship in Geneva, however, it is enough to describe how these various ministers were involved in the liturgy, because there has been some question about the case of lay leaders sharing in the distribution of the cup at the Lord's Supper.

The claim is that Calvin wanted only ministers, i.e., pastors to administer the Lord's Supper, and that he compromised his teaching when he tolerated the Genevan custom of allowing elders and deacons and even others to participate in leadership by offering the cup. Christian Grosse considers even the statement in the *Ecclesiatical Ordinances* which authorizes "none to give the cup but the elders (*comys*) and deacons with the ministers"[39] to be a compromise. To support this judgment he cites various sources in the reformer's writings, both ecclesiastical texts such as the 1537 *Articles* and letters of the Company of

---

37 *Ordinances*, OS II, p. 327. *Inst.* 4.3.4-9. See McKee, *Elders and the Plural Ministry*, part II, esp. chap. 6.

38 See McKee, *John Calvin on the Diaconate*, chap. 9, esp. pp. 213-17.

39 *Ordinances*, OS II, p. 344: "Que les ministres distribuent le pain en bon ordre et avec reverence, et que nul aultre ne donne le calyce sinon les anciens (*comys*) ou diacres avec les ministres…" That Calvin wrote the text is evident in the fact that he calls the men "elders" and "deacons" but the Senate substituted the word "comys" for "anciens."

Pastors, and theological statements such as the Geneva Catechism and the *Institutes*.[40] Grosse says that, although Calvin essentially claimed the authority of scripture and the early church for his reforms, in this case he did not have their support.[41]

It seems there may be some confusion here – confusion to which Calvin himself certainly contributes. One point is context. In the 1537 *Articles* Calvin does argue for administration by ministers of word and sacraments, but he expresses this as desired and not as a requirement. For the sake of "the greatest possible dignity… it seemed to us the better idea that the ministers of the word… distribute the bread and wine."[42] However, it may be noted that in 1537 there was no other office of ministry established: that is, Calvin's teachers, elders or deacons had not yet been introduced. Therefore his expressed wish might have undergone development when these other offices were available.

A second source of confusion is language. A variety of sources from different dates can help to clarify this point. First is the use of the word "minister." In fact, when it is not qualified by some other phrase (e.g., "de la parolle") the word "minister" can be used for any of the four offices, not just the pastor. For

---

[40]   Grosse discusses at length Calvin's "compromise" on this matter. He identifies "ministers" as those called to preach and, citing the 1537 *Articles*, objects that according to Calvin's theology only "ministers" (i.e., pastors) were allowed to serve communion, but contrary to this in Geneva laymen were appointed. During the years 1538-41 when there were few preachers in the city, the Senate authorized several of its members and the hospitalier to do this; Grosse emphasizes that this was not simply a response to an emergency since the pattern continued after Calvin's return. Although he cites the *Ecclesiastical Ordinances'* regulation qualifying both elders and deacons to serve in this role, Grosse identifies this as a "compromise between Calvin's ideas and Genevan usage." He says further that in the 1540s men who were neither elders nor deacons were appointed by the Senate to offer the cup. It was not until Dec. 21, 1553, that the consistory took over the task of appointing communion servers, and it was still possible for the hospitalier and consistory secretary and even a professor at the Academy to be given this role.

[41]   Grosse, *Les rituels de la Cène*, pp. 125-26, 208, 219-23. p. 221: "Il est clair qu'en la matiére, Calvin a dû composer avec l'usage établi à Genève. Il n'a jamais rien écrit qui défende cet usage, qui tente d'en dégager les fondements scripturaires ou d'en conforter la légitimité en référencee aux pratiques de l'Eglise primitive." Grosse goes on to cite the *Institutes* and the Geneva Catechism to support his point and concludes that this was an example of Calvin's acceptance of an *adiaphoron*, p. 221; see n.170, which quotes from 4.17.43. For a different reading of both *Institutes* and Catechism, see following notes.

[42]   *Articles*, OS I, p. 371: "Affin qu'il n'y ayt rien de contemptible, mays que ce hault mistere soyt traicté en la plus grande dignité que possible sera, il nous a semblé aduis le meilleur que les ministres de la parolle, desquelz proprement l'office est d'administrer tout ce que apartient aux misteres de Dieu distribuent le pain et le vin, figures et sacremens du corps et du sang de nostre Seigneur."

example, Calvin explicitly applies this name to deacons, both in the *Institutes* and in his exegesis and preaching on Acts 6:1-6.[43]

> This word here (deacon) means simply "minister"; those who have the responsibility for serving in the church, whether to distribute alms or to preach, are well named "ministers," and all the apostles had this name in common. All those who have the task of ministering in the churches are well named "ministers of the word of God," but the church calls all those [ministers] who are charged with the care of the poor "deacons" without further qualifying words.[44]

The language of the Strasbourg liturgies may contribute to the picture of Calvin's teaching. In 1542 the text refers to both minister and deacon, and in 1545 it explicitly says that the deacon offers the cup.[45] By this point Calvin had clearly expressed his understanding of the deacon as a minister who cares for the poor, so it is highly unlikely that he would use the term deacon for an assistant minister[46] (assuming that Calvin was responsible for the exact wording of the Strasbourg edition).

A third factor in sorting out this confusion is that, while Calvin does not claim scriptural authority for allowing deacons to participate in administering the Supper, he does explicitly cite the early church. The first exposition of the Lord's Supper in the 1536 *Institutes* refers to the deacon giving the cup.[47] It is possible though not probable that this means "deacon" as assistant minister, but even if that should be the case, later in the sermons on Acts in 1550 there is absolutely clear evidence that Calvin affirms the propriety of the deacon of the poor offering the cup in the Supper.

---

[43]   *Institutes* 1536, chap. 5, OS I, p. 219: "En diaconorum officium: pauperum curam gerere illisque ministrare; unde et nomen habent; sic enim vocantur, quasi ministri." Further on in this 1536 paragraph he describes the kinds of liturgical acts of Roman "deacons" and denies that these are diaconal duties. The language is slightly altered in later editions but the sense remains the same; cf. 4.3.9. See also the Commentary on Acts 6:1-6, OC 48:120, 122. Calvin also emphasizes the fluidity of New Testament names for church offices; see *Inst.* 4.3.7-8.

[44]   *Sermons on Acts*; sermon on 6:1-3, S VIII, pp. 197-98.

[45]   *La forme des prières*, OS II, pp. 48-49: "Cela faict le Ministre recoipt, puis le dyacre…[1545 le Ministre]… reçoit le premier le pain et le vin, puis le donne au Diacre et consequemment à toute L'eglise…. Et le Diacre presente le Calice en disant… "

[46]   The later somewhat revised version of this liturgy published by Valerain Poullain describes deacons explicitly as collecting alms, but it also calls an assistant minister "deacon"; Poullain, *Liturgia Sacra*, pp. 60-63, 92-93, 230-31.

[47]   *Institutes* 1536, chap. 4, OS I, p. 161: "In manum accipiant fideles nec ne, inter se dividant an singuli quod sibi datum fuerit edant, calicem in diaconi manu reponant an proximo tradant, panis sit fermentatus an ayzmus, vinum rubrum an album, nihil refert." Grosse, *Les rituels de la Cène*, p. 222 n.172, quotes this from the French, which substitutes "Ministre" for "diaconi" and thus loses the distinction, while in fact proving that the words can be used interchangeably.

> As for the early church, the deacons …. were to consider that they did not
> hold a profane or worldly office but that it was a spiritual charge. And for
> this reason it was given to them to offer the cup in the Supper of our Lord
> Jesus Christ: those who were responsible for the poor were there joined
> with the ministers of the word of God.[48]

Thus, even if there may have been some ambiguity in Calvin's earliest references
to "deacon," he soon clarified his approval of the patristic practice of deacons
giving the cup in the Supper.

Two other sources might seem to support the idea that only pastors may
distribute communion. The Geneva Catechism does affirm that the sacraments
are to be administered by those who have the public responsibility of teaching
in the church, i.e., the pastors.[49] Although this could be understood to exclude
anyone but pastors from any role in the Supper, when the text is read in the larger
context of Calvin's theology, it can be seen that the intent was to exclude anyone
but pastors from celebrating the sacraments. The force of the statement was
probably directed particularly at the sacrament of baptism because the Reformed
were determined to eliminate emergency baptisms and prevent women (midwives) or other laity from baptizing babies.[50] In the case of the Supper, the point
was the proper teaching and consecration of the elements: no one could lead the
Supper celebration except a pastor. That is not the same as excluding all assistants.
A second source which sounds opposed to elders and deacons participating in the
Supper is a letter of the Company of Pastors written in 1563 in response to a
situation faced by the church of Lyons. The Genevan pastors identify the assis-

---

[48] *Sermons on Acts*, S VIII, p. 200: "Quant est de l'Eglise ancienne, les diacres avoient le soing de
tout ce qu'il luy apartenoit, et tout ce qui estoit donné à l'Eglise, leur estoit commis. Et nous
voyons comme il leur estoit commandé estroictement de cheminier comme devant Dieu, de
considerer qu'ilz n'estoient point en ung office prophane, ne mondain, mais que c'estoit une
charge spirituelle. Et pour ceste cause mesmes on leur faisoit bailler le calice, quand ce venoit à
la cene de nostre Seigneur Jesus Christ, que ceulx qui avoient la charge des pauvres estoient là
conjoinctz avec les ministres de la parolle de Dieu, affin qu'on les congneust comme ayans
charge en l'Eglise, et qu'eulxmesmes congneussent qu'il leur failloit cheminer droictement pour
dire: 'Nous ne sommes plus à nous, mais il nous fault dedyer du tout au service de Dieu.'" See
McKee, *John Calvin on the Diaconate*, pp. 151-57.

[49] *Catechism*, OC 6:131-33: "Le ministre: A qui appartient il tant de baptizer, que d'administrer la
Cene? L'enfant: A ceux qui ont charge publique en l'Eglise, d'enseigner. Car ce sont choses
conjoinctes que de prescher la Parolle, et distribuer les Sacrements. Le ministre: N'en y a il pas
certaine probation [scripturae testimonio]? L'enfant: Oui bien. Car nostre Seigneur donne
specialement la charge à ses Apostres de baptiser, comme de prescher (Math. 28, 19). Et
touchant la Cene, il commande que tous la facions à son exemple. Or il avoit faict office de
Mnistre pour la donner aux autres."

[50] *Inst.* 4.15.20-21.

tance of elders and deacons in the Supper distribution in Lyon as a concession to the lack of pastors – although they do not consider this as wrong, since "the deacons and elders are the arms and hands of the ministers." French Protestants were debating whether administration of the sacraments should be reserved to pastors, and this advice should be seen in that context. The description of what was happening in Lyons gives more nuance to the question. It appears that the elders and deacons in Lyons were administering both bread and wine, not just the latter; the crowds attending worship were too large for the pastor to reach so after he had consecrated the elements, his assistants carried these to the people further away. [51] The Genevan pastors' hesitation might perhaps have been focused on the idea that the Lyons deacons were administering the bread, something never done in Geneva, and allowing this may be what they viewed this as a concession. Whether or not that holds true, this judgement by his colleagues at the end of Calvin's life must be weighed against his own explicit statements.

It is clear then that Calvin approved of the idea that elders and deacons would serve the cup, as the *Ecclesiastical Ordinances* ordered. (He had drafted the legislation; this provision was not an addition by the Senate.) On the surface, the addition of elders goes beyond the patristic authority for deacons which he cited, but Calvin understood these elders to be included in the category of "presbyter" along with pastors and teachers. [52] Teachers, the second order of the *Ecclesiastical Ordinances*, were not named in the serving of communion probably because those who served as theology professors were not only presbyters but were already held to be under the same discipline as the pastors, regarded as potential pastors, and participated in the Company of Pastors' meetings. [53] That there were occasions in

---

[51] For charge, see Grosse, *Les rituels de la Cène*, p. 222 n. 172. Letter, OC 20:500: "Sur la question qui a été faite à nos Freres de Geneve: *Si les Pasteurs seulement distribueroient le Pain et le Vin au Peuple, à la Table du Seigneur.* Ils ont répondu, qu'il seroit beaucoup mieux s'ils le faisoient, et qu'ils le pussent faire commodément en tous temps: mais que la chose paroissant impossible à present, et encore plus impraticable pour l'avenir, si Dieu multiplioit le nombre des croïans, les Pasteurs étant si rares: qu'aussi les Diacres et les Anciens étant les bras et les mains des Ministres, il n'y avoit nul inconvenient qu'ils distribuassent les especes Sacramentelles aux Peuples plus éloignés du Ministre, lorsqu'il les auroit consacrees."

[52] For a full picture of Calvin's teaching on the Biblical character of elders as presbyters, see McKee, *Elders and the Plural Ministry*, part 1.

[53] For teachers in the *Ordinances*, OS II, pp. 398: "Le degree plus prochain au ministere et plus conioinct au gouvernement de l'esglise est la lecture de theologie…"; 399: "Que touz ceulx qui seront là soient subiectz à la discipline ecclesiastique comme les ministres. … Que nul ne soit receus s'il n'est approver par les ministres…" See chap. 2 at nn.21ff; for example, in 1543 when the ministers were considering whom to send to the plague hospital, the teacher Castellio volunteers; even though he later backs out, it is obvious that he was considered qualified; cf. chap. 7 at n.94.

the early years when the Senate appointed men who were not either elders or deacons (the hospitalier was counted among the latter) would on the face of it constitute a conflict with Calvin's teaching. However, he apparently tolerated these instances as temporary substitutes, and this did not contradict his general rule that all the presbyters and (male) deacons were fit to be appointed to offer the cup in the Supper. Calvin did not have a theory of ministerial "indelible character" and the main point was that the people who served should be morally and spiritually capable and properly appointed. [54] This would apply even to the civil authorities in rural parishes who helped the pastors, since they functioned as the appointed lay leaders, in the same way that the elders and deacons in the city were appointed.

Thus it can be concluded that Calvin's teaching and practice were coherent. The ministers of the church were understood to be patterned on scripture and the inclusion of other offices along with pastors in specific aspects of public worship followed the model of the early church.

III: The Worship Books of Geneva

Protestants changed many things about corporate worship. Use of the vernacular is one of the most obvious. [55] Related to this was the way that the whole body of worshipers was invited and expected to engage together in a single, focused service. For this purpose, in addition to a move from Latin to French or Italian or Spanish or English (the languages of public prayer in Calvin's Geneva), the materials for congregational participation were necessary. With the help of the expanding printing business, Protestants quickly began publishing the vernacular

---

[54] There was no ordination ceremony in Geneva, even for pastors, but a proper appointment with prayer and presentation to the people. The way that elders were appointed was rather less formal than Calvin might have liked, but it was orderly; for his teaching about the apostolic example of laying on hands for pastors and teachers and deacons, see *Inst.* 4.3.16. However, this sign is not essential; the calling and authorization are, and Calvin explains these in 4.3.10-15, including inward and outward calls; 4.3.14-15 says that it is normal for human beings to appoint ministers (the outward call) and for the people to approve. 4.3.15, *Institutes* McNeill-Battles, p. 1066 : "We therefore hold that this call of a minister is lawful according to the Word of God, when those who seemed fit are created by the consent and approval of the people; moreover, that other pastors ought to preside over the election in order that the multitude may not go wrong either through fickleness, through evil intentions, or through disorder." OS V, p. 56.

[55] Calvin's preface to the Psalter illustrates this. OS II, p. 13: "[N]ous avons le commandement expres du sainct Esprit, que les oraisons se facent en langue commune et congneue au people. Et dit l'Apostre, que le peuple ne peult respondre, Amen, à la priere qui a esté faicte en langue estrange [1. Co. 14]. Or est-il ainsi que puis qu'on la faict au nom et en la personne de tous, que chascun en doit estre participant."

materials which their congregations needed for corporate worship.[56] The Reformed communities, beginning in Strasbourg, were the most active in creating orders of service, while Luther's followers took the lead in song. The growing wealth of Lutheran hymns took their place alongside a selection of Psalms, while the Reformed concentrated on Psalm singing; Strasbourg had a complete German metrical Psalter by 1538.[57] The earliest liturgies and song books were often soon replaced with more complete and/or fixed texts, and it is helpful to bear in mind that for some years, at least in the orbit of Strasbourg, what was available for lay people to read or sing was frequently changing.

Regions and languages gained a stable base of Protestant worship at different times, and in French-speaking communities this was later than in German-speaking ones. For Geneva, as for most "Calvinist" Reformed, the fully developed printed books which served for public and private worship included three key pieces: *La forme des prieres 1542* (with the liturgies for Sundays and other special services, e.g., the day of prayer, the sacraments, marriage, instructions for visiting the sick) 1542, the Psalter 1539-62, and the catechism 1542. Christian Grosse, in his impressive book, *Les rituels de la Cène. Le culte eucharistique réformé à Genève (XVIe-XVIIe siècles)* (2008), has provided an excellent overview of the way these texts developed. The earliest forms of all three books were in the hands of parishioners by 1542, although the Psalter continued to grow over the years. By the 1550s these necessary sources for piety and worship (often supplemented by smaller items such as the brief question-and-answer form used for examining students before admission to communion) had begun to be combined into a kind of fixed service book, usually simply called "the Psalter."[58] To grasp the detailed form of public worship it is helpful to trace the development of the elements of this collection, beginning with the liturgy.

---

[56] For Calvin's conscious advocacy of printing liturgy and Psalms in his preface to the Psalter see quotations of OS II, p. 12 & p. 15, in this book's introduction at nn.48ff.

[57] See Bornert, *La réforme protestante du culte*, pp. 110-21; Hughes O. Old, *The Patristic Roots of Reformed Worship* (Zurich: Theologischer Verlag, 1975), discusses the many stages of liturgical development. Note that Lutherans did not have a complete Psalter until 1573, Ambrosius Lobwasser's translation of the Reformed metrical Psalter. Lutheran music is too well known to need comment and the bibliography too extensive to make references easy. It is perhaps simplest to point to Luther's own involvement in translating some Psalms, writing hymns and music, and prefaces to hymnbooks, which began to appear in print before his first vernacular liturgy in 1526 and continued throughout his life.

[58] Grosse, *Les rituels de la Cène*, pp.159-76; p. 174, he indicates that such a service book was not common among Protestants (he compares Reformed and Lutheran practice but does not include English-language options).

The Liturgies of Geneva

The First French Liturgy

Farel, whose *La maniere et fasson* appeared in 1533, was the first to publish a Protestant liturgy in the French language. His text was also the basis for the earliest Protestant worship in Geneva, and apparently continued in use until replaced by Calvin's new liturgy in 1542. *La maniere et fasson* included orders for the services of baptism, marriage, the Lord's Supper, and for preaching, with an additional note about visiting the sick.[59] The preaching service demonstrates a strong influence from the Zwinglian tradition[60] especially in the order. Farel begins with the prayer of intercession (based on the interpretation of 1 Tim. 2:1-2: "First of all I beseech you to make prayers… for all people…"); this petition concludes with the Lord's Prayer. He next moves to the scripture and sermon; the latter is an exposition of a Biblical text which leads into application with a strong emphasis on obedience to rulers and rulers' responsibility to their people. Then follows a series of exhortations and catechetical pieces: instructing the people to keep the commandments and recite the Decalogue, and to confess their sins (as in the Supper service). The Lord's Prayer is recited again, and the Apostles' Creed, followed by more prayers (1 Tim. 2:1 appears again) and a benediction.[61] One element of Farel's service which deserves a comment is the confession of sin, because Grosse indicates that Farel has an absolution and thus Calvin's reference to it being an innovation in his day is not credible. As expressed in the Supper service, the form of the absolution in Farel's liturgy is an exhortation in the second person plural ("therefore believe…"). This would have sounded quite different to sixteenth-century former Catholics from the first person singular ("I absolve you") which they had heard from priests – and resented as a manifestation of clerical power.[62]

---

[59] *La maniere et fasson*, 1533. E-rara.ch. For English see "Liturgical Practices and Forms (1533)," pp. 195-223.

[60] Zwingli, "Ein kurtze gmeine form, kinder ze touffenn, die ee ze bestäten, die predig anzefahen und zuo enden, wie es zuo Zürich gebrucht wirdt." The third section: "Ein form des bittens nach der leer Pauli, 1. Timoth. 2[1-7], die man yetz Zürich brucht im anfang der predigen" [different printing has Predigtgottesdienstes]; this appeared in 1526 and several later printings; critical edition in CR 93, part 5; *Huldreich Zwinglis Sämtliche Werke*, 6:5, p. 431.

[61] *La maniere et fasson*, pp. E3r-E7r. "Liturgical Practices and Forms (1533)," pp. 217-19.

[62] The issue of why the Geneva 1542 liturgy does not include an assurance of pardon has been debated, and Calvin himself claimed that it would have been an innovation; see n.149 below. The point here is whether or not Farel's liturgy had one, as Grosse claims, *Les rituels de la Cène*, pp. 146-47. It is not clear that Farel's liturgy had an absolution after the confession of sin, at least not in the traditional language. There is a form in the Lord's Supper service which is also used in

When *La maniere et fasson* was reprinted in 1538, there were a few changes. The introductory essay for the Supper added a reference to the issue of a more frequent celebration, and the sequence of services was reordered to place the two sacraments together (moving the Supper liturgy to follow that for baptism). Grosse sees these as possible evidence of Calvin's influence.[63] When Calvin came to Geneva he followed the good work already begun, as he says in preaching on Corinthians. In 1 Cor. 3:10 Paul speaks of the foundation which he laid and on which others should build, and this leads Calvin to one of his extremely rare personal references. In discussing the relationship of the apostle to his successors, he gives the negative example of a proud mason who insists on tearing up a good foundation before working on a cathedral just so that he can say that he has both started and finished the building.[64] Then he applies this to his own context.

> What would have happened when we came here if [we] had wanted to destroy everything? (As there are rogues in our time who have wanted to do, so that it was necessary to fight vigorously against them.) Now if through empty glory or ambition I had said: We have to start a new building here. And what would that have been except serving the devil? And finally what would have become of the church of Geneva?[65]

---

the preaching service, but it is not precisely what is usually meant by an absolution. (It also does not appear at the beginning of the service in either case.) In the Lord's Supper section the minister says: "Et nous a promis ce bon sauveur/ que tous ce que nous demanderons en son nom nous l'obtiendrons/ & que si nous pardonnons aux aultres leurs pechez/ les nostres nous seront pardonnez du pere. Croyez donc qu'en demandant mercy à dieu au nom de nostre seigneur Jesus/ en pardonnant de bon cueur unng chascun à son prochain/ que nostre seigneur nous pardonne : & que par la foy que nous avons en JesuChrist noz cueurs sont purgez." *La maniere et fasson*, 1533, p. D7v.; cf. "Liturgical Practices and Forms (1533)," pp. 214, 217-19. Grosse cites an absolution in one of Farel's sermons in 1556 phrased as "je vous annonce l'absolution de vos péchés," *Les rituels de la Cène*, p. 147 n.115. The form found in the Strasbourg 1542 [1545] liturgy is "je denonce l'absolution [des pechez estre faicte]," OS II, p. 19 [brackets for 1545]. The words used in *La maniere et fasson*, an exhortation in the second person plural, would have had a very different sound from an affirmation in the first person singular. Thus Calvin's later claim that some Genevans considered the introduction of an absolution such as he had used in Strasbourg an innovation would be true.

63   Grosse, *Les rituels de la Cène*, pp. 123-24.

64   Manuscript sermon #19, f155b.

65   Manuscript sermon #19, f155b. "Qu'eust on gaigné quand nous sommes venus icy qu'on eust volu tout ruyner comme il s'est trouvé des canailles qui l'ont volu faire de nostre temps tellement qu'il a fallu bataillee vertueusement à l'encontre? Or si par vayne gloire ou par ambition j'eusse dict, il fault commencer icy ung nouveau bastiment, et qu'eust ce esté sinon servir au diable? Et en la fin que fust ce de l'eglise de Geneve?"

Calvin's autobiographical comments in public contexts can almost be counted on the fingers of one hand, so (although very brief) this instance of the preacher using himself as an example to clarify a text is worth remarking. While spoken many years later, this short sentence expresses well how Calvin worked with Farel and other senior colleagues, and his adopting and adapting their liturgies is a key expression of this respect for good foundations.

The Origin of Calvin's Liturgy: *La forme des prieres*

As he had used Farel's liturgy in Geneva, when he moved to Strasbourg Calvin worked with and learned from Bucer's liturgical creativity. The influence of the Alsatian reformer on Calvin's ecclesiology has long been recognized, and this is clearly evident in the shaping of what has come to be considered the Calvinist pattern of public worship.[66] The earliest extant form of Calvin's service book appeared in 1542 in two versions, one in Strasbourg entitled *La manyere de faire prieres...* (sometimes called the Pseudo-Romana because of its claim to have been published in that city) and one in Geneva called *La forme des prieres*. Both texts are usually identified by the latter name, but to avoid confusion here only the Genevan version will be called *La forme des prieres*. Scholars normally consider the Strasbourg publication a second edition of a lost text which Calvin used with his refugee congregation in that city, although there is some dispute about the contents of this probable first edition.[67]

For practical purposes, analysis of Calvin's own liturgical work usually starts with a comparison of the two editions published in 1542, and it is common to point out some easily identifiable differences between the two, particularly the fuller form of the Strasbourg version. One of the changes most often remarked is the omission in Geneva of the words of absolution spoken after the confession of sin. Another significant one is the essay which introduces the Lord's Supper in the Strasbourg *La manyere de faire prieres* and which is not found in the Genevan book; as noted above, this text provides Calvin's one reference to almsgiving in a liturgical document (as distinct from a theological or exegetical one). In 1545 a new Strasbourg printing of the liturgy (now entitled *La forme des prieres*) produced a third form which combined elements of the two texts from 1542. For the present study the primary focus is worship in Geneva, and thus the Strasbourg liturgies

---

[66] Calvin's words in his farewell statement express his own sense of dependence with regard to the Sunday service, cf. OS II, p. 403-02. See Dora Scheuner's comments in her preface to the critical edition of *La forme des prières*, OS II, pp. 1-4. Bornert, *La réforme protestante du culte*, pp. 192-201. For the most recent assessment of the influence of Bucer and the Strasbourg liturgical tradition, as well as the earlier Swiss (Basel, Bern, Farel), see Grosse, *Les rituels de la Cène*, pp. 129-32.

[67] See Scheuner, preface to *La forme des prières*, OS II, p. 2.

will be considered only insofar as they cast light on Calvin's work after he returned to Geneva.

The differences between the Strasbourg and Genevan liturgical traditions have been variously weighed. Some liturgical scholars regard the Genevan service book as a poor relation of the Strasbourg one, as if there were only omissions in the Genevan order. In fact, as will be seen in the discussion of the day of prayer, there was a very significant addition to the parallel text in Geneva.[68] Some early modern historians, on the other hand, have pointed out the particular strengths of the Geneva tradition. The most detailed recent study of Calvin's liturgy is found in Grosse's *Les rituels de la Cène*. For Grosse, the Geneva liturgy has a notably greater coherence than its Strasbourg sibling.

> As a whole, the structure of *La forme des prieres* is more coherent than that of the Pseudo-Romana. The different liturgies are gathered at the end of the volume, while in the Strasbourg one the Lord's Day liturgy was separated from the others by the collection of Psalms and a short catechism. The pivotal function of the sermon in the corporate liturgical life, so that the liturgy is defined in the liturgy for Sunday worship, is given greater weight here. The title of this service gives its name to the whole book. In addition, the liturgies for the different services [e.g., baptism, marriage] show exactly how each one is related to the liturgy for the sermon, which was not the case in the Pseudo-Romana. This coherence is particularly evident in the way that *La forme des prieres* integrates the Lord's Supper liturgy with the Lord's Day worship, so that they overlap closely.[69]

Pointing to the way that the Supper prayer is printed juxtaposed to the Sunday morning prayer of intercession in *La forme des prieres*, Grosse cites Markus Jenny's conclusion that "the Protestant liturgies of the Swiss-Alsatian region work to keep a close tie between the preaching service and the Eucharistic service" and concludes that the order of *La forme des prieres* is the "result of Calvin's theological conceptions."[70]

Grosse then goes on to identify changes between the two forms of the liturgy published in 1542: the omission in Geneva of the words promising forgiveness after the confession of sin, alterations in the singing of the Decalogue and Song of

---

68 For an example of criticism, see James White, *Protestant Worship: Traditions in Transition* (Louisville: Westminster/ John Knox, 1989), p. 67. For the day of prayer, see chap. 4, pp. ___ at nn.134ff.

69 Grosse, *Les rituels de la Cène*, p. 144.

70 Grosse, *Les rituels de la Cène*, p. 145; citing Jenny, *Die Einheit*, pp. 130-31, 137-42.

Simeon, the prayer "for illumination," and when the Lord's Prayer was recited. Together these had the effect of shortening the Genevan service.[71] On the other hand, some points were filled out in Geneva; for example, in Strasbourg a rubric instructed the minister to make an exhortation before communion but Geneva provided a text, which Grosse considers to be one of the high points of this liturgy.[72]

The Genevan *La forme des prieres* was reprinted at intervals with relatively few changes. The following overview combines some personal observations with the fuller work of Grosse. In 1952 the preface to the critical edition prepared by Dora Scheuner for the *Opera Selecta* outlined the pre-history of the liturgy, the editions of 1542 and 1545, and then some later printings of the Geneva 1542 in 1547, 1549, and 1559; of these the second was not available to her so the edition is based on 1542, 1547, and 1559.[73] In the interval since this volume of the *Opera Selecta* was published, other printings of *La forme des prieres* have become accessible, and there it is evident that a number of the changes in the Sunday and day of prayer intercessions which Scheuner attributed to 1559 had in fact been introduced in 1552. There were some verbal alterations in earlier editions, but the point of significant textual change in the prayers, particularly the addition of petitions for persecuted fellow believers, came in 1552.[74]

Grosse's study is based on the most complete collection of editions of *La forme des prieres*, and his first appendix provides a text for the Sunday and day of prayer services and the Lord's Supper liturgy which now supersedes the *Opera Selecta* version as the best critical edition of these texts.[75] Grosse notes that for the first ten years, 1542 to 1552, the liturgies for preaching, the Supper, and the day of prayer, were retouched in a number of ways, primarily through modifications to the wording of prayers. These were not radical changes and they did not have a significant effect on the structure, but they did "alter the tone of the whole"[76] since they smoothed the French and made it clearer. Grosse details the specific verbal additions in the prayers of intercession in 1547 (extending the list of

---

[71] Grosse, *Les rituels de la Cène*, pp. 145-47.

[72] Grosse, *Les rituels de la Cène*, pp. 148-49.

[73] Scheuner, preface to *La forme des prières*, OS II, pp. 1-10.

[74] See McKee, "introduction" to the Lord's Day and day of prayer services, in *Writings on Pastoral Piety*, pp. 99, 158. Additions to the prayers, which are marked "1559" in *Opera Selecta*, appeared in print in 1552.

[75] Grosse, *Les rituels de la Cène*, p. 151 n.135 ; esp. Appendix I, pp. 633-52, plus bibliography, pp. 652-57.

[76] Grosse, *Les rituels de la Cène*, pp. 152-52.

afflictions) and 1548 (naming enemies explicitly), and then the much more significant ones that Calvin requested in late 1551 and that appeared in 1552, which explicitly prayed for those suffering for the faith. As Grosse points out, these important additions to the prayers were a response to the increased persecutions in France, where the largest number of executions for heresy came between 1545 and 1549. "The sufferings and martyrdom of their fellow believers thus became, especially through the liturgical prayer, an element of the collective Reformed consciousness."[77] Grosse considers 1552 the point at which the liturgy was essentially fixed, although in 1553 one further change replaced the paraphrase of the Lord's Prayer with its recitation in some versions of the day of prayer intercessions.[78]

The rubrics in the Genevan *La forme des prieres* had never been very extensive and they did not change, so an examination of the liturgy itself would make it appear that the sequence and experience of the prescribed services did not vary beyond the wording of some prayers. Partly in reaction to the forms of the Mass where the priest's actions were minutely ordered, many Protestant service books included very sparse instructions about their performance, which makes it especially important to look for other indications outside the liturgy itself. When the latter are taken into account, not only do the movements and the embodiment of the worship become clearer, but it is also apparent that some aspects of the liturgy, and the people's experience of it, did expand over time. This was particularly true for the singing of Psalms. To understand what Sunday worship was like in Calvin's Geneva, it is necessary to go beyond the printed liturgies.[79]

Psalms and Singing in Genevan Worship

Congregational singing was one of the key Protestant innovations in public worship. Outsiders, both reformers and critics alike, remarked on this phenomenon.[80] Particularly the participation of girls and women raising their voices in

---

77 Grosse, *Les rituels de la Cène*, pp. 152-58, quotation p. 156. There is some question about how often the Lord's Prayer was used in the liturgy. In 1549 the Senate demanded that it be recited more often, to which Calvin replied that it was being used twice in the service every time and anything more would be like a magical charm and he would rather die than allow that; see discussion in chap. 4 at nn.5ff. Lambert reads the phrase "rather die" as referring to adding more services; cf. *Preaching, Praying, and Policing*, p. 286.

78 Grosse, *Les rituels de la Cène*, p. 157. For examples, see *Writings on Pastoral Piety*, pp. 158, 175.

79 Grosse's fine book does this at some length, and I have benefited from its great wealth of detail. In a number of instances, however, my reading of the sources is somewhat different.

80 Letters from Gerard Roussel in Strasbourg Dec. 1525 to friends in Meaux; #167 to bishop of Meaux: "octava vero hora, aut eo circa contio fit in majori templo, adjunctis cantionibus in

public liturgies was shocking to some and delightful to others. Calvin explicitly defended this, citing patristic support.

> Chrysostom exhorts men as well as women and little children to accustom themselves to sing [the Psalms], in order that this may be, as it were, a meditation for associating themselves with the company of angels.[81]

The story of Calvin's work to insure that his church could sing appropriately in worship is well known, but it is useful to provide an overview of the content and practice. Here the Psalms are considered as the sung prayers of the church; in a later chapter some of their other roles in prayer will be treated.[82]

Introducing Singing in Corporate Worship

During his first years in Geneva, Calvin wanted to introduce congregational singing of Psalms. This goal figures prominently in the *Articles*, the church order which he prepared for the city in 1537.

> Moreover it is very necessary for the education of the church to sing some Psalms in the form of public prayer, Psalms by which they can pray to God or sing His praises so that the hearts of all may be moved and incited to shape common prayers and offer common praises and thanks to God with the same feeling.[83]

---

commune linguam ex hebraico psalterio transfusis, ubi mire assonant mulieres viris, ut jucundum sit audire." The same idea is repeated in another letter the same month, A.-L. Herminjard, ed. *Correspondance des Réformateurs dans les pays de langue française* (Paris: H. Georg, 1878), vol. 1, pp. 406-07, 411-13. Cathelan, Geneva 1552-53, *Passevent Parisien*, p. 27 (quoted n.116). Florimond de Raemond, *L'histoire de la naissance, progrez et decadence de l'heresie* (Rouen, 1623), Book 8, chap. 10, p. 1010: "La pratique de l'ancienne & sage Chrestienté estoit-elle semblable au jeune & fol Calvinisme, qui permet à la femme de chanter dans l'Eglise? Qu'elle se taise, dit S. Paul: qu'elle chante, dit Calvin. Il n'y a point, disent-ils, de distinction selon sainct Paul, de l'homme & de la femme. C'estoit le mesme passage que certains Heretiques des premier siecles produisoient, pour prouver que les femmes pouvoient & devoient prescher de mesme que les hommes. Mais, & ces vieux, & ces nouveaux ne consideroient pas que sainct Paul ne parle en ce lieu de prier ny de prescher mais seulement que tout & de l'un, & de l'autre sexe, sont appellez esgalement à la foy Chrestienne, & à la vie eternelle."

[81] *Writings on Pastoral Piety*, p. 96. OS II, p. 17.

[82] Chap. 7 at nn.8ff.

[83] *Articles*, OS I, p. 369: "D'avantage c'est une chose bien expediente à l'edification de l'eglise de chanter aulcungs pseaumes en forme d'oraysons publicqs par les quelz on face prieres à Dieu ou que on chante ses louanges affin que les cueurs de tous soyent esmeuz et incités à former pareilles oraysons et rendre pareilles louanges et graces à Dieu d'une mesme affection."

Here Calvin clearly expresses both the character of Psalm singing as prayer and praise, and the role of unison words to bring all the worshipers into united voice and heart. Later in the same text he amplifies this statement with some pointed application to the situation at hand; singing Psalms would provide a counter to the "coldness" of worship.[84] The practice of singing was sufficiently important for Calvin to include it among the fourteen Articles that listed issues the Genevan church needed to address, which he sent to Bullinger in May 1538.[85] However, at this time there did not yet exist collections of metrical Psalms in French.

In Strasbourg, Calvin was able to begin to remedy this problem. Having gotten copies of some translations by the famous French lyric poet Clement Marot (before they were officially printed), Calvin set about publishing them. The thirteen Marot Psalms available (1-3, 15, 19, 32, 51 ["50]", 103, 114-15, 130 ["129"], 137, 143 ["142"]) did not, however, include some that the pastor really wanted, so he made his own translations of six others: 25, 36, 46, 91["90"], 113, 138, and the Song of Simeon, the Decalogue, and the Apostles' Creed.[86] The Strasbourg liturgies, both 1542 and 1545, prescribe Ps. 138 to be sung during communion, which suggests that Calvin's decision to translate it was prompted at least in part by his feeling that it was better to provide specific Psalms for worship than to wait for the best poetry. Recognizing, however, that metrical verse was not his gift, he evidently supported having his versions replaced as Marot's and Beza's became available.

When Calvin returned to Geneva in 1541 music was incorporated into worship. The *Ecclesiastical Ordinances* prescribed congregational singing of Psalms, led by the children until the rest could learn the songs, and the Sunday and day of prayer services called for singing a Psalm at one point in the service.[87] When *La*

---

84 *Articles*, OS I, p. 375: "Nous ne povons concepuoyr l'advancement et edification qui en procedera, sinon apres l'avoyr experimenté. Certes commme nous faysons, les oraysons des fidelles sont si froides, que cela nous doyt tourner à grand honte et confusion." A polemical note is heard, as Calvin objects to the way that "le pape et les seins ont privé l'esglise, quant il ont applicqués les pseaulmes, qui doibvent estre vrays chants spiritual, à murmurer entre eux sans aulcune intelligence."

85 Letter 111, OC 10b:192: "Alterum ut ad publicas orationes psalmorum cantio adhibeatur."

86 Pidoux, *Psautier huguenot*, vol II, p. 3 n. 7, indicates that it is uncertain whether Ps. 113 and the three catechetical pieces are Calvin's translations, but all except 113 reappear in Geneva [so that conclusion is likely].

87 *Ordinances*, OS II, p. 345: "Il sera bon d'introduyre les chantz ecclesiastiques pour mieulx inciter le peuple à pryer et louer dieu. Pour le commencement on apprendra les petiz enfants, puys avec le temps toute l'esglise pourra suyvre." Later, in December 1561, it was noted that the children coming out of catechism were making a great noise and confusion which was scandalous to visitors arriving to attend the Sunday afternoon service (in mid-winter at 2 p.m.) so it was ordered that the children be organized to sing before the service in order to teach the people the newly published Psalms. Dec. 25, 1561, OC 21:769 (RC 56 f282v).

forme des prieres was printed in 1542 it was part of a combined liturgy-Psalter, which now included thirty-six Psalms (Ps. 1-15, 19, 22, 24-25, 32, 36-38, 46, 51, 91, 103-104, 113-115, 130, 137-138, 143), plus the Song of Simeon, the Lord's Prayer, the Decalogue, and the Apostles' Creed in metrical form. [88] Calvin wrote a preface to the Psalter for this publication where he expresses clearly his understanding of music in worship.

> As for the public prayers, there are two kinds: the first are made with the word only, the others with song. And this not a thing invented a short time ago. For from the first origin of the Church, this has been so, as appears from the histories. And even Saint Paul speaks not only of praying aloud, but also of singing (Col. 3:16). And in truth we know from experience that song has great force and vigor to arouse and inflame people's hearts to invoke and praise God with a more vehement and ardent zeal. [89]

Having affirmed forcefully that sung prayers are Biblical and ancient Christian practice, and thus grounded the role of music in worship, Calvin goes on to assert that the kind of music must be appropriate to the purpose. [90] Later in the essay he addresses explicitly the matter of suitable texts and cites Augustine's words that the only songs worthy of God are those which have come from God. Thus, the Psalms are the ideal texts for believers to sing because they were given to David by the Holy Spirit. [91] Although he does not state that here, Calvin accorded the same status to any other texts from scripture, and (like other Protestants) included the Apostles' Creed as the summary of Biblical teaching.

In 1543 the rest of Marot's Psalms were published, along with his versions of the other commonly used texts such as the Song of Simeon and the Decalogue. The next printing of *La forme des prieres* in 1543 introduced the new Marot texts, Ps. 18, 23, 25, 33, 36, 43, 45, 50, 72, 79, 86, 91, 101, 107, 110, 118, 128, 138, although the fact that the "angelic salutation" (Ave Maria) was included led the

---

[88]   *La Forme des Prières et Chants Ecclesiastiques Genève 1542.* Fac-simile de l'édition originale, avec une notice par Pierre Pidoux (Kassel & Bâle: Bärenreiter, 1959). Hereafter *La Forme des Prières 1542/ 1959.* See p. i6v (OS II, p. 20).

[89]   *Writings on Pastoral Piety*, p. 94. OS II, p. 15.

[90]   *La forme des prières*, OS II, p. 15: "Il y a toujours à regarder, que le chant ne soit pas legier et volage: mais ait pois et majesté, comme dit sainct Augustin, et ainsi il y ait grande difference entre la musicque qu'on faict pour resjouyr les hommes à table et en leur maison: et entre les psalmes, qui se chante en l'Eglise, en la presence de Dieu et de ses anges."

[91]   *La forme des prières*, OS II, p. 17: "Or ce que dit S. Augustin est vray, que nul ne peut chanter choses dignes de Dieu, sinon qu'il ait receu d'iceluy: parquoy quand nous aurons bien circuy par tout pour cercher çà et là, nous ne trouverons meilleures chansons ne plus propres pour ce faire, que les Pseaumes de David: lesquelz le sainct Esprit luy a dictz et faitz."

Senate to order this song removed.[92] The 1543 printing also provided Calvin with an opportunity to add a further section to his preface; one new point was an emphasis on the use of the Psalms in daily life.

> And how much more widely the practice of singing may extend! It is even in the homes and in the fields an incentive for us, and, as it were, an organ for praising God and lifting up our hearts to Him, to console us by meditating on His virtue, goodness, wisdom, and justice, something which is more necessary than one can say.[93]

Calvin emphasizes that music is "either the first or one of the principal" means of human recreation so it should be rightly used as God's gift.[94] Over the course of the next nearly twenty years the Psalter was enlarged twice more; in 1551 it reached eighty-three and in 1562 the full one hundred fifty Psalms.[95] The sheer volume of printed copies of the text demonstrates that it was desired and bought by many. Estimates place the number of examples of the 1562 Psalter at many thousands, so that it has been called "the run-away best-seller of the century in France."[96] In Geneva copies were even supplied to those living on public welfare, so that poverty would not prevent anyone having access to the prayer book of the church. Probably devout Genevans brought their Psalters to worship at least until they learned all the Psalms; a visitor, Piero Paulo Vergerio, commented in 1550 on seeing both men and women singing from books.[97]

Before they could actually sing in worship, however, the people of Geneva needed more than the texts; they needed musical education. This had already begun several months before Calvin's arrival in 1541, when Guillaume Franc had been hired to teach the children music. The following year the city considered hiring a second teacher but Calvin did not believe the man was sufficiently qualified and told the Senate that between them, the school teacher and the ministers would do what was needed for teaching the children. In mid-1545

---

92 Pidoux, *Psautier huguenot*, vol. II, p. 25. June 9, 1543, OC 21: 313 (RC 37 f121).

93 *Writings on Pastoral Piety*, p. 94. OS II, pp. 15-16.

94 *Writings on Pastoral Piety*, p. 94. OS II, pp. 15-16.

95 Pidoux, *Psautier huguenot*, vol II, p. 53 for 1551; pp. 132-33 identifies the multiple places where the 1562 edition appeared (Geneva, Lyon, Paris, Caen, St. Lo).

96 Grosse, *Les rituels de la Cène*, p. 174, says "plusieurs dizaines de milliers d'exemplaires." Lambert, *Preaching, Praying and Policing*, p. 342 quotation.

97 Grosse, *Les rituels de la Cène*, p. 176 ; Pier Paulo Vergerio, *Epistola del Vergerio, nella quale sono descritte molte cose della Cità, e della Chiesa di Geneva* (Geneva: Badius, 1550), p. 11 : "Tutto il populo, huomeni & donne con i loro libricini in manu suole avanti, & do po le prediche cantare nelle chiese, & canti di salmi nella sua lingua, com si legge che nella primitiva chiesa fare si soleva."

Louis Bourgeois came to join and then replace Franc, and headed the music program until his departure in January 1553.[98] Apparently the choice of Psalms for the day's worship was not organized in the early years. However, in May 1546 the ministers and Bourgeois proposed to the Senate that a "table" be posted on the church doors to tell the people what Psalm would be sung at each service.[99] No copy of this "table" is extant, but the reprint from 1549 (which figured now as an addition to the Psalters)[100] indicates that the Psalms were distributed over seventeen weeks. Henceforth devout Genevans could prepare before worship by reading or meditating on the Psalm to be sung at that service, or at the least they could be expected to find the song quickly in their Psalters since it was both printed in their book and posted at the church door as they entered.

Expanding Singing in Genevan Worship

Among the important factors related to the expanded repertoire of Psalms and the increasing competence of Genevans to sing them was the addition of a second time of singing during services (Sunday morning and afternoon and the day of prayer) which had previously only had one. When exactly this happened is not clear, but the first dated instance comes from November 1545, in a day of prayer service which was printed early the following year. Here the editor, Jean Cousins, who had copied down Calvin's sermon and was now publishing it, explained that the congregation sang the first four verses of Ps. 79 before the sermon and the rest afterwards.[101] Grosse considers this evidence that the practice was already established, but he does not give further evidence. In addition, he also affirms that the addition of a third time of singing was a relatively early phenomena; it began "already in the beginning of the 1550s, or

---

[98] June 17, 1541, Franc employed. June 16, 1542, Pierre Bochi called Servandi, not hired. July 14 & 18, 1545, hiring of Bourgeois. See Pidoux, *Psautier huguenot*, vol. II, pp. 5, 11, 28.

[99] Pidoux, *Psautier huguenot*, vol. II, p. 32. On p. 44 Pidoux gives this first extant table, 1549, putting in the numbers of the Psalms rather than the titles; in doing so he makes a mistake, copied from one of the early tables. The table in at least some of the 1549 tables, e.g., *Pseaulmes Cinquante de David mis en vers françois par Clement Marot*, à Lyon chez Godefroy & Marcellin Beringen, 1549, prints the final Ps. for Wed. as "64" when in fact it is "46." At this point 64 had not yet been translated into metrical form, while 46 (which had been available since 1549) is not found elsewhere in the table. Evidently Pidoux copied the numbers from the table but did not check them against what was actually in verse form.

[100] Pidoux (previous note) indicates that it was not possible to determine whether it was systematically included in the Psalters or added by the owner, but Grosse affirms that it was the regular practice; *Les rituels de la Cène*, p. 164 n. 184.

[101] See discussion of context in chap. 4 at nn.149ff.

at least by 1562."[102] Pierre Pidoux, who has studied the Genevan Psalter in great depth, provides much information and many helpful quotations from primary sources,[103] but he does not treat the specific patterns of singing in worship. The following discussion draws on these sources with some independence and combines them with further research.

Exploring exactly how often Genevans sang Psalms in church and when the practice of singing twice and then three times was introduced might seem a kind of excursus. It is in fact, however, a lacuna in the story of worship in Geneva and a significant point in tracing the development of liturgical practice over the course of Calvin's ministry, particularly with regard to the extent of active participation by the people in the pew. The Strasbourg liturgy of 1542 included two times of singing, near the beginning and at the end of the service, although only one was a Psalm. The first song was the Decalogue, which was divided into two parts; the first table was sung after the confession of sin and assurance of pardon; then followed a prayer and the singing of the second table while the minister went up into the pulpit to preach. The second time of singing was a Psalm which came after the sermon and prayer of intercession and just before the benediction. In the parallel Genevan *La forme des prieres* the weekly use of the Decalogue on Sunday morning was dropped (although it apparently figured regularly in the catechism lessons), and it was probably sung by the whole congregation at the Supper services.[104] In sung form, this basic text soon became well known to the urban population – sufficiently

---

[102] Grosse, *Les rituels de la Cène*, p. 183 : "On sait que depuis 1545 au moins, le chant intervient à deux reprises dans le culte dominical; la deuxième partie du psaume peut être remplacée par le chant du décalogue. Au début des années 1550 déjà, en tout cas en 1562, on chante à trois reprises puisque le culte commence alors par un psaume." pp. 165-66 : "Dans sa version modifiée de 1562, la table indique en second lieu que le chant d'assemblée n'intervient pas seulement comme prévu par le formulaire entre confession des péchés et sermon, mais aussi à la suite de la prédication, proba-blement après la prière d'intercession et le Notre père. L'ensemble du culte comprend ainsi trois séquences de chant: en introduction, avant et après le sermon. La table enregistre en fait une pratique genevoise antérieurs à 1562 : un recueil de deux sermons prononcés par Calvin lors du service de prière, en novembre 1545, précise que l'on 'chanta en l'assemblée le Psaume 79 prenant une partie au commencement du sermon, réservant le reste pour la fin'. Cette pratique a été officialisée par les ordonnances ecclésiastiques adoptées le 13 novembre 1561 (soit l'année précé-dant la modification de la table dans les psautiers), qui ordonnent 'd'introduire les chants Eccle-siastiques tant devant qu'apres le sermon, pour mieux inciter le peuple à louer et prier Dieu'." It appears in Grosse's various comments (see also n.117 below) that the exact time is not a particular concern for him; in the several places where he discusses this point, he either generalizes or collapses the addition of the second and third times of singing. The issue is a minor one for his large canvass.

[103] Pidoux, *Psautier huguenot*; vol. I *Les melodies*. vol. II *Documents et Bibliographie*.

[104] For singing of Decalogue, see note in Psalter table. Since that is the only explicit evidence, the practice may date from the mid-1540s when the tables were first prepared, but it seems more likely that the Decalogue had been part of the Supper service before. *La forme des prières*, OS II, p. 20.

that the youth could parody it. Perhaps the omission on non-Supper Sunday mornings was partly to simplify the liturgy for the people; starting and stopping the singing several times could have been confusing to people who had never before participated in congregational song. Thus Geneva in 1542 had only one time of singing and it was a Psalm except on Supper Sundays. Over time, urban Genevans did learn their Psalms and at least a good number adapted to this new form of active participation enough to be upset when some Psalms were changed (printers' errors "corrected") in 1551.[105]

The introduction in 1546 of tables to show which Psalm to sing in each service is a very important clue to clarify practice and was certainly helpful in smoothing it. Rather than having the music leader announce the Psalm or leave people to identify it when he and/or the children began to sing, now everyone could anticipate what was coming. From 1546 until 1562, the tables provide one column for each of the three services when there was singing: Sunday morning, Sunday afternoon, and the Wednesday day of prayer.[106] In 1546/49 there were different Psalms for each of seventeen weeks, after which the cycle began again. A second, updated version of the table was published in 1551.[107] This incorporated the newly available metrical Psalms and provided for twenty-eight weeks, but still had only one column per service and no accompanying rubric. In these tables the specific text to be sung in a service is noted by number and the incipit for that service, which is not always the beginning of the Psalm, in the case that one Psalm is divided between two services. When a complete Psalm is not sung, the end point is also identified, so that the congregation will know where to stop.[108] See Figure 1. (Pidoux's transcription of the tables gives the Psalm numbers with verses instead of the incipits, which can be useful although sometimes confusing because verses can be of varied lengths.) The new table was printed and attached to the doors of the three parishes; St. Pierre and St. Gervais each received three posters, La Magdeleine two.

---

[105] For parody, see Lambert, *Preaching, Praying and Policing*, p. 343; the text he names is actually the metrical Decalogue, which was probably one of the first things catechism students learned to sing; cf. below at n.138. For conflict over changes, see Pidoux, *Psautier huguenot*, vol. II, pp. 52-53, Dec. 1551 (RC entries for Dec. 3, 4, 14, 15, 31).

[106] In 1549 and 1551 the tables are printed as a single page for each service, 11x7 centimeters of print; in 1562 there are two pages for each service, 15x8 centimeters of print. When lined up, the pages represent columns, and so they are described here.

[107] Pidoux dates this to 1552 (*Psautier huguenot*, vol. II, pp. 55, 62), but Grosse (*Les rituels de la Cène*, p. 164) indicates that he has found this table already in 1551 Psalters.

[108] If the end of the singing is the end of the Psalm, the table will say sing "the rest of the Psalm" but if the end point is earlier, it will give the incipit of the next verse after where the congregation stops singing: sing "up to ____." See Figure 1, e.g., Sunday morning #10, 12, 25-28.

TABLE DES PSEAVMES

Le Dimanche au matin.	Le Dimanche au soir.	Le Mecredi iour des prieres.
1 Veu que du. 11 Le fol. 14	1 Qui au conseil. 1 Qui est ce qui. 15	1 O Seigneur qde. 3 Quand ie t'inuoque. 4
2 Seigneur, le Roy s'esiouyra. 21	2 Pourquoy font bruit. 2	2 Aux parolles que ie. 9
3 Du malin les. 36 Sois moy Seigneur. 16	3 O nostre Dieu & Seigneur 8	3 Ne vueilles pas ô Sire.
4 Seigneur entend a mon bon. 17	4 Les cieux en chacun lieu. 19	4 Mon Dieu i'ay en toy esperance. 7
5 Enfans qui le. 113 Le Seigneur ta. 20	5 Mô Dieu me paist, 23 La terre au. 24	5 De tout mon cœur. 9 Iusqu'a Chantez en.
6 Seigneur garde mon droit 26	6 Vous tous princ. 19 L'Omnipotent. 110	6 Chantez en exul. Reste du 9
7 Le Seigneur est la clarté. 27	7 Propos exquis faut que de. 45	7 D'ou vient cela. 10
8 Seigneur puis que m'as retiré. 30	8 Quand Israel. 114 Or sus tous hu. 47	8 Iusques a quand. 13 Or peut bien, 114
9 I'ay mis en toy mon esperance. 31	9 Tes iugemens, Dieu veritable. 72	9 Ie t'aimeray. 18 Iusqu'a Certes Seig.
10 Si est-ce que. 73 Iusqu'a Lors chacun.	10 Lors chacû. Reste du 73 Vouloir m'est pris 101	10 Certes Seigneur. Reste du 18
11 O combien. 133 Il faut que. 138	11 Bien-heureux est 128 Seigneur ie n'ay 131	11 Mon Dieu, mon. 22 Iusqu'a D'humeur ie.
12 Resueillez-vous. 33 Iusqu'a Le Seigneur,	12 Le Seigneur Eternel, Reste du 33	12 D'humeur ie suis. Reste du . 22
13 I'ay dit en moy de pres. 39	13 Aleph Bienheur. 119 Beth. Comme pourront	13 A toy mon Dieu, mon cœur 25
14 Apres auoir constammént. 40	14 Gimel. Espans tes. Daleth. Ie suis helas,	14 O Dieu qui es. 28 Dés ma ieunesse. 129
15 Or auons-nous de nos. 44	15 He. Ie te suppli' Vau. Fay moy sentir.	15 O bien-heureux celuy dont les. 32
16 Le Dieu le fort l'Eternel. 50	16 Zain. Souuienne toy. Heth. O Dieu tu es	16 Deba contre mes debateurs. 35
17 Tu as esté, Seigneur, nostre. 90	17 Teth. Seigneur, tu as. Iod. Tes propres mains	17 Las en ta fureur. 38 Iusqu'a Ceux qui a.
18 Qui en la garde du haut 91	18 Caph. De ton salut. Lamed. En ce haut.	18 Ceux qui a ma mort. Reste du 38
19 Sus louez Dieu mon ame. 103	19 Mem. O que ta Loy. Nun. Ta parolle est.	19 O bien-heureux qui iuge. 41
20 Non point a nous, non. 115	20 Samech. I'ay tousiours. Ain. Droit & bon iuge	20 Ainsi que la biche ree. 42
21 Iamais ne cesseray de magnifier. 34	21 Pe En tes edits. Sade. Seigneur tu es	21 Reuenge moy. 43 Estans assis. 137
22 Vers les monts. 121 Incontinent. 122	22 Coph. Ie t'ay prié. Res. Voy la misere.	22 Dés qu'aduersite nous 46
23 A toy, ô Dieu. 123 Or sus seruit. 134	23 Schin Les princes. Tau. A toy mon Dieu.	23 Misericorde au poure vicieux. 51
24 Du fond de. 130 On a beau. 127	24 Tout homme. 125 Alors que de. 16	24 Les gens entrez sont en ton heritage. 79
25 Ne sois fasché. 37 Iusqu'a Leur main.	25 Leur main sera. Reste du 37	25 Mon Dieu preste moy l'oreille, 86
26 Sus, sus, mô am. 104 Iusqu'a Que diray	26 Que diray plus? Reste du 104	26 Alors qu'affliction. 10 Donné secours. 12
27 Dônez au Seig. 107 Iusqu'a Ceux qui.	27 Ceux qui dedans. Reste du 107	27 Vueilles Seigneur estre recors. 132
28 Rendez a Dieu. 118 Iusqu'a De l'Eternel	28 De l'Eternel. Reste du 118	28 Seigneur Dieu oy l'oraison mienne. 142

Chap. 3, Fig. 1. Table for finding the Psalms to be sung in 1551.
Texts are divided to be sung in two parts, before & after the sermon. Source is *Les Pseames de David* printed with *La Bible*, etc., Geneva by Nicolas Barbier & Thomas Courteau, 1559.

In 1562 a new table was prepared which included the now complete series of metrical Psalms distributed over twenty-five weeks. Significantly, this table had two columns for each day. In some printings each of the columns was headed with a rubric: one for singing at the start of the service: "after the second ringing of the bell," the other for singing "before and after the sermon."[109] Some tables, however, give rubrics only for the new column and leave the old (now second) one exactly the same as before: "Le Dimanche au matin au presche" or "Le Dimanche au soir au presche" or "Le Mecredi jour des prieres au presche."[110] There is no reference to "before and after" the sermon, yet the listing of Psalms is the same as in the tables where that is spelled out. Furthermore, the way this second column identifies the appropriate Psalm did not change; it was exactly the same pattern as before, i.e., without any specific indication about what would be sung before and what after the sermon. This demonstrates that Genevans did not need the specific instructions about dividing the single column of Psalms into two times of singing and thus the practice could long antedate the explicit rubrics in some of the 1562 tables.

---

109   The notes in the table of Psalms in 1562 say: "Pour le Dimanche au matin [le Dimanche au soir, etc.], apres le second coup de la cloche," Facsimile of *Les Pseaumes*, 1562; for the second column, see below at n.114 and Figure 4. Cf. Pidoux, *Psautier Huguenot*, II, p. 134.

110   See the table printed in the Psalter bound with the Bible, liturgy, catechism, and short examination for admission to Supper, printed in 1566. MHR 04e (566).

Chap. 3, Fig. 2. An illustration of Psalm divisions in the 1562 Genevan Psalter.
The stars and "pause" marks on this page illustrate the division of a longer Psalm into sections. In 1551 this Psalm was divided at the "pause" for singing (even before the mark appears in the printed book); see Figure 1 above, in the Wednesday day of prayer column for weeks 9-10. The assignment of the portions of Psalms might change. In 1562 the first part of this text is used on the Sunday afternoon of week 1, the second part on Wednesday of week 1, both times at the beginning of the service; see table in Figure 4. Source is *Les pseaumes de David* printed with *La Bible*, etc. Geneva by Zacherie Durant, 1566.

Before examining the tables more closely, it is important to look at the Psalters themselves, that is, at how the texts are printed. In 1542 and 1551 (the two major stages of expansion in the number of metrical Psalms available) there are no markings in Geneva printings to divide the Psalms. The Strasbourg publication in 1553, however, does have a certain number of clearly marked breaks labeled "PARTIE II" (in one case "PARTIE III"), which demonstrate that the French metrical Psalms being used by Calvinist Reformed churches were being divided into sections at least by 1553. There is no "table" to indicate how the Strasbourg French congregation assigned the singing of the Psalms but it is revealing that a number of these divisions correspond to those which would appear in Geneva in 1562. In several places where the divisions are different, a hand-written ink "X" has been added in the copy of the Strasbourg 1553 which I examined to mark where the 1562 Geneva divisions appear, as is seen at the second line of p. 63 in the photograph. Apparently the owner of the Strasbourg book knew what was being practiced in Geneva when divisions were added to those Psalters.[111] See figure 3. These ink additions in the Strasbourg book extend only through the first several divided Psalms, which suggests that the French congregation in Strasbourg did not adopt the Genevan practice even if at least some members knew of it.

---

[111] Pidoux, *Psautier huguenot*, vol. II, pp. 64-66 describes this volume, but he does not notice the divisions of the Psalms which I observed in the copy that I used in La Salle Senebier, Bibliothèque de Genève, under the signature "Bb 2368 res." The exact comparison with Geneva 1562 is as follows:
Ps. 7 marks "LA II. PARTIE" after « les fons des cueurs, je t'en requiers. » And before « C'est Dieu qui est mon asseurance » p. 28. Ps. 9 marks « LA II. PARTIE » p. 37 at point where 1562 Psalter has « Pause » [Su 830] before « Chantez en exultation ». Ps. 18 has « LA II. PARTIE » p. 63 mark "x" at the point in the Psalm where Geneva 1562 has its breaks (stars correspond with X pp. 61, 65, & pause p. 63) [LA II PARTIE is not at one of the Genevan breaks]. Ps 19 has ink "X" p. 67 at Genevan stars. Ps. 22 has "LA II. PARTIE" p. 78 where Genevan has stars although the translation a bit different. Ps. 25 has "LA II. PARTIE" p. 90 – not exactly where Genevan has stars but the translation is different. Ps. 33 has "LA II. PARTIE" p. 102 where Genevan has pause, but no ink marks for Genevan stars. Ps. 37 has "LA II. PARTIE EN AUTRE MELODIE" p. 113 with music following ; the break is one stanza later than Genevan pause. Ps. 38 has "LA II. PARTIE" p. 122 at same place Genevan has pause. Ps. 51 has "LA II. PARTIE" p. 146 one stanza later than Genevan stars [no pause in this Ps]. Ps. 103 has "LA II. PARTIE" p. 175 at the same place Geneva has stars [no pause in this Ps.]. Ps. 104 has "LA II. PARTIE" p. 180 and « LA III. PARTIE » p. 183 but these do not correspond to Genevan stars and pause [Geneva has three breaks : stars, pause, stars ; Strasbourg only two]; Strasbourg 6 stanzas for I, 5 stanzas for II, 6 stanzas for III. Ps. 107 has "LA II. PARTIE" p. 192 which is where Geneva has pause (though Geneva has two sets of stars to divide it into 4 pieces). The law and Nunc dimittis are provided with music; the law is divided with similar language between tables "LA II. TABLE" p. 238.

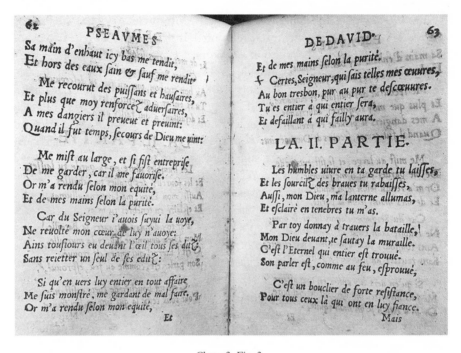

Chap. 3, Fig. 3.

Two pages of the 1553 Strasbourg Psalter, with the division of a Psalm clearly marked. On p. 63 at line 2, there is an ink "x." This corresponds with where the starred division would be intro-duced in the 1562 Genevan Psalter. Source is *Pseaumes de David,... dans l'eglise Francoyse de strosbourg. ..* 1553. [BGE Bb 2368 res]

When division markings were introduced in the Genevan Psalters in 1562, they were accompanied by a table, and combining information from the Stras-bourg and Geneva sources illuminates the practice of singing. In the 1562 Genevan Psalters there are two kinds of marks dividing sections of Psalms; a group of stars is the most common, while the word "pause" is found much less often but not infrequently. Inspection reveals that the Psalms which the 1562 "table" assigns for "before and after" the sermon are divided into two sections which correspond to the stars or stars and pause marks in the printed Psalter. Short Psalms are not divided at all, and they appear "whole" in the table, i.e., incipit and number. Medium-length Psalms have stars at approximately the mid-point, dividing the Psalm in two. (On some rare occasions the stars come in the middle of a verse!) Long Psalms have two or three divisions. Commonly there will be three: stars, pause, stars, indicating that from the beginning to the pause is one assignment, to be divided in half at the stars, and from the pause to the end is another assignment, also to be divided at the second stars. [112] Some medium long Psalms will have two divisions, with stars once and a pause. The exception to all these rules is Ps. 119, which is divided by letters of the Hebrew alphabet, and one assignment is two letters (sixteen Biblical verses).

Checking the 1562 table against texts of Psalms shows that the table always divides the assignment (what is to be sung) at one of the star or pause marks. The simplest assignments are two short Psalms, [113] a medium-length Psalm divided into two parts by stars, or one half of a long Psalm divided into four sections by stars/pause/stars. In these cases, two whole short Psalms are sung as one assignment, or two consecutive sections of a divided Psalm can be sung as one assignment. It becomes more complicated, however, if the divided Psalm is assigned in a different way, e.g., the first section (of three or four) sung as half of one assignment and then the second and third paired as another assignment. (If there are four divisions, the fourth will then become half of another assignment.)

What emerges from this analysis is a way to see how corporate Psalm singing was organized in Genevan worship. As noted above, the 1562 table is the only one to provide more than one column or assignment for each day, and its headings cast light on the practice. At least sometimes the second column is labeled "Table for finding the Psalms which are sung immediately before and after the sermon Sunday morning" (or "Sunday afternoon" or "Wednesday the day of prayer") [114]. With very few exceptions, every single assignment in these three columns is made up of two parts, either two short Psalms or a divided medium length Psalm or the two-part half of a long Psalm. Thus it is apparent that the assigned Psalms were easily capable of being divided between two points in the service: immediately before and after the sermon.

There are two exceptions, places in which a single Psalm (without the stars to mark a division) serves as one complete assignment. This constitutes something of a challenge to the modern reader, but it probably did not disturb the Genevans too much because the likelihood is that they were accustomed to using a book printed without internal divisions in the Psalms while they still broke the singing into two parts. The 1562 table does not explicitly say anything about dividing the assigned Psalm(s), but the rubric at the top of the column does indicate that there

---

[112] Once there are three sets of stars instead of two and a pause, but the function appears the same.

[113] Once there are three very short Psalms (112. 114. 117) assigned together, at the beginning of the Wednesday service in the 19th week.

[114] "Table pour trouver les Pseaumes qu'on chante incontinent devans & apres le sermon le Dimanche au matin [au soir, etc.]," Facsimile of *Les Pseaumes*, 1562. see Pidoux, *Psautier huguenot*, II, p. 134.

AVTRE TABLE POVR TROVVER LES
PSEAVMES SELON L'ORDRE QV'ON LES
chante en l'Eglise de Geneue, tant le Dimanche au
matin & soir, que le Mecredi.

Le Dimanche au matin, apres le second coup de la cloche.		*Le Dimanche au soir apres le second coup de la cloche.*	
1 Ne vueille pas, o Sire	6	1 Ie t'aimeray en 18. ius. Certes Seigneur,	
2 Seigneur, le Roy s'esiouira	21	2 Mon Dieu, mon Dieu 22. ius. D'humeur	
3 Vous tous Princes 29. I'ay mis 31. ius. Entre		3 Entre tous ceux-la qui me reste du	31
4 Sus, ie te reste du 35. Ne sois 37. ius q. Mais		4 Mais les benins du 37. ius. Les bien-Viuans	
5 Tant me fait du 38. ius. Vien donc: car		5 Vien donc reste du 38. Or auons 44. ius. En	
6 Propos exquis faut que de mon	45	6 C'est en sa tressaincte Cité	48
7 Exauce, o mon Dieu, ma priere	55	7 Aye pitié, aye pitié de moy	57
8 O Dieu, qui nous as deboutez	60	8 O Dieu, ie n'ay Dieu fors que toy	63
9 Dieu nous 67. Que Dieu 68. ius. Lors		9 Lors que ton du 68. ius. C'est Dieu	
10 Helas, Seigneur 69. ius. Approche-toy		10 Approche-toy en mon aduersité reste du 69	
11 Outre ta louange ordinaire reste du	71	11 Tes iugemens Dieu veritable	72
12 O Seigneur 75. Sois enten. 78. ius. Ce non-obst.		12 Ce nonobstant dere. du 78. ius. A tenter	
13 Mais il reste du 78. O Pasteur 80. ius. Iadis		13 Iadis ta reste du 80. Chantez 81. ius. Ouure	
14 O Dieu ne 83. Du Seigneur 89. ius. C'est		14 C'est toy qui as du 89. ius. l'establiray	
15 Chantez à Dieu chanson nouuelle	96	15 Or est maintenant 99. Vous tous qui	100
16 Que diray plus? la claire reste du	104	16 Sus qu'vn chacun 105. ius. Lors fit Israel	
17 Louez Dieu: car 106. ius. Mais ils oublierent		17 Mais ils oublierent du 106. ius. A Baalpeot	
18 Donnez au Seigneur 107. ius. Ceux qui		18 Ceux qui dedans galees reste du	107
19 Sois sa race ostee du monde reste du	109	19 Du Seigneur Dieu en tous endroits	118
20 119 Aleph. 1. Bien-heureuse Beth 2. Comme		20 Gimel 3. Espan tes Daleth 4. Ie suis, helas	
21 Zain 7. Souuienne-toy Heth 8. O Dieu		21 Theth 9. Seigneur, tu Iod 10. Tes propres	
22 Mem 13. O que ta Loy Nun 14. Ta parole		22 Samech 15. I'ay tousiours Ain 16. Droit &	
23 Coph 19. Ie t'ay prié Resch 20. Voy la		23 Schin 21. Les princes Thau 22. A toy, mon	135
24 O combien 133. Or sus, seruiteurs du		24 Chantez de Dieu le renom Vous tous les	148
25 O Dieu, tu cognois 139. O Dieu donne	134	25 O Seigneur, a toy 141.	
	140		

Le Dimanche au matin au presche.		*Le Dimanche au soir au presche.*	
1 Mon Dieu, i'ay en toy esperance	7	1 Qui au conseil 1. Qui est ce qui	15
2 Veu que du tou: 11. Donne secours	12	2 Pourquoy font bruit	2
3 Sois moy, Seigneur, ma garde &	16	3 O nostre Dieu, & Seigneur	8
4 Seigneur, enten à mon bon droict	17	4 Les cieux en chacun lieu	19
5 A toy, mon Dieu, mon cœur monte	25	5 Le fol malin en 14. La terre au Seigneur	24
6 Seigneur, garde mon droit	26	6 Mon Dieu me paist 23. Or sus tous	47
7 Le Seigneur est la clarté qui m'adresse	27	7 Peuples oyez, & l'aureille prestez	
8 O Dieu qui es 28. Du malin le	36	8 Dés qu'aduersité nous offense	46
9 Seigneur, puis que m'as retiré	30	9 Le Dieu le fort	50
10 Resueillez-vous 33. ius. Le Seigneur		10 Le Seigneur eternel regarde reste du	31
11 Iamais ne cesseray 34. ius q. Dieu tient		11 Dieu tient son reste du 34. Enten à ce	62
12 I'ay dit en moy, de pres ie viseray	39	12 Mon ame en Dieu tant	62
13 Apres auoir constamment attendu	40	13 O Dieu des armees	84
14 Si est-ce que Dieu 73. ius. Lors chacun		14 Lors chacun reste du 73. Chantez à Dieu	92
15 Tu as esté, Seigneur, nostre retraite	90	15 Qui en la garde du haut Dieu	91
16 Seigneur enten ma 102. ius. En registre		16 En registre sera mise reste du	102
17 Sus, louez Dieu, mon ame en toute	103	17 O que c'est chose belle de	92
18 Rendez à Dieu 118. ius. De l'Eternel		18 De l'Eternel la main adextre reste du	118
19 I'aime mon Dieu	116	19 Non point à nous, non point	57
20 Mon Dieu mon Roy	145	20 L'Eternel est regnant	97
21 Vouloir m'est 101. O Dieu tout	54	21 Dieu pour fonder 87. L'Omnipotent	110
22 Le Seigneur ta priere 20. Alors que de		22 Enfans qui le 113. Estans assis aux	137
23 On a beau 127. Bien-heureux est qui.	126	23 Sus mon ame qu'on benie	146
24 Du fond de ma 130. Il faut que de	128	24 Louez Dieu, car c'est	147
25 Vers les monts 121. Incontinent que	138	25 C'est en Iudee 76. Dieu est regnante	98
	122		

Le Mecredi apres le second coup de la cloche.			Le Mecredi iour des prieres au presche.	
1	Certes, Seigneur, qui scais telles *reste du*	18	1 O Seigneur que 3.Quand ie t'inuoque	4
2	D'humeur ie suis comme tuile *reste du*	22	2 Aux paroles que ie veux	5
3	Deba contre 35.*iuf.* Sus ie te beniray		3 De tout mon 9. *iuf.* Chantez en	
4	Les bien-viuans *reste du* 37. Las, en 38. *iuf.* Tant		4 Chantez en exultation *reste du*	9
5	En Dieu gift toute nostre *reste du*	44	5 D'ou vient cela, Seigneur,	10
6	Di-moy mal heureux 52. Le fol malin	53	6 Iulques à quand 13.Reuenge-moy	43
7	Entre vous conseilliers qui estes	58	7 O bien-heureux celuy dont	32
8	Or fus, Iouez Dieu tout le monde	66	8 Ainsi qu'on oit le cerf	42
9	C'est Dieu, & non autre *reste du*	68	9 Misericorde au poure vicieux	51
10	O Dieu, ou 70. l'ay mis 71.*iuf.* Outre		10 O bien-heureux qui iuge sagement	41
11	D'ou vient, Seigneur, que tu nous	74	11 Misericorde à moy poure	56
12	A tenter Dieu, du 78.*iuf.* Mais il quitra		12 Mon Dieu l'ennemi m'enuironne	59
13	Ouure seulement *reste du* 81.Dieu est	82	13 Enten à ce que ie veux dire	64
14	I'establiray sa race à perpetuité *reste du*	89	14 A Dieu ma voix i'ay haussee	77
15	Sus, fus, mon ame 104.*iuf.* Que diray		15 Les gens entrez sont en ton heritage	79
16	Lors fit Israel son entree *reste du*	105	16 Mon Dieu, preste moy l'aureille	86
17	A Baalpeor neantmoins *reste du*	106	17 O Dieu eternel mon	88
18	Mon coeur 108. O Dieu 109.*iuf.* Soit sa		18 O Eternel Dieu des vengeances	94
19	O bien-heu. 112. Quâd Israel 114. Toutes 117		19 Auec les tiens, Seigneur 85. Alors qu'af.	129
20	He 5. Ie te suppli *Van* 6. Fay-moy sentir		20 A toy, o Dieu 123.Or peut bien	124
21	Capb 11. De ton salut *Lamed* 12. En ce haut		21 Tout homme qui 125.Dés ma ieunesse	129
22	Phe 17. En tes edicts *Zade* 18. Seigneur, tu		22 I'ay de ma voix 142. Sus, esgayons-nous	95
23	Seigneur, ie 131.Vueilles, Seigneur	132	23 Seigneur Dieu, oy l'oraison mienne	143
24	Louez Dieu tout hautement	136	24 Loué soit Dieu, ma force	144
25	Chantez à Dieu 149.Or soit loué	150	25 O Dieu la gloire qui t'est deuë	65

On chante les commandemens de Dieu(Leue le coeur, ouure l'aureille, Exo. 20.) apres le Sermon le iour qu'on celebre la saincte Cene de nostre Saueur Iesus Christ:laquelle on celebre quatre fois l'an:assauoir, à Pasque, à la Pentecoste, au premier Dimanche de Septembre, & au plus prochain Dimanche de la Natiuité de Iesus, On chante en l'action de graces le Cantique de Simeon:Or laisses Createur. Luc 2.

Chap. 3, Fig. 4. The Table for Finding the Psalms to be Sung:
from one printing of the 1562 Genevan Psalter.

In this printing the second column of the table does not state "before & after" the sermon, but the table is identical with Psalters which do so. Some assignments are the same as those in the 1551 table though not always the same sequence since more Psalms were added; e.g., Sun. morning week 4, Sun. afternoon week 2, Wed. weeks 5-6 (instead of weeks 4-5). For an example of a Psalm moved from one day to another, see Fig. 2 above. Source is *Les pseaumes de David* printed with *La Bible*, etc. Geneva by Zacherie Durant, 1566.

are two times when singing occurs, once on either side of the sermon. One might say that in the case of two short Psalms, it is easy to see what was meant: one is sung before the sermon and the other afterwards. However, the fact that many assignments are a single Psalm which is supposed to be used in the same fashion, combined with the fact that this Psalm has an internal division marked at the midpoint, makes clear what is intended. The table assumes that the people reading the list know how to interpret it; when a single Psalm is assigned, they know to sing the first part up to the division mark (usually stars) before the sermon and the second part after.

This decoding of the 1562 table makes it possible to read the earlier tables in a new way. The earlier tables (1546/49 and 1551) had only one column of assignments for each service, and no rubric about the time of their use. Probably the reason for making explicit in 1562 when to sing the Psalms ("before and after the sermon") was that a second column had been added to the table for each service; now there were two columns for Sunday morning, two for Sunday afternoon, two for the day of prayer. The new columns give the Psalm assignment to be sung at the beginning of each service, and thus it was appropriate (if not necessary) to label the (customary) practice "before and after the sermon" to distinguish it from the newly introduced occasion for song at the start of worship. When this evidence is combined with that from the Strasbourg Psalter of 1553, it becomes plain that internal divisions in the printing of metrical Psalms did not refer to religious content but to church practice: the marks showed where the congregation was supposed to begin and end the musical part of a particular service.

When Geneva began to sing twice during a service, i.e., when the practice of having a Psalm before and after the sermon was introduced, can now be more precisely defined. That this was the case even before 1562 is reasonably certain, although the evidence is circumstantial. The first in time comes from the pamphlet of the day of prayer service held on Nov. 4, 1545 (noted above), where Jean Cousins, the publisher, states that the congregation sang Ps. 79, the first half before the sermon and the second half afterwards. In the 1562 Psalter this Psalm is marked with stars to divide it into two parts exactly at the point where the break was made at the day of prayer service in 1545. Cousins does not appear to regard the division of the Psalm as an innovation; his only explicit comment has to do with the fact that Ps. 79 had just recently been translated into metrical form so he provides a printed copy because it was not included in the published Psalters then available. This pamphlet included also the sermon and Psalm 9 from the day of prayer service a week later, Nov. 11, although here it is not specifically said that the Psalm was sung in two parts. This Psalm 9 was well-known to Genevans, because it had been a part of their repertoire since 1542, and since Cousins' audience was ostensibly his fellow Genevans, comment on its use would not be needed. It seems likely that both Psalms were sung in two sections, before and after the sermon, and the reason for describing the division of Ps. 79 was the fact that the text, not the practice, was new.

The second form of circumstantial evidence that Calvin's liturgy had begun to include two times of singing, long before this was made explicit in 1562, is how closely the table in 1562 resembles the earlier assignment of Psalms to be sung on specific days. Many of the actual assignments are identical to those in 1551, and a significant number are also identical to 1549, although sometimes they are listed for use at different services. (The main change between 1549 and 1551 is the expanded repertoire of Psalms available at the later date, but a good portion of the Psalms which were the complete assignment for "before and after the sermon" in 1562 already appeared in that column much earlier, before the rubric was added.)

A third suggestive point is based on a comparison of the two columns of the table in 1562, one of which gives the texts sung "before and after the sermon" and the other (completely new) which assigns Psalms for the beginning of the service. The addition of a second list of texts was possible because the edition of 1562 almost doubled the metrical versions available (from 83 to the complete 150). In fact, the number of verses or pages assigned for singing at the start of worship (column one) is often nearly equivalent to what is assigned to be sung before and after the sermon (column two). The way that the Psalms are assigned is sometimes different, however. Because the singing at the beginning of worship was uninterrupted, there was no need to insure that the Psalm could be more-or-less evenly divided. So, for a number of days the initial song time is made up of three divisions of a Psalm (divided by stars or stars and pause), which would have been confusing if the congregation had been expected to divide the Psalm between two times of singing. When this practical observation is compared with the assignments in the second column (the "original" one which identified the Psalms for before and after the sermon), it becomes obvious that the latter was planned to be used in divided form. To put this another way, in the single column per service in 1546/49 and 1551, as well as the one labeled "before and after the sermon" in 1562, the assigned Psalm or Psalms are presented as two more-or-less neatly organized parts, while the new column assigning texts for the start of the service in 1562 does not always meet this standard. Thus, the way that the Psalms are assigned contributes to the circumstantial evidence for interpreting what the "original" column meant even before 1562 when the words "before and after the sermon" were added.

A fourth indication that Psalm singing happened at two points in the worship service, at least by 1546 (or 1549), is the confusing point about where the Decalogue appears in the Lord's Supper service. A note at the bottom of the 1549 table (which it is assumed is a reprint of the no longer extant 1546) states that when the Supper is celebrated, the Decalogue will be used "in place of the Psalm which should be sung according to the order of the present table."[115] The liturgy

---

115 "Le jour qu'on célébre la saincte Cène de nostre Seigneur Jesus Christ selon son ordonnance, après icelle on chante pour action de grâces le cantique de Symeon," Pidoux, *Psautier huguenot*, II, p. 44.

itself (as was noted earlier) establishes only one Psalm, to be sung before the sermon. The Decalogue, however, was associated with the Lord's Supper and thus logically sung in that part of the Lord's Day service, after the sermon. If Geneva had in fact begun to sing a Psalm text after as well as before the sermon, then this instruction would make perfect sense and the Psalm to be replaced by the Decalogue would be the one after the sermon.

This combination of various pieces of circumstantial evidence strengthens the hypothesis that Genevans were already singing Psalm texts at two points in their worship service (probably long) before this was officially stated in 1562. The practice was almost certainly present by 1545, when the special day of prayer service publication speaks of dividing Ps. 79 to sing half before the sermon and half afterwards. The marks printed in the Strasbourg 1553 Psalter demonstrate that indications of where longer Psalms would be divided could be found in published texts of another French Reformed church nearly a decade before those were printed in Geneva.

When the third time of singing was introduced into the Genevan service is a further aspect of the matter to be considered. As was noted above, Grosse affirms that this was the case by 1562, but he also suggests that it began rather earlier ("already by the beginning of the 1550s"). The apparent basis for this extrapolation is a sentence from Cathelan's *Passevent Parisien*, a description of worship in Geneva and French Switzerland about 1552-53. "Twice a week (only in the city) before the sermon they sing a Psalm or a part of one, all together: men, women, girls, and children, all seated."[116] Grosse identifies the two days as Sundays and Wednesdays. This is the only evidence he offers as grounds for thinking that singing at the beginning of the service (and therefore at two times before the sermon) "probably antedates 1562."[117] This seems an unwarranted interpretation. The fact that Cathelan does not mention singing after the sermon might call into

---

[116] Cathelan, *Passevent Parisien*, p. 27: "Et deux fois la sepmaine (aux villes seulement) devant le sermon ilz chantent un Psalme, ou une partie d'iceluy tous ensemble: hommes, femmes, filles, et enfans, tous assis."

[117] Grosse, *Les rituels de la Cène*, p. 662 n.13 : "Le chant d'un psaume en ouverture du service de prière est attesté par la 'Table pour trouver les psaumes selon l'ordre qu'on les chante en l'Eglise de Genève' publiée dans les psautiers à partir de 1562 (Pidoux, *Psautier huguenot*, f. II, p. 134-135). Une brève note d'introduction à ce tableau précise que le chant intervient notamment 'après le second coup de cloches', c'est-à-dire au tout début du service. Cet usage est probablement antérieur à 1562: Cathelan, qui se trouvait à Genève en 1553, décrivant les usages liturgiques genevois, signale que 'deux fois la sepmaine (aux villes seulement) devant le sermon ils chantent un Psaume, ou une partie d'iceluy' (*Passevent Parisien*, f. 15v) ; ces deux jours correspondent sans aucun doute à ceux que mentionne la 'Table', c'est-à-dire au mercredi et au dimanche."

question even two times of singing in the service. The very high probability of the latter has already been demonstrated, so it is clear that Cathelan's comment cannot be read as a description precise in all details. What he does reveal is his amazement at the participation of every person present, and his observation that the texts sung were not always complete Psalms. The 1561 revision of the *Ecclesiastical Ordinances* makes explicit that Psalms would be sung before and after the sermon, but it does not note any other times. A printing of the complete Psalter, the one made by Jean-Baptiste Pinereul for Antoine Vincent in 1563, simply tacks the new columns for singing "after the second bell" onto the end of book. The three columns for singing before and after the sermon are placed together, first, as if they had already been part of the book, and the new addition to the table, with Sunday morning and afternoon, and Wednesday, are grouped in the last three pages. Most printings set the two columns for Sunday morning, the two for Sunday afternoon, and the two for Wednesday, in sequence, but this Pinereul-Vincent one suggests that the old table of before and after the sermon had already been a part of the production and so it was not recomposed but merely extended by the inclusion of the new "after the second bell" time of singing.[118] While that does not categorically exclude the idea that singing right at the start of worship on Sundays and Wednesdays had begun before 1562, it certainly does not offer any support to the claim for such a thing. In fact, it suggests that the addition of a third congregational Psalm had not yet been instituted in 1561. It was the publication of the complete Psalter the next year which both allowed and mandated the expanded place of music in worship.

Over time Genevans in the city learned the Psalms well, although their country neighbors were not as able. According to the notes of Pastor Charles Perrot of Moens and Genthod, written about 1564 to guide his successor, the number of different Psalms the village people knew was quite limited, and he continued to have singing in only two places rather than the three which had recently been introduced in the city.[119] Nonetheless, slowly even rural Genevans were developing an acquaintance with the prayer book of their church in song, and that included the basic articles of faith.

---

[118] *Ordinances*, OS II, p. 345. See *Les pseaumes de David...* par Jean-Baptiste Pinereul pour Antoine Vincent. (BGE Su 4939 Res)

[119] See Lambert, *Preaching, Praying and Policing*, Appendix 4, pp. 539-48; p. 541: "On chante au sermon ces pseaumes: 1, 3, 15, 24, 119 Aleph et Beth, 129, 130, 128 [sic] et quelquesfois les Comandemens. On partit chesque pseaume en deux pour l'entree et l'issue du sermon. On chante à la Cene le 23 tout du comencement et le Cantique de Symeon tout à la fin, asçavoir devant la derniere priere et action des graces."

Catechisms and Catechesis

Understanding one's faith was a crucial factor for Protestants. Thus, in addition to translating public worship into the vernacular and putting both liturgy and Psalms into the hands of the congregation, one of the key genres of text which reformers published was the catechism. The process of catechesis was not new, but the intensity with which it was pursued was. In the expanding role that educating the faithful played in humanist-influenced Europe, Protestants pioneered the practice of regular, clergy-led classes and the production of a new form of text, the question-and-answer catechism. Almost the first thing which Calvin published in Geneva was a catechism, and one of his conditions for returning to the city in 1541 was that (obligatory) catechesis would be instituted.

Catechisms

There are a number of catechetical texts associated with Calvin's name and/or used in Geneva. These include both "full catechisms" and shorter versions intended to summarize or test the minimum of knowledge required for admission to the sacraments, especially the Lord's Supper. (Both sacraments were implicated, however, because Geneva also required that parents and godfather know the catechetical elements in order to present a child for baptism. [120]) The texts will be treated in two groups, each chronologically arranged.

Calvin himself wrote and published two "full" texts called catechisms. The first was the prose form which appeared in French in Geneva in 1537 and in Latin the following year, a text often considered a kind of summary of the first *Institutes*. As Olivier Millet has convincingly argued, the vernacular was a translation of the Latin and not very well adapted to the purpose of instructing the relatively uneducated audience in Geneva; it was still too close to the Latin to be easily understood. Millet goes on to demonstrate, by comparing some of Calvin's writings between 1536 and 1541, how the reformer developed the great clarity of thought and expression which would make him the master of the French language that he became. With regard to purpose and form, in 1537 Calvin did not really distinguish between the two genres of texts which contain the points of Christian belief, i.e., a catechism for teaching the basics of Christian belief, and a confession of faith for the purpose of witness to those convictions. However, his next catechism would show that he had learned the style for instructing in the faith as distinct from a statement of faith. [121]

---

[120] See chap. 5 at nn.172, 216.

[121] "Instruction et confession de foy," OS I, pp. 378-426. A major recent study is John I. Hesselink, *Calvin's First Catechism: A Commentary: Featuring Ford Lewis Battles' Translation of the 1538 Catechism*

The Genevan Catechism, which is usually described as Calvin's second catechism and is certainly much the best known, was published in 1542 in French. No example is extant but the text was reprinted in 1545, the same year that a Latin translation was published. Millet has praised this substantial theological text as a kind of summary of the most important points of the 1541 *Institutes*, remarkably orchestrated to educate believers in the faith. This catechism includes various model prayers, as well as a short introductory essay added in 1545 which explains Calvin's understanding of the role of catechesis in uniting the church. [122] The style is question-and-answer; at times it can appear more of a conversation than an examination, because sometimes the master supplies the content and the student simply says "yes." The catechism was primarily used by the ministers in teaching the faith, and students were not expected to memorize it. (After the founding of the Genevan Academy in 1559, with its more advanced students and rigorous form of instruction, there was more concentrated school-time use of the catechism.)

There is a second kind of catechetical text which played an important role in Calvin's work, and this was the summary used in testing or professing the faith. In 1542 *La manyere de faire prieres* published in Strasbourg included a relatively brief catechism in dialogue form which provided a basic question-and-answer treatment of the Apostles' Creed, the Lord's Prayer, and the Decalogue. This was a translation of one of Bucer's texts, which Calvin may well have used in his Strasbourg congregation; according to the editors of the *Opera Selecta*, it continued to serve the French parish in Strasbourg until at least 1545. There has been some debate about whether Calvin brought it back to Geneva, but Millet provides reason to conclude that he did not. [123]

Geneva already had a kind of primer which Pierre Robert Olivetan had first published in 1533 under the title *The Instruction of Children, containing the way to pronounce and write in French. The Prayer of Jesus Christ. The Articles of the Faith. The Ten*

(Louisville, KY: Westminster/ John Knox Press, 1997). See Olivier Millet, "Le premier 'Catéchisme' de Genève (1537-1538) et sa place dans l'oeuvre de Calvin," *Catéchismes et confessions de foi* (Montpellier: Université Paul Valéry, 1995), pp. 209-29.

[122] *Catechism*, OS II, pp. 73-51, gives the Latin. OC 6:1-146, provides the French and Latin in parallel columns. For further discussion of the model prayers, see chap. 7 at nn.31ff.

[123] *La manyere de faire prières*, pp. 123-31; "Institution puerile," OS II, pp. 152-57. In the introduction to the catechism in OS II, the editors attribute this to Calvin and say there is evidence that it continued to be used in Strasbourg. They also suggest that Calvin used it in Geneva when he returned in 1541 (before the Geneva Catechism was available) and that he continued to use it for examining those preparing to receive the Lord's Supper, since Geneva did not have a short formulary until 1553; OS II, pp. 60-61. Millet, however, demonstrates that this short text was a translation from Bucer, "Rendre raison de la foi," p. 192.

Commandments. The Angelic Salutation. In 1537 Jean Girard reprinted this, reversing the order of the Lord's Prayer and the Decalogue in the title but not changing the body of the text. Rodolphe Peter has examined various "ABC" books, setting this first French Protestant catechism published in Geneva in its larger context. [124] Girard's book presents the alphabet with pronunciation guide (using Biblical names), the Lord's Prayer, the Apostles' Creed, the Decalogue, and Luke 1:28-31 & 42 and Matt. 1:21. (The most surprising thing here is the way that the two tables of the Decalogue are divided between the fifth and sixth commandments, so that honoring parents is counted under the first table.) The greater part of the book is taken up with scripture quotations carefully chosen to "comment" on each phrase of each catechetical text. To give an idea of the kind of interpretation Genevans found here, it is worth noting a couple of examples. One is the many subsections which appear under the Creed's "one holy catholic church," detailing a rather full ecclesiology. [125] A second is the way that the Decalogue concludes with a significant New Testament section on Christ as the end and fulfillment of the Law, while also indicating the continued use of the law (e.g., the importance of assemblies for worship). [126] The booklet concludes with a list of the books of the Bible (naming "Les Apocriphes" in a separate section), a letter to the reader, and some final primer elements (e.g., numbers).

Besides the book published by Girard, Peter lists several publications entitled "L'ABC," including one printed in 1551 by Jean Crespin which contains two

---

[124] Peter, "L'abécédaire genevois ou catéchisme élémentaire de Calvin," pp. 175-76. Girard also printed it again in 1539, cf. RC IV, p. 520 (Nov. 21, 1539).

[125] *L'Instruction dés enfants, contenant la maniere de prononcer et escrire en françoys. L'oraison de Jesus Christ. Les articles de la Foy. Les dix commandemens. La salutation angelique.* [Genève: Jean Girard, 1537] ; e-rara. ch accessed Jan. 29, 2013. Under "L'Eglise universelle, la communion des sainctz," p. 49, there are headings: "Des deux signes sacramentaux de l'Eglise, instituez par Jesus Christ. Du Baptesme" p. 52; "De la table & Cene de nostre Seigneur," p. 53; "De l'excommunication, & des clefz, puissance de l'Eglise," p. 54; "De l'estat & office de l'Eglise, tant en particulier que en general. Du Surveillant, autrement dict Evesque, & ministre de la parolle," p. 59; "Du ministere de l'Eglise, autrement dict Diacre et proviseur; De la Principauté & Magistrat," p. 57; "Des Anciens; Des Jeunes," p. 60; "Des mariez en general," p. 61; "Des maris; Des femmes," p. 63; "Des vierges & continens," p. 67; "Des peres," p. 68; "Des enfans; Des serviteurs & servantes; Des Seigneurs & maistres; Des paouvres & des riches," p. 69; "De toute l'Eglise; Fin des estatz & office d'un chascun en l'Eglise de Dieu," p. 70.

[126] *L'Instruction des enfans*, section on Jesus Christ, two great commandments, etc., pp. 124-29; "Le commandement que Dieu fait de garder & faire garder sa Loy à tous; Premierement aux chefz & gouverneurs du peuple, pour l'intimer et recommander," p. 129; "Item au populaire, notamment aux peres et maistres de familles, affin qu'ilz la proposent et enseignent, principalement à leurs domestiques," p. 130 ; "Comment il ne faut adjouster ne diminuer à la Loy & Parolle de Dieu," p. 131; "Des promesses à ceux qui gardent les commandemens de Dieu," p. 132.

anonymous short texts generally attributed to Calvin. One is a "Short Treatise Necessary for Those who Want to Commune in the Holy Supper of Our Lord" which, after an introduction about honoring and trusting God who is known through Jesus Christ, provides a brief guided tour through the Apostles' Creed, the Decalogue, the Lord's Prayer; and a Calvinian summary about faith ("certain knowledge of God's good will toward us...") and explanation of the two sacraments which "the Lord ordained because of the weakness of our faith." This last section makes up about one-third of the whole. The "short treatise" of catechetical reminders was probably intended for personal use in preparing for communion. The other ABC text in Crespin's booklet is about the same length but organized as an exchange between a minister and child, and entitled "The Way of Questioning the Children Whom You Wish to Receive at the Supper of Our Lord Jesus Christ." The question and answer format is very economical in words, and does not even include the recitation of the three catechetical tools.[127] Beginning in 1552, this text came to be a regular part of the Psalter as service-book and was printed following the Genevan Catechism. It was successively lengthened, first and immediately by recitation of the Creed, Decalogue, and Prayer plus a little more elaboration of each, and later by a considerably fuller form which was still couched with great succinctness. The three forms of this text are published in the *Opera Calvini*.[128] Thus it is clear that there were several possible short texts which teachers in the little vernacular schools of Geneva could use for their beginning students, and which the ministers probably did employ for testing whether the youth – and others! – were ready to be admitted to the Lord's Supper.

Calvin's two main catechisms have been studied a number of times and their teaching is well known. In recent years attention has also been given to the very short forms in the "ABC" primers, although it has not apparently been remarked that the Olivetan text launched Genevans on an untraditional division of the Decalogue. The purpose here is not to examine these texts in any depth but to make some observations about the practical place of catechesis in the worship life of Geneva.

Catechesis in Geneva

It is well known that the main reason that Farel wanted to detain "that young Frenchman" in Geneva was because the newly declared reformation needed to be organized. One part of putting this plan into effect was implementating regular catechesis, and the church order of 1537 indicates that this was included among

---

[127] Peter, "L'abécédaire genevois ou catéchisme élémentaire de Calvin," pp. 171-205.

[128] "La maniere d'interroguer," OC 6:147-60. The editors of OC consider the third version unworthy of Calvin and include it only because they grant that he knew of it, 6:147-48.

the key reforms. It is first stated as a norm which would apply to children, [129] and later explained more fully as the patristic pattern of instruction "in the basics of the Christian religion" so that the children could "come to testify to the church their faith to which they could not give witness in their baptism." [130] The church order goes on to describe the plan for teaching the children, advising that a brief catechism be prepared. The tradition of instruction in the home is continued, although any mention of godparents is omitted and the responsibility is laid on the parents. When the children were considered ready, they should be brought to the ministers for examination and further instruction, until their knowledge was judged sufficient. The text seems to anticipate that the pastor would become involved at intervals, since it requests that the Genevan authorities make the parents "present themselves to the ministers at the times to be appointed." [131] The frequency of this catechesis is not specified. The patristic practice had been to have (adult) catechetical training for specific periods of time before baptism, and some Protestant reformers like Zwingli adopted that schedule at first (before adding weekly classes). Zurich changed to a weekly rhythm but Basel continued this looser format for many years, [132] so this may have been what Farel recommended and Calvin accepted.

---

[129] *Articles*, OS I, p. 369: "Tiercement il est fort requis et quasi necessaire pour conseruer le peuple en peureté de doctrine que les enffans des leur jeune eage soyent tellement instruicts que ilz puissent rendre rayson de la foy affin que on ne laisse deschoyr la doctrine evangelique, ains que la sentence en soyt diligemment retenue et baillee de main en main et de pere en filz."

[130] *Articles*, OS I, p. 375: "Le 3ᵉ article est de l'instruction des enfans, lesqueulx sans doubte doibuent à l'esglise une confession de leur foy. Pour ceste cause anciennement on avoyt certain catechisme pour instituer vng chascun aux fondemens de la religion crestienne, et qui estoyt comme vng formulayre de tesmoignage dont vng chacun usoyt pour declairer sa crestienté, et nommement les enfans estoyent enseignez de ce catechisme pour venir testiffier à l'esglise leur foy dont il n'auoyent peu rendre tesmoignage à leur baptesme."

[131] *Articles*, OS I, p. 376: "L'ordre que nous avons advisé de y mettre, c'est qu'il y aye une briefve somme et facile de la foy crestienne, laquelle soyt apprinse à tous les anfans et que certaynes fassons de l'anne ils viennent par devant les ministres pour estre interroguez et examinez et recepuoyr plus ample declaration selon qu'il sera besoing à la capacité d'ung chacun d'eux, jusques à ce qu'on les aye approuvez estre suffisamment instruicts. Mays que vostre playsir soyt fere commandement aux parens de mettre payne et diligence que leurs enfans apprennent icelle somme et qu'il se presentent aux ministres aux temps qu'il sera dict."

[132] Twice a year is what is proposed in Zwingli's *Usslegen und Gründe der Schlussreden* of 1523 (CR 89, p. 123) but in the 1532 *Züricher Prädicantenordnung* preachers were expected to give weekly catechism lessons; cited in Old, *The Shaping of the Reformed Baptismal Rite*, pp. 183-84 and nn.11-12. Burnett, *Teaching the Reformation*, pp. 55, indicates that something like this was the early practice in Basel; the children learned catechism in school, and were to be examined by the pastors four times/ year. Luther also practiced a similar form, with two weeks of concentrated instruction four times per year.

In Strasbourg, however, weekly Sunday catechism classes had been instituted in 1526, and in 1534 a quarterly examination day was begun.[133] This was not intended to replace education in the home, but it was a significant complement which would give a certain standard to the catechetical task. It was this practice of weekly clerically-taught, parish-based services which Calvin brought back to Geneva in 1541, and something very similar to the Strasbourg organization was introduced almost immediately. The *Ecclesiastical Ordinances* define the basic practice, including the distribution among the parishes.

> For sending the children to catechism… the boundaries of the parishes will be observed as much as possible. … All citizens and residents must bring or send their children to the catechism at noon on Sundays. A certain form will be prepared as the basis for their instruction. Along with the teaching they are given, let them be questioned about what has been said, to see if they have understood it well and retained it.[134]

The following year, 1542, the new Geneva Catechism was published and this became the standard text for the regular weekly services. The children of Geneva are named as the (normal) students of the catechism, but in fact servants and others who did not know the basics of the faith were also required to attend. City servants often came from rural areas, including neighboring Catholic villages, so church leaders made a concentrated effort to see that these residents of the community were properly instructed, and all masters or mistresses were expected to see that every member of their household was taught, one way or another.[135]

There is no outline or description of the Geneva catechism service in these years, but a contemporary text from Strasbourg, the *Ministers' Agreement* (*Concordia* 1542) provides a glimpse of Bucer's practice.

> At the beginning, the children sang a Psalm; then, they recited a prayer adapted to their intellectual level; next, one or another child repeated aloud the text which had been announced the previous time and which

---

[133] Bornert, *La réforme protestante du culte*, pp. 60, 174, 501-02.

[134] *Ordinances*, OS II, p. 337: "Pour envoier les enfans au cathechisme et pour recevoir les sacremens, que en tant qu'il se pourra faire on observe les limites des paroysses." p. 356: "Que touz citoyens et habitans ayent à mener ou envoyer leurs enfans le dymanche à mydy au cathechisme, dont il a esté parlé. Qu'il y ait ung certain formulaire composé sur lequel on les instruyse. Et que avec la doctrine qu'on leur donnera, qu'on les interroge de ce qui aura esté dict, pour veoir s'ilz l'auront bien entendu et retenu."

[135] See chap. 7 at nn.204, 209 (La Donne Polliere's servants). In terms of age, children were probably about eleven or twelve when they completed catechism; see the Consistory's use of catechism as a gauge of age for marriage, chap. 5 n.75.

was going to be explained at the present lesson. The pastor gave an explanation of this text, in the form of a sermon; the children were questioned about this explanation. The text for the next time was read aloud; the class ended with the singing of a Psalm and the benediction. [136]

Although published the year after Calvin left Strasbourg, if this summarized or codified an existing practice (which is possible or even probable), the young French reformer must have known it and might have had it something similar in mind. [137] For Geneva the first known description of how the catechism service was structured or what it included was written in 1564 by Perrot about his rural parishes.

> I ... [began] by singing the Commandments with men and women or girls, every Sunday one table at the beginning and the other at the end, except when it was very cold I would divide the tables into two parts; afterwards I made a little confession and prayer, and then read the article of the Creed, the Lord's Prayer, or the Commandments where I had left off. As for the treatise on the sacraments, I had not yet started it, and I would have explained it the most easily and briefly I could, in three or four Sundays, because there are questions and teachings in the Catechism which cannot easily be told to the people for fear of confusing them. So I treated the article (which was to be explained) as it was set out in the Catechism, at least somewhat adequately and then I summarized it in a sentence or two at most, and then questioned them. I made the boys and [male] servants, and [then] the girls and [female] servants say this, twice, one after the other (because these [children and servants] are the ones who are explicitly supposed to come to catechism). After the questioning, I made the last prayer and signaled for specific children to say the *Our Father*, the *I believe*, and *Hear, Israel*, as is done in Geneva. ... Then we completed singing what we began [at the start of catechism], either a half table of the Commandments or an entire one, and then the benediction, as in the weekday sermons in the city. [138]

---

136 Bornert, *La réforme protestante du culte*, p. 502. "Selon l'*Accord des ministres* de 1542, cette instruction devait se dérouler de la façon suivante: au début, les enfants chantaient un psaume; puis, ils récitaient une prière adaptée à leur niveau d'intelligence; ensuite, l'un ou l'autre enfant répétait à haute voix le texte qui avait été annoncé la fois précédente et qui devait être expliqué à la leçon présente; le pasteur donnait, sous la forme de sermon, une explication de ce texte; les enfants étaient interrogés sur cette explication; le texte à commenter la prochaine fois était lu à haute voix; la classe se terminait par le chant d'un psaume et la bénédiction."

137 Old, *The Shaping of the Reformed Baptismal Rite*, p. 196: "Whether the catechetical services included prayer and psalmody is not clear, but there is some evidence that they did."

138 Lambert, *Preaching, Praying, and Policing*, Appendix 4, pp. 543-44, gives Perrot's description of his larger or more able congregation at Moin or Moens: " J'y tenois cet ordre qu'une heure et demye ou environ apres le sermon je l'allois faire, començant par chanter avec les hommes et femmes

As he notes in the summary of his simpler catechetical efforts at his second village, Perrot began with the Psalm phrase used in all Genevan services: "Our help is in the name of the Lord who made heaven and earth." [139] Although he only refers to the practice "in the city" in two places, Perrot probably modeled his service on what his colleagues were doing in the other Genevan parishes. The broad outlines are similar to those planned for Strasbourg. The details may well have varied, but the order was relatively analogous to other services: singing, opening sentence, prayers (including a confession of sin); the reading of the catechism text for the day and a "sermon" of explanation, with a concluding summary; questioning of the students in groups, with the requirement that they recite the basic words of the text (presumably the phrases of the Creed or Prayer or Decalogue set for the day); another prayer; recitation of the three texts by designated students (probably those who were closest to being ready to make their own profession); a second time of singing; and a benediction. The reference to the weekday sermons probably means that, since there was no prescribed order

ou filles les Command[ements], tous les dimenches une table au com[mencement] et l'autre à la fin ormis qu'au grand froit je partissois les tables en deux apres je faisois une petite confession et priere, [p. 11] et puis lisois l'Article de la Creance, priere de Notre Seigneur ou Commandemens auquel j'estois demouré. Quant au traité des sacremens, je n'y estois point encores entré, et je l'eusse exposé le plus facilement et brefvement qu'il m'eust esté possible, comme en trois ou quatre dimenches. Car il y a des questions et doctrines au Catechisme que l'on ne peult aisement declarer au peuple de peur de les confondre. Ainsy je traittois l'article à exposer selon qu'il estoit declaré dedans le Catechisme au moins mal et puis je recueillois en une ligne ou deux au plus et lors demandois et faisois dire à tous les garsons et serviteurs, filles et servantes deux fois l'un apres l'autre, car ce sont ceulx-la qui se doivent trouver expressement au Catechisme. Apres lesdittes demandes, je faisois la derniere priere et les enfans à qui je faisois signes disoient *Notre Pere, Je croy, Escoute Israel*, comme à Genesve. Je les faisois prononcer au moins mal, car il les fault supporter beaucoup, mesques en la substance ils ne corrumpent rien, et y fault prendre garde. Apres on acheve de chanter ce que l'on a comencé ou une demy table des Com[mendemens] ou une entiere, et puis la benediction, comme aux sermons des cours sur semeine à la ville. En esté, que l'on fait le Catechisme apres disné, je prenois au bout ou devant le temple les petitz enfans et taschois à leur faire bien prononcer *Notre Pere* et *Je croy* et à leur aprendre quelque chose des Commandemens."

[139] Lambert, *Preaching, Praying, and Policing*, Appendix 4, pp. 548. Perrot: "Au catechisme de Gento que je faisois, estant descendu de la chaire, les petitz enfans se treuvent et je m'assies sur un ban et lors je commence ou leur faire commencer à un à dire 'Nostre ayde soyt au nom de Dieu qui a fait le c[iel] et la terre' et puis comment fault-il prier Dieu. Tous les petitz pononcent 'Nostre Pere' et fault bien s'arrester à la pronunciation et puis on leur demande la Creance pareillement et puis les commandemens à ceulx qui les sçavent. Cela fait, on expose plus simplement qu'à Moin l'article de l'Oraison ou des Com[mandemens] ou de la priere et puis on fait respondre comme à Moin aux plus grands des garçons ou des filles. Et ainsy par chesque dimenche, car jusque icy je n'ay peu faire d'avantage. On tasche aussy à apprendre aux grandetz 'Leve le coeur' en demy couplet à chesque fois. Cela peut durer une demy[e] heure au plus. Au bout je faisois une petite priere en forme d'exhortation de deux ou trois lignes."

for catechism, Perrot followed the practice of extempore prayer (as did Calvin in his *Exposition* of the Catechism). It may be noted that Perrot identifies the Decalogue by the words "Hear, Israel," the title printed in Marot's metrical setting "Aude Israel" and found in the 1562 Psalter, but in the catechism at his second village he refers to the Decalogue as "Leve le coeur," the actual incipit. Evidently both phrases were current, although the latter was probably more common. [140]

The Geneva Catechism presented a mature summary of Calvin's theology. By 1549 the text had been divided into 55 sections, with the intent that one section would be explained every Sunday. [141] It was the task of the ministers who taught or preached at the catechism classes to explain the week's text and require some participation by the students in reciting and responding. Experienced men like Michel Cop also taught catechism, but often the ministers assigned to do catechism were new preachers, [142] presumably since the fixed subject matter would logically be easier to teach than doing the full exegesis and application of a Biblical passage. Evidently there were some pastors who found it difficult to convey the substance of the Catechism to their young parishioners, and late in his life Calvin himself provided them with an example. Only one of his lessons, that for Section

---

[140] For prayer concluding catechism, see Calvin's *Exposition*, see chap. 6 at nn.122. For the "Aude Israel," see Facsimile of *Les Pseaumes* 1562. This was not used in the 1551 edition; see facsimile of *Pseaumes octantetrois*. Also nn.165, 170 below. For common use of "Leve le coeur" as parody, see Lambert n.105 above. Poullain provides a description of Strasbourg's French congregation some years later during its English and then its Frankfurt exiles; *Liturgia Sacra*, pp. 96-99. Here the French, pp. 97 & 99: "Apres le disner à une heure tous les Dimanches l'Eglise s'assemble pour le Catechisme: assavoir ou que les petitz et rudes sont instruictz en la Foy. Premierement l'on chante l'un des Octonaires du Psalme. 119. et puis l'on interrogue les petitz, selon leur degré, qui sont ainsi assis en leur rangs. Les ungs recitent l'oraison, les autres le Symbole, les autres le decalogue, et les derniers recitent ce qu'ilz ont apprins, par toute la sepmaine hors la confession de la Foy, que tous sont tenuz de sçavoir par cueur, aussi bien les grans que les petitz. Ceste confession est mise en la fin de ce livre. Le ministre en expose par chascun Dimanche quelque partie, autant que les petitz en pourront apprendre au long de la sepmaine. Et puis invoque la grace du sainct Esprit sur ces enfans, et faict fin." The various printings of the Latin text give the time as noon or 1 p.m.; the description of the proceedings is shorter but concludes by saying the whole should only take one hour (pp. 96 & 98). It may be noted that these instructions must have been formulated no earlier than 1551 because that is when the metrical version of Ps. 119 was published. Poullain's catechism class must have sung something else before 1551, as the first Latin text (1551) simply says a Psalm, while later printings add the precision of Ps. 119, p. 96. The Latin also indicates that the explanation of the catechism focuses on the articles which are more familiar to the children and more accessible and engaging to the people ("carnosius nervosiusque," pp. 96-98). The instruction to begin with Ps. 119 is a rather apt parallel to the decalogue.

[141] Millet, "Rendre raison de la foi," p. 202. Although obviously there were three divisions more than Sundays, there is no explicit explanation for this.

[142] See chap. 2 at nn.76, 90f, *et passim*.

43 on the concluding petition of the Lord's Prayer, was preserved through publication. This catechism sermon will be examined in the context of Calvin's preaching. One important fact, which must have reassured even the preachers, and certainly the students, was that no one was expected to memorize the whole Geneva Catechism. It was the basis of education but not of examination.

The *Ecclesiastical Ordinances* of 1541 required only that each child "solemnly recite the summary of what is contained [in the catechism] and also make a profession of his faith [*chrestiente*] in the presence of the church."[143] This examination or profession did not include any attempt to assess inward piety; the goal here was objective knowledge, since conviction would come through the Holy Spirit.[144] The public occasion was conducted according to the very short "The Way of Questioning the Children Whom You Wish to Receive at the Supper of Our Lord Jesus Christ," which essentially required only the ability to recite the three main texts: Apostles' Creed, Decalogue, and Lord's Prayer, plus answer some relatively straight-forward questions about the sacraments. The catechetical examination was held the week before the celebration of the Lord's Supper; this was called the "Sunday of proclamation" because it announced the coming sacramental occasion and it was the logical time to admit those who were deemed ready to participate in the Supper. When the examination was first instituted in

---

[143] *Ordinances*, OS II, p. 356: "Quant ung enfant sera suffisamment instruict pour se passer du cathechisme, qu'il recite solennellement la somme de ce qui y sera contenu: et aussi qu'il face comme une profession de sa chrestienté en presence de l'esglise." The reforming work of Valerain Poullain, Calvin's successor in Strasbourg and pastor of the French refugees in London, and that of Johannes a Lasco, leader of the Strangers' Church in London, both discuss the examination of catechumens but do not describe the outline of the catechism service. See Poullain, *Liturgia Sacra*, pp. 217, 219; A Lasco, *Opera*, vol. 2, pp. 91-100. A Lasco appears to include an explanation of the catechism in the Sunday afternoon service following the sermon, and says the boys recite it in the vernacular according to their ranks or orders, and then a Psalm is sung before the benediction, pp. 91, 98. The make-up of the Strangers' Church as communities of religious refugees was notably different from Calvin's Genevan situation, and both Poullain and A Lasco could reckon with more committed members. This is evident in the fact that A Lasco outlines two catechetical procedures for different ages of children. The first was for children of five or six who would learn the Lesser Catechism, i.e., to recite the Lord's Prayer, Apostles' Creed, and Decalogue; they are taught by their parents and then examined by the ministers on two occasions during the year, pp. 94-97. The second catechism for adolescents or young adults involved a weekly explanation of the more advanced teaching during the Sunday afternoon service. The students were taught by their parents or (other) teachers, and the Sunday afternoon occasion appears to be more of a public demonstration, including explaining the scriptural bases for the teachings, than the primary locus of instruction, pp. 97-98.

[144] For a fuller picture of the context of this profession of faith in Calvin's understanding of the marks of Christians, see introduction at nn.10ff. For Calvin's teaching on the work of the Holy Spirit, see *Inst.* 1.7.4, 3.2.33-37; also excerpts from sermons quoted in chap. 6 at nn.203ff, esp. nn.207ff.

1542, this meant the addition of a second hour to the regular noon catechism on the day of the catechetical test. In mid-1556, however, it was decided to drop the regular lesson on this day, effectively reducing the ministers' work at least slightly. Three years later in the baptismal records, Jean Macar once identifies this service as the "sermon d'examen."[145]

IV: The Lord's Day in Geneva

The centrality of Sunday for the Reformed tradition is well-known and obvious from the discussion above. The way that Geneva observed this special day, with multiple services at various hours and the prohibition of ordinary work, is also generally common knowledge. There are details of the liturgical practice, however, which have been neglected and which, in context, fill out the picture of the Lord's Day worship in Calvin's Geneva.

Sunday Morning Worship in Calvin's Geneva

The Sunday morning service in Geneva could take one of two forms, and it developed somewhat over the course of Calvin's ministry. The two forms were the Lord's Day service with the Lord's Supper, which was celebrated four times per year, and the Lord's Day service without the sacrament.[146] While it is clear that Calvin wanted to hold the Supper much more frequently than the Genevan government allowed, for most Sundays of the year the service was essentially focused on the Word, so the service will be outlined as it was practiced both with the sacrament and without. The structural changes over time will be incorporated into each form of the service. Since in early modern Europe it was virtually impossible for all members of a community to gather at the same time, Geneva dealt with this situation by scheduling worship services at two different times on the most important days. The description of Sunday morning applies in principle, therefore, to both the dawn and the main service at 8 a.m.

---

[145] Jean Macar, March 19, 1559, St. Gervais: "au sermon de l'examen" in baptismal records. Aug. 18, 1556; OC 21:645 (RC 51 f268v): "De l'examen qui souloit estre faict apres le cathesimes le dimenche devant la cene a esté mis en avant que se fist de heure en avant ledit examen au lieu dudit cathesimes que checune dimenche devant checune cene, etc. Az este arresté qu'il es trouvé bon que se face de heure en avant comme sus dict est."

[146] The source for this is a combination of Grosse, *Les rituels de la Cène*, and personal examination of the texts. Grosse provides an annotated table of all the services, pp. 658-65; this has been very useful to me, though at some points my interpretation is different.

The Organization in 1542

The Sunday service began with the ringing of the bells which called the people to worship. [147] All were supposed to enter and sit down quietly (without the traditional genuflecting). In time the question of precedence and arguments about seating would become a very serious issue, but in the beginning what was most noticeable was the fact that, contrary to medieval practice in which most of the faithful moved around freely, everyone was seated. [148] When the minister entered and went up into the pulpit, the people would kneel while he said the opening words: "Our help is in the name of the Lord, who made heaven and earth," then a sentence of invitation inviting the people to confess their sins, and the confession, for which a text was printed in the liturgy. [149] The people might respond with "So be it" or "Amen" as they promptly began to rise to their feet to resume their seats. Then the congregation, led by the children, [150] sang a Psalm.

---

[147] Various regulations indicate that the bells would begin ringing half an hour or an hour before the service; then they were rung a second time to announce the start of the service. On Sept. 27, 1548, Calvin's servant identifies the time one Sunday afternoon as "come le second coup du sermon sonnoit du vespre," *Consist.* IV, p. 141. See above at n.109 & below at n.169 for reference in table of Psalms. Other examples: see Lambert, *Preaching, Praying, and Policing,* pp. 290-91, nn.23, 24. Grosse, *Les rituels de la Cène,* p. 165.

[148] Grosse, *Les rituels de la Cène,* pp. 272-77, 579-84. Cathelan, *Passevent Parisien,* p. 27, "Tu demandes s'ilz prient en commun ou en particulier, non: mais tout incontinent qu'ilz sont entrez dedens l'église, chacun prend garde de choisir place et s'assoir, comme dedens une escolle, et là attendant que le prêcheur se monstre, chacun se met à genoilx, sauf luy mesme qui est de bout en priant, teste descouverte, à mains joinctes, et faict une oraison composée à sa fantasie, la concluant par le *Pater noster,* sans *Ave Maria,* le tout en François, et le peuple tout bas respond: *Ainsi soit-il.*"

[149] Late in his life Calvin responded to a question about the lack of an assurance of forgiveness, *Consilium,* Aug. 12, 1561, OC 10:213: "Confessioni publicae adiungere insignem aliquam promissionem, quae peccatores ad spem veniae et reconciliationis erigat, nemo nostrum est qui non agnoscat utilissimum esse. Atque ab initio hunc morem inducere volui: sed quum offensionem quidam ex novitate metuerent, nimium facilis fui ad cedendum. Ita res omissa est. Nunc vero non esset opportunum hic quidquam mutare: quia, antequam ad finem confessionis ventum fuerit, magna pars incipit surgere. Quo magis optamus, dum vobis integrum est, populum vestrum ad utrumque assuefieri." English in *Calvin's Ecclesiastical Advice,* pp. 95-96. This corroborates Cathalan's note about kneeling. The issue of why the Geneva 1542 liturgy does not include an assurance of pardon has been debated. Grosse claims that this would not have been an innovation because Farel's liturgy had one (see n.62 above), and goes on to give a brief overview of theories advanced by scholars, including the idea that the Lord's Supper was a kind of enacted absolution, or that it would contradict the self-examination called for in the Supper service. Grosse, *Les rituels de la Cène,* pp. 145-47.

[150] In the city, music education was provided by special teachers, although in village churches the minister usually had this responsibility; see the comments of Perrot on singing at catechism, quoted above at n.138. See also his reference to leading Sunday worship in the more able parish of Moens: "Je ne chantois pas volontiers au sermon quant il n'y avoit nul homme qui m'aydast,

The minister offered a prayer for understanding and receiving the teaching of the scripture. Liturgical scholars normally call this a prayer for illumination, but the text does not give it any title, and according to Calvin's theology this could more appropriately be named a prayer for illumination *and sealing*. There are two aspects of the work of the Holy Spirit, one affecting the mind and the other the heart; Calvin prayed for both the opening of the understanding and the heartfelt reception (sealing). [151] Unlike the Strasbourg liturgy, which gave a text for this prayer, in Geneva the minister was free to compose his own, although it is probable that most pastors developed a fairly fixed form for their own use. This prayer concluded with a recitation of the Lord's Prayer, which may have been recited by the minister or may have been spoken also by the people, who certainly were expected to know it and at least to follow along silently. [152] Then the minister read the next section of the Biblical text he was currently expounding, beginning where he had left off the previous Sunday, and preached his sermon. Immediately there followed the prayer of intercession. This was attached to the

---

mais bien avec un homme quand il n'y eust point eu de femmes ou filles pour ayder. [names some parishioners who can sing, including visitors from the city]," Lambert, *Preaching, Praying, and Policing*, Appendix 4, pp. 541-42.

[151] Various forms of Calvin's prayers along with those of other preachers are found in the third appendix of Grosse, *Les rituels de la Cène*, pp. 666-69. See also Calvin's preface to the Psalter, OS II, p. 13, describing active worship: "Ce n'est pas une chose morte ne brutifve, que bonne affection envers Dieu : mais est un mouvement vif, procedant du sainct Esprit, quand le cœur est droictement touché, et l'entendement illuminé." *Inst.* 3.2.7 for definition of faith which gives the language: essentially knowledge of the gospel "which is revealed to our minds and sealed on our hearts by the Holy Spirit." OS IV, p. 16: "divinae erga nos benevolentiae firmam certamque cognitionem, quae gratuitae in Christo promissionis veritate fundata, per Spiritum sanctum et revelatur mentibus nostris et cordibus obsignatur." A vernacular form of this is found in his sermons on 1 Cor.; see chap. 6 at nn.208f.

[152] It is not clear whether the congregation recited the Lord's Prayer aloud with or after the minister. Grosse, *Les rituels de la Cène*, p. 191, leaves this open. However, there are examples of public occasions which include the recitation of the Lord's Prayer as part of the opening procedure. On Nov. 25, 1537, when the General Council gathered to discuss business with Bern, the record begins: "Ainsin que cela est esté leu et dicte l'oraison dominicale, chescung se taisant, A. Chap. Rouge a dict..." RC II, p. 398. Here it is not clear to what the "se taisant" refers; the officials in charge may have spoken everything, but it is also possible that the whole assembly might have recited the Prayer and then become silent for Chapeau Rouge to speak. On a similar occasion two years later, it appears that the whole body did recite the Prayer. On Nov. 16, 1539, the General Council "avant toutes choses, l'on az invoquer l'ayde du vrayct Saulveur, disant, tous de cueur: 'Nostre Pere quil est aut ciel etc.'" RC IV, p. 510. This probably means "by heart" or from memory, although that does not guarantee that all were speaking. On May 9, 1544, a woman says she goes to church "à la bonne intence en priant Dieu apres le pregiory"; *Consist.* I, p. 367 n. 293 explains that "pregiory" probably means preacher or one who prays. It is possible that the woman is reciting the Prayer aloud after the preacher, but it is more likelz that she means she followed his words while being silent herself, cf. Beza in n.156 below.

sermon itself by a fairly brief "individual" petition linked to the sermon thematically, which led into the formally established prayer printed in the liturgy. This long intercession gives particular attention to specific petitions for many groups of the faithful (a practice shaped by Reformed exegesis of 1 Tim. 2:1-2),[153] and a paraphrase of the Lord's Prayer. The Apostles' Creed followed,[154] and the service concluded with the benediction from Num. 6:24-26.

When the Lord's Supper was celebrated, the Lord's Day service became the full form of word and sacrament. The first part, up through the sermon, remained the same. Then the prayer of intercession was expanded by the insertion of a specific eucharistic text, followed by the Apostles' Creed. This may have been recited by all the people but was probably spoken by the minister in their name, although certainly all were expected to know it and follow along silently.[155] Probably at this point the minister would descend from the pulpit and take his place at the tables, facing the people. The tables were not a fixed furnishing of the churches in Geneva but were set up and prepared for the service each time the Supper was celebrated. There were two tables, because men and women were expected to present themselves separately, each line walking forward to its table.[156] The tables would be covered with white cloths, and large wafers of unleavened bread would be placed at one end, and large cups for wine at the other end. At the beginning of the reform Farel had introduced the use of ordinary bread. However, in 1538 unleavened bread was re-adopted as part of the Bernese "ceremonies," although it was stipulated that the wafers must be large enough to be broken into pieces to allow for the *fractio panis* or

---

153 See McKee, "Calvin Never Changed His Mind," pp. 18-36.

154 Grosse, *Les rituels de la Cène*, p. 663 n. 21, indicates that although none of the French versions of the liturgy include this, the Latin translation published by Estienne in 1563 (*Rudimenta fidei Christianae,vel Rudis et elementaria quaedam institutio : quam Catechismum veteres appelarunt*, p. 293), does so. Personal examination indicates also that this text gives the Sunday and day of prayer liturgies in Greek and Latin on facing pages; following the prayer of intercession, before the section added on Supper Sundays, there is a rubric. "Posthaec recitatur Apostolorum symbolum" (p. 293).

155 Grosse, *Les rituels de la Cène*, pp. 199-20, indicates that it is uncertain. See the comments of Theodore Beza, *Cours sur les Épîtres aux Romains et aux Hébreux, 1564-66*, edd. P. Fraenkel & L. Perrotet (Geneva: Droz, 1988), p. 182 on Rom. 10:9: "Requiritur ergo *confessio* non frigida, sed quae *ore* procedat. Ennunciatur [!] singulari etiam numero, ut intelligamus, nostro ore, *non* alieni virtute *confiteri*. Singulis dedit, non tamen facias hoc pro tota ecclesia. Praeit pastor. Ecclesia non audire debet, sed sequi – non alta voce, ne tumultus fiat in ecclesia."

156 Grosse, *Les rituels de la Cène*, pp. 217, 203. That the pastor would face the people was the common Protestant practice, different from the traditional Roman priest's stance with his back to the people so that he could face east. *Ordinances*, OS II, p. 344: "Que les tables soient pres de la chaire, affin que le mistere se puysse mieulx commodement exposer pres des tables."

breaking of the bread. [157] When Calvin returned in 1541 he tolerated the continuation of unleavened bread as a secondary matter (*adiaphoron*). The wine could
be either red or white; the only requirement was that it should be pure wine of
good quality. (In the celebration of the Mass wine and water were mixed, but
Protestants generally rejected this idea. The one practical exception Calvin
would allow was a situation in which there was not enough wine to serve the
whole church, in which case water might be added simply to assure that all could
participate.) [158] Large containers of wine were placed under the tables, so that the
cups could be refilled as needed. All the equipment was simple but good: made
of tin or pottery. [159]

At the table the minister spoke the text of 1 Cor. 11:23-29 and the exhortation
to communion prepared in the liturgy. Then the designated ministers joined him.
The pastor was the only one who could offer the bread, but in Geneva elders or
deacons (and occasionally a theology professor) were honored with the assignment to offer the cup. First the ministers received the bread and wine, then the
people. During the distribution of the elements, the liturgy called for the singing
of Psalms or reading some appropriate scripture. It is possible that Psalms were

---

[157] Breaking the bread was part of the practice but not a matter of great moment in Geneva; later it
would become one of the most noted symbols by which the Reformed churches in Germany
distinguished themselves from Lutherans. There was of course no marking on the wafers.
Grosse, *Les rituels de la Cène*, pp. 225-29.

[158] Insisting that Christ's teaching alone must be followed, Calvin rejected the tradition of mixing
water with wine which the Roman church based on its interpretation of I John 5:6 and John 19:
34. Calvin makes a practical exception: if there is not enough wine, one can add water to make it
sufficient for the service! *Consilium* April 5, 1558; OC 10: 212: "Si penuria sit vini, exiguum quod
suppetet aqua diluere, ut toti ecclesiae sufficiat, minime absurdum erit. Si religio iniicitur, ac si
necessaria foret mixtio, superstitione hoc non caret."

[159] Grosse, *Les rituels de la Cène*, pp. 217-19. See the description by Cathelan, *Passevent Parisien*,
p. 74: "Par trois ou quatre fois l'année selon le vouloir des Seigneurs et Princes, deux tables
sont dressées en l'église, et chacune est couverte d'une nappe, et puis au bout de vers main
gauche sont à force d'oblies, et à l'autre bout de main droicte sont trois ou quatre tasses, ou
verres, et au dessouz des tables force potz d'estain à frein, pleins de vin blanc ou claret
indifféremment. Et après le sermon le prédicant descend de la chaire, et se va mettre au bout de
la table, du costé des oblies, et à teste descouverte tout debout en baille à chacun un morceau
en sa main, disant: *Qu'il vous souvienne que Jésus-Christ est mort pour vous*, et ainsi chacun en
mengant son morceau d'oblie marche à l'autre bout de la table, pour prendre à boire de la main
d'un des Seigneurs, ou autre à ce député, sans rien dire, et les sergents servent de verser à boire
à teste descouverte, et fournir des oblies s'ils deffaillent, et ce pendant un autre lit en chaire en
langage vulgaire, teste descouverte, l'Evangile Sainct Jean, depuis le commencement du
treizième chapitre, et continuant jusques à ce que chacun ait prins son morceau tant hommes
que femmes, chacun en sa table différente, et les enfans et filles de l'aage de huict à dix ans
pour le moins, et après que telle collation est achevée chacun s'en va disner s'il en a, sinon qu'il
en cherche."

sung but the only explicit evidence involves reading;[160] either the appointment of specific persons (often teachers) to do this, or an indication of the text of a passion narrative (one visitor claims it was the Gospel of John, beginning at chapter 13).[161] In 1542, as he delivered the piece of bread into each person's hands, Calvin was probably speaking the words "Take, eat, this is the body of Jesus which was broken for you; do this in memory of Him." Later he would discontinue the practice because it was impractical since as the line moved forward no one person was before him long enough to hear the complete sentence.[162] When all had communed the minister spoke the thanksgiving prayer printed in the liturgy, and gave the benediction.

In principle, an offering for the poor was intended to complete the Lord's Supper service, as a sign of the love of neighbor which Calvin believed the sacrament should and would increase. In Strasbourg in his small poor refugee

---

[160] Grosse, *Les rituels de la Cène*, p. 233, says that reading and singing alternated; p. 234 n.243, he cites Henri Vuilleumier, *Eglise réformée au Pays de Vaud*, tome 2, p. 429, as saying that in the Vaud singing and reading alternated and that this practice was inspired by Genevan usage.

[161] Here Grosse has hesitations regarding the personnel similar to those about the elders and deacons helping to serve communion; see *Les rituels de la Cène*, pp. 232-33. In fact, the Thomas Genod whom Grosse names as an example, applied on Dec. 6, 1538, to become a deacon, i.e., assistant minister to visit the sick, baptize, marry, make announcements, as well as read the passion for the Supper. The Senate's response was to stick with "les nostres" and not ask "estrangiers" but they also decide to inquire of the ministers whether Genod would be suitable to be a deacon, RC III, p. 512. The point was not that the passion could not be read by a non-minister but that this man was not employed by the city. Within a few weeks, on Dec. 23, 1538, the Senate asked the school teachers to do this – apparently essentially because they were "les nostres" and qualified by their education, cf. chap. 2 at n.24. Even former Catholic clergy were acceptable, although those questioned about this (because they did not do it) explained that no one gave them the book and they were too poor to own the New Testament; April 20, 1542, *Consist.* I, p. 40. The point is that reading the scripture during communion was not assigned to a particular office in Protestant Geneva.

[162] Calvin's letter of counsel Aug. 12, 1561: "In administering the Lord's Supper I have sometimes used Paul's words, but I preferred to stop doing this because the words could not be repeated to each individual without a long delay; and if numbers of people went across [in front of him as he gave the bread] during the recitation, scarcely one in ten understood what I wanted understood, and no one grasped the entire meaning" (OC 10:213), *Calvin's Ecclesiastical Advice*, p. 96. The Strasbourg liturgy of 1545 gives the words "Prenez, mangez, le corps de Iesus, qui a esté livré à la mort pour vous"; Pauline words in the 1542 Genevan text of 1 Cor. 11:24: "Prenez, mangez, cecy est mon corps, qui est rompu pour vous: faictes cecy en memoire de moy." *La forme des prières*, OS II, pp. 49, 46. Given the Strasbourg example, it seems probable that Calvin would not say "my body" but "the body of Jesus." See n.159 above where Cathelan affirms that a phrase was said when he visited Geneva, though obviously he would not have received communion to hear it. Cathelan does not actually say that it was Calvin who spoke the words; his informant might have referred to another pastor, or it might be that Calvin was still trying to use the words in 1552.

congregation he probably practiced such a collection on the day of the monthly Lord's Supper,[163] but the situation in Geneva was different. In practice, such offerings seem to have been found in Geneva's territory but not regularly in the city parishes for many years. There is evidence that in 1542 Satigny set up a box in which the people were to deposit their alms, and on the Supper Sunday Pastor Bernard urged them to contribute as they were able. When this did not prove very effective, starting on Easter in 1554 he began to have the guards (more-or-less the rural equivalent of deacons) rise and walk about the church to collect an offering while he, the minister, moved from the pulpit to the table for the sacrament. In the city it was ordered that alms boxes be installed in the churches in 1545, but this did not actually happen until 1568. That year, after some debate, the Senate ordered boxes to be put in each church at the door and men to be chosen from each parish to stand at the doors at the exit from the Sunday sermons to urge the people to contribute; five men are named for each of the three parishes. Apparently the alms offering became the general practice by 1580, usually every Sunday although in some parishes it was only the day of the Lord's Supper.[164]

The Mid-1540s to 1562

The order of the Sunday morning service experienced a change, probably in the mid-1540s, when a second time of Psalm singing was added, after the long prayer of intercession and the Creed. According to the table of Psalms to be sung, by 1549 or (if it is assumed that the first table was identical) already by 1546,[165] on the day when the Lord's Supper was celebrated, the singing of the Decalogue replaced the second Psalm.[166] The minister probably descended from the pulpit

---

[163] McKee, *John Calvin on the Diaconate*, chap. 2, esp. 38ff for Reformed, pp. 50-63 for Calvin and Geneva; pp. 58-60 quotes the organization of the church boxes and collection in 1568. The deacons of the French congregation in London did collect an offering during the service and at the door, according to Poullain, *Liturgia Sacra*, pp. 60-63.

[164] Grosse, *Les rituels de la Cène*, pp. 237-39; quotation of text by Pastor Bernard of Satigny, p. 238.

[165] "Ce mesme jour de la saincte Cene, on chante communement les Commandemens de Dieu, au lieu du Pseaume qu'on devoit chanter suyvant l'ordre de la presente table. Exod. 20. Leve le cœur." Facsimile of *Les Psaumes* 1562, ed. Pidoux. Pidoux, *Psautier huguenot*, vol. II, p. 44, gives this instruction but it was not found in all the tables; see *Pseaumes Octantetrois de David* printed in Geneva by Jean Crespin in 1551 which lacks it.

[166] There is some argument about whether the decalogue came before or after the creed, and when the minister moved from pulpit to table. Jenny, *Die Einheit*, pp. 132-133, discusses the two together; the decalogue could be either after the [prayer &] creed, or immediately after the sermon, before the intercessory prayer [& creed]. He says the former solution suggests that pastor comes down from pulpit during the singing of the Decalogue, the latter solution leaves this movement unclear. Jenny's reason for preferring second solution is theological: it puts the three catechetical pieces in the Supper service one after the other, in Biblical order: Decalogue,

during the singing, and went to the tables to read 1 Cor. 11:23-29 and the exhortation which led into the communion itself. The same table of Psalms also included a rubric stating that the singing of the Song of Simeon would be "au lieu de" the prayer of thanksgiving in the liturgy.[167] It is quite possible that here "in the place of" is more a reference to the location of the singing than an indication that it actually replaced the spoken prayer, because there is evidence that both sung and spoken prayer were or could be used.[168]

By 1562 the order for Sunday morning had expanded to include a third time of singing, at the very beginning of the service immediately after the bells,[169] which was the only change in the first half of the service since 1542. On the day of the Lord's Supper, the order was the same as in previous years since the tables of Psalms had been introduced. Now the instructions about the Decalogue and the Song of Simeon were expanded by the indication of which days Geneva cele-

---

prayer, creed. From this order he concludes that these are part of Supper liturgy and since the pastor could not change places in midst of that liturgy, he must remain in pulpit until after excommunication and exhortation (see Jenny's table, pp. 116-117 n.6). On p. 131 he says the earliest the preacher could leave the pulpit was after the creed. However, though Jenny mentions the connection of the prayers with sermons (p. 130), which terminate immediately in prayer, with no gap, even on Supper Sundays, he does not seem to take this seriously. It contradicts the evidence of Calvin's sermons to say that a Psalm or song could be introduced between the sermon and the prayer,* which means the decalogue must come after the prayer. Grosse makes the same observation about sermon and prayer in his discussion of Jenny, and adds that the 1576 revision of the *Ordinances* clarifies this point: the pastor comes to the table after the full sequence from prayer-scripture-sermon-through prayer-creed, cf. *Les rituels de la Cène*, p. 202. *The exception is the probability that the pastor makes announcements between sermon and prayer, as it is clear happens when there are special events like the reconciliation of sinners; see below at nn.171f.

167 "Le jour qu'on celebre la saincte Cene de nostre Seigneur Jesus Christ selon son ordonnance, apres icelle on chante pour action de grace le cantique de Symeon. Luc. 2. Or laisse createur." Pidoux, *Psautier huguenot*, vol. II, p. 44, gives this note but it was not found in all the tables; see *Pseaumes Octantetrois de David* printed in Geneva by Jean Crespin in 1551.

168 Grosse indicates the uncertainty about whether the Song of Simeon replaced the prayer, and cites the practice of Charles Perrot for an example of the combination of the two, *Les rituels de la Cène*, p. 167 cf. n. 196. About 1564, when he was preparing instructions for his successor in a village church, Perrot wrote: "On chante à la Cene le 23 tout du commencement et le Cantique de Symeon tout à la fin, asçavoir devant la derniere priere et action des graces," Lambert, *Preaching, Praying, and Policing*, p. 541. It should be noted that in his introduction Perrot says that he received from his predecessors most of what he passed on, so his evidence may well antedate his own years in this parish: "De ma part je apprins et receu de mes predecesseurs et mesmement de feu Mons. Maubué la plus [grande partie?] de ce que j'ay receuly cy-apres." Lambert, p. 540.

169 "Pour le Dimanche au matin, apres le second coup de la cloche." Facsimile of *Les Psaumes* 1562, ed Pidoux.

brated the Lord's Supper: Easter, Pentecost, the first Sunday in September, and "the Sunday closest to the nativity of our Lord Jesus."[170]

Announcements

It is well known that public worship was the place for community announcements, and many of these were directly related to the liturgical or ecclesiastical life of the people. Exactly when these happened in the order of worship is somewhat unclear. It is possible that there was not a single fixed place for all of them, but this seems unlikely since it would contribute to confusion to have the pastor interrupt the service more than once. Normally the contents might be such routine matters as banns for marriages or the less frequent but roughly analogous public notices necessary for dissolving an engagement or marriage, and may well have included baptisms: that is, telling the congregation to stay seated after the apparent end of the service in order to witness a baptism! Although there is no explicit evidence, it is possible that deaths in the community were also announced at this time. One visitor writing about the early 1550s says that marriage banns were made before "the sermon" (which may mean before the whole service or before the prayer-and-scripture-and-sermon). According to one country pastor, in his parish these might come after the concluding prayers.[171] At least some liturgies published for the French congregation in London explicitly placed all announcements between the sermon and the intercessory prayer,[172] and this may have been the case in Geneva.

---

[170] "On chante les Commandemens de Dieu (Leve le Coeur, ouvre l'aureille, Exode 20) apres le sermon le jour qu'on celebre la saincte Cene de nostre Sauveur Jesus Christe : laquelle on celebre quatre fois l'an: asçavoir, A Pasque, A la Pentcoste, Au premier Dimanche de Septembre, & au plus prochain Dimanche de la Nativité de nostre Seigneur Jesus. On chante en l'action de graces le Cantique de Simeon. Or laisses, createur, Luc. 2." Facsimile of *Les Psaumes* 1562.

[171] cf. Cathalan, *Passevant Parisien*, p. 75, the deacons [he means assistant ministers, not Calvinist deacons] "dénoncent les fiancez tous les dimenches, avant le sermon seulement." cf. Charles Perrot's account of his country parish @1564; if he has something to communicate at a weekday sermon, he does it before the benediction because after it the people leave too quickly; Lambert, *Preaching, Praying, and Policing*, Appendix 4, p. 543: "Quant j'avois quelque chose à proposer aux paroiciens, je les en advertissois au bout des prieres pour faire arrester les maistres d'autant qu'apres la benediction ilz s'en vont trop viste." Grosse, *Les rituels de la Cène*, p. 390, gives examples of excommunication, although without indication of the point in the sermon. In Reformed liturgies perhaps the best known example of the announcing of deaths is Zwingli's Sunday liturgy, cf. "Ein kurtze gmeine form, kinder ze touffenn, die ee ze bestäten, die predig anzefahen und zuo enden, wie es zuo Zürich gebrucht wirdt." The third section: "Ein form des bittens nach der leer Pauli, 1. Timoth. 2[1-7], die man yetz Zürich brucht im anfang der predigen" [different printing has Predigtgottesdienstes]; this appeared in 1526 and several later printings; critical edition *Huldreich Zwinglis Sämtliche Werke*, vol. 4, p. 688.

[172] Poullain, *Liturgia Sacra*, p. 61 : "Et acheve son sermon en une heure. Et puis il faict les prieres en la forme qu'il s'ensuit, apres avoir advisé et admonesté l'Eglise, s'il y a quelque chose de nouveau

Besides the day-to-day business of banns or baptisms, there were other types of less frequent and arguably more important communications – particularly regarding elections and presentations of new pastors or elders in the city or the reconciliation of penitent apostates – and there is evidence for when these were done. The extant examples from late in Calvin's life indicate that at least these special notices would be inserted between the sermon and the long intercessory prayers. In the case of new ministers they would be introduced at St. Pierre in the morning, and in the afternoon at St. Gervais, so that they were formally recognized by both sides of the city. The Company of Pastors records this for Jean Macar and Louis Enoch on May 10, 1556, but unfortunately Calvin's sermon for that day is missing, because he collapsed in the pulpit and could not finish.[173] However, the procedure is visible in the records of his sermons on the Gospel Harmony. By 1560 this presentation of the church's new ministers was extended to include the elders; in the service on Sunday morning, Feb. 11, 1560, Calvin introduced the men who had been elected the previous week to serve on the consistory. According to the way his sermon is printed, it is clear that this took place immediately after the sermon, before the preacher began the prayers, which fits with Calvin's teaching in other places about the importance of making special intercessions for these very significant occasions in the life of the church.[174] Some months later at the end of sermon #59 the preacher announced the election of Jean-Reymond Merlin to be pastor in Geneva and invited the people to report if they had any reason to think he was not fit. The following Sunday morning in the

---

survenu, Si comme pour les paovres, et pour les malades demandans les prieres et aide de l'eglise : puis s'il y a quelque mariage, il le denonce semblablement." Also in Latin, p. 60 : "Concionem horae spatio absolvit, ac subiecta precatione concludit. Admonet autem prius Ecclesiam, si qua sunt digna aut necessaria. Nempe si sponsalia sint, si baptismus, si quis pauper, aut aegrotus se commendat precibus Ecclesiae, et caetera eiusmodi." Here baptisms are included among the announcements. Since this list is not exhaustive, presumably deaths were also included, at least by Poullain. What might have been named in Geneva is unclear, although baptisms are likely (if the people needed to be told to remain in their seats after the intercessory prayer).

[173] RCP, II, p. 67 ; cf. chap. 7 at n.219.

[174] *Les sermons sur l'harmonie evangelique...*, #29, pp. 526-27, OC 46:361-62. Note that the editor of these sermons includes after #28 preached on Feb. 4, 1560, the exhortation which Calvin made at the General Council meeting, but it is printed after the Sunday morning sermon *and* its prayer, confirmation that it was not included in the service itself; pp. 506-08, OC 46:347-48. The appropriateness of signaling civic elections to the people in the context of worship is seen in various places. One such is Calvin's sermon on 1 Cor. 7:3-5, where he indicates that the early [model] church practiced prayers and fasting when there was some significant task such as electing ministers of the church. When Calvin goes on to apply this to Geneva, he adds the election of magistrates ("seigneurs de justice") as another such occasion. See sermon #42, Ms.fr. 26, f347v-348r. See chap. 4 at nn.118, 129.

last part of his sermon (#60) Calvin spoke of the call of Merlin and asked the
people to pray for their new minister, before he himself began the major intercessory prayer.[175]

Besides presenting new ministers, the Sunday morning service became the key
place for the reconciliation of sinners. Perhaps the earliest Protestant service to
demonstrate this was in June 1536, although since that was a case of Roman
priests asking forgiveness for saying Mass it may well have been an isolated event.
At least by 1542 it had become customary for rituals which marked the resolution
of quarrels to be formally held after worship services at the church door, but this
was not strictly a liturgical act.[176] However, by 1560 Calvin and his colleagues had
begun a formal rite of reconciliation for those who had committed the most
serious sins, particularly apostasy. After such individuals had proved their contri-
tion to the consistory, they made a formal act of repentance and received the
welcome back into the fellowship – now at the Sunday morning service. What
appears to be the first recorded instance of this rite of reconciliation was held
probably on March 10, 1560, and the notes about the act are included in Calvin's
sermon for the day. Again, the place in the liturgy was between the sermon and
the prayer of intercession.[177]

Sunday Afternoon Worship in Geneva

The Sunday afternoon service in Geneva has often been overlooked or
sometimes misconstrued by scholars. One common assumption is that the
afternoon was the same as the morning, except that the Lord's Supper was
never celebrated then. In fact, it is not entirely clear what the form for the
afternoon was, but it was not identical to the morning. *La forme des prieres* nowhere
says explicitly what the order for Sunday afternoon is. The Sunday rubric refers
only to the morning; the heading of the service in Strasbourg 1542 (which seems
not to have been copied in *Opera Selecta*) says "Pour le dimanche matin"[178] and *La
forme des prieres* gives a rubric "For Sundays in the morning (les Dimanches au
matin), the form which follows is commonly used."[179] The shape of the Sunday
afternoon service must be deduced from other liturgical sources. The most

---

[175] *Les sermons sur l'harmonie evangelique...*, OC 46:361-62, 748 & 760.

[176] See chap. 2 at n.152.

[177] *Les sermons sur l'harmonie evangelique...*, #33, pp. 595-97; OC 46:410-412.

[178] *La maniere de faire prieres...* [Rome] 1542, p. 4.

[179] OS II, p. 18; cf. Facsimile of *La Forme des Prières 1542*, p. i6r : "Pour les Dimanches au matin, on use communement de la forme qui s'ensuit."

obvious of these is the Psalter with its tables for Psalm singing, which from the beginning includes a column for Sunday afternoon.[180] Other evidence is found in the prayers with which Calvin concluded his sermons on Sunday afternoons, which identify the opening words of the "fixed part" as different from what is printed in *La forme des prieres*.[181] A further category of sources which cast light on the Sunday afternoon service are the various liturgies printed for the French Reformed congregation in exile in London. These provide explicit evidence that this body used a prayer for Sunday afternoons and weekdays that was different from the one for Sunday morning.[182]

Sunday afternoon worship in 1542 almost certainly began with the same invocation as Sunday morning, and probably included the sentence of invitation

---

[180] The form is the same as for Sunday morning and the day of prayer, changing each time those do. This contributes to the probability that the Sunday afternoon service also began with the exhortation to and confession of sins, since once the third time of singing was added in 1562 there would have been no break between the first Psalm time (as soon as the bell stopped ringing) and the regularly scheduled one before the pastor's prayer for illumination-and-sealing, scripture reading, and sermon.

[181] Some aspects of Calvin's sermon prayers will be examined in chap. 6 at nn.134ff.

[182] There were at least two printings of *La forme des prières* in French by refugee congregations in 1552, the one edited in Poullain's *Liturgia Sacra* and a different text, a copy of which is now preserved in the Bodleian (here designated "Bodleian"). There were also at least three printings of the Latin translation by Poullain, in 1551, 1554, 1555, also edited in *Liturgia Sacra*. The 1551 Latin (*Liturgia Sacra*, p. 98) only gives a rubric: the "Liturgia Vespertina" begins at 4 p.m., includes two Psalms, one before the sermon and one after; the sermon is *lectio continua*. This text leaves the prayer after the sermon to the minister's discretion and specifies one hour for the whole; it does not provide a model prayer. The French of 1552 (*Liturgia Sacra*, pp. 98 & 99-103) says that the service begins after the catechism, specifies that the pastor is preaching from the New Testament in sequence, and then speaks of the prayer after the sermon: "et à la fin conclud par quelque priere à sa discretion: ou il use de ceste icy," p. 99. Then follows a rubric "Priere Au sermon du Dimanche apres disner, et aux sermons quotidians" and a long prayer, pp. 101, 103. The other 1552 printing of *La forme des prieres* (Bodleian) is different from the one edited in *Liturgia Sacra*, as both title and contents make clear, but it was evidently intended for use in England because it includes prayers for the king like those in *Liturgia Sacra*. It is notable that this petition is found in the Sunday afternoon and weekday prayers (*Liturgica Sacra*, p. 103, Bodleian *La forme des prières*, p. 13r), with the main difference that the one *Liturgia Sacra* is slightly fuller, and the rubrics in the two books are different. A more significant divergence between the two French texts is that *La forme des prières* in the Bodleian print gives two different prayers for Sunday afternoon and weekdays (pp. 10r-13v); the one like *Liturgia Sacra* is the second (pp. 12r-13v) and it is introduced with the rubric "Oraison prinse en partye du chapitre 9. de Daniel le prophete" (p. 12r). This is significantly different from Calvin's. The first prayer is not the same as Calvin's but has some common elements, including a form of the Lord's Prayer and the recitation of the Apostles' Creed; the Prayer is a paraphrase (the same idea but not identical to Calvin's Sunday morning one, whereas on Sunday afternoons and weekdays he simply recited it).

leading to the confession of sin itself.[183] The Psalm would follow and then the prayer for illumination and sealing, scripture, and sermon. This prayer before the scripture was left to the minister and Calvin used the one for ordinary weekdays. At the point of the long prayer of intercession, he went from the short fluid paragraph which reflected the sermon, to the prayer he usually used on ordinary weekdays[184] (not the Sunday morning or day of prayer texts printed in the liturgy). The words were left to the individual minister; there was no prescribed form, although as Calvin's sermons illustrate, the preacher was likely to forge his own pattern and stick to it. This prayer concluded with the words of the Lord's Prayer and was followed by the recitation of the Apostles' Creed. The Sunday afternoon service probably ended with the same benediction used in the morning.[185]

When the Psalm tables began to be published, the Sunday afternoon service experienced the same changes as the Sunday morning. In the mid-1540s a second time of singing was added after the sermon and the prayer of intercession with its recitation of the Lord's Prayer and Creed. By 1562 a third time of singing, at the very beginning of the service after the bells finished ringing, made the final change in the Sunday afternoon service during Calvin's ministry. It is this fact which offers circumstantial evidence for the afternoon service following the basic order for Sunday morning and the day of prayer, because if there were no confession of sin the first Psalm and the Psalm before the sermon would be immediately juxtaposed. (That is, the sentence of invitation and confession of sin were the main features of the liturgy before the original first Psalm. If there were no prayer, there would be no action or interval between the singing newly added in 1562 and the Psalm before the sermon.) It can be deduced, therefore, that the Sunday afternoon service basically followed the order of the morning, but it did not use the prayer for illumination-and-sealing or the intercessory prayer of the morning.

---

[183] This part of the service is speculative. Poullain's afternoon service seems to begin with the Psalm and go directly to the prayer for illumination-sealing; *Liturgia Sacra*, pp. 98, 99. There were a number of differences between the Poullain's liturgy and the Geneva one (e.g., the former provides for communion for the sick/dying), so it cannot be assumed that silence in Geneva should be filled in with information from London. However, with regard to the Sunday afternoon prayer being the same as that for ordinary weekdays, the London text merely makes explicit what is visible in Calvin's own prayers.

[184] For convenience these are designated "extempore #1," "extempore #2" and "extempore #3"; see chap. 6 at nn.134ff.

[185] The *La forme des prières* found in the Bodleian spells out the Creed; on the other hand, it gives a different benediction: "La grace de nostre Seigneur Jesus Christ. La charité de Dieu & la communication du sainct Esprit soit avec nous tous. Amen." (pp. 11v-12r).

V: Calvin's Teaching on the Lord's Supper in Historical Context

The theological debates over the Lord's Supper have been rehearsed and argued many times and the Calvinist Reformed teaching on discipline has long been a subject of legend. For the purposes of this examination of worship in Geneva, however, the main object is to provide an overview of how these issues affected the practical implementation of reform. Therefore the doctrinal arguments will be sketched as a context for Calvin's teaching and how that shaped the sacramental practice in Geneva.

The Historical Situation Sketched as a Paradigm

It is always dangerous to attempt to summarize anything as complex as the sixteenth-century Supper Strife. This short introduction to Calvin's thought offers itself only as a rough paradigm of the kinds of issues which must be considered. As the young Frenchman himself stated in 1536, the central locus of explicit arguments was the problem of Christ's presence in the Eucharist, more specifically in the elements per se. In Calvin's view this obscured the larger and more important question of the purpose for which Christ instituted the sacrament; disputes about how He was present missed the point of what the Supper was supposed to do.[186] While certainly not intended to put words in Calvin's mouth, the following paradigm can illustrate how his position was related to those of his senior colleagues.

The Purpose of the Lord's Supper and its Relationship to Salvation

The purpose of claiming "presence" was closely connected to concepts of access to salvation and understanding of Christology. Is it necessary for Christ to be present bodily in the sacrament in order to give the faithful access to saving grace, even if this requires defining the communication of properties to allow the ubiquity of His resurrected flesh? Lutherans answered yes. Or does the claim for ubiquity in fact contradict the reality of the resurrection by changing the humanity of the True God-True Man into some *tertium quid*? Grace is given by the Holy Spirit to the human spirit but is not connected to the Supper. This Zwinglian stance was intended to protect salvation by identifying the sacrament as thanksgiving, pledge, and memorial of the work of the resurrected Christ who is at God's

---

[186] *Institutes 1536*, OS I, p. 139: "Si haec vis sacramenti pro dignitate excussa expensaque esset, satis superque habebat, unde nobis satis fieret, nec excitatae essent horribiles istae dissensiones, quibus tum olim, tum nostra etiamnum memoria, ecclesia misere vexatat est; dum volunt curiosi homines definire, qomodo in pane praesens adsit Christi corpus."

right hand. In effect, the question of presence was so intensely argued because it focused the relationship between the Eucharist and access to grace. For both Protestant positions, grace is vitally important: for Luther, it must come through the real body and blood "in, with, and under" the sacrament (to use the language of the Augsburg Confession); for Zwingli it must come through the Spirit. Calvin agreed with Luther that the sacrament is a means of grace, but he denied that this required local bodily presence. He agreed with Zwingli that Christ's resurrected body is at the right hand of God and not ubiquitous, but he was equally insistent that this did not mean separating grace from the Supper. Believers truly receive the spiritual body and blood with the elements because the Holy Spirit lifts them to communion with Christ.

Ecclesiology and the Lord's Supper

The debate about the function of the Eucharist consumed much attention, leaving a second cluster of issues related to the doctrine of the church and actual practice of the sacrament to receive a more piecemeal response. Who are the people who share the Lord's Supper, how do they prepare, and how often do they celebrate? The Roman church had long required the sacrament of penance before communion, and every person was supposed to confess to his or her priest at least once a year before receiving the host, usually during Holy Week. The Mass itself was held daily, of course, but only the priest was obliged to commune and normally lay people observed (devoutly or not, according to their own level of preparation or attention). Protestants all insisted that this division was intolerable; the sacrament must not be a "private" act of the priest, and should not be held except with the participation of the faithful in the communion. Bearing in mind that a long tradition emphasized that eating (and drinking, which was not offered to laity in the late middle ages) unworthily would lead to damnation, this Protestant stance on the Lord's Supper required at least three further important decisions: how to determine worthiness, how frequently to celebrate, and what level of participation was expected of the people.[187]

For Protestants, worthiness was essentially defined in terms of faith, trusting in Christ's forgiveness and not in one's own works, recognizing oneself as a sinner

---

[187] The views and practices of Radical Reformers/ Anabaptists are not included here. The classical "Evangelical Anabaptist" paradigm identifies worthiness with an adult confession of faith for baptism, separation from the world, and a community of believers who share in a fellowship meal possible because they are baptized and unified (as assured by the practice of fraternal admonition). While participation and frequency are linked in ways similar to Calvin's ideas, other key factors (such as the purpose of the sacrament and the definition of the church) are different.

who could not possess any actual righteousness to merit God's acceptance but only receive Christ's imputed righteousness. This justifying faith was fundamental to salvation and not related in any exclusive way to the Lord's Supper, but it was also linked to the sacramental context in very tangible ways. Frequency of the Supper would be influenced by what it was believed to do. Was it a means of grace? Then it should be celebrated often. Was it a confession of faith and obedience to Christ's command to "do this," a memorial and thanksgiving and pledge? Then the frequency could be determined differently. A third question would naturally follow from each of these specific answers: If the Supper was a means of grace and therefore offered often, could individuals decide when they were ready to receive it and abstain at other times? If it was a pledge of the faith and obedience which the whole church shares, then must all participate or else be understood to deny their place in the community? The answer to both these questions was yes, but the practical consequences for the life of the church were quite different. The first position: frequent celebration and individual decision about communing, characterized Martin Luther's and other Lutheran liturgies (it is also explicit in Thomas Cranmer's first *Book of Common Prayer* and implicit in the second), and the answer was that the Supper could be celebrated weekly, since it was not obligatory that everyone commune every time.[188] The second position: a pledge and obedience which are needed only at intervals but which are required of the whole church, is characteristic of Zwingli's sacramental theology, and this fitted well with a Supper service four times per year, at which everyone was expected to commune. In neither case was ecclesiastical discipline theoretically linked to participation in the sacrament.[189] For the Calvinist Reformed, on the

---

[188] See Luther, *Formula Missae*, 1523, WA 12, pp. 215-16; Ernestine Saxony, *Gemeine verordnung und artikel der visitation in Meissen*...1533: Sehling I, p. 192: no Mass without communicants. Albertine Saxony, *Kirchenordnunge zum anfang, für die pfarherrn... 1539*, Sehling I, p. 272: "Communio. Wenn man communicanten hat, sol man... Wenn aber keine communicanten sein, so lass man..." *General-Artikel und gemeiner Bericht*, 1557, Sehling I, p. 318: "Von der communion,...Und so oft etzliche person der communion begeren, sol auch die communion also gehalten..." Leipzig, *Kirchenordnung... 1539*, Sehling, I, p. 593: "Auf alle festage und sontage. Soll in beiden kirchen die communion gehalten warden, zu S. Thomas und zu S. Niclas, so often communicanten vorhanden." Wolfenbüttel, *Kirchenordnung 1569*, Sehling VI/1, p. 143 "wenn communicanten vorhanden sein..." *Book of Common Prayer* 1549: "so manye as shalbe partakers of the holy Communion, shall tary still in the quire,... All other (that mynde not to receive the said holy Communion) shall departe out of the quire..." 1552: "al those that are mynded to receyve the holy Communion)," in *Liturgies of the Western Church*, ed. Bard Thompson (Cleveland & New York: Collins World, 1961/ 1975), pp. 254, 278.

[189] See "Action oder bruch dess nachtmals, gedächtnuss oder dancksagung Christi, wie sie uff ostren zuo Zürich angehept ist im jar 1525," *Huldreich Zwinglis sämtliche Werke*, ed. E. Egli & G. Finsler [Leipzig, 1904-90], vol. 4, p. 692: "Demnach tragind die verordneten diener das

other hand, there was a link between discipline and participation, but while that fact is well known, it is often not well understood. The conviction that there is such a link helps to illuminate the arguments over the (in)frequency of the celebration of the Supper, despite Calvin's expressed desire to the contrary. But that is getting ahead of the story.

A Summary of Calvin's Teaching

Calvin's teaching on the Lord's Supper is both too large a subject to encompass in a few pages (or even chapters) and also not the focus of the present work. However, it is helpful to note the key factors in his doctrine because the pastor's convictions guided ecclesiastical decisions just as civic and liturgical practice shaped the theology that the people in the pew received and (increasingly) accepted.

Sources of Calvin's Teaching

The Institutes of the Christian Religion provides Calvin's first clear presentation on the Supper.[190] Much of the text is devoted to arguing against Roman, Lutheran, and Zwinglian teaching, but the key affirmation regards the positive purposes of the sacraments as confirming or sealing the faith of believers, and secondarily serving as a pledge or confession of faith. Over the years the discussion of these two points would be further developed but the purposes themselves did not change – and both would have important consequences for practice. Sealing faith meant that participation in the Lord's Supper would strengthen believers by granting them a tangible support for the word of the gospel which they heard. It is the same gospel and yet in some way more real, adding touch to hearing, because human beings are weak and God graciously meets that need for something more than words. The sealing function of the sacrament not only confirms faith/trust in God but also incites believers to thanksgiving and gratitude to God and love for their neighbors. The secondary purpose Calvin names, as a confes-

---

ungeheblet brot harumb, und nemme ein jetlicher [jeder] glöubiger mit siner eygnen hand einen bitz oder mundvoll darvon, oder lasse im dasselbig bieten durch den diener, der das brot harumb treyt. Und so die mit dem brot so vil vorggangen sind, das ein yeder sin stücklin gessenn habe, so gangind die anderen diener mitt dem tranck hinnach und gebind glycherwyss einem yetlichen se trincken." This was begun by dividing the population into three groups, the young people on Maundy Thursday, middle aged on Good Friday, and old people on Easter, and instructions were given for celebration at Easter, Pentecost, autumn, and Christmas; cf. vol. 4, pp. 15-17. For how this was put into practice under Zwingli's successor Bullinger, see chap. 4 at n.29.

[190] See *Institutes 1536*, pp. 139-68; OS I, pp. 136-62.

sion of faith, both expresses and even in some sense defines the human, visible church, and the recognition of the individual as a member of the body of Christ. From the beginning, Calvin's discussion of the sacraments demonstrates his understanding of the relationship between the marks of the church and the marks of Christians. The Church is made visible and identified by the word purely preached and heard and the sacraments rightly administered. Insofar as the earthly church needs to know who should be counted as its members, Christians are known and established as members of the body of Christ by professing the faith, acting in accordance with it, and confessing the same through participation in the sacraments.

This basic teaching never changed, but it was elaborated in various ways. For present purposes, the most useful summary is Calvin's very pastoral *Short Treatise on the Lord's Supper*, written at virtually the same time as the French translation of the *Institutes*, the *Ecclesiastical Ordinances*, and *La forme des prieres*. The five sections of the *Short Treatise* cover the key points. [191] First Calvin explains the purposes of the Supper as God's loving gift; foremost is to sign and seal the promises which the gospel proclaims, then to incite believers to recognize God's goodness and respond with praise, and thirdly to exhort them to love their neighbors. Next Calvin expounds these same points with considerable fervor under the rubric of how the Lord's Supper benefits Christians. In the Supper God presents Christ and all He offers to Christians with the bread and wine; as God's instruments by the power of the Holy Spirit, the elements both present and represent. For those who trust in Christ for everything, the tangible elements with the audible promises are made effective signs by the internal action of the Spirit. The third section on the right use of the sacrament includes emphasis on the only true worthiness as trust in Christ, which entails repentance and reconciliation with God and neighbors. This point will be examined further below, as it relates to practical preparation for participation in the Supper. The fourth and fifth sections of the treatise instruct Calvin's readers about the errors of the traditional teaching and the complicated disagreements among Protestants. Here the teacher both praises his predecessors Luther and Zwingli and gently (by sixteenth-century standards) points out where he thinks they have failed. Luther's fault is language which does not adequately distinguish his intent from transubstantiation, Zwingli's is a failure to provide a positive interpretation of what the Supper actually does.

Later, of course, the development of the Lutheran doctrine of ubiquity would be strongly attacked by Calvin, and his own teaching on the spiritual real presence

---

[191] *Short Treatise*, OS I, pp. 503-30.

would be expressed less than clearly in the *Consensus Tigurinus* (with Heinrich Bullinger and the Zurich church) which brought about the joining of the "Zwinglian" and "Bucer-Calvinist" branches of Protestantism to form the "Reformed" tradition. For the purposes of this study, however, those developments may be left aside. The polemics might continue to echo in Geneva for some years, but the shape of the teaching and practice of the Supper was already set by 1542 and had begun establishing its own significant "tradition."

Purpose, Preparation, and Frequency

For Calvin, the Lord's Supper was a means of grace which should be celebrated as often as the whole church was prepared to commune. Two texts explain the implications of this for somewhat different audiences. The Latin *Institutes*, beginning in 1536, gives more attention to the task of the pastors; the French *Short Treatise on the Lord's Supper* in 1541 has in view primarily lay readers. Ideally, following the apostolic practice as seen in Acts 2:42, the Lord's Supper should be held whenever the Church gathered, as Calvin wrote in the 1536 *Institutes:* "no meeting of the church would take place without the Word, prayers, partaking of the Supper, and almsgiving."[192] The value of celebrating evidently required no demonstration, and the apostolic church was (apparently) always so well prepared that they could commune at each assembly. The following ages showed decline, but Calvin describes what should have been the standard practice.

> [T]he Lord's Table should have been spread at least once a week for the assembly of Christians, and the promises should have been declared to feed us in it spiritually. None indeed should have been forcibly compelled, but all should have been urged and aroused; also the inertia of indolent people should have been rebuked. All, like hungry people, would have flocked to such a bounteous repast.[193]

Here the words indicate how the clergy should have encouraged people to frequent participation and expresses the conviction that the response would have been positive.

However, when he became a pastor, Calvin recognized that the ideal frequency of the apostles would be virtually impossible in the circumstances he faced. The long tradition of communing once a year after carefully prescribed acts of penance, and the inbred terror that unworthy eating and drinking would lead to

---

[192] *Institution 1536*, p. 153; OS I, p. 149, see at nn.32ff above.

[193] *Institution 1536*, p. 154 [slightly altered: "men" to "people" because the Latin is simply "*omnes*" without gender]; OS I, p. 150.

damnation, were deeply ingrained in his age and his flock. Reforming the practice required a balance between emphasizing the value of participating and the ways of (re)defining worthiness, and it was lay people who most needed this kind of encouragement. Both of these issues are addressed in the *Short Treatise on the Lord's Supper*; the benefits of communing have been noted above, although Calvin weaves this theme into the question of preparation and frequency.

The major issue was right preparation for celebrating the Lord's Supper. There were two parts to implementing this: an inward personal dimension and an external corporate one. The first and inward part was naturally not accessible to the view of the church, but it was not neglected. The ideal description in the 1536 *Institutes*, cited above, rejected compulsion, and in the *Short Treatise* Calvin allowed that at times an individual might abstain from communion temporarily for some legitimate reason such as a troubled conscience.

> As to the time of using [the Supper], it cannot be fixed certainly for every person. For there are sometimes specific hindrances which excuse a person if he abstains. Moreover, we do not have an explicit command to compel all Christians to use the Supper every day that it is presented to them. [194]

These notes were probably directed against the Zwinglian requirement that all must participate every time the Supper was celebrated. The permission voiced here is presented as an exceptional situation, which suggests that Calvin also has in view the "Lutheran" position, something which becomes clear in the next sentences of the *Short Treatise*. A troubled conscience should not be taken as permission to stay away any longer than necessary, and such a person should take steps to resolve the problem as soon as possible and rejoin the church's communion, which is where the believer finds comfort.

> For the more that weakness presses upon us, the more often we need to practice what can and should serve to confirm us in faith and further us in purity of life. Thus, all well ordered churches should have this custom of celebrating the Supper as often as the people are able to bear it. And each individual should prepare himself to receive it as often as it is

---

194 *Short Treatise*, OS I, p. 515: "Quant est du temps d'en user, on ne le peut pas limiter à tous pour certain. Car il y a aucunesfois des empeschemens particuliers qui excusent l'homme s'il s'en abstient. Et d'avantage, nous n'avons pas de commandement expres de contraindre tous Chrestiens à en user chascun jour qu'elle leur est presentée. Toutesfoys, si nous regardons bien la fin à laquelle le Seigneur nous meine, nous congnoistrons que l'usage en doibt estre plus frequent que beaucoup ne l'ont."

administered in the congregation, unless there is some great impediment
which constrains him to abstain. [195]

Given the fact that experiencing the benefits of communion should encourage
people to seek it more often, Calvin goes on to address some of the hesitations
which they might have about frequent celebration of the Supper. The first, their
own unworthiness, he acknowledges as a concern. However, he promptly turns
this around and asks how they can be content to go so long without calling upon
God?

> I ask of [those] who hide under their unworthiness, how their conscience
> can bear to remain more than a year in such a bad state as not to be able to
> invoke God rightly? For they will confess to me that it is audacious to call
> upon God as our Father if we are not members of Jesus Christ. That
> cannot be, unless the substance and truth of the Supper is fulfilled in us.
> Now, if we have the reality, we are so much more capable of receiving the
> sign. You see then that the one who wants to excuse himself from taking
> the Supper because he is unworthy, excludes himself from praying to
> God. [196]

Fundamentally, prayer demands the same relationship to Christ as participation in
the sacrament, and are Christians willing to forego praying for a year or more?
Obviously Calvin expects a negative answer; so here he explains in simple terms
what is required for communion: justifying faith which allows the believer to
address God as Father. The preparation for participating in the sacrament has
changed from a certain set of actions (doing penance) to an attitude of heart
(trusting in Christ's forgiveness) which underlies the most basic Christian act,
prayer. This puts more responsibility on the individual, of course, who must
examine herself, himself every time he or she prays. The Supper is, in a way, only a
more emphatic expression of that preparation for engaging face to face with God.
The pastor then prescribes what the anxious person should do.

---

[195] *Short Treatise*, OS I, p. 515: "Car d'autant que l'imbecilité nous presse, nous avons mestier de
nous exerciter tant plus souvent en ce qui nous peut et doibt server à nous confermer en Foy et
advancer en pureté de vie. Pourtant, ceste coustume doibt estre en toutes Esglises bien
ordonnées, de celebrer souvent la Cene tant que la capacité du peuple le peut porter. Et un
chascun particulier à son endroit se doibt preparer à la recevoir toutes les foys qu'elle est
administrée en la congregation: sinon qu'il y ait grand empeschement qui le contraingne de s'en
abstenir."

[196] *Short Treatise*, OS I, p. 516.

If there is legitimate reason which hinders, I do not deny that it may be legitimate to defer [participating]. I only want to show that no one should allow oneself for a long time to abstain from the Supper because of his unworthiness; since in doing so he deprives himself of the communion of the Church in which lies all our good. Rather, let him push himself to fight against all the hindrances which the devil sets before him, so that he may not be excluded from such a great good, and thus from all the graces which follow from such deprivation. [197]

The pastoral instruction emphasizes not only the person's relationship with Christ as an individual but makes clear that communion in the Supper is also with Christ's body the Church. (Although Calvin does not say so here, it is worth noting that withdrawing from the sacraments is a way of erasing one of the marks of a Christian.)

The second reason which people might claim for refraining from communion is the idea that one should not participate with wicked people. Calvin explains that although this might seem so, in fact individuals may not judge others; even pastors may not exclude someone who is unworthy until the proper church body has made the judgment. Paul's injunction is that each should examine him or herself, not others. Although the faithful should warn those who do not live as they should and will not accept rebuke, they themselves should not withdraw from the church because of such people. Until the proper ecclesiastical process has been carried out, one must tolerate those who are not demonstrating worthiness, praying for God to cleanse the church of scandals and awaiting the final judgment when the wheat and chaff will be separated.

The third excuse for not participating in the Supper is that it is unnecessary to do this very often, and to this Calvin answers with a very sharp negative. Those who say that having once received Christ, they do not need to return frequently, are just wrong.

This spiritual bread was not given to us so that we might be replete at one sitting, but rather so that, having had a taste of its sweetness, we might desire more and use it whenever it is offered to us. ... Jesus Christ is never communicated to us in such a way that our souls may be completely satisfied, but He wants to be our continual nourishment. [198]

---

[197] *Short Treatise*, OS I, p. 516.

[198] *Short Treatise*, OS I, p. 517.

All the church should be eager to participate frequently in the Lord's Supper to reconfirm their faith continually, to have the visible words of the sacrament strengthening the preached word.

Frequency and preparation were closely connected for each member of the church, and if the internal readiness was too long in coming, the leaders of the community were obligated to seek out the lost person and inquire into the impediments preventing him or her from full communion with the body of Christ. In the *Short Treatise* the pastor is speaking to the people about their responsibility. In the 1536 *Institutes* quoted above, the reformer was addressing the leadership who should use exhortation and even rebuke to bring the lazy to a proper awareness of their need to commune. Over time, one of the pastoral difficulties which Calvin and his colleagues had to address was the need to bring back into the fold those who had withdrawn from the sacrament, and thus from full communion.[199] This is the point at which inward and outward preparation meet: when the individual does not make the appropriate effort to get back into right fellowship with the whole body of the church, then the leaders of the church must do more than exhort the community... they must address the individual in person.

This second part of implementing preparation for celebrating the Supper is more external, and requires a great deal more effort on the part of the larger church body, effort which could not practically be compressed into a short time. Calvin believed that a certain level of knowledge and observable behavior were required of all who wanted to participate in the Lord's Supper – these were two of the marks of Christians. Teaching the catechetical basics was one of the pastors' major tasks; insuring that the catechism had been learned was one of the consistory's important responsibilities, along with its more obvious role in guiding, rebuking, and recon-

---

[199] Usually this concerned those who had been suspended from the Supper, but it also included those who withdrew on their own. Examples of those who excused themselves because their consciences would not allow them to commune are fairly frequent, cf. Grosse, *Les rituels de la Cène*, pp. 515-23. The issue of conscience was actively claimed by Antoine Saunier and his assistant teachers in December 1538 when they were asked/ordered to help with the Christmas Supper; see chap. 2 at n.24. On Friday, Dec. 14, 1548, Calvin came before the Senate saying that the Supper is approaching and many abstain from taking communion; he names various ones and says he fears that they have some bitterness against him. He wants a reconciliation before the Supper so a meeting is called for the following Monday, Dec. 18. The key figure, Ami Perrin, says he holds no bitterness, and as for abstaining from Supper "que c'est une chose sainne et libres parquoy cella est en sa conscience et aussy que quant il sera en estre et dispost de la recepvoir qui la recepvra." He insists that he is not at odds with anyone and pardons those who have done him wrong and he "prestend à l'aide de Dieu estre en bonne volunté et aussi de recepvoir la cene, si est dispost à ce noyel prochain." OC 21:442, 443 (RC 43 f265 & f267v). For a full examination of this, see Jung-Sook Lee, *Excommunication and Restoration in Calvin's Geneva, 1555-1556* (Princeton Theological Seminary, Ph.D. dissertation, 1997).

ciling openly sinful behavior. Insuring that Genevans achieved both of these marks led logically to the third one, their participation in the sacraments.

As the research of Robert Kingdon has demonstrated, one of the main occupations of the Consistory was mediating quarrels and inter-personal conflicts, with the goal of bringing all the people into concord to share in the common life of faith, especially the Lord's Supper. This "compulsory counseling service" was concerned not only with actions but also with their roots in enmity. The intent of discipline-teaching was to bring people to the point of recognizing their sin – whether it was wife-beating or obvious bitterness against another person – so that they might forgive or seek forgiveness, in order to be reconciled with God and their neighbors. Most consistory cases were concluded with admonitions, and the cases which did reach the point of suspension from the Supper were just as likely to be family quarrels as sexual misbehavior. [200] Even when the Consistory suspended persons from receiving the Supper, if they manifested repentance or learned their catechism, they were quickly welcomed back. Grosse indicates that as many as 37% of those suspended never in fact missed a Supper, and most others were suspended only for one or two celebrations. [201] The problem cases were essentially those (relatively) few who refused, after repeated invitations and counsel, to recognize their fault and seek forgiveness and reconciliation with God, Church, and neighbor.

Because so much was involved in preparing the people as a whole to share in communion, Calvin concluded that monthly celebrations of the Lord's Supper were the best accommodation to the circumstances. In the Geneva *Articles* of 1537 he proposed a monthly Supper (in the city), rotating among the three churches then in use so that it was celebrated in each church every quarter, with the proviso that anyone could participate in all three parishes. If enacted it would have meant that those who wished could receive commune every month, [202] but the proposal was not implemented. When he came to Strasbourg Calvin was able

---

[200] One example: Robert M. Kingdon, "Calvin and the Family: The Work of the Consistory in Geneva," in *Calvin's Work in Geneva*, ed. R. C. Gamble (New York: Garland, 1992), p. 96.

[201] Grosse, *Les rituels de la Cène*, pp. 392-93.

[202] *Articles*, OS I, p. 371: "Mays pour ce que l'infirmité du peuple est encore telle qu'il y avoyt dangier que ce sacre et tant excellent mestere [mystere] ne vint en mespris s'il estoyt si souvent celebre. Ayant esgard à cela il nous a semblé bon que en attendant que le peuple qui est encores aucunement debile sera plus confermé, cest saincte Cene soyt usitee une foys chascun moys en l'ung des troys lieux ou se fonte maintenant les predications, C'est à sçauoir St. Pierre, Rive ou St. Gervays. Tellement que l'ung des moys elle se face à Sainct Pierre, l'aultre à Rive et l'aultre à Sainct Geruays et ainsi revienne par ordre apres avoyr acheué le tour. Toutefoys ce ne sera pas pour ung quartier de la ville mays pour toute l'esglise."

to practice a monthly Lord's Supper, as was the custom in that city's parish churches.[203] When he returned to Geneva in 1541 and drafted the *Ecclesiastical Ordinances*, he again stipulated a rotating monthly Supper, this time based on the newly defined parish system. Again the Genevan authorities refused this idea, substituting their preferred schedule of four times per year, and adding the restriction that every person was bound to commune in her or his own parish.[204] In the 1561 revision of the *Ordinances* this restriction is tacitly dropped, so that in principle people were no longer obliged to commune in their own parishes, but because the Supper was still celebrated on the same days in every parish, the freedom to move around did not mean access to more frequent communion.[205]

Later in his life, in responding to questions from correspondents about aspects of the liturgy, especially the Lord's Supper, Calvin commented on his desire for monthly celebrations, but only when these were rightly done.

> It pleases us greatly that the Supper is being celebrated every month [in your church], provided the more frequent use does not occasion carelessness. When the greater part [of the congregation] abstains from communion, the church is in a measure fragmented.[206]

One notable thing here is the concern with gathering the whole church; that is, if people stay away, the purpose of the Supper in bringing the body of Christ together is seriously hindered. Calvin was apparently cautioning this correspondent not to sacrifice unity for the sake of frequency. While he continued to protest against the small number of times the sacrament was offered, the pastor accepted

---

[203] Calvin's letter to Farel, OC 10b:279. Bornert, *La réforme protestante du culte*, pp. 537-39, indicates that the Supper was at first celebrated every Sunday in each city church; by the time Calvin arrived, it was still every week in the cathedral but usually once per month in the parish churches, on a rotating basis so that there were always several Supper celebrations every Sunday. The Supper was usually held every month in the villages, also. Basel had a similar custom, cf. Grosse, *Les rituels de la Cène*, pp. 286-87.

[204] *Ordinances*, OS II, p. 344. The only difference between the *Articles* of 1537 and Calvin's draft in 1541 is that he says that at Easter, Pentecost, and Christmas it will be celebrated in all three parishes and therefore the rotation will be interrupted so that the Supper will only be celebrated once in the month. The civil authorities inserted in the *Ordinances* their decision that the Supper would be held "quatre foys l'annee, assavoyre à noel, pasques, penthecoste et le premier dymenche de septembre en aulthone"; p. 337 requires that the sacraments be received according to parish boundaries; cf. quotation in n.134.

[205] See *Ordinances*, OC 10:20 in 1541, disappears in 1561, OC 10:99-100.

[206] *Calvin's Ecclesiastical Advice*, p. 96. *Consilium*, Aug. 12, 1561, OC 10:213: "Iam vero singulis mensibus coenam celebrari maximo nobis placeret: modo ne usus frequentior negligentiam pariat. Nam dum maior pars a communione abstinet, quodammodo dissipatur ecclesia."

this accommodation as preferable to a conflict which might destroy the church. [207] He chose his battles and determined to take his stand on preparation and unity.

Frequent communion was very desirable, but it was not mandatory, and it was essential that when the Supper was held, it was with a community that was prepared and united to share in the sacrament. Although some people ignored the laws requiring everyone to attend worship on Sunday, the day the Lord's Supper was celebrated came very close to fulfilling Calvin's teaching that the whole people should commune together. One evidence for this is the way that, already by 1545, the government began to take defensive precautions at the time of the main Supper service, for fear that an enemy might attack while the great majority of the population were at worship. The guards were instructed to attend the dawn service on the Supper Sunday so that they might be in their places when the rest of the people were in church, and this arrangement became the regular practice. [208]

VI: The Practical Implementation of the Lord's Supper in Geneva

Implementing the Reformed Lord's Supper

In the first Protestant period following the abolition of the traditional liturgical calendar, the Supper was celebrated several times each year at somewhat irregular intervals. [209] After the Bernese "ceremonies" were introduced in April 1538, the practice was apparently fixed at three times a year: Christmas, Easter, and Pentecost. When Calvin returned to Geneva in 1541, the *Ecclesiastical Ordinances* decreed that it would be celebrated on Easter, Christmas, Pentecost, and the first Sunday in September. The choice of this date for the fourth celebration was natural, since it was approximately what Zurich practiced, but it is likely that the immediate catalyst was Calvin's dismay that there was such a long gap between the Pentecost and Christmas communions. [210] Almost immediately after Calvin's arrival, a first

---

[207] *Consilium*, Aug. 12, 1561, OC 10:213: "Malimus tamen singulis mensibus invitari ecclesiam, quam quater duntaxat in singulos annos: ut apud nos fieri solet. Quum huc primum veni, non distribuebatur nisi ter quotannis: et quidem ut inter coenam Pentecostes et Natalis Christi, septem toti menses intercederent. Mihi placebant singuli menses; sed quum minime persuaderem, satius visum est populi infirmitati ignoscere, quam pertinacius contendere. Curavi tamen referri in acta publica vitiosum esse morem nostrum, ut posteris facilior esset ac liberior correctio."

[208] Grosse, *Les rituels de la Cène*, pp. 329-31.

[209] On Fri. Oct. 5, 1537, the Supper is announced for Oct. 14; on Thurs. Jan. 3, 1538, reference to a celebration scheduled for the next Sun. Jan. 6. OC 21:215 & 219 (RC 31 f69, f146).

[210] See n.207 above.

Supper service was announced on Oct. 30, with an order by the Senate on Friday, Nov. 4, and then it was held on Nov. 6, 1541. It is notable that for this occasion the plan called for "twice at St. Pierre and twice at St. Gervais."[211] That is, there would be services at dawn and mid-morning (probably 8 a.m.) in the two parts of the city, but this time not at La Magdeleine. (It may be that La Magdeleine was still not entirely ready for occupancy, or simply that four services were considered sufficient for the moment.)

Over the next several years, the records of the *Registres du Conseil* include fairly regular orders about the Supper during the week or so before it was to be celebrated, and the *Registres du Consistoire* provide fuller details. Usually the Senate notes are very brief, a simple statement of the fact and day, although occasionally there are some other details. The consistory organized the assignments of those who were to serve the cup alongside the pastors, and usually who would read the passion. These instructions make it possible to reconstruct aspects of the practice. All three parishes were in use for the Christmas Supper service, according to the Senate order on Dec. 23, 1541, and the celebration was held on Sunday the 25th. This meant that there was no need to debate whether it would be Sunday or the 25th, as would happen the following year, when the Senate wavered back and forth before settling on Monday the 25th.[212] On April 6, 1542, planning for the Easter celebration on April 9, the consistory listed the assignments. They named five men "for the two Suppers" at St. Pierre and also five for St. Gervais, although the reference to two services is not repeated. La Magdeleine was assigned only three men, which would be appropriate for a single service in a large parish. The consistory instructions also included naming readers although there are some lacunae. In addition every church was supposed to have a syndic, indicating that the highest civil offices were to be visibly engaged in the services. The instructions include times: the men are to be present at 4 a.m. for the first service and at 7:30 a.m. for the second (apparently arriving early for the more crowded 8:00 a.m. services).[213] The consistory records do not name those assisting for Pentecost but

---

[211] OC 21:284 (RC 35 f370). Nov. 6, OC 21:285 (RC 35:f379): "Ordonné que dymenche prochaien laz cene de Monseigneur soyt célèbre 2 foy az S. Pierre et 2 foys az St. Gervex."

[212] See RC 35 f442v; quoted in *Consist.* I, p. 34 n.158 : "soyt célèbre et administree dymenche en troys lieux assavoyer St. Pierre, laz Magdeleine, St. Gervex, et que les Seigneurs deputés du Consistoyre doybjent destribuyr le vin"; also archives@etat.ge.ch, accessed Feb. 11, 2013. For Christmas 1542, cf. *Consist.* I, p. 156, n. 639, see hesitations about day, i.e., Sun. 24th or Mon. 25th.

[213] *Consist.* I, pp. 34-35. "Pour Saintz Pierre pour les deux Cenes: le Seigneur Birbel, Mychiel Varod d'Orsieres, Jehan Coquet, Pierre de Rages, Checand. Pour lecteur__. Pour Saintz Gervays: le Seigneur Hudriod Du Mollard, le S. Pierre Britillion, Blandin, Loys Dufour, Emoz Tacon, pour lecteur le Procureur General. Pour la Magdeleine: Jehan Pictiod, Fontannaz, hospitalier, Pen-

the Senate minutes ordered the sacrament to be held in the three churches and the "deputies" to attend according to the ordinance.[214]

In 1542 for the September Supper there was apparently still some confusion about specific details, particularly the preparation expected of the men assisting in the Supper. It seems that (at least while the procedure was still new), those designated to assist the pastors were expected to participate in some training. The consistory met twice (Tues. Sept. 5th and Thurs. Sept. 7th) as was the custom the week before the Supper, and made the same assignments for men to serve as had been named for Easter. However, three of the latter did not come to the preparatory meeting as they were supposed to do.[215] Evidently, appearing before the consistory prior to the day they were to assist in worship was expected by the institution but not yet ingrained in the men. There is no further reference to this delinquency but the arrangements for the Supper went ahead. The next day, Friday Sept. 8, the Senate ordered the Supper to be held on the following Sunday, Sept. 10, again stating that it would be celebrated in all three parishes.[216] Since the new schedule of an autumn celebration of the Supper had not yet been fixed in actual practice, it is probable that celebrating on the second rather than the first Sunday did not disturb the people in the pew unduly. In fact, there continued to be a degree of flexibility about the exact timing of this Supper service. In 1543 the September sacrament was delayed a week because there was a foreign army

---

sabin. Et par tout ung Seigneur Sindique. Et entrer en chayre à 4 heures pour le premier et pour le second à VII heures et dymi." As Grosse says, cf. n.40, several of these men were not elders or deacons. However, most were or had been (e.g., Chiccand, just recently retired as hospitalier), and the ones who were not were among those devoted to Farel and Calvin. The reference to the pulpit is not clear, because even if the instruction was intended for the reader, he would not begin reading until the second part of the service, after the preacher left the pulpit. The time must therefore signify something else, probably the time of the pastor's arrival, and an indication that those assisting should be very prompt! This note suggests that the seasonal time change actually began on Easter, because the dawn service is listed at 4 a.m.

214 There were consistory meetings twice in the week before May 28, but these were held on Thurs. 25th and Fri. 26th instead of Tues. and Thurs. as usual. *Consist.* I, pp. 66-74. The Senate notes for May 24, 1542, order the celebration of the Supper in the three temples "& les deputés doybjent assistye comment l'ordonance est esté par cy devant faycte." The dinner for the ministers and deacons (after the mutual censures) is to be prepared at the hospital. RC 36 f23v. archives@etat. ge.ch accessed Feb. 11, 2013.

215 Sept. 7, 1542, *Consist.* I, p. 113: "Sur la resolution de la sainte Cene, les Seigneurs ontz ordonné comme paravant ci-devant az esté fayt. Et furent demandés les seigneurs assistants ici apres escripts. Et premierement led. jour sept de septembre : Monsieur Girbel, le Seigneur Hu. Du Molard, d'Orsieres, Britillion, Pensabin, Tacon, Forchet, Blandin, Rages. Rages, ny Du Molard, ny Orsieres ne furent point presents bien qu'il fussent demandés."

216 RC 36 f115, "Ordonné qu'elle soyt celebree dimenche prochain aux troys temples." This is Friday Sept. 8, 1542 [not Monday, as OC 21:302 says] archives@etat.ge.ch accessed Feb. 11, 2013.

passing nearby on the first Sunday of the month,[217] so the city was on high alert and the Senate thought it better to attend to defense.

The organization for serving communion continued to be polished with regard to assigning elders, deacons (and readers), although the instructions at times seem something less than precise about details. For the Easter Supper in 1543 the Senate ordered the Supper to be held twice in all three churches, but the corresponding minutes of the consistory do not seem to support this. St. Pierre is again listed as "two Suppers" with four men assigned to serve; St. Gervais again lacks the note about the number of services but also has four men (implying two services), while La Magdeleine is only assigned three.[218] Given the fact that from all the other evidence there was no dawn service at La Magdeleine, the Senate note was probably an error written in haste and there was only one service at La Magdeleine.[219] It appears that the names of those who served communion were set at Easter for the rest of the year. The preparations for Pentecost 1543 refer back to Easter, but the September and Christmas Suppers in the consistory minutes repeat the same names for the same parishes, along with an additional note that there should be a syndic in each church.[220] The consistory records assigning men to assist with the Easter Supper in April 1544 include for the first time the reference to two services at St. Gervais as well as St. Pierre, thus signaling the pattern of five Supper services, two at St. Pierre and St. Gervais at dawn and 8 a.m., and one at La Magdeleine at 8 a.m.[221] For Pentecost the consistory simply

---

[217] Fri. Aug. 31, 1543, *Consist.* I, p. 256.

[218] March 22, 1543, *Consist.* I, p. 207: "Pour Saint Pierre pour les Deux Cene: Seigneur Pernet de Fosses, Mychiel Varod, Pierre d'Orsieres, Michiel Morel. Pour la Magdeleine: Jehan Chautemps, P. Vernaz, Pensabin. Pour Saint Gervays: Claude Du Pan, Loys Dufour, Blandin, Amed Gervays." This time there is no mention of readers, though someone must have been assigned. Again, most of these were either elders or deacons. The Senate record for March 23 is given p. 207 n. 185: "celebree à ces Pasques, assavoyer deux foys aux troys temples St. Pierre, la Magdelene et St. Gervex" (RC 37 f41v).

[219] In Dec. 1541 the Senate mentioned all three churches without identifying the number of services (n.212 above). Although there were certainly two services at St. Pierre, the Sunday dawn service at St. Gervais was not begun until Aug. 1542 (see chap. 1 at n.159). Here again the same "one size fits all" approach applies the practice at St. Pierre and St. Gervais to Magdeleine.

[220] For Pentecost, September and Christmas Suppers, see May 10, 1543, Aug. 30, 1543, and Dec. 20, 1543, *Consist.* I, pp. 242, 254-55, 292-93. For Pentecost the Consistory simply says "fust ordonné comme à Pasques dernier passé," p. 242. The Senate notes for Pentecost say that the names of the men assigned to serve were read but does not record them, cf. May 11, 1543, RC 37 f89. archives@etat.ge.ch accessed Feb. 11, 2013

[221] April 10, 1544, *Consist.* I, p. 360: "Et premierement pour les deux Cenes au temple Saint Pierre: les Seigneurs Pernet de Fosses, Mychiel Varod, Pierre d'Orcieres, et ___. Pour la Cene à la Magdaleine : Jehan Chautemps, Pierre Vernaz, Jehan Pensabin. Pour les deux Cenes à Saint

reaffirmed the Easter order, and the Senate notes were equally brief.[222] For the autumn Supper in 1544 the celebration was scheduled for the first Sunday in September, and the Senate record indicates that the names of "ministers and deacons to serve at [the sacrament]" were read but the list is not given. The routine orders for Supper services appeared a few more times in the Senate records, but then only when there was some particular change.[223] There is a lacuna in the consistory minutes in 1544-45 from July 3, 1544, the last entry made by the first secretary, to Oct. 8, 1545, when the new secretary actually began his register. As the editors of the consistory records note in the introduction to the second volume, one reason for this break may have been the considerable ravages of the plague, which was especially virulent in 1544 and 1545. When the records resume, they no longer regularly include assignments for serving communion.[224] Perhaps that was because those who assisted the pastors in this way were elders or deacons and special arrangements were not necessary, or the system was sufficiently well established that regular participants no longer required specific instructions.

For the Christmas Supper in 1546 the consistory asked the Senate to elect "deacons" to help the ministers serve communion, according to the edicts (*Ordinances*); the Senate told them to leave matters as they were for the moment and they would review the edicts.[225] It is not perfectly clear what is meant. Grosse believes the consistory was asking to have only the official elders and deacons be named, as the *Ordinances* specified. At this point it was the Senate which chose the

---

Gervaix : Claude Du Pain, Loys Dufour, Mermet Blandin, Amed Gervaix. Et partout ung seigneur sindique." The blank indicates an incomplete list ; the fourth name is missing. For the number and times of services, see chap. 1 at nn.159ff.

[222] May 29, 1544, *Consist.* I, p. 376. May 30, 1544 (RC 38 f229): "dimenche prochain venant jour de penthecoste." archives@etat.ge.ch accessed Feb. 11, 2013

[223] Sept. 5, 1544 (RC 38 352v): "esté leu l'ordre des ministres & dyacres pour servye à icelle." Dec. 19, 1544 (RC 39 f75v): "jour de noel prochain." April 3, 1545 (RC 40 f71): in three temples. archives@etat.ge.ch accessed Feb. 11, 2013.

[224] *Consist.* II, pp. XVI-XVII. See, however, March 20, 1554, IX:1 (IX, 30) where men are named to serve the Supper "dimenche prochain."

[225] Dec. 21, 1546, *Consist.* II, p. 359, n. 1456 quotes RC entries for Dec. 23 & 24, RC 41, f268 & 269. The request on Dec. 23 says: "diacres pour servyr à la Ste Cene joux les esdictz." On Dec. 24 the note reads: "Des dyacres que doybvent servyr en la Ste Cene. Et semblablement led. ministres ont proposer que, joux les esdictz, il doybve avoyer des dyacres du Consistoyre, requerant fere observé lesd. esdictz. Resoluz que pour à present l'on demore à ce qu'est faict, toutesfoys que cy-appres l'on visitera les esdictz." Given the reference to the edicts and the fact that there is no hint that the city was planning to increase the number of ministers of word and sacraments, these are probably elders and deacons by Calvin's definition (not distinguishing between the two offices even though only elders would have been seated in the consistory).

men to participate; it was not until 1553 that the consistory itself had that authority. [226]

Besides the organization of the celebration of the Lord's Supper for the whole community it is also possible to glimpse at least a little of the personal experience of some individuals. Particularly in the early years when the consistory habitually asked all those who came before it about their church attendance and knowledge of the catechetical basics, there is fairly frequent mention of how people participated in the Supper. Normally a person would go to only one service; one woman affirms that she was at the dawn service for communion and offers confirmation for this by naming another woman – probably near her in the line walking up to the table to receive the bread and wine. Another woman said she received the Supper from Master Henri (de La Mare) and heard the passion but does not remember what the preacher said. [227] Evidently the familiar story of the passion stuck in her memory while the sermon did not! Sometimes an individual appears to have attended both Sunday morning services, but received the Supper at only one. (Did he abstain when the Supper was offered at dawn, in order to participate at 8 a.m.?) The man said that he went to the dawn service but could not hear because he was sitting where the bells were ringing, so he went to the "grand presche" and took communion there. He was before the consistory to answer questions about his Supper participation. There were two points. He had not taken the sacrament this time in Jussy, his home parish (a rural church), but the man explained that he had been retained in Geneva on business. He had also not received communion at Christmas at all, but he explains that it was because he had to stay home and guard the house and not because of some scruple (which needed to be worked out). The consistory admonished him to be more assiduous in receiving the Supper and not to blaspheme, but when he recited both Prayer and Creed acceptably they seemed satisfied. [228]

People who abstained from participating in the Supper offered various excuses. In Sept. 1542 one man said that he did not know the Lord's Prayer and Creed [229] – evidence that he had assimilated one of the key requirements for receiving the Supper much more quickly than he had the content of the Prayer or

---

[226] Ordinances, OS II, p. 344. Grosse, *Les rituels de la Cène*, p. 222.

[227] On May 8, 1544, *Consist.* I, p. 367, Pernon, wife of Anthoyne Valloz, says she received the [Easter] Supper at St. Pierre with the servant of M. Velluti "au premier sermon" and "fust dymenche au premier sermon." March 29, 1544, p. 209: "receupt la Cene à Pasques par Monsieur Henri à la Magdeleine et oyt le sermon et la passion et ne scet qu'il fust ditz."

[228] March 29, 1543, *Consist.* I, p. 210.

[229] Sept. 14, 1542, *Consist.* I, p. 116.

Creed. This was not the kind of reasoning most Genevans applied, however; normally those who stayed away explained that their consciences would not allow them to commune. In some instances this was clearly an excuse, though it might be rather creative, as in the case of Jane, wife of Claude Pignier, examined two days after the Christmas Lord's Supper in 1543. (She was the only person on the docket that day, and her examination covers almost two pages of the modern edition of the consistory records.) In 1537 Jane Pignier had been imprisoned and then exiled for her Anabaptist convictions but readmitted in 1538 at the petition of her neighbors because she was their daughters' school teacher. When questioned she said that she did not have scruples about infant baptism. On the Supper, however, she cited no less than Master Viret as her teacher; "he told her that it was much better for her not to receive than to live thus." ("Thus" is not explained clearly but Jane Pignier stated that she had not taken communion for two or three years, and she was busy with child care and no one knew her heart.) Questioned further, she repeated what Viret had told her and added that "she had been taught that it was not wrong not to receive the Supper," though she does not attribute this to Viret. The discussion continued and Mme Jane acerbically said that one had to believe what the preachers said even if they told you there was no water in the Rhone (River)! With regard to the Christmas Supper, she said she did not take it because she had been called to the consistory "the other Thursday." In effect her name was on the list to come before the consistory on Dec. 20 in preparation for the Supper but she had not appeared,[230] and thus had not been approved in order to receive the Supper. Jane Pignier's case illustrates that some Genevans might use the consistory's own investigations as an excuse to avoid the Supper.[231]

Geneva's "Sacramental Seasons"

For the Calvinist Reformed tradition, the practice of the Lord's Supper was much more than a single service on certain Sundays of the year; it was the central high point of liturgical time. There were a number of distinctive factors about the celebration of this sacrament as it developed in Geneva. One was that by 1550 it

---

[230] Dec. 27, 1553, *Consist.* I, pp. 292-94. For record of her being called to the Consistory, p. 404.

[231] Occasionally there are oddities in the Consistory records, which may owe more to the secretary's inattention than to the facts. For example, one woman appears to say that she took the Supper at vespers (the Sunday afternoon service). Jan. 4, 1543, *Consist.* I, pp. 165-66: "fust dymenche au sermon à Saint Pierre à matin et au vespre à la Cene." It seems probable that she was listing: morning, afternoon, and Supper, but the secretary missed the conjunction and ran the second and third together.

came to be held only on Sundays; this development will be traced in the next chapter dealing with the "four feasts." Another was the characteristic relationship between the Lord's Supper and teaching/discipline in Geneva that led to a pattern of liturgical time which distinguished the Calvinist Reformed into the modern era. This was a distinctive liturgical rhythm which later generations would call "sacramental seasons." Christian Grosse has investigated this complex and neglected issue in great detail and provided a very fine picture of what this practice was and how it developed.[232] Thus a brief summary here is sufficient to outline the process which he has brought to light.

In effect the four celebrations of the Lord's Supper shaped four seasons of special religious devotion. The Supper and its importance are illuminated by the rituals which came to be associated with it. These manifest an intensified attention to faith and practice on the part of the whole of Geneva for the week or even two before and sometimes after the actual service itself. Formally, there was supposed to be an announcement of the Supper on the previous Sunday, with some (limited) exposition of the meaning of the sacrament. Although at least sometimes this was not done explicitly in the sermon, no one who was paying attention would have failed to mark the time. That same Sunday before the Supper there was regularly an examination of the catechism for students who were considered ready to profess their faith. During the week there would be at least one more consistory meeting than was usual (Tuesday[233] as well as Thursday), and sometimes even an additional day if business ran over on Thursday. (There are occasional Saturday or Friday meetings.) This made a total or two or three times when those who had been suspended might come to demonstrate their knowledge of the basic teachings (reciting the Lord's Prayer and Apostles' Creed was the most common test) or their readiness to confess their sin and be reconciled.

---

[232] Grosse, *Les rituels de la Cène*, esp. chap. 5: "Le temps liturgique." Cf. p. 283: "Le rythme que construit l'enchaînement des services divins tente d'imprimer ainsi au temps social une direction, celle d'un processus d'élévation spirituelle. En observant comment la Réforme genevoise redéfinit le temps liturgique, c'est-à- dire la fréquence selon laquelle ce rappel de la signification religieuse du temps intervient dans le temps social, et plus particulièrement comment la périodicité des célébrations de la cène exerce une emprise sur le cours du temps social, c'est cette spiritualisation du temps que ce chapitre cherche à saisir." Chapters follow on other aspects du process : #6 on correction ("Le glaive spirituel de la parole"), #8 on appropriate communal knowledge ("'Le sainct accord de la foy' communion et unité religieuse"), #9 on reconciliation ("Le 'lien de la charité' communion et reconciliation").

[233] What may have been the first such instance was ordered by the Senate on April 4, 1542; see citation in Lambert, *Preaching, Praying, and Policing*, p. 446 n.125. However, it became a regular practice, as the consistory records demonstrate.

In 1550 a pattern of house-to-house visitation was introduced at the ministers' request. At first it was intended to precede every Supper, then to be held before the Christmas and Easter services, and finally it apparently settled into an annual pre-Easter event. This involved a pastor, one or two elders, and the dizainier (civic official of the neighborhood who would know everyone), and the visits began some weeks before Easter in order to cover the whole city. The *Registres de la Compagnie des Pasteurs* sets out the order for 1556, organizing it about a month before the date of Easter, April 5.

> Thursday March 12 it was decided at the consistory, and afterward appro-ved by the Senate, that the visitation would be done throughout the city, to learn [the state of] the people so that the Lord's Supper was not profaned, and to exhort each one to do his duty toward God and to hear His holy word. With two elders there will be one minister, together with the dizainier of each dizaine. There are 25 dizaines so it was ordered that the each minister would do four, since there are only six ministers to do the visitation, and the fifth dizaine would be done by the one who finished his four first. [234]

The primary purpose of the visit was to check on ignorance (e.g., discover whether servants hired from rural Catholic villages had been properly instructed and/or sent to catechism),[235] and general household readiness for the Supper

---

[234] RCP II, p. 66.

[235] In 1564, Charles Perrot described how he practiced the pre-Easter visitation in one of his two village churches; note the emphasis on catechetical basics. Lambert, *Preaching, Praying, and Policing*, pp. 544-45: "Les quatre ou cinq premiers dimanches devant la Cene de Pasques, j'advertissois les gens de se trouver au temple à l'heure du Catechisme au lieu duquel je les interroguois, asç[avoir] en les priant de penser à rendre compte de leur foy, sans autre forme expresse de priere sinon quelques fois en un mot à l'entree et au [sic] sortie. Je les apellois aud. lieu et heure du Catechisme pource que je ne les pouvois commodement assembler sur semeine par les maisons à Moin. Car ceulx de Magny je les assemblois sur semeine à une fois ou deux ches Tombeti le couturier. Je commence par faire prononcer la priere, Creance, Command [emens] à un mesme ou plus[ieu]rs au reng des hommes, principalement à ceulx qui semblent estre plus ignorans. Et s'il y a trop grand default de memoire, je leur conseille de se faire recorder les Command[emens] et tascher à les aprendre avant que de venir à la Cene, au moins leur fais-je dire la sommaire et tasche a leur donner crainte pour gaigner quelque chose. Les femmes suivent apres les hommes et si cela dure une heure ou une heure et demye, c'est assez pour une fois, car le Catechisme, au lieu duquel on interroge ne doit durer en tout plus de trois 4 d'heures. Quant à la forme d'interroger, je suis librement celle qui est au Catechisme, ou bien unne que j'ay recueillie tout expres. Ceulx qui respondent assés bien sont receus; ceulx qui ont quelque bon sentiment sont supportés aussy. Ceulx auxquelz rien de cela ne se voit sont advertis de ne s'y presenter ainsy ignorans. Neantmoins si le ministre ne le raporte à la ville, il ne leur refusera la Cene s'ilz y viennent."

(e.g., no known quarrels unresolved). The visit was (usually) conducted outside the house, which meant that neighbors might lend their "assistance" in bringing up issues of "mauvais ménage."[236] A young boy from Basel, Andreas Ryff, was apprenticed in Geneva during the last years of Calvin's life, and he describes the experience of these ministerial visits.

> It was the custom of the ministers in Geneva to go to all the houses every three months. They gathered together all the residents, young and old, from more-or-less six or eight houses, to question and examine them, to make them give an account of their faith and to catechize them before they took the Supper, which is only celebrated every three months. For that purpose, my master had taught me so that I could give satisfactory answers to the ministers' questions.[237]

Ryff's positive memory may be owed in part to distance, since he wrote this narrative many years after his experience in Geneva. That may also account for the fact that he associates a visit with every one of the four yearly Supper services, although other sources indicate that there were usually only two at most and soon only one just before Easter.[238]

The ordinary citizens were not alone in being examined for the Lord's Supper; a regular time of mutual censures was part of the pastors' duty as described in the *Ecclesiastical Ordinances*. They also took very seriously the need to be reconciled with other members of the community. In 1548 Calvin came before the Senate to seek their help in organizing his meeting with various people, especially Ami Perrin, and in 1552 he did the same with Jehan Troillet so that he/ they would be fit to share in the sacrament together.[239] Preparation for the celebration of the

---

[236] Grosse, *Les rituels de la Cène*, pp. 400-07 (urban; pp. 408-12 rural); p. 405: "Les habitants sont interrogés par le ministre non pas à l'intérieur de leur domicile, mais de manière publique."

[237] Ryff, "Un jeune Bâlois à Genève," p. 415: "A ce propos, je dirai que c'est la coutume des ministres à Genève d'aller tous les trois mois dans toutes les maisons. Ils réunissent ensemble les habitants, jeunes et vieux, de six, de huit maisons, plus ou moins, pour les interroger, les examiner, leur faire rendre compte de leur foi et les catéchiser avant qu'ils prennent la cène, laquelle n'est distribuée que tous les trois mois. Pour cela mon patron m'avait instruit lui-même, de manière que je pus répondre de façon satisfaisante aux questions de Messieurs les ministres ; et cela fut pour moi un moyen d'édification dont je puis me réjouir en priant Dieu tout-puissant qu'Il daigne par sa grâce me maintenir dans cette foi comme j'en ai fait profession, et telle qu'elle est contenue dans notre confession bâloise, qu'Il m'accorde en outre une fin bienheureuse en Jésus-Christ notre seul Sauveur et Rédempteur. Amen!"

[238] Grosse, *Les rituels de la Cène*, pp. 401-02.

[239] *Ordinances*, OS II, p. 335. For reconcilation with Perrin, see above n.199; for Troillet, Aug. 28, 1552, OC 21:516 (RC 46 f262v).

Supper led to the development of a number of formal arrangements for censures: times to bring any festering problems to the surface and cleanse the body of Christ of conflicts among those who had to work together. In 1557 the Senate instituted its own schedule of mutual corrections in preparation for the Supper, and other groups of leaders later followed suite. [240] The seriousness of the Supper preparation might seem draconian to modern ears, but it was less foreign to people of the sixteenth century, who participated actively in correcting each other even when there were no ecclesiastical or civic officials present. Grosse cites examples of ordinary Genevans rebuking neighbors for such things as blasphemy, and even requiring the offenders to demonstrate repentance (in the traditional way by kissing the ground) on the spot. Furthermore, such acts committed in the season of the Supper: before, after, or especially on the day, were regarded as particularly heinous. [241]

The period around the Supper came to have a special character, making four high points in the year. While this did not correspond to Calvin's ideal in frequency, it came close to expressing the more essential part of his vision of the unity of a people prepared to share together in communion with the body of Christ as the body of Christ.

---

[240] Grosse, *Les rituels de la Cène*, pp. 316-22. A humorous example is found in the consistory minutes for Tues., March 20, 1554, IX, 25: a man (tongue in cheek?) explains that he did not kiss the ground because he could not find it under the two feet of snow.

[241] Grosse, *Les rituels de la Cène*, pp. 415, 327, 331.

CHAPTER FOUR

WEEKDAY WORSHIP AND THE DAY OF PRAYER

Sunday was the fundamental fulcrum of liturgical time in Geneva, but it was not the only day of worship. Far from it. In fact, at least in the city, there were regular services on every weekday. There were also, however, some weekdays which received special attention, times when Genevans were expected to gather for particularly significant liturgies. The better known of these "holy days" were the "four feasts" of Christmas, Circumcision, Annunciation, and Ascension, which Geneva adopted to please its protector and patron Bern. These holy days were the continuation of an annual liturgical cycle, and it has long been assumed that when this tradition was abolished nothing was put in its place. There were, however, two ways that the Calvinist Reformed tradition created its own distinctive sense of liturgical time. One of these was the seasonal pattern of four annual celebrations of the Lord's Supper which was discussed in the previous chapter. The second was the day of prayer, a remarkable creation which Calvin very consciously and deliberately fostered, as will be seen below.

The words "abolish" and "abolition" have commonly been used to describe what happened to the traditional liturgical cycle in Geneva, but these terms are frequently employed in an ambiguous fashion. What exactly was "abolished"? Before examining the development of the practice of any of the holy days, therefore, it is important to note in what that observance consisted and thus what could be changed or "abolished." Four aspects of practice can be identified: the form of the liturgy, the Biblical text and content of the sermon, the number of services held on the day, and whether work was permitted or whether holiday status was obligatory.[1] For the "four feasts" two of these points, the form of the liturgy and the number of services, are rather obscure; on the other hand, the intended content or topic of the sermon and the holiday status are clear. For the day of prayer, the form of the liturgy and the usual content of the sermon are clear, while the two-services per day may have been a bit uncertain just at first, and holiday status in fact changed over time.

The simple liturgy used on most weekdays will be described briefly as a preface to the special weekday services. Then the Genevan story of the more "traditional" liturgical year will be traced from 1536 to its official abolition in 1550. The day of prayer expressed Calvin's own vision of the key complement to the Lord's Day worship, and it completes the regular pattern of corporate worship which he planned, so the major portion of this chapter will be devoted to examining this distinctive service in detail.

I: The Ordinary Weekday Liturgy

Reaffirming the centrality of the Lord's Day and elevating its value in tangible practice was the single most wide-spread change in liturgical time which Protestants made. The centrality of Sunday did not mean that this day was intrinsically more important, and so the corollary was to emphasize that all days can be equally holy – set apart to God. Like many others, Calvin interpreted this to mean that daily worship is right even if it is not required. That fact, combined with consternation about the ignorance of the people, led Protestants to institute regular preaching services as frequently as possible.

Weekday Services

Thus in the city of Geneva there were daily services of preaching and prayer on every weekday. (In rural areas usually there were services only on the special days: Sunday and the day of prayer.) In the three urban parishes, services were held in at least two places every day: St. Gervais and (usually) La Magdeleine. Greater Geneva also had an additional time of worship on three weekdays, Monday, Wednesday, and Friday, at St. Pierre. As will be seen below, the Wednesday services followed the printed day of prayer liturgy, whether they were at dawn or later. However, for the ordinary weekdays the *La forme des prieres* gives only a brief instruction.

---

[1]   Calvin had already expressed his view about people being able to go to work after worship in his letter to Bullinger in 1538 where he stated his willingness to accept the four feasts: see Letter 111, OC 10b:191. Grosse, *Les rituels de la Cène*, p. 129.

> For the work days, the minister makes an exhortation to prayer as seems good to him, accommodating it to the time and to the matter which he treats in his sermon. [2]

This very concise note is followed by a rubric introducing the Sunday liturgy. In itself the instruction here indicates that daily worship included prayer and preaching, but the form is left to the minister. The phrase about "accommodating it to the time" does not refer to fitting the petitions to the liturgical season but rather that the preacher should pay attention to the length of time he speaks, in order to keep within the hour allotted for the service. [3]

The picture of ordinary weekday worship can be filled out a little by examining Calvin's practice as it was recorded at the end of his life by those who published some of his sermons. There it becomes clear that the preacher opened with a prayer for illumination and sealing which included the Lord's Prayer, read his scripture text (picking up where he had left off the previous time), and gave his sermon. At the end of this Biblical exposition the pastor moved directly into a short petition reflecting the sermon text and then added an intercessory prayer of his own making[4] which concluded with the recitation of the Lord's Prayer and then the Apostles' Creed. The liturgy's instruction about "accommodating [the prayer] to the... matter which he treats in his sermon" appears to refer to the first individualized part of the intercessory prayer.

Reciting the Lord's Prayer in Worship

In 1549 an argument over the frequency of reciting the Lord's Prayer (and the Decalogue) in worship developed between the Genevan Senate and the ministers. Since the weekday sermons were the most unscripted and therefore the ones at the center of this debate, it is appropriate to provide evidence for the

---

2   *La forme des prières*, OS II, p. 18: "Les jours ouvriers, le Ministre fait telle exhortation à prier, que bon luy semble: l'accomodant au temps et à la matiere, qu'il traicte en sa predication."

3   The German translation of *La forme des prières* made in 1563 for Heidelberg in fact alters this rubric slightly to make it refer to the time in the sense of season; apparently in Germany where the most Protestants continued to follow the traditional Christological cycle, the translator misunderstood Calvin's intent. "An wercktagen thut des Prediger ein vermanung zum Gebet/ nach dem er für gut erkent/ die sich schickt auff die zeit/ oder auff die fuergenommene predigt. Am Sontage aber des morgens / wirdt gemeiniglich solchen form gebraucht/ wie folget." *Ordnung der Evangelischen Kirchen in Franckreich/ so gehalten wird im Gemeinen Gebet/ Reichung der Sacrament/ Einsegnen der Ehe/ Besuchung der Krancken. Und Christlichem Catechismo* (Churfuerstlichen Stadt Heydelberg/ durch Johannenm Mayer, 1563).

4   For the various extempore prayers (illumination-sealing, intercession, etc.), see chap. 6 at nn.134ff.

statement above that the Prayer was in fact said twice. According to two editors of Calvin's sermons, Jacques Bourgeois (1561) and Antoine Vincent (1563), both Calvin's prayer for illumination-and-sealing and his weekday intercessory prayer concluded with the recitation of the Lord's Prayer, the latter followed by an invitation which led to reciting the Apostles' Creed.[5] The presentation of evidence goes in stages in reverse chronological order, from the most certain evidence to the least substantiated.

If Bourgeois is speaking exactly, then at least by 1561 the Lord's Prayer was being recited twice (in the prayers before and after the sermon) and the Apostles' Creed once (after the intercessory prayer) on every ordinary weekday. There might be some question, however, about when the recorded practice began. However, the incipits of the intercessory prayers printed by both Bourgeois and Vincent match the evidence from the earliest regularly transcribed sermons which the stenographer Raguenier made in 1549. This indicates that at least by that time the Lord's Prayer was being recited at the end of the prayer after the sermon and probably the Creed as well. To go further back in time and to trace the first recitation of the Prayer it is necessary to turn to other sources.

In the Senate records for October 1549 there are a number of sharp debates, if not an actual battle, between the council and the ministers over liturgical matters. The focal point of the conflict was the Senate's demand that the preachers provide daily services at dawn, in addition to weekday sermons at the ordinary time of 6 a.m. or 7 a.m.[6] There were ancillary issues as well, and one of these was the magistrates' desire to have the Lord's Prayer and the Ten Commandments recited more often in the worship services "as they were at the beginning." (Although both texts are mentioned, apparently the argument centered on the Prayer because that is the item which is found in both versions of the minutes.) Calvin and the ministers objected. First, they reminded the Senate that the Lord's Prayer was being repeated twice on Sunday, twice at every service and at catechism. Secondly, they insisted that to add more repetitions of the Prayer would be to treat the recitation as a kind of sorcery or charm, in the way that reciting John 1:1ff (*In principio*) at the end of the Mass had traditionally been regarded. To make it clear that they considered this wrong, the ministers said that they would rather

---

5   OC 23 :756-57: "Nous le prierons de toutes ces choses ainsi que nostre bon Maistre et Seigneur Jesus Christ nous a enseigné de prier, disant Nostre Père qui es és cieux, etc. Nous prierons aussi ce bon Dieu nous donner vraye perseverance en sa sainte foy, l'augmenter de jour en jour en nous de laquelle nous ferons confession, disant: Je croy en Dieu le Pere, etc. *La benediction sur le Peuple apres le Sermon.* La grace de Dieu le Pere, et la paix de nostre Seigneur Jesus Christ par la communication du sainct esprit demeure eternellement avec vous, Amen."

6   See chap. 1 at nn.113ff.

be dead than give in on this point.[7] Clearly the Lord's Prayer was being recited twice in each service by 1549. However, from the council's viewpoint it sounds as if this represented a reduction.

The Senate's reference to "at the beginning" probably meant the first years of Farel's ministry. *La maniere et fasson* in fact seems to provide for the Prayer to be recited twice in the regular service, along with the Decalogue (and Apostles' Creed) once; if the Lord's Supper was celebrated at the same time, that would have added another recitation of the Prayer (and a second Creed). Since the sacrament was infrequent, it is not clear how often the Prayer would have been said three times.[8] On the other hand, it is obvious that although in 1549 the Decalogue was sung only at the Supper service (and almost certainly at catechism), under Farel it had been repeated more often, every Sunday in fact, so the Senate had reason to remember multiple recitations "in the beginning." One might speculate that at least one reason the ministers focused on the Lord's Prayer in this argument was that here they were on firmer ground in claiming that they were providing sufficient repetitions, whereas the frequency of the Decalogue was another matter. However, it would have been much harder to make a charm out of the Ten Commandments, not only because of their content but because they had never acquired such a reputation as the Lord's Prayer. Conceivably the latter could easily be in danger of becoming the Protestant replacement for the popular Ave Maria or *In principio*. Be that as it may, Calvin maintained that that early practice had been confused and he rejected the precedent; twice in each service was enough.

It is helpful here to look at Calvin's own liturgy. In particular the Strasbourg versions offer some insight into what he might have considered for Geneva. As noted in an earlier chapter, the Strasbourg service provided a fuller Sunday service. Both editions, 1542 and 1545, included a printed prayer for illumination-and-sealing which ended with the Lord's Prayer. The 1542 order also called

---

7   Oct. 28, 1549, OC 21:457 (RC 44 f250): "Et aussy leurs avoit esté commandé de faire l'oraison dominicale plus souvent et dire les commandementz de nostre Seigneur comme estoit au commencement: Surquoy il dictz que cella ne doibt estre faict, car il avoit esté faict estoit confus, et que quant ainsi seroit que il aymeroit myeulx mourir d'aultant qui sembleroit estre sorcerie et enchantement et que il estoit quasi que l'on faisoit du passé etc. Arresté que remonstrance luy soyent faictes," archives@etat.ge.ch accessed Aug. 16, 2013. A second version or recension of this day's debate was located by Lambert, *Preaching, Prayer, and Policing*, p. 328 n.111: "Quant au pater que l'on le dictz deux fois les dimanches deux fois [sic] à chascunes sermontz et aussi au cathezimes et que de faire aultrementz que cella seroit ung enchantement & ung charme comme aultreffois l'on disoyt In principio eratz verbum." RC 44 f268c (out of order). archives@etat.ge.ch accessed Aug. 16, 2013.

8   For *La maniere et fasson*, see discussion, chap. 3 at nn.59ff.

for the Prayer to be recited at the conclusion of the intercessory prayer, while the 1545 used the paraphrase of the Lord's Prayer which Calvin prepared for Geneva in the 1542 *La forme des prieres*. The latter only prescribed the paraphrase for the Sunday and day of prayer intercessions after the sermon. However, as Bourgeois and Vincent show, it is clear that the Lord's Prayer appeared in the prayer for illumination-and-sealing on Sundays and all weekdays, and in the intercessory prayer also on all weekdays.

When Calvin said to the Senate in 1549 that the Lord's Prayer was said "twice at each sermon and catechism" it is probable that he meant twice at every service. The argument then lines up the certain evidence: 1) the model of the Strasbourg liturgy of 1542 where the Lord's Prayer is used twice; 2) the similarity between this edition and the prayers for illumination-and-sealing and the weekday intercessory prayer recorded by Bourgeois and Vincent much later in Geneva, where again the Lord's Prayer is found twice; 3) the fact that the Bourgeois/ Vincent intercessory prayer was in regular use by 1549; and 4) Calvin's reference to two recitations of the Prayer in each service as the usual practice in 1549. It seems a logical deduction that the prayers Bourgeois and Vincent published were already the normal practice in Geneva in the 1540s, and thus the Lord's Prayer was used twice at every service. It was recited two times at every service except on Sunday morning and the day of prayer when the intercessory prayer in *La forme des prieres* called for the paraphrase, and then it would be recited once and paraphrased once.[9] In addition to the regular Sunday and weekday services, the Lord's Prayer was of course recited in the baptismal liturgy. When that sacrament was celebrated, the Prayer would be said three times. One can understand why Calvin objected to anything more. What all of this makes plain is that the Lord's Prayer was recited more often and much more consistently than *La forme des prieres* indicates, and its presence in worship was a constant. Calvin's extempore prayers not only served the theological edification of his congregation at the time but also provide modern scholars with very helpful clues to the history of worship in Geneva.

The basic daily worship in Geneva was extremely simple from a liturgical viewpoint and extremely didactic. It was intended to be edifying; participation by those in the pew consisted in being able to understand the whole service because it was now in the vernacular (instead of Latin). The form of these services was

---

[9]   It has been noted that the paraphrase was changed to recitation on the day of prayer in some editions of the liturgy beginning in 1552; see chap. 3 n.78. One might speculate that this was a concession to the Genevan Senate, but it is more likely to have been simply a way to shorten the service, especially given the ministers' version of "over my dead body."

stable – not to say monotonous, although naturally each preacher gave his own impress to the language of prayer as well as the sermon.

The common view of worship in Calvin's Geneva has been one of stark didacticism, and that is most nearly true for weekday services. However, the form of daily worship was not restricted to this basic pattern. There were two manifestations of more elaborate weekday liturgical observances: one was concerned with the remaining "four feasts" of the traditional Christological cycle which fell on weekdays, and the other was the Calvinist Reformed day of prayer. In terms of the development of these practices one might speak of two directions: the revision (down) of the inherited patterns until they were no longer observed as weekday celebrations, and the introduction and building up of a very distinctive weekly prayer service which gave liturgical expression to the characteristic Calvinist Reformed sense of God's providence.

II: The Traditional "Four Feasts," Passion Sermons, and Weekday "Holy Days" in Geneva

Although all Protestants gave renewed emphasis to Sunday and eliminated the veneration of saints and observance of most saints' days, many traditions retained a greater or lesser number of other holy days which celebrated particular events of Christ's life. The observance of Easter and Pentecost was not questioned,[10] but the Reformed tradition generally dropped many features of the traditional Christological cycle, such as Advent and Lent. However, most Reformed churches either retained or reintroduced the practice of four specific feasts: Christmas, Circumcision, Annunciation, and Ascension, and some gave particular attention to Christ's passion even if they did not restrict the observance to one day (Good Friday). Before examining how Geneva's practice fits into this story, it is helpful to summarize Calvin's reflections on the issue of special weekday "holy days."

Calvin's Reflections and Advice on the Christological "Holy Days"

In the previous chapter Calvin's discussion of religious time in the *Institutes of the Christian Religion* was examined. In 1536 he spoke of "other solemn days" focused on the events of salvation history as if these were normal, but in 1539 he personally rejected them, while still allowing that other churches might use such occasions appropriately. In the 1542 essay about the Lord's Supper published in

---

10 Scottish Presbyterians and English puritans became an exception to this general Reformed practice when they rejected the idea of marking these Sundays in a special way, e.g., with the celebration of the Lord's Supper.

the Strasbourg liturgies, Calvin in effect lists the occasions which he considered
appropriate to mark in a special way.

> We must greatly praise and exalt the memory of Jesus Christ and of all His
> benefits, that is, of His Incarnation, Passion, Resurrection, Ascension, the
> sending of the Holy Spirit, His Coming (again) to judge the world, and
> finally all that He has done for us. [11]

Although he uses the word "Incarnation," it is virtually certain that Calvin means
here the first coming of Christ which would be celebrated as the Nativity, and not
the "Conception" or "Annunciation" on March 25, since he repeatedly and
strongly objected to that observance because it was commonly associated with
the veneration of Mary. What remains, then, is a selected list of Christological
events which corresponds exactly to the occasions named in the book of his
sermons published in 1558 with the title *Some Sermons of John Calvin concerning the
Divinity, the Humanity, and the Birth of our Lord Jesus Christ: also concerning His Passion,
Death, Resurrection, Ascension, and Last Coming. Then concerning the Descent of the Holy
Spirit on the Apostles and St. Pierre's First Sermon.* [12] It is not surprising that it was these
"holy times" (minus the Last Coming, naturally!) which would eventually become
the key observances in Geneva.

In addition to these public theological affirmations there are a number of more
occasional reflections on Christological observances by Calvin in the context
of debates about the "four feasts." Most of these are found in correspondence,
letters of advice or explanation. This subject has been of special interest to editors
of Calvin's sermons, and use has been made here of two of the recent scholarly
discussions, by Erwin Mülhaupt (1981), [13] and Willem Balke and W. H. Th. Moehn
(1994). [14] The debate is somewhat complex; it will be divided into several parts. First

---

[11]   *La forme des prières*, OS II, p. 44: "Finallement nous enseignons/ qu'il fault rendre graces au
    Seigneur JHs pour ces grandz benefices icy de cueur/ de parolles/ et de faict, et qu'il nous fault
    grandement louer et exalter la memoire de JHsChrist et de tous ses benefices c'est à sçavoir de
    son Incarnation Passion Resurrection/ Asçencion/ de la mission du sainct Esprit/ de son
    Advenement pour juger le monde, et finallement de tout ce qu'il est qu'il a fait pour nous/ et
    ordonné en nous." Capitalization in the translation reflects the French, since it appears that
    these are intended to mark special "feast" days.

[12]   See chap. 6 at nn.69ff.

[13]   Mülhaupt, "Einleitung," S. VII, pp. xlii-xlvii. Mülhaupt gives a brief overview of the situation in
    Geneva when Calvin arrived, the theological impetus from Luther, and the further develop-
    ment of the rejection of the liturgical year (which he considers fanatical as well as evidence of an
    admirably high regard for the Bible, p. xlvi).

[14]   Balke & Moehn, "Introduction," S. VIII, pp. ix-xi. Balke and Moehn devote most attention to
    the ways Calvin discussed the feast days in correspondence; I am grateful to their work for
    alerting me to these texts, though I have also consulted the latter independently.

is Calvin's correspondence with colleagues, before 1550 and then after that date; this will be followed by scholars' discussion of Calvin's position.

Correspondence before 1550

Over the years Calvin wrote about the practice of Christological holy days on a number of occasions. When he and his colleagues were obliged to leave Geneva in April 1538 because they would not accept the Bernese "ceremonies," Calvin sent to Heinrich Bullinger a list of responses to the issues he considered involved in the conflict and the ecclesiastical situation generally. Of the fourteen articles, one deals with the feast days. There the young Frenchman explains to his colleague in Zurich that the problem is not a principled objection to the feasts per se but Bern's "extremely domineering declaration" ordering the institution of the feasts (as if they were essential). He thought that this declaration must be removed and the regulation of the four observances must not require an obligatory holiday for the full day, but those who wished should be free to go to work after worship.[15] In effect, Calvin was reflecting here something like his position in the 1539 *Institutes*: the feasts might be observed by (other) churches provided they are recognized as *adiaphora* and not raised to the level of the Sabbath command. Here he concedes that he would accept the practice of weekday holy days for the sake of ecclesiastical peace, provided the feasts are not accorded the same rank as Sunday with its complete rest as ordained by God's word.

Much the same principle guided other comments which Calvin made about the feasts. In October 1543 he responded to questions from the ministers at Montbéliard about Lutheran liturgical practices which their prince was considering, among which was the (re-)introduction of various holy days. Calvin noted that this should be resisted more firmly than some other things (e.g., ringing of bells) but that the ministers should not fight over matters of lesser importance; the principal thing was to resist what was unedifying or superstitious (which here meant the content of specific holidays).

> And you have plausible grounds for refusing, for in the papacy they worship with great solemnity the Conception and the Assumption of the Virgin. What will the servant of Christ have to say if he mounts up

---

[15] Letter 111, OC 10:191: "In feriis plurima laboramus perplexitate, quemadmodum semper sumus professi, neque alia conditione concedere possumus istas quatuor institui, nisi ut tollatur nimium imperiosa earum indictio, ac liberum sit iis qui volent post concionem ad opus se conferre. Non tamen fenestram audemus aperire tot turbis, quas emersuras iam prospicimus si aliter fiat."

into a pulpit on those days, except to ridicule the foolishness of those who invented such festivals?[16]

The exchange between Calvin and the ministers in Montbéliard about these issues continued, and the next year his advice to them listed the three main superstitions which they should avoid.

> Regarding the ringing of bells and feast days, we think it is better for you to bear these foolish matters than to desert the station in which the Lord has placed you. At the same time you will show that you do not approve and also be free to reprove diligently the superstitions which come from these points, as you ought to do. However there are three principal points: distinguishing one day from others; defining these holidays as the worship of God; observing the days not so much in honor of God (which the Jewish practice itself was), but also for the sake of people.[17]

Clearly, tolerating the religious bells and holy days was better than leaving their pastoral duties, provided the ministers maintained the right to rebuke superstition. For Calvin, the real problem was not the ceremony of having liturgical feast days but the danger of the theological implications which so easily flowed from setting any day (except Sunday) apart. People might think that one day was more holy than another; they might believe that feast days were essential for or constitutive of the worship of God; and they might conclude that observing specific days for worship was actually doing something for God rather than serving the needs of the human community (polity). This advice distinguishing *adiaphora* and essentials expresses in different words the points Calvin had already made in the *Institutes*.[18]

---

[16] Letter 506, OC 11:625: "De campanae pulsu nolim vos pertinacius reclamare, si obtineri nequeat ut princeps remittat: non quia probem, sed quia rem contentione non dignam arbitror. In festis non recipiendis cuperem vos esse constantiores, sic tamen ut non litigetis de quibuslibet, sed de iis tantum quae nec in aedificationem quidquam factura sunt, et superstitionem prima ipsa facie prae se ferunt. Et habetis plausibilem recusandi materiam. Nam in papatu magna celebritate conceptionem et ascensionem [Assumption] Virginis coluerunt. Quid habebit servus Christi quod dicat, si suggestum conscenderit illis diebus, nisi ut eorum stultitiam rideat qui tales ferias excogitarunt?"

[17] May 8, 1544; Letter 547, OC 11:707: "De pulsu campanarum et diebus festis ita sentimus, ferendas potius esse vobis has ineptias, quam stationem in qua estis a Domino collocati deserendam: modo ne approbetis, modo etiam liberum vobis sit reprehendere quae inde sequentur superstitiones, atque in eam rem diligenter incumbatis. Sunt autem tria potissimum capita: quod dies a die discernitur, quod cultus Dei constituitur in feriis, quod non in Dei tantum honorem, quod ipsum iam foret iudaicum, sed hominum quoque dies observantur. " Quoted also in Balke and Moehn, "Introduction," S VIII, p. x. I have preferred a slightly more literal translation.

[18] See chap. 3 at nn.9, 13f, 19, 31.

Correspondence after 1550

After Geneva's decision to abolish the weekday feasts at the end of 1550, Calvin wrote a number of explanatory letters to colleagues in other places, exculpating himself from responsibility. Whether this is a case of protesting too much, as some scholars think, will be considered below. What is of interest at the moment is the content of his letters. The first two were written to a minister in Buren and to Johannes Haller in Bern early in January 1551. The substance of the two letters is similar but Calvin gives the minister of Buren a fuller explanation. First he denies the rumor that Geneva had abolished the Lord's Day, and explains that they have changed the celebration of the birth of Christ to the nearest Sunday. In the next section of both letters Calvin claims that he was not responsible for the abrogation and gives a brief summary of the history of the holy days in Geneva, from his perspective. In writing to Haller he emphasizes the relationship to Bern.

> Before I ever entered the city [Geneva], there were no festivals but the Lord's day. Those celebrated by you [in Bern] were approved of by the same public decree by which Farel and I were expelled; and it was rather extorted by the tumultuous violence of the ungodly, than decreed according to the order of law. Since my recall, I have pursued the moderate course of keeping Christ's birthday as you are wont to do. On other days when there are extraordinary occasions of public prayer the shops are shut in the morning, and every one may return to his work or other activities after dinner. [19]

Calvin goes on to indicate to Haller that the problem which had developed was that some people would not accept the "common custom" by which (other) people returned to work after the morning observances. He considered the diversity of behavior (some keeping a full holiday, others going back to work after worship and the mid-day meal) to be completely unacceptable, and asked the

---

[19] *The Letters of John Calvin*, vol. 2, p. 288. Letter 1428, OC 14:5: "Priusquam urbem unquam ingrederer, nullae prorsus erant feriae praeter diem Dominicum. Quae apud vos celebrantur, eodem plebiscito acceptae sunt, quo ego et *Farellus* fuimus expulsi: idque improborum violentia tumultuose extortum magis fuit, quam legitimo ordine decretum. Ex quo sum revocatus hoc temperamentum quaesivi, ut Christi natalis celebraretur vestro more: aliis autem diebus extraordinariae supplicationes tabernis mane clausis fierent, a prandio ad suas operas aut res agendas quisque rediret. Erant tamen interea praefracti quidam, qui praepostera quadam malitia a communi more dissiderent. Ea varietas quum in ecclesia rite composita tolerabilis non foret, atque etiam apud exteros suspicionem gigneret, non bene civibus inter se convenire: senatum hortatus sum, ut commodo remedio in posterum hoc dissidium tolleretur. Verum simul illa, quam hactenus coluerant, moderatio disertis verbis ac nominatim a me laudata est."

Senate to remedy the matter. Calvin criticized the person he believed had spread the negative report (i.e., that Geneva had abolished Sunday); this was the Bernese minister whom he considered responsible for the original problem in 1538. In the process the Genevan pastor reveals his own sense of liturgical priorities. "When I once asked him [the Bernese man] why circumcision had a right to more honour than the death of Christ, he was compelled to be silent." Writing to the minister in Buren about the same point, Calvin is more forceful. Giving circumcision precedence over Christ's death is "preposterous" – putting the cart before the horse, one of his favorite expressions for disordered priorities.[20] It is clear that, while he did not consider remembering Christ's circumcision superstitious as such, Calvin definitely saw the observance of Christ's passion as more important in the scope of what he had called "solemn days, wherein the mysteries of our salvation are called to mind." As he concluded his letter to Haller, Calvin reiterated his claim not to have initiated the liturgical changes in Geneva. While he did not regret them, he insists that "if I had got my choice, I should not have decided in favour of what has now been agreed upon."[21]

In a letter to Viret written only a few days after the one to Haller in January 1551 Calvin mentions the issue of liturgical days but does not discuss it at length. In another note to Viret several weeks later Calvin indicates his pleasure that Haller had responded moderately.[22] In April Calvin felt compelled to write again about the liturgical changes, this time to Bullinger, in response to the latter's question about the (persisting?) rumor that Geneva no longer observed Sunday but had changed to the sixth day (Saturday).[23] Calvin hastens to assure his Zurich colleague that these are silly rumors, and then proceeds to recount the same

---

[20] Letter 1428, OC 14:5: "Quum olim ex ipso sciscitarer quo iure circumcisio plus haberet honoris quam mors Christi, obmutescere coactus est." *The Letters of John Calvin*, vol. 2, p. 289. For use of "preposterous" elsewhere, e.g., *Inst.* 1.7.4 "Praepostere tamen faciunt qui disputando contendunt solidam scripturae fidem adstruere."

[21] Letter 1428, OC 14:5: "Ego tametsi neque suasor, neque impulsor fui, sic tamen accidisse non moleste fero. Quod si statum ecclesiae nostrae aeque compertum haberes, non dubitares meo iudicio subscribere. Hoc tamen testatum esse volo, si mihi delata optio fuisset, quod nunc constitutum est non fuisse pro sententia dicturum." *The Letters of John Calvin*, vol. 2, p. 289. The reference to "solemn days" is the phrase in the 1536 *Institutes* which was dropped in subsequent editions; see chap. 3 at n.13.

[22] Letters 1429 & 1441, to Viret on Jan. 4 and 24, 1551; OC 14:6-7, 27-28.

[23] April 3, 1551, Bullinger to Calvin, letter 1476, OC 14:95: "S. D. Mirus spargitur de vestra ecclesia rumor quem omnino vanum esse contendo, abrogatam esse ex nescio qua contentione diem dominicam, imo non abrogatam sed translatam in sextam feriam. Spero autem te (nisi te invito aut nesciente id factum sit) huiusmodi innovationibus, quae plurimum incommodi nihil utilitatis habent, non delectari."

history that he had told Haller,[24] although at considerably greater length and with some more details. He explains that one reason for the (false) stories might be the fact that the celebration of Christ's birth had been moved to the nearest Sunday. He denies, however, that this was his wish and so disclaims responsibility if Bullinger disapproves.[25] Calvin also adds that he could have asked for the abolition of the feast days as a condition of his return to Geneva, and he had not done so. Here he notes (again) that he considers it preposterous to celebrate the Circumcision and not the Passion of Christ,[26] and adds a sharp criticism of the feast of the Annunciation.

> Hitherto because the common people worship the day of the conception of Christ under the name of Mary, I have sharply spoken against this superstition every year. For in their language the French call it the feast of Our Lady in March and the day is commonly considered sacred to her.[27]

Obviously in Calvin's eyes there were differences among the various feasts. He has nothing particularly negative to say about Circumcision, although he believed it had been inappropriately elevated above the remembrance of Christ's passion. The Annunciation, however, he considered superstitious because it was

---

[24] Letter 1482, OC 14:105: "S. Quod frivolis illis sermonibus de abrogato apud nos die dominico fidem non habueris prudenter abs te factum est. Nam eiusmodi fabulae portentis sua absurditas fidem omnem derogat. Quod autem fiducia nostrae modestiae fretus graviter repulisti calumniam quae nobis inurebatur, in eo amici et fratris officium nobis praestitisti. Nam certe plus quam insanus essem si inepta hac et frivola novitate turbarem bonos, improbos armarem, omnium me exponerem ludibrio. Et quid de me loquor?" "Verum id quoque inadvertentia potius quam pervicacia accidit. Antequam urbem hanc primo adventu ingressus essem abrogati erant dies festi omnes praeter dominicum. *Farello* et *Vireto* hoc utile visum fuerat: ego receptae consuetudini libenter acquievi. Eandem quoque rationem nova haec Bernatium provincia sequuta initio fuerat. Surrexit *Contenus*, nec minus tumultuose pro diebus festis quam olim Victor Romanus pro suo paschate pugnavit. Ex quo autem fuimus expulsi quatuor festi dies cum aliis quibusdam ritibus instituti sunt."

[25] Letter 1482, OC 14:105: "Fortassis res una fabulae materiam praebuit, quod festus dies qui Christi natali dicatus erat in proximum diem dominicum translatus est. Rectene an secus, meum non est pronunciare, ac per me licet ut libere tuo id iudicio improbes. Quando enim factum est me nec autore nec conscio, mihi imputari non debet. Miraberis nostros inconsultis pastoribus receptum in ecclesia ordinem ita subito mutasse."

[26] Letter 1482, OC 14:105: "Reversus, quum momento possem quidquid me absente actum erat magnae partis applausu convellere, placide quievi: nisi quod dissimulare non poteram, praepostere celebrari Christi circumcisionem praeterito mortis die."

[27] Letter 1482, OC 14:105-06: "Iam quod diem conceptionis Christi sub Mariae nomine plebs colebat, acriter in eam superstitionem quotannis invectus sum. Galli enim sua lingua festum Nostrae Dominae in Martio appellant, ac proinde dies illi sacer esse vulgo creditur. Sic tamen mihi temperavi ut compescerem ex adverso qui dies illos prorsus tollendos esse clamitabant."

commonly regarded as a Marian feast. Having clarified his position on the feast days as such, Calvin then goes on to explain to Bullinger what he did want: the abolition of their obligatory holiday status. After the worship services in the morning and dinner, work should be permitted.

> A middle way would have pleased us, so that there might be holiday in the morning and the shops would remain closed, and after dinner people might go about their ordinary work. This was ordered nine years ago. But nevertheless by this means the strife was not quieted. For diversity in having shops open or closed produced shameful discord. When neither end nor remedy was found, last year I went to the Senate, and I asked them in their prudence to think of some way to maintain the people in better agreement. I did not speak expressly about abrogating [the feasts]. Indeed I have praised the Senate that heretofore it has endeavored to foster peace by accommodating itself to the Bernese custom. When I heard that these days had been abrogated by the vote, it was completely unexpected so that I was almost stunned. Certainly if I were asked about this decision I would say nothing else except that I would hardly have ventured to establish (things) in this manner. [28]

Several points are noteworthy. One is that a significant focus for Calvin was the obligatory observance of a full holiday. A second point is his claim that the law requiring this had been changed "nine years ago," i.e., in 1542, so that the ordinary work and commercial life of the town would be prohibited only in the morning before dinner. As will be seen below, Calvin's memory for the date of this action seems to have been off by two years; he requested it at least by 1544 and did persuade the senate to sponsor a partial holiday for the day of prayer. Along with this Calvin gives another date: the previous year, when he had spoken to the Senate about what he would later call the "scandal" of discordant behavior in Geneva. Here his memory appears to have telescoped time, since the recorded request came as early as 1548. The final point is Calvin's weak statement about not having requested the abrogation of the feasts explicitly, his claim to be completely

---

[28] Letter 1482, OC 14:106: "Media ratio nobis placuerat, ut mane clausis tabernis feriae agerentur, a prandio conferrent se ad ordinarias operas. Id ante annos novem statutum fuit. Neque tamen hoc modo sedata fuerunt certamina. Varietas enim in clausis vel apertis tabernis turpe dissidium prodebat. Quum nec finis nec remedium inveniretur, anno proxime elapso veni in curiam, rogavi senatum ut modum aliquem pro sua prudentia excogitaret quo populus in meliore consensu retineretur. De abrogatione nominatim loquutus non sum. Quin potius laudavi quod hactenus fovendae pacis studio se ad Bernatium morem accommodasset. Quum plebiscito audivi abrogatos esse dies illos, adeo res erat inexspectata ut propemodum obstupuerim. Certe si sententiam rogatus essem, nihil aliud dico nisi quod vix ausus essem ita statuere."

surprised, and his further comment that what was done was not what he would have chosen. It does appear that he "protests too much."

At this point a brief excursus may be permitted with regard to the comparative practices of Bullinger's Zurich and Calvin's Geneva. This illumines in a new way more precisely what Calvin was actually arguing with Bullinger, and reveals that the similarities between the two cities were as remarkable as their differences. In Zurich, the "Christmas" Lord's Supper service took place on Sunday, not on Dec. 25, and the "Pentecost" Supper was celebrated on the previous Sunday (i.e., the Sunday after Ascension). December 25th and Ascension and Pentecost – as well as the next following day each time – were maintained with the traditional lections and holiday status, but the Supper was not a part of the observance.[29] It is clear that Bullinger could not object to holding the Lord's Supper service on the Sunday closest to Christmas-Dec. 25 because that was what Zurich did. His own practice does imply that the celebration of the Lord's Supper was not seen as an integral part of the major Christological observances; it would be held on an appropriate Sunday in proximity to the feast day three out of four times per year. Assuming that Calvin knew of this Zurich schedule for the Supper, it is not surprising that his response to Bullinger focuses on the problem of the civic holiday status of these traditional holy days. In point of fact, what Geneva was now doing was in some ways like the Zurich practice of celebrating the sacrament only on Sundays. Zurich had apparently dissociated the Lord's Supper from the Christological feast day, and kept the latter on whatever day the date (e.g., Dec. 25) fell. When the Bernese ceremonies were re-introduced in 1538, Geneva followed the tradition of keeping the feast day observance and the sacrament

---

[29]   See Engammare, "Reformed Preaching in the Sixteenth Century," p. 212 lists the sermons in Bullinger's series for the special holy days of the year 1555, beginning with Circumcision. This includes "the Sunday after Ascension when the second Lord's Supper of the year was celebrated (*'Sermo de coena. 26. Maii 1555'*), Pentecost morning (*'In Festo Pentecostes. 2. Junii 1555. De missione Spiritus Sancti. Ex Actorum 2'*) and evening (*'Concio vespertina. Explicatio Psalmi 113'*), the day after Pentecost (*'Postera Pentecostes. 3. Junii 1555. Ex Johan. 3. Et sicut Moses exaltavit serpentem in deserto etc.'*).... the Lord's Supper before Christmas (*'Sermo de Coena Domini. 22. Decembris 1555'*), Christmas (*'In Festo Nativitatis Domini 1555. Ex Lucæ .2.'*), Christmas evening (*'Concio vespertina. Titum III. Apparavuit enim gratia dei saluti fera etc.'*) and the day after Christmas (*'Postera Nativitatis 1555. Ex Lucæ .2. De pastoribus'*)." While this set of sermons comes from a particular year, after Geneva's change of the feast days, there is no reason to believe that 1555 was in any way exceptional; Zurich had probably been following this organization for "Christmas," "Easter," "Pentecost" Suppers for many years. Zwingli introduced the new sacramental liturgy in Holy Week 1525, and the celebration was held on three successive days to accommodate the whole population, but obviously that was an initial action (cf. Chap. 3 at n.189) and when Bullinger moved back to a stronger emphasis on the traditional liturgical year, he apparently separated the Supper from the actual feast day.

together, even if that meant celebrating the Supper on a weekday. Now Geneva maintained the tie between the feast and the sacrament, but moved both to Sunday. What Calvin may have meant when he said this was not his idea was that he would have been content to have kept Christmas-Dec. 25 as an observance, provided it was not a required day of rest like Sunday and provided everyone knew and followed this "weekday" status. For Geneva to move the Lord's Supper celebration to Sunday was in fact to follow Zurich practice so Calvin had no need to offer an apologia to Bullinger. On the other hand, Calvin could perhaps honestly say that he had not asked to have the observance of Christmas-Dec. 25 moved to the nearest Sunday, as long as celebrating it during the week did not require any more "holiday" status than was established for the day of prayer.

Some Scholars' Discussion and Analysis

As Balke and Moehn point out, Calvin's protests that this was not what he would have done has been noted by various scholars, who "feel that Calvin is not as innocent in this abolition as he appears to be." Balke and Moehn go on to give a balanced summary of the question of the four feasts.

> We can only establish that Calvin was not strictly opposed to the liturgical year. He would not have abolished Christmas. He did not think much of Circumcision Day, and the Mary-feast was in his eyes complete superstition. The fact that the day of the death of Christ was not honoured, he considered a matter of ignorance. At Easter and Whitsun, he always interrupted his sermons in the *lectio continua* and addressed the "feast matters." He also interrupted his weekday sequential material in order to address the history of the passion. Social care was an important issue to Calvin. The weekly rest day is a gift of God, but too many days off would lead to lawlessness, idleness, alcohol abuse and all kinds of immorality. [30]

The "holy days" marked by specific interruptions in Calvin's *lectio continua* practice will be considered further below. For the moment it is worth considering, in light of the totality of the reformer's comments on the "other solemn days," what exactly is meant by Balke and Moehn's helpful summary and interpret it further.

Of the six special feasts, five are mentioned: Christmas, Circumcision, Annunciation, Easter, and Pentecost; Ascension is not named. One point of confusion about this summary is that Balke and Moehn apparently use "abolish" ambiguously and do not distinguish between Calvin's view of the content of the

---

[30] Balke & Moehn, "Introduction," S VIII, p. xi.

celebration and the relationship of a day's observance to its "holiday" status. In fact Geneva continued to observe the Nativity (the subject matter of Christmas was not abolished), so what Balke and Moehn seem to mean by "abolish" is that Calvin would not have changed the celebration from Dec. 25 to the nearest Sunday, if it was clear that people could attend to their ordinary business after the morning worship and dinner. With regard to Circumcision and Annunciation, however, Balke and Moehn appear to be considering the content of the two days, which were effectively "abolished" as observances. They rightly indicate that Calvin would (probably happily) have passed over the special content of Circumcision day on Jan. 1, but was much more strongly opposed to preaching on the subject of the Annunciation on March 25 each year. (In both cases, he naturally treated these passages in the ordinary course of his *lectio continua* sermons on Luke 2.) These scholars appropriately point out that Calvin honored the subject matter of Easter and Pentecost regularly on the Sundays when those feasts had traditionally been observed, but these two celebrations were not part of the argument over the four feasts so they will be discussed later, along with the question of Ascension and the Passion. What Calvin's 1551 letters to various colleagues reveal is his own understanding of the relative values of (week)day feasts which could or should be appropriately observed.

Balke and Moehn appropriately note that there is a moral and social consideration in Calvin's desire to eliminate "too many days off," but at least in the materials they cite the reformer does not refer to that well-known problem. What he does express is concern for the witness of a united community, in which times allotted to daily work and times reserved for corporate worship (to be undisturbed by ordinary business) must be commonly agreed upon. In 1548 he was probably accurate in reporting that he had asked for the full implementation of a regulation about keeping shops closed until after morning services, followed by a return to ordinary work for everyone. As will be seen below, what was objectionable in the content of the four feasts was probably well on its way to being curtailed by the mid-1540s. The main difficulty remaining in 1550 was the confused state of practicing the "holiday" aspect. It is likely, as Calvin wrote to Haller, that the change (once made) was more acceptable to him than he expressed to Bullinger. However, it is also possible that he would not have made the change in the way that it was done... for fear that it might jeopardize the day of prayer which was very important to him and for which he had fought to achieve the status of a partial holiday. That is, he would probably have been content to limit the holiday status of the four feasts (while removing the "superstitions"), rather than jeopardize the day of prayer. To grasp fully Calvin's position on liturgical time and the

observance of feasts, it is necessary to understand his creation of this special
worship occasion.

In order to complete the discussion of the four feasts, however, it is helpful to
trace the development of Geneva's practical regulations for weekday worship,
before examining more closely Calvin's explicitly affirmed sense of liturgical time
in Sunday worship and the day of prayer.

(Re-)Shaping the Liturgical Calendar in Geneva

Scripture shaped liturgical time for Geneva and the Calvinist Reformed
tradition in a number of ways. Besides the dominant role given to Sunday
worship, there were two other interrelated aspects of this Biblical reform of
time: the way that texts for preaching were chosen and the weighing and then
rejection of much of the liturgical and devotional tradition. As is well known,
many Reformed preachers chose to follow the practice of *lectio continua*, which
meant preaching straight through a Biblical book in order to explain the
individual passages in their context and to teach the whole content of scripture,
the Old Testament as well as the New. To do this required dropping most of
the medieval religious calendar which had coordinated specific selected readings from scripture (mostly of course the New Testament and Psalms) with
particular holy days. The old calendar of Christological holy days and saints
days was also rejected for theological reasons. The veneration of the saints and
the whole concept of especially holy people were incompatible with the Protestant understanding of holiness and the teaching of the first commandment
about worshiping God alone. In addition, the Reformed tradition also regarded
many of the holy days in the Christological cycle of the Roman church as
unbiblical.

Here the re-shaping of Geneva's liturgical calendar from 1536 through its
fully developed form in 1550 will be outlined. A key point is the question of rest
or work. Traditionally holy days were holidays from daily work, they distinguished sacred time from profane. Over the years the status of specific religious
observances would be measured by whether or not work was allowed on that
day.

The Liturgical Year in Protestant Geneva from 1536 to 1541

The "abolition of the liturgical year" for which Calvin is (in)famous in fact
antedated him. When Farel and his allies gained control of Genevan worship
practices in 1536, they persuaded the city to do away with all the holy days except
Sunday. In this sense they were not innovating but following the precedent of a

number of other Reformed cities, especially Strasbourg,[31] but also their powerful neighbor Bern.[32] On March 23, 1536, the Senate ordered that no feasts would be celebrated except Sundays. A few months later in June this was repeated, along with an order about holidays related to monthly fairs.[33] Within a few days a more detailed proclamation instructed everyone to work six days per week and decreed there should be no holidays except Sundays, when people should come to worship.[34] Various other changes in "ceremonies" were also made, such as removing baptisteries and celebrating the Lord's Supper with leavened bread.[35] Thus, when Calvin arrived, and for the whole course of his first ministry in Geneva, Sundays were the only days of religious observance and the only holidays when shops were closed (apart from the specific "secular" fair days). From 1536 to 1538 the orders against keeping the traditional medieval feasts were repeated, along with increased penalties.[36] This seems to have influenced the dates when the Lord's Supper was celebrated, setting them at irregular intervals. There are notes on Oct. 5, 1537, for

---

31 Bornert, *La réforme protestante du culte*, pp. 136, 337-38. In 1525 Strasbourg abolished all holy days except Sunday, according to Bucer's plan. The saints days were eliminated and Christological feasts were remembered on Sundays. By 1530 Bucer even expressed the desire to drop the Christological feasts, but by 1536 he was ready to re-establish those which had been observed by the early church. By 1548 the liturgical legislation prescribed a new form of liturgical year, with Christological holy days and even some commemoration of the saints as members of the body of Christ, although Sunday still had primacy.

32 Mülhaupt, "Einleitung," S VII, p. xliv, gives an overview. Bern had abolished the various ceremonies at the beginning of its reform, but after the fateful defeat of the Protestant cantons in 1531, they had gradually moved in a more conservative direction in religious practice. In December 1537 they reintroduced the use of baptisteries, unleavened bread for communion, and the four feasts.

33 June 13, 1536, RC I, p. 35: "(De festis) Ibidem fuit loquutum de festis et feriis, et arrestatur quod nulla festa, preter Dominico, solemnizentur, ferie messis dumtaxat per mensem, a festo Baptiste ad Magdallennam."

34 June 16, 1536, RC I, p. 37: "(Cride) ... Item quod omnes artem habentes debeant per sex dies laborare, non ferare nisi Dominico; inmo per dictos sex dies apperire buthecas, diebus Dominico cessantes veniant ad sermonem et expectatur donec argumentari decesserint, pena 3 solidorum."

35 Baptisteries were removed in the early months of iconoclastic fervor; for their re-introduction in 1538 and final removal, see chap. 1 at nn.22ff. For changes in the bread of communion, see Grosse, *Le rituel de la cène*, pp. 225-28.

36 July 13, 1536, RC I, p. 69: increased fine from 3 to 5 sols. Jan. 16, 1537, RC II, p. 23: close shops when the last bell for the Sunday sermon is rung, do not hawk pastries during the sermon. March 30, 1537, RC II, p. 127: lieutenant must hold court every week day and not observe feasts. June 1, 1537, RC II, p. 203: person punished for observing feast the previous day (Corpus Christi). June 4, 1537, RC II, p. 208: ordinance against observing feasts, with graduated fines. Dec. 25, 1537, RC II, p. 447: dizeniers told to go through their district to mark those who are observing the feast and write their names down for punishment.

the sacrament on the next Sunday, Oct. 7; and on Jan. 3, 1538, for the following Sunday, Jan. 6,[37] dates which either had no role in the liturgical tradition or a more subordinate one (Epiphany of less stature than Christmas).

Meanwhile, however, Bern decided to change its liturgical plan to follow the organization of Zurich. The Zwinglian reform had retained four of the main Christological holy days which fall on weekdays: Christmas, Circumcision, Annunciation, and Ascension, as well as the Sundays of Easter and Pentecost. When the Genevan Senate received a letter from Bern regarding various liturgical practices which had been discussed at a church synod on March 31, 1538, the council decided to re-adopt these holy days (along with certain other ceremonies related to the Lord's Supper and baptism) and required the ministers to implement the plan.[38] This order came on Friday, April 19, two days before Easter. Farel, Calvin, and their colleague Corauld asked to postpone discussion of the changes for a few months until the synod of Reformed churches scheduled after Pentecost.[39] The Genevan authorities insisted on adopting Bern's practices instantly by celebrating the Easter communion with unleavened bread, without waiting to work out a reconciliation of the liturgical diversity, and told the ministers they could not preach if they would not follow the new liturgical forms.[40] The ministers felt they had no options; they could not in good

---

[37] References in RC to the Lord's Supper being ordered by the Senate at the ministers' request: Oct. 5, 1537, RC II, p. 345: "dimenche prochain en vuyt jours." Jan. 3, 1538, RC III, p. 4: "dimenche prochain." NB these are not fixed feasts.

[38] April 19, 1538, RC III, pp. 226-227: "Recyue une missive de Berne touchant du seynne [synod] tenus az Laussane [on March 31, with purpose of making Reformed Lord's Supper liturgy uniform], pour adviser si voullons observer les ceremonies comprises en ycelle, lesquelles az esté resoluz d'observer, selon de grand Conseyl general. Nonobstant az esté advisé de monstré ladte missive az Faret et Caulvin, predicans, autquieulx leur az esté lyseuz et leur az esté fayct les remonstrances voyr si veullent observer lesdtes ceremonies aut non, et leur az esté donner terme pour responder. Resoluz que l'on doyge suyvre az laz forme de ladte missive, special- lement touchant laz Cenne." P. 228: "Az esté resoluz que laz Cenne se fasse, s'il est possible fere, az laz forme de ladte missive, cart az icelle l'on se veultz tenyr." The same day, perhaps anticipating Farel's resistance, the council told Henry de La Mare to preach at St. Gervais and give the Lord's Supper, p. 226. (St. Gervais was Farel's parish.)

[39] April 19, 1538, RC III, p. 227: "Lesdictz predicant on prié de non poient volloyr fere chose de noveau, jusqu'az laz Penthecoste, et que entre cy et là se tiendraz ung seyne az Churyt et Estrabour" [Zurich & Strasbourg]. De La Mare also asked not to preach [at St. Gervais] because his colleagues objected, but the Senate insisted, and he was given a license to preach [also] in Bernese territory, according to the Bernese liturgy, pp. 227, 228. Meanwhile, Corauld was prohibited from preaching because he had been criticizing the magistracy, pp. 227, 228.

[40] Corauld was jailed on Sat. April 20 because he preached, contrary to orders, and Farel and Calvin with various Senate members and supporters petitioned the council to release him and let him preach. At the same time, the ministers were asked again about following Bern's liturgy and

conscience share the communion when the church was so divided. Defying Senate orders, they insisted on preaching on Easter Sunday, April 21, 1538, but refused to celebrate the Lord's Supper. Within hours the council reacted angrily and arranged a meeting of the Two Hundred for the next day,[41] which was followed by a General Council on Tuesday the 23rd; Farel, Calvin, and Corauld were ordered to leave within three days, and they departed immediately.[42] Taking over the ecclesiastical order, the Senate decided that the sacrament would be celebrated the following Sunday with the ministers who remained, but in view of the fact that there were only two pastors left, the Supper would be held in only two rather than three churches.[43]

For Calvin and his exiled colleagues, neither the observance of holy days nor even the use of unleavened bread was the sticking point. It was instead the issue of control of the church and respect for the religious conditions necessary for right participation in the Lord's Supper. The ecclesiastical-civil power struggle is too well known to need detailed explanation. The factors surrounding preparation for the Supper have been fully examined by Christian Grosse and very briefly summarized in the previous chapter, although it is sometimes forgotten that this conflict in the community was a significant issue for the ministers in 1538. (They not only objected to civil pressure to conform to Bern's ways, but they considered the disunity and fighting a primary hindrance to sharing in communion.) The point here is to unfold the changes in liturgical time in Geneva.

Having rid themselves of their uncooperative preachers, the Genevan government introduced the regular practice of following Bernese customs, including the

---

refused: "... lesquel predicans on responduz que il n'en veullent fere, synon selon ce que Dieu leur az comandé." RC III, p. 230. The Senate met again later on the same day, Sat. April 20, and reiterated their stance: "(Cennaz) Az esté resoluz de fere demaien laz Cenne, selon laz lectre envoyé de laz part de Messrs de Berne. (Predicant) Az esté resoluz, encore une foys, d'aller prier Faret et Calvin, voyr si veullent preché demaien et donné laz Cenne az laz forme de laz missive, synon, en cas de reffus, qui se doyjent deporter de precher demaien, cart l'on en troveraz d'aultres. Et az esté envoyé monsr le soultier vers eulx. Luy estant revenus, az refferuz qu'il n'avoy trové que Calvin, lequel az responduz que l'on n'avoy pas observer le contenus de ladte lectre. Nonobstant, de fere laz Cenne coment est contenus en ycelle, n'az fayct nulle responce certainne. Et allors, ledt soultier l'az deffenduz laz predication et qu'il s'en dyussent deporter etc." RC III, p. 231.

41 April 21, 1538, RC III, p. 232: "Az esté proposé coment Faret et Calvin, oultre les defenses az leur faycte de non poient precher az cause de ce qu'il ne veullent pas optemperer az laz missive envoyé de Berne, lesqueulz, oultre ladte deffence, en meprisant laz justice, sont aller precher, Calvin à Sainct-Pierre et Faret az Sainct-Gervays." H.de La Mare says he cannot preach because Farel and Calvin have forbidden it and he will be excommunicated if he does.

42 April 22, 1538, RC III, p. 233 (Ironically, the council of Two Hundred says that Farel and Calvin can remain until the city finds replacements for them). April 23, 1538, RC III, pp. 235-36.

43 April 21 & 26, 1538, RC III, pp. 232, 239; see chap. 1 at n.15.

celebration of Ascension, "Incarnation" (Annunciation), Circumcision, and Christmas.[44] It is worth noting that in December 1538 the ministers raised the question whether the Lord's Supper should be held on Dec. 25 or on the Sunday before or after; the Senate said Dec. 25 but referred the matter to the Two Hundred. The latter also decided for that day, although they allowed those who had objections to speak up and left it to the Senate to determine whether or not to punish anyone who did not commune at Christmas.[45] On the 27th there were indeed some culprits who gave various excuses for not having shared in the sacrament, including referring to the commandment which teaches that one should work six days and their objection to making Christmas "a feast day."[46] Clearly the reforms introduced by Farel and his colleagues had taken root in some Genevans. Most of their fellow citizens seem to have accepted the Bernese-influenced change. On March 25, 1539, there is a note in the *Registres du Conseil* indicating that they were celebrating the Annunciation and their meeting would be postponed to another day. On Dec. 25, 1539, the date is marked in the *Registres* but nothing is entered under it. On Dec. 31, 1540, the council discussed whether they should work on the fortifications the next day, which was Circumcision, and concluded to keep to what had already been decided[47] (i.e., observing this day as a holiday free of work).

---

[44] May 29, 1538; RC III, p. 289: "Resoluz de fere cryes az voex de trombete, que ung chescon doyjent fere les quattre feste de l'an, coment l'Ascension, l'Incarnation, Circoncission, et jour de Noe, coment az esté arresté en Petit, Grand et General Conseyl, de observer, az laz forme des ceremonies arrestés de tenyr az Lausanne, et fermé le buctiques, et ce sus laz poienne de LXs."

[45] Dec. 3, 1538; RC III, p. 507: "Messrs les predicans ont proposé coment laz feste de Noel s'approche et qu'il est neccessayre fere laz saincte Cenne de Jhesuscrixt; et que, selon l'ordonance qu'il playraz az Messrs de fere, il ministreront laz Cense ledtz jour de Noel aut laz dymenche devant aut après. Resoluz de fere laz Cennaz ledtz jour de Noel; toutefoys remys l'affere en Grand Conseyl." Dec. 5, p. 510: "…et voyer si az persone quil vollie alleguer que cella ne ce doyge fere, qu'il le dye. Et puys az esté regarder de desbacstre en Peti Conseyl, voyr si l'on mecstraz poienne de venyr prendre la Cennez aut non. Nulli ne az allegué chose du contrayre raysonable."

[46] Dec. 27, 1538; RC III, pp. 538-39; p. 539: "… leur excuses, pourquoy est-ce qu'il n'avyent pryns ladte Cennaz, les ungs pour ce qu'il n'estyent pas dispos de leur conscience, les autres pour ce qu'il dist aut comadement de Dieu : 'Six jour tu travallieras' et que l'on avoyt fayct le jour de Noel feste, les aultres pour ce qu'il disyent que les predicans avyent dist que l'on avoyt fayct ung faulx seyrement de juré laz confession et observé les comandement, et plusieurs aultres excuses."

[47] March 25, 1539, RC IV, p. 128: "Mardy 25 de mars. Az esté fayct feste de l'Yncarnation de Jesu-Cryst et remys le Conseyl ordinayre az ung aultre jour." Dec. 25, 1539 ; RC IV, p. 586. Dec. 31, 1540; RC V, p. 720: "(Circoncision) Icy az esté parlé voyer si demaen l'on travallieraz aux terraulx de laz ville aut non. Arresté que pour az present l'on ne doyge rien inover."

Calvin's Return and Geneva's Calendar in 1541

When Calvin was invited back to Geneva in 1540-41, he made no reference to holy days; his conditions were more fundamental: church order and catechism. This did not mean that he considered the traditional observance of Christmas, Circumcision, Annunciation, and Ascension to be fitting for a fully reformed city, but they were certainly *adiaphora*, secondary matters. Calvin also distinguished among the holy days; it was proper to commemorate the Nativity and the Ascension, even though he wanted to reform specific features of the feasts.[48] The other two "ceremonies" were a different matter. Circumcision was not particularly important, but Annunciation, even when it was called "Incarnation," still reflected its interpretation as a Marian feast.

Parallel with Calvin's gradual reforming of the weekday feast days in Geneva in the 1540s was the institution and growing significance of the one weekday service which the reformer established and resolutely fostered, the day of prayer. The character of this distinctively Reformed liturgical creation will be examined below. However, since its practical manifestation in civic life was interwoven with that of the four feasts, it is appropriate to consider all the weekday services in tandem over the period 1541-1550 until the Genevan liturgical system reached its final organizational stability in 1550. At that point the "four feasts" were definitively reformed, a restrained observance of the passion was in place, and the celebration of the day of prayer was recognized as the preeminent weekday observance.

Status of the "Four Feasts"

There were two main distinctions of the four Christological feasts adopted from Bern. One was their status as full holidays when shops closed for the day; that would change over the course of the 1540s, but it was the base line when Calvin returned. The second fixed point about the "four feasts" was the subject matter of the sermon on those days; to honor the Christological event required an interruption in the *lectio continua* series that the preacher was following. (There was no obligation to approve the topic, however, and Calvin's later letters indicate that he denounced the superstitious character of the traditions about Annunciation "yearly.") Two other points are less clear: what liturgy was used, and how many services were held and/or at what times. Both of these issues have a bearing on the status of the particular celebration.

---

[48] It is quite probable that here Calvin was influenced by conversations with Bucer, who had at different times advocated various options, from observing Christological occasions on Sundays, to eliminating all special attention to the events of Christ's life on predetermined days (i.e., not in the sequence of the Biblical text being expounded), to re-introducing patristic celebrations. Bornert, *La réforme protestante du culte*, pp. 337-38.

What can be known – or rather, discerned – about the liturgical form of the "four feasts," and how many services were held on those days? The liturgy being used is nowhere defined, which is significant, because Calvin published orders of service for Sunday and the day of prayer. It is clear that Christmas followed the form for Sunday, since the Lord's Supper was celebrated that day. For the other three feasts: Circumcision, Annunciation, and Ascension, only circumstantial evidence is available. Logically the liturgies for the four days would have been alike, i.e., following the order for Sunday, and that is likely what had been the case before Calvin returned to Geneva. The only reference in the *Ecclesiastical Ordinances* which could be extended to cover weekday feasts is the instruction that "[i]f the need of the time requires some extraordinary service, the form for Sunday will be used."[49] This was added by the Senate to replace a reference to "the day of prayer" in one of the drafts. The change in language makes it clear that the Senate did not wish to be bound (exclusively) to Calvin's desired day of prayer, but the wording does not explicitly connect with the "four feasts." Later negotiations which intertwine the feasts with the development of the day of prayer support the idea that the Sunday liturgy was used for these weekday holidays.

> Calvin explained that next Tuesday [March 25, 1544] will be the day called Annunciation, to ask if the prayer will be made on that day or not: ordered that the prayer will be held on the said Tuesday and for the following three Tuesdays.[50]

Since sermons and prayers were held every day of the week Calvin was obviously not asking if there would be a worship service. He meant the day of prayer liturgy, and he was apparently inquiring whether it would be moved to Tuesday to accommodate the special service of the Annunciation. If the point was simply the subject matter of the sermon, that would not require a change in the liturgy; thus it seems probable that there was a special liturgy for the "four feasts." Moving the day of prayer to Tuesday for the Annunciation rather than simply adding the Annunciation to the week itself was probably prompted by the desire not to have the two special (and inevitably slightly longer) services on successive days. However, the liturgy used for the Annunciation would probably be that for Sunday rather than the day of prayer. The only difference between the two was

---

[49] *Ordinances*, OS II, pp. 337-38 note e: "Si ce faict quelque priere extraordinaire pour la necessité du temps, on gardera l'ordre de dymenche." Also in OC 10:22.

[50] March 21, 1544, OC 21:332 (RC 38 f131): "Sur ce que leditz M. Calvin a exposé que mardy prochain est le jour appellé annunciacion et voyer si tel jour sera faycte la priere aut non: ordonné que leditz mardy soyt faycte la priere et consequemment troys mardy apres."

an orientation toward repentance in the long prayer of intercession on the day of prayer, and it is likely that the alternate Sunday prayer would be used for a celebratory "holy feast."

An important factor in honoring a holy day was providing worship services at several times, so that no one need miss the occasion because he or she had to stay home to keep house, and/or setting the hour of the service later as was the custom for Sundays. It is probable that the "four feasts" were at first accorded the special treatment of two services, and it may have been the first "status-symbol" of the feasts to be changed. A Senate order on Dec. 19, 1544, indicates that the feast days will be accorded only one sermon. This seems to have been intended at first for the immediate context of Christmas and Circumcision weeks, but a marginal note extended the application beyond that to the rest of the four feasts. Reducing the number of services would constitute an important difference between the four feasts and the two liturgical observances which Calvin advocated, Sunday and the day of prayer, on which worship was normally held at several different times so no one had to miss the service for practical reasons.

The matter of a special time for the "four feasts" is also obscure, but there is some evidence that the (main) service was set at a later hour on that day. On Thursday, May 17, 1548, Aima wife of Claude Veyron is questioned by the consistory about what she was doing on Ascension (the previous week). She says that she was at the sermon at 8 a.m. and then went to ask for some money [owed to her] by a merchant; she states that she did not go into his shop but stayed outside talking with another woman. (Apparently the problem was suspicion of immoral relations with the shopkeeper. Witnesses testify that she did not go into the shop but the consistory admonishes her to be more careful not to cause gossip.)[51] Here the point is that the service on Ascension was at 8 a.m., later by two hours than the ordinary time for that season of the year, and that the date was still being observed in a special way. It is also noteworthy that the consistory is not concerned with a failure to observe the holiday, since there is no rebuke either to Aima or the merchant for doing business on Ascension – after the service.

Establishing the Day of Prayer and Its Status

The day of prayer was a distinctive Calvinist Reformed liturgical creation. The character and importance of this service will be explored below; here it is enough to identify its "status-markers" and trace its civic establishment. The day of prayer

---

51 *Consist.* IV, p. 67: "A esté apellee pour sçavoir d'elle où elle fust le jour de l'Assension. Laquelle ha respondu qu'elle fust au presche de 8 heures et puis fust demandé d'argent cheux André Duc et n'entra pas en sa moyson, ains demora là devant avecq la Silmandie."

was one of the two services for which Calvin wrote and published a liturgy, a liturgy which was in fact almost identical to that for Sunday. There was no instruction about the content of the sermons; the normal *lectio continua* preaching continued except when a rare interruption was made because of some big event, and then the choice of text was made by the preacher.

The day of prayer also received higher practical rank by having the biggest bell rung and being accorded services at two times, and then by achieving partial holiday status. The bell was significant, since it placed the day of prayer on the same level as Sunday morning. (It is probable that the four feasts also had this distinction at first.) At first the dual service times may have happened only in one church, and been something of an accident (at least from the Senate's perspective, if not Calvin's) because the chosen weekday, Wednesday, was one of the three on which there was already a dawn service scheduled at St. Pierre. So, from the beginning there were two times of worship in Greater Geneva. As the importance of the observance became increasingly felt by the city (Calvin's influence), and it became expected that people would attend this service if they did not go to church on any other weekday, a dawn service on Wednesday was begun at St. Gervais. This may well have been the case very shortly after the day of prayer was instituted, but it is likely that at least it was in place by the end of 1544 because a note in Dec. 1544 suggests the reduction from two services to one for a particular reason and time; this did not refer to changing the schedule of dawn services as such. Certainly by the time the baptismal records bring the schedule of sermons to full visibility, having two services on the day of prayer was an established practice in both St. Pierre and St. Gervais. The main (second) service was also set at a later hour which usually rotated with the seasons.[52]

The third and most significant aspect of the civic status of the day of prayer, its honored place as a partial holiday, developed over time.[53] At first it seems to have been a matter of clearing time for the service, so people were allowed (encouraged?) to keep their shops closed until after the second sermon. Later it would become obligatory to keep shops closed until after worship, and people were expected to come to church and then go to work.

---

[52]   See chap. 1, at n.145 for instructions about Wed. sermon at 7 a.m. winter, & presumably 8 a.m. summer.

[53]   One other mark of the significance of the day in civil terms was the fact that public discipline might be associated with it. On June 8, 1556, the Senate ordered punishment of fornicators after the day of prayer service. OC 21:639 (RC 51 f173v): "Quant aux paillardes: arreste quelles soient detenues en prison pour la premiere foys jouxte la coustume et oultre cela seront menées devant S. Pierre le mescredy au partir du sermon et soient mises au colier." The reasoning was that this was the weekday the most people would be at worship so the punishment would be most public.

Although its official place in Genevan life developed over time, the day of prayer services were actually begun almost immediately after Calvin's return in Sept. 1541. First it was a special request on Oct. 26 to celebrate a service of intercession for fellow Christians suffering in various ways.

> The preachers have explained how the Christian churches are suffering greatly from the plague as well as persecution by the Turks, and that we are bound to pray to God for each other. So it would be good to turn back to God with humble intercession and prayers for the increase of the honor of the holy gospel. ... This was passed.[54]

The same day, Oct. 26, Calvin went on to request a regular day of prayer for more general intercession, which he thought should be announced by the ringing of the largest bell in St. Pierre.

> It is proposed that one day per week the big bell will be rung for the sermon, to assemble the people in order to pray to God that He might please to preserve us by His grace. Let the Sixty and Two Hundred and heads of households be alerted.[55]

The Senate apparently decided to consider this matter further, and a few days later, on Monday November 7, they made their decision. "It is ordered that all the dizeniers must alert those in their dizene to come every Thursday from now on to the public preaching, and after that is over each one should go to work."[56] Although the subject matter of the service is not named, this order appears to establish a regular day of prayer, that is, a weekday when people were expected to attend worship. Also, it is understood that this service does not create a holiday but it entails a delay in the start of the work day, although there is no legal prohibition on opening shops and carrying on business during the sermon time. In this first proposal the chosen weekday is one when there was no dawn service.

---

[54]   OC 21:284, Oct. 26, 1541 (RC 35 f370): "*Les predicans* Lesquieulx hont exposé comment les eglises cristiennes sont fort molestees tant par peste que par la persecution du turch, et pource que nous sumes tenus de prier Dieu les ungs pour les aultres qu'il seoyt bon se retourner az dieu avecque humble supplication et prieres pour l'augmentation et honneur du sainct evangile... ce que az esté ainsy passé."

[55]   Oct. 26, 1541, OC 21: 285 (RC 35 f370): "Az esté advisé que ung jour de la sepmaienne l'on doybje sonné le sermon à laz grosse choche pour assembler le peuple affin prier dieu qu'il luy playse par saz grace nous perserver et que le 60 200 et chiefz de moyson en soyent advertys."

[56]   Nov. 7, 1541, OC 21:285 (RC 35 f383): "Ordonné que tous dizenyers doybjent advertys cieulx de leur dizenne de venyr tous les jeudy des icy en là az laz predication publique et estant parachevé icelle ung chascun doybje allé travailler."

Meanwhile, the *Ecclesiastical Ordinances* had been drafted and were being debated. One paragraph of the draft was altered in committee to include a reference to the day of prayer; the draft read: "and as for the day of prayer, they must come to the sermon at St. Pierre on the day that the big bell is rung"[57] – a phrase which essentially picks up Calvin's request on Oct. 26 for the ringing of the bell and also names a place for the service. The Senate, however, made certain alterations in the *Ordinances*, including replacing this phrase with the one quoted above: "[i]f the need of the time requires some extraordinary service, the form for Sunday will be used."[58] Although this slightly cryptic phrase did not imply a regular day of prayer it did allow for occasional ones. Despite the ministers' protests about various revisions (it is not clear that this was one of them), on Nov. 9 the Senate voted that no further changes would be made in the *Ordinances*, and on Sunday Nov. 20 their version was passed by the General Council.[59] It has sometimes been assumed that this meant that the day of prayer was not officially established in Geneva.[60]

However, two days after the Senate apparently eliminated the day of prayer from the *Ordinances* (and before the latter was voted into law), they themselves ordered the practice of the day on their own authority. On Friday November 11, the instructions issued on Monday Nov. 7 were reiterated, with some practical alterations and additions.

> It is ordered that every week one day there must be the general prayer in St. Pierre, and it will be done next Wednesday and after that we will propose the other days; and there will be prayers of intercession for the lords of Bern, Basel, Zurich, Strasbourg, and other allied cities suffering from plague. Let there be two candles in the church to provide light for the people.[61]

---

[57] *Ordinances*, OS II, p. 337: "*et quant au jour de la priere l'on doybje venyr au sermon au temple sainct Pierre le jour qu'il sera sonné à la grosse cloche.*" Also in OC 10:21 n.1

[58] *Ordinances*, OS II, pp. 337-38 note e: "Si ce faict quelque priere extraordinaire pour la necessité du temps, on gardera l'ordre de dymenche." Also in OC 10:22 n.b.

[59] Nov. 9, 1541, OC 21:286 (RC 35 f384v): "Sur ce que les Srs. predicans desyrent voyer les reparacions sus les ordonnances de l'eglise: ordonné que az eulx n'appartient les revoyer, et que l'affere soyt mis aux deux cens aujourdhuy." Nov. 20, 1541, OC 21:287 (RC 35 f406).

[60] cf. Peter, "Introduction," S VI, pp. xxv-xxvi.

[61] "Ordonné que toutes les sepmaiennes ung jour de la sepmaienne l'on doybje fere la priere general aut temple S. Pierre et qu'il soyt mercredi prochaien et puys l'on adviseraz des aultres jours et qu'il soyt faycte priere en faveur des seigneurs Berne Basle Zurich Estrasbourg et aultres villes alliés lesquelx sont persecutés de peste, et que audit temple le matin soyent mys 2 chandoyles pour allumer le peuple." Nov. 11, 1541, OC 21:286 (RC 35 f385)

Obviously the Senate had no principled objection to the regular weekly practice of the day of prayer as a particularly significant service, even if they had chosen to remove explicit language about it from the *Ordinances*. This order changes the weekday from the Thursday proposed on Nov. 7 to Wednesday, when there were de facto two times of worship at St. Pierre. However, the Senate expresses a certain ambivalence (which would recur at intervals for many years) about the day of the week, and this is where the intertwining with the "four feasts" becomes evident.

Disestablishing the "Four Feasts," Adding Passion Week, and Elevating the Day of Prayer, 1541-1550

Over the course of the years 1541-1550 Geneva's weekday calendar of special services was revised in several ways. The gradual diminution of importance of the "four feasts," leading to their official abolition in 1550, is what has been most commonly noted. Alongside this, a new observance of Passion Week was added. The third and most important factor was the increasing weight given to the day of prayer until it was confirmed as the only weekday special liturgy, with status as a partial holiday.

Circumcision and Ascension: Content Accepted, Holiday Rejected

For practical purposes, it is useful to deal first with the uncontroversial feasts, Circumcision and Ascension. These two, especially Circumcision, seem not to have raised any real discussion regarding content, and thus the only issue was the holiday status. Genevans themselves do not appear to have been deeply attached to Circumcision, as is evident in the debate in Dec. 1540 about whether they should observe it as a holiday instead of doing needed repairs to the city walls. (Note that Circumcision is *not* a celebration of a "new year"[62] nor should it be called that, despite the fact that it occurs on January 1. In fact, Geneva had had the tradition of starting the new year on Dec. 25th. In the early sixteenth century this was beginning to waver; while some sources continue to identify the celebration of Christmas as the new year, others do not,[63] but the fact is that what was

---

62   Grosse, *Les rituels de la Cène*, pp. 127, 227

63   After the reform, secretaries of the Senate continued to hesitate between this date and the end of the month; RC I, p. 282: "le vingt et cinq de decembre. L'on est de coustume changer l'an pour ainsin se comence l'an de la Nativité." RC II, p. 446, n.44, on Dec. 25, where the editors note that the secretary wrote in the margin "annus 1537 mutatur in 1538" and also signals the year change on Dec. 30 (p. 450); he was clearly undecided about which to adopt. The same is true on Dec. 23, "1550" = 1549. The Senate meeting on Dec. 25 is marked "L'an de la Nativité naissance Jesus Crist 1549 est change à l'an 1550 ce vingt et cinq de decembre," RC 44 f292v, and the dates following, Dec. 27-Dec. 31 are marked "1550," RC 44 f293r, 293v, 295r.

observed on January 1 was Circumcision, not new year's. Circumcision naturally came eight days after Dec. 25th because Jewish boys were circumcised on the eighth day, so it was only a coincidence that this was January 1.)

Ascension was of more importance to Calvin than Circumcision, as his essay on the Lord's Supper in 1542 and his sermons on the Acts of the Apostles in 1549 demonstrate. In later years, when a collection of his "feast day sermons" was published, four for Ascension were included along with those for the Nativity, Passion Week, Easter, Pentecost – and the Second Coming (!). Calvin was not involved in the sermon publication, but his earlier essay (which names incarnation, passion, death, resurrection, ascension, sending of the Holy Spirit, and second coming) makes clear that he was content to have Ascension marked out by name as significant to be remembered in a way which did not apply to Circumcision. The published sermons also illustrate, however, that there was no special focus on the day traditionally labeled Ascension because all four sermons in the "feast day" book are simply lifted out of Calvin's *lectio continua* series on Acts which was preached in the autumn of 1549. As a New Testament book, Acts was treated on Sundays. One of the "Ascension" sermons happened to fall on the first Sunday in September and thus was accompanied by the celebration of the Lord's Supper, but the rest were not marked by any special observance, and even this "Ascension" sermon was not preached on the traditional day.

The setting apart of Circumcision and Ascension as weekday observances was not formally abolished until 1550. They continued to be practiced as legal holidays, and the sermon might well have formed a break in the *lectio continua*, but the evidence is only circumstantial because the time of service continued to be the later hour marking a special occasion. So completely was Circumcision forgotten that when Calvin preached on this passage in 1559, he never even alluded to the tradition of observing it as a holy day. [64] As already noted, the extant sermons labeled "Ascension" were not preached on that special occasion. Before the changes in 1550 there was probably an interruption in the *lectio continua* on the traditional date of Ascension, but there is no concrete evidence either for or against, and no sermons identified as given on that occasion have been preserved.

---

archives@etat.ge.ch accessed Aug. 5, 2013. Transcripts of Calvin's sermons illustrate the date change at the 25th as late as the 1550s. For Calvin's sermons, see #20 on 1 Cor. 3:12-15, preached on Sunday, Dec. 22, 1555, but marked 1556 [obviously it was not necessarily Dec. 25th but the day the Nativity was celebrated!]; or #41 on Gen. 8:20-22, preached on Monday, Dec. 25, 1559, marked 1560. Engammare, "Introduction," *Sermons sur Esaie Chapitres 52,1/-59,21*, p. xxv, cites evidence for the new year beginning on Jan. 1. In this period the precise point was apparently in flux.

[64] Sermon #26 on Gospel Harmony, on Luke 2:21-22, cf. OC 46:311-24.

Christmas and Annunciation: The Lord's Supper and "Superstition"

The other two holy days: Christmas and Annunciation, were a different matter. The content of the Nativity was never in question, but the proper way to celebrate it was, especially since Christmas was the only one of the "four feasts" which was normally elevated to the highest rank in Genevan life by being the occasion of one of the four Lord's Supper services. While Calvin had no real objection to holding the Supper on a weekday, he thought that the traditional way that the Christmas feast was celebrated created a very inappropriate context for the sacrament. As regards the last of the "four feasts," Annunciation, it was the way the content was interpreted which made this day controversial. Traditionally, Annunciation or Conception (as it was often called in Geneva) was celebrated as a Marian feast and Calvin considered it superstitious.

It is useful to trace the development of the practice of the four feasts with the issues of content and holiday status in mind. During the first years after his return, Calvin made some effort to change Genevan observance of these days but did not press the issue. In May 1542 he brought up the question of celebrating the Ascension, and on May 19 the Senate ruled that all would remain the same "in order that the whole city should follow the same course."[65] The decision points to a concern for a uniform worship practice; there is no question about content. The matter of observing the feasts came up again two years later, on March 21, 1544, as the Annunciation approached and, as was noted above, the Senate ordered "la priere" (the day of prayer) moved to the Tuesday of Annunciation to continue there for a month.[66] In effect, this functioned as a displacement of the regular day of prayer on Wednesday, but the attention to the content of the Annunciation would naturally be confined to March 25, and the other weeks presumably the day of prayer liturgy and *lectio continua* would be in place.

Passion Week

In fact, the Senate responded to Calvin's question about Annunciation in March 1544 by asking for a further development of liturgical observance, i.e., a

---

65 May 19, 1542; OC 21:296 (RC 36 f18): "Affin que l'on suyve ung mesme cours en la ville ordonné que quant à la feste appellé assencion ne soyt rien fayct de nouveaulx pour apresent."

66 March 21, 1544; OC 21:332 (RC 38 f131): "Sur ce que lediz M. Calvin a exposé que mardy prochain est le jour appellé annunciacion et voyer si tel jour sera faycte la priere aut non : ordonné que lediz mardy soyt faycte la priere et consequemment troys mardy apres." The final instruction probably intended to cover the rest of the weeks until Easter on April 13, assuming the Tuesday of March 25 was read as the first of the three. It is possible that this was meant literally, i.e., including the first Tuesday after Easter, but while it would make sense to keep the change until a specific important date, it was not particularly logical to extend it past that date and "en huict jours" often meant one week, e.g., Sunday to Sunday.

special worship time just before Easter. "[It is] ordered that the preachers should preach on the Passion through the whole week before Easter."[67] This order did not involve changing the liturgy or adding holidays, but it did require an interruption of the *lectio continua* course of sermons. That is, the question of having sermons with a special content at a particular time in the liturgical year was raised by the Senate and apparently approved by the ministers. It formed an addition to the special Christological observances in Geneva. Since preaching on the Passion during the week before Easter did not alter the form of the services or the civic status of the days, this practice does not fit precisely the criteria for "holy days" even though it does represent a significant element of the (re)defined liturgical year in Geneva. Calvin did not introduce this, but he considered remembrance of Christ's Passion and death to be much more important than Circumcision, so he was willing to have the *lectio continua* interrupted for preaching on the Passion before Easter.

Apparently, it was enough that there be at least one series of expositions on the Passion each year, and parishioners could attend these seasonal specials or continue with the regular series they usually heard on weekdays. This is evident from the fact that at least one year (1555) when Calvin was preaching the week before Easter, the book was Deuteronomy, his current weekday text. The reason he was continuing his weekday *lectio continua* was, however, that he had been out of town at the beginning of the week and returned in time to preach only the last several days. It was probably agreed among the pastors that the one(s) doing the passion should be available the whole week, so someone else was assigned and Calvin simply went on with his regular text when he got back to Geneva. Some years he may not have preached at all the week before Easter because it was his alternate's turn. However, even when it was not his week he sometimes did the Wednesday day of prayer, as was the case in 1551 and 1554.[68] If the city's chief pastor did not do the Passion week series, it might have been partly to give his colleagues the opportunity to preach on these special texts. It is possible that the Passion week sermons were less highly ranked by Calvin and his colleagues than the day of prayer, for which the Company of Pastors was prepared to make special arrangements in order to keep their best preacher in the pulpit. It is pure

---

[67] March 21, 1544; OC 21:332 (RC 38 f131) "Ordonné que les predicans tout aut long de la sepmainne devant pasques ayent à precher la passion."

[68] An examination of his extant sermons reveals that he preached on the synoptic gospels or John in some years, although the only extant ones are two complete series on the synoptic sequence of the passion from late in his life (1558 and 1562). For Calvin's preaching, see chap. 6; for passion week sermons, including specific Wednesdays when it was not his week, see chap. 6 at nn.70ff.

speculation to attempt to determine how many sets of Passion sermons there might have been on a regular basis. Certainly the minimum was one series at the "ordinary" hour of 6 a.m. and there may well have been two, so that there was at least one on each side of the city, in St. Gervais and in Greater Geneva.

For present purposes, it is enough to note that the Passion Week practice in Geneva formed an interruption of the *lectio continua* which Calvin willingly accepted, since it was one way of expresssing his view that it was appropriate to mark Christ's death in a special way. The sermons were fitted into the liturgical order for weekdays and the day of prayer, and they were never observed as holidays, so there were none of the difficulties presented by the "four feasts" introduced under Bernese influence.

Modifying the Observance of the Four Feasts

One of the main issues for many people was the holiday status of the four feasts. On May 22, 1544, as Ascension approached, Calvin returned to the Senate with a proposal for modifying the regulation about maintaining the days as holidays.

> Calvin explained that it would be very useful to eliminate all superstitions regarding the four feasts which the General [Council] voted to keep. It would be good to preach each of these days in the morning and then after dinner people should be free to work or to rest. Ordered that this be considered further in the small, large, and general councils. [69]

Plainly Calvin had no problem with the remembrance of the content of the Ascension, but he was asking that the four special feast days no longer be accorded the rank of obligatory full holidays. The issue was brought to the Two Hundred on May 26, where it was said that the ministers should be consulted, and then the matter should go before the small, large, and general councils. [70] No further mention of the subject is found over the course of the following weeks, so it is probable that the ministers' request went no further.

---

[69] May 22, 1544; OC 21:334-35 (RC 38 f209v): "M. Calvin ministre. Lequelt a exposé qu'il seroyt fort utile pour oster toutes superstitions et que touchant les quattres festes que fere passé par le general de fere: il seroyt bon de presché ung chascun jour d'ycieulx de matin: et appres disné qu'il fust en liberté de travallié ou reposé. Ordonné que cella soyt advisé plus oultre en petit grand et general conseyl."

[70] Nothing is found in the Annales (OC) ; a cursory survey of the *Registres du Conseil* for this period (May 22 to June 2, archives@etat.ge.ch , accessed Jan. 8, 2013) turned up only the following note, RC 38 f216: "Des 4 festes de l'an. Pource que aulchongs sont en dubies si l'on fera lesdtes festes aut non. Ordonné d'en confronter avecque les predicans pour il mectre quelque bon ordre selon la parolle de Dieu. Toutesfoys soyt en appres passées par petit, grand & general conseyl." Also quoted in Lambert, *Preaching, Praying and Policing*, p. 195 n.91.

Late in 1544 Calvin suggested a temporary modification in the schedule which serves to cast more light on the practice of the holy days. On Dec. 19 he proposed that, in view of the fact that Christmas would fall near the middle of the week, the day of prayer should be changed.

> Regarding next Christmas day: The minister Calvin explained that, for good order in the church, and seeing that Christmas day is on Thursday, the prayers should not be held on Wednesday; and it should be like the four other feasts; and it will be enough to preach once on those days. [It is] ordered that the said order should be kept.[71]

The central feature of the Christmas service was the Lord's Supper, which was celebrated at two times on that morning, and (at least in one parish, St. Pierre, perhaps also St. Gervais) the day of prayer also had worship at two times.[72] Thus, Calvin was suggesting that rather than have two morning services on each of two successive weekdays, it would be enough to have one sermon on the day of prayer as was done on the "four feasts." A marginal note seems to have had the purpose of clarifying what was meant by "those days." Next to the reference to the "four feasts" it says: "Regarding the next Circumcision day and thereafter the other feasts which are four in number."[73]

What does this mean? Although it is not certain, the reference to preaching "once on those days" appears to be an innovation, which might imply that the special holy days had previously been honored with two services but probably indicates that for the duration of the stipulated period one sermon was enough for the day of prayer. So on Wednesday, Dec. 24th, before Christmas on Thursday, and on Wednesday, Dec. 31st, before Circumcision on Thursday, Jan. 1, 1545, the day of prayer liturgy would be used but there would be one service each day instead of two. This would imply that there was already the tradition of having two services on the day of prayer, and argues for the possibility that this was true at

---

[71] Dec. 19, 1544 (RC 39 f75): "Le jour de Noel prochain. Le ministre Calvin a exposé qu'il seroyt bon ordre en l'eglise que voyeant que le jour de Noel est pour judy, que les prieres cessent le mecredy et soyt faict semblable des aultres quattre festes et que il sera assés de presché une foys lesd. jours. Ordonné que led. ordre soyt observé." Quoted in Lambert, *Preaching, Praying and Policing*, p. 195, n. 91.

[72] This means twice in a given parish, except for La Magdeleine, which at this period usually had only catechism, with the addition of a Sunday service on the days when the Supper was celebrated; cf. chap. 1 at n.167 and chap. 3 n.221.

[73] Dec. 19, 1544 (RC 39 f75): Margin: "Du jour de la circoncision prochain et consequement des aultres festes que sont en nombre 4." Quoted in Lambert, *Preaching, Praying and Policing*, p. 195, n. 91.

St. Gervais as well as St. Pierre because otherwise it would be simpler to say "we will not cut the dawn service at St. Pierre." This service was one of a three-part plan in the original *Ordinances* for weekday services for servants and so was not specifically related to the day of prayer. However, to avoid multiplying services, it was probably moved to the next day and practiced as a Supper service for Christmas. St. Gervais had not originally had any weekday dawn services, but it is very likely that its Wednesday dawn service, which is clearly in view when the baptismal records begin in 1550, had in fact been begun in the early 1540s. (It is difficult to guess whether this might still have been held at its regular time because people were accustomed to it; if not, one can imagine an inattentive father and godfather showing up with a baby for baptism, not remembering that the schedule had changed for these weeks.)

If there had been two services on the four feasts, the application of this order was meant make it permanent that henceforth on those days it would be sufficient to preach once a day. That seems to be the intent of the marginal note, and it is how Lambert interprets the instruction, although he is under the misapprehension that this applied also to the day of prayer.

> That December [1544], Calvin succeeded in getting the Council to suppress the Christmas prayer service, Christmas falling on a Thursday, and to make do with just a sermon. The council also agreed to do the same for the other feasts.[74]

Here Lambert reads "the Christmas prayer service" as another name for the special observances reintroduced under Bernese influence in 1538. This is natural, since the day of prayer has not been recognized as a liturgical entity in its own right. Part of the present purpose is to distinguish the "four feasts" from the day of prayer. In fact, Calvin was not in the least interested in "suppressing" the day of prayer; on the contrary, he was vigorously fostering it. However, he had to tread carefully because of the inherent competition between these two categories of weekday special observances.

In December 1544 the change probably had more to do with sheer practicality, to limit the number of services. Since everyone had to come on Christmas for the Lord's Supper, and they would probably attend on Circumcision, both of which fell on Thursdays, it was almost certain that no servants would be seeking dawn services in addition to those on the major feasts. Besides this, Calvin's proposal probably had in view the burden of preaching which having multiple services two

---

74   Lambert, *Preaching, Praying and Policing*, p. 194, n. 91.

days in a row would impose on the six or seven ministers. Remember, there were three parishes, and the schedule for Christmas would require two services in St. Pierre and St. Gervais, plus one at Magdeleine for the Lord's Supper celebration. The day of prayer at this time had at least three services and more likely four (assuming a dawn service on Wednesday had already been added at St. Gervais).[75] In the mid-1540s the regular daily schedule for a Wednesday was four services, two at St. Gervais and two in Greater Geneva; the regular schedule for a Thursday was two services, one on each side of the river. When Christmas was celebrated on Thursday, this would add three more services: at dawn at St. Pierre and St. Gervais, and morning at Magdeleine, to the regular two for that day.

Even changing the day of prayer to one sermon, Calvin and his five colleagues would have been looking at an impossible eight days, from Sunday, Dec. 21 through Sunday, Dec. 28. On Dec. 21, there would be nine services = four at St. Pierre, four at St. Gervais, and catechism at Magdeleine; on Dec. 25, five = two at St. Pierre, two at St. Gervais, and one at Magdeleine; plus three each on Monday and Friday, two each on Tuesday and Saturday; and then on Sunday, Dec. 28, again nine. This comes to thirty-three services in eight days. Furthermore, the examination of the catechism students on Sunday Dec. 21, in preparation for their first participation in the Lord's Supper at Christmas would add three more hours of pastoral work because at this point the examination was held in the hour after the regular catechism. In fact, ministers not doing the catechism were often present for the profession of faith before admisison to the Supper, so this might have meant an extra hour for more than the three who were teaching.[76] Thus, when Calvin proposed dropping the day of prayer on Dec. 24, he was omitting only two sermons, the dawn ones at St. Pierre and St. Gervais; but even that would be a help: thirty-three plus three examinations, instead of thirty-five plus three. If the preaching were evenly divided among the six ministers and the catechism exams are included, that would be six services for each within eight

---

[75] By 1550 such a service was well-established; it was not listed in the *Ecclesiastical Ordinances* of 1541 but it was added sometime in the 1540s, perhaps by 1545. Certainly it had been begun well before 1549, because otherwise it would have formed one of the concessions which the ministers made when the Senate asked for daily dawn services. It is notable that the 1549 argument named the day of prayer service at the Magdeleine as one issue, although Greater Geneva already had two services that day at two different times. If St. Gervais had not had a dawn service that day, it would probably have been included among the desiderata. cf. chap. 1 at n.150.

[76] Calvin would often be present even though he was not the one responsible for catechism. For the service schedule on which this is based, see chap. 1 at n1.159ff ; for Calvin's own work, see chap. 6 at nn.105ff.

days. Unless it was his alternate's week to preach, Calvin would bear the heaviest load, and even if it happened to be his colleague's turn for the daily sermons, Calvin would be preaching extra times because he had to be in the pulpit on Christmas-Dec. 25th even if it was not his week and even if it was not Sunday.

Lambert identifies December 1544 as in some sense a turning point for the celebration of the four feasts of Christmas, Circumcision, Annunciation, and Ascension. The tide was slowly shifting in the direction of Calvin's views, as would become evident when the next feast day arrived. In 1545 Annunciation, March 25, actually fell on a Wednesday, the day of prayer. Several days before, on March 20, the Senate acted. "The feast of the Conception will be held, although it is superstitious. [It is] ordered that the said day will be done as on the day of prayer."[77] (It is noteworthy that the day of prayer was such a well-known factor by 1545 that it could serve as a standard.) Precisely what is meant by keeping the Annunciation the same way as the day of prayer is not clear. The possibilities to consider are the liturgy, the number of services, and holiday status. If the Sunday liturgy was being used for the "four feasts," the change would not refer to that – unless it was intended that the day of prayer intercession be used, thus giving the whole liturgy its usual penitential character. It is more likely that the Senate was referring to holding two services, which was the normal day of prayer practice. That is, since in the previous December the Senate had ordered one service per feast day, it is now clarifying that because Annunciation falls on the day of prayer, both of the usual day of prayer services will be held (even if the topic of the sermon would still be the Annunciation). This note probably also refers to the holiday status. It was no longer obligatory to refrain from all work, and after the service people might go about their business if they wished, as they would ordinarily do on the day of prayer. (See similar language comparing the day of prayer with Sunday, in the Sept. 4, 1544 order below.)

Bringing together the Senate's decisions in December 1544 and March 1545, Lambert says that Geneva "abolish[ed]" the feasts in 1545.[78] He does not define clearly what such abolition meant, however. Apparently he considers the Dec. 1544 order to "suppress" the day of prayer and have only a sermon on the four feasts a *de facto* end to their observance. Since this culminated in the

---

77 March 20, 1545, OC 21:349 (RC 39 f59): "La feste de la conception combien que c'est superstition se fayct. Ordonné que ledit jour l'on fasse ainsin que le jour de la priere."

78 Lambert, *Preaching, Praying, and Policing*, p. 195 n.91: "The important point is that by 1544 the Council had clearly come around to Calvin's position in calling the feasts 'superstitious,' despite the fact that the Bernese continued to celebrate them. The Council did not, however, *abolish* these 'superstitions' until 1545." The reference to superstition does not appear in 1544 but in 1545, and it is clear that Geneva did not "abolish" the feasts until 1550.

Senate's pronouncement in March 1545 that the Annunciation was superstitious, he considers this equivalent to abolishing it and the other feasts. In fact, however, the official discontinuation of the feasts came only in 1550. By "abolishing" Lambert appears to mean that the feasts were accorded only a sermon (as was the practice on ordinary weekdays) and, since their subject matter was regarded as "superstitious," the content of the sermon was changed. The first point is based on a misunderstanding of the day of prayer, which was definitely more than just a sermon. The second point is ambiguous. Calling the subject "superstitious" would certainly have been a mark of dishonor, but it might or might not have implied a discontinuation of the sermons focused on the particular holy day topic. In his April 1551 letter to Bullinger (quoted above), Calvin said that he had preached on the superstitious character of the feasts every year ("quotannis"). Thus it is likely that what the Senate meant when it said that the Annunciation would "be held" refers to the content of the sermon.

The Senate decisions in December 1544 and March 1545 seem to signal a move toward what Calvin had requested in 1544, i.e., a loosening of the obligatory holiday status for the four feasts. There does not appear to be any explicit regulation on this subject, but there were changes in the civic status of the day of prayer. Although it had been presented as a partial holiday from the beginning, this was made an official order on Sept. 4, 1545.

> M. the syndic Des Ars explained that yesterday at the Consistory meeting they talked about those who do not come to the sermon, so that on the day of prayer the streets are full: and asked that this be put in order. [It is] ordered that the cries be renewed and Wednesdays be made like Sundays until after the sermon. [79]

Renewing the cries probably refers to the orders for people to attend worship on Wednesdays as well as Sundays. If (as seems likely) the earlier legislation was only permission or encouragement to delay the opening of shops and not a legal requirement, at this point the matter was clear. Now businesses could not open until after the second of the day of prayer services, which meant that for most of the morning ordinary work was restricted as it was on Sundays, although the day of prayer was not a full holiday like Sunday.

---

[79] Sept. 4, 1545, quoted in Lambert, *Preaching, Praying, and Policing*, p. 307 n.57: "Suyvant ce que le Monsr. Le sindicques Des Ars a exposé que estant hier au Consistoryre, il fust parler de ceulx qui ne vont point au sermon, dont les jours de la pryeres sont pleine les rues, requerant il mectre ordre. Ordonné que les cries soyent renouvellee et que le mescredi soyt faict comme la dimanche jusques apres le sermon." From RC 40, f231 (r) archives@etat.ge.ch, accessed Jan. 8, 2013.

By 1545 the day of prayer apparently had a status close to that of the "four feasts," but some important differences remained. The four feasts were still full holidays and legally could supersede the day of prayer. On Tuesday, Dec. 15, 1545, the Senate made plans for the next two special observances, a practical repetition of 1544. "The Supper [is] to be celebrated at Christmas, and until then the Wednesday prayers are suspended, and the same will be done on the day of Circumcision."[80] The ruling affected three weeks; on the Wednesdays of Dec. 16, 23, and 30, 1545, there would be no prayer service, because on Friday, Dec. 25, 1545, and Jan. 1, 1546, there would be special services and holidays. The number of services would be determined in part by the holy day and in part by the rhythm of Geneva's on-going worship life. The Christmas Lord's Supper would insure that Dec. 25 had five services at two times: two at St. Pierre, two at St. Gervais, plus one at Magdeleine. The fact that Circumcision fell on Friday when St. Pierre already had a dawn service would mean that this day also had two services at least in Greater Geneva (St. Pierre at dawn and Magdeleine at 7 a.m.), plus one at St. Gervais. The Sunday liturgies for Christmas and Circumcision pre-empted the day of prayer liturgy, but the loosening of the absolute holiday status for Dec. 25 and Jan. 1 moved these feasts in the direction of the day of prayer. That is, because the holiday status was not strictly enforced for Christmas and Circumcision, it could resemble the day of prayer with its partial holiday status.

The final step was to eliminate the obligatory holiday status of the four feasts. The practical initiation of this may have dated from 1545, since the way had been left open for those who chose to return to work. Apparently, increasing numbers of Genevans opted for this possibility and a significant portion of the city was no longer observing the complete holiday, so that by the spring of 1548 the difference between those who did and those who did not was causing public disturbances. (Perhaps there was a particularly egregious confusion on Ascension, May 10, the date that Aima wife of Claude Veyron went to the merchant's shop?) On May 14, 1548, Calvin came before the Senate to complain about the situation, because "some people open their shops and others do not, which is a scandal."[81] In theological terms, a scandal is a stumbling block to faith, something

---

[80] Dec. 15, 1545, OC 21:367 (RC 40 f327): "La cene à celebrer à noel et jusque là les prieres de Mercredy suspendues et le semblable soyt faict le jour de la circoncision." Lambert (*Preaching, Praying, and Policing*, p. 194 n.91) interprets this to mean "no special observance" but that is because he does not distinguish the day of prayer as a special observance independent of the four feasts.

[81] May 14, 1548, OC 21:426 (RC 42 f89): Calvin "semblablement a prié il advise sus les quattre festes que sont esté publiés out les ungs ovrent leur buctiques les autres non qu'est scandalle. Ordonné que l'on en aye conference avecque les ministres."

which can cause religious problems; in this case, the idea was that having some people doing regular business and others enjoying an (often rowdy) holiday produced confusion and disunity in the community and that dishonored God. The Senate decided to consult with the ministers, but apparently no change was made. In November 1550 the whole matter was brought up again and this time there was a resolution of the entire question of the four feasts. One of the main concerns was the matter of civic practice, i.e., making all weekdays work days.

> Regarding the feasts: because it is a scandal to have diversity of practice about the feasts, it is ordered that from now on for the future such feasts will no longer be held but each one opens his shop, and the prayers will no longer be changed from Wednesdays but will remain then no matter what feast may follow. [82]

The main point was changing the obligatory holiday status for the weekday holy days of Dec. 25th/Christmas, January 1st/Circumcision, March 25th/Annunciation, and Thursday/ fortieth day after Easter-Ascension. It is possible that what was "superstitious" in the content (especially of the Annunciation) had already been diminished or eliminated (unless Calvin was still preaching against it), since the debate about that disappears after 1545. The use of the Sunday liturgy on a weekday was also implicitly rejected. The intent of the order was not to get rid of all remembrance of the events of Christ's life, however, but to provide for a Biblical observance.

> And because, when the Supper is celebrated on a feast day it causes the people to have a party after dinner, it is ordered that at the feasts when the Supper has been celebrated, the Supper will be held on the Sunday closest to the feast day. [83]

---

[82] Nov. 11, 1550; OC 21:470 (RC 44 f125): "Sus ce que M. Calvin a remonstré de la diversité du people quant aux festes à cause de ce que aulcungs ovrent leurs boutiques les autres non qu'est une division scandaleuse." The council responded: "Sus les festes pource qu'il est chose de scandale que de estre en diversité d'usaige des festes, est arresté que des icy à l'advenir telles festes ne ce fassent plus mais chescung ovre sa bouticque et les prieres ne soyent plus changees du mescredi mais il demourent quelque feste qui ensuyve." The 1561 *Ecclesiastical Ordinances* explicitly name Wednesday for the day of prayer but allow for future revision, and after Calvin's death the debate was reopened and finally Thursday was definitively chosen. (OS II, pp. 337-38 n.4 or OC 10:99). Against the pastors' objections, a change to Thursday was proposed by the Senate in 1578-1579 and finally carried out in 1581.

[83] Nov. 11, 1550; OC 21:470 (RC 44 f125): "Et pour ce que la senne celebree le jour des festes cause que les gens apres disne suyvent à faire feste : est arresté que advenans les festes où se celebre cene que l'on la celebre le dimenche plus prest du jour de la feste et que l'ong face advertir le peuple par les dizeniers."

The minutes of the Senate meeting do not indicate whose idea this was. As seen above, Calvin denied that it was his, although he certainly did not object to controlling the holiday partying. The matter was approved by the Two Hundred on Nov. 14, and passed by the General Council on Sunday, Nov. 16, 1550. [84] As it is summarized in the minutes of the Company of Pastors, this is called "an edict of abrogating all the feasts, except the day of the Lord, as was ordained by God." [85] In actuality, this absolute statement must be understood in its larger context.

What was abolished was the holiday status of the four feasts reintroduced in 1538, along with a formal end to any observance of the Lord's Supper (and the Lord's Day service) on a weekday. The annual recognition of Christ's birth would still be celebrated on the Sunday closest to Dec. 25. Thus the observance of Christmas could be said to continue, though it was now moved to the weekly day of rest so activities on that day would be guided by the teaching about how one should behave on Sunday and the day of the Supper. The edict also made official the end of any special religious content on Jan. 1 or March 25. The day of Ascension also was no longer observed on its traditional Thursday, that is, the content of the day no longer interrupted the *lectio continua* preaching. In fact, in this case the subject may not have been particularly highlighted at all, either on the weekday or the following Sunday; on Thursday, May 23, 1555, Calvin continued his exposition of Deuteronomy, and on Sunday, May 26, 1555, he followed his regular sequence of Second Timothy. [86] In neither case does he mention the Ascension. However, the text of the Sunday sermon is a confession of faith, 2 Tim. 2:8-13, which speaks of Christ's death and resurrection, and Calvin expounds both of these and Christ's exaltation, so there is an indirect allusion to the Ascension. [87] The Biblical event might not have received marked attention

---

[84] Nov. 14 & 16, 1550; OC 21:470-71 (RC 44 f127, 128).

[85] RCP II, p. 74: "Le dimenche 16 jour de novembre oud. an 1550, ... fut aussi prononcé un edict de l'abrogration de toutes les festes, reservant le jour du dimenche, comme il est ordonné de Dieu."

[86] See sermon #23 of Deut. (4:19-24), for May 23, 1555; OC 26:147-159. Sermons #10-11 on 2 Tim. 2:8-10, 2 :8-13, for May 26, 1555; OC 54 :113-140. Although the sermons are not dated, they are identified as the week before Pentecost because in the morning #10 Calvin refers to the celebration of the Lord's Supper the next week, OC 54:125-126; he also indicates that this is the morning by a reference (OC 54:125) to continuing his point in the afternoon sermon. The same appears to be true in 1558, the next date for which Sunday sermons before Pentecost are available; see #2-3 on Ephesians.

[87] For example, see OC 54:126: "Et de nostre part advisons à nous, que nul ne se presente pour recevoir la Cene de nostre Seigneur Iesus Christ, qu'il n'ait ceci devant les yeux: c'est de contempler le Fils de Dieu qui a esté du tout aneanti pour nous, qui a esté mis en extremité d'opprobre, et est descendu jusques aux abysmes d'enfer, et que de là il a esté exalté en gloire,

at a specific time of the year, but its importance in the larger picture of Christian teaching was never in doubt, as is clear from Calvin's own preferred list of Christological observances and the book of sermons mentioned above.

The edict of 1550 brought to a close the changes with regard to the weekday celebrations of the four feasts. The way it was phrased also reiterated the two key aspects of Calvinist Reformed liturgical time. The primacy of Sunday, with its unique Biblical and holiday status, was re-enforced. The edict also provides evidence for the importance of the day of prayer, in that it was now no longer subject to being upstaged by any other occasion. Although it was secondary to the Lord's Day, this special observance had become the second fulcrum of the week in Geneva.

III: The Day of Prayer

The Calvinist Reformed day of prayer was a distinctive and significant develop-ment of traditional themes, a development which both expressed and shaped piety and practice in characteristic ways. The importance and liturgical role of the day of prayer has largely been neglected or misinterpreted, and thus to understand its place in the broader picture of Reformed worship it is necessary to set this special practice in historical context. The following presentation of the day of prayer begins with a brief summary of medieval and German Protestant antece-dents, then outlines Calvin's teaching and Genevan practice, concluding with a short consideration of the uniqueness of this development for the Calvinist Reformed sense of liturgical time.

---

afin que nous soyons en la fin receus avec luy,…. et que nous soyons invincibles pour surmonter tous les combats que Satan nous suscitera, et qu'avec toute humilité et crainte nous aspirions à ceste constance de foy, de nous élever là haut aux cieux, et de contempler Jesus Christ qui a le regne en sa main, auquel toutes creatures sont sujettés, et que nous tendions tousiours à ceste vie celeste, passans tellement par ce monde, que nous y soyons estrangers, n'ayans point de repos asseuré, sinon en ceste heritage celeste qui nous est appresté, et où nous attendons ceste couronne de gloire qui nous a esté acquise par le Fils de Dieu." At 54:121 there is a reference to the Roman church which may be an allusion to the kinds of liturgical plays enacted at Ascension : "Les Papistes se diront assez Chrestiens à pleine bouche: mais cependant on voit comme ils aneantissent tout la vertu de nostre Seigneur Jesus Christ, entant qu'en eux est. Or au contraire, quand ils auront joué toutes leurs farces, quand ils auront usé de tous leurs masques, quand ils auront tasché à se transfiguré que le diable leur aura soufflé toutes les finesses et ruses qu'il est possible pour nous esblouir les sens, que nous ne laissions pas de nous tenir à l'Evangile."

Historical Context

It is well known that the medieval west was strongly influenced by the Biblical tradition of associating suffering with punishment for sin and blessing with God's mercy. In individual lives this was manifested as a pervasive penitential culture, which rose to corporate expression in times of disaster such as plague or famine, or occasions of public rejoicing such as military victory or the long-awaited birth of a royal heir. The liturgical or devotional form which embodied these manifestations of personal or communal response to the workings of God varied; it might be confession and penance or a gift to the church or the poor by an individual, or a penitential procession by the parish or proclamation of national celebration for a principality. (It may be noted that the only known clerical act by the young Calvin was participating in a chapter meeting of Noyon clergy held on Aug. 23, 1533, to arrange for special public prayers on account of the plague ravaging the city.[88]) What all these traditional responses to punishment or blessing had in common was their occasional character. They were responses, and thus their occurrence was determined by the events that Christians and their communities experienced. There were no fixed or prescribed rhythms.

Protestants shared the Biblical heritage of identifying the good and the bad in their lives with God's mercy or punishment, and they were equally heirs of the strong penitential culture of the late middle ages. It is natural, therefore, that Protestants adapted or created forms to express repentance and thanksgiving.[89] For present purposes, the individual practices will be passed over, in part because the focus here is public worship, but also in part because many Protestants

---

[88] Doumergue, *Jean Calvin*, vol. 1. *La jeunesse de Calvin*, p. 304, citing Lefranc, *Jeunesse*, p. 107, and *Pieces justificatives*, p. 200.

[89] Simons, *Die evangelische Buß- und Bettagsfeier*, and several other short articles by the same scholar are the basic treatments of this topic. A theological critique of the practice seems to be as important as historical research; e.g., Simons feels compelled to defend the Protestant tradition against the accusation of having renewed a penitential attitude which had weakened in the later Middle Ages. He claims that not only did the Reformation give the Bußtag a different character but that it was drawing on a medieval form and name, p. 3. Later in the article he characterizes various aspects of the medieval practice negatively, for its superficiality and its Jewish orientation, pp. 23-25. Besides the perspective of his day, Simons' sources were also more limited than those available now; however, the extent of his canvass was greater, as he described all the German Protestant church orders he had at hand. Individual cities which were vital in this movement have now received more focused attention from modern scholars, e.g., Bornert for Strasbourg, Burnett for Basel, although this topic is not central to their studies. Simons remains, therefore, an initial guide to the big picture, even though his study must be used with considerable caution.

shifted the weight of attention from private to corporate. Whereas the medieval sacrament of penance meant individual confession, Protestants often replaced this with a corporate confession of sin. Each person was expected to confess directly to God, of course. In addition, Lutherans encouraged (or sometimes required) confession to the minister, but this was no longer the one required liturgical mode for acknowledging sin.[90] In the Reformed tradition, individual confession to another person became an occasional practice for the relief of a burdened conscience or when one had wronged another;[91] the main focus was the corporate confession of sin which played an important role in most public liturgies.

The first generation of German-speaking Protestants began to develop several observances of public confession of sin and repentance. The most obvious was of course a kind of continuation of the medieval idea of special response to particular circumstances such as war or plague. The origin of these has been attributed to Bucer, and his work was certainly seminal. In August 1532 the Strasbourg magistracy set a day of special prayer for the war against the Turks. There were other such occasions later, including days of prayer because of bad weather in Oct. 1535, as intercession before the colloquies of Worms and Ratisbon, because of the plague in 1541, or in face of the war which set the Schmaldkald League against Charles V in 1546.[92] Strasbourg was not the only place to respond to the crisis of the Schmalkald war with a special day of intercession; in 1546 Heinrich Bullinger prepared a prayer specifically for this occasion.[93] These special times of response to crises could take various forms, some more elaborate than others. For example, in Strasbourg in response to these last two occasions, a "great prayer day" was celebrated with preaching at the normal Sunday morning hour (not the daily earlier time), the Lord's Supper, and a command to everyone to stop work,

---

[90] Albertine Saxony, *Kirchenordnungen zum anfang, für die pfarherrn... 1539*, Sehling I, pp. 268-69: "Wie mit den leuten in der beicht zu handeln. ... Forma der absolution." *General-Artikel und gemeiner Bericht*, 1557, Sehling I, p. 318: "Von der privat-absolution. Es soll niemand zum hochwirdigen sacrament ... zugelassen warden, er habe denn zuvor bei seinem ordentlichen pastor oder deacon die privat-absolution gesucht..." Leipzig, *Kirchenordnung... 1539*, Sehling, I, p. 593: "Auf alle festa und sontage. ... Und auf den abend zuvor von zwei uhr bis umb vier deren, so communiciren wollen, gewartet werden. Und sollen an idem ort solcher verhörung, tröstens, underrichtens und der absolution warten..." Hoya, *Kirchenordnung, 1584*, Sehling, VI/2, p. 1145.

[91] Calvin expresses this from the first edition of the *Institutes*, OS I, p. 180; becomes *Inst.* 3.4.12-13.

[92] Most of these occasions are named by Simons, "Die evangelische Buß- und Bettagsfeier," pp. 3-4, and/or Bornett, *La réforme protestante du culte*, p. 186. For the council note on Oct. 25, 1535, referring to a special service on the following Monday, cf. Brant's *Annales*, in BSCMHA 19 (1899), #5111, p. 253.

[93] Bächtold, "Gegen den Hunger beten," pp. 9-10.

close the shops, and come to worship.[94] Sometimes the services could be held in the afternoon or evening. They might be practiced once or a number of times during a crisis and Bornert says that "little by little" they could eventually lead to more regular prayer services.[95]

A different form of continuity with the medieval tradition is found in the most common Lutheran forms for repentance. Here the main text was Luther's litany, adapted from medieval sources.[96] This series of petitions could be used in the Sunday service or it could be added to a weekday one; in some places it was ordered on Wednesdays or Fridays.[97] The litany might be substituted for the sacrament when there were no parishioners who wanted to commune.[98] Besides medieval borrowings there were also mutual influences among German Protestants in this area, particularly the practice of combining the Lutheran use of the litany with the Reformed preference for a sermon. For example, the church order

[94] Bornert, *La réforme protestante du culte*, p. 186: "En règle générale, [la grande journée de prière] avait lieu un mardi: le matin, les fidèles étaient invites à se rendre à des services de prière et de prédication spéciaux, parfois suivis de la cène; la journée était normalement chômée." P. 186 n.90 gives the text of the order on Sept. 24, 1541: "... einen gemeinen bettag zu halten, und nemblichen bis zinstag nachkünfftig zu acht horen vormittag, soll und wirdet man in diszer und allen anderen Pfarrkirchen das Wort Gottes predigen, christenliche ermanungen zu sollichem gemainen gebet und dann dasselbig gebett thun, auch des herren nachtmal halten ... Es sollen auch zu zeiten sollicher predig und ämpter und bisz dieselben in allen pfarren volbracht seindt, alle eusserlichen arbeiten, gewerb und händel, auch unser Statt werkh underlassen, die gäden, läden und werkstätten beschlossen bleiben, und niemand zeitlich arbait thun, bisz sollicher gottgefelliger handel und dienst in den kirchen auszgericht ist, alsdann mag ain jeder sein gebürende arbait und handttlerung widerumb ür handt nemmen."

[95] Bornert, *La réforme protestante du culte*, p. 186 : "Puis, peu à peu, les journées de prière devinrent une coutume. Elles étaient régulièrement fixées le mardi. Dans l'après-midi ou dans la soirée, une prédication spéciale avait lieu. Aux heures correspondantes, le travail cessait."

[96] WA 30, III, pp. 20-21 for Luther's adaptation of medieval litanies; pp. 35-36, for some collects to conclude the litany.

[97] Ernestine Saxony, *Gemeine verordnung und artikel der visitation in Meissen…*1533: Sehling I, p. 192: "Letanei. Die letanei kann man halden under der vesper am sontag, oder am sonnabend zum vesper, und die wochen ein tag, wen das folk am meisten darbei sein kan." Albertine Saxony, *Kirchenordnungen zum anfang, für die pfarherrn... 1539*, Sehling I, pp. 272-73: "Litania. Wiewol das volk bei allen emptern in der kirchen zum gebet sol vermanet und angehalten warden, doch sol man auch zu sonderlichen bestimpten zeiten, das gemeine gebet der litania halten, als auf die vier quatember eine wochen-lang, in den stedten alle mitwochen oder freitage in der wochen, nach der predigt. Auf den dörfern, uber den andern sontag ein mal, zu gelengener stunde." P. 273 n. 1 provides the litany and collects to go with it. Use on Sunday or feast day, Lüneberg, *Kirchenordnung 1564*, Sehling, VI/1, p. 543. Hoya, *Kirchenordnung, 1584*, Sehling, VI/2, p. 1189.

[98] Grubenhagen, *Kirchenordnung 1544*, Sehling, VI/2, p. 1033: "Alle wochen, entweder am Mittwochen oder Freytage, und am Sondage oder feyrtagen, wen keinen communicanten vorhanden sind, so sollen die pfarner und ihre pfarkinder die letanien, welche man vormaln die bettmessen geheissen, singen und halten."

written for Calenberg-Göttingen by Anton Corvinus in 1542 ordains a sermon with the litany on Wednesdays and Fridays,[99] and Corvinus adds a substantial polemical instruction about the differences between the old use of the litany in Rogation (Ascension week) and the proper practice.[100] (Apparently some Lutheran areas retained the medieval practice to which Corvinus objected.) The project for the reform of Cologne which Bucer and Melanchthon prepared for Archbishop Herman von Wied in 1543 also combines "Lutheran" and "Reformed" elements, with a monthly prayer day and weekly recitation of the litany.[101]

For the Reformed tradition shaped by Martin Bucer and John Calvin, the practice of regular repentance had some similarities with but also some differences from medieval and Lutheran uses. The most important characteristic was probably the way that the idea of recognizing historical events as manifestations of God's just judgment was conceived as a regular, special service with a sermon.

---

[99] Corvinus had been an advisor to Philip of Hesse before he served Elisabeth of Braunschweig. Calenberg-Göttingen, *Kirchenordnung 1542*, Sehling, VI/2, p. 797: "Von predigttagen in der wochen. Aber auf den Mittwochen und Freitag sol anstadt des capitels, so man dem volke die anderen tage fürlieset, ein predigt geschehen und nach der predigt die wittembergische letaney gesungen werden, und sollen die pfarherrn das volk, solche bettage vleissig zu ersuchen und in die kirchen zu kom, bitten und ermanen." pp. 811-12: "Von der letaney. [cites 1 Tim. 2:1f] …ihr wöllet ja mit dem gemeinen gebete anhalten und auf die bestimpte tage, nemlich den Mittwochen und Freittag, die letaney mit aller andacht singen lassen; denn weil sich umb unser sunde willen allenthalben Gotts zorn mit pestilenz, theurer zeit und furcht des krieges ereuget, fordert die hohe not, das wir ihm zu fuss fallen und ohn unterlas, das er die wolverdiente straffe gnediglich von uns abwende, zu bitten nicht aufhören." The Wolfenbüttel, *Kirchenordnung 1569*, Sehling VI/1, p. 153, shows a similar plan "Es soll auch in der wochen auf den Mittwochen oder Freytag, nicht allein in den stetten, sondern auch in den dörfern, ein gebettag gehalten werden, an welchem die litania gesungen und von der ganzen gemein Gott dem Herrn alle noth und anligen der christenheit fürgetragen. Und soll das volk durch die pastorn ernstlich vernmanet werden, das sie sich mit allem vleiss zu solchem gemeinem gebet verfügen und sich ihr arbeit daran nicht verhindern lassen, welche durch solch gebet gesegnet und gefürdert wird." The preacher is also warned to keep the whole service to one hour. Here the intercessory element of the day of prayer receives more attention.

[100] Calenberg-Göttingen, *Kirchenordnung 1542*, Sehling, VI, p. 812: "Es haben etwa die alten solchs gebets halben eingesetzt die kreuzwochen. Es ist aber der teufel balde dazukomen und hat solche wolmeinung beschmeisset mit merklichem missbrauch, nemlich das man mit den fanen und heiligen hin und wider gelaufen und des rechten gebets darüber ganz und gar vergessen hat. Wollen derhalben, das solch affenspiel mit der procession gar abgeschafft, aber nichtdestoweniger solche bettage mit predigen, sacrament reichen und der letaney des morgens früe ehrlich gehalten werden, nicht das das gebet an sondere zeit gebunden sein solle, sonder das wir noch ein zeitlang den schwachgleubigen damit mit [!] zu dienen furhaben. Es sol aber die letania nicht wie in vorigen zeiten, da man sang: Sancte Petre, ora pro nobis! Sonder auf weise und masse, wie sie zu Wittemberg gedruckt und ausgangen ist, gehalten werden."

[101] cf. Simons, "Die evangelische Buß- und Bettagsfeier," p. 18.

What may be the first concrete evidence for this is found in the church order which Bucer prepared for Kassel in 1537.

> Concerning special prayer days. Every month there should be a day planned when the people are seriously exhorted to come more diligently. There [the pastor] should make a communal exhortation to repentance, with an urgent declaration about God's rods, those partly already sent upon us and partly still threatening. After such a sermon the people should be faithfully exhorted to prayer, almsgiving, and the right kind of fasting. After each one has prayed individually for the needs which have been lifted up, the pastor should read in German a common collect in which such prayers are summarized in an orderly way and, after they sing what is appropriate to the occasion, bless the parish and dismiss them. Such prayer days should be held more often at times of greater need and anxiety. [102]

The intention here was to establish special days of sermons and prayer each month. It is noteworthy that Bucer speaks of looking back at experiences of punishment as well as forward to ward off the need for God's disciplinary action. The concluding collects which were printed in the later Erfurt version of this Kassel church order came from the Lutheran books, [103] another example of the mutual borrowing which was common in this liturgy as in many others.

For Strasbourg, 1542 is identified as the year when the day of prayer practice was regularized. The chronicler Daniel Specklin describes this organization as a (simpler) day of prayer on three Tuesdays and then a "great day" on the fourth Tuesday, when a service like that on Sunday was held in all the churches. [104]

---

[102] Bucer, *Kasseler Kirchenordnung*, BDS 7, p. 294: "Von besonderen betetagen. Allen Monat sol man einen tag fürnemen, darzu man das volck, fleissiger zukommen, ernstlicher weiss vermanen sol, und da ein gemeyn ermanunge zur buosse thun, mit ernsten ermeldunge der Ruote Gottes, so uns zum teyl schon zuogeschickt, zum theyl noch warlich geträwt werden. Nach sollicher predigung sol man das volck zum gebet, Almuosen und rechtem Fasten trewlich vermanen. Und nach dem ein jeder bei ime selbst gebettet für die fürgehalten notturfft, sol der Pfarher ein gemeyn Collect zu teutsch verlesen, darin sollich gebet ordentlich summiert werden, Und die gemeyne nach dem gesang, dass sich darzu reimet, und segen lassen hingehen. Solche gebet tage, wo grösser not und anfechtungen fürfielen, sol man öffter halten."

[103] Bucer, *Kasseler Kirchenordnung*, BDS 7, pp. 294-95.

[104] Bornert, *La réforme protestante du culte*, p. 186 n.91 by Daniel Specklin, *Collectanées*, n. 2362: "Anno 1542 ward auch zu Strassburg von Bucero und den geistlichen angestelet, auch von der obrigkeit gebotten, dass man alle zinstag sollte einen bettag anstellen, aber alle vier wochen einen grossen bettag, also dass man in allen kirchen betten solte und predigen wie an einem sontag, gott anzuruffen, damit er seine kirche wolle erhalten." Bornert goes on to say that the practice of a weekly day of prayer, with a special monthly "great day" which sometimes included the Lord's Supper, became customary in Strasbourg until the major liturgical revisions of 1598, p. 186.

Specklin was writing some sixty-plus years after the events he describes (which occurred before he was born), and Bornert does not give further information to indicate what he means by saying "little by little" the practice became customary. Thus it is not clear precisely how the day of prayer developed during the period when Calvin was in Strasbourg, though it seems fairly certain that it was still in the formative stages.[105] It did not have a set liturgy and (if Specklin's date can be trusted) it did not become a regular practice until 1542. The length of the plague which began in 1541 probably helped establish an occasional service as a regular one; something similar apparently happened in Basel.

In 1541 the city of Basel began a time of penitential prayer with a sermon on Tuesdays.[106] Amy Nelson Burnett says: "In 1541, during a severe outbreak of the plague, an additional service of prayer and repentance on Tuesday morning was instituted in each of the parish churches and the Tuesday sermons remained a fixed feature after the plague subsided."[107] The ministers Oswald Myconius, Andreas Bodenstein von Karlstadt, Marcus Bertschi, and JakobTruckenbrot asked to have a "communal devotional prayer" held "every Tuesday as a penitential (Buss) sermon in the four parish churches."[108] It may be noted that Basel

---

[105] In letter to Farel #238 which the editors of OC date in Sept. 1540, Calvin mentions in passing, in the context of his poor health, that he preaches on Tuesdays; OC 11:83: "Antequam illinc discederem catarrhus me corripuit, qui continuo fluxu usque ad diem Martis admodum me vexavit. Eo die quum de more haberem concionem et magna in loquendo difficultate laborarem...". Lacking other information it is not possible to determine whether this regular weekday sermon had any connection with a nascent day of prayer; that is possible but perhaps unlikely since, if this date is accurate, the regular practice of the day of prayer had not yet begun and Calvin speaks of this as his custom.

[106] Simons, "Die evangelische Buß- und Bettagsfeier," p. 4, wonders whether Basel might have influenced Strasbourg but decides against this idea because he believed the Basel practice was discontinued. His source for Basel is a personal communication of an archival note from a colleague, which does not correspond to Burnett's careful research.

[107] Burnett, *Teaching the Reformation*, p. 56. This was held in each parish church, in addition to the daily 5 a.m. sermon in two places (Franciscan church and St. Clara, the two parts of the city).

[108] According to a private letter from Prof. Burnett, the archival basis for this was accidentally omitted from her book, but it is "a document in the Basel UB, from one of the several volumes from the church archives now housed in the manuscript dept., MsKiAr 23a, no. 94, fo. 279-80, which is listed in the index as 'Gemeine andectige Gebett, so man alle zinstag zur Busspredig in der vier Pfarrkirchen zu Basel haltet: Myconius, Carlstadt, Bersius & Truckenbrot (1541).' ... This is the earliest reference I've found to the Tues. sermon. There's very little specific evidence about any of the worship services from the first 2/3 of the century. Even the liturgical agendas include only the portion of the service for celebrating the Lord's Supper, and there's nothing for regular preaching services, whether Sun., Tues., or the early morning services. I don't have any documentary evidence to support this, but I think that once the service was instituted, it simply continued after the outbreak of the plague was over (since it lasted for over nine months, I suspect people got used to it.)." My thanks to Prof. Burnett for this helpful information.

lost several of its key preachers (Karlstadt, Grynaeus) in this same 1541 plague [109] (as Strasbourg lost Wolfgang Capito and others), so the request must have come before the full severity of the epidemic was experienced. The latter continued for nine months and Burnett thinks "that once the service was instituted, it simply continued after the outbreak of the plague was over." The content of this service is not specified until 1583; edicts about attendance at the Tuesday as well as Sunday services were issued in September 1582 and March 1584. [110] In keeping with the epidemic which originally prompted it, the prayer day in 1541 was focused on repentance, since the ravages of the plague were understood as punishment for sin. Given that the day chosen in Basel was the same as that in Strasbourg, and Bucer's work in Basel is well known, [111] it is quite possible that Basel's practice was influenced by its sister city further down the Rhine.

These "special" responses to disaster seem to have been the catalyst for some people to adopt a regularly recurring day of prayer. They were not, however, at the root of the Calvinist Reformed vision of the day of prayer, which included concern for a less spectacular set of circumstances. Some scholars recognize that, even before they faced war or the threat of war, the Strasbourg reformers were interested in a regular day of prayer, one not provoked by a special crisis but responding to the concrete situation of the church in its daily life. In February 1531 Bucer and his colleagues began to ask the magistrates for permission to establish a day of prayer because the people needed to be stirred up to more spiritual fervor. Their request does not seem to have been connected to a particular threat, and there was apparently no action until such a danger appeared (obviously the magistrates were following the older idea of such prayers as a response to particular circumstances). Bucer continued express his desire for days of prayer and repentance; for example, on Feb. 2, 1534, he was back before the magistrates on this matter. However, it required the severe outbreak of plague before days of prayer came into regular practice. [112]

---

[109] Burnett, *Teaching the Reformation*, p. 81.

[110] Amy Nelson Burnett, personal letter: "It's not until the 1580s that there is more information about what is said and/or done during this or any other service. There is a printed document, 'Ein Buss Gebet nach der Zinstag Predigt zu halten' from 1583 (Basel UB, MsKiAr 22a, no. 116, fo. 592v-593r) .... and there are edicts from Sept. 1582 and again from Mar. 1584 requiring attendance at both the Sun. and Tues. services…"

[111] Burnett, *Teaching the Reformation*, pp. 49-50.

[112] Cf. Bornert, *La réforme protestante du culte*, p. 185: "Dès le mois de février 1531, les prédicateurs réclamaient auprès du magistrat l'introduction de «journées de prière commune » (*gemeine Bettage*), parce que le people était «tiède et rude et qu'il montrait de moins en moins d'intérêt pour les exercices spirituels.»" Cf. QTG 7, #244, pp. 327-28. For the 1541 plague, see above after n.105.

Bucer describes his ideas most clearly in the Kassel church order in 1537 quoted above. The form which developed in Strasbourg was somewhat different: a weekly observance which emphasized one Tuesday per month along with a much less elaborate practice for the other Tuesdays. There are no complete outlines for this, much less written liturgies, but only limited references in the council minutes or a chronicler's account. Bucer's liturgical genius led the way to what became the characteristic Reformed practice of a regular day of prayer, but it was Calvin who brought this development to its full and lasting form.

Calvin's Teaching on the Day of Prayer

The day of prayer developed by Calvin built on the Strasbourg heritage but made it something more, something distinctive and defined. It became the liturgical expression of an integral aspect of his theology, the teaching on providence. His ideas about the practice developed over time, as the reformer moved from more general Biblical-theological observations to the practical implementation of his teaching in Geneva.

The 1539 Institutes and Strasbourg

The first clear formulation of the idea is found in the 1539 *Institutes of the Christian Religion*, completed shortly after his arrival in Strasbourg in 1538. In the chapter on penitence-repentance Calvin gives the fullest description in the context of explaining Joel 2:12-13.

> But although perhaps sackcloth and ashes better fitted those times, we do not deny that there will be a very suitable use among us for weeping and fasting whenever the Lord seems to threaten us with any ruin or calamity. When he causes some danger to appear, he announces that he is ready and, after a manner, armed for revenge. Therefore, the prophet does well to exhort his people to weeping and fasting – that is, to the sorrow of accused persons, for he had just stated that their evil deeds were brought to trial. Pastors of the church would not be doing ill today if, when they see ruin hanging over the necks of their people, they were to cry out to them to hasten to fasting and weeping; provided – and this is the principal point – they always urge with greater and more intent care and effort that "they should rend their hearts and not their garments." There is no doubt whatsoever that fasting is not always closely connected with repentance, but is especially intended for times of calamity.[113]

---

[113] *Institutes* McNeill-Battles, 3.3.17, p. 611; OS IV, p. 74. (minor changes because of differences between 1539 & 1559). *Institutio 1539*, Wevers (5:6:13-27): "Quanquam autem, cinis et soccus illis forte temporibus magis conveniebant: fletus tamen et ieiunii valde oportunum fore inter

Calvin goes on to explain that what is intended here is a public fast and prayer related to extraordinary times of disaster. It is important, however, to note that he clearly indicates that acts of repentance are more frequent than responses to the great calamities which should also include fasting. The suggestion about practicing acts of repentance more often could be a general allusion, since repentance is a normal part of Reformed worship, but one might wonder if Calvin is thinking of something more specific such as the concept of regular days for repentance. More pointed is his advice that pastors should be watching to warn their people before the actual disaster arrives, since "impendentem" suggests that the ruin is imminent but not actual. At the least it is clear that responsibility for interpreting the signs rests on pastors and this explains why Calvin and his colleagues took the initiative in calling their people to pay attention, and in establishing a day of prayer.

In this same edition of the *Institutes* (1539) there is another reference to the idea of a day of prayer, this time in the chapter on prayer. It follows a discussion on public and private prayer where Calvin says that for corporate prayer the church must agree upon times and places for worship so that things may be done with decency and order. "But this does not preclude any church from being both repeatedly stirred up to more frequent use of prayer and fired by a sharper zeal if it is alerted by some major need." [114] Here the occasional nature of the day of prayer is still the primary point. It may be noted, though, that Calvin seems to think in terms of frequent additional times of special assemblies, which suggests that the cause would not have to be a terrible (and thus probably more rare) disaster but could be anything outside the ordinary. This text does not indicate whether the cause of special prayer is within the specific church itself or not, but it leaves open the possibility that intercession might be needed for those beyond the local community. That aspect would be explicitly addressed in actual practice, as will be seen below.

---

nos usum non negamus: quoties cladem aliquam, aut calamitatem nobis minari visus fuerit Dominus. Se enim ad ultionem apparari et quodammodo armari denunciat, ubi periculum apparere facit. Bene igitur propheta, qui suos ad fletum et ieiunium, hoc est, ad reorum moestitiam cohortatur, de quorum flagitiis, constitutam quaestionem paulo ante dixerat. Nec male hodie fecerint Ecclesiastici pastores: si dum impendentem suorum cervicibus ruinam vident, ad ieiunium et fletum properandum vociferentur, modo quod est praecipuum maiore et intentiore cura et opera semper urgeant, scindenda scilicet esse corda, non vestimenta. Extra dubium est, non semper poenitentiae cohaerere ieiunium, sed calamitosis temporibus peculiariter destinari, unde et cum luctu coniungitur a Christo, dum Apostolos ab eius necessitate absolvit, donec suo praesentia orbati, moerore conficerentur, de solenni ieiunio loquor."

114 *Institutes* McNeill-Battles, 3.20.29, p. 891. OS IV, p. 338. *Institutio 1539*, Wevers (9:16:23-26): "Sed enim istud nihil obstat, quo minus unaquaeque ecclesia, cum subinde ad frequentiorem precationum usum se extimulare, tum maiore aliqua necessitate admonita, acriore studio flagrare debeat." See McKee, "Calvin 'Never Changed His Mind.'"

It is helpful to consider Calvin's words from the angle of what causes prompt such "extraordinary" manifestations of prayer. In the first case the focus is the association of suffering with punishment for sin, corporate or individual; in the second, it is the more neutral sense of uncontrollable circumstances which press upon the church. Other allusions in the 1539 *Institutes*, especially in the chapter on the Christian life, provide echoes of both of these themes, along with instruction on the appropriate attitude. Calvin exhorts and assures the faithful that rather than rebel and complain about afflictions such as illness, they should consider "the righteousness and goodness of the heavenly Father" and see these as chastisements to lead them to patience.[115] In speaking of bearing the cross, as Christ did to teach us patience, Calvin cites Paul's words about all God's children being conformed to Christ and says that this should be the source of a unique consolation: "in enduring all the miseries which people call bad and contrary, we may share in Christ's cross so that, as He has passed through an abyss of evils to enter into heavenly glory so also we may by various tribulations come there."[116] Some of these changes in the 1539 *Institutes* are clearly related to pastoral concerns of one who had to counsel people in difficult circumstances. This is natural because this was the first edition to appear after Calvin had gained some personal pastoral experience.

Development in the Institutes and the Question of Fasting

The additions to the *Institutes* in 1543 were particularly focused on ecclesiastical issues and in fact the issue of fasting, which is related to the day of prayer, is greatly expanded. The section which became book four, chapter twelve in 1559, on the organizational discipline of the visible church, is almost all introduced in this third edition. A significant part of the new material concerns fasting; there is some limited reference to prayer, but the central concern is right and especially wrong uses of fasting. Calvin begins the section with a general comment.

> The remaining part of discipline, which is not properly contained within the power of the keys, is where the pastors, according to the need of the times, should exhort the people either to fasting or to solemn supplications, or to other acts of humility, repentance, and faith – of which the time, the manner, and the form are not prescribed by God's Word, but left to the judgment of the church.[117]

---

[115] *Institutio 1539*, Wevers (17:10:14-18). 3.7.10; OS V, p. 160.

[116] *Institutio 1539*, Wevers (17:11:13-17). 3.8.1; OS V, p. 161-62.

[117] *Institutes* McNeill-Battles, p. 1241. 4.12.14; OS V, p. 224.

Calvin continues by explaining that this practice was customary in the early church (which employed it "as it was useful" [*utilis*]), but it was also modeled on the law and prophets. He emphasizes several times that this observance was based on a kind of utilitarian principle: "what would be useful" (*utile*) to the people. It is clear that the concept or teaching is Biblical, but matters of implementation: time, manner, and form, are *adiaphora*, to be decided by the church. Calvin also extends the various occasions which could call forth such a special public response of prayer and fasting.

> To sum them up: whenever a controversy over religion arises *which ought to be settled by either a synod or an ecclesiastical court,* whenever there is a question about choosing a minister, whenever, finally, any difficult matter of great importance is to be discussed, or again when there appear the judgments of the Lord's anger (as pestilence, war, and famine) – this is a holy ordinance and one salutary for all ages, that pastors urge the people to public fasting and extraordinary prayers. If anyone declines to accept the testimonies which can be cited from the Old Testament, as if inappropriate to the Christian church, the fact remains that the apostles also followed the same practice.[118]

In his French translation of this passage in 1545, Calvin substitutes "which involves great consequences" in place of the reference to synod and ecclesiastical court,[119] evidence that he was adjusting his counsel to the situation of the scattered Christians in France – who were not yet organized as churches, even though they were certainly "under the cross." The variety of occasions for which special prayer and fasting would be appropriate can include, therefore, any significant issue in the life of the church, whether internal to its functioning or related to God's chastisement. Calvin explicitly states that this practice is based on scripture, both the Old Testament and the apostolic practice (e.g., Acts 13:2-3), and affirms that Biblical examples were intended as part of the *bene esse* of the church, to be applied "for all ages."

The next sentence of this summary adds an interesting note. "Concerning prayers, however, I think scarcely anyone will be found who would raise a

---

118 *Institutes* McNeill-Battles, p. 1241. 4.12.14; OS V, p. 225.

119 4.12.14; OS V, p. 225, n.a. French of 1545 substitutes "qui tire grande consequence" in place of the reference to synod and ecclesiastical judgment which is here marked with *. In preaching on 1 Cor. 7:3-5, after discussing the election of ministers, he adds a reference (somewhat in passing) to the election of magistrates; cf. below at n.129. This is a common theme in sermons, e.g., those on the election of widows (the second kind of deacon) in #39 on 1Tim. 5:7-12, OC 53:474-75. chap. 3 at n.174.

question." Calvin effectively states that the references to prayer are uncontroversial. Then he proceeds to spend the rest of this quite long section of chapter twelve (paragraphs 15-21) on fasting. He begins by explaining the three uses of fasting.

> We use it either to weaken and subdue the flesh that it may not act wantonly, or that we may be better prepared for prayers and holy meditations, or that it may be a testimony of our self-abasement before God when we wish to confess our guilt before him. [120]

Calvin identifies the first use of fasting as essentially private, because the physical strength of human beings varies and nothing can be legislated for all. The second and third uses are both private and public, so Calvin examines these in more detail. Fasting in preparation for prayer is simply to make people more ready, and he provides examples from Acts 13:3, 14:23, Luke 2:37, and Neh. 1:4. (This is one of the few places where there is a later addition to this passage in 1559 to provide another example, 1 Cor. 7:3-5.) [121] The other private and public use is the one named for the day of prayer.

> Again, if either pestilence, or famine, or war begins to rage, or if any disaster seems to threaten any district and people – then also it is the duty of the pastors to urge the church to fasting, in order that by supplication the Lord's wrath may be averted. For where he causes danger to appear he warns that he is ready and, so to speak, armed for vengeance. [122]

Clearly Calvin considers fasting joined with prayer as a Biblical and appropriate response to signs of God's judgment, and the call to repentance which he institutionalized in the day of prayer. This is perhaps the most common cause for fasting: repentance and petition for help in time of disaster.

However, while he plainly defends the appropriateness of fasting ("an excellent aid for believers today"), Calvin indicates that there are considerable difficulties with its practice. For clarity, he begins by explaining what he means by a fast (when it is used rightly). First he affirms that in all things Christians should exercise restraint and moderation; however, a fast is something more. It is a temporary withdrawal "from the normal regimen of living" which is done to carry out the specific purpose (e.g., in order to pray), and by eating simpler food

---

[120] *Institutes* McNeill-Battles, p. 1242. 4.12.15; OS V, p. 225.

[121] *Institutes* McNeill-Battles, p. 1242-43. 4.12.15, 16; OS V, p. 225-26.

[122] *Institutes* McNeill-Battles, p. 1243. 4.12.17; OS V, p. 226.

and less of it. He then turns to refute what he regards as superstitious: trust in external ceremony alone, honoring fasting as meritorious or as a way to worship God, and extreme measures in fasting. Observance of Lent is identified as one of the ways that people have been deceived into thinking they are doing something for God. The traditional (Roman) practice of fasting has also been turned into a time of feasting on delicacies in disregard for the poor; the rich avoid meat but instead eat all kinds of dainties, yet if anyone touches "bacon fat or rancid meat with dark bread" he is regarded as totally impious. [123] In the French *Institutes* in 1545, Calvin adds here: "Indeed, even if a poor man who has nothing else does it" [124] (eats some fat or meat drippings). Obviously for his vernacular audience the reformer wanted to include a reference to the kind of injustice which issued from the application of church laws without regard for the destitution of the poor. What is immediately relevant here, however, is Calvin's caution about public fasting.

> For it would be much more satisfactory if fasting were not practiced at all, than diligently observed and at the same time corrupted with false and pernicious opinions, into which the world repeatedly falls, unless the pastors meet it with the highest faithfulness and prudence. [125]

It is clear that in theory Calvin had a high regard for the value of fasting as a Biblical and patristic practice. He did not regard it as a necessary thing, however, and in the circumstances of his own day considered the risks to be very serious.

This teaching in the *Institutes* is partially echoed in the sermons, and it is worthwhile to see how Calvin explained the Pauline passage in 1 Cor. 7:3-5 to the people in the pew. (In this passage couples are given permission to withdraw from marital relations for a time of special prayer and fasting – but not as a constant state.) Calvin firmly situates the special occasions of prayer and fasting of this Biblical passage in the context of constant daily prayer and moderation ("our life should be like a continual fast"). He seems anxious to be sure that his congregation does not make the mistake of thinking that a "big occasion" is the only time they should turn to God and pray. Human life is very fragile, we are always surrounded by so many dangers: "we should be a hundred thousand times more moved [to pray] than we are," and the preacher goes on to give examples. It is

---

123 *Institutes* McNeill-Battles, pp. 1244, 1247. 4.12.17-21; OS V, p. 226-31.

124 *Institutes* McNeill-Battles, p. 1247. 4.12.21; OS V, p. 230 n.g "Voire mesme si un povre homme qui n'a autre chose, le faict."

125 *Institutes* McNeill-Battles, p. 1245. 4.12.19; OS V, p. 228. The French of 1545 adds: "Voicy donc les remonstrances qui nous sont necessaires pour bien user du jeune."

not only earthly life but the more urgent needs of eternal life… [126] Having emphasized the context, Calvin then addresses the occasions of "extraordinary prayer"
which Paul treats here. He names the usual dangers: plague, threat of war or
famine; and then adds the less obvious or more private ones: signs of God's wrath,
a sense of our sins, or some significant business either general or personal. [127]

The next part of the sermon applies the teaching to the Genevans. Here the
preacher seems to be concentrating on what the *Institutes* identified as the second
use of prayer and fasting, i.e., preparation for a major task. He exclaims: "we are so
stupid God cannot drag a prayer out of us, at least not one in good conscience and
without pretence." [128] People pay no attention when there are "great afflictions in
the church and in a public estate" – they say "Alas" but will not hear of calls to
prayer. This is contrary to the example of the early church. When that model
church gathered to attend to business which concerned the state of the church,
such as electing ministers, there were public prayers and fasting, and "the prayers
were even done in the temple." The fact that Calvin highlights that this practice
received such a mark of status from the apostles suggests that he thought his
hearers needed to recognize the importance of these special prayers, and his next
words imply that the Genevans still have much to learn.

> Yet today they do not think of that when it is a question of instituting fasts
> or extraordinary prayers in the election of the lords of justice, in the
> election of ministers. It seems [to them] that this is like the meritorious
> devotional minutiae of the papacy. [129]

---

[126] Sermon #42, f347a.

[127] Sermon #42, f347b: "Et c'est quand nous sommes affligez de peste, ou qu'il y a quelque menace
       ou de guerre ou de famine, que nous voyons la main de Dieu qui desja nous presse ; quand il y a
       quelque apparence que Dieu est courroucé contre nous, alors nous avons besoing de souspirer
       et de gemir comme povres malfaicteurs qui viendront demander pardon à leur juge, et ainsi fault
       il que tousjours nous recourions à Dieu et en ardeur plus grande quand il nous a donné quelque
       signe de son ire ou quand noz pechez nous redarguent ou que nous sommes en quelque affaire."

[128] Sermon #42, f347b: "D'aultre costé quand nous avons quelque affaire soit en general soit en
       particulier nous sommes si stupides que Dieu ne peut arracher une oraison de nous, voire à bon
       escient et sans feintise."

[129] Sermon #42, f348a: "Mais aujourd'huy on n'y pense point quand il seroit question d'instituer
       jeusnes et prieres extraordinaires en l'election des seigneurs de justice, en l'election des minis-
       tres. Il semble que ce seroit comme une bigottise de la papaulté." The word *bigottise* is equivalent
       to the modern French *bigoterie*, defined as "devotion étroite et pointillieuse" in *Le Quillet
       Flammarion dictionnaire usual* (Paris: Quillet Flammarion, 1963), p. 190. Calvin uses it in other
       sermons to express meritorious devotion. See Edmond Huguet, *Dictionnaire de la Langue
       Française du seizième siècle*, vol. 1 (Paris: Ancienne Librairie Edouard Champion, 1925),
       pp. 581-82. (Definition of *bigotise* includes citations of Calvin's sermons.)

Calvin thinks the Genevans' reluctance to participate in fasts and special prayers is a part of their reaction against traditional Roman practice, here probably including the power of the clergy and regulation of every detail of liturgical life. It is the end of the sermon and Calvin concludes with another repetition of his main point.

> When we are in some perplexity or have some business which presses on us, let us run back to God and let us have extraordinary prayers. For when we have some public business, it is as if [God] is waking us up. When we have something which concerns the common state of the church let us pray to God that He may be pleased to take care of it as is necessary. [130]

In this final summary, Calvin makes no further mention of fasting, but reiterates his conviction that Christians must pay attention to what is unfolding around them. He adds that this applies to individuals as well as the larger community. However it is clear, from the fact that he introduced the corporate public dimension into the explanation of a text in which the instruction could have been considered purely personal (between husband and wife), that one of his key concerns was the life of the church as a body.

The subject of fasting in Calvin's Geneva may be concluded with a few comments. First, it is clear that Calvin defended the principle of fasting, but it appears that he did not have a particular determination to put it into practice. Partly that may have been because it was in his eyes secondary to the prayers with which it was associated in scripture and patristic sources, and partly because it was so much compromised by medieval tradition. He also was aware that it retained negative Roman associations for Genevans. Given his own hesitations about superstition, he probably did not consider this point worth a battle, even if he might cite critically his congregation's reluctance to follow precisely the Biblical model. It is also significant that fasting does not seem to have been implemented in a formal corporate fashion in Calvin's Geneva. [131] The Annales, the day-to-day

---

[130] Sermon #42, f348a: "Quand nous sommes en quelque perplexité, que nous avons quelque affaire qui nous presse, que nous recourions à Dieu et que nous ayons des prieres extraordinaires, car c'est autant comme s'il nous esveilloit; quand nous aurons quelque affaire public, que nous aurons quelque chose qui concerne l'estat commun de l'eglise, que nous prions Dieu qu'il luy plaise d'y provoir comme il fault, qu'il y besogne et qu'il y mette la main. Car sans cela tout ce que nous pourrons faire ne sera que confusion."

[131] Eduard Simons, *Fasttage in den alten calvinistischen Kirchen* (Marburg: Univ.-Buchdruckerei von Joh. Aug. Koch, 1912) treats Calvin's day of prayer which he had omitted in his earlier text cited above. He does not distinguish between fast days and prayer days, and considers

schedule of Calvin and Genevan life collected by the editors of the *Opera Calvini,* does not record any orders for a general fast[132] nor does the contemporary chronicle of Michel Roset mention such a thing. Christian Grosse, who has made the most recent and exhaustive study of Genevan rituals, also does not refer to the prctice of fasting until 1567.[133] However, the practice of special corporate public prayers – a day of prayer – was another matter entirely.

The Liturgy of the Day of Prayer

The earliest full liturgy for the day of prayer was published by Calvin in 1542. While in Strasbourg he had probably followed the gradually developing practice of the Tuesday day of prayer services, although there is no explicit evidence for that. (This is not surprising, since the practice itself was probably just then developing an organized form.) The only collection of liturgical texts used by Calvin's French-language congregation in Strasbourg is no longer extant. The fact that the Pseudo Romana (1542), which most scholars regard as a republication of that text, does not include any liturgy for the day of prayer is not conclusive for Calvin's practice either way, since there was no printed German liturgy for the practice of this rite in the Strasbourg churches,[134] but it does support the idea that there was no Strasbourg liturgy for this observance. The surprise is all the greater, then, that Calvin produced a full liturgy for the day of prayer in the Geneva 1542 *La forme des prieres,* and in addition explicitly made this a regular weekly service. In fact, he had already written the special prayers for the

---

Genevan practice to have been shortlived. "Schon bald scheint man auf wöchentliche sich wiederholende Fasttage verzichtet und mit einem Tag begnügt zu haben," p. 3. He goes on to discuss the fast day invitation which Geneva issued to its sister churches after the St. Bartholomew's massacre, and other similar occasional fasts. The basis of Simons' discussion of Geneva's day of prayer seems to have been the *Institutes'* positive association of prayer and fasting. He also notes (p. 2) that even in an instance where the scriptural text mentions only fasting, as in Matt. 9:15, Calvin adds a reference to prayer. (In fact, this suggests that Calvin was much more interested in prayer than fasting; at least, he could not imagine fasting without prayer.) Because of Simons' confusion that prayer days and fast days were identical, he fails to understand what in fact Calvin's day of prayer was. He says (p. 4) that Valerand Poullain's idea of a weekly hour of prayer on Thursday made a rule of what was an exceptional case for Calvin.

132 The only reference to "jeune" or "ieune" is found in an excerpt from the consistory for May 15, 1550, in which a girl and her aunt fasted on Good Friday ("le Grand Vendredi"); OC 21:464. See *Consist.* V, p. 93.

133 Grosse, *Les rituels de la Cène,* p. 300. It was begun in 1567 and there were about fifteen between that date and 1620, on an occasional basis. They became a regular feature from 1640 in conjunction with the annual fast established by the Swiss Reformed churches.

134 *La forme des prières,* OS 2, p. 2, and Strasbourg 1542/Pseudo-Romana (photocopy preserved in IHR).

November 1541 services of intercession for the cities suffering from the plague and war[135] – so his liturgical work on the day of prayer began almost immediately after he arrived in Geneva.

Among the most significant things about Calvin's liturgy for the day of prayer are that it was published in his *La forme des prieres* in 1542, that it was obviously modeled on the Sunday morning service, and that it was intended to be a weekly event. As seen above, other communities who practiced a penitential prayer hour were content to use a revision of the traditional medieval litany published as an independent prayer and attached to another service. Those who established a prayer day did not publish a complete liturgical form; at most there might be a description in a church order. The content and the timing of these services were also rather variable. The Kassel order quoted above featured an exhortation to repentance and a collect. Although the "great prayer day" in Strasbourg seems to have been modeled on the Sunday liturgy, the lesser weekly one was not, and the Basel service was word and prayer. While the Kassel order envisioned a monthly service, the legislation which established the services in Strasbourg and Basel was not explicit about its permanence. Thus, the fact that Calvin published a liturgy for the day of prayer, modeled it on the Sunday service and planned it as the only other fully defined order of worship, and insisted that it be held every week, makes his day of prayer distinctive. That he would successfully work to achieve its status as a partial holiday with services at two times, and as the only special weekday observance in the Genevan Reformed calendar, gives his day of prayer particular significance.[136]

The order of the day of prayer liturgy closely follows that for Sunday so the basic outline can be summarized. In 1542 there was the opening salutation, followed by the invitation and confession of sin, a sung Psalm, prayer for illumination and sealing concluding with the Lord's Prayer, Biblical text and sermon. This led into the individual prayer for the day and the special prayer of intercession which included a paraphrase of the Lord's Prayer, (perhaps the Apostles'

---

135 In a letter written at the end of January 1542, probably to Sebastian Münster, Calvin says: "Quoniam pestis in Germania saeviebat et alter ex parte bellum, feci ut supplicationes extraordinariae decernerentur. Precationes quibus in iis uteremur conscripsi," Herminjard, *Correspondance*, vol. 7, p. 409; letter 1090. My thanks to Grosse for bringing this text to my attention; *Les rituels de la Cène*, p. 141.

136 The day of prayer even took precedence over the Sunday afternoon service by having a distinctive prayer of intercession. This has also not been observed by later scholars, who assume that Calvin used the Sunday morning prayer also that afternoon, but the evidence from his sermons demonstrates that the Sunday afternoon prayer was the extemporaneous one the preacher used for most weekdays, i.e., all except the day of prayer. See chap. 3 at n.182.

Creed?[137]), and benediction. By the mid-1540s a second time of singing had been introduced after the sermon. In 1552 there were important additions to the prayers of intercession, prompted by the persecutions in France, and after 1553 the form of the Lord's Prayer in the intercession could be either paraphrased or recited. By 1562 a third time of singing was introduced, at the beginning of the service. Fuller discussion of the Sunday order is found in the previous chapter. Here the distinctive aspects of the day of prayer will be emphasized.

From a theological viewpoint, the explanatory preface to the day of prayer is especially significant. The other services in the Geneva *La forme des prieres* do not have such prefaces but only some comments at the end of each sacrament to defend the Protestant changes.[138] At the least, Calvin's choice to give a theological rationale for the day of prayer service suggests that he thought that the reasons for the regular weekly practice of a day for repentance would not be obvious to the parishioners. This preface itself has two principal themes. The first combines the Biblical teaching that admonitions like plague and war are God's punishment for sin, with instructions on the appropriate response.

> Inasmuch as scripture teaches us that plagues, wars, and other such adversities are visitations of God by which He punishes our sins, when we see such things approaching we must recognize that God is angry with us and then if we are truly faithful, we must recognize our offenses, be grieved with ourselves, turning back to the Lord in repentance and amendment of life, and pray to Him in true humility in order to obtain pardon.[139]

The language suggests that Calvin is beginning with the statement of a well-established tradition: the experience of adversity as punishment for sin and a call to repentance. Based on this understanding of God's will, the reformer goes on to draw an untraditional conclusion, i.e., Christians should not wait for God to punish them but should be alert to repent. That is the second theme of the preface.

---

[137] Grosse maintains that even though there is no written evidence, the Apostles' Creed was probably recited at this point in the service, because it was found in all the other liturgies; *Les rituels de la Cene*, pp. 199, 663. This is certainly possible or perhaps probable, but it must be marked as hypothetical.

[138] There are little essays in the Strasbourg1542/ Pseudo-Romana before the sacraments, brief before baptism, longer before the Supper liturgy, but these are not in the Genevan text. OS II, pp. 30, 39-44, 38, 49-50. Grosse, *Les rituels de la Cène*, pp. 141-42, maintains that the preface to the Psalter was intended to have an explanatory section on the Lord's Supper, but this was omitted, and it was also not directly parallel to the introduction to the day of prayer.

[139] *Writings on Pastoral Piety*, p. 159; OS II, p. 26.

> For this reason, if we sometimes see that God threatens us, in order not to try His patience but rather to submit before His judgment falls on us – judgment which otherwise we see ready to be manifest – it is good to have a set day each week in which there may be special exhortation about these things, and on which we may make prayers and supplications according to the need of the time. [140]

Note that at least in this rationale Calvin's view is focused forward; the text of the intercessory prayer later in the liturgy will recall previous sin or punishment, but here the point is a watchful attention for what is coming. It is too much to say that the past has been dealt with in the confession of sin at the beginning of the service but it is notable that the emphasis here is on preparing for the Christian life ahead. The motif of the day of prayer might be summarized as "pay attention to look for providence – God's active presence – in everything that is happening in human society." [141]

It is important to note that the day of prayer was distinctive in two ways. First, it was markedly different from the ordinary weekday services which consisted of scripture and sermon and prayers. By contrast, the day of prayer liturgy was very much like that for Sunday, with sung Psalms as probably the most notable aspect for the people in the pew. Secondly, however, the day of prayer was slightly but significantly different from the Sunday morning liturgy because it had its own printed intercessions (something not even Sunday afternoon had), and of course it was never joined with the Lord's Supper. Singing Psalms has already been discussed in the previous chapter so a few words will be sufficient; then more attention will be given to the remarkable prayer of intercession.

The singing of Psalms was understood in Calvin's teaching as part of prayer, and it is significant that he wanted the vocal participation of the congregation on the day of prayer as well as on Sundays. This was perhaps the most memorable feature of the liturgy for the Genevan congregation. The Psalms to be used on Wednesdays were chosen with an eye to their appropriateness; the petitions were allocated to the day of prayer and Psalms of praise and thanksgiving designated for Sundays. Within these categories, the Psalms were generally though certainly not always arranged in canonical sequence. [142]

---

140 *Writings on Pastoral Piety*, p. 159; OS II, pp. 26-27.

141 The preface concludes with a brief admonition to the pastor to exhort the people before beginning the intercessory prayer ; cf. OS II, pp. 26-27.

142 Pidoux, *Psautier huguenot*, p. 61 (for 1551 list which he identifies as 1553): "Considerans que le jour du Mecredy est ordonné pour les prieres solennelles, nous avons choisi entre les Pseaumes, ceux qui contiennent prieres et requestes à Dieu plus expresses pour chanter en ce jour: reservant ceux qui contiennent action de graces et louanges du Seigneur nostre Dieu et de ses oeuvres, au jour du Dimanche…"

Besides the congregational Psalm-prayers, there were also the printed texts spoken by the minister. The long prayer of intercession which distinguishes this liturgy from that for Sunday morning echoes the penitential theme but expresses also trusting gratitude for past benefits. Framed in the first person plural, it begins with a recognition of sin which is also accompanied by the command to pray and the reason that God will hear such prayers: "because by Your infinite mercy it has pleased You to command us to call upon You, even from the depths of hell" and, "You have promised to hear our prayers and supplications" through Jesus Christ. Therefore "renouncing trust in all things human, we take courage from Your goodness alone to address You and invoke Your holy name, in order to obtain mercy." Next, after briefly acknowledging the gifts common to all people, the prayer expresses thanks for special graces to Christians, particularly the knowledge of the gospel. Following this is a confession of past sin and its punishment (with the affirmation that much more was deserved). Having recalled such experiences, the prayer affirms the similarity of the present situation to those earlier times when God had chastised sin: "now we see Your hand again uplifted to punish us, because the swords You are accustomed to use to execute Your vengeance are now deployed…"[143]

The next part of the prayer expresses the relationship of the people with God, beginning with a lyric passage reaffirming that tie.

> And yet, Lord, You are our Father, and we are only earth and clay; You are our Creator, and we are the work of Your hands. You are our Shepherd, and we are Your flock; You are our Redeemer, and we are the people whom You have ransomed; You are our God, and we are Your heritage. Therefore, do not be angry against us, to correct us in Your wrath. May You not remember our iniquity to punish it, but may You chastise us gently according to Your loving kindness.[144]

Following this is a brief evocation of the historical relationship of the people of God with God by allusion to the stories of mercy to Israel. Using the pastor's voice, the community then gladly affirms their own even better covenant in Christ and makes a plea to God to accept Christ's intercession and give the Holy Spirit.[145] The next part of the prayer is devoted to fairly detailed intercessions for other people: individuals by name, and all churches and peoples afflicted with plague, war, and other ills, as well as the more general petitions for rulers and

---

[143] *Writings on Pastoral Piety*, pp. 173-74. OS II, pp. 27-28.

[144] *Writings on Pastoral Piety*, p. 174. OS II, p. 28.

[145] *La forme des prieres*, OS II, pp. 28-29.

pastors and others which is the same as for Sundays.[146] Additions to this prayer in later printings of *La forme des prieres* demonstrate that the shaping of the special intercessions of the day of prayer continued to be a matter of special interest to Calvin. In 1552 new references to those suffering for the proclamation of the gospel were added here (as well as in the prayer for Sunday morning).[147] This is one of several new liturgical intercessions for the churches under the cross as the situation of French Protestants in particular became ever more difficult. The prayer indicates that Calvin the pastor was continuing to follow his own earlier admonition (in the *Institutes*) to ministers to observe the ills God sends and to respond appropriately by alerting their people to afflictions about which they should be praying.

The aspect of explicit intercession for fellow believers seen in Calvin's Geneva liturgy seems to be characteristic of Protestant day of prayer services. This is stated in the proclamation by which Geneva established the first celebration to intercede for "Bern, Basel, Zurich, Strasbourg and other allied cities which are persecuted by plague"[148] (quoted above). However it is notable that while special prayer days were called and established in other cities or territories in response to their own immediate experience of plague, Calvin's Geneva first took this step even though it was not personally suffering disaster at the time. This concern for mutual intercession is expressed even more forcefully and explicitly in Calvin's first published sermon preached on Nov. 4, 1545, one of the rare recorded special days of prayer, one which gave particular attention to a specific act of God.

Special Days of Prayer

For Calvin, the day of prayer was a weekly feature of worship life but, like the larger tradition, he also acknowledged that there were specific times when a special observance was appropriate. For these times, the liturgy, the day, and the number of services remained the same, but the text of the sermon was chosen in consideration of the nature of the historical situation (intercession, thanksgiving) and thus formed an interruption in the preacher's *lectio continua* series. It is probable that the special prayer days were a very secondary aspect for Calvin, since the number recorded during his ministry is extremely limited, but it is important to include these occasions because the sermons offer helpful insight into the purposes of the day of prayer. A few later examples will be sketched

---

[146] *La forme des prieres*, OS II, pp. 29-30.

[147] *La forme des prieres*, OS II, pp. 29-30. This is identified as 1559 [OS II, p. 29], but it is actually 1552, in a printing by Jean Crespin [identified by anchor printer's mark] which the editors of OS did not know. For addition to Sunday, see chap. 3 at n.74.

[148] Nov. 11, 1541 (RC 35 f385) ; see above at n.61.

below. Events in November 1545 led to the only completely documented examples of special days of prayer in Calvin's Genevan ministry. The historical situation and two sermons, preached on the Wednesdays of Nov. 4 and Nov. 11, 1545, can illumine this unusual occurrence. The texts of the sermons were transcribed by Jean Cousins, who also recorded the Psalms sung on these occasions and published the little booklet early the next year. [149]

The presenting cause for these special prayer days was the situation in Germany, where Protestant and Catholic princes were fighting. Yet when Calvin preached these two sermons Geneva itself was experiencing a very difficult time, and its chief pastor was extremely busy with other problems than the German war. Probably most obvious to the citizens of Geneva – Calvin's congregation – was the severe visitation of the plague in which many people were dying, including one of the ministers. Arguments among the pastors over who would go to the Plague Hospital, and over the dismissal of one of their number, Aimé Champereau, for misconduct, contributed to the tensions. When Champereau complained to Bern, Geneva's traditional patron and constant critic, a further layer of exasperation was added to Calvin's effort to provide Geneva with good pastoral leadership. [150] As if all this were not enough, almost certainly one of the most distressing things to the reformer himself was the harsh persecution of Protestants in France. Officials of Francis I had descended on the people of Provence in 1544 and 1545 because these subjects had had the audacity to write a Protestant confession and refuse the services of their priests, although they still dutifully paid their tithes. Hundreds of these poor French people were killed, enslaved in the galleys, wounded, raped, and driven out. Calvin had persuaded Geneva to welcome the refugees, and had also spent not a little time and energy over many previous months working to get Swiss and German diplomatic intercession for these persecuted fellow believers. [151] Besides all of this trouble near at hand, there was the bad news from Germany, which Genevans might consider far away but which Calvin (like his mentor Martin Bucer) regarded as closely related, because every local community of the church is part of the whole body and responsible for mutual prayer and mutual care as much as possible.

---

[149] This is actually the first evidence for two times of Psalm singing in the service; it is also evidence for the introduction of a new metrical Psalm between printings of the Psalter; see chap. 3 at nn.101.

[150] For plague, see chap. 7 at nn.93ff. For Champereau, Naphy, *Calvin and the Consolidation*, pp. 70-71.

[151] See Bruce Gordon, *Calvin* (New Haven: Yale, 2009), pp. 182, 198-99; there is a summary in McKee's introduction to some of Calvin's letters, *Writings on Pastoral Piety*, pp. 315-20.

From the viewpoint of history, the conflict between Philip of Hesse and the Duke of Braunswig was a fairly small matter. Therefore it might be asked why Calvin thought that these events were so important that a special day of prayer should be held. Examination of his sermon will offer some theological clues, but there were also some practical considerations prompting the decision by both the reformer and the Genevan Senate.

Among the latter was a letter from Simon Sulzer, Calvin's friend in Bern. Besides commenting on the activities of Champereau seeking Bernese redress for his dismissal from Geneva, Sulzer writes that the Bernese ministers are exhorting their churches to prayer and repentance in face of the afflictions in Germany, as he also expects that Calvin is doing.[152] (It should be remembered that Bern did not have a regular day of prayer, and later they would accuse Calvin of establishing a new saint's day because Geneva celebrated this liturgy weekly. This will be examined below.) Thus Sulzer's letter should be understood to mean that the leaders in Bern thought that the news from Germany was significant enough to follow the old tradition of a special intercessory act in a time of affliction. Given this prompting and since it built on a liturgy that was already so important to him, it is no surprise that Calvin apparently asked the Genevan authorities to proclaim a special day of prayer.

A second reason for giving the news from Germany high visibility may have been the Genevan need to please Bern in every way they could without mortgaging their independence. When they knew the Bernese plans, they were probably only too happy to follow suit. Since this is also the year that Calvin had persuaded the city government to scale back the celebration of the "four feasts," he and they both may have thought that it was appropriate to respect Bern's judgment and follow its lead on the seriousness of the German situation. By logical extension, if the great danger to fellow believers called for special intercessions, then naturally when news of the victory came, God's wonderful delivery must also be celebrated with thanksgiving. At least, that was Calvin's conclusion and apparently the Senate agreed, because they approved when he asked for the second day of special observance at the next regular weekly day of prayer time.[153]

---

152 Sulzer to Calvin, Oct. 27, 1545; #719, OC 12:202: "Ecclesias ergo nostras ad preces hortamur et poenitentiam: quod et te facere nihil ambigo, uti adflictis rebus adsit misericorditer Christus ipse, qui solus verbo sedat maria frementia exitiumque minitantia."

153 Nov. 5, 1545, OC 21:364 (RC 39 f283): News of victory, "Surquoy M. Calvin a prier luy oultroye licence de rendre graces à Dieu avecque mecredy prochaien de telle victoire. Resoluz que sa requeste luy soyt oultroye et que les dizenniers allent moyson par moyson fere commandement de venyr aut sermon."

On the first special day of prayer Calvin chose to preach on Ps. 115, concentrating on the first three verses: "Not to us, Lord, not to us: but to Your name give the glory, for the sake of Your gracious goodness and truth. Why should the nations say: 'Where now is their God?' For our God is in the heavens, He does whatever He pleases." This is not a traditional penitential text, but it fits the context of intercession extremely well. Calvin begins with a word about why people suffer, explaining that there are various reasons.

> Sometimes there is nothing which moves [God] to [afflict people], except that it pleases Him that His truth may be confirmed by the patience of His servants. Or indeed when He has put them in some danger and He delivers them, in that also He wishes to be glorified. Or there may be some other outcome; sometimes He chastises them for their offenses. [154]

While the idea that God may afflict people might seem to call into question God's goodness, it reflects Biblical teaching such as the testing of Abraham and other examples of parental discipline (e.g., Gen. 22:1-14, Heb. 12:5-11). One significant point, however, is that Calvin does not assume that all suffering is punishment, even though – as he goes on to explain – that is always deserved.

The exegesis of Ps. 115 shapes the first part of the sermon. There is an extended discussion of the psalmist's appeal to God for help based on God's own name and glory ("Your gracious goodness and truth") and not on the merits of the petitioners. Calvin begins by imagining a dialogue with God and then points to the Biblical grounds.

> "See, all that we claim of You is not that You are obligated [to us], not that we have deserved something from You, not at all. May it never happen that we presume to allege our merits! You are not bound to us. But it is Your goodness, You are good, that is the reason that You acknowledge us as Your people." Truth is joined with goodness, and not without reason, that is the common usage in scripture. For just as the promises of God are founded on His pure gratuitous mercy, so also their support comes from His truth. [155]

Calvin then deals with the problem presented by verse 2 and the derision of enemies ("Where is their God?"). The next verse provides the "shield." As the pastor explains, the taunts of foes are a temptation, and the faithful may not know

---

[154] *Writings on Pastoral Piety*, p. 161. OC 32:455.

[155] *Writings on Pastoral Piety*, p. 163. OC 32:457.

how to answer. "God arms us. When we are attacked by unbelievers and it looks as if we are done for, we must take this shield: 'Our God is in heaven, He does whatever He pleases.'" Calvin goes on to emphasize the personal relationship with God who is "our God." This is a very practical pastoral response. "If there were a God in heaven with whom we had no acquaintance, what good would that do us? But instead it is said: 'our God.' This is reciprocal; He is our God and He acknowledges us for His children."[156]

In the next section of the sermon, Calvin applies the text to the Genevans. First he points to the terrible situation of the church; the enemies have reason to attack because the lives of the people who claim the gospel do not meet the appropriate standard. Thus the faithful must repent and entreat God to consider the honor of His name. From this the preacher turns to the situation of the German Christians whose danger has prompted this special day of prayer.

> Today is the time to make the prayer written here; although it is for any time, nevertheless when the need is urgent we should make use of it. We should well have greater zeal. We [act as if we] know nothing about the union our Lord wanted there to be among His members. Are we the church? We must have a spiritual connection with all the faithful. ... We all have the same gospel, we are surrounded by enemies. Should we separate [from each other]? Should we say: "Those [people in Germany] are far from us?" Not at all. They are of the church, and we are its members; because we have the same Father in heaven, let us have a brotherhood together which is indeed more than fraternal! Let us reflect that what happens to one member of the church happens to us. Behold troubles everywhere! ... We should not be thus nonchalant. This is the time to seek God. We should forget everything else; we cannot help them [the German Protestants] with our hands, but we ought to pray to God for them as for ourselves: the condition of the church is not the [concern of only] one member. Moreover, let us fear that in a short time the storm may roll over our heads.[157]

Calvin's words show the sense of Christians' mutual responsibility: here that of Genevans for fellow Christians in Germany. Even though their specific statement of faith is different, these Lutherans are clearly fellow believers. Furthermore, Genevans should learn from others' experience of God's judgment in order not to call the same down upon themselves.

---

156 *Writings on Pastoral Piety*, p. 164. OC 32:458. See introduction to this book, at n.9.

157 *Writings on Pastoral Piety*, p. 166-67. OC 32:460-461.

The preacher then reminds the congregation of the purpose of the day of prayers.

> This day has been established to offer prayers. Therefore let us be more diligent than is customary, not only to come and present ourselves [here], but let us be moved to humble ourselves before our God, asking Him to convert our hearts and change our lives, that He may not allow His poor church to be exposed to the fury of the wicked. [158]

Further application to the Genevans comes as exhortation to repent from the heart, and not simply in words. This applies to "all of us," Calvin says, as he goes on to emphasize corporate responsibility; he quotes the prayer of Daniel who, although he had lived faithfully in his Babylonian exile, still associated himself with the sin of the whole people. The preacher adds a bit of polemic, contrasting Daniel with the traditional Roman practice of "solitary" individual penance. The Reformed sense of corporate sinfulness expressed in the opening confession of sin echoes in this brief aside, as it does in the constant use of the first person plural throughout the sermon. [159] The preacher's final word is another note of comfort provided by (Ps.115) verse 3.

> [This is] for us a shield to withstand every evil thought – thoughts such as wondering whether our God can aid us at need, something which troubles the wicked. This must be imprinted in our memory: our God will aid us. The reason: nothing can prevent Him. And He has declared to us that it is His good pleasure never to fail us at need. Let us conclude therefore that nothing can happen to us outside His will. (The prophet does not speak of the secret will of God but of that which He has revealed to us in scripture, which is contained in His open promises.) Let us take and hold to this will [to save]. Then let us think about the power of God, and let us put that power into effect. God does everything that He wants; let us therefore comfort ourselves in our adversities. And if God does not help us at first, let us wait on Him, we will not be disappointed. Our God will come, and when? He knows when it will be time. There we have the sum of this verse, and how we should apply it to our own use. [160]

The German problems which led to calling a special day of prayer figure in Calvin's sermon as an exhortation to intercession, but most of the text is directly related to the more immediate concerns of the Genevans and those refugees who

---

[158] *Writings on Pastoral Piety*, p. 167. OC 32:461.

[159] *Writings on Pastoral Piety*, p. 170. OC 32:464.

[160] *Writings on Pastoral Piety*, p. 172. OC 32:465-466.

were beginning to appear at their gates. The sermon also provides one of the best pictures of how Calvin would apply the day of prayer in concrete circumstances.

By the week following this sermon Geneva had received news of the Protestant victory and Calvin asked for another special service to give God thanks. The sermon on Ps. 124 which he preached on Nov. 11 is a rather complex combination of exegetical application and contextual application, aimed at showing the Genevan people how this text and the German situation which prompted the special day of prayer are immediately relevant for them. In the course of the exposition it becomes clear how the pastor guides his people in looking for God's providence.

Since the day of prayer is a regular event, Calvin begins by explaining what distinguishes this service. For one thing, the choice of a special text, interrupting the usual *lectio continua*, would be notable.

> First it must be explained to us why we have come together, and then that we may benefit from the present Psalm. There is certainly reason, when our Lord declares that He is so good to us, for us to be obliged to recognize His mercy, and that from our side we may not keep our mouths closed but may offer Him praise. [161]

He then describes the events in Germany in hyperbolic fashion, and speaks of the great importance of giving particular thanks and praise for this victory. Germany was a long way away from the daily lives of the Genevans, however, and they were fully occupied with many other problems, so why should they care about those foreigners? Furthermore, the announced purpose of the day was to celebrate a victory, but Calvin's description of the German situation does not really focus on the military events. He sets this battle in a broader ecclesiastico-political context to show what is at stake for the gospel more generally. He explains that the Catholics are moving their forces around to prevent different Protestants from assisting each other. However, he gives most attention to the vexing issues of church politics. First is the Catholic opposition to Herman von Wied, the archbishop of Cologne, who was trying to reform his territory with Bucer's assistance and counsel, opposition which Protestants saw as leading toward the "destruction of the gospel" in von Wied's land. That is not all, however. The effort to strengthen the Catholic control of the empire included not only deposing von Wied but also insuring that a solidly loyal son of Rome (and, not so incidentally, of the Hapsburg family) was established at

---

[161] OC 32:467.

Mainz. [162] The events in Germany are thus defined as a religious struggle in both military and ecclesiastico-political forms.

Then Calvin explains how his text, Ps. 124, applies to the various events in Germany so that God's providence is revealed. The psalm recounts the destruction which God's people would suffer from their enemies if God did not protect them, and celebrates the contrasting protection which God provides. Calvin regards this Psalm as particularly apt for the present situation: "It seems that the prophet may have composed this psalm on purpose to teach us about what we see today by experience." [163] The first three of the four images of disaster in Ps. 124 are violent: being swallowed up in the earth, drowned, or torn by wild beasts, and Calvin applies these to the destruction of the gospel by force. The fourth and last danger is subtle, a danger of trickery: the hunter who sets snares for unwary birds, and this is the one which Calvin applies to the ecclesiastical and imperial efforts to dislodge von Wied. Perhaps since, despite the military victory, he still sees so much danger for the church in Germany, Calvin steps back a little to put the present situation in perspective. The presence of God to protect His people is not something new: far from it, and Calvin briefly summarizes for the Genevans the past twenty or thirty years of Reformation history. [164] Although the enemies have indeed cruelly persecuted many believers, yet by a "miraculous providence" God has restrained them from swallowing up the Church or tearing it to pieces, even when they have tried to do by craft what they could not accomplish by violence.

> On the other hand, see if they are not like hunters, that is, do they not spy out by tricks, by wicked practices all the ways they can find to destroy us? Have they not employed this before, when our Lord did not allow them to use violence against us? For in truth in this place we have seen a miraculous providence of God, that already for a long time He has driven them. [165]

---

[162] OC 32:467-468: "C'est que d'un costé on consulte de tirer un Electeur en jugement tyrannique, pour le condamner sans audience, asavoir l'Archevesque de Coulongne. Voila un Electeur mis bas, et par consequent sera l'Evangile ruiné en son pays. Nous mettrons là un tyrant qui tiendra ferme. Il y aura un autre lieu d'Electeur, asavoir l'Archevesque de Magonce [Mayence], qui sera bien convenable au filz du Roy des Romains: il sera là ordonné. Or son pere Ferdinand l'a fait jurer sur toutes ses idoles de jamais ne renoncer au Pape. Puis la guerre ouverte d'un costé, prester gens de main en main. Ce sera tousjours pour amuser les autres, empescher les Protestans en leurs maisons, à ce qu'ilz n'ayent pas loysir de subvenir à persone. Si nostre Seigneur leur eust donné quelque avantage, que fut il advenu?"

[163] OC 32:469.

[164] OC 32:469-470.

[165] OC 32:471.

By God's "driving the Catholics," Calvin appears to mean the conflicts among Catholic factions which have contributed to Protestant security, because he goes on to cite the Biblical story of the Midianites, enemies of Israel whom God blinds and leads to kill each other rather than fight God's people (Judg. 7:22). The implication is that from past instances of "miraculous providence" the people can draw confidence for the future.[166]

Having dealt with the German situation, Calvin turns to an immediate application of the Psalm for Genevans. Calvin knows that his congregation thinks all of these events in Germany are far away: "What have they to do with us? It is not our victory." There are two responses to this. One is that defeat for the Lutherans would have threatened the gospel everywhere – and would bring the danger of destruction down upon Genevan Protestants, too.

> Think of the danger we were in. But the chief thing is to think about the consequences. They would not have affected only Germany; Satan would not have been satisfied to destroy the Gospel in Germany – the fall out would have reached us here. That would have encouraged all the papists. What would they have said? "These Lutherans are conquered everywhere; we must destroy the rest, we must crush the seed." The devil would have reigned everywhere; we would have felt it more than we can express in words.[167]

A Catholic victory in Germany would not only threaten Geneva's religious security. Equally important to Calvin, if not to his congregation, is the conviction that all the church is one, and each and every Christian must recognize God's activity for others as being also for themselves.

> The prophet [David] speaks to all the faithful who are the Israel of God. He appeals to and calls all. Now we cannot all be assembled together (in one place), but each body of the church must do its duty. Our Lord has delivered us. Let us sing His praise. "Blessed be the Lord who has not let us be prey in the teeth of our enemies." ... He speaks to all. We must not think this is only an individual matter but all of us together must offer a solemn thanksgiving, as we have seen in the Psalm [9] which we sang at the beginning of the sermon. We must celebrate the Lord. How? In the assembly of all the faithful.[168]

---

[166] OC 32:471.

[167] OC 32:472.

[168] OC 32:472.

Repeatedly Calvin emphasizes that the psalm being expounded is addressed to each and every person. A victory for "our brothers" is a victory for our salvation as well. An attack on believers because they follow the gospel is an attack on Jesus Christ.

> In that our Lord has given victory to our brothers let us recognize that it is also for our salvation, that is, for all His church. Moreover, are we not members of the church? Have they not made war on our Head Jesus Christ? When it is a matter of our Captain, our King, when it is a question of His word in which consists all our good, our glory, our happiness, when they persecute our brothers, should that not affect us?[169]

Given this providential victory, Calvin asks his congregation how they can fail to give thanks? The right response is to praise God both individually and in common together.

Part of the preacher's task is to stir up his congregation to act. One way he does this is by reminding them what their Catholic foes would do: they would celebrate all the way to Spain and throughout Italy with fireworks, "sacrifices to their idols," and processions.[170] To highlight this point, Calvin puts mocking words in the mouths of Roman opponents.

> They say: "These wretches have been victorious, and instead of being in great distress, they have rest. And look! They act as if nothing has happened. They are like pigs. Now if it had been us, we would have made processions."[171]

Then the preacher gives his answer. First he takes to task his own people – some of whom would be quite content to consider what has happened as unimportant: "it is no great thing, it is the fortunes of war, no need to extol it so much."[172] To this Calvin responds with a description of all that God has done, adding a warning that ignoring such a great blessing is the way to anger God so that He might not help another time. The preacher does allow that the worst has been prevented, but

---

[169] OC 32:475-476.

[170] OC 32:268, 273.

[171] OC 32:476.

[172] OC 32:476: "Si on allegue, ce n'est point si grande chose, c'est une fortune de guerre, il ne la faut pas tant extoller. Advisons de ne point supprimer les benedictions de Dieu. Il s'en trouvera bien de si meschans, qui seroyent contens que les graces de Dieu fussent supprimées, afin que son ire s'augmentast de plus en plus contre nous. Or ne pensons point que nostre Seigneur ne s'en vengeasse, de passer un tel benefice sans protester, et recognoistre que nous l'avons receu de sa main. Une autre fois il pourroit dire, vous n'estes pas dignes que je vous face du bien."

that, he thinks, should make us even more grateful. It is notable that Calvin frankly approves the Roman idea that such a victory calls for significant thanks, even as he distinguishes the right way to offer a "solemn thanksgiving" from the traditional Catholic practices. In Calvin's eyes, not only did the Roman church divide the honor of the victory between Christ and their saints, but Catholics even gave so much credit to themselves that the religious ceremonies per se were "pure hypocrisy." [173]

What then is the right way to praise God? Naturally Calvin turns to scripture and gives what may be his fullest expression of the special thanksgiving service. The primary Biblical text is Exod. 15.

> Let us see how all God's servants have proceeded from the beginning. When the people of Israel had been drawn out of captivity and Pharaoh had been plunged into the Red Sea with his army, then Moses and the elders began to sing, as it is written in Exod. 15. Moses is named first, as the principal leader, then the elders. That is, those who had the governing of the polity: they also had to give an example to the others. Thus when we have received a particular benefit from God's hand, the elders ought to go before, they should not wait for others to go ahead. That is the first thing to note in this story. [174]

Everyone should join in thanks to God but Calvin gives special responsibility to the leaders of the community to set a good example. In keeping with his understanding of God's providence, the preacher insists that such praise and thanksgiving are due not for this one deliverance but because God's protection continues forever "to the end," and cites the Biblical warrant for making liturgies of thanksgiving a regular thing.

> This protestation [of thanksgiving by Moses and others] was not a singular act, but there always was such an order in the ancient church. When our Lord gave some victory, there was a kind of sacrifice which was called "peace-offering." When the people had had some affliction or war or famine or plague, after they had been delivered they made a solemn festival, they announced that the people should assemble, then they made acknowledgement to God. This was done especially for a victory. Following the idea which we must consider here, when an enemy rose up and was repulsed by the people, they made a festival to acknowledge God's beneficence. [175]

---

[173] OC 32:473.

[174] OC 32:473-474.

[175] OC 32:474.

This exposition of Exod. 15 is followed by a reference to Ps. 68. Calvin explains explicitly that in this psalm David expresses praise to God for his victories, which the king and his people know are owed only to God and not to their own might. [176] (The reformer's commentary on Exod. 15 echoes some of this homiletical application. [177])

Giving thanks for the victories which God grants to His church is always right, but in November 1545 Geneva was not able to think only of that blessing. Although the good news from Germany had prompted the special day of prayer, Calvin's sermon repeatedly mentions those believers who were continuing to suffer persecution, including (especially) those in France. Emphasizing the obligation to thank God for the blessings received and the assurance that He will continue to protect His people does not cause the preacher to forget those still being killed for their faith, as he reminds the Genevans that the "blood of His martyrs is a seed to multiply the number of the faithful." German Christians are not alone in experiencing violent opposition. As Calvin says, "there is no need to wait for the post" to know that the faithful are being treated with barbarous cruelty all over France, and he exhorts the Genevans to pray for those who are suffering. He acknowledges that the church "is still in great danger," but claims the victory for Christ, "our Captain." [178] In effect, as the preacher reminds his congregation, providence is not (primarily) safety, when that is granted, but it is God's presence even in the midst of persecution.

There are relatively few later special day of prayer services which can be clearly identified. These are essentially various kinds of military situations which threatened the Protestant church, either internationally or near at hand. The Schmalkald war was one of the former. On Jan. 17, 1547, the ministers ask the Senate to encourage special attendance at worship "especially on Sundays and the day of prayer to pray for God's help in view of the trouble in God's church and the machinations [of the enemies] against the faithful" and the council agrees and imposes a small fine on those who do not come to services. In December 1563 a threatened conspiracy by Geneva's Roman neighbor Savoy brought the need for a special day of prayer closer to home, but this time to recognize God's mercy. On Dec. 20 the ministers request a day of thanksgiving on the next Wednesday in gratitude for God's deliverance of the city from the recent dangers threatened by

---

[176] OC 32:474-475.

[177] OC 24:157-162; cites many Psalms, including Ps. 68 (24:162), although the focus is the musical instruments which Calvin regards as part of the old law that should no longer be used.

[178] OC 32:476-478.

Savoy. Dizeniers are ordered to tell the people to attend worship and guards will be posted at the gates for safety "as on the Supper days."[179]

Savoy was responsible for considerable anxiety over the years. One of the best attested instances of a special day of prayer in later years gives a more detailed idea of how Calvin responded when Geneva itself faced danger. It also illustrates the fact that he did not always interrupt his *lectio continua* series for this service. In mid-October 1557 the soldiers of the Duke of Savoy brought war to the borders of Geneva, and the preacher had no need to explain to the people why special prayers were in order. In fact, the council ordered both spiritual intercessions and practical preparations for a siege.[180] Since Calvin's weekday series had reached Isa. 37:1-4, in which Hezekiah faces the approach of the Babylonian army, the regular text was entirely appropriate for the circumstances of this special day of prayer. His sermon on Wednesday, Oct. 13, weaves together the Biblical passage and the current situation, including the common themes of repentance, intercession, and trust.

The full sermon cannot be examined here, but some key points may be noted. First, while Calvin repeatedly emphasizes the importance of constant prayer, he also recognizes that particular situations call for special efforts. He then explains the educational purpose of calamities. God teaches both by the word and by signs of rebuke; the scripture preached and read should be enough, but when people are slow and inattentive, "God does His office of judge."[181] Hezekiah manifested his repentance by sackcloth and ashes, so the application of the text to Christians requires some clarification. The preacher cites Joel 2:13, to rend the heart and not the clothes; "the ceremonies are nothing before God" but the true repentance of heart is necessary, and like Hezekiah, we should humble ourselves, using everything which can teach us to repent. Hezekiah consulted the prophet Isaiah, but God's people today do not need any further revelation because "we have the universal witness that God has given us that those who hope in Him will never be abandoned or confounded."[182] Part of the sermon naturally focuses on repen-

---

[179] See the ministers' request: "specialement les dimanches et le jour des prieres affin de prier Dieu qui nous assiste, voyeant le trouble qu'est en l'eglise de Dieu et la machination dressé contre les fidelles." Jan. 17, 1547, OC 21:394 (RC41 f288). Dec. 11 indicates word of a conspiracy against Geneva by Savoy, and Dec. 20, 1563, is the response of thanksgiving for danger averted; OC 21:810 (RC 58 f131, 137).

[180] S. III, sermon 33/165 on Oct. 13, 1557. I am indebted to the editors for pointing out this situation. See Parker, Higman, Thorpe, "Introduction," S III, p. xi. They cite Gautier, *Histoire de Genève*, IV, 142, quoting RC, 53 f355, 356, 358, for Oct. 12 & 13, 1557.

[181] S. III, sermon 33/165, pp. 306, 308, 310, quotation p. 308.

[182] S. III, sermon 33/165, pp. 310-11, 312.

tance, but Calvin gives practically equal time to address the fears of the faithful and exhort them to trust in God.

> Let us know that our Lord, who reached out His hand to deliver His servant Hezekiah, has not forgotten His nature today. He has not changed His will. His power also is not lessened, His reach is not shortened, His ears are not dulled. There is nothing which hinders us from being heard and helped by Him, unless our sins put up a barrier...[183]

There are two dangers: paying no attention to God's rebukes or collapsing in despair. Hezekiah does not do either. The instance of despair Calvin cites is the terror which his hearers might feel in seeing the terrible suffering of God's people; believers in France are naturally among those in view. In face of this the preacher speaks strongly of compassion for those who are persecuted; the concern for Christians beyond Geneva is clear, echoing the intercessory character of the day of prayer. However, at the end Calvin returns to the fears of his congregation; "although we are afflicted [because of our sins] nevertheless our Lord will not cease to have pity on us."[184] The day of prayer was not only a response to international crises but also a form of consolation for the special fears that Genevans faced.

Summary of the Importance of the Day of Prayer

In many ways the Calvinist Reformed day of prayer in Geneva came to have a rank just below that of Sunday. Schedules and locations are one demonstration. There were services at two times on the day of prayer so that no one in the city would be excluded simply because he or she must stay home to keep house. At first this was not unique to the day of prayer, because dawn services were held at St. Pierre on three week days: Monday, Wednesday, and Friday, in addition to the "ordinary" sermon at 6 a.m. or 7 a.m. in both parts of the city. However, probably well before 1550, perhaps even by the early 1540s, a dawn service on Wednesday had been added at St. Gervais, on the other side of the river. Then both parts of the city had worship at two times on the day of prayer so that households could more easily go to church in relays on Wednesdays as they did on Sundays. Furthermore the time of the second service was delayed an hour or two so that it might have a dignity similar to that of Sunday. (There was some variation: at first it was set at 7 a.m. or 8 a.m. depending on the season, later it was fixed at 8 a.m. like the Sunday service.) During the 1540s and certainly before 1549 it also

---

[183] S. III, sermon 33/165, p. 310.

[184] S. III, sermon 33/165, p. 315.

became customary to hold the second day of prayer service in Greater Geneva at St. Pierre, even though the rest of the regular weekday services in that part of the city were held at La Magdeleine.[185] Larger crowds were expected on the day of prayer because it was the one weekday when all Genevans who could do so were supposed to attend worship, and St. Pierre was the logical place for a large crowd.

The importance of the day of prayer to the Company of Pastors can be seen in the ways they organized themselves to insure that these services were provided with the best preaching. Calvin was of course considered the best, and apparently his colleague Abel Poupin, with whom he alternated weeks doing the daily sermon, was also well regarded. When Poupin became ill in 1553, however, and could no longer do his full range of services, the Company asked Calvin to change his schedule to make certain that the day of prayer was given its due. Instead of preaching Monday through Saturday in one week, while his alternate did the same days the following week, Calvin would do Monday through Friday in his own week and Wednesday of the other week, while another minister would take Calvin's Saturday sermon. Evidence for this routine is found in the records of the Ezekiel and Deuteronomy sermons in 1553-1556. A similar kind of care for the day of prayer is seen in Viret's sermons preached in March 1559 during Calvin's long illness; the four sermons which were preserved were given on Sundays and Wednesdays, March 5, 8, 12, and 15.[186] When a substitute was needed for their chief minister, those were the specific occasions he was asked to preach, and apparently he was expected to do every Wednesday.

A similar sign of the special importance of the day of prayer is found in the records of Calvin's sermons on the Passion during the week before Easter. Some years he preached the whole week (these were times when it was his week to do the daily sermons), but in some years when the week before Easter was not his regular preaching assignment, Calvin nevertheless did one sermon on the Passion on Wednesday.[187] Plainly, Geneva's pastors thought that the day of prayer deserved special effort on their part, even if it meant making some (significant and inconvenient) changes in the organization of their pulpit schedules.

---

[185] Baptismal records, e.g., rotation 7 a.m./ 8 a.m. in 1550, only 8 a.m. in 1562. No baptisms on Wednesdays at La Magdeleine. See Appendix One.

[186] See chap. 2 at n.69, after n.87; chap. 6 at n.134. Appendix Eight Part One: Old Testament Sermons. For fuller discussion of Viret's sermons, see chap. 6 at n.37.

[187] See above, at n.68; also Appendix Eight Part Two: New Testament Sermons.

A Distinctive and Influential Liturgy

The idea of a regular observance of repentance and prayer was beginning to develop in some German-speaking lands before Calvin became a pastor. The idea of a weekly day of prayer (not just a litany attached to another service) was taking shape in Strasbourg while Calvin was there, and it spread to Basel the same year he introduced it in Geneva. However, neither of these services began as a distinct liturgy, and both were responses to the presence of the plague at home. Thus, when Calvin established a special liturgy on a regularly weekly basis it is perhaps not a complete surprise that some of his close contemporaries thought that this day of prayer was his invention. Some criticized, while others freely copied him and spread this distinctive liturgy widely through the Reformed churches.

Controversies over Calvin's Day of Prayer

The identification of Calvin as the author of the day of prayer comes to historical visibility through controversy. In the early and mid-1550s he was accused of having created a new feast or a kind of saint's day. The criticisms surface in at least three places. The first of these is an interrogation of the French Protestant martyr Richard le Fevre in 1554 as reported in Jean Crespin's *Martyrology* that same year. Another is a book by Sebastian Castellio, the *Contre le libelle de Calvin*. This was the response to Calvin's 1554 answer to Castellio's own famous book *On the Burning of Heretics*; although written in 1554 Castellio's response was published only posthumously in 1612.[188] The third place this issue appears is Calvin's correspondence in 1555, where he replies to the accusations in a letter to the senate of Bern. These will be discussed in chronological order.

The story of Richard le Fevre, tried and executed in Lyons on July 7, 1554, was added at the end of Crespin's first edition and expanded later to include two earlier examinations in Grenoble. The account of the second interrogation in Grenoble begins with an accusation that Geneva in effect contradicts itself and legislates things not in the Bible, and the example given is the day of prayer. Le Fevre had said that the pope was not allowed to impose laws binding the conscience, and the priests draw on the evidence of his own Psalter to insist that Geneva has made such laws: Wednesday is elevated above the other days as being more holy. The word used is "notice" (*advertissement*) but this is probably a reference to the table of Psalms to be sung on that day.[189] Le Fevre then begins an

---

188 Barilier, "Introduction," *Sebastien Castellion*, p. 25.

189 Crespin, *Histoire des vrays Tesmoins de la verite de l'evangile* [1570], p. 282r: "D'avantage, que mesme à Geneve il y a des loix qui ne sont point contenues en la parole de Dieu; me remonstrant par mes

extended refutation, explaining that the observance of Wednesday is just a civil law for the purpose of "brotherly union" and citing the historical practice of Christian princes. His key argument is Biblical: these rules were made not to bind consciences but rather to ease them, something the apostles did according to Jesus' teaching, and a number of scripture texts are cited.[190]

The outlines of this story are in fact very much like the accusation by Castellio's in *Contre le libelle de Calvin*. In the small world of Swiss Protestantism, Castellio certainly had heard (and expressed) many criticisms of Calvin, and he apparently knew that the Bernese called the Genevan day of prayer "the feast of Calvin."[191] He might also have remembered the day of prayer practice from his own time in Geneva. Castellio's book is cast in dialogue form; he lifts citations from Calvin and then gives his own response under the name "Vaticanus."

> Calvin: "But if one fabricates worship [acts] in his own fashion or by chance, and claims to make others honor this lie, the more pains he takes to do it, the more guilty he is. None will applaud superstition."
> Vaticanus: "Worship [acts] in his own fashion? That is what Calvin himself does with his Wednesdays: he who requires that certain Psalms be sung on such days, not to speak of other ceremonies. I am not against a certain order, without which the crowd cannot be contained, but I see also what superstition presides in that order."[192]

Pseaumes, & par l'ordre du jour des prieres, que le Mecredy estoit plus sainct en la sepmaine, l'ayant trouvé par les Pseaumes en l'advertissement. " [He asks and is granted permission to speak.] "Et ayant regardé l'advertissement contenu aux Pseaumes, que ce Cordelier tenoit en main, luy monstray le Mecredy estre seulement une police civile, sans obligation de conscience, & pour convenir en union fraternelle : & que les Rois anciens ont tousjours gardé quelque police, pour entretenir le peuple à la cognioissance & obeissance de Dieu, & du service qu'on luy doit rendre."

[190] Crespin, *Histoire des vrays Tesmoins de la verite de l'evangile* [1570], p. 282r. He cites Rom. 15[18]; 2 John [10]; Gal. 1[8]; John 10[8-9], 18[37] & 20[21], 1 Pet. 4 =5[2-4]. That Roman church authorities in France recognized the day of prayer as a special time of Reformed worship is later seen in the fact that Wednesdays, like Sundays, became primary occasions for attacks on Huguenot communities; e.g., Wed. May 6, 1562, as well as Sun. March 1, April 12, and May 17, 1562. See OC 21:775, 777, 778, 779.

[191] Castellio, *Contre le libelle de Calvin*, p. 126 n. 2.

[192] Castellio, *Contre le libelle de Calvin*, pp. 126-27 : "Calvin 43b. Mais si l'on fabrique un culte à sa guise, ou au hasard, et qu'on prétend faire honorer ce mensonge par autrui, plus on se démène, plus on est coupable. A la superstition, nul n'applaudira. Vaticanus Un culte à sa guise? C'est ce que fait Calvin lui-même avec ses mercredis, lui qui exige que certains psaumes soient chantés tels jours, sans parler d'autres cérémonies. Je ne suis pas contre un certain ordre, sans lequel la multitude ne peut être contenue. Mais je vois assez quelle 'superstition' préside à cet ordre-là."

Castellio wants to accuse Calvin out of his own mouth, saying that he is doing the same superstitious thing which he attacks. Here the emphasis of the criticism falls on the content of the day of prayer and, although the matter of the date is mentioned, it seems a lesser point. Castellio's comment about "certain Psalms" probably refers to the Genevan practice of posting the list of the Psalms to be sung at each service on Sunday and Wednesday. [193]

It is important to remember that when Castellio wrote this book he had been living in Basel for many years, and he must have known about the Tuesday service in that city's worship life, which was also fixed on a specific day and included a sermon and special prayers for repentance. Thus in order to make his criticism stick, he may have felt he needed to identify something else as the primary objection to the Genevan practice, and the "legalism" of a list of Psalms would serve that purpose nicely. It is also possible that the Psalm singing which he derides was the practice which made the day of prayer liturgy most memorable to lay people. That is, every weekday Geneva had a service with a sermon and prayers, and lay people would be unlikely to notice particularly whether there was a printed liturgy (such as *La forme des prieres* provided for the day of prayer) or not (as on other weekdays). In that case, the singing of Psalms would probably be the most memorable factor for them and in Castellio's eyes it perhaps served as the best way to mark the elevation of the day of prayer to near-Sunday status and so made it a better stick to beat Calvin.

It is noteworthy that the tenor of the argument is practically identical in these two attacks on Calvin's day of prayer and their occurrence is virtually simultaneous. While French authorities might have seen the Psalter independently of Castellio, since they use Le Fevre's own Psalter to challenge him it seems likely that they had heard of Castellio's argument, whether from him or from others. It is unclear how widespread this story was, but it was evidently making the rounds in certain circles, and the Catholic interrogators were no doubt happy to exploit intra-Protestant conflicts.

Calvin's own response does not seem particularly anxious. The day of prayer figures as one minor point among the ecclesiastical ceremonies and festivals which were named in the controversy between Calvin and the authorities in Bern, according to his letter to them in early April 1555. The chief issue was Calvin's doctrine of predestination. However, there was also a brief rehearsal of long-standing differences in liturgical practice between Geneva and Bern, including the ways that the "feast day" observances had developed, especially after Geneva abolished them in 1550. It is in this context that Calvin mentions the day of prayer once.

---

[193] See chap. 3 at nn.99ff *et passim.*

I am reproached with having created a new feast on the Wednesday. In this I am sadly wronged. For the magistracy of Geneva have indeed, by my exhortation, set apart one day in the week to offer up extraordinary prayers, as necessity and the exigencies of the times should require it. And on that day we pray for you and the other churches who are in need of it. But we carry on our usual labours on that day; and besides we have not so constantly established a certain day as not to select now one, now another, just as the magistrates shall deem proper for their convenience. [194]

Calvin goes on to deal with the "more serious rumour" that he wanted to transfer the Lord's Day to Friday. It appears, then, that he did not consider the accusations about a new Wednesday holy day as bad as some others which were also circulating.

Calvin's defense of the day of prayer treats three points. One is the content, i.e., intercession for other churches, something itself not controversial. At least the traditional sound of "necessity and exigencies of the times" would be familiar enough perhaps to smooth over the reference to "one day in the week" – especially since at least the clergy in Bern must know that something of the kind was practiced in neighboring Basel. The other two points of his defense deal with whether this day of prayer is a workday and whether its observance is set on a specific day. Calvin counters the last point by indicating the contingent and fluctuating day of the service, which had in fact been changed a number of times before 1550. In other words, the observance was not established on a specific date, like traditional saints' days. His reference to it being a workday was somewhat disingenuous, since shops were closed until after the second service so it might count as a partial holiday, but it was certainly not a holiday in the traditional sense of a day without any work (such as the Strasbourg "great day" of prayer was). After Calvin's death the debate would be opened again. Against the pastors' objections, a change to Thursday was proposed by the Senate in 1578-1579 and finally carried out several years later. Wednesday was market day and the prohibition against opening shops until after the second service on the day of prayer was interfering with commerce. [195]

---

194 *John Calvin's Letters*, vol. 3, p. 164-65 (where it is dated March 1555 because of the instruction from Genevan authorities on March 28th for the mission to Bern). Letter #2173 to Senate of Bern, OC 15:540: "On m'a reproché que j'avoye faict une feste nouvelle, le mercredy, en quoy on m'a faict grand tort. Car Messieurs de Genefve, à mon exhortation, ont bien ordonné un jour la sepmaine pour faire des prieres extraordinaires, selon la necessité et exigence des temps; et là nous prions Dieu pour vous et les aultres Eglises qui en ont besoing. Mais ce n'est pas qu'on ne besongne ce jour là, comme les aultres. D'aultre part on n'a pas estably tellement un certain jour qu'on n'ait prins maintenant l'un, maintenant l'aultre, selon que les seigneurs en ont advis' pour leur commodité. Qui plus est, on a bien semé le bruict que je voulais translater le dimanche au vendredy …"

195 Engammare, *On Time, Punctuality, and Discipline*, p. 72.

The Significance and Spread of the Day of Prayer

One thing which the various rumors and accusations and Castellio's criticism make clear is that the Genevan day of prayer was in some ways distinctive from that practiced elsewhere. If any other Reformed city had had a special liturgy with Psalms, or had accorded the day of prayer such full recognition as Geneva, this practice would not have constituted an issue which Calvin would need to explain and defend. In view of the fact that after 1550 Geneva did not celebrate any other weekday "holy days," the day of prayer took on a greater significance than perhaps any other Protestant churches' fast-or-prayer day regulations (concerning the use of litanies or other regularly scheduled expressions of worship focused on repentance or intercession). The Calvinist Reformed day of prayer combined a distinctive (new) practice, with the theological emphasis on providence which churches under the cross would feel particularly acutely, to shape a characteristically Reformed sense of liturgical time.

Calvin's text and its derivatives seem to be the first actual liturgies for the Reformed day of prayer service, and perhaps the only ones for many years. Some idea of the spread of the liturgy and its practice can demonstrate who found the day of prayer appealing. Besides its use in Geneva (by refugee groups of various languages as well as the native inhabitants), Calvin's liturgy spread beyond the city. Naturally the day of prayer liturgy become a regular part of practice in France, since *La forme des prieres* was normally used there. It is not surprising that the day of prayer service appears in the 1545 Strasbourg printing of *La forme des prieres*. However, it is notable that by 1553, the French-speaking congregation in Strasbourg had begun to alter its service book in certain ways; one of those changes was the addition of a rubric explicitly placing its day of prayer service on Tuesday (like that of its German-speaking host).[196] The teaching and practice were the same as in Geneva but the historical situation was not: adaptation had begun.

The liturgy and practice of the day of prayer began to spread beyond the French language and/or to experience some minor modifications besides just the day of the week on which it was used. In 1551 Valerain Poullain, the leader of the French congregation in the London Strangers' Churches, made a Latin translation, *Liturgia Sacra*, with a weekly day of prayer, which was now set on Thursday and called a "Liturgia poenitentiae."[197] Given the number of changes which Poullain introduced into the liturgy as a whole, such as the addition of simple funeral rites, it is significant that he maintained Calvin's "new" day of prayer

---

[196] *Pseaumes de David....* Published by Jean Garnier, 1553. [Bb2368 res], p. 282: "Prieres pour les Mardis, jour des prieres."

[197] Poullain, *Liturgia Sacra*, pp. 104-18. For funeral rites, see chap. 7 at nn.151ff.

virtually as it appeared in Geneva, including the explanatory essay. There are only two changes, one in the text and one in the rubrics. The rubric indicates that the preacher might follow his *lectio continua* text or the elders might choose a text appropriate for the time and situation.[198] In effect, Poullain was making explicit the possibility of interrupting a Biblical series for a "special day of prayer" occasion but ascribing the choice of text to the elders, not the pastor. The same thing is found in the French liturgy which Poullain published in 1552 in Frankfurt.[199] The real change comes in the long prayer of intercession which, like its Sunday counterpart, changes the language for the civil authorities from the city-state magistrates of Geneva to fit the location in England, naming the king and other officials of the kingdom.[200] The French *La forme des prieres* printed in London in 1552 and preserved in the Bodleian is an exact copy of the Genevan text as far as the rubrics are concerned but also adopts a locally specific petition for rulers. The language is slightly different from Poullain's prayer, being extended to name various other civil and ecclesiastical personages.[201]

In 1556 Calvin's *La forme des prieres* was translated and adapted by John Knox for the English-speaking refugees in Geneva and then taken back to Scotland, where the day of prayer service was ordered at least for urban contexts.[202] In 1563 the complete Genevan French book was translated into German in Heidelberg, and the day of prayer liturgy was naturally included.[203] Other branches of the Reformed tradition developed their own special prayer day traditions.[204]

---

[198] Poullain, *Liturgia Sacra*, p. 106: "Postea, aut perget in libro quem explicandum antea sumpserit, vel seniores certum aliquem locum scripturae temporibus aut hominum moribus accomodatissimum hic concioni praescribent."

[199] Poullain, *Liturgia Sacra*, p. 107.

[200] Poullain, *Liturgia Sacra*, p. 65: "Nous te prions, donc, Pere celeste, pour tous Princes et Seigneurs tes serviteurs, ... singulierement, pour le Roy de ce royaume N. et tout le sang Royal, Messeigneurs du Conseil privé, et tous les gouverneurs de ce lieu..."

[201] [Bodleian] *La forme des prières*, p. 10v, includes: "Des dames du Sang Royal, De tout le sang du Roy... Du Maire... Des Evesques et Pasteurs..."

[202] John Knox, *Works* (Edinburgh, 1855), vol. 6, pp. 156, 186.

[203] *Ordnung der Evangelischen Kirchen in Franckreich/ so gehalten wird im Gemeinen Gebet/ Reichung der Sacrament/ Einsegnen der Ehe/ Besuchung der Krancken. Und Christlichem Catechismo.* Churfuerstlichen Stadt Heydelberg/ durch Johannem Mayer. 1563, pp. b [i]r –. [MHR A27, 3 (63)]

[204] One of these privileged the response to special occurrences which had a certain continuity with the longer history, but seems to have adopted the Protestant sense that such occasions could or should be more frequent. This is found in the work of Johannes a Lasco, the Polish nobleman and reformer who was the senior minister of the Strangers' Churches in London. After the refugee congregations moved to Frankfurt, a Lasco published *Forma ac Ratio* (1555), a Latin elaboration of his plan of worship. His discussion of the day of prayer is focused essentially on the special occasions, and includes explicit reference to times of thanksgiving for God's mercies

It is clear, however, that Calvin's particular shaping of the day of prayer became a significant and widespread part of the Reformed tradition, dominant in French language contexts and very influential in English ones, but also a presence in some German-speaking communities. At least some contemporaries considered this special liturgical observance a creation for which Calvin was responsible... and they did not approve. The fact that the Genevan day of prayer established a specific temporal rhythm and distinctive content for a weekday service made it an original liturgical creation in Reformed circles which was all the more visible because of the quite spare calendar in most Reformed churches. After 1550 the only "holy day" tradition in Geneva gave principal place to the Lord's Day and a not-insignificant second rank to the Wednesday day of prayer, alongside the "sacramental seasons" of the Lord's Supper. These were the corporate patterns of time. There were other personal liturgies which were celebrated in the context of the community but on an individual schedule. These will be examined in the next chapter.

---

as well as repentance in the face of calamity. Johannes a Lasco/ Jan Laski, *Forma ac Ratio*, in *Opera II*, pp. 239-49: gives the heading: "De publicis Ecclesiae supplicationes"; then "Argumentum concionis in publica Ecclesiae calamitate" and "Supplicatio gratiarum actoria pro publicis beneficiis in Ecclesiam collatis" followed by "Argumentum concionis post collatum in Ecclesiam publicum aliquod beneficium." Given the thoroughness of a Lasco's preparations, it is very likely that he expected the day of prayer liturgy to be used relatively frequently, even if this form of the tradition dropped one of the key characteristics, i.e., the weekly rhythm. In 1571 Heinrich Bullinger led Zurich in establishing a regular day of prayer, a special liturgy in response to famine; Bächtold, "Gegen den Hunger beten," pp. 9-44. Bullinger was not influenced by Geneva so much as by the larger historical tradition – and perhaps the practice of other Swiss German churches. Basel's leaders gave their long-standing Tuesday service new attention and a published prayer text in the early 1580s; see above at nn.106ff.

CHAPTER FIVE

THE PUBLIC RHYTHMS OF PERSONAL RELIGIOUS LIFE: BAPTISM AND MARRIAGE

While worship in Geneva was fundamentally corporate, there were important liturgies which were also very personal and planned in accordance with individual or family life rhythms. The two most significant were baptism and marriage. Baptism was a sacrament, marriage (for Protestants) was not; however for Reformed Christians both became public, congregational events in a new and special way. Whereas traditionally both marriage and baptism had been essentially private family occasions, for Calvinist Reformed churches these kinship religious celebrations were brought out into the larger community which would be the extended Christian family to support both new couples and their children.

As one of the two sacraments, baptism was more important to church life, and it usually receives more theological attention than marriage. Since the Calvinist Reformed tradition affirmed infant baptism, the teaching and practice of marriage were intimately related to the teaching and practice of baptism because it was the parents who would make the promises to teach their children the faith. Therefore it is helpful to present Calvin's understanding and the Genevan practice of marriage first, and then the teaching and practice of baptism. The chapter is divided into three parts. The first treats marriage, the second baptism, and the final very brief summary shows how the regular celebration of these liturgies worked out in real time and space in Geneva's city parishes.

I: Marriage

The word "marriage" evokes many things, and it can encompass many dimensions of human life. Thus it is appropriate to state plainly that the intent here is selective, narrowing the focus to the public, liturgical aspects of the teaching and practice of marriage in Calvin's Geneva, in its historical context. First the essentials of the medieval background and some of the literature on the subject of marriage in Geneva are sketched. The second section presents an overview of Calvin's teaching about marriage, especially as expressed in pastoral terms. The third part addresses the re-shaping of the Genevan experience of marrying, particularly its public, corporate, liturgical character.

Historical Context and Historiographical Comments

As fundamental institutions of human societies, marriage and the family have been extensively studied, not least with regard to their expressions – religious, legal, economic, cultural, gender-related, and more – in early modern Europe. The first purpose of this introduction is to identify the main features of the religious and social organization of marriage in the late medieval Latin world in which the Calvinist Reformed tradition was born. The second is to indicate briefly some of the relevant literature on the Genevan reform of marriage.

The Historical Religious Context
Marriage in the medieval Latin church was one of the seven sacraments and as such it was understood to mediate grace. Theologically, marriage was affirmed as holy because it is the human expression of the great mystery of Christ's union with the church. Practically, the main purposes of marriage were the procreation of children and serving as a remedy for sinful and immoral behavior. Since the ideal of Christian holiness was virginity, married life was considered a lesser rank than celibacy, although it was the vocation open to most people.

Marriage was one of the two sacraments which could be performed by lay people, that is, a priestly blessing was not required for validity. For this as well as other reasons, the question of consent became a critical factor shaping medieval canon law on marriage; protecting consent was a main concern of the work of Pope Alexander III (elected in 1159). He defined a valid marriage as "free and voluntary exchange of present consent between persons of legal age who were free to marry each other or free and voluntary exchange of future consent... ratified by subsequent sexual intercourse." A minimum age was also established (girls at least twelve years old and boys fourteen). While theologically consent alone was vital, canon lawyers gave a particular weight to sexual intercourse. A marriage between minors which had been consummated could not be dissolved, and the same was true of other circumstances (e.g., future consent or conditional marriage was made binding by consummation). Sexual intercourse with someone closely related to the prospective bride or groom also constituted an impediment to a valid marriage between the couple. Alexander tried to balance the protection of consent (and thus greater individual action) with an insistence that a marriage without witnesses was anathema, but he stopped short of making this public character necessary for the act's validity. In principle banns were to be published for three weeks before the wedding and a priestly blessing was required, but although without the banns and benediction the marriage was regarded as sinful, it was still valid.[1] Thus Alexander's influence in canon law made clandestine marriage much easier and led to one of the major issues which later generations deplored. Besides the importance of consent, marriage required that the two persons be free to contract this union. The question of who might marry whom was complex, since not only blood ties had to be considered but also the relationships of spiritual affinity which were created when individuals became godparents to a child in baptism, as well as the very unspiritual ties of intercourse. There was no divorce, but annulment (on the grounds that it had never been a valid marriage) or separation was possible by ecclesiastical dispensation under the authority of the pope.

Many couples, especially those without substantial financial resources to pay for a special service, simply exchanged vows at the church entrance before the priest and a few witnesses. Even this much ceremony was not obligatory. However, those who could afford it would usually include as part of their celebration a nuptial Mass, which might be held in the personal chapels of nobility or in the parish sanctuary itself after the promises witnessed at the church door. The ceremony had to be scheduled at an appropriate time in the liturgical calendar, since marriages were not allowed at specific holy seasons, particularly Advent or Lent. Usually weddings were a (private) family affair, the liturgy being arranged with the priest at a time convenient for the couple and their relatives, and whenever possible it would be followed by merry-making with guests.[2]

The practice of marriage among Protestants was in many ways similar to that of the late middle ages but there were also some significant differences, both in teaching and in practice. Theological perspectives on marriage played an important role in reshaping social ideals. Marriage was no longer a sacrament and civil rulers took over many of the functions previously handled by an episcopal court.

---

1   James Brundage, *Sex Law and Marriage in the Middle Ages* (Brookfield, VT: Ashgate, 1993), pp. 332-37; quotation, p. 334. My thanks to Gordon Govens for pointing me to this book.

2   For a recent summary, see Karant-Nunn, *The Reform of Ritual*, pp. 9-13.

Protestants revised the understanding of the liturgical year and no longer consi-dered certain seasons too holy for the blessing of marriages.[3] The gradual, humanist-influenced cultural shift toward the civic ideal of a society based on solid families was now joined with religious conviction which reversed the cult of virginity in favor of elevating marriage as the normal pattern of Christian vocation. Protestants rejected vows of celibacy as a denigration of the vows taken by all Christians in baptism, as a spurious claim to a higher holiness, and as a contradiction of the Biblical teaching on marriage, including marriage of the clergy.[4] This new scriptural ideal did not mean that all men and women married; economic constraints prevented the poorest from being able to establish their own households. It did, however, make the household gathered around a married couple the normative lifestyle even for the unmarried or widowed.

Specific legal changes were also characteristic of Protestants generally. Jeffrey Watt identifies the three primary ones as the abolition of secret marriages and requirement of parental permission and witnesses; the reduction of the numbers of impediments to a valid marriage; and the legitimizing of divorce, with remar-riage allowed for the innocent party.[5] Virtually all communities aimed to make the whole marriage process more publicly visible in legal terms, but the Reformed carried this further with a particularly determined effort to make marriages a part of the parish worship life of the community. Not only were public banns issued, but it also became customary (or, in Calvin's Geneva, even a requirement) that no marriage could take place except in the context of a public service with preaching.

Some Historiographical Comments

The literature on family and marriage in early modern Europe is far too extensive for even a limited sketch here.[6] It is appropriate, however, to note

---

[3] For an example of horror at the way that Protestants changed the rules, see Jeanne de Jussie, *Le Levain du Calvinisme*, p. 115, regarding a wedding on Maundy Thursday. Grosse, *Les rituels de la Cène*, pp. 72-82, describes actions of this kind which expressed and effected "separation" from the traditional practices.

[4] For a lively contemporary treatment of this from a woman's perspective, see Katharina Schütz Zell's 1524 apologia for her husband : *Entschuldigung... M. Matthes Zellen*, in Katharina Schütz Zell, *The Writings. A Critical Edition* (Leiden: Brill, 1999), pp. 21-47, translation in *Church Mother* (Chicago, 2006), pp. 62-82.

[5] Jeffrey Watt, *The Making of Modern Marriage: Matrimonical Control and the Rise of Sentiment in Neuchâtel, 1500-1800* (Ithaca: Cornell Univ. Press, 1992), pp. 39-40.

[6] Influential examples on different sides of the interpretative divide include Steven Ozment, *When Fathers Ruled: Family Life in Reformation Europe* (Cambridge, MA: Harvard, 1983); Lyndal Roper, *The Holy Household: Women and Morals in Reformation Augsburg* (Oxford: University Press, 1989). For specific liturgical aspects, see Karant-Nunn, *The Reform of Ritual*.

some of the significant items relating to the history of marriage in Geneva and its neighbors which have been consulted for this work. A helpful survey of some of the trends in the history of marriage is found in Jeffrey Watt's fine book, *The Making of Modern Marriage: Matrimonial Control and the Rise of Sentiment in Neuchâtel, 1550-1800* (1992), with its long view of the institutions which Calvin's colleagues originally shaped. More immediately useful for Geneva are several other publications. One is the volume edited by John Witte and Robert M. Kingdon, *Courtship, Engagement, and Marriage* (2005), the first volume of *Sex, Marriage, and Family in John Calvin's Geneva*. Witte and Kingdon's selected primary source excerpts and chapter introductions provide a rich collection of detail along with overviews of the key aspects of the process from engagement through marriage, including much information about the varied impediments Genevans recognized. Robert M. Kingdon's *Adultery and Divorce in Calvin's Geneva* (1995) uncovers some of the stories about what was perhaps the most notorious aspect of Protestant reforms, the legitimacy of divorce. Cornelia Seeger's extremely detailed *Nullité de mariage, divorce et séparation de corps à Genève, au temps de Calvin. Fondements doctrinaux, loi et jurisprudence* (1990) examines the legal grounds for dissolving marriage at any stage, including Calvin's views on the matter as well as Genevan law. These scholarly works have been helpful for the present study, although the focus here is somewhat different. The object of this study is to examine briefly the theology which guided the views of marriage in Geneva and then more fully the characteristic and surprisingly public and corporate shape that weddings assumed.

An Overview of Calvin's Teaching on Marriage: Part I: *Institutes* and Liturgy

Calvin's teaching on marriage presents an illuminating example of the mutual influences of the reformer's key identities: exegetical theologian, trained lawyer, and life-long pastor. The following sketch is not intended to be exhaustive but simply to provide the broad contours of the reformer's thought in its historical and ecclesiastical development, giving particular attention to the aspects of marriage which he felt compelled to emphasize in speaking to the people in the pew.

Marriage in the *Institutes*

Calvin's earliest writing on marriage as a young Protestant was essentially a reaction against what he considered the traditional abuses. The 1536 *Institutes* discusses marriage in two places. One is the brief exposition of the seventh commandment against adultery. It is notable that Calvin calls this a prohibition of fornication, a wider category than adultery. One important purpose is to vindicate God's approval for marriage and refute the traditional denigration of marriage and elevation of virginity.

> These people [Roman theologians] dare to call "pollution" the matrimony which God deigned to establish, which He pronounced to be honorable for all people, which our Lord Christ sanctified by His presence, which He esteemed worthy to grace with His first miracle. They do this only so they may give marvelous praises to some kind of celibacy ... [which] they call an "angelic life."[7]

Turning from the theologians to the bride and groom themselves, Calvin affirms that the couple may consider themselves "wedded in the Lord" if they act "with sobriety and modesty."[8] The second place where marriage is treated is the chapter on false sacraments; the only positive statement is significantly approving but rendered tepid by its context.

> Marriage is a good and holy [bona ... sancta] ordinance of God. And farming, building, shoemaking, and barbering are lawful [legitimae] ordinances of God; nevertheless they are not sacraments.[9]

There is a distinction between marriage and the other examples of earthly activities, all of which Calvin will later name as "vocations." While all of these are established by God, the adjectives qualifying marriage as "good and holy" set it apart as more valuable. In this context, however, most of the reformer's attention is devoted to attacking the idea of marriage as a sacrament, although he also names various practices (such as clandestine marriages) which were sore points for reformers and moralists of all churches. This 1536 discussion of the false sacrament of marriage is taken over as is into the next edition of the *Institutes* and does not really change later.[10]

However, the exposition of the seventh commandment was much extended in 1539, giving a fuller picture of marriage, including its positive character. Here the 1541 French version is cited, not because it is different but because this is what

---

[7] *Institutes 1536*, chap. 2, OS I, p. 50.

[8] *Institutes 1536*, chap. 2, OS I, p. 51.

[9] *Institutes 1536*, chap. 5, OS I, p. 220; cf. 4.19.34-37 (OS V, pp. 467-71).

[10] See *Inst.* 4.13.3 in the chapter on vows, which comes mostly from 1543 & 1559. Seeger, *Nullité de mariage*, pp. 91-95, remarks on the very limited attention which Calvin gives to matrimonial law in the *Institutes*; more must be uncovered in his commentaries. She does not focus on the seventh commandment.

Calvin's parishioners would have been able to read. Characteristically, the teacher begins with the larger frame of the meaning of the commandment.

> The purpose of this commandment is that because God loves purity and chastity we should stay far away from all impurity. The summary then will be that we should not be stained with any fleshly filth or intemperance. The positive command corresponds to this: that our life should be ordered to chastity and sobriety or continence in all its actions. [11]

Calvin then gives the purpose of marriage in a nutshell.

> Because people were created with the condition that they might not live alone but that one might have a helper like himself [Gen. 2:18] and since moreover they were subjected to this need even more because of the curse of sin, the Lord gave us a sufficient remedy for this by establishing marriage; and after ordaining it by His authority, He sanctified marriage by His blessing. [12]

The note about people being created to live together (Gen. 2:18) is very significant; Calvin always sets marriage in the context of human society. As will be seen below in his later exposition of Genesis, the reformer's strong sense of the priority of the corporate over the individual is a marked factor in shaping his understanding of marriage.

A considerable part of the discussion of marriage deals with the value of this institution over against traditional claims for celibacy. In the course of the argument Calvin cites various church fathers in favor of the holiness of marriage.

> We will be content with one testimony from St. Chrysostom, seeing that he is not suspected of having favored marriage too much but on the contrary was too inclined to value and magnify virginity. Now he speaks in this way: "The first degree of chastity is unspotted virginity. The second is marriage loyally kept." The love of the husband and wife, when they live well in marriage, is a second kind of chastity. Now if married people recognize that their union is blessed by God it ought to exhort them not to contaminate it by dissolute intemperance ... ruling themselves so that they do not do anything contrary to the holiness of marriage. [13]

---

11   *Institutes 1541*, p. 149; cf. 2.8.41.

12   *Institutes 1541*, p. 149; cf. 2.8.41.

13   *Institutes 1541*, p. 152 ; cf. 2.8.44 & 4.12.28.

Set in the context of an attack on Rome's requirement of clerical celibacy, the quotation from Chrysostom here is understood to support also the appropriateness of marriage for ministers (as its location in the 1559 edition demonstrates).

In the third edition of the *Institutes* Calvin adds a substantial paragraph and several shorter comments to his treatment of the seventh commandment. The main focus is an expansion of the questions about celibacy, i.e., under what circumstances good Christians may appropriately abstain from marriage. The teacher insists that each person must weigh his personal gifts; continence is a special gift and may be given only for a limited time.

> Let no one rashly condemn marriage as something either useless or superfluous for himself; let no one aspire to celibacy unless he is able to be without a wife. Let him also not consider the ease or convenience of the flesh, but rather that being free of this marriage bond he may be more quick and ready for all the duties of piety. [14]

For Calvin, neither celibacy nor marriage is more holy in itself. Permanent celibacy is not within the power of most people, but insofar as someone is able to remain unmarried, the purpose should be greater dedication to serving God. By this third edition of the *Institutes* the discussion of marriage is essentially complete as regards theology. However, there are two other very important sources for understanding Calvin's teaching on marriage: his liturgy and his Biblical exposition, especially the sermons.

Calvin's Liturgy

Calvin's marriage liturgy was largely influenced by the one that Farel published in 1533. The basic order of Farel's text and (much of) its contents were taken over in Calvin's two Strasbourg and his Genevan liturgies. The 1542 Strasbourg edition contains more rubrics and less liturgical prayer than its Genevan counterpart, while Strasbourg 1545 combines both versions published in 1542. The Geneva *La forme des prieres* did not really change after 1542 (apart from very minor verbal alterations), but was essentially simply reprinted. [15] Both Strasbourg editions

---

[14] *Inst.* 2.8.43, OS III, p. 382.

[15] OS II, pp. 50-56. See the 1552 printing by Jean Crespin. Verbal changes: "il" (OS p. 51) drops out, p. 43; "honorable" & "qui ne se peuvent contenir &" (p. 52) drop out, p. 44; "de mariage " drops out, "en ce noble estat" (OS p. 54) is replaced by "ensemble d'un commun accord" p. 47; "en ce sainct estat de" (OS p. 55) becomes "au sainct," p. 47; "& vivant purement" (OS 55) drops out, p. 48. Grosse did not include the marriage service when he prepared the critical edition of the Sunday, Lord's Supper, and day of prayer liturgies; however, this is similar to the changes he noted in the early years of those rites; *Les rituels de la Cène*, pp. 633-52; pp.151-54.

include a brief introductory essay not found in the Genevan text. However, the content of the first prayer in Geneva covers the same material as the Strasbourg essay (which means that in 1545 this expository passage effectively appears twice).

The main purpose of the first prayer of the wedding service in *La forme des prieres* was to ground marriage in scripture, and Gen. 2:21-22, Matt. 19:5, Eph. 5:28ff, Col. 3:18, I Tim. 2:12, 1 Pet. 3:1, Heb. 13:5, I Cor. 3:17 & 6:15 & 7:1ff, all appear in one form or another. This was the exposition heard by the Genevan congregation on a regular basis. In effect, Calvin's marriage liturgy was both a blessing of the couple's promise to live together in faithfulness before God and the community, and a clear instruction in the Biblical teaching on that "holy estate." A fuller order of the service will be presented below, as it would have been experienced in the context of worship.

An Overview of Calvin's Teaching on Marriage: Part II: Exegesis

Calvin's exegetical treatment of the Biblical texts he considered relevant to marriage is a rich although also somewhat repetitious source for understanding his teaching and practice. Particularly in its homiletical form, this scriptural instruction gives important glimpses of Calvin the pastor and allows modern readers to overhear what he told his congregation. For that reason, the primary focus of this section is the reformer's sermons on especially pertinent passages. Two of these, Genesis 2 and First Corinthians 7, are among the manuscript sermons which have been unknown or unavailable to scholars since the sixteenth century.[16] Their use here may illustrate the rich contribution of the reformer's sermons to expanding the interpretation of Biblical texts from exegesis to practical application.

Calvin published his commentary on First Corinthians in 1546; he preached the parallel sermons on Sunday mornings and afternoons in 1555-56, beginning on Oct. 20, 1555. The commentary on Genesis first appeared in 1554, based on lectures started in 1550; Calvin began the extant sermons on Sept. 4, 1559, and preached on this book on weekdays in alternate weeks for several years. (There is some evidence that Calvin was either preaching or lecturing on Genesis early in his second Genevan ministry, but these expositions were not recorded, as will be discussed in a later chapter.)[17] Since the Old Testament passage, Gen. 2:18-24,

---

16 The two volumes of *Sermons sur la Genèse*, ed. by Max Engammare, in *Supplementa Calviniana* 11, present the critical edition of Gen. 1:1-20:7. The sermons on the first nine chapters of First Corinthians are found in Ms.fr.26, which I am presently editing for the *Supplementa Calvinians* series.

17 Peter & Gilmont, *Bibliotheca Calviniana* I, pp. 214-16, 519-23. S XI/1 p.1; Ms.fr. 26, f1a. For Calvin's earlier work on Genesis, see chap. 6 at n.102.

expounds the establishment of marriage in a relatively straight-forward fashion, this material will be examined first. The New Testament, especially 1 Cor. 7, complicated the picture for Calvin (and other Protestants) because it leans toward promoting the unmarried state. Thus 1 Cor. 7 provides an intriguing perspective on how Calvin reconciled text and application when the written words of scripture (Genesis and Corinthians) seemed to conflict.

Genesis 1-2

The sermons on Genesis express essentially the same teaching as the commentary, but in the presentation to the congregation there is considerably less theological argument and much more application. For Calvin, Gen. 2:18-24 is a more detailed explanation of the account in Gen. 1:26-27 in which God "created man in his own image, male and female." The preacher is quite clear that both sexes express fully that image. For his congregation Calvin briefly sketches the nature of the soul. As the most valuable part of a person, a soul has reason, intelligence, and will. [18]

> There are reason and intelligence in the man, and these are also found in the woman; there is will, there is the ability to distinguish good and evil. In short, there is what pertains to the image of God [in the woman as well as the man]. [19]

Genesis here presents male and female as equal before God, but since all scripture must fit together, Calvin stops to harmonize this passage with 1 Cor. 11:7, which refers to woman as the image of man. In both commentary and sermons Calvin explicitly states that the subordination of woman to man is only in the context of earthly "polity," [20] and in the Genesis sermon he goes on to cite Gal. 3:28 that in Christ "there is neither male nor female... and we are all made participants" in His grace. [21] The good creation of the first man and first woman leads to the establishment of marriage, as expounded in Gen. 2:18-24.

However, for Calvin, marriage must be understood in the context of its significance for the creation of human society. The preacher seems to marvel at the manifestation of God's goodness in making man and woman from the same flesh and bone, which produces "a holy joining of all the human race... like a tie of

---

[18] *Sermons sur la Genèse*, S. XI/I, pp. 125, 58.

[19] *Sermons sur la Genèse*, S. XI/I, p. 62.

[20] *Sermons sur la Genèse*, S. XI/I, pp. 62-63. Commentary on Gen. 1:26, OC 32:27.

[21] *Sermons sur la Genèse*, S. XI/I, p. 63.

mutual love so each one knows that he is bound to his neighbors."[22] As his sermon unfolds, it becomes apparent that the creation of Adam and Eve defines not just marriage but ideal human society. Calvin states as an obvious fact that human beings were formed to live in community.

> For there is nothing more contrary to our nature than solitude, as each one knows. If we had everything we could wish, if there were a table in front of us all day long, our bed ready for us to sleep, if we had both supplies and all necessities; if then each one had an earthly paradise on condition that he had to live there alone, would that life not be full of sadness and like being half dead? We could only languish in the midst of such felicity – each one knows that. God's inestimable goodness and His more than fatherly care are demonstrated in this place, when He did not want man to be alone but wanted him to have company. This order was established in such a way as to warn us by the creation of Eve that, all of us being so formed from our father Adam and procreated of his seed, we must truly be one, and each person must recognize his neighbors as his flesh and bone and his very substance.[23]

Marriage is both the completion of the person and the pattern and nursery of truly human life. The commentary states that without his wife Adam was half a man [*dimidius*] and with her he was complete [*integrum*]; the sermon's parallel says "man is complete [*parfait*] ... by means of marriage."[24] This necessity for mutual completion extends to the whole human race.

> When God decided it was not good for us to be alone, it was not only so that each husband would have his wife, but so that we should by this means be held (together) in concord and unity.[25]

The goodness of marriage was greatly obscured by Adam's fall, so that now it is not the blessing which God created it to be, but Calvin insists that this is the fault of human beings, and marriage remains God's gracious gift.

> [If Adam had not fallen] we would see that God reigns over marriage: He is the Author of it and so blesses the whole that it would be like an angelic

---

22 *Sermons sur la Genèse*, S. XI/I, pp. 125-26: "afin qu'il y eust une conjunction saincte en tout le genre humain, et que cela soit comme un lien d'amour mutuelle, et que chascun se congnoisse estre tenu à ses prochains, veu que tous sont prins d'une seule personne."

23 *Sermons sur la Genèse*, S. XI/I, p. 126.

24 Commentary on Gen. 2:21, OC 23:49. *Sermons sur la Genèse*, S. XI/I, p. 127.

25 *Sermons sur la Genèse*, S. XI/I, p. 127.

melody between husbands and wives. And that would be so not only for
each married couple themselves, but the neighbors would help each other,
and each woman would draw her neighbors and relations to do their duty,
and each husband the same. [26]

Another aspect of this communal vision is visible in the way Calvin treats the
subordination of wives to husbands. Eve was created to be Adam's help-mate,
and so in marriage and in the world (earthly polity), men and women are not equal;
men are to lead and women are to be the helpers. The preacher then immediately
extends this observation to unmarried men and women: that is, even those who
are not married are still obligated to live in community with their neighbors. [27]
(Quite a number of people in early modern Europe were too poor ever to marry,
which may help to explain why Calvin puts so much emphasis on how Genesis
applies to their place in the whole society.) [28]

The sermon deals also with other issues regarding marriage, including other
Biblical texts which must be harmonized and the various problems of marrying
now in the state of sin. Calvin insists that God created one wife for Adam and this
means that polygamy is wrong. Briefly the preacher addresses one of the scriptural
challenges related to this issue, i.e., the multiple wives of the patriarchs and kings
of Israel, including those models of faith, Abraham and David. He explicitly
regards it as a very serious fault that these Old Testament leaders took many
wives. [29] Even when only one man and one woman are involved, however, there
are other problems which come from human sin. Sometimes marriages are
contracted on false grounds or from inappropriate motives or excessive passion,
and afflicted with various troubles. [30] However, Calvin sharply reproves disrespect
for the institution of marriage when he identifies the popular defamation of

---

[26]   *Sermons sur la Genèse*, S. XI/I, p. 129.

[27]   *Sermons sur la Genèse*, S. XI/I, p. 134.

[28]   In order to marry two people had to have the means to establish their own household. For
        some, this was possible through family wealth given by the parents, for others by inheritance of
        the parents' possessions, for others by working and saving sufficient money for themselves.
        There were always some who had none of these sources, and they remained life-long in the
        households of others, usually their employers. About 10-15% of early modern people in
        northwestern Europe (where Protestants became dominant) never married. The work available
        for women, whether unmarried or widowed, was usually poorly paid and the households they
        headed were "the poorest in any city," Merry Wiesner, *Women and Gender in Early Modern Europe*
        (Cambridge: Univ. Press, 1993), pp. 56-63; quotation p. 62. Poor rural women who could not
        marry often had to seek work in the cities where there was the possibility of paid labor, p. 88.

[29]   *Sermons sur la Genèse*, S. XI/I, pp. 135, 144-46.

[30]   *Sermons sur la Genèse*, S. XI/I, pp. 130, 131.

women as the work of the devil. Men toss around proverbial sayings: "O, woman is an evil one can't avoid" or "It would be good if there were no women in the world" – to which he retorts: "And if your mother had not existed, where would you be?"[31] At the end of this sermon the preacher summarizes once more the gift of marriage.

> When marriage was instituted and God pronounced this sentence "it is not good for man to be alone," He was not considering the corruption which we have today in our flesh, but it was because marriage was useful to the man and woman and that they should live together in concord. And there would be a correspondence and a melody, each one would recognize his flesh and bone, and the husband would know that his wife is a part of him, and the wife would know that she was taken out of her husband to be joined to him. That was the first institution of marriage.[32]

Calvin concludes that "our Lord wanted to be glorified in holy marriage... and already in this world we have a mirror to see the angelic concord which is in heaven."[33] Marriage as a mirror of angelic concord?! Although by 1559 Genevans would have been accustomed to hearing that marriage was God's good gift, they might still have been surprised to have the old language which exalted celibacy ("angelic life") re-purposed in praise of marriage.

First Corinthians 7

The sermons on 1 Corinthians 7 particularly take up the challenges to the value of marriage. The whole chapter itself seems objectively weighted in the opposite direction from Genesis 2. Paul's words favor the unmarried state and this provides considerable scope for Calvin to exercise his determination to harmonize Old and New Testaments and to praise the goodness and original purpose of marriage as God's good gift of human companionship.

Defending the Goodness of Marriage

Part of the preacher's task was to explain why Paul spoke of marriage as he did. The Corinthians were convinced that to seek the "angelic" life they should reject everything earthly and that marriage was not fit for Christians.[34] Having esta-

---

31 *Sermons sur la Genèse*, S XI/1, p. 131-32.

32 *Sermons sur la Genèse*, S XI/1, p. 137.

33 *Sermons sur la Genèse*, S XI/1, p. 138.

34 Sermon 41, Ms.fr. f333r: "Car si ung homme se vouloit exempter de toutes les necessittés de la vie presente soubz umbre de mener une vie angelicque, il tentera Dieu. ... il leur sembloit que le mariage estoit une chose repugnante à la foy et à l'estat des enfans de Dieu."

blished the context, Calvin then addresses the apparent contradiction between Paul's statement that it is better for a man not to touch a woman (1 Cor. 7:1) and the words of "Moses" (Gen. 2:18) that it is not good for man to be alone. Since Paul could not be in fundamental disagreement with Moses, Calvin points out what has intervened between the two texts, and that is the fall.

> (Gen. 2:18 quoted) Let us note that if we had remained in the integrity of Adam and had not been corrupted by sin, this phrase would be so for us: that the true human happiness in this mortal life would be for each to live with his wife, and we would see a much greater blessing in marriage than we can now perceive. [35]

Calvin maintains that marriage still bears marks of the fact that God is its Author, although the effects of sin are very evident. Paul's teaching about a man not touching a woman deals with the dangers which sin introduced into the relationship established by God, but the preacher feels the need to emphasize that the original order for marriage was good.

> It is certain that the companionship of man and woman was happy in everything and every way, there was nothing in marriage to cause anything except for them to rejoice and bless God's name with full voice; there were no quarrels, discontents, sorrows, nothing of all that, but there was an angelic rest and contentment. [36]

The word "companionship" [*compagnie*] includes sexual union – and yet – the true married life was "angelic." (The continuing emphasis on this inverted application of traditional language suggests that the preacher thought his hearers, including many refugees recently come to Geneva from Roman lands where the monastic ideal was still strong, needed to understand a Protestant view of 1 Cor. 7.)

Sexuality before and after the Fall is a significant part of Calvin's wrestling with the Corinthians passage because it seems to contradict Genesis. In the commen-

---

[35] Sermon 41, Ms.fr. f334v: "Or notons que si nous feussions demourez en l'integrité d'Adam et que nous n'eussions point esté corrompus par le peché, ceste sentence auroit lieu en nous que la vraye felicité des hommes en ceste vie caducque seroit de vivre chacun avec sa femme, que nous verrions une benediction beaucoup plus grande au mariage qu'on ne la peult point aujourd'huy appercepvoir." Quotations of Gen. 2 :18 – f334v, f335v.

[36] Sermon 41, Ms.fr. 26, f335r-v: "Il est certain que la compagnie de l'homme et de la femme eust esté heureuse en tout et par tout, il n'y eust eu occasion en mariage sinon de s'esjouyr et de beneir le nom de Dieu à pleine bouche. Il n'y eust nulles riottes, nulles facheries, nulz chagrins, rien de tout cela, mais il y eust eu ung repos et ung contententement [! contentement] angelicque."

tary on 1 Corinthians he briefly refers to the difference between marital relations before and after the fall,[37] but in the sermons he spells this out for his congregation in a way they could easily grasp. In the original state of innocence ("integrity") sexual relations between man and woman were without any sin.

> For when God ordained that it was not good for man to be alone, Adam could have lived with his wife without sin or vice, for they were still in that integrity of nature in which they had been created. But now, since there has come the corruption which is in us and which we all get from our father, it is certain that our desires go beyond the right bounds.[38]

After the Fall sexual desires, like all others, have been corrupted. However, God graciously counts marriage as a cover which sanctifies the relationship, provided that men and women recognize the sinfulness of their inordinate desires and strive to live together modestly in the fear of God. The obligation of fidelity rests on both partners equally; neither one may betray or cheat the other.[39] While recognizing the problems caused by sin, Calvin clearly rejects the traditional solution of total sexual abstinence and the papal definition of chastity enshrined in monastic vows; a couple living in fidelity and harmony are chaste.[40] In fact, Paul even tells married couples to sleep together except when for a limited time and by mutual agreement they abstain in order to devote themselves to fasting and prayers.[41] The preacher notes that such instruction about sex might be considered surprising and inappropriate language from the pulpit, but it was intended to correct those who thought that marriage was not fitting for Christians. Despite

---

37 Commentary on 1 Cor. 7:1, OC 49:401-02.

38 Sermon 44, Ms.fr. 26, f353r: "Car quand Dieu a ordonné qu'il n'estoit pas bon que l'homme fust seul, Adam pouvoit bien habiter avec sa femme sans peché ne vice, voire, car ilz avoyent encores ceste integrité de nature en laquelle ilz avoyent esté creez, mais maintenant despuis la corruption qui est en nous et que nous tirons tous de nostre père, il est certain que tous noz appettis sont desbordez, et quand l'homme est assemblé avec la femme cela encores est vicieux, si on l'examine à la rigueur."

39 Sermon 42, Ms.fr. 26, f341v-343r, explains that this is not simply sexual fidelity but love and devotion.

40 Sermon 42, Ms.fr. 26, f343v: "Or au contraire voicy Dieu qui prononce que les hommes et les femmes vivront chastement et que leur vie sera pure et honnorable devant luy moyennant qu'ilz tiennent ung mesnage sainct et pur et que chacun s'acquicte fidellement de son debvoir." Cf. Sermon 43, f354r.

41 Sermon 42, Ms.fr. 26, f345v-346r on temporary abstinence from the marriage bed for prayer; on f346v Calvin explains that this does not refer to ordinary prayers which should be continual: "Car non seulement nous debvons prier par chacun jour mais soir et matin," and moderation in food and drink are also continual. This instruction is for particular occasions of affliction, etc. f347r-348r.

humanity's sin-induced frailty, marriage does not separate people from God or hinder their prayers, and a faithful couple may "invoke God" together in good conscience. [42]

This discussion of marriage fits consciously and explicitly into Calvin's wide-ranging doctrine of the goodness of creation and the right use of God's bounty, before and after the Fall. [43] Marriage is in many ways very much like every other good gift of God, such as food and drink. The preacher reminds his hearers that, after the fall, these wonderful gifts also require effort and are not unalloyed blessings, and he describes at some length the challenges fallen humans face in getting enough to eat: bread or meat or wine. [44] Not surprisingly, this analogy is repeated a number of times. Calvin compares marriage to food, drink, and also sometimes to sleep, all of which are expressions of God's goodness to human beings. After the Fall, all of these have been abused – he offers the example of gluttons and drunkards [45] – but that is the fault of human sin, not of the Creator.

---

[42]   Sermon 43, Ms.fr. 26, f350r: "Cecy pourroit estre trouvé estrange que S[ainct] Paul ordonne aux marys d'avoir compagnie avec leurs femmes quant au lict, car il ne semble pas que ceste doctrine là soit pour estre preschee en chaire." Cf. f343v & 351r. f350r: "Il a fallu que ceste admonition fust donnee pour declairer que l'estat de marriage encores qu'il emporte distraction n'est pas toutesfois pour nous faire aliener de Dieu. Et combien que cela monstre la fragilité qui est en nostre nature que l'homme ayt sa femme et la femme son mary, toutesfois que Dieu approuve cela et qu'ilz le peuvent invocquer tous deux en bonne conscience."

[43]   The classic statements, *Inst.* 3.19.7-13, from 1536 (OS I, pp. 226-31). and *Inst.* 3.10.2-3, from 1539. The first (which becomes part of 3.19) discusses the third part of Christian freedom: all things (like food and drink) which are not defined by God in scripture are to be used freely according to the purpose for which God gave them. This means no scrupulous effort to do something extra to please God; Calvin gives the humorous example: "If he boggles at sweet wine, he will not with clear conscience drink even flat wine, and finally he will not dare touch water if sweeter and cleaner than other water," *Institution 1536*, p. 245 [3.19.7]. Christians must also take care not to hurt others by the way they use their freedom. The 1539 addition (which becomes part of 3.10), discusses the right use of the present life. Calvin explains that God gave the good gifts "not only to provide for necessity but also for delight and good cheer" and then goes on to list as examples food and clothing, wine and beauty. "Has the Lord clothed the flowers with the great beauty that greets our eyes, the sweetness of smell that is wafted upon our nostrils, and yet will it be unlawful for our eyes to be affected by that beauty, or our sense of smell by the sweetness of that odor?... Did he not, in short, render many things attractive to use, apart from their necessary use?" However, people must never abuse the gifts, e.g., by gluttony or drunkenness, etc. *Institutes* McNeill-Battles, p. 721 [3.10.2].

[44]   Sermon 41, Ms.fr. 26, f334v-335r. In this little reflection on the human state, Calvin also describes various kinds of good and bad weather.

[45]   Sermon 43, Ms.fr. 26. Eating and drinking are good but people must thank God and not abuse them; the same applies to marriage, f336r-v. Exercise sobriety in eating and drinking but use these in order to fulfill one's duty; people cannot do their work without sleeping and so sleep is necessary. The same principle applies also to marriage, f337v. In several places Calvin gives

Besides sex, food and drink and sleep were the main forms of self-denial practiced by Roman monks and nuns, and Calvin's polemical note would not be lost on Genevans. While the most obvious form of abuse of God's bounty which the preacher criticizes is excessive indulgence, in the context of balancing Gen. 2 and 1 Cor. 7, he also works to make it clear that refusal to appreciate God's gifts is another form of sin.[46]

Along with vindicating the goodness of marriage as God intended it, Calvin has to deal with various other issues raised by 1 Cor. 7 and its traditional interpretations. He readily acknowledges that the Fall added a second purpose to marriage, i.e., in addition to its original intent as the ideal form of human association, marriage also serves sinful humanity as a remedy for inordinate desires. Calvin does not give a great deal of attention to the need for the remedy: that is self-evident. However, another issue requires many more words, since Paul expresses his preference for Christians to follow his example and remain unmarried. For a Protestant it was necessary to balance this instruction with the scriptural affirmation of marriage by explaining the context of Paul's words and the conditions under which faithful people might legitimately not marry. Calvin develops 1 Cor. 7: 7 where, while telling married couples not to deny each other the appropriate sexual fulfillment, Paul says that Christians have different gifts. The preacher emphasizes this idea, essentially equating it with individual vocations; one special gift is continence, but for those who do not possess this gift, the only faithful choice is to marry. For those who do have the ability to remain chaste in single life, the choice should be made for the purpose of serving God better and not from some false idea of special sanctity or desire to have an easy life.[47]

---

sarcastic examples about exaggerated applications of refusing to use natural gifts well; refusing to eat bread but instead eating dates, or refusing to sleep [in beds] but sleeping on the ground, f337r. He adds that some ancient heretics rejected marriage, and the church condemned them … but then turned around and did the same thing, reviling marriage, f338r. Sermon 43, Ms.fr. 26, f352r, for example of gluttons and drunkards. The commentary also makes the comparison of marriage with food, drink, and sleep; 1 Cor. 7:1, OC 49:401.

46 Sermon 43, Ms.fr. 26, f352r, all foods are good and allowed but they are meant to be used soberly. A little later Calvin repeats this idea and then gives a glimpse of his own time and place. Living in the world as it is, one must recognize the condition and thankfully make use of the aids which God gives; saying one can do without the remedies God gives is like saying one can do without food or drink. Speaking of God's good gifts, the preacher points to the coming of spring [this sermon was preached in late March], the new green of the fields, the beauty God created for human pleasure with liberality beyond satisfying any necessity, but people never keep to their proper limits and use God's gifts as they should, f355v.

47 Sermon 43, Ms.fr. 26. There is first a long passage explaining the gifts common to all Christians, things which have to do with their vocation as Christians: renewal by the Holy Spirit, fear of

Brief Excursus on the Pauline Privilege

Among the key practical issues raised by 1 Cor. 7:10-16 were the possible reasons or conditions under which husband and wife might separate. Given the emphasis on the permanence of marriage, especially the Roman teaching that it is a sacrament, this issue had long been a source of argument. Several different scenarios are presented by the Biblical text; in vv.10-11 it is separation without identifying a particular cause, while vv. 12-16 treat separation because one spouse is an unbeliever. Traditionally the second circumstance was called the Pauline privilege. It was generally agreed that the "privilege" applied only to a marriage already contracted; in the early church the situation would arise with the conversion of one half of a "pagan" couple. In this case, Paul's counsel is that the two should stay together unless the pagan rejects the tie, in which case the Christian is freed from the marriage. By the twelfth or thirteenth century, the religious landscape and so also the shape of "unbelief" had changed; now theologians had to deal with the question of a marriage between an orthodox person and a heretic (i.e., someone baptized but not orthodox). If not yet accomplished, such a marriage was prohibited; if one partner of a "heretical" couple converted, the marriage remained valid and the orthodox could not claim the Pauline privilege. He or she could separate from the heretic but was not free to remarry. [48]

Calvin on the Permanence of Marriage

One of the significant themes of Calvin's teaching, especially but not exclusively on 1 Cor. 7:10-16, is a vigorous defense of the permanence of marriage. He rejects the easy divorces which he saw as common in the ancient world and among the Jews. He equally explicitly argues against the Roman theology which praised a married couple who chose to vow celibacy and separate. The preacher insists that marriage was meant to bind a couple together for their whole lives, and leaving a spouse is rebellion against God, resisting the order which God esta-

---

God and illumination by faith, providing charity and help for neighbors, living a sober and honest life with patience in afflictions, taking refuge in God, f353v; this is followed by a discussion of individual gifts such as continence or not, with polemic against papal vows, f354r-v. He gives the example of a young girl being forced into a convent for lack of a dowry, despite the fact that she does not understand what her vow means, and this ignorance compounded by the fact that she has to make the promise in Latin!

[48] Seeger, *Nullité de mariage*, pp. 47-48, 58-61. Seeger points out that the case of a pagan marriage and a Christian marriage-sacrament differed. If one partner of a pagan marriage converted and the other refused to cohabit, the convert could dissolve the marriage because it had not been a sacrament. The same would not be true for a marriage between a Christian and a heretic, i.e., it was a sacrament and could not be dissolved.

blished to be inviolable (citing Gen. 2:18, 23).[49] To be sure his congregation does not misunderstand, Calvin clarifies that Paul is not discussing adultery, which scripture regulates in other places. What is meant in 1 Cor. 7:10-16 is the case of a man or woman leaving the other spouse, and in such a situation, the person must live as a widow(er) or be reconciled to the partner. A man or woman who marries someone else while the abandoned spouse is alive commits adultery and cuts himself or herself off from God. Since Paul's text speaks of a woman abandoning her husband, the preacher identifies the problem as a cruel man who abuses his wife. With the magistrate's permission the wife must be aided, but the marriage is not broken and therefore the woman is not free to remarry.[50] (Calvin's contemporary situation is evident in this appeal to the magistracy and, given the number of cases of wife-beating which came before the consistory, it is no surprise that the preacher identifies a husband's abuse as the reason for a woman to leave, but he does not deal with this question at length in the sermons.[51])

The second scenario, separation because one person is not a believer, was a more difficult issue in a world sharply divided by religious confession. In the sermons Calvin distinguishes two situations of a marriage between a Christian and an unbeliever: one contracted when the difference of faith is known, and one in which the change in faith follows after the marriage. Calvin explains that Paul is not discussing the first situation here; he treats that elsewhere (2 Cor. 6:14-15). To be sure his people do not misunderstand, the preacher explicitly says that by deliberately marrying an unbeliever the believer tempts God, profanes himself, and cuts himself off from the church. (In this instance, it is the church visible which Calvin means, but rejecting the church where the true marks are found is choosing to reject the salvation God offers.)[52] In the text at hand, 1 Cor. 7:12-16, the issue is a change in the religious stance of either the husband or the wife. The point for Calvin is not validity but whether the marriage receives the blessing which is only

---

[49] Sermon 44, Ms.fr. 26, f361r-362r. For rejection of separation in order to vow celibacy, see Sermon 42, Ms.fr. 26, f344r.

[50] Sermon 44, Ms.fr. 26, f362r-364r.

[51] For two examples of wife-beating from this same month, see chap. 7 at nn.164, 171. The consistory did whatever it could to get the husband to stop the abuse but also to reconcile the couple. To modern eyes the protection was far from adequate, but the lack of other resources for a battered woman even led a seriously injured wife to take the blame and petition for mercy for her husband, lest he abandon her and her children; see example for Aug. 17, 1542, *Consist.* I, pp. 104-05.

[52] Sermon 44, Ms.fr. 26, f364r-v. For cutting self off from church which has the marks, see *Institutes* 1536, OS I, p. 92; clear expression 1543, *Inst.* 4.1.19. For examples of families arranging marriages of a daughter or sister with a Catholic and the consistory arguing strongly against this, see Witte & Kingdon, *Courtship, Engagement, and Marriage*, pp. 374-77.

given to Christian marriages. In effect, when Paul says that the unbelieving wife is sanctified by the believing husband and vice versa, it means that as long as the two remain together the marriage as such is a true one (as distinct from a pagan marriage which is legal but not true), and this has implications for the children.[53]

It is evident here that Calvin agreed with the tradition that a marriage between a believer and a heretic is still a valid marriage. While the canonists allowed separation in view of this confessional difference, Seeger says that Calvin made the regulation stricter. Such separation should be contingent on severe bodily harm from the unbeliever; not only does the marriage remain in force but the separated partner should return when there was no longer physical danger.[54] Although less immediately related to the situation of native Genevans, this Biblical passage and the resulting teaching were of considerable importance to many French Protestants, especially women who had converted "to the gospel" but whose husbands were adamantly opposed to their change of confession. The husband had the right to determine the residence of a couple, so a man who became a Protestant could insist that his wife follow him, but a woman was supposed to stay with her Catholic husband. There are examples of men being strongly encouraged by the consistory to bring their wives to Geneva, but obviously the reverse was much more difficult. On rare occasions a married woman was able to take refuge with the permission of the consistory: there is a case the very month of Calvin's sermon in March 1556, but many were still suffering for their faith and their faithfulness.[55]

Despite the fact that the great majority of his correspondents in these trials were women, Calvin's homiletical examples are primarily of men whose wives reject the faith. Besides his cultural custom of making the male the standard, the reformer may have been influenced by the contemporary and very significant case of Marquis Galeazzo Caracciolo. The most prominent Italian refugee in Geneva

---

[53] Sermon 44, Ms.fr. 26, f364v-365r.

[54] Seeger, *Nullité de mariage*, pp. 131-32.

[55] For an example of Calvin's advice to these women, see his letter to Mme de Cany, June 7, 1553, whose endurance would finally have the result of converting her husband (OC 14:556/58; *Writings on Pastoral Piety*, pp. 305-07). For general correspondence, Charmarie Jenkins Blaisdell, "Calvin's Letters to Women." *Sixteenth Century Journal* 13 (1982): 67-84. For Jeronime Patron being told by the consistory to bring his Catholic wife to Geneva, see April 12 & May 24, 1548, *Consist. IV*, pp. 45, 69; on May 28 the Senate enforces this with an order to bring her within one month (p. 69 n.390). For the woman who, after much effort on her part and abuse on his, was allowed to remain in Geneva without her Catholic husband, see chap. 7 at n.172. For an earlier example, see April 6, 1542, *Consist.* I, p. 32; in this case, the woman was a long time resident of Geneva who had apparently converted along with the city; her husband refused to join her and the consistory allowed her to remain.

and one of the highest ranking Italian converts to Protestantism, Caracciolo was in the process of trying to work out ways to reunite his family without giving up his faith. Since his wife refused to join him or even to live with him in a neutral place, their case must have seemed to Calvin like a classic example of 1 Cor. 7:12-16. [56]

Expounding 1 Cor. 7 in the context of religious conflict meant not only teaching what the people should do but also responding as a pastor to their anxieties or perplexities (within the limits of cultural views about men's and women's relative independence). Part of Calvin's attention in the sermons is given to reassuring the believing spouse that living with the unbeliever does not compromise the goodness of marriage. "Since marriage was instituted by God, one who uses it with a good conscience will not be tainted by another's sin." [57] In addition, Calvin follows Paul in affirming that if the unbeliever is determined to separate, the Christian is not bound, "because God has called us to peace." The preacher then treats at some length the various aspects of what it means to be called to peace, setting marriage (the specific issue of his Biblical text) in the larger contemporary context of confessional conflict. [58]

In 1 Cor. 7:16 one question is whether the believer can win the unbeliever to faith; the preacher identifies two major dangers and one great honor. The first loyalty must be to God; keeping the peace must not mean lessening fidelity to God in order to please the spouse. Further, Paul's words are not meant to open the door to (groundless) accusations that one's spouse is an unbeliever so that one may divorce him or her. That is hypocrisy, and the marriage remains binding. However, when the believer properly follows the apostle's instructions and uses all legitimate means to persuade the partner, he or she is described as working "to save" the spouse. Calvin hastens to clarify that this does not mean usurping Christ's role but being the instrument of saving another person. However, such an honor should move us with "great zeal to do everything in our power to win those who are alienated from Christ." [59] Was Caracciolo listening? He was doing his best to win his wife.

---

[56] Kingdon, *Adultery and Divorce*, chap. 6; see pp. 152-54 for Galeazzo's activities in 1555-56 while Calvin was preaching these sermons.

[57] Sermon 44, Ms.fr. 26, f365r: "D'autant que le mariage est institué de Dieu, celuy qui en use en bonne conscience ne sera point souillé par le vice d'aultruy."

[58] Sermon 45, Ms.fr. 26, f368r-369r. Opponents claim that all the troubles of the church would be resolved if the Protestant "heretics" would come back to Rome. Calvin insists that such a thing would be apostasy, not seeking peace.

[59] Sermon 45, Ms.fr. 26, f369r-371r ; f370v: "Puis qu'ainsi est aprenons d'estre tant plus esmeuz d'ung zele ardent à faire tout ce qui sera en nous et tant que nostre faculté le portera de gaigner ceux qui estoient alienez de nostre Seigneur Jesus Christ."

Calvin's Autobiography

Although Calvin makes no specific reference to marrying a former unbeliever who is now a believer, that kind of situation might have been in the back of his mind... because he had done this himself. It is often said that Calvin married an Anabaptist and sometimes the conclusion is drawn that he did not object to marriages with Anabaptists.[60] This is simply not true. He married a *former* Anabaptist whom he had brought, along with her husband, to embrace his (Protestant) understanding of the faith and specifically infant baptism.[61] Following their conversion this couple joined Calvin's parish in Strasbourg. After Idelette de Bure was widowed Calvin evidently came to realize that she embodied the virtues he had been seeking and was the right companion in faith for him. To see what that marriage became one has only to read the letters by the grieving widower written to his best friends to tell them of Idelette's death and his sorrow at losing "the best companion" of his life.[62] The point here is that Calvin would have considered marrying an Anabaptist a contradiction of scripture and, although he certainly did not convert Idelette de Bure in order to marry her, the similarity between what had happened and what Paul taught would probably not have been lost on him.

Comment

In concluding this sketch of Calvin's teaching on marriage it is worth noting its effect on the traditional discussion of the purposes for marriage. There are some distinct differences, both in what is dropped: procreation, and what is added: true companionship. For Calvin the procreation of children does not make the list of Biblical reasons for marriage. Neither in Genesis (even in Gen. 1:28 in which Adam and Eve along with the animals are commanded to multiply), nor in 1 Cor. 7:14 (which talks about the children of Christians) is the birth of children named as a purpose of marriage. Of course the institution of marriage is the place or context in which children are supposed to be born, but it is significant that Calvin does not make procreation a reason to marry and that instead he stresses the social companionship. In fact, this was also true in the wedding liturgy. Every time a couple came to church in Geneva to be married, the whole congregation

---

[60] One of the most recent is Witte & Kingdon, *Courtship, Engagement, and Marriage*. The editors affirm that Calvin married "an Anabaptist widow" (p. 99), but the main problem is the conclusions which they draw. They say that Calvin did not object to marriages with Anabaptists because he "married an Anabaptist widow"; and they comment that they do not know of any disputes between Calvin and Idelette de Bure over the baptism of their infant son, p. 358 n.22.

[61] See Colladon, OC 21:79, for conflict with Anabaptists and their conversion. See Balke below at n.120.

[62] OC 13:228-29, 230-31; cf. *Writings on Pastoral Piety*, pp. 52-54.

heard the affirmation of the two Biblical purposes which Calvin taught: companionship and a remedy for sin. Procreation is not named.

Although at times the affirmation of the goodness of marriage might seem to be drowned out by attention to fighting the effects of the fall in human sexual behavior, Calvin's parishioners were hearing a new kind of language about marriage. It is an "angelic" vocation?! Couples came to worship and found that the preachers were turning up-side-down texts like 1 Cor. 7 which had shaped their sense of being second-class Christians. Calvin spoke explicitly and forcefully about marriage as a manifestation of God's bounty and goodness equal to the nourishment which sustains human life! Old and young, men and women, everyone sitting in the pews in Geneva on a regular basis witnessed weddings, that "holy estate" in which a couple promised to live together, loving each other purely, edifying their neighbors, and rearing any children in God's service.

The Practice of Marriage in Geneva

Marriage and family are fundamental social institutions and thus changes in views of ecclesiastical-civil relationships in early modern Europe had important implications for both marriage and family. For centuries the Roman Church had claimed jurisdiction over all matters related to marriage, but Protestants generally regarded this as usurping the prerogatives of civil rulers at least in part, if not wholly. The Genevan re-form of marriage can be examined in three parts: the development of the laws which governed the new order, including the *Ecclesiastical Ordinances*; the experience of a wedding and character of the liturgy as it was enacted in the city parishes; and the evidence for the ordinary or regular practice as found primarily in the marriage records which were begun in 1550.

The Legal Establishment Governing Marriage Matters

The laws and authorities which re-shaped the practice of marriage in Geneva were of several kinds. The first concern of the government was to assume the oversight of marriage and family which had been a major part of the business of the episcopal court, and one of the key reasons for establishing a consistory was to handle these issues. In areas influenced by Zurich, a consistory in the shape of the Marriage Court was a function of the civil government whose members might and often did consult the clergy but who kept the reins in their own hands.[63] Bern adopted this general pattern, and in the early years of its dominant role in Geneva

---

[63] See the classic study, Walter Köhler, *Zurcher Ehegericht und Genfer Konsistorium*, vol. 1, (Leipzig: Heinsius,1932). Strasbourg instituted a modified form of this before Calvin's arrival there; cf. Bornert, *La réforme protestante du culte à Strasbourg*, pp. 551-69.

the Bernese urged their neighbors to follow their example. In discussing this advice in January 1540, the Genevan Senate referred to the idea as a proposal for a "consistory" and declined the advice on the grounds that theirs was a small territory and they as the council could handle it themselves, using whatever consultation with the ministers they wished.[64]

Already in the *Articles* of 1537, Calvin and his colleagues had protested against the reigning confusion about marriage and called for its regulation, beginning with an ordinance prepared jointly by a commission of Senators and ministers. In August 1538 a petition from the ministers then in Geneva repeated the call for a marriage ordinance and a consistory for marital issues (the presenting occasion was a clandestine marriage of minors with bribery as a factor), but despite the public confusion about the new order, no action was taken.[65] However, several years later the authorities changed their minds, a process helped no doubt by their determination to get Calvin back. On April 5, 1541, the Senate proposed to the Two Hundred that a consistory be established with oversight of marriage and some other matters. On April 22 it was decided to experiment with the idea before establishing an official ordinance, and then in November this practice was legally enacted in the *Ecclesiastical Ordinances*.[66] Although there was obviously a longer history, the fact that church discipline was one of Calvin's conditions for returning must have swayed the Genevan government; they agreed to the idea of a consistory during negotiations with their former and future pastor, even though the implementation awaited his coming. As is well known, the consistory was claimed by Calvin as the court of the church, with jurisdiction over much more than just marriage. However, he also frankly believed that many aspects of marriage were civil matters;[67] the work of the consistory in this area was therefore essentially pastoral, with the ministers serving mostly a consultative or monitoring

---

[64] Jan. 12 & 13, 1540; RC V, pp. 36, 40, 42.

[65] *Articles*, OS I, p. 376: "pour ce que le pape a tant brouillé les causes de marriage…" Calvin appealed to the Genevan government; note that this is a separate part of the *Articles* from the proposal for a kind of discipline system (not yet called a consistory) which is described on pp. 373-74. Senate minutes, Aug. 20, 1538; RC III, p. 373.

[66] April 5 & 8 & 22, 1541; OC 21:235 & 277, 278. *Ordinances*, OS II, pp. 339-40.

[67] For Calvin's understanding of the consistory, see *Inst.* 4.3.8 *et passim.*; McKee, *Elders and the Plural Ministry*, part 1. A glance at the *Registres du Consistoire* illustrates the wide-ranging work of the consistory, and the many fine studies by Robert M. Kingdon and his students have shown how this institution actually worked. For a collection which gives consistory examples especially focused on marriage, see Witte and Kingdon, *Courtship, Engagement, and Marriage*. Seeger, *Nullité de mariage*, p. 94, says that Calvin does not give much attention justifying the role of civil government because he was a second generation reformer and this had effectively been settled by the first generation.

role.[68] As regards the public liturgical part of marriage which is the focus here, the consistory dealt mostly with sorting out contested marriage promises, i.e., the necessary prerequisite to the official banns, or the less common determination of a desertion, which would also entail announcements to the public in worship.[69]

The development of regulations about marriage in Geneva was at first piece-meal. Specific legislation was a project jointly led by the ministers and the Senate, with the former usually proposing and the latter deciding what would be law. In January 1537 the Senate's summary of the ministers' *Articles* included a brief regulation of marriage: there should be a respectable man to sign the papers in recognition that the two parties were legitimately free to marry, banns should be announced for three Sundays, and weddings were allowed every day in worship.[70] In April 1540 the Senate ordered marriages to be held at the beginning of the service, with guards available to insure silence for the liturgy.[71] The *Ecclesiastical Ordinances* in 1541 included basic regulations about weddings.

> After the customary announcement of the banns the wedding will be held when the parties decide, Sundays as well as workdays, provided that it is at the beginning of the service. It will be good, though, that they abstain from celebrating weddings on the day of the Lord's Supper out of respect for the sacrament.[72]

(Although not celebrating weddings on Supper Sundays was phrased as a wish, in fact this appears to have been the practice, since there are none listed on those days in the marriage records.) The next ordinance which defined the process came in January 1543 in the order about the civil officers which regulated the details of legal "licenses." This required the first syndic to sign the marriage banns before they were announced from the pulpit.[73]

---

[68] Example of monitoring, *Consist.* I, July 20, 1542, p. 90, the consistory asks Andri Arnod & Janatez Ponarde who married them and who signed the announcement; they answer Champereaulx (minister) and Curtet (syndic).

[69] *Ordinances*, OS II, p. 345. For examples of announcements in worship, see chap. 3 at nn.171ff, chap. 7 at n.174.

[70] Jan. 16, 1537; RC II, p. 23.

[71] April 13, 1540; RC V, p. 238.

[72] *Ordinances*, OS II, p. 345. It may be noted that this is one point on which the Senate did not make any changes – except orthographic – to Calvin's draft. In fact, there were no major changes in 1561, when elements of the language changed to become more explicit: 1) "face les espon-sailles" becomes "on celebre et benisse le Mariage en l'Eglise" and 2) the instruction about avoiding the day of the Lord's Supper is reformulated.

[73] Witte & Kingdon, *Courtship, Marriage, and Engagement*, p. 84. *Sources du Droit de Genève*, vol. 2. #807.

Within a few years of his return to Geneva, Calvin became convinced that the city needed more specific and extensive marriage legislation, but the city government was slow to recognize this as an urgent matter. In November 1545 the pastor drafted a full text, dealing particularly with the complex questions of who might marry whom (especially the rejection of spiritual affinities)[74] and by whose permission (the freedom of adult couples, the rights of parents or guardians[75]), how marriage promises were to be made and what constituted valid promises, how engagements should be licensed and announced and weddings celebrated, what was expected of married couples as a household, and for what cause(s) marriage could be declared null or divorce might be granted. The ministers together seem to have revised Calvin's text slightly,[76] but the Senate refused to act on this legislation.

It is clear from the marriage registers begun in 1550, however, that even without official sanction Calvin and his colleagues followed the provisions of his plan in the spheres over which they had control, such as the services at which they were willing to perform weddings. This included limiting Sunday weddings

---

[74] This involved clarifying what relationships did constitute an impediment to marriage. Genevan regulations, like those of other Protestants, on this matter intended to follow Biblical and classical guidelines. In addition, there was some attention to what might shock the ignorant unnecessarily. For example, they prohibited marriages between first cousins "for the present," i.e., these were not considered immoral but introducing the practice should be delayed until people were more accustomed to the new ways. One of the few recorded criticisms of the new customs was a blasphemy case before the consistory on Feb. 27, 1550, while the marriage legislation was being debated; several people affirmed that they heard a certain Valentin say that the ministers wanted to let brothers and sisters and [first] cousins marry each other. *Consist.* V, pp. 13 & 14.

[75] The regulations included stipulated ages at which young men and women could contract marriage (sons at 20, daughters at 18 though Calvin would have preferred 24 and 20); this was intended to prevent young people from taking matters into their own hands before they were of age (OC 10:36, 105). In fact there were occasions when parents had to be reprimanded for betrothing their children before puberty, especially peasant girls. On Sept. 1, 1558, the consistory handled the problem of defining the earliest possible time parents could make such promises for their children as the point when a child was first admitted to take the Lord's Supper, but even then there might be objections if the girl was very young. OC 21:702.

[76] Nov. 10, 1545, OC 10:33-44, for Calvin's draft. (This is also found in OS II but it is combined with 1561 so it is more difficult to read.) The ministers' revision (published in RCP 1, pp. 30-38) essentially consists of reordering some of the items in Calvin's texts along with some minor verbal changes. The editors of RCP (p. 37 n.1) indicate that the ministers added four paragraphs under the provisions for annulling a marriage, concerning what should be done if a man or woman promises marriage and then leaves town and does not return to fulfill the promise, but in fact these are also in Calvin's draft under the provisions for annulling an engagement (10:36-37). The editors of RCP date this ministerial version shortly after Calvin's draft and not later than 1546 or 1547 (p. 30 n.1) and this is the form which was inserted into the *Ordonnances* in 1561. The ministers seem to have presented their version to the Senate in Feb. 1550 (cf. Feb. 24, 1550, OC 21:461).

to the dawn or afternoon services, i.e., not the main morning time or noon catechism.[77] In September 1549 Calvin raised the issue of marriage regulation again, especially because couples promised marriage and then dragged out the engagements for many months. In January and February 1550 the ministers repeated their complaints about the disorder in marriage practices.[78] Finally, when problems over long delayed weddings brought Calvin before the Senate again in May 1551, it was agreed that the marriage ordinances should be completed.[79] There is no record that this was in fact done at this time, but eventually the regulations (according to which at least the ministers had consistently been working) were incorporated into the revised *Ordonnances* in 1561.[80]

The Process of Engagement (and Disengagement) and the Celebration of Marriage

The process governing the public establishment of a marriage involved the larger worshiping community at a number of stages, and thus it is appropriate to outline how a couple in Calvin's Geneva would be guided and overseen – literally, looked upon – as they became a new household in the family of the church.

The Process of Engagement (and Disengagement)

In a simple engagement which moved smoothly from promise to wedding, there were a number of steps at which the couple interacted with the civil and ecclesiastical authorities.[81] After a man and woman promised marriage in the presence of witnesses, the man came to the first syndic for the "license." If either person was not known to the community, reliable witnesses must testify that there was no impediment to the marriage: no wife or husband, no promise of

---

[77] cf. OC 21:206, Jan. 16, 1537 (RC 30 f151). OC 10:40 (1545): "Qu'il soit loisible de celebrer tous les jours les mariages: assavoir les jours ouvriers au sermon qu'il semblera bon aux parties, le dimenche au sermon de l'aube du jour, et de trois heures apres midy, exceptés les jours qu'on celebrera la cene, afin que lors il n'y ayt aucune distraction et que chascun soit mieux disposé à recevoir le sacrement." One evidence of the neglect of attention to the relationship between worship services and marriage is the fact that Parker assumes that all weddings listed in the *Opera Calvini* were performed at the main morning hour unless otherwise stated; cf. *Calvin's Preaching*, appendix 2, p. 165.

[78] Sept. 12, 1549; Jan. 20, & Feb. 17 & 24, 1550; OC 21:455-56, 460, 461 (RC 44 f212, 306v, f329v). The discussion may have become public knowledge early in 1550, because some Genevans commented on the ministers' views on consanguinity, although these comments might have referred to rules already in practice; cf. above n.74.

[79] May 1, 1551, OC 21:480 (RC 45 f266).

[80] OC 10:105-14.

[81] cf. OC 10:39 (1545), 10:107-108 (1561): length of engagement, signing of certificate and witnesses, number and times of announcements, report of impediments if any.

marriage elsewhere. (Between the commercial activities of Genevans and the growing refugee population, the issue of determining whether both parties were free to marry was not a mere formality.)[82] When approved, the announcement was brought to the minister(s) of the couple's home parish(es), and the pastor(s) announced the engagement from the pulpit at the main morning service on three Sundays. In the case of a bride and groom from different Genevan parishes, the minister of the parish where the marriage was not being performed must notify his colleague that the announcements had been made, and whether or not objections had been forthcoming.[83] These public notices could be three weeks in succession, or at intervals of two weeks. During this time, anyone who knew a valid impediment to the marriage was supposed to bring it to the authorities. Care should be taken, however, to insure that no objections offered by an unknown person were allowed to disrupt the process. Once a marriage was performed, those who moved to a new place (e.g., to Geneva from France) were also expected to provide evidence of their marital state.[84]

Various difficulties might arise in the course of an engagement, however. One common problem was an argument over whether a legitimate promise of marriage had been made, and the consistory dealt with a significant number of such cases. In some instances it was concluded that there was no binding promise, in others there was a breach of promise and the marriage must be carried out, in others involving minors the parents' refusal of permission was invoked.[85] The

---

[82]   *Consist.* I, May 17, 1543, p. 243, concerning the marriage of M. Bastien de Villa & Jane, daughter of Mathieu Milliaud; the consistory notes that they have information from the consistory of Gex [in reply to an earlier request] that there is no impediment, so the ministers send the couple on to the Senate, along with the witnesses [so they can get their signed license for banns].

[83]   For the place of announcements, see chap. 3 at nn.171ff. The *Ordinances* do not explicitly note the announcement in the other parish, but this is clarified by the 1564 report of Charles Perrot for his successors: "Les annonces doivent estre proclamees les trois dimanches precedents au grand sermon. Si c'est pour un mariage qui se celebre en un[e] autre paroisse, j'escrivois en latin comme c'est la coustume: *Proclamatio tridominico...* Si c'estoit pour ma paroice et qu'il y eust une des parties de un[e] autre paroice, fault aporter lors pareilles attestations du ministre de ce lieu-la; fault que le chastellain ait aussy signé premierement les annonces." Lambert, *Preaching, Praying and Policing,* appendix 4, p. 547.

[84]   *Consist.* I, May 4, 1542, pp. 58-59, gives an example of attestation required for husband Jaques Pernod but describes the proper procedure for wife Tevena with signed witness of announcements and wedding; p. 60, gives the text of an attestation a marriage properly carried out for Laurence Viongiere and Anna Coppier.

[85]   A few examples: *Consist.* I, Feb. 16 & 23, 1542, pp. 3-4, 6, 7-8; *et passim.* For the order to fulfill the promise on pain of prison, cf. *Consist.* I, June 22, 1542, p. 81, Pierre Magnin (first mentioned Feb. 16, p. 3); p. 81 n.373 indicates that the Senate carried out the threat and eventually Magnin must have agreed to do his duty in order to be freed.

marriage legislation made provision for annulling a promise for legitimate reason (such as physical inability),[86] but this was not the usual issue. Two common difficulties (from the viewpoint of the pastors) were a delay in celebrating the wedding and/or consummating the marriage, or premarital cohabitation, since some couples apparently confused the written announcement with full legal marriage.[87] At times also there was concern about some laxity on the part of the official required to insure that both parties were free to marry, and his acceptance of unreliable witnesses.[88] It might happen that one party to the engagement, usually the man, left town and did not return. In such circumstances, the fiancée would bring the matter to the authorities; inquiry would be made to discover if there was some legitimate reason for the absence and to admonish the man to return by a set date. If he complied, the marriage would be performed as soon as possible; if he did not, the announcement requiring him to return would be made three times at two week intervals in the main Sunday morning worship service, and if there was still no response the fiancée would be free of her promise. If there was legitimate reason for the absence, known to the woman, then she must wait for a year before proceeding. In the case of a woman leaving the city before the marriage, the man would follow the same procedure but would not be compelled to wait for a year unless he had given his permission and known that the reason for the journey would require an extended absence.[89]

---

[86] cf. OC 10:36. Witte & Kingdon, *Courtship, Engagement and Marriage*, pp. 270-72.

[87] For delays, cf. *Consist.* I, June 15, 1542, p. 77, Loys Franch is dragging his feet about marrying his fiancée (as is his brother Claude also, p. 77 n.351); for ministers' objections, see above n.79. Problem with cohabitation, cf. OC 10:39 (1545), 10:108 (1561). Witte & Kingdon, *Courtship, Engagement and Marriage*, chap. 12.

[88] Even after the regulations were commonly known, Geneva experienced some difficulty with the reliability of witnesses who should testify that someone was free to marry (in order for their banns to be signed) or on the contrary that there were impediments. Nov. 16, 1556, OC 21:654-55 (RC 52 f98): Calvin complains about the strangers who come to be married in Geneva but are not in fact free to do so, and asks the syndic in charge to write the names of their witnesses (i.e., Genevans) so that the latter may be shamed if they testify falsely. May 30, 1558, OC 21:696 (RC 58 f197): Calvin returns to the Senate to protest that the previous year's ordinance is not being observed, and asks that it be enforced: when strangers come to ask for their certificates they must have witnesses.

[89] cf. RCP 1, p. 37; OC 10:113-14 (1565). Instances which required these measures were known well before, cf. *Consist.* I, May 11, 1542, p. 61, La Gervayse asking to be freed of a promise to the former servant of Laurent Maigret because he has disappeared without sending any word, to which the consistory consents. March 9, 1542, p. 14, and June 22, 1542, pp. 80, 82, for the case of Francoyse Reys against Pierre Favre, asking to be freed of her promise because he has not come back.

Although a great deal more complicated, from an ecclesiastical viewpoint the process of divorce had many similarities to that of breaking off an engagement. The Calvinist teaching on marriage rejected the traditional idea of annulling a marriage which had been consummated, except in the case of physical incapacity which had not been known or acknowledged before the wedding. It did, however, introduce the possibility of divorce and remarriage in certain very strictly controlled circumstances, and in this aspect of marriage granted to women rights (very nearly) equal to those of men.[90] Although a great deal of the consistory's time was spent on family arguments, including conflicts between spouses, wife beating, and other domestic abuse, every effort was made to reconcile couples. If finally that was not possible, in the face of proven adultery or abandonment, then divorce could be granted. Divorces were pronounced by the authorities after the proofs had been accepted and no further reconciliations were possible. In the case of abandonment, there was a somewhat different process. The length of time involved varied with the nature of the case, but in most instances, when all efforts had failed to bring the missing spouse back, public announcements were made from the pulpit at the main Sunday morning service three times at intervals of two weeks to allow the parties one final chance and to make the matter public for the community, and then if there was no response the divorce was declared final.[91]

---

[90]   OC 10:40-44 (1545), 10:110-114 (1565), first the causes for declaring null, then those for which a valid marriage could be ended.

[91]   If a man on a business trip did not return and there was no news of him, his wife must wait ten years before being declared free. If, however, a man known for his bad behavior abandoned his wife, and, after being convoked would not return, the wife had recourse. The announcement that he must appear would be made three times at two week intervals, from the pulpit at the main Sunday morning service and in the civil court, and several of his relatives would be notified. If he still did not appear, he would be declared banished and his wife would be released from the marriage bond. If a man abandoned his wife repeatedly and did not reform, she could also be released after his third punishment produced no change. In the case of man of bad conduct whose whereabouts were not known, the woman had to wait for a year, then she and the man's relatives must swear that they did not know where he was, and again the proclamations would be made from the pulpit in the same fashion as for other cases. If a woman left her husband, she should be notified in the same way as an absent husband; if she returned, and her husband suspected her of bad behavior further inquiry would be made to determine if there were grounds for divorce. If she did not return by the set date, the procedure would be same as for a husband who abandoned his wife. cf. OC 10:41-44, 10:111-113, 114. For an example of a man being ordered to return to answer to accusations of adultery (blasphemy, etc.), see RCP II, p. 68; on Aug. 6, 1556, Mme de Boi(n)ville asked to have her husband summoned "par trois quinzaines de venir responde sur plusieurs pointz" and the secretary goes on "et le dimanche suivant, 9e dudit mois, la premiere denunciation en fut faicte publicquement en chaire, au sermon de 8 heures, comme on a acoustumé." (For an earlier stage of M. de Boiville's behavior before the consistory, see chap. 7 at n.174.)

The Celebration of a Wedding in the City of Geneva

Among the most visible changes which the Reformed tradition made in the practice of marriage was the insistence on its communal character, and this applied to the liturgy as much as to the engagement. In Geneva, perhaps even more than elsewhere, this meant that every wedding, like every baptism, took place in the context of a regular service of the preaching of the word. Since weddings were allowed on almost any day at almost any service where there was preaching, couples had a wide range of choices in the city. (There were considerably fewer alternatives in a rural parish simply because there were fewer services.)[92] From the viewpoint of the rest of the parishioners at St. Pierre or St. Gervais or La Magdeleine, the requirement of a public rite in the context of the ordinarily scheduled worship meant that faithful members of the congregation would find themselves attending weddings much more frequently than in the past, even though they would not participate in the rest of the occasion's festivities unless they were specifically invited. For the bride and groom, there was a new experience of having their vows heard by anyone and everyone in their neighborhood who was in church at the time.

Couples were required to present themselves before the final bell at the beginning of the service because the wedding liturgy would precede the rest of worship. Anyone coming late would have to postpone the wedding until another service and usually to another day. While this might sound harsh, it was as much practical as disciplinary. The service began promptly after the bells, and the minister would not interrupt it to go back and do the wedding liturgy. There were rules about appropriate dress and festivities for weddings, such as the kind of headdresses virgin or widowed brides might wear and what musical fanfare was allowed: the wedding party should not be accompanied by musicians and "Swiss tambourines or other instruments."[93] A contemporary description of a wedding comes from the pen of a Catholic visitor, Antoine Cathelan, who spent some months in Geneva and Lausanne in 1552-53. First he gives a rather full picture of the festive procession.

> Carrying branches of rosemary or bouquets, the groom and his party come to find the bride at her residence, and they wait there. The bride is dressed as is customary here, i.e., if she is a widow she has her head covered and if a

---

92 Weddings in rural parishes were relatively infrequent; Charles Perrot indicates that he had only performed one during the several years he was in the villages of Moens and Genthod; Lambert, *Preaching, Praying, and Policing*, Appendix 4, p. 457. Given the paucity of weekday services, weddings were probably usually celebrated on Sunday mornings or the day of prayer.

93 OC 10:39-40 (1545), 10:108 (1561). For a description of the instruments see Cathelan quoted below in n.96.

virgin she has her hair loose. In either case she has a crown of flowers on her head and her companions each have a bouquet in their hand or bosom and then they go to the sermon when the bell rings. All the men go first as the vanguard, two by two, then the groom holding his bride by the hand for fear of losing her, and then at the end follow the women, two by two, as the rearguard. [94]

The hint of sarcasm heard in "for fear of losing her" increases when Cathelan begins to describe the service, contrasting it with his own (true) Roman fashion.

In this way they come to the door of the church (which they call the temple) and then each one takes his place, waiting for the preacher to begin. After the sermon the groom takes his bride by the hand again and leads her before the door of the choir, or where the great altar should be, and there the deacon, or when he is absent the minister, standing with head uncovered facing the people, joins them together using ceremonies as long as or longer than ours. [95]

Following the service the wedding party leaves the church in similar fashion and returns to the groom's home for dinner and, if they do not care what Calvin and his friends think, enjoy dancing or games. [96] Cathelan concludes his description

---

[94] Cathelan, *Passevent Parisien*, pp. 70-71: "Le fiancé avecques ses conviez, chacun tenant une branche de rosmarin, ou un bouquet en sa main, vont trouver la fiancée à son logis, qu'il attend là, avecques ses conviées. Et est accoustrée comme de par deçà, c'est à sçavoir si elle est veufve, en teste couverte, et si elle est pucelle, en tête deschevelée, avecques un chapeau de fleurs en teste, tant la veufve que la pucelle, et les femmes de sa compaignie chacune avecques son bouquet à la main ou au sein, et puis s'en vont au sermon qui sonne. Premièrement tous les hommes deux à deux au devant, pour faire l'avangarde, et puis le fiancé menant à la main sa fiancée pour peur de ne la perdre, et tout au dernier suivent les femmes deux à deux, pour faire l'arrière garde."

[95] Cathelan, *Passevent Parisien*, p. 71: "Et en tel ordonnance s'en vont jusques à la porte de l'eglise (qu'ilz appellent le temple) et puis chacun prent sa place, attendant que le prédicant commence, et après le sermon le fiancé reprend sa fiancée par la main, et la meine devant la porte du coeur, ou degrez là où souloit estre le grand autel: et là est le diacre, ou le ministre en son absence, tout debout à teste descouverte, sa face vers le peuple, les conjoinct par ses cérémonies aussi longues ou plus que les nostres, en protestant qu'il ne faict tout ce qu'il faict, sinon pour ratifier leur promesse (en présence de leur Eglise) jà au paravant faict entre eux."

[96] Cathelan, *Passevent Parisien*, p. 71: "Et puis au mesme ordre tous s'en retournent à la maison du fiancé, et après disner, chacun se retire pour faire place aux espousez pour deviser de leurs secretz privez, et ainsi le mariage et nopces sont consommez tout par ce moyen: et ceux qui ne ce soucient pas beaucoup de Calvin ny de ses compaignons, font tout le semblable que dessus, et davantage vont et retournent à l'église avecques un tabourin de Suysse, ou bien autres instrumentz, et après disner dansent ou jouent en chambre, et bien secrettement sur peine d'estre appellez en Consistoire."

with a comment on the wedding festivities – allowed or not. Placing the liturgy at the end of the service is the critical observer's accidental confusion of Genevan practice with that of Lausanne, where in 1551 weddings were moved to the end of the service.[97] It is also clear that this account does not include registering the marriage in the parish book (a formality which would have followed the service and delayed the departure Cathelan describes). These points further contribute to the impression that this Catholic visitor does not present an exact picture of Genevan practice.

In Geneva the order of the service would be as follows. After the final bell sounded, the minister probably went to stand before the couple at the front of the church. The service then began with the usual opening invocation, the same heard on Sunday mornings and at the beginning of the baptismal service.[98] A Biblical description of marriage followed, then a series of questions and answers to the couple about their intention to marry, to the gathered congregation about any impediments, then to the groom and the bride individually. Next the minister confirmed that the couple were married, exhorted them with Biblical texts and concluded the ceremony with a prayer and blessing, and began the ordinary service planned for that hour. The couple was of course obliged to remain for the entire service until the benediction at the end of worship: that was the point of having the wedding at a preaching service. According to the ministers and consistory, this rule applied also to the rest of the wedding party, although the Senate did not enact it as law until 1560.[99] Occasionally, newly-weds would find themselves obligated to stay even beyond the end of the regular service if there was a baptism after the preaching...!

---

[97] See Witte & Kingdon, *Courtship, Engagement, and Marriage*, p. 448 n.13, citing Henri Vuilleumier, *Histoire de l'Eglise réformée du Pays de Vaud sous le régime bernois* (1927-33),1:346; Philip Benedict, *Christ's Churches Purely Reformed* (New Haven: Yale, 2002), pp. 491-92.

[98] *La forme des prières*, OS II, pp. 51-56.

[99] There is no record of the parishioners who had come to worship that day wandering out during the wedding, to return later for the service, as they did at baptisms. However, the reverse was sometimes true: some members of the wedding party might come to the wedding liturgy, leave during the regular service, and return to bear the happy couple company back to the festivities. The Senate had been persuaded to legislate that all who came to a baptism must attend the whole service, and the consistory tried to extend the same rule to weddings. See rebuke of Jaques Papa on March 20, 1550, *Consist.* V, pp. 40-41: "Auquel furent faictes les remonstrances que Messieurs ont esté faict ung editz que tous ceux qui yront encompagnés, tant aux mariages que en batesme, faut ouy le presche." The editors say that an edict requiring people coming to the church with the wedding or baptism party to stay for the service was (finally) issued in 1560 but was not very effective; p. 41 n. 281.

The Frequency and Distribution of Wedding Services

From the beginning of the reform the ministers had proposed that written marriage (and baptismal) records should be kept. This provision appears in Farel's liturgy and again in Calvin's Strasbourg liturgy in 1542, as well as in pastors' requests to the Senate in Dec. 1538 and Feb. 1540.[100] However, nothing concrete happened in the city parishes of Geneva until December 1549. Then a new command was issued along with instructions for making chests in which to keep the baptismal and marriage records, and a book registering both rites began promptly on January 1.[101] It appears that in the interest of simplicity, there was only one physical book, with baptisms recorded at one end and marriages at the other. One turned the book upside down in moving from one rite to the other, so that in both cases the entries would read from the top left.[102] The books for St. Pierre, St. Gervais, and La Magdeleine have been examined for eight years of Calvin's ministry: 1550-51, 1553, 1555, 1557, 1559, 1562, and 1564 for St. Pierre and St. Gervais, and all the years 1550-1564 for La Magdeleine. Tabulations are found in Appendix Two. The fruits of this "counting operation" make it possible to identify patterns of practice in the three parishes from 1550 to 1564.

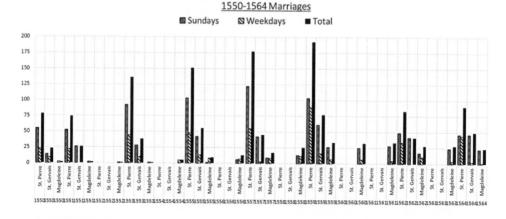

100 Farel, *La maniere et fasson*, p. C4v. OS II, p. 56. Dec. 10, 1538, RC III, p. 515; Feb. 23, 1540, RC V, p. 137. The village parish of Satigny actually began its baptismal records in 1542; cf. Spierling, *Infant Baptism in Reformation Geneva*, p. 148.

101 Dec. 23, 1549, OC 21:459 (RC 44 f290v); Senate agrees "pour ce que nous somes au commecement de l'annee." archives@etat.ge.ch accessed Aug. 5, 2013. In effect, the new year would begin in two days; see chap. 4, at n.63. Evidently action was taken immediately because the first baptism is recorded on Wed., Jan. 1, 1550, at St. Pierre at 8 a.m. by Fabri; one is recorded on Jan. 2 at St. Gervais [at the ordinary time of 7 a.m.] by Des Gallars; see Appendix One: Baptismal Records.

102 My thanks to Jeannine Olson for this information. The records are now filmed and access to the originals is restricted, so I used the filmed version.

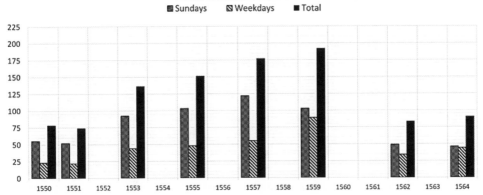

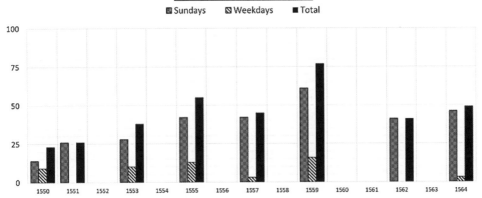

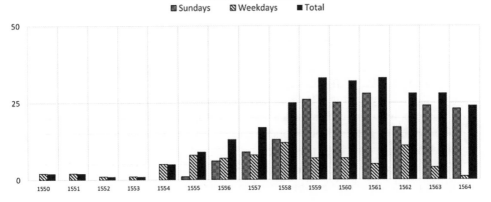

The marriage books reveal that Sunday dawn and Sunday afternoon were the most popular times for weddings, with Monday mornings as the third favored time. In fact, almost all marriages were celebrated at these services, with only a small handful left for later in the week. The consistency of this pattern, and the limited number of weddings recorded for La Magdeleine after the records began in 1550, lead to some interesting conclusions about the practice of marriage in Greater Geneva. It can be extrapolated that in the 1540s, when La Magdeleine had only one service on Sunday and that was catechism, there were no Sunday weddings in that parish. When the main morning service was established as a regular thing in 1549, this did not change; there are no Sunday weddings recorded for La Magdeleine after the registers begin in 1550. Only in mid-1555, when the Sunday afternoon service was begun in this parish, did weddings begin to appear; the first was celebrated on the afternoon of Sept. 22, 1555. This means that until the middle of 1555 all the Sunday weddings in Greater Geneva were performed at St. Pierre. The logical corollary is that persons did not legally have to be married in their home parish, although that was probably the normal custom in most places. Furthermore, only eleven (weekday) weddings are recorded for La Magdeleine for the five years 1550-1554, even though this was the most populous parish before the Reformation and hundreds of baptisms were celebrated at La Magdeleine (which, since those had to be held in the home parish, demonstrate that this was still a very busy church community). In fact, more babies were baptized at La Magdeleine than at St. Pierre, fairly clear evidence that the limited number of weddings at La Magdeleine was owed to the fact that the couples of this parish regularly went to St. Pierre to be married, often by Calvin.

Probably people living in Greater Geneva were married there, and those living in St. Gervais were married there, but it seems that engaged couples might consider which minister they wanted to have perform their wedding. They could even schedule such a thing, at least indirectly. The ministers who were going to preach at any given service were organized without regard to the wishes of the parishioners, but the wedding liturgy did not have to be performed by the preacher; another pastor who was present could officiate. Normally, most couples probably came to their parish church on the day and at the time which suited them best; after all, the liturgy was the same, no matter where they went. They would be married by whichever minister was preaching at that service. Others might choose to come to a particular worship time in order to have the minister who was scheduled there perform their wedding. This seems to have been the case quite often for Calvin at Sunday afternoon services. It was much less common for a couple to ask a specific pastor to come to a specific service to marry them, but it did happen in the case of family or close friends. For example, Calvin performed the wedding of his dear friend Laurent de Normandie to Anne Colladon at St. Pierre at dawn on Sunday, Sept. 14, 1550, although he was certainly not preaching at that service. Another example was a wedding Calvin celebrated on Sunday afternoon at La Magdeleine on Oct. 27, 1560, although he had not been preaching regularly in that parish for over a year (and had never done Sunday afternoons there). [103]

While many wedding liturgies were held for a single bride and groom, it was also not at all uncommon for two or more couples to be married at the same time. The service would be the same: the prayers would not be repeated more than once, but (presumably) each couple would be asked individually for their assent. At least five times in the recorded instances of his ministry Calvin married four couples at once, on Sunday afternoons in the mid-1550s. [104] This was the second most popular time; Sunday dawn was likely to be chosen by even more couples, and thus the chance of being the only bride and groom at one's own wedding liturgy was even less then.

For services which were popular for weddings, there were some practical considerations for the whole community. Modern readers might think first of the response of the couples to sharing their wedding with other pairs, but this was probably less of an issue in the strongly corporate society of early modern Europe than it would be today. However, given the Reformed insistence on celebrating marriages at parish worship, many more people than the couple were affected by the addition of weddings to the regular services. From the viewpoint of the rest of the parish who were present at Sunday dawn or on Sunday afternoons, one might consider how a wedding – especially if conducted for four or five couples – would extend the worship service, right at the beginning. In particular, would this affect the length of the sermon? For some pastors it no doubt did so and they probably abbreviated their expositions. However, a very limited sample suggests that there does not appear to be a correlation between the length of Calvin's sermons and the marriages he performed on those days; that is, he does not seem to have shortened what he was going to say. [105] If he did not limit the length of his sermon

---

[103] See Appendix Five for Calvin's weddings.

[104] See Appendix Five for Calvin's weddings.

[105] Occasions when Calvin does both wedding and baptism: Sat. June 13, 1551, in La Magdeleine, but there is no extant sermon. On Sun. Feb. 12, 1553, in St. Pierre, the sermon #6 on Ps. 119:41-48, the length of the sermon seems average. Mon. Sept. 6, 1557, in La Magdeleine, the sermon on Isa. 32:17-20, which is slightly shorter than others but in fact not the shortest (Wed. Sept. 1 is shorter.) Others: Nov. 2, 1559, and Dec. 18, 1559, at St. Pierre; the Nov. 2 sermon was preached but not recorded.

when he married one or more couples, then there must have been a number of days when the service ran over time!

To put in perspective the frequency with which parishioners and preachers would find their services extended by weddings, it is worth noting the relatively limited number of days which did not include this liturgy. In 1555, a year for which we have extant sermons for Calvin on almost every Sunday afternoon, it can be seen that he performed weddings nineteen times for a total of thirty couples, leaving thirty-one Sunday afternoons when he was preaching but there was no wedding. In this same year, pastors Cop and Bourgoing were alternating at St. Pierre's dawn services; Cop performed weddings on eighteen Sundays for a total of thirty-two couples, while Bourgoing did fifteen services for thirty-five couples. Cop also did two weddings for two couples and Des Gallars did one wedding for four couples, all on Sunday afternoons when Calvin was preaching. Almost half of all couples married on Sundays had their weddings at dawn (67) in 33 services; the remaining group (36) were married in 22 weddings in the afternoon. The weekday numbers for this same year 1555 at St. Pierre were 48 couples in 38 services, most at the Monday dawn service (39 couples in 29 services) with significantly smaller numbers on Wednesday (7 couples at 7 services) and Friday (2 at 2).

When one considers that everyone who came to hear Geneva's most famous preacher was also necessarily present for all of the marriages on Sunday afternoon when Calvin was in the pulpit, and that everyone who fulfilled their Sunday duty of attending worship at dawn was also in attendance for the weddings at that hour, it becomes clear how large a part this "personal" liturgy played in the common worship life of a parish. By the same token, a couple planning their wedding day would also have to be prepared to share that special service with at least one other bride and groom, if not more. At 27 of the 55 marriage services at St. Pierre on Sundays in 1555, there were at least two couples and in one case as many as six (March 24 by Cop), once five (March 17 by Bourgoing), and three times there were four (Feb. 17 by Bourgoing, June 16 by Calvin, and Aug. 18 by Des Gallars) and six times there were three couples. On weekdays a bride and groom were more likely to have a wedding service of their own, but even on weekdays this was not a foregone conclusion; the Monday dawn service at St. Pierre in 1555 included eight times when there were two couples and once when three were married at the same time. The experience of celebrating weddings in Calvin's Geneva was very definitely communal!

II: Baptism

Baptism, as one of the two Protestant sacraments and the traditional mark of entrance into salvation, was very important both theologically and practically. The continuities between medieval and Protestant ideas about baptism were greater than in the case of the Lord's Supper, as is evident particularly by contrast with the "radical" ways of the Anabaptists and Spiritualists. There were two fronts on which Protestants had to define their teaching and practice; in Geneva, the inherited weight of the Roman doctrine and tradition was stronger than Anabaptist challenges, but the reverse was true in Calvin's Strasbourg congregation and thus he had experience as pastor to people influenced by both perspectives. The focus here is Geneva but the issues raised in Strasbourg will also be considered in passing.

There are three main parts of this discussion of baptism in Calvin's Geneva. The first is an overview of the historical religious context. The second part provides a summary of the development of Calvin's teaching and then examines the issues loosely related to the theory and practice of baptizing illegitimate babies and the role of godfathers. The third section provides a picture of the day-to-day rhythms of baptism "on the ground" in Geneva's three main city parishes.

The Historical and Historiographical Context

Virtually no one in early modern Europe questioned that baptism was the foundation of the Christian life. Thus, precisely what it signified or did, and how it was practiced, were matters of intense importance not only for theologians but also for every devout person in the whole society. For Calvin and for Protestants generally, baptism was reformed in various ways from medieval teaching and practice, yet it also maintained significant continuities. A brief outline of the tradition can illumine the religious issues at stake in the changes introduced in sixteenth-century Europe.

The Historical Religious Context

According to Roman doctrine, the sacrament of baptism was understood to wash away the original sin with which every child is born, and thus the rite of baptism was essential for salvation. Without it the unbaptized infant would go to limbo. Therefore, baptism was the one vital sacrament and it could be performed by anyone; all that was necessary was the Trinitarian formula, water, and the intent to baptize as a Christian.[106] Naturally, midwives were regularly in the position of

---

[106] It has been noted that theology and liturgy followed rather different lines. For example, theologians did not consider exorcism necessary but this had become one of the key aspects of the baptismal liturgy; Old, *The Shaping of the Reformed Baptismal Rite*, pp. 10-16, esp. p. 15.

baptizing newborns if it appeared that their deaths were imminent. A stronger baby could wait a day for a church baptismal liturgy, which included much more than the three basics which anyone could do. Among the possible additional ceremonies were multiple exorcisms, "blessing" salt and water, breathing in the child's face and anointing it with spittal and later with chrism, presenting a lighted candle, a white robe, and other symbolic actions; the exact details often varied according to the region.

The institution and role of godparents was quite significant on many levels. [107] Becoming a godparent established a spiritual kinship, *compaternitas*, between the person and the whole family of the infant, and this was important socially as well as spiritually. Usually there were at least two or three godfathers and godmothers, and often (many) more. Naming and presenting the baby for baptism was the prerogative of godparents. Normally parents did not participate in the baptism itself; the mother had usually not yet recovered from childbirth, and the father was occupied with the festivities of the baptismal party to which family and friends were invited. In fact, the guests were not expected to attend the liturgy in the church. Even if the father was present, he was not considered fit to present his baby, because it had been conceived in carnal sinfulness and the father, as a participant in that conception, was disqualified from the holy state necessary to offer the baby to God. Godparents had no such sinful relationship to the infant and therefore they could establish a spiritual relationship through baptism.

As with other aspects of faith and religious practice, Protestants combined a sharp reaction against what they saw as the errors of the Roman church with the insights which they believed they had learned from the Bible. The latter usually came first and led to the rejection of what seemed to contradict scripture. The chronological order was preaching to instruct the people in the true Biblical meaning and then, when at least a significant number of laity had been convinced, action was taken to change the liturgical practices.

Theologically, Protestants began by attacking the idea that the rite of baptism in itself is essential and effective for salvation. Lutherans would gradually move back to a much greater emphasis on the necessity of the baptismal act, while the

---

[107] Much has been written on the social context and practice of godparentage; for one well-known exponent, see Bossy, *Christianity in the West 1400-1700*, pp. 13-19; Bossy notes the interwoven history of the roles of families and church in naming babies for saints (including liturgical insistence on this), p. 17. Idem., "Godparenthood: the Fortunes of a Social Institution in Early Modern Christianity" in *Religion and Society in Early Modern Europe 1500-1800*, ed. K. von Greyerz (London: German Historical Institute, 1984), pp. 194-201; note the exclusion of natural parents, p. 195. A very helpful recent overview, oriented to Geneva, is found in Spierling, *Infant Baptism in Reformation Geneva*, chap. 4.

Reformed firmly denied this point and its corollary of limbo for unbaptized infants. Inextricably tied to this issue was the question of the appropriate or possible agents of the sacrament. Those (like the Reformed) who rejected the idea that the ritual act as such was necessary for salvation, insisted on baptism by pastors in the context of public worship and strongly opposed baptism by midwives or any other laity. Protestants retained the basic doctrine that baptism is constituted by the Trinitarian formula, water, and the intent to baptize as a Christian, but they generally discarded or outright denied any need for the ceremonies which had made the Roman liturgy a complex ritual. Again, the degree of change varied; for example, Lutherans continued to practice an exorcism while the Reformed did away with this entirely.[108] One of the key continuities between Protestants and the traditional teaching and practice was the affirmation of infant baptism. This guaranteed a clear and visible difference between Protestants and the various Radical reformers, whether the latter practiced believer's baptism or spiritual (immaterial) baptism.

For all who broke with Rome, the question of faith became a significant factor in defining the grounds for baptism because of the primary affirmation that salvation is by faith alone. Part of the developing diversity therefore had to do with the definition of faith. Luther, for whom the key aspect of faith was trust, taught that infants do in fact have faith, although he put increasing weight on other issues in defending infant baptism.[109] Some Anabaptists tended to define faith as a personal act of confession, and thus both it and baptism were only possible for "adults" (those who could think and speak for themselves). The Reformed developed the teaching that the faith of the covenant people is the foundation for baptizing the children of believers. For Calvin, faith is certain knowledge of (including trust in) God's good-will toward us, founded on the truth of the free promises in Christ, which are revealed to the mind and sealed on the heart by the Holy Spirit.[110] This definition includes both cognitive and

---

[108] See Luther's *Taufbüchlein*, in WA 12, p. 42. Farel's liturgy explicitly rejects "salt, oil, and spit," *La maniere et fasson*, p. B5r. "Liturgical Practices and Forms," p. 203. Salt and spit were associated with exorcism; Old, *The Shaping of the Reformed Baptismal Rite*, pp. 9-13.

[109] Old, *The Shaping of the Reformed Baptismal Rite*, pp. 134, n.68, cites Lorenz Girönvik, *Die Taufe in der Theologie Martin Luthers* (Abo: Abo Akademi, 1968), pp. 154-72.

[110] *Inst.* 3.2.7. The exact wording is "Nunc iusta fidei definitio nobis constabit si dicamus esse divinae erga nos benevolentiae firmam certamque cognitionem, quae gratuitae in Christo promissionis veritate fundata, per Spiritum sanctum et revelatur mentibus nostris et cordibus obsignatur." From 1539, this remains unchanged to the end; cf. OS IV, p. 16. Here "trust" expresses "persuasion," cf. 3.2.14 *et passim*. For another lay-oriented version of this definition, see chap. 6 at nn.203ff.

existential dimensions; with regard to what is outwardly visible, however, what can be tested is only the confession of faith (an act of intellect and will) and the behavior befitting that profession. Personal acquaintance with and trust in God are vital for salvation, but the context in which people come to faith is normally the visible church, and the church covenant was made with the whole people of God. For that reason, the confession of faith required for baptism can be made by parents (or guardians) who are members of the church, for their infant children. The covenant relationship is based on the Old Testament sacrament of circumcision, and those who make the baptismal promises affirm that covenant, and vow to rear the children in it so that they can make their own profession.

This Reformed defense of infant baptism has often been regarded as at least inconsistent, if not a contradiction of the claim to be reformed according to scripture alone. Debating or even examining the merits or defects of the Reformed defense of infant baptism is not the purpose of the present work. However, Calvin's exposition of Genesis 17 sketched below may offer some further evidence for his own conviction that baptizing the newborn children of Christians, in the context of the covenant community, was indeed established by clear Biblical teaching.

Some Historiographical Comments

The subject of baptism and the debates about infant baptism fill many books. Even those relating to Calvin's theology and practice are too numerous to list here. Since the primary purpose of the present study is to examine the relationship between Calvin's teaching and Geneva's worship practice, or to place the two in conversation, the discussion of secondary literature on theology is reduced to a minimum, and citation of works on the wider implications of baptism in Geneva are limited. Among the most useful secondary sources for this study are Karen Spierling's very helpful *Infant Baptism in Reformation Geneva* (2005), parts of William Naphy's *Calvin and the Consolidation of the Genevan Reformation* (1994) and Hughes O. Old, *The Shaping of the Reformed Baptismal Rite in the Sixteenth Century* (1992). Because the object here is to explore what was happening in worship in Geneva and how that was shaped by its key architect, Calvin, the reformer's writings, the baptismal records, and the minutes of various councils or other bodies are the main sources for this study.

Calvin's Teaching

John Calvin was the chief architect of the Genevan church, but his work was clearly influenced by the fact that he was a second generation reformer. This is perhaps particularly true with regard to the discussion and practice which shaped baptismal teaching and liturgies. Much of the work had already been done by his predecessors, defining Biblical teaching against traditional or new errors and translating and revising liturgies. This is not to say that Calvin did not set his own mark on the Reformed sacrament of baptism, but it is sufficient to survey his stance on the common issues before exploring some of the ways that his teaching was heard, and Genevan worship was experienced, by those in the pews.

An Overview of the Development of Calvin's Teaching on Baptism

As with most aspects of Calvin's theology, the chronological as well as logical place to begin is the *Institutes of the Christian Religion*, but this is not the only important source and it also underwent significant development on the question of baptism. It is useful to distinguish the stages of teaching and the various sources in which it was presented.

The *Institutes* of 1536 and Catechism of 1537

The first edition of the *Institutes* names and explains the purposes of the sacrament, how to receive and use it, and identifies and argues against the most dangerous (or prevalent) errors currently in Calvin's view. The first and longest section discusses the two purposes: serving believers' faith before God, and their confession before the world, and includes anonymous critiques of common errors which the knowledgeable would recognize as Roman, Lutheran, or Zwinglian. Calvin explains that baptism is a sign to confirm the forgiveness of sins. It consoles believers by showing them a sure testimony of being integrated into Christ's death and new life, to share in all His blessings. Baptism is not merely a token or pledge. It assures believers that their condemnation has been removed by the imputation of Christ's righteousness even though they are never free of sin. On the other hand, the water as such does not have power to accomplish anything and the baptismal rite does not have the power to wash away original sin or to save. It is given once to be effective for the entire life, baptism into lifelong mortification and vivification. The second section on baptism explains how this sacrament should be received and used, and concludes with an extended and explicit polemic against Anabaptist ideas. [111] Before discussing the *Institutes* further, however, it is worthwhile to examine Calvin's first French exposition of baptism for the Genevan church.

In 1537 the first Geneva catechism summarized Calvin's teaching. After naming the two purposes of baptism, the greatest part of the text is devoted to the first one: serving the believer's faith before God.

---

[111] *Institutes 1536*, OS I, pp. 127-36.

> Baptism specifically represents two things: ... purification ... and morti-
> fication of our flesh... we are buried in His death so that we may walk in
> newness of life. These things do not signify that water is the cause or even
> instrument of purification and regeneration, but only that the knowledge
> of such gifts is received in this sacrament, since we are said to receive and
> obtain what we believe is given to us by the Lord, either that we first come
> to know this or that, having previously known it, we are more certainly
> persuaded of it. [112]

Calvin's final statement suggests that he is thinking of the community which is
present at the sacrament, whether it is their child or someone else's who is being
baptized. The faith of all those who hear is strengthened when they are reminded
by the rite of baptism of the grace that God gives them throughout their lives.

The second and shorter section of the 1537 treatment of baptism deals with
confession before the world and concludes with the one sentence affirmation of
infant baptism.

> Likewise it serves our confession before men, for it is a mark by which we
> publicly make profession that we want to be numbered among God's
> people, so that with all the faithful we may serve and honor one God with
> the same worship [*religion*]. Since this is so, that it is chiefly by baptism that
> the Lord's covenant is confirmed with us, it is right that we should baptize
> our children, who are participants in the eternal covenant by which the
> Lord promises that He will be God, not only to us but also to our
> descendents (Gen. 17:1-14). [113]

The second purpose of the sacraments, public confession, is very plainly linked
with the baptizing of believers' children. This appears to be Calvin's indirect
response to Anabaptist ecclesiology, affirming a different understanding of
membership in the visible church. To those who insisted on believer's baptism
as public witness and confession of faith to constitute the true and visible church,
Calvin answers with the public confession of the whole community which is
grounded in the "eternal covenant" (initiated with the family of Abraham, to
which Christians and their children now belong) and manifested in the baptism
of believers' infant children. This is affirming the church which already exists as
a given, God's gift. Calvin rejects the "Anabaptist" claim for baptism as marking
the elect. For him it is a mark of the church; participation in it is a mark of
Christians and that mark belongs to the body of those who confess the faith.

---

[112] *Institutes 1536*, OS I, p. 412.

[113] *Institutes 1536*, OS I, p. 412.

Developments on Baptism in the *Institutes*: Latin and French

The period between 1536 and 1539/41 was one of the most important times of growth for Calvin the theologian, as he became a full-time pastor with daily responsibility for an increasing number of parishioners. [114] By 1539 and especially by the time he translated this edition of the *Institutes* into French in 1541, Calvin's teaching on baptism in particular had been forced to grapple with various pastoral issues. The one chapter on the sacraments in 1536 becomes three in 1539: a general discussion of the sacraments, baptism, and the Lord's Supper. The 1536 treatment of baptism is expanded in various ways, but the most obvious factor is additional material on infant baptism; this is so extensive that it would become a full chapter in 1559, almost all dating from 1539 (except a section written in response to Servetus). Others have treated this matter from several viewpoints; Willem Balke, *Calvin and the Anabaptist Radicals* (1973/81) and John Riggs, *The Development of Calvin's Baptismal Theology 1536-1560* (1985). [115] Here what is of particular interest is the form of this teaching as expressed in the first French *Institutes*. [116]

In 1541 Calvin published the translation of his *Institutes* into French for the first time, in the same years when he was also writing the *Ecclesiastical Ordinances* and *La formes des prieres*, the two texts which would shape the experience of worship in Geneva. While the French *Institutes* was essentially a translation of the Latin, it was also consciously and visibly fitted to its vernacular audiences. A comparison of the 1539 and 1541 editions makes this very clear. [117] Calvin deliberately made small but significant changes and/or additions or deletions to accommodate his different readers. He did not alter the theology, but he did re-touch the way he wrote in order to communicate to a less educated audience, people to whom he was as much pastor as teacher. It is notable that the most

---

[114] It is perhaps worth noting that Calvin's great older contemporary Martin Luther was not a regular parish pastor for most of his life. He did serve as pastor at times, both before he broke with Rome and after, but most of his life as a reformer he was involved in the leadership of his local parish primarily by preaching once on Sundays, and sometimes he did not do that. (There was a period beginning in 1530 when he almost completely stopped preaching; cf. Paul Glaue, "Der Predigtmüde Luther," *Luther* 11 (1929), pp. 68-81; cf. pp. 77-78.) This is not to question Luther's pastoral character but only to point out that he did not have the same routine parish responsibilities which Calvin carried throughout his adult life.

[115] Balke, *Calvin and the Anabaptist radicals*, esp. pp. 101-08. John Riggs, *The Development of Calvin's Baptismal Theology, 1536-1560* (Ph.D. dissertation, Notre Dame University 1985).

[116] Calvin/Millet, *Institution de la religion chrétienne (1541)*. Calvin/McKee, *Institutes-1541 French Edition*. (For clarity these are identified by the editor or translator plus title.)

[117] Elsie Anne McKee, "The First French *Institutes*: Calvin's Pastoral Voice," *Princeton Seminary Bulletin* (n.s. 2009-2010), pp. 161-79, esp. 165ff.

extensive differences between 1539 and 1541 are found precisely in the chapter on baptism.[118] Many examples could be cited; for present purposes it is enough to point out that Calvin twice explains the controversial text Acts 19:4-5 about Paul "re-baptizing" some disciples. In the 1539 *Institutes* this is discussed only once, and later editions of both Latin and French drop the second treatment, but in 1541 Calvin felt the need to emphasize how he believed the Anabaptists had misunderstood this passage and so he discussed it twice.[119]

The theologian-pastor's context in Strasbourg at the time suggests some reasons: his parish was made up of French-speaking religious refugees who included a number of (former) Anabaptists. Radical religious views were hardly surprising since refugees, whether Anabaptist or not, were almost certain to be very committed to their convictions if they had been driven out by persecution for their faith, or chosen exile to escape it and be able to worship as they believed scripture teaches. A literalist approach to the Bible was also natural for less educated people. Hence it was important if one wished to convert such people from Anabaptism to explain specific "stumbling block" texts in a way which made sense to a literalist mind-set. In fact, whether it was the material which went into the French *Institutes* of 1541 or his preaching or other means, Calvin's efforts were evidently fairly successful because he managed to "convert" at least a number of them (including a couple named Jehan Stordeur and Idelette de Bure!).[120]

The 1539 and (further developed) 1541 *Institutes* chapter on baptism not only shows how Calvin expanded his teaching, but it serves as one place where development in his thought becomes visible. (The old legend says that he never changed his mind, but he certainly did learn and develop, and sometimes even change particular details.[121]) In the course of the discussion of baptism in 1536, Calvin denied that baptism is an instrument of grace (italics added).

---

[118] The *Opera Selecta* editors believe that this chapter might have begun as a separate treatise, parallel to the *Short Treatise on the Lord's Supper*; cf. OS V, pp. 303-04 n.i. Olivier Millet and others reject this idea, but do affirm that the translation is rather looser in this section than in others; cf. Calvin/Millet, *Institution de la religion chrétienne (1541)*, pp. 1270-71 n.54.

[119] See Calvin, *Institutio 1539*, Wevers, pp. 273-74 (11.10.43-78); p. 287 (11.25.60-61). Calvin/Millet, *Institution de la religion chrétienne 1541*, pp. 514, 542. Calvin/McKee, *Institutes-1541 French Edition*, pp. 519, 542-43. Cf. OS V, notes on pp. 303-06; French 1560.

[120] See Beza's biography; this section is copied by Colladon. OC 21:31-32, 62. Balke discusses Calvin's contacts with Anabaptists both in Geneva and in Strasbourg, including Jean Stordeur; see *Calvin and the Anabaptist Radicals*, pp. 80-84, 127-38.

[121] McKee, "Calvin Never Changed His Mind," pp. 18-36.

> For this analogy or similitude is the most certain rule of the sacraments, so that in physical things we may see and consider spiritual ones when by means of these figures God was pleased to represent them to us. Not because such graces are enclosed in or bound to the sacrament, *or because the sacrament is an organ or instrument* [of such graces] by which they are conferred on us, but because by these tokens God testifies His will to us, namely that He wishes to lavish all these things on us. [122]

It is notable that the italicized phrase disappears in 1539 although the rest of the passage does not change (bar substitution of synonyms), and this revised form is carried through 1559. [123] A second point of development is the issue of infant faith. In 1536 Calvin affirmed that because no one is saved without faith, infants have faith in common with adults, [124] but in 1539 he revised this view. Having backed off from saying that the faith of grown people and babies is the same, Calvin still wants to refute what he calls the Anabaptists' claim that God "cannot manifest Himself" to babies in some fashion. To say that is to denigrate God's power. In the Latin Calvin goes on to explain that he does not affirm that infants have faith "as we know it"; he prefers to leave that undetermined. [125] In the 1541 French he changes to the first person plural and makes it clear that he believes God acts but refuses to be more specific; "we do not want to affirm that babies have faith because we do not know how God works in them," [126] but that God does work is clearly implied.

After his exposition of the purposes of baptism, Calvin deals at length with various arguments against infant baptism, explaining his interpretation of the disputed scriptural texts and refuting attacks. It is worth highlighting another example of a slight but interesting difference between the 1539 Latin and the 1541 French. The Latin simply says that the truth of circumcision (like that of baptism) is the testimony of a good conscience. The French recasts this to make the meaning clearer for lay readers; even though it was given to babies, circumcision "was still a sacrament of the righteousness of faith, a sign of repentance and

---

122 OS I, p. 133; cf. *Institution 1536*, p. 134.

123 *Institutio 1539*, Wevers, p. 272 (11.9.12). *Inst.* 4.15.14, OS V, p. 295.

124 OS I, p. 136: "Quare manet fixa sententia, nullos nisi fide salvos fieri, sive pueri sint, sive adulti."

125 *Institutio 1539*, Wevers, p. 283 (11.20.79-83): "Non quod eadem esse fide praeditos temere affirmare velim, quam in nobis experimur (quod in suspenso relinquere malim) verum ut istorum stolidam arrogantiam paululum coerceam: qui prout inflata illis bucca fuerit, secure quidvis aut negant aut asserunt." *Inst.* 4.16.19, OS, p. 323, n .f.

126 Calvin/ McKee, *Institutes-1541 French Edition*, p. 535. Calvin/Millet, *Institution de la religion chrétienne 1541*, p. 1297: "Non pas que nous veuillons affermer que les enfans ayent Foy, d'autant que nous ne scavons comment Dieu besongne en eux."

regeneration."[127] The whole discussion concludes with a strong affirmation that attacks on infant baptism "diminish the comfort that the Lord wanted to give us by His promise, and by so much obscure the glory of His name," with the consequence that people will be ungrateful and neglect to educate their children in the faith.[128] The pastoral intent is obvious; fidelity to scripture is essential, but attention to the people for whom the Holy Spirit spoke is the necessary corollary. For that reason, it may be worthwhile to elaborate a little on the doctrine in the 1541 *Institutes*.

Calvin begins the section on infant baptism with a pastoral explanation for his teaching. Bearing in mind the need to address literalists and the fact that his simple and unwary readers may be confused by the fact that the Anabaptists appeal to scripture and reject infant baptism as a human invention, Calvin proceeds to give a thumbnail lesson on how to read scripture. First he reiterates that he has already proved that the baptism of believers' children is Biblical; he then explains that it is not enough to understand the rite but one must grasp the teaching of the promises which are given in baptism, all of which are based on Christ. Since everyone who is saved is saved through Christ, the promises made to Abraham and his descendants were the same as those to Christians and thus circumcision and baptism have the same function though different forms. Having proved (at least to his own satisfaction) that infant baptism is Biblical, Calvin turns to the benefit which this sacrament gives to both parents and children. It seals and witnesses God's goodness in adòpting believers' children "to the thousandth generation." The act of baptism to seal the promise is God's generosity to human weakness.[129] In Calvin's discussion of the disputed scriptural texts, one important addition here is the affirmation that the act of baptism is not essential for salvation if there is a legitimate hindrance. At this point the argument is more hypothetical: if a child who was instructed died before the rite it would of course be saved.[130] The question of unbaptized babies would be one of the significant pastoral concerns in later editions of the

---

[127] *Institutio 1539*, Wevers, p. 284 (11.22.41); Calvin/Millet, *Institution de la religion chrétienne 1541*, p. 1307: "Car la Circoncision, pourtant si elle estoit baillée aux petis enfans, ne laissoit point d'estre Sacrement de la justice de la Foy, signe de Penitence et regeneration." Calvin/McKee, *Institutes-1541 French Edition*, p. 540. *Inst.* 4.16.21, OS V, p. 326 n.e.

[128] Calvin/McKee, *Institutes-1541 French Edition*, pp. 544-45. Calvin/Millet, *Institution de la religion chrétienne 1541*, pp.1315-16.

[129] Calvin/McKee, *Institutes-1541 French Edition*, pp. 520-27. Calvin/Millet, *Institution de la religion chrétienne 1541*, pp. 1269-83.

[130] Calvin/McKee, *Institutes-1541 French Edition*, pp. 527-45. Calvin/Millet, *Institution de la religion chrétienne 1541*, pp. 1283-1316.

Institutes, along with other words of comfort. In 1543 Calvin adds that when the devout are troubled in conscience they can recall their baptism for reassurance of the unique and perpetual absolution in Christ's blood; this is an expansion of an idea touched on in 1536. In 1559 there is a stronger affirmation of baptism as an instrument of the promised grace as far as God works through external means.[131]

Several additions over the course of the years seem to have in view particularly the situation of scattered Christians in France. This is manifest in various ways, especially with regard to the relationship between baptism and the wider society. In 1536 Calvin had given qualified approval to the Roman baptism which he and others received before they were converted (to the reformed faith), in order to refute the Anabaptist claim for rebaptism. Like other Protestants Calvin said that the sacrament was not harmed by the impious priests who performed it.[132] In the following years he added several further nuances to this, primarily to deal pastorally with the fears of parents faced with a sickly newborn. In the 1543 Latin and the French translation of 1545 he applies what he had already said about the act of baptism not being essential for salvation to the context of his fellow believers under the cross. The first issue is to insure that baptism is treated with appropriate respect, and that normally involves receiving it in the church which God ordained to administer it.

> For when we do not treat [the sign] with contempt or carelessness, we are free of all danger. That is why the best thing is to give such honor to God's ordinance that we do not take the sacraments anywhere except where He has placed them. Now He has given their distribution to the church. Therefore when we cannot receive them from the church, let us not think that the grace of the Holy Spirit is so tied to the sacraments that we cannot obtain its power by the word of God alone.[133]

When church baptism is not possible, God's grace is still available. Calvin continued to try to make his point clearer, both to Latin audiences (1545) and French (1551). Believers' babies are baptized not to make them God's children but to declare that they already are members of Christ's body. The seal of baptism does not give power to God's promise (which does not need such help) but confirms

---

[131] OS I, p. 128 = *Inst.* 4.15.4, 14 & 15.

[132] OS I, p. 133 = *Inst.* 4.15.16.

[133] *Inst.* 4.15.22; this paragraph added in 1559, except for the 4 concluding sentences from 1545 & 1543. *Institution de la Religion chrestienne 1560*, vol. 4, p. 337.

the promise to us. The French repeats this personal application: it is "to make us more certain of it."[134]

In 1559 Calvin the pastor explicitly repeats that infants are not excluded from the kingdom of heaven if they happen to die before the act of baptism. In another addition to this final edition of the *Institutes* the pastor also seeks to defend the right way of administering this sacrament, that is, in the gathering of the believing community, while refusing to make this a condition for baptism to exist. Returning to his 1536 statement that those baptized in the papacy were truly baptized, Calvin adds a statement which expresses how he would qualify the validity of Roman baptism.

> [The Anabaptist] objection that baptism ought to be celebrated in the assembly of the godly does not have the effect of extinguishing the whole force of what is only partially faulty. For when we teach what ought to be done in order that baptism may be pure and free of all defilement, we do not abolish God's ordinance, however idolaters may corrupt it.[135]

In 1536 Calvin the theologian had been primarily concerned to refute the Anabaptist claim that Roman infant baptism was invalid and thus to reject any need for rebaptism. By 1559 Calvin the churchman had an additional ecclesiological concern, which apparently had in view the issue of private or emergency baptism. He wanted to make clear that he agreed with the Anabaptist principle that baptism should be celebrated in the context of "the assembly of the godly" but he still wanted to insist that (although it was "partially faulty"), failure to follow this proper way did "not abolish God's ordinance."

Although Calvin does not explicitly say so, the significance of these additions may well be related to the struggles of small communities in France and elsewhere, the "churches under the cross" for which a formal gathering with an ordained minister would not be regularly possible. Some light may be cast on what the reformer wanted to convey by examining briefly an issue with which he struggled in December 1549 in a response to a letter from Laelius Socinus. One point the latter raised was interreligious marriages, another was baptism. First Calvin deals with the consequences for the children born to a couple one of whom is Roman.

---

[134] *Inst.* 4.15.22. The Latin gives "sed eam duntaxat nobis confirmet" but the French 1551 adds "afin que nous la tenions tant plus certaine," as if Calvin were determined to make the reassurance, the *pro nobis* aspect, quite clear to his lay readers; cf. *Institution de la Religion chrestienne 1560*, vol. 4, p. 337.

[135] *Institutes*, McNeill-Battles, p. 1316, slightly altered; Battles has "assemblies" for the singular *conventu*, and Calvin is speaking of the generic worship assembly. *Inst.* 4.15.16, OS V, p. 297.

> If of two evils the lesser should be chosen, I judge that those living under the papacy cannot do otherwise than to offer their children for baptism, however corrupted. If they detest the corruptions that conflict with the command of God, they act piously and according to the duty of Christians. There is indeed mortal danger present; but that constancy more greatly deserves praise that is not shaken by fear, however great, from making a confession worthy of its piety. Whoever deprives his children of baptism commits more than a double offense. Therefore I have not advised this. [136]

Here the situation Calvin addresses is the consequence of a prior wrong choice by a believer (marrying outside the faith). He concludes that baptism in the Roman community is the lesser of two evils, i.e., better than refusing to present one's child for baptism. On the other hand, this is apparently only to be considered as a last resort, on condition the parents "detest the corruptions that conflict with the word of God," and recognize the "mortal danger" of what they are doing in participating in Roman worship. Nonetheless, depriving one's children of baptism entirely is worse, so Calvin has not advised French believers to do this.

The next section of the letter treats baptism in more detail. First Calvin states the agonizing dilemma that believers in France face: "not to be able to offer their children to Christ without prostituting them to corruptions of the Antichrist, and yet not able to omit the use of baptism without incurring reproach for scorning the mark of Christianity." He emphasizes that baptism was instituted by Christ's command and therefore despite the many corruptions of the papal practice, when rightly done it is still the "testimony of regeneration." [137] Calvin goes on to provide an explanation for his willingness to allow baptism in the Roman church as better

---

[136] Witte & Kingdon, *Courtship, Engagement, and Marriage*, p. 371. See letter #1323, OC 13:486: "Ego si ex duobus malis eligendum sit levius, facere aliter non posse arbitror qui sub papatu degit, quam ut liberos suos ad baptismum quamvis adulteratum offerat. Si corruptelas, quae cum Dei mandato pugnant, detestetur, pio et ex christiani hominis officio faciet. Praesens sane mortis periculum : sed eo plus laudis merebitur constantia, quod nullo metu frangetur quisquis erit, quominus confessionem pietate sua dignam edat. Liberos si quis baptismo privet, plus duplo pariet offensionis. Itaque hoc non consulerem."

[137] Letter #1323, OC 13:486 . "Hoc vere est inter sacrum (ut loquuntur) et saxum premi, non posse Christo liberos suos offerre, quin ad inquinamenta Antichristi prostituant: et tamen non posse usum baptismi praetermittere, quin contempti christianismi notam in se suscipiant. ... Tantum enim respicienda est institutio, et continuus usus: qui a Christi mandato, tanquam ex fonte fluxit. Certe non heri primum coepit baptizandi ritus. Eum nec papistae, nec idololatrae alii excogitarunt. Perperam itaque eum aestimas, nisi ad originem suam revoces. Utcunque autem multis pravis accessionibus vitiatus fuerit, semper tamen stetit hoc fixum, baptizari Christi mandato, in nomen patris, filii, et spiritus sancti; ut sit regenerationis testimonium. Hic est finis quem considerandum doceo."

than no baptism. Even with all of Rome's faults, there are "the remains of a church in the papacy" and this does not mean just the elect who are scattered there but also that the church exists there, in a ruined state.[138] Having dealt with that extreme position, however, Calvin goes on to correct Socinus' accusation that he does not allow baptisms in the private homes of the devout, in effect, that he forbids house churches in France to practice baptism. First it must be clear that the form is correct: "baptism is administered purely according to Christ's rule." Then the circumstances are taken into account. "For this kind of baptism, which is not permitted among us and indeed is covered by law, I allow more readily than than that papal one infected with such filth."[139]

To return to the 1559 *Institutes*: It is notable that Calvin does not touch on the extremely difficult case which Socinus had presented, but he emphasizes again that God's ordinance is greater than the power of human superstition. It is possible that one point the pastor wanted to reiterate to his French readers was that there was no emergency which required baptism to save a baby's life, and thus no reason why parents should despair if their child died without the sacrament (or anxiously administer the rite themselves). The proper place for baptism is in the church community, but the fundamental point is that what God has ordained cannot be destroyed by human sin or sudden death. God's promise to adopt the children of the covenant community can be trusted as long as their parents actively affirm that covenant. Whatever counsel Calvin could give for the exceptional situation of the churches under the cross, it is plain that he was convinced that celebrating baptism in the gathered church was a vital point. In Geneva there

---

[138] Letter #1323, OC 13:487. "Quod ecclesiae reliquias manere in papatu dico, non restringo ad electos, qui illic dispersi sunt: sed ruinas dissipatae ecclesiae illic exstare intelligo. Ac ne mihi longis rationibus disputandum sit, nos Pauli autoritate contentos esse decet, qui Antichristum in templo Dei sessurum pronunciat (2. Thess. 2, 4). Quanquam et hoc rationibus satis validis me probasse puto, ecclesiam licet semiruptam, imo si lubet diruptam ac deformem, aliquam tamen manere in papatu."

[139] Letter #1323, OC 13:487. "Atqui non patior, ut in privatis pii hominis aedibus baptismus pure iuxta Christi regulam administretur. Facilis responsio est. Nam huiusmodi baptismum, qui apud nos non permittitur, ac iure quidem vetitus est, facilius tolerarem, quam papalem illum tot sordibus infectum. Verum hic non agitur, quid ego probem. Quod autem baptismum pro nihilo me ducturum putas, quem e fratribus meis quispiam forte intra privatos parietes administraverit, hoc nunquam mihi venisse in mentem, Deum et homines testor. ..... Timiditatem, qua fit ut cautius vivant quidam, quam ut in suspicionem veniant tyrannis, simpliciter damnare non est meum. Unus enim legislator et iudex, cuius ore non video damnari." To put this in context, a baptism had to be in the church with a sermon; even a minister could not baptize without those. On Dec. 3, 1562, the consistory records a rebuke to a minister who was accused of administering the sacraments improperly: baptism without the congregation or a sermon, and the Supper in private or without prior catechesis; OC 21:794.

were no circumstantial hindrances, so parents had no excuses; the *Ordinances* of 1541 reiterated the earlier decrees requiring baptism in the regular worshiping community.

The Liturgy and the Genevan Catechism

Ordinary Genevans experienced Calvin's teaching in a language they heard on a regular basis in daily life or worship. Most persistent was the baptismal liturgy. The basic form was published by Farel in 1533; Calvin adapted and developed this in his *La forme des prieres* 1542. The teaching in the ritual is positive; it explains the purposes and benefits of the sacrament generally as well as what pertains specifically to infant baptism, and includes the confession which the parents promise to teach their child. In Geneva 1542 the liturgy was followed by a polemical paragraph directed against traditional Roman ritual practices, especially the elaborate ceremonies.[140] The text for baptism did not change much over the years. There were some verbal alterations, the same kind of polishing of the French which occurred in the Sunday service and Lord's Supper liturgy. The main scriptural text, Matt. 19:13-15, Jesus' command to allow the little children to come to Him, is printed in full from 1547, and the doxology of the Lord's Prayer is added beginning in 1552 (although occasional printings still omit it).[141] One significant change is found in 1547 in the minister's long initial explanation of baptism, where "presents" replaces "represents"; "there God represents to us our renewal" becomes "there God presents to us our renewal, which consists … in the mortification of our flesh and the spiritual life which he produces in us."[142] This

---

[140] OS II, pp. 31-38 ; see rejection of "le cresme, luminaire, et telles aultres pompes" as human inventions, p. 38. This was not balanced by warnings about Anabaptist errors, probably because the point here was liturgical and Anabaptists had discarded the ceremonies as well, and did not usually publish liturgies. Hubmaier's baptismal liturgy, in German, was practically the only printed Anabaptist liturgy; cf. Balthasar Hubmaier, "Ein Form" in *Balthasar Hubmaier Schriften*. ed. Torsten Bergsten and Gunnar Westin (Gütersloh: Gerd Mohn, 1962), pp. 349ff.

[141] Some minor variants marked in printings of 1547-52. 1547 (OS II). French doubles drop out (as in Sun. liturgy), and Mt. 19:13-15 recited in full (p. C1v, not just opening words as in 1542); LP recited without doxology (p. C3v). 1549 (MHR O6e [1549]). Mt. 19:13-15 recited in full (p. C1v); LP recited without doxology (p. C3v). 1552 [J. Crespin] n.p. A few verbal changes ("car" becomes "et de faict" p. 29; "ses enfans" becomes "siens" p. 29, "Judaique" becomes "des Juifs" p. 30, "pour le faire participant de tous les biens" becomes "afin qu'il soit faict participant des biens" p. 31). LP recited has doxology added, p. 32. Also adds "N." [name] to baptismal formula, p. 34. 1553 Adam & Jean Riveriz (BGE Bb 662 Res.). Same verbal changes as 1552, with one difference that LP has no doxology. 1561 Jean Rivery (BGE Bd 1928 Res). Same as earlier, with addition of doxology to LP (p. 21).

[142] OS II, p. 32: "Puis apres, il nous y represente nostre renouvellement…" p. 32 n.k: "Puis apres, il nous y presente nostre renouvellement, lequel gist, comme dict a esté en la mortification de nostre chair, et la vie spirituelle, laquelle il produict en nous." This change is maintained.

obviously parallels the development evident in the changed language elsewhere (the 1536-37 denial that baptism is an instrument which dropped out in 1539, and the use of "presents" in speaking of the action of the Lord's Supper) to emphasize the reality of the grace: it is offered, it is not merely pictured.[143] A fuller outline of the baptismal liturgy will be presented below, in the worship context in which it was practiced.

Like the liturgy, the Genevan Catechism concentrates on the positive teaching about baptism. As in his other writings, Calvin begins with the general discussion of the sacraments as seals of the promises and "secondary instruments" which God uses, although they are made effective only by the work of the Holy Spirit. The meaning of baptism is forgiveness of sins and regeneration; these come only from the blood of Christ. However, they are sealed by the sacrament, which is a symbol to which the reality is attached and so both are offered and received in baptism, by faith. From the purpose and benefits of baptism Calvin proceeds to the case of infant baptism, again explaining this by circumcision. The promises to Israel are now spread through the whole world; since the children of Abraham were included and the coming of Christ extends the promise more fully, how could the children of Christians be excluded? To take baptism away from such children would be to lose a powerful witness to God's mercy and confirmation of His promises and great consolation.[144] Note the strong pastoral emphasis; comfort and reassurance are plainly a vital part of the liturgy's purpose.

Biblical Expositions

Calvin's formal teaching about baptism included of course his extensive exegetical writings and preaching. His Biblical exposition grounded the *Institutes* and the two developed in tandem, but the commentaries and sermons often provide a more accessible expression of the theology. This is particularly true for such issues as election and the covenant which figure in important ways in the understanding of baptism, especially as based on passages of Genesis, Romans, and First Corinthians. There is no intention here of discussing the doctrines of election or covenant in themselves; the point is to draw out some of Calvin's scriptural comments to illumine aspects of the explanations of their church's practice which Genevans heard from the pulpit. The specific issues which are of interest here are points raised by "mixed-marriages" in 1 Cor. 7:14, and the practice of godfathers which may be related to Gen. 17:7-26. When in 1546

---

[143] See above at nn.122f; chap. 3 after n.191.

[144] Questions 309-20 on sacraments generally, 324-39 on baptism (333-39 for infants), OS II, pp. 130-37.

Calvin published the commentary on 1 Cor. 7:14, he referred the reader to what he had said about Romans 10 and 11, [145] and thus brief attention to that passage is helpful as context.

In Romans, his first commentary, published in 1540, Calvin clearly outlines the corporate understanding of God's adoption on which infant baptism was based. In dealing with Rom. 11:28-31, Calvin refers to the covenant with Abraham and the promise to his descendants in Gen. 17:7; the holiness of the people as those set apart to belong to God is not contradicted by the falling away of individuals, even a great number or the majority of the people. This election of Abraham's "race" has been extended to other nations by Christ who has broken down the wall dividing gentiles from the chosen people, and thus others are engrafted into the people of the promise. [146] Here it is helpful to recall the distinction between the church known to God (the elect) and the church visible on earth; Abraham's covenant included all his descendants and household as the church visible on earth, but this is not coterminous with the elect. For Calvin, the people of the covenant promise have a special status as the corporate body of Christ, visible according to the marks of the church. All those who manifest the marks of Christians, i.e., confession of faith, life according to that profession, and participation in the sacraments, belong to the church as far as human beings can charitably judge. [147] That belonging – being set apart as God's people – by parents extends to their babies until the children grow up to the point of being able to make their own profession and become fully practicing members who share in the Lord's Supper.

Some Questions about "Limits" and Calvin's Homiletical Response

Two particular points related to the practice of baptism in Geneva can be illumined by Calvin's preaching on 1 Cor. 7:14 and Gen. 17. These issues may be seen as "liminal" cases of one kind or another. What is the baptismal status of a child born to a mixed marriage, or parents who are not married, or a child whose father is unknown or one who is a foundling? Calvin does not address all of these cases directly, but the combination of his preaching and Genevan practice casts light on some puzzling questions, including possibly the rationale for godfathers in a Reformed church.

---

[145] Commentary on 1 Cor. 7:14, OC 49:413.

[146] Commentary on Rom. 11:28-31, OC 49:228-29.

[147] *Inst.* 4.1.8-9; cf. introduction to this book, at n.10.

Baptizing Illegitimate Babies

Traditionally, any infant, legitimate or not, was baptized immediately because the sacramental rite was necessary for salvation and it was irrelevant whether the parents were married, or even known. Anabaptists rejected the baptism of babies, whether their parents were believers or not. Protestants maintained infant baptism but had to identify the grounds. For the Reformed, who rejected any idea of the efficacy of the rite as such, the foundation for giving the sacrament to children was the status of their parents as members of the covenant people. The question was whether the parents had to be married to each other in order to be members of the covenant.

First it is important to discuss briefly the fine chapter which Karen Spierling devotes to the baptism of illegitimate babies. She begins with a case study of a baby presented by the grandfather-godfather under the name of his step-daughter's husband, although the actual father was a man whom the mother knew before she married. Spierling then examines many facets of the question about baptizing illegitimate babies, including Calvin's theology and the ways that Geneva dealt with the parents; the insistence on paternal responsibility for every child, whether born in wedlock or not; and the conflicted relationship with people who had their children baptized by Catholics (usually, in the case of an unwed mother, because the birth took place outside Geneva).[148] The purpose here is more limited than Spierling's larger investigation of the baptism of illegitimate children. It addresses a point she notes as puzzling: how could Calvin justify baptizing children if their parents were not behaving as faithful members of the covenant community?

> [Calvin's argument for infant baptism] presupposed that the parents presenting their children to be baptized were themselves faithful Christians acting out of their commitment both to God and to the care of their children's bodies and souls. ... But if that child was the offspring of parents who had violated the bound of that community by having extra-marital sex, and by attempting to conceal that fact or refusing to admit or repent for it, how was that child connected to the Reformed of Geneva?[149]

As Spierling notes, however, instead of the "strictly logical consequence" of requiring that parents repent and be reconciled with the church before baptism could proceed, "godparents and grandparents came to the forefront in these

---

[148] Spierling, *Infant Baptism in Reformation Geneva*, chap. 5.

[149] Spierling, *Infant Baptism in Reformation Geneva*, p. 165.

situations, substituting for absent fathers as faithful Christians in good standing."[150]

It is in this context that one must examine a curious, even an anomalous event which occurred in Geneva during Calvin's exile in Strasbourg. On Feb. 23, 1540, the Genevan authorities decreed that illegitimate babies should not be baptized. "[It is ordered] to command the preachers that they not baptize bastards and they must ask the name from the mother." (This ambiguous note means ask the mother to name the father.) This regulation is confirmed by the contemporary chronicler Michel Roset although he dates the decree two days earlier.[151] Such an act seems very strange. There does not appear to be any precedent in the practices of neighboring cities such as Bern or Basel.[152] The Senate gives no reasons for the prohibition. No means of redress (such as the marriage of the parents) is named, and there is no explanation about the extent of this ban (e.g., as applying to all babies born out of wedlock or only to babies born of adultery, because that parent would not be free to marry his partner in crime and regularize the relationship).

Explicit notice of a reversal of this puzzling regulation is not found, but after Calvin's return Geneva certainly did baptize illegitimate babies. The instructions about baptism in the 1541 *Ecclesiastical Ordinances* refer to bastards, not to forbid the sacrament but to instruct the pastors to alert the civil authorities to the fact of an illegitimate baby.[153] (Obviously it was assumed that the child would be baptized, but the parents who were at fault would face proper punishment.) There

---

[150] Spierling, *Infant Baptism in Reformation Geneva*, p. 165.

[151] Feb. 23, 1540, RC V, p. 137: "De leur fere comandement, aux predicants, qu'il n'ayent az baptizer bastard et qu'il doygent demander le nom de laz mere, escripre les marriages et avoyer des lyvres des mors." Roset, *Les chroniques de Genève*, chap. 36, p. 272: "Le vingt & ungme dudict moys fut deffendu de ne baptizer les bastards."

[152] See Alfred Ehrensperger, *Der Gottesdienst in Stadt und Landschaft Bern im 16. Und 17. Jahrhundert* (Zürich: TVZ, 2011), pp. 258-60, 314-17, deal specifically with baptism, with no mention of any prohibition of baptizing illegitimate babies. Ehrensperger indicates (p. 314) that in Bern three godparents were the norm and since most godparents came from the family's neighborhood (which often included Catholics in villages which bordered Catholic territories), they allowed families to choose godparents who were not Reformed. Also, at the beginning, Bern followed Zwingli's acceptance of lay baptisms in an emergency, although this was rejected by the First Helvetic Confession in 1534. Alfred Ehrensperger, *Der Gottesdienst in Stadt und Landschaft Basel im 16. Und 17. Jahrhundert* (Zürich: TVZ, 2010), pp. 144-45, 226-28, deal specifically with baptism, again with no reference to refusing illegitimate babies baptism. Ehrensperger states (p. 227) that the questions ("do you want to baptize this child?" "what is the name?") were directed to the godparents, not the father! He goes on to indicate (p. 228) that even in the later Reformation ministers complained that baptism was not treated with respect, and fathers were often (still) absent.

[153] *Ordinances*, OS II, p. 343.

are notes about the baptism of illegitimate babies in criminal cases [154] and consistory records, [155] even before the baptismal records began in 1550, and the latter identify the "bastards" who are baptized. [156] The fact that Genevan practice changed twice, first to ban giving the sacrament to illegitimate infants and then to reverse that prohibition, suggests that the decision to baptize babies born out of wedlock was a conscious choice and not merely a concession to the desire of families to have their illegitimate offspring recognized as members of the church community.

The anomaly in Genevan practice during Calvin's absence can easily be passed over – and has been – but it poses several questions, not the least being why the reformer supported the baptism of illegitimate babies to the degree that he would at least cooperate with, if not advocate, the reversal of the current law. The rationale for the original ban be can hypothesized, based on Genevan politics and relevant Biblical texts and theological ideas current in the early Reformation. It is entirely possible that the prohibition in 1540 was simply political expediency: refusing to baptize a baby could coerce the mother into naming the father and enable the authorities to compel the father to support his child. As noted above, the *Ecclesiastical Ordinances* required pastors to inform the civil authorities when a bastard was baptized. There continued to be concerted efforts to uncover the paternity of nameless babies. Occasionally there might be a short delay in carrying out the sacrament, but usually the child was baptized fairly quickly. On

---

[154] Examples: Procès criminels PC series 2. #726 for Thurs. Nov. 24, 1546, Jean-François Ramel was sent to the court by the consistory because he got a servant pregnant; the consistory asks the Senate to identify the servant's master and investigate why the baby died without baptism ("informer de quelle gens lad[icte] fille est. et s'il est point cause que l'enfant est expiré sans batesme"). #861 July 11-29, 1550, the case of a servant who claimed the illegitimate child of his master, born to a woman servant. Now a year later after the master's death there is an investigation. One of the issues is the baptism of the baby, which the man who claimed the child recounted, identifying the godfather and location (f2v). Under questioning the man answers that he never said he got the servant pregnant but that this was assumed because he said the baby was his. See next note.

[155] See June 5 & 19, July 10, 1550, *Consist.* V, pp. 118-27 n.817, p. 157 (the issue is changed testimony over where a baby was baptized). *Consist.* V, pp. 127 n.887, 152, 156 (Claude Bonna appears as the father in a dispute about who had the baby baptized as a Catholic). Catholic baptism of illegitimate babies, see p. 160 n.1103; pp. 247, 258, 264, 289. *Consist.* V, pp. 209 & 309, Sept. 11, 1550 & Jan. 22, 1551 (the case of a couple of servants: the second entry indicates that the baby needs material support and is unbaptized; the consistory decides that inquiry should be made but they allow the baby to be baptized as a bastard).

[156] See Appendix One. Illegitimate babies are identified at St. Pierre on Aug. 24, 1550, & May 26, 1553, & Feb. 24, 1557; at St. Gervais on Aug. 26, 1551; at La Magdeleine on May 2, 1553, & June 15, 1557.

the other hand, if there was a theological logic behind the 1540 order not to baptize bastards, it might have been related to conflicting interpretations of 1 Cor. 7:14. Some people read this text, or 2 Cor. 6:11ff, to mean that mixed marriages between believers and unbelievers (here "heretics," not "pagans") were not valid and their children were not fit to be part of the covenant people. By extension, it might be argued that those who had children out of wedlock or by adultery were not practicing believers and so their offspring should be refused baptism – but Calvin cites 1 Cor. 7:14 in his liturgy as one part of the Biblical basis supporting infant baptism. [157] The reformer's preaching on this text may provide some insights into how he came to the conclusions he did, which allowed if not espoused the baptism of illegitimate babies.

It is necessary to say first that the reformer does not address this question directly, as that is nowhere found in the texts he was expounding. The passage in 1 Cor. 7 deals with varied aspects of married and single life; verses 12-16 focus on a mixed marriage between a believer and an unbeliever. If one partner is a believer and the other is not, the choice about continuing is with the unbeliever; if he or she will remain in the marriage, the believer should do so. The unbeliever is set apart as holy by the faithful partner; "otherwise your children would be impure; but now they are sanctified." As Calvin explains, this does not mean that the unbeliever is saved, but the children are reckoned as members of the church. If the unbeliever determines to leave, the believer is not bound and the marriage is dissolved. [158]

One of the issues addressed is what makes a marriage "legitimate" and how this affects the children. In the commentary Calvin explicitly says that the point is not to invalidate the legitimacy of unbelievers' marriages, but to show that these are lawful by human polity and not as a fulfillment of God's intention in establishing this fundamental social institution. Only the faithful have truly legitimate marriages, in the sense that these are lived in right relationship to God as originally established at the creation. [159] The concept of legitimacy was apparently somewhat confusing, because in the sermons Calvin explains his interpretation in other

---

[157] In both commentary and sermons Calvin refers to those who think 1 Cor. 7:14 deals with the legitimacy of marriage as such and denies that claim; OC 49:412; Sermon 44, Ms.fr. 26, f364v, 366r-v. For liturgy, see OS II, p. 33. That this was a matter of controversy is evident in Beza's explicit refutation in annotations on vss 13-14; cf. *Iesu Christi D. N. Novum Testamentum, siue Novum foedus* (Geneva: Henricus Stephanus, 1565), f253f.

[158] Sermon 44, Ms.fr. 26, f364v-365r: cf. Sermon 45, Ms.fr.26, f369-370. Calvin is more concerned with keeping the couple together than allowing the unbeliever to leave; the key for him is whether the unbeliever is leading the believer away from the faith.

[159] OC 49:412.

words. The holiness of Christian marriage does not come from the couple but from God's special blessing. All Christians are born sinners, just like everyone else, and every child is born a sinner. However, marriage was God's good creation and therefore for those in right relationship with God it regains its original (religious) legitimacy, i.e., sexuality can be used with a good conscience by those who are married with God's blessing. For this reason children born to believers, or even to a couple of whom only one is a believer, are born into a religiously legitimate marriage and are therefore heirs of the covenant promise. [160] (Calvin does not discuss the status of an infant whose unbelieving parent has left because the primary focus of the text is the mixed marriage, and the situation of the children is effectively a side issue intended to encourage the Christian partner not to leave the unbelieving one. However, as will be seen below in his sermons on Gen. 17 he makes it clear that one believing parent is enough.)

In preaching on this passage, however, Calvin makes an interesting comment which contributes to answering the question about baptizing illegitimate infants. The context is God's mercy.

> [God] adopts the children of the faithful to the thousandth generation and claims them as His and declares that they are separated from the common curse of the human race. … [Because of our sin] we are mortal enemies of God, we will find that there is only condemnation and vengeance upon us, yet nonetheless we have been adopted by God inasmuch as He has poured out His grace on our fathers. Or, if indeed our fathers were unbelievers, His promise extends further, i.e., to a thousand generations; it does not say only to the first or second degree but to a thousand generations. [161]

While this remark was made in passing, it suggests that a child could properly be baptized if the grandparents were believers, even if the parents were not. However illegitimate birth fits into the equation, this would mean that a Genevan couple could present their grandchild for baptism. This did in fact happen on occasion. The case study presented by Spierling demonstrates that even when the

---

[160] Sermon 44, Ms.fr. 26, f365r-v.

[161] Sermon 44, f365b: "Il adopte les enfans des fidelles en mille generations et les advoue pour siens et declaire qu'ilz sont separez de la malediction commune du genre humain… que nous sommes ennemiz mortelz de Dieu, nous trouverons qu'il n'y a que condemnation et vengeance sur nous mais ce pendant nous ne laissons point d'avoir esté adoptez de Dieu, d'autant qu'il avoit espandu sa grace sur noz peres, ou bien si noz peres ont esté incredules sa promesse s'estend plus loing, c'est asçavoir en mille generations. Il n'est point dict seulement jusques au premier ou au second degré, mais il est dict en mille generations."

baby was proved to be illegitimate there was no question about the sacrament, although the baptismal records had to be corrected to identify the actual father, and the grandfather's lie about paternity was punished. [162] The point here, though, is that for Calvin the right to be numbered among the covenant people was not dependent on the parents themselves being members of the church in good standing – or even believers! – as long as believing family took responsibility for rearing the baby in the faith.

One factor which contributes to this conclusion is the Reformed conviction that baptism does not guarantee salvation, it does not overrule God's election. It has to do with membership in the visible earthly church.

> The babies are accepted by God and received in the hope of salvation. … [Calvin speaks of election which overrules all human acts] But nevertheless the promise of this adoption which He makes is not vain, when He offers salvation to all who were circumcised in the time of the law, and to those who are baptized today. When He declares that He is their Father and receives them as members of His household that is not in vain for, until they have made themselves unworthy, they are household members of the church, recognized and claimed as the flock, if they are not cut off by their ingratitude and ill will. So let us note well that all those who come forth from a holy lineage are blessed by God and are exempt from Adam's curse, not by nature (as we have said) but by a special privilege. That is why baptism is the mark of God and of His grace. [163]

The emphasis on belonging to the church unless or until the person deliberately breaks that tie demonstrates the gift of infant baptism in Calvin's eyes: the

---

[162] Spierling, *Infant Baptism in Reformation Geneva*, p. 158 *et passim*.

[163] Sermon 44, f365a: "Le fruit [du mariage] en est bon, il s'ensuyt donc que la racine en est bonne quand et quand, d'autant que les enfans sont acceptez de Dieu et qu'ilz sont receuz en l'esperance de salut. Et pourquoy ? A cause qu'ilz sont engendrez du mariage legitime." f366a: "Quand Dieu sanctifie par sa promesse ceulx qui sont engendrez de pere ou de mere fideles, ou de tous les deux, qu'il ne s'oblige point tellement qu'il n'ayt son ellection libre par dessus et que ceulx qu'il a choysis devant la creation du monde sont seulement siens, ... car son election domine par dessus en toute liberté... mais ce pendant si est ce que la promesse de ceste adoption qu'il faict n'est point frustratoire, quand il offre salut à tous ceulx qui estoyent circoncis soubz le temps de la loy, à ceulx qui sont aujourd'huy baptisez. Quand donc il se declaire estre leur pere et qu'il les reçoit comme de sa maison, cela n'est point frustratoire, car jusques à ce qu'ilz s'en soyent rendus indignes ilz sont domestiques de l'eglise, recogneuz et advouez du trouppeau, s'ilz n'en sont retranchez, voire par leur ingratitude et malice. Et ainsi notons bien que tous ceulx qui sont procedez d'ung lignage sainct sont beneictz de Dieu et qu'ilz sont exemptez de la malediction d'Adam, non pas de nature (comme nous avons dict) mais d'ung priviliege special, et voila pourquoy le baptesme est la marque de Dieu et de sa grace qui apparoist en nous."

covenant lifts the original curse of alienation from God and puts the children of believers in a privileged position to hear the word and share the sacraments. Perhaps another way to say this is that there are not two levels of holiness in the visible church: members and unbaptized children. All are members because they all join together to receive the marks of the church according to their ability, and they all strive to manifest the marks of Christians according to their ability. This is obedience to God's earthly, ordained means of bringing human beings to salvation. Because it proclaims the gospel in word and sacraments, this earthly visible church is part of the church visible only to God; to be in the visible church is therefore to be located within the ordained means for knowing the gospel. Baptism is the mark of God's covenant grace, for the children of believers as well as for themselves. A child could be baptized on the basis of the grandparents' faithful participation in the covenant community because the inheritance of the covenant relationship is not tied simply to the baby's immediate ancestry but to the larger active family in the church who will rear the child.

Finding a Godfather for an Illegitimate "Nameless" Baby

If the baptism of illegitimate children can be considered at least arguably justified by the appeal to earlier forebears in the covenant, on what grounds might a foundling be baptized? What about other situations which produce an infant without the requisite covenant ancestry, such as the baby of a Roman Catholic mother or one whose father was unknown? What theological rationale should be applied for baptizing or not baptizing such a baby? Virtually all these situations occurred in Geneva, and the fact that they appear in the records indicates that they raised questions which had to be answered. In the case of the Catholic woman who gave birth at the General Hospital in November 1550, she was ordered to take her baby back to its Catholic father unbaptized.[164] Plainly, the baby could not be given the sign of the covenant because its family did not belong to the visible church. In addition, any child who was going to be reared in the Roman church could not be baptized in the Reformed church because the latter could not fulfill the promised educational duties.

The situation was noticeably different in the case of a baby of unknown paternity who was understood to be Genevan. One very difficult and long drawn out process was that of a foundling discovered in May 1550 whose parents

---

[164] Nov. 11, 1550, OC 21:470: A poor mother from Viectra (over the border in France) had a baby at the General Hospital (welfare center). Viectra was a Catholic area so the question came to the Senate about baptizing the baby: "pour ce que son pere et sa mere sont de Viectra out il [où ilz] demeurent quant la mere sera relevee qu'elle emporte son enfant au pere qu'il le nurrisse et fasse baptizer."

could not be identified. On July 30, Jean de St. André, minister of Jussy, brought this case to the consistory. Two months previously the baby had been found near the Château du Crest, the home of Louise de Roverée, Mme du Crest, and this lady wanted Pastor St. André to baptize the baby (although she did not claim that it was hers). St. André refused, saying that the father was unknown. In theory the baby was not claimed by anyone. The fact that Mme du Crest was asking for the sacrament for this "foundling" was apparently considered suspicious, and she was called before the consistory multiple times (Aug. 21 & 28, Dec. 18 & 22, 1550, Aug. 20, 1551) to explain about the baby. However, she never appeared. (Several years later she and a Catholic priest in her household were suspected of adultery – probably the suspicions began with this baby.)[165] On Dec. 18, 1550, some months after the baby was found, a certain Loys Lechiere told the consistory that Mme du Crest had given him the child to care for, and he did not know whether it was baptized or not. The consistory's response was to ask the Senate to deal with Mme Du Crest's disobedience, put things in order, identify the father and get the baby baptized because the failure to do this was a scandal.[166] The case dragged on and on, however, until in August 1551 it was joined by an even more notorious instance.

Sometimes the abandoned infant was not actually unknown but unclaimed, i.e., a bastard whose parentage was disputed. Spierling discusses the case of a newborn discovered in a basket near the home of Pierre de La Mare in the rural parish of Foncenex in August 1551. A note with the baby identified the father as de La Mare's brother Philibert. Pierre de La Mare called the local official, Martin de Loerme, the châtellain's lieutenant, who investigated the case (his job) but who was also saddled with caring for the baby. A considerable process ensued among the consistory, Senate, and various people involved, because Philibert de La Mare refused to come to the consistory to claim the child and the ministers refused to perform the sacrament without knowing the father. Finally on Aug. 14 the Senate ordered the baby to be baptized; Martin de Loerme presented her to the minister

---

165 July 30, 1550; *Consist.* V, p. 158-159 and n. 1092, which details the summons to the consistory and the later adultery.

166 *Consist.* V, p. 270, Dec. 18, 1550: "Advis: qui [sic] Messieurs y pourvoisse tant de la desho-beyssance de lad. dame, semble d'i mettre oddre; et sçavoir le pere et pourvoistre à baptizé led. enfant, qu'est matiere scandaleuse." Cf. *Consist.* VI, p. 139 n. 850, p. 149 n. 908, Aug. 6 & 20, 1551. p. 149: "Sus ce que Messieurs n'ont prins information de l'enfant que futz remis à Marcelli dans le chasteau y a environ sept moys et ne sçayt-on à qui il est et s'il est batizer. Et ont bien commander de le batizer sans sçavoir la verité. Qu'i p[l]aise à monsieur Calvin soy transporté vers Messieurs et faire responde en Consistoire lad. dame de Marcelli." Spierling, *Infant Baptism in Reformation Geneva*, pp. 89-90, indicates that Calvin complained that the baby might already have been baptized.

at Foncenex, but the latter insisted on deferring the sacrament. Four days later the Senate repeated its order that this baby and the other foundling be baptized, and this time it was done. [167] For present purposes, one of the important factors here is that the Genevan official who had been charged with the child was the one who was told to present her for baptism. Apparently, the fact that she was in his household was grounds for his being the godfather.

Another similar though less complicated case confirms this hypothesis. It was quite possible for a child to have no known father, and for the person(s) in the case to be of a class in which that was not unusual. A poor expectant mother might come to the General Hospital (welfare center) for charity. When her baby was born the authorities would try to discover the father so that he could be held accountable for supporting his offspring, but at least occasionally the baby would be baptized before its paternity was known. One such case is recorded on May 28, 1557. It is noteworthy that a man of high rank, Jean Collondaz, the Hospitalier and a "deacon" in Calvin's church order, [168] stood as godfather to this "nameless" charity case and promised his guardianship. The baptismal liturgy was held on a Friday at the main weekday service in the parish of La Magdeleine, where Calvin's alternate Nicholas Des Gallars was preaching that week. [169] Normally the father would choose the godfather, although no doubt the mother often had some influence on the decision. [170] In this case, there was no known father. It is conceivable that the poor woman who had been forced to rely on public welfare to see her through childbirth would dare to ask a prominent stranger to stand as godfather to her illegitimate baby, but that is very unlikely. Even if she did, there would have to be some compelling reason for that important person to agree. The logical conclusion is that it was either Collondaz's choice to take on spiritual responsibility for this newborn waif, or it was expected of him as head of the household in which the infant was living. As Hospitalier he already had responsibility for the baby's material well being – at least until the father could be found and made to fulfill his obligations – and thus to add spiritual responsibility might make sense. It should be noted that this occurred in

---

[167] Spierling, *Infant Baptism in Reformation Geneva*, pp. 89-90. For the consistory's side of the matter, see *Consist.* VI, pp. 139 n. 850, 145 n. 882, for Aug. 6 & 13, 1551. R.C. entry for Aug. 14, 1551, OC 21:486 (RC 46 f35v-36).

[168] Cf. *Ordinances*, OS II, pp. 340-41.

[169] See baptismal records for La Magdeleine in Appendix One.

[170] For example, the godfather for Abel Poupin's first son Benjamin, baptized at La Magdeleine on April 10, 1544, was the brother of the baby's mother. (Poupin's three children are the only baptisms recorded in the books before 1550; evidently when the register was begun, Poupin retroactively listed his sons. See chap. 1 at n.150.)

1557, when Calvin's leadership was unquestioned, so this kind of act must have had his approval.

Why might Martin de Loerme, why might Jean Collondaz, take the spiritual responsibility of a godfather for a foundling or a charity case living in his household, to which he had no tie except the fact that he had been entrusted with the physical care of the baby? Was there some teaching which would make this a natural conclusion for a man in Calvin's Geneva?

It is quite clear that godparents are never mentioned in the Bible, and Calvin does not discuss them anywhere in the *Institutes* or other treatises. Some Protestants in the early years of the Reformation (e.g., the Zells in Strasbourg) completely rejected the idea of godparents,[171] although most reformers (except of course Anabaptists) retained the practice in one way or another. In Calvin's Geneva, the form that the institution took was distinctive: the number was reduced to a single person and that person was a man. The responsibilities and qualifications of the godfather were briefly set out in the *Ecclesiastical Ordinances* in 1541.

> Strangers should not be received as godfathers (*comperes*) except faithful people who are of our confession (*communion*), since others are not capable of making the promise to instruct the children as is appropriate [to the godfather's role].[172]

From Calvin's viewpoint, a godfather must be a person known as a faithful member of the church because his task was to second the father to insure that the child received proper religious education. In effect, he served as an alternate father who would take over responsibility for the spiritual (and, if necessary, sometimes the physical) nurture of the child until the latter could make his or her own profession of faith. In the baptismal liturgy, the father and godfather made the promises and affirmed or recited the confession in which the child would be reared. To return to Martin de Loerme and Jean Collondaz, the civil official and the Hospitalier who stood as godfathers to "nameless" babies who were living in their households: on what grounds might they have done this, according to Calvin's theology?

At least for the Reformed tradition, the most important Old Testament text relating to baptism was Gen. 17:7, God's promise to Abraham to be both his God and the God of his descendants, a promise sealed with circumcision. Calvin's

---

171 See Elsie Anne McKee, *Katharina Schütz Zell. Vol. 1: The Life and Thought of a Sixteenth-Century Reformer* (Leiden: Brill, 1999), pp. 93-94.

172 *Ordinances*, OS II, p. 343.

sermons on this passage provide a significant exposition of infant baptism, the more noteworthy since it is the only extant exegetical context for an extended discussion of this subject for his Genevan congregation.[173] A few sentences of summary may be useful. The importance of the sacrament to strengthen the weak faith of believers is emphasized, and Calvin can go so far as to say that to keep God's covenant both the word and the sacraments must be held together, and his hearers are admonished to appreciate the generosity which provides the assurance of a tangible confirmation. The actual rite is not essential, however; there is no danger to a baby who dies without the rite because the child of a believing father or mother is sanctified from the womb.[174] There is one important caveat, however. If the parent refuses to bring the baby for baptism; then both are cut off from the church.

> The children were not cut off unless the fathers despised baptism, rejected it and mocked it as something frivolous and worthless. When the fathers are so wicked, it is certain that they and their children are cut off and banished from the church, and consequently from all hope of salvation.[175]

Here, being cut off from "hope of salvation" was not because the baby was not baptized but because the parents rejected God and abandoned the church which proclaimed God's promise of salvation. Deliberate self-exclusion from the visible church and from God's promise of forgiveness and reconciliation is action characteristic of reprobation. (The earthly church does not decide the person's eternal fate but it pronounces on the visible signs which are the measure given to it for practical purposes.) This point clarifies why Calvin and his colleagues were so emphatic about insisting that fathers must be known and take responsibility: if they refused to acknowledge their children and bring them into the visible church community, they were effectively rejecting that promise of salvation. Thus, beyond the practical need for paternal support of the babies, which was the primary concern of the civil authorities, the ministers were determined that fathers re-affirm their own commitment to the faith by presenting their children for baptism.

---

[173] Calvin's sermons on Matt. 19:13-15, the passage read in the baptismal liturgy, were not recorded because the stenographer who transcribed sermons had recently died.

[174] *Sermons sur la Genèse*, S. XI/II, pp. 915, 917, 918.

[175] *Sermons sur la Genèse*, S. XI/II, p. 919: "les enfans n'ont point esté retranchez, sinon qu'on ait rompu l'alliance de Dieu, c'est à dire que les peres ayent desdaigné le baptesme, qu'ilz le repoussent et qu'ilz s'en moquent comme d'une chose frivolle et qui n'apporte nul profit. Quand donc les peres sont si vilains, o il est certain qu'eulx et leurs enfans sont retranchez et banniz de l'Eglise, et par consequent de toute esperance de salut."

For present purposes, however, the main focus is on a much neglected aspect of the larger passage, Gen. 17:10-14, in which Abraham is told to circumcise all the males in his household, whether born or bought. That is, Abraham is to give the seal of the covenant promise to every male he "owns," of any age or actual parentage. Outsiders are not to be circumcised, but anyone who belongs to him must be, whether he is a son or a slave: not just descendants but all those for whom Abraham is the head of household. In his sermons on this passage, Calvin begins by praising God's goodness to Abraham in accepting those who were considered scarcely human. The preacher states that "in those [Old Testament] times" the condition of the "serfs" was dreadful; they were despised, and regarded like cattle. Yet circumcision, the sign of God's adoption, made them His children and heirs of heavenly life.[176] (The preacher's language about the status of those whom he calls "serfs" was certainly intended to highlight God's generosity; it is worth noting that even though he calls these people by a contemporary term, he distinguishes their lot from servants in Geneva.) For Calvin, such an act of adoption expresses the extent of God's will to confirm Abraham's faith; it also warns this master of his responsibilities to "take care that all his house may be a temple of God, where great and small will adore Him in common accord."[177] Then this is applied to the Genevans.

> So there is good reason for each one to busy himself in teaching not only his children but also both wife and men and women servants, so that God may have the mastery which He reserves to Himself and all people may be under Him. ... [T]he more that God shows us how much He loves and values us, when He is pleased to gather with us all those whom He has given into our charge, [the more] there is a mutual obligation, i.e., that we take pains to keep this good (blessing) pure and whole, and that those whom He has willed to gather with us and to whom He has joined us in the hope of salvation, that they may be truly dedicated to Him and we may apply all our effort to that.[178]

---

[176] *Sermons sur la Genèse*, S. XI/II, pp. 911, 912.

[177] *Sermons sur la Genèse*, S. XI/II, p. 912: "Dieu n'a rien obmis ny oublié de ce qui appartennoit, pour confermer la foy de ses eleuz et de ses enfans. Or ce pendant Abraham a esté adverty de son devoir, c'est de mettre peyne que toute sa maison fust un temple de Dieu, et que là il fust adoré de grandz et de petis, d'ung commun accord. Or ceste mesme exhortation appartient aujourdhuy à tous fideles."

[178] *Sermons sur la Genèse*, S. XI/II, p. 912: "Ainsi donc c'est bien raison que chacun s'employe à enseigner non seullement ses enfans, mais aussi et femme et serviteurs et chambrieres, tellement que Dieu ait la maistrise qu'il se reserve, et que tousjours les hommes luy soyent inferieurs. ... Voylà donc ce que nous avons à retenir, que d'aultant plus que Dieu monstre combien il nous aime et nous prise, quand il luy plait de recueillir avec nous ceux qu'il nous a donnez en

Calvin continues the application in a sharper vein, saying that this is not practiced as it should be. Householders are content as long as they are comfortable and do not care whether their servants have all kinds of vices or whether God is revered in their homes. Abraham's example teaches that all those "in his house had to range themselves in order and also be counted in this number and company of the children of God."[179] The whole house must live according to the commitments of faith made by the head, and the head must see that this is done.

Obviously in these sermons Calvin says nothing about godparents, but it is equally clear that he makes Abraham effectively the "godfather" to every male in his household, the one who must present these boys and men for the sacrament of circumcision. The record of Martin de Loerme and Jean Collondaz, civil official and Hospitalier, presenting the "nameless" infants living in their households, could easily be seen as modeled on Abraham's circumcising all the males of his "family." After all, the babies in the villages and city of Geneva, especially the charity cases at the General Hospital, were just as much members of their keepers' households as the people in Abraham's tents were of his. At the very least, this Biblical passage offers some suggestive indications of what might have shaped Calvin's thinking in allowing and even sponsoring the institution of godparents in Geneva. Most godfathers never took their godchildren into their own house-holds, but that was certainly a possibility.

In any event, in the absence or death of the father, the godfather should and did step in to see that the baby was reared in the faith which father and godfather had professed and promised in the baptismal liturgy. Calvin himself gave an example of this in the case of the baby son of the English refugee William Stafford who had brought his family to Geneva to escape the reign of Queen Mary.[180] Stafford had actually become a "bourgeois" and apparently intended to stay in the city. Shortly after the baptism of his baby son John, William died. The widow, Dorothy Stafford, and her brother-in-law wanted to move the family to France, but godfather John refused to agree. He said that he could not prevent the mother

---

charge, qu'il y a obligation mutuelle, c'est asavoir que nous mettions peine que ce bien soit gardé pur et entier, et que ceux, lesquelz il a voulu assembler avec nous, et ausquelz il nous a conjoinctz en l'esperance de salut, que ceux là vrayement luy soyent dediez, et que nous appliquions là tout nostre estude."

[179] *Sermons sur la Genèse*, S. XI/II, p. 913: "Et notons ce qui est dit, que les serviteurs qu'aura achapté Abraham, combien que de race ilz ne soyent pas sanctifiez, mais qu'ilz soyent gens polus, toutesfoys, d'aultant qu'ilz habitent en sa maison, il fault qu'ilz se rangent et qu'ilz soyent comprins aussi bien en ce nombre et en ceste compaignie des enfans de Dieu."

[180] Summary of the story in Spierling, *Infant Baptism in Reformation Geneva*, p. 105. However, because the point here is Calvin's reasoning, further notes are included.

from returning to the papacy but he was obligated to see that baby John would have a proper Christian education as he had promised God and William Stafford.[181] The Genevan government accepted their pastor's argument and would not agree to the departure of the Staffords[182] until the family changed its destination from France to a Reformed city, which happened to be Basel.[183] Several points are important: one is the seriousness with which Calvin took his obligation to insure that the promises he made in baptism would be carried out, one way or another. A second is the city's readiness to insist that its ecclesiastical laws took precedence over family wishes. These various cases of specific godfathers illuminate what the Calvinist Reformed institution meant and the complex way that Calvin's teaching about baptism and Genevan church life were intertwined in practice.

---

181 April 22, 1556, OC 21:640 (RC 51 f192): "M. Calvin disant qu'il est bien marry du conseil que la dite vefve a prys de se retirer de l'evangile pour retourner es soullieures du monde desquelles par le moyen de son feu mary elle avoit esté retiree, mais quant à cela qu'il ne l'en peult garder: totesfois qu'il parlera pour l'enfant lequel il a porté au baptesme en estant requys par le feu pere lequel mesmes pour la grande affection qu'il luy portoit desiroit luy imposer nom Calvin, ce qu'il ne volut faire pour chose du monde, mais le nommant et tenant fit le serment et promesse solennelle accoustumee faire en ceste Eglise ensuyvant la reformation evangelicque par laquelle il a promys d'instruyre à l'evangile ledit enfant tellement que maintenant en deffaut du pere il en est obligé."

182 April 26, 1556, OC 21:641 (RC 51 f196): "l'exposition de M. Calvin est bonne d'aultant que le serment presté par M. Calvin de instruire ledit enfant en deffault du pere est venu en effect et que la volunté du pere est assez declairee en ce qu'il se fit recevoir icy habitant pour luy et ses enfans pour vivre selon l'evangile: en quelle volunté il a perseveré jusque à la mort mesmes qu'on a entendu icelluy avoir commandé et declairé au lit de sa maladie qu'il ne voloit point que on emmenat sez enfans d'ycy mais qu'ilz y fussent nourrys et instruys. Quant à ce qu'lz ont requys tochant de donner coadjuteur à la tutrice: Arresté que le Sr. Lieutenant provoye sus cela par election façon accoustumee et comme de raison pour le bien et preservation des pupilles et de leurs biens." The last point is the Senate's provision for a guardian for the Stafford children, according to the usual Genevan practice (because women were legally minors in certain respects). This must have made Dorothy Stafford's brother-in-law livid, since it virtually stated that he was not fit to do this. The whole issue, however, demonstrates that the godfather was clearly distinguished from the financial guardian, even if in some cases the same person might have both responsibilities.

183 On Aug. 24, 1556, OC 21:645-646 (RC 51 f277), Dorothy Stafford sent a request to the Senate that she wanted to move her children to a Reformed city and promised on oath see that they would be reared in the faith, and after consulting Calvin the Senate gave her permission to leave since the promise made in baptism would be kept.

The Practice of Baptism in Geneva

Continuity and discontinuity marked the practice of baptism in Geneva, but discontinuity was more evident. A brief comparison of the old and the new may set the stage for an examination of how the public forms of baptism developed in Geneva.

Although the teaching about infant baptism may not have seemed as different to Genevans as that of the Lord's Supper, the changes in practice were probably just as evident and almost certainly had even more personal impact. Perhaps the most important transformation in the experience of the sacrament was its location: religious and social as well as (to some extent) physical. The celebration of baptism was no longer a family affair; it belonged to the church as a whole. The participation of parents – at least the father – and the action of a minister were required; presence at the liturgy could not be left to the godfather, and the administration of the sacrament by a midwife was not allowed. [184] Traditionally baptism might be celebrated in the parish church or a family chapel, but it did not have to have any special place and might well be held in private even if there was no emergency. When the full Roman baptismal liturgy was carried out, it did not include a sermon. For Reformed Christians, baptism must be celebrated in the gathered church and in Geneva it was essential that the liturgy be part of a regular preaching service, which the father and godfather must (and the whole baptismal party should) attend from beginning to end. Furthermore, the liturgy itself was quite different from the traditional ritual: much simpler, seeming bare and unadorned by comparison with the long-established ceremonies.

The Development of Baptismal Practice in Protestant Geneva

Most of the changes in baptismal practice, which included both liturgical and practical issues, were introduced by the first reformers. Farel's 1533 liturgy explicitly eliminated exorcisms, salt, spit, oil and other ceremonies, and substituted "pure water" for what he called "enchanted" water. Babies should be presented by "those most closely associated with [them]" and baptism should be performed "in the full congregation of the faithful" although no specific time or place was required. [185] The 1537 *Articles* made these provisions laws: baptisms were done "in the congregation," where they could be performed on any day. (It is not clear whether this happened at the beginning or the end of the regular service.) The baptisteries were removed from the churches and a simple bowl was used to

---

[184] See below at n.186 for regulations. *Inst.* 4.15.20 (from 1543 against laity, male or female, baptizing); 4.15.21 (from 1559 against women baptizing).

[185] Farel's liturgy translated in *Early French Reform*, pp. 197-199, quotations on p. 199.

provide water for the sacrament, part of clearing the buildings of the old "holy" objects. Besides the various changes in worship, the agents of baptism were restricted; midwives were prohibited from carrying out this rite [186] — something which probably had as much impact on the experience of the people as the liturgical innovations.

The Place and the Liturgy

In the spring of 1538, under the influence of Bern, Geneva readopted some traditional sacramental usages, and these included the reintroduction of baptisteries for baptism. Apparently the actual practice was less urgent than affirming the use, because it took the city a good many months to re-install the baptisteries. The old ones had been broken or destroyed, and acquiring new ones was not at the top of the Senate's to-do list; however, by the end of 1538 baptisteries had been brought back into the city parishes, even if it took longer in some rural ones. [187] Calvin did not make this an issue when he returned in 1541, although in February 1544 he unsuccessfully proposed removing them; [188] and baptisteries continued to be used for some time. How long, is not clear. In the consistory records, on May 29, 1544, a man says that he brought water to the baptism at La Magdeleine. [189] (Although it can only be inferred that this was the water for the sacrament, it is difficult to imagine what other purpose there could have been in associating water with baptism… perhaps to fill the baptistery or…?) However,

---

[186] Jan. 16, 1537; RC II, p. 23: "que le batesme se doege faire tous les jours en la congregation … que l'on deffende aux femmes obstretrices de ne baptizer point." The baptisteries were removed along with other objects; Roset, *Les chroniques de Genève*, book 4, chap. 22, p. 255, says simply "au commencement de la réformation."

[187] May 16, Dec. 3 & 10 & 24, 1538; RC III, pp. 267, 507-08, 515, 532, 534. The Dec. 24 entry indicates that Jussy and Satigny do not yet have baptisteries.

[188] Feb. 4, 1544; cited by Lambert, *Preaching, Praying, and Policing*, p. 210 n.130.

[189] May 29, 1544; *Consist.* I, p. 373. Jehan Favre, carpenter of Longemale before the consistory: "A cause de quelque vin roge qu'il ballia au baptesme du derrier. Respond qu'il az troys enfans et ne scet quel temps il i a et n'avoy point de bonne femme que se trova, car elle estoyt allé aultre part. Et fust porté d'aygue à la Magdalene et qu'il n'est pas son office de porter du vin car la Boniface [note identifies as probably midwife] avoyt receup l'enfant. Et ne scet dire que porta celluy vin sinon qu'il fusse la femme de Jehan Collomb et qu'il ne s'en vutz rien." Here the point is that a man involved in a baptism brought water to the church for the occasion. That is not the reason he was called before the consistory, but the cause is rather confused. It appears that wine was brought to the baptism, though that had no part in the sacrament itself, obviously; it is possible that the wine was part of the baptismal festivities after the service or a gift to the midwife. Here Favre implies that the wine was associated with the job of the midwife and identifies another woman, the wife of another carpenter, Jehan Collomb, as the one who brought the wine. Evidently these women were part of the baptismal party and one was responsible for the gift of wine.

the description of a baptism by the Catholic critic Cathelan, reporting on Geneva about 1552-3, includes the note that the midwife carries a "bowl full of water." That would not be the case if a baptistery filled with water was a part of the church furnishings. Certainly by the time Michel Roset had finished his *Chronicle* in 1562, these reminders of traditional "holy water" receptacles were a thing of the past in Geneva. [190]

The *Ecclesiastical Ordinances* (1541) and *La forme des prieres* (1542) both provide instructions about the practice of baptism. First is the order about when, where, and by whom the sacrament might be celebrated. The *Ordinances* say "only at the hour of preaching" by ministers or "coadjuteurs" (assistant ministers). This law also orders the baptisteries to be set near the pulpit "so that the reciting of the mystery and usage of baptism may be better heard." [191] *La forme des prieres* gives more detail.

> They should bring babies for baptism either on Sunday at the catechism hour or on the other days at the sermon, so that since baptism is a solemn reception into the church, it may be done in the presence of the assembly. After the sermon, they present the child, and then the minister begins to speak. [192]

Whereas the *Ordinances* do not distinguish any specific services on Sunday, Calvin evidently wanted to link baptism with catechism, which is logical, since the completion of baptism would be the grown child's own confession of the faith taught in the catechism. *La forme des prieres* was not the same kind of legal text as the *Ordinances*, however, and this instruction appears to have been ignored; as the baptismal records indicate, the sacrament could be and was celebrated at any of the four Sunday services, although catechism was one of the favorite times. [193]

The baptismal liturgy was a specific rite but, like the Lord's Supper, it was not a separate service; it was always attached to the end of a regularly scheduled "sermon." After the concluding prayers of the regular service, the minister would come down from the pulpit to the baptistery (or appropriate place, after that piece

---

[190] For Cathelan, see below at n.200. Roset, *Les Chroniques de Genève*, book 4, chap. 16, p. 249.

[191] *Ordinances*, OS II, p. 343: "Que les pierres ou baptistaire soit aupres de la chaire: affin qu'il y a meilleure audience à reciter le mystere et l'usaige du baptesme." The instruction also includes an order to register the names of the children and parents.

[192] OS II, p. 31: "Il est à noter qu'on doit apporter les enfans pour baptiser, ou le Dimanche, à l'heure du Catechisme, ou les aultres jours au sermon, afin, que comme le Baptesme est une reception solennelle en l'Eglise, qu'il se face en la presence de l'Assemblée. Le sermon achevé, on present l'enfant. Et lors le Ministre commence à dire."

[193] See Appendix One: Baptismal Records.

of furniture was removed). The father, and godfather carrying the baby, and the person with the bowl of water (at least by the 1550s) would come to meet the minister and the liturgy would begin. There were the same opening words used at every worship service, and the question: "Are you presenting this baby to be baptized?" This was followed by a long didactic exposition of baptism, first in general and then with specific focus on infant baptism which included a reading of Matt. 19:13-15 in which Jesus commands the disciples to bring the little children to Him. Then there was a prayer, concluding with the Lord's Prayer. Next came the promise made by the father and godfather to teach the baby the faith, "which is received by God's people as it is summarized in the confession of faith which we all have: I believe in God the Father..." The minister goes on to amplify what this means.

> You promise then to take pains to instruct him in all this teaching, and generally in all that is contained in the holy scriptures of the Old and New Testaments, so that he may receive this as the certain word of God coming from heaven. Also, you will exhort him to live according to the rule which our Lord gave us in His law, which is summarized in these two points: that we love God with all our mind, our heart, and power, and our neighbor as ourselves. Likewise, according to the admonitions He gave by His prophets and apostles, that renouncing himself and his own desires (*concupiscences*) he may dedicate and consecrate himself to glorify the name of God and of Jesus Christ, and to edify his neighbors.[194]

The minister then asks the baby's name and baptizes it with the Trinitarian formula.

Over the years the baptismal liturgy underwent some changes, some marked in the text itself and others found in its practice. Early editions often give only the incipit of a familiar piece, but beginning in 1547 the texts of Matt. 19 and the Lord's Prayer are printed in the liturgy. (The doxology usually recited with the Prayer is omitted although it appears in some 1552 and 1561 publications.)[195] After 1552 it became the norm for the Lord's Prayer and the Creed to be printed in larger type and/or a different font. For example, the edition brought out by Jean Crespin 1552 sets off these two catechetical pieces in italics, double-spaced, as well as larger print then the rest of the text, and an analogous demarcation is found in many printings, especially after 1559.[196] This visual change in the material culture may be a clue to altered practice.

---

[194] *La forme des prières*, OS II, pp. 36, 37.

[195] *La forme des prières*, OS II, p. 34. The editors mark the Prayer as 1559, but both are quoted in full in 1552 Jean Crespin's edition (see next note).

[196] [J. Crespin's anchor], *La forme des prieres*... 1552, pp. 32, 33.

By the later 1540s or at least by the 1550s it is probable that the Lord's Prayer and Apostles Creed were recited by the father and godfather. When exactly this was introduced is not clear. On Aug. 30, 1546, in the midst of the first conflict over baptismal names, Calvin asked the Senate to require the (father and) godfather to speak the words themselves. "It would be good that instead of the minister making the confession, the godfather ought to do it in order to show what he is held to." The Senate told Calvin to persevere with the status quo.[197] However, beginning in 1552 there are some visual clues that the tide was turning in the direction Calvin desired, because publishers changed the font or size of the type in which the Lord's Prayer and Apostles' Creed were printed so that these passages stood out in the liturgy. In Crespin's 1552 edition of the liturgy, which seems to have been planned with laity in view, the Prayer and Creed appear in italics and larger letters than the rest of the text – something for which there is no other logical reason except that he wanted these to be easy to see and mark.[198] Over the next years many other publishers changed the appearance of the Prayer and Creed in the baptismal service, normally without altering the script for anything else.[199]

---

[197] Aug. 30, 1556, OC 21:387 (RC 40 f186): "M. Calvin a exposé de fere les remonstrances à ceulx qui portent leurs enfans batizé et leurs mectent plusieurs et divers nom qui ne sont point de l'escripture: dont il seroyt bons que au lieu que le ministre faict la confessions que le parains la dheubz faire affin de monstrer à quoy il est astraint. Ordonné qui luy soyt faicte les remonstrances que il soyt perseveré ainsi comme par avantz et à cause de ce que plusieurs en seroyent trobler et qui soyt dictz que il ne mectent point de nom sinon de l'escripture et que celluy qui ne sera *(saura)* saz fayt ne porte point." The OC editors suggest this is intended for the godfathers, but it seems plausible that the requirement of being able to recite the Prayer and Creed could refer also to fathers.

[198] [J. Crespin], *La forme des prières...* 1552, pp. 32, 33. The Sunday and day of prayer intercessions are printed separately, rather than expecting the people to know where to go in order to find the section of prayer which was common to both days and which had first been printed only once. Since this common text included the paraphrase of the Lord's Prayer, which was a very long piece to repeat twice, and since the ministers could hardly be thought to need this aid, it seems obvious that Crespin was concerned that his lay readers be able to follow exactly. See [Crespin], pp. 9-11, 20-22. (In the 1542, the single printing of the part used both times is k1r-k2v). See OS II, pp. 29, 23.

[199] The following is not intended to be an exhaustive list, but simply illustrative and only the baptismal services of the liturgy are noted. Almost always these are bound with the other usual elements of the Psalter, and often with New Testaments or full Bibles. Here Bibles/ NT are listed in chronological order, then service books the same. Bible 1559 (Geneva, Nicolas Barbier & Thomas Courteau) LP and Creed in larger print (pp. 3v, 4r of separate pagination). NT 1562 (Geneva, Nicolas Barbier & Thomas Courteau), LP and Creed in italics (p. Z3v). NT/ Psalms 1562-63 (Lyon/ Geneva, Francoys Jaquy pour Antoine Vincent), larger print (pp. 17, 18 = B1r-v). Bible 1566 (Geneva, Zacharie Durant) LP and Creed in larger print (pp. A3v, A4r). Bible 1567 (Geneva, François Estienne) LP and Creed in italics (pp. Hh8r-v). NT 1570 (Geneva/ Lyon, Sebastian Honorati), LP and Creed in italics (p. Y2r). Service book 1561 (Geneva, Jean

In Geneva's city parishes there were very often two or more babies baptized at the same service. Occasionally there were as many as six (Pastor Chauvet on Aug. 28, 1554, at La Magdeleine where Calvin was preaching), and four or five at once were not uncommon, especially at La Magdeleine. This meant that when the practice changed there would be several fathers and godfathers all speaking the Prayer and the Creed at the same time. The babies would of course each be named separately, but that may have been the only part of the liturgy which was individualized.

The description by Antoine Cathelan provides a sketch of the baptismal service by a critical visitor.

> After the sermon, the preacher or the deacon of the place stands with head uncovered, and recites four or five prayers ordained by Calvin, [a liturgy] which contains more than our baptism. The others are each in his seat according to their fancy [i.e., worship ordered like a school-room]. Even if there are several babies, they say "I baptize you" only once, and then throw a hand full of water on the faces of the children, water which they took from the hand of the midwife. At their baptisms they have only one godfather or one godmother, who carries the baby in front, and after comes the midwife who carries a bowl full of water and a towel to dry the preacher's or deacon's hands.[200]

Rivery), LP and Creed in italics (pp. 32, 33). Service book 1562 (Lyon, Jean de Laon pour Antoine Vincent), LP and Creed in larger print (pp. 8, 9). Service book 1562 (n.p., Antoine Danodeux & Lucas de Mortiere pour Antoine Vincent), LP and Creed in larger print (pp. ccc2v-ccc3r, pp. ccc3r-v). Service book 1563 ([Geneva], Jean Crespin), LP and Creed in larger print (p. 16). Service book 1563 (Geneva, Stephanus), LP and Creed in larger print (pp. 34-36). Service book 1563 (Geneva, Jean-Baptiste Pinereul pour Antoine Vincent), LP and Creed in italics (p. bb6v). Liturgy 1563 German translation of *La forme des prières* (Heidelberg, Johanne Meyer) has LP and Creed in larger font, pp. "37" = 38-39, 39-40. Service book 1565 (Caen, Simon Mangeant) LP and Creed in italics (p. K2v). Exceptions: Psalter 1549 (Lyon, Godfrey & Marcellin Beringen); Liturgy 1553 (Geneva, Adam & Jean Riveriz); New Testament 1563 (Caen, Pierre le Chandelier). The Strasbourg liturgy published by Garnier in 1553 calls for the father to take a much more active role, expecting him to speak an extended confession, pp. 294-303.

200 Cathelan, *Passevent Parisien*, p. 11: "Après le sermon, le prêcheur ou diacre du lieu tout debout, teste descouverte, il recite quatre ou cinq oraisons jà ordonnées par Calvin et autres, chacun en son siége selon leur fantasie, contenant plus que nostre baptesme. Et combien qu'il y ait plusieurs enfans, ilz ne dient qu'une fois *Je vous baptise*, et puis jettent de l'eaue leur plaine main, sus le visage des enfans, laquelle ilz ont prise de la main de la sage femme. Ilz n'ont en leurs baptesmes qu'un Parrain, ou une Marraine, qui porte l'enfant tout au devant, et après vient la sage femme, qui porte une aiguière pleine d'eau, et une serviete pour sécher les mains au prédicant ou diacre. Et après suivent les hommes, et puis les femmes deux à deux, comme si un seul homme, ou une seule femme pouvoit engendrer, qui démonstre bien leur sottise et ignorance de l'institution du Parrain et Marraine." Spierling, *Infant Baptism in Reformation Geneva*,

Cathelan then describes a baptismal procession, men two by two and women the same, which he says demonstrates the [Reformed] ignorance of the institution of godparents (because in his Catholic tradition godparents were supposed to be paired like physical parents, not separated by sex). For the Reformed, the godparents were not supposed to symbolize a couple, of course, and in Calvin's Geneva, a single godfather was the norm. In the early years the rural parish of Satigny registered a number of godmothers (about 15.8%), but this traditional practice had disappeared by 1555, and in the city of Geneva only godfathers are recorded.[201] (Perhaps Cathelan the visitor had an informant who described the practice in Satigny where there had been godmothers?)

Cathelan indicates that the whole congregation remained seated until the end of the baptismal liturgy, since for Calvin the object of holding it at a regular preaching service included both the necessity of the proclamation of the word with the act of the sacrament, and the presence of the gathered church. However, at least at first many Genevans apparently did not grasp the importance of both aspects. Members of the baptismal party and even godfathers fairly often would come to deposit nurse and baby at the church and then leave to do something else, before returning in time for the baptism at the end of the service.[202] Ordinary

---

p. 119, reads this as saying that the godfather would hand the baby to the midwife who would in turn hand it to the pastor. That appears to read "laquelle" as referring to the baby but the feminine pronoun goes with "l'eau." In fact, it would have been impractical if not impossible for the minister to take and hold every baby being baptized, when there were often several and sometimes as many as six. Poullain's 1552 & 1554 Latin and 1552 French liturgies instruct the minister to take the baby in his arms to baptize; *Liturgi Sacra*, pp. 144, 145. The Strasbourg liturgy printed in 1553 also instructs the minister to do this, p. 306. However, the 1552 French liturgy preserved in the Bodleian does not include this (cf. p. 17v) nor does Poullain's 1551 Latin (p. 144).

[201] See Spierling, *Infant Baptism in Reformation Geneva*, pp. 112-14, referring to registers for the years 1550-57, comparing Satigny and St. Pierre, part of chap. 4 on godparents. Prescriptive evidence indicates that at least urban Genevans were told to expect only a godfather as early as Dec. 10, 1538, when the pastors requested a book in which to record baptisms and explicitly list godfather "paren"; RC III, p. 515. This language is repeated in the *Ordinances*, OS II, p. 343 (quoted above at n.172). For context, it may be noted that Farel's liturgy which calls for recording baptisms and marriages mentions only the babies and the couples and the dates; *La maniere et fasson*, p. C4v.

[202] Jan. 20, 1550, OC 21:460 (RC 44 f306v) the Senate agreed to have the dizeniers tell the people not to leave during the sermon. April 24, 1550 (same point) and Sept. 30, 1550, cited in *Consist.* VI, p. 155 n.948; for Sept. (R. Publ. 2, f 18): "...tous les parens ou parrains en portant baptiser les enfans, ilz doibgent assister au sermon et baptesme sans partir jusques après que le baptesme soit faict et achevé à poienne de cinq soldz pour une ch[es]cune foys." *Consist.* VI, p. 155, Aug. 20, 1551: case of Jean de Miribello who brought a baby to La Magdeleine but left to go do some business before returning for the baptismal liturgy at the end of the service.

parishioners who happened to be present at the service where a baptism was celebrated often did not feel compelled to stay, or they might get up and walk about the church while the liturgy was being celebrated.[203] The reasons for this were varied, including the difficulty of changing the religious culture which said that baptisms were family affairs and no obligation of the larger community. However, one other factor was the possibility that the sacrament might extend the worship time by some minutes (ten?). (The question of timing will be addressed below.) There were so many baptisms in the city parishes that virtually all Genevans were likely to experience this rite fairly frequently. Calvin and his colleagues tried to persuade the magistrates to make people stop moving about the church during baptisms but it took considerable time and effort. As the city became better adapted to its new confessional practices the people in the pew learned to remain there to witness baptisms, and the persons actually involved conformed to the requirement to be present for the whole preaching service.

Baptismal Names

One of the well-known problems related to baptism in Geneva was the conflict over appropriate names.[204] In fact, regulation of names was becoming the practice in various parts of early modern Europe, but the Genevan situation has attracted the most attention.[205] Traditionally it was the godparents' privilege to name the child and normally the main sponsor gave the baby his or her own name. Saints' names were very common and in Geneva the local saint, Claude, was the most popular; it has been estimated that before the Reformation this was the third most popular name in Geneva, for many girls as well as boys. The conflict over names has received considerable notice recently, so a brief summary is sufficient. Beginning in 1546 there was a concerted effort by the

---

[203] July 1, 1549, excerpt from R.C. published in *Consist.* IV, pp. 218-19: "Ayant entendu Maystre Jehan Calvin, ministre de [Genève] qui a proposé aut nom du Consistoyre pour mecstre ordre à cyeulx que ce pourmenent par l'eglise pendant que l'on administre le saint sacrement du baptesme et d'autres qui viennent accompagnyé cyeulx qui apportent baptissé les enfans jusque à la porte du temple et puys s'en retournent, requerant il avoyer advys. Resoluz qu'i soyent deputés des guex pour deffendre à cyeulx qui ce pourmenent par l'eglise de non ainsi ce pourmener et la rest est layssé comment de coustume."

[204] See Naphy, *Calvin and the Consolidation*, pp. 144-52. Spierling, *Infant Baptism in Reformation Geneva*, pp. 140-52. The present summary is a combination of these sources and independent reading.

[205] Spierling, *Infant Baptism in Reformation Geneva*, pp.142, 143, citing Monter and Roget. There are various views about the causes of this baptismal conflict. Naphy considers it essentially a reaction of native Genevans against their (overbearing) foreign clergy; cf. *Calvin and the Conso-lidation*, pp. 144-52; others reject or modify this identification of the cause. Spierling provides an overview of the debate; *Infant Baptism in Reformation Geneva*, pp. 140-44.

pastors to change the custom of giving babies "superstitious" names. The first notable outbreak came in August 1546 when a minister refused the name Claude and baptized the child "Abraham," to the great dismay and indignation of the gathered family and friends. [206] This was followed by another disturbance in November which led to the formulation of a list of prohibited names, such as those of saints: Claude, Caspar or Melchior or Balthasar (traditional for the three wise men); or names of offices ("Baptist") or of God ("Savior"); or other such names ("Cross" or "Sunday"). [207] The problem flared up again more seriously in 1548; on May 27 at the St. Pierre catechism service Pastor Cop refused to name a baby Balthasar as the father and godfather wanted, and the family and at least some of the parishioners in attendance joined in the protest. [208] The tide of the argument went up and down. The use of some of the disputed names temporarily reappeared and was accepted, e.g., Gaspard(e) or Balthazard(e) in the 1550s, [209] but over the years Genevans apparently came to terms with the restrictions on baptismal names and these traditional favorites also disappeared.

The changing practice of naming children in Geneva reflects a shift in the Calvinist Reformed understanding of godparents away from the traditional idea of identifying the baby with the sponsor. Examination of the baptismal registers in the later 1550s reveals that a number of Genevan godfathers who had perfectly fine (sometimes Biblical) names, in fact gave their godchildren different ones. In 1558 at St. Gervais, Guillaume Chappuis named his goddaughter Jehanne (Jan. 23), Antoine du Four named his godson Abraham (Feb. 14), Jehan Coricheron (?) named his Isaac (March 23), Maturin Periguet named his Jheremie (May 22). Visible evidence that the tempo increased over time is seen in the baptisms at St. Pierre in the first eleven days of January in 1562. Denis Lassone presented his godson with the name David, Michel Roset called his Samuel, Nicholas Colladon named his Nathanael, François Guarin presented his goddaughter Elizabeth, Jehan Jesse his goddaughter Susanne, Pierre Chopin his godson Jacob, Loys Voland called his godson Jehan, and François Paris named his godson Abraham. A glance at Calvin's recorded acts as godfather illustrates

---

[206] Naphy, *Calvin and the Consolidation*, pp. 146-52.

[207] See the ordinance on names, OC 10:49-50.

[208] *Consist.* IV, pp. 73-75, May 31, 1548. This is Thursday at consistory, describing the previous Sunday, with statement of the issue and then of the witnesses.

[209] Baptismal records for Balthazard Bonna, Feb. 26, 1553; Gaspard Fichet, Sept. 27, 1553; Balthazard Delaporte, Oct. 1, 1553; Gaspard Rousset, Oct. 10, 1553; Balthazarde Paris, Oct. 14, 1554; Gaspard Philibert, July 21, 1554; Balthazarde Mutin, March 25, 1555; Gasparde Simon, April 15, 1555; Gaspard Riguot, Oct. 31, 1555; Gasparde Mercier, March 7, 1557; Gaspard Fourjod, May 2, 1557.

the same thing; while there are many more variants on Jean or Jehanne/ Anne than any other name, there are also a number of other baptismal names apparently chosen by Calvin: Jacqueline, Samuel, Jaques, David, Paula, Marie, Sara, Judith, Elizabeth, and Pierre. In the next generations the Reformed tradition would become known for the frequency and popularity of Old Testament baptismal names, a custom clearly becoming visible in these examples from Geneva in Calvin's later years.[210]

The Daily Practice of Baptism

Geneva was a large city to have only three parish churches; a growing population produced many babies and this meant that baptisms were a part of many worship services. In the city dawn and catechism were the favorite times for this sacrament, at least from 1550 on, as the baptismal records show. Given the steady pattern manifested in these registers, it is more than likely that dawn and catechism had always been the most popular, especially because the liturgy actively encouraged the catechism hour. Calvin evidently discouraged baptisms at the main 8 a.m. Sunday morning time when he was preaching, probably because that was a key time for announcing banns, which would already lengthen the service before a baptism was held. The same was true for Sunday afternoon services because that was one of the most important times for weddings.[211] However, baptism was permitted and actually took place at least occasionally at every service on Sundays or weekdays, except the mornings when the Lord's Supper was celebrated.

---

210 For Calvin's acts as godfather, see Appendix Six. This orientation toward OT names was already apparent to Cathelan in the early 1550s; cf. *Passevent Parisien*, pp. 12-13.

211 See above at n.192 for catechism; chap. 3 at nn.171ff for banns; above at nn.70ff for weddings.

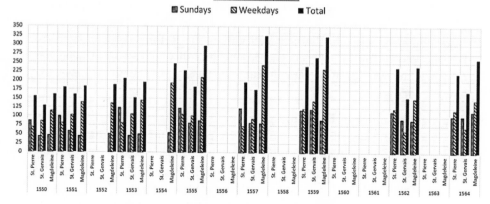

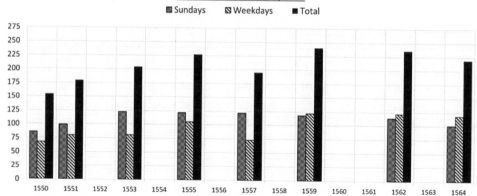

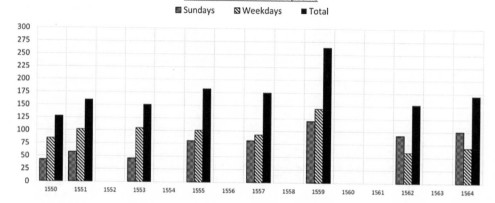

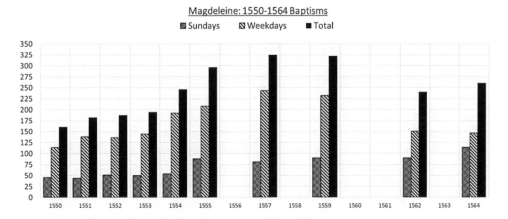

Genevans were supposed to receive the sacraments in their home parishes,[212] so a couple with a baby to present for baptism would go to a service in their own local church. For parishioners at St. Gervais, this was simple and they had many choices of times: dawn, 8 a.m., catechism, or 3 p.m. on Sundays, and once each weekday morning, plus a second time on Wednesday, the day of prayer (probably by around 1545). For most of Calvin's ministry, those in Greater Geneva had a somewhat more complicated system. A couple in the parish of St. Pierre had the same four Sunday options as at St. Gervais: dawn or catechism (or, sometimes 8 a.m. or 3 p.m.), but the weekday choices were limited to one of the dawn services on Monday, Wednesday, or Friday, or the second worship time on Wednesday. Until June 1559 there were no other weekday services in St. Pierre. In the parish of La Magdeleine, the possibilities were (mostly) different. La Magdeleine was never intended to have a dawn service on any day (and never did, except for a few months in 1559-60). Thus, one of the most popular times for baptisms did not exist at La Magdeleine. For a number of years (until 1549) there was no 8 a.m. Sunday service except on days the Lord's Supper was celebrated, and for even longer (until 1555) there were none on Sunday afternoon. The only regular Sunday service at La Magdeleine in the 1540s was catechism, so that was the time for Sunday baptisms in this parish. However, until 1559 La Magdeleine hosted most of the weekday worship in Greater Geneva. There were services at the "ordinary" hour of 6 a.m. in summer and 7 a.m. in winter, Monday through Saturday (except Wednesday when the day of prayer service moved up the hill to St. Pierre).

Usually Genevans brought their infant children to church for baptism within a few days, or a week, of birth. According to Reformed teaching, which most of them apparently came to accept, a newborn who died before the actual rite of baptism was not eternally lost since it was already an heir of the covenant promise because its parents were. Nonetheless virtually no one except suspected Anabaptists delayed in presenting a baby in church for the sacrament, unless there were some unusual circumstances. In the consistory records for May 27, 1544, a woman and her husband affirm that their six week old baby had been baptized seven days previously at La Magdeleine. (The child was born when the woman was visiting her mother in a Catholic village and she was too ill to know if it had been baptized. However, she and her husband had the sacrament properly done in Geneva, with a godfather from the faithful community. The seriousness of this couple was demonstrated when they added that because the wife refused the "papist" baptism desired by her mother, the latter had disinherited her.) [213] In the registry for La Magdeleine there is an entry for May 31, 1562, of a man from one of Geneva's rural villages, Tonne, who brought his baby to the city for baptism because there had not been a pastor in his parish for three weeks and he did not want to wait longer. Obviously the city minister understood the problem because the baby was baptized, even if La Magdeleine was not the parents' home parish. Again, the Roman visitor Cathelan provides a critical perspective: "some wait for Sunday, others only until after the [weekday] sermons, and others at three in the afternoon" [214] (this last must mean Sunday afternoon). What Cathelan saw as a sign of confusion and discord because he did not understand or approve the varied hours of services was almost certainly not viewed as divisive by the Genevans once they became accustomed to the new schedule of worship.

In the parish of St. Pierre well over half of the parents brought their babies for baptism on Sunday, especially at dawn or catechism, and usually about one-quarter to one-third came for the sacrament at the dawn services on Monday, Wednesday, or Friday. Occasionally there were actually more baptismal liturgies on weekdays, even if the number of babies was greater on Sunday owing to multiple children receiving the sacrament in the same service. For example, in 1551 there were 65 services on Sunday at which 99 babies were baptized, while there were 67 services on weekdays at which 80 babies received the sacrament. Beginning in 1559 when a daily service at the "ordinary" hour was introduced at

---

[213] *Consist.* I, p. 371, May 27, 1544.

[214] Cathelan, *Passevent Parisien*, p. 12: "Les uns attendent le Dimenche, les autres seullement après les sermons, et des autres à trois heures de soir: qui démonstre bien leur division et discord ensemble." Obviously he considers the variety of worship times when baptisms could be performed as an evidence of disagreement, but the point here is that some parents would bring their babies to the weekday services soon after birth, others would wait for Sunday worship. Probably most were baptized any time from a day or two after birth to six days later.

St. Pierre in addition to its three weekday dawn services, the numbers of babies baptized on weekdays became larger than those on Sunday. This was logical, since now there were actually nine weekday services and still only four on Sunday. See Graphs.

In the 1540s parishioners at La Magdeleine brought their infants to the Sunday catechism or on one of the weekdays. By the time the baptismal records began in 1550, the main 8 a.m. Sunday service had been added and before long the Sunday baptisms came to be divided more evenly between catechism and 8 a.m. at La Magdeleine. (In the early 1550s, Poupin, the minister who usually did the morning service, did not mark the times when he baptized and so it is not always clear whether a baptism was at 8 a.m. or catechism. Later other ministers did give the time.) Even after a Sunday afternoon service was added and some baptisms were celebrated then, that was the least popular time. In La Magdeleine the great majority of baptisms took place on weekdays; this was not surprising, since there were always more services then than on Sundays. From 1550 to 1555 when La Magdeleine had two Sunday and five weekday services, there were often more than double or triple the number of babies baptized on weekdays as on Sundays, but this was done in three to five times as many liturgies. For example: in 1550 there were 32 services with 46 babies on Sundays, and 94 services with 114 babies on weekdays; in 1551 there were 29 services with 44 babies on Sundays, and 100 services with 138 babies on weekdays. Even after the third Sunday service was added, the proportions remained fairly much the same, with the great majority of babies being baptized on weekdays. In 1557 there were 53 services with 81 babies on Sundays, and 169 services with 243 babies on weekdays; in 1559 there were 61 services with 90 babies on Sundays, and 155 services with 232 babies on weekdays. By the early 1560s the totals fell and the disproportion between Sundays and weekdays diminished, although the latter still had the majority of services and babies.

At St. Gervais the parish organization which was established when Calvin returned to Geneva in 1541 held steady. There were more baptisms on weekdays than on Sundays because there were more opportunities: six (in 1542) or seven (well before 1550) services during the week compared to four on Sunday. About one-third to slightly less than one-half of the children in St. Gervais were baptized on Sundays. In 1550 there were 39 services with 43 babies on Sundays, and 72 services with 85 babies on weekdays; in 1551 there were 45 services with 58 babies on Sundays, and 80 services with 102 babies on weekdays. In 1557 there were 67 services with 82 babies on Sundays, and 75 services with 93 babies on weekdays; in 1559 there were 83 services with 120 babies on Sundays, and 119 services with 144 babies on weekdays. See Graphs.

Several general observations may be made. La Magdeleine had been the most populous parish before the Reformation, and it remained so in Calvin's day. In the early 1550s St. Pierre had about equal numbers of baptisms but by 1555 La Magdeleine was clearly ahead, and both usually had more babies and baptisms than St. Gervais. It appears that, all things being equal, Sundays were preferred for baptisms, even though more babies received the sacrament at the weekday services. It can regularly be observed that the Sunday baptismal services account for more babies per liturgy; or to put it another way, on a weekday one baby might well receive baptism by him or herself, while on Sunday there was a higher likelihood of sharing the liturgy with one or more other infants and their families. Obviously parents were willing to double-up in order to have a Sunday baptism. One reason for the higher profile of Sunday might simply have been convenience, since everyone was required to attend worship on Sunday, even if there was no specific penalty for an occasional absence. Thus if there was some question about your chosen godfather not wanting to take time off from work to come to a weekday baptismal service in your parish, the prudent father might opt for a Sunday service. Especially when it became accepted that the godfather could not drop off the child and return for the baptismal liturgy at the end of the service, it might have seemed sensible to plan a Sunday baptism when all the people involved would have another reason besides the sacrament to be in church.

III: Pastors and Coordinating the Rhythms of Marriage and Baptism in the Parish

Imagine being a pastor or a parishioner at worship in Calvin's Geneva. How would the rhythms of personal religious occasions fit into their larger context as liturgies in the community's worship life?

Parishioners in Geneva made choices about their weddings and baptisms, the two religious services which affected their lives as individuals. To a considerable degree, if they were following approved patterns, their weddings would be celebrated about six weeks after their engagements were formally recognized. They could choose the service and probably had some freedom about the parish, at least if they lived in Greater Geneva. The two most popular times for weddings were dawn and afternoon services on Sundays in St. Pierre or St. Gervais. Usually if a couple wanted the public visibility of being married by chief minister Calvin, as some people of status no doubt did, they would choose Sunday afternoon. (Between 1546 and 1552 Calvin was preaching at St. Gervais on most Sunday afternoons but not all; he regularly did weddings at St. Gervais as well as occasional ones at St. Pierre. Before and after this period he was at St. Pierre on Sunday afternoons, until in old age he no longer preached twice on Sundays.) Other couples might choose a dawn service; this would probably appeal to less socially prominent Genevans, or to those who desired a less crowded service or wanted to be home from church early to have the rest of the day for their wedding party. The marriage records indicate not only that the great majority of weddings were celebrated on Sundays but also that most of the remaining ones were held on Mondays at the weekday services. Very few weddings were performed later in the week, although there are at least a few examples on every day.[215]

Planning a baby's baptism was of course not entirely in the parents' hands, but there was still considerable flexibility possible. The chosen godfather and others could be alerted when the mother-to-be went into labor and the organization of the baptismal party would probably already be in hand before the actual day and time of the sacrament could be fixed. Probably the father and godfather would agree on when they wanted to have the service and would inform anyone else who needed to be present, e.g., the midwife who carried the water. The mother usually was still too unwell to leave her bed and so mothers did not often attend their children's baptisms. The father (or perhaps the godfather?) would probably tell the pastor when they would be bringing the baby to church, although it is entirely possible that on occasion a father and godfather would turn up with the baby just before the service and say they wanted a baptism at the end.

One further issue in planning a baptism was insuring that all the participants were in good standing with the church. Those who were guilty of fornication or, worse, adultery, would be subject to discipline. If they were suspended from the Lord's Supper, then they were also barred from presenting an infant for baptism until the suspension was lifted. Although this was not legislated until the *Ecclesiastical Ordinances* were revised in 1561, it began to be practiced long before, by the late 1540s at least.[216] The common difficulty was a godfather who was feuding with the consistory and thus prevented from presenting a child, although on occasion it might be the father who was suspended from the Supper. Since being a godparent was an important social honor, many Genevans considered this ruling

---

[215] See Appendix Two: Marriage Records.

[216] For one early example see Jehan Bandiere, questioned on this matter on Sept. 24, 1548, OC 21:434 (RC 43 f220v). Spierling, *Infant Baptism in Reformation Geneva*, pp. 129-40, discusses this issue fully. The 1552 French liturgy published by Poullain for the refugee congregation in London and Frankfurt explicitly affirms that one must be in good standing not only to participate as father or godfather in a baptism but also to be married (both bride and groom). See Poullain, *Liturgia Sacra*, p. 219.

very unfair, while the ministers insisted that someone who was not fit to take the Lord's Supper was not fit to make and carry out the promise to teach a godchild the faith. However, assuming that both father and godfather were faithful, communing members of the church, and there was no argument about giving the baby an unacceptable name, the family had made their preparations for the baptism and it could go forward.

From the pastor's viewpoint, the coordination of baptisms and weddings was a rather different matter. There was no real surprise about weddings; the minister of the parish had been announcing the banns at intervals for six weeks. The groom(s) who wanted to be married on a given day had almost certainly informed the officiating preacher. Again, it is possible that a couple might appear without warning the minister at that specific service, e.g., coming to St. Pierre at dawn or on Sunday afternoon when the minister on duty that day only knew that their banns had been completed and the wedding was in order. In any case, the couple had to be early enough to take their places before the final peal of the bell, so that the service could begin on time. Since the marriage liturgy was performed at the beginning of worship, those coming late would have to reschedule their wedding because the minister would already have begun the regular preaching service.

Coordinating baptisms could be more of a problem than doing weddings, however, and not just because there were so many more babies to baptize than couples to marry. Probably a father would inform his pastor when a baby was born, and the minister would then be prepared to expect a baptism. When two men were alternating in a pulpit, as was often true in the city parishes in Geneva, it is not clear whether both would be told about the baby's arrival. In any event, it was less urgent that the pastor know ahead of time that he needed to celebrate a baptism than in the case of a wedding, because the baptism was at the end of the regular preaching service. When the people with the newborn baby arrived at church as the bells were ringing, they would only need to be sure that the minister registered their presence. Then, when the sermon and prayers were finished, the baptismal party would come forward to meet the pastor near the pulpit and the liturgy could proceed.

For the ministers of Geneva's three urban parishes, weddings and especially baptisms were fairly common occurrences. In fact, on some days the pastor would marry one or several couples at the start of the service, and baptize one or more babies at its conclusion. Then each couple, and each baby with its parents and godfather, had to be registered in the appropriate book (sometimes there were mistakes, and baptisms got into the marriage records and vice versa), along with the name of the minister and the date. Besides having to carry out two more rites along with the sermon he had planned, the pastor had to fit all of these together in the single hour allotted for that service. Each of the special liturgies: wedding or baptism, would take about ten to fifteen minutes, and if there were multiple couples who had to respond or babies who had to be named, that would extend the process. Even if the minister cut short his sermon, it is not surprising that the service might overrun the designated time, and if he did not abbreviate his sermon, it was virtually certain that this would happen. The congregation would complain and, since baptisms were celebrated at the end of worship, they might vote with their feet and get up and leave, disrupting the sacrament and raising the ire of the pastors – and perhaps of the baptismal party. The Senate occasionally rebuked the preachers and told them to keep to the time limit,[217] but the problem was not necessarily that the sermons were longer than usual on those days, but that the services incorporated more different liturgies. After Calvin's death there was a push to move baptisms (as well as weddings) to the beginning of the service so that the preacher would know how much he had to abbreviate his sermon to insure that the service got out on time, but the ministers resisted because this would compel them to cut their services in half – from one hour to half an hour for the whole thing: prayers, possibly Psalms (depending on the day) as well as the sermon.[218]

Weddings and the even more frequent baptisms were a significant part of public worship life in Protestant Geneva. The ways the teaching and practice of marriage and baptism were reformed have been studied from a number of viewpoints. It is illuminating, however, to observe the effect of transferring these personal family liturgies into the ordinary rhythm of the city's public religious experience. The character of the "private" family rituals was changed in significant ways by having these services lived out in the context of any neighbors and fellow parishioners who happened to be in church when a groom and bride presented themselves to be married, or parents brought their newborn baby for baptism. Equally important and perhaps less often noted is that the texture of the community's experience of worship was changed by having the public vows of married couples and the public promises of fathers and godfathers set before the eyes of the whole parish on a regular basis. Last but not least, the implementation of the many services which the ministers had fought to establish was naturally affected; planning a rotation of preachers was not enough – they had to be flexible about the daily order in the pulpit to incorporate weddings and

---

217 Aug. 31, 1552, OC 21:516 (RC 46 f265v): "pour ce que l'heure est tard à cause du sermon arresté que l'on remect l'affaire à demain."

218 See discussion in 1573, RCP III, p. 98 n. 5, cited in Lambert, *Preaching, Praying, and Policing*, p. 291.

baptisms into the hour allotted and still have time for the sermon and prayers. Sermons were integral to the experience of corporate worship in Geneva and that dimension of the story: i.e., setting the preaching of the word in the context of the daily, weekly, annual rhythm of worship, is the necessary complement to the patterns of sacramental and marriage liturgies.

PART THREE

Preaching in Geneva and Calvin's Sermons

Expository Biblical preaching was arguably the single most prominent, if not most important, feature of Reformed worship, and its place in Calvin's Geneva and his own theology is well established. Usually, however, the actual relationship between the reformer's sermons and his pastoral ministry has not been fully appreciated. A focused examination of the preacher in the daily life of his church can thus be illuminating for both.

Preaching in Calvin's Geneva was part of both a longer history and a larger Protestant practice. Calvin himself has long been famous as a theologian who also preached. In keeping with the purpose of this book to explore what was happening "on the ground," Part Three examines the reformer's homiletical work in context, with special attention to his sermons as part of the nuts and bolts – or pulpits and pews – of Genevan worship practice.

CHAPTER SIX

CALVIN THE PREACHER OF GENEVA

This chapter has four main divisions. The first section is contextual; it begins with a brief overview of the historical context, particularly the ways that Protestants shaped the tradition of sermons and preaching that they inherited, and then sketches the Genevan situation in Calvin's day. The second section is a four-part exploration of Calvin's homiletical activity, which identifies where he preached, what is known about his Biblical subject matter and what is missing, and concludes with an examination of his catechetical work. The third section investigates the reformer's sermons themselves: how they were copied down and how they can be dated. The final section explores some aspects of what can be learned from the sermons about Calvin's audiences: what they can reveal about the preacher's knowledge of and accommodation to his hearers, and how his preaching was received by varied audiences.

I: Sketching the Historical Context of Preaching

The Protestant Reformation is often seen as a revival of preaching, although in fact it was rather a very distinctive part of an on-going movement. To understand Calvin's Geneva it is important to note briefly what ordinary parishioners before the Protestant reform would have known or expected in the way of preaching and where and how they received it.

Preaching and Sermons in the Late Middle Ages

Monastic meditation on scripture has a long and continuous history, but preaching to laity, especially regular sermons in ordinary parish churches, had been uncommon for centuries before the high middle ages. Then the rise of universities and the cry for preaching – which produced "heretics" like the Waldensians – brought about a growing interest in preaching; parish clergy, however, were not well equipped to respond to this new demand. (It must be remembered that sermons were not a means of grace as the sacraments were, and preaching was not a required part of a Mass or any other sacramental liturgy. Thus, a parish priest could still do his job even if he could not preach.) It was the thousands of Dominicans, Franciscans, and other mendicant orders who took up the challenge and spread preaching across western Europe, particularly in the towns and cities.

Late medieval urban Genevans had access to a considerable number of sermons from the religious orders, both by members of local houses and experts brought in from outside, on alternate Sundays at the Franciscan and Dominican monasteries. At least until the later part of the fifteenth century there was little or nothing from their parish clergy. (In this Geneva lagged behind cities like Strasbourg and especially Basel, where those in charge of parishes were probably better educated and resident.)[1] In 1455 an agreement among the heads of the Dominican and Franciscan houses and Geneva's city councilors was made that the religious orders would provide public sermons every Sunday in the year in perpetuity. Over time this apparently shifted to the right to choose the preachers for the special Advent and Lent sermons, in alternation and with the concurrence of the bishop and the cathedral chapter. Sometimes there were conflicts about inviting outsiders instead of the local preachers. In 1484, although it was the Franciscans' turn, both religious orders invited special guests for Lent and appealed to the city council to decide who should give way. The fact of the appeal is significant for the council's increasing power, but its members wisely referred this matter to the cathedral chapter. The latter ordered the Dominican to preach at his convent on Sunday morning and the Franciscan would preach after mid-day dinner in the open court before St. Pierre; the two would then maintain

---

[1]   Manetsch, *Calvin's Company of Pastors*, pp. 147-48, describes the late medieval situation in Geneva, both the monastic and the parish sermons. For the latter he cites Binz; p. 147: "In his careful study of the visitation report of the Diocese of Geneva from 1378 to 1450, Louis Binz found not a single instance of a priest or curate preaching in his parish." See Binz, *Vie religieuse et reform ecclésiastique*, 1:390-92. See Burnett, "A Tale of Three Cities," p. 110, for comparisons among these three cities which would become leading Reformed churches.

this same program for the rest of the Sundays of Lent. As for weekdays, sermons were allowed but the bells could not be rung to signal them.[2]

A witness from the early sixteenth century affirms that there was regular preaching in the religious houses but public sermons were limited. Jeanne de Jussie, a member of the prominent St. Clare Sisters and author of an account of her house in this period, noted that there were sermons in the convents every Sunday and feast day. She also refers occasionally to sermons in public contexts, but it is unclear with what regularity these were held and which might have been provided by parish clergy.[3] If the priests in Geneva's parishes did preach they might become involved in polemic. The populous parish of La Magdeleine belonged to an absentee canon who had appointed a vicar. Conflict between the secular priest in this church and the neighboring religious orders erupted in 1516 and the city council got involved. The plan had been for the Franciscans and Dominicans to continue alternating to choose the Lenten preacher. However, the priest at La Magdeleine was in his pulpit calling the people "stupid," and when the bishop's vicar did nothing, the city council acted to import a noted Dominican preacher. La Magdeleine continued to ring with polemic, however, as the priest attacked the Franciscan women as prostitutes, leading to immediate action by city leaders to defend the Sisters of St. Clare.[4] In summary, there were regular (or semi-regular) opportunities to hear preaching in the religious houses in Geneva, but it was unlikely that sermons would be available in the parish church. Or at least, some doubt that what was found there would be edifying – which raises the question of the sermons themselves.

The preaching revival included both elite and common audiences, and sermons were usually fitted to the hearers. The language for the educated or clergy was Latin, for the majority of laity it was their vernacular. Generally speaking, sermons took one of several forms: thematic exposition of a word or idea from the text or focus of the day, shaped by university educated preachers for an elite audience; the old homily meditation still popular in some monastic (and heretical) circles; and popular sermons to lay people. John O'Malley identifies the most influential pattern of preaching to laity as the Franciscan motto "to preach vice and virtue, punishment and glory."[5] Since all church teaching was regarded as

---

2   Naef, *Les Origines de la Réforme*, vol. I, pp. 156-57. The following pages give further examples of the increasing involvement of the city council in the organizing of the special sermons.

3   see chap. 2 at nn.2ff.

4   Naef, *Les Origines de la Réforme*, vol. I, pp. 160-62.

5   John W. O'Malley, "Introduction: Medieval Preaching," *De Ore Domini: Preacher and Word in the Middle Ages*, ed. T. L. Amos et al. (Kalamazoo: Medieval Institute, 1989), p. 6.

authoritative, sermons could be based on any one of a number of sources: Biblical texts (either the lectionary, which was essentially New Testament texts; or popular Old Testament stories), church dogma (e.g., the sacraments), saints' lives (especially miracles), catechetical materials (often with mnemonic devices to make it easier for an oral culture to remember, such as *seven* deadly sins, *twelve* points of the creed), and other moral instruction (particularly sermons *ad statu*, or how each estate in society should behave). Jeanne de Jussie provides an idea of the topics offered to the Genevans during Lent: penitence and confession, the "sacrament of the altar," pardons and indulgences. In the instance she cites, the Dominican who had preached in Advent was asking to do the 1534 Lenten sermons and offered these headings.... only to be told by the Senate that he should stick to the gospel.[6] The times were changing!

Many books of sermons and sermon aids were published to help parish clergy as well as friars. The language and origin of these handbooks is significant. Traditionally texts produced by scholars were usually in Latin, and preachers who wanted to use them were expected to translate the sermons they needed if they could not prepare their own. If scholars intended to publish any sermons they had preached in the vernacular, these were commonly turned back into Latin and almost always polished before being circulated. The pre-publication editing of homiletical material might range from a preacher giving fuller form to his own (Latin) notes, through transcription by educated clerical listeners, to the formal writing out of a sermon which had never been preached in that specific fashion. In the case of transcriptions made while the sermon was being preached, the process might result in a macaronic text, a mixture of the spoken language and Latin, because clerical hearers were ordinarily accustomed to thinking theologically in Latin and that vocabulary would come to mind more readily than the less precise descriptive equivalents used with laity.[7] Until the later middle ages, most serious sermon literature remained in Latin. Vernacular texts by responsible scholars were beginning to be published by 1500, when German expositions of the lectionary were produced in more sophisticated

6   Jeanne de Jussie, *Le Levain du Calvinisme*, p. 90: "Penitence, & Confession sacramentelle. Le second du S. Sacrement de l'Autel. Le troisiesme, des Pardons & Indulgences."

7   G. R. Owst, *Preaching in Medieval England, an introduction to the sermon manuscripts of the period c. 1350-1450* (Cambridge: Univ. Press, 1926) pp. 223ff, notes examples of vernacular sermons recorded in Latin and then transposed back into the vernacular and describes how a sermon would be recorded. These practices continued in the Reformation. See examples of Luther (transcriptions by others, sometimes macaronic texts; and/or with revisions), in n.19. Johannes Oecolampadius (transcription by others) and Oswald Myconius (written out by himself) in Burnett, *Teaching the Reformation*, pp. 57, 61.

urban contexts like Strasbourg, and by learned preachers like the famous Geiler von Kaisersberg.[8]

However, scholars were not the only men producing homiletical aids. Books of sermons in the vernacular which dealt with topics used in popular preaching were current from the fourteenth century. To see what was available in Geneva before the new reforms it is worth mentioning briefly two books which were printed there in the late fifteenth century. One, *Le Livre de sapience*, appeared in October 1478; it was destined for priests who did not know Latin or the Bible, and gave them simple explanations of such things as the Creed, the Lord's Prayer, the Decalogue and the church laws, along with miracle stories intended to teach people to avoid the sins described (sins from which the saint rescued the sinner). The second book published in Geneva in 1480, *Le Livre des bonnes meurs*, had five parts: sermons on the seven deadly sins, on clergy, on princes, on common people, and on death. Each chapter heading served as a topic (for example: "How one should live soberly: gluttony is the nursing mother of several other evils and sins, and engenders several physical and spiritual diseases") and was followed by examples from which to construct a little sermonette. As will be seen later, at least a few Genevan priests had books they called postils, but these were probably not common.[9]

Protestant Preaching and Sermons

Protestants were rooted in the preaching revival of the late middle ages, but they brought their own very distinctive reforms to the movement. The best-known characteristics are the insistence on scripture alone as the source for sermons and the general rule that sermons must be part of every Sunday service. There would be no more sermons on church dogma that Protestants saw as human invention – no more preaching on indulgences, or the seven deadly sins in carefully detailed stories,[10] and no more Sunday Masses without a Biblical

---

8   See Old, *The Medieval Church*, pp. 538-39, for the "Strasbourg Plenarium" as kind of late medieval postilla c.1500, which provided an exposition of the gospels and epistles; another example was Geiler von Kaysersberg's Plenarium, the *Evangelia mit Auslegung*, published posthumously in 1517.

9   Naef, *Les origines de la Réforme*, pp. 171-73. See below at n.87.

10 Badius gives an example of the categories of preachers and sermons as Protestant polemic saw them, in his preface to *Plusieurs Sermons*, OC 35:587-88. "Cependant au lieu de repaistre le simple peuple de vraye et saine doctrine, l'instruisoyent à je ne sçay quels badinages et vaines ceremonies qu'ils invertoyent [!] outre la parolle de Dieu. Autant en font de nostre temps nos grans docteurs Sorbonistes, et tous ces criars de Moines, desquels les uns,… neantmoins ne font que conter des fables vaines et sottes, ou s'amusent à des questions curieuses et plenes de sophis-

sermon. Most urban reforms included some kind of weekday worship, which might be primarily prayer, but also could – and in Geneva did – include preaching. However, the Lord's Day or any day when the Lord's Supper was celebrated *had* to have a sermon and ministers in charge of a parish *had* to be able to preach, one way or another.

For content and purpose, the teaching of the text of scripture and Biblical doctrine were key. The approach to scripture might be essentially expository or it might combine explanation of a text with significant attention to drawing out its key doctrines, a kind of *loci communes*. Of course Protestants also preached on the basic catechetical tools: the Lord's Prayer, the Apostles' Creed, the Decalogue. Amy Nelson Burnett provides a very helpful overview of the development of Protestant homiletics in *Teaching the Reformation: Ministers and Their Message in Basel, 1529-1629* (2006). The new, humanist-influenced movement seeking to teach pastors how to preach naturally drew on classical rhetorical sources. Understanding a Biblical text in its relationship to the rest of scripture and the (recovered) "apostolic teaching" was necessary, as was communicating this to people of many different intellectual backgrounds – and often through less-than-well-educated preachers. The main factors in developing a Protestant homiletics were dialectic and rhetoric, with the former increasingly identified with exegesis and the latter with sermon composition and delivery. Eventually the different emphases became identified with confessions, with Lutherans building on Melanchthon's topical method and inclined to the *loci* approach and Reformed (usually) more strictly expository.[11] Noting with appreciation Burnett's attention to the form of sermons, Max Engammare points out that scholars have given relatively little attention to this question in the early Reformation, before treatises on homiletics began to be published. He outlines the three main patterns available: the traditional lectionary system, a "*loci communes*" order, and *lectio continua*, and then builds on this to illustrate that many Reformed communities practiced a variety or combination of forms.[12] The object here is not to develop this intriguing subject

---

terie, et à mille subtilitez qui ne servent d'aucune edification. Les autres preschent, au lieu de la parolle de Dieu, les constitutions et ordonnances qu'eux mesmes ont faites pour establir la tyrannie du Pape, vray Antechrist et ennemi de la verité: les autres aussi escument en chaire, et desgorgent propos arrogans contre les enfans de Dieu, et ceux ausquels Jesus Christ s'est revelé en ces derniers temps, les appelans Lutheriens, seditieux, et controuvans mille mensonges à l'encontre d'eux, au lieu de nourrir de vraye pasture de la parolle de Dieu leurs povres brebis affamees, qui hument telles poisons en guise de la nourriture spirituelle de leurs ames."

[11] Burnett, *Teaching the Reformation*, chap. 7; see esp. pp. 157-58, 160, 162-63. For Calvin's comparison of Luther's postils with what Westphal advocated, see n.15 below.

[12] Engammare, "Reformed Preaching in the Sixteenth Century," pp. 195-200.

further but to give an overview of the wider Protestant practice in which to situate Calvin's work, so that its distinctive character can be more clearly seen.

Naturally, one of the ways Protestants conveyed their new Biblical preaching was in the traditional form of expositions of the one-year selected lectionary. Late medieval reformers had already begun to publish humanist-inspired vernacular exegesis of the lectionary readings, and Lutherans maintained both the traditional Christological calendar and the lectionary system of epistles and gospels as the basic form of scriptural selection. Beginning with his Advent Postilla written in the Wartburg in 1521-22, Luther and his colleagues published expositions which could be read to the people just as they had been printed. As time passed, the shaping of these sermons became more of a *loci* pattern, highlighting the essentials without insisting on every detail. (In addition to the New Testament selected lectionary, Luther had envisioned a continuous reading of the Old Testament on Sunday afternoons, but this did not become a common or regular practice among Lutherans. [13]) In 1524 French-language reformers associated with Meaux and led by Jacques Lefèvre produced a volume entitled *Epistres et Evangiles pour les cinquante et deux dimenches de l'an;* a revised version of this augmented with six more sermons was published by Pierre de Vingle in Neuchâtel about 1535 and circulated in Protestant territories. [14]

Reformed theologians, who also stripped away most of the traditional liturgical year, are usually thought to have chosen the scripture for preaching using a variant of the *lectio continua* system which they considered characteristic of the early church, [15] or a combination of this with more traditional forms. The object of

---

13   See Luther's *Formula Missae et Communionis*, in WA 12, p. 216. The *loci* method was fully set out in the treatise by Andreas Hyperius in 1553, which was translated into French and published in Geneva in 1564; cf. Engammare, "Reformed Preaching in the Sixteenth Century," p. 197.

14   See G. Bedouelle & F Giacone, *Jacques Lefèvre d'Etaples et ses disciples. Epitres et Evangiles pour les cinquante et deux dimanches de l'an. Texte de l'édition Pierre de Vingle* (Leiden: Brill,1976). Neuser, *Johann Calvin – Leben und Werk*, pp. 118-33. De Boer, *Genevan School of Prophets*, pp. 52-53. The other three editions were two by Simon du Bois, and one by Etienne Dolet in Lyon 1542 which would also have been accessible to Genevans. Following Neuser, pp. 141-42, De Boer, p. 53 (citing OC 21:303) believes that the minister of "Grandson" asked the Genevan Senate to allow Jean Michel to print this book. In fact, however, the Annales report is not entirely reliable; when checked against the original it is evident that it was not the Meaux volume but one composed by the minister himself which the Senate rejected. See below at n.88.

15   Calvin's *Secunda Defensio* to Westphal, OC 9:104: "Quod ad sectiones spectat, satis ex omnibus veterum scriptorum homiliis constat scripturae libros uno contextu ad plebem fuisse expositos. Ut aliquid ex Evangelio et apostolicis lectionibus recitandum excerperent quod tempori congrueret, mos inolevit. Hinc sectiones istae pro quibus Westphalus non secus ac pro aris et focis dimicat: quas tamen inepte, nulloque iudicio factas esse lectio coarguit. Certe si fragmenta sumi oportuit, quae singulis diebus dominicis legerentur, longe alio delectu opus

using *lectio continua* was to insure that all of scripture was covered and that it was explained in context. One innovative result of this was the introduction of regular preaching on the Old Testament as well as the New, something which became a marked characteristic of the Reformed tradition in all its branches. In fact, readings from the Old Testament were included as "epistles" in the Zurich lectionary![16]

However, as Max Engammare has shown, there was considerable variety in the ways that Reformed pastors organized their homiletic work. Because so much attention has focused on Calvin and Geneva, it has not been recognized that most of his German-speaking colleagues practiced a rather less radical break from the tradition. For present purposes, and with apologies to the preachers of Zurich, the object is to highlight the kind of world in which Calvin worked and the surprises that his reform must have afforded to his contemporaries. Engammare has discussed the situation in Basel in the first generation of the reform; here a brief summary of the first Protestant century must suffice.[17] Basel both followed the *lectio continua* pattern and maintained the use of a lectionary for selected traditional holy days. Many printed sermons in the sixteenth and early seventeenth centuries took the form of continuous exposition, but there were also publications of sermons on Christmas, New Year's-Circumcision, and other days, including – by 1608 – on "the veneration of Mary."[18]

Engammare's fine overview of the Zurich Reformed homiletic practices provides a particularly helpful context for grasping the peculiarity of Calvin's Geneva. As Engammare so perceptively states, form is not neutral.

> [T]he models of preaching are not neutral, either for the preacher or for the listener, or for the political and ecclesiastical authorities which legislated. Beyond the model of preaching, we can distinguish the figure of the

---

fuit. Nec modo perperam et inconsiderate lectiones distribuit quisquis ille fuit sector, sed medias interdum sententias nescio qua socordia abrupit. Ne quis tamen putet Westphalum de nihilo excandescere, monitos esse volo lectores, de postillis esse sollicitum. Quid enim sine postillis factura esset bona pars eorum, quibus se venditat? Luthero, qui rebus adhuc incompositis se ad morem vulgatum accommodavit, danda venia est: imo quod ad evangelium spargendum hoc usus est compendio, laudanda est eius industria et sedulitas. Sed praepostero ingenio est Westphalus, qui data opera in eodem luto semper haerere volens, Lutheri rudimenta praetexit." My thanks to Janse, "Calvin and Westphal," pp. 160-61, for directing me to this reference.

[16] See below in n.21.

[17] Max Engammare, "Les modèles de prédication protestante au XVIe siècle en Suisse : le cas de Bâle à l'époque de Joannes Œcolampade et juste après sa mort (1520-1546)," *Theologische Zeitschrift*, Basel, 2013, 1-23.

[18] Engammare, "Reformed Preaching in the Sixteenth Century," p. 198, esp. n.14 citing Johann Jakob Grynaeus, Oct. 9, 1608.

preacher *urbis et ecclesiæ*, to the City and to the Church, wished for by civic and religious authorities, and portrayed by the Reformers.[19]

Engammare then proceeds to outline a century of sermonic practice in Zurich. Although Zwingli began his ministry with straight *lectio continua* preaching through the Gospel of Matthew, there was no explicit instruction for determining the way that Zurich pastors should choose the scripture for the sermon until 1628.[20] Zwingli's sixteenth-century successors in fact developed a much more varied combination of sermonic practices. In c.1542 Leo Jud published a *Postilla Teütsch*, a version of Erasmus' *Paraphrases,* presented explicitly as a lectionary of epistles and gospels, and this was very popular, serving for pastors who might want to preach these, as well as for lay reading. There were Old Testament texts included in the list of "epistles" (clearly a Reformed rather than Erasmian orientation).[21] Bullinger himself presented and published *lectio continua* sermons, especially on the Old Testament, but he also followed the more widespread Basel-and-Lutheran influence of preaching and printing sermons on the traditional Christological holy days. It is well-known that the *Decades*, which are explicitly theological topics, followed a *loci* structure, but in fact Bullinger's Biblical sermons also demonstrate this form. In addition, Zurich observed certain civic occasions with special sermons, including until 1597 the annual festival of the consecration of the Gross Münster.[22]

In this wider context of neighboring Reformed churches Calvin's emphasis on *lectio continua* stands out as distinctive. While the others generally combined various patterns for choosing the scripture texts for preaching, he practiced an exact course reading which normally did not skip any verse, or even part of a verse. Not only was his form consistent in its almost pedestrian determination not to omit anything – there was no *loci* approach to the text – but it also applied equally to the Christological "interruptions" in the book-long sequences. Calvin certainly gave particular emphasis to any doctrinal or moral points in the verses he was explai-

---

19 Engammare, "Reformed Preaching in the Sixteenth Century," pp. 199-200.

20 Engammare, "Reformed Preaching in the Sixteenth Century," pp. 200-201. By this point, a century after Zwingli's death, the Zurich church was tired of the loci-commonplaces model and instituted the *lectio continua* pattern for Sundays, at just about the time that their Genevan counter-parts were moving in the opposite direction, from worn-out *lectio continua* to commonplaces, cf. p. 203.

21 Engammare, "Reformed Preaching in the Sixteenth Century," pp. 203-205. Engammare does not explain how the Old Testament "epistles" were chosen, though he indicates that "only the beginning and the end of the pericope are given without any Erasmus' commentary, because he did not paraphrase the Old Testament," p. 204.

22 Engammare, "Reformed Preaching in the Sixteenth Century," pp. 206-208, 211-213, 224.

ning, but he did not shape the sermon as a series of commonplaces; virtually every verse received at least some explicit notice. It is not possible to know if every one of his Genevan colleagues was so careful, but surviving records of the *congrégation* exercises demonstrate that they must have been fairly close to Calvin's practice. (Whether or not the traditional selected lectionary was ever read in Protestant Geneva will be examined below.)[23] Besides the *lectio continua* sermons, the one prescribed-text sermon series practiced in Geneva was the exposition of the catechism, a popular form among Protestants. Calvin himself only preached through the Geneva Catechism at the request of his colleagues and of those lessons only one was preserved, but several of his associates published explanations of the Catechism.[24]

Although specifics varied, the Reformed patterns for choosing the Biblical readings for worship fitted well with their much altered liturgical calendars, which usually only interrupted the sequential exposition of the Bible for the major Christological feasts. The type of handbook which would serve this kind of preaching naturally was a commentary, i.e., a continuous explanation of a Biblical book which concentrated on exegesis and might well not give attention to application. Full books of *lectio continua* sermons were also published, and there the exegesis was applied, i.e., addressed to a particular audience.

Whatever the ways that homiletical aids were planned by Protestants, there were some similarities and certain differences between their publications and those of their medieval predecessors. One difference was linguistic. Preaching in the vernacular had long been common, but publishing serious theology in the language of the laity had not. Although there continued to be some Latin sermons as a form of clerical education, the orientation had shifted.[25] Protestants consciously chose the ordinary speech of their regions as the medium for many of their

---

[23] See the work of Erik de Boer, both his analysis of the institution and practice of the *congrégations* and the new edition of texts; de Boer, *Genevan School of Prophets*, and *Ioannis Calvini Varia: Volumen I. Congrégations et disputations*. For traditional lectionary, see below at nn.82ff.

[24] For Calvin, see below at nn.105ff. Colleagues : François Bourgoing, *Paraphrase ou briefve exposition sur le catechisme* (1564), Niccolò Balbani, *Il catechismo di messer Giovan Calvino* (1566). Cited in de Boer, *Genevan School of Prophets*, p. 193. Peter & Gilmont indicate that these were complete paraphrases, *Bibliotheca Calviniana* II, [63/10] p. 1001.

[25] There were sermons published in Latin, because that remained the international language of the educated, but these texts were usually commentaries or theological instruction in a different form. Bullinger published a number of Biblical sermons in Latin; those on the Apocalypse are a kind of *lectio continua*, and in addition he published series on Jeremiah, Daniel, and Isaiah, plus some sermons on the Christological feast days. His most famous sermons are the topically ordered *Decades*, which appeared in both Latin and the vernacular, and in English became the theological textbook for ministers in Elizabeth's church.

homiletical aids. That gave every literate person access to these expositions, and in fact, since it was normal to read aloud, one member of a family or village who could read the local spoken language could edify many others. For Calvin, commentaries were the preferred form of preaching aid and he made a concerted effort to see that his Latin commentaries were quickly translated into French. Ironically, considering his principles, later some of the Genevan reformer's own sermons would be used as handbooks to help French pastors preach.[26]

There was a significant similarity between medieval and early modern preachers which has apparently passed mostly unnoticed: the conviction that, if they were to be published, sermons should be polished and edited first. That is, virtually no preacher wanted his extempore words to be circulated. For most men, this was not a danger; normally sermons were not recorded. But Luther was the (first) great exception. He wrote out his early *Postils*, and even when the later ones were taken down by students and colleagues as he spoke, the preacher wanted the results to be edited before printing. The degree of touching up varied, as did the precision of the original transcription (a number of Luther's sermons were preserved in the traditional macaronic fashion of German-and-Latin because that was easiest for his secretaries).[27] Like his great German senior colleague, Calvin was also an exception to the rule that sermons usually went unrecorded, but he was if anything more unwilling than Luther to have extempore texts printed. As one of his editors said, "he wanted the writings which he published to appear with all their ornaments."[28] On the other hand, Calvin was

---

26 For Farel's objections to postils, below at n.87; for Calvin's sermons as homiletical aids below at nn.276f. The translation of Calvin's commentaries, starting with the Pauline epistles, had begun by 1547; the remaining New Testament epistles were published in 1551, and then all were assembled in 1556. See Peter and Gilmont, *Biblitheca Calviniana*, II, p.598.

27 Some of the Postils were edited by Luther himself, but many were prepared by his colleagues from his spoken words. It appears that Stephen Roth was the most faithful to what Luther actually said, but the reformer "was dissatisfied with Roth's work and commissioned Caspar Cruciger to replace it" with a more literary edition of his words. In fact, Luther remarked appreciatively "that after Cruciger had finished editing a sermon for his postil, it was far better than anything that Luther himself had said"; quoted in Lowell Green, "Justification in Luther's Preaching on Luke 18:9-14," *Concordia Theological Monthly* 43 (1973), p. 733 n.3 and p. 734 (citing WA *Tischreden*, vol., 3, No. 2869b). See Old, *The Age of the Reformation*, p. 5, on Luther's "stenographers"; pp. 8-9 n.11 refers to a sermon writer who was not a trained stenographer. It is worth observing that when Des Gallars served as Calvin's secretary for the Commentary on Isaiah, although he heard sermons in French he made his notes in Latin; he also recast the text enough that Calvin was not satisfied with it; cf. Peter & Gilmont, *Bibliotheca Calviniana* I, p. 405.

28 See Badius in the preface to sermons on the Ten Commandments, quoted below at n.238. For fuller discussion of how his sermon editors interpreted Calvin's dislike of publishing his extempore sermons, see below, pp. 545 ff.

more fortunate than Luther in his secretaries. The Frenchman's preaching was transcribed consistently by one trained stenographer for over eleven years (1549-1560), which gives his homiletical corpus a surprisingly untraditional and even unique character. It also provides a remarkable set of sources on early modern preaching, ideal for contributing to a fuller picture of worship in Calvin's Geneva and especially of the reformer's own pulpit ministry.

Preaching in Calvin's Geneva

The sermons regularly presented in each pulpit of a Reformed church in early modern Europe were normally intended for a specific congregation and not considered worth recording. They were believed to be a powerful instrument of religious teaching; it was hoped that they would be effective, not that they would be preserved. Even for someone as prominent as Calvin, there are no precise contemporary references to his early preaching, much less careful transcripts. That would change definitively in 1549, but this view of sermons as local and "ephemeral literature" helps to explain why there is so little detail available for what was actually spoken from the pulpit in Geneva (and most other places). Some occasional anecdotal evidence suggests that at least in the early years Geneva's ministers preached mostly on the more familiar books: the New Testament and Psalms. [29]

When Calvin had gathered his better qualified corps of ministers by about 1546, they included a significant number of highly educated men. Three others besides Calvin himself were authors of some international repute, even before Theodore Beza arrived, and these preachers more often ventured into the Old Testament. The most prolific of these early colleagues was Nicholas Des Gallars, who published both his own writings and others in collaboration with Calvin, for whom he was secretary, translator, and sometimes pseudonym. [30] The most

---

[29] Here the point is Biblical texts, not polemic. Some references from the *Registres du Conseil*: 1) 1 Cor. 7:12-15 preached by Jaques Bernard on May 10, 1538, RC III, p. 262. The Gospel of John & Ps. 4, preached by de La Mare, Sept. 27 & 29, 1540; RC III, pp. 549, 562 (see below at n.99). Later more examples appear in the *Registres du Consistoire*: The beheading of John the Baptist, Nov. 9, 1542: Jana, wife of Jaques Symond, "fust au sermon hier et prescha de la decollation saint Jehan." (There is no reference to the preacher or the parish, and the sermon on the decapitation of John the Baptist was on a weekday, so it is probable that this was preached by one of Calvin's colleagues and it could have been on any of the gospels.) The Lord's Prayer by H. de La Mare on Nov. 30, 1542. *Consist.* I, pp. 137, 144.

[30] Peter & Gilmont, *Bibliotheca Calviniana* I, pp. 190f (Latin translation of *Short Treatise on Supper*), pp. 199f (book defending Farel against Caroli was a collaboration with Des Gallars and appeared under the latter's name), pp. 211f (Latin translation of treatise *Against the Anabaptists*),

important of the collaborative works was Calvin's first commentary on Isaiah, published in 1551 (although so much of this was shaped by the secretary that the results were apparently not really satisfactory to the principal author).[31] Some of Des Gallars' writings were polemical, e.g., a response to Johannes Cochlaeus in 1549.[32] Others were constructive: in 1559 he published a commentary on Exodus and later a church order-and-liturgy for the French refugee congregation in London, as well as participating in the French Bible projects being done in Geneva.[33] François Bourgoing wrote an explanation of the Catechism, and works on religious history: an *Ecclesiastical History* drawing on the Magdeburg Centuries, and a translation of Josephus.[34] Michel Cop produced two commentaries on wisdom literature, Proverbs in 1556 and Ecclesiastes in 1557, and there exist a few unpublished sermons.[35] Raymond Chauvet was highly regarded in French Protestant circles before he came to Geneva and would become more so in later years.[36] It is notable that only a few of these publications were

p. 259 (Latin translation of *Treatise on Relics*), pp. 436f (French translation of first Isaiah commentary), p. 456 (edition of Calvin's *Opuscula omnia* as of 1552), pp. 624, 630 (one of three secretaries for Psalms commentary but Peter & Gilmont, p. 631, note that Calvin nowhere indicates that he used Des Gallars' notes), pp. 696, 723, 1018 (prefaces by Des Gallars).

31 Peter & Gilmont, *Bibliotheca Calviniana* I, pp. 403-06. On p. 405, they quote Des Gallars' comment that he made the notes after Calvin's sermons and lessons, "en usant cependant de mon jugement et de mon style." There was considerable independence.

32 Peter & Gilmont, *Bibliotheca Calviniana* I, p. 239. A complete list of Des Gallars' works will be found in Jeannine Olson's biography which is presently being written.

33 "Des Gallars, Nicolas" in *Dictionnaire de Biographie Française*, vol. 10, col. 1353-54. On Sept. 11, 1559, OC 21:721 (RC f105) Crespin asks the Senate for permission to print Des Gallars' commentary on Exodus.

34 "Bourgoing, François" in *Dictionnaire de Biographie Française*, vol. 7, col. 1500.

35 "Cop, Guillaume" in *Dictionnaire de Biographie Française*, vol. 9, col. 555. The article includes his father Guillaume and brothers. On March 13 & 23, & Nov. 5, 1556, OC 21:631, 632, 653 (RC f48, f70, f83), Cop's commentary on Proverbs is presented, with a request for publication; Calvin is asked to check it and on receiving his favorable report the Senate approves publication. In November Cop presents a copy to the Senate. A year later, Dec. 3, 1557, OC 21:680 (RC f444), Cop presents a properly bound copy of his commentary on Ecclesiastes to the Senate; they thank him but tell him that the printer is supposed to give each of them a paper-bound copy "according to custom." (One wonders if they actually read the copies they were customarily given?!). There are a few of Cop's sermons in Ms.fr. 40b, which I have not yet been able to read but plan for a later work. Manetsch, *Calvin's Company of Pastors*, p. 52, gives a short summary of Cop's ministry, but he does not include biographies of these other three early recruits.

36 "Chauvet, Raymond" in *Dictionnaire de Biographie Française*, vol. 8, col. 914-15. Naphy, *Calvin and the Consolidation*, p. 73, n. 99, cites this article for evidence that Chauvet published, but the article does not name any specific work.

exegetical texts and, while no doubt based on these pastors' preaching or at least the research for it, Des Gallars' Exodus, Cop's Proverbs and Ecclesiastes, and Bourgoing's Catechism lectures were certainly revised and edited for publication. That leaves Calvin as *almost* the only preacher whose real-time voice in the pulpit can be heard.

"Almost" the only one because there are also four extant sermons on Isaiah 65 by Viret, preached in Geneva in March 1559 and transcribed by Calvin's stenographer. These were published in the twentieth century, and while they provide a very limited basis for comparison they also raise some quite interesting questions. The editor, Henri Meylan, affirms clearly that Viret's preaching was very much like Calvin's, with certain exceptions. The most notable of these is that, while Calvin plunges directly into his text, Viret follows a version of the medieval homiletic tradition of using a quotation from some other source as his thematic introduction. It is evident, however, that Viret is Protestant; his "protheme" is a Biblical verse rather than some unrelated author. (Meylan gives the example of a celebrated late medieval preacher who began every Lenten sermon on the gospels with a quotation from Roman law.) [37] One of the points on which Meylan does not comment is the significance of the fact that Viret's Isaiah sermons were preached on Sundays as well as Wednesdays: Sunday March 5, Wednesday March 8, Sunday March 12, and Wednesday March 15, 1559. This is clear evidence that an Old Testament text could be preached on Sunday in Calvin's Geneva, even if the only ones he himself chose were Psalms. It also illustrates afresh the status of the day of prayer; Viret was in the pulpit for the two most important worship days.

Books can be and have been written about Calvin's preaching and sermons, and thus it is appropriate here to identify the purpose of the present investigation. The present goal is not to describe Calvin's theology or rhetorical style, important as those are. It is to place his preaching in the context of worship in Geneva and of Calvin's pastoral ministry as the architect and most prominent representative of the preachers. For this purpose, identifying what and when Calvin preached is the main interest. Along with this is why and how his sermons came to be preserved,

---

[37] Viret, *Quatre sermons*. Editor Henri Meylan comments that one might imagine that Viret picked up where Calvin left off; he adds "cette hypothèse séduisante se heurte à de très réelles difficultés" (p. 7), without explaining what those might be. In fact, Calvin's last sermon before his illness was on Isa. 61:6-8, and when he returned he took up at Isa. 61:10-11; sermons 9/309 and 10/310 in Engammare, *Sermons sur Esaie chapitres 60,1-66,4* (S IV/2), pp. 580ff, 590ff. In Appendix Seven: Calvin's Sermons, numbers 53 & 54. Viret's sermons cover Isa. 65:8-12, one or two verses at a time, each sermon overlapping the contiguous ones; beginning on pp. 15, 35, 60, 84. See Meylan, "Introduction," pp. 7-11, including discussion of the great length of Viret's sermons, supplemented with quotations from Bullinger who offers apologies for preaching for two hours! For a comment on Viret's prayers, see below in n.134.

which may provide at least a partial view of how they were perceived and cast some light on issues of his style from the standpoint of his audience.

A Short Historiographical Overview of Calvin's Preaching

Calvin's sermons were of great interest to some of his contemporaries, but they then fell into near oblivion for centuries. Modern attention to these texts began seriously in the first part of the twentieth century, with the concerted effort to publish all of the remaining manuscripts in the series *Supplementa Calviniana,* which was established under the aegis of the World Alliance of Reformed Churches. The scholars who have written about the reformer's preaching have usually been editors of these manuscripts. This is true for two of the most prominent interpreters, Edwin Mülhaupt and T. H. L. Parker. That literature has been cited in an earlier chapter and will only be touched on briefly here. [38] The best-known secondary examinations of Calvin's preaching in German and English are Mülhaupt's *Die Predigt Calvins. Ihre Geschichte, Ihre Form und Ihre Religiösen Grundgedanken* (1931) and Parker's *Oracles of God. An Introduction to the Preaching of John Calvin* (1947), along with Parker's slightly updated volume *Calvin's Preaching* (1992). Each of these men has written other books and articles which focus on specific sermons or topics. A number of other scholars have examined portions of Calvin's homiletical work, for example Peter Opitz on Ps. 119; or have made use of sermon texts in a variety of ways, e.g., Rodolphe Peter, Richard Stauffer, Max Engammare, Erik de Boer, Wilhelmus Moehn, Elsie McKee. [39] The most common and natural question has been what the sermons reveal about

---

[38] See chap. 1 at nn.67ff. The original editorial committee of the *Supplementa Calviniana* was gathered by James I. McCord in 1954, with Erwin Mühlhaupt as main editor, and Georges A. Barrois, Jean Daniel Benoît, Willem Frederik Dankbaar, Bernard Gagnebin, Henri Meylan, Barnabas Nagy, Thomas H. L. Parker, Hanns Rückert, and Richard Stauffer as members. Later, as it became evident that the task was more time-consuming than anticipated and some of the original group were not able to complete their assigned texts, other editors were added: Willem Balke, Erik de Boer, Max Engammare, Olivier Fatio, Francis M. Higman, Elsie Anne McKee, Wilhelmus H. Th. Moehn, Rodolphe Peter, and Lewis Thorpe.

[39] Here only representative examples: Opitz, "Ein Thorapsalm als ABC des christlichen Glaubens." Rodolphe Peter, "Rhétorique et prédication selon Calvin," *Revue d'Histoire et de Philosophie Religieuse* 55 (1975-2), pp. 249-72. Richard Stauffer, *Dieu, la création et la Providence dans la prédication de Calvin* (Berne: P. Lang, 1978). Max Engammare, "Calvin connaissait-il la Bible? Les citations de l'Ecriture dans ses sermons sur la Genèse," *Bulletin de la Société d'Histoire du Protestantisme Français,* 141 (1995), pp. 163-84. Erik de Boer, "Jean Calvin et Esaie 1. Edition d'un texte inconnu, introduit par quelques observations sur la différence et les relations entre congrégation, cours et sermons," *Revue d'Histoire et de Philosophie Religieuse* 80 (2000), pp. 371-95. Wilhellmus Moehn, *"God Calls us to His Service." The Relation between God and His Audience in Calvin's Sermons on Acts* (Genève: Droz, 2001). McKee, *John Calvin on the Diaconate,* chap. 3, 6, & 7.

Calvin's thought, although some, like William Naphy, have also drawn on these texts to illuminate political events in Geneva.[40] The purpose here is to provide a study of the sermons as material evidence of Calvin's work as a pastor.

II. Calvin the Preacher of Geneva

Although Calvin would not approve of the elevation of his extempore expositions to the role of *the* sermons of Geneva, the fact is that his homiletical work was the most prominent in his day and it remains the most abundant witness to what was preached in the city pulpits. It is therefore appropriate to focus on Calvin as *the* preacher of Geneva, the more so because he was in fact active in every parish and his legacy offers a perspective on the Biblical breadth of what was expounded to the people. This section has four parts; the first uncovers where Calvin actually was when preaching. The remaining three give an overview of what he was saying, beginning with the evidence from the recorded and published Biblical sermons. A hypothetical reconstruction of what is missing follows, and the last part is a short example of his rare catechetical teaching which was offered for the edification of his fellow pastors and may or may not have been delivered to laity.

Calvin in the Pulpits of Geneva

The role of Calvin as the chief minister of Geneva has placed him in the pulpit of (the former cathedral of) St. Pierre, but that logical assumption was not in fact a regular reality until the last five years of his life. For most of his ministry, Calvin preached in both of the two parishes of Greater Geneva, but he also served in St. Gervais for a number of years at the Sunday afternoon service, and thus could be heard from any one of three different pulpits.

The specific evidence about Calvin's preaching in the 1540s is very limited, as regards both place and choice of Biblical texts. The latter will be discussed below; here the focus is where the reformer was. It is not possible to be sure exactly where Calvin preached when he joined Farel in 1536. Since the leading ministers often had responsibility for the two sides of the city, one might have been identified with St. Gervais and the other with St. Pierre or Greater Geneva. Farel ceded intellectual leadership to Calvin, so it is probable that the latter was in St. Pierre on a regular basis. What is certain is that when the argument over Bernese ceremonies broke out in April 1538, Calvin was preaching at St. Pierre and Farel at St. Gervais for the Easter morning service which was the catalyst for

---

[40]   Naphy, *Calvin and the Consolidation*, examples pp. 156-60.

their exile, and Calvin was at the Rive that afternoon.[41] Thus it is probable that these were their usual Sunday assignments. St. Pierre was used primarily on Sundays, so weekday preaching in Greater Geneva was in the Rive for these early years, and Calvin was there at least part of the time.[42]

The picture is much clearer after Calvin's return in 1541. The organization of the plan is explained first, then a summary of the weekday preaching, followed by the much longer and more complex investigation of where Calvin was on Sundays. In 1541 he was assigned to the parish of St. Pierre and Viret to St. Gervais, until Viret went back to his long-term appointment in Lausanne in July 1542.[43] The first known instructions about Genevan pulpits come from early 1542, before Viret's departure. According to this, Calvin and Viret would alternate at La Magdeleine for the weekdays, while Henri de La Mare and Jacques Bernard did the same at St. Gervais and Aimé Champereau had the dawn services at St. Pierre. Calvin was at St. Pierre on Sunday, with Viret most probably at St. Gervais. The personnel changed considerably in mid-1542, but Calvin's assignment remained essentially the same; on weekdays he preached at La Magdeleine in alternate weeks opposite Champereau, while other pairs did the services at St. Gervais and the dawn ones at St. Pierre.[44] Calvin was, of course, at St. Pierre on Sunday mornings and probably also on Sunday afternoons, except for a (short) time when he was relieved of the second sermon to work on the city's legal code. It is unlikely that Calvin taught catechism, since his regular assignment was already heavier than his colleagues': he had twenty sermons every four weeks over against about sixteen on average for the others.[45] (Catechism was later one of the typical assignments for a new member of the pastoral company; there is no good reason to think that this idea was an innovation in the 1550s so it was probably the most recent additions to the pastoral corps who did usually did it.[46] That would naturally exclude Calvin.)

---

41 April 21, 1538, RC III, p. 232; Roset, *Les Chroniques de Genève*, p. 252; both quoted in chap. 1 n.50.

42 If the later plan of alternating weekday sermons was in practice, he and Farel may have taken turns at the Rive. However, it is more likely that pairing alternates was a development shaped by Calvin after his return.

43 Nov. 7, 1541, OC 21:285 (RC 35 f383), quoted in chap. 2 n.9.

44 See chap. 2 at nn.35ff.

45 See chap. 1 at nn.85f; chap. 2 at n.36 & after n.67. De Boer, *Genevan School of Prophets*, p. 193, and others believe Calvin did teach catechism.

46 Other colleagues (perhaps Champereau, Calvin's weekday alternate) would be doing this since La Magdeleine did not have a Sunday morning service except on the days when the Lord's Supper was celebrated, and thus Champereau would not have a Sunday assignment unless he was doing catechism.

For weekday services Calvin preached regularly at La Magdeleine from the time he returned to Geneva in 1541 until mid-1559. The one exception was the Wednesday day of prayer service which was located in St. Pierre. The assignment of preachers in the instructions about weekday preaching beginning in early 1542 defines this for the 1540s, and careful analysis of the baptismal and marriage records demonstrates it for the period 1550-59. [47] In 1557, when the new (fourth) parish was opened at St. Germain because of the ever-increasing numbers of French refugees crowding the city's churches, Calvin offered to move his week-day preaching to the new site. Apparently the Senate refused. [48] Perhaps they did not approve of "wasting" their premier preacher on the new parish because they were accustomed to worshiping at La Magdeleine and wanted to keep Calvin there. Calvin's final move came in 1559. When daily services at the "ordinary" hour of 6 a.m. or 7 a.m. began at St. Pierre in June of that year, Calvin became the "preacher of St. Pierre" full time, i.e., all his scheduled sermons were delivered at St. Pierre.

Perhaps the most surprising aspect of Calvin's pulpit ministry is the fact that in the mid-1540s he started preaching regularly at St. Gervais on Sunday afternoons, although with some exceptions. The beginning of this practice can be dated by arguments which turn up in the city government records. In 1545 there was a problem at St. Gervais because the minister, Pierre Ninault, was unpopular, and the Senate ordered the pastors of the two parts of the city to work out an exchange of pulpits so that those from Greater Geneva would preach at St. Gervais occasionally, and vice versa. [49] While it cannot be proved that this was the reason that Calvin came to St. Gervais, there is evidence that he was preaching in that pulpit on Sunday afternoons by early 1546. On the afternoon of Sunday, March 28, 1546, a certain Amyed Alliod, a baker, caused a public incident at St. Gervais by attacking some of Calvin's remarks in recent sermons. The "guest preacher" had criticized the people who stayed out in the streets rather than attend worship, and apparently this was not a single rebuke. In the course of the Procès Criminel that resulted, the words of Alliod and the witnesses make it clear that not only was Calvin preaching at St. Gervais that Sunday afternoon, but he

---

[47]   For the move to St. Pierre, see chap. 1 at nn.151f, chap. 4 at n.61.

[48]   July 19, 1557, OC 21:670 (RC 53 f241): "Aussi pource que le temple S. Germain est bien pres preparé qu'il plaise à Messieurs adviser en quel ordre se debvra prescher par les temples sçavoir s'il seroit pas bon qu'il preschat sa sepmaine à S. Germain. Arresté qu'on commet deux Seigneurs pour conferer avec M. Calvin." The result of this consultation was evidently the decision not to move Calvin, because he continues to do baptisms at Magdeleine. archives@ etat.ge.ch accessed Aug. 7, 2013 [to see if there were any further comments].

[49]   See chap. 2 at nn.46ff.

had been doing this for at least a month and probably more. Alliod says that Calvin "had already made three sermons on the people of St. Gervais," which indicates that the minister of St. Pierre had in fact been in the pulpit of St. Gervais for some time.[50] This provides an initial date. The chronicler Michel Roset confirms that the practice was (still) true in 1551. He says that on Sunday March 8, "towards evening, Calvin, having just preached at St. Gervais" encountered "some dissolute persons" on the Rhone bridge, which led to a fracas in which a Frenchman and one of the rowdy men were injured.[51] Clearly, Calvin was walking home to Greater Geneva from St. Gervais after his Sunday afternoon sermon.

Further evidence for Calvin preaching at St. Gervais is found in the marriage records,[52] and this provides a probable terminal date. In the first years that these records were regularly kept, 1550-52, Calvin performed most of his weddings at St. Gervais on Sunday afternoons. (Weddings, like baptisms, were recorded in the specific parish in which they were celebrated.) There are six wedding liturgies by Calvin at St. Gervais in 1550, with four at St. Pierre, all Sunday afternoons (plus a single weekday at La Magdeleine). In 1551 Calvin performed eleven weddings at St. Gervais and one at St. Pierre on Sunday afternoons (and one weekday at La Magdeleine). However, in 1552, there is only one wedding by Calvin at St. Gervais, on April 3, and thereafter all the Sunday weddings (i.e., the great majority) are registered at St. Pierre. Calvin could not have done a wedding at St. Gervais at 3 p.m. and then gone to preach at St. Pierre that same afternoon. Not only was it mandatory to remain for the whole service when one attended a

---

50   Procès Criminels, 2 #695; "Calvin avoit desja faict trois sermons sur ceulx de sainct gervais." See discussion below at nn.195ff. There are several other small signals that Calvin was at St. Gervais. On April 1, 1546, the son of Jehan Romani is before the consistory regarding disrespect for his father and is asked about his attendance at worship; "Interroguer que prescha yer, ne sçayt, et dimenche à St-Gervays, ditz que se futz Monsieur Calvin, se que n'estz, et est menteur,"*Consist.* II, pp. 184-85. Evidently the boy had heard that Calvin was preaching at St. Gervais on Sundays and did not get the details, so when he claimed to have been present (probably assuming that the crowd would have been sufficient to hide him) he was caught. Since this is the consistory after Sunday March 28 when there was the uproar and Calvin certainly was at St. Gervais in the afternoon, the boy probably was talking about Sunday morning, not realizing that Calvin would be present only in the afternoons. Another sign that Calvin was not at St. Pierre is the fact that his alternate, Poupin, was probably in that pulpit on at least some Sunday afternoons during this period. See the criticism of Poupin's preaching about God's judgment as recorded in the consistory minutes for April 12, 1548, *Consist.* IV, p. 45.

51   Roset, *Les Chroniques de Genève*, p. 337, "Le dimenche huictiesme de mars [1551] fut renouvelé le serment de la combourgeoisie en Conseil Général comme de coustume. Le mesme jour devers le soir, Calvin, venant de prescher de S. Gervaix, estant hurté sus le pont du Rosne par quelcuns des débaulchez, leur remonstre que le pont estoit assez large…"

52   See Appendix Five: Calvin's Weddings.

wedding (and the last person who would have broken the rule was Calvin), but it was also physically impossible to get from one side of the city to the other on foot in the given time. Thus, it is clear that Calvin was preaching at St. Gervais on Sunday afternoons regularly, though not every week, probably from early in 1546 until spring 1552. After April 3, 1552, there are only three more weddings by Calvin at St. Gervais, on the Sunday afternoons of July 18, 1557, and May 12 and June 9, 1560. The first of these Calvin might have been preaching but the Sunday sermons from this period are missing so it is not possible to say. For the two dates in 1560 there are extant sermons on Ps. 46 and 48. By that year he was no longer regularly preaching twice on Sundays because of his health, so a colleague was probably in charge of St. Pierre in the afternoons and Calvin was free to lead worship – and do weddings – elsewhere. [53] So it seems that although the spring of 1552 marked his return to Greater Geneva full-time, even thereafter he occasionally preached at St. Gervais on an ad hoc basis.

The organization of Calvin's sermons in these years also contributes to the picture of his dividing his Sundays between St. Pierre and St. Gervais, and provides a glimpse of how he organized his work to accommodate moving between two sides of the city. According to his biographer Nicolas Colladon, describing 1549, the reformer was preaching on one book in the morning and another in the afternoon; then in 1554 Calvin began to expound the same book morning and afternoon.

> That year [1549] he was preaching on the Epistle to the Hebrews on Sunday morning, and when he finished that he took up the Acts of the Apostles, which he began at the same hour on Sunday, Aug. 25, 1549. At the Sunday afternoon service he preached on the Psalms.... In 1554, as for the Sunday sermons, morning as well as afternoon, having then completed the Acts of the Apostles he began the Epistles to the Thessalonians on March 25. [54]

---

[53] See the summary by Beza, who gives a more nuanced account of Calvin's preaching twice on Sunday: "Outre ce qu'il preschoit tous les jours de sepmaine en sepmaine, le plus souvent et tant qu'il a peu il a presché deux fois tous les Dimanches..." OC 21:33. It seems logical that this reflects the time Beza himself was a pastor in Geneva, when there are very few Sunday afternoon sermons recorded for Calvin, and it is probable that he did not preach then on a regular basis.

[54] See Colladon, OC 21:71: "Ceste annee-la [1549] il preschoit les Dimanches au matin l'Epistre aux Hebrieux, et l'ayant achevee il print les Actes des Apostres, lesquels il commença à prescher à la mesme heure le Dimanche 25 d'Aoust audit an. Au sermon du soir les Dimanches il preschoit les Pseaumes prenant seulement ceux qui n'estoyent pas encore traduits en rythme (car desja auparavant il avoit presché les autres), et en estoit au 40. Les autres jours de la sepmaine il preschoit le Prophete Jeremie." OC 21:76: "Audit an 1554, ... quant aux sermons des Dimanches, tant du matin que du soir, ayant lors achevé les Actes des Apostres, il commença les Epistres aux Thessaloniciens le 25. Jour de Mars."

The evidence that the Acts sermons were essentially preached in the morning and Psalms in the afternoon is supported by Denis Raguenier, Calvin's stenographer. He says he began transcribing Acts sermons on Aug. 25, 1549, but what he recorded was "not sequential," i.e., there were gaps. Calvin never skipped anything, so the lacunae were sermons which Raguenier missed, not ones the reformer failed to preach. [55] As noted above, during the years Calvin was regularly at St. Gervais he still preached occasionally on Sunday afternoons at St. Pierre. In the first, non-sequential set of Acts sermons from 1549-51, there are a few sermons marked "après midi" or identifiable as afternoon sermons by their prayer incipits or other words, but the great majority were preached in the mornings. Since the two volumes of the second half of Acts are missing, it is not clear exactly when Calvin changed to preaching on the same book in the morning and afternoon. Because he was back in Greater Geneva regularly by spring 1552, it is possible that he decided to do this when he had completed expositions of the Psalms. Colladon mentions that on the first Sunday in September 1553, Calvin was expounding Acts 20:31-32 (+?) as a continuation of his morning sermon. [56] If the preacher did turn to explaining the same scriptural book morning and afternoon while he was still working on Acts, this timing would make sense, because on July 2 he had concluded the series of twenty-two sermons on Ps. 119 which had occupied him on Sunday afternoons since January. There were probably a few more Psalms to be covered but these would likely fit into the rest of the summer, leaving the preacher free to change to a morning-and-afternoon pattern for the remainder of Acts. Six months after this September sermon Calvin would move on to Thessalonians on Mar. 26, 1554, so he almost certainly needed morning and afternoon to preach through the last eight-plus chapters of Acts. [57]

---

55 There is a documented example of this in the Ezekiel sermons for Wed. Jan. 11, 1553, when the schedule changed so that Calvin began preaching every Wednesday... evidently someone failed to tell Raguenier the first day and that sermon was not recorded, although it was preached.

56 See Colladon, OC 21:71, quoted above in n.54. The occasion was the battle with the Senate over their re-admitting Philibert Bertellier to the Supper. In the morning sermon Calvin had refused to give communion to those to whom the consistory had forbidden it. OC 21:78: "Et au sermon d'apres disner le mesme jour, suivant son texte des Actes des Apostres, chap 20, qui est le sermon de sainct Paul aux Anciens de l'Eglise d'Ephese sur ces mots de l'Apostre: Parquoy veillez, ... Car il remonstra qu'il ne savoit si ce seroit point son dernier sermon à Geneve, puis que ceux qui avoyent la puissance, le voulyent contreindre de faire une chose qui ne luy estoit licite selon Dieu. ... Il faut donc (disoit-il) que je parle à vous d'un mesme stile qu'a parlé sainct Paul: Frere, je vous recomande à Dieu et à la parole de sa grace."

57 The Ps. 119 sermons are clearly dated in the contemporary printings, and even though the words "après midi" are not found, both the prayer formula and the fact that Calvin was preaching on Acts in the morning indicates that they were on Sunday afternoons; see Appendix Ten Part Three for all the calculations of the Psalms sermons.

Raguenier's catalogue shows that he began recording Calvin's Psalms sermons on "Nov. 17, 1549, Sunday afternoon." That this did not mean that only the initial sermon was in the afternoon is confirmed by Colladon's general statement quoted above. This volume of 72 sermons is one of those lost in 1805. The sermons were not consecutive Psalms; as Raguenier explains, that was (at least partly) owed to the fact that he was ill from late spring to mid-summer.[58] However, the preacher was also skipping some Psalms, since this is the only book for which he did not follow a regular *lectio continua* pattern (see below). Contrary to the commonly accepted theory that Calvin never chose anything except the New Testament for Sunday mornings, there are at least two instances of extant Psalm sermons preached on Sunday mornings in 1554 and 1555 and possibly as many as four.[59] However, such an event was extremely rare, and so it is probable that (virtually) all of the lost sermons on Psalms from 1549-52 were heard on Sunday afternoons. That would fit with the evidence of the surviving Acts sermons as morning ones and the fact that the sermons on Ps. 119, which are dated, were preached on consecutive Sunday afternoons. Thus, it is possible to state that most of the time Calvin focused on Acts in the morning and Psalms in the afternoon during this period, at least until late summer 1553. It is also clear that the program of explaining two books concurrently was in effect for some years. (Colladon does not appear to know anything about the preacher's earlier pulpit ministry before the Colladon family arrived in Geneva in the late 1540s.[60] When

---

[58] See above at n.54; below at nn. 130f. Weekday sermons on most of Jonah, all of Nahum, and four chapters of Daniel were not recorded. Since Calvin's schedule was very regular at this point, his weeks to preach can be calculated from the last sermon on Jonah on April 2 to the first on Daniel on July 18. Thus the weeks beginning Monday April 11 through Saturday July 9, 1552, were not recorded, and thirteen or fourteen Sundays are missing. See Raguenier's catalogue in Gagnebin, "L'histoire des manuscrits des sermons de Calvin," S. II, p. xvi.

[59] For the claim that Psalms were only Sunday afternoons, see Parker, *Calvin's Preaching*, pp. 63, 165, 166, 168. Psalms were preached on Sunday mornings on Sun. Sept. 30, 1554, on Ps. 148:1-14; and Sun. July 14, 1555, on Ps. 149:4-9. The evidence is circumstantial. First, the concluding prayers of these Psalms sermons begin with "Dieu tout puissant" which is the Sunday morning fixed prayer. Parallel to this the sermons of Calvin's contemporary *lectio continua* series, #4 & #5 on 1 Tim., #21 & #22 on 2 Tim., begin with the weekday-Sunday afternoon phrase "Que non seulement," i.e., they are marked as two sequential Sunday afternoons. The other two Psalms, 147:12-20 and 65:6-14, which might have been preached on a Sunday morning because they have the prayer incipit "Dieu tout puissant" are harder to verify because the surrounding *lectio continua* series is no longer extant. See Appendix Seven: Calvin's Sermons.

[60] Members of the Colladon family had been in Geneva since the late 1540s; Germain and Léon Colladon became habitants on Aug. 28, 1550, but Léon's son Nicolas himself did not arrive until 1553. *Consist.* V, p. 316 n.2124. Both Beza and Colladon, Calvin's first biographers, had to rely on others for information about the period before the late 1540s, and it is quite possible that, since the books on which the reformer was preaching were not recorded, the rhythm would also not have been passed down in the local lore.

Calvin began explaining one book both morning and afternoon Colladon presents this as if it introduced something new, but it was almost certainly a return to Calvin's pre-1546 practice.) The point here is that the orderly-minded pastor knew that when he was moving between the two parts of the city it was important to have two separate books, one for each place, so that those who attended one parish church regularly would in fact hear a whole sequence.

Obviously, then, Calvin was well known in all three pulpits of Geneva. Not only did he alternate with a colleague for weekday services at La Magdeleine from 1541 until 1559, but he also moved between the two other parish churches on Sundays, at least for about seven years, early 1546 until spring 1552. Although he was officially designated the pastor of the parish of St. Pierre from 1541 until his death, the leading minister of Geneva must have been very well known as a preacher by all the city residents. In addition his movements among the three pulpits demonstrate his full participation in the orderly plan of collegial exchanges which began officially in 1542.

Calvin's Recorded Sermons

Calvin preached on books of both the Old and New Testaments. However, which books and in what order can be clearly defined only beginning in 1549, when both some sermons and Denis Raguenier's catalogue are available, and when Colladon's biography discusses the reformer's preaching and teaching more precisely. It is helpful in filling out the details of Calvin's work to identify patterns and exceptions in the way the reformer (and no doubt his colleagues) organized their preaching.

The *Lectio Continua* Pattern

The foundation of Calvin's preaching practice was *lectio continua*, working straight through a book; this was a principle to insure covering the whole text of the Bible and explaining each passage in its context. For the historian, knowing that there should be a regular sequence can provide a guide for ordering sermons which have no dates, as well as for extrapolating the organization of ones which no longer exist. For practical purposes of reconstructing Calvin's preaching, the dreadful loss of the folio volumes sold as old paper in 1805 (see below) means that dating even his extant sermons can be difficult, particularly for the early years of the stenographer's work when the latter was not yet functioning like clock-work. Here follows the basic picture of the books through which Calvin preached, as provided primarily by Raguenier, with some information from Colladon and modern scholars.

After (nearly) finishing Psalms by late summer 1553, Calvin probably began to preach on the same New Testament book morning and afternoon on Sundays, following this plan in order to complete Acts by mid-March 1554. Thereafter the flow of Sunday sermons was interrupted only on the regular occasions of a specific Christological holy day or the very rare times when a crisis seemed to call for a special Psalm. When there was a break in the *lectio continua* for the Nativity, Easter, or Pentecost, it was only for the morning service, and the regular sermon series continued on those Sunday afternoons.[61] These exceptional cases will be examined below but here the known sermons are listed. First Thessalonians began on the afternoon of March 26, 1554, followed by 2 Thessalonians; of these 46 sermons, all except a single one are lost. Then Calvin was ready to start 1 Timothy on the morning of Sept. 16, 1554, for a total of 54 sermons, and then 2 Timothy and Titus beginning on April 21, 1555, together making 47 sermons. There were only a couple of interruptions for specific Psalms. On Oct. 20, 1555, in the morning Calvin began the 110 sermons on 1 Corinthians, followed by 66 on 2 Corinthians beginning on Feb. 28, 1557. Galatians was next, beginning on the afternoon of Nov. 14, 1557, and counting 43 sermons; then Ephesians, again with the first sermon on the afternoon of May 15, 1558. The 48 sermons on Ephesians were interrupted for a good many months by the preacher's very serious illness, from mid-October 1558 until the following summer. When he took up preaching again on June 11, 1559, Calvin no longer preached twice on Sundays except on rare occasions. He completed Ephesians by mid-July; he next chose the Gospel Harmony (the synoptics) for his Sunday sermons and this would occupy him for the rest of his life.[62]

Colladon noted that Calvin was working on Jeremiah in the summer of 1549, followed naturally by Lamentations, and the next weekday sermons were more prophets. Over the course of several years, November 1550 to the spring of 1552, Calvin worked through eight of the minor prophets: Micah began on Nov. 12, 1550 (28 sermons), Zephaniah on Feb. 6, 1551 (17 sermons), Hosea on April 2,

---

[61] For examples, see Appendix Seven: Calvin's Sermons, #18 & #19 on 1 Corinthians, for Dec. 15 and Dec. 22, 1555 (Nativity on the morning of Dec. 22), sermons #44 & #45 on 1 Corinthians, for March 29 & April 5, 1556 (Easter on the morning of April 5). The same can be extrapolated for other sermons, as the Appendix shows for sermons #11 & #12 on Galatians in Dec. 1557, and sermons #3 and #4 on Ephesians in May 1558.

[62] For this and the following paragraph, see Raguenier's catalogue, supplemented by Gagnebin, "L'histoire des manuscrits des sermons de Calvin," S. II, p. xvii, with the addition of notes from Colladon on the date of Judges OC 21:91. Note that Raguenier says 55 sermons on 1 Tim. and 31 on 2 Tim., but in fact there are only 54 and 30, respectively. He also that 2 Tim. begins on the morning of April 21 but it was almost certainly the afternoon. See Parker's discussion below at nn.151ff. Colladon's dating of 2 Samuel is not accurate (21:95).

1551 (65 sermons), Joel on Sept. 5, 1551 (17 sermons), Amos on Oct. 28, 1551 (43 sermons), Obadiah on Feb. 5, 1552 (5 sermons), Jonah on March 28, 1552 (only 6 recorded), and Nahum. Then it was back to the major prophets: Daniel, Ezekiel. Raguenier missed the second part of Jonah, all of Nahum, and the first four chapters of Daniel because he was ill, so his records of Daniel pick up on July 18, 1552 (47 recorded). Ezekiel, which took more than a year, was begun on Nov. 21, 1552, and filled 174 sermons. This was finished by Feb. 26, 1554, when Calvin began to preach his 159 sermons on Job, and then Deuteronomy beginning on March 20, 1555 (200 sermons). The Isaiah sermons which came next, starting on July 16, 1556, kept the preacher busy for more than two years (343 sermons!), although they also suffered a long break when Calvin was ill from October 1558 to mid-June 1559. After he returned to the pulpit, he finished Isaiah and on Sept. 4, 1559, took up Genesis (123 sermons recorded by the time of Raguenier's death, but this certainly was not all that were preached). On Feb. 3, 1561, Calvin began Judges, and then 1 Samuel (107 sermons), starting on Aug. 8, 1561, followed by the 87 sermons on 2 Samuel, dated Feb. 23, 1562, through Feb. 3, 1563, and then he was occupied with First Kings until his death.

The Exceptions

Normally Calvin worked through each book, verse by verse. There were two exceptions. One was the book of Psalms, the other the sermons preached on special Christological holy days. Before turning to the puzzle of his sermons during the "missing years" it is important to complete what is known of his preaching on these two topics.

Psalms

First to be considered will be the sermons on Psalms, which is the only book for which Calvin's order of preaching deliberately did not follow the sequence of "chapters." When Colladon consistently begins to identify the reformer's texts in mid-1549, the biographer explains how Calvin chose the pattern of his expositions of Psalms.

> For the afternoon sermon on Sundays he preached on the Psalms, taking only those which had not yet been translated into meter (because he had already preached on the others), and he was up to Ps. 40.[63]

Colladon's words reveal one significant reason for the fact that Calvin did not preach straight through the book of Psalms, i.e., the texts had not been translated

---

[63] See Colladon, OC 21:71, quoted above in n.54.

into meter in canonical order and these were the ones he explained first when he began a concentrated series of sermons. Furthermore, the reformer would choose appropriate Psalms for specific occasions. On the special day of prayer services in November 1545 he selected Ps. 115 to express intercession for fellow believers, and Ps. 124 to give thanks for their deliverance by God's goodness. Another example is Ps. 90, which he probably explained in 1546. This sermon is not extant, but it seems to have been the text on the memorable afternoon in March 1546 when Alliod made the disturbance at St. Gervais. Alliod criticized Calvin's preaching on "the song of Moses," which is how the reformer (and others) commonly identified Ps. 90.[64] There is thus good reason to believe that sometimes Calvin took special Psalms out of order, even before they were available for singing.

It may be taken as given that Colladon was correct in affirming a connection between the Psalms in metrical form and Calvin's preaching in the years the biographer was describing, i.e., prior to mid-1549. The pastor explained those which the congregation was singing, so that they would understand their prayers, and then he moved on to Psalms which were not in the Psalter. For this second method of selection Colladon implies that the preacher proceeded in *lectio continua* order (skipping the ones already done). A hypothetical reconstruction of Calvin's earlier practice will be proposed below. Here the question is what else may be extrapolated from Colladon's information to identify Calvin's work in the period the biographer was describing. Did the preacher change his mind about the order when the next set of metrical Psalms appeared in 1551, i.e., did he continue the canonical order or change to explain the texts newly published in the Psalter? Perhaps he did both. He had been following the canonical order, skipping those in meter, and this almost certainly continued until the new Psalter was published. At that point or at least not too long afterwards he may have done (most of) the new

---

[64] For Ps. 115 and 124, see chap. 4 at nn.154ff. Several times when referring to this Psalm Calvin calls it "the song of Moses"; e.g., sermon 200 on Deut. 34:7-11, OC 29:218, as well as in the commentary on Ps. 90 itself (OC 31:832 *et passim*.). This is what Alliod also calls it, see below at n.215. This is also the title in the Vulgate, so naming it this way was standard practice. The phrase "cantique de Moise" can be used for various texts, probably most often for Deut. 32. The texts of Exod. 15 and Deut. 32 appear along with a number of other "canticles" in a Latin volume entitled *Liber Davidis Psalmorum* published by Robert Stephanus (Geneva, 1556), pp. 507-12. (Other canticles are Judg. 5, Isa. 5, Hab. 3, Luke 1-2 [Magnificat, Benedictus, Simeon's song], and the prayer of Daniel, Dan. 9. None of these are metrical.) The earliest metrical version appears to be Marot's Deut. 32 in *Cinquante deus pseaumes de David* (Paris, Guillaume le Bret, 1548), pp. 76r-79r. François Estienne's French Bible 1567 reprints this (pp. Hh2r-Hh3r). In 1559 N. Barbier and T. Courteau printed a Bible with the service book with French metrical versions of some canticles, including Deut. 32 by Accasse d'Albiac. For Calvin's presence at St. Gervais, see chap. 2 at nn.46ff; his criticism of the situation, see below at n.213.

metrical texts, before finally returning to the canonical order for Psalms which would not be published for singing until 1562. It is not possible to know, but perhaps a hypothesis can be sketched on the basis of the sermons which are extant.

There are 37 (or 38) sermons from scattered sources and periods.[65] Of these, three on Ps. 16:4, 27:4, 27:8, plus an exposition on Ps. 87, were edited and published by the reformer himself in 1552. The rest were transcribed as preached: one each on Ps. 124 and part of 115 from 1545; one each on Ps. 80 and part of 89 in or about 1551; twenty-two on Ps. 119 preached on Sunday afternoons in 1553; one on part of Ps. 147 in Nov. 1553, one on Ps. 148 in Sept. 1554 and one on part of Ps. 149 in July 1555; one on Ps. 65 in May 1557, two each on Ps. 46 and 48 preached in May and June 1560. The correlation between the dates (definite or approximate) of these sermons and the metrical versions in the Psalters reveals that some of these expositions preceded the sung versions, while others did not. Most of the extant sermons on Psalms were preached before the texts appeared in metrical form. For example, the 72 sermons which Raguenier recorded in 1549-52 almost certainly included Ps. 80, 87, and 89, but these were not printed in the Psalter until 1562. Colladon says that Calvin had reached Ps. 40 in the summer of 1549. Then these three Psalms would fit very well in the canonical sequence of texts which had not yet been put into meter.

On the other hand, all the verses of Ps. 119 were published in the 1551 Psalter. They also appeared in the table printed that same year which assigned Psalms to Sunday mornings and afternoons and the day of prayer. However, it was well over a year before Calvin began to preach on all twenty-two sections of Ps. 119, on Sunday afternoons from January through the first week of July 1553.[66] It may be that he decided to leave this (admittedly very time-consuming) commitment until he had done at least most of the remaining Psalms, both those newly introduced into the Psalter and those in canonical sequence up to Ps. 119. At least, as Appendix Ten: Part Three illustrates, there were relatively few Psalms in the canonical sequence after Ps. 119 which had not been translated into meter by 1551. They were Ps. 135-136, 139-142, 144-150. These may have occupied Calvin once he finished the last of Ps. 119 on July 2, 1553. Perhaps he did not complete all of them immediately, given the fact that there are sermons on Ps. 147 on

---

65 The exposition of Ps. 87 which Calvin published was not technically a sermon, but it can be included here. The dating is based essentially on Mülhaupt, "Einleitung," S. VII, p. xxxviii, plus notes by Peter & Gilmont, *Bibliotheca Calviniana*. For full discussion, see Appendix Seven at n.37.

66 See chap. 3 Fig. 1 for the 1551 table; Appendix Ten, Part Three for records and calculations about Psalms texts.

Nov. 12, 1553, Ps. 148 on Sept. 30, 1554, and Ps. 149 on July 14, 1555. With so many variables unknown, it is impossible to pin down exactly when the reformer expounded each Psalm, but it is safe to say that he had preached on all of them at least once by the mid-1550s.

It is evident that Calvin preached on some Psalms more than once. For example, the sermons on Ps. 65 (in 1557) and 46 and 48 (in 1560) were at least a second time through these texts. Ps. 46 had been in the Psalter since 1539 – because Calvin had translated it himself the first time![67] – and according to Colladon the preacher had already expounded such texts by 1549. (In the section below on pre-1549 preaching the question of when Calvin began to concentrate on the Psalms will be explored.) Ps. 48 and 65 would not appear in metrical form until 1562, but they would follow in the canonical sequence not long after Ps. 40, which the preacher had reached in the summer of 1549. The conclusion is that there must have been a number of Psalms on which Calvin preached at least twice. There is nothing surprising about this; as the preface to the contemporary English translation explains, the re-appearance of Ps. 46 in May 1560 was owed to rumors that Geneva would be attacked following the failure of the Conspiracy of Amboise.[68] A particular danger led Calvin to take up again a Psalm which fit the circumstances. Indeed, the association of Psalms with times of intense spiritual crisis or joy had been established at least as early as the special day of prayer services in November 1545. This Biblical book could be seen as applicable in the most diverse circumstances.

Christological "Holy" Days

The second kind of exception to the regular series of *lectio continua* sermons, which Calvin preached straight through whole books, were the partial expositions for designated special occasions. These comprised the regular Passion Week sermons on the gospel narratives, and those preached on the individual "feast days" of Christmas-Nativity, Easter, and Pentecost, which included the main Lord's Supper celebrations. There are three sources for knowing what Calvin preached on these special days. One is a volume of feast day sermons collected by Raguenier during the period 1549-1555; unfortunately, the texts have disap-

---

[67] See Pidoux, *Psautier Huguenot*, II, p. 3; the editors of OC 6:211 give the text but say it is copied from the 1542 version (they did not have access to the 1539). This was later replaced by Marot's version. For discussion of Ps. 115 and 124 in Nov. 1545, see chap. 4 at nn.154ff, 161ff.

[68] See Peter & Gilmont, *Bibliotheca Calviniana* II, p. 963. The publisher was Rowland Hall, one of the English exiles, who left Geneva to return to England just after the sermons were preached and took copies of them with him. Calvin's letter #3215 (written by Beza) to Bullinger in June 1560 describes some of the situation in France (OC 18:115).

peared, but at least the table of contents survived. The second is a book published in 1558 which provides a number of different sermons for these same kinds of occasions. Usually identified by the first two words of the title, *Plusieurs sermons*, the full title is revealing: *Some Sermons of John Calvin concerning the Divinity, the Humanity, and the Birth of our Lord Jesus Christ: also concerning His Passion, Death, Resurrection, Ascension, and Last Coming. Then concerning the Descent of the Holy Spirit on the Apostles and St. Peter's First Sermon.* The first item in this collection is a weekday "Bible study" (*congrégation*) on John 1:1-5, which was evidently added late in the process because it is separately paginated,[69] but it corresponds to the emphasis on divinity in the book title. The last section is made up of seven sermons on Isaiah 52-53 that the table of contents calls "of the mystery of the passion of Christ taken from Isaiah." These were excerpted from the *lectio continua* series Calvin was preaching when this volume was published. Apart from the *congrégation* and the Isaiah section, the rest of the sermons will be described below. The contents of *Plusieurs Sermons* and the lost volume, plus a few texts which remained in manuscript until modern times, provide an entrée into Calvin's preaching on "feast days" when he interrupted his *lectio continua* series for special occasions. Each sermon or set of sermons will be discussed in order.

The missing volume for which only the table of contents remains included sermons on the passion and Easter and Pentecost from 1549 taken down by Maistre André de la Chesnaye, and others on Christmas, and/or "passion et resurrection," and/or Pentecost recorded by Raguenier for every year between 1550 and 1555 except 1552.[70] (He gives the dates in the traditional style, according to which Dec. 25 was counted as the first day of the next year.) It is perhaps clearest to analyze the list topically. Calvin preached a single sermon on Luke 2 on Christmas-Nativity in 1549, 1553, and 1554.[71] For Pentecost in 1549, 1554, and 1555 he preached a single sermon on Acts 2. The sermons on the passion and/or resurrection are slightly more complicated because there were different gospel texts from which to choose, although only two are named: Matthew (which stood

---

69   See de Boer, *Genevan School of Prophets*, pp. 35, 146, 150.

70   See the "table of contents" published by Mülhaupt, "Einleitung," S. VII, pp. xlvii-xlviii, which gives the topics of 34 sermons by Calvin. For further discussion, see next note.

71   The text says 1550, or 1554, 1555, but Raguenier used the old style of dating which made Dec. 25 the first day of the next year. That these are actually 1549, 1553, and 1554 is clear from the fact that they are listed before the passion and resurrection sermons dated 1550, 1554, and 1555; otherwise they would follow the Easter listings for 1550, 1554, and 1555. Note also that the sermon for "1550" is labeled "mercredi, 25. jour de Decembre" [i.e., 1549], and the celebration of the Nativity would not have been held on Dec. 25 after 1549 unless that date fell on a Sunday. See Mülhaupt, "Einleitung," S. VII, p.xlix.

for the synoptics) and John. For 1549, the passion-and-resurrection sequence was seven sermons on Matthew, from the Sunday before Easter through Easter, April 21. The next year Calvin preached eight sermons on the Johannine passion and resurrection in the week of March 31-April 6, 1550. The following year he treated the passion from John 18-19 in a single sermon on Wednesday, March 25, 1551 (the day of prayer, the one weekday he often preached when this was not his regular week). For two other years, 1553 and 1554, the texts of the passion and resurrection sermons are not named. In 1553 the number of sermons is listed as eight (Sunday March 26 through Sunday April 2), and three in 1554 (of which the two Sundays are named, March 18 & 25, and the third must have been preached on Wednesday March 21). There was a single sermon on Matthew for Easter, April 14, 1555. (This is the year when Calvin was out of town for the first half of Passion Week. When he returned, he continued his weekday *lectio continua* series on Deuteronomy in the last weekdays before Easter and so did not preach any passion sermons.)

The New Testament sermons in *Plusieurs sermons*, the collection of Calvin's "feast day" preaching printed in 1558, have now been published in a critical edition with a fine introduction by W. H. Th. Moehn in the new *Opera Omnia Denuo Recognita*, Series V.[72] Moehn's introduction provides the best discussion of the dates of these nineteen sermons,[73] one on Christmas, nine on the passion and resurrection, four labeled "Ascension," four more on "Pentecost," and one on the last coming. The original editor of the *Plusieurs Sermons* labeled the first sermon: "Sermon de la Nativité de Jesus Christ, fait le jour de Noel, auquel se célèbre la saincte Cene du Seigneur," and the text is Luke 2, as always on the Nativity. As Moehn argues, since the title identifies the day as "the day of Christmas," i.e., Dec. 25, and it had to be a Sunday because the Lord's Supper was celebrated at this service, the year must be 1552 because that is the only time in this period that the traditional Christmas date fell on a Sunday. (That this text comes from early in Raguenier's work is confirmed by the shorter length of the

---

[72]   Moehn does not include either the *congrégation* on John 1:1-5 or the Isaiah sermons of the original *Plusieurs Sermons* in his critical edition.

[73]   See Moehn, "Introduction," *Sermones*, pp. xxviii-xxxv. For distribution of these sermons through the years of Calvin's preaching, see references to *Plusieurs sermons* at specific points in Appendix Eight Part Two. In the case of the Passion-Resurrection sermons, which Moehn identifies as 1557 or 1558, I have tentatively narrowed the date to 1558 because in 1557 Passion Week was not Calvin's regular week to preach whereas in 1558 it was; see Appendix Eight Part Two at 1558, and Appendix Three: Ministerial Rotations, for Calvin 1557. (Easter was April 18, 1557; other ministers do baptisms for Calvin in the following week, April 19, 20, & 22, showing that this was his week to preach and therefore Passion Week was not.)

sermon.) [74] The passion and resurrection are represented by a set of sermons on Matthew 26-28 which were preached in 1558. This series is unusual because there are nine separate expositions: two from the Sunday before Easter (morning and afternoon), one for each weekday, and the final one on Easter morning. The four sermons on the "Ascension" were not in fact preached on the traditional day of Ascension but excerpted from the series on Acts which Calvin began preaching in the late summer of 1549. The four sermons which follow next are identified as "Pentecost" sermons, although only the first was actually preached on that day in May 1558, while the rest were excerpted from the series on Acts preached in 1549. [75] The final sermon is labeled "on the last coming of our Lord Jesus Christ" and the text is 2 Thess. 1:6-10, from the series preached in the summer of 1554. (Calvin began 1 Thessalonians in March and completed 2 Thessalonians in September, so this particular sermon probably comes from mid or late summer.)

What this anthology, *Plusieurs sermons*, offers is some examples of sermons actually preached on special days: Christmas 1552, Passion Week and Easter 1558, Pentecost 1558, as well as others which fitted the "feast day" subject. That it was not a collection only of the days Geneva celebrated in some special fashion is evident from the addition of the *congrégation* on John 1 and the final sermon on the second coming. However, it corresponds exactly to Calvin's list of the key Christological events as he named them in his essay about the Lord's Supper in his Strasbourg liturgies of 1542 and 1545. [76] It also highlights the main acts of salvation history which were given prominence in Geneva.

In addition to these two collections of "feast day" sermons, whether extant or lost, whether on the day or about the topic, there are some other excerpts from Calvin's preaching which treat the theme of the special Christological days. One is the only other extant set of Passion Week sermons, six in number, also on the synoptics, which comes from 1562. In addition there are three separate sermons, two on the Easter passage Matt. 28:1-10 from 1559 and 1560, and one on Acts 2:1-11 from Pentecost 1560. These had remained in manuscript but were finally printed in the twentieth century in the *Supplementa Calviniana* series. [77] Of these, only the sermons from 1562 were not recorded by Raguenier, who had died the previous year.

There are a few comments to be made about the preservation of Calvin's sermons on feast days, and then about what conclusions can be drawn from these records. First, turning to the table of contents of the lost sermons, it is notable that

---

[74] Moehn, "Introduction," *Sermons*, pp. xxix-xxx, xxxv.

[75] Moehn, "Introduction," *Sermons*, p. xxxiii-xxxv.

[76] See chap. 4 quoted at n.11.

[77] Mülhaupt, *Psalmpredigten. Passions-, Oster-, und Pfingstpredigten*, S. VII, pp. 83-169.

1552 is the only year for which not a single sermon is listed. However, Moehn has shown that the Christmas text published in *Plusieurs Sermons* comes from that year. The feast day sermons which survived in manuscript form were preserved in bound collections that included a wide variety of topics,[78] which implies that the individual sermons had been kept unbound originally and were assembled in a somewhat hap-hazard fashion. Together these observations suggest that Raguenier had been collecting feast day sermons for many years, and that the ones put together in the lost volume were assembled some time after the *Plusieurs Sermons* book was published in 1558.[79] That is, no special sermons for 1552 were named in the surviving table of contents, but this might have been because the one for Dec. 25, 1552, had already been printed. All the Nativity sermons mentioned would have been celebrations of the Lord's Supper, including the one on Wednesday, Dec. 25, 1549. However, if the Christmas sermon in *Plusieurs Sermons* was originally part of this collection, it might well have been chosen for publication because it combined the traditional date with the sacramental celebration, which would maintain but avoid emphasizing Geneva's idiosyncratic practice of keeping Christmas only on Sunday.

Examining records of Calvin's sermons marking special "feasts" leads to some conclusions about his practice, particularly his preaching on Passion Week. First, it clear that he always interrupted his *lectio continua* series for the Christmas-Nativity, Easter, and Pentecost Lord Supper services. The evidence for Passion Week is somewhat more confusing. It may be noted that the years 1550 and 1551 in the lost book of sermons are the only two times the passion from John is explicitly mentioned. Since none of these sermons are extant, it is not possible to compare Calvin's treatment of this passage from the pulpit with the synoptic version, which survives in two sets of sermons from 1558 and 1562. Raguenier's table of contents lists sermons on the passion and resurrection in 1553 and 1554, without identifying the specific gospel. It is virtually certain that Calvin preached

---

[78] Mülhaupt, "Einleitung," S. VII, p. xv.

[79] Mülhaupt, "Einleitung," S. VII, pp. xlviii-xlix, proposes a date for this table of contents before 1557 because it is not included in the proper place in Raguenier's catalogue, but then goes on to discuss why this collection might have been omitted from any contemporary mention, including in Beza's 1564 list of Calvin's unpublished sermons. The first notice of this collection is the catalogue of 1697 (citing Gagnebin, "L'Histoire des manuscrits des sermons de Calvin," p. xix): "sur l'histoire de la nativité, passion et résurrection de J. C. et sur le c. 2 des Acts, un volume." Given the argument that the Christmas sermon in *Plusieurs Sermons* came from this collection, it seems probable that Raguenier kept this book separate. Mülhaupt suggests that this book remained in Raguenier's possession (i.e., was not handed over the *Bourse française* as the other sermons were) either because it included sermons by other preachers and not just Calvin, or because the feast sermons might seem to contradict Geneva's *lectio continua* tradition somewhat.

on the passion story more often than the instances on record, but there is no evidence to determine when he followed which gospel or exactly how frequently he did the Passion Week sermons. It is probable that he preached on the passion most years, even if sometimes it was not his week to preach and he did only the Wednesday day of prayer service (as was the case in 1551 and 1554). The one year when he is known to have maintained his *lectio continua* series is 1555, but that is an exception which may prove the rule. Calvin was out of town on business for part of the two weeks before Easter. Knowing this, the ministers must have assigned someone else (likely Calvin's alternate) to take the Passion Week sermons. As the records of his sermons indicate (see Appendix Eight: Part One), when Calvin returned, about mid-week, he did preach daily because it was his regular week, but he did not take the Passion Week subject; instead he picked up Deuteronomy where he had left off before he went out of town.

A Hypothetical Reconstruction of Calvin's Early Preaching (1536-1548/9)

While a remarkable amount can be known about the Biblical texts on which Calvin preached, there are some significant lacunae which have apparently passed almost unnoticed, even though some of these involve the reformer's favorite Biblical books.[80] Furthermore, the early years of the reformer's preaching are usually passed over with only a few suggestive comments. Perhaps that prudence would be the better part of wisdom... but the absence of sermons or even of any reference to sermons on such books as the Gospel of John is very intriguing and worth at least some educated guesswork. The present essay is an attempt to offer a hypothetical reconstruction of what Calvin's preaching before 1549 might have been. The discussion is ordered from most probable to least, or the greatest circumstantial evidence to the most limited.

The Intriguing Questions
What is Missing?

There are not only no sermons on the Gospel of John, arguably the gospel Calvin most valued, but also there is not even any mention of such a series. The same is true for various epistles, including some by Paul, the key apostle for most

---

80 As early as 1539 in the *Reply to Sadoleto* Calvin identified his habit of devoting more time to teaching things he considered necessary for his hearers' salvation; OC 5:409. Gary Hansen, *John Calvin and the Non-Literal Interpretation of Scripture* (Princeton Theological Seminary Ph.D. dissertation, 1998), p. 16, has pointed out that the Pauline epistles, John, and Hebrews were keys in Calvin's theology because of his "explicit practice...of commenting first on the books that have the greatest clarity on the most important subjects." In pp. 16-21 Hansen examines the vital role of Paul, John, and Hebrews in the development of Calvin's theology.

Protestants. There are no sermons on Romans or Philippians or Colossians (or Philemon), none on the Petrine letters or James or 1 John. (Calvin did not write commentaries on 2 and 3 John or Revelations, so he may indeed not have preached on them.) The fact remains, however, that the omission of the Gospel of John, and Romans, Philippians, Colossians, and First Peter is startling, since all of these, especially the gospel, were at least as important as the "minor" prophets or Samuel or Kings. If he could preach on Isaiah twice, then he could not have skipped the Gospel of John or Romans.

It is only in the last century that Calvin's sermons have again received sustained attention. The common question has been what he taught in them, and so the focus has been on the sermons that are extant. There are occasional references to what the reformer might have been preaching in the years before 1549. Naturally, one of the few missing books to attract attention has been Romans, and some scholars suggest in passing that Calvin probably preached on this during his first Genevan ministry.[81] There has been no real effort, however, to look carefully for what is not there. To draw as full a picture of Calvin the pastor of Geneva as possible, it is worthwhile attempting to fill in the gaps in the list of what he preached before his sermons began to be recorded.

Lectionary Sermons?

First, however, it is appropriate to note Wilhelm Neuser's thesis that there are in fact six early sermons which can be attributed to Calvin. These are the expositions which were added to the *Epistres et Evangiles pour les cinquante et deux dimenches de l'an* in the edition published by de Vingle in 1535. The texts are Matt. 1:1-17 and 5:1-12, John 15:17-25 and 12:24-26, Mark 12:33-37, and Luke 19:1-9. Neuser's primary argument for Calvin's authorship rests on the similarity between these sermons and the preface to the New Testament which Calvin is thought to have provided for Olivétan's Bible in 1535.[82] It is not the purpose of the present work to

---

[81] T. H. L. Parker mentions this in passing, in the "Introduction" to his critical edition of the Commentary on Romans, *Iohannis Calvini Commentarius in Epistolam Pauli ad Romanos* (Leiden: Brill, 1981), p. ix. Parker, *Calvin's Preaching*, p. 58, says there is no information about Calvin's preaching 1536-38 "except that he called the City Council 'a council of the devil,'" and adds that there is nothing about Strasbourg. He goes on (p. 62) to suggest that Calvin might have preached on the Catholic Epistles after his return to Geneva, because there is no other record of them.

[82] Neuser, *Johann Calvin – Leben und Werk*, pp. 134-43. See also Wilhelmus H. Neuser, "The first outline of Calvin's theology: the preface to the New Testament in the Olivétan Bible of 1535," in *Koers. Bulletin for Christian scholarship* 66 (2001), pp. 1-38. Neuser, *Johann Calvin – Leben und Werk*, pp. 141-42, cites an incident in 1542 as evidence that Calvin no longer liked the collection of *Epitres et Evangiles*. However, the incident he cites is the one discussed below at n.88, where on Oct. 17, 1542, the Senate refused to publish such a book; as stated there, this was not the same collection.

examine in detail the question of the provenance of these sermons, but it is worth noting that Frans van Stam has convincingly demonstrated that the preface *A tous amateurs* was actually written by Olivétan himself, and thus similarities between it and the sermons cannot be used as proof of Calvin's authorship of the latter.[83]

If these sermons were by Calvin, that would strengthen the likelihood that Geneva might have been open to some kind of use of the traditional lectionary. This is the claim of Erik de Boer, who suggests that Geneva was still using the selected lectionary in some form during the early years, between 1536 and perhaps as late as 1550.[84] Based on Farel's being influenced by Zurich, where "the *lectio continua* was followed in preaching [but] the readings from the Epistles and Gospels – in this sequence –were maintained," de Boer believes that Geneva might have continued the use of the old lectionary.[85] A "good argument can be

---

83 Frans van Stam, "Olivétan, not Calvin the author of *A tous amateurs*, a preface to the oldest French protestant Bible," in *Calvin – Saint or Sinner?* ed. Herman J. Selderhuis (Tübingen: Mohr Siebeck, 2010), pp. 66-81.

84 De Boer, *Genevan School of Prophets*, pp. 51-56. His argument is based partly on a misinterpretation of the April 3, 1536, note, which he reads as "a number of priests were presented to the Council by representatives of the villages to serve as ministers of the Word," p. 53. (see below). Other evidence cited is the Council's determination on May 19, 1542, to keep Ascension as usual, and the introduction in 1544 of the Passion Week sermons. He goes on to suggest that the lectionary may have continued in use until the feasts of Annunciation and Circumcision were abolished in 1550. "It could very well be that on Sundays the lectionary had been in place as late as 1550." There are several ways that "lectionary" can be used; traditionally this referred to the one-year cycle of epistles and gospels of the Latin church. Calvin's Geneva definitely did not follow this. They did have a kind of informal "lectionary" which consisted of regularly planned interruptions in the use of the *lectio continua* for specific occasions. This was not a set of readings (traditional or new) but it meant that the preaching text of the day changed for that specific service. Thus, Luke 2 was used on the morning that the Nativity was celebrated; Acts 2 on the morning of Pentecost; one of the gospels (usually Matt. 28 or John 20) on Easter morning. Passion Week might begin on the previous Sunday morning or it might begin on the Monday; it might focus on Matthew/ the synoptics or John.

85 De Boer, *Genevan School of Prophets*, p. 53. He cites Calvin's familiarity with the traditional epistles and gospels in letters written in May 1542 which refer to "the letter of the first Sunday in Advent," and "proves that Calvin was very much aware of the liturgical calendar and readings of the Roman Catholic church of his youth," *Genevan School of the Prophets*, p. 52. In fact, the letter is written to some believers in Lyon to put them on guard about a monk who used to preach to them and wanted to be ordained in Geneva but would not submit to examination. The Genevans recognize that the monk's preaching has been fruitful: "Car à la verité pource qu'il avoit pleu au Seigneur de se servir par dela de ses predications, et que quelque edification s'en estoit ensuyvie, nostre vouloir et desir totalement estoit de ne le point rejecter." However, Calvin says they do not want to receive him as a minister until he meets certain conditions: less pride, more trust in God, and better knowledge to teach purely. It is in this context that he gives the example of the monk's ignorance, evident in his contribution when the *congrégation* was discussing the passage of the epistle for the first Sunday in Adent. He uses this language because it would be familiar to his audience as a way to identify the passage. Letter #397, OC 11:402.

made for the hypothesis that in the 1540s some form of a lectionary was still in place in Geneva, either as a set of pericopes to be read in Church or as a preaching program for the occasions connected to the festivals."[86] Arguing for the use of the lectionary is a minor point for de Boer's purpose, since his main concern is to explore the links between the *congrégations* and the new patterns of training for Protestant preachers which the Reformation had made necessary. However, in the present context it appears that the evidence which he cites about Genevan acceptance of the old lectionary, especially the reference to the priests who spoke of a postil in April 1536 and a proposed publication on the lectionary in 1542, may be more complicated than appears on the surface.

First, the 1536 "postil." On April 3, 1536, Farel appeared before the Senate along with a number of village priests who were being questioned about their adherence to the new teaching. The priests basically explain that they want to follow their predecessors but see their neighbors changing and wish to do as they do. One of the men is accused of having a book by which he leads the people astray, literally "seduces" them. To this he answers that he has a postil of the gospels ("une pastille sur l'evangille") to which Farel takes exception. "[Farel] said to him that they should hold to the gospel rather than to the postil." (It is interesting to observe that the Senate's secretary feels he needs to explain what a postil is, because he adds "pastille vault dire après cela," which suggests that the language is not familiar and thus the object itself was probably not commonly known to Genevan laity.) Farel goes on to exhort the village priests, to which one of the priests answers for the rest "what you say is true" but he requests another month for them "to read the gospel" and consider. The Senate then agrees that the priests can come back in a month to say whether they accept the "evangelical teaching preached in this city" or not. Meanwhile they are forbidden to do any priestly function until they can prove to the Senate that it is "ordered by scripture," and they are told to attend gospel preaching (by the new Protestant ministers).[87] So far from proving that a postil was being used in Geneva, this seems to indicate that a few traditional priests owned them but laity did not know

---

[86]   De Boer, *Genevan School of Prophets*, p. 54.

[87]   April 3, 1536, OC 21:198 (RC 29 f.65r-v). "Alors par la bouche dudit Claude Savoye est esté dict audit Don George Putex qui il ha des livres par lesquelz il seduyt le people. Surquoy il a respondu que il a une postille sur l'evangille. Alors Maistre Guillaulme Farel luy ha dict que l'on se doibt tenir à l'evangille plustost que à la postille (postille veult dire apres cela) et luy leur a faict plusieurs belles remonstrances le dit Farel, auquel il hont respondu par la voix de celluy de Malva que ce qu'il dict est vray mais toutefffois il supplient que l'on les laisse encore pour ung moys prochain pour puysse lire sur l'evangille, affin une aultreffois il puysse plus franchement et myeulx respondre." Archives@etat.ge.ch accessed Aug. 9, 2013.

them and Farel wanted nothing to do with them. It is hardly more likely that Calvin would have accepted them, especially if (as is probably the case) the sermons on the lectionary which Neuser attributes to him were actually written by Olivetan.

The other case cited by de Boer is a note in the Genevan Senate records in October 1542 which he reads as a republication of the de Vingle book. In fact, it was the product of a local minister. The Annales citation is incomplete, and recourse to the original record reveals that the point was this minister's request for permission to publish his own "book on the 52 Sundays." The council denied the request because the contents "are not very edifying" and not apparently because the concept of a lectionary was objectionable.[88] However, Geneva's pastors do not seem to have approved of the concept.

Preaching Before 1549

What might Calvin have been preaching in his early years as a pastor? After brief attention to the first Geneva sojourn and the Strasbourg ministry, the main focus will be 1541-49, from Calvin's return until his sermons were being recorded and his biographers were including this information in their accounts of his work. The first task, however, is a bit of a numbers game: attempting to determine how much time it would require to expound a given book.

Calculating Ratios of Biblical Verses Per Sermon

One way to determine how long a sermon series might require is to calculate the average number of Biblical verses Calvin covered in each sermon, and approximately how long it might have taken him to complete his *lectio continua* exposition of each book. To the raw numbers must be added the recognition that there were also interruptions, times when Calvin missed his regular day in the pulpit. Appendix Ten outlines first the dated New Testament and then the dated Old Testament sermons, giving the average ratio of verses to sermon for Calvin's extant sermons and adding the periods of time which the reformer actually took to preach them. This reveals that in general the number of verses per sermon in the extant New Testament letters ranges from 2.092 in 1 Timothy to 3.519 in 1 Corinthians, while the expositions of the Acts – a rather different genre – average 4.409 verses per sermon. For the Old Testament, the prophetic books appear to range from 3.345 in Isaiah up to 6.91 for Ezekiel; the books of the law

---

[88] De Boer, *Genevan School of Prophets*, p.53. Oct. 17, 1542, RC 36 f146: "Predicant de Grasson lequel a prier de permerstre à Jehan Michel d'imprimer un livre qu'il a composé nomé les 52 dymanches. Surquoy resoluz pource qu'il n'est pas de grande ediffication que leditz livre luy soyt restitué." Archives@etat.ge.ch accessed Aug. 9, 2013.

and history range from 4.695 for Deuteronomy to 7.54 for 2 Samuel. The sermons on Psalms are a special case; very few are extant, so determining the ratio of verses to sermon is rather more like guess work, but an approximation of 7 seems to fit.

When these calculations are applied to missing Biblical books, it is possible to hypothesize about the probable number of sermons Calvin may have preached on each one. From that can be estimated the approximate time period that he might have spent on each book, assuming that he did preach through each one following a fashion similar to his extant sermons. All the numbers in the following passages are based on calculations found in Appendix Ten. The sequence of known or extant sermons is found in different forms in Appendix Seven (Biblical order) and Appendix Eight (Part One: Old Testament, Part Two: New Testament and Psalms, in the chronological order in which Calvin preached them).

1536-41

There is some quite limited evidence about Calvin's preaching in the first years. It is very likely, if not certain, that he began with some of the Pauline epistles, particularly Romans, during his first ministry. It is known that he was lecturing on these books, and Romans was the logical place to begin and would be the subject of his first commentary. Working from the probable ratio of verses per sermon, Romans might have required 165 sermons. If Calvin was treating this book on Sundays, morning and afternoon, he might not have completed it in the approximately eighteen months between fall 1536 and April 1538.[89] What he might have preached on weekdays is difficult to guess. It is possible that the Genevan ministers had already begun to expound the Old Testament books on weekdays, but they may well have concentrated particularly on the New Testament. The number of New Testament books that are not mentioned anywhere else in Calvin's corpus requires the historian to consider the possibility that some were expounded on weekdays in the reformer's first Genevan sojourn. Incidental references during the period 1538-41 suggest that those who took over after Farel and Calvin were exiled generally kept to books of the New Testament and Psalms, so if there had been Old Testament preaching it was almost certainly dropped.[90]

---

[89] The printer Oporin wrote to Calvin on 25 March 1537 that he heard Calvin was commenting on Paul, and he asks Calvin to put those lectures into commentary form; cited Peter & Gilmont, *Bibliotheca Calviniana* I, p. 76: "L'Epître aux Romains a probablement fait l'objet de ses premières leçons." See Appendix Ten.

[90] For the New Testament books Calvin might have explained at this time, see below at n.103. For sermons during 1538-41, see references to John, Psalms, etc., in n.98f.

There are no clear indications of the subject of Calvin's sermons in Strasbourg, 1538-41. However, it is known on the testimony of Johannes Sturm, the long-time defender of the French congregation, that its new pastor was lecturing on the Gospel of John. In Strasbourg Calvin was almost certainly not preaching every day. A passing reference to his Tuesday sermon in a letter to Farel in 1540 makes it clear that he preached regularly on (at least) one weekday as well as Sunday but also suggests that he did not attempt more than that.[91] It is logical to imagine that Calvin was preaching either on Paul or John because those favorite books would also be important in his work to convert Anabaptists.

When Calvin returned to Geneva in 1541 he explicitly said that he took up his preaching where he had left off in 1538 but he does not identify what he had been explaining.[92] Perhaps it was still Romans? If so, the preacher probably soon moved on to other New Testament books. Rodolphe Peter has classified the little French commentary on Jude published in 1542 as a "sermon" in content, if not form, which leads Parker to suggest that Calvin may have preached on the Catholic Epistles during these years.[93] The evidence for Jude early in this time is fairly strong, and the rest of this group probably did fit in the period after Calvin's return, but perhaps not immediately.

1542-49: (Almost) Certain

The circumstantial evidence for the subject matter of Calvin's preaching in 1542-49 can be approached from two directions. One is tracing what can be determined about the later years of this period by extrapolating back from explicit information provided by Colladon and Raguenier. For his morning sermons Calvin finished Hebrews in the summer of 1549 and began Acts on Aug. 25. On Sunday afternoons he was working through Psalms and had completed all

---

91 De Boer, *Genevan School of Prophets*, p. 149: "The first author Calvin exposited was the Gospel of St. John." He is quoting Sturm, *Quarti antipappi tres partes priores* (Neustadt: Mattheus Harnisch, 1581), p. 20. Sturm was a major defender of the French congregation in Strasbourg in his role as Bucer's close colleague; later Sturm's opposition to the strict Lutheran leadership of the church that included Johannes Pappus led to a long-drawn out battle for a more "Reformed" orientation in the city. Bornert, *La réforme protestante du culte*, pp. 60-61, 76, 244, 247, 323. For letter to Farel about Strasbourg preaching, see chap. 4 n.105.

92 Letter #384 to an unnamed correspondent, January 1542, OC 11:366.

93 Peter cited in notes by Gilmont, *Bibliotheca Calviniana* I, p. 110: "De plus cet ouvrage est rédigé directement en français contrairement aux autres travaux d'exégèse. Dans une note inédite, R. Peter range cette exposition parmi les sermons de Calvin: 'bien qu'elle n'ait pas la forme d'une prédication, elle nous en donne la substance'. Il remarque que le commentaire de la même Épître publié ultérieurement propose une exégèse plus serrée et un texte plus dense." Parker, *Calvin's Preaching*, p. 62.

those in the current Psalter plus the others up to Ps. 40. The weekday services on Jeremiah and Lamentations were finished before Calvin began Micah in November 1550. Since Colladon picks up his account by referring to the texts Calvin was then explaining, it is necessary to estimate at what point the preacher actually began his work on each one. One way to do this is to note the date the preacher finished each Biblical book and interpret that in light of his homiletical habits.

Take the Old Testament first. According to his catalogue, Raguenier recorded 91 sermons on Jeremiah, beginning on Tuesday, Nov. 12, 1549. These were probably not the entire number from this period because Raguenier notes that they were not consecutive; the preacher did not skip anything, so the secretary must have been absent some of the time. Even before he began officially in the autumn of 1549, however, it is known that Raguenier had actually already transcribed some sermons. For this weekday series, there are 25 sermons on Jer. 14:19-18:23 dated from June 14 to Aug. 16, and these are extant even though they were not listed in his catalogue.[94] Furthermore, Calvin continued to preach between Aug. 16 and Nov. 12. The average of verses per sermon in the 25 extant texts suggests that the preacher might have covered between six and seven chapters during these three months. So when Raguenier began the sermons which are listed in his catalogue, Calvin would have been nearly halfway through Jeremiah. Working backwards, it is clear that he had already preached on nearly fourteen chapters when he reached Jer. 14:19 on June 14, 1549. Given his typical pace of exposition, it is likely that Calvin began Jeremiah sometime in later 1548, perhaps around the beginning of October. So what came before Jeremiah? Max Engammare has found evidence that Calvin first preached on Isaiah in this period, starting on Jan. 27, 1546. It is quite possible, or even likely, that these sermons continued into 1548. Since the extant series on Isaiah lasted from July 16, 1556, to Aug. 26, 1559 (with a nearly seven-month interruption for illness), something over two years would be reasonable for the first set.[95] The relatively limited time of about five or six months between the two major prophets might have served to

---

[94] Raguenier's catalogue, see Gagnebin, "L'Histoire des manuscrits des sermons de Calvin," S. II, p. xvi. "Premierement sus le livre des revelations du Prophete Jeremie, 91 sermons ... non reliez, et non suivans l'ung l'aultre, commenceant le premier d'iceulx le Mardi 12. jour de Novembre 1549." There are other similar gaps in the first sermon series, e.g., Acts. The 25 on Jer. 14:19-18:23, preached from June 14 to Aug. 16, 1549, are edited in S. I. See Appendix Ten on sermon calculations.

[95] See Engammare, "Introduction," *Sermons sur le Livre d'Esaïe*, S. IV/I, p. xxv. For the beginning date, see Raguenier's catalogue, Gagnebin, "L'Histoire des manuscrits des sermons de Calvin," S. II, p. xvi.

cover the four minor prophets, Habakkuk, Haggai, Zechariah, and Malachi, which are not accounted for in Raguenier's catalogue when the other eight are listed. There is no other mention of sermons on these books, but it is very unlikely that Calvin would have skipped them, particularly such a text as Malachi, with its strong Christological associations.

Then take the Sunday sermons, which included Psalms as well as the New Testament, and work backwards from Colladon's information. In this period the reformer was preaching at St. Pierre on Sunday mornings and St. Gervais most Sunday afternoons. Colladon says Calvin completed Hebrews in late summer 1549, followed by Acts, beginning on Aug. 25, 1549. Both books were preached essentially on Sunday mornings (i.e., one sermon per week). Acts lasted until mid-March 1554 but the final chapters may have been given on both mornings and afternoons. However, it is known that Calvin had reached Acts 20:31 by Sept. 3, 1553, which means approximately four years (Aug. 25, 1549 to Sept. 3, 1553) to preach through twenty chapters, although there were undoubtedly many inter-ruptions. It is best to make an estimate based on the one section of Acts which is extant and sequential. The sermons on Acts 2:36-7:60 extended from Dec. 22, 1549, to Jan. 11, 1551, and covered 192 verses in 43 sermons. The thirteen chapters of Hebrews contain 260 verses. There is evidence that sermons on the epistles normally covered fewer verses than those on Acts, so Hebrews probably required about 86-87 sermons. If 43 sermons on Acts filled just over a year, and the interruptions while he was preaching on Hebrews were comparable, Calvin would need at least two years for the sermons on Hebrews on Sunday mornings, and perhaps longer. He probably began this book in the summer of 1547.[96]

The Psalms which occupied the reformer on Sunday afternoons continued at least until July 1553, when Calvin completed Ps. 119, and probably for several more months. The organization of the reformer's preaching on Psalms has been sketched in some detail above. The question here is when he began work on this book. It is clear that Calvin considered Psalms appropriate for all kinds of "extraordinary" occasions, such as special days of prayer which marked "provi-dential" interruptions in the *lectio continua* sequence. It might be that he also consi-dered this book – which does not have an internal linear structure – a good choice for other times which did not exactly fit into his regular pulpit rhythm. It is known from other sources that Calvin was in fact preaching at St. Gervais on most Sunday afternoons for some years, but this could not be as fixed a schedule as his work at St. Pierre. Thus, it seems natural that the reformer chose this spiritually

---

[96] For Colladon's various comments, see above at nn.54ff. For calculations see Appendix Ten, Part One.

very important yet also easily interrupted book for St. Gervais. He was certainly expounding it there in 1549. So when might he have begun the Psalms sermons?

According to Colladon, by the summer of 1549 Calvin had explained all those which had appeared in the Psalter (Genevans were still working with the 1543 collection) and had also covered all those up to Ps. 40 which had not yet been versified for singing. How many Psalms would that be and approximately how many sermons? There were thirty-six metrical Psalms in the 1542 Psalter. Fifteen more by Marot appeared in 1543 and these were incorporated into the repertoire found in the first extant table of Psalms to be sung on Sundays and Wednesdays.[97] In 1549 there were thirteen psalms between #1 and #40 which had not yet appeared in the Psalter. This means that by the summer of 1549 Calvin had explained about sixty-four (or sixty-six, including Ps. 124 from Nov. 1545 and Ps. 90 from March 1546). It required 22 sermons to cover Ps. 119, stretching through all the Sunday afternoons of the first six months of 1553, so covering sixty-six Psalms might very well have required three and a half years. There are too few extant sermons on Psalms to make definite claims. However, following the loose guestimate of verses per sermon outlined in Appendix Ten, Part Three, it is very likely that Calvin began "regular" work on the Psalms when he started his "regular" work at St. Gervais in early 1546.

To summarize: in the later 1540s the Biblical books on which Calvin preached were Hebrews on Sunday mornings beginning in the summer of 1547, Psalms on Sunday afternoons (probably from 1546), and Jeremiah beginning about October 1548 and preceded by Isaiah from late January 1546, with some minor prophets between them.

The other approach for filling in the period 1542-49 starts from 1542, bringing together incidental evidence found in Genevan records such as the Senate or consistory minutes with inferences from Calvin's characteristic approach. It seems virtually certain that Calvin expounded the Gospel of John some time in these early years of his second ministry in Geneva, and he probably began it shortly after he arrived. He could not have skipped it, and there is no other period in which to fit this book; it must have been before 1549. Especially since he had been lecturing on it in Strasbourg, this would be a natural sequence, and that seems borne out by anecdotal evidence in the consistory records.

---

[97] Since there is no extant edition of the 1543 Psalter, there is some dispute about its exact contents. Cf. Pidoux, *Psautier huguenot*, vol. II, pp. 24-25. The publication of the sermons on Ps. 115 and 124 in 1545 includes the form of Ps. 79, as if this were new, though it was one of Marot's second group, so perhaps the transcriber and editor of these two sermons thought that not everyone had access to it; see chap. 3 at n.101.

On April 4, 1542, Pierre the Barber was being questioned about his attendance at worship. He said that on Sunday morning the sermon was on "St. Jehan" and he thought Calvin was preaching; the afternoon was also on John, though he did not know who was preaching.[98] It is not certain from this whether Pierre the Barber meant sermons on a Biblical person named John or John the Biblical book. However, considering the way he refers to "St. Jehan" or "Jehan," it seems probable that it was the book, especially since he speaks of morning and afternoon sermons as if their substance formed a single subject matter or a series. (If he recognized Calvin in the morning he ought to have done so in the afternoon, but since he seemed dubious about the identity of the preacher in the morning, he may not have been paying much attention to who was in the pulpit. If he was at St. Pierre in the morning, then he was also there in the afternoon because there was no other Sunday afternoon service in Greater Geneva at this time.) Even if the reference were to John the Baptist, it would probably have come from the Gospel of John. The sermons on the synoptics, the only other logical place for a reference to John the Baptist, were not preached until the last five years of Calvin's life. It is possible that there was a missing set of synoptic sermons in the early years, but this seems extremely unlikely simply for reasons of time. There were not enough Sundays to allow the slow and deliberate way Calvin worked through a book, if the 1540s had to account for the exposition of New Testament texts he preached through later, as well as the other missing epistles.

Besides the consistory note, there is also other circumstantial evidence from the council records to support the hypothesis that Calvin was preaching on the Gospel of John, i.e., he needed to correct the incompetence of his early colleagues. Apparently John was a popular book for pastors in Geneva and some of what they said about it was at the least controversial if not in fact wrong. On Sept. 27, 1540, just before the Genevan Senate decided to invite their former pastor to return, Ami Porral, one of the leaders of the council and a supporter of the exiled ministers, got into a dispute with minister Henri de La Mare over his sermon on John. Porral said that it was poison and that the preacher turned St. John upside down. The argument continued on Sept. 29, with de La Mare repeating his complaint about Porral's criticism of "St. Johan" and adding that Porral also called his preaching on Ps. 4 "poison." Porral responded that he approved the explanation of St. John by minister Aimé Champereau. The accu-

---

98 *Consist.* I, April 4, 1542, p. 28: "Az respondu qu'il vaz aux sermons et ce fust dymenche à matin et cuyde que ce fust Calvin et qu'on prescha de Sainctz Jehan; et apres dyné ne scet lequel, sinon qu'il prescha de Jehan."

sations led to a sharp altercation between Porral and the preachers de La Mare and
Jaques Bernard (who took his colleague's part), a falling out not healed until
Porral's deathbed two years later.[99] Clearly, there was good reason for Calvin to
think a careful exposition of this gospel was needed in Geneva. Combining these
points: Calvin's lecturing on the Gospel of John in Strasbourg, problems in the
interpretation of this vital book in Geneva during his absence, and Pierre the
Barber's comments about "St. Jehan," provides very strong circumstantial
grounds for identifying this book as the reformer's key text for Sunday sermons
after his return to Geneva.

Therefore, although the hypothesis must remain tentative, it is likely that
Calvin was preaching on the Gospel of John in 1542. That he was following
the format he would (re)introduce in 1553 or 1554, of using the same Biblical
book for Sunday morning and afternoon, seems probable not only from the
account of Pierre the Barber but also from another consistory record the following year. On April 26, 1543, a man says that he attended church twice the
previous Sunday and Calvin preached, which means it was morning and afternoon
at St. Pierre. Calvin had to be at St. Pierre in the morning and there is no evidence
that the barber went to St. Gervais for the afternoon service, so he must have
returned to St. Pierre. At this point Calvin had no reason to expound parallel
books because he was in the same pulpit all day on Sunday,[100] so he was preaching
on the same Biblical book morning and afternoon. If the reformer's early expositions were like the recorded sermons and assuming an average of 2.5 verses per
sermon (half-way between the averages for Ephesians and 1 Timothy), he might
have preached as many as 351 sermons on the Gospel of John. This would
probably need almost four years of Sundays. If Calvin completed Romans at
the end of 1541 and then preached on Jude for a month, the Gospel of John could
fill the time from winter 1542 up to 1546. In fact, this book may have taken
longer, because during the spring of 1545 Calvin was traveling on his mission to
other Reformed churches to obtain their diplomatic intercession for the persecuted Protestants in Provence. His absence was significant enough that Viret was

---

[99] Sept. 27, 1540, RC V, p. 549: "Lequelt se complaient de monsr le secretayre Porralis que,
　　autjourduy apprès laz predication, az dist que saz doctrine n'estoyet que poyson et qu'il
　　ranversoyt laz saincte Escrip[tu]re quant sus ung passage sus sainct Johan, et que totallement
　　il veult maientenyr ce qu'il az presché estre veritable..." Sept. 29, RC V, p. 552: "Maystre Henry,
　　predicant, se complaent de Porralis,... Puys daventage quil c'estoyt poyson de qu'il havoyt
　　presché le psaulme 4 « cum invocarent »..." "Responce de Porralis: confesse il dist az maystre
　　Champereau qu'il havoyt bien declayré le passage sainct Johan..." For reconciliation, see
　　Calvin's letter to Farel on June 16, 1542; #402, OC 11:409; chap.7 at nn.108ff.

[100] *Consist.* I, p. 233.

brought in as a temporary replacement.[101] So it may be that Calvin finished John early in 1546, at which point he was free to begin to divide his Sundays between St. Pierre and St. Gervais.

On weekdays in the 1540s Calvin was working through Old Testament books. As noted above, he began a first set of sermons on Isaiah on Jan. 27, 1546. Since he preached on this book again about a decade later, this is the clearest evidence for a second series on the same Biblical text, and so also supports the likelihood that the reformer repeated other favorite books. Genesis is a case in point. Correspondence shortly after Calvin's return suggests that he may have been working on Genesis at this time, and this fits with a brief note in the consistory records for Thursday, March 15, 1543. A man who was being questioned about his attendance at worship says he was at La Magdeleine "today" and Calvin preached about "Joseph's departure" – probably Gen. 38:13-17.[102] Sermons on Genesis soon after he returned to Geneva would not be surprising, given the role of this history for establishing the first "church" in Abraham's family, and Genesis was a particularly significant choice for proving Reformed ideas of infant baptism against Anabaptist challenges. As for how long this series would take: considering how many months were required for the extant Genesis sermons, September 1559 perhaps to August 1561 (the beginning of 1 Samuel), it is likely that the first series filled at least a year and a half or more. Since apparently Calvin had reached Gen. 38 by March 1543, he might have completed the book by late summer or early autumn in 1543. In view of the likelihood of interruptions, it seems logical to guess that it could have been autumn.

To summarize: Soon after his return to Geneva Calvin may have preached on the little epistle of Jude, but he almost certainly then began a four year sequence of morning and afternoon sermons on the Gospel of John. Alongside this was an exposition of Genesis on weekdays, bringing Sunday sermons up to 1546 and daily ones to later 1543. This leaves a period between the beginning of 1546 and the middle of 1547 in the Sunday morning sermons, and between autumn 1543 and late January 1546 in the weekday preaching, for which there are very few clues.

---

[101] For the Gospel of John calculations see Appendix Ten. For Calvin's travels and the Senate's invitation to Viret, see chap. 2 at nn.49f.

[102] See Peter & Gilmont, *Bibliotheca Calviniana* I, p. 521, citing Herminjard, *Correspondance*, tome 8, pp. 80-81, Calvin's response to Farel in a letter of July 28, 1542, in which he refers to "mes remarques sur la Genèse" and his concern about his auditors "je n'ai pas grand espoir." *Consist.* I, p. 195: "Az esté aujourd'huy au sermon à la Magdeleine et a presché le S. Calvin et de Joseph az partie." The editors of the consistory records identify this as Gen. 38:13-17 or possibly Gen. 38:12, p. 195 n.144. See Max Engammare, "Introduction," S. XI/I, p. ix.

Guesswork, or What Else is Missing?

What else Calvin was expounding to the people in the pews becomes much more like guess-work, and the timing is equally uncertain. It is possible, however, to return to the question: What else is missing? The other important New Testament books for which there is no mention of sermons are Philippians, Colossians, Philemon, 1 and 2 Peter, James, and 1 John. Beginning in early 1546 (probably after completion of the Gospel of John) Calvin was preaching at St. Pierre regularly only on Sunday mornings; by the summer of 1547 he may well have begun Hebrews on Sunday. This leaves a period of about a year and a half on Sunday mornings, and these "missing" New Testament books are the natural subject for that time. They could not all be fitted into this space, so it is likely that Calvin had already expounded some of them during his first Genevan ministry. Perhaps he was preaching mostly on Paul on weekdays as well as Sundays in those first months of the Protestant reform. (It would be logical to focus in a concentrated fashion on the New Testament at the beginning, and leave the Old Testament for a time when the hearers had a better grasp of the new teaching of the gospel.) [103] What can be said is that since Calvin could not have skipped such significant epistles as Philippians or 1 Peter of 1 John, they were probably fitted into one of these periods: 1536-38 or Sunday mornings in the mid-1540s.

For the Old Testament, it is not so obvious what might have been "missing." The prophets are almost fully covered in Calvin's known preaching, and all are included if the four missing minor ones were preached in 1548 between Isaiah and Jeremiah. Job and key books of the Pentateuch, Genesis and Deuteronomy, are extant, and various historical books such as Judges, Samuel, and Kings appeared in later years. Some of the books not named for daily sermons in any other context are reasonable choices, particularly Joshua, which was the subject of the *congréga-tions* late in Calvin's life. While it is pure speculation, it seems possible that books like Erza or Nehemiah might also have found their way into Calvin's list of pulpit texts as he tried to (re)build the church in Geneva. [104] It is also quite possible that Deuteronomy might have appeared for a first time in the early years, or Exodus might have followed the first series on Genesis, since the exposition of the

---

[103] See above at n. 90.

[104] For Joshua see; de Boer, *Genevan School of Prophecy*, pp.194-205. On Nov. 26, 1537, when the Genevans make objections to subscribing the confession of faith, etc., Farel answers with a reference to the assemblies in Nehemiah and Jeremiah; RC II, p. 416. It seems possible that these books about the rebuilding of the temple might have had a particular resonance in Geneva in the early years of the reform.

Decalogue was such a vital interest in the Reformed tradition, and the institution of Passover would have been an important occasion for explaining the Lord's Supper.

Whether this scenario, based as it is on various kinds and weights of mostly anecdotal or circumstantial evidence, is accepted in detail or not, it does offer hypothetical answers to two very real questions. What was Calvin preaching? And, more importantly, what about glaring gaps in the record of his exposition of the Bible for the people in the pew in Geneva? There are no sermons on Romans, the Gospel of John, and a number of other New Testament books, and some Old Testament prophets, which Calvin could not well have completely omitted. The fact that none of his contemporaries felt any need to reconstruct this part of his ministry before 1549, although presumably they could have asked still-living auditors, and the fact that Calvin scholars have not worried about the lacunae, may be attributed to the relatively lower level of importance which extempore sermons have held in comparison to the reformer's consciously planned and carefully written corpus. While there is no shadow of a doubt that Calvin considered preaching a very central pastoral task (if not indeed *the* most essential), he himself thought that the fruit should be seen in the hearts and minds of his congregation and not in print. Some of the preacher's friends and colleagues disagreed with him about the importance of this "ephemeral literature" and began to preserve, and then even to publish selections of it. The fruits of that work will be examined below.

Practically all of the reformer's homiletical work was the exposition of Biblical texts, but at least once in his life he taught catechism and this was recorded and partially preserved. Since it is normally overlooked in discussions of Calvin's preaching, yet provides some insight into what Genevans called the "sermon de midi," it is appropriate to include a short notice here, before analyzing the preservation and publication of the sermon corpus.

Calvin Teaches Catechism

The place of catechism as one of the regular Sunday "sermons" in Geneva has sometimes seemed puzzling, but an examination of one of Calvin's model lessons gives a sense of how this weekly exposition fitted into the preaching or teaching which Genevans received. For most of his life the reformer did not have time to do the catechism, something which was usually assigned to new preachers. However, in the last years of the reformer's life when he was apparently not in the pulpit on Sunday afternoons, probably for health reasons, he was asked to do these catechism sermons. In this series Calvin covered the whole Genevan Catechism, but only one lesson, on the petition of the Lord's Prayer which deals with "deliver us from evil," was immediately published (1563) and so has survived.

According to Rodophe Peter, the first modern editor of the extant lesson, it is probable that Calvin gave these "sermons" at a gathering of the Company of Pastors because he was doing the lessons in response to his colleagues' request for guidance in teaching the text.[105] Erik de Boer has studied the work of the Company, particularly the *congrégations* or French-language Bible lessons which were presented on Friday mornings and were open to the public. He has just completed a new critical edition of the *Exposition* along with the texts of extant *congrégations* most of which come from 1562-63. According to de Boer, there is not sufficient space in the schedule of the *congrégations* to allow for this catechism project, which would take about a year, and he suggests that Calvin presented these "in the Friday *afternoon* sessions of the Company of Pastors."[106] Logically all of his colleagues would want to be present; even if old hands like Chauvet and Cop had no need for such a review, they might still attend.

However, it is possible that Calvin did actually preach these lessons in some kind of public context, even if it would have been difficult for all of his colleagues to gather. The evidence for this is primarily an inference from the concluding prayer of the *Exposition,* which follows the regular Sunday afternoon and ordinary weekday pattern. (Prayer patterns will be discussed fully below.) This Catechism prayer is different from those recorded at the end of the *congrégations*. While it is possible that a special series at the Company of Pastors meetings could have used the ordinary intercessory prayer, it does seem a little odd to have a formal prayer (which included recitation of the Lord's Prayer and the Creed) at a business meeting, especially if such was not the practice at the *congrégation* sessions.[107]

---

[105] Peter, "Introduction," *Deux Congrégations et Exposition du Catéchisme*, p. xxvi, esp. n.93. In n.92 Peter quotes Calvin, *Supplex exhortatio ad Caesarem* [OC 6:490] in the French translation of 1544 in the *Recueil des Opuscules* (Geneva: J. Stoer, 1611), 2 ed. col. 608: "De notre côté, s'il trouve quelques ministres qui ne soient guère savants, toutefois nul n'y est reçu qu'il ne soit pour le moins moyennement propre à enseigner." De Boer, "Introduction," to "8. Exposition du Catéchisme," p. 409, points out that the 1561 *Ecclesiastical Ordinances* made explicit that the doctrine which the ministers were to teach was "sur tout selon le contenu du Catéchisme."

[106] De Boer, "Introduction," to "8. Exposition du Catéchisme," *Varia*, p. 409.

[107] Compare the final prayers for the other *congrégations*. The one on John 1:1-5 from 1550 does not preserve a prayer (p. 56); the one on predestination from 1551 has a distinctive one (pp. 128-29); the one on Exod. 1:1-8 from 1559 does not preserve one (p. 151). The two on Galatians (the series was Nov. 1562 to May 1563), do have prayers (pp. 178-79, 195-96), and the 23 comments on Joshua from June 4, 1563, to Jan. 7, 1564 (pp. 217-18, 235, 238-39, 245-46, 252-53, 258-59, 263-64, 271-72, 278-79, 282-83, 289, 296-97, 311-12, 318, 323-24, 328, 332-33, 344, 349-50, 355-56, 364-65, 379-71, 379-80), and one on Isa. 1:1-3 on Jan. 24, 1564 (pp. 402-03) also. Almost all of these prayers have a clear pattern, even though the words vary; usually there is first

There is very little direct information about Geneva's catechism services, but the one contemporary description by Charles Perrot, a village pastor writing in 1564, indicates that he concluded the catechism service in the same way as the weekday prayers in the city.[108] Furthermore, other circumstances would support the likelihood that Calvin did preach these catechism lessons publicly. For one, it was physically possible; during most of these last years of his life he was probably not preaching regularly on Sunday afternoons. Also, from the viewpoint of Genevans, it might seem like a waste of their best pastor's work if the ordinary people did not have a chance to hear him.

It is possible, therefore, that Calvin did present these lessons in the catechism service. If so, he might well have begun with a prayer for illumination-and-sealing, then read the Catechism text and explained it, and followed that with the short prayer fitted to the text and concluded with the long intercessory prayer used on Sunday afternoons and ordinary weekdays. With this hypothesis in mind, the object here is to show how the *Exposition* functioned as a sermon. The means is to construct an analogy between the *Exposition* and the *Institutes*. Scripture is explained in an academic way as commentary and in a pastoral way as sermon. Here the Catechism plays the role of the Biblical text, the *Institutes* that of a commentary, and this *Exposition* serves as the parallel sermon.

Calvin's *Exposition* provides a glimpse of what he wanted his preachers to know or do, as they were teaching the catechism students. He begins by referring back to the previous material, as was his common practice in his sermons; here the prior lesson dealt with the petitions for daily bread and forgiveness. He then turns to the day's "text": "lead us not into temptation but deliver us from evil." Having set the context by explaining that after pardon for past sins we also need God's restraint to

---

a paragraph about the word of God and its right reception, followed by a paragraph which focuses on the "povres freres" in situations of persecution where they do not have such access to God's word. Clearly there are common themes between these prayers and the intercessory prayers in public worship, but the prayers in public worship are more broadly couched. It is almost as if the Company is primarily thinking of their fellow ministers whom they have been sending "into the lion's den" in France. This would be entirely natural. The fact remains that it is a different emphasis than the wide-ranging intercessions for the more general context. The *Exposition* prayer, on the other hand, is shaped exactly like the Sunday afternoon or ordinary weekday intercession: i.e., it is not self-contained, as are the *congrégation* prayers which each have a conlusion. The *Exposition* ends with the first words of the intercessory prayer and then "etc.," meaning that something else was to follow... and that prayer included the recitation of the Lord's Prayer and Apostles Creed, which would hardly be necessary for the Company of Pastors.

108 Lambert, *Preaching, Praying and Policing*, p. 544: "Apres on acheve de chanter ce que l'on a comencé ou une demy table des Com[mandemens], on [! ou] une entiere, et puis la benediction, comme aux sermons des cours sur semeine à la ville."

keep from falling in future, Calvin reads the three short catechism exchanges which initiate this petition, and begins his exposition. The rest of the lesson completes the explanation of the Lord's Prayer.[109] Here Calvin takes the questions and answers one at a time. His explanation for each section of the *Exposition* is approximately 1 1/3 to 2 1/3 pages of modern print, making 13 pages (or 15 in the critical edition) in all, in place of the 30 pages of the original tiny format. While the points Calvin makes are similar to those in the discussion of the Prayer in the *Institutes* (3.20.46), the exposition is much longer and its application is more immediate and personal – very much like the relationship between a Biblical commentary and a sermon on the same passage, which is in fact what might be expected.

A few examples of the application can illustrate how the reformer brought the substance of his thought down to the level of his audience – at least, the more mature listeners! Twice in the course of this lesson Calvin speaks of the need "to descend into ourselves." This is a significant phrase for self-examination found in the *Institutes* from the beginning, particularly in the context of the law and the Lord's Supper but also in contrasting the redemption of Christ with human sinfulness.[110] The phrase is notably absent from the exposition of the Lord's Prayer in the *Institutes*. Here the experiential orientation – Calvin is instructing himself and his hearers to act – contributes to giving his exposition for the catechism class more emotional impact than the academic discussion. Another theme here is God's work in the believer, expressed in the simplest of terms.

> In summary then, this prayer contains that God changes us… in such a way that instead of our being inclined to evil and given over to it – indeed, that we run after it and are full of sin – that He renews us and puts in us such an impression of His goodness and fear that we may hate evil and love the good to which we must be conformed. And how does that happen? By the power of His Spirit.[111]

---

[109] *Deux Congrégations et Exposition du Catéchisme*, pp. 32-33; explanation of these initial three questions, pp. 33-36. De Boer, "8. Exposition du Catéchisme," *Varia*, pp. 411-14.

[110] In the chapter on law, OS I, p. 39 (which would become 2.8.1); in the discussion of the Lord's Supper in chapter 4, OS I, p. 147 (4.17.40). In 1539 a second reference is added in the chapter on law, OS III, p. 345 (2.8.3). In 1559 there are two additional references, OS III, p. 483 (2.16.1), OS IV, p. 124 (3.2.32). There is a somewhat similar idea expressed in 1539 in the chapter on Christian life, as believers descend from considering the goodness of the present life as God's gift to the recognition of "miserrimam eius conditionem," OS IV, p. 173 (3.9.3).

[111] *Deux Congrégations et Exposition du Catéchisme*, p. 35. "8. Exposition du Catéchisme," *Varia*, p. 415: "Ceste priere donc en somme contient que Dieu nous change … Ceste requeste donc contient en somme que Dieu nous change en telle sorte qu'au lieu que nous sommes enclins au mal et y sommes addonnez, voire que nous y courons et que nous sommes confits en peché, qu'il nous renouvelle et mette en nous une telle impression de sa bonté et de sa craincte, que

This point, at least, demonstrates that Calvin could speak in a way that even children could grasp, whether or not they were his actual audience.

For Calvin, application of the Catechism to his Genevan context also meant dealing with hard questions. This included some polemic against traditional ideas of the Lord's Prayer which his hearers might still retain. He criticizes constant repetition of the Pater Noster (in Latin) by people who do not comprehend what they are saying and who, more seriously, think that they have the free will to choose between good and evil. [112] The allusion to followers of Rome is clear. But Calvin is also frank in addressing the failings of a Protestant audience; to repeat this petition (in French) without understanding what temptation means is to profane it. [113] He goes on to explain that there are temptations which come from outside and others from within; the former are those in which the devil uses God's good creation to awaken sin, and the latter those which arise from sinful desires inside a person. The preacher offers several examples of external temptations which might be very familiar to his hearers. A person sees a handsome house or field and the devil lights the fire of covetousness. A man looks at a beautiful woman with "a chaste eye" but the devil uses this sight to awaken lust and fornication.

> In short, God's creatures as they are, both high and low, cannot of themselves hurt us, and they are useful to us, but the devil makes us stop there in order to misuse these good creatures, so that what is beneficial to us and which we ought to use as God's blessing become so many nets (traps) to lead us to ruin. [114]

---

nous haïssions le mal et que nous aimions le bien auquel il nous faut aspirer. Or comment cela se fait-il? Par la vertu de son Esprit." Note that in extempore speaking Calvin repeats himself almost word-for-word in the same paragraph, something he would probably not do in writing unless for rhetorical effect.

112 *Deux Congrégations et Exposition du Catéchisme*, p. 37. "8. Exposition du Catéchisme," *Varia*, pp. 416-17: "Voyla mesmes les Papistes: … Il est vray que ceux qui parlent latin et n'auront jamais esté à l'escole ne sçavent qu'ils disent, tant hommes que femmes, mais quoy qu'il en soit, si est-ce que cela viendra en conte. Car ils se font à croire qu'ils ont leur franc-arbitre pour se conduire ou bien ou mal." The polemic suggests that Calvin thinks his audience still has to deal with this fallacy.

113 *Deux Congrégations et Exposition du Catéchisme*, p. 39. "8. Exposition du Catéchisme," *Varia*, p. 419: "car il y en a beaucoup et possible en ceste compagnie qui ont prié Dieu qu'il ne les induist point en tentation et n'ont jamais sceu qu'ils demandoyent à Dieu. Or c'est profaner l'oraison que nostre Seigneur Iesus Christ nous a donnée." This is the phrase both editors cite as identifying the Compagnie des Pasteurs as the audience; cf. above nn.105f.

114 *Deux Congrégations et Exposition du Catéchisme*, p. 39. "8. Exposition du Catéchisme," *Varia*, p. 419: "Brief, les creatures de Dieu autant qu'il y en a, et hautes et basses, d'ellesmesmes ne nous peuvent nuire et nous sont utiles, mais le diable nous y fait arrester à fin d'en abuser, tellement que ce qui nous est profitable et de quoy nous devons user comme d'une benediction de Dieu sont autant de filets pour nous mener à perdition."

Here are echoes of Calvin's teaching on the right use of God's good creation. In itself it is all good, but the preacher points to the obvious temptations related to abusing the good things. It is worth noting that Calvin does not suggest to his Genevan hearers the two more abstract forms of temptation which he mentions in the *Institutes*: great riches, power, honor, and the opposite: poverty, afflictions, disgrace. Nor does he expound the more subtle point made in the *Institutes* that God uses temptation – even though differently from the way the devil does – and believers should not pray to feel no temptation.[115] Evidently Calvin considered both of these ideas inappropriate for the immature Christians who would be learning the basics of the faith. The sections of the *Institutes* on the Lord's Prayer come from the earliest edition, and the *Exposition* was the fruit of Calvin's old age. Perhaps some of the difference in tone should be attributed to the experience of the pastor's many years of ministry. Or maybe he had lowered his expectations?

The next question of the Catechism addresses the most difficult point, the respective roles of God and the devil in temptation. (Here, in the more colloquial, spoken lesson, unlike the *Institutes*, there is no hesitation in calling "evil" the "devil" without qualification.[116]) The answer in the Catechism poses the difference between those on whom God has mercy and those whom God hands over to the devil. First Calvin acknowledges that this seems an unreasonable and difficult prayer because it appears to attribute to God what is instead appropriate to the devil. He begins with a scriptural quotation (Jas.1:14) and then a pastoral response, which does not really answer the question but emphasizes that his hearers are among those on whom God has mercy and effectively they do not need to concern themselves about the reprobate (though he does not use that term).

> But we must come to God's secret judgments, which we must finally adore when we cannot fully understand; for it is enough that we know in part what is appropriate for our salvation, and that God keeps the rest for the last day, when we will see Him face to face. For we see how God guards His faithful, and each person senses this by his own experience.[117]

---

[115] *Institutes*: 3.20.46, see OS IV, p. 362.

[116] *Institutes* 3.20.46, OC IV, p. 363: "Maligni nomine Diabolum an peccatum intelligamus quam minimum refert."

[117] *Deux Congrégations et Exposition du Catéchisme*, p. 41. "8. Exposition du Catéchisme," *Varia*, p. 421: "Or il est vray que de prime face ceste façon de parler semble dure; mais il nous faut venir aux jugemens secrets de Dieu, lesquels finalement et pour conclusion il nous faut adorer quand nous ne pouvons pas parvenir jusques à une cognoissance entiere, car c'est assez que nous cognoissions en partie ce qui est propre à nostre salut et que Dieu reserve le reste au dernier jour, là où nous le contemplerons face à face."

The allusions to the revelation of "what is appropriate for our salvation" and to their own experience serve as an appeal to his hearers to assure them that they know what is needed. Scripture and experience both witness that they are among those God has called into the communion of faith. Then the reformer's second response is polemical. Because this petition for God not to lead us into temptation "seems strange at first sight," there are madmen who would like to erase from scripture the passages about God blinding or hardening people's hearts. However, Calvin declares, these texts describe God as just judge, and "God's judgments are a profound abyss."[118] This is God's secret judgment which we must adore without understanding. The preacher concludes by insisting that, while God uses human corruption and the devil's action, He is not responsible for sin.

(The Catechism lesson gives considerably more space to those whom God has rejected than is found in the parallel section of the *Institutes*. In fact the reference to God's "secret judgment" is added to the *Institutes'* treatment of the Lord's Prayer in 1559, probably only a few years before Calvin preached this exposition of the Catechism. [119] It is noteworthy that the Catechism itself, unlike the *Institutes*, never addresses reprobation directly. It discusses the elect under the Apostles' Creed but skips the reprobate as not relevant to the people of faith who are reciting the Creed. [120] Thus, in explaining the Catechism, questions raised by Biblical references to God hardening Pharaoh's heart must be treated – or at least raised! – in other places, and the reference to evil in the Lord's Prayer provides an occasion.)

The Catechism lesson concludes with the doxology of the Lord's Prayer, which Calvin interprets as both an affirmation that all prayers are based on God's glory, righteousness, goodness, and power, and as a way of teaching believers to end every prayer with thanks. In the first case, the doxology is a

---

118 *Deux Congrégations et Exposition du Catéchisme*, pp. 40-42. "8. Exposition du Catéchisme," *Varia*, pp. 420-23; p. 41/422 : "mais il nous faut revenir là, que les jugemens de Dieu sont abysmes profonds et ainsi que Dieu induit en tentation ceux qu'il luy plaist. Et en quelle sorte? non seulement d'autant que le mal procede de nous, mais c'est qu'il condamne ceux qu'il a delaissez et rejettez pour estre vaincus de toutes tentations."

119 *Institutes* 3.20.46, OS IV, pp. 363-64. The only other part of this paragraph which is not 1536 or, in lesser measure, 1539, is the introductory sentence, added in 1559. In effect, the exposition of this petition is essentially from 1536, with two very short additions from 1539, and two somewhat longer ones from 1559 placed at the beginning and the end of the paragraph.

120 One question in the Catechism, under the Apostles' Creed, addresses this issue and explains the omission. "Le ministre: Pourquoy donc est-il seulement parlé de la vie eternelle, et non point aussi bien d'enfer? L'enfant: Pource qu'il n'y a rien couché en ce sommaire, qui n'appartienne proprement à la consolation des consciences fideles; il nous recite seulement les biens que Dieu fait à ses serviteurs. Et ainsi, il n'y est faict nulle mention des iniques, qui sont excluz de son Royaume." OC 6:43.

means of assurance that God will hear prayers. Using imagined dialogue, Calvin speaks to his hearers' likely situation of doubt, and then answers with the reassurance that "our petitions are not founded on what we bring ….[because] …we always change in a minute."

> So when we want to be certain that our prayers have not been in vain, that we have not been frustrated in our effort but that we have obtained everything that we have asked, then let us come to this: "How have you prayed it?" "I confess that He is all powerful and that my requests, being founded on that, cannot be without effect and fulfillment."[121]

Our assurance is based on the conviction of God's power and God's command to pray and God's promise to hear, and thus we can be sure of being heard. With a final insistence on the thanksgiving which should conclude every prayer, Calvin then ends this sermon on the Catechism in the same way that he would any other sermon: that is, with a prayer which touches on the content of the exposition which he has just made (extempore #2), and then the text of the fixed prayer which he used on Sunday afternoons and ordinary weekdays (extempore #3).[122] This longer intercessory prayer ends with the recitation of the Lord's Prayer followed by the Apostles' Creed. Given the fact that this was the "sermon" part of the catechism "service," one might say that if this was the standard of teaching, it is easy to see why a young minister would feel challenged by being responsible for catechism in Calvin's Geneva!

III: Calvin's Sermons: How and When

Records of extempore sermons from medieval and early modern periods are very uncommon, and yet many of Calvin's were not only copied down as he preached but also preserved and valued. Given the kind of "literature" sermons

---

[121] *Deux Congrégations et Exposition du Catéchisme*, p. 43. "8. Exposition du Catéchisme," *Varia*, p. 424: "Or nostre Seigneur nous declare que nos requestes ne sont point fondées sur ce que nous apportions, car qui sommes-nous? et qu'est-ce que nous apportons? Et encores que nous fussions les mieux disposez du monde de prier, il est certain que tousjours nous voyla changez en une minute. … Quand donc nous voudrons bien estre certifiez que nos prieres n'ont pas esté vaines, que nous n'avons pas esté frustrez de nostre attente, mais que nous avons obtenus tout ce que nous avons demandé, que nous venions là: comment l'as-tu prié? Et c'est que je le confesse tout-puissant, que toute vertu luy appartient, que mes requestes estans là fondées ne seront point sans avoir leur effect et accomplissement."

[122] *Deux Congrégations et Exposition du Catéchisme*, p. 44. "8. Exposition du Catéchisme," *Varia*, p. 425: "Or nous nous prosternerons devant la majesté ... Que non seulement il nous face ceste grace, mais à tous peuples et nations de la terre, etc."

were and the ways they were used, however, the friends and colleagues who collected and published Calvin's sermons left a challenging legacy for anyone who would like to date exactly when the reformer preached which texts. This section retells the story of how the sermons were recorded and preserved and then engages in detective adventures to work out at least approximately when these were presented in the pulpits of Geneva.

The Recording (Preservation?!) of Calvin's Sermons

Recording preaching as it happened was not traditional, so how and why were Calvin's sermons preserved? The short answer is that some of his hearers thought that what he said would be valuable not only for themselves but also for those who could not be present. A fuller answer will be given later. Here the object is to (re)tell the story of how it happened.

It is probably no surprise that it was French refugees in Geneva who conceived the plan to take down all the reformer's sermons, beginning in 1549. Several years earlier one educated hearer, Jean Cousins, had recorded and published the two sermons on Ps. 115 and 124 which Calvin had preached at special day of prayer services. However, when the refugee community hired their fellow exile Denis Raguenier to use his stenographic training in this project on a day-by-day basis, something new was begun. From the summer of 1549 until his death before March 1, 1561, and except for times when he was incapacitated by illness, Raguenier attended and took down virtually every sermon Calvin preached. There was a break at Raguenier's death, and then other scribes carried on his work, but none were as skilled as he and some sermons were not recorded at all.

The fixed procedure was for Raguenier to write down the sermon in shorthand and then dictate it to a scribe who would make a fair copy. Sometimes the stenographer himself made the finished version, but there were a number of other scribes who worked with him. Each sermon was normally written on large sheets of paper folded in half to make eight, ten, or occasionally more folio pages, usually filled on both sides (although sometimes the final side or occasionally even the last full page might be blank). Apparently the main variable in terms of the space needed was the handwriting of the different scribes.[123] The individual sermons

---

[123] Balke and Moehn, "Introduction," S. VIII, p. xiii, note that sometimes the scribe miscalculated the number of pages needed and left some blank. Max Engammare, "Introduction," *Sermons sur la Genèse*, S. XI/I, p. xi, describes the differences for the Genesis sermons (beginning 1559), which might extend the number of pages to 14. Engammare has edited more sermons than any other person, and is the most experienced in this work. My own count for 1 Corinthians 1-9 (beginning 1555) indicates that eight to ten pages is normal. Although the number of words per

were collected together but not bound until a significant number were copied; this meant that some specific sermons might be borrowed for reading or printing and not returned to their proper place. Commonly, however, when an appropriate number were collected, they were bound. Sometimes the sermons from several shorter books might be grouped together, e.g., some of the Old Testament minor prophets. On the other hand, the sermons preached on longer and more significant books frequently became too many for a single binding; for example, Isaiah required six volumes, Acts was bound in four, Deuteronomy in three, First Corinthians in two.[124] If a set of sermons was printed, the manuscripts were discarded. Having examined the process, it is appropriate to see just what Raguenier and his successors recorded.

Calvin's regular schedule was two sermons on Sundays and six on the weekdays of alternate weeks. Sunday texts were from the New Testament or Psalms, weekday ones (as far as is known) were from the Old Testament. Apparently Raguenier started recording in mid-1549, although he did not officially begin work until Sept. 30. As noted above, during the summer Calvin was preaching on Hebrews and Psalms on Sundays; by the end of August he had finished Hebrews and begun Acts.[125] The weekday book in 1549 was Jeremiah, which Raguenier says that he started on Nov. 12, although he had already "practiced" during the summer months: hence the 25 extant sermons which cover Jer. 14:19-18:23, dated June 14-Aug. 16, 1549. By November Calvin was probably about half way through the prophet. A vignette from Colladon's biography gives a glimpse of one of the last sermons on Jeremiah; in August 1550, when high-ranking visitors from France passed through Geneva on their way back from Rome and stopped to hear him, the preacher was treating Jer. 51:38.[126]

In fact, none of the first sermon series transcribed by Raguenier were complete. Perhaps he was not yet available on every day, so some where not recorded. It is also possible that some individual sermons which were actually written down

---

sermon increased, a sample of sermons from 1549-51, 1555, and 1559 indicates that this does not appear to have affected the number of pages in a predictable way, but a more precise count would be needed to determine this definitively.

[124] See Raguenier's catalogue, Gagnebin, "L'histoire des manuscrits des sermons de Calvin," S. II, pp. xv-xvii.

[125] See Colladon, OC 21:71.

[126] See Raguenier's catalogue. See Colladon, OC 21:72: "L'an 1550, au mois d'Aoust, un prince et avec luy certains seigneurs du pays de France revenans de Rome passerent par Geneve, et ouirent tout au long un sermon de Calvin, qui lors avoit un fort beau texte au 51. Chapitre de Jeremie, verset 38 … lequel il deduisit d'une grande grace, vehemence et simplicité, à sa maniere accoustumee, sans ostentation."

began to circulate and were not returned, as those who had commissioned the stenographer sampled the wares. Unbound sermons (even those which might be restored to their proper place) could be temporarily separated from their set.[127] At this early date Raguenier was also not yet able to get every word. Comparison of the lengths of sermons from 1549-51 with those from six or seven years later demonstrates that the earliest recorded sermons, the ones on Jeremiah in 1549, averaged 4,000 words; Acts sermons preached in 1549-51 increased to 5,300 and the sermons on Micah beginning in November 1550 reached 5,500 words. By the time Calvin was expounding Isaiah in 1557, the sermons could be as much as 7,000 words. When a new secretary took over after Raguenier's death, the number of words actually recorded diminished; 2 Samuel in 1562 has about 6,000 words per sermon.[128] For eleven years the gifted French stenographer transcribed Calvin's words; the last New Testament ones he produced were 65 on the Gospel Harmony, from Matt. 1:1 up to the point where the preacher was beginning Matt. 5 and parallels. No records exist for the continued recording of these Sunday sermons. After Raguenier's death, Calvin's sermons on Judges, 1 and 2 Samuel, and 1 Kings were taken down by another secretary but only those on Samuel survive to show his work. Although it seems odd that some weekday preaching would be recorded and not the Sunday gospel texts, perhaps it was considered more important to transcribe the Old Testament ones because Calvin had not written a commentary on these as he had on the gospels. The last time the frail but determined old reformer preached on a weekday was Wednesday, Feb. 2, 1564; the last Sunday sermon was Feb. 6, 1564.[129]

Recording sermons did not actually mean preserving them, as it turned out. Some of Calvin's homiletical work was published in his own day, as will be seen below, but about two-thirds or more remained in manuscript form. These were stored as forty-four folio volumes in what became the University of Geneva library.[130] In 1805 the director of that library ordered the sale of all second copies of books on the shelves, and added to these doubles forty-three of the forty-four volumes of Calvin's manuscript sermons. They were sold by weight as old paper!

---

[127] Engammare, "Introduction," *Sermons sur la Genèse*, S. XI/I, p. xiv, traces the case of a sermon which, from physical evidence of wear and tear, was obviously separate from the rest before they were bound.

[128] Francis Higman, T.H.L. Parker, "Introduction," *Sermons sur le livre d'Esaie, chapitres 13-29*, S. III, p. xxiii; W.H.T. Moehn, "Introduction," *Sermones*, p. xxxv.

[129] See Colladon, OC 21:96.

[130] Gagnebin, "L'histoire des manuscrits des sermons de Calvin," S. II, pp. xiv-xxviii, provides the basic story.

Some years later, in 1827 when several theology students found their purchases being wrapped in Calvin's sermons, there was a hue and cry, and some few volumes were recovered. The librarian of that day wrote a piece in the newspaper to explain what had happened, emphasizing that this act had been a deliberate choice, not an accident, and offering the likely rationale. "They did not attach a very great importance to the sermons" in 1805 since they were not in Calvin's own hand, "were very difficult (not to say impossible) to decipher," and the library owned quite a number of other, autograph manuscripts by the reformer. Other apologists have provided further reasons: a need for room on library shelves, the sense that it was unnecessary duplication to have both sermons and commentaries, and the idea that one tome was sufficient witness for the large and space-consuming set.[131]

By 1887 twelve of the lost folio tomes had been recovered, and all that have been recovered are being edited. In recent years some more of Calvin's sermons have been found, in the shape of manuscript copies of Raguenier's originals which he and his circle made for people leaving Geneva who wanted to take some of Calvin's preaching with them. In 1995 Max Engammare discovered volumes of Isaiah which add 87 of the lost sermons to the number now extant; they were in the library of the French refugee congregation of London once served briefly by Nicholas Des Gallars.[132] The lost sermons on Genesis have been partially completed with duplicates of the originals prepared by Raguenier at the request of Thomas Bodley, one of the English refugees in Geneva and father of the founder of the Bodleian Library.[133] Even with the amazing finds which have been made, the disappearance of the main body of transcriptions of Calvin's recorded sermons remains a scholar's nightmare come true.

Calvin's Extempore Prayers and Dating the Sermons

The prayers of public worship in Calvin's Geneva were partly set by the published liturgy and partly left to the ministers to formulate for themselves. Most attention has naturally focused on the printed ones because they are available in *La forme des prières*. Even if exploring the extempore prayers is a worthy project, it might seem to fit more in a liturgical context than in a chapter on the

---

[131] Gagnebin, "L'histoire des manuscrits des sermons de Calvin," S. II, p. xxi; the librarian quoted was Charles Bourrit, March 23, 1826; Gagnebin adds the other reasons.

[132] Engammare tells the story in "Des sermons de Calvin sur Esaie découverte à Londres," in *Calvin et ses contemporains*, ed. O. Millet (Genève: Droz, 1998), pp. 69-81. He has now edited these sermons for the S. IV, *Sermons sur Esaie Chapitres 60,1-66,24*, 2 vol. (2012).

[133] Engammare, *Sermons sur la Genèse*, 2 vols., S. XI (2000).

reformer's sermons. However, the present purpose is not an analysis of the theological content but an examination of the insights into Calvin's preaching for which the extempore prayers are the evidence. In fact, it is thanks to their connection with the printed sermons that records of the reformer's extempore prayers have been preserved, and the prayers themselves serve as a way to help date the sermons. It is first important to examine what can be known about the extempore prayers and then explore the dating of sermons.

Calvin's Extempore Prayers

There were several kinds of extempore prayers used in Genevan pulpits. Generally these have been passed over by scholars, except for the related matter of how often the Lord's Prayer would be recited in worship because that evoked an argument in October 1549 which shows up in the Senate minutes. It is helpful to begin by defining when prayers were left to the Genevan ministers' discretion, and what evidence is available for Calvin's own practice. Because no other corpus of sermons and prayers has survived, all examples here are drawn from Calvin's work with the exception of the limited information in Viret's four sermons recorded by Raguenier.[134]

There was no printed liturgy for the ordinary weekday services, and each pastor was free to create his own prayers for both before and after the sermon. Naturally, a minister was likely to develop a pattern which, though it might vary, was usually fairly stable. These "extempore" prayers were of three types, or rather came at three points in the service. One was the prayer for illumination-and-sealing before the reading of the day's scripture text (extempore #1); no matter what the day of the week, and even if he had several personal forms, this was left to the preacher.[135] The other two extempore prayers came immediately after the sermon. The first of these was a short "individual" prayer at the end of each sermon, which was usually about two or three sentences and supposed to reflect in some way the sermon theme (extempore #2). Every one of Calvin's sermons had this, no matter what day of the week and (as will be seen below) it is the initial phrase of this prayer which Mülhaupt used to calculate the dates of the reformer's

---

134   The evidence of Viret's sermons is somewhat confusing; the sermons on Sun. & Wed. March 12 & 15, 1559, do conclude with the phrase "Dieu tout puissant," Viret, *Quatre Sermons*, pp. 83, 108. The previous two, for Sun. & Wed. March 5 & 8 do not follow this pattern, although on the 8th it is not far off ("Seigneur Dieu, Pere eternel, etc.," p. 59). Sun. March 5 reads: "Or nous le prierons tous qu'il nous face ceste grace et qu'il luy plaise nous pardonner ce en quoy nous avons failly etc.," p. 34.

135   The Strasbourg liturgy gives a printed form, but the Genevan liturgy left it to the minister's discretion; OS II, pp. 19-20.

sermons. This individual sermon prayer was followed by a long intercessory prayer. The fixed form of this intercession to be used on Sunday morning and the day of prayer was printed in *La forme des prières*. For Sunday afternoons and ordinary weekdays, the wording of this intercession was left to the minister; that long prayer which followed the individual one (extempore #2) is here called extempore #3.

Sunday afternoons? Yes. As noted in an earlier chapter, there was in fact no rubric in *La forme des prières* to define the liturgy for Sunday afternoons. Generally it has been assumed that the afternoon was like the morning and, as regards the order of service it probably was, but the same is not true of the prayers. Before developing this further, it is necessary to examine the texts of Calvin's extempore prayers.

Several publications of the reformer's sermons late in his life include a guide to his "extempore" prayers. The three sermons on Abraham's sacrifice of Isaac published by Jacques Bourgeois in 1561 and the popular series on Job which Antoine Vincent brought out in 1563 are the best known, but the Gospel Harmony of 1562 edited by Conrad Badius also includes extempore prayers. Beza's Latin translation of the Job set also includes these prayers for before and after the sermon. Their incipits are important for dating sermons. The prayers for the Abraham and Job sermons, with their rubrics, are copied in *Opera Calvini*.[136] Rodolphe Peter indicates that there are some minor differences of detail between these prayer texts and the first editions because the editors of *Opera Calvini* used later editions, so he provides both forms in parallel columns in his introduction to the sermons on Jeremiah and Lamentations.[137] For present purposes, both the texts of Calvin's prayers and the sixteenth-century editors' rubrics are important. Each type of extempore prayer will be treated in order.

---

[136] Bourgeois' rubrics for Abraham, see p. 6 (1561 printing) or OC 23:741: "La Priere ordinaire de l'Autheur, sur le commencement de ses Sermons en la semaine." P. 7 (1561) "Ceste Priere suivante, se dit aussi par l'Autheur apres qu'on a chanté le Pseaume, tant le Dimanche que le Mercredi, jour des Prieres." P. 36 (1561) or OC 23:755: "L'Autheur fait aussi ceste Priere à la fin de ses predications du Lundi, Mardi, Jeudi, Vendredi, et Samedi." Except for orthography, these are the same as the original printing. Vincent's rubrics for Job, see OC 33:15-16: "Priere que fait ordinairement M. Jean Calvin au commencement de ses sermons." For Beza, see *Ioannis Calvini Operum Omnium Theologicorum, Tomi Secondi Pars Altera* (Genevae: Iohannem Vignon, Petrum & Iacobum Chouet, 1617), pp. iii(v)-iv(v).

[137] Peter, "Introduction," S. VI, p. xxix. These differences do not affect the incipits and so are not relevant to the present argument.

Extempore #1

Bourgeois, the editor of the three Abraham sermons (1561) provides a full picture of the preacher's "extempore" prayers, but examples from Vincent's and Badius' publications fill out – or complicate – the picture. In Bourgeois's book, the first two rubrics introduce the prayers customarily spoken at the beginning of the sermons. On weekdays it says: "The author's ordinary prayer at the beginning of his sermons during the week." Then the special liturgies read: "This following prayer is also said by the author after they have sung the Psalm, both Sunday and Wednesday, day of prayers." Naturally, each rubric introduces a different prayer although there are some common themes. It is interesting to note that the prayer for illumination-and-sealing for Sunday and Wednesday in Bourgeois' collection does not include a confession of sin, which all the others do. Even the one actually written for and published in the Strasbourg liturgy (1542), which is otherwise fairly similar, has a phrase about repentance. [138] It is tempting to speculate that late in his life Calvin chose to remove the penitential phrase from the prayer for illumination-and-sealing on Sunday and Wednesday, to distinguish it more clearly from the actual confession of sin which preceded it. By the same token, since there was not a separate confession of sin on weekdays, retaining the language there made sense.

Where Bourgeois has two, Vincent and Badius provide only one prayer for illumination-and-sealing. These two editors give the same form, which is slightly different from Bourgeois' one for the weekdays. Their rubrics are two variants with the same meaning: Badius' "the author's ordinary prayer at the beginning of the sermon" or Vincent's "the prayer which M. Jean Calvin ordinarily makes at the beginning of his sermons." [139] There is no designation of day. However, since the Job sermons were preached only on weekdays and the Gospel Harmony only on Sundays, this form must be associated with both. Its appearance with the New Testament sermons poses a problem for Jean-François Gilmont, who regards the publication of this prayer as out of place because he identifies it as (only) for the weekday [140] since he was not aware that Sunday afternoon prayers were the same as ordinary weekdays.

---

138 See Grosse, *Les rituels de la Cène*, Appendix 3, pp. 666-68. He prints the text for Strasbourg Sunday (as found in OS II, pp. 19-20); then the rubrics and texts for the two different forms found in the Abraham sermons, and the form printed in the Job sermons.

139 For Vincent, see above n.136; for Badius, f6v [vi(v)].

140 Peter & Gilmont, *Bibliotheca Calviniana* II, [62/22] p. 954: "Il est à remarquer que la prière imprimée f *6v n'est pas à sa place, car il s'agit de la prière que Calvin faisait au commencement de ses sermons de semaine et qu'il avait une autre prière pour les sermons de dimanche." When the 1562 printing of the Gospel Harmony is examined, the heading on f6v [vi(v)] says "Priere

Extempore #2

At the end of each sermon Calvin added a short individual prayer, "extempore #2." The substance of this varied from day to day, although there were some themes which recurred so regularly that they can be catalogued. The initial phrase of this extempore prayer was standardized, varying only slightly through the years. Edwin Mülhaupt has argued that the examination of these tiny variations offers a way to assign undated sermons to different periods. He divides the prayers into three groups according to these phrases, the first attributed to the period beginning in 1549, the second to approximately five years later in 1554, and the third to three or four years after that, about 1557-58. [141] More recently other scholars have recognized that this pattern is not entirely reliable. While it can be a generally helpful guide, there are exceptions. Wilhelmus Moehn's introduction to the first set of sermons published in the new *Opera Omnia Denuo Recognita* (discussed above) gives a good overview of this debate. [142] My own observation supports Moehn's caution; one example may suffice. The sermons on Daniel, preached in 1552, provide relatively numerous examples of exceptions to the phrase which Mülhaupt considered indicative of this period. [143]

Extempore #3

It is the third type of extempore prayer which is the most interesting for the present study. In the Bourgeois publication, the first sermon on Abraham's sacrifice (Gen. 21:33-22:2) concludes with the short prayer individually fitted to this particular Biblical exposition (extempore #2). This is followed by the rubric: "The author also makes this prayer at the end of his sermons on Monday, Tuesday, Thursday, Friday, and Saturday," [144] and then the text of the prayer.

---

ordinaire qui se fait avant la predication." This is the same prayer that is printed in OC 33:15-16 in the sermons on Job and identified there as "Priere que fait ordinairement M. Jean Calvin au commencement de ses sermons."

[141] See Mülhaupt, "Einleitung," S. VII, pp. L-LII.

[142] Moehn, "Introduction," *Sermones*, pp. xxviii-xxxv.

[143] Of the 47 sermons on Daniel, *Quarante sept sermons de M. Iean Calvin sur les hvict derniers chapitres des propheties de Daniel* (La Rochelle: Barthelemi Berton, 1565), the great majority begin with the phrase Mülhaupt identifies, "Suivant cette saincte doctrine nous nous prosternerons devant la face de nostre bon Dieu." However, sermons 6 & 18: "devant la majesté de nostre bon Dieu"; sermons 15 & ["18"]17: " devant la haute et souveraine majesté de nostre bon Dieu"; sermon 29 omits: "Suivant cette saincte doctrine," and sermon 45 is completely different: "il faut donc que nous prions Dieu que cette doctrine soit imprimee."

[144] Bourgeois on Abraham, p. 36 or OC 23:756: "L'Autheur fait aussi ceste Priere à la fin de ses predications du Lundi, Mardi, Jeudi, Vendredi, et Samedi." Prayer itself is pp. 36-38 or 23:755-57.

Vincent's rubric for the Job sermons is rather less helpful, or more confusing. The "prayer which M. John Calvin ordinarily makes at the end of each sermon."[145] In effect, Vincent is concerned only with weekday prayers, but it is noteworthy that he does not distinguish the ordinary weekdays from the day of prayer service for which *La forme des prières* provides a printed text. Perhaps he assumed that the role of the printed prayer was such common knowledge that it did not need to be stated; both the liturgy itself and the day of prayer had been standard practice since 1542. Whatever the reason, Vincent is less precise than Bourgeois, who thus emerges as the most detailed guide to Calvin's extempore prayers.

Bourgeois' rubrics introduce an "extempore #3" prayer text; that is, the form of Calvin's "free" intercessory prayer used on ordinary weekdays and Sunday afternoons. Here the initial words are significant.

> Et que non seulement il nous face cette grace, mais à tous peuples et nations de la terre, reduisant tous povres ignorans de la captivité de l'erreur et tenebres à la droicte voye de salut. Que pour ce faire il lui plaise susciter de vrais et fideles ministres de sa parole...
> And may He give this grace not only to us, but to all peoples and nations of the earth, drawing back all the poor ignorant ones from the captivity of error and darkness to the right way of salvation. To do this, may He be pleased to raise up true and faithful ministers of His word...[146]

Both French and English are given here because it is useful to have the incipits or introductory phrases in mind, as tags for identifying the prayers. Most common is "Que non seulement" but sometimes this is missing and the initial phrase is the second sentence of this prayer: "qu'il lui plaise susciter de vrais et fideles ministres." The content of the prayer has much in common with the one for the day of prayer published in *La forme des prières*, including the fact that both give marginal notes indicating that the sick may be mentioned by name. "Here prayer is explicitly made for someone who is detained [at home] by illness, who commends himself to the prayers of the church."[147]

For present purposes it is this incipit, "Que non seulement" (or "vrais et fideles pasteurs"), at the beginning of the "extempore" prayer which is of interest.

---

[145] Vincent on Job rubric and prayer, OC 33:17-18: "Priere que fait ordinairement M. Jean Calvin en la fin de chacun sermon."

[146] Abraham sermon, p. 36 or OC 23:756-57. Texts in Peter, "Introduction," S. VI, pp. xx1x-xxx. Grosse, *Les rituels de la cène*, Appendix 3, pp. 666-69.

[147] "Ici se fait priere expresse pour quelcun qui est detenu de maladie, qui se fait recommender aux prieres de l'Eglise," Bourgeois, p. 37, also quoted in Peter, "Introduction," S. VI, p. xxx. For day of prayer equivalent, see OS II, p. 29.

Unlike the initial phrase for the extempore #2 prayer which Mülhaupt studied, the incipit for this intercessory prayer for ordinary weekdays and Sunday afternoons does not change throughout Calvin's life, as an examination of all of his extant sermons demonstrates. Thus, it is possible to use this incipit to help identify the day of the week of his sermons and so to contribute to fixing patterns of dates. There is one more not so minor challenge to studying Calvin's sermon prayers, however. Not only did many printed sermons omit the dates, but also the *Opera Calvini* dropped almost all the individual sermon prayers (extempore #2), which always conclude with the incipit of the long intercessory prayer (extempore #3). Therefore the only way to determine which prayer a sermon had is to consult either the manuscripts or the early modern printings, which almost always retained the prayers.[148]

Dating Calvin's Sermons

Calvin's sermons were taken down by Raguenier and transcribed by a scribe, who wrote the date and day of the week on each one. On Sunday afternoons the date was followed by "après midi" to distinguish it from the morning sermon, so normally a dated sermon without that addition was almost certainly delivered in the morning. Frequently when the sermons were printed all information about their location in time was omitted. To establish a (tentative) pattern for undated sermons it is necessary to combine various kinds of details or observations. An analysis of Calvin's typical preaching schedule provides a useful pattern. A second approach is ferreting out all possible clues which can contribute to assigning dates to undated sermons despite inconsistencies in the preacher's actual schedule. The basic plan was fairly predictable: twice on Sundays and once on every weekday in alternate weeks. This schedule was a regular template for Calvin's preaching but it was not an inflexible grid. In the nature of daily life, there were interruptions which mean that undated texts cannot be dropped into the pattern as if it were absolutely unchangeable.

To determine dates for unmarked sermons it is helpful to begin with an overview of the most common variations in the pattern of Calvin's schedule as those are revealed by an examination of the dated sermons and their prayer incipits. Here it is seen that there are sometimes Sunday mornings without Sunday afternoons to correspond, or vice versa. Or it is clear that there are weekday sermons on alternate days or skipping a day here or there, or a single sermon in

---

[148] The sermons on Galatians and the few excerpts from the Genesis sermons which were published in the 16th c. are practically the only exceptions to this rule.

one week instead of the six that would customarily be expected.[149] Sometimes there are logical reasons for something missing. Take for example the Sunday sermons. When Calvin was preaching from different books in the morning and afternoon, gaps in either series may be attributed to an absence. However, beginning in 1554 (when Calvin was preaching through the same book twice on Sunday, morning and afternoon) there would be a break in the *lectio continua* schedule but not in the sequence of that Biblical book text on the day when the Nativity or Easter or Pentecost was celebrated. The reason is that in the morning Calvin would preach on Luke 2 or the resurrection or Acts 2, and then on the afternoon of the festal Sunday he would take up again his current *lectio continua* book where he had left off the previous Sunday afternoon. On the other hand, the weekday sermons have fewer predictable reasons for a skip in the sequence, and sometimes there is nothing obvious. For example, one finds a Monday-Thursday-Saturday sequence, or a Monday-Wednesday-Friday sequence, when Calvin would normally preach Monday through Saturday. Sometimes when there are extended breaks, the reason can be traced to an absence or an illness: a diplomatic trip to Bern, a serious fever (Calvin traveled more in the early years, he was sick more in the later years). The dated sermons show all these kinds of breaks in the expected pattern of two Sunday sermons and six weekdays in alternate weeks.

Kinds of Evidence for Dating Sermons

While it is useful to know the typical kinds of variations in the grid, especially for Sundays, this serves more as a caution than as a guide for determining the dates of unmarked sermons. Some other sources can provide additional bits and pieces of data. Raguenier's catalogue supplies the day, month, and year (and time, if it is a Sunday afternoon sermon) of the beginning of a series, but that is often the only fixed date available. Language used in the sermons themselves provides evidence of greater or lesser precision, whether it refers to a specific occasion such as the Lord's Supper, or to a time such as "this morning" or "yesterday." Prayer

---

149 For afternoons without corresponding mornings, see I Corinthians, sermons #18 & #19 for Dec. 1555 before and after Nativity Lord's Supper, or sermons #43 & #44 & #45, where the two mornings are missing because they were probably replaced by a passion and a resurrection sermon for Easter 1556. For a morning without an afternoon, see sermon #24 for Jan. 12; there is no explanation for the lack of an afternoon sermon that day, but there is no gap in the texts so it is clear that Calvin did not preach on 1 Cor. that afternoon. For weekday gaps in unexpected ways, see Ezekiel #49, #50, #51, when Calvin preaches only on Wednesdays for three weeks; on the other hand he sometimes does sermons which are not his week, e.g., Ezekiel #15 & #16. See also the sermons on Deuteronomy, especially in the first weeks, show absences even before Calvin left town for a trip to Bern, and reveal that he took up preaching in the middle of the week when he returned. Appendix Seven: Calvin's Sermons.

formulae also can contribute in various ways. Information in the baptismal and especially the marriage records can be helpful, since there were certain fixed practices of the ministers such as refusing to perform weddings at the main Sunday morning service or catechism. Weddings on Supper Sundays were excluded by the *Ordinances*. Before laying out how I believe this works, it is appropriate to see what has been done by others.

A number of scholars have formulated patterns or experimented with dating the sermons. The pattern proposed by Edwin Mülhaupt for using prayer formulae (extempore #2) has been described above. Here it must be noted that he also looked for other general patterns, which led him to assign all Psalm texts to Sunday afternoons. As seen above, this fits with Colladon's general description of Calvin's preaching beginning in 1549 but carries it further. In fact, as the incipits of the prayers demonstrate, making this common practice an absolute rule goes too far.[150]

T. H. L. Parker, the other scholar who has devoted the most attention to dating sermons, has approached the dating project from a slightly different angle, focusing his work on some specific sermons in order to assign exact dates to each one. Parker's special example is the Pastoral Epistles, although he also gives some attention to Job because Calvin preached on that book simultaneously. Parker's work is very helpful in many ways. He has created a table to identify dates; to do this he draws on various sources, including both internal and external evidence. Many of his suggestions, such as pointing out the usefulness of "this morning/ ce matin" or "yesterday/ hier," are very helpful. Some others provide good insights but can be confusing in the way they are expressed. In one place Parker says that there were only 54 sermons on 1 Timothy; several pages later he rejects Raguenier's explicit statement that the sermons on 2 Timothy began in the afternoon.[151] The missing step is the explanation that, even though Raguenier lists 55 sermons on 1 Timothy, he must have miscounted. Since the sequence of sermons does not omit any text, it seems clear that the stenographer confused the number. There were only 54 sermons on 1 Timothy and thus 2 Timothy must have begun one service earlier, on the morning of April 21 rather than the afternoon. Raguenier also lists 31 sermons on 2 Timothy when there are only 30 extant and these are all

---

[150] Mülhaupt, "Einleitung," S. VII, pp. liii-liv, assigns all the Psalm expositions to afternoons, since he does not recognize the prayer phrases indicating Sunday morning, although only certain ones of the sermons are actually marked "apres midi" or "afternoon," pp. 40, 48, 56, 73. For Colladon, see above at n.54; for carrying too far, see analysis of incipits of sermons on Ps. 147, 148, 149, 65 in Appendix Seven.

[151] Parker, *Calvin's Preaching*, Appendix 2, pp. 163-78; esp. pp. 163-64, 169.

sequential so it is very unlikely that anything is missing. (Despite the mistakes in counting these sets of sermons, as far as can be determined other counts are correct.) [152] As is evident in Appendix Seven, the examination of the intercessory prayer incipits for the sermons on the Pastoral Epistles demonstrates that Raguenier was wrong and Parker was right about the time of day when the 2 Timothy sermons began – even if Parker did not clearly explain why he dismissed Raguenier's statement.

There are, however, difficulties with some of the assumptions on which Parker bases his assigning of dates to the Pastoral Epistles. While reasonable, these assumptions do not correspond with the facts. For example, he proposes in a rather off-hand manner that Calvin sometimes preached on a topic, such as "a wedding sermon," or might not have preached at all when he had to do four weddings. Parker also assigns all the weddings listed in the *Opera Calvini Annales* to Sunday morning services unless they are explicitly labeled afternoon. [153] There is no evidence anywhere that Calvin ever preached "a wedding sermon" – or one on any other specific topic as such, apart from the rather different context of the Friday *congrégations*. In addition, both the *Ecclesiastical Ordinances* and *La forme des prières* state that marriages were to be performed at a regular preaching service, so if Calvin married anyone it would be in the context of his ordinary role in the pulpit. (The one exception would be a marriage he performed for a friend at a service when he was not preaching, but that would still be a normal service with a sermon by a colleague and not an occasion of a wedding without a sermon, as Parker's words suggest.) In addition, although the marriage laws were not legislated until 1561, they were written many years earlier in 1545 and these show that Calvin and his colleagues did not want to perform weddings at the 8 a.m. Sunday service. Without examining the marriage records themselves, Parker could not ascertain that the ministers actually followed their own marriage ordinance before it was enacted. However, attention to the draft marriage ordinance would reveal that performing weddings on Sunday morning was contrary to Calvin's wishes,

---

152 See Raguenier's catalogue in Gagnebin, "L'histoire des manuscrits des sermons de Calvin," S. II, p. xv. See above at n.62.

153 Parker, *Calvin's Preaching*, pp. 164-67; p. 166: "We proceed to 2 Timothy, which we have shown to have begun on the afternoon of April 21, not morning, as the Raguenier Catalogue." P. 167 "The Registers tell us that on that day 'Calvin married four couples in S. Pierre' (CO 21.609). May it be that he then preached a wedding sermon which went unrecorded or has been lost? But he had three weddings on June 9 and still preached twice. Or was it that four weddings was too much even for him, and he did not preach? However that may be, it is hard to see how the sermons on 2 Timothy and Titus can be arranged any differently from the following charts." Parker also follows Mülhaupt in assigning all Psalm sermons to afternoons.

and therefore making this the default choice for such liturgies is an unlikely interpretation.

Both Mülhaupt and Parker have brought good ideas and creative imagination to the question of trying to date Calvin's sermons. There is still something to be done, especially in defining more precisely the uses of each kind of evidence and taking into account information these pioneering scholars did not consider.

The types of evidence which can play a part in uncovering dates for undated sermons are varied and have different weights of accuracy or precision. The following discussion identifies specific categories and demonstrates how they can be used. The main means, apart from limited facts such as Raguenier's record of the first sermon of each series, is by discerning and developing patterns seen in the clear evidence of dated sermons. Exceptions must be noted, of course, but the paradigms can then be used to narrow the possible range of dates for undated sermons. A second key element of organizing undated sermons is to attend to the various ways that other rules or customs shaped Calvin's preaching and Geneva's worship life. These would include such things as the fact that Calvin did not preach "topical" sermons (the only breaks in *lectio continua* were for the special Christological holy days), and Genevan custom regulating when marriages could be celebrated.

Prayer Incipits for Weekdays

When Calvin's sermons are examined with an eye to the incipit of the intercessory prayer text, it becomes possible to determine something about the day of the week on which the sermon was preached. Take a catalogue of the endings of his Old Testament sermons. It is seen that (unless the scribe made a mistake), when the concluding intercessory prayer begins with "Que non seulement" (or sometimes "Vrais et fideles ministres") it means the sermon was preached on a Monday, Tuesday, Thursday, Friday, or Saturday. One might ask: why not a Wednesday? Because the day of prayer liturgy in *La forme des prières* specified a printed prayer of intercession which begins with the phrase: "Dieu tout puissant, Pere celeste"; weekday sermons which conclude with this formula were preached on Wednesdays. (In a minority of cases, the scribe goes directly to "Pere celeste" but it is obviously the same prayer.) Examinations of *dated* sermons such as Genesis, 2 Samuel, Isaiah, Jeremiah, Micah, the first part of Ezekiel and the later part of Deuteronomy, reveal that this pattern holds true almost perfectly. On only five occasions is the ordinary weekday prayer incipit found at the end of a Wednesday sermon, probably because the scribe was so accustomed to it that he, or perhaps Raguenier himself, forgot what the day was.[154] (Since five days out of six "Que non seulement" was used, it is natural that once in a while there would be a mistake.) On the other hand, the Wednesday prayer formula "Dieu tout puissant" is almost never found on one of the other weekdays; a single instance on a dated text is March 26, 1556. (It was much less likely that the more rare "Dieu tout puissant" would be misapplied than "Que non seulement," which was heard day in and day out.)

Examining dated weekday sermons according to their intercessory prayer incipits provides the first part of a pattern for identifying dates for undated sermons. The simplest format is "the regular" one, in which there are five sermons ending in "Que non seulement," followed by one ending in "Dieu tout puissant," followed by another five with "Que non seulement" and another single "Dieu tout puissant." In this case the "Dieu tout puissant," which is Wednesday, allows the group to be divided neatly; the first three "Que non seulement" are the Thursday-Saturday of one week, and then two "Que non seulement" are Monday-Tuesday of the next week of preaching, with "Dieu tout puissant" for Wednesday and then three more "Que non seulement" for Thursday-Saturday, followed by "Que non seulement" for Monday-Tuesday and so forth. This pattern is clearly visible in dated sermons on Jeremiah, Micah, the first part of Ezekiel, the end of Deuteronomy, Isaiah, Genesis, and 2 Samuel (listing in chronological order). It also works almost perfectly for the undated sermons on Daniel which come between Micah and Ezekiel, because while preaching on Daniel Calvin seems to have been able to follow the regular format without many interruptions. The full picture is set out in Appendix Seven.

There was another "official" pattern for Calvin's preaching for more than three years in the 1550s. As explained in chapter two, because of the illness of his alternate, Pastor Poupin, Calvin was doing all the day of prayer services in Greater Geneva from January 1553 until March 1556; most of the time a colleague took the Saturday of Calvin's usual week. This meant that the normal pattern for these years was Monday through Friday of his own week and Wednesday of the following week which (as a week) was assigned to his alternate.[155] In terms of incipits, this produces two "Que non seulement" for Monday-Tuesday of his own week, followed by one "Dieu tout puissant" for Wednesday and then two more "Que non seulement" for Thursday-Friday of his week, and then another "Dieu tout puissant" for the Wednesday of his alternate's week, before repeating the

---

154 Genesis sermons #62 & #79, Deuteronomy sermon #77, Isaiah sermon #57, Micah sermon #1.

155 See chap. 2 at nn.69ff; the Deuteronomy sermons demonstrate that Calvin had to add Saturday as well part way through 1555, and to continue this until a new pastor was chosen to replace Poupin. Appendix Seven: Calvin's Sermons.

series. The pattern is explicit in the later part of the dated Ezekiel sermons preached in this period (Jan. 16, 1553-Feb. 21, 1554) and the first part of Deuteronomy (March 20, 1554-March 18, 1556). After Poupin's death and the election of his successor, Calvin could return to the normal pattern. This analysis confirms the accuracy of recognizing "Dieu tout puissant" as a sign of a Wednesday sermon, even when it appears to be out of sequence. In the case of undated sermons, then, at least the Wednesdays are fixed. This pattern helps to order the undated Job sermons which come from this same period when Calvin was doing virtually all the Wednesday services in Greater Geneva. [156]

Prayer Incipits for Sunday Afternoons

Prayer incipits are also critically important in identifying Sunday afternoon sermons. Although these have not previously been treated as a separate category, there is good reason to distinguish them from the morning ones. Finding sixteenth-century indications which can serve to identify the characteristic intercessory prayers for Sunday afternoons is less easy than for weekdays. [157] However, there is some circumstantial evidence. First is the fact that Badius published the "weekday" prayer for illumination-and-sealing in his volume on the Gospel Harmony which was comprised solely of Sunday sermons. As noted above, the presence of this prayer in a book of texts preached on Sunday puzzled Jean-François Gilmont, but unless this "weekday" text was used on Sunday afternoons, there would be no point in providing it in a book of Sunday sermons. Secondly, as discussed in an earlier chapter, the liturgy of the French-speaking refugee church in London explicitly identifies the intercessory prayer "for Sunday afternoon and weekdays," which means that the practice of having one intercessory prayer for both Sunday afternoons and ordinary weekdays was officially ordered in of one of the closest offspring of the Genevan liturgy. [158]

So, it is virtually certain that the prayers in the Genevan parishes – both those for illumination-and-sealing and for intercession – were different on Sunday afternoons from those in the mornings. This can be verified for the intercessory prayers through examination of dated Sunday sermons of a series where morning and afternoon are clearly marked; there it is seen that the concluding phrases for

---

[156] In the Ezekiel sermons there are some exceptions, when at various points Calvin did a full week and no extra Wednesday, although no reason is given for this change. The tentative reconstruction of Job dates is fitted into this pattern, in Appendix Seven: Calvin's Sermons.

[157] Moehn, "Introduction," *Sermones*, pp. xvi-xvii, is the only source which states that the Sunday afternoon prayer began with "que non seulement" and indicates that this is the weekday prayer form, but he does not give evidence to support this.

[158] See Poullain, *Liturgia sacra*, pp. 99, 101-03, and discussion in chap. 3 at nn.182ff.

the two are not the same. Sermons preached in the morning end with the initial words of the Sunday and day of prayer intercessions, "Dieu tout puissant." Sermons preached on the afternoons of the same Sundays conclude with the ordinary weekday formula "Que non seulement." The practice is consistent for the sermons on 1 Corinthians, chapters one through nine, the only Sunday set which is dated and has both morning and afternoon sermons on the same book. The other extant New Testament sets which follow this morning-and-afternoon pair pattern (Galatians, Ephesians, Timothy and Titus) lost their dates when they were printed in the sixteenth-century. The ones on Acts which are dated were preached essentially as Sunday mornings plus only an occasional afternoon, as was also the case for the Gospel Harmony. The dated Corinthians sermons clearly demonstrate, with only one exception (which appears to be a mistake on the part of the scribe[159]) that the morning intercessory prayer was the one prescribed in *La forme des prières* and the afternoon one was Calvin's extempore #3 used on weekdays. This pattern can thus be applied to Galatians, Ephesians and the Pastorals, the other undated series of sermons which the reformer preached in morning-and-afternoon pairs, to help identify the afternoon ones.

The sermons on First Corinthians also provide an example of a "predictable" interruption of the series and the incipit pattern helps define the situation when there was only one recorded sermon on a given day. Normally special Christological observances required an interruption in the *lectio continua* series (unless Calvin was preaching on a book which fit the special event). At these given points a *lectio continua* series demonstrates a pattern of two consecutive sermons concluding with the incipit "Que non seulement." For example, in December 1555, Calvin was working through 1 Cor. 2:11-3:19. The Nativity Lord's Supper was celebrated on the morning of Dec. 22, so there are sermons on Dec. 15 morning ("Dieu tout puissant") and afternoon ("Que non seulement"), and then on the afternoon of Dec. 22 ("Que non seulement"), followed by Dec. 29 morning ("Dieu tout puissant") and afternoon ("Que non seulement"). The Nativity sermon, almost certainly on Luke 2, was not preserved, but the text of First Corinthians does not skip any verses between the afternoons of Dec. 15 and Dec. 22, clear evidence that the intervening sermon was not from this book.[160] It also explains why there are two afternoon sermons in succession.

---

[159] In fact, this mistake happens once in the dated sermons on 1 Corinthians, chapters 1-9, comprised of 58 sermons; on the Sunday afternoon of Nov. 17, 1555, although clearly marked as afternoon, the morning prayer incipit is used: "Dieu tout puissant." See Appendix Seven: Calvin's Sermons.

[160] See sermons #18 & #19 on 1 Corinthians, Appendix Seven: Calvin's Sermons.

Other Language Clues

There are other clues in Calvin's sermons themselves which can help in identifying relationships or, occasionally, actual dates. One common form is a reference to special temporal occasions. In the afternoon service on Dec. 15, 1555, Calvin announced that the Lord's Supper would be celebrated the following Sunday. (Such a notice was supposed to be given the week before the sacrament to help the people prepare.) Alternatively, on the day itself the preacher might devote particular attention to the Supper, or at least speak about it briefly to invite the congregation to participate. Sometimes the actual day of the celebration is missing, since many of the feast day sermons which interrupted a *lectio continua* flow are no longer extant, but usually the sermon for the September Lord's Supper is available, because this one time out of the four yearly celebrations did not interrupt the usual Biblical sequence. Calvin did not always include such a declaration or exposition (for example, when he had been preaching on the passion the week before Easter), but when he does mention the sacrament "next week" or "today" in a sermon it can help to locate the latter in the larger cycle of the year. [161] Besides Corinthians, the dated Acts sermons include such an exhortation the Sunday before Christmas in 1549 and before the September Supper in 1550. [162] Such indications can help fix the dates of at least certain ones of the undated sermons: on 1 Timothy for the Nativity Supper in 1554, on 2 Timothy for Pentecost 1555, and on Titus for the September Supper 1555. The Ephesians sermons show this pattern for Pentecost and September 1558; and the Gospel Harmony for September and the Nativity 1559 and for Easter, Pentecost, and September 1560. [163]

There is other language, heard much more frequently, which provides a way to relate sermons to each other. For the Sundays, the most obvious is a reference in one sermon to what was said "ce matin/ this morning," [164] which shows which two sermons form a pair; on the other hand, two sermons may form a day's pair without that identifying phrase. A similar kind of linkage is found in the weekday

---

[161] Grosse, *Les rituels de la Cène*, pp. 191-92.

[162] See Appendix Seven: Calvin's Sermons. Note that Sermon #17 on Ps. 119 which was preached on the afternoon of March 26, 1553, the week before Easter, mentions the Lord's Supper (although this is not a case of naming it with a time, it does confirm that Calvin might draw in the sacraments on a day when the Supper was being announced, even if the text did not go in that direction); this appears to be the only mention of the Supper in this set of sermons.

[163] See Appendix Seven: Calvin's Sermons.

[164] See dated 1 Corinthians: sermons #1 & #2, #9 & #10, #11 & #12, #13 & #14, #17 & #18, #22 & #23, #25 & #26, #27 & #28, #31 & #32, #35 & #36, #37 & #38, #41 & #42, #48 & #49, #53 & #54. Another obvious one is a reference to "last Sunday" in sermons #22 & #48.

sermons with the word "hier/ yesterday," which (as long as it refers to what is being preached and not to some local event) indicates that the sermon in which it appears came one day after the previous one. [165] Again, the absence of "hier" does not mean a gap between two sermons but only that Calvin is not explicitly linking what he says one day with the previous day's text. Sometimes on Sundays Calvin will say "last week" which indicates the interval since the previous sermon.

A less reliable but still helpful clue is some variation on "cy devant/ previously" or "cy dessus." One of these formulations usually indicates an interval of time or text between the sermon in which it appears and the one to which it refers. It is not uncommon to find Calvin beginning a sermon with a sentence including "cy devant" when the previous sermon in the sequence was several days or a week earlier; the sermons on 1 Corinthians, chapters 1-9, offer a number of examples for Sundays, and those on Genesis provide a sample for weekdays. [166] (However, sometimes this phrase refers to an earlier action by a Biblical character and not to a sermon per se, so simply noting its presence is not enough.) Still, attention to words like "cy dessus" can contribute to building up a picture of the temporal relationship between two consecutive but undated sermons. Because of their relative infrequency by comparison with the incipits of the intercessory prayers, clues such as "ce matin" or "cy devant" or "hier" are less useful for determining patterns of undated sermons, but together all of these tiny signs can provide a certain level of assurance.

Patterns and Extrapolation for Weekdays

The organization of Calvin's preaching was orderly but not a rigid grid, or at least, the "regular" patterns did not always hold true. Sometimes the sermons give evidence that Calvin missed a day even when the usual five or six days per week format was functioning. For example, there are occasional sermons missing in the dated Genesis series (several on Thursdays, one on Saturday); and Deuteronomy (several Mondays and Tuesdays as well as the expected Saturdays because in 1553-56 Calvin was doing all the Wednesdays and not the Saturday of his assigned week). Although in general the Isaiah sermons are regular, they provide examples

---

[165] See dated Genesis: sermons #3, #14, #16, #19, #25, #28, #32, #43, #44, #46, #47, #50, #51, #53, #55, #56, #57, #63, #65, #67, #69, #70, #72, #73, #74, #76, #79, #80, #81, #82, #87, #88, #89, #90, #93, #97.

[166] See 1 Corinthians: sermons #5, #13, #17, #20, #29, #31, #33, #39, #43, #47, #51. Genesis, sermons #7, #18, #24, #52, #70 are all at the beginning of a week, when it would have been an interval of days (usually10) since the last sermon. Examples in which this phrase refers to some earlier aspect of the Biblical text and not to an interval of time between sermons, see Genesis, sermons #20, #34, & #40 [marked in the list as "es" for earlier sermon].

of even more scattered absences or additions. In one week in May 1557 Calvin preached Tuesday-Thursday-Saturday, and other times he preached "extra" sermons on Mon. June 7, 1557, and several Wednesdays later that year.[167] (The "extra's" might have been to cover the illness of his alternate, but the omission of Monday-Wednesday-Friday does not make any obvious sense…) However, the point here is that since there are exceptions in the dated sermon series, those are also to be expected in the undated ones.

This information about unexplained temporal skips when there is no gap in the sermon series can be applied to the undated sermons. The logical deduction is that a similar pattern means that Calvin did not preach on one of the ordinary weekdays; that is most often Saturday, but it could also be another day. This pattern can be applied with some hesitations to the sermons on 1 Samuel. The first step in attempting to date the undated sermons is to center the weeks on the Wednesday incipit "Dieu tout puissant" in order to have a fixed point in the pattern. Say there are four "Que non seulement"; the "Dieu tout puissant" will be Wednesday; the four "Que non seulement" will be some combination of four of the next five weekdays when Calvin would preach (Thursday-Friday-Saturday-Monday, or Thursday-Friday-Monday-Tuesday, or Friday-Saturday-Monday-Tuesday, or Thursday-Saturday-Monday-Tuesday); and then the next "Dieu tout puissant" will mark the following Wednesday. Next, one looks to see if there may a reference to "hier"/ "yesterday" somewhere in a sermon, to see if one or more sermons form a sequence that can be linked up temporally.[168]

Even when it is possible to identify whether a sermon was on a Wednesday day of prayer or another weekday, and to establish a sense of alternate weeks, there are other factors which must be considered in attempting to date Calvin's weekday preaching accurately. One of these is accounting for his longer absences or illnesses. There are times when the dated sermons show that Calvin missed a week; this is visible in sermons on Ezekiel and Isaiah. In early September 1553, there is a three week interval between sermons 2 and 3 of Ezekiel, from Sept. 2 to Sept. 25; there is similar hiatus in the Isaiah sermons between Feb. 26 and March 21, 1558, and again between March 26 and April 18, 1558. In none of these cases is there any break in the exposition of the Biblical book.[169] It is assumed that Calvin's alternate preached during the week missing from his pattern in those instances. (The system of pastor pairs and alternation in a specific pulpit at a given time made it relatively easy to cover absences – or at least clear how that should be

---

[167] See Appendix Seven: Calvin's Sermons.

[168] See Appendix Seven: Calvin's Sermons.

[169] See Appendix Seven: Calvin's Sermons.

done.) In attempting to determine when undated sermons were preached it is helpful to be reminded that from time to time Calvin missed his regular week to preach without any obvious explanation. That means he produced fewer sermons than the sheer number of days that he was scheduled to preach according to the typical routine. Thus undated sermons may not fill the full time between the day Raguenier identifies as the first for that Biblical book and the day when the next series began.

The schedule of Calvin's sermons might also change even if the fundamental rhythm did not, however. For example, he might not preach for two or four weeks and this could result in exchanging "regular weeks" with his alternate. This is visible in the sermons on 2 Samuel in the fall of 1562. All was going normally through September, and Calvin's next week would begin on Oct. 5, 1562; that day he preached the Monday sermon of his week, but then was ill. Instead of waiting for his next regular week, he took up his preaching again on the following Monday, Oct. 12, which would originally have been his alternate's week, and the rhythm between them was re-established in different weeks.[170] Then comes the question: how to determine such a change in the weeks one would expect Calvin to have, in cases where the sermons are not dated? Here it is possible to add another category of evidence.

External Information

Information drawn from other sources besides Calvin's sermons can be helpful in adding further clues about gaps in his preaching. One obvious place to look is any notes about the reformer's travels or illnesses, and sometimes when neither of these is explicitly stated, absences from consistory meetings can also suggest business or health reasons that he might not have been in the pulpit.[171] Seeing how these play out in dated sermons offers some ideas for tracking undated series which do not fill all the available days between their initial date (given by Raguenier) and the beginning of the next Biblical book.

One of the most helpful external pieces in the puzzle is supplied by the baptismal and marriage records. First it is necessary to identify what can be

---

170 Sermons #54-#59, which show that the schedule changed: Calvin's rhythm had been weeks beginning Mon. Sept. 7, Sept. 21, Oct. 5, Oct. 19, Nov. 2. He got as far as Oct. 5 and became ill, so he began again on his alternate's rhythm, Oct. 12, Oct. 26, Nov. 9. Apparently he was ill also the week of Oct. 26, but the new rhythm continued when he picked up preaching again on Nov. 9. See Appendix Seven: Calvin's Sermons. See also Ezekiel sermons #15 & #16 which show that Calvin might fill in for his alternate without that changing their rhythm.

171 See Appendix Seven: Calvin's Sermons, where any information about travel or illness or consistory absences found in the Annales or RCP is noted. I have not combed all the correspondence for every mention of illness.

learned from such data. Normally one would expect that when a minister cele-brated a wedding or a baptism, he was also preaching. This was generally true for most Genevan pastors; Calvin was the exception. He performed many weddings and in that case he was most likely to be preaching himself. This means that a record of the marriages he did is fairly good evidence that he was in the pulpit, although it is not conclusive because he could also perform the ceremony for special friends when he was not preaching. Sundays were the most popular day for weddings, which were allowed only at dawn services (which Calvin did not do) or in the afternoon, which was when he performed the most marriages. [172] In his last years after his long illness in 1558-59 he rarely preached on Sunday afternoon, but especially during the earlier 1550s it is sometimes possible to line up undated sermons with weddings. [173]

On the other hand, Calvin rarely baptized babies even when he was preaching; a colleague usually did it for him, as is evident when his dated sermons are correlated with the general baptismal records for the parishes where he was in the pulpit. [174] Some examples can give a sense of this practice. In December 1550 Calvin's alternate Poupin did many baptisms in his own week at La Magdeleine; however, he also did one on Dec. 22, which was not his week and when in fact there is a dated sermon by Calvin on Micah. In that same week, Bourgoing (who was not Calvin's alternate but had come to hear him preach) did baptisms on Dec. 25 and 27, while the Micah sermons were continuing. This pattern is repeated many times, as can be seen in a few further examples from other parishes and different years and ministers. Pastor Chauvet from St. Gervais did a baptism

---

[172] See Appendix Five: Calvin's Weddings, to identify the full listing of weddings correlated with sermons. The weddings for which sermons are not identified are essentially those dates for which the sermons are no longer extant. A few examples of weddings when he was not preaching are Sept. 14, 1550, at dawn for the marriage of his close friend Laurent de Normandie to Anne Colladon.

[173] For example, the wedding recorded on July 24, 1558, practically requires that Calvin be preaching, but this also counters the notice of an illness which might have explained why a Sunday is missing between Pentecost and the September Supper in this series of sermons. It is just possible that Calvin did the wedding for friends when someone else preached.

[174] See Appendix Four: Calvin's Baptisms, to identify the ones correlated with sermons. The baptisms for which sermons are not identified are essentially those dates for which the sermons are no longer extant. See Appendix Three: Ministers' Rotations; underlined dates in the baptismal acts of Calvin's colleagues indicate that there are dated sermons by Calvin, underlined italics are dates of undated sermons which are tentatively correlated. In fact this practice antedates the regular baptismal records, as can be seen in the three occasions in 1544, 1546, and 1548 when Poupin's sons received the sacrament; at least the Sunday morning and probably the other two were days Calvin was preaching but he does not do any of the baptisms. See chap. 1 at n.151.

at St. Pierre at 8 a.m. on Sept. 28, 1550, when Calvin was preaching on Acts. Pastor Fabri, also from St. Gervais, did one on Jan. 8, 1551, at La Magdeleine when Calvin was preaching on Micah. Bourgoing, who worked in Greater Geneva at dawn and catechism services, did one the next day, Jan. 9, at La Magdeleine where the Micah sermons were continuing. Skip to 1553: St. André was the new minister who was helping cover for Poupin, and he worked in all the parishes. He baptized on Sunday afternoons at St. Pierre on Feb. 5 and 26, 1553, when Calvin was preaching on Ps. 119; he also did baptisms frequently in January through April, September through December 1553, at St. Pierre on Wednesdays, on other weekdays at La Magdeleine, when Calvin's book was Ezekiel. The next year 1554, Chauvet and St. André did baptisms at La Magdeleine in January-February, hearing the last of Calvin's Ezekiel sermons. (By this point, however, St. André was Calvin's alternate, so he was doing most of the baptisms in La Magdeleine on weekdays.) St. André continued this in 1555, and in the later part of the year Chauvet was still coming over from St. Gervais to do quite a few baptisms at La Magdeleine while sitting in on Calvin's sermons on Deuteronomy. And so forth.

Why would it matter who was doing the baptisms? The answer is that, once undated weekday sermons have been grouped by weeks (according to the prayer incipits), it is necessary to assign them to a place in the months between the date Raguenier began recording that set and the date he started the next Biblical book. Since Calvin preached in alternate weeks, the groups of sermons must be fitted into a tentative pattern by assigning them to actual dates. Although Calvin did not do enough weekday baptisms and weddings to make it easy to trace his weeks of preaching, the liturgies done by his colleagues can illuminate the picture and thus help narrow the field for undated weekday sermons. Baptisms at La Magdeleine or St. Pierre on weekdays before June 1559, or at St. Pierre from that date until his death, by ministers who were not his alternate, can identify Calvin's weeks. For example, when Chauvet (who was the chief minister at St. Gervais and doing regular weekday preaching there) is found doing baptisms in Greater Geneva in 1550 or 1554, it is clear that he was not preaching but listening to Calvin. On the other hand, tracing the baptisms (and weddings) by his alternate can help to identify Calvin's own weeks by contrast. This is a long way around to locate dates for sermons, but when this strategy is applied it is possible to see if there is any change in the schedule of weeks when Calvin was in the pulpit and thus to have one more tool to help narrow how undated sermons can be fitted into their hypothetical places.

In particular, this can serve to help find some fixed points in the most difficult undated sermons, those on 1 Samuel, which have the distinct disadvantage of having been translated into Latin and lost some concluding prayers in the process. This series began on Aug. 8, 1561. Taking into account the fact that Calvin did the full week of Passion sermons only when it was his turn to preach, and adding the fact that there are dated sermons on Matthew 26-27 for March 23-27, 1562, one can conclude that Calvin was not preaching in the weeks on either side of Passion Week.[175] This means there should be a three week break in the 1 Samuel sermons around Easter in 1562. The next step is to look at Calvin's three recorded weddings for weekdays, on Feb. 2, April 7, and May 18. This reveals that the first wedding belongs in one schedule of alternating weeks – before Easter – and the other two in a different one – after Easter. Somewhere there is a change…[176] These clues can then be combined with records of baptisms and weddings by Calvin's alternate, Jean Merlin, which in turn provide a fairly clear idea of what weeks he was on duty as preacher. Merlin's weeks are seen to change between January and March in a way which would fit if he and Calvin had exchanged weeks. Merlin's schedule had been weeks beginning Mondays Dec. 29, 1552, and Jan. 12, Jan. 26, Feb. 9, Feb. 23, 1553. However, it is obvious from the baptisms that Merlin continued to be in charge the week following Feb. 23, i.e., starting on Monday March 2, 1553; he then skipped a week, now to be on a different schedule: March 2, March 16, March 30, April 13, April 27, May 4…[177] This evidence means that Calvin's weddings fit in weeks when he was preaching. While this does not guarantee that the dates of the 1 Samuel sermons can be made exact, it does illustrate that the rhythm Calvin and his alternate followed could change and allows the pieces to be fitted together so that there is somewhat greater clarity about when Calvin was preaching and where 1 Samuel fits.

Appendices Seven and Eight

What all these detective strategies do is provide a better idea of the times Calvin preached and how to distribute the texts of his sermons in their appropriate places. While the result is a pattern with various levels of certainty, there are enough fixed markers to make a fairly reliable over-all picture of the reformer's preaching: Sundays and weekdays, mornings and afternoons, special Christological holy days, days of prayer, and the "ordinary" sermon fare which Calvin provided for the people in the pew, day by day, week by week, year by year. The fruit of combining all these clues can be seen in the schedules of Calvin's sermons found in Appendices Seven and Eight. Seven gives all the extant sermons in

---

[175] See Appendix Seven: Calvin's Sermons.

[176] See Appendix Five: Calvin's Weddings.

[177] See Appendix Three: Ministers' Rotations

Biblical order. The two parts of Appendix Eight set out the Old Testament (minus Psalms) and the New Testament and Psalms sermons, each in the chronological order in which Calvin preached them.

IV: Calvin's Sermons and His Audiences

The people in the pew in Geneva changed over the years of Calvin's ministry. At least by the time his sermons were being recorded there were both native Genevans and increasing numbers of religious refugees. It is of course not possible to know what most of them thought about the preacher's words. However, several ways of approaching the existing evidence can be illuminating. The most subjective is an effort to deduce from sermons themselves the character and/or composition of the congregation as the preacher saw it and accommodated his words to the understanding of the people in the pew. Another somewhat indirect set of known reactions are those of hearers who turn up in the public records for objecting to what they heard from the pulpit. A third form offering the most articulate response comes from the men – and women! – who chose to publish one or more of Calvin's sermons, explaining why they valued these and setting out how they understood their use.

Calvin's View of and Accommodation to the People in the Pew

What the preacher says is certainly not the same as what the people hear or think, but the way the preacher explains his text can shed some light on how he views the people in the pew and who he thinks may be present. In particular, the way Calvin accommodated his exposition to the identity and needs of the people before him, as he understood those, can be glimpsed in his sermons. For practical purposes, only a small sample can be included here.

The test case is nine sermons on 1 Cor. 2:6 through 1 Cor. 3:19, preached on the Sunday mornings and afternoons of the month of December 1555. The audience included not only Genevan-born members but also increasing numbers of well-educated religious refugees. While most of the latter were from France, there were also others, like high-ranking English exiles and some Italians, who knew enough French to follow the preaching of the famous leader who had drawn them to Geneva. In addition, his colleagues among the Genevan pastors often attended Calvin's sermons when they were not preaching elsewhere.[178] To

---

[178] See evidence from baptismal records in Appendix Three: Ministers' Rotations. McKee, "Calvin and His Colleagues as Pastors," p. 38. De Boer, *Genevan School of the Prophets*, p. 50, affirms that the ministers attended each others' sermons.

help discern the preacher's awareness of who was sitting before him in St. Pierre in December 1555, the content of the nine sermons has been compared with that of the corresponding commentary on First Corinthians, published in 1546, almost a decade before the sermons were preached.

Time and space constrain the number of examples which can be presented here. The object is to provide a few of the most prominent categories of evidence for Calvin's awareness of who his hearers were. One theme is the preacher's perception of the intellectual or geographic diversity within the congregation. Another is the kind of traditional language which the reformer uses, noting when he thinks explanation is needed – and when it is not. A final section sketches theological and devotional themes which Calvin apparently thought required emphasis. To put these observations in context, it may be said that the last of these nine sermons, the one preached on the afternoon of Dec. 29, does not offer any specific clues to Calvin's view of his hearers. There he expounds the meaning of being God's temple in a manner which might apply to any congregation: or, to put it another way, without overt indication that this was fitted to a particular audience. Apparently he thought that sometimes it was enough to explain and apply the text in a fairly undifferentiated manner, since all his hearers needed the same instruction. The evidence here, therefore, is drawn from the eight sermons preached from the morning of Dec. 1 to the morning of Dec. 29, 1555, where some accommodation to his audience comes into view. A preliminary reminder: since it is the nature of Calvin's preaching to add a considerable amount of application and exhortation to the exposition of each line of scripture, that particular difference between commentary and sermons is acknowledged here and will be taken for granted in what follows. That is, the fact of application is a given; the focus here will be the specific ways in which the application gives clues about the identities of the people in the pews.

Addressing the Learned and the Simple

Calvin was clearly aware of diversity among his auditors in St. Pierre, and intellectual ability or education was a significant factor. Often signs of this are indirect. For example, Calvin knew that some hearers were well-educated humanists like himself, or at least people whom he expected to look for very careful attention to the words of the Biblical text and their context. In these sermons he shows great sensitivity to how the New Testament writer Paul uses the Old Testament source which is identified as Isaiah. Referring to the quotation in 1 Cor. 2:9, Calvin indicates that Paul is not citing Isaiah "word-for-word," but the preacher assures his hearers that the apostle is not wrong to call on the prophet in this place and insists that Paul does not misapply his quotation. Calvin goes on to point out that the New Testament writer adds something which is not in Isaiah; and then the apostle says explicitly something which his Old Testament source mentions only in passing. The pastor concludes that the two Biblical authors use different words but their meaning comes to the same thing.[179]

When this passage is compared with the commentary, there seems to be a greater level of tension in the sermon, despite the preacher's confident insistence that Paul has not misappropriated Isaiah. The commentary begins by dealing with whether this is actually a quotation from Isaiah, but concludes by agreeing with the scholarly view common in Calvin's day that it is. However, then Calvin points out two apparent difficulties in the way that Isaiah is applied by Paul, which he goes on to resolve to his own satisfaction.[180] The sermon does not allow for such academic detail, and so it seems that the preacher gives extra emphasis to the accord between Old Testament and New. Such repetition logically has in view educated people who would have read both Paul and Isaiah yet might well not know how Calvin reconciled the textual differences, and thus would need assurance of the agreement between the two Biblical writers.

Not only the learned but the illiterate were in the preacher's view. In expounding 1 Cor. 2:12 from the pulpit, Calvin says that when it comes to matters of the kingdom of God "poor simple people who have never been to school" compare favorably with the highly educated who think they know everything.[181] This acknowledgment of the uneducated is naturally lacking from the commentary, which is addressed to scholars, but it is evidence that the preacher is conscious that many of his hearers fall into the category of "simple people."

Sometimes Calvin explicitly addresses the different educational levels of his congregation. When he expounds 1 Cor. 3:2 on feeding the people with milk, the pastor says that everyone must continue to be God's pupil throughout life. Some "who have heard preaching and have also attended lectures" think they have no

---

179 Ms.fr 26, sermon #13, f103a = "il est vray qu'il n'y a point ainsi de mot à mot au prophete" ... "il l'approprie tres bien ce tesmoinage"; f103b = "concluons que non sans cause S[ainct] Paul a prins ce tesmoinage"; f104a = "n'est point sans cause que S[ainct] Paul n'a point faict scrupule de dire..." "S[ainct] Paul n'a point mal applicqué le tesmoinage du prophete..." f104b= "Or Sainct Paul adjouste ce qui n'est point contenu au texte du prophete"; f105a = "il est vray que le prophete Isaye use du mot de faire... or S[ainct] Paul declaire plus expressement ce qui est touché comme en passant par le prophete"; f105b = "le prophete dict que 'c'est à ceulx qui attendent Dieu' et S[ainct] Paul mect 'qui l'ayment' mais tout revient à ung."

180 Commentary on 1 Cor. 2:9, OC 49:339-40.

181 Ms.fr 26, sermon #14, f111a = "voire que les povres idiotz, qui n'ont jamais esté à l'eschole, soient plus sçavans quant au royaulme des cieulx que ne sont pas les plus habiles, ceulx qui sont si ayguz que merveilles, quand ilz parlent il semble qu'ilz ayent mesme forgé le monde en leur boutique."

more to learn.[182] The "lectures" here are the public teaching in Geneva. They might be the *"congrégations,"* French scripture studies held on Friday mornings, which were fairly popular with the upper ranks of the city – and even some artisans who were not so highly educated. It is equally or more likely that Calvin meant the more academic Latin lectures on which his commentaries were based, since he goes on to refer to "clerks or literate" people, in which case the audience he had in view would be the elite.[183] The preacher then bluntly objects to the idea that he might ignore the majority of the congregation in order to serve "a handful" of learned people. He says that the latter must recognize that the preacher needs to speak in a way that the simple people can understand, so they are not left with "the wind, when things [being spoken] are obscure to them." He goes on to criticize the educated. "We see a great many who are angry when you don't bring them some novelty…[they say] 'you could make such a point in one word … you don't need such a long explanation.'"[184] Calvin reminds his hearers that the learned may in fact be less perfect in knowledge than they think, but then concedes that even if they do not need his repetitions, they should bear these lessons patiently because the church is one body.[185] The preacher illustrates his point with a little word picture.

---

[182] Ms.fr 26, sermon #16, f128a = "et ainsi ne soyons point si grans docteurs que nous ne demourions tousjours escholiers tout le temps de nostre vie; comme nous en voyons beaucoup quand ilz auront cheminé quelque temps en la craincte de Dieu, qu'ilz auront ouy les predications et auront aussi frequenté la lecture il leur semble qu'il n'y a plus que redire en eulx."

[183] For the *congrégations* see De Boer, *Genevan School of the Prophets*. De Boer tells the story of Aymé Du Nant, pp. 95-96. This is a fascinating story of an artisan who had been attending the congregations, but was ridiculed by another man of his own rank for "wasting" so much time on a work day (essentially, doing what upper classes who had some leisure could do), OC 21:431-432, Aug. 16, 1548. De Boer sets this story in context, see chap. 4, especially pp. 95-96. For the possibility that Calvin was referring to his Latin lectures see the next note.

[184] Ms.fr 26, sermon #16, f128b-129a: "Il n'y a celuy d'esprit si excellent qui ne doibve se ranger à Dieu pour estre l'ung de ses disciples mais ce pendant si ne fault il pas que nous laissions la plus grande part du monde pour servir à une poignee de gens, à ceulx qui sont clercz, qui sont lettrés, et que le menu peuple ce pendant et ceulx qui n'auront point hanté les escholes, que ceulx là soient delaissez ou qu'ilz demeurent tousjours abrutiz ou qu'ilz n'ayent que du vent quant les choses leur soient obscures." Was Calvin perhaps chiding some colleagues who thought they did not need to attend ordinary sermons regularly because they were hearing sophisticated lectures?

[185] Ms.fr 26, sermon #16, f129a: "Ceulx qui viennent pour ouyr la parolle de Dieu doibvent penser que si une chose leur est superflue ce n'est pas à dire pourtant qu'ilz ne la doibvent recevoir paysiblement. Car nous en verrons beaucoup qui sont faschez quand on ne leur apporte rien de nouveau, 'et je scay bien tout cela, et ung tel propos doibt estre declairé en ung mot, il ne falloit que le toucher en passant; d'en faire une si longue deduction il n'estoit ja de besoing.' Quand ceulx qui parlent ainsi regarderont à eulx ilz trouveront qu'ilz ont plus grand besoing d'estre enseignez qu'ilz ne pensent, mais encores prenons la cas qu'ilz s'en peussent passer, si est ce que nous sommes comme ung corps et fault que les membres supportent les ungz les aultres."

> If there is someone strong enough to walk and there is a little child, when I am in their midst if I take the hand of the little child and I conform my step to his because I would break his legs and neck if I wanted to force him to walk too fast; and if the other person complains and says 'I would walk faster if I wanted' – yes, but pay attention to the company. So therefore let us learn to behave in such a way that we can profit from the teaching when it is not distributed to us according to our capacity, and let us recognize that the majority are still simple and frail. [186]

Highly educated refugees might feel cheated; they came to Geneva for Calvin's brilliance. But the pastor reminds them that their needs can be met just as well (if not so elegantly) when the preaching fits the level of the whole body. Having remarked on the fault of the learned, Calvin is equally explicit about the failings of (some of) the self-acknowledged unlearned. There are people who claim to be too ignorant to understand their faith but they are sharp enough to remember, months after they loan out money, exactly how much the debtor owes them. [187] Obviously the teacher thinks these individuals are not really trying to learn what is being preached. The Biblical text on feeding the people with milk naturally lends itself to contrasting different educational levels, but in the commentary Calvin simply indicates that "a wise teacher has the responsibility of accommodating himself to the comprehension of those whom he undertakes to teach, so as to begin with first principles when instructing the weak and ignorant, and not to move any higher than they can follow." [188] The way he speaks of the educated and the simple in the sermons seems to go beyond applying the text to a general audience. It gives the sense that Calvin was very much aware that the people before him had quite different levels of intellectual preparation for listening, and the majority needed the long explanations which bored the small number of learned.

---

[186] Ms.fr 26, sermon #16, f129a: "Comme si quelcun est desja assez robuste pour cheminer et qu'il y ayt ung petit enfant, quand je seray au milieu si je prens la main du petit enfant et que je me conforme à luy pour ce que je luy ferois rompre et les jambes et le col avec si je le voulois par trop efforcer. Si l'aultre se plainct pour dire, 'Et je marcherois plus viste si je voulois.' Ouy, mais regarde la compagnie. Ainsi donc apprenons de nous supporter en telle sorte que nous puyssions faire nostre proffit de la doctrine quand elle ne nous sera point distribuee selon nostre capacité, que nous cognoissions que la plus part sont encores rudes et fragiles."

[187] Ms.fr 26, sermon #16, f130a: "'Je n'ay point esté à l'eschole et puis j'ay ung esprit si pezant et si lourd que ceste pitié.' Mais ilz ne laisseront point d'avoir beaucoup de finesses, ilz ne se laisseront pas tromper s'ilz ont à faire ung compte de cent florins de deniers à deniers, de fortz à fortz ou de quartz à quartz, ilz ne se tromperont jamais et au bout d'ung mois ou de quatre si on leur ramentoit ilz sçauront tousjours bien trouver leur compte. Mais quand se vient à la doctrine de salut ilz ne cognoissent rien."

[188] *The First Epistle... to the Corinthians*, pp. 65-66, on 1 Cor. 3:2. OC 49:347.

Genevans and Refugees

A second kind of diversity which comes to expression in the sermons is geographic; or rather, it is clear that in December 1555 Calvin knew that he was addressing not only Genevans but also religious refugees from lands under the papal church. In the passage 1 Cor. 3:13-15 Paul speaks of the day which will reveal how each person builds on the foundation of Christ which his preaching has laid: whether with gold, silver, and fine stone, or wood, hay, and stubble. He also names the fire which will test each building. This text was traditionally used to support the doctrine of purgatory. Calvin naturally rejects that idea. The fire is not a test of human actions to determine whether they are good or bad but it is God's way of testing teaching to determine whether it is true or false. In the commentary he refers to the day of testing without giving a temporal identification, though he says that it is will be "in [God's] own time."[189] In the sermons, however, the preacher rejoices in his own age as a time when the false teaching of the traditional church has been tested and is being burned away. Contrasting the situation "fifty years ago" with the present, he exults that the light of the gospel is now known.[190]

In this context, when Calvin goes on to speak of how a person might remain faithful even while living under the Roman church, it is almost certain that the refugees would have known that the preacher was particularly addressing them. Religious exiles from France, England, and Italy knew that there were people of faith at home who had been enlightened by the gospel but could not leave their places. Some refugees might have rejoiced that Calvin recognized and celebrated that fidelity with them. Others no doubt thought that their own exile placed them higher than those whom they had left behind, and made their faith better. The preacher first refers to the passage in 1 Kings 19:18 in which God tells Elijah that there are seven thousand in Israel who have not knelt to Baal. It is likely that he is reminding the refugee exiles in Geneva not to think that they are the only people of faith. The preacher goes on to affirm that there are (some) faithful where there is no visible sign of the church.[191]

---

[189] *The First Epistle... to the Corinthians*, p. 76, on 1 Cor. 3:13. OC 49:355.

[190] Ms.fr 26, sermon #20, f165b: "Et de faict qui eust esperé jamais qu'on eust eu une clarté si grande comme aujourd'huy elle nous est offerte? Il y a cinquante ans que la theologie qu'on enseignoit pour lors estoit pour ravir ceulx qui en ouyoient parler. Or il n'avoit qu'ung petit nombre de gens qui en eussent cognoissance et ceulx là estoient appelez messieurs noz maistres et sembloit qu'ilz eussent esté comme raviz par dessus les nues. Toutesfois qu'on regarde ce qu'ilz ont dict et on trouvera des resveries si lourdes que jamais on ne pourroit croire qu'il y eust jamais eu de telles sottises au monde."

[191] Ms.fr 26, sermon #20, f165a: "Comme nous voyons qu'Elie en a esté de son temps, les choses estoient en telle dissippation que luy pensoit estre seul en l'eglise de Dieu. Il est vray qu'il luy est

And so now, when it happens that things are torn apart (as we have well deserved) and when God sends us terrible confusion: those who have dwelt in integrity will always now have the light of the sun [i.e., the gospel] to be well guided. Like those who are in the papacy. Behold a person who is faithful to God; he lives in this cave of hell. Now, even though there is nothing there but lies, tricks and errors still one who has known the truth of the gospel will withdraw apart, he will withdraw and separate himself from the abominations of Satan and dedicate himself, body and soul to God. In the midst of darkness that person does not cease to be illuminated as in full midday.[192]

Here Calvin celebrates the knowledge of the gospel which has been brought back to light after so long. He almost certainly had Luther and other Protestants in mind, but given the reference to "fifty years" he probably included Erasmus and Lefèvre d'Etaples and other earlier Biblical scholars. He also recognizes that individuals can hear their call into the visible church even in the midst of "the cave" of Rome. To the various refugees, these words from the pulpit may have been both comfort and challenge: comfort as they thought about friends and relatives at home, and challenge as they weighed the choice they had made to leave. Calvin's next words about not following the blind into darkness would have offered some reassurance about their exile: just because it was possible to live faithfully under the Roman Church did not mean one should plunge into that situation.[193]

The pastor was aware, however, that most of his hearers were Genevans, and at least once he seems to appeal to their memory of the beginning of the reform in their city. In explaining 1 Cor. 3:10 on the foundation laid by Paul on which his

---

respondu que Dieu en avoit encores reservé sept mille mais tant y a que si nous regardons l'estat du peuple d'Israel pour lors il estoit comme ruyné, il n'y avoit plus nulle apparance d'eglise. Or Elie ne laissoit pas toutesfois d'aller son chemin. Ainsi en sont les aultres fidelles car ilz estoient esclairez, ilz avoient le jour au milieu des tenebres."

192 Ms.fr 26, sermon #20, f165a-165b: "Et ainsi maintenant quand il adviendroit que les choses seroient dissippees comme nous le meritons bien, et que Dieu nous envoyast d'horribles confusions, ceulx qui demoureroient en leur integrité auroient tousjours maintenant la clarté du soleil pour estre bien conduictz, comme ceulx qui sont en la papaulté. Voila ung homme qui sera fidelle à Dieu, il habite en ceste caverne d'enfer. Or combien que là il n'y ayt que mensonges, tromperies et erreurs, toutesfois celuy qui aura cogneu que c'est de la verité de l'evangile se retire à part, il se recueille et se separe des abominations de Satan et se dedie à Dieu corps et ame, celuy là au milieu des tenebres il ne laisse pas d'estre esclairé comme en plain midi."

193 Ms.fr 26, sermon #20, f165b: "Mais tant y a qu'il ne fault point qu'on s'abuse à ce qu'on void pour dire, 'Et comment chacun faict ainsi?' 'Et comment chacun?' Voire mais voila de povres aveugles qui vont en tenebres et les veulx tu suyvre?"

successors must build, Calvin gives a negative example of a proud mason who insists on tearing up a good foundation before working on a cathedral just so that he can say that he has both started and finished the building.[194] Then he moves from his imagined story to concrete Genevan history and alludes to how he faithfully followed Paul's instructions to build on the work of those who first taught the Gospel.

> What would have happened when we came here if [we] had wanted to destroy everything? (As there are rogues in our time who have wanted to do, so that it was necessary to fight vigorously against them.) Now if through empty glory or ambition I had said: "We have to start a new building here." What would that have been except serving the devil? And finally, what would have become of the Church of Geneva?[195]

This anonymous reference to the work of Farel and Viret in establishing "the gospel" would have been clear to most Genevans, as the preacher expressed his respect for his pioneering senior colleagues. Calvin's personal autobiographical comments in public contexts such as the pulpit can almost be counted on the fingers of one hand, so although very brief, this instance of the preacher using himself as an example to clarify a text is worth remarking. For present purposes, however, this respectful reference to the first Protestant preachers can be seen as an appeal to those Genevans who remembered the beginning of the reform and as a means to confirm their pastor's own obedience to Paul's teaching. Naturally, in the commentary on this same verse there is no mention of this local history. The allusion to their own story serves nicely to illustrate the preacher's claim that his words were meant for specific hearers.

---

[194] Ms.fr 26, sermon #19, f155a-b: "Si ung masson par envye ou pour se faire valloir ne daignoit mectre / la main à l'ouvraige quand il verroit ung beau fondement et bon et bien posé, sinon qu'il remue toutes les pierres et qu'il face nouveau mourtier et qu'il donne nouvelle forme afin de dire c'est celuy là qui a commencé et accomply, c'est luy qui a faict toute la besogne. Et si ung masson consumera l'argent de celuy qui l'employe, et puis il le retardera qu'il ne soit point logé. Et ainsi voila Dieu qui declaire que par la predication de l'evangile son temple est basty et quand il envoye gens qui sont pour avancer sa verité il dict qu'ilz sont les maistres massons qui commencent. Or des aultres viendront et rien ne leur plairra, et pourquoy? O il fault qu'ilz soient les premiers et qu'est ce à dire sinon de tout pervertir?"

[195] Ms.fr 26, sermon #19, f155b. "Qu'eust on gaigné quand nous sommes venus icy, qu'on eust volu tout ruyner, comme il s'est trouvé des canailles qui l'ont volu faire de nostre temps tellement qu'il a fallu bataillee vertueusement à l'encontre? Or si par vayne gloire ou par ambition j'eusse dict, il fault commencer icy ung nouveau bastiment, et qu'eust ce esté sinon servir au diable? Et en la fin que fust ce de l'eglise de Geneve?"

Traditional Religious Language and Explanations

Another approach to delineating Calvin's audience can be found in the ways his sermons reveal what level of religious knowledge he expected would be understood. What kind of more "academic" language does he employ, especially when he does not appear to explain it? One example is the phrase "inferior means," used three times within these eight sermons. In discussing the use of eloquence in proclaiming the gospel (1 Cor. 2:12-13), Calvin denies that this gift has to obscure God's grace, but he says that "people always abuse the inferior means." He goes on to add that God "wants His power to be recognized above all the inferior means which He gives us." [196] Similarly, regarding the role of pastors (1 Cor. 3:5) Calvin affirms that God could do without "inferior means" but chooses to use human preaching. [197] It may be that he thought the context would convey the meaning. However, this assumption that hearers will understand a learned "tag" contrasts somewhat with the preacher's reference to the "grace of meriting." Calvin reminds his hearers that "the papists... have another error which they call the state of grace of meriting, that if a person is worthy to be received because of his good works, God acknowledges him as one of His own." [198] Evidently this scholastic definition about grace and merit was not something the preacher expected all his hearers to know, although he anticipated that they would understand when he briefly explained or recalled it to them.

Somewhat more subtle is the way that Calvin draws on the traditional language of piety while giving it a different sense, apparently confident that his hearers would know the familiar terms and grasp the changed nuance. This is particularly visible in the sermons just before and just after the celebration of the Lord's Supper; these echo with "sacrificial" language while simultaneously the context redefines the traditional Mass terminology. The timing of what is said in these two sermons is no accident. In 1555 the Nativity was celebrated on Sunday, Dec. 22. The practice of *lectio continua* was interrupted for this observance so Calvin's

---

[196] Ms.fr 26, sermon #14, f114b: "Et comme les hommes abusent tousjours des moyens inferieurs." f115a: "Nostre Seigneur veult que sa vertu soit cogneue par dessus tous les moyens inferieurs qu'il nous donne."

[197] Ms.fr 26, sermon #17, f137b: "Sans aulcun moyen inferieur mais il a volu que l'evangile se presche, que nous soyons enseignez et il a constituez les homes à cela."

[198] Ms.fr 26, sermon #14, f113b: "Voila comme les papistes parlent, ... ilz ont une aultre erreur qu'ilz appellent estat de grace de meriter que si ung homme est digne par ses bonnes oeuvres d'estre receu, Dieu l'advoue des siens." It is not absolutely clear whether Calvin refers to condign or congruent grace, but in either case the problem was the human being claiming to merit acceptance by God.

sermons on 1 Corinthians skip from Sunday afternoon Dec. 15 to Sunday afternoon Dec. 22. The week before any celebration of the Supper there was an exhortation to the congregation to prepare for the sacrament; in this case that day fell on the afternoon of the 15th. Thus, the two sermons which cover 1 Cor. 3:8-16 happen to form a parenthesis around the Supper. Although the Biblical text does not refer to the sacrament or sacrifice, the language of sacrifice appears in the sermon on the afternoon of Dec. 15, the designated day for preparing for the Lord's Supper. Here Calvin clearly explains the nature of the right kind of sacrifice.

> It is to offer [God] voluntary sacrifices without being forced or cons-
> trained; to obey Him purely; and in that, all the devotions of the world
> must be destroyed, for all that God asks is that we be taught to conform
> our lives to His word... [199]

Here the "devotions of the world" include everything humanly devised, meaning in this context papal ceremonies. It is notable that Calvin does not refer to the sacrifice of the Mass directly, which suggests that he did not think explicit polemic was needed. It was enough to define the right sacrifice of free obedience to God according to the teaching of God's word.

The following Sunday afternoon, Dec. 22, after the morning's celebration of the Lord's Supper, the text was 1 Cor. 3:16, which refers to believers as God's temple. Calvin describes that as "where He may be served and adored as is right, and the where 'spiritual hosts' [*hostie spiritual*] which He asks may be sacrificed to Him." [200] The word "hostie" means "victim" or sacrifice, but its traditional use to name the consecrated bread of the Mass makes this language significant. The Protestant preacher carefully qualifies this "host" with the word "spiritual" and locates it in the exposition of right teaching and obedience to God's word which happens in the church (the gathered people, not the building). The prayer at the end of this sermon echoes this thought of "offering [God] the sacrifices of praise

---

[199] Ms.fr 26, sermon #18, f149b: "Et ainsi retenons qu'il ne nous fault point estre inutiles quand Dieu envoye ainsi des laboureurs pour nous cultiver. Et que le fruict que nous luy appourtons ne doibt point estre amer, mais qu'il doibt estre tel qu'il le demande, c'est de luy offrir sacrifices volontaires sans estre forcez ne contrainctz à luy obeir purement. Et en cela toutes les devotions du monde doibvent estre abbattues car tout ce que Dieu demande c'est que nous soyons enseignez de conformer nostre vie à sa parolle."

[200] Ms.fr 26, sermon #19, 155b: "Que ceulx qui leur succedent regardent de ne se point complaire en leurs phantaisies mais de poursuyvre tousjours afin que l'eglise de Dieu s'avance et qu'il habite en ung lieu et qu'il ayt là son temple dressé où il soit servy et adoré comme il appartient et qu'on luy sacrifie les hosties spirituelles qu'il demande."

which He asks from us."[201] It appears that Genevans were sufficiently accustomed to speaking of "the bread of the Supper" (even though the actual wafer still looked rather like the old "host"[202]) that Calvin could use "spiritual host" for faithful worship and obedience according to the right teaching of God's word, without explicit polemic against the Mass. Since this was a Supper Sunday, he was drawing on the resonance of the traditional words with a changed referent. Particularly the religious refugees might hear the contrast with the papal contexts from which they had recently come.

Religious Anxieties and Continuing Education

Although members of his congregation brought different intellectual backgrounds, Calvin knew that they shared many common religious experiences. The older adults and the immigrants from Catholic lands had grown up in the traditional Roman theology and many people were still in greater or lesser contact with those who followed the pope. This meant that much of Calvin's preaching wove together instruction in what he understood to be the true meaning of the Biblical text, with pastoral and polemical concerns about its application. The polemic is obvious. Here the point is identifying the pastoral purpose.

One of the issues which Calvin addresses at greater length in the sermons than in the commentary regards the certainty of salvation. The preacher seems to believe that his hearers are troubled by a terrible anxiety about their salvation. One theme he repeatedly addresses is the gift of faith: trusting in God alone and no human free will or meritorious work. As he explains 1 Cor. 2, particularly verses 10-13 regarding the gift of the Holy Spirit who enables God's children to understand the gifts God gives them, Calvin contrasts what he means about the gift of faith with what his congregation would have been taught as children in the Roman Church.

> Faith is not an opinion, as the papists imagine; or even some persuasion that there is a God and that we must fear and honor Him. But it is that we are fully assured that He loves us, in such a way that we may come to Him and seek there all our good, and we may not ask anything except to belong to Him, seeing that it is the height and fullness of all happiness for us to be joined to Him… The entrance to salvation is by faith.[203]

---

[201] Ms.fr 26, sermon #19, f160b. "que nous luy servions de vrays temples où il soit adoré non point en feintise mais en telle integrité que nous luy offrions les sacrifices de louange qu'il demande de nous."

[202] See Grosse, *Les rituels de la Cène*, p. 28.

[203] Ms.fr 26, sermon #13, f106a-b: "Et ainsi nous voyons ce qu'emporte la foy. Ce n'est pas une opinion comme les papistes imaginent, ou bien quelque persuasion qu'on ayt qu'il y a ung Dieu

As Calvin goes on to repeat, God "wanted to give us an infallible certainty," a certainty of faith which is the special gift of illumination from on high, and which "we will not have [...] until God gives it to us."[204] The preacher acknowledges that certainty is not a new idea but the Roman teaching has made it an act of hubris to claim such a thing.

> For when the papists speak of faith they say rightly that it must be certain, but still they want each person to remain in suspense because it is presumptuous (they think) for people to assure themselves that they are in God's grace.[205]

Calvin flatly insists that God intends for the faithful to be certain that they have been received into God's grace, and this assurance extends even beyond death.

> [T]he certainty of which Paul speaks extends through the whole course of this life and beyond death. That is also indeed against what the papists say that people cannot be assured of final perseverance, because they think that, if people ought to be in doubt, they should never be assured about what their end will be.[206]

---

et qu'il le fault craindre et honnorer, mais c'est que nous soyons pleinement certifiez qu'il nous ayme, voire en telle sorte que nous venions à luy et que nous cerchions là tout nostre bien et que nous ne demandions sinon d'y adherer, veu que c'est le comble et la plenitude de toute felicité que nous soyons conjoinctz à luy puis qu'il contient tous biens en soy. Maintenant donc nous voyons ce que nous avons à noter de ce passage du prophete Isaye mais il fault venir plus oultre si nous voulons faire nostre proffit de ceste doctrine. Car nous avons veu que les hommes ne de leur veue ny de leur ouye ny de toute leur intelligence et raison ne peuvent parvenir aux secretz de Dieu, ilz n'ont mesme nul approche. Et que sera ce maintenant: nous sommes forcloz de toute esperance de salut.[106b] Or l'ouverture nous en est faicte par foy."

[204] Ms.fr 26, sermon #14, f109a: "Dieu nous a volu retirer de toutes ces vanitez qui sont en l'oppinion humaine et nous a volu donner une certitude infallible." 110b-111a: "Et en premier lieu il monstre que nous pourrions avoir toute la sagesse qu'il est possible de soubhaiter mais nous n'aurons point certitude de foy jusqu'à tant que Dieu nous la donne et qu'il ayt mis ceste signature en noz cueurs."

[205] Ms.fr 26, sermon #14, f113b: "Quand les papistes parlent de la foy ilz diront bien qu'elle doibt estre certaine mais si veullent ilz qu'ung checun demeure en suspend pour ce que c'est presomption si leur semble de s'asseurer qu'on soit en la grace de Dieu, qu'ung homme se dise estre en estat de grace et quel orgueil? Voila comme les papaistes parlent."

[206] Ms.fr 26, sermon #14, f114a: "Concluons donc que la certitude dont il parle s'estend jusques tout au long du cours de ceste vie et oultre la mort. Et c'est aussi bien contre ce que les papistes ont gazouillé que les hommes ne se peuvent point asseurer de la perseverance finale. Car ilz concluend que si les hommes doibvent estre en doubte qu'ilz ne doibvent point aussi estre asseurez que ce sera d'eulx en la fin."

The polemic rings in a familiar way. The Biblical text invites attention to the question of faith and certainty, of course, but the emphasis which Calvin gives the subject suggests that this is one of those points he believes must be said over and over, even if that repetition annoys the handful of learned hearers. In the next sermon he elaborates on the Holy Spirit's work, reminding the people that God has a double way of Self-revelation: through the word and through the Spirit. The word which is preached must be made effective by the Spirit, who works both illumination and conviction-sealing, both understanding and certainty. [207] Calvin's characteristic theological emphases echo through this passage. Later, in explaining 1 Cor. 3:11, he returns to the definition of the certitude of faith in a way which clearly connects this instruction with his concern to reach every listener, including the ones who need their theology in simple (pre-digested) form.

> I will take a definition not from books but [use] a rough expression, because now it is a question of chewing the matter so that each may know what is required of us. So faith is a certainty we have about the truth of God, in order that we may know that He is our Father, He has adopted us as His children, that we know how to trust in Him and know also how we ought to call upon Him, and also how we ought to serve and honor Him: That is what faith means. And where do we find all of that? In Jesus Christ. [208]

Calvin goes on to repeat that "it is not enough to have the letter, that is, that we know what God requires, but the principal point is that we are renewed by the Holy Spirit" whom we receive "by participation in the resurrection of our Savior

---

[207] Ms.fr 26, sermon #15, f120a: "C'est asçavoir quand les fidelles sont illuminez de l'esprit de Dieu non seulement ilz recepvent en obeissance la doctrine de l'evangile mais ilz y sont arrestez, ilz ont une foy qui est tellement resolue que si puis apres on tasche à les debauscher, qu'on leur presente cecy ou cela, ilz rejectent tout, voire sçaichant bien qu'il n'y a qu'une pure verité et simple. Et c'est ce que dict nostre Seigneur Jesus Christ au 10.ᵉ chapistre de S[ainct] Jehan, que les brebis oyent la voix du pasteur et ce pendant rejectent celle des estrangiers." #15, f121a: "S [ainct] Paul dict que l'homme spirituel juge tout. En somme cognoissons que maintenant si Dieu nous a revelé sa volonté par sa parolle, et que ce n'est point seulement pour ce qu'elle nous est presché mais qu'il l'aura seelee en noz cueurs par son S[ainct] Esprit, qu'il aura esclairé noz ames tellement que nous comprendrons ce qu'il nous a envoyé."

[208] Ms.fr 26, sermon #19, f156b: "J'en prendray une definition non point des livres mais grossierement pour ce que maintenant il est question de mascher les choses afin que chacun en apprenne ce qui nous sera requis. La foy donc est une certitude que nous avons de la verité de Dieu afin que nous cognoissions qu'il est nostre pere, qu'il nous a adoptez pour ses enfans, que nous sçachons comme il nous fault fier en luy, que nous sçachons comme nous le debvons invocquer, que nous sçachons aussi comme nous le debvons servir et honnorer. Voila qu'emporte la foy. Or où est ce que nous trouverons tout cela? En Jesus Christ."

Jesus Christ."[209] The echoes of the *Institutes'* famous definition are obvious: faith is certain knowledge of God's good will to us based on the truth of the freely given promises in Christ, illuminated in our minds and sealed on our hearts by the Holy Spirit (3.2.7). However, here Calvin pre-chews the theological food into a form that every listener can understand. Then he adds a polemical note about "the stupidity" of the Roman claims for Peter as the foundation of the church… What kind of certainty can a mortal and unstable man be?[210] The preacher seems to feel no need to explain the papal claim (Matt. 16:18), but simply recalls and ridicules it.

The central importance of assurance of salvation and the gift of faith for Calvin are seen not only in the repetition of this teaching but also by contrast with some other traditional doctrines which he apparently did not regard as much of a problem for his hearers. When preaching on the fire which will test all that humans build (1 Cor. 3:13-15), Calvin spends some energy disputing the traditional Roman use of this passage to support the doctrine of purgatory, but his tone is a combination of academic and ironic. The exegesis may well have interested his learned hearers, but the exposition does not suggest that anxiety about purgatory lingered among the Genevans. The point which would probably have connected with many of his congregation was the anti-clerical humor. The preacher sarcastically indicates that, if this text were a proof of purgatory, only clergy would go there… Why? Because in this passage Paul is not talking about all the faithful but about ministers and the kinds of teaching which they build upon the foundation of Christ. The fire will test all teaching and burn up what is wrong.[211] So the hearers are left to choose between Calvin's explanation that

---

[209] Ms.fr 26, sermon #19, f157a: "Ce n'est point assez d'avoir la lettre, c'est à dire que nous sçachions que Dieu demande, mais le princippal est que nous soyons renouvellez par son S[ainct] Esprit. Or comment obtiendrons nous ce S[ainct] Esprit? Quand nous participperons à la resurrection de nostre Seigneur Jesus Christ. Nous voyons maintenant que toutes les parties de nostre foy sont en Jesus Christ."

[210] Ms.fr 26, sermon #19, f157b: "Nous voyons quelle bestise c'est en la papauté d'alleguer que S[ainct] Pierre est le fondement de l'eglise: 'Car sur ceste pierre j'edifieray mon eglise.' Et quelle est ceste pierre là? Ilz entendent ung homme mortel et caducque que despuis a renoncé Jesus Christ, et nous sçavons qu'il estoit du tout desesperé, car si Jesus Christ ne l'eust receu à mercy qu'estoit ce? Voila ung fondement qui est bien ferme. Et puis d'aultre part il a tasché d'empecher la redemption du genre humain: 'Ja n'advienne (dict il), Seigneur, que tu t'esposes ainsi à la mort, il te fault espargner.' Voire, que Jesus Christ s'espargne, et pourquoy? Pour nous laisser tous en damnation eternelle."

[211] Ms.fr 26, sermon #20, f163b: "Icy S[ainct] Paul a parlé du fondement qui doibt estre en l'eglise, c'est asçavoir de nostre Seigneur Jesus Christ. Or les papistes ont tellement falsifié les motz de S[ainct] Paul* [* margin = du purgatoyre] qu'ilz ont fondé leur purgatoire cy dessus. Car il n'y a ung seul mot ny sillabe en l'escripture saincte qui soit pour approuver le purgatoire sinon ce qu'ilz en ont pretendu en ce lieu. Or regardons quelle apparence il y a, ilz disent 'le feu

the fire tests teaching and not people, and the implications of the traditional interpretation of the verse which would lead to the conclusion that purgatory is reserved for priests! One can imagine that the people in the pews on this day may have sat up in surprise. Whether or not they needed the reassurance of the Holy Spirit and faith, they probably thought this was a good joke on the clergy and were unlikely to have found the sermon boring.

Objections to Calvin's Preaching

Negative reactions to Calvin's preaching naturally appeared when certain ones of his hearers protested against what he said. Most often they took exception to criticisms which they believed were false and/or a personal affront. Here the purpose is not to make a full summary, much less an exhaustive list, but only to provide a few examples. In his study of the reform in Geneva, Lambert cites a number of cases, pointing out that Genevans were divided; one reason that some of the objections became known was because fellow worshipers took the Calvin's critics to task. [212]

The case of Amyed Alliod the baker whose protest led to a disturbance at St. Gervais on Sunday afternoon March 28, 1546, demonstrates one of the better documented instances. Leaving the church (on Sunday afternoons probably several weeks before) Calvin had seen many people of St. Gervais relaxing in the streets [213] and the next week he rebuked them from the pulpit. This particular afternoon things heated up when the "guest" preacher defended his earlier remarks. Alliod took great exception to this, and something he said led to a disruption of the service and thus to the courts. On Monday March 29 the investigation began by deposing the main witness, Pierre Poyent (probably from the parish of La Magdeleine). [214] Poyent summarized what had happened:

---

approuvera' et bien, est ce le feu de purgatoire? Et puis 'il sera sauvé, mais comme par le feu.' Or il ne fauldroit sinon les prescheurs qui allassent en purgatoire, car S[ainct] Paul ne traite point icy de tous fidelles."

[212] Lambert, *Preaching, Praying, and Policing*, pp. 367-90, for discussion of responses to sermons; one perhaps tongue-in-cheek criticism (p. 380) is by a man who said that the ministers preached many things which are not in scripture, such as the pope (evidently meaning that the pope is not in the Bible); pp. 384-88 for example of one hearer rebuking another.

[213] PC series 2, #695. testimony dated April 1, 1546, page 3: "....dimenche passé estant de vespres au sermon à sainct gervais et estant là le Sr. Jehan Calvin avoit presché qui avoit vheu passé par le bour de feur trois centz bestes." This example was copied from the Procès Criminels records in the Archives d'Etat de Genève, October 2013.

[214] Pierre Poyent or Payan, was from Vaucluse in Provence ; he had come to Geneva about 1539, was admitted as bourgeois on Nov. 28, 1541, and married the daughter of Furjod du Molard

"The preacher said that 'he had come to maintain what he had said before and not to explain, because he was not preaching what came from himself but from the word of God.'" [215] (Obviously this was not the first occasion of criticizing the people of St. Gervais, and Calvin was offering a defense rather than an apology for what he had previously said.) Poyent continued his testimony, identifying the substance of the preacher's remarks: "When he [Calvin] was coming out of preaching, he found 'more than a hundred, indeed more than three hundred who resembled beasts [rather than people] because they made no account of coming to the sermon to hear the word of God.'" Poyent recounted that when Alliod heard this from the pulpit, he said in a loud voice: "It is not true, we are not beasts," which greatly scandalized the witnesses and others. Then after the sermon Alliod came and talked to Poyent (apparently seated next to him in the church) and others, saying: "You were murmuring, but don't worry, you know well he is only a foreigner." [216] (Was Alliod implying that Poyent was anxious about the uproar, and so he patronizingly reassured his neighbor that Calvin was not a citizen and therefore negligible?)

On Tuesday March 30, it was Alliod's turn. [217] According to his story, he spoke quietly in the ear of Pierre: "Alas, we are not beasts," adding that he said this

---

and evidently lived near the latter. His first appearance before the consistory, March 2, 1542, seemed routine, verifying his recent marriage and his knowledge of the faith; since he is simply told to continue to live well according to the word of God, his examination was obviously satisfactory; *Consist.* I, pp. 9, 10. The second appearance, on May 24, 1547, seems to have been as witness for the behavior of his in-laws; *Consist.* III, pp. 101, 108. Alliod identifies him as "pierre le couroyeur deriers la magdalene," PC series 2, #695, March 30, 1546, page 2.

[215] PC series 2, #695 testimony dated March 29, 1546, p. 1: Pierre Poyent's textimony: "par son serment esté vray que hier que fust dimenche 28 au temple de Sainct Gervaix ainsi que monsieur Calvin prechoyt sus le vespres et en son sermon menoyt les ca[n]ticques de moyse et certain passaiges, leurs faissant les remonstrances que ilz (!) estoyt là venuz pour maintenir ce que auparavant ilz avoit prescher et que non pour ce declaré car ilz ne preschoyt point de soyt mesme meis ce qu'estoyt de Dieu." (Throughout this section the plural "ilz" is used for Calvin; it is marked only the first time.)

[216] PC series 2, #695 testimony dated March 29, 1546, p. 1: Pierre Poyent: "Disant que alors quant ilz (!) preschoy que en sortant ilz avoit trouver plus de cent voyre troys centz qui resembloyent plus bestes d'aultant que ne faissoyent conte de venir à la predication et ouyr la parolle de Dieu. [then Alliod said] à aulte voix devant chastungs ilz n'est pas vray et si ne sommes nous point bestes. Surquoy led[ict] tesmoings et plussieurs aultres ayant ouoyt lesdictes parolles furent grandement scandallizé. ... touteffois que apres lid[ict] serment led[ict] Amyed vient à prendre à parolles led[ict] tesmoings, luy disant c'este toy que murmeroient mes ne te chaille, toy sçay bien que ce n'est que ung extroigner.'"

[217] PC series 2 #695 testimony dated March 30, 1546: The Senate states the case as they know it: "interogué si ainsy que spectable Maistre Jehan Calvin preschoit le dimanche xxviiie du present mois à sainct gervaix et en son sermon menoit les cantiques de moise et certains passaiges leur

"because the said Calvin had already made three sermons about the people of St. Gervais." Alliod denied that he had said: "It is not true." He claimed that what happened was that when he spoke quietly to Poyent the latter cried out loudly: "Go speak to Master Calvin yourself, go correct him, you others of St. Gervais." Then there was a "great tumult" and Alliod told Poyent after the sermon: "It was not well done of you to want to make a tumult in the middle of the sermon. I will make the report to Messieurs [the Senate] myself."[218] Clearly Alliod wanted to blame Poyent for the uproar. The incident ended up in the Procès Criminels, where Alliod was identified as being responsible for the problem and eventually punished. It is difficult to ascertain the rights of the story. Evidently, however, even though Calvin was not everyone's favorite preacher, the council would not allow a public tumult in worship. One thing which is notable here is the division among the members of the congregation. Pierre Poyent was from Greater Geneva and must have been strongly attached to Calvin's preaching because he had evidently followed him across the city to hear the afternoon sermon. He distanced himself from the people of St. Gervais and objected to Alliod's actions as an attack on his pastor.

The ordinary people were not the only ones who did not like some of what Calvin said; on a considerable number of occasions he was rebuked by the Senate. One example may suffice here. On Monday, July 9, 1548, Calvin was called to account for his sermon the previous day; this was the period of the battles over baptismal names. He himself was accused of talking about a certain "crusade" and the fact that someone had defaced the Psalm listed to be sung. The pastor who had preached at St. Gervais in the afternoon had accused the "enfants de Genève" of wanting to bring down the gospel and chase out the ministers. (Evidently on that Sunday afternoon Calvin was not at St. Gervais.) The Senate

---

faisant les remonstrances qu'il estoit là venu pour maintenir ce que au paravant il avoyt presché et non pour ce desdure car il ne preschoit point de soy mesmes mais ce qui estoit de dieu et si ainsy que led. Alliod disoit que en sortant il avoyt trouvé plus de cent voire trois cens qui ressembloyent plus bestes d'aultant quilz ne faisoyent compte// de venir au sermon et aouir la parolle de dieu."

218 PC series 2, #695 testimony dated March 30, 1546, p. 3: "Lequel a dict et respondu que ainsy que led spectable Calvin preschoit avyant qu'il appelloit bestes dist tout bellement et à basse voix en l'aureille de pierre le couroyeur deriers la magdalene, helas nous ne somme pas bestes, disant qu'il dist cela par ce que led Calvin avoit desja faict trois sermons sur ceulx de sainct gervais, disant n'avoir point dict il n'est pas vray, disant que ainsy qu'il hont dict lesdz. parolles aud. couroyeur icelluy couroyeur es cria à haulte voix, 'allez parler à monsieur Calvin, allez le corriger vous aultres de sainct gervaix,' [et fust gros tumulte et c].... Disant d'avantaige ded. Alliod que appres le sermon il dis aud. couroyeur, 'ce n'est pas bien faict à vous de voulloir esmouvoir ung tumulte au meillieu du sermon, j'en feray le rappport à messieurs mes seigneurs."

called both ministers to remonstrate with them, saying they should bring problems of insults to the council first and only preach about them if the Senate did not act. However, the council also promised to investigate and punish the person who had defaced the Psalm.[219] The following week, July 16, the discussion of this complaint continued. The Senate tried to calm matters and ordered both accusers and ministers to acknowledge each other as "gens de bien" (honorable people) but Calvin refused. He in turn explained that in his reference to a crusade he had not meant something like the papal crusade. He was objecting to the party badges ("marques et enseygnes") that groups had taken up (and were wearing) without the Senate's permission, which Calvin said would lead to divisions between those who wore them and those who did not. As for bringing all the insults to the Senate first, he objected that this would require witnesses and legal processes and they should let him carry out his office freely; in this case, however, he wanted redress for the calumny. The record ends with the Senate again ordering an act of reconciliation… apparently more successfully now that their angry preacher had had his say.[220] Obviously being members of Calvin's congregation was often as trying as it was edifying…

Publishing Calvin's Sermons

There were a significant number of people, however, who were deeply impressed by Calvin the preacher and eager to share the riches heard from his pulpit. The publication of the reformer's sermons began as the special project of particular individuals who personally valued what they were hearing and believed it was important that others should have access to it. Before examining who these people were and why they made the considerable effort to get the reformer's sermons into print, it may be useful to give an overview of what was published. An appendix will provide the full story, including reprints and translations. Here it is only the first editions which will be noted. For this, a major "merci beaucoup" is in order. Any discussion of the publication of Calvin's corpus must begin by acknowledging a great debt to Rodophe Peter and Jean-François Gilmont, the editors of the *Bibliotheca Calviniana, Ecrits théologiques, littéraires et juridiques,* volumes which meticulously catalogue every printing of these texts (though not such items as Psalters), and provide wonderful notes. As will be clear in what follows, these scholars have been sure guides in the process of uncovering more about Calvin's sermons as they appeared in the sixteenth century.

---

[219] July 9, 1548, OC 21:429 (RC 42 f131).

[220] July 16, 1548, OC 21:429-30 (RC 42 f137).

The Choice of Sermons

The main focus in the early years was printing selections of sermons, a few of which had been preached on special occasions but most of which were excerpts from one or another *lectio continua* series. Most of these early sermons appeared not long after they were preached. The first were: *Two Sermons Given in the City of Geneva* (Ps. 115 and 124), preached on Nov. 4 and 11, 1545, and printed early in 1546. The next publication was the *Four Sermons Very Useful for Our Times with an Exposition of Ps. 87*, on four Psalms and Heb. 13:13, which appeared in 1552, and was the only sermon publication which Calvin himself sponsored. In 1554, the year after they were preached, the twenty-two sermons on Ps. 119 were published, and in 1555 there were two sermons on 1 Tim. 2:4-5 selected from Calvin's current Sunday series. Next, in 1557, was a book of sixteen sermons on the Ten Commandments excerpted from the recently completed series on Deuteronomy. This was followed in 1558 by *Plusieurs Sermons*, the collection of texts preached on or related to special Christological holy days (discussed above), and then the sermons on chapters ten and eleven of the First Corinthians series which had been preached several years before. In 1560-61 there were a number of selections from the two series which were Calvin's current books, Genesis and the Gospel Harmony, and some brief excerpts from the earlier series on Timothy and Isaiah. One entitled *Eighteen Sermons which unfold the History of Melchisedek and the Matter of Justification* included ten from Genesis and eight essentially on the hymns in Luke 1-2. Another, expounding the stories of Jacob and Esau, was entitled *Thirteen Sermons on God's Gratuitous Election*. Two short selections of four sermons on Isaiah chap. 38 and two on 2 Tim. 1:8-10 were published in 1560. This was followed in 1561 by a single sermon on 1 Tim. 2:9-11 and a third short excerpt from the Genesis series called *Three Sermons on Abraham's Sacrifice*.

In 1561 the big event in publishing Calvin's sermons was the printing of the first full series, the *Sermons on the Epistles to Timothy and Titus*. Soon, there were two further more-or-less complete series: all the sermons on Ephesians and the sixty-five on the Gospel Harmony which Raguenier had transcribed before his death. The one other new publication in this year was some expositions of Psalms 46 and 48 in English (of which the one on Ps. 46:1-5 is now extant only in English). In 1563 there were two new series, the sermons on Galatians and those on Job. Three more series appeared after Calvin's death: the existing sermons on Daniel in 1565 (*Forty-Seven Sermons on the Last Eight Chapters of the Prophecies of Daniel*), the whole of Deuteronomy in 1567, and a Latin translation of the sermons on First Samuel in 1604 (as with Ps. 46, the French original is no longer extant).

Calvin and His Editors, or Issues of Form and Principles of Value

The publication of his sermons was practically the project of Calvin's colleagues, although he had a small part. Here a word of explanation is necessary. As one fruit of his work on the *Bibliotheca Calviniana*, Jean-François Gilmont produced a very illuminating book, *Jean Calvin et le livre imprimé* (1997), which includes a helpful overview of the publication of the sermons. [221] Although it was prepared independently, the present essay overlaps with Prof. Gilmont's work in a number of ways. Here the focus is rather on the books in the context of historical homiletical aids, and the reception of the sermons by those who chose to publish them: how they understood their task, how they argued for it, what they believed they must explain to their audience. Thus, while this presentation has much in common with Gilmont's discussion, it is shaped by a somewhat different point of view.

One of the striking things that an overview of the reformer's published sermons brings to the fore is the fact that only one publication was sponsored by the preacher himself. When this is correlated with the observation that the set of sermons which he produced is also the only one which was edited and polished, while all the others remained in their extempore form, it is worth considering whether there is something more than a difference of form involved. In fact, one of the themes woven through the whole discussion of publication is the issue of form and the related question of what values would outweigh a poor style to tilt the balance in the direction of making public something of limited literary merit. The discussion can be divided into several parts, although in effect they are really different ways of looking at the same material. For the sake of clarity, the order here will begin with an examination of Calvin's principles as those can be discerned through what he said and did, and what his editors report about his stance on publishing his sermons.

Calvin's Part and Principles

What role did Calvin have in this enterprise? It was actually a rather small one. He himself only published the *Four Sermons*, which he had edited and revised for print with the goal of addressing the theological problem of Nicodemism.

> Although I have previously written two treatises sufficiently extensive to show that it is not allowed for a Christian who lives under the papacy, and who knows the pure doctrine of the gospel, to do anything which appears to be consent or adherence to the abuses, superstitions, and idolatries which reign there: Nevertheless every day there are people who ask me afresh for

---

[221] Jean-François Gilmont, "L'oeuvre imprimé. 5. La publication des sermons," in *Jean Calvin et le livre imprimé* (Genève: Droz, 1997), pp. 106-14.

counsel, as if I had never spoken. I understand that there are others who do not cease to make their retorts and offer subterfuges against what I have written about this. So, in order to cut short those who ask about what ought to be known and notorious, and those who think to cover themselves with a wet sack against the judgment of God [excuse themselves], I have thought it expedient to revise and put in order a sermon which I preached on this subject, of which a summary was taken down. [222]

In fact, there were four sermons and one further exposition (Ps. 87). Perhaps Calvin thought that the homiletical format, the exposition of specific Biblical texts, would reach those who ignored or seemed impervious to treatises. In any event, he not only published these in French but sponsored their translation into Latin the next year, and certainly must have approved of the Italian and English translations which appeared even before the Latin. [223]

The limited part Calvin played in publishing his sermons was owed primarily to his conception of the purposes of preaching. In principle sermons were intended for a local congregation, the proclamation of the gospel to specific people in a particular place; application should fit the hearers and different people in other places would not be well served by what was presented in Geneva. In fact, Calvin knew that what his friends wanted to print was extempore and unrevised material, which may have disturbed him (nearly) as much as offering one people's spiritual food to others. The reformer's repeatedly recorded reluctance about having such texts printed was of course a standard rhetorical ploy, but in the case of his sermons it may well have been more than that because it offended his humanist sensibilities to allow unpolished work to appear. The response of his good friend Farel to the appearance of the first two sermons on Psalms 115 and 124 must have been confirmation of this anxiety. "I much enjoyed reading your sermons, even though I wished you had set out your discourse with a little more care as you usually do. But it is enough that nothing be lacking in the meaning, even if the reading is not as pleasing as it could have been." [224] These sermons

---

[222] Calvin, OC 8:373-374.

[223] See notes in Peter & Gilmont, *Bibliotheca* I, pp. 465-66, 479. In a presentation at the Sixteenth Century Society and Conference in New Orleans, Oct. 15, 2014, entitled "Beyond the Nicodemite: the Twofold Audience of John Calvin's *Quatre Sermons* (1552)," Mr. Kenneth Woo suggested that Calvin's audience was domestic as well as French.

[224] Letter from Farel to Calvin on Feb. 25, 1546, OC 12:302: "Tes sermons me furent très agréables, bien que j'aurais voulu que tu élabores ton discours avec un peu plus de soin, comme tu en as l'habitude. Mais il suffit que rien ne manqué au sens, même si la lecture ne sera pas aussi agréable qu'elle aurait pu l'être." Quoted in Peter & Gilmont, *Bibliotheca Calviniana* I, p. 219.

were not transcribed by a trained stenographer but taken down in the traditional way by an educated listener, which makes them different from the later texts done by Raguenier. However, what both secretaries recorded was still extempore. Farel's comments may thus give an idea of what other senior colleagues probably thought about Calvin's apparent willingness to buck the tradition that texts were supposed to be edited and polished before publication, and the criticism must have reinforced his reluctance to repeat the experiment.

In fact, the custom of editing before publication applied generally, and what Calvin says about his Latin lectures can be illuminating for his vernacular sermons, even if in the case of the Latin texts his reluctance was probably mostly rhetorical. In the preface to the lectures on Hosea, the first to be published as they were transcribed by his auditors, Calvin the humanist-turned-Biblical exegete makes a clear distinction between freely spoken lectures and commentaries he either wrote or revised. Speaking from experience, he reflected that, if people criticized the texts prepared (in the study) when he had time to think and organize and make the expression concise, he anticipated being attacked as presumptuous for printing ones "more freely spoken in my [Bible] lessons according to the time and occasion." [225] Leaving aside the defensiveness, real or rhetorical, what is more important here is the fact that Calvin repeatedly made an explicit distinction between things he prepared for the press and unpolished ones that he was persuaded to allow to be printed. In this same preface the reformer goes on to explain two reasons why he had agreed to let his friends publish the lectures on Hosea. He could not refuse to allow publication unless he could promise to write a commentary himself, something he did not have time to do. Secondly, his colleagues thought he was too severe in critiquing his own works and said he was wronging the churches to deprive them of this good. [226] Whether or not he agreed about the severity, Calvin could not in good conscience refuse to do something which they were convinced would serve the church.

The preacher voiced similar reasons for giving in to pressure to publish his sermons: no time to write something better and the need of the church. Here, though, there was an additional reason for hesitation. His sermons were meant for the people in Geneva for whom he was pastor, and not for a wider audience. In correspondence with the church in Poitiers in 1555 Calvin wanted it plainly understood that he had not written out the sermons on Psalm 119 in his study

---

[225] Calvin, quoted in Peter & Gilmont, *Bibliotheca Calviniana* II, p. 622: "plus librement pronouncés en mes leçons selon que le temps et l'occasion se presentoit."

[226] Calvin, see Peter & Gilmont, *Bibliotheca Calviniana* II, p. 623. Evidently one must have some significant reason to override the custom against publishing extempore texts.

but he affirms that they give an example of "our ordinary style and fashion of teaching."[227] His pulpit expositions were emphatically products for a local audience.

Traditional Sermon Handbooks, Rhetoric, and Calvin's Preaching

A considerable number[228] – though not all[229] – of the editors who published first editions of Calvin's sermons included in their prefaces references both to the preacher's objections and an apologia for the deficiencies of style or arrangement. Sometimes this is coupled with a defense of the way in which that very simplicity made its own contribution. In part because this raises the important question of Calvin and rhetoric,[230] in part because it illuminates some of the differences which the preacher's contemporaries saw between the traditional sermon handbooks and what he was doing, it is appropriate to examine what Calvin's editors said about the form of his sermons. To identify what made their product distinctive, and worthwhile or even better, publishers of the Genevan reformer's sermons had to address at least two kinds of expectations. One was skepticism about extempore sermons. The common homiletical aid was handbooks which had been written or revised explicitly for publication, so someone presenting untraditional extempore sermons would need to acknowledge the differences of his product and demonstrate the value of such material. A second and related

---

227 For fitting it to the local scene, see below at nn.231, 233, 238, 239. Calvin's letter to Poitiers, Feb. 25, 1555, OC 15:446: "Je n'ay point escrit en chamber les vingt deux Sermons sur le Pseaulme octonaire, mais on les a imprimez naifvement come on les avoit peu recueillir de ma bouche au temple. Là vous voiez nostre style et façon ordinaire d'enseigner." Quoted in Peter & Gilmont, *Bibliotheca Calviniana* I, p. 541.

228 It seems to be the ones close to Calvin, especially the first editors, who were the most sensitive about his reluctance. See Girard, Badius, Roux, Vincent, quoted below at nn.233, 235, 238, 241. One oddity is presented by Jean de la Haize, who published the pirated sermons on Daniel. He says "l'autheur les ait supprimés et contenus, enclose et serrés comme en prison," but in his notes on this Gilmont indicates that it is very unlikely that La Haize meant Calvin himself whom he called "sainct personnage" so it was probably the deacons of the Bourse Française to whom Calvin had assigned the rights. See Peter & Gilmont, *Bibliotheca Calviniana* III, pp. 82-84.

229 A few exceptions: the anonymous preface to the *DixHuict Sermons* (Gen. & Luke) published in 1560 by Jean Bonnefoy & Etienne Anastaise says permission "il nous a accordé facilement pour l'edification de l'Eglise," OC 23:636. The anonymous preface to the Ephesians sermons in 1562 does not mention this; OC49, pp. xii-xiii. Jacques Bourgeois' preface to his edition of 3 sermons on Abraham's sacrifice of Isaac, 1561, also does not note it, Peter & Gilmont, *Bibliotheca* II, p. 866; nor does the anonymous preface to the sermons on predestination, OC 58:13-14.

230 The seminal and very influential work is Olivier Millet, *Calvin et la dynamique de la parole: étude de la rhétorique réformée* (Genève: Slatkine, 1992). However, this fine work does not really examine the sermons. The intent here is not to offer a rhetorical analysis of the latter, but simply to note what Calvin's editors explain about this question.

expectation was the humanist habit of applying classical rhetorical criteria to published works. This was an expectation Calvin himself shared, so here his editors' apologia had to function internally as well as to the larger public.

It is noteworthy that Calvin himself does not discuss the form of traditional sermon handbooks, although he does sharply criticize the content of traditional preaching. Some editors of his sermons, however, especially Conrad Badius, give repeated attention to distinguishing the work of the Genevan preacher from the products their audiences would have previously known or known about. One common way that this concern appears is by explicit contrasts between Calvin's preaching and pre-packaged sermons where "one size fits all," as Badius calls them in the preface to the Christological collection *Plusieurs Sermons*.

> [Calvin's sermons] are not ready made, or bought by the dozen, but are duly premeditated and well fitted to the capacity of his sheep, keeping the benefits of the Lord Jesus Christ always before the eyes [of the hearers] so as to engrave them vividly in their souls. They are not "common places" already digested, nor sermons which he has up his sleeve to make them serve for all passages of scripture like a shoemaker's model "one size fits all."[231]

Badius' comments make explicit the preacher's intent to fit his words to his hearers. This theme is frequently paired with an insistence on the difference between Calvin's sermons and the traditional ones. Often editors remark on the contrast between written and extempore expositions; it is sometimes a general comparison, because sermons "prepared at leisure" or "in the study" were traditionally the rule. The point appears as early as the first sermons to be published, in 1546, as Jean Girard explains in his preface.

> It is also good that people be informed that the author did not write these sermons but that we are publishing them according to what could be taken down as he spoke from the pulpit. This notice will serve two purposes: [the first is] that the reader may excuse it if matters are not expressed as precisely as one could wish and the words are not well polished, considering that these are sermons spoken once, not composed to be published to the world.[232]

Already the rhetorical issues which would become more prominent later appear here. The contrast between written and extempore sermons is still explicit in

---

[231] Badius, *Plusieurs Sermons*, OC 35:587-588.

[232] Girard, OC 32:549-552.

Jacques Roux's preface to the sermons on Isaiah 38 published in 1562, near the end of Calvin's life.

> I present to you [Hezekiah's song] with its true explanation, faithfully drawn from the sermons of John Calvin, loyal minister of Jesus Christ, as he preached them publicly, without anything being added or taken away. However I confess that I did not get his permission to publish without great difficulty, as also all who know him personally will easily recognize, since they know well that he has only wanted to serve the flock which God has committed to him, by teaching them in a familiar (accessible) way, and he has not wanted to make Homilies at his leisure to set before the eyes of the whole world. [233]

Despite Calvin's focus on his own flock, his editors seemed determined to create a new path, even though sermons written out in the study were the norm for their preacher as well as the tradition. [234] In fact, once it is Calvin's own publication of the *Four Sermons* which serves as the contrasting model for Badius in his preface to the Sermons on the Ten Commandments.

> [Calvin] did not want to permit the publication of any sermons, except four for the comfort of the poor faithful who seek the liberty of the gospel and yet find so many hindrances that they cannot disentangle themselves. He did this in part to fulfill a promise that he had made that someday he would publish some sermons. The others [including those which Badius is presenting] which have since then been added to the four have been published rather with a forced permission, or more importunity than his free will and consent. [235]

Badius addresses head-on the fact that these were extempore sermons, because his audience would expect published texts to be polished and he knows Calvin would be mortified if his readers thought that these represented his best work!

---

[233] Jacques Ruffy or Roux, OC 35:543-544.

[234] The preface of second printing of 13 sermons on Gen. 25-27 (which appeared without the name of the publisher or place) speaks of the difficulty of the subject (predestination) and the need for something "liquidee et vuidee avec facilité"; since the treatise on predestination was available in French, it is clear that this editor thought the sermons were easier to understand. The first edition of these sermons had appeared with the treatise but this editor apparently thought that was too complicated. Peter & Gilmont, *Bibliotheca Calviniana* II, p. 963.

[235] Badius, quoted in Peter & Gilmont, *Bibliotheca Calviniana* II, p. 650, OC 25:597-598 (*Bibliotheca* mistakenly says OC 35).

> These (like all the others which he preaches) were gathered under him by the usual secretary without his having set hand to them or revised them in any way. I say that because one might think that he had outlined and polished them at home completely at his leisure in order to make a good showing. But I assure you that they are just as God gave him to pronounce them publicly, without a word added or subtracted. [236]

The matter of word-for-word precision has been examined by several scholars and it is clear that there were in fact some minor changes made between the manuscript and printed versions, and also perhaps at the earlier stage before the fair copy of the text. These consisted of usually small stylistic changes, which did not affect the substance of either the language or the form. [237] Thus, while certainly interesting for a detailed study of the editorial process, for present purposes they can be omitted because by the standards of early modern sermon transcription they are barely worth notice.

What did concern Calvin's editors were the preacher's own literary criteria for publication, and how these were being compromised. The five basic categories drawn from classical rhetoric were invention, arrangement, style, memory, and delivery. In Calvin's distinctive approach to sermons on the Bible, there was no question about finding the basic subject. The *lectio continua* practice erased the idea of a daily choice of text or topic within scripture except in the rare instances when the course reading was suspended. (Critics could object that Calvin did not even lighten the tedium by using the *loci* system to produce a satisfying beginning and end of each day's preaching.) His memory was also excellent, if not always perfect. His capacity to make himself heard from the pulpit, and to speak so as to be understood by a population which used a different kind of French, were probably the key concerns in pronunciation, which will be considered later. The categories of style and arrangement receive the most attention in the prefaces to the printed sermons – naturally, because those were the two categories most vulnerable to criticism by readers, who could not, of course, judge the delivery. Conrad Badius, himself well-educated, paid careful attention to appropriate style and arrangement of text. He addresses both points in the preface to the first sermons he published, the ones on the Ten Commandments, in explaining Calvin's reluctance to allow publication.

> The whole of his purpose is that the works which he brings to light should appear with all their elegance (ornaments), so he does not like it if what he

---

[236] Badius, quoted in Peter & Gilmont, *Bibliotheca Calviniana* II, p. 650, OC 25:597-598.

[237] Francis Higman cited by Peter & Gilmont, *Bibliotheca Calviniana* II, p. 952.

has preached in a simple and bare fashion, to accommodate himself to the ignorance of the people, speaking without dressing it up and without graceful arrangement, is suddenly brought to light – as if he thought that everything he said should be spread everywhere and the world filled with his writings. [238]

As seen here and elsewhere, references to style are frequently related to the character of Calvin's accommodation to his audience. Badius repeats this with even more detail the next year in the preface to *Plusieurs Sermons*.

But he did not want his preaching to reach further than his flock, because they [the sermons] were made especially for his sheep to whose capacity he accommodates himself as much as he can, and because it seems to him that a different order and arrangement would be required for them to be put before the eyes of all the world. [239]

The pastor was determined to meet his hearers at a level they could grasp, even if that meant constant repetitions and sermons which often did not have a real beginning or end because a verse might spill over from one sermon to the next, or

---

[238] Badius, quoted in Peter & Gilmont, *Bibliotheca Calviniana* II, pp. 650-51: "Ce qu'il faut aussi que je confesse de ceux-ci, car jamais ne m'eust permis les imprimer, en ayant desjà esté requis d'autres fois, sinon que je l'eusse pressé, et souvent importuné. Non qu'il soit si chagrin et difficile de sa nature; mais d'autant que toute son entente est à ce que les œuvres qu'il met en lumiere, sortent avec tous leurs ornemens, il luy fait mal que ce qu'il a presché simplement et nuement pour s'accommoder à la rudesse du peuple, sans appareil ni disposition exquise, soit subit mis en lumiere, comme s'il affectoit que tout ce qu'il dit soit incontinent semé par tout, et que le monde soit rempli de ses escrits. Voylà pourquoy il a tousjours fait refus que tant ses leçons que ses predications fussent imprimées. Cependant il est si debonnaire, qu'il ne peut si bien se defendre des importunitez de ceux qui sont autour de luy…" OC 25:597-598.

[239] Badius, preface to *Plusieurs Sermons*, OC 35:589-590: "Vray est (comme j'ay desja donné à entendre en la preface des sermons sur le Decalogue) que ce n'est ne du gré ne du consentement de l'autheur: non qu'il veuille empescher le bien et le fruit qu'en peut recevoir l'Eglise, mais il desireroit que ses predications ne s'estendissent pas plus loin que sa bergerie: tant pource qu'elles sont faites specialement pour ses brebis, à la capacité desquelles il s'accommode le plus qu'il peut: pource qu'il luy semble qu'un autre ordre et disposition y seroit bien requise pour estre ainsi mises à la veue de tout le monde: mais de les revoir pour les polir, outre ce qu'il n'a pas le loisir, il ne s'y voudroit jamais occuper. Car quand il voudroit en mettre en avant, il sçauroit bien faire des homilies toutes nouvelles et mieux labourees, sans remanier une chose par luy ja prononcee sur le champ. Neantmoins voyans le grand fruit qui peut revenir de telles predications ainsi publiees, nous n'avons pas craint de luy desplaire et desobeir aucunement en cest endroit, afin de vous faire participans des excellentes richesses desquelles nous jouissons en ce petit anglet hay et detesté du monde comme pernicieux et maudit, mais cependant precieux devant Dieu. Vray est que ce qui nous a donné ceste hardiesse, c'est la liberalité de nos magnifiques et treshonorez Seigneurs, qui desirant l'avancement de l'Eglise de Dieu, nous ont donné permission et privilege de les imprimer."

a logical break in the text might come in the middle of the day's reading.[240] The arrangement of his sermons was not because Calvin could not do better but was a form of accommodation to getting his congregation through the entire Bible. That meant his sermons were unlike the selected lectionary postils and totally different from the topical handbooks most common in the middle ages. In Calvin's hands *lectio continua* was even different from the *loci* orientation of colleagues like Bullinger. Badius' preface to the Pastoral Epistles in 1561 expresses this clearly.

> If you do not find such an arrangement as could be required in some premeditated or carefully ordered writing, do not blame the author, who simply spoke as God's Spirit gave him utterance, without special attention [to style] but giving total attention to the meaning and true interpretation of the scripture and accommodating himself to the ignorance of his flock and to the capacity of the weak. Also he did not preach with the intention that these would be brought to light, and in fact I dare say that it is not his will that that happen; he is not so lacking in graceful speech that he could not have enriched them with the arrangement appropriate to such homilies as are written at leisure.[241]

Along with the defensive stance came a positive affirmation of Calvin's own ordering, as Badius describes in his preface to the set of sermons on the Ten Commandments. "But his [Calvin's] custom is to follow a thread [of thought] and tenor [of the text] which tends toward edification, omitting nothing which makes for the honor of God and instruction of his hearers."[242] These words suggest that it was necessary to emphasize the value of *lectio continua* preaching, and especially the fact that it does not skip anything. Calvin believed everything written in scripture is there "for the honor of God and instruction of his hearers" and thus should be heard attentively. Badius' summary comes at the end of polemic which defines Calvin's preaching in contrast to that of his opponents.

> [But his sermons are] true, pure expositions, bare [of clutter] and suited to the text he has to explain. He does not fill them with extraneous exhorta-

---

[240] For Calvin's sense that some part of his congregation was very impatient with his repetitions, see above at nn. 182ff. For examples of sermons which divide a verse or change chapters in mid-sermon or indicate that the preacher cannot finish what he had planned to say. OT: #13 on Micah 3:11-12 (S V, p. 112); #4 & #15 on Ezek. 1:26-2:4 & 3:25-4:3 and #54 & #55 on Ezek. 14:12-13 & 14:13-23 (Ms.Fr.21); #17 on 2 Sam. 6:6-12 (S I, p.141). NT: #27 & #28 on Acts 7:1-4a &7:4b-6 (S VIII, p. 243); #30 on 1 Cor. 4:21-5:2 (Ms.Fr.26).

[241] Badius, preface to Pastoral Epistles, OC 49, p. xvii.

[242] Badius, preface to *Plusieurs Sermons*, OC 35:587-588.

tions or invective born of ambition. For, even though we greatly need to have the word of God daily fight against superstitions of the papacy, to efface them from our hearts like a strong odor which we have drunk in from our youth, yet if the passage is not formally (intentionally) against such abuses, he [Calvin] does not go out of his way in the interpretation to speak out against that abuse the way the papists, on every occasion and without cause, bark like mastiffs against the gospel which has been renewed in the world in recent days.[243]

Badius' words are not an objection to polemic as such, but it is notable that his focus here is defending Calvin against the accusation that he was not being faithful to his avowed intention of explaining scripture. Indeed, the preacher is so concerned to stick to the text that he does not include even useful arguments against (or attacks on) traditional errors! The arrangement is given by the Bible itself, and Calvin follows his text verse by verse in order to edify his hearers.

Whereas Badius' defense praises Calvin for not digressing, the anonymous preface to the collection of sermons from Genesis and Luke published in 1560 implicitly contrasts the reformer with his opponents more specifically on their exegesis and application. Protestant preachers are described as ordained by God "rightly to cut the bread of doctrine for all the faithful, just as a father, who distributes bread to his children, cuts it in pieces for each according to what he sees each needs."[244] The anonymous editor then explains what this feeding of the flock means for Protestant pastors, with Calvin specifically in view.

> For instead of tangling it [this scriptural bread] up in complete confusion in the spirits of their hearers, [gospel pastors] explain it in familiar fashion in detail and with a marvelous order. Instead of trimming it, tearing it in pieces, twisting it to another meaning, and stopping at the crust rather than penetrating to the interior, [these pastors] offer it [scriptural bread] in its entirety, in its perfection and truth, in full reverence without disfiguring it, and they nourish our souls with its marrow.[245]

The central point here is the content and the claim that Calvin (unlike his opponents) does not pick and choose (trim, tear in pieces) or misrepresent (twist) or rest satisfied with a superficial crust. Indeed, instead of confusion, the hearers receive an accessible, detailed, and straightforward discussion. This praise for Calvin's preaching reflects the editor's appreciation for *lectio continua*, since the "marvelous

---

243 Badius, *Plurieurs Sermons*, OC 35:585-586.

244 Anonymous preface to sermons on Gen. and Luke, OC 23:635-636.

245 Anonymous preface to sermons on Gen. and Luke, OC 23:635-636.

order" of the sermons he was publishing was in fact the sequence of the Biblical text and not a particular arrangement. Apparently at least some people did not think that disregarding classical rhetorical categories was a serious problem.

Others, like Badius, not only gave attention to style and arrangement but also considered points related to pronunciation. They recognized that one significant lack in printed sermons was the missing animation of the preacher's presence. Since there were already concerns about style and arrangement to address, doing without the "in-person" aspects of rhetorical delivery was even more of an issue. The first to speak of this was Girard, the publisher of the first sermons, in the context of explaining that these were extempore texts. The fact that what he offered had been copied out while the preacher was speaking should make "the argument treated here ... the more efficacious, as it should be if the readers think that they are there at the presentation." [246] The effectiveness of the subject matter is increased if the readers imagine themselves present before the pulpit. Years later other editors echo this in different ways. Jacques Bourgeois refers to Calvin's "ordinary sermons" which he prints "in order that you may get the taste like those who were touched and moved by his living voice." [247] In Badius' preface for the Pastoral Epistles there is an even more explicit awareness of the role of "the living voice in which a majesty full of efficaciousness is seen to shine" [248] and gestures of the preacher to impress the scripture on the hearers. He cautions readers that the verbatim accounts must be supplemented with an awareness of the contribution that the act of preaching makes to the meaning as well as the vividness of the sermon.

> Seeing this [the fact that the sermons were extempore] if you find some sentences short and some thoughts cut, reflect that the gestures made when speaking help a great deal in understanding the thoughts, which when read often do not have the grace they did when spoken. Also, when one is accustomed to a pastor's style and way of teaching, one understands with half a word (so to speak) what he means. Therefore do not pay so much attention to the external arrangement as to the purity of teaching. [249]

---

[246] Girard, OC 32:449-452, also printed in Peter & Gilmont, *Bibliotheca Calviniana* I, p. 219.

[247] Bourgeois, Abraham sermons, 1561. Peter & Gilmont, *Bibliotheca Calviniana* II, p. 866: "lesquelles ont esté si dextrement amplifiés et ingeniusement representées comme au vif, par nostre fidele ministre M. Jean Calvin traitant le dit passage en ses sermons ordinaires, que j'ay pensé faire chose agreable, te communiquant ceux qui en auroyent esté recueilliz, afin que tu y puisses prendre le goust tel qu'on senti ceux qui ont esté touchez et esmeuz de sa vive voix." Preface not found in OC.

[248] Badius, OC 49, p. xvi.

[249] Badius, OC 49, pp. xvii-xviii.

Badius has to concede that the style is not perfect but he reiterates that the key is doctrine. This reference to the effect of gestures in preaching is not to say that Calvin was a dramatic preacher in the theatrical sense, but simply to indicate that someone present for the sermon would have found it more engaging and clear.

Badius' preface to the sermons on the Gospel Harmony spends some time defending the preacher against criticisms and mockery by those hearers who compared him unfavorably with actors. They complained about the faults of his delivery.

> Here I mean particularly a bunch of restless fastidious ones with ears eager to be courted, who come to the preaching of God's Word more to observe the face and pronunciation of the minister, in order to find reason to criticize and matter to chatter about with those like them, than in order to be filled with the teaching of salvation. It seems to such profane people that there is no more to preaching the gospel than declaiming some secular (profane) harangue or acting a farce on the stage. So that, no matter how pure his teaching, if a pastor does not have gestures which please them or a tongue the same, they mock him and take no account of him [or what he says].[250]

Gesticulation in the pulpit was not a positive thing and preachers were supposed to behave with "modesty" so it was not surprising that Calvin did not gesture a great deal, only pointing to his head or his heart,[251] and that his editors felt on good grounds in defending him. Badius goes on to compare Calvin with Paul, who had to deal with the same kind of attack about weak delivery in the letters to the Corinthians. The editor affirms: "God's word ought to be treated in a different style than human sciences and what seems folly and weakness to human sense is wisdom and strength before God."[252] Paul defended himself not from

---

250 Badius, quoted in Peter & Gilmont, *Bibliotheca Calviniana* II, p. 956: "J'enten yci parler princi-palement d'un tas de curieux et fretillans, qui ayant les aureilles chatouilleuses, frequenteront plus les predications de la parole de Dieu, pour contempler la contenance et pronunciation des ministres d'icelle, afin d'y trouver à redire, et avoir de quoy deviser avec leurs semblables, que pour estre repeus de la doctrine de salut. Or il semble à telles gens profanes qu'il n'y a non plus d'affaire à prescher l'Evangile, qu'à declamer quelque harangue profane, ou bien à jouer une farce sur un eschaffaut; tellement que si un pasteur, quelque pureté de doctrine qu'il ait, n'ha les gestes à leur plaisir, et la langue affilée de mesme, ce sera à s'en mocquer, et n'en faire conte." This preface is not found in OC.

251 Lambert, *Preaching, Praying, and Policing*, pp. 374-75, touches on this briefly. On p. 375 n. 224 Lambert cites Max Engammare as affirming that Calvin pointed to his head or heart; Engam-mare, "Le Paradis à Genève. Comment Calvin préchait-il la Chute aux Genevois?" *Etudes théologiques et religieuses* 69 (1994, n.3), p. 344.

252 Badius, quoted in Peter & Gilmont, *Bibliotheca Calviniana* II, p. 956.

self interest but for the sake of his apostolic calling and (implicitly) Calvin has the same task if not the same rank. Then Badius goes on to explain why (since he does not consider Calvin's delivery to be a problem) he still presents this argument. It is because some people are upset that extempore sermons are being published.

> Thus they are giving the simple a distaste for reading [these sermons], because they sometimes find in them repetitions, or sentences which are short and obscure. That happens when one speaks without writing and long premeditation but according as God's Spirit gives one to speak, in view of the subject and matter which one is treating. So, because the curiosity of [these detractors] is not satisfied, they want what does not please them to displease the whole world. [253]

Exasperated, Badius sharply says that the detractors, who could not do nearly as well themselves, pay no attention to the doctrine which is the primary concern. [254] A few years later in the preface Jacques Roux wrote for some sermons on Hezekiah (Isa. 38), he added his enthusiastic description of Calvin's teaching. Although he mentions "the living voice," he seems to place the effectiveness in the content. What he heard was "led and guided by the Holy Spirit, without deceit or adornment of human eloquence but pure and simple, yet lively and penetrating." [255] The point is that Calvin's editors recognized that the sermons lost some of their vividness and perhaps some clarity when they were printed, but in the same breath they maintained that the extempore origins in fact serve a purpose in making the exposition more dynamic and immediate than if Calvin's words had been polished at leisure. More to the point, the fundamental need as they saw it was the pure preaching of the Biblical text, and that was what compelled them to publish the sermons.

Calvin's Contemporary Editors and Their Purposes

Most of the editors and sponsors of Calvin's sermons were Geneva-based men with significant theological background, and/or personal engagement, because the majority were French refugees themselves. It is this existential context which helped to shape both what they published and how they explained their purpose. The first sermons were published by Jean Girard. The expositions of Psalms 115 and 124 copied out by Jean Cousins in on Nov. 4 and 11, 1545,

---

[253] Badius, quoted in Peter & Gilmont, *Bibliotheca Calviniana* II, pp. 956-97.

[254] Badius, quoted in Peter & Gilmont, *Bibliotheca Calviniana* II, p. 956.

[255] Roux, quoted in Peter & Gilmont, *Bibliotheca Calviniana* II, p. 952. OC 35:523-24.

appeared early in 1546; and then in 1554 came the twenty-two sermons on Ps. 119 transcribed by Raguenier in 1553. In both cases Girard himself gives explanatory notes, touching on Calvin's reluctance but then turning to the over-riding considerations which led to the publication. For the first two sermons the stated purpose was to supply people in Geneva, i.e., his own flock, so the preacher could not really object that the audience was different from those who could have been present on the day he spoke.

> Because the author is not accustomed to having his sermons published, it is good that everyone be informed why we have published these two sermons. The reason is that, a number [of people] having seen that the content and argument were worth remembering, asked for copies, so that it would have been a great deal of trouble to copy it out so many times. Along with that is the fact that the truth of the teaching would be beneficial to all, as much for the teaching as for the knowledge of the story which is touched on there, in which we see clearly how God has helped His church in its need.[256]

When Girard speaks of "the teaching" he means the Biblical doctrine which would naturally be expected to be valuable. When he names "the story," however, he almost certainly has in mind the situation in Germany which had occasioned these special day of prayer sermons, the first one pleading for God's help for embattled fellow Christians, the second offering praise and thanks for God's wonderful answer to prayer.[257] The sermons then were a witness involving both Calvin's congregation (the local church acting in obedient intercession and thanksgiving) and the church universal (God's providence manifested for the Lutherans in Germany). The latter point might have mollified the preacher about this publication; although the booklet was intended for Genevans as the original sermons had been, if it was spread abroad at least it showed that Calvin's church explicitly expressed concern for fellow Christians.

Girard's preface for the second publication, which appeared in 1554, elaborates a little on the preacher's attitude about publication, since for the first time there was no claim for purely local use. This time extempore sermons were being

---

256   Girard, OC 32:449-452, also printed in Peter & Gilmont, *Bibliotheca Calviniana* I, p. 219.

257   The full title tells the story: *Deux sermons de M. Jean Calvin, faitz en la ville de Geneve. L'un le mecredy quatriesme de Novembre 1545 jour ordonné pour faire prieres extraordinaires: apres avoir ouy nouvelles que les Papistes avoyent esmeu guerre en Allemaigne contre les Chrestiens. Le second, le mecredy prochainement suyvant, auquel par l'ordonnance et authorité de Messieurs de la ville, on rendit à Dieu action de graces solennelle, apres que nouvelles furent venuës que Dieu avoit donné victoire aux siens, et brisé la force des ennemis.* See chap. 4 at nn.149ff.

directed to those beyond Geneva. Girard explains that publishing these expositions of Ps. 119 was not just his own idea but some anonymous "good faithful
people" had joined with him to persuade Calvin to permit this so that "the profit
of them might extend further." The preacher's answer indicated his sense of the
difference between commentaries and sermons.

> [Calvin] objected, preferring to print some short commentary when the
> occasion lent itself to that, rather than fill paper with such long matter as
> one unfolds in the pulpit: nevertheless, since he cannot hope to do that
> [the commentary] for a good while, given the small amount of leisure
> which he has, and meanwhile the world would be denied the great
> usefulness which reading these sermons – just as they are – could provide,
> I thought it was better to publish them. If God pleases to allow the author
> to make a work more polished and perfect, nothing will be lost if the
> children of God have been edified by the holy teaching which they will
> find here. [258]

Girard apparently voices one of Calvin's objections to publishing sermons instead
of commentaries: the sermons are longer. The real difference, however, is not
length but genre. Preaching requires many more words than exegesis because the
text is being applied to the local congregation in the pew and thus it is repetitious
or diffuse. Implicitly Calvin indicates that this application is not appropriate to
distribute to a wider public. However, even though the preacher was at work on
his Psalms commentary, Girard was not willing to wait. (In fact, no more sermons
on Psalms were published in French in the sixteenth century, so perhaps Calvin
and the printer came to an agreement? The former would get on with the
commentary and the latter would refrain from publishing extempore sermons
on Psalms.) Girard's purpose was edifying people who could not be present to
hear Calvin, and it is interesting to observe why he chose Ps. 119. It was "because
this Psalm ... contains an argument in which all Christians ought to be exercised

---

[258] Girard: "Je l'ay prié [Calvin], estant requis aussi de plusieurs bons fideles, qu'il souffrist que ses
sermons comme ils ont esté recueillis de sa bouche fussent publiez: afin que le profit s'en
estendit plus loing. Or combien qu'il en ait fait difficulté, aimant mieux faire imprimer quand
l'opportunité s'y addonneroit, quelque brief commentaire, que de remplir le papier de si longs
propoz qu'ils se desduisent en chaire: toutesfois, n'esperant pas que cela se peust faire de long
temps, veu le peu de loisir qu'il a, et cependant que le monde seroit frustré d'une grande utilité
que pourra apporter la lecture desditz sermons selon qu'ils sont couchez, j'ay pensé que le
meilleur seroit les publier. S'il plaist à Dieu donner grace à l'Autheur de faire un ouvrage plus
poly et exquis, il n'y aura rien de perdu que les enfans de Dieu ayent esté edifiez de la saincte
doctrine qu'ils trouveront icy." Peter & Gilmont, *Bibliotheca Calviniana* 1, p. 540. Text not found
in OC.

night and day." [259] To modern readers, the more devotional character of the earlier Psalm texts (115, 124) seems a natural reason for publication. However, to early Protestants the instructive value of the Psalms (as witnessed in the *Four Sermons* as well as this presentation of Ps. 119) was a significant concern. Peter Opitz calls these sermons a kind of ABC of faith, and the number of early modern translations and editions witnesses that this "Torah-Psalm" had considerable appeal for Calvin's contemporaries. [260]

The last book of sermons which Girard published for Calvin, the little collection of two expositions on 1 Tim. 2:4-5 (Christ as Mediator), was printed in 1555. The brief note about the importance of this text indicates that it was again theologically motivated.

> After having heard these two sermons, and considered the teaching contained in them, it seemed to me good to bring them to light for the purpose that such a treasure might not remain hidden but might benefit the whole church, not only among the papists but also those who profess the gospel. [261]

Girard implies that this exposition of basic Christological teaching is needed by Protestants as well as those who had not committed themselves to "the gospel"; maybe the lingering arguments over Servetus were a concern. Although it is always difficult to interpret such public notes to the reader, the apparently personal character of this short commendation is significant for Girard's own appreciation of Calvin's teaching. Perhaps others felt the same way, because the stenographer Raguenier himself added a little poem at the end of this booklet.

Whoever wants to have God for Savior And does not want to return to Him empty
But to find in Him all grace and favor; He must have Jesus Christ for his guide;
Because otherwise a person, poor and timid, Would not dare approach his God
If Jesus Christ did not intervene between To grant him favor, access and grace.
So let us not seek salvation somewhere else Than in Jesus and his pure grace.
    I hope for good. [262]

---

259 Girard, quoted in Peter & Gilmont, *Bibliotheca Calviniana* I, p. 540: "Pource que le pseaume, qu'on appelle les octonaires, contient un argument auquel tous chrestiens se doivent exercer nuicts et jours, et qu'il avoit esté familierement exposé par Maistre Jean Calvin en autant de sermons qu'il y a de huictains." Text not found in OC.

260 Opitz, "Ein Thorapsalm als ABC des christlichen Glaubens." See Appendix Nine: Sermon Publication in the Sixteenth Century.

261 Girard, quoted in Peter & Gilmont, *Bibliotheca Calviniana* I, p. 585.

262 Raguenier, quoted in Peter & Gilmont, *Bibliotheca Calviniana* I, p. 585.

The personal religious experiences of the stenographer and editor expressed here are significant in explaining why unpolished, extempore sermons were considered worth printing. Although Calvin's carefully edited *Four Sermons* had been printed by Robert Stephanus,[263] Jean Girard appears to have been one of the few printers who was committed to publishing the extempore sermons in the early years. Several other printers re-issued some of the books which Girard brought out first, and his work led the way for others to publish more of the untraditional, unpolished texts.

Girard's most important successor in producing these fruits of Calvin's pulpit ministry was Conrad Badius, the outstanding editor of collections of sermons as well as of the first series. Badius was working with and for Laurent de Normandie, the reformer's close friend who devoted a good part of his considerable wealth to supporting publication of Calvin's works.[264] In 1557 Badius produced the sermons on the Ten Commandments excerpted from the series on Deuteronomy, and reprinted this the following year (with the addition of two more sermons). In 1558 he published two chapters (10-11) of First Corinthians from that series, plus the collection of special-occasion Christological sermons discussed above, and in 1561 he was the first to bring out an entire series, the 101 sermons on the Pastoral Epistles. This was followed the next year by the 65 sermons on the Gospel Harmony (all that were available before Raguenier's death).[265] Virtually all that Badius published was explicitly intended to help persecuted French Protestants. This is prominently in view in the preface to the Ten Commandments, which turned out to be one of the most popular sets of Calvin's sermons.

> Because all the poor faithful, who are scattered about in the countries in the world and places where the pope still has dominion, cannot enjoy every day this precious gift [of preaching], I thought that I would give them great comfort if, using the beneficial character of my art [of printing], I let them see on what kind of pasture we are nourished and in what simplicity, purity, truth, reverence and zeal God's word is proclaimed to us by those whom the Lord Jesus has commissioned as pastors for His poor flock in this country.[266]

---

[263] Stephanus produced the first French (with a second edition in 1555 by Zacharie Durant), Crespin produced the Latin and Italian translations of the *Four Sermons*; see Peter & Gilmont, *Bibliotheca Calviniana* I, 52/9 & 55/10; 53/4 & 53/3.

[264] Moehn, "Introduction," *Sermones*, p. xxvii. Peter & Gilmont, *Bibliotheca Calviniana* II, pp. 599 *et passim*.

[265] See Peter & Gilmont, *Bibliotheca Calviniana* II, 57/10 & 58/10; 58/9; 58/5; 61/24.

[266] Badius, quoted in Peter & Gilmont, *Bibliotheca Calviniana* II, p. 650. OC 25:595-98.

It is a testimony to Calvin the pastor dominating Calvin the humanist that he could be persuaded to allow the publication of expositions to serve those whom his editor considered to be suffering in a spiritual wilderness.

> For if the desire of every faithful person should be that all should come to the knowledge of the truth, and all participate in the same heavenly riches which [God] gives, who is there – seeing that there are so many poor members of Jesus Christ in the world (detained in worse servitude under the Roman antichrist than in Egypt or Babylonia), people who are languishing and parched for lack of this spiritual pasture – who would not be induced to give them succor? [267]

These are Badius' words, explaining why he badgered his friend and pastor to let him publish the sermons. Calvin's prayers, both in the liturgy and at the end of the *congrégations,* make it very clear that he himself shared the concern for the French Protestants, [268] even if his preferred prescription to help would not have been the publication of his extempore sermons.

The same concern for the French believers is evident in Badius' preface to the sermons on Christological observances when the Lord's Supper was celebrated. The first point is the importance of providing nourishing teaching to the people and guidance to their preachers.

> [I publish these sermons] because all cannot live in this church to participate in the heavenly pasture which this good shepherd has been administering for twenty years and continues to do; and because it is necessary that those who are newly come to this charge [of preaching] see his manner of teaching in order to follow it. [269]

Badius turns from the French believers to their Roman context. He addresses the people who considered Geneva's premier preacher a heretic and rabble rouser.

> Likewise so that those who think that [Calvin] does nothing in the pulpit but slander and cry out against the pope and his followers, and thunder against their traditions without otherwise explaining scripture, or indeed that he does not cease to lead people into carnal liberty and unsettle the yoke of kings and princes and all authority: let them read his sermons in which they can see that it is all wrong to accuse him of such blasphemies... [270]

---

267 Badius, quoted in Peter & Gilmont, *Bibliotheca Calviniana* II, p. 651. OC 25:597-598.

268 See above n.107, and chap. 3 at nn.74ff.

269 Badius, quoted in Peter & Gilmont, *Bibliotheca Calviniana* II, p. 678; OC 35:589-590.

270 Badius, quoted in Peter & Gilmont, *Bibliotheca Calviniana* II, p. 678; OC 35:589-590.

Whether Badius actually thought that opponents would read the sermons or not, he knew that French Protestants could use this support to counter the slanders of their faith. His caution might also be intended subtly to remind the more radical French Protestants that Calvin did not approve of rebelling against properly constituted political authority. Having vindicated the preacher, Badius goes on to explain why he chose sermons from sacramental occasions.

> For the rest, we have considered to choose, as much as possible, sermons which were preached on all the days when the Holy Supper of the Lord is celebrated in this church, as much because they are naturally more vehement and intense, as because the purpose of the sacrament is always explained.[271]

From the viewpoint of publishing extempore sermons it was strategically appropriate to choose ones which would most easily awaken a response in the readers. These would have an inherent intensity and emotional resonance which would offset the lack of in-person gestures. From the viewpoint of content it was very important that good access to the essential and controversial subject of the Lord's Supper be available for French Protestants. This first book of sermons preached on Supper Sundays was probably particularly significant for "internal" or devotional use. In the preface to this collection of feast day sermons, however, the editor set out a program of publishing

It is certainly no accident that the sermons on Badius' list included the two chapters of First Corinthians which focus on the Lord's Supper. Teaching on the sacraments was not only a key part of Reformed theology and practice; it was also particularly needed in France. The confusion bred by the on-going Supper strife in western Europe, and the fact that most French Protestants did not have organized churches or pastors to guide them in these matters, made an accessible form of Calvin's teaching imperative. In this set of sermons it is likely that the controversial aspect of the knowledge was as important as or more so than the devotional.

> We thought it would be very suitable to bring to light the sermons of our faithful pastor John Calvin on the tenth and eleventh chapters of the first epistle of St. Paul to the Corinthians, where among other matters the Supper is treated in an accessible (*familierement*) way. It is true that in his *Christian Institutes*, and in a treatise which he wrote expressly on the *Lord's Supper*, and similarly in the *Accord on the sacraments, their nature and right usage, agreed upon between the doctors and pastors of the Church of Zurich and those of this city*

---

[271] Badius, quoted in Peter & Gilmont, *Bibliotheca Calviniana* II, p. 679; OC 34:591-592.

of Geneva, one may well see that he [Calvin] does not detract in the least from the pure and true ordinance of our Lord Jesus Christ, and that he faithfully declares what we ought to know about this sacrament. Nevertheless, because he is more accessible (*familier*) in his sermons, we thought it good to publish these, so that it might be clear to everyone that we bear as much honor and reverence for the Supper of the Lord as anyone alive, and that we seek what Jesus Christ presents to us there, that is, His body and His blood as food for our souls, but not in a carnal way but a spiritual one. [272]

Even though other works by Calvin on the sacrament were available in French, Badius considered the more accessible (less elitist) presentation in the sermons to be sufficient reason to publish them. It is worth emphasizing that the editor wanted to arm his readers also with a reminder that the Reformed Christians in Geneva honored and revered the Lord's Supper, and believed that Christ's body and blood are *presented* there. Badius lists the Zurich Consensus as one of the texts in which to find Calvin's sacramental teaching, but it is clear that he also wishes to distinguish this doctrine from Zwinglian as well as Roman interpretations.

The next project on Badius' publication program was the Pastoral Epistles, and in 1561 he brought out the first complete series of sermons, a fat book on Timothy and Titus. Constantly before his eyes are the persecuted French believers who have few preachers; it is they who have in fact prompted this brother now living in Geneva to make available texts which focus so much on the ministry of pastors and other offices.

And because you do not yet have such a freedom in the preaching of the gospel as we do, and because God has only begun to gather some little flocks here and there in France – flocks which are daily in fear of the wolves – and because the pastors to whom they have been entrusted do not yet minister the pasture of life to them except in secret, surreptitiously (*en cachette et comme à la desrobbee*), the faithful there have thought that the publication of these sermons would be extremely useful. [273]

Badius' thumbnail image of the situation of the newly forming French churches under the cross is vivid. Undoubtedly he had a fairly good idea of the struggles of the little groups who were constantly writing to Geneva for pastors, and the men whom the Company of Pastors commissioned to respond to these

---

[272] Badius, quoted in Peter & Gilmont, *Bibliotheca Calviniana* II, p. 690-91. OC 49, pp. xiv-xv. Note the emphasis on "familiar."

[273] Badius, quoted in Peter & Gilmont, *Bibliotheca Calviniana* II, p. 869. OC 49, pp. xvi-xvii.

needs.[274] There were never enough qualified ministers to meet all the requests, so the publisher was offering his assistance through print.

The following year Badius continued his program of publishing Calvin's sermons, although with a change, presenting the first sixty-five sermons on the Gospel Harmony instead of the Galatians he had originally projected. Here he makes explicit the role of the sermons not only as models for inexperienced preachers but also as "mute teachers" when ministers are lacking.

> I beg you to consider the contribution to the progress of the church of God which has resulted from the sermons of our good Master John Calvin which have been published to date. Although he did not have the leisure to revise these sermons and we were obliged to bring them to light just as they were taken down, nevertheless they have served as mute teachers to those who, deprived of the freedom to hear the living voice, have enjoyed reading these sermons, and have been brought to a knowledge of the truth by that means. And likewise [they have served as] a form for a number of those who in these times of visitation (trial) have been called to the ministry of the gospel and who, being conformed to this manner of teaching: pure, simple, and far from all ostentation and affectation of human eloquence, today are fishing for souls in great heaps, to dedicate and consecrate them to their Lord and Shepherd.[275]

In Badius' eyes, the sermons from Geneva were already proving their worth in France, as proclamations of the gospel for people who had not heard or been persuaded, as well as help for new preachers. (They were a means of the light of the gospel shining on a person living in the cave of papal teaching, as Calvin had identified it in his 1 Corinthians sermon cited above.) Given a choice, Calvin himself would have certainly preferred that ministers use his commentaries. However, Badius was probably rather closer to the situation on the ground,

---

[274] See Robert M. Kingdon, *Geneva and the Coming of the Wars of Religion in France, 1555-1563* (Genève: Droz, 1956).

[275] Badius, preface to Gospel Harmony, 1562, quoted in Peter & Gilmont, *Bibliotheca Calviniana* II, p. 957: "[J]e vous prie de considerer l'avancement que l'Eglise de Dieu a receue jusques icy de la publication des Sermons de nostre bon Pasteur M. Jean Calvin, lesquels combien qu'il n'ait eu le loisir de remanier, et que nous ayons esté contraints de les mettre en lumiere selon qu'ils ont esté recueillis, toutesfois ont servi de docteurs muets à ceux qui, privez de la liberté d'ouir la vive voix, ont eu la jouissance de la lecture d'iceux, et par ce moyen sont parvenus à la cognoissance de verité." Not found in OC. In 1554 Girard had begun the tradition of noting that the sermons had already proved useful; OC 32:453-54: "Et pourtant pour toute recommandation tant de l'autheur que de l'Oeuvre, je ne proposeray autre chose, sinon le fruit, lequel desja ont recueilly ceux qui les ont leuz, et que pourront rapporter ceux qui les liront: car on peut bien penser, qu'il n'y a rien qui rende l'homme plus heureux, que la meditation vive et continuelle de la Loy saincte et bonne volonté de Dieu."

at least in his sense of what could be expected of the pastors in the field and what would be beneficial for them, and he thought sermons were more accessible than commentaries. In practice, Calvin's sermons were becoming a kind of new handbook for French pastors, a fact noted later by Theodore Beza as well as by various ministers themselves.[276] Shortly after the appearance of these sermons Badius himself left Geneva for France, to be a pastor there for only some months before his ministry was cut short by the plague. When he was serving his church Badius must have drawn on his own publications of sermons and commentaries as well as his memories of Calvin's preaching.

After Badius' departure, Laurent de Normandie turned to others to continue bringing out Calvin's extempore sermons,[277] and there were also other publishers who had started producing some new sermons or reprinting others. Since the purpose here is to show what motivated his editors and how they presented the texts to their readers, it will be sufficient to note only a few more prefaces. Significant among these are the Job sermons printed by Jean de Laon for Antoine Vincent in 1563. The story of Job is easily read but the "the assistance of a good expositor is very helpful to the more learned, and necessary to the common people, to know and understand better the varied content and to profit from the teaching contained in the book."[278] Vincent then explains why, among the learned explanations of Job, he has chosen to publish Calvin's sermons.

> Besides the fact that they are in the common language French, the way of treating the teaching is so simple and within the grasp of the most ignorant (so to speak), yet without omitting what is necessary. Moreover, here and

---

[276] Beza's preface to the Latin translation of the Job sermons, OC 33:13-14: "*Editae sunt igitur iam pridem gallicae istae conciones, non ipsius certe Calvini voluntate, qui illas sibi velut extorqueri testabatur, sed collegarum ipsius iudicio, et eorum qui loquentem illum audierant efflagitatione. Neque id vero temere factum fuisse res ipsa mox ostendit, maximo cum remotissimarum etiam gallicarum ecclesiarum fructu, quibus usque adeo privatim et publice placuerunt ut plurimis in locis, quibus quotidiani pastores deerant, conciones istae in communi coetu ex pulpito recitatae pastorum vice fuerint, et nunc quoque asper rimis istis temporibus plurimae in Gallia tum ecclesiae tum familiae eorum confirmatione mirifice confirmentur.*" Minister Ambroise Faget of La Rochelle in a letter to Colladon requesting the Genesis sermons; Peter & Gilmont, *Bibliotheca Calviniana* II, p. 749.

[277] Sermons on Galatians, see Peter & Gilmont, *Bibliotheca Calviniana* II, p. 1033.

[278] Vincent, OC 33:5-6: "Cependant il n'y a point de doute que l'aide d''un bon expositeur ne soit chose fort utile aux plus savans, et comme necessaire au commun, pour tant mieux cognoistre et entendre les matieres diverses, et faire son profit de la doctrine qui y est contenue. C'est ce qui a esmeu aucuns bons personnages à mettre en lumiere ceste année ces sermons du fidele serviteur de Dieu et de son Eglise Maistre Jean Calvin sur ce livre de Job: jaçoit que lui mesme qui en est l'autheur, et de la bouche duquel ils ont esté recueillis, y resistast en tant qu'en lui est: comme il a fait quant à ses autres sermons."

there they are applied to the present age, so that all who are willing to judge rightly and without ill-will, still (now) will find a good help and what will satisfy them. To show that, there is no need to make here a summary of the book or the main points of doctrine and their various uses, because besides the fact that it would be better to learn this here and there by reading the sermons, the first one contains an overview which is sufficient and yet short enough to be easily remembered. [279]

Calvin's sermons on Job are not only accessible because they are in the vernacular and easy to grasp, but they are also a special help in understanding and facing the difficulties of the present day. Vincent's audience is believers and unbelievers in war-torn France, although it is not the fighting so much as the many other trials and temptations which loom large in his mind. For the persecuted French Protestants, the sermons will give "means to profit more in the knowledge of God and our Lord Jesus Christ, but chiefly to be confirmed in right patience in their afflictions." For unbelievers "the teaching of this book, prepared for easy digesting" will lead them to awaken by seeing God's "extraordinary judgment in the person of Job." [280]

Like his predecessor Badius, the writer of this preface has in view strengthening believers and drawing to the gospel those who have not heard or responded. Where Badius spoke gladly of people who had come to faith by reading Calvin's sermons, Vincent – referring to "the things which have happened this year," 1563 – sees a bleaker picture, even as he exhorts his readers to recognize God's providence and judgment. [281] Among the readers who took this appeal to

---

[279] Vincent, OC 33:5-6.

[280] Vincent, OC 33:5-6: "Quoi qu'il en soit, si ceux qui liront le tout, sont gens qui ayent desja laissé les idolatries, pour s'addonner à la doctrine de l'Evangile, ils trouveront ici à profiter tousjours d'advantage en la cognoissance de Dieu et de nostre Seigneur Jesus Christ: mais principalement à se confermer en droite patience en leurs afflictions. Que si ce sont gens, lesquels n'ayent pas encore sceu, ou voulu discerner la vraye religion, pour s'y ranger en laissant les fausses: quelque occasion qui les ait empeschez, estans advertis par la doctrine de ce livre, ainsi maschee comme ils la trouveront, et principalement resveillez par ce jugement extraordinaire en la personne de Job, qu'ils y verront deduict et declaré au long: ils seront preparez à mieux penser à eux-mesmes, et à faire leur profit de tant d'adversitez qu'on voit aujourd'hui parmi le monde, et de plus grandes encore, desquelles il est bien à croire que Dieu menace les hommes, pour le grand et manifeste mespris de l'Evangile."

[281] Vincent, OC 33:5-6: "Car combien que les choses qui sont advenues ceste année, tant en ses jugemens sur les meschans et ennemis de Jesus Christ, qu'en ses chastiemens sur les fideles, soyent bien espouvantables: si est-ce que d'autant que bien peu s'amendent, et au contraire plusieurs s'enveniment tant plus à batailler contre Jesus Christ, aucuns ayans commencé à bien faire, s'anonchalissent: voire mesmes de revoltent…" The admonitions continue at length, OC 33:7-8.

heart was Admiral Coligny, whose biographer reported that he had a great love for these sermons and read one every morning and evening.[282] Calvin might object to the application he intended for local use being read in other contexts, but evidently some people thought that precisely the contemporary application was one of the strengths of the sermons for their own audiences.

It is appropriate here to add only two more figures because of what they illustrate about the surprises in studying the publication of Calvin's sermons. Like Girard and Badius and many others, these two were also refugees for their faith. Unlike the earlier editors of Calvin's sermons, however, these two were women.

One was originally from France, Marie Dentière (or D'Ennetières). Dentière had been a nun and when she came to the "gospel" she brought a higher level of education than was common for women. She first worked in Strasbourg, where she married and was widowed; then Dentière moved to Geneva with her second husband Antoine Froment. She was active – and preaching – in the city before Calvin came; the couple moved away in 1537 when Froment was called to another ministry, but they remained in close contact with affairs in Geneva.[283] In 1561, Dentière published a separate edition one of Calvin's sermons on 1 Timothy which Badius had printed a few months earlier. At least, this exposition of 1 Tim. 2:9-11 is signed M.D. and the attribution to Dentière has been accepted by a number of scholars, supported by the fact that it is not the only text from her pen and is in character with her reforming concerns.[284] Dentière's preface explains the importance of making a defense against vices which can lead the faithful astray. In keeping with the Biblical text (that women should "adorn themselves in modest apparel, with shamefastness and sobriety; not with braided hair, and gold or pearls or costly raiment," etc), she focuses on "extravagant clothing," to which she considers women particularly prone. Besides appeals to "St. Cyprian" and various classical figures, and an allusion to a medical metaphor, Dentière closes with a commendation of Calvin.

> Let us listen to the Apostle speaking to Timothy and to the man who preached about that passage, a man who because of the purity of his

---

[282] Cited from François Hotman's 1575 biography by Peter & Gilmont, *Bibliotheca Calviniana* II, pp. 1036-37.

[283] Calvin and the couple Froment were often on the opposite sides of arguments. One particularly heated dispute was in fact related to earlier publications; rebukes to Froment about his wife, Sept. 21, 1537, RC II, p. 330; May 6 & July 25, 1539, RC IV, pp. 203-05 *et passim.*, p. 337.

[284] See McKinley, "Introduction," *Epistle to Marguerite of Navarre*, pp. 22-23, 32-34. Peter & Gilmont, *Bibliotheca Calviniana* II, pp. 855-56, note the attribution by Théophile Dufour but question its feasibility.

teaching deserves to be heard among all the ministers and faithful pastors in Europe today.[285]

For a woman to select the topic of women's dress as a publication may be rather surprising to modern readers, and (assuming this was by Dentière) it suggests that gender issues in the sixteenth-century reformation were more complex than is often assumed. At the least, Dentière's positive appreciation for both a difficult Biblical text and a reformer usually remembered as very strict about morals indicates that Calvin's sermons could speak to more audiences than one might guess.

A second woman editor, Anne Vaughn Lock, was also one of the first translators of some of Calvin's sermons. Like several others who began the diffusion of the extempore sermons in English, Lock was among the Marian exiles in Geneva and she probably heard Calvin preach the sermons which she later translated. The ones she selected were four on Isaiah 38, the story of King Hezekiah's illness and healing, and unlike Dentière's edition, Lock's translation in 1560 was the first time these sermons appeared in print.[286] The booklet is dedicated to Katharine, Duchess of Suffolk, who had also been an exile from Queen Mary's rule, and Lock's words explain both why she chose this particular text and how she saw Calvin's role. The importance of the example of Hezekiah is evident in the medical analogy which Lock applies to the spiritual ills which English exiles had suffered.

> [T]he peines and diseases of minde and soule are not only the most grievous, and most daungerous, but also they onely are peinfull and perilous... He then, that cureth the sicke minde, or preserveth it from disease, cureth or preserveth not onely minde, but bodye also...[287]

Although some might consider this an astonishing over-statement: spiritual ills are more dangerous than physical ones (English Protestants had been burned at the stake just a few years earlier!), the point Lock wanted to make is clear: that the spiritual disease of not knowing the gospel is damning. Her appreciation for Calvin is evident in the extended medical metaphor which shapes the whole of Lock's preface, linking God, the Bible, and the preacher. People are very grateful for someone who provides knowledge of how to treat physical sickness; how much more they owe to someone who has a recipe ("receipt") to restore health of mind and body!

---

[285] See Dentière, *Epistle to Marguerite of Navarre*, pp. 93-94.

[286] Lock, *Collected Works*, pp. 2-61. See Peter & Gilmont, *Bibliotheca Calviniana* II, p. 771.

[287] Lock, "preface," *Collected Works*, p. 4.

> This receipte God the heavenly Physitian hath taught, his most excellent
> Apothecarie mast[er] John Calvine hath compounded, and I your graces
> most bounden and humble have put into an Englishe box, and do present
> unto you. My thankes are taken away and drowned by the greate excesse
> of dutie that I owe you: Master Calvine thinketh his paynes recompensed
> if your grace or any Christian take profit of it: bicause how much soever is
> spent, his store is neverthelesse. And for God, recompensed he can not
> be: but how he is continually to be thanked, your graces profession of his
> worde, your abidyng in the same, the godly conversation that I have sene
> in you, do prove that your selfe do better understand and practise than
> I can admonishe you. [288]

Here the former refugee, now back at home, sets out her spiritual medical
treatment: God the Physician, Calvin the apothecary, herself the box-maker, to
provide the gospel teaching-medicine for a friend and patron who knows how to
appreciate such a gift and will use it well. While Calvin might not have called
himself an apothecary, it is probable that he would have found this metaphor very
apt, and certainly he would appreciate the point about being recompensed for his
labor if Christians profited from his preaching.

It is clear that whether they pictured his sermons as necessary teaching for
every person, or model sermons for beginning preachers, or mute ministers where
no human ones were available, or medicine to heal spiritual disease, or just a
simpler way to grasp a difficult subject, or a moving record of prayer for the wider
church, a remarkable range of people, both pastors and lay leaders, thought
Calvin's vernacular expositions of scripture were well worth preserving, publishing, and propagating through translations.

Calvin the preacher: this pulpit ministry was arguably the most constant part of
his vocation as pastor in Geneva. It was a major part of pastoral care as Protestants conceived it, since communicating the gospel day in and day out was the way
that ministers served as instruments of the Holy Spirit's work. Anne Lock's image
of Calvin the preacher as an apothecary was very apt. The application of God's
"physic" to the ills of Geneva's people was focused in the pulpit. It was certainly
not restricted to it, however. Pastoral care included bringing scripture and prayer
to the people in the pews also when they went home, as the next chapter will
illustrate.

---

[288] Lock, "preface," *Collected Works*, p. 5.

PART FOUR

Worship and Pastoral Care in Daily Life

The marks of the Church for Calvin are "the word purely preached and heard and the sacraments rightly administered" and these are essentially corporate actions. The teaching and practice of worship in Geneva were therefore primarily focused on what the people who are the visible church do when they are gathered together before God. However, the church continues to live in God's presence (*coram Deo*) wherever they as individual members may be; every day and every moment Christians have to do with God (*negotium cum Deo*) and that relationship must find expression in appropriate ways. Obviously "praying without ceasing" cannot be corporately manifest, but in Calvin's Geneva structured aids to that end were not restricted to public services of worship. Pastors have certain responsibilities for individual teaching and pastoral care, but shaping the daily prayer of people where they live – in households – is essentially the domain of the priesthood of believers. Part Four therefore explores several facets of Geneva's worship practices beyond the services in the parish churches.

CHAPTER SEVEN

WORSHIP IN PRIVATE SPACES
AND THE DAILY ROUND
FOR PEOPLE AND PASTORS

The major part of Geneva's visible worship took place in corporate public spheres, but a significant number of more private acts of worship were also liturgical, that is planned and guided by the church community. The two most important of these were household prayers and pastoral care for the sick and dying. The first two parts of the present chapter give an overview of these dimensions of worship. The third part sketches out "a month in the life of Pastor Calvin" to provide a glimpse of how the leadership of worship shaped the life of a pastor in Geneva, as he and his people followed the daily round of devotion in an early modern city. This includes the reformer's responsibilities for public services as well as what he was doing in ministry with individuals, and thus may provide a bridge between pastoral work in the pulpit and beyond it.

I: Household Worship and "Private" Prayer

Praying and learning how to pray were a central part of the Christian life for all Genevans. In itself, this was neither surprising nor novel, but the specific forms of prayer as a Protestant city had both similarities to and differences from the tradition. A brief word about notable changes in prayer and devotional life will be followed by an examination of the teaching and patterns, texts and contexts, of the practice of prayer in the lives of Genevans.

A Word about the Tradition and Protestant Changes

The historical tradition of prayer in Latin Christendom can generally be divided into clerical and lay domains. Monastic prayer was the holiest ideal: ceaseless prayer. Lay prayer was usually (at least somewhat) different in content and almost always embedded in a different context. Monastic prayer has long been studied, and popular piety has become much better known in the past generation. Here the object is to identify some important features of devotional life which Protestants and the Reformed in particular changed. Orders of monks and nuns were essentially abolished (particularly in Reformed areas) and the lay community became central. Besides rejecting the idea of any privileged intercessors in favor of the priesthood of believers, Protestants significantly altered the texts or patterns of prayer to be used by that lay community. Among the most obvious changes were the elimination of prayers to Mary and the saints, and the insistence on intelligibility: prayer in a language the person offering it could understand. This applied to all prayer, in every time or place. In addition, there was a new prominence given to praying because a great deal (if not all) of the other traditional forms of personal piety were discarded: there were no more pilgrimages, no more obligatory fasts, no more saints' days to observe, no more holy water or signing with the cross, and so forth.

On the other hand, there was now a greater emphasis on corporate prayer and a significant degree of continuity between worship in the gathered parish community and worship in "private" spaces. Protestant liturgies and prayers and Psalms and hymns in the vernacular which were prepared for public corporate worship were not only available to the laity but also the latter were encouraged and expected to use them in their homes in one way or another. Over time more individual emphases in prayer regained a role in various Protestant communities, but in others, especially among the Calvinist Reformed, the hegemony of the Psalter maintained a strong continuity between parish and home or personal worship.

Like their medieval predecessors, Protestants believed in the value of teaching people how to pray, the importance of having the faithful learn to pray. If anything, this determination to instruct the people in the right way to pray was even stronger among Protestants, because the Biblical standard for teaching both set specific limits and required a vigorous struggle against unacceptable prayer and devotional forms. The primary focus was naturally the Lord's Prayer; this was certainly not new, but it stood out distinctively when it was recited in the vernacular and stripped of its constant companion, the Ave Maria. Psalms and hymns formed the other main catechetical prayer texts for Protestants. Usually some individual or corporate model prayers made up the third and subordinate group of texts for Protestant usage.

Calvin's Teaching on Prayer in the Home

Biblical Prayers

The Lord's Prayer and the Psalms, as the Biblical texts of prayer par excellence, were central to daily prayer as well as corporate worship. In view of the purpose of the present study it is impossible to give adequate attention to the reformer's work on either of these subjects; however, it may be worthwhile to note just a few points about Calvin's teaching which probably had some importance for ordinary Genevans. With regard to the Lord's Prayer, three things may be highlighted, in ascending order of visibility. One, which the people in the pew and home may not have consciously examined, was the fact that when they said "Our Father" they were supposed to remember that they were praying for all people. From the first *Institutes* to the end, Calvin states clearly that this petition involves the believer in praying for all God's people... present and possible.

> Just as one who truly and deeply loves any father of a family at the same time embraces his whole household with love and good will, so it becomes us in like measure to show to his people, to his family and lastly, to his inheritance the same zeal and affection we have toward this Heavenly Father. For he so honored these as to call them the fullness of his only-begotten Son [Eph. 1:23]. The prayer of the Christian ought then to be conformed to this rule in order that it may be in common and embrace all who are his brothers in Christ, not only those whom he at present sees and recognizes as such but all people who dwell on earth. For what the Lord has determined concerning them is beyond our knowing, except that we ought to wish and hope the best for them. Yet we are to be drawn with a special affection to those, above others, of the household of faith, whom the apostle has particularly commended to us in everything [Gal. 6:10].[1]

Praying for "all people who dwell on earth"?! The evidence for Calvin's application of this in practice appears in the intercessory prayers of the liturgy, which include a section specifically shaped by this teaching.[2] It is no accident that

---

[1] *Institution 1536*, p. 105; OS I, p. 107. The translation is slightly modified: *hominis/homines* as "people"; Calvin makes a distinction between *homo* and *vir* which indicates that he does in fact intend *homo* to include women as well as men. See McKee, "The First French *Institutes*," pp. 165-66.

[2] OS II, pp. 21-22: "Apres, nous te prions, Dieu tresbening et Pere misericordieux, pour tous hommes generallement, que comme tu veulx estre recongneu Saulveur de tout le monde, par la

versions of this language reappear in some of the model prayers that Genevans were invited to add to their morning and evening devotions.[3]

A second aspect of the Lord's Prayer, one which was more likely to have been significant to ordinary Genevans, was the petition for daily bread. Traditionally this had often been interpreted as referring primarily to the Mass, the heavenly food.[4] Calvin, following Bucer and his favorite patristic exegete Chrysostom, taught that "daily bread" included all that God's people need for their life in this world.

> By this petition we ask of God all things in general that our bodies have need to use under the elements of this world [Gal. 4:3], not only for food and clothing but also for everything God foresees to be beneficial to us, that we may eat our bread in peace.[5]

It must have been comforting for lay people (for whom communion had normally been infrequent although they were taught to share it spiritually by presence at the Mass) to be assured that Christ was not in this place talking about the Lord's Supper but explicitly meant for them to ask for what they needed for their very concrete day-to-day existence.

The third point which undoubtedly did get the attention of lay people was the petition "forgive us our sins as we forgive." As became clear in their preparations for the Supper, Genevans were very conscious of the danger of communing when they had not forgiven someone, or still harbored resentment. In fact, the consistory records include the case of a man who got up and left the service when it came to the point of reciting the Prayer because he would not perjure himself and

---

redemption faicte de ton Filz Jesus Christ, que ceulx qui sont encores estranges [estrangiers] de sa congnoissance, estans en tenebres et captivité [d'erreur] et ignorance, par l'illumination de ton sainct Esprit, et la predication de ton Evangile, soyent reduictz à la droicte voye de salut: qui est de te congnoistre seul vray Dieu, et celuy qui te as envoyé Jesus Christ. Que ceulx que tu as desja visité par ta grace, et illuminé par la congnoissance de ta parolle, croissent journellement en bien, estans enrichis de tes benedictions spirituelles: afin que tous ensemble t'adorions d'un coeur et d'une bouche, et donnions honneur et hommage à ton Christ, nostre Maistre, Roy et Legislateur."

3   See below at n.44 and Appendix Eleven.

4   See McKee, "John Calvin's Teaching on the Lord's Prayer," in *The Lord's Prayer: Perspectives for Reclaiming Christian Prayer*, ed. Daniel L. Migliore (Grand Rapids, MI: Wm. B. Eerdmans, 1993), pp. 88-106, for summary of the medieval tradition and Luther, who began by interpreting daily bread as the Eucharist and preaching, and then in his catechism in 1528 added a reference to ordinary bread.

5   *Institution 1536*, p. 109; OS I, p. 110.

would not/ could not forgive.[6] (Calvin quite well understood the seriousness of this issue, even if he rejected the choice to run away. In the *Short Treatise on the Lord's Supper,* when he addresses the anxious soul who feels unworthy of communing, the pastor points out that participating in the Supper and praying to God require fundamentally the same relationship.[7]) Even if most people probably did not equate reciting the Lord's Prayer with preparing for communion, praying these words was still a serious matter in Geneva!

The second and much larger corpus of Biblical prayers which Calvin was determined to teach Genevans was of course the book of Psalms. In the amazing preface to his commentary on Psalms, written relatively late in his life after years of experience in praying and preaching and teaching these prayers, Calvin the believer speaks from the heart. The Psalms are "an anatomy of the soul."

> For there is not an emotion of which any one can be conscious that is not here represented as in a mirror. Or rather, the Holy Spirit has here drawn to the life all the griefs, sorrows, fears, doubts, hopes, cares, perplexities, in short, all the distracting emotions with which human minds are wont to be agitated. … the prophets themselves, seeing they are exhibited to us as speaking to God, and laying open all their inmost thoughts and affections, call, or rather draw, each of us to the examination of himself in particular.[8]

As Calvin saw it, since the Psalms set out inspired prophetic practice, and express the full range of human situations and people's fluctuating feelings, these texts make the best guide for prayer in all circumstances. They are God's invitation to pray and God's assurance that nothing in the human heart is too terrible to bring to the Lord.

> Only it appeared to me to be requisite to show in passing that this book makes known to us this privilege which is desirable above all others that not only is there opened up to us familiar access to God, but also that we have permission and freedom granted us to lay open before Him our infirmities which we would be ashamed to confess before other people.[9]

---

6   See chap. 3 at nn. 229ff. Grosse, *Les rituels de la Cène,* chap. 8; example of Tivent Pape who got up and walked out when it came time to say the Lord's Prayer, p. 521; citing June 5, 1550, *Consist.* V, p. 117: "Mesme que le jour de la Cene, quant il fut dictz au sermon que l'on priasse Dieu, allors y se sorti du sermon. L'a confessé." Grosse also cites an earlier case of Claude Curtet, who refused to take communion and also did not say the Lord's Prayer because of his bad will toward his brother ("ne ditz pas son Pater pour cause qu'il veult mal à son frere"), April 27, 1542, *Consist.* I, p. 48. For other examples, see Claude Vuarin, Oct. 26, 1542 (*Consist.* I, pp. 133-34); Anry Bully, Feb. 5, 1551 (*Consist.* V, p.326); hostess of the Ours, Aug. 5, 1546 (*Consist.* II, p. 267).

7   See chap. 3 at n.196.

8   *Writings on Pastoral Piety,* p. 56; OC 31:15-16.

9   *Writings on Pastoral Piety,* p. 57; OC 31:17-18.

In effect the Psalms are an accommodation to the human condition under sin, voicing self-examination and self-revelation to God. That is certainly not all, however. Calvin explicitly celebrates the positive counterpart; the Psalms are the guide to "the right manner of offering to God the sacrifice of praise" and the richest expression of God's goodness and deliverance. "In short there is no other book in which we are more perfectly taught the right manner of praising God, or in which we are more powerfully stirred up to the performance of this exercise of piety."[10] One of the objects of using the Psalms as their prayer book was to insure that God's people learned how to speak with God in a way that would both please the Lord and meet their own needs.

It was a novelty for the entire population to be offered – and expected to learn – the whole Psalter. Although traditionally devout laity had learned at least some Psalms in Latin, the complete book was usually regarded as a prerogative of monastic prayer. The Reformed idea of putting all 150 Psalms into the mouths of ordinary people in meter was first intended to enable the whole congregation to praise God together, and it certainly served that purpose. However, after Calvin returned from Strasbourg and introduced the first metrical Psalms to the Genevans for use in corporate worship, the pastor apparently continued to develop his understanding of the role of these pre-eminent Biblical prayers in daily life. In 1543 he added a section to the Psalter preface which he had published the previous year, and one aspect he emphasized here was the role of singing these sacred songs "in the houses and fields" as well as in formal worship.[11] For Calvin, singing the Psalms and reciting the Lord's Prayer were clearly the primary Biblical patterns of prayer for the people of God.

Times and Themes of Prayer in Daily Practice

Biblical texts were central but they were not the only factors which shaped Protestant teaching on prayer. Two other questions which Calvin addressed were the principles for organizing a rhythm of domestic or private prayer and the practical corollary of providing guidance for that practice. The first of these: regular household devotions, had to take into account the fact that the intended pray-ers were lay people and by definition active in the world. For Protestants, an explicit issue in prescribing weekday times of prayer was the role of work, which was part of the Christian's vocation and therefore dedicated to God; it also filled the daylight hours six days out of seven. The second principle was the conviction

---

[10]   *Writings on Pastoral Piety*, pp. 57-58; OC 31:19-20.

[11]   *Writings on Pastoral Piety*, p. 95; OS II, pp. 15-16 (OS marks this as 1545, but it actually was added in 1543). See Grosse, *Les rituels de la Cène*, pp. 167-68. Also chap. 3 at n.93.

that every household was or should be a "little church" and therefore the home should be the primary locus of corporate worship outside the services in the parish church.[12]

Calvin's teaching on the times of prayer is defined clearly if briefly in the first *Institutes* in 1536. He begins with the affirmation that Christians should pray without ceasing, but because of human weakness, they should set specific times.

> These hours should not pass without prayer, and during them all the devotion of the heart should be completely engaged in it. These are: when we arise in the morning, before we begin daily work, when we sit down to a meal, when by God's blessing we have eaten, when we are getting ready to retire. But this must not be any superstitious observance of hours, whereby, as if paying our debt to God, we imagine ourselves paid up for the remaining hours.[13]

Regular times for prayer each day are necessary, and Calvin lists five which would be natural in the ordinary life of lay people because these are related to daily activities. These distinct occasions are an accommodation to human limitations and must not be considered as satisfying the believer's duty to God; however, with that condition understood, the designated times provide a basic structure.

In his sermons Calvin returns to the question of prayer rather frequently. The two key factors are the Biblical text and the perceived needs of the people in front of him. Naturally, one necessary part of the preacher's job is to interpret perplexing passages of scripture. He must also give attention to the right attitude for prayer and practical instructions about times and contents, as well as correctives for wrong or inappropriate forms. Since Calvin attended to virtually every point in the Biblical texts as he preached, he was obliged to make clear to the people in the pews why the scriptural instructions about specific hours of prayer (third hour/ mid-morning, sixth hour/ noon, ninth hour/ mid-afternoon) no longer applied to them. For example, when preaching on Luke 2:36-38, the story of the prophetess Anna, which was a key text for supporting women's religious orders, the preacher explains that the Jews rightly kept those hours before Christ came but now such regulations have come to an end. In the process, of course, he characterizes the monastic practices of Rome as "stupid devotion" because those who observe them think that they are keeping the world from falling apart, they are appeasing God's wrath by their

---

12   For work, see chap. 3 at n.27 et *passim.*; for family, see discussion of baptism, especially Abraham, chap. 5 at nn.176ff.

13   *Instruction 1536*, pp. 115-16. OS I, p. 116.

prayers.[14] The preacher concludes that Christians should not copy the Jewish order now that Christ has come. However, it is apparent that the reason for his criticism is not an objection to specific hours but to the human claim to share the sacrificial role of the one Mediator; those who do that are refusing to recognize that Christ's advent has made human priests not only unnecessary but wrong.

Preaching on I Tim. 5:4-5, Calvin sets out a picture of the right ways and times to pray. This includes a sharp criticism of the "laziness" of the contemplative life but its primary object is to clarify how Protestants can fulfill the injunction to pray without ceasing (1 Thess. 5:17) if they reject the traditional monastic hours.

> Let us learn to practice praying in such a way that when we have begun in the morning, we continue, and the night responds to the day, and there is a corresponding melody in our whole life so that we always honor God. It is true, as I have said, that we should not make a business of praying as we have seen those excessively scrupulous people do who wanted a contemplative life.... [polemic against monastic practice]... St. Paul did not want to introduce such a superstition among the children of God, but he wanted to show how the faithful ought to begin whatever they have to do by invoking God's name. As we cannot move a finger without His help, so let us learn to begin with that, so that He may govern us. Have we begun in that way? Let us continue in eating and drinking, and then in taking our rest let us always look to God. But let each one apply himself to this according to his vocation and the estate of his life.[15]

---

14   Gospel Harmony, sermon #34, OC 46:419: "Car dont est venue ceste folle devotion en la Papauté, qu'on chantera matines, et puis qu'il y aura les primes, et tierces et sextes, et nonnes, et vespres, et complies, et tous ces badinages-là? Voyla les prestres, et les moines, et toute ceste canaille qui sont à louage, et font à croire qu'ils soustiennent le monde par leurs prieres, et que le ciel tomberoit sans que leurs devotions entreveinssent, et qu'ils fussent devots pour appaiser Dieu. Et sur quoy se sont-ils fondez? Pource qu'anciennement au Temple il y avoit des sacrifices de soir et de matin. Il y avoit l'oblation des premices qui se faisoit. Il y avoit puis apres les heures de sexte, de tierce, de nonne, comme midi, et trois heures, et ainsi du reste, comme on le peut veoir par l'Escriture: mais ils n'ont point regardé que Dieu avoit establi alors ce qu'il cognoissoit estre bon et propre pour les Juifs, devant que nostre Seigneur Jesus Christ fust manifesté. Maintenant il y a une raison toute diverse quant à nous. Et mesmes quand les Papistes ensuyvent les Juifs, non seulement ils sont fols, et s'en vont là comme des grües sans entendre nulle raison. Mais il y a un blaspheme en toutes leurs devotions folles. Et pourquoy? Car il faut regarder l'intention de Dieu, et son conseil pour bien juger."

15   1 Timothy, sermon #38, OC 53:464-65. Calvin goes on to add (465): "Et au reste, selon que chacun aura loisir de s'exercer en prieres et oraisons, et frequenter les sermons, et lire l'Escriture saincte, qu'il cognoisse, Voici Dieu qui m'oblige tant plus à venir à luy: car il y a un lien tant plus estroit quand il me donne une telle liberté. Il faut donc que j'approche de luy, que je l'invoque tant plus songneusement, et que je m'addonne du tout à cela. C'est en somme ce que nous avons à retenir de ceste doctrine de sainct Paul."

Praying without ceasing means that life is conformed to prayer so that in every-thing and every moment God's people honor Him. This is exercised practically not in sitting and reciting words all day but in recognizing that each separate activity should begin with a prayer and be governed by God. There is no fixed regulation; Christian freedom is expected and each individual applies the general rule to her or his own situation. (It may be noted that in the course of this exhortation, Calvin mentions each of the specific times which he had listed in the *Institutes*: morning and evening, work, and meals.) When the preacher empha-sizes the continual attitude of prayfulness he may also chide the people; Calvin thinks that his people consider morning and evening prayers sufficient and feel that they have done their duty with that minimum...[16]

However, as long as there is no false confidence of having paid God off with two short prayers, Calvin can use the terms "morning and evening" to cover the times or rhythms of prayer. One connotation is what would for lay people be the most regular times of personal prayer: literally, rising in the morning and going to bed at night. Sometimes this schedule is particularly focused on entrusting all of life to God's care.

> And so let us learn to be content with our lowliness, provided that God gives us rest, that is: that we may rise in the morning and after having prayed, live the day; and in going to bed at night, commit our life into God's care and protection, and that it is enough for us to be governed by Him. Let us consider that rest [in God] to be a good beyond price by comparison with all the happiness which the world so greatly values.[17]

God's covenant is rest and, enjoying that divine protection, God's people should acknowledge God's goodness with praise and thanks.[18] When believers recognize God's goodness they are emboldened to express in their prayers what they need;

---

16 Gospel Harmony, sermon #61 OC 46:766: "Il nous semblera que nous ferons beaucoup quand de matin et de soir nous prierons Dieu, que nous aurons quelque devotion, encores qu'il y ait beaucoup de traverses pour nous en destourner." [Lest they think it is only Christ who prays so, Calvin cites David and Paul.]

17 Gospel Harmony, sermon #27, OC 46:331-332: "Et ainsi apprenons de nous contenter de nostre petitesse, moyennant que Dieu nous donne repos, c'est à dire que nous puissions nous lever de matin, et apres l'avoir prié, passer la journee: et en nous couchant le soir, remettre nostre vie en sa garde, et en sa protection, et qu'il nous suffise d'estre gouvernez par luy. Estimons (di-je) ce repos-là comme un bien inestimable, au pris de toutes les felicitez que le monde magnifie tant."

18 Ephesians, sermon #33, OC 51:664: "Car ne devrions nous pas et soir et matin, et jour et nuict penser à la grace qui nous est faite en nostre Seigneur Iesus Christ, qui est le soleil pour nous esclairer?" Eph. #39, OC 51:743: "Car ne devroit-on pas et soir et matin reduire en memoire la grace qui nous a esté faite à la venue de nostre Seigneur Jesus Christ?"

God has provided in the past, God will hear their prayers for their continuing necessities.[19] Morning and evening prayers should also include petitions for the salvation of the whole world – all those who dwell on earth.[20] In addition, the phrase "morning and evening" often has to do with self-examination.[21]

Calvin names the importance of hearing God's word, God's voice, morning and evening.[22] The means to this end was a guided approach rather than a simple individual reading of the Bible. The preacher could speak of meditating on God's law in various forms; that probably included singing the Decalogue and metrical texts like Ps. 119.[23] In the catechisms, the section of model prayers was often

---

[19] 1 Timothy, sermon #16, OC 53:186: "Voilà donc en quoy il nous faut exercer, apres que nous aurons cognu le bien si grand et si infini que Dieu nous a faict de nous donner liberté de le prier, c'est que nous soyons diligens à cela, que nous ayons ceste solicitude et soir et matin de crier à nostre Dieu, veu que les necessitez nous pressent à chacune minute de temps, voyans aussi que ses promesses nous rompent journellement les aureilles, qu'il nous solicite de venir à luy ou par paroles, ou de faict."

[20] 1 Timothy, sermon #11, OC 53:126: "Maintenant nous voyons quelle est l'intention de S. Paul en ce passage: c'est asçavoir de monstrer à quoy les enfans de Dieu se doyvent employer: c'est à ne point travailler en vain, et sans aucun profit: c'est à invoquer Dieu, et en le priant avoir le soin du salut de tout le monde: et que soir et matin ils s'appliquent à cela." See Appendix Eleven, part one.

[21] Galatians, sermon #13, OC 50:427: "Que soir et matin nous pensions que nous avons à rendre conte de toute nostre vie." Gal. #23, OC 50:564: "Mais quand nous serons resveillez pour penser que c'est de rendre conte devant Dieu, que soir et matin il nous souviendra qu'il est le juge du monde, et qu'il ne peut pas quitter son office: apres que nous entrons en nousmesmes pour faire examen de nos pechez, il est certain qu'il nous faudra estre en frayeur et comme gens transis: et si nous n'avions quelque remede pour nous soulager, il faudroit que nous fussions abysmez en desespoir, mais ayons nostre refuge au Baptesme, et que nous sçachions que ce n'est pas en vain que Dieu nous a appelez pour estre participans de la pureté de son fils unique, et que nous sommes faits un avec luy." Gal. #43, OC 51:125: "Que donc chacun s'adjourne et soir et matin, et que quand nous regarderons à nos pechez..." Eph. #14, OC 51:417: "Mais cognoissons, puis que nous n'avons nulle heure certaine, que c'est nostre office de nous adjourner et soir et matin devant Dieu, faire un bon examen de nos pechez pour gemir et pour estre du tout confus." Eph. #28, OC 51:604: "Que de bonne heure nous cheminions en crainte et solicitude, et que soir et matin, et à chacune heure nous souspirions en nos vices, pour n'estre point ainsi endurcis." 1 Cor. 10-11, #6, OC 49:650: "Mais cependant ce n'est pas que nous ne devions et soir et matin regarder quelle est nostre infirmité." 1 Cor. 10-11, #14, OC 49:755: "Il faut donc que soir et matin nous entrions en conte."

[22] 1 Corinthians, chap. 10-11, sermon #4, OC 49:623: "Et pour que cela nous est presché et soir et matin, Dieu nous espargne pour un temps." Sermon #19, OC 49:821: "Et c'est un passage que nous devons bien noter et recorder, et reduire en memoire soir et matin."

[23] Galatians, sermon #21, OC 50:542: "Et puis que la Loy nous picque et nous solicite, quand nous serons froids, qu'il y aura telle paresse et tardiveté en nous, que nous ne pourrons venir à Dieu, qu'un chacun regarde bien à soy, et que soir et matin nous reduisions en memoire les commandemens de Dieu, à fin de nous redarguer." Note the addition of the Decalogue to the daily household prayer published by Simon Mangeant; Appendix Eleven, part one. The character of Ps. 119 would make it an appropriate parallel to the Decalogue; cf. chap. 6 at nn.129f.

provided with Biblical verses for edification, which were usually fairly well-known passages, especially quotations from the Psalms.[24] Extensive Bible reading was normally located in the public contexts of school or church where the people could be guided in their study. Genevan presses did specialize in smaller format Bibles which were more affordable, and households (including inns) were expected to buy and read these instead of playing games like cards.[25] However, Bible reading apart from the collection of texts in the Psalter service book was not strongly emphasized as part of family devotional lives. Calvin seems to have felt the need to balance several issues. He can speak as if reading scripture at home goes along with attending worship, but he was also evidently concerned that people might think they could do it all themselves, without the help of the gathered church.[26] According to Christian Grosse, the caution about individual Bible study appears to have won out; he indicates that this was not encouraged until long after Calvin's day. At home the Psalter and catechism texts were the central Biblical focus to shape the prayer lives of Genevans.[27]

---

[24] 2 Timothy, sermon #29, 54:326-27: "Et pour ce faire que nous sçachions qu'il ne faut point que nous demeurions le bec ouvert, mais que nous advisions d'user des moyens que Dieu nous donne. Que nous frequentions les sermons, que nous ayons la lecture de la parole de Dieu pour recommandee, que nous desirions d'estre edifiez par bons propos et saincts, que nous ne cessions ne soir ne matin d'apprendre quelque bonne sentence, qui soit pour nous rafreschir la memoire de ce que nous pourrions avoir oublié, et de ce qui nous pourroit advancer en la cognoissance que Dieu nous a donnee de sa verité. Et sur tout que ceux qui ont la charge d'enseigner les autres regardent bien à eux: car quelques habiles qu'ils soyent, il s'en faut beaucoup qu'ils approchent de sainct Paul." For example, verses from Ps. 119[9, 18, 34], 25 [14], 104[27], and "118" =117[1-2], along with Deut. 7[3] are found in selection of model prayers in the catechism section of the Psalter printed by François Jaquy for Antoine Vincent.

[25] For the focus on reading in the school setting and the production of small format Bibles, see Francis Higman, "La présentation typographique des Bibles genevoises du XVIe siècle et pratiques de la lecture (1998)" in *Lire et découvrir. La circulation des idées au temps de la Réforme* (Genève : Droz, 1998), pp. 573-82. Here pp. 573-75. See examples in *Consist.* I, March 2, 1542, p. 10, where a woman is told to buy a Bible to read instead of playing cards, etc. The same day another woman is told to buy a Bible to show to the guests in their establishment (an inn).

[26] For an example of the assumption that Bible reading is part of home devotions in some form, see Sermon 33/165 on Isa. 37:1-4, Oct. 13, 1557: S. III, p. 310: "Ainsi donc toutesfois et quantes que nous venons au Sermon et qu'un chacun aussi en sa maison list l'Escriture sainte, que nous soions tout preparez pour recevoir les remonstrances que Dieu nous fait de noz pechez." The insistence that private Bible reading is not sufficient is usually expressed in a polemic context in which Calvin is combatting rejection of the public ministry of the word through human beings, e.g., *Inst.* 4.1.5.

[27] Grosse, *Les rituels de la Cène*, p. 176: "Le psautier encadre encore la manière dont le fidèle se nourrit des Ecritures. Médiateur privilègié – avec la prédication – de l'accès à la parole divine, il propose une sélection de textes bibliques à portée normative, du point de vue de la foi

Many of the preacher's homiletical exhortations to pray were prompted by the scriptural texts he was explaining, but the theme of prayer was never out of season, and in fact, there were organized, published means for daily individual or household prayers available to Genevans.

Household Prayer in Calvin's Geneva

Teaching the people to pray took many forms. Although Reformed church leaders tended to begin with preparation of texts for public worship, they soon had to take into account the need for more individual or private forms. [28] Rosaries and books of hours as aids to personal devotion were common in the late middle ages and various forms of these continued to be found in Geneva. The newly reformed city prohibited selling or wearing rosaries, but the old devotional ways certainly lingered for a time. [29]

Most Genevans learned the new rules even if they interpreted them in their own ways. For example, in 1550 one woman was accused of continuing to read her book of hours but explained to the consistory that all she did with it was to say the Latin gospels (i.e., she stuck to the Biblical texts even if she used the old language). A few years later a number of printers were before the consistory for including "superstitious" prayers in their almanacs, prayers which attributed

---

(Symbole des apôtres, Confession de foi, catéchisme), de la conduite (décalogue), et de la piété (psaumes, Notre père). L'usage des Ecritures auquel il incite passe donc par la pratique cultuelle plutôt que par la lecture, que les Réformes protestantes ne favorisent guère avant la fin du XVIIe siècle."

[28] See for example the very articulate lay woman reformer, Katharina Schütz Zell, who identified this problem more quickly than most of her clerical colleagues and set out to fill the gap for her friends in Strasbourg by publishing an edition of the Bohemian Brethren hymnbook. She supplied a preface explaining her purpose and annotations on almost every hymn to guide the lay readers in teaching themselves and their households while they sang. For the text of her preface, see "Von Christo Jesu unserem säligmacher..." in *Katharina Schütz Zell. The Writings*, pp. 58-64; English in *Church Mother*, pp. 92-96. For a full study of this project, and for a transcription of the annotations, see Elsie Anne McKee, *Reforming Popular Piety in Sixteenth-Century Strasbourg: Katharina Schütz Zell and Her Hymnbook*. Studies in Reformed Theology and History 2:4 (Princeton, N.J.: Princeton Theological Seminary, 1994). Appendix with annotations, pp. 69-82.

[29] For March 8, 1537, OC 21:209, the editors of OC say "chapelets" are prohibited but no source is cited. However, there is a Senate order on Oct. 5, 1537; the ministers have complained that there are still people who have rosaries and the council responds "faire lever et oster tous les chappelletz," RC II, p. 345. The order is repeated on Jan. 30, 1543, now with a fine, OC 21:307 (RC 36 f225v). Early consistory examinations include questioning about rosaries ("chapelets"); on April 4, 1542, a woman denies that she has one, *Consist.* I, p. 28. Cathelan, *Passevent Parisien*, pp. 27-28, remarks on this prohibition.

salvation to Mary.[30] The most humorous of these is the case of the Genevan merchants who were called before the consistory in October 1559 for selling rosaries at the fair at Briançon. Under questioning they explained that they had also sold some relics which they had had left over for a long time (*superrestees des long temps!*). Since they sold "instruments of idolatry" even though they knew better and knew it was against Genevan law to have such, the merchants were told to collect all the rosaries ("paternosters") to be burned and they were suspended from the Supper.[31] Evidently the thrifty merchants saw no problem in selling off old Roman devotional items to those who could appreciate these things, despite the fact that they themselves did not see religious value in such items. One can only wonder if this cache of ancient merchandise had been kept hidden away in case it might someday be useful. The men had given up on selling it in Geneva but they were ready to make a profit from the benighted. Obviously the leaders of Geneva thought it was necessary to replace the old manifestations of traditional piety: rosaries, books of hours, etc. By 1559 (and probably long before) Genevans themselves were perfectly aware that these things were "superfluous" as well as superstitious... even if they still regarded them as merchandise. It is appropriate to see what had replaced them.

Model Prayers

The first texts planned by Calvin appeared very shortly after his return to Geneva in 1542 with the inclusion of some model prayers in the catechism. Over the years the teacher added a few more to the general repertoire, and late in his life more special prayers were published. By comparison with medieval and some contemporary resources, these little collections were very limited. The main reason was that for the French Reformed (and those influenced by the Genevan pattern of devotion), the Psalms played such a large role in personal devotion. As Grosse has pointed out in his helpful discussion of the Psalter, by 1556 these books began to include indices to guide those seeking God's help for individual matters. The first list was published in a Parisian edition, entitled "Index to find the Psalms according to the 'current events' (*l'occurrence des afaires*) which God's

---

30 May 15, 1550, Claudine the niece brought the charge (along with saying that her aunt taught her to fast on Good Friday). Bertollomee the aunt says she will stop reading the Latin gospels because it displeases the consistory; she denies that she taught her niece to fast on Good Friday but did tell her to fast on the Saturday before Easter (!), *Consist.* V, pp. 93-94. For printers' almanacs "l'honneur de Jesus Christ en ceste pallette est transferé à la vierge Marie" and furthermore it gives a false place of publication: Lyon instead of Geneva. Oct. 12, 1553, OC 21:555 (consistory).

31 Oct. 19, 1559, OC 21:722.

church or a private person may encounter; in which consists the true use of the Psalms." Twenty years later this kind of personalized guide to suitable texts began to be printed in Genevan editions of the Psalter.[32]

In Calvin's Geneva it was assumed that Psalms would be sung in daily life but there was no formal instruction about when or how, perhaps because this was deemed to be so obvious. There were other texts, however, which were recommended for particular times or activities. As will be seen below, both the Lord's Prayer and the Creed became a regular part of the household worship practice of devout Genevans.[33] The main focus here, however, is the model prayers prepared by Calvin and later by his circle of friends to serve the people for the specified times when they were exhorted to pray: morning and evening, before and after meals, and before beginning school or work.

In the Genevan Catechism (1542) model prayers for these five times were published. The ones for meals were voiced in the plural, while the morning, evening, and school prayers were in the singular. Soon published in Latin as well as French, this group of prayers was directed in the first place to children, with the Latin catechism and prayers intended for the school boys studying in that language and the French for the rest of the population.[34] In 1551 Jean Crespin

---

[32]   Grosse, *Les rituels de la Cène*, pp. 167-68. "Indice pour trouver les pseaumes selon l'occurrence des afaires, esquelles l'Eglise de Dieu, ou bien la personne privee se peut trouver : en quoy consiste le vray usage des Pseaumes," p. 167.

[33]   For the Lord's Prayer in public worship, see chap. 3 at nn.61, 71, 78, 152ff, 185; chap. 4 at nn.5ff, 137; chap. 5 at nn.136, 189ff. For Creed, see chap. 3 at nn.61, 86, 154f, 166; chap. 4 at nn.5ff, 137. For Decalogue, see chap. 3 at nn.61, 71, 86, 104,115, 166. Here are not included the references to these three texts (prayer, creed, commandments) in the context of catechesis. Below at n.40.

[34]   Candaux, *Le Psautier de Genève*, pp. 86-90, provides a brief introduction to these prayers. He begins by noting that the collection as a whole has never been studied and then takes as his point of departure the complete Psalter 1562-63. He identifies eighteen different prayers, beginning with the five from Calvin's catechism. Three others which he also indicates come from Calvin are the two prayers before work and the one for captives. Three other prayers for before reading scripture, thanksgiving for reading and preaching of the word, and a prayer for visiting the sick, come from the collection entitled "Le régime domestique des Chrestiens," which Candaux says may be attributed to Christophe Fabri, Maturin Cordier, or Theodore Beza. (p.86) [see at n.38 below.] Candaux goes on to discuss the household prayers found in the edition of the Psalter by Jean Crespin (1563), and a similar collection published by Davodeau & Mottière in 1562. He suggests that three prayers in Crespin's book may be his own (see n.37 below). Candaux outlines the two collections on p. 89. After this point, according to Candaux, no more new prayers were added until 1643, and the prayers in various printings of the Psalter between 1562 and 1643 ranged from none to the full eighteen; pp. 86-87. Candaux does not appear to include the earliest forms of the household devotions, as found in Jean Rivery 1561, and he does not analzye the origin of the prayers or consider their use (singular, plural forms). In this chapter, the purpose is the development of these prayers rather than Candaux's summary overview of the completed project.

published a small catechism, *L'ABC françois*, which gave four of the prayers along with further short options for several of the specific times, but Crespin substituted one for "before going to work" for the one for school, thus making the series more appropriate for adults. [35] Among the most common additions were multiple alternatives for before and after meals; this begins at least as early as *L'ABC françois*. Note that all six of these categories of petitions are activity-related, in fact corresponding to Calvin's list, and they appeared in the catechisms with considerable regularity. These times are not fixed like the monastic hours but are linked to daily activities, a functional lay orientation to keeping "holy time."

In 1552 there was something new in the model devotional prayers: Crespin's publication of the liturgy added a long intercession for use by a captive, voiced in the first person singular. This was not time-specific although it was situational, and it appeared in *La forme des prières*, not the catechism. Several scholars point out that this new prayer was related to the increased persecutions in France; it is similar to sentences added to the Sunday and day of prayer intercessions, which supports the probability that the prayer came from Calvin's pen. [36] This model prayer was soon added to editions of the liturgy published by others, e.g., the Rivery brothers in 1553, Robert Estienne the same year, and it became a fixed part of the Psalter-service book used by the French-language Reformed for the next century. [37] The prayer for captives was the only new prayer added in the 1550s, but by 1560 the model prayers were expanding, with most appearing in the catechism but some in the liturgy. By 1561 there was at least one more version of the prayer before beginning work, now in *La forme des prières*, [38] and in 1563 Crespin published a catechism with a prayer "on going out of the house" and one "Before going back to work after a

---

35 See Peter, "L'abécédaire genevois," pp. 182-88. It has three short prayers before meals and three after, plus a second short one for the morning, in addition to the four original ones and the prayer before work. For translation of the last, see Calvin, *Writings on Pastoral Piety*, p. 214. Candaux attributes this prayer for work to Calvin, *Le Psautier de Genève*, p. 86.

36 See Grosse, *Les rituels de la Cène*, pp. 170-71; citing also Candaux, *Le Psautier de Genève*, chap. 15. For Sunday prayers, see chap. 3 at n.77.

37 *La forme des prières*, "Oraison," [Jean Crespin printer's mark], 1552, pp. 52-54. *La forme des prières*, Adam & Jean Rivery, 1553, pp. 56-59. Robert Estienne published it in 1553, also, adding to the title: "Oraison que font les captifs sous l'Antechrist," see Grosse, *Les rituels de la Cène*, p. 170, who affirms that this appears for about a century in the service-books, annexed to the liturgy. For text see OS II, pp. 150-51 (where it is dated 1559 and associated with the Bible, because the OS editors did not have the earlier liturgies to trace its origin). English translation in Calvin, *Writings on Pastoral Piety*, pp. 215-16.

38 *La forme des prières*, by Jean Rivery in 1561, pp. 54, 54-56. [BGE Bd1928 res]

meal."[39] Some other specific foci, such as prayers to use before and after reading scripture or hearing the sermon, or in visiting the sick, also came to be included.[40] Since by the 1550s the liturgy and catechism were beginning to be bound with the Psalter as a Reformed "service book," the model prayers might migrate between the catechism and liturgy, and the choice of both place and selection of texts was up to the publisher.[41]

Household Devotions

One of the most interesting developments, the publication of corporate household prayers, came late in Calvin's life. He may well not have been directly responsible for it, although there is good reason to suppose that he approved because in effect it was simply a re-purposing of his own public texts for a smaller "family church" context. This might have been in practice earlier, as well, if devout households crafted their own versions informally.

What appears to be the first printed instance of this development of a household liturgy for daily devotion was published by Jean Rivery in 1561, and varied versions followed in the next several years. Rivery's rubric sets the stage: "The practice of the father of the family and all his household to pray in the morning." Then follows the exhortation and confession of sin which Calvin used on Sunday mornings, and the model morning prayer now voiced in the first person plural, with the addition of the Lord's Prayer and Apostles' Creed as those would have been part of the public liturgy at the end of the regular weekday prayer

---

[39] Catechism in the service-book collection (Psalter, liturgy, etc.) published by Jean Crespin in 1563 [BGE Su 830]; pp. 91-92: "Toy, Seigneur, qui as tousjours esté nostre seure guide & garde à l'encontre de tous nos ennemis, nous te requerons de nous faire aussi la grace de t'en rendre les louanges qui t'appartiennent: & estre tellement conducteur & protecteur de nostre chemin, que rien ne nous puisse nuire. Mais singulierement nous te supplions de dresser tellement nos pas en la voye de tes saincts commandemens, que nous marchions & courions droictement en icelle, non obstant tout rencontre si que tu en puisses estre glorifié, & nos prochains edifiez, par nostre Seigneur, &c." Plus one "avant de vaquer à aucune chose apres le repas." See Grosse, *Les rituels de la Cène*, pp. 170-71 n.210, for various publications, including one by Jean de Laon for Antoine Vincent in 1562 which has: "priere à Dieu pour donner benediction à nostre labeur."

[40] An example of this can be found in the large composite collection called *Instruction des Chrestiens. Ou recueil de plusieurs passages de la sainte Escriture… avec quelques autres traitez* (Geneve, François Jaquy pour Guillaume Fournet, 1562), pp. 228-29. ZURICH e-rara.ch. suggests Cordier, Calvin, Christophe Fabri as authors. One section is entitled *Le regime domestiques de chrestiens*, pp. 223ff. This book also includes a variety of prayers for various estates: those about to marry, husbands, wives, children, masters, servants, et al., along with a flood of Biblical quotations. Peter, *L'abécédaire génévois*, pp. 176-77, briefly describes this work. Cf. Candaux, *Le Psautier de Genève*, n.32 above.

[41] My own observation; see also Grosse, *Les rituels de la Cène*, pp. 162-63, 170-74.

(extempore #3).[42] This household format was soon taken up in some publications in both Geneva and France, and the texts were elaborated in various ways. The earliest new form seems to be the text printed by Françoys Jaquy for Antoine Vincent in 1562,[43] soon followed by Jean-Baptiste Pinereul for Antoine Vincent in 1563,[44] Jean Crespin in 1563,[45] and Pierre le Chandelier at Caen in 1563 and Simon Mangeant in Caen in 1565.[46]

The household devotions published by Antoine Vincent in 1562 and 1563 provide a liturgical pattern which can apparently be applied either in the morning or the evening. The text of this set of prayers is provided in an appendix.[47] The title is simple: "Prayer to say in the evening" but it then begins with an exhortation in the plural: "My brothers..." which is actually a form of Calvin's invitation to the confession of sins, (borrowed from? or) at least like Rivery's morning prayers in 1561. The long prayer which follows inserts the model evening prayer (now in the plural) into a variant of Calvin's prayer for illumination-and-sealing used on weekdays (extempore #1). The petition to be illumined by the Holy Spirit to

---

42 *La forme des prières* and Catechism published together by Jean Rivery in 1561 [BGE Bd1928 res]. The catechism has "L'exercice du pere de famille, & de tous ses domestiques pour prier au matin," pp. 180-83, with the form in the plural (exhortation, confession, prayer concluding with Lord's Prayer and Apostles' Creed). Then other prayers: two before and after meals (in plural), and evening prayer in the singular, pp. 183-87. A translation of the household devotions is found in Calvin, *Writings on Pastoral Piety*, pp. 217-19.

43 *Les pseaumes mis en rime françoise...* de l'imprimerie de Françoys Jaquy pour Antoine Vincent, 1562 Avec privilege du roy. This appears in the catechism section, pp. 96-100. [This was reissued with the New Testament by Jaquy in Geneva, 1563 = MHR O4e (563)]. See Appendix Eleven, part one.

44 *Les pseaumes mis en rime françoise...* par Jean Baptiste Pinereul pour Antoine Vincent, 1563. (The prayer for captives is placed after the instructions for visiting the sick.) The catechism has prayers for the morning (singular), two before work (plural), one before school (singular), before and after meals (one each, both plural), then one in the plural for the evening as liturgy, with another long intercessory prayer to be used after morning and evening prayers, plus one for visiting the sick, pp. cc5r-dd3r. [BGE Su 4939 Res]. See Appendix Eleven.

45 *Les Pseaumes mis en rime françoise...*, published as service book with liturgy, catechism, by Jean Crespin 1563 [BGE Su 830]. The Catechism has family prayers for morning "L'exercice du pere de famille & de tous ses domestiques, pour prier au matin" p. 90-91; a prayer "en sortant de la maison," pp. 91-92; plus ones before and after meals and evening, in the plural.

46 *Cent cinquante pseaumes de David...* a Caen, par Pierre le Chandelier, 1563 [MHR O4e (563)a]. It includes Psalter, liturgy, catechism, short formula for examining children, and the French confession of faith, and is also bound with New Testament. The catechism gives the morning household devotional liturgy, pp. I3v-I4v, plus the rest of the usual prayers in the singular. *Les pseaumes mis en rime françoise...* a Caen, chez Simon Mangeant, 1565. [MHR O6e (565)]. This appears in the catechism section, pp. M3v-M4v. See Appendix Eleven, part one.

47 Specific page numbers are not given for these comments, since all are visible in the texts printed in Appendix Eleven, part one.

know God's will is a creative adaptation of the prayer for understanding God's word. (The French version published by le Chandelier actually inserts the reference to "ta Parole.") It is followed by the rubric: "General Prayer for the needs of the church that can be added after the morning or evening prayer." This introduces an even longer intercession, a composite drawn from various sources, particularly elements of the Sunday and day of prayer intercessions as well as Calvin's extempore weekday prayers. It includes as well a few other points not found in Calvin's texts. One of these is a petition specifically for those whose business requires them to travel in papal lands, and another is a reference to those "who are deprived of this heavenly pasture of Your word which is daily ministered to us by Your grace, who do not have the freedom to invoke Your holy name publicly as we have." The language here echoes the prefaces which Conrad Badius supplied for Calvin's sermons, so it is possible that he may have been involved in crafting these prayers. [48] The long intercessory prayer is followed by the recitation of the Lord's Prayer and the Apostles Creed. Occasionally, the recitation of the Decalogue might be added, as in the edition by Simon Mangeant published in Caen in 1565. [49]

Although these particular versions of the devotional prayers do not explicitly give a liturgy for household morning prayers they clearly presuppose such a thing and thus confirm that there were forms for morning and evening family devotions. This very limited sample of texts suggests that household prayer in the morning may have been more common than in the evening, but both were strongly recommended.

A contemporary description of the devout Genevan household comes from the pen of a young German Swiss boy from Basel, Andreas Ryff, who lived in Geneva for three years. In 1560 (at about age eleven) he was sent by his father to Geneva to learn French, but things did not go well in the first family with whom he lived. He was unable to keep up with his studies in a foreign language and did not apply himself since no one gave him proper oversight or instruction. In June 1562 Ryff's father moved young Andreas to the devout household of Jean Du Molard the younger, a spice merchant. Du Molard the father was a brother of the syndic Hudriod Du Molard, and more importantly for the present purpose, one the earliest elders on the consistory, first elected in 1543 and continuing to serve for years thereafter. [50] Thus the boy from Basel got some experience of a family headed by a Genevan Protestant who had been reared by

---

[48]   See Appendix Eleven, part one, and chap. 6 at nn.266, 269.

[49]   See Appendix Eleven, part one.

[50]   Feb. 15, 1543, *Consist.* I, pp. 180-81; Feb. 18, 1546, *Consist.* II, p. 141 n. 171.

one of Calvin's strong supporters. Ryff said that Du Molard (the younger) was a harsh master, but his wife was very good to the young boy, and both of them took care to provide him with an excellent religious education. According to Ryff, the master sent the whole household to worship every morning (apparently in their parish church, although of course it could have been any one of the three places in Geneva where there were daily services by 1559).[51]

Regular attendance at public worship was vital but it was not all, however. The household was gathered every morning and evening for devotions.

> Each morning and also each evening, Master Jean, his wife, his brother-in-law, and all the household knelt down in the main room and there Madame made the prayers in a very loud voice, thanking God with acknowledgment of His gifts and benefits, and praying with fervor for Him to pour out His Spirit, protection, blessing and mercy on us.[52]

It is noteworthy that it was the mother who led the prayers. The head of the family was in charge and present, but he delegated leadership, not only to his wife but also to other members of the household. He took seriously his obligation to instruct all the members well, and when Ryff was properly educated – by Du Molard – it became his turn to lead the prayers.[53] Certainly not all households were like this, but the fact that such a practice existed among the native Genevans, and not merely among those (like religious refugees) who

---

51 Ryff, "Un jeune Bâlois à Genève," p. 415 "Tous les matins, à cinq heures, il envoyait tout son monde à l'église, et quand il avait l'intention de me fustiger, il me faisait rester à la maison ... Malgré cela, je ne me suis jamais plaint, parce que je me trouvais bien chez mon maître, et que je sentais que je tirerais bon profit de cet apprentissage. D'ailleurs, autant maître Jean se montrait sévère, autant sa femme me témoignait d'attachement, et je remercie Dieu particulièrement de m'avoir conduit dans leur maison, parce qu'il y régnait une discipline parfaite et une police bien ordonnée." The reference to 5 a.m. is a little puzzling, since Ryff arrived in the DuMolard household in mid-summer, when the dawn service would be at 4 a.m. and the "ordinary" one at 6 a.m. There were dawn services only on Mondays-Wednesdays-Fridays at St. Pierre and on Wednesdays at St. Gervais, but daily sermons at 6 a.m./7 a.m. in all the parishes. It is probably a slightly confused memory of the schedule, because Ryff is more likely to have remembered the daily rhythm than the exact time. See chap. 1 at nn.145ff.

52 Ryff, "Un jeune Bâlois à Genève," p. 415: "Chaque matin et aussi chaque soir, maître Jean, sa femme, son beau-frère et toute la maisonnée s'agenouillaient dans la salle du poêle, et là la Dame faisait la prière à très-haute voix, remerciant Dieu avec recueillement pour ses grâces et ses bienfaits et le priant avec ferveur, pour qu'il répandît sur nous son esprit, sa protection, sa bénédiction et sa miséricorde."

53 Ryff, "Un jeune Bâlois à Genève," p. 415: "Plus tard, ce fut moi que mon patron chargea de cette fonction de faire la prière, lorsqu'il m'eut un peu enseigné; je crois avoir acquis par ce moyen une ferveur sincère pour la religion."

might be expected to be receptive to Calvin's teaching, is significant evidence for the development of "private" worship patterns in the daily lives of the people. [54]

II: People and Pastors Facing Sickness and Death

Households were the normal site of another key aspect of worship: pastoral ministry to the sick. Visiting and providing spiritual care for the ill and dying were very important parts of the pastors' responsibility and the people's expectation. The shape that such ministry took in Reformed circles was rather different from many traditional practices, at least in significant ways, although there were also continuities between medieval and Protestant or (more narrowly) Reformed ways. The present purpose is not to discuss the large question of death and dying in the late medieval and early modern world – a topic on which much ink has flowed – but simply to provide a summary context in which to understand Calvin's Geneva.

The Tradition and Protestant Changes

Sickness and death were a very present part of daily life in medieval and early modern Europe. It was commonly believed that no one could be certain of her or his salvation except by a special revelation, and thus anxiety and lack of assurance were significant problems. (There is considerable debate about the extent of this fear, but it is clear that this was a serious issue for quite a number of people.) Along with anxiety about salvation there was also the conviction that a major reason for illness was sin: the disease was punishment. Combined with what was, by modern standards, a limited scientific knowledge of "natural causes," this gave particular prominence to the need for spiritual remedies. Illness did not always lead to death, of course, but that was usually a real danger, and in some cases such as plague it was nearly certain. Pastoral care for the sick was therefore usually addressed in the awareness that death was as much a possibility as healing.

An important focus of late medieval piety was the fear of sudden death. Not being ready would make the danger of hell much graver, because repentance and the last rites were essential; a common theme in prayers to Our Lady was to be

---

[54] *Consist.* I: on Nov. 23, 1542, p. 142, the mother of M. Hugoz says she goes to the sermon "tous les jour" and makes her apprentices go. On Dec. 28, 1542, p. 159, Mercet Michallet says that he goes to the sermon on Sundays and when he can but those for whom he works do not want him to go to sermons.

spared a sudden death.[55] Some of the most popular books published (before and after printing became possible) were the *ars moriendi* literature; these were handbooks to guide lay people in preparing for their own deaths or, because death was communal, helping family and friends assist a loved one in his or her last days. In ordinary life in the middle ages the intensity of concern about salvation naturally varied from person to person, but it is clear from the literature that on the deathbed nearly everyone focused on trying to find assurance.[56] The *ars moriendi* gave considerable attention to dealing with the fears about salvation, the *Anfectungen*. A "good death" in which the person was able to receive the sacraments and demonstrate a certain peace and acceptance was considered an important sign of ultimate salvation and much desired. A "bad death" of terror, rage, and doubt, death without benefit of the last rites, left behind the fear that the newly dead relative might well be headed for damnation. Although by the later middle ages laity were taking a greater role in helping their family or friends achieve a good death, the ministry of the clergy was necessary, if at all possible. The last rites: confession, communion, extreme unction, could only be properly

---

[55] Popular examples of such prayers found in many books of hours include "Obsecro," in *Time Sanctified. The Book of Hours in Medieval Art and Life*, ed. Roger Wieck (New York: George Braziller, 1988), pp. 163-64; p. 164: "And at the end of my life show me your face, and reveal to me the day and the hour of my death. Please hear and receive this humble prayer and grant me eternal life. Listen and hear me, Mary, sweetest virgin and Mother of God and of mercy. Amen." Dietrich Kolde, "A Fruitful Mirror," in *Three Reformation Catechisms*, ed. D. Janz (Toronto: Mellon, 1982), pp. 64-97, for examples of instruction about prayer; pp. 84-85: "In the morning when you awake from sleep, you should wait and think or speak thus: O almighty, eternal, compassionate God, how I waste my precious time, how lazy and indolent I am, how I will have to burn in purgatory for having lost my precious time so miserably. Further, during the night all spiritual hearts sang and read praise to God, and I slept. And there was also great joy in heaven, and I did not think about working so that I too might find joy. And there was also great lamentation and distress in purgatory, and I did not pray about it. And also, many a person died during the night and God let me live. Further, after this you should get up cheerfully and think eagerly about making up for past omissions, and go get on your knees and speak as follows: O dear Lord Jesus Christ, I thank you for all the bitter suffering that you suffered during the night of your passion and suffering: when your soul was grieved until your death: when you begged your heavenly Father and he did not hear you: when you sweat water and blood in fear of death: when you were captured and bound and thrown to the ground: when you were struck in your most holy, beautiful, loving and dear face in Anna's house: when you suffered monstrously in Caiphas' house: when you were forsaken by your disciples. I beg you, O dearest Lord, not to let your bitter suffering be lost on this poor sinner, and please convert all sinners, male and female, and console the poor souls in purgatory and all grieving hearts, and protect me from all sins today and all the days of my life. Amen. Further, then say an Our Father and the creed."

[56] Bornert, *La réforme protestante du culte*, p. 581, notes that even someone as worldly wise as Sebastian Brant linked sin and sickness, and said that it is a good idea to confess to the priest before seeking out the doctor.

performed by a priest, and only a priest could celebrate a Mass for the dead. Such Masses were an ever-increasing feature of the religious landscape. More and more men were ordained not for parishes but for altars, to supply the sacramental grace which anxious people desired for themselves and their loved ones, and more and more Masses were being accumulated by those who could afford them in order to ward off the terrors of hell and shorten purgatory.

Protestant Modifications and Changes

Protestants revised these traditional responses to sickness and death in various ways. Obviously Masses for the dead were one of the first things to go. As has frequently been noted, the sense of close connection between living and dead underwent a significant rupture because Protestants did not believe that human action could affect the state of those who were no longer living on earth. The focus therefore shifted to accompanying and consoling the sick up to the point of death, and then comforting the bereaved; beyond the grave everything was entrusted into God's hands.[57] The forms of accompaniment and comfort also underwent some change, although many aspects of the care for the sick and dying continued even as they were also modified or re-defined. The traditional *ars moriendi* were replaced with rewritten or completely different texts, the rites for the communion of the sick and funerals were revised more or less radically, and the tradition of burial within churches or hallowed ground was reformed.

Protestants varied among themselves with regard to the exact shape of the care for the sick and dying. Austra Reinis' recent book, *Reforming the Art of Dying: The ars moriendi in the German Reformation (1519-1528)* (2007), provides a fine discussion of the earliest German Protestant approaches to pastoral care of the dying.[58] Her careful and detailed analysis of sermons and handbooks (loosely called *Sterbebücher*) by Luther and a number of other leaders, points out continuities and discontinuities.

> The most important theological difference between the dying person of the *ars moriendi* and the dying individual of the Reformation *Sterbebücher* is that the latter can be certain of his salvation even as he faces *Anfechtung*.[59]

---

[57] One well-known example of the emphasis on the community between living and dead in the late middle ages is Bossy, *Christianity in the West*, pp. 26-34 For a summary of the break between living and dead and how this affected Protestants, see Bornert, *La réforme protestante du culte*, pp. 580-82.

[58] Reinis, *Reforming the Art of Dying*, gives a good recent picture of the relationship between *ars moriendi* literature and Protestant developments in early Lutheranism. Chap. 2 in particular outlines the "uncertainty of salvation in the late medieval ars moriendi" and chap. 3 examines Luther's *Eyn Sermon von der bereytung zum sterben*, 1519, the first Protestant *ars moriendi*.

[59] Reinis, *Reforming the Art of Dying*, p. 140.

The teaching on justification by faith alone changed the perspective on what humans can contribute to their salvation and thus had important consequences for how one prepared for death. Trust in Christ's all-sufficient grace meant that one could be certain of salvation. This also made teaching that doctrine a critically important aspect of preparing for death. Rituals which had had a central place at deathbeds were no longer the essential focus, especially for the more radical reformers. Some of the traditional means of reassurance which continued in one form or another were deathbed sacraments provided by the clergy and participation in prayers and comfort offered by family and friends in the dying process: death remained a communal experience. However, the re-defined preparation for death put less emphasis on the final hours and more on life-long teaching ("a bad death" was not a sign of reprobation). The degree of continuity or discontinuity with late medieval practice varied among Protestants; Lutherans were more inclined to modify and Reformed more likely to break with aspects of the tradition.

This is visible even in the early years. As Reinis concluded from her study of the first Protestant writings about preparing for death, in their sermons and manuals Lutherans continued to make use of late medieval aids such as the crucifix, prayers to Mary and a role for the saints.[60] On the other hand, Johannes Oecolampadius, the one Reformed voice in her survey, did not. Reinis discusses three of the Basel reformer's works: a sermon, a liturgical manual for clergy, and a litany for lay use, and her overview of these three texts gives a starting place to describe Reformed pastoral care of the dying. Oecolampadius' sermon, entitled *Nunc Dimittis* (1521), is essentially an exposition of Luke 2:29-32 which was directed to both monastics and lay people; Reinis suggests that the author may have intended his work to invite "his hearers to embrace the Reformation."[61] It was clearly an exposition of a text – indeed the text which later Reformed congregations, including those in Geneva, sang at the conclusion of the Lord's Supper. Oecolampadius' *Lettaney* (1520 or 1523) comes from the same period as the sermon, and provides an order which lay people might use with the dying: the Kyrie (in Greek), the Lord's Prayer, the Ave Maria, the Creed, a long litany of 110 petitions (preceded by another Kyrie but this time in German), a paraphrase of Rom. 8:32, and a didactic collect.[62] As Reinis points out, Oecolampadius draws on some medieval forms but carefully distinguishes his litany by replacing references to Mary, the saints, and angels with ones which dwell on Christ's life. The

---

[60] Reinis, *Reforming the Art of Dying*, pp. 142, 143-59, describes a particular Lutheran book which also includes unction and other traditional acts.

[61] Reinis, *Reforming the Art of Dying*, pp. 84, 85. (Full discussion, pp. 83-104)

[62] Reinis, *Reforming the Art of Dying*, pp. 160-64; outline pp. 160-61.

Form und Gestalt (1525 or 1526) was Oecolampadius' first liturgy for the Church in Basel. The section on care for the dying includes confession and absolution, with Psalms, the Gloria, a litany (not the same as the previous one), the Lord's Prayer, a reading from the Lukan passion and related exhortation, the Lord's Prayer again and Creed, and then the words of institution and administration of the Lord's Supper, followed by an exhortation on its meaning and the final blessing.[63]

Amy Nelson Burnett's fine study of Basel extends the discussion of Oecolampadius' early views and the ways they were changed over time. As she explains, the first form for visiting the sick included both a kind of private confession and the invitation to commune. The revised liturgy allowed the sick person to ask the minister questions about the faith but the rest of the family could remain present and there was no mention of confessing sins. With regard to the sacrament, the rubrics were altered to indicate that if the sick person had not received it for a long time and "wished to testify to Christian unity, he or she should not be refused. Those who had communed recently, however, were to be told that they did not need the sacrament."[64] All of Oecolampadius' writings concerned with the sick and dying express plainly the importance of knowing the faith. Despite the traditional practices in the initial versions, the early Reformed texts were clearly different from the medieval *ars moriendi* and even from those of their Lutheran contemporaries. And more radical revisions were coming, although not all Reformed would follow them.

The teaching and practice of Strasbourg was of course a very important influence on Calvin. Bucer's practice is discussed by René Bornert in his massive and detailed examination of all aspects of Strasbourg's Protestant liturgical reforms. Bornert's discussion is relatively brief, however, since he notes that visiting the sick was related more to pastoral care than to liturgy (his subject), particularly since Protestants removed much of the traditional (liturgical) ritual. In Strasbourg's first reforms in 1524, unction was dropped, and the sick were at first encouraged to come to church to receive the sacrament. By 1534 sickbed communion was defined, and in 1537 pastors were given more precise instructions for visiting the sick. They were to console them by reading scripture; the Biblical texts that are suggested view illness as a trial and the consequence of sin, but in this suffering the hope of eternal life is already glimpsed. This scriptural reading is followed by exhortation, private counseling if that is needed, prayer with the family and then the celebration of the Lord's Supper with the group present.[65]

---

[63] Reinis, *Reforming the Art of Dying*, pp. 164-69; outline p. 165.

[64] Burnett, *Teaching the Reformation*, pp. 51-52 (quotation p. 52).

[65] Bornert, *La réforme protestante du culte*, pp. 580-83.

When it came to funerals, at first Strasbourg clearly took the more radical step of virtually eliminating them. According to the earliest practice in 1524, the burial took place without even the presence of a minister; the family and friends carried the body directly from the home to the cemetery. From 1527 on, cemeteries were located outside the city walls; burial in the city and thus in its churches was forbidden. In 1537, shortly before Calvin arrived in Strasbourg, this extreme simplicity (which many considered disrespectful) was modified; a minister would accompany the funeral cortege to the cemetery and there he would speak to the people for the consolation of the living. Various Biblical texts were suggested for this purpose, to be followed by an exhortation to comfort – and instruct – the bereaved, including the reminder that all people live in sin, from which death comes, and all must direct their lives to die to sin. The burial concluded with a silent prayer and then a collect by the minister.[66] An example of what the consolation and exhortation might sound like is found in a very unlikely source: the words of a woman at the grave of her husband. In January 1548, after Bucer gave the official sermon for his colleague Matthew Zell, Katharina Schütz Zell preached... and then (apparently) went home and wrote it down! According to reports from those who heard her, including one highly educated humanist, she did a good job and friends cared enough to pass down her text.[67]

When the Strasbourg French-language congregation which Calvin had once led was established in London it seems to have followed a pattern similar to the form developed by Bucer and his colleagues. Valerain Poullain's liturgies (printed in Latin in 1551 and French in 1552), give a fairly fully developed picture of the simple service. This included a graveyard sermon about death and resurrection, mention of the deceased's virtues to edify the church, and a (probably long) prayer. After thanking God for delivering the person from this miserable life and allowing him to die in true faith, the minister would exhort the people to meditate on death and prepare for their own, and then conclude with the prayer that all might come to the resurrection and share in the joyful immortality of Christ's reign. A final word instructed those present to give the deacons alms for the poor as they departed.[68] Plainly, although bare by traditional standards, this Reformed funeral had come some distance from the first Strasbourg radical changes. In fact,

---

66 Bornert, *La réforme protestante du culte*, pp. 586-87.

67 "Klag red und ermahnung," in *Katharina Schütz Zell : The Writings*, pp. 70-94. English in *Church Mother*, pp. 103-23.

68 Poullain, *Liturgia Sacra*, pp. 166-69. A Lasco, *Forma ac Ratio*, in the *Opera* II, pp. 272-77, provides a rite for burial with sermon and prayers. As Engammare points out, this includes a service in the church itself; cf. "L'inhumation de Calvin," pp. 276-78,

on the subject of what was appropriate, various theologians differed. Viret published his *Disputations chrestiennes* in 1544 and then a completely revised version in 1552. Along with vigorous polemic against traditional Roman practices and learned references to antiquity, Viret also seems to have engaged in some intra-Reformed critique. In the 1552 edition of the book, he objects to recounting the life (and virtues) of the deceased on the grounds that God's word is enough "to incite [people] to virtue and honorable behavior."[69] Might he have been taking aim at Poullain's liturgy or at least that line of thought?

It is not possible to say what Calvin practiced during his ministry in Strasbourg, but it is quite probable that he had a very simple form of sermon at the graveside. For one thing, it was his usual pattern to follow his senior colleagues' liturgical patterns (since all those with whom he worked shared basic agreement on principle and varied only with regard to *adiaphora*). In this case, it is also true that Calvin expressed a qualified approval of the idea of an exhortation at the graveside. As Max Engammare has pointed out, several letters from 1543 affirm this. In the first, Oct. 7, 1543, Calvin responds to a question from the pastors at Montbéliard; there should not be any funeral service in the church but he sees no objection to a graveside exhortation to the people. A month later, the same subject appears in a letter to Viret; Calvin says that "if a minister is asked to do so, he may lead the procession to the grave, and there he will give some words of exhortation (*horta-tiunculam*) to console the friends."[70] It is clear, then, that Calvin had no principled objection to a graveside sermon, nor to a minister being involved at the request of the family. There is no evidence that this was practiced in Geneva, however.

Calvin Preaches on Moses' Death

Before examining what is known about Geneva, it may be helpful to see how Calvin dealt with this subject in preaching on a significant Biblical instance of death and mourning in the final chapter of Deuteronomy. There are two sermons; the second is the focus here. What he says about Deut. 34:7-11 offers a guide to the way Calvin shaped the pastoral response to what was a very frequent experience in early modern life.[71]

The text gives the simple facts of Moses' age, health, and death, and the thirty-days mourning practiced by his people, concluding with the transfer of leadership

---

69　Engammare, "L'inhumation de Calvin," pp. 278-79, quotation p. 279. Citing Pierre Viret, *Disputations chrestiennes touchant l'estat des trepassez faites par dialogues, desquelles la premiere partie est intitulée Les Enfers* [Genève : Jean Girard, 1552], pp. 89ff.

70　Engammare, "L'inhumation de Calvin," p. 274, citing Herminjard, *Correspondance*, vol. 9, #1291, p. 65, and #1305, p. 104.

71　Sermon 200 on Deut., OC 29:218-232; notes will be given only for direct quotations.

to Joshua. First the preacher notes what a gift it was to Israel that God granted Moses such a long life, for their sakes: 120 years or "six 20s." There seems to be more than a touch of weary amazement in Calvin's words as he contrasts Moses' age with his own experience and his own world. Even strong people begin to fail when they pass sixty, and "it is a great thing when a person reaches that age with full vigor." (The preacher cites the "Song of Moses," i.e., Ps. 90, apparently considering that if seventy is the usual limit of life, those who reach sixty are close to the end.) [72] He goes on to emphasize that God gave Moses such a long life in order to provide leadership through the forty years of wilderness wandering which Israel brought on itself by sin and disobedience. Now they are at the entrance to the promised land but Moses cannot accompany them because he also failed to obey God. Before going further, Calvin repeats that the fact Moses retained his strength and was able to lead the people (at an age when others are decrepit) is a measure of God's care for Israel. He adds a note of application: when God does this "for us" we should recognize that it is evidence of God's kindness for which we should be grateful.

The preacher devotes considerable attention to the appropriate burial and mourning practices. First he deals with some more general questions about what is fitting. Calvin begins by saying that it is natural for people to mourn a death. He explains that it is usually the members of the family and close friends who do this, but in the case of an important public figure like Moses it was all the people, for whom he had been a caring father. Then the preacher addresses the issue of whether mourning is not a contradiction of faith in view of the fact that life and death are in God's hands. Calvin explains that one must pay attention to the purposes of mourning; he then proceeds to explain two main aspects. One is that when the believer sees that a person has died, he or she knows that this is a mirror of God's curse on human sin – not on one person or several but on all humankind. "Whence does death come, except that we are alienated/ separated from the source and fountain of life?" [73] Thus when we weep at a death we are weeping for our own sinfulness. The preacher observes that in his day this reason for mourning is almost completely forgotten: when people cry at a funeral they are not thinking about this. The second cause for mourning is the loss of good leaders. Calvin points out that this is a kind of chastisement by God, but then he also affirms that in the case of the righteous they are taken away so that they may rest and escape some imminent disaster. (Although he does not cite the passage, the preacher is almost certainly thinking of Isa. 57:1-2.) He does quote

---

72   Sermon 200 on Deut., OC 29:218.

73   Sermon 200 on Deut., OC 29:220.

Heb. 11:38, and adds that weeping for the loss of the ministry of such leaders is right.[74]

Then the preacher deals with the manner of mourning, drawing out both the wrong and the right ways.

> St. Paul remonstrates with us when we weep at the death of our friends or relatives or those who serve God's church; we must not be like unbelievers (he says), who have no hope and so cannot console themselves with that [Eph. 2:12]. In this passage St. Paul does not say that it is sinful to weep; he does not condemn it at all. But he shows us that we must moderate our tears since God gives us consolation when He calls us to the hope of the heavenly life where we will be renewed.[75]

The pastor continues, referring to the experience of death and decay; it even appears as if souls vanish and as if everything is lost.

> Nevertheless we must always come back to this: that God of His infinite goodness still has pity on us and does not want us to perish in death, but that it may be for us like a passage to eternal life. That hope is intended to make us rejoice in the midst of our sorrows, or at the least it may be a bridle to restrain our tears so that they may not pour out beyond bounds and we may not come to the point of defying God [as the unbelievers do].[76]

Calvin exhorts his hearers (including himself) not to give way to despair as if God could not care for them in face of the loss of someone who could be very helpful. He adds "[God] could even raise up stones [Lk. 19:40], if that seemed good to Him."[77]

Why should the church not follow these practices of mourning? The preacher explains that what Deuteronomy recounts was characteristic of the ceremonies of the Jewish people. While appreciating that these were right for the Old Testament people whom God treated as little children, Calvin expresses his conviction that the coming of Jesus Christ has made these obsolete. This leads to a sharp note of polemic against Roman funeral traditions which the reformer identifies as (too) similar to those of the Old Testament people. For Israel, these mourning practices were God's accommodation to the situation before Christ's resurrection was

---

[74]   Sermon 200 on Deut., OC 29:220.

[75]   Sermon 200 on Deut., OC 29:221.

[76]   Sermon 200 on Deut., OC 29:221.

[77]   Sermon 200 on Deut., OC 29:221.

visible, but now that that vital assurance of eternal life is plainly known in the gospel, the old ways must pass away.[78]

Pastoral Care in Sickness and Death in Geneva

The focus in Geneva was on ministry to the sick and dying, and there were no formal funerals as such. Both the liturgy and the church order included instructions about how pastors and people should behave in face of illness, but only the *Ecclesiastical Ordinances* gives orders about burial. This point will be considered briefly later. Here it is important to note what was prescribed and then the more anecdotal evidence for actual practice.

Instructing Pastors and People

The earliest Protestant forms for pastoral care of the sick in Geneva are found in Farel's liturgy, *La maniere et fasson* (1533).[79] The order can be summarized. First there is a basic Biblical reference: Christ and the apostles taught not only in public but also from house to house. Then the minister is provided with material for a (long) exhortation to the sick person to emphasize trust in God's goodness and remembrance of Christ's bitter pain and death, because His suffering was much worse than that which the sick person now bears. The patient should commit himself into God's hands and "do to his neighbor as he would like done to him"; he should put his affairs in order so that if he dies there will be no conflict among his relatives. After these general points, Farel counsels the minister to speak according to what the sick person needs: admonition if he is trusting in his good works, comfort in God's promises if he is fearful of God's anger. Then there is a practical note about providing any physical help which he can: "bread, wine, fruits, or anything else, he shall spare nothing, showing to all a true example of love."[80] The penultimate paragraph instructs the pastor about what to do after the person dies, and includes a polemical note.

> After the death, he must, by holy exhortations, give courage to those left behind, that they praise God and conform themselves to his holy will. In place of former times when the poor desolate widow who had lost her husband was made responsible for the whole cost of singing and eating while she wept and fasted (as also for the orphans), we must, as our Lord

---

78   Sermon 200 on Deut., OC 29:222.

79   Farel, *La maniere et fasson*, pp. E7r-F4r. For English, see *Early French Reform*, pp. 220-23.

80   Farel, *La maniere et fasson*, pp. E4r-F2v. For English, see *Early French Reform*, pp. 220-22.

gives us the ability, have pity on them and help them with advice and goods so as not to add insult to injury.[81]

The polemical allusion refers to the expenses of funeral practices which the family must bear, e.g., food for the mourners, payment for singing, and alms for the priest and Mass. Farel concludes with a note on the Christian instruction of the orphans.

When Calvin wrote *La forme des prières*, it was still addressed essentially to the pastors but there were some notable changes from Farel's liturgy. The most obvious difference is the considerable shortening of the instructions; the long hortatory section disappears and much of the rest is abbreviated. The reference to good works, to setting one's affairs in order, the polemical note, all are gone. Anecdotal evidence elsewhere, however, indicates that if it is appropriate, i.e., if the dying person is wealthy, pastor and elders may encourage him to leave alms for the poor in his will.[82] This does not appear in Calvin's written liturgy, where instead he reflects on the trials of sickness.

> The greatest need anyone ever has of the spiritual teaching of our Lord is when he is visited with affliction by God's hand: whether of illness, or other troubles. This is especially so at the hour of death, because it is then that he feels more strongly than any other time in his life the suffering in his conscience, as much [anxiety about] God's judgment before which he will soon be called, as about the attacks of the devil, who then exercises all his efforts to beat down the poor person and cast him down and destroy him in disorder. And therefore it is the duty of a minister to visit the sick and comfort them with the word of the Lord.[83]

After a reminder of God's "good providence" and the conviction that God "does not send anything to His faithful except for their good and salvation," Calvin distinguishes between (ordinary) sickness and life-threatening illness.

> And if he sees that the illness is serious, the minister will give the sick consolations which go beyond this, according to how he sees them moved in their feelings. That is, if he recognizes that they are terrified by the

---

[81]   Farel, *La maniere et fasson*, pp. F3r-v. For English, see *Early French Reform*, p. 222. In fact some people continued to give gifts after a death, and this was rebuked, March 22, 1555, OC 21:599 (RC 49 f34).

[82]   On Jan. 4, 1549, the Senate notes that Sr. de Falais is sick but has not made any provision for the poor so it orders two councilors/ elders and Calvin to visit de Falais to ask him to contribute to the General Hospital, OC 21:444 (RC 43 f275v).

[83]   *La forme des prières*, Calvin, *Writings on Pastoral Piety*, p. 292; OS II, pp. 56-57.

horror of death, he may exhort them that there is no cause for the faithful, who have Jesus Christ as their guide and protector, to be desolated by death, by which He will lead them to the life into which He has entered. And by such exhortations he may relieve them of the fear and terror they have of the judgment of God.[84]

The next section briefly indicates the two situations which Farel had treated: those who need to be reminded of their sins, and those with troubled consciences who need to have the mercy of Christ presented to them "au vif" ("to the life)." The wise minister has to determine what is needed in each situation. A final sentence instructs the pastor to offer such physical assistance as may be possible.[85]

The *Ecclesiastical Ordinances* gave the second official Genevan text regarding care for the sick and these instructions gave particularly directed to the parishioners. No one who has a serious illness (who is bedridden more than three days) should fail to notify a minister, and if the sick person does not do it, then the family or friends should. The reason given is that, when they are ill, many people do not seek God's consolation from His word. The clear assumption is that scripture is the fundamental comfort in any distress. It is apparent that, at least in 1541 when the *Ordinances* were written, it was also expected that lay Christians would not be able to provide each other with adequate Biblical consolation. That is, the need for a minister is not absolute but circumstantial. A properly educated layperson could in principle offer Biblical consolation, but few were sufficiently fluent in scriptural knowledge to fill this role well. Further, the text of the *Ordinances* instructs people to call the ministers "at a convenient hour in order not to distract them from their work which they do in common for all the church."[86] Here the point is not to prevent calling the pastor when there is an emergency but to take into account that he has other responsibilities, particularly preaching. It is another way of emphasizing that one should not wait until he or she is at the moment of death to send for the minister. One might ask why the burden of notifying the minister of illness was laid on the parishioners, and in fact the dizeniers and their rural counterparts were also supposed to provide such information to the pastors.[87] The simple fact was that in a city as large as Geneva, with only a handful of ministers, the latter required help to keep up with who was

---

84 *La forme des prières*, Calvin, *Writings on Pastoral Piety*, p. 292; OS II, p. 57.

85 *La forme des prières*, Calvin, *Writings on Pastoral Piety*, pp. 292-93; OS II, pp. 57-58.

86 *Ordinances*, Calvin, *Writings on Pastoral Piety*, p. 293; OS II, pp. 355-56.

87 See Perrot's reference to the guards telling him about the sick, Lambert, *Preaching, Praying, and Policing*, Appendix 4, p. 542: "Apres le sermon le ministre se repose un peu avec les deux gardes pour sçavoir s'il y en a eu d'absens, s'il y a des malades à visiter, et des scandaleux à apeller."

ill or needed a visit. It may be noted here that there is no reference to respecting parish boundaries, something which had been a fairly significant problem in the old system. While naturally family would appeal to the minister(s) they knew best, in the context of the city church at least parishioners might turn to any one of the pastors, and if the sick or dying persons were of some status (and therefore known beyond their own local diziene) they might well have been visited by several ministers, as was the case with Ami Porral described below. [88]

Although knowledge of illness would naturally lead to a pastoral visit, there was also another context in which information about a sick parishioner should be shared. Either a family member or the dizenier was invited to tell the preacher about illness in order to have the sufferer included by name in the public intercessory prayers. There was a special place explicitly marked for this in the day of prayer liturgy, but it was also included on other weekdays and Sunday afternoons; Calvin's extempore #3 prayer has a place for the insertion of specific names so that the whole parish might remember the sick before God. [89]

Visiting the Sick: Vital and Challenging Work

The main means of pastoral care in Reformed Geneva was preaching, and to modern eyes that seems very limited, if not skewed. Thus it is important to emphasize that tending the sick was a very significant part of a minister's duty and sometimes a deadly one. In November 1542 when a village pastor was disciplined for not doing his job, "negligence and failing to visit the sick" were the two issues named. (No sexual or financial misconduct is identified, which highlights the fact that not visiting the sick was considered a serious dereliction of duty.) In July 1557 a village minister with a two-point charge asked to be moved to another parish because his bad foot made it difficult for him to visit the sick in their scattered homes. [90] Care for the ill was equally essential in the city, of course, even if getting to the parishioner-patient was much easier. In 1543 the head of the General Hospital (welfare institution) complained that the ministers were neglec-

---

[88] For medieval parish boundary problems, see Binz in chap. 1 at n.4. For Porral, see below at nn.110ff.

[89] Day of Prayer liturgy, OS II, p. 29; see chap. 4 at n.146; ordinary weekday, chap. 6 at n.147.

[90] Nov. 27, 1542; OC 21:305 (RC 36 f178). July 2, 1557, RCP II, p. 76 : Jean Melrey "qu'à cause de son pied il ne se pouvoit acquicter de son devoir là où les maisons de ses parrochiens estoyent fort esparses et eslongnees l'une de l'autre, et qu'il ne pouvoit pas se transporter aisement d'un village en l'autre pour visiter un malade." (The 1561 revision of the *Ordinances* would give this a more prominent place in the list of the ministers' duties when they described the tasks of rural pastors. See *Ordinances* 1561, OS II, p. 336: "Quartement, pour savoir si le Ministre est diligent tant à prescher comme à visiter les malades, et admonester en particulier ceux qui en ont besoin, et à empescher qu'aucune chose se face au deshonneur de Dieu.")

ting the sick and the Senate promptly decided to rebuke them. On April 26, 1543, a man being questioned by the consistory denies that he had said that the ministers do not want to visit the sick – clearly this was a serious complaint.[91] It is probable, however, that pastors actually spent a fair amount of time responding to the needs of those who were sick or imprisoned (often a related category, since those being visited in prison might well be awaiting execution), even if this pastoral attention was not as much or as often as parishioners wanted.[92]

One of the most terrifying early modern illnesses was naturally the plague, in part because it was usually deadly and in part because it spread so widely and mysteriously that it was often associated with malevolence and witchcraft. No one was immune, but in urban areas the pastoral challenge was greater than in the country simply because the epidemic flourished in the crowded towns and cities. Geneva maintained a special hospital outside the city walls for plague victims, and the minister called to that "parish" often died in service to his people.[93] There were major eruptions of the disease in the early 1540s, and in October 1542 Pierre Blanchet bravely offered to move his residence outside the city close to the plague hospital to serve for that time. Apparently matters were not too grave yet and Blanchet was able to return to the city; the brunt of the epidemic was yet to come.

In May 1543 the Company of Pastors was again faced with finding a minister for the plague hospital. At first Sebastian Castellio (a teacher member of the Company) agreed to do it, while others were frankly saying they would rather go to the devil than the plague hospital, but then Castellio changed his mind and would not go. Pastor Blanchet again agreed to go and within three weeks he had died of the disease.[94] Now there was a further problem; the Senate refused to allow Calvin to take this duty, and no one (else) volunteered. Finally on June 5 Matthieu de Geneston stepped forward; on Aug. 3 it was reported that he had caught the

---

91 Oct. 2, 1543, OC 21:321, citing Roget II, p. 74. April 26, 1543, *Consist.* I, p. 232.

92 On April 19, 1548, Pierre Ameau says that he has not been to church because he has been sick for four months, and did not come to sermons because the minister always attacked him. He also complains that when he was in prison instead of helping him clear up the problems Calvin went off to Thonon. Calvin apologizes and says he never thought of such a thing and Ameau must not suspect him of such cruelty, and the latter accepts the apology and asks pardon for his suspicion. *Consist.* IV, p. 49. It is not perfectly clear but the issue seems to be Calvin's failure to visit Ameau in prison, or at least his (apparent) neglect of a parishioner in need. It is possible that the issue of visiting also concerns the time when Ameau was ill, but if so Calvin's answer is not appropriate.

93 Some discussion in Manetsch, *Calvin's Company of Pastors*, pp. 284-89. Summary in Naphy, *Calvin and the Consolidation*, pp. 68-69.

94 Oct. 23 & 25, 1542; OC 21:304 (RC 36 f151v, 153v). May 1 & 2 & 11, June 1, 1543; OC 21:312, 313 (RC 37 f80, f82, f89, f110, f113, f117).

plague and his wife had died of it. This time the pastor survived; he was relieved of his task and supplied with what he needed for physical recovery.[95] Two years later, however, in August 1545, de Geneston again caught the disease and this time he did succumb, although at this point he was not serving at the plague hospital. (Nicolas Des Gallars was responsible for that hospital at the time, but he managed to escape infection and the epidemic was beginning to subside.)[96] Meanwhile at least one other city pastor was brought down by the plague and one village minister; Abel Poupin contracted it in Nov. 1544 yet recovered, but Pastor Regalis and his wife both died of plague in May 1545.[97] Obviously, one did not have to be assigned to the plague hospital in order to minister to the victims and contract the disease, but that was certainly the most dangerous post for a pastor.

Praying with the Sick

Toward the end of Calvin's life, some editions of the Psalter-catechism-liturgy service book and other devotional materials began to print model prayers to add to the simple description of what a person ministering at a sickbed should say.[98] Several versions are known. The present study is not exhaustive but probably sufficiently representative to give an idea of what was being said.[99]

---

[95] June 2 & 5 & Aug. 3, 1543; OC 21:314, 318 (RC 37 f113, f117, f169).

[96] Death of de Geneston, Aug. 11, 1545; OC 21:359 (RC 39 f212). Des Gallars recalled to the city, Aug. 31, 1545; OC 21:361 (RC 39 f227v).

[97] Poupin has plague and asks for assistance, Nov. 25, 1544; OC 21:345 (RC 38 f51). Regalis and wife have died, June 1, 1545, OC 21:354 (RC 39 f124v)

[98] A prayer for the sick is found in the edition of *La forme des prières* published in Strasbourg in 1553, immediately after the instructions about visiting. It is preceded by a short rubric emphasizing the sick person's need of forgiveness and citation of Jas. 5:14, and followed by a paragraph of instructions about burial. See *Pseaumes de David, mis en rime francoyse, par Clement Marot, avec plusieurs cantiques, comme on les chante dans l'eglise Francoyse destrosbourg. ... La forme des prieres...* Strasbourg, 1553. [BGE Bb 2368 res], pp. 362-64. This prayer is rather different from those used in Geneva; it also does not appear in the edition of this liturgy published by Valerain Poullain in 1552, which does however have the burial instructions (see above at n. 63). Evidently the prayer was added to the Strasbourg 1553 text by the editor of the preface dated April 10, 1553 after Poullain and his group left for refuge in England.

[99] It should be noted that in the liturgy the instruction for visiting the sick is sometimes followed by a prayer which is not clearly labeled, but turns out to be the 1552 prayer for or by a captive, not one for use with the sick (although evidently the themes might overlap). For an example see *Les psaumes mis en rime francoise....* Psalter, liturgy, catechism, published in Genève by Nicolas Barbier & Thomas Courteau for Antoine Vincent, 1562, pp. Aa1r-Aa2r. [BGE Bb2006 or 2007 Res] Bound with New Testament. *Les psaumes mis en rime francoise...* François Jaquy pour Antoine Vincent, 1562, with a new title page for the New Testament in 1563 which names only Jaquy but gives the place of publication as Geneva. [IHR O4e (563)]. This book has the prayer for or by a captive in the liturgy (pp. 28-30) right after the instructions about visiting the sick.

What was likely the first Genevan prayer for visiting the sick appeared in a publication by François Jaquy for Guillaume Fournet in 1562. It is entitled *Instruction des Chrestiens, ou Receuil de passages de la saincte Escriture, accordans à l'oraison Dominicale, aux articles de la Foy, & aux dix Commandemens de la Loy. Avec quelques autres traitez, lesquels trouverez en la page suyvante.* This composite work presents a collection of catechetical and devotional items, some of which (such as the short formula used to test catechism students before admission to the Lord's Supper) appear as part of the larger Genevan liturgical resources. As was common in such cases, the editor probably made the choice of contents.[100]

Several publications of the Psalter service book provide other forms of prayer to be used with a sick person, and these are set in the usual places for individual prayers, i.e., at the end of the Geneva Catechism or more rarely at the end of *La forme des prières* after the instructions about visiting the sick. In 1563 *Les pseaumes mis en rime françoise* produced by Jean Baptiste Pinereul for Antoine Vincent includes a prayer for visiting the sick in the catechism section.[101] In 1570 Sebastian Honorati produced a service book which has the prayer in identical form and location as Pinereul-Vincent.[102] For present purposes this shorter version is here identified as the "Genevan" form since, despite the references to the king's privilege and Lyon, the publishers were actually working in Geneva. Alongside this form of the prayer, in 1563 Pierre le Chandelier in Caen published a slightly but significantly different version, which he placed in the liturgy itself after the instructions about pastoral visits.[103] Before examining more closely the shorter "Genevan" version, it is worthwhile to look briefly at the others.

---

[100] The first part appears to be a republication of part of the *Instruction des enfants* which Girard produced in 1537 (although with the two tables of the commandments now properly divided, p. 19). Among the other familiar Genevan formulae is "La maniere d'interroguer les enfans qu'on veut recevoir en la Cene." cf. chap. 3 at nn.124ff.

[101] See *Les pseaumes mis en rime francoise...* Jean Baptiste Pinereul pour Antoine Vincent, 1563, "avec le privilege du roy pour dix ans." [BGE Su4939 Res]. This publication has two prayers, which can be confusing. In the liturgy there is the prayer for or by a captive (pp. cc4r- cc5r) immediately after the instructions for visiting the sick. In the catechism there is a prayer for the sick (pp. dd2r-dd3r) after the other occasional or household prayers. The visual presentation is the same as that by Jaquy for Vincent.

[102] *Les pseaumes mis en rime françoyse par Clement Marot & Theodore de Beze,* A Lyon pour S. Honorati, 1570, pp. cc8v-dd1v. Bound with *Le Nouveau Testament* which identifies place of publication as Geneva. [IHR O4e (570)].

[103] *Cinquante psaumes de David* published by Pierre le Chandelier in Caen, 1563, prayer for the sick is in the liturgy, pp. C3v-C5r.

The *Instruction des Chrestiens* provides a very long and wandering form of prayer for visiting the sick. [104] Pierre le Chandelier, on the other hand, uses the "Genevan" form but adds a number of sentences or phrases; the most interesting of these refers to the preaching of the gospel at the bedside of the sick followed by a reminder of the person's participation in the sacraments in the gathered company of the church. [105] In fact, the *Instruction des Chrestiens* may have been a source for this particular thought. However, while le Chandelier puts the words in the pastor's mouth, consistent with his locating the prayer in the liturgical instructions to clergy, the *Instruction des Chrestiens* makes no reference to the minister but indicates that the speakers are "nous" – obviously leaving the door open for this prayer to be used by lay people. The way le Chandelier inserts this idea into the "Genevan" form is much smoother than its place in the rambling text printed in the *Instruction des Chrestiens*. The latter, however, is the only version which includes an explicit petition for the caregivers – presumably family or others to whom the sick person is dear – and then for their consolation in the event of bereavement. [106] Both of these features and other language suggest that this form of the prayer was written either by or at least for laity.

While it is not possible to identify the source of the "Genevan" prayer, it is very likely that Calvin was in some way responsible, or at least approved. A fairly limited number of prayers were added to the catechism after his initial set of five and (as noted above with regard to the household devotions) these were often based on his words from other liturgical contexts. The form of the "Genevan" prayer for visiting the sick is shorter and more sober than the others of this genre, and includes some of Calvin's typical rhetorical language. In content it also accords well with what he himself said about the consolation of trust in Christ and the way of understanding death and mourning. Thus, although there is no

---

[104] *Instruction des Chrestiens*, pp. 239-45. For present purposes the most interesting quotation is p. Q2r =243: "lequel se presente maintenant à cette povre personne malade, par tes promesses que nous luy annonçons selon ta Parole, laquelle il a frequentee en ton Eglise avec nous, & ainsi l'usage des Sacremens que tu y as establis pour la confirmation de la foy de tous tes fideles."

[105] *Cinquante psaumes de David... le Chandelier*, p. C4v: "lequel [Christ] mesme maintenant luy [sick person] est en ce lieu offert par le ministere de la Parole preschée, & l'usage des Sacremens, qu'il a frequentez avec nous en la congregation & Eglise de tes esleuz & fideles: que cela luy soit pour une defense invincible contre les bruits de sa conscience qui l'accuse si fort, & contre les ruses & finesses du diable." For the context in the larger prayer, see Appendix Eleven.

[106] *Instruction des Chrestiens*, p.Q3r=245 : "fortifie par ta grace ceux qui se sont travaillez pour exercer tout acte d'humanité en servant ce povre malade, afin qu'ils ne defaillent point par trop grand & continuel labeur : mais qu'il (!) puissent tousjours poursuyvre franchement & de bon coeur leur devoir envers iceluy. Et si tu le retires d'avec eux que tu les consoles par ta bonté, afin qu'ils portent patiemment une telle separation, & qu'ils te remercient de tout."

claim that this is directly from Calvin, it certainly represents the kind of pastoral ministry to the sick and dying which was (at least in later years) normal in his community.

The prayer opens with a general statement which speaks of God's goodness that calls us (the pastor speaks in the first person plural throughout) to awaken from sin. The present suffering is a kind of forerunner of death, and the last judgment and life eternal which will follow it, either in glory and blessedness or shame and damnation.[107] Then the prayer continues focused on the sick person with whom those present are united as human beings and as Christians.

> We poor sinners who await this same hour of adversity according to our human nature, humbly pray with this poor sick person that You may not exercise rigorous judgment on him, as he has deserved. But rather, kind Lord, look upon him with Your eyes of mercy and, considering him as redeemed, grant him grace and steadfast courage by which he may receive peaceably this gracious correction and fatherly visitation [cf. 1 Pet. 2:12].[108]

The prayer continues with recognition of the severity of the sick person's trials, both physical and spiritual, and a strong affirmation of salvation through Christ's death and resurrection.

> Aid him in all his adversities and worries and be his protection against the danger which is so close to him. And especially if his conscience, uncovered [to his sight], accuses him of his inward sins [cf. Rom. 2:15-16], Lord full of goodness, set over against this the great torments and willing sacrifice of your beloved Son Jesus Christ, who bore our infirmities and endured the pain that we ourselves deserved, having become sin for us, when for our sins and offences He suffered death [cf. Isa. 53:4-5, 2 Cor. 5:21, 1 Pet. 2:21, 24]. He washed our sins with His blood and, rising from the dead, He has been made our righteousness and perfect redemption [cf. 1 Cor. 1:30].[109]

The words are filled with scriptural echoes and allusions. Then there is the fruit of Christ's work for the sick person which is received through faith.

> May the poor sick person sense the fruit and power of these benefits, by faith, and being pressed down with this anguish, may he receive for his

---

[107] *La forme des prières*, Pinereul pour Antoine Vincent, 1563, p. dd2r, see Appendix Eleven, part two.

[108] *La forme des prières*, Pinereul pour Antoine Vincent, 1563, p. dd2r-v.

[109] *La forme des prières*, Pinereul pour Antoine Vincent, 1563, p. dd2v.

consolation a very great treasure of joy, i.e., the forgiveness of his sins because of Your Son Jesus Christ. May this faith be for him like a shield by which he may repel the terrors of death [cf. Eph. 6:16] and may walk bravely, to come to the eternal and blessed life; and when he has apprehended it may he rejoice in it eternally. [110]

The next passage bears the marks of Calvin's typical rhetorical grace.

> O our good God, in this way, because he is ill, You will heal him; he is slipping down, You will lift him up again; he is weak, You will strengthen him; he recognizes his impurity and spots and filthiness, You will wash him; he is pierced to the heart, You will apply Your holy and good medicine; he is seized with fear and trembling, You will give him good courage. [111]

Having offered comfort and reassurance, the minister goes on to face directly both possible outcomes, life and death, and affirm that they are in God's hands. If the sick person dies, may he be given life with Christ in glory, and if it is God's will that the sick person recover ("still have some profit in cultivating Your vineyard in this mortal life"), may he be conformed to Christ's example. The minister then clearly says "Your will be done" and expresses trust in "the only Lord Jesus Christ, Redeemer, Physician, and Savior of poor sinners" who took the thief with Him to paradise as an example and consolation to sinners. He concludes with a Trinitarian invocation. [112]

Whether it was written by Calvin or not, the prayer conveys a sense of his teaching, and may perhaps be a surprising contradiction to the legend of the predestinarian. That conviction is mentioned, but only at the beginning and in passing, as the pastor gives voice to the Biblical comfort which stands behind Calvin's preaching and passionate call to all Genevans to put God first and find their joy and peace in Him.

A "Good Death" in Calvin's Geneva

If these are the themes of ministry to the sick, it is also possible to see the pastor in action. In Calvin's correspondence there are several rather detailed descriptions of his presence at the bedside of dying parishioners. One is preserved in a letter to Farel written on June 16, 1542, which recounts the death of the syndic

---

[110] *La forme des prières*, Pinereul pour Antoine Vincent, 1563, p. dd2v.

[111] *La forme des prières*, Pinereul pour Antoine Vincent, 1563, p. dd2v. See close parallels in the day of prayer intercession, OS II, p. 29; and *Inst.* 3.7.1 (which comes from 1539).

[112] *La forme des prières*, Pinereul pour Antoine Vincent, 1563, p. dd2v.

Ami Porral. The latter, although he was a supporter of the ministers, had been one of the key figures in the factionalism which caused so much trouble in the 1530s.[113] The length and detail of Calvin's story are probably owed to his desire to share the very surprising "conversion" of Porral, who preached to everyone who visited him on his deathbed in a fashion which filled his clerical hearers with amazement as well as joy.

The focus of the account is the intelligent faith manifested by the dying man, and his ministry to the pastors as well as others. The first visit by both Calvin and Viret came the day after Porral became ill, when the latter said that the disease was usually fatal in his family. They had a long conversation which showed the patient to be perfectly sound in mind. Over the course of his fairly short illness, Porral apparently acted as counselor to his visitors; Calvin says he "applied to each individual what was best adapted to his circumstances, and most likely to be of use to him."[114] Both leading ministers were visiting again the day of Porral's death, arriving about 9 a.m. Several long quotations are justified by the light they cast on what Calvin saw as a very remarkable witness to the gospel (and modern readers might enjoy as a case of the preacher being preached to).

> When I had spoken a few words, to set before him the cross, the grace of Christ, and the hope of eternal life, – for we were unwilling to weary him with tedious addresses, – he replied, that he received God's message as became him; that he knew the efficacy of the power of Christ for confirming the consciences of true believers. Thereupon he spoke in such a luminous manner on the work of the ministry, and all the benefits which accompany or flow from it as the means of grace, that we were both of us in a sort of stupor of astonishment; and whenever it recurs to my memory, even yet I grow bewildered. For he spoke in such a way, that it seemed to reflect some discourse by one of ourselves after long and careful meditation. He concluded this part of his address by declaring that the remission of sins which we promised on the authority of Christ, he received just the same as if an angel had appeared to him from heaven. After that he spoke of the unity of the church, which he commended with marvelous praise: he bore testimony that, in his own experience, he had found no better or more certain source of consolation, in the struggle of death, than from having already been confirmed in the assurance of this unity.[115]

---

113 See Naphy, *Calvin and the Consolation*, pp. 26-27, 37, 40-41.

114 Letter to Farel translated as #LXXVI in Bonnet, *Letters*, vol. 1, pp. 331-35. #402, OC 11:408-10. Here Bonnet, p. 332; OC 11:408.

115 Bonnet, *Letters*, vol. 1, pp. 332-33. #402, OC 11:408-09.

Remarkably, the recent convert to Protestant ways seems entirely confident in his salvation based on the promises of forgiveness, and in spite of the lack of any of the traditional rites. It is small wonder the pastor was impressed!

Calvin breaks off the account of Porral's words to say that the dying man had called two of the ministers, De la Mare and Bernard, to be reconciled with them. Several years before he had criticized De la Mare's theology and when Bernard supported his colleague, the difference had developed into a quarrel. (In point of fact, the opinions in question were unacceptable to Calvin.) [116] Porral decided that it would leave a bad example if he died without being reconciled with these two men; as he told Calvin and Viret, "Since the public edification of the church compels you to bear with them as brethren, why might not I acknowledge them as pastors?" [117] The bemused Calvin then turns back to recount the rest of Porral's speech for Farel.

> Turning himself to those who stood around [obviously the ministers were not the only visitors], he exhorted every one to prize very highly the communion of the church; such of them as are superstitious in the observance of days and ceremonies, he advised to lay aside their perverse opposition, and to agree with us, for that we better understood, and saw more clearly what was the prudent course than they did; that he had himself, also, been rather obstinate in these things, but that his eyes were at length opened to perceive how injurious contention might become. After that he made a short, serious, as well as sincere and luculent confession. Thence he proceeded to exhort us both, as well regarding the other departments of our charge as ministers, as also to constancy and firmness; and when he discoursed at some length on the future difficulties of the ministers of the gospel, he seemed inspired with the foresight of a prophet. [118]

Clearly Porral saw his role as a dying believer to be a kind of ministry – a vivid evidence of the priesthood of believers. In view of the reference to the "observance of days" it appears that Porral was now on Calvin's side in regarding the traditional liturgical year practices as "superstitious." After a few more words, the bemused pastors, Calvin and Viret, prayed with Porral and left.

However, the letter continues with an account of how the dying man received Idelette de Bure when she went to visit him the next day, and then sketches Calvin's final visit. When Mme Idelette arrived, Porral assured his pastor's wife that she should know that "she had not been rashly led hither, but brought by

---

[116] See Naphy, *Calvin and the Consolidation*, p. 60. See chap. 6 at n.99.

[117] Bonnet, *Letters*, vol. 1, p. 333. #402, OC 11:409.

[118] Bonnet, *Letters*, vol. 1, p. 333. #402, OC 11:409.

the wonderful counsel of God, that she also might serve in the gospel." He repeated the song of Simeon and applied it to himself: "I have seen... and have touched with my hand, that saving merciful Redeemer." Calvin returned about 4 p.m. with the syndics; Porral could not speak but Calvin assured him that "his confession [of faith] was abundantly satisfactory." The pastor added a few more words to which the dying man "hearkened with a very composed and tranquil countenance" and shortly after the visitors left, Porral "gave up his pious soul to Christ."[119] This letter reveals that some Genevans had made the new faith their own and were ready to give that testimony of a "good death" in a remarkable way. Porral repeatedly offered a strong confession of faith, expressed his trust in the word delivered by the ministers, drew on appropriate Biblical words (the Song of Simeon which concluded the Lord's Supper service), took conscious thought for reconciliation for the sake of the church community, testified to those who visited him, and faced death peacefully. It is worth noting, given the challenges which Genevans offered the "foreigners" who were their pastors, that this man could affirm that even his pastor's wife had been brought to the city by God's providence and she also had a ministry to perform!

Calvin's letters include another account of a deathbed, this time of a woman, a French refugee, Anne de la Vaquerie de Normandie. Dated April 29, 1549, the letter is addressed to Mme de Cany, a devout woman who had been instrumental in converting Mme de Normandie's father "to the gospel."[120] Normally the details of ministry which Calvin records here would never have been written down, but in this case the pastor felt a strong obligation to provide a full account for the sake of Mme de Normandie's father. The latter had only recently come to share his daughter's (Protestant) faith and he would be very much shaken if he did not have the reassurance that she had died a "good death." That is, he needed to know that the new faith was secure and saving even at the end, despite the absence of traditional last rites – because one powerful form of Roman propaganda against "the heretics" was that they all came to a bad end.[121] The death itself would not be a great surprise because Mme de Normandie was already ill when she and her husband came to Geneva as religious refugees, but it was essential that the testimony she expressed should be shared with her family at home.

---

119 Bonnet, *Letters*, vol. 1, p. 334. #402, OC 11:409.

120 OC 13:244-48, *Writings on Pastoral Piety*, pp. 305-07.

121 In fact, opponents invented many scenarios describing the Protestant reformers dying "bad deaths" in great torment. Doumergue assembles those which began to circulate immediately after Calvin's death. See *Jean Calvin, Tome 7, Le triomphe* (Neuilly-Sur-Seine: La Cause, 1927), pp. 471-74.

Calvin's account of Mme de Normandie's deathbed first describes the weeks before her death; although hoping to recover she also prepared for death because she knew her illness was terminal. Along with all medical attention, she was supported with "what she prized most highly… pious admonitions to confirm her in the fear of God, in the faith of Jesus Christ, in patience, in the hope of salvation," to which her response was strongly faithful: "in her discourse you could see that she had the whole deeply imprinted upon her heart." [122] Then came the last days, when Mme de Normandie also preached by "exhorting her people" and telling her attending servant not to return to Rome and its idolatry but to live a holy life where God had led him to "a Christian Church" in Geneva. [123]

Through the last night in great pain the dying woman did not complain but prayed and shared in the fellowship of family and pastors who surrounded her. She asked that God "would have pity upon her, and that He would deliver her out of the world, vouchsafing grace to persevere always in the faith which He had bestowed." [124] About 5 a.m. Calvin came to visit, offering fitting teaching, to which she responded with a strong affirmation of faith.

> The hour draws near, I must needs depart from the world; this flesh asks only to go away into corruption; but I feel certain that my God is withdrawing my soul into His kingdom. I know what a poor sinful woman I am, but my confidence is in His goodness, and in the death and passion of His Son. Therefore, I do not doubt of my salvation, since He has assured me of it. I go to Him as to a Father. [125]

While Mme de Normandie was speaking, other members of the community came into the room; they prayed for her as they saw she needed and Calvin continued to intersperse words that seemed suitable. The dying woman again confessed her sins and the certainty of her salvation "putting her sole confidence in Jesus and having her whole trust in Him," and then began to sing Ps. 51 in the metrical version used in Genevan worship. This was difficult (apparently for lack of breath) but she persisted, and Calvin "seeing the pleasure she took in it" responded by making a short summary of the whole Psalm. She took his hand and expressed her deep gratitude for being able to die in a land where she could speak of her faith and hear it expounded to confirm her trust. When she was overcome with pain, Calvin assured her of God's presence and she answered "I do so believe

---

[122] OC 13:245-46, *Writings on Pastoral Piety*, p. 302.

[123] OC 13:246, *Writings on Pastoral Piety*, p. 302.

[124] OC 13:246, *Writings on Pastoral Piety*, pp. 302-03.

[125] OC 13:246, *Writings on Pastoral Piety*, p. 303.

and He makes me feel His help." [126] Throughout M. de Normandie was beside his wife, deeply grieved but giving a great testimony to his faith. Calvin, who had just months before lost his own wife, describes the husband's part.

> For while possessed with such grief as I know it to have been, and weighed down by extremity of sorrow, he had so far gained the mastery over self, as to exhort his better part as freely as if they were going to make a most joyful journey together. [127]

All this time the dying woman was in great pain, but finally after some hours that eased and she began again to praise God and express her trust in Christ. Even after she could no longer speak, she continued to listen to the prayers and exhortations of those gathered around her bed. When it appeared that she was gone, Calvin said "Now let us pray God that He would give us grace to follow her." The dying woman's eyes turned to him "as if charging us to persevere in prayer and in consoling her" and soon "she passed away so gracefully that it was as if she had fallen asleep." [128]

The letter concludes with Calvin's words of comfort to the grieving father, to be transmitted by Mme de Cany as seemed appropriate. Alluding to Rom. 12:15 about weeping with those who weep, he affirms that "if we are Christians, we ought to have such compassion and sorrow for our neighbors that we should willingly take part in their tears and thus comfort them." Then the pastor again speaks of the comfort that witnessing this death should be.

> But the great consolation is the example which she has afforded to him [her father] and to all of us, of bowing to the will of God. And thus, seeing that she has presented herself so peaceably to death, let us herein follow her, willingly complying with the disposal of God; and if her father loved her, let him show his love in conforming himself to the desire which she exhibited of submitting herself to God. And seeing that her dismissal has been so happy, let him rejoice in the grace of God vouchsafed to her, which far surpasses all the comforts we can possess in this world. [129]

All the elements of a "good death" are evident in Mme de Normandie's falling asleep in the faith to pass (as she and Calvin and the community believed) into the fullness of life in Christ. There was the preparation of faith during the lifetime: she

---

[126] OC 13:246-47, *Writings on Pastoral Piety*, p. 303.

[127] OC 13:247, *Writings on Pastoral Piety*, pp. 303-04.

[128] OC 13:247, *Writings on Pastoral Piety*, p. 304.

[129] OC 13:247-48, *Writings on Pastoral Piety*, pp. 304-05.

not only learned "the gospel" but also went into exile in order to live according to her convictions. There was the concern for those remaining behind, to exhort them to faithfulness: a powerful witness because deathbed words were always valued in a special way. There were repeated confessions of sin and of trust in salvation through Christ, expressed in her own words and in the words of the church — through the singing of the psalm. There were the presence and participation of family and pastors, all sharing the same faith and offering teaching and prayers and exhortations to confirm and comfort and uphold her. There was the testimony of the one nearest to her, her husband, and of the community, to their conviction that she was going on a journey to a better place and that she was also giving them an example to follow.

This is the fullest deathbed description from Calvin's pen, but it was not the most personal. Only a few months earlier, the pastor had been the husband at the bedside. A small glimpse of his own experience is found in his letters written early in April 1549 to Farel and Viret, his two closest friends, about the death of Idelette de Bure. [130] In one, Calvin also gives a picture of the deathbed with various ministers as well as her husband (and probably other family) gathered around. Again, the account includes several days before the death, as well as the actual day. "On Tuesday" March 26, 1549, the ministers were gathered at Calvin's home and joined together in prayer for his dying wife. Abel Poupin, one of Calvin's good friends (and his alternate in the preaching schedule), spoke for all in exhorting Mme Idelette and she responded briefly, and then husband-pastor John added an appropriate exhortation. He was concerned that she did not mention her children (his stepson and stepdaughter), so he brought up the matter and promised to care for them like his own. She said she had committed them to God; he replied that this was not to hinder him doing his part, and she effectively said that it was the same thing: "If the Lord shall care for them, I know they will be recommended to you." [131] Later, a woman visitor raised the subject again and Calvin said he (over) heard his wife say something similar: "Assuredly the principal thing is that they live a pious and holy life. My husband is not to be urged to instruct them in religious knowledge and in the fear of God. If they be pious, I am sure he will gladly be a father to them; but if not, they do not deserve that I should ask for aught in their behalf." [132] While this might sound harsh to modern ears, it is clear that Mme Idelette shared her husband's convictions about what was essential in life and in rearing children. She had been willing to take them into exile for the

---

[130] OC 13:228-29, 230-31, *Writings on Pastoral Piety*, pp. 52-54.

[131] OC 13:228-29, *Writings on Pastoral Piety*, p. 52.

[132] OC 13:230-31, *Writings on Pastoral Piety*, p. 54.

sake of following the gospel, giving up material security for them as well as for herself; this was a fitting conclusion to that life-long teaching.

The last day came. Calvin records the witness of the dying woman's faith. Around noon one of the ministers, Francois Bourgoing, exhorted her, and Mme Idelette's response was a strong affirmation of her trust. "O glorious resurrection! O God of Abraham, and of all our fathers, in thee have the faithful trusted during so many past ages, and none of them have trusted in vain. I also will hope."[133] Calvin explicitly says that these were her own meditations, not suggested by anyone else. He himself had to leave the room at 6 [p.m.] (probably he did not realize this was her last day, and he had another duties), but returned an hour later. His wife asked all to pray: "Let us pray, let us pray. All pray for me." Seeing that she seemed troubled but could no longer speak, Calvin offered "a few words about the love of Christ, the hope of eternal life, concerning our married life, and her departure" and then prayed. He affirmed that she could hear and attend to the words, and then very quietly she died.[134]

Besides the description of the deathbed, in both letters the widower speaks of his intense grief, the effort of friends to help, his trust in God.

> I do what I can to keep myself from being overwhelmed with grief. My friends also leave nothing undone that may minister to my mental suffering… which would certainly have overcome me had not He who raises up the prostrate, strengthens the weak, and refreshes the weary, stretched forth His hand from heaven to me.[135]

The grieving widower also expressed his great respect and love for the wife who had been his partner in faith and ministry.

> And truly mine is no common source of grief. I have been bereaved of the best companion of my life, of one who, if anything more difficult had befallen me, would not only have been the willing sharer of my exile and indigence, but even of my death. During her life she was the faithful helper of my ministry.[136]

It may be remembered that Idelette de Bure was, like Calvin, an exile for her faith. In Strasbourg they had had a rather precarious existence financially, and had been obliged to take in paying boarders to maintain the household. (This was a common

---

133 OC 13:229, *Writings on Pastoral Piety*, pp. 52-53.

134 OC 13:229, *Writings on Pastoral Piety*, p. 53.

135 OC 13:228, 229, *Writings on Pastoral Piety*, p. 52, 53.

136 OC 13:230, *Writings on Pastoral Piety*, pp. 53-54.

way for clergy to make ends meet and was welcomed as a means of mentoring young students, but the Calvin household in Strasbourg seems to have been in particularly straitened circumstances and Mme Idelette would have been hard-pressed to put enough food on the table.) Plague had also swept through their home, carrying off two of the household and scattering the others – and Calvin had been away at the time attending to church business (the colloquy of Ratisbon) so more responsibility fell on the mistress of the house. Then came the move to Geneva: the salary was much better, but it could not have been an easy life. Their only clearly attested baby died shortly after birth, and Mme Idelette may well have suffered at least one more miscarriage.[137] There were also the conflicts which swirled around her husband all the time, and the attacks on the French in the city. Yet through the years the couple had shared everything. Not only did the pastor mourn for his wife; he never remarried, although that was the normal thing for a widower to do, and he had to explain – if not defend – his action.[138]

---

[137] Calvin writes to Farel and Viret in July 1542, letters #407, #409, OC 11:418, 420, about his wife's dangerous labor and the premature birth of their son. #416 to Viret on Aug. 19, 1542, expresses their grief at the death of their "filioli" (OC 21:430) "Jacques." A number of scholars have suggested that Calvin and Idelette had other babies, e.g. see Engammare, *Sermons sur la Genèse*, vol. 2, pp. 817-18 n. 30, commenting on sermon 73 on Gen. 15:15-16, preached on March 20, 1560. Also Witte & Kingdon, *Courtship, Engagement, and Marriage*, pp. 99-100. Witte / Kingdon suggest that the other children were daughters, because Calvin explicitly says that he had only one son (in *Responsio ad Balduini Convicia*, OC 9:576). Engammare goes into some detail about references to children in Calvin's correspondence. Engammare cites a letter from Calvin to his friend de Falais in March 1546: "Je vous remercie humblement de l'offre tant gratieuse que vous me faites pour le baptesme de nostre enfant"; nothing further is heard of this baby so the mother probably miscarried or the child was stillborn. In a letter to Farel of uncertain date Calvin speaks of the fever of his little daughter ("mea filiola"). This would indicate a living child (could it have been his step-daughter Judith?). A letter in Feb. 1544 from Christophe Fabri to Calvin speaks of the death of a child, calling her "puella." Emile Doumergue, however, believes that this language does not refer to an infant and considers the general expression very strange in a letter of consolation to parents who have lost a child; *Jean Calvin*, vol. 2 *Les premiers essais*, p. 471. If it were not an infant, it could not be the child of Calvin and de Bure, since Fabri wrote early in 1544, only some 20+ months after Jacques' birth and death. The evidence for more than one living child born to Calvin and de Bure is therefore quite uncertain, although it is very likely that Idelette experienced several pregnancies which may not have come to live births.

[138] Remarriage was usually necessary in order to care for children and run the household; Calvin had no children and his stepchildren were nearly grown, so he moved into his brother Antoine's home. One of his very rare personal notes in a public context regards why he did not remarry. The context was a sermon on 1 Tim. 3:1-4. Here and elsewhere, the Pastoral Epistles describe the bishop as the husband of one wife; in the Roman tradition of celibate clergy the "wife" was interpreted as church or parish, but Protestants naturally took the text literally and made marriage for pastors a norm. However, early in the Reformation this passage raised the issue of whether a widower could remarry, a question which was generally answered in the affirmative. Perhaps the most visible example of the remarriage of widowers involved the story of Wibrandis

The Question of Communion for the Sick and Dying

It may be noted that in none of these deathbeds is there any mention of the sacraments. In the longer version of the prayer for visiting the sick, published by Pierre le Chandelier in Caen, there is a reference to the services of the sacraments as something which the sick person and those gathered around the deathbed would have shared in the gathered community – i.e., not at the place and time the prayer was being offered. In fact, the *Ecclesiastical Ordinances* forbade the celebration of the Supper anywhere except in the church "until a more favorable occasion (*meilleur opportunité*)."[139] The purpose was to prevent any "private Mass" or practice of the sacrament elsewhere than the gathered community. In addition and not incidentally, the Reformed Church sharply rejected the idea of a reserved host. The celebration of the Supper does not change the elements; the words are spoken to the people, not to the bread and wine. This means that there is no value in taking "consecrated" elements anywhere.[140]

Wim Janse has analyzed Calvin's thought on the subject of communion for the sick. His fine article, which draws together many of the relevant sources with an illuminating commentary,[141] has contributed greatly to the present discussion, along with personal research. Janse is primarily interested in the reformer's teaching, and thus does not take into account the pastor's deathbed descriptions discussed above.

Rosenblatt and her four husbands. Widowed as a young woman in Basel, she subsequently married Oecolampadius in his first marriage and after his death, she married the Strasbourg reformer Wolfgang Capito in his second marriage and after his death, she married Bucer in his second marriage. Each time Mme Wibrandis cared for the widower's household (and according to Bucer, keeping Capito's in order was something of a challenge) and all the children: yours, mine, and ours. See Roland Bainton, "Wibrandis Rosenblatt," in *Women of the Reformation in Germany and Italy* (Boston: Beacon, 1971), pp. 79-96. In his sermon #21 on 1 Tim. 3:1-4 (OC 53:255) Calvin explains that some people think it is a virtue that he is not married but in fact not marrying would be a fault if by doing so he could serve God better. He expresses a concern for whether a woman could live with him, and says he remains as he is because he is freer to serve God. Evidently there was enough attention to Calvin's failure to remarry that he had heard about it, but he would not have spoken in a sermon if his action had not seemed to call into question the interpretation of the passage and the Protestant theology of marriage.

139 For le Chandelier's additions see underlined words in the prayer for visiting the sick, in Appendix Eleven. *Ordinances*, OS II, p. 344.

140 In the preface to the Psalter where he discusses the importance of intelligible worship, Calvin states that it is superstitious to address the water, bread, and wine, in baptism and the Supper, as if the inanimate objects could be affected by words, while the people do not understand anything said. "Car il [Christ] ne dict pas au pain, qu'il soit fait son corps: mais il adresse sa parolle à la compagnie des fideles..." OS II, p. 14. Cf. *Inst* 4.17.35-37 for rejection of objectifying the host, adoring it, carrying it in procession, etc.

141 Janse, "Controversy and Concordance," pp. 158-78,

It is clear from Calvin's correspondence with other reformers that he himself did not object to communion for the sick. He thought it would be good if it were properly done, i.e., in the context of a service of worship in a small community of the faithful around the sick person. Perhaps he had also followed this practice in Strasbourg, since it was the custom when he lived there and it was certainly a practice of the French-language congregation in later years (as Poullain's London publication demonstrates [142]). Calvin's appreciation for the value of communion for the sick also apparently increased over the years. His first extant statement is found in a response in 1543 to questions from ministers in Montbéliard where the ruler wanted to establish Lutheran practices. Calvin affirms that celebrating communion with the sick should be "freely" allowed according to need and opportunity, and if requested could also be done for condemned criminals before their execution, as long as it was a "true communion, that is, that the bread be broken in some gathering of the faithful." [143]

Three other statements come from late in Calvin's life and these all indicate a stronger desire to have a Supper service at the bedside of the gravely ill person. The first is a reply to questions from the Lutheran pastor Wenceslaus Zuleger in 1558. To him Calvin the pastor says that he does not like the Genevan custom of forbidding the communion of the sick and he disclaims responsibility, but explains that it is too strong a custom to change, although he wants to register his objection for the sake of posterity. [144] In effect, this was an acknowledgment of a negative situation. The fact was that Geneva had followed its Swiss neighbors, Zurich and Bern, in forbidding the communion of the sick, and Calvin did not want a battle. [145] (It should be remembered that the reformer came to a similar conclusion about the frequency of the public celebration of the Lord's Supper, and in neither case did he consider the issue to be worth causing a destructive conflict.)

The second text is ecclesiastical advice to what was probably a small church in a largely Roman context. In replying to their question in August 1561, Calvin expresses more positively how communion of the sick might be done, since here he did not have to excuse local practice.

> There are many and weighty reasons which compel me to think the Supper should not be denied to the sick. I see that this can lead to a downhill slide

---

[142] Poullain, *Liturgia Sacra*, pp. 166, 167, which required a celebration in the context of a group of the faithful.

[143] Letter #506, OC 11:624-25.

[144] Letter #2549, Aug. 29, 1558, OC 17:311-12.

[145] See Janse, "Controversy and Concordance," p. 168.

into many abuses which should be countered prudently and carefully, for unless there is communion [not simply offering the reserved host], it is a wrongful turning away from Christ's holy institution. There should therefore be some gathering of relatives, household and neighbors so that there can be a distribution [of elements] according to Christ's command. Then the act may be joined with the explanation of the mystery, so that nothing will be different from the ordinary procedure of the church. [146]

Calvin explicitly rejects carrying "consecrated bread" around – something which would be a significant theological problem for their Protestant witness if his correspondents lived in the midst of traditional Roman practices where such an action would easily be read as a reserved host. He also adds that this communion of the sick should only be allowed to those in danger of death,[147] perhaps because a sick person who recovers could take communion again with the rest of the church when it was next celebrated. The main point is that the pastor-theologian sees this celebration of the sacrament as similar in all essentials to the one in the regular assembly: both include the word explained to the church (the people, including more than just the dying person) as well as the sacramental communion.

The third letter was written to Caspar Olevianus on Dec. 1, 1563. Here the Genevan pastor gives a fuller presentation of his mature views on offering communion to the sick.

> From the nature, purpose, and use of the mystery [i.e., the sacrament] I think I may justly conclude that those who are suffering from a long illness or are in mortal danger should not be robbed from such a great benefice. (…) Receiving the Eucharist provides us with the weapons for the spiritual battle we have to wage. Now, if a pious person sees he will have to depart this world, he will certainly be beleaguered and tormented by many temptations, and he will rightly wish to arm himself in order to hold his

---

146 Aug. 12, 1561, OC 10:213-14: "Cur coenam aegrotis negandam esse non arbitror, multae et graves causae me impellunt. Video interea quam proclivis in multos abusus sit lapsus, quibus prudenter seduloque occurrendum esset. Nisi enim sit communicatio, perperam deflectitur a sacra institutione Christi. Conveniat ergo aliquis coetus oportet ex cognatis, familiaribus et vicinis, ut fiat distributio ex mandato Christi: deinde coniuncta sit actio cum mysterii explicatione: nec quidquam a communi ecclesiae ratione diversum." This translation differs from that provided by Beaty and Farley, *Calvin's Ecclesiastical Advice*, p. 96, who for some strange reason give the last sentence as "There should then be the canon, combined with an explanation of the mysterious sacrament…"

147 OC 10:214: "Promiscue etiam huc et illuc deferre, valde periculosum est. Atque hic difficillimum est cavere, ne alios superstitio, alios ambitio et vana ostentatio ad petendum sollicitet. Itaque iudicio opus esset ac delectu, ne quibus daretur nisi in magno vitae discrimine. Panem tanquam sacrum e templo afferri praeposterum est: gestari vero in pompa nullo modo tolerabile."

ground. Should he be denied this unique aid (*singulare adiumentum*)? (...) [That] is harsh and constitutes a bad example. (...) Although there is no lawful Eucharist without the community, the communion given to the sick should not be judged a desecration: it will not be a private celebration. For it is definitely a part of or appendix to the public action (*pars vel appendix publicae actionis*).[148]

What Calvin says in these more private contexts clearly demonstrates that he wished to be able to celebrate a Lord's Supper service with those who were gravely ill.

Janse has examined the evidence to explain why Calvin's public statements in the controversy with Joachim Westphal contradict this personal view about the value of communion with the sick. In arguing against Westphal, Calvin practically adopts a kind of spiritual eating, a remembering of the communion which the sick person has shared with the community.[149] Janse appropriately identifies this spiritual eating as a Zwinglian idea, and goes on to say that in fact Calvin's treatment of the Supper with the sick as expressed in non-polemical contexts is fairly close to that of Westphal. Janse identifies various constraints which probably influenced Calvin's polemical stance. Besides the practical reasons for not publicly contradicting Genevan and Swiss practice, the Genevan reformer was influenced by the theological situation ("rising gnesio-Lutheranism") and his "distrust of anything that could lead to magic, superstition, adoration of the sacrament..."[150] It remains true, however, that Calvin personally greatly valued the privilege of participating in the Lord's Supper, and had himself carried to church in a chair for the Easter communion on April 2, 1564. He also abided by his choice to live in the Genevan system when he remained quietly at home on May 21, the Pentecost celebration just before his death on May 27, because he was too frail to be brought to the church to share the sacrament.

Burial and Life Everlasting

The main work of ministers was to the sick, but it also included the bereaved, although in a rather different way from the tradition. As noted above, Calvin's Geneva did not have funerals as such. This fact has been viewed negatively both by contemporaries and by later critics. Bernard Roussel has suggested that the experience of the Lord's Supper was (at least part of) the reason there was no funeral service.

---

[148] Janse, "Controversy and Concordance," p. 169; letter #4051, OC 20:200-201.

[149] Janse, "Controversy and Concordance," pp. 158-78.

[150] Janse, "Controversy and Concordance," pp. 162-63, 170-72.

The first French Reformed prohibited any funeral rite. This stunning proposition quickly proved to be intolerable and impracticable. An explicit reason for this proposition was the break with Catholic beliefs and practices. But the emergence of a prescription like this also presupposes the belief that physical death did not destroy anything in the order of salvation which had begun before this, and that there was nothing left to be completed, nothing else to do. The Supper is the occasion for the believer to begin *to live in his Savior*. Death does not interrupt this union. The absence of a funeral rite contributes to making explicit the figurative meaning of the expression: *this is my body*, which calls for the belief in the life of *us in Him*. The original Reformed ritual system is coherent.[151]

It was mentioned above that the first published Reformed sermon on dying was called the Nunc Dimittis, the Song of Simeon. It is notable that the text which Oecolampadius chose to express comfort for the dying also figured so prominently in Reformed Lord's Supper liturgies like Calvin's: every time the sacrament was celebrated Genevans and others sang Simeon's prayer expressing his – and their – readiness for death. Porral's deathbed as recounted above demonstrates that some people understood and practiced it that way.[152] Calvin might well have asked: what more do you need, except a decent burial and comfort for the family?

The Practice of Burial

According to the *Ecclesiastical Ordinances*, burial was to be held between twelve and twenty-four hours after death. The body would be carried to the graveyard outside the city walls (there was no more "hallowed ground"). The undertakers were required to swear not to allow "superstitious" actions and also not to carry out the interment at "an inappropriate hour" (probably meaning at night).[153] The funeral cortege was composed of family, friends, and neighbors. In the case of well-known leaders, such as magistrates or pastors, it might well include not only notables but also a large portion of the population; a brief description of Pastor

---

151 Bernard Roussel, "Comment fair la Cène? Rite et retour aux écritures dans les églises réformées du royaume de France au XVIe siècle," in *Les retours aux écritures. Fondamentalismes présents et passés*, ed. Evelyne Patlagean & A. Le Boulluec (Louvain-Paris: Peeters, 1993), pp. 195-216. Quotation, p. 213.

152 See above at nn.59, 114; chap. 3 at n.167.

153 *Ordinances*, OS II, p. 355. Some examples of superstition continued to be reported, especially in the villages. On March 15, 1548, a woman was accused of kneeling on her husband's grave, praying, "requisescant in pace, amen," and other women with her; *Consist*. IV, p. 15. Giving gifts to the children of the dead is forbidden as a "papist" practice, March 22, 1555, OC 21:599 (RC 49 f34). A brother and sister went to the hospital to pray for the dead and are sent to the Senate by the consistory, Dec. 6, 1557, OC 21:681 (RC 53 f445).

Abel Poupin's burial will be seen later in its context in the daily round of Calvin's pastoral life. As indicated above, some Reformed communities such as Strasbourg had a sermon at the graveside: not really a traditional eulogy but a preaching of the gospel. There is no evidence that Geneva did this, much to the horror and disgust of (at least some) Roman critics. [154]

Calvin's Teaching and Preaching on Death, Union with Christ, and Resurrection

For Calvin, burying the dead in an appropriate fashion was a part of ecclesiastical decency;[155] death, however, was not to be understood as destruction but as a passing into the fullness of life. While he clearly recognized the fear of dying, he emphasized the unbreakable union with Christ which transcends both life and death. This conviction apparently guided him from the very beginning. Michael Walker's fine new study of Calvin's first theological work, the *Psychopannychia*, shows that this very enigmatic treatise makes sense when read as working out a pastoral problem rather than a philosophical one. By the way the young theologian marshals the arguments and his Biblical texts, he defends the crucial religious claim that the believer is never separated from Christ even when passing through death. The union with Christ in faith is unbroken even by the end of the bodily life; there is no sleep of the soul because that would be an interruption of the conscious union with Christ. [156] What Calvin addresses in his first treatise as a Protestant is at the core of his life-long religious focus on the secure gift of unending life in union with Christ.

---

[154] See Strasbourg above at nn.61f. See the horrified observation by Cathelan, *Passevent Parisien*, pp. 72-73: "Tu me proposes maintenant un article le plus pitoyable qui puisse estre en toute nature humaine, car tout incontinent que l'homme ou la femme est trespassée, ceux de la maison les font accoustrer s'ilz veulent, et puis advertissent leurs autres prochains parens et voisins pour les accompaigner, et ceux qui sonnent les cloches pour le sermon seulement, qui est l'office de porter et ensepvelir les morts, et faire la fosse au lieu député, comme s'ensuit: les deux députez susdits portent sus leur col le trespassé, comme entre nous se portent les reliquères aux processions, couvert d'un drap ou linge, puis suivent les hommes deux à deux, et après les femmes en mesme ordre: les uns rient, les autres pleurent, et ainsi le vont jetter à la fosse sans rien dire, ny faire aucune cérémonie non plus que pour un chien, ou cheval. Et puis s'en retournent tous ceux qui ont accompaigné jusques au logis du trespassé et à la porte chacun dict aux plus prochains, *Dieu vous conserve en vie*, et eux respondent, *Et vous aussi*. Et si hardy de faire quelque prière ny aulmosne pour l'ame du trespassé, sur peine d'estre appellez en leur Consistoire, et estre tenus pour un Papiste et idolâtre."

[155] *Insti.* 4.10.29, originally from 1536, slightly modified in 1543; cf. chap. 6, OS I, p. 256.

[156] Michael Ryan Walker, *The Progress of the Kingdom of Christ in John Calvin's Psychopannychia* (Ph.D. dissertation at Princeton Theological Seminary, 2011). Walker sets Calvin in the context of his fellow French Evangelicals as the young reformer tried to defend them against the dangers of a movement which he believed threatened the foundation of the gospel. Paying attention to Calvin's rhetorical context and his two prefaces as well as the body of the work, Walker

While the *Psychopannychia* seems obscure, the articles of the Apostles' Creed, especially the descent into hell, provide a very clear locus for Calvin to treat death-to-everlasting life. The *Institutes* is naturally where one would look for more about how the Christian faces death in union with Christ and what Calvin says about His "descent into hell." According to the reformer's understanding of the seriousness of the separation from God caused by sin, the death of the Mediator's body on the cross would not have been enough. As the young reformer wrote in 1536 and expanded in 1539, Christ had to experience "the severity of God's vengeance... [to] grapple hand to hand with the armies of hell and the dread of everlasting death." The reason was "so that in death we may not now fear those things which our Prince has swallowed up."[157]

However, a fuller and more accessible expression of encouragement for the Christian facing death is found in Calvin's preaching on the passion. This sermon comes from late his life, in 1562. It should be noted that although he read the story from Matthew, the preacher understood his text as the synoptic harmony, and also felt free to call upon the Johannine passion. In expounding the cry of dereliction (Matt. 27:46), Calvin explains that physical death is fearful, but it is spiritual death – being abandoned by God – which is the most terrible thing.

> We see how our Lord Jesus Christ not only suffered in His body but also in His soul. In fact, it would be a great absurdity to say that He was the savior only of our bodies. To bring about our salvation He had to pay the debt of our sins and the corruption of our offenses was upon Him, to reconcile us to God, as Isaiah says. And we know that our bodies are not culpable in themselves; they are muddied with the sins we commit, but still the root of every sin is in the soul. Thus it was necessary for our Lord Jesus Christ to bear the spiritual punishment to gain acquittal and absolution for us from God. That is why He was put in such anguish besides the suffering of death.[158]

Christ was sinless but humans are only too sinful. Thus, besides physical death, Christ had to suffer the anguish of bearing human sin in order to be the assurance

---

demonstrates how the treatise can be understood as the young reformer's positive teaching about the gospel and then his refutation of his opponents' arguments. The abstract sums up the fruit very succinctly. "The result is a new clarity in our understanding of the reformer's teaching in the Psychopannychia and, by extension, a new appreciation for the centrality of the progress of the Kingdom of Christ as the practical concern motivating Calvin's first treatise and as the chief hermeneutical lens through which the young Calvin read the scriptures."

157 *Institutes* McNeill-Battles, p. 515. OS I, pp. 82-83; 2.16.10-11, OS V, pp. 495-97.

158 *Writings on Pastoral Piety*, pp. 182-83. *Psalmpredigten*, S. VII, pp. 153-54.

His people need that they are never abandoned. Calvin explains that, despite all appearances, Christ continued to pray, experiencing human feelings but continuing to act in hope that God was still with Him.

> [Christ] adds: *You have abandoned me*, according to human feeling, but that does not prevent Him from always hoping in God. And see why it is also said that we must hope beyond all hope,... Now it was necessary that He come to that point, so that we might be assured that we will never be abandoned by God. ... We must be reformed to be like Him and let us never lose courage nor cease to pray to God; when it appears that He is opposed to us and even armed to thunder against us, let us not cease to return to Him and to call Him our God. [159]

In expounding Christ's "second cry," the words of Ps. 31:5 as found in Luke, Calvin speaks of the blunt fact of death. While living on earth "still we can hope in some way that God will have us in His keeping and we will be protected by His power. But in death all will fail if we take the counsel of human feelings." Christ spoke these words for us, "in order to put in our mouths the same words, and for us to call upon God at the point of death and for us to commit ourselves into His hands," which Calvin understands to emphasize the continuity of life in God. Although we die we will live forever, "inasmuch as if we die in this world and to visible sight, God will not cease to be our Father, and thus our life will rest in His mercy, that is, it will endure always." [160]

Most particularly the death and resurrection of Christ assure believers that they will never face their own deaths alone, or in vain.

> If God had delivered Him from [death], what would that be to us when we are dying? We would be like lost people. But when our Lord Jesus Christ goes before us even when we are dying, in that lies our hope, see how we can persevere in calling upon Him. Let us note well then that our Lord Jesus Christ not only died ... but He was raised so that we might be completely and everywhere united and joined with Him, and we might willingly follow Him to death, with the true hope that we will share in His death and His resurrection to experience their fruit, because by that [death-resurrection] the devil is overcome. [161]

---

[159] *Writings on Pastoral Piety*, p. 184-85. *Psalmpredigten*, S. VII, pp. 154-55.

[160] *Writings on Pastoral Piety*, p. 191. *Psalmpredigten*, S. VII, pp. 158-59.

[161] *Writings on Pastoral Piety*, p. 192. *Psalmpredigten*, S. VII, p. 159.

Speaking in 1562, the preacher knew that his own death might come at any time, and perhaps his words were more passionate because of that. However, it is likely that he had expressed these same thoughts at the bedsides of many parishioners.

Not only has Christ experienced everything that a person can face, even apparent abandonment by God, but also union with Christ is not threatened even by death. Because that union is through faith which, by the power of the Holy Spirit has accompanied the person through life, the Christian does not need to fear sudden death, or even a death in anguish. No last minute preparations are required. On the other hand, the whole course of the believer's life is preparation for death in a distinctive way (not like the patterns prescribed in the *ars moriendi*) because it is life-long exercise in faith. In preaching on 1 Cor. 2:11-13 Calvin the pastor explicitly affirms that the certainty of this faith continues beyond death.

> St. John… says that we have certainty, and that is the reason God has given us His Holy Spirit, for until we are resolute to be able to call on Him in full confidence, there is no faith in us … The certainty of which St. Paul speaks extends through the whole course of this life and beyond death. [162]

Paradoxical as it might sound, there is a clear coherence to Calvin's understanding of the union with Christ through faith which defines earthly life, enables the believer to face her own death with prayer and trust despite fear, and gives strength and hope to the bereaved in the certainty that God will never abandon those who are in Christ through the Holy Spirit. Never.

Comforting the Bereaved

The pastor faced not only his own death but far more often he faced the deaths of others. Even when he had prayed with them and watched with them until the believer passed into the next life, he still had to comfort those who must go on living. One more letter may suggest how Calvin addressed the bereavement of a faithful Christian. Although it comes from early in his ministry and may not be his most mature thought, the letter which he wrote to M. de Richebourg in 1541 gives a good sense of how the pastor and teacher spoke in this situation. M. de Richebourg's two sons and their tutor were living in Calvin's household in Strasbourg when the plague ravaged that city, and one of the boys, Louis, and the tutor Claude Féray both died, and there was danger to the whole house. Calvin was on church business at the Colloquy of Ratisbon, and understandably worried about his new wife, his brother, and all the rest of those for whom he was responsible. [163] When

---

162 Ms.fr 26, sermon #14, f114a, quoted in chap. 6 at n.206.

163 *Writings on Pastoral Piety*, pp. 293-94. Letter #295, OC 11:188-89.

he wrote to this French follower of the gospel, the young pastor must have known that the loss of his gifted young son was a testing of the father's confidence in the new form of teaching. In fact, Calvin says he has asked two of his colleagues, Philip Melanchthon and Martin Bucer, to send their words of consolation, also.[164] De Richebourg was a socially prominent and well-educated man who knew the teachings of the faith, so obviously there is no word of Masses for the dead. However, in the Roman context in which he lived, he would have seen that traditional sort of comfort staring him in the face. What could the Protestant minister say to him? What could he offer instead?

It is significant that Calvin begins his letter by expressing his own very real grief over the deaths of Louis de Richebourg and Claude Féray. He explains that news of the loss of his good friend Féray and one whom he "loved as [his] own son" came with the added anxiety for the rest of the household, some of whom were ill and all were scattered. His particular concern, however, was the remaining de Richebourg son, Charles, who would be deeply saddened by losing his brother. Calvin says that he writes these personal feelings so that the father will know that the pastor does not observe this grief from outside but has experienced some of the same affliction. It is thus that he can offer "the remedies I took advantage of and which were of greatest benefit to me in the midst of such a sorrow." He alludes to the common places of philosophical comfort which he says are usually offered in these circumstances, but Calvin acknowledges that de Richebourg already knows these.[165] The minister goes on to add that the other man also knows the truths which the gospel teaches, but he believes that it is worthwhile to repeat them. Then follows a full and nuanced passage of religious reflection. Christians do not rail against fortune because all of life is in God's hands, which means death is not by chance. God's providence is our comfort; the frantic exclamation: "Why?" is only rightly asked when we have failed in our duty.[166] (Perhaps the point is that for the one who believes that all is in God's hands "why?" is not relevant unless we have been irresponsible.)

The next section turns to the more personal part and heart of the letter. Calvin speaks of how this death does not hurt the beloved son but can even be seen as a blessing to him who is taken away before the greatest temptations of life could threaten him, yet when he had already shown that he had come to a real knowledge of faith. Along the way, the teacher cites Gen. 17:7,[167] usually asso-

---

[164] *Writings on Pastoral Piety*, p. 300. Letter #295, OC 11:194.

[165] *Writings on Pastoral Piety*, pp. 294-95. Letter #295, OC 11:189-90.

[166] *Writings on Pastoral Piety*, pp. 295-96. Letter #295, OC 11:190-91.

[167] *Writings on Pastoral Piety*, p. 297. Letter #295, OC 11:191.

ciated with baptism because it is the covenant with Abraham extended to his children. Clearly, Calvin thought that de Richebourg would be comforted by knowing that he had seen the fruit of this baptismal promise in Louis' own profession of faith. Later he explicitly affirms that God does not make mistakes in calling home even those whom we consider too young.

> However brief, therefore, either in your opinion or in mine, the life of your son may have been, it ought to satisfy us that he has finished the course which the Lord had marked out for him. Moreover, we may not reckon him to have perished in the flower of his age, who had grown ripe in the sight of the Lord. For I consider all to have arrived at maturity who are summoned away by death; unless perhaps we would contend with Him, as if He can snatch anyone before his time. This, indeed, holds true of everyone; but in regard to Louis, it is yet more certain on another and more peculiar ground. For he had arrived at that age when by true evidences he could prove himself a member of the body of Christ: having put forth this fruit, he was taken from us and transplanted. Yes, instead of this transient and vanishing shadow of life, he has gained the real immortality. Nor can you consider yourself to have lost him, whom you will recover in the blessed resurrection in the kingdom of God. For they had both so lived and so died, that I cannot doubt but that they are now with the Lord; let us, therefore, press forward toward this goal which they have reached. [168]

The foster father repeats more fully his own joy in having known Louis and his tutor Féray, and his own grief, adding "nor would I desire now to be free from all this sorrow at the cost of never having known them. I hope to hold their memory ever sacred to me, and even sweet and comforting, to the end of my days." He also speaks at some length of the comfort de Richebourg should have in knowing such a fine son as Charles still lives, the kind of son, Calvin says, that he and "all" would want to have. [169]

The conclusion of the letter offers some words about how to express grief. Calvin explicitly says that Christ does not teach "any such philosophy as requires us to put off that common humanity with which God has endowed us": we feel grief, we are not stones. Thus believers will feel and show their sorrow and shed tears. They will not, though, "give way to senseless wailing." [170] Calvin is emphatic that Christians must not be like blocks of wood or stones; they experience sorrow

---

[168] *Writings on Pastoral Piety*, p. 298. Letter #295, OC 11:192-93.

[169] *Writings on Pastoral Piety*, pp. 298-300. Letter #295, OC 11:192.

[170] *Writings on Pastoral Piety*, p. 300. Letter #295, OC 11:194.

and they experience it fully. Nonetheless, Christians remember that they are not only God's children while on earth but also they already live in union with Christ on whichever side of the grave they stand, and they look forward to eternal life with the Lord.

III: A Month in the Life of Calvin the Pastor of Geneva

The ordinary work of a pastor in Calvin's Geneva can be a surprising as well as illuminating window on early Reformed pastoral ministry and worship. While it is certainly true that Calvin was not your ordinary minister in terms of his influence or the amount which can be known about his life and work, nevertheless his daily round was in many ways typical of the church leaders he led and taught.

The time chosen is a month early in the year 1556, chiefly because the wealth of sources allows for a fuller picture than some other periods of the reformer's life. These sources include Calvin's sermons, records of the acts of the Company of Pastors and the consistory and the Senate, information drawn from marriage and baptismal records, the reformer's correspondence and other materials from his writings. This time was also chosen to coincide with preparations for Easter, which was arguably the most intense period of preparation for the service of the word and the Lord's Supper because it was preceded by the (annual) house-to-house visitation by teams of pastors and elders. [171] In an effort to make the story more fluid without sacrificing authenticity, the chronological sequence has been maintained but some details (e.g., contents of sermons) have been limited. The story text follows Calvin through each day for something over a month, beginning on Sunday, March 1, 1556, emphasizing aspects (such as consistory meetings) which have not been treated in any depth in earlier chapters. [172]

Calvin's ordinary schedule began at dawn and closed about 9 p.m. The bells rang in Geneva at 4 a.m. to sound the beginning of the day. [173] The household

---

[171] See chap. 3 at nn.234ff.

[172] Except for specific citations which have not previously been mentioned, notes are kept to a minimum.

[173] For this paragraph see Engammare, *On Time, Punctuality, and Discipline*, pp. 19-25. For Colladon, see OC 21:105-06; for references to meals, see OC 21:103-05 et passim. For Calvin's salary, see Oct. 4, 1541: "Lequelt est home de grand sçavoyer et propice az la restauration des eglises chrestiennes et supporte grandes charges des passans. Surquoy resolus que il aye de gage pour an cinq cens florins douze coppes de froment et deux bossot de vin," OC 21:284 (RC 35 f352). The caveat about how often Calvin stayed home in bed working and the statement that at least some of the time he must have attended worship when his colleagues were preaching is my own, based on the evidence that his colleagues came to hear him preach and his own well-known habit of expecting of himself as much or more than he did of others.

probably gathered for morning prayers, and then if it was his week to preach Calvin left for church. Beza and Colladon recount that when it was not his week to preach, Calvin worked from his bed, beginning at 5 a.m. or 6 a.m. to read and dictate to his secretaries. Since this biographical note comes in the midst of an account of the constantly over-worked pastor's various illnesses and the ways he dealt with them, it seems likely that the practice was common but not necessarily constant. (On some days it may have lasted only an hour, before the ordinary sermon time. It is virtually impossible that the model preacher regularly skipped worship when his colleagues were preaching, although he might well have done so more often as his health grew worse.) Calvin had always eaten moderately and in time this was reduced to one meal a day in the evening, but such suppers were often times of fellowship with friends and colleagues. In fact, at least in earlier years meals were probably busy social times, since it was customary for pastors to receive not only personal friends but also important guests on behalf of the city. This was recognized by the Senate when they assigned their chief minister a large salary. During his marriage Idelette de Bure no doubt managed most of this work. While there might have been changes after her death when Calvin lived with his brother, there is no reason to think that the task of hospitality competely disappeared. Thus, along with the rest of his schedule, it must be assumed that meal times and conversations of business as well as fellowship punctuated Calvin's days.

Week One

On Sunday morning March 1, 1556, Calvin went as usual to St. Pierre for the service at 8 a.m. ("mid-morning" by the early modern clock). This was the second sermon in St. Pierre; one of his colleagues had preached at 5 a.m. Calvin's text was 1 Cor. 6:9-10 (sermon #37), and he picked up the exposition of First Corinthians where he had left off the previous Sunday afternoon. His practice was to take the Greek text (or Hebrew, if he was preaching on the Old Testament) into the pulpit and translate into French the number of verses he thought he could explain in approximately an hour.[174] While he was in the pulpit Calvin might well have announced wedding banns; since he would be marrying two couples that afternoon, he could have made the third announcement of their banns in the morning service. His next task was preaching again at the 3 p.m. service, taking up where he had stopped in the morning, so his text was 1 Cor. 6:11-13. Before beginning the regular liturgy, however, he married the two couples.

---

174 See Engammare, "Introduction," S XI, pp. xliv-vi, for the best recent discussion of Calvin's use of the original languages.

This week was not Calvin's turn to preach at the daily service but on Monday March 2 he would have been at La Magdeleine at 7 a.m. to attend worship led by his alternate. Probably a good part of the rest of the morning would be spent in preparation for his 2 p.m. lecture on Hosea, the book through which he was then working his way, verse by verse. [175] While he preached in French, of course, Calvin lectured in Latin, to anyone who wished to attend, though naturally most of his hearers were his fellow ministers and any educated residents or visitors to the city who were interested. By 1556 the latter would have included a number of religious refugees, e.g., the theological leaders of the Italian and English-language congregations as well as the more numerous French refugees. Also by 1556 the lectures were being held in the chapel of Our Lady the New, now called the Auditoire, next to St. Pierre. Decommissioned at the Reformation, this had recently been re-opened for worship to provide space for refugee congregations like the Italians and English. Their services were held in the mornings, so the space was free in the afternoon for other purposes.

Lecturing on the Bible to prepare ministers to preach was one of the most influential tasks of the leading reformers, and Calvin was particularly well organized in this regard, producing works on almost the entire New Testament and much of the Old. In his teaching as in his preaching Calvin skipped nothing, but his exposition was also distinguished from that of some of his colleagues by its more "practical" character, in that he tried to give what he considered essential for understanding each verse, without citing everything he had read. The point was to provide what a pastor would need to know both to explain scripture to his congregation and to defend Biblical teaching against misinterpretation. In typical humanist fashion, Calvin dealt with linguistic points on how best to interpret particular words, commonly consulting Erasmus for the Greek and Sebastian Münster for the Hebrew. The explanation normally included a concise survey of disputed issues in the exegetical history of the verse, especially if there were points of controversy between Roman and Protestant theologians that were based on patristic comments or arguments. Calvin's first commentaries had been both spoken to students and written down and polished by the reformer himself. Gradually it became clear that the busy pastor did not have time to do it all himself so a new system had to be found and his colleagues were eager to help him. They would copy down what he said in his lectures as fully as possible; often several would collate their notes to prepare a text for Calvin to correct and polish before publication. By 1556 it had become too much for him even to do this polishing; the Hosea lectures would be the first to be published still in the lecture

---

[175] See Peter & Gilmont, *Bibliotheca Calviniana* II, #57/3, pp. 622-24.

format as he had spoken them, complete with the prayers with which he began and ended his lessons.[176]

Before or more likely after his lecture on March 2, Calvin wrote a long letter to the Lutheran church leaders in Frankfurt about several rather delicate issues of potential friction between Lutheran and Reformed Protestants. Since he did not personally know the men to whom he wrote, Calvin excuses himself for addressing them but appeals to the concern for the church which they and he share, and then explains two matters which he requests them to consider. One is a question about Joachim Westphal's *A Just Defense against the False Accusation of a Certain Sacramentarian* (July 1555) which had been published in Frankfurt. This was directed at Calvin but formed part of the on-going polemic between Reformed and Lutheran theologians over the Lord's Supper. Since some of the Frankfurt church leaders also rejected Calvin's teaching on the Lord's Supper, he offers to travel to visit and talk with them in person. The other issue he treats is the state of the recently arrived Reformed congregation, as he intercedes on their behalf. Frankfurt was Lutheran, but they were willing to accept religious refugees when they were assured by some of their own leaders that these people were theologically acceptable. This was the case with the French-speaking congregation – originally from Strasbourg but coming now from exile in England. The problem was that there were internal disagreements in the Reformed congregation which Calvin feared might jeopardize their welcome and he asks the Lutheran leaders' forbearance with the faults of their refugee guests.[177] The conflict with Westphal was, of course, an issue throughout this period and recurs repeatedly in Calvin's correspondence. The matter of the French church in Frankfurt was a different kind of problem, which would personally occupy Calvin for many months of this year. Thus the themes of this letter reflect ways that the pastor in Geneva continued to interact with the larger European church scene in the midst of the daily duties which occupied most of his time.

Tuesday March 3 was much like Monday: attending worship, seeing to other duties and preparation for the lecture at 2 p.m. In addition, part of the day was spent writing more letters to Frankfurt, this time to members of the French church itself, people whom Calvin knew personally and for whom he felt a special responsibility because of his earlier ministry with them. The problem he needed to

---

[176] See Peter & Gilmont, *Bibliotheca Calviniana* I, #52/3, p. 442, for Acts written as commentary; #51/6, pp. 404-05, for Des Gallars' explanation of how he produced the first edition of the commentary on Isaiah from his notes but in his own style; Calvin was not satisfied and completely revised the text in 1559; *Bibliotheca Calviniana* II, #57/3, pp. 622-24 for Hosea.

[177] See OC 16:53-54, letter #2401.

address was internal arguments about the choice of a new minister after the recent death of one of the church's two pastors; this was complicated by irregularities in the election of the other surviving pastor. As the French church's senior counselor, he writes to attempt to move this situation in the direction of mutual understanding and resolution as well as to offer them help in finding a replacement for their deceased minister.[178] Along with his other specific tasks, Calvin would also have spent time during these days visiting his dying colleague Abel Poupin, joining with fellow ministers in Geneva to pray with their friend and his family through his last hours. Prayers and exhortations, Psalms and edifying conversation, pastors and family present with the dying man: his colleagues gathered or took turns at his bedside during these last hours.

Wednesday March 4 was another full day for Calvin. Since Poupin had fallen ill at the beginning of 1553, Calvin had been preaching every Wednesday for the day of prayer, so although it was not his usual week to be in the pulpit, he would be there today.[179] As he walked to St. Pierre for the service at 8 a.m. Calvin might have been reminding himself of the names of the sick, including Pastor Abel, to be included in the day's intercessions on this day of prayer. His text was Deut. 27:16-23 (sermon #151), taking up where he had left off the previous Friday. Normally when he preached on a week day Calvin would not be lecturing also, but because of the change in schedule so that he could do the sermon on the day of prayer every week, there were times when he did both. Thus 2 p.m. found Calvin back in the Auditoire lecturing on Hosea. Then he would go again to Poupin's bedside.

March 5 began with Poupin's death at 7 a.m., with at least some of his colleagues – likely including Calvin – gathered around him. Before his burial the church still had its regular business to do, and so by later in the morning all the ministers and the city elders were gathered for the usual consistory meeting. On this day[180] the most time-consuming business was a continuing investigation into the behavior of Guillaume Lecointe, sire de Boiville (sometimes Boinville), and a number of witnesses: servants, neighbors, and others, gave accounts of what they knew about his blasphemy and sexual improprieties. The case was not resolved until much later in the year, but at this point one of the women involved with M. de Boiville is judged to be guilty of fornication; she is suspended from taking the Lord's Supper until she manifests repentance, and remanded to the Senate for punishment because her behavior was contrary to civil moral laws. A minister and

---

[178] See OC 16:55-56, letter #2402.

[179] See chap. 2 at n.69 *et passim*.

[180] *Registres du Consistoire*, transcription of XI:2, 5v-7v.

an elder, Calvin and Guillaume Chicand, are charged to convey this decision to the council, and at the same time to request permission for the annual pre-Easter house-to-house visitation. (Senate authorization was necessary as a matter of policy but also because the dizeniers, the civil officers of each district who knew everyone in their area, must accompany the ecclesiastical representatives.) After the business with de Boiville, several shorter cases were heard: a husband and wife who were fighting, a conflict between two brothers and their mother also involving "blasphemy," a couple who had promised marriage but wanted to dissolve the engagement, and guards who were fighting. (The last was referred to the appropriate civil authority.) In the case of the quarreling couple, the problem had almost certainly been causing tensions in their neighborhood for some time; the rebellious sons and the complaints of their mother would also have been common knowledge.

Calvin's day was far from over. The burial of Poupin took place that afternoon, and naturally, a great part of the city turned out to accompany the ecclesiastical and civil leaders who went with the family to bury "Pastor Abel."[181] Probably in the evening, tired though he might be, if he had a messenger waiting Calvin would push himself to complete his correspondence for Frankfurt. This time he wrote letters to individuals: one to the Lutheran merchant Johannes Clauburger, a leading layman who had befriended and protected the French congregation, the other to Valerain Poullain, the irregularly elected minister of the congregation who was a part of the controversy (some members supported him, others did not). Both letters were part of on-going correspondence, and the one to Poullain responded to his praise for Calvin's most recent book against Westphal (*Second Defense*, Jan. 1556).[182] In both letters Calvin gives counsel about the church conflict.

Friday March 6 began with worship as usual. The next thing on the schedule was the *congrégation*, a kind of Bible study held every Friday by the ministers and open to the public.[183] One of the purposes was to give ministers practice in expounding Biblical texts in the vernacular; all their theological education was in Latin, but they must preach in French. In addition, this study-and-preaching session provided a chance for them to critique each other, since one person

---

181 For practice in Reformed Strasbourg, see the records of burial for Matthew Zell, in McKee, *Katharina Schütz Zell. Volume One*, pp. 125-29; and *Volume Two. The Writings*, chap. 4. Geneva's burial of Abel Poupin is briefly recorded in the RCP II, p. 66.

182 OC 16:58-65 for letters #2404 and #2407. For information about the *Second Defense*, see Peter & Gilmont, *Bibliotheca Calviniana* II, #57/4, p. 608.

183 De Boer, *Genevan School of the Prophets*, provides a full study of this important institution.

would explain a chosen text, followed by others who would offer their shorter comments, and normally Calvin would then give his exposition (almost another sermon, as Beza wrote in his biography[184]). Finally lay people might also speak, usually to ask questions; they did not attempt to explain the text. In 1556 the book being expounded was probably a continuation of the Psalms begun in the previous year.[185]

After the Friday *congrégation*, the next engagement was the meeting of the Company of Pastors, which usually took place at 2 p.m.[186] Generally this time was occupied with the business of organization, e.g., making preaching assignments for specific men to be in specific pulpits at specific hours, or proposing and examining candidates for the ministry, attending to matters of overseeing the schools, mutual corrections, correspondence with ecclesiastical leaders in other places, and so forth.[187] On this day there is no explicit record of the agenda but it is almost certain that, besides the remembrance of Poupin, one topic would have been the problem with Pastor Jean Fabri which had reached a crisis point. The next day, Saturday March 7, after worship at 7 a.m., the consistory gathered for an extraordinary session to discuss this case. There were public claims of his having made sexual advances to, if not actually seduced, a married woman, and gossip accused him of getting his serving girl pregnant (although this was apparently only gossip). The consistory dealt with witnesses and Fabri regarding the relationship with the married woman (who also testified), and despite his denials of wrongdoing Fabri was deposed and dismissed.[188] Along with the death of Poupin, this meant that the city was short two pastors. Poupin had been unable to preach except occasionally for some time, so the pastors had already doubled-up their duties, but a more permanent solution was needed now that two places were vacant.

Week Two

The new week began, and on Sunday March 8 Calvin was back in the pulpit at St. Pierre, preaching on 1 Cor. 6:13-17, and in the afternoon at 3 p.m. on the

---

[184] Beza, OC 21:33.

[185] See de Boer, *Genevan School of the Prophets*, p. 159.

[186] See Engammare, *On Time, Punctuality, and Discipline*, p. 21, quoting a letter from Calvin to Matthieu Wattel of Sept. 25, 1562, #1395, OC 19:547. This indicates that the Company of Pastors met at 2 p.m. and finished at 3 p.m. Though the information comes from late in the reformer's life, it is unlikely that the schedule had changed significantly over time.

[187] See *Ordinances*, OS II, pp. 332-35 for institution, and RCP for on-going activities.

[188] Transcription of *Registres du Consistoire*, XI:2, 7r-v. For gossip, XI:2, March 31st, 12v-14v. Report to Senate and decision, *Annales*, OC 21:630; RCP II, p. 66.

following verses, 1 Cor. 6:18-20. At the morning service he might also have announced the banns for other marriages which were planned. This week was Calvin's turn to do the regular daily sermon, and Monday morning at 7 a.m. he was at La Magdeleine, taking up the Deuteronomy sequence where he had left off the previous time (Wednesday's day of prayer); it was sermon #152 on Deut. 27:24-26. At 8 a.m. he and elder Chicand went to the regular meeting of the Senate to lay before them the consistory matters with which they had been charged: the report on M. de Boiville and the woman in the case, the request to begin the annual visitation, and the report on the decision about Fabri. The Senate decided to give de Boiville and the woman a hearing at a called meeting after the noon meal to determine how they should deal with this situation, and the deposition of Fabri. They also informed the consistory that the pastors and elders might begin the visitation with the help of the dizeniers. [189]

Tuesday March 10 Calvin preached on Deut. 28:1-2 at La Magdeleine at 7 a.m. Specific activities for this day are not recorded but he would have a certain number of other responsibilities such as visiting the sick. Following the instructions of the *Ecclesiastical Ordinances* that as much as possible the sick should call for pastoral visits when this would not disrupt the pastor's other duties, it is probable that days when Calvin did not have other urgent business would be used in part for pastoral visits. [190] He might also have returned to comfort the members of Pastor Poupin's family. There was also always reading and writing to do, and during this time Calvin received several letters from colleagues outside Geneva. Wednesday March 11 would be much like Tuesday, except that because it was the day of prayer Calvin would be preaching at St. Pierre that morning at 8 a.m. on Deut. 28:2-8.

Thursday March 12 began with preaching the next sermon on Deut. 28:9-14 at La Magdeleine at 7 a.m., and much of the rest of the morning would go into hearing cases at the consistory. [191] Six ministers (all that were left in the city) and the elders in attendance dealt with a number of fairly ordinary cases. Pastor D'Anduse (D'Airebaudouze) from the village of Jussy presented a man to be installed as guard. A man returned to the consistory after rebuke but since he was not repentant for his disorderly behavior was suspended from the Supper and referred to the Senate for punishment for his civil misdemeanors. A quarreling couple were admonished and the husband was warned about beating his wife. A man suspended for financial impropriety comes to demonstrate that he has corrected his behavior and requests and receives restoration to Supper fellowship.

---

[189] March 9, 1556, OC 21:630 (RC 51 f41v, f42)

[190] *Ordinances*, OS II, pp. 355-56.

[191] Transcription of *Registres du Consistoire*, XI:2, 7v-8r.

A couple who married very young were rebuked for premarital sex (their baby was born four months after the wedding), suspended from the Supper and remanded to Senate for the civil offense of living together before marriage. Another man admitted to the charge of blasphemy, asked forgiveness and was pardoned on condition of not repeating the offense. Two men came regarding a dispute over slander and they are told to return next week because witnesses and further information are needed. The consistory also made arrangements to assign pastors and elders to do the pre-Easter visitation (probably as much as possible according to the districts in which they resided).

Friday March 13 found Calvin again in the pulpit of La Magdeleine at 7 a.m. to preach on Deut. 28:15-24. The *congrégation* proceeded as usual with exposition of the Psalms continuing, and then the Company of Pastors met. One item was almost certainly a complaint about the school system. The appointed teachers in the Latin school attended the Company of Pastors because they were regarded as the doctors, one office of the church's educated leadership; they were subject to the same clerical discipline as pastors and new ministers were often drawn from this group.[192] The custom was for the teachers to transmit their concerns to the Senate through the pastors, and that was probably on the agenda this day. The main recorded matter of business for the Company was organizing the visitation from the ministers' side. Geneva had twenty-five districts and there were only six pastors so they decided that each pastor must take four districts and the first one to finish his four would do the last one.[193] Probably each of the six was assigned to four specific districts, where he would accompany the designated elder and the local dizenier from place to place, or house to house, or (according to Ryff's description) from one group of families to another. Although the visitors questioned individuals of one or several households, the corporate character of the preparation for communion is demonstrated by the fact that the questioning might well take place outdoors where there was enough room for a sizable group. The members of the household were called out by the dizenier who knew the district, to meet the pastor-and-elder team, and the other people present could hear what was said – while they awaited their turns. Everyone was involved in the communal process, including probably witnesses who helped their neighbors

---

[192] See chap. 2 at n. 21. Evidence for their presence at the Company of Pastors' meeting is found in incidental cases, e.g., when in 1543 Castellio first volunteers for the plague hospital and then changes his mind; above at n.89.

[193] For teachers, see the introduction of this book at nn.35f; chap. 2 at nn.21ff. The reason for supposing that this matter was presented at this meeting is that Calvin conveys the message to the Senate the following week. RCP II, p. 66.

keep to the facts, since the whole street knew what was happening in every family's quarrels.[194] The pastor-elder team would check that every person knew the Lord's Prayer and the Apostles' Creed in French (possibly also the Decalogue, since all were supposed to learn this, but it may be that some inadequacies on this were tolerated, since the consistory records indicate that the first two were the chief concern). Besides identifying ignorance, the object was to see that there were no unresolved quarrels or other spiritual or moral impediments to hinder a person from coming to the Supper in a state of trust in God and reconciliation with family and neighbors. Over the course of the following weeks the fruits of these visits would be seen in the large number of cases brought before the consistory for problems discovered during the visitation.

Saturday March 15 Calvin was not preaching (since he did the Wednesday day of prayer sermon in what was supposed to be his free week), though he almost certainly was at worship as usual. The rest of the day he may have spent in study or reading. On Friday the Senate had given Calvin a copy of his colleague Cop's exposition of Proverbs, which as senior minister he was asked to examine and approve before it could be published. He might also have been dealing with correspondence: letters received during this period include one from Nicholas Zerkintes in Bern about church matters, others from Bullinger and Johannes Utenhove in Zurich particularly on the Westphal controversy, and a note from Viret in Lausanne.[195]

Week Three

The new week began as usual, with Calvin preaching at 8 a.m. Sunday morning at St. Pierre, the text being 1 Cor. 7:1-2. He may have announced banns again also because at the 3 p.m. service, before preaching on 1 Cor. 7:3-5, he married three couples. (The final reading of the banns could be part of the actual rite of marriage, but it is probable that at least several of these announcements were made at the main morning service in order to reach the largest number of people.) Monday continued regular activities: attending morning worship and the regular lecture on Hosea at 2 p.m. in the Auditoire, but also probably the visitation had begun.

Tuesday after morning worship Calvin went to the Senate meeting at 8 a.m. to put before them some problems in the schools which had probably come to his attention at the Company of Pastors' meeting the previous Friday. There were

---

[194] See Grosse, *Les rituels de la Cène*, pp. 400-07; p. 405 says the questioning was held outdoors.
[195] For Cop's book, OC 21:631; see chap. 6 at n.28. Letters #2403, 2406, 2407, 2409, OC 16:56-58, 65-70, 71-72.

many little schools in Geneva, usually the small projects of individual men or sometimes women who set themselves up as teachers. This was legal but, as Calvin's report indicated, in some cases there was not much teaching happening, so the school masters of the official Latin school sent a request by Calvin to have some changes. The recommendations were: 1) a fixed number of these little schools, 2) an examination for the teachers to see if they were fit to instruct the children, 3) a ruling that these little schools be open only to small children who were not yet capable of being taught in Latin, and 4) all the masters of these little schools be obliged to bring their pupils to the official school every Wednesday for common instruction (which would also serve as a check on how the children were being taught). Besides school business, the rector of the main school requested more space for his family, indicating that there were some unoccupied rooms beside his house which he would like to use. Obviously, Calvin's responsibilities as the main spokesman for the teachers as well as the pastors involved him in matters large and small, of every kind. The Senate agreed to the recommendation about the little schools; it deferred an answer about the rector's request for more space but deputized a syndic to investigate and make a recommendation. [196] The normal schedule continued; Tuesday afternoon Calvin lectured on the next passage of Hosea at 2 p.m. in the Auditoire. Then he wrote to Farel about all the recent news: Poupin's death, Fabri's case, the on-going controversy with Westphal. [197]

Following the schedule of preaching established to insure a good sermon on the day of prayer, the next morning March 18 Calvin was at St. Pierre at 8 a.m. to continue the exposition of Deut. 28:25-29. In the afternoon he gave the next Hosea lecture and probably part of the day was also devoted to visitation.

Thursday March 19 after 7 a.m. worship most of Calvin's morning was probably filled with consistory business. [198] As the Easter celebration of the Lord's Supper approached, the number of cases increased, and this time there were seventeen, which also included matters brought to the consistory's knowledge by the visitation process. Several cases were men who had been suspended from the Supper, who requested to be restored to fellowship; one was deemed repentant, a second not so, and a third was told to return the following week. There are various instances of domestic problems: a man who does not manage his household well, a couple quarreling (over his wasting money and beating her, and her responding with

---

[196] Regulations on the school system in *Ordinances*, OS II, pp. 338-39 (which tries to limit the little schools for boys, and orders girls' education to be separate). March 17 & 19, 1556, OC 21:631, 632 (RC 49 f52v, 55v).

[197] Letter #2412, OC 16:75-76.

[198] Transcription of *Registres du Consistoire*, XI:2, 8v-10v.

rudeness), a widow and her stepdaughter who were called to account for the girl's pregnancy, another man ordered to come and answer regarding the pregnancy of his servant. There were other moral issues: a man and married woman engaged in improper behavior, two unwed mothers (one of whom was a wet nurse in a city family and who was charged with having slept with the children rather than in the attic), a very involved story about a man escorting a woman after dark (the claim being that she needed security, the charge improper behavior). There were other quarrels: two women were told to come for reconciliation after worship next Thursday or else reappear before the consistory if they will not reconcile.

Another problem was more complex: the husband of a quarreling couple was accused of taking food to his buddy who was in prison serving his (short) sentence for fornication. The problem was not the food per se but the fact that this turned into a noisy party on Saturday night, which also involved the prison guards; Calvin and elder Lullin are charged to report this to the Senate. One man came to the consistory from prison where he was serving a sentence decreed by the council for his insolence during the visitation; he was still unrepentant so he was not readmitted to communion. One woman who fled from an earlier summons three years before now appeared and was told to return the next week after the consistory looked up the old records. Another man tried to explain his behavior (blasphemy and frequenting taverns against the consistory's explicit prohibition), for which he asked pardon. However, these were not the only matters in his case; word had it that he had denied the resurrection of the dead, which he admitted but he affirmed that he now believed in it, and said that he attends worship at St. Gervais and La Magdeleine.

What modern readers might consider one of the most interesting cases on this Thursday is the story told by a woman who said that she had come to Geneva for religious refuge seven years before. Then her husband had persuaded her to return home in papal territory and she went, evidently hoping to convert him and regain her children. (Her husband had apparently sold her property!) She confessed that while she was with her husband she attended Mass but she was repentant; her husband persecuted her (for her faith) and she returned to Geneva with two children. The consistory concluded that this story was trustworthy and the woman was dismissed without penalty. As is clear from a number of Calvin's letters to French women, it was common practice to encourage wives who had become converts to the gospel (Protestant faith) to remain with their "unbelieving" husbands as long as this was possible, so the fact that this woman returned to papal territory would not be considered such a serious fault as it would have been if she had been either a man or a widow (i.e., her own master). The fact that she left her husband again would be excused if she felt that her life was in danger; it is possible that her actions both in returning to her husband and in leaving again were influenced by the desire to save her children, also.[199] The day's agenda was not quite over, either; the consistory had to consider a book on Christian Liberty which the ministers were asked by the Senate to examine, and one of the consistory elders was commissioned to report to the council the following week.

The rest of the week included regular worship Friday and Saturday mornings, with the *congrégation* and the Company of Pastors on Friday. The pastors probably spent a considerable amount of time weighing possible replacements for their two colleagues just recently lost, as well as concerns uncovered in the on-going visitation. Apparently the prison was one place on the list for visitation during this week, perhaps as a response to the issue raised by the man who took food to his buddy for a party in jail. It is not stated that Calvin himself made this visit, but that is the logical inference: both because he and elder Lullin had been charged to bring the matter to the Senate, and because of the way Calvin recounted the matter the following Monday: he tells the council that the jail was "full of" people from St. Gervais who had come to banquet with the fornicator.[200] Sometime during this period Calvin also would be handling correspondence, part of the network of letters which linked him with many people beyond his day-to-day world in Geneva.

Week Four

The new week beginning March 22 was certainly filled with the heightened tension of preparation for Easter and the need to complete the city-wide visitation. There is no extant sermon recorded for Calvin at 8 a.m. on Sunday and it is known that Farel was in town, so it seems probable that the latter was in the pulpit at St. Pierre. Calvin was back in St. Pierre at 3 p.m. on Sunday afternoon with the next sermon on 1 Cor. 7:6-9, taking up where he had left off the previous Sunday afternoon. At the same time Farel was at La Magdeleine where he did a wedding and probably also preached.[201] The presence of his good friend was certainly a

---

[199] Transcription of *Registres du Consistoire*, XI:2, 8v. See chap. 5 at nn.54f.

[200] March 23, 1556, OC 21:632 (RC 49 f60v).

[201] OC 21:632 indicates that Farel did a wedding at La Magdeleine on this date. Since there were no weddings at the morning service, the marriage must have been at dawn or afternoon, and the famous visiting pastor would have been welcomed at the afternoon service (rather than the dawn). La Magdeleine had begun Sunday afternoon services only the previous year; cf. chap. 1 at n.169. When Farel or Viret visited they were usually asked to preach; on July 23, 1550, Calvin wrote to Viret saying that since the latter would be in Geneva he himself would go to visit one of the village churches; cf. #1387, OC 13:603, cited in Balke & Moehn, "Introduction," CS 8, p. xviiii n.67.

pleasure for Calvin; it might even have given him an opportunity to attend worship on Sunday morning instead of preaching – unless he had to fill another pulpit, because Geneva was so short of qualified ministers.

Monday Calvin preached at La Magdeleine at 7 a.m. on Deut. 28:29-35 and then at 8 a.m. he and Lullin went to the Senate with their report from the last consistory meeting. The key issue was the evidence that conditions in the prison needed attention, since not only did a visitor bring a prisoner supplies for a party, but the jailor and his wife joined in the fun instead of doing their job. Calvin and Lullin also recounted their visit to the prison and the Senate took the matter in hand, punishing the jailor and his wife and putting the prisoner on bread and water. Calvin reported back positively on Pastor Cop's commentary on Proverbs and the council approved publication. One of the elders – a different one – added his report that the pastors had approved the book on Christian Liberty for publication. [202]

Tuesday March 24 Calvin preached as usual at 7 a.m. at La Magdeleine on Deut. 28:36-48, and Wednesday at 8 a.m. at St. Pierre for the day of prayer on Deut. 28:46-50, then Thursday back at La Magdeleine on Deut. 28:49-58. (The repeated verses show that when Calvin felt a text had not been fully treated one day, he continued the thought in the next sermon. [203]) The main work of the week was the visitation, and that process augmented the number of people before the consistory on Thursday morning: [204] cases of fornication or drunkenness; a number of family quarrels or general "mauvais ménage" (either new problems or further witnesses in on-going investigations). Several were instances of people who came (perhaps reluctantly) to confess that they had been communicant members in Geneva some years before but had spent the intervening time in papal territory and attended Mass, and now they wanted to return to the faith. For the most part these individuals were apparently judged to be not yet truly repentant, they were suspended or their earlier suspensions from the Supper were renewed, and they were remanded to the Senate. One man who returned from his time in the papal lands had demonstrated his repentance and now his suspension was lifted and he was restored to fellowship. Likewise a man who had served his penalty for fornication and was repentant was restored. Some cases the consistory dealt with this morning were the result of ignorance or popular "superstition" uncovered during the visitation. La Donne Polliere was accused of holding to the Mass, she uses the sign of the cross to chase away the devil, objects to eating meat

---

[202] March 23, 1556, OC 21:632 (RC 49 f60v, 70r).

[203] See chap. 6 at n.240.

[204] Transcription of *Registres du Consistoire*, XI:2, 10v-12r.

on Friday, and has stayed away from the Lord's Supper (although the consistory claims that she was suspended). In addition, her two serving girls do not know anything about the faith ("do not know if the Mass is bad"). One by one, each case received the attention of the consistory, working witness by witness or person by person to sort out the facts and decide what response was appropriate.

Friday continued the regular work. Calvin preached at La Magdeleine at 7 a.m. on Deut. 28:39-64, followed by the regular *congrégation* and the meeting of Company of Pastors. At this gathering one subject would probably be preparation for the special observances before Easter, since at least one minister would interrupt his usual *lectio continua* series to preach on the passion during the week before Easter. This year it would not be Calvin, because it was not his turn to preach during that week.[205] Saturday March 28 he again preached at the regular 7 a.m. service at La Magdeleine on Deut. 28:65-68. The responsibility for an extra day had been given to him since the pastors were obliged to divide up the work that the deposed minister Fabri had been doing.

Passion Week

Sunday March 29 marked the beginning of the week before Easter, the high point of the year. There is no sermon recorded for Calvin for Sunday morning March 29 at 8 a.m., but it is probable that he was in the pulpit preaching on the passion – choosing between John and Matthew (i.e., the synoptics). According to the liturgical instructions, the sermon probably included words of exhortation to prepare the people for the Lord's Supper the next Sunday.[206]

Following the morning service and noon catechism, Calvin would attend the examination of the candidates considered ready to make their own profession of faith. This was a second hour of catechism at which the youth who were ready would be expected to answer a simplified series of questions which included reciting the Lord's Prayer, the Apostles' Creed, and the Decalogue. (The double catechism class on the Sunday before the Supper was becoming cumbersome and

---

[205] See chap.4 at nn.67f; chap. 6 at nn.70ff.

[206] See chap. 6 after n.71 & after n.79. See Appendix Eight Part Two for April 1549; March-April 1550; March 25, 1551; March 1554. These lost sermons often begin on the Sunday before Easter; in 1550 there are eight, Sunday morning, the six weekdays, and then Easter Sunday morning. In 1549 there is the same pattern except apparently one weekday is missing because there are only seven sermons. In 1553 there are nine sermons, two on the Sunday before Easter, one each weekday, and then Easter; this is the longest series known. In 1551 there is only the Wednesday; evidently it was not Calvin's week to preach but he did the day of prayer. In 1554 there are Sunday morning, Wednesday, and Easter morning; again, not his week to preach but he does a series of three.

later in 1556 it was decided that on these four Sundays each year the regular catechetical exposition would be omitted in favor of having the examination an hour earlier. This day, however, the old pattern was still in force.) It is probable, though not certain, that Calvin would have participated in the catechism at St. Pierre. [207] If the examination went quickly, he might have had a short break before his afternoon service at 3 p.m., where his text was 1 Cor. 7:10-14.

Monday March 30 began with worship at 7 a.m. as usual, although Calvin was not preaching. He probably gave his regular lecture, still on Hosea, at 2 p.m., unless perhaps the visitation work might have hindered this. (It is not clear what events Calvin allowed to interrupt his lecture schedule, but it is possible that there were occasions when that happened. Normally only severe illness or absence from Geneva was permitted to interrupt his preaching; the same may have been true for his teaching, although it was less urgent that these special classes be held than that regular sermons continue.) On this day Calvin wrote a letter to Viret, recounting the death of Poupin, the deposing of Fabri, and the various candidates who would be desirable as replacements. These included Jean Merlin (who might not be available), as well as Claude Baduel and Pierre Le Duc, two teachers who were being considered for the vacant posts. [208]

Tuesday after morning worship the consistory gathered, because during the week before the Lord's Supper celebration two consistory meetings were held in the effort to bring back into the fellowship as many as possible of those who had been temporarily suspended. [209] The docket was full, and this pre-Easter period involved not only the cases already known but also new ones reported by the pastor-elder visitation teams. Today that included the two servants of La Donne Polliere who had been named the previous week. Despite a ten-year residence in Geneva, the one named Loyse only knew the Lord's Prayer and the Apostles' Creed in Latin – a scandal because it meant that her mistress had not sent her to catechism and somehow she had escaped notice in previous visitations. The other servant, Michee, could not say what was wrong with the Mass (i.e., did not know anything about the Reformed teaching on the Lord's Supper). Both young women were suspended from communion and told to attend catechism, and then return to the consistory before the next Supper celebration at Pentecost to demonstrate that they now knew the basics of the faith in their own language. The

---

207 See chap. 3 at n.145. Discussion of wider practice, Grosse, *Les rituels de la Cène*, pp. 466-98.

208 Letter #2418, OC 16:85-86.

209 Transcription of *Registres du Consistoire*, XI:2, 12v-14v. For increase in cases before the Lord's Supper, see Grosse, *Les rituels de la Cène*, pp. 416-23, graphs pp. 417, 419; for cases involving ignorance, graph on p. 499.

visitation had also revealed that a very elderly woman was still praying as she had been taught as a child in catholic Geneva and could not say the Lord's Prayer or the Creed in French; however, she had been receiving the Supper. No rebuke is recorded but the old lady was told not to take the sacrament this time but to study and come back before Pentecost. One whole family was cited for ignorance; another woman failed at the first words in her attempt to say the Lord's Prayer; another man was repentant and restored but then suspended because he said that he took the Supper "for the profit of his soul" (apparently indicating lingering ideas of transubstantiation).

Various kinds of insolence or other bad behavior at the visitations were also noted and now were dealt with, including a woman who said that she did not come (i.e., obey the call to come out and answer the questions) because she thought that the persons calling her were neighbors and did not realize that they were the consistory visitors. (One wonders if perhaps this was a convenient fiction to avoid answering unwelcome questions; it might have saved her responding in front of the neighbors but it got her a summons to the consistory.) Cases of fornication and family quarrels and problems among neighbors were numerous this day. One man who confessed that he had been guilty of fornication when he was in Lyon (papal territory) now said that he had repented; the consistory apparently considered that he was repentant and left it to his conscience to decide whether or not to commune in the Supper. After this long consistory meeting Calvin might still have had his 2 p.m. lecture.

Wednesday April 1 was the day of prayer during this most special week, and Calvin almost certainly was preaching at St. Pierre at 8 a.m. on the passion. There is no recorded sermon, but it was the pattern for him to lead the day of prayer every week in this year, and in other years his day of prayer sermon during this special week was often on the passion. If he was also doing his regular lectures in this busy week, he would have been at the Auditoire at 2 p.m. for the next section of Hosea.

Thursday April 2 after worship at 7 a.m. came the regular consistory meeting, although again most of the agenda was related to preparation for the Supper.[210] A number of cases concerned issues such as blasphemy, drunkenness, ignorance of basic teachings, participation in the Mass or other papal practices while living in foreign lands. One repentant man was pardoned for his blasphemy but, when he was examined on his knowledge of the faith, he was then suspended until Pentecost because he said that Jesus Christ's passion was in the sacrament (evidently some variation of transubstantiation). The case of M. de Boiville was

---

[210] Transcription of *Registres du Consistoire*, XI:2, 14v-17r.

brought up, not for completion but to note that he was suspended, so that he would not try to take the Supper when he was unfit. The last item of business was for the consistory to decide which elders would serve communion in which parishes.

This was the last of the consistory meetings before Easter, but preparations for the celebration of the Supper were far from over. Friday April 3 after worship Calvin went before the Senate at its 8 a.m. meeting regarding a problem with Jean Troillet. Several years before, in 1552, there had been a controversy between the two men when Troillet had attacked Calvin's teaching on predestination. That had been resolved, but Calvin had just received word that something written by Troillet about the issue was circulating in Bourgogne and this text did not give the actual conclusion of the controversy which vindicated the teaching in the *Institutes*. While affirming that he was not upset on his own account, Calvin said that he must object to this text by Troillet for the sake of the faith and the honor of Geneva. He brought this to the Senate because he felt he should not hide it, lest it be said after the Supper that he had kept this in his heart (i.e., that he was not reconciled with the whole community). Troillet was called and questioned, and denied having written or sent such a text to Bourgogne.[211] This apparently odd visit by Calvin to the Senate was not only prompted by a desire to vindicate his teaching, although that was obviously part of it. The timing and explanation indicate that he was applying to himself the same standards that he was convinced that all believers should meet, the standards which had been recognized in one way or another for ages: a Christian must not approach the sacrament while harboring resentment in his heart, without having confessed any rancor which separated him or her from full fellowship with neighbors. As the consistory worked to learn the rights of any case, it also labored to be sure that every Genevan was reconciled with every other. Here Calvin applied to himself the same requirement, which meant airing and resolving a conflict before sharing in the Supper, so that it might be evident that he was practicing what he preached about seeking a clear conscience in harmony with his neighbors as preparation for communion.[212] The action suggests that he had been angry with Troillet and no doubt other people knew it, so he needed to make sure there was a very public reconciliation.

Normally on Friday the Bible study congrégation would take place during the morning. It is assumed that this would be true also this Friday before Easter, but

---

[211] April 3, 1556, OC 21:633 (RC 49 f79r-v).

[212] See chap. 3 at nn.197, 199, after n.229 *et passim*. Grosse, *Les rituels de la Cène*, chap. 8, esp. pp. 515-25 for people's hesitations about communing and consistory efforts to bring as many as possible to restoration.

one wonders if it might possibly have been omitted. The Company of Pastors did hold its meeting, and this would have been longer than usual because it was the appointed day for mutual censures when each member of the company spoke his criticisms of his fellows and submitted to theirs. (These might include such things as neglecting to visit the sick, bad study habits evident in sloppy preaching, problems of reputation – if people were gossiping about a minister because of some less than discreet or appropriate words or behavior.) These mutual censures involved not only the city pastors but also those from the country parishes. One session of mutual censures would involve the pastors and the deacons who cared for the poor, sick, and needy and ran the General Hospital. After this airing of mutual corrections among these officers of the church, the pastors and deacons would share a dinner at the hospital. [213]

Saturday morning April 4 meant regular worship at 7 a.m. It might also include visits to the prison, since Saturday afternoon was the appointed time for pastors, accompanied by civil officials, to visit persons in special confinement for serious crimes. Deacons would be seeing to the preparation of bread and wine for the communion next morning. [214]

Easter Sunday April 5, and the main focus was the morning celebration of the Lord's Supper. This would take place twice at St. Pierre and St. Gervais and once at the Magdeleine, since the sacrament was held at the dawn service at 4 a.m. at St. Pierre and St. Gervais, as well as in all three churches at 8 a.m. Calvin preached on the resurrection at St. Pierre and celebrated the Lord's Supper. At the time for communion, the people would come forward in two lines; the pastor would give each person a piece of bread and then the elder standing beside him would offer the cup. There were two elders and two pastors serving, at least at the main service, because the pattern was to have two tables side-by-side in the space before the pulpit, one for the men and one for the women. [215] During the communion, there would be a continuous reading from the passion, perhaps usually from the gospel of John because it was Calvin's favorite and full of theological reflection. [216] In the afternoon, the regular schedule resumed, and Calvin was back to preaching on 1 Cor. 7:15-17.

---

[213] *Ordinances*, OS II, pp. 332-35. Grosse, *Les rituels de la Cène*, pp. 316-19.

[214] *Ordinances*, OS II, p. 356. Grosse, *Les rituels de la Cène*, pp. 230-31.

[215] See chap. 3 at n.156.

[216] For translation of a full Easter Sunday service, see *Writings on Pastoral Piety*, pp. 111-34.

The Next Months

At Easter Geneva moved to its summer schedule, with the dawn service at 4 a.m. and the regular weekly preaching at 6 a.m. instead of 7 a.m. So Monday April 6 found Calvin in La Magdeleine at 6 a.m., continuing his sermons on Deut. 29:1-4. This day, when he arrived at the church he would see a baptismal party: father, godfather, and a nurse with the baby [217] and so the day-to-day life of a pastor in Geneva continued. Besides the usual round of preaching, teaching, visiting the sick, meetings with consistory and colleagues and Senate, the next weeks would include the task of examining and installing new pastors, dealing with the further results of the visitation, and picking up more of his correspondence. In fact, during the previous week Calvin might well have begun the long letter – really, a short treatise – against the Anabaptist Menno Simons, which he addressed to Martin Micronius about this time. [218] And neither the controversy with Westphal nor the situation in the French church in Frankfurt had been resolved. Calvin was working so hard that on May 10 – the day he was also supposed to present two new ministers to the city, at St. Pierre at 8 a.m. and St. Gervais at 3 p.m. – he collapsed in the pulpit while preaching his Sunday morning sermon and was confined to his bed for nearly three weeks, before he could take up all his regular duties again. His alternate, Des Gallars, smoothly took over the service on May 10 and continued the sermon on Calvin's very text! [219] And no doubt he did much of the rest of Calvin's preaching during this illness: the pastoral rotation worked, and although Calvin was the most prominent preacher, he was not indispensable. In his farewell to his colleagues, the dying reformer thanked them for supporting him in the task of preaching. [220] The pastoral

---

217 See chap. 5 after n.215; see Appendix Four: Calvin's Baptisms.

218 *Consilia*, OC 10:167-76.

219 Colladon's description, OC 21:81: "Le second accez [of the illness] venoit au Dimanche 10 jour de May, et lors en son sermon devoyent estre presentez au peuple deux nouveaux Pasteurs, au lieu de deux autres, dont l'un estoit mort, et l'autre avoit esté deposé pour malversation. Or luy ne pensant point à sa fievre, ou n'y voulant point penser (tant il prenoit grand plaisir de servir l'Eglise) un bien peu devant qu'il sortist de sa maison pour aller au temple, on apperceut à ses doigts quelque signe de l'accez venant. Mais il dissimula cela, et monta au chaire, et apres la priere et le chant du Pseaume, commença son sermon, et s'efforça de continuer, faisant apporter pour son soulagement une selle [siege] dedans la chaire, afin de s'assoir. Mais la force des frissons le pressant tousjours, il fut contreint finalement de s'excuser envers l'assemblee, et se retirer en sa maison, n'ayant fait qu'une partie de son sermon. Pour suppleer au defaut, et afin que l'acte ne demeurast imparfait, un des ministres là presens, assavoir M. Nicolas des Gallars, acheva le sermon, poursuivant fort bien à propos le text qu'avoit commencé à exposer ledit Calvin."

220 Beza's account of the farewell includes: "et remercia, comme souvent il avoit fait, de ce qu'on avoit soutenu sa charge quant à prescher," OC 21:44.

ministry, especially in worship, was carried out by a corps of movable parts so that the continuing edification of the people would be reliable, no matter who was in the pulpit.

CONCLUSION

REFLECTIONS ON PASTORAL MINISTRY AND WORSHIP IN CALVIN'S THEOLOGY AND PRACTICE

For Calvin, and the Reformed tradition more generally, re-forming the life of worship – and the worship in life – was crucial. The marks of the church, defined as the word purely preached and heard and the sacraments rightly administered, were central to knowing and honoring God and thus to finding the goal and joy of human life. These marks of word and sacraments also had to be embodied in actual liturgical forms and human actions. While clearly never salvific in themselves, the concrete forms must be fitting for their purpose and as close to God's will as practicable in the actual time and place of the people who are the visible church. At the conclusion of a book full of the detailed examination of the many individual parts of worship in Calvin's Geneva, it is both appropriate and challenging to attempt a summary. This reflection-in-guise-of-conclusion will focus on two clusters of comments which may highlight some of the fruits of the previous chapters. The first cluster is institutional, the second is theological.

I: Where, What, Who, and When

The reform of worship and pastoral ministry in sixteenth-century Geneva was a significant change in both public worship, and the nature of the work and collegial organization of those who led it. It is fitting to begin with the people in the pew: where and when, what and who.

For parishioners, the places they worshiped and especially what they did there changed dramatically. There were only three regularly used buildings. These looked rather different on the inside without the color and form of paintings and statues and side altars; instead there were (virtually) bare walls and a prominent pulpit facing ranks of chairs and benches. The times of services had multiplied, and the schedule was very much changed. There was still worship at the hour which had been traditional for the weekday Mass, but now there were two specific times on some days, with dawn services on Mondays, Wednesdays, and Fridays at St. Pierre and Wednesdays at St. Gervais in addition to the "customary" daily time of 6 a.m. or 7 a.m. The traditional Sunday morning time was still practiced but now there were dawn and afternoon sermons (usually 3 p.m.) as well, plus catechism at noon. More startling no doubt was that the whole annual schedule had been revised: all the saints' days and most of the other holy days except Sundays were gone. The year was shaped by the four high points when the Lord's Supper was celebrated, and three of these were the key Christological feasts of the Nativity, Easter, and Pentecost. The week was shaped by the prominence of Sunday and the lesser but still very important Wednesday day of prayer.

As for what the services were like and what they were expected to do: that was very different! For one thing, worship was now an extremely didactic and strongly corporate activity. The main course was expository preaching, on a Biblical book except at catechism, and it was *lectio continua* except on the limited number of special Christological observances. The whole service was in the vernacular and everyone was supposed to sit still and participate by listening and, on Sunday and the day of prayer, singing Psalms. The practice of the Lord's Supper involved (virtually) every person in the city on the same day, which was at least three times per year more often than had been traditional. Those who had communed more frequently than medieval law required would almost certainly have done so on an individual basis, and thus the Easter duty would have been the only time a person joined in the sacrament with the whole parish. Now there were four "Easters." Even more surprising, however, was the fact that the entire congregation shared the sacrament of baptism and the rite of marriage with all the families who presented their babies for baptism or themselves to be wed. Worship was now tangibly a gathering of the whole community on a regular and frequent basis. It demanded more time and attention and preparation. It offered more intellectual and (usually) edifying fare for anyone who seriously cared about knowing the contents of God's word, although much of the color was missing without the saints' miracles and other popular morality stories.

For pastors in Geneva, the reform of worship had major implications for education and collegial expectations. Not surprisingly, requiring university training as well as "conversion to the gospel" limited the candidates for ministry and so almost all the new preachers were foreigners, some former priests but most not. Prominently featured in the new job description for urban pastors was the obligation to preach at least four sermons per week and often more. It also included – and this was more unusual still – the willingness to work as a team, in pairs whose pulpits might and did change much more frequently than had ever been the case for traditional parish clergy. The novel practice of having alternates for regularly scheduled services was begun in part to insure that all the people in the pew heard a variety of preachers. From the viewpoint of the ministers it was a necessary means to insure that pulpits were always filled, even when a pastor fell ill or had to be absent for some other reason. The collegial organization did not presume that every minister liked every other, but it did make cooperation in leading worship a bedrock requirement of pastors in Calvin's Company.

The shape of public corporate worship in Geneva can be summarized briefly. In the early years (before 1541), the buildings used were St. Gervais on one side of the Rhone, and St. Pierre and the Rive in Greater Geneva. There were five services on Sundays: one dawn at St. Pierre, at least one in the afternoon at the Rive, and three others distributed between the two sides of the city. There was a main morning service at St. Gervais, and probably one each at the Rive and St. Pierre (although the exact organization may have changed during these years). There were also two daily sermons on each weekday, at the Rive and St. Gervais. When the *Ecclesiastical Ordinances* came into effect in 1541 there were three parishes: St. Pierre and La Magdeleine, which functioned in symbiosis until 1559 in Greater Geneva, and St. Gervais. St. Pierre and St. Gervais hosted most of the Sunday services: dawn (4 a.m. or 5 a.m. according to the season), 8 a.m., catechism at noon, and 3 p.m. (2 p.m. in deep winter). Until 1549 La Magdeleine had only weekly catechism, plus a morning service on Sundays when the Lord's Supper was celebrated. Then a weekly 8 a.m. service was added in 1549, so with catechism there were two until 1555, when an afternoon service was added. (There was a short-lived dawn sermon in 1559-60.) Weekdays La Magdeleine and St. Gervais hosted services at 6 a.m. or 7 a.m. depending on the season, on all six days except the Wednesday day of prayer. Then St. Gervais had also a dawn service and the second service was later (7 a.m. or 8 a.m.) and La Magdeleine had none until 1555 because the one scheduled for La Magdeleine actually happened at St. Pierre, again at the later hour. At St. Pierre there were regularly three dawn services on Monday-Wednesday-Friday; in 1559, with the large influx of refugees crowding the city, a full set of six at the ordinary time (6 a.m./7 a.m.) was begun.

Ministers in these city parishes worked in pairs, usually defined by the weekday sermons at the ordinary time at St. Gervais and La Magdeleine, and dawn at St. Pierre. Sunday services were less clearly fixed; in Greater Geneva catechism was usually done by alternates but in St. Gervais it might be assigned to one man who also did the two dawn services. Sunday morning at 8 a.m. was led by the specifically designated chief pastors; at St. Pierre that was of course Calvin. At

St. Gervais where the two assigned pastors were on a more equal footing most of the time, the ministers usually alternated. The arrangements at La Magdeleine were more complicated because its morning service was held only four times per year until 1549. Calvin's alternate may have been the usual Sunday morning preacher until his illness at the beginning of 1553, when major shifting around meant that no one's schedule remained exactly fixed. In general, throughout Calvin's ministry, Sunday afternoon was the most flexible time. Often it was linked with the morning but it was also sometimes used as a key time for pulpit exchanges across the city. For much of his life Calvin did both morning and afternoon at St. Pierre. However, in an effort to link the two sides of the city and reassure the people of St. Gervais that they were not being neglected, Geneva's chief preacher made the trek across town to St. Gervais on most Sunday afternoons from early 1546 until spring 1552.

The public office of a pastor centered on corporate worship, which meant preaching and the administration of the sacraments and the rite of marriage. One form of sermon was explaining the catechism at the regular weekly services in each parish and this was usually the first assignment for new pastors because the content was presumed to be quite familiar. The more frequent and challenging preaching was the exposition of a Biblical book in sequence. For this Calvin's lectures and the resulting commentaries and the French-language *congrégations* were probably key resources, although Calvin's sermons must also have been useful since his colleagues frequently came to hear him. The liturgies for the sacraments and the rite of marriage were printed in *La forme des prières*, which also provided certain prayers for Sunday mornings and the day of prayer. Other prayers were left to the ministers' own gifts, although some may have borrowed from each other – or Calvin. Besides their regularly scheduled public worship, pastors were expected to visit the sick and remember them before the church in pastoral prayers, to participate in the work of the consistory and the Company of Pastors, and other services for the church. Among the latter was filling in for colleagues who were prevented from providing their appointed sermons!

In describing the daily duties of ministers in Geneva a great deal of attention has been focused on such tasks as discipline. However, it is worth remembering that the weight of assuring that all the people were fed with the word of God may have been the most time-consuming task of the pastoral ministry. Certainly, given the very limited numbers of qualified men and the staggering schedule of preaching in urban Geneva, conceiving and then executing the plan for establishing alternates and their rotation as preachers throughout the city may rank as one of the most impressive organizational feats achieved by their leader John Calvin.

II: The Rhythm of Religious Time

While worship is fundamentally rooted in the heart and not subject to time constraints, the practice of worship – what Calvin calls the *officia pietatis* or duties of piety[1] – must be embodied in space and time. Reformed views of the physical place of worship have usually been examined in relationship to the question of the visual arts. Calvin himself says very little about this matter with the exception of two key points: any location where worship is held must not be regarded as intrinsically different from other buildings (it is the people who are the church); and whatever edifice is used should be appropriate to its purpose.[2] The second criterion includes not only a space free of distracting images but also a place where the people can hear what is said. Although critics objected to the "school" or "auditorium" character of Reformed churches, Calvin would probably have considered that description a kind of compliment.[3] By comparison with the amount of attention to the character of the Reformed relationship with the visual arts, scholars have devoted much less energy to questions of time. At least, Calvin's sense of time in relation to worship has usually been discussed in a somewhat piece-meal and/or theoretical fashion. The foregoing comprehensive picture of how worship was actually being practiced in Calvin's Geneva can contribute to illuminating the coherence between what might seem like abstract theology and practical piety.

The largest temporal span for worship is the entire Christian life: every moment the believer justified by faith alone is in God's presence and should in principle praise and worship the Lord. One corollary of this is that all time is hallowed insofar as it is dedicated to God; or to put it another way, no time is sacred or profane in itself but only as a function of the relationship to God of the person who worships (or does not). This is the reason that Calvin insists there are

---

1   See McKee, *John Calvin on the Diaconate*, chap. 10.

2   The debates on use of images or other visual arts are both extensive and well known. For Calvin's objections, a good summary is found in *Inst.* 1.11.12-14. His meager comments on the place of worship are summarized in *Inst.* 3.20.30, in a passage from 1539/41. "Particularly, since God's word ordains public prayers among the faithful, it is necessary for there to be temples assigned for that. ... [W]e must be on guard agianst considering them the proper dwellings of God and places where our Lord gives us a more attentive ear... or ascribing to them some secret holiness which makes our prayer better before God," *Institutes 1541*, p. 474. See introduction to this book at n. 20.

3   Calvin insists on the necessity of intelligible worship; his main point is people being able to understand the language but another aspect of this is sheer audibility; see the preface to the Psalter, OS II, p. 12, quoted in the introduction at n.50. For Roman critics, see Cathelan and Raemond, in chap. 2 at n.144.

no days holy in themselves, and so the details of the way the visible church orders the duties of piety are a matter of polity. God's word teaches that human beings must have one day out of seven for the purpose of public corporate worship, and the early church tradition provides guidance that the day of resurrection should be chosen. In fact, daily worship would be good, so it is fitting to set aside a specific time every day for the church to gather. It is logical that Calvin and Protestants generally made Sunday, the Lord's Day, the central marker of religious time, and it is no surprise that they sought to organize daily services as much as possible.

There are several other aspects of religious time which Calvin and the Reformed tradition developed in special ways. The negative side of this reform is widely recited: they abandoned the liturgical year and Calvin went so far as to "abolish" Christmas. There is a certain truth in the charge of abandoning the medieval liturgical calendar, although it is wrong to say that Calvin abolished Christmas. He rejected the traditional date of Dec. 25 (nowhere indicated in scripture) but quite explicitly maintained the observance of the Nativity with the full solemnity of the Lord's Supper. He also did not object to the practice of Christological holy days by other church communities, as long as doing this was not understood as marking an intrinsic difference between days. The positive side of the Calvinist Reformed sense of liturgical time has long been overlooked. The truth is that Calvin had a distinctive sense of religious time and a liturgical creativity which embodied his theology: the day of prayer. To understand this, it is necessary to take into account the doctrine of providence as well as the teaching on Christology.

The Lord's Day is the fundamental marker of salvation history for Christians, pointing to what God has done in Jesus Christ for the redemption of the world. Nevertheless the incarnation is far from God's only involvement with human beings; from the beginning God has been present and active. The Reformed tradition in general and Calvin in particular have long been associated in a special way with emphasis on the doctrine of providence, God's constant active engagement in God's world at every minute. The immediacy of the divine governance in the world is not restricted to God's engagement with believers but it has a specific meaning for them.[4] Without the faith acquaintance with Christ the Mediator, human beings may know God as a just and good Creator but they

---

[4]   Calvin's first extensive discussion of providence appears in 1539, as the second part of chap. 8; the fact that this follows predestination instead of preceding it expresses the theological order of knowing salvation first and then trusting God's governance of the world. In 1559, providence becomes *Inst.* 1.16-17. Calvin goes so far as to say: "[I]t is the greatest misery that a person can have not to know God's providence and, on the other hand, it is a singular blessing for him to know it well," *Institutes 1541*, p. 455 = 1.17.11.

cannot have confidence that God has saving good will toward them personally. Christians believe that the *pro nobis/ pro me* character of God is revealed in Jesus Christ by the power of the Holy Spirit.

One corollary of this conviction is that only Christians can recognize God's providential work for what it is: the engagement of their Savior God with them in the present. Why? Because providence encompasses things which are "bad" in human eyes as well as those they consider "good." Only when the character of God *pro me/ pro nobis* is known through Christ can the otherwise "random" events happening all around be reckoned as coming from a good God. Calvin was convinced that by definition the God known in Christ is *for us* and therefore no matter what happens on earth it cannot do us ultimate harm. In fact, some of what seems "bad" to us may be a form of "tough love," God's action to bring God's people back into the right way. "Providence" does not mean that no physical injury will come but that whatever happens, whatever God sends, cannot separate us from God, whom to know is the purpose of our creation and our highest good. That relationship cannot be destroyed by good or bad experiences on earth, which can all work together for the good of God's children. Therefore nothing can separate us from God and our true good except sin, which Calvin defines ultimately as unbelief, refusing to trust God's good will in Christ.[5] Union with Christ through faith by the power of the Holy Spirit gives believers the confidence to face whatever happens, because the God who rules the universe is the same One who died to save them. In Christ the character of God is known as *pro nobis/ pro me*. Trusting that all is in God's hands for their ultimate good does not mean Christians do nothing. They continue to call upon God for help and guidance, and they act as careful stewards of all God's gifts; but they do not panic as if they were abandoned in a dangerous world. Such is Calvin's doctrine of providence.

The liturgical manifestation of this understanding of God's providence is the day of prayer. For Calvin, God not only acted in Jesus Christ in a unique way but God's Spirit always has been and always will continue to be active in the world and the church. The Old Testament patriarchs and prophets saw the signs and interpreted them for the people of their age. The ministers of the gospel have the same calling and their people have the same need. In Calvin's world everyone agreed that this was so when great events, especially disasters or victories, brought the church up short or surprised it with mercy. What Calvin developed is the

---

5   See *Inst.* 2.1.4 (unbelief as original sin); 3.2.6 (necessity for knowing God's attitude toward us/ *pro nobis*, dating from 1536); 3.2.18 (conflict between faith and unbelief, dating from 1539). For discussion of faith, see chap. 6 at nn.203ff.

teaching that the faithful would do better not to wait for great punishments to recall them to repentance, but should keep alert to see what is imminent. Calvin was convinced that God's purpose is good: God not does want sinners to die but to repent, so if they recognize their sin and repent, chastisement will not be needed. (Humans are always sinful and deserve discipline, but the goal is right relationship with God born of acknowledging who we are and who God is, not achieving a perfection impossible in this life.) By the same token, although this receives less emphasis, Calvin would say that people need to be roused to see manifestations of God's "marvelous providence" protecting the church, even when such manifestations may be at a distance. Gratitude and praise are always owed to God but at some times these are even more immediately fitting.[6] Hence in order to assure regular attention to what God is doing in the world, there should be a weekly service dedicated to that purpose. Most of the time the trials and joys will be less extreme, at least for the church as a whole; for example, some people ill, some imprisoned, healthy babies born or sick persons healed, but being part of one body means mutual attentiveness and intercession. When larger, community-wide or international situations arise, e.g., plague or war or victory, the church through its pastors can lead the whole community in particular responses on the appropriate scale.

For Calvin then, the weekly day of prayer functions as a kind of balance to Sunday. The Lord's Day is the marker for the unique work of Christ which is the center of liturgical time. The day of prayer is the marker for the on-going providential presence of God in the world and with the church, and serves as a second-level but very important influence on the Calvinist sense of liturgical time.

Two other aspects of liturgical time or space are focused on the sacraments and marriage. While Calvin wanted the Lord's Supper to be celebrated frequently because it is a means of grace, he was equally clear that the people must be prepared. That means all the people, because the Supper is given to the church as a body, and when people stay away or refuse to commune they are breaking the fellowship. For Genevans who were accustomed to annual reception, the increase to four times per year was a significant challenge, and the Senate made this number the limit. Calvin had hoped for a monthly celebration but he compromised on frequency in order to insure preparation. In practice this meant that a kind of "sacramental season" developed in Geneva and involved the whole city in a considerable ritual for at least one to two weeks each time the Supper was held. Often the period of heightened religious attentiveness could be rather longer, since the examination of knowledge of faith and community reconciliation occu-

---

6   See his sermon on Nov. 11, 1545; chap. 4 at nn.162ff.

pied a serious amount of time and energy when house-to-house visitation was included. Although not spaced at exactly equal intervals and never precisely the same two years in a row (because Easter and Pentecost are moveable feasts, and the dates of the Sunday closest to Dec. 25 and the first Sunday in September changed year by year), the four celebrations of the Lord's Supper created a significant liturgical rhythm for the whole of Geneva.

There was another rhythm of worship, however: the individual timing of baptisms and weddings. These naturally did not fit any larger schedule, since there were no longer any holy seasons when marriages were prohibited. There were certain constraints on weddings: they could never be performed on Supper Sundays and (by custom or law) never at the main Sunday morning service or catechism. Baptisms could be celebrated at any service, although for practical reasons there were none at the Lord's Supper service, and usually not on Sunday afternoons because that was a favorite time for weddings. What made these liturgies a special part of the common religious calendar was their presence in the regular worship life of the entire parish. Baptismal and marriage liturgies had to be held as part of services with sermons, and the whole wedding or baptismal party must be present for the full service. Liturgical time and space in Calvin's Geneva were corporate. Some of the most personal family religious rites were necessarily shared with the body of the church.

This makes the radical Genevan response to death even more evident, since there were no funeral services. In Calvin's view, while death is something humans naturally dread, it is not itself a break in the life of a Christian. The union with Christ established while dwelling in the earthly church is maintained through the death of the body so that the Christian is never cut off from Christ. Calvin's Geneva had a proper and decent burial, with comfort offered to the bereaved, but not a special religious service. If the focus is *liturgical* time, death was not included. If the focus is religious *ministry*, however, pastoral care for the sick, the dying, and the grieving was an important aspect of the daily work of the pastors. Visiting the sick, praying with and for them, offering counsel according to the individual's needs, bearing witness to the faith with the dying and of the dying: these were necessary parts of daily ministry. Calvin would have liked to celebrate the Lord's Supper with the gravely ill and those members of the church gathered around the deathbed, but this was not permitted in Geneva and the Swiss Reformed Churches.

The reform of personal piety went hand-in-hand with the changes in public worship in Geneva. As organized patterns of ritual life, household and individual prayer schedules were second to the corporate worship, not because they were not important but because in terms of liturgical form they were derivative. The principal shape of the church's worship is as a gathered body, but the size of the assembly may vary. For each believer, the primary locus of worship is the heart. However, the practical form of individual or household prayer was fitted to key times or circumstances: rising and going to bed, before and after meals, before work or school, when in captivity or special affliction or illness. The rhythm of set prayers at specific times was not meant to constrain the believer but to provide a practical framework for all Christians to orient their "praying without ceasing."

And that brings this reflection on worship in Calvin's Geneva full circle to what the reformer and his colleagues saw as their vocation: to be apothecaries of the medicine of life delivering the gospel day in and day out to the whole body and to individuals. It brings to the fore also what they expected of the whole priesthood of believers: to trust in God, learn God's word, and act on that in corporate worship and household prayer and daily life and work as fully as possible. This book may stand as an exploration of Calvin's conviction that, while all of time belongs to God, at regular and frequent intervals God's people act through specific human forms of worship to embody their adoration and allegiance. The pastors both lead and participate in this rhythm of daily, weekly, and lifelong worship which is the calling of the whole church, the people of God living on earth.

Bibliography

Abbreviations

OC   *Ioannis Calvini opera quae supersunt omnia.* Ed. Baum, Cunitz, Reuss. Brunsvigae: C.A. Schwetschke, 1863-1900. 59 Vol. (in *Corpus Reformatorum.* Vols. 29-87).

OS   *Ioannis Calvini opera selecta.* Ed. P. Barth, W. Niesel, et al. München: Christian Kaiser, 1926-62, 5 Vol.

S   *Supplementa Calviniana.* Ed. Erwin Mülhaupt, Georges A. Barrois, et al. Neukirchen-Vluyn: Neukirchener Verlag, 1936-

WA   *D. Martin Luthers Werke; kritische Gesamtausgabe.* Weimar: H. Böhlau/ Nachfolgers, 1883-

Bibliography

PRIMARY

Calvin, Jean

Institutes and Treatises

1536 *Christianae Religionis Institutio.* OS I, pp. 19-283.

1559 *Institutes of the Christian Religion of John Calvin 1539. Text and Concordance*, ed. Richard F. Wevers. Grand Rapids: Meeter Center for Calvin Studies, 1983. Cited as *Institutio 1539*, Wevers.

1541 *Institution de la religion chrétien (1541)*, édition critique par Olivier Millet Genève: Droz, 2008. Cited as Calvin/ Millet.

1559 *Institutio Christianae Religionis.* OS III-V. cited as *Inst.*

"Petit traicté de la saincte Cene de nostre Seigneur Iesus Christ," OS I, pp. 503-530.

Commentaries and Sermons (alphabetical)
Modern Editions

Iohannis Calvini Commentarius in Epistolam Pauli ad Romanos, edit. T. H. L. Parker. Leiden: Brill, 1981.

Ioannis Calvini Sermones. Volume VIII. *Plusieurs sermons de Jean Calvin*, edit. Wilhelmus H. Th. Moehn. Geneve: Droz, 2011.

Predigten über das 2. Buch Samuelis, hg. Hanns Rückert. *S. I* Neukirchen-Vluyn, 1961

Psalmpredigten. Passions-, Oster-, und Pfingstpredigten, hg. Erwin Mülhaupt. *S. VII* Neukirchen-Vluyn, 1981.

Sermons on the Acts of the Apostles, edit. By Willem Balke & Wilhelmus H. Th. Moehn. *S. VIII.* Neukirchen-Vluyn, 1994.

Sermons sur la Genèse, Chapitres 1,1-11,4; Sermons sur la Genèse Chapitres 11,5-20,7, edit. Max Engammare. *S. XI/1 & XI/2* Neukirchen-Vluyn, 2000.

Sermons sur le Livre d'Esaïe, chapitres 13-29, pub. Georges Barrois. *S. II.* Neukirchen-Vluyn, 1961.

Sermons sur le Livre d'Esaïe, Chapitres 30-41, pub. Francis Higman, T. H. L. Parker, L. Thorpe. *S. III.* Neukirchen-Vluyn, 1995.

Sermons sur le Livre d'Esaïe, Chapitres 52,1-66,24, 2 volumes, edit. Max Engammare. *S. IV/I & IV/II.* Neukirchen-Vluyn, 2012.

Sermons sur les Livres de Jérémie et des Lamentations, pub. Rodolphe Peter. *S. VI* Neukirchen-Vluyn, 1971.

Sermons sur le Livre de Michée, pub. Jean Daniel Benoit. *S. V.* Neukirchen-Vluyn, 1964.

Sermons sur le Livre des Revelations du prophete Ezechiel Chapitres 36-48, edit. Erik Alexander de Boer & Barnabas Nagy. *S. X/3.* Neukirchen-Vluyn, 2006.

Early Modern Prints

Deux sermons faitz en la ville de Genève, l'un le 4 Nov 1545, le second le mercredy suyvant. Genève: Jean Girard, 1546.

Iohannis Calvini Operum Omnium Theologicorum. Tomus Secundus: continens Homilias in 1. Librum Samuelis & conciones in Librum Iobi. Genevae. Apud Iohannem Vignon, Petrum & Iacobum Chouet, 1617.

Quarante sept sermons sur les huict derniers chapitres des propheties de Daniel. La Rochelle, Barthelemy Berton, 1565.

Quatre sermons fort utiles pour nostre temps avec exposition du Pseaume 87. Geneva: Robert Estienne, 1552.

Sermons de Jean Calvin sur l'epistre S. Paul Apostre aux Ephesiens. Genève: Jean Baptiste Pinereul, 1562.

Sermons de Jean Calvin sur l'epistre S. Paul Apostre aux Galatiens. Genève: François Perrin, 1563.

Sermons de M. Jean Calvin sur le livre de Iob. Genève: Jean Bonnefoy, 1563.

Sermons sur les deux Epistres à Timothée et sur l'Epistre à Tite. Geneva: Conrad Badius, 1561.

Sermons de M. Jean Calvin sur le V livre de Moyse nomme Deuteronome. Genève: Thomas Courteau, 1567.

Sermons sur le 10ᵉ et 11ᵉ chap. de la premiere Epistre aux Corinthiens. Genève: Michel Blanchier, 1563.

Soixante cinq sermons de Iean Calvin sur l'Harmonie ou Concordance des trois Evangelistes, S. Matthieu, sainct Marc, & S. Luc. Genève: Conrad Badius, 1562.

Trois sermons sur le sacrifice d'Abraham par M. Jean Calvin. Genève: Jacques Bourgeois, 1561

Manuscripts

Sermons sur la premiere Epistre aux Corinthiens, chapitres 1-9. Ms.fr. 26, Genève, BGE.

Sermons sur le Livre des Revelations du prophete Ezechiel Chapitres 1:1-15-8. Ms.fr.21, Genève, BGE.

Sermons sur le Livre des Revelations du prophete Ezechiel Chapitres 23:1-35:15. Ms.fr.22, Genève, BGE.

Sermons sur le Livre d'Esaïe, chapitres 42:1-51:23. Ms.fr.19, Genève, BGE.

Church Orders, Catechisms

Articles concernant l'organisation de l'église et du culte à Genève, proposés au Conseil, par les ministres, le 16 janvier 1537, OS I, pp. 369-377, OC 10:5-14.

Le catechisme de l'église de Genève, OS II, pp. 59-157, OC 6:1-146.

Deux Congrégations et Exposition du Catéchisme, Rodolphe Peter. Paris: Presses Universitaires de France, 1964.

Instruction des Chrestiens. Ou recueil de plusieurs passages de la sainte Escriture… avec quelques autres traitez. Genève, Francois Jaquy pour Guillaume Fournet, 1562. e-rara.ch [Zurich]

Ioannis Calvini Varia. Volumen I. *Congrégations et disputations*, edit. Erik A. de Boer. Genève: Droz, 2011.

"La maniere d'interroguer les enfans qu'on veut recevoir à la Cene de nostre Seigneur Iesus Christ," OC 6:147-160.

"Ordinances ecclesiastiques," OS II, pp. 325-364, OC 10:15-146.

Liturgies, Psalters with Catechisms (in order of publication) [1]

La manyere de faire prieres aux eglises Francoyses…[Strasbourg 1542]/ *La forme des prieres et chantz ecclesiastiques…* [Geneva] 1542, OS II, pp. 1-58, OC 6:161-224.

La forme des prieres et chants ecclésiastiques, Genève 1542. Facsimilé, ed. Pierre Pidoux. Kassel: Bärenreiter, 1959.

Cinquante deux pseames de David… par Clement Marot… à Paris chez Guillaume le Bret, 1548. [MHR O6e (548)]

Pseaulmes Cinquante de David mis en vers francois par Clement Marot, à Lyon chez Godefroy & Marcellin Beringen, 1549 [MHR O6e (549)]

Pseaumes octantetrois de David… Genève: Iean Crespin, 1551.

La forme des prieres… [London] 1552 [preserved in the Bodleian Library, as "Anon" STC – 165723-1688].

Pseaumes de David, mis en rime francoyse, par Clement Marot, avec plusieurs cantiques, comme on les chante dans l'eglise Francoyse destrosbourg.… La forme des prieres… Strasbourg, 1553. [BGE Bb 2368 res]

Liber psalmorum Davidis Translatio duplex Vetus & Noua… [Geneva] Rob. Stephani, 1556 [MHR O6d (556)]

La Bible… with *Pseaumes de David… La forme des prieres… Le catechisme…* [Geneve] par Nicolas Barbier & Thomas Co,urteau, 1559 [MHR Oe (559)]

La forme des prieres.… Le catechisme… etc. Geneve par Jean Rivery, 1561 [Bd1928 res]

Les pseaumes mis en rime françoise… La forme des prieres… Le catechisme… etc. Iean de Laon pour Antoine Vincent, avec privilege du roy, 1562 [BGE Bb 2153]

Les pseaumes mis en rime françoise… La formes des prieres.… Le catechisme… par Antoine Danodeux & Lucas de Mortiere pour Antoine Vincent avec privilege du roy, 1562 [BGE Su 5053]

Le nouveau Testament… with *Pseaumes de David… La forme des prieres… Le catechisme…* Geneve par Nicolas Barbier & Thomas Courteau, 1562 [BGE 2007 Res.]

Les Psaumes en vers français: avec leurs mélodies. Fac-similé de l'édition genevoise de Michel Blanchier, 1562; intro. de Pierre Pidoux. Genève: Droz, 1986.

Les pseaumes mis en rime françoise… de l'imprimerie de Françoys Jaquy pour Antoine Vincent, 1562. Avec privilege du roy.

Reissued with *Le nouveau Testament…* à Genève par Françoys Jaquy, 1563. As *Le nouveau Testament… Les pseaumes… La forme des prieres… Le catechisme…* [including family devotions, etc.] [MHR O4e (563)]

Rudimenta fidei Christianae, vel Rudis et elementaria quaedam institution: quam Catechismum veteres appelarunt. [Geneva] Henri Stephanus, 1563 [BGE Bd217]

---

1   Distinguishing these printings is very difficult, so the call numbers of examples used are provided.

Les pseaumes mis en rime françoise... La forme des prieres... Le catechisme.... par Iean Baptiste Pinerevl pour Antoine Vincent, 1563 Avec privilege du roy1563 [BGE Su 4939 Res]

Les Pseaumes mis en rime françoise... La forme des prieres... Le catechisme... avec privilege [extraict du Privilege] du Roy, Jean Crespin, 1563 [BGE Su830]

Le catechisme... La forme des prieres... [with Greek & Hebrew catechisms] [Geneva] Robert Estienne, 1563 [BGE Bd74 res]

Le nouveau Testament... Cent cinquante pseaumes de David... La forme des prieres ecclesiastiques... Le catechisme... à Caen, par Pierre le Chandelier, 1563 [MHR O4e (563)a]

Ordnung der Evangelischen Kirchen in Franckreich/ so gehalten wird im Gemeinen Gebet/ Reichung der Sacrament/ Einsegnen der Ehe/ Besuchung der Krancken. Und Christlichem Catechismo. Churfuerstlichen Stadt Heydelberg/ durch Johannenm Mayer. 1563 [MHR A27, 3 (63)]

Les pseaumes mis en rime françoise... à Caen, chez Simon Mangeant, 1565. [MHR O6e (565)]

La Bible... with *La forme des prieres, Le catechisme, Les pseaumes...* Genève, Zacharie Durant, 1566 [MHR Oe (566)]

La Bible... with *Les pseaumes... La forme des prieres... Le catechisme...* [etc.] [Genève] par François Estienne, 1567 [MHR Oe (567)]

Le nouveau testament... à Genève pour Sebastien Honorati, 1570 [MHR O4e (570)] bound with *Les pseaumes mis en rime françoise...* à Lyon pour Sebastien Honorati, 1570.

English Translations cited (alphabetical)

Bonnet, Jules, compiler. *Letters of John Calvin*, trans. M. R. Gilchrist, New York (reprint) Philadelphia: Presby. Board of Pensions, 1858) 1858, 4 vol.

Calvin's Ecclesiastical Advice, trans. M. Beaty & B.W. Farley. Louisville: Westminster-John Knox, 1991.

Calvin: Theological Treatises, ed. J. K. S. Reid. Philadelphia: Westminster, 1954.

The First Epistle of the Apostle Paul to the Corinthians, trans. J. W. Fraser. Ed. D.W. & T. F. Torrance. Edinburgh: T&T Clark, 1960.

Institution of the Christian Religion, trans. F. L. Battles. Atlanta: John Knox, 1975. Cited as *Institution 1536*

Institutes of the Christian Religion. The 1541 French Edition, trans. Elsie McKee. Grand Rapids: Eerdmans, 2009. Cited as Calvin/ McKee

John Calvin, Institutes of the Christian Religion, ed. J. T. McNeill, trans. F. L. Battles Philadelphia: Westminister, 1960. Cited as *Institutes* McNeill-Battles

John Calvin: Writings on Pastoral Piety, trans./ ed. Elsie McKee. Mahweh, NJ: Paulist, 2001. Cited as *Writings on Pastoral Piety*

The First Epistle of the Apostle Paul to the Corinthians, trans. J.W. Fraser. Ed. D.W. & T. F. Torrance. Edinburgh: T&T Clark, 1960.

* * * * * * * * * * * * * * *

Beza, Theodore. *La vie de Calvin*. OC 21:21-50.

Bucer, Martin. *Kasseler Kirchenordnung*, Martin Butzer Deutsche Schriften, vol. 7, *Schriften der Jahre 1538-1539*, ed. R. Stupperich. Gütersloh: Gerd Mohn, 1964, pp. 279-97.

Castellio, Sebastian. *Contre le libelle de Calvin*, trans from Latin, Etienne Barilier. Carouge-Genève: Editions Zoé, 1998.

Cathelan, Antoine. *Passevent Parisien respondant à Pasquin Romain de la vie de ceux qui sont allez demourer à Genève, et se disent vivre selon és réformation de l'Evangile*. Paris: I. Liseux, 1875.

Colladon, Nicholas. *La vie de Calvin*, OC 21:51-118.

Compagnie des Pasteurs. *Registres de la Compagnie des Pasteurs de Genève au temps de Calvin, tome premier 1546-1553*, ed. J-F. Bergier. Genève: Droz, 1964.

Conseil de Genève. *Registres du Conseil de Genève à l'époque de Calvin.* Publiés sous la direction des Archives d'Etat de Genève. *Tome I du 1ᵉʳ mai au 31 décembre 1536 (volume 30, f. 1-139).* Texte établi par Paule Hochuli Dubuis. Genève: Librairie Droz, 2003. *Tome II du 1ᵉʳ janvier au 31 décembre 1537,* P. H. Dubuis et Sandra Coram-Mekkey. Droz, 2004. *Tome III du 1ᵉʳ janvier au 31 décembre 1538,* S. Coram-Mekkey, avec P. H. Dubuis et Gilles-Olivier Bron. Droz, 2006. *Tome IV du 1ᵉʳ janvier au 31 décembre 1539,* S. Coram-Mekkey et C. Chazalon, avec Catherine Santschi. Droz, 2009. *Tome V du 1ᵉʳ janvier au 31 décembre 1540,* S. Coram-Mekkey, G.-O. Bron et C. Chazalon avec C. Santschi. Droz, 2011. Cited as RC.

Consistoire de Genève. *Registres du Consistoire de Genève au temps de Calvin. Tome I (1542-1544).* Publiés par Thomas A. Lambert et Isabella M. Watt sous la direction de Robert M. Kingdon avec J. R. Watt. Genève: Librairie Droz, 1996. *Tome II (1545-1546).* T. A. Lambert, I. M. Watt, et Wallace McDonald. Droz, 2001. *Tome III (1547-1548).* T.A. Lambert, I. M. Watt. Droz, 2004. *Tome IV (1548), avec extraits des Registres du Conseil, 1548-1550,* T. A. Lambert, I. M. Watt. Droz, 2007. *Tome V (20 février 1550-5 février 1551),* T. A. Lambert, I. M. Watt. Droz, 2010. *Tome VI (19 février 1551-4 février 1552),* I. M. Watt & J. R. Watt. Droz, 2012. *Tome VI (25 février 1552-2 février 1553),* I. M. Watt & J. R. Watt. Droz, 2013. Cited as *Consist.* Transcription by J. & I. Watt, G. Sunshine, D. Wegener, & T. Lambert, supervised by R. M. Kingdon. Financed by the H. Henry Meeter Center of Calvin College & Calvin Theological Seminary & the Univ. of Wisconsin-Madison. Microfilm: Geneva: Etat de Genève. Service de Micro-Copie, 1937. Cited as *Transcription.*

Crespin, Jean. *Histoire des vrays Tesmoins de la vérité de l'Evangile.* Facsimile of Geneva 1570. Liège: Centre National de Recherches d'Histoire Religieuse.

Evangelische Kirchenordnungen des XVI. Jahrhunderts, hg. Emil Sehling. Leipzig: O. R. Reisland, 1902-

Farel, Guillaume. *La maniere et fasson qu'on tient en baillant le sainct baptesme en la saincte congregation de Dieu: et en espousant ceulx qui viennent au sainct mariage, et à la saincte Cene de nostre seigneur, es lieux lesquelz dieu de sa grace a visité...,* [Neuchatel], 1533. E-rara.ch.

—. "Liturgical Practices and Forms (1533)," in *Early French Reform: The Theology and Spirituality of Guillaume Farel,* ed. Jason Zuidema & T. Van Raalte. Farnham: Burlington, VT: Ashgate, 2011.

Froment, Antoine. *Les actes et gestes merveilleux de la cité de Genève...,* ed. G. Revilliod. Genève: Fick, 1854.

Girard, Jean. See Olivetan.

Herminjard, Aimé-Louis. *Correspondance des Réformateurs dans les pays de langue française.* Genève: H. Georg, 1878-97.

Jeanne de Jussie. *Le levain du Calvinisme, ou commencement de l'heresie de Geneve.* Genève: Jules-Guillaume Fick, 1865.

Lasco, Johannes a. "Forma ac ratio tota ecclesiastici ministerii," *Opera: tam edita quam inedita recensuit vitam auctoris,* Abraham Kuyper. 2 vol. Amsterdam: Frederic Muller, 1866.

Lock, Anne Vaughn. Preface to the "Sermons... upon the Songe that Ezechias made after he had been sicke," *The Collected Works of Anne Vaughan Lock,* ed. S. M. Felch. Tempe, AZ: Arizona Center for Medieval and Renaissance Studies, 1999, pp. 3-8.

Luther, Martin. Deutsch Messe, Taufbüchlein, WA.

Olivetan, Pierre Robert. *L'instruction des enfans, contenant la maniere de prononcer et escrire en françoys. Les dix commandemens. Le articles de la Foy. L'oraison de Jesus Christ. La salutation angelique....* [Genève: Iean Girard,] 1537.

Poullain, Valerain. *Liturgia Sacra (1551-1555),* ed. A.C. Honders. Leiden: Brill, 1970.

Ryff, Andreas. "Un jeue Bâlois à Genève au XVIe siècle (1560-1563)," ed. Ad. Gautier, in *Mémoires et documents* 17 (1872), pp. 412-416.

Roset, Michel. *Les Chroniques de Genève,* pub. Henri Fazy. Genève: Georg, 1894.

Saunier, Antoine. *L'ordre et maniere d'enseigner en la Ville de Genève au College*. Genève par Jehan Gerard, 1538. facsimile by E. A. Betant, *Notice sur le College de Rive*. Genève: Jean-Guillaume Fick, 1866.

Schütz Zell, Katharina. *Church Mother: The Writings of a Sixteenth-Century Reformer*. Chicago: Univ. Press, 2006.

—. *Katharina Schütz Zell: Volume Two. The Writings, A Critical Edition*, ed. Elsie Anne McKee. Leiden: E. J. Brill, 1999.

Viret, Pierre. *Quatre sermons français sur Esaïe 65 (mars 1559)*, ed. Henri Meylan. Lausanne: Peyot, 1961.

Zwingli, Ulrich, "Ein kurtze gmeine form, kinder ze touffenn, die ee ze bestäten, die predig anzefahen und zuo enden, wie es zuo Zürich gebrucht wirdt," *Huldreich Zwinglis Sämtliche Werke*, ed. E. Egli & G. Finsler [Leipzig, 1904-90], CR 92 = vol. 4

SECONDARY

Bächtold, Hans-Ulrich. "Gegen den Hunger beten: Heinrich Bullinger, Zürich und die Einführung des Gemeinen Gebetes im Jahre 1571," in *Vom Beten, vom Verketzern, von Predigen*, ed. H.-U. Bächtold, R. Heinrich, K. J. Rüetschi. Zug: Achius, 1999, pp. 9-37.

Balke, Willem. *Calvin and the Anabaptist radicals*, trans. W. Heynen. Grand Rapids: Eerdmans, 1981.

Balke, Willem & Wilhelmus H. Th. Moehn, "Introduction," *Sermons on the Acts of the Apostles*, ed. Willem Balke & Wilhelmus H. Th. Moehn. S *VIII*. Neukirchen-Vluyn: Neukirchener Verlag, 1994, pp. vii-xli.

Barilier, Etienne, "Introduction," *Sebastien Castellion, Contre le libelle de Calvin*, Genève 1998.

de Boer, Erik A., *The Genevan School of the Prophets. The congrégations of the Company of Pastors and Their Influence in Sixteenth-Century Europe*. Genève: Droz, 2012.

Bornert, René, *La réforme protestante du culte à Strasbourg au XVIe siècle (1523-1598). Approche sociologique et interprétation théologique*. Leiden: Brill, 1981.

Bossy, John. *Christianity in the West 1400-1700*. Oxford: Oxford University Press, 1985.

Burnett, Amy Nelson. "A Tale of Three Cities: Parishes and Pastors in Basel, Strasbourg, and Geneva," *Calvin and the Company of Pastors*, ed. David Foxgrover. Grand Rapids: CRC Product Services published for the Calvin Studies Society, 2004, pp. 95-124.

—. *Teaching the Reformation. Ministers and Their Message in Basel, 1529-1629*. Oxford/ New York: Oxford Univ. Press, 2006.

Candaux, Jean-Daniel. *Le Psautier de Genève, 1562-1865. Images commentées et essai de bibliographie*. Genève: Bibliothèque publique et universitaire, 1986.

Dentière, Marie. *Epistle to Marguerite of Navarre; and Preface to a Sermon by John Calvin*. Chicago: Univ. of Chicago Press, 2004,

Dictionnaire de Biographie Française, sous la direction de J. Balteau, M. Barroux, M. Prévost et al. Paris: Letouzey et Ané, 1933-94.

Doumergue, Emile. *Jean Calvin: Les hommes et les choses de son temps*, vol. 1. *La jeunesse de Calvin*. Lausanne: G. Bridel, 1899. Vol. 2 *Les premiers essais*, 1902. Vol. 3. *La ville, la maison et la rue de Calvin*. 1904.

Engammare, Max. "L'inhumation de Calvin et des pasteurs Genevois de 1540 à 1620," *Les funérailles à la Renaissance*, ed. Jean Balsamo. Genève: Droz, 2002, pp. 271-93.

—. "Introduction," *Sermons sur la Genèse, Chapitres 1,1-11,4; Sermons sur la Genèse Chapitres 11,5-20,7*, edit. Max Engammare. S. *XI/1 & XI/2* Neukirchen-Vluyn, 2000, pp. vii-lxiii.

—. "Introduction," *Sermons sur le Livre d'Esaïe, Chapitres 52,1-66,24*, 2 volumes, edit. Max Engammare. S. *IV/I & IV/II*. Neukirchen-Vluyn, 2012.

—. *L'ordre du temps. L'invention de la ponctualité au XVIe siècle.* Genève: Librairie Droz, 2004.

—. *On Time, Punctuality, and Discipline in Early Modern Calvinism,* trans. by Karin Maag. Cambridge: Univ. Press, 2010.

—. " Reformed Preaching in the Sixteenth Century: The use of lectionaries in Zurich," *Zwingliana,* 42 (2015), pp. 195-224.

Gagnebin, Bernard. "L'histoire des manuscrits des sermons de Calvin," *Sermons sure le Livre d'Esaie, chapitres 13-29,* ed. Georges Barrois, S. II, pp. xiv-xxviii,

Grosse, Christian, *Les rituels de la Cène. Le culte eucharistique réformé à Genève (XVIe-XVIIe siècles).* Genève: Droz, 2008.

Janse, Wim. "Controversy and Concordance between Calvin and Westphal on the Communion of the Sick," *Calvinus clarissimus theologus,* ed. Herman J. Selderhuis. Göttingen: Vandenhoeck & Ruprecht, 2012, pp. 158-78.

Jenny, Markus. *Die Einheit des Abendmahlsgottesdienstes bei den elsässischen und schweizerischen Reformatoren.* Zurich: Zwingli Verlag, 1968.

Karant-Nunn, Susan. *The Reform of Ritual. An Interpretation of Early Modern Germany.* London, New York: Routledge, 1997.

Kingdon, Robert M. "Was the Genevan Reformation a Revolution? The Case of Geneva," *Transition and Revolution: Problems and Issues of European Renaissance and Reformation History,* ed. Kingdon. Minneapolis: Burgess, 1974, pp. 53-76.

Lambert, Thomas A. *Preaching, Praying and Policing the Reform in Sixteenth-Century Geneva.* Ph. D. Dissertation at the University of Wisconsin-Madison, 1998.

Manetsch, Scott. *Calvin's Company of Pastors: Pastoral Care and the Emerging Reformed Church, 1536-1609.* New York: Oxford Univ. Press, 2013.

McKee, Elsie Anne. "'Calvin Never Changed His Mind' – Or Did He? Evidence from the Young Reformer's Teaching on Prayer," *John Calvin: Myth and Reality,* ed. Amy Nelson Burnett. Eugene, OR: Wipf & Stock, 2011, pp. 18-36.

—. "Calvin and His Colleagues as Pastors Some New Insights into the Collegial Ministry of Word and Sacraments," *Calvinus Praeceptor Ecclesiae. Papers of the International Congress on Calvin Research. Princeton, August 20-24, 2002,* ed. Herman J. Selderhuis. Geneva: Droz, 2004, pp. 9-42.

—. *Elders and the Plural Ministry.The Role of Exegetical History in Illuminating John Calvin's Theology.* Geneva: Droz, 1988.

—. *John Calvin on the Diaconate and Liturgical Almsgiving.* Geneva: Droz, 1984.

—. *Katharina Schütz Zell. Volume I: The Life and Thought of a Sixteenth-Century Reformer.* Leiden: Brill, 1999.

McKinley, Mary B. "Introduction," *Marie Dentière, Epistle to Marguerite of Navarre; and Preface to a Sermon by John Calvin.* Chicago: Univ. of Chicago Press, 2004, pp. 1-39.

Moehn, Wilhelmus H. Th. "Introduction," *Ioannis Calvini Sermones.* Volume VIII. *Plusieurs sermons de Jean Calvin,* edit. W. H. Th. Moehn. Genève: Droz, 2011, pp. xiii-lxxxix.

Millet, Olivier. "Rendre raison de la foi: Le Catéchisme de Calvin (1542)," *Aux origins du catechism en France,* ed. P. Colin et al. (Desclée, 1988), 188-203

Mülhaupt, Erwin. *Die Predigt Calvins, ihre Geschichte, ihre Form und ihre religiösen Grundgedanken.* Berlin & Leipzig: Walter de Gruyter,1931.

—. "Einleitung," *Psalmpredigten. Passions-, Oster-, und Pfingstpredigten,* hg. Erwin Mülhaupt. *S. VII,* Neukirchen-Vluyn: Neukirchener Verlag, 1981, pp. vii-liv.

Naphy, William G. *Calvin and the Consolidation of the Reform in Geneva.* Louisville: Westminster John Knox, 1994.

Naef, Henri. *Les origines de la réforme à Genève.* Genève: Droz, 1968.

Neuser, Wilhelm H. *Johann Calvin – Leben und Werk in seiner Frühzeit, 1509-1541.* Göttingen: Vandehoeck & Ruprecht, 2009.

Old, Hughes O. *The Reading and Preaching of the Scriptures in the Worship of the Christian Church.* Grand Rapids: Eerdmans. Vol. 3 *The Medieval Church,* 1999. Vol. 4 *The Age of the Reformation,* 2002.

——. *The Shaping of the Reformed Baptismal Rite in the Sixteenth Century.* Grand Rapids: Eerdmans, 1992.

Opitz, Peter. "Ein Thorapsalm als ABC des christlichen Glaubens – Beobachtungen zu Calvins Predigten über Psalm 119," *Calvin's Books, Festschrift for Peter de Klerk,* ed. W. Neuser et al. Heerenveen: J.J. Groen, 1997, pp. 117-31

Parker, T. H. L. *Calvin's Preaching.* Louisville: Westminster John Knox, 1992.

——. *The Oracles of God. An Introduction to the Preaching of John Calvin.* London & Redhill: Lutterworth, 1947.

Peter, Rodolphe. "L'abécédaire genevois ou catéchisme élémentaire de Calvin," *Regards contemporains sur Jean Calvin.* Paris: Presses Universitaires de France, 1965, pp. 171-205.

——. "Introduction," *Sermons sur les Livres de Jérémie et des Lamentations,* pub. Rodolphe Peter. *S. VI* Neukirchen-Vluyn, 1971, pp. vii-lxi.

Peter, Rodolphe & Jean-François Gilmont, *Bibliotheca Calviniana.* Les oeuvres de Jean Calvin publiées au XVIe siècle. Vol. 1: *Ecrits théologique, littéraires et juridiques, 1532-1554.* Vol. II. *Ecrits théologique, littéraires et juridiques, 1555-1564.* Vol. III. *Ecrits théologique, littéraires et juridiques, 1565-1600.* Genève: Droz, 1991, 1994, 2000.

Pidoux, Pierre, *Le psautier Huguenot du XVIe siècle: mélodies et documents.* Vol. II. *Documents.* Bâle: Edition Baerenreiter, 1962.

Reinis, Austra. *Reforming the Art of Dying: The ars moriendi in the German Reformation (1519-1528).* Aldershot, UK/ Burlington, VT: Ashgate, 2007.

Scheuner, Dora. "Introduction," OS II.

Schreiner, Susan. "Church," *The Oxford Encyclopedia of the Reformation.* New York/ Oxford: Oxford Univ. Press, 1996, vol. 1, pp. 323-27.

Seeger, Cornelia. *Nullité de mariage, divorce, et séparation de corps à Genève au temps de Calvin: fondaments doctrinaux, loi et jurisprudence.* Lausanne: Société de l'histoire de la Suisse romande, 1989.

Simons, Eduard. *Die evangelische Buß- und Bettagsfeier in Deutschland bis zum dreißigjährigen Krieg.* Separatabdruck aus Philotesia für Paul Kleinert. Berlin: Trowitzsch & Sohn, 1907.

Spierling, Karen E. *Infant Baptism in Reformation Geneva: The Shaping of a Community, 1536-1564.* Aldershots, Eng., Burlington, VT: Ashgate, 2005.

Stauffer, Richard. *L'homilétique de Calvin.* Th.M. Thesis, Union Theological Seminary, 1953.

——, "Les sermons inédits de Calvin sur le livre de la Genèse," *Revue de Théologie et de Philosophie* 98:1 (1965), pp. 26-36.

Witte, John, Jr., & Robert M. Kingdon. *Sex, Marriage, and the Family in John Calvin's Geneva.* Vol. 1 *Courtship, Engagment, and Marriage.* Grand Rapids: Eerdmans, 2005.

APPENDIX ONE: BAPTISMAL RECORDS

<u>Baptisms in St. Pierre and St. Gervais</u>
<u>for Eight Years: 1550, 1551, 1553, 1555, 1557, 1559, 1562, 1564</u>
<u>and in La Magdeleine for Ten Years: 1550-1555, 1557, 1559, 1562, 1564</u>

1550 ST. PIERRE SUNDAYS TOTAL 60 services, 86 (87) babies[1]

<u>Dawn</u>: 32 services, 52 babies. One dawn service with regular seasonal rotation 4 a.m. or 5 a.m. **Cop** (18 services, 31 babies; Jan. 5, Feb. 2[4] & 16[3], March 16[2] & 30 at 5 a.m.; April 13[2], May 4 & 11, June 8, July 6[2], Aug. 10[3]& 24, Sept. 21 at 4 a.m.; Oct. 5 & 19 [3], Nov. 2[2] & 16 & 30 at 5 a.m.; alternates weeks opposite Bourgoing except May 4; in mid-Aug. changes weeks for the rest of the year). **Bourgoing** (13 services, 20 babies; Feb. 9 & 23, March 9 at 5 a.m.; April 20, June 1[3] & 15[2] & 22 & 29[2], July 13 & 27[2], Aug. 17 & 31[2] at 4 a.m.; Oct. 26 at 5 a.m.; alternates weeks opposite Cop except June 22; in mid-Aug. changes weeks for the rest of the year). **Chauvet** (1 service, 1 baby; July 20 at 4 a.m.).

<u>Eight o'clock</u>: 4 services, 4 babies. **Poupin** (1 service, 1 baby; June 15). **Chauvet** (1 service, 1 baby; Sept. 28). **Bourgoing** (2 services, 2 babies; Oct. 12 & 26). It is probable that Calvin was preaching in the morning, so these baptisms would have been done by colleagues after his concluding prayers.

<u>Catechism</u>: 18 services, 21 or 22 babies.[2] **Fabri** (9 services, 11 babies; March 23, April 13 & 27, July 13, Sept. 28[2], Oct. 19[2], Nov. 16 & 30, Dec. 14). **Des Gallars** (8 services, 8 or 9 babies; April 20, June 1 & 8 & 22, July 27, Aug. 24, Nov. 9, Dec. 7). **Cop** (1 service, 2 babies; May 11). Rotation is not clear; apparently Fabri and Des Gallars have chief responsibility, and at times their baptisms rotate weeks, but a precise pattern is not certain.

<u>Afternoon</u>: 3 services, 3 babies. **Cop** (1 service, 1 baby; April 6). **Bourgoing** (2 services, 2 babies; July 20, Sept. 7). Too few instances to determine any pattern.

<u>Other</u>: 3 services, 6 babies, no times listed. **Bourgoing** (2 services, 5 babies; May 18, Oct. 12). **Poupin** (1 service, 1 baby, Aug. "9" = 10[3]). Bourgoing's were probably dawn, Poupin's probably 8 a.m.

Baby baptized by **Des Gallars** on Aug. 24 was illegitimate; parents and godfather in attendance.

---

1   Brackets beside a date indicate the number of babies baptized in that service.

2   The record appears to add a second name one day, but this is not perfectly clear.

3   There is 1 service (1 baby) listed as Aug. 9 by Poupin, but it is entered after Sun. 10th.

1550 ST. PIERRE WEEKDAYS TOTAL 57 services, 68 babies

Mondays: 7 services, 7 babies. One dawn service with regular rotation 4 a.m. or 5 a.m. **Cop** (6 services, 6 babies; April 7, June 30, Aug. 11, Sept. 8 & 22 (all listed "between 4 and 5" except Aug. 11), Dec. 29 at 5 a.m.; alternates weeks opposite Bourgoing). **Bourgoing** (2 services, 2 babies; Feb. 3 du matin, Dec. 22 at 5 a.m.; alternates weeks opposite Cop).

Tuesdays: none.

Wednesdays: 38 services, 47 babies. Two services with regular rotation: dawn at 4 a.m. or 5 a.m.; later service at 7 a.m. or 8 a.m. Sometimes two on the same day indicate two services even if the time for one is not named, e.g., "21" = Jan. 22 Bourgoing did services at 5 and 8 a.m.; July 23 Bourgoing did services at 4 and 7 a.m.; Sept. 3 Cop did 4 a.m. and Bourgoing 7 a.m.; Sept. 17 Bourgoing did 4 a.m. and Poupin did another [probably 7 a.m.], July 30 Cop did 4 a.m. and Poupin another [probably 7 a.m.], Oct. 22 Cop did 5 a.m. and Poupin did another [probably 8 a.m.].[4]

Dawn: 19 services, 23 babies. **Cop** (9 services, 9 babies; Jan. 29, March 12 at 5 a.m.; April 9, May 21, July 30, Sept. 3 & 24 at 4 a.m.; Oct. 22, Dec. 17 at 5 a.m.; alternates weeks opposite Bourgoing except Sept. 3). **Bourgoing** (10 services, 14 babies; Jan. "21" = 22 "du matin"; March 19[2], April 2[2] & 30 at 5 a.m.; May "15" = 14[2], June 4 & 25, July 23 [2], Aug. 20, Sept. 17 at 4 a.m.; alternates weeks opposite Cop except June 4.)

Later service: 19 services, 24 babies. **Poupin** (10 services, 12 babies; only once marked "au grand sermon" on Jan. 29, but that was almost certainly his usual time; Jan. 15 & 29, Feb. 26, May 7, June 18, July 30, Sept. 17, Oct. 22, Nov. 5[3], Dec. 3; alternates weeks opposite Bourgoing's baptisms at the later service, except Sept. 17). **Fabri** (1 service, 1 baby; Jan. 1 at 8 a.m.). **Chauvet** (1 service, 1 baby; Oct. 1 at 7 a.m.). **Bourgoing** (7 services, 10 babies; Jan. "21" = 22, March 5 at 8 a.m.; July 23[2], Sept. 3 & 10[2] at 7 a.m.; Nov. 26, Dec. 24[2] at 8 a.m.; alternates weeks opposite Poupin except Sept. 10.)

It appears clear that Cop and Bourgoing regularly alternate for the dawn service, as they do on Mondays and Fridays. On Wednesdays the second service was done by Calvin or Poupin, with one of the other ministers (here usually Bourgoing, occasionally Fabri or Chauvet), apparently standing by to do the baptisms on days when Calvin preached, in order to spare him.

Thursdays: [5]

---

4   Where multiple babies are baptized by one person at a single service, after the first entry, which is usually introduced with "le __ du mois" or "[day of the week] le __ du mois," the rest are introduced by the word "item" or "audict sermon" or "au mesme sermon." Thus consecutive listings by one person which are introduced with the usual formula and not "item" or its equivalents mean different services.)

5   There is a dawn service listed on May 15 (2 babies) by Bourgoing, following two entries for Sun. May 11 at catechism by Cop, before three on Sun. May 18 by Bourgoing for which no time is given. The May 15 is almost certainly an error for May 14; there are no baptisms listed for this date, though most Wednesdays did have them. May 14 would have been Bourgoing's turn at the dawn service on Wednesday, rotating with Cop, and it is not uncommon for the ministers to mix up dates and even times. For example, after Easter on April 6 the dawn service would move from 5 a.m. to 4 a.m.; Cop's entry for April 9 demonstrates this ("entre 4 et 5 heures"), but on April 30 Bourgoing is still writing "de cinq heures" by accident, while on Friday March 28 Cop

<u>Fridays:</u> 12 services, 14 babies. One dawn service with regular rotation at 4 a.m. or 5 a.m. **Cop** (4 services, 4 babies; Jan. 17 at 5 a.m.; March 28, July 4 at 4 a.m.; Dec. 5 at 5 a.m.; alternates weeks opposite Bourgoing). **Bourgoing** (6 services, 7 babies; Feb. 7 & 21 "du matin/ 5 a.m.," June 6, Sept. 19[2] at 4 a.m.; Nov. 28 and Dec. 26, no times given, but probably 5 a.m.; alternates weeks opposite Cop except June 6). **Fabri** (1 service, 1 baby; June 20 at 4 a.m.). **Chauvet** (1 service, 2 babies; Sept. 5).

<u>Saturdays:</u> –

1551 ST. PIERRE SUNDAYS TOTAL 65 services, 99 babies

<u>Dawn:</u> 24 services, 44 babies. Regular seasonal rotation: 4 a.m. or 5 a.m. **Cop** (13 services, 23 babies; Feb. 8[3] & 22, March 8[3] at 5 a.m.; April 5 & 19[2], May 31 [2], June 28[3], July 12 & 26 at 4 a.m.; Oct. 18, Nov. 15[3] & 29, Dec. 13 at 5 a.m.; alternates weeks opposite Bourgoing). **Bourgoing** (11 services, 21 babies; Jan. 4[4] & 18 [2], Feb. 15[2] at 5 a.m.; June 21, Sept. 13[2] at 4 a.m.; Oct. "10" = 11[2] & 25[3], Nov. 8 & 22, Dec. 6 & 20[2] at 5 a.m. [though Oct. 25 says "du matin" instead]; May 24, no time given but entry before his own at 8 a.m.; alternates weeks opposite Cop).

<u>Eight o'clock:</u> 11 services, 13 babies. **Fabri** (9 services, 10 babies; April 12, May 3[2] & 10[6] & 31, July 19, Aug. 30, Oct. 25, Nov. 1, Dec. 20). **Cop** (1 service, 2 babies; April 5). **Bourgoing** (1 service, 1 baby; May 24).

<u>Catechism:</u> 19 services, 25 babies. **Fabri** (6 services, 7 babies; Jan. 11 & 25, May 24, July 5, Oct. 4[2], Dec. 13). **Des Gallars** (12 services, 16 babies; Jan. 4 & 18, March 1[2], April 5[2] & 19[2], May 3[7], June 7 & 14, July 19, Aug. 9[2], Oct. 11, Dec. 6). **Bourgoing** (1 service, 2 babies; Sept. 27). Fabri and Des Gallars generally alternating; they alternate exactly Jan. – March; then in April they apparently switch weeks, continuing alternation for the rest of the year, though with several specific instances in which Des Gallars apparently had two weeks in a row (early June, perhaps mid-July).

<u>Afternoon:</u> 4 services, 4 babies, all by **Cop** (Jan. 4 at 2 p.m.; March 1 & 29, Oct. 25 at 3 p.m.).

<u>Other:</u> 7 services, 13 babies, no times listed. **Bourgoing** (6 services, 12 babies; Feb. 1, March 15, April 12, May 10, June 7, July 5. These are Sundays which would have been his rotation for the dawn service). **Poupin** (1 service, 1 baby; April 26, which may have been at 8 a.m.?).

had already accidentally changed and written "entre 4 et 5 heures." In view of the fact that this is the only baptism listed for a Thursday and there are none on Tuesdays or Thursdays or Saturdays until mid-1559, it is certain that Bourgoing means May 14 (or possibly 16?) and so this baptism is included with those for Wed. the 14th.

6   The May 10 entry comes from the Marriage records; since it is not crossed out there or re-entered in the baptisms, it is included here. Calvin was the godfather.

7   This May 3 entry comes from Marriage records. Ministers often made mistakes about the book into which to enter baptisms or marriages; usually these are crossed out, but in this instance that is not the case, so the record has been entered here.

1551 ST. PIERRE WEEKDAYS TOTAL 67 services, 80 babies

Mondays: 14 services, 14 babies. One dawn service with regular rotation 4 a.m. or 5 a.m. **Cop** (5 services, 5 babies; Jan. 26, March 9 at 5 a.m.; May 18 at 4 a.m.; Nov. 30, Dec. 28 at 5 a.m.; alternates weeks opposite Bourgoing). **Bourgoing** (6 services, 6 babies; Feb. 2, March 30 at 5 a.m.; June 22 at 4 a.m.; April 27, May 25, Nov. 9, no times given; alternates weeks opposite Cop). **Des Gallars** (1 service, 1 baby; April 20). [**Poupin** 1 service, 1 baby; April 6.] [8] [**Fabri** 1 service, 1 baby; May 18.] [9]

Tuesdays: none.

Wednesdays: 44 services, 57 babies. Two services, regular rotation, dawn 4 a.m. or 5 a.m.; later service 7 a.m. or 8 a.m. Sometimes there are two services same day: Jan. 14 Cop 5 a.m. and Poupin __?; March 11 Cop 5 a.m. and Poupin __?; May 20 Bourgoing and Poupin, neither with times; Sept. 2 Bourgoing 4 a.m. and Chauvet 7 a.m.; Nov. 4 Cop 5 a.m. and Poupin __?; Dec. 9 Bourgoing 5 a.m. and Fabri 8 a.m.

Dawn: 23 services, 29 babies. **Cop** (10 services, 13 babies; Jan. 14 & 28, Feb. 11, March 11[2] at 5 a.m.; April 22, July 1 at 4 a.m.; Oct. 7[2], Nov. 4[2] & 18, Dec. 2 at 5 a.m.; alternates weeks opposite Bourgoing). **Bourgoing** (12 services, 15 babies; June 10, Sept. 2 at 4 a.m.; Nov. 25, Dec. 9 at 5 a.m.; Jan. 7[2], Feb. 4, March 18, April 15, May 20 & 27, July 8, Aug. 19, no times given; alternates weeks opposite Cop except May 20). **Des Gallars** (1 service, 1 baby; Sept. 23 at 4 a.m. in Cop's schedule).

Later service: 21 services, 28 babies. **Poupin** (12 services, 16 babies; Jan. 14 & 28, March 4 & 11, May 20, July 1 & 15[2] & 29, Aug. 12, Oct. 21, Nov. 4[2], Dec. 30[3]; no times identified but probably later service since Poupin was Calvin's alternate; alternates weeks). **Calvin** (1 service, 1 baby; April 1, no time given but almost certainly the later service when he would be preaching; opposite Poupin's schedule). **Fabri** (7 services, 9 babies; March 25, at 8 a.m.; April 29, July 22, Aug. 5[2], at 7 a.m.; Sept. 30, Dec. 9[2] & 23 at 8 a.m.; alternates weeks opposite Poupin except March 25). **Chauvet** (1 service, 2 babies; Sept. 2 at 7 a.m.), in Calvin's cycle.

Thursdays: none.

Fridays: 9 services, 9 babies. One dawn regular rotation 4 a.m. or 5 a.m. **Cop** (3 services, 3 babies; April 10 at 4 a.m.; Nov. 6, Dec. 18 at 5 a.m.; alternates weeks opposite

---

8   This April 6 entry and the one for March 4 under Wednesdays were by Poupin and come from the Marriage records. Poupin often confused the two books. Since the entries are not crossed out in the marriage book, nor re-entered in the baptismal records, they are transferred here from the marriage records.

9   On May 18 Cop lists a baptism at 4 a.m. Following this there is a regular entry by Bourgoing for May 20. In between these two Fabri later inserted a cramped entry marked "ce mesme jour" and gives the time as 8 a.m.; Calvin is the godfather named here. It is not precisely sure what Fabri means; there is no later service on Mondays. If he meant to refer to Bourgoing's entry for May 20, the time would still be slightly off for the second service (8 a.m. instead of 7 a.m. for summer time), but that is an error Fabri makes frequently [perhaps because he is thinking of the end of the service?]. In any event, either this baptism was on Monday and the time is totally wrong because there was no second service, or – more probably – this baptism was held at the second service "the same day" as Bourgoing's Wed. baptism. Another possibility is that Cop wrote May 18 for May 17, but he almost never makes any mistakes, and May 17 was Pentecost, and baptisms were almost never done at the same service with the Lord's Supper.

Bourgoing). **Bourgoing** (4 services, 4 babies; Oct. 2 at 4 a.m.; April 3, June 12, Sept. 4, no times given; alternates weeks opposite Cop). **Des Gallars** (1 service, 1 baby; Jan. "22" = 23). **Fabri** (1 service, 1 baby; April 24 at 4 a.m.).

<u>Saturdays:</u> none.

<u>COMMENT</u> on 1550-51: Total services 117 + 132 = 249; total babies 154 (155) + 179 = 333 (334). On Sundays there were four services, as the *Ordonnances* mandated. The dawn services at 4 a.m. or 5 a.m. were the most popular for baptisms, accounting for more than the other three services put together. Catechism was the most popular of these three services and Sunday afternoons the least. The number of babies increases signficantly from 1550 to 1551, a total of 25.

For the weekdays, there were no services on Tuesdays and Thursdays and Saturdays. On Mondays and Fridays there were dawn services at 4 a.m. or 5 a.m. according to season; though on some days times of baptisms are not identified, only once (and that appears to be a mistake for Wednesday) is any time named except dawn, which indicates that there were only dawn services those days. Wednesdays were the big days, with services both at dawn and at 7 a.m. or 8 a.m. Wednesdays were also the most popular days for baptisms, with about equal numbers of babies baptized at the dawn and at the later service. Calvin himself did not baptize on Wednesdays except once, but other ministers baptized on the days when he preached. He may have been more reluctant than his colleagues to combine other liturgies with the day of prayer, but in any event, no matter what day of the week, he usually left the baptisms to his colleagues.

It appears that two ministers had responsibility for the dawn services both on Sundays and during the week. In these two years they were Cop and Bourgoing, who alternated Sunday dawn services each week, and took alternate weeks of the three dawn services during the week. The first half of 1550 the one who had Sunday dawn did not have the daily services that week, but beginning about the end of July (when Cop and Bourgoing switched weeks), and continuing through 1551, the one who did Sunday dawn also had the daily services (evidently leaving the other free that week – though the alternate apparently attended a service and did baptisms for Calvin). Two other ministers normally did the catechism services; in these years they appear to be Des Gallars and Fabri from St. Gervais. Calvin was preaching at the Sunday 8 a.m. service every week, though he was preaching at St. Gervais on Sunday afternoons. It appears that Calvin and Poupin regularly alternated to do the second (later) service on Wednesdays, the day of prayer, which was moved from their usual weekday preaching place at La Magdeleine.

1553 ST. PIERRE SUNDAYS TOTAL 83 services, 123 babies

<u>Dawn:</u> 22 services, 37 babies. Regular seasonal rotation, 4 a.m. or 5 a.m. **Cop** (15 services, 28 babies; Jan. 1[3], Feb. 12[2] & 26[2], March 26 at 5 a.m.; May 7, June 25[2], July 2 & 16[2] & 30[2], Aug. 13[2], Sept. 24[2] at 4 a.m.; Oct. 8[2], Nov. 5 [3] & 19, Dec. 31[2] at 5 a.m.; alternates weeks opposite St. André or Bourgoing, except June 25). **St. André** (2 services, 2 babies; April 2 at 5 a.m.; May 14 at 4 a.m.; alternates weeks opposite Cop). **Bourgoing** (2 services, 4 babies; Sept. 17 at 4 a.m.; Oct. 1[3], no time given; alternates weeks opposite Cop.). **Poupin** (3 services, 3 babies; July 23, Nov. 12, Dec. 10, no time given but entries before 8 a.m. service).

Eight o'clock: 13 services, 17 babies. **Calvin** (3 services, 4 babies; Feb. 26,[10] Aug. 20 [2], Dec. 10. **St. André** (10 services, 13 babies; [April 30 before catechism], May 14[2], July 2 & 23, Aug. 27[2], Sept. 24, Oct. 1[2] & 8, Nov. 12 & 26).

Catechism: 28 services, 35 babies. **St. André** (22 services, 28 babies; Jan. 1 & 15 & 22 [2], Feb. 5 & 12[2] & 26[3], March 26, April 30, May 14, June 25, July 9[2], Aug. 6 & 13 & 20, Sept. 24, Oct. 1 & 8, Nov. 5[2] & 12 & 26, Dec. 17 & 31). **Cop** (2 services, 2 babies; March 12, April 23). **Bourgoing** (4 services, 5 babies; Sept. 10, Oct. 29[2], Dec. 3 & 10). No particular patterns evident.

Afternoon: 7 services, 7 babies. **St. André** (4 services, 4 babies; Feb. 5 & 26, Aug. 20, Sept. 17). **Calvin** (1 service, 1 baby; Feb. 12). **Fabri** (2 services, 2 babies; May "20" = 21, Sept. 3).

Other: 13 services, 27 babies, no times listed. **St. André** (3 services, 6 babies; March 5[3], April 16[2], July 16). **Poupin** (7 services, 16 babies; Jan. 8[3], March 5[4] & 19, June 11[2], July 23, Oct. 15[3]; Plus: Oct. "21" = 22[3][11].] **Des Gallars** (1 service, 1 baby; March 19). **Bourgoing** (1 service, 1 baby; Sept. 10). **Chauvet** (1 service, 3 babies; Dec. 24[3]).

1553 ST. PIERRE WEEKDAYS TOTAL 67 services, 81 babies

Mondays: 8 services, 8 babies. Regular seasonal rotation 4 a.m. or 5 a.m.. **Cop** (5 services, 5 babies; Feb. 20; Aug. 21, Sept. 4 at 4 a.m.; Nov. 27, Dec. 25 at 5 a.m.; alternates weeks). **Des Gallars** (1 service, 1 baby; Jan. 2). **Poupin** (2 services, 2 babies; May 29, Nov. 6).

Tuesdays: none

Wednesdays: 47 services, 57 babies. Two services, regular rotation, dawn 4 a.m. or 5 a.m. and later service 7 a.m. or8 a.m. Cop and St. André at different times on the same day several times (Jan. 11, May 10, Nov. 29; and probably Nov. 15).

Dawn: 15 services, 19 babies. **Cop** (10 services, 12 babies; Jan. 11, Feb. 8[2] at 5 a.m.; May 10, July 12, Aug. 23 at 4 a.m.; Oct. 18, Nov. 1[2] & 15 & 29, Dec. 13 at 5 a.m.; alternates weeks except May 10). Most of Cop's baptisms are at dawn; the ones at the later service do not seem to fit any pattern, as would be natural since he would not be preaching at both services. **Bourgoing** (1 service, 1 baby; Oct. 4).[12] **St. André** (2 services, 3 babies; March 8[2], Sept. 27[13]). **Poupin** (1 service, 1 baby; June 28 probably dawn because listed before St. André at 7 a.m.). **Des Gallars** (1 service, 2 babies; Jan. 4, no time given but probably dawn because he did dawn on Mon.).

---

[10] Balthasar son of Jehan Philibert Bonna & Humberte, presented by Balthasar Sept. This was probably at 8 a.m. because there are two baptisms by Cop at the 5 a.m. service recorded just before Calvin's entry, and two baptisms by St. André at catechism recorded just after his entry.

[11] Poupin lists 1 service, 3 babies for Oct. 21, but this seems almost certainly an error of date, since there are no Saturday services at St. Pierre until mid-1559. There are also no baptisms on Sunday Oct. 22; this is the only entry between Oct. 18 and 25. Therefore it is assumed that he intended Oct. 22.

[12] The child being baptized was Michel Cop's son, and it seems probable that it would have been done at the service where Cop himself preached rather than at the later service.

[13] No times are given, but they may have been dawn since St. André marked all the other Wed. baptisms at the later service and these dawn services fit large gaps in Cop's schedule.

Later service: 32 services, 38 babies. **St. André** (19 services, 23 babies; Jan. 11 & 25[2], Feb. 1 & 8 at 8 a.m.; Feb. 15 at 7 a.m., April 26, May 10[3] & 17, June 28, July 5, Aug. 2 & 16 at 7 a.m.; Oct. 11 & 25, Nov. [6 =] 8 & [13 =] 15[2] & 29, Dec. 6 & 27 at 8 a.m.[14] There is no clear picture of alternation. Probably St. André normally performed baptisms at the services when Calvin preached, and at least early in this year Calvin was probably preaching every Wed.). **Fabri** (7 services, 8 babies; Feb. 22, May 3, May 31, June 14, July 26, Aug. 9[2], Sept. 20 at 7 a.m.; alternates weeks). **Poupin** (5 services, 6 babies; Jan. 18, March 1, May 24[2], June 7 & 21, no time given, probably 8 a.m.). **Cop** (1 service, 1 baby; July 19, Sept. 13 at 7 a.m.)

Thursdays: none

Fridays: 12 services, 16 babies. Regular seasonal rotation 4 a.m. or 5 a.m. **Cop** (3 services, 4 babies; April 7, June 16 at 4 a.m.; Dec. 29[2] at 5 a.m.; alternates weeks opposite Poupin). **Poupin** (7 services, 10 babies; Feb. 17[3], March 17 & 31, May 26 [baby illegit.], June 9 & 30, Aug. 4[2]; alternates weeks opposite Cop except June 30). **St. André** (2 services, 2 babies; May 12 at 4 a.m.; Oct. 6 at 5 a.m.).

Saturdays: none.

COMMENT on 1553: TOTAL: 150 services, 204 babies. Sundays as usual have four services, with regular seasonal rotation for dawn; dawn and catechism are preferred times for baptisms, although there are occasional morning and more often afternoon baptisms. The number of babies has increased fairly significantly since 1551, a total of 25.

Calvin was preaching both morning 8 a.m. and afternoon services. Cop continues to be responsible for the dawn service on Sunday, with perhaps either St. André or (less likely) Bourgoing as his alternate. It is probable that St. André had responsibility for catechism. The days when St. André does baptisms for which no time is given are usually in alternate weeks, though in July the rhythm changes. Dates of St. André's 8 a.m. services are in rhythm with Calvin's three baptisms at 8 a.m., and Calvin's morning and afternoon services are on the same rhythm. St. André's baptisms alternate with the dates of Poupin's baptisms (i.e., which are opposite weeks from Calvin's). On Wed., the only day with two services, the second has become more popular for baptisms. (Poupin himself was no longer preaching at La Magdeleine because of his "broken voice" but he was quite capable of doing baptisms.)

Weekdays continue to have services only three days, Mon./ Wed./ Fri. at dawn, with regular seasonal rotation. There is a second service on Wednesdays is at 7 a.m. or 8 a.m. It appears that Cop is the main one responsible for the dawn services here as well as Sundays, but it is not sure who his alternate is. For the second service on Wednesday

---

14   Unlike his usual care, St. André appears to have made several mistakes. On Feb. 15 he writes 7 a.m. instead of the expected 8 a.m. On Nov. 6, he follows Poupin saying "ledict jour" but gives the time as 8 a.m. It seems probable that St. André did not exactly note the date, and intended Nov. 8, a Wed., because otherwise there is no record of a second service at a later hour on Mondays in St. Pierre until mid-1559. Later he inserts entries marked Nov. 13 at 8 a.m., after one by Cop on Nov. 15 at 5 a.m.; it seems probable that here St. André mistakenly wrote 13 instead of 15? Here it is assumed that the incorrectly written entries should be Wednesdays. Fabri also makes one of his frequent errors about time, giving 7 a.m. for Feb. 22 before the service would have changed from winter schedule.

Calvin had been asked to do all the day of prayer services, Poupin's as well as his own, with Fabri to take Calvin's Saturdays at La Magdeleine.[15] It appears that St. André did baptisms when Calvin preached.

1555 ST. PIERRE SUNDAYS TOTAL 90 services, 122 babies

Dawn: 35 services, 52 babies. Regular seasonal rotation 4 a.m. or 5 a.m. **Cop** (22 services, 36 babies; Jan. 13, Feb. 10[3], March 10[2] & 24[3], April 7 at 5 a.m.; May 5 & 19, June 16 & 30[2], July 14 & 28[2], Aug. 11 & 18 & 25, Sept. 8[4] & 22 at 4 a.m.; Oct. 6[3] & 20[2], Nov. 3 & 17, Dec. 1[2] & 29 at 5 a.m.; alternates weeks opposite Bourgoing except Aug. 18). **Bourgoing** (13 services, 16 babies; Feb. 17, March 3[2] & 31 [2], April 28, May 12, June 9, July 7, Aug. 4, Sept. 15 & 29, Oct. 13 & 27, Dec. 8 "du matin"; alternates weeks opposite Cop).

Eight o'clock: 15 services, 17 babies. **Fabri** (8 services, 9 babies; May 19,[16] June 9, Aug. 18, Oct. 13 & 20[2] & 27, Dec. 8 & 29). **Chauvet** (4 services, 5 babies; April 28, Aug. 11, Nov. 3 & 17[2]). **Bourgoing** (2 services, 2 babies; March 10, July 14). **Cop** (1 service, 1 baby; Sept. 15).

Catechism: 27 services, 37 babies. **Cop** (20 services, 28 babies; Feb. 3 & 17 & 24, March 24 & 31, April 21[2] & 28, May 19 & 26[3], June 16, July 21 & 28, Aug. 11 & 18[4], Sept. 29[3], Oct. 27, Nov. 10, Dec. 1 & 8 & 29; no pattern [evidently taking extra ones when Bourgoing elsewhere?]). **Bourgoing** (5 services, 6 babies; March 10, April 7, Nov. 17[2] & 24, Dec. 15; alternates weeks except Nov. 24, opposite his dawn schedule). **Calvin** (2 services, 3 babies; Aug. 25[2], Sept. 22).

Afternoon: 9 services, 10 babies. **St. André** (4 services, 4 babies; Easter April 14, June 2 & 9, July 7). **Cop** (1 service, 1 baby; Feb. 3 at 2 p.m.). **Bourgoing** (1 service, 1 baby; March 31). **Chauvet** (2 services, 3 babies; Sept. 8, Dec. 22[2] at 3 p.m.[!]). **Fabri** (1 service, 1 baby; Sept. 1).

Other: 4 services, 6 babies, no times listed, all by **Bourgoing** (Jan. 6[2] & 20[2], Feb. 3, March 17: these would have been his dawn rotation.)

1555 ST. PIERRE WEEKDAYS TOTAL 73 services, 105 babies

Mondays: 11 services, 13 babies. Regular seasonal rotation at 4 a.m. or 5 a.m. **Cop** (4 services, 6 babies; June 10, July 8[2] & 22 at 4 a.m.; Dec. 23[2] at 5 a.m.; alternates weeks opposite Bourgoing). **Bourgoing** (7 services, 7 babies; Feb. 25, June 3, Sept. 23, Oct. 7 & 21, Nov. 18, Dec. 30 "du matin"; alternates weeks opposite Cop).

Tuesdays: none
Wednesdays: 46 services, 73 babies. Two services, dawn 4 a.m. or 5 a.m.; later 7 a.m. or 8 a.m.[17]

---

15   RCP 1, p. 150.

16   Fabri May 19 no time given, but entered between dawn and catechism; Oct. 13 no name given but it is in Fabri's hand. Also marriage by Calvin on Feb. 10 apres midi, 2 couples, listed here by accident.

17   Here several ministers: Calvin, St. André, Fabri, do not distinguish the seasonal times of the second service; all list the time as 8 a.m., even during the summer hours. However, Bourgoing

Dawn: 15 services, 21 babies. **Cop** (7 services, 10 babies; dawn service: March 6 at 5 a.m.; March 20 "matin"; June 26[2], Aug. 21[3], Sept. 18 at 4 a.m.; Nov. 27, Dec. 25 at 5 a.m.; alternates weeks opposite Bourgoing). **Bourgoing** (7 services, 10 babies; dawn: Jan. 2 [no time given but before entry by St. Andre at 8 a.m.], Feb. 27, March 27, June 5, "Wed. Sept. 9" = Sept. 11 & 25[2], Oct. 9[3], all "du matin"; alternates weeks opposite Cop). **Colladon** (1 service, 1 baby; Oct. 2 at 5 a.m.).

Later service: 31 services, 52 babies. **St. André** (19 services, 31 babies; Jan. 2 & 9 & 16, Feb. 27, March 6[3] & 27[2], April 3, May 8 & 15 & 22, June 19[2] & 26, July 10[3] & 24, "Wed. Aug. 13" = Aug. 14 & 21[3], Oct. 30[2] at 8 a.m.; Jan. 30[2], May 1[3], no time given, probably later service. **Calvin** (1 service, 2 babies; Sept. 11[18] at 8 a.m.) **Fabri** (5 services, 7 babies; July 31, Oct. 9[2], "Oct. 15" = Oct. 16[19][2], Oct. 23, Nov. 20 at 8 a.m.). **Chauvet** (2 services, 6 babies; March 20[3] at 8 a.m.; July 3, no time given). **Des Gallars** (1 service, 1 baby; "Wed. Dec. 13" = Dec. 11 at 8 a.m.) **Cop** (1 service, 2 babies; March 13[2] at 8 a.m.) **Bourgoing** (2 services, 3 babies; Sept. 25[2] at 7 a.m.; Feb. 20, no time given but not his dawn rotation.)

Thursdays: none

Fridays: 16 services, 19 babies. Regular seasonal rotation at 4 a.m. or 5 a.m. **Cop** (6 services, 6 babies; March 22 at 5 a.m.; April 19, June 28, Aug. 9 & 23 at 4 a.m.; Nov. 1 at 5 a.m.; alternates weeks opposite Bourgoing). **Bourgoing** (10 services, 13 babies; March 1[2] & 29 [no time given], May 10, July 5, Aug. 2[3] & 16 & 30, Sept. 27, Oct. 25, Nov. 8 "du matin"; alternates weeks opposite Cop).

Saturdays: none

COMMENT on 1555: TOTAL 163 services, 227 babies. Sundays continue to have four services with regular seasonal rotation for dawn, which has clearly become the most

---

does give the seasonal time on Sept. 25 as 7 a.m., which would be just before it was due to change to 8 a.m. Although it might be assumed that it is Bourgoing who makes the mistake, there is no other evidence that the second service had yet been given a fixed time; in 1557 and 1559 it is still alternating between 7 and 8. However, there are a significant number of errors, which suggests that either "huict heures" had come to be the designation of the service in some people's minds, or that they sometimes reckoned from the time of the end of the service, which is when they were actually performing the baptisms.

18 Bourgoing wrote "ce mercredi 9" but Wednesday was Sept. 11. Calvin's entry reads "Le mesme jour a huict heures..." Sept. 9 is Monday, but usually the day of the week is more accurate than the date of the month. Also St. Pierre had two services on Wednesdays but only one on Mondays, which would mean this would have to be Wednesday. Presumably, if Calvin only glanced at the record before his, the longer word would be easier to spot than the number. Calvin's time may be in error; usually the change to winter schedule comes at the end of Sept. Alternatively, it may be that "huict heures" had come to mean the second service, even when it was held at 7 a.m. or, since Calvin baptized more rarely, he forgot what the seasonal time was. OC 21:614 reads this as Mon. 9th, not knowing that Calvin was preaching atLa Magdeleine most week days and that there was no 8 a.m. service on Mon. anywhere in Geneva.

19 Fabri does not say "mercredy" as do the others which are misdated (cf. St. André, Bourgoing, Des Gallars), but this must be a mistake because there were no services anywhere in French at 8 a.m. on Tuesday.

popular time for baptisms; catechism is not too far behind in numbers of services, although there are many more babies at dawn. The number of baptisms at the main morning service is approximately the same, with a few more in the afternoon. The weekday schedule remains the same, with dawn services having a regular seasonal rotation on Mon., Wed., and Fri., and a second service on Wed. at 7 a.m. or 8 a.m. Here the second service is the more popular one, with approximately equal numbers for the Mon., Wed., and Fri. dawn services. The number of babies has increased since 1553 by 23, nearly the same in raw figures but a smaller percentage than in earlier years.

The ministers responsible continue a similar alternation. Cop now shares the dawn services, Sundays and weekdays, with Bourgoing. Cop also apparently shares with Bourgoing the catechism, though in this year Cop seems to have done most of it. Calvin preaches on Sundays, morning and afternoon, though others do most of the baptisms.

1557 ST. PIERRE SUNDAYS TOTAL 85 services, 122 babies

Dawn: 29 services, 35 babies. Regular seasonal rotation 4 a.m. or 5 a.m. **Cop** (15 services, 18 babies; Jan. 10[2] & 24, Feb. 7 & 21, March 7 at 5 a.m.; May 2 & 9 & 16, June 13 & 27, July 25 at 4 a.m.; Sept. 19, Oct. 3 & 31[3], Nov. 14 at 5 a.m.; alternates weeks opposite Macar except May 9). **Macar** (12 services, 15 babies; Jan. 17, Feb. 14 & 28 [2], April 11 at 5 a.m.; May 23, June 20, July 4[2], Aug. 1[2] & 22, Sept. 12 at 4 a.m.; Sept. 26, Oct. 24 at 5 a.m.; alternates weeks opposite Cop except Aug. 22). **Des Gallars** (1 service, 1 baby; April 4 at 5 a.m.). **Bourgoing** (1 service, 1 baby; Aug. 29 at 4 a.m.).

Eight o'clock: 10 services, 12 babies. **Macar** (6 services, 8 babies; Jan. 24, Feb. 21[3] & 28, June 20, Oct. 3, Dec. 5). **Enoc** (1 service, 1 baby; May 2). **Bourgoing** (1 service, 1 baby; Aug. 29). **Dupont** (1 service, 1 baby; Sept. 19). **Colladon** (1 service, 1 baby; Dec. 12).

Catechism: 33 services, 59 babies. **Cop** (16 services, 27 babies; Jan. 17[2] & 31, Feb. 14, March 14[2] & 28[2], April 11 & 25[2], May 2[2] & 9 & 16, June 20, Aug. 15 [3], Oct. 10, Nov. 7[2] & 21, Dec. 5[4]; alternates weeks opposite Macar except May 2 & 16; this is also opposite Cop's own dawn services). **Macar** (13 services, 25 babies; Jan. 10 & 24[2], Feb. 21[3], March 7, April 4, June 13 & 27[2], Aug. 1, Sept. 19[4], Oct. 17[3], Nov. 14[3] & 28[2], Dec. 12; alternates weeks opposite Cop except for Aug. 1; this is also opposite Macar's own dawn services). **Calvin** (1 service, 1 baby; Aug. 22). **St. André** (1 service, 1 baby; Jan. 3). **Morel** (1 service, 4 babies; July 25). **Bourgoing** (1 service, 1 baby; Aug. 29).

Afternoon: 10 services, 13 babies. **Calvin** (2 services, 2 babies; Nov. 7; his April 11 is almost certainly afternoon because it comes after catechism baptism). **Macar** (5 services, 7 babies; Sept. 5[2] & 12, Oct. 10 & 24, Dec. 19[2]). **Enoc** (2 services, 3 babies; Feb. 28, March 7[2]). **Colladon** (1 service, 1 baby; Aug. 29).

Other: 3 services, 3 babies, no times listed. **Calvin** (1 service, 1 baby; May 23[20]). **Des Gallars** (1 service, 1 baby; July 18). **Macar** (1 service, 1 baby; May 2). An interesting note: Bourgoing baptized a baby at each of three different times on Aug. 29 (dawn, 8 o'clock, and at catechism); almost certainly he was not preaching at all those services, and he might not have preached at any of them, because Cop and Macar generally alternated dawn and

---

[20] Either 8 a.m. or 3 p.m.; it follows an entry by Macar for a baptism at 4 a.m. and there are no others recorded on this day to narrow the identification of time.

catechism, and Calvin usually did the morning and afternoon services. Unfortunately, there are no extant Sunday sermons by Calvin for Aug. 29, 1557, although there are Isaiah ones from Sat. Aug. 28 and Wed. Sept. 1, so he was not ill or absent from the city. It is possible Bourgoing was substituting at the dawn service but simply attending Calvin's services and helping out with the baptisms.

1557 ST. PIERRE WEEKDAYS TOTAL 54[55] services, 73[74] babies

Mondays: 3 or 4 services (one possibly crossed out), 3 or 4 babies. Regular seasonal rotation, 4 a.m. or 5 a.m. **Cop** (1 service, 1 baby; June 7 at 4 a.m.). **Macar** (3 services, 3 babies – or 2 and 2; Aug. 23 at 4 a.m. crossed out; April 19, Sept. 6, no times given). Dates given indicate alternation of weeks by Cop and Macar.

Tuesdays: none.

Wednesdays: 45 services, 64 babies. Two services 4 a.m. or 5 a.m., and 7 a.m. or 8 a.m. Times are listed by all ministers on one day or another. Dawn services named sixteen times and later service seventeen times. In many cases (e.g., Feb. 24, March 24, May 19, June 23, July 28, Sept. 8, Nov. 3) these are pairs, with times named in order to distinguish the services. In most instances, both services are done by the same person, e.g., Feb. 24 at 5 a.m. and 8 a.m. by Macar, March 24 at 5 a.m. and 8 a.m. by Macar, May 19 at 4 a.m. and 7 a.m. by Macar, July 28 at 4 a.m. and 7 a.m. by Macar, Sept. 8 at 4 a.m. and 7 a.m. by Macar, Nov. 3 at 5 a.m. and 8 a.m. by Macar; but on June 23 the 4 a.m. is Cop, 7 a.m. is Des Gallars. There are two entries for Jan. 20, at 5 a.m. for Cop and no time listed for Des Gallars, but his was probably 8 a.m. and this is also a pair. The same is true for Feb. 10 (Bourgoing says "au premier sermon," Enoc does not list a time).

Dawn: 18 services, 24 babies. **Cop** (7 services, 8 babies; Jan. 20 at 5 a.m.; June 23, Sept. 1 at 4 a.m.; Sept. 29, Nov. 10[2], Dec. 8 & 22 at 5 a.m.; alternates weeks opposite Macar). **Macar** (10 services, 15 babies; Feb. 24[2, one illegit.], March 24 at 5 a.m.; May 19, June 16[2], July 28[2], Sept. 8 at 4 a.m.; Oct. 20, Nov. 3[3], Dec. 15 at 5 a.m.; Dec. 1, no time given but fits his rotation; alternates weeks opposite Cop. Macar is the central figure here; on one day (Aug. 25 at 7 a.m.) Macar baptized five at once. Correlation with dates of Calvin's sermons indicates that Macar was almost certainly preaching only the dawn service but was on duty to perform baptisms after services at which Calvin was preaching). **Bourgoing** (1 service, 1 baby; Feb. 10 "au premier sermon").

Later service: 27 services, 40 babies. **Des Gallars** (10 services, 13 babies; March 17[2] at 8 a.m.; June 23 at 7 a.m.; Jan. 20[2], Feb. 3 & 17, March 31, April 28[2], May 26, June 9, Aug. 4, no time given, though probably at least one more was the later service; alternates weeks opposite Macar's later baptisms). **Macar** (13 services, 22 babies; Jan 13, Feb. 24, March 24 at 8 a.m.; May 5 & 19, July 28, Aug. 25[5, includes girl-boy twins], Sept. 8 at 7 a.m.; Sept. 22[2], Oct. 6[2] & 13[3], Nov. 3 & 17[2] at 8 a.m. Alternates weeks except Oct. 13; these are the same weeks as he does the dawn service, and on a number of days he has baptisms at both services; these later services alternate weeks with Des Gallars. **Enoc** (2 services, 3 babies; Feb. 10, March "9" = 10[2], no times given but Feb. 10 almost certainly 8 a.m. after Bourgoing's earlier entry for dawn). **Bourgoing** (1 service, 1 baby; Oct. 28 at 8 a.m.). **Morel** (1 service, 1 baby; July 21 at 7 a.m.).

Thursdays: none.

Fridays: 6 services, 6 babies. Regular seasonal rotation 4 a.m. or 5 a.m. **Cop** (4 services, 4 babies; Jan. 29 at 5 a.m.; July 23, Aug. 6 at 4 a.m.; Oct. 1 at 5 a.m.; alternates weeks opposite Macar except Jan. 29). **Macar** (2 services, 2 babies; Jan. 15, Aug. 27, no times given; alternates weeks opposite Cop).

Saturdays: none.

COMMENT on 1557: Total services 139 (140?), total babies 195 (196?). Sundays continue to have four services and baptisms at all of these. Catechism has become the most popular time, with dawn as second, and there are approximately equal numbers for morning and afternoon services (less than a third the number of baptisms at the catechism services and about one fifth of the number of babies). There are still no services on Tuesdays, Thursdays, or Saturdays, and on Mondays and Fridays the only times given are for dawn services. A few babies are baptized on Mondays or Fridays, but most baptisms are on Wednesdays, when there are two services, dawn and 7 a.m. or 8 a.m., continuing to have more at the later service. In terms of the number of babies, there is a significant drop of 31 babies from 1555, but this is probably because the new parish of St. Germain had eased the pressure.

On July 23, 1557,[21] the Company of Pastors assigned Cop and Macar as the weekly preachers at St. Pierre for "le matin," evidently meaning the dawn services three days/ week. This did in fact hold true, according to the evidence of the baptismal records, but it was probably a continuation of their previous assignments, not an innovation. The Company also assigned Calvin and Des Gallars to do the weekly services at La Magdeleine, which apparently (continued to be) moved to St. Pierre for the second service on Wednesday, thus Des Gallars did baptisms when he was preaching, i.e., in alternate weeks from Calvin's services, and Macar and others stood by to do the baptisms when Calvin preached. Examination of the dates of Calvin's sermons on Isaiah in 1557 indicates that he was preaching on the Wednesdays when baptisms are recorded for Macar at the second service (including occasionally when Calvin preached on consecutive Wednesdays, e.g., Oct. 13 as well as Oct. 6 and 20), and that on the contrary Des Gallars' baptisms at the second service at St. Pierre on Wednesdays are almost always the opposite week, except when once he does two services in a row, probably one on Calvin's preaching day. On Aug. 16 Des Gallars left to serve the church in France, but the St. Pierre baptismal records do not indicate who took over the weeks opposite Calvin; the records at La Magdeleine suggest that it was Bourgoing.

1559 ST. PIERRE SUNDAYS TOTAL 72 services, 118 babies.

Dawn: 24 services, 37 babies. Regular seasonal rotation 4 a.m. or 5 a.m. **Cop** (10 services, 15 babies; Feb. 5, March 5[2] & 19[5] at 5 a.m.; May 28, June 11 & 25, July 9, Aug. 6, Sept. 17 at 4 a.m.; Oct. 15 at 5 a.m.; alternates weeks opposite Colladon). **Colladon** (14 services, 22 babies; Jan. 1 & 15[3] & 29[3]; April 9, May 7, June 4[22] & 18,

---

[21]   cf. RCP 2, pp. 77-78.

[22]   On June 4 no minister is named but the handwriting is Colladon's and it would be his rotation.

July 16, Aug. 27[2], Sept. 10 & 24[2] at 4 a.m.; Oct. 8[2] & 22, Dec. 31[2] at 5 a.m.; alternates weeks opposite Cop).

Eight o'clock: 8 services, 9 babies. **Colladon** (5 services, 6 babies; March 19[2], July 16, Sept. 10, Oct. 8 & 15). **Macar** (2 services, 2 babies; July 9, Sept. 24). **Enoc** (1 service, 1 baby; Aug. 27).

Catechism: 31 services, 58 babies. **Cop** (15 services, 28 babies; Feb. 12[2] & 26[4], March 12, April 23[2], June 4[2] & 18, July 2 & 30, Aug. 20[2], Sept. 10[2], Oct. 1[4] & 8, Nov. 5[2] & 19[2], Dec. 3; alternates weeks opposite Colladon except Aug. 20, Oct. 1; also opposite his own schedule for dawn baptisms). **Colladon** (13 services, 25 babies; March 5 [2] & 19, April 16 & 30, June 11 & 25[3], July 9[3] & 23, Aug. 6[2] & 13[3], Sept. 17[3] & 24, Nov. 26[3]; alternates weeks opposite Cop except Aug. 13, Sept. 24; also opposite his own schedule for dawn baptisms). **Des Gallars** (1 service, 1 baby; Jan. 8). **Morel** (1 service, 3 babies; Oct. 22). **Macar** (1 service, 1 baby; April 2).

Afternoon: 6 services, 8 babies. **Colladon** (3 services, 5 babies; April 14[2], July 9 & 23 [2]). **Macar** (2 services, 2 babies; March 19, June 4). **Enoc** (1 service, 1 baby; Aug 13).

Other: 3 services, 6 babies, no times listed. **Enoc** (1 service, 1 baby; April 30). **Morel** (1 service, 3 babies; Oct. 15). **Macar** (1 service, 2 babies; Oct. "28" = 29).

1559 ST. PIERRE WEEKDAYS TOTAL 96 services, 122 babies.

For Mondays, Wednesdays, and Fridays there is one service with seasonal rotation at dawn all the year. In mid-summer a second service is added at the hour of the "ordinary" sermon (not the same time as the second service on Wednesday the day of prayer). There is regular seasonal rotation for each service: 4 a.m. or 5 a.m. three days/ week, and 6 a.m. or 7 a.m. five days/ week with the second Wed. service still later. Times begin to be listed in mid-summer, at the same point that Tuesday, Thursday, and Saturday services are begun.[23]

Mondays: 13 services, 17 babies. One service, 4 a.m. or 5 a.m. until mid-summer, then two, with second at 6 a.m. or 7 a.m.

Dawn: 6 services, 6 babies. **Cop** (4 services, 4 babies; Dawn: Aug. 21 at 4 a.m.; Oct. 9, Nov. 6 at 5 a.m.; Jan. 30, no time given but must be dawn because no later service in Jan.; alternates weeks except for Aug. 21). **Colladon** (2 services, 2 babies; Oct. 16 at 5 a.m.; Dec. 18 no time given but his rotation).

Later service: 7 services, 11 babies. **Cop** (2 services, 2 babies; Aug. 28, Sept. 11 at 6 a.m.) **Colladon** (1 service, 3 babies; Dec. 25 at 7 a.m.) **Macar** (2 services, 4 babies; June 26[3], Aug. 21, no time but probably later). **Enoc** (2 services, 2 babies; Aug. 14, Sept. 4). When the second "ordinary" service begins, Calvin moves from La Magdeleine to St. Pierre, where he alternates with another minister, probably Viret, although neither of them do many of the baptisms.

Tuesdays: 13 services, 14 babies. After mid-summer, one service at 6 a.m. or 7 a.m.; the first date of a baptism is July 11. (Often in the early records the day of week as well as the date is given, suggesting that this is an innovation.) **Colladon** (3 services, 3 babies; Sept. 12 at 6 a.m.; Dec. 12 & 19, no times given). **Macar** (3 services, 3 babies; July 11,

---

23 Because of the crowding at St. Germain, this new daily sermon at the "ordinary" hour was transferred to St. Pierre; see chap.1, at n.154.

Oct. 31, Dec. 26). **Enoc** (4 services, 5 babies; Aug. 1, Sept. 5, Oct. 24, Nov. 14[2]). **Cop** (1 service, 1 baby; Sept. 26). **Des Gallars** (1 service, 1 baby; Nov. 28). **Viret** (1 service, 1 baby; Nov. 7).

<u>Wednesdays</u>: 36 services, 50 babies. Two services, at 4 a.m. or 5 a.m. and at 7 a.m. or 8 a.m. [Macar and Colladon appear to have made errors in the times of the second service on April 12, and May 2 & 31, putting this at 8 a.m. in summer, though the rotation for the rest of the year is accurate.] Several times there are two baptismal services at different services/ times the same day: Feb. 8 Colladon at 5 a.m. and Macar at 8 a.m.; June 28 at 4 a.m. and at 7 a.m. both by Colladon; Aug. 2 at Cop at 4 a.m. and Colladon at 7 a.m.; Aug. 9 Colladon at 4 a.m. and Enoc __?

<u>Dawn</u>: 11 services, 14 babies. **Cop** (3 services, 3 babies; Jan. 4 at 5 a.m.; April 26, Aug. 2 at 4 a.m.; alternates weeks opposite Colladon). **Colladon** (8 services, 11 babies; Feb. 8, March 8[2] at 5 a.m.; June 28, Aug. 9, Sept. 6 at 4 a.m.; Nov. 29 at 5 a.m.; alternates weeks opposite Cop. For June 21[3], Aug. 16, no time given but fits dawn rotation.)

<u>Later service</u>: 25 services, 36 babies. **Cop** (1 service, 2 babies; Dec. 6[2] at 8 a.m.) **Colladon** (10 services, 14 babies; May 3 & 31 at 8 a.m.; June 28, July 5, Aug. 2 & 30, Sept. 27[2] at 7 a.m.; Dec. 27 at 8 a.m. Alternates weeks, same schedule as dawn until end of June, then changes weeks, except Dec. 27. For Nov. 15[3] no time given but fits later service rotation; Dec. 20[2] no time given; fits dawn rotation but that week he appears to be doing later service regularly so it is assumed to be later service. He makes some errors of time for May 3 & 31, because the summer schedule had already begun.). **Macar** (8 services, 10 babies; Feb. 8, March 22[2], April 12 at 8 a.m.; June 7, July 12 & 26[2], Oct. 4 & 18, no times given; alternates weeks except April 12, June 7). **Enoc** (5 services, 8 babies; July 19 [3], Aug. 9, Sept. 13[2] & 20, Nov. 8). **Chauvet** (1 service, 2 babies; March 29 at 8 a.m.).

<u>Thursdays</u>: 10 services, 12 babies. After mid-summer, one service (at 6 a.m. or 7 a.m.); the first date of a baptism is June 22. (Often at first day of week as well as date given, suggesting that this is an innovation.) **Colladon** (1 service, 2 babies; June 22). **Macar** (4 services, 4 babies; Sept. 21, Oct. 5, Nov. 2, Dec. 14; alternates weeks [opposite Enoc & Colladon]). **Enoc** (4 services, 5 babies [24]; July 20, Sept. 7 & 28[2], Nov. 9; alternates weeks except Sept. 7). **Morel** (1 service, 1 baby; Nov. 30).

<u>Fridays</u>: 12 services, 13 babies. One service, 4 a.m. or 5 a.m. until mid-summer, then two, with second at 6 a.m. or 7 a.m.

<u>Dawn</u>: 8 services, 8 babies. **Cop** (2 services, 2 babies; July 7 at 4 a.m.; May 12, no time given.). **Colladon** (6 services, 6 babies; Jan. 13, Feb. 24, March 24 at 5 a.m.; Aug. 4 & 25 at 4 a.m.; Oct. 6 at 5 a.m.; alternates weeks opposite Cop except Aug. 4.)

<u>Later service</u>: 4 services, 5 babies. **Colladon:** (1 service, 1 baby; Sept. 15 at 6 a.m.). **Macar** (2 services, 2 babies; June 30, Aug. 11). **Enoc** (1 service, 2 babies; Nov. 24).

<u>Saturdays</u>: 12 services, 16 babies. After mid-summer, one service at 6 a.m. or 7 a.m.; the first date of a baptism is 29 July; no times given. (Often at first day of week as well as date given, suggesting that this is an innovation.) **Cop** (4 services, 5 babies; Aug. 5[2], Oct. 14, Nov. 25, Dec. 9; alternates weeks). **Colladon** (2 services, 3 babies; Sept. 2[2] & 16). **Macar** (2 services, 3 babies; Sept. 23[2], Nov. 4). **Enoc** (2 services, 3 babies; Aug. 26 [2], Oct. "27" = 28). **Des Gallars** (2 services, 2 babies; July 29, Dec. 30).

---

24   Once minister's name is not given but it is Enoc's hand.

It appears that Cop and Colladon alternate for dawn at least first part of the year. When the second service added, then it appears that Macar does this most often; he might be Calvin's alternate but it is not certain.

Comment on 1559: Total services 168; total babies 240. Sundays continue to have four services, with baptisms at all, catechism being the most popular, dawn second, and few at morning or afternoon. The number of babies has increased from 1557 by 44, but this is only 13 higher than 1555; 1557 marked a dip, perhaps because of the new parish of St. Germain.

The weekdays are the same (services at dawn on Mondays, Wednesdays, and Fridays, with a second on Wednesdays), until about mid-summer. Beginning in mid-June, there is a notable change; services are added on every weekday except Wednesdays (which already had two), so that there is at least one on every day and two on Mondays, Wednesdays, and Fridays. Mondays and Fridays have services at 4 a.m. or 5 a.m. and 6 a.m. or 7 a.m., depending on season; Tuesdays, Thursdays, and Saturdays now have services at 6 a.m. or 7 a.m.; Wednesday remains the same as before, with services at 4 a.m. or 5 a.m. and 7 a.m. or 8 a.m. The change was effected by council order on June 19, because of overcrowding in La Magdeleine where Calvin and Viret were preaching and the heat was oppressive.

It was intended to be a temporary change, during the heat of the summer, but evidently daily services at the "ordinary" hour continued to be held at St. Pierre. This was officially ordered in the *Ecclesiastical Ordinances* of 1561, and baptismal records indicate that it remained constant at least throughout the rest of Calvin's life. Cop and Colladon appear to have done most of the dawn baptisms; Cop had always been assigned dawn services, and it is probable that Colladon was his alternate. Calvin was ill for the last months of 1558 and first half of 1559, so there were two others doing the second service on Wednesdays, before Viret came. By the time the daily services are begun in mid-June Viret appears to be Calvin's regular alternate.

There is one curious point about dawn services. On Nov. 7, 1559, Calvin "propose que au lieu de sermon qu'on fait le matin à S. Pierre à cause du grand froid il seroit bon de prescher à la Magdeleine et à S. Germain. A esté arresté qu'on declaire audit Sr. Calvin quil advise comme la chose sera mieux et que ainsi soit fait" (OC 21:724, RC 55 f141). It is not clear which dawn services are intended, weekday or Sunday or both, or for how long this regulation was to last. There is a gap in the Sunday dawn baptisms at St. Pierre between Oct. 22 and Dec. 31, 1559, but these resume at the end of the year when presumably it would still be very cold: Sun. Jan. 14, 1560 Colladon at 5 a.m.; Feb. 4, 1560 Cop at 5 a.m.; Feb. 11, 1560 Colladon at 5 a.m.; Feb. 18, 1560 Cop at 5 a.m.; Feb. 25, 1560 Colladon at 5 a.m.; March 10, 1560 Colladon at 5 a.m.; March 24, 1560 Colladon at 5 a.m.; April 7, 1560 Cop at 5 a.m.

If the reference is to weekdays, this seems contradicted by the fact that Colladon performs a baptism at 5 a.m. at St. Pierre on Wed. Nov. 29, 1559, then Dec. 31, 1559, and this also continues in the new year: Wed. Jan. 3, 1560, Cop at 5 a.m. (and also two more at 8 a.m.), and probably Wed. Jan. 31, 1560, Des Gallars (no time given, but followed immediately by Colladon's entry for that day at 8 a.m.). Other weekdays: Mon. Feb. 19, 1560, Colladon at 5 a.m. (followed by Colladon at 7 a.m.); Fri. April 5, 1560 Colladon at

5 a.m.; Fri. April 12, 1560 Cop at 5 a.m.; Mon. April 15, 1560, Colladon at 5 a.m. (followed by Macar, no time given but probably 7 a.m.).

However, it appears that dawn services at La Magdeleine may have been begun at this time. The evidence for the end of 1559 is limited. There is a dawn baptism on Wed. Dec. 20, 1559, by Colladon at 5 a.m. There are marriages by Morel on Sundays probably at dawn (as well as afternoon), on Nov. 28, Dec. 17, and Dec. 31 (the evidence for dawn is circumstantial, not explicit). By 1560 the evidence for marriages at dawn on Sundays at the La Magdeleine is explicit: by Colladon on May 26, 1560, at 4 a.m.; by Morel on July 21, 1560, "sermon du matin," and possibly 3 others by Morel on March 3, April 28, June 9.

Thus, although it is not entirely clear that dawn services at St. Pierre ceased in the last six weeks of 1559 – there is at least one baptism at dawn during this time – it is apparent that dawn services were begun at La Magdeleine. When the record for St. Pierre becomes full again at the turn of the year (Dec. 31, 1559; Jan. 3, 1560 in succession) and it is evident that dawn services on all the regular occasions (Sundays, Mondays, Wednesdays, Fridays) are being practiced again, still there continue to be dawn services at La Magdeleine, until Sept. 5, 1560, when Calvin requests that they be dropped for lack of pastoral personnel.

1562 ST. PIERRE SUNDAYS TOTAL 85 services, 114 babies

Dawn 26 services, 35 babies. Usual seasonal rotation 4 a.m. or 5 a.m. **Cop** (16 services, 24 babies; Jan. 11[2], Feb. 1, March 15[2] at 5 a.m.; April 12, May 24[2], June 7 & 21, July 19, Aug. 2 & 30 at 4 a.m.; Sept. 27[2], Oct. 11 & 25[2], Nov. 29[3], Dec. 6 & 13[2] at 5 a.m.; alternates weeks opposite Colladon except Jan. 11, Nov. 29, Dec. 13; opposite Cop's own catechism schedule). **Colladon** (9 services, 10 babies; March 8 & 22[2], April 5, May 3, June 14 & 28, July 26, Oct. 4, Nov. 15 "l'aube du jour[25]"; alternates weeks opposite Cop; opposite Colladon's own catechism schedule). **D'Airebaudouze** (1 service, 1 baby; Aug. 9 – time not named but entered before his next record of baptism at 8 a.m.).

Eight o'clock: 20 services, 23 babies. **Colladon** (6 services, 6 babies; Jan. 4, Feb. 15, March 8, Sept. 20, Dec. 6 & 13). **Merlin** (10 services, 13 babies; Jan. 11, Feb. 1, April 5[3], May 24, July 12, Aug. 30, Oct. 4, Nov. 1[2] & 8, Dec. 20). **Chauvet** (3 services, 3 babies; June 7, Aug. 2, Sept. 27). **D'Airebaudouze** (1 service, 1 baby; Aug. 9).

Catechism: 26 services, 38 babies. **Cop** (15 services, 24 babies; Jan. 25[2], Feb. 22, March 8, April 19, May 31, June 7[2], July 26[2], Aug. 9[2] & 23[2], Sept. 20, Oct. 4 & 18, Nov. 15[3] & 29[3], Dec. 13; alternates weeks opposite Colladon except June 7; opposite his own dawn schedule.). **Colladon** (10 services, 13 babies; Jan. 18, Feb. 15[2], March 15, April 12, July 5, Aug. 2[2] & 30, Sept. 27, Oct. 11, Dec. 6[2]; alternates weeks opposite Cop; opposite his own dawn schedule). **D'Airebaudouze** (1 service, 1 baby; March 1).

Afternoon: 7 services, 9 babies. **Merlin** (7 services, 9 babies; Jan. 4[2] at 2 p.m.; Feb. 1 & 15, May 17, Sept. 6, Nov. 15 at 3 p.m.; Dec. 20[2] at 2 p.m.)

Other: 6 services, 9 babies, no times listed. **Enoc** (1 service, 3 babies; Jan. 11, no time given but after 8 a.m.). **Merlin** (3 services, 4 babies; April 26, Oct. 25, Dec. 27). **Colladon** (2 services, 2 babies; May 10, Sept. 20).

---

25   Colladon indicates the service, but when he refers to the earliest one he regularly says "l'aube du jour" and does not give a time, so it is not possible to verify seasonal rotation from his entries.

1562 ST. PIERRE WEEKDAYS TOTAL 103 services, 122 babies

Mondays: 13 services, 15 babies. Two services at 4 or 5 a.m., and 6 or 7 a.m.[26] Once two services in sequence (Oct. 19: Cop at 5 a.m., Merlin at 7 a.m.).

Dawn: 6 services, 6 babies. **Cop** (5 services, 5 babies; April 6, Aug. 24, Sept. 21 at 4 a.m.; Oct. 19, Nov. 2 at 5 a.m.; alternates weeks). **Merlin** (1 service, 1 baby; May 18 at 4 a.m.)

Later service: 7 services, 8 babies. **Merlin** (6 services, 7 babies; Aug. 3 at 6 a.m.; Aug. 31, Oct. 19[2], Dec. 28 at 7 a.m.; Nov. 16, Dec. 21[2] no times given, but usually Colladon is Cop's alternate at dawn). **Chauvet** (1 service, 1 baby; Nov. 9).

Tuesdays: 19 services, 22 babies. One service at 6 a.m. or 7 a.m. **Calvin** (1 service, 1 baby; Feb. 17). **Cop** (1 service, 1 baby; June 2). **Merlin** (10 services, 11 babies; Feb. 10, March 3[2], April 28, May 5, Aug. 18, Sept. 1, Oct. 6, Nov. 3 & 17; Dec. 29). **Chauvet** (3 services, 3 babies; Jan. 6, Nov. 10, Dec. 8). **D'Airebaudouze** (3 services, 5 babies; April 21[2], Aug. 11[2], Sept. 8). **Enoc** (1 service, 1 baby; Dec. 22).

Wednesdays: 33 services, 41 babies. Two services; dawn on a regular seasonal rotation, the later service now consistently at 8 a.m. Some days two services in sequence (Jan. 21, Colladon at dawn and Chauvet later; March 4 & 18, Colladon at dawn and Merlin later; April 8, Cop at dawn and D'Airebaudouze later).

Dawn: 10 services, 10 babies. **Cop** (2 services, 2 babies; Jan. 28 at 5 a.m.; April 8 at 4 a.m.; alternates weeks opposite Colladon's dawn baptisms). **Colladon** (8 services, 8 babies; Jan. 21, Feb. 4, March 4 & 18, June 24, Sept. 30, Nov. 11 "l'aube du jour"; Aug. 12 no time given but fits dawn rotation; alternates weeks opposite Cop).

Later service: 23 services, 31 services. **Merlin** (11 services, 17 babies; March 4 [no time given but after dawn entry by Colladon]; March 18, April 1, May 13[2], June 17[2], Dec. 2[2] & 16 at 8 a.m. For April 15[3], Aug. 5 & 19[2], Nov. 4 no time given, probably later service). **Chauvet** (3 services, 5 babies; Jan. 21 at 8 a.m.; Feb. 18, Dec. 23 no times given). **Gaigneulx** (3 services, 3 babies; Sept. 16 at dawn; Aug. 26, Sept. 9 at 8 a.m.). **D'Airebaudouze** (2 services, 2 babies; April 8, Sept. 23 at 8 a.m.). **Colladon** (3 services, 3 babies; Jan. 7, March 25, May 6 at 8 a.m.) **Enoc** (1 service, 1 baby; Oct. 28). [The popularity of baptisms at the later service suggests that more people came to hear Calvin and his alternate than came to the dawn service.]

Thursdays: 19 services, 23 babies. One service at 6 a.m. or 7 a.m. **Cop** (2 services, 2 babies; May 7, June 18). **Colladon** (2 services, 2 babies; July 30, Aug. 27). **Merlin** (11 services, 14 babies; Jan. 1[2] & 15, March 19, April 16 & 30[2], May 14[2] & 28, July 9, Aug. 20, Nov. 5 & 19; alternates weeks except Jan. 1 & 15, Nov. 5 & 19). **Chauvet** (2 services, 2 babies; Feb. 19, Dec. 10). **Gaigneulx** (2 services, 3 babies; Sept. 10 & 24[2]).

Fridays: 5 services, 5 babies. Two services, though only dawn time named, 4 a.m. or 5 a.m.

Dawn: 4 services, 4 babies. **Cop** (1 service, 1 baby; June 19 at 4 a.m.). **Colladon** (3 services, 3 babies; Jan. 9, March 6, Aug. 21 "l'aube du jour").

Later service: 1 service, 1 baby. **Merlin** (May 29 no time given, but fits his usual time).

---

26   There appear to be occasional errors of entering the times, however; on Aug. 31 Merlin writes "sept," though in theory that date would still be on the summer time of 6 a.m., as Cop's entry for Sept. 21 at 4 a.m. indicates.

Saturdays: 14 services, 16 babies. One service at 6 a.m. or 7 a.m. **Colladon** (3 services, 4 babies; Feb. 7[2], July 4, Dec. 12). **Merlin** (8 services, 9 babies; Jan. 17, March 21, April 25, May 16, June 27, Sept. 5, Nov. 21, Dec. 5[2]). **D'Airebaudouze** (2 services, 2 babies; March 14, Aug. 29). **Chauvet** (1 service, 1 baby; Feb. 21).

COMMENT on 1562: Total 188 services, 236 babies. The Sundays continue to have baptisms at all four services, with dawn and catechism about equally popular but the main morning service beginning to catch up. (Afternoons remained few, probably because that was the most popular time for weddings.) The number of babies is approximately the same as 1559, having dropped only by 4.

Weekdays now have services on every day, with two services on three days. There is a dawn service at 4 or 5 a.m., on Mondays, Wednesdays, and Fridays. On Mondays, Tuesdays, Thursdays, Fridays, and Saturdays there is a regular service at 6 or 7 a.m. On Wednesdays the second service is now consistently at 8 a.m. throughout the year, so that the Wednesday morning schedule at St. Pierre is exactly like that of Sunday mornings. The format follows almost exactly what the 1561 *Ordonnances* stipulated. The difference is that the second service on Wednesdays is not at the regular hour assigned for the "ordinary" sermon, 6 a.m. or 7 a.m[27]. Evidently the brief reference to the day of prayers in the *Ordinances* covered a slight deviation from the plan.

It is certain that Calvin is preaching at the daily 6 a.m. or 7 a.m. service, and other ministers stand by to do the baptisms. It is not apparent from the baptismal records who was his alternate; Des Gallars had gone to England in 1560 and Macar had died in September; Viret had left for France at the end of Sept. 1561 and Bourgoing early in November.[28] Beza spent much of this time in France. Merlin is the most logical possibility; he had been with Coligny in France for much of 1561, but came back in October and was retained in Geneva, despite requests from Coligny that he return to France. Merlin was certainly the one assigned to do the daily sermon at St. Pierre (apparently opposite Calvin) somewhat later, because early in 1564, after he had been gone for much longer than expected in France, Colladon was assigned to do the regular daily service in place of Merlin.[29] If this held true earlier, he would have been opposite Calvin; by 1564 he was opposite Beza.

1564: ST. PIERRE SUNDAYS TOTAL 76 services, 101 babies

Dawn: 23 services, 31 babies. Regular seasonal rotation 4 a.m. or 5 a.m. **Cop** (8 services, 13 babies; Jan. 16[2] & 30[2], March 12 & 26[3] at 5 a.m.; May 7, June 4[2] at 4 a.m.; Oct. 22 at 5 a.m.; July 2 no time; alternates weeks opposite Colladon, then Maubué). **Colladon** (6 services, 7 babies; Jan 9, Feb. 6 & 20, March 5[2] & 19, April 30 "l'aube du jour"; alternates weeks opposite Cop until @May when assigned to weekday daily). **Maubué** (3 services, 4 babies; May 28, July 9[2] & 23: no time given, but he was assigned to dawn hour when Colladon changed to daily[30]; alternates weeks opposite Cop).

---

27   OC 10:99-100.

28   RCP 2, pp. 91-92. Sept. 29 & Nov. 6, 1561 OC 21:762, 765.

29   Oct. 23 & 27, 1561, OC 21:764. RCP 2, pp. 101-102.

30   RCP 2, p. 102.

Des Bordes (3 services, 4 babies; Aug. 20, Oct. 1 at 4 a.m.; Oct. 15[2] at 5 a.m.; alternates weeks apparently opposite Cop). **Chauvet** (1 service, 1 baby; Nov. 5 at 5 a.m.). **Enoc** (1 service, 1 baby; Oct. 29 at 5 a.m.). **Perrot** (1 service, 1 baby; Dec. 17).

Eight o'clock: 16 services, 24 babies. **Beza** (8 services, 9 babies; March 12, April 30, May 7[2] & 14, June 18, July 2 & 16 & 23 [some of these times are not marked, but entries located before catechism or between those for dawn and catechism, and this was Beza's regular time, replacing Calvin]). **Des Bordes** (1 service, 2 babies; Jan. 9). **Chauvet** (2 services, 4 babies; Jan. 30, Dec. 3[3]). **Gaigneulx** (2 services, 2 babies; Feb. 6, July 9). **Cop** (1 service, 3 babies; March 19). **Merlin** (1 service, 3 babies; Oct. 8). **Colladon** (1 service, 1 baby; July 30).

Catechism: 22 services, 29 babies. **Cop** (6 services, 8 babies; Feb. 20, June 25, July 2 & 9[2] & 23[2], Sept. 17; alternate weeks opposite Colladon except July 2; opposite his own dawn schedule). **Colladon** (7 services, 10 babies; Jan. 16, Feb. 13, March 12[2], April 9 & 23[2] & 30[2], May 7; alternates weeks opposite Cop except April 30; opposite his own dawn schedule). **Maubué** (4 services, 4 babies; June 18, July 16 & 30, Dec. 10; alternates weeks opposite Cop except Dec. 10; opposite his own dawn schedule). **Des Bordes** (2 services, 2 babies; Sept. 10 & 24; opposite Cop). **Enoc** (2 services, 3 babies; Nov. 19, Dec. 3[2]). **Beza** (1 service, 2 babies; Nov. 26). During the first half of the year, Cop and Colladon appear to do baptisms at catechism in alternate weeks from those in which they do the dawn service. Beginning in June, Des Bordes and Maubué (except for Dec. 10] appear to fit into the rhythm that had been Colladon's, opposite Cop.

Afternoon: 8 services, 9 babies. **Colladon** (2 services, 2 babies; April 2, May 21 "du soir"). **Cop** (1 service, 1 baby; May 7). **Des Bordes** (1 service, 1 baby; March 26). **Merlin** (2 services, 2 babies; Aug. 20, Sept. 24). **Gaigneulx** (2 services, 3 babies; Nov. 26, Dec. 24 [2] at 2 p.m.).

Other: 7 services, 8 babies, no times listed. **Beza** (6 services, 7 babies; March 5[2], May 28, Aug. 27, Oct. 29, Nov. 12 & 26). **Chauvet** (1 service, 1 baby; April 9 before catechism). Beza is probably preaching at the 8 a.m. service every week, at least from the beginning of March; although he does not do all the baptisms, he does rather more than Calvin had.

1564: ST. PIERRE WEEKDAYS TOTAL 98 services, 118 babies

Mondays: 18 services, 21 babies. Regular rotation at 4 a.m. or 5 a.m. and 6 a.m. or 7 a.m.

Dawn: 4 services, 4 babies. **Cop** (2 services, 2 babies; Feb. 21, Oct. 2 at 5 a.m.). **Maubué** (1 service, 1 baby; June 5 at 4 a.m.). **Des Bordes** (1 service, 1 baby; Sept. 11 at 4 a.m.) Limited information, but Cop appears to alternate weeks, with Maubué as his opposite.

Later service: 14 services, 17 babies. **Beza** (7 services, 8 babies; March 6[2 girl-boy twins], April 24, May 22, Aug. 14 & 28, Nov. 6, Dec. 18; alternate weeks except March 6). **Colladon** (2 services, 3 babies; April 3, June 26 at 6 a.m.). **Merlin** (2 services, 3 babies; Aug. 21 at 6 a.m., Sept. 4[2]). **Chauvet** (1 service, 1 baby; Sept. 25). **Enoc** (1 service, 1 baby; Dec. 4). **Gaigneulx** (1 service, 1 baby; Dec. 25 at 7 a.m.). Colladon and Merlin appear to alternate with Beza, Colladon for the first part of the year, Merlin for the second.

Tuesdays: 10 services, 13 babies. One service 6 a.m. or 7 a.m. **Beza** (5 services, 6 babies; Feb. 22 at 8 a.m. [should be 7]; Jan. 25, Feb. 8[2], April 25, May 23 no times given). **Colladon** (3 services, 3 babies; Feb. 29, June 13, Aug. 8). **Gaigneulx** (2 services, 4 babies; Dec. 12[2] & 26[2]).

Wednesdays: 28 services, 37 babies. Two services, at 4 a.m. or 5 a.m. and second at 8 a.m. Example of two baptisms at different services the same day: Aug. 23 Cop at 4 a.m. and Merlin at 8 a.m.

Dawn: 13 services, 17 babies. **Cop** (4 services, 5 babies; Dawn: March 8 at 5 a.m.; April 5[2], June 28, Aug. 23 at 4 a.m.; alternate weeks). **Colladon** (1 services, 2 babies; Feb. 2 & 16 at "l'aube du jour"; alternates weeks opposite Cop for dawn until summer.). **Maubué** (2 services, 2 babies; Aug. 2 at 4 a.m., Dec. 13; alternates weeks with Cop for dawn from mid-summer on). **Chauvet** (6 services, 8 babies; March 1 at 5 a.m.; Jan. 5 & 19 [2], April 12, Nov. 8 & 22[2] no time given; alternate weeks on Colladon/ Maubué's dawn schedule).

Later service: 15 services, 20 babies. **Beza** (10 services, 15 babies; Feb. 23[3], March 8 [2] at 8 a.m.; June 7 at 7 a.m. [should be 6]; Jan. 26, Feb. 16, March 29, May 24[3], June 21, July 5, Aug. 16 no times given; alternates weeks, changes weeks @end March). **Colladon** (3 services, 3 babies; June 28, July 26, Aug. 9 at 8 a.m. [31]). **Cop** (1 service, 1 baby; Sept. 13 at 8 a.m.). **Merlin** (1 service, 1 baby; Aug. 23 at 8 a.m.). Colladon and Merlin appear to alternate weeks with Beza, Colladon in the first part of the year, Merlin later. [32]

Thursdays: 20 services, 21 babies. One service 6 a.m. or 7 a.m. **Beza** (10 services, 11 babies; Jan. 13, Feb. 10[2] & 24, April 13, May 25, Aug. 3, Sept. 14, Oct. 12 & 26, Dec. 21; alternates weeks, changes weeks @end of March). **Colladon** (5 services, 5 babies; Feb. 17, March 16, June 1, July 13, Aug. 10; alternates weeks opposite Beza, changes @end March). **Merlin** (3 services, 3 babies; Aug. 24, Sept. 28, Oct. 5; alternates weeks opposite Beza except Sept. 28). **Gaigneulx** (2 services, 2 babies; April 20, Dec. 14).

Fridays: 7 services, 7 babies. Two services, 4 a.m. or 5 a.m. and 6 a.m. or 7 a.m. It appears that all of these baptisms are dawn. **Cop** (2 services, 2 babies; Feb. 25 at 5 a.m., Aug. 11 at 4 a.m.). **Colladon** (1 service, 1 baby; May 12 "l'aube du jour"). **Maubué** (2 services, 2 babies; July 7, Dec. 1). **Des Bordes** (1 service, 1 baby; Sept. 1 at 4 a.m.). **Enoc** (1 service, 1 baby; Dec. 22 at 5 a.m.).

Saturdays: 15 services, 19 babies. One service 6 a.m. or 7 a.m. **Beza** (7 services, 10 babies; Jan. 15, April 1[2] & 29, June 10[2], Aug. 19, Sept. 2[2] & 16; alternates weeks, changes @end March). **Colladon** (3 services, 3 babies; July 1 & 29, then Aug. 12 at 6 a.m.; alternates weeks opposite Beza). **Merlin** (1 service, 1 baby; Oct. 21). **Cop** (2 services, 3 babies; Feb. 26, Sept. 30[2 = twins]). **Trembley** (1 service, 1 baby; March 25). **Pinault** (1 service, 1 baby; Nov. 11).

COMMENT: TOTAL 174 services, 219 babies. Sundays have baptisms at all four services. Dawn and catechism continue to be primary times, but there are now more at

---

[31] June 28 is Colladon's distinctive writing, though no name is given.

[32] Colladon is sometimes opposite Cop at dawn, but probably @early May he is assigned to the daily service which was Merlin's job, until latter returns [RCP 2, pp. 101-102]; in fact, Colladon had probably been doing this already, provisionally.

the main morning service than previously; apparently Beza did not share Calvin's general aversion to having baptisms at the main Sunday service when he was preaching. The weekdays continue the pattern developed in 1562, with services on every day of the week, and at two times on three of those days, i.e., Mon., Wed., Fri. The "ordinary" service time for Mon.-Tues., Thurs.-Sat. rotates between 6 a.m. and 7 a.m. according to season. On Mon., Wed., and Fri. there is also a dawn service at 4 a.m. or 5 a.m. On Wed. the second service is at 8 a.m. year-round. Though there appear to be somewhat fewer services and children baptized on Sundays, there are somewhat more weekday services. The number of babies is lower by 21 than in 1562, probably marking the fact that refugees were leaving Geneva.

The dawn services were anchored by Cop, as usual. The first part of the year he alternated opposite Colladon; beginning probably about the middle of May, Charles Maubué was called in from the village of Moins to help preach the dawn services, though of course various other preachers also occasionally performed baptisms at these times. The main daily service at 6 a.m. or 7 a.m., which was held all six days, was the one for which Calvin had been responsible in alternate weeks. It is not perfectly clear, but it appears that when Calvin could no longer preach, at the beginning of February, other arrangements were being made, at first in a somewhat temporary fashion because many hoped that he would recover from this time of illness and continue his work. Probably by late March it was becoming evident that this would not be so. Beza had apparently become Calvin's alternate, with Merlin perhaps as designated substitute. Merlin was in France for an extended time, longer than anticipated. When it became clear that Calvin would not recover, probably sometime early in May, on Calvin's advice the Company of Pastors decided to replace Merlin with Colladon, that is, move Colladon from the dawn service assignment to the regular daily sermon schedule (opposite Beza), and call Charles Maubué from his village Moins to take over the dawn assignment (opposite Cop), [RCP 2, pp. 101-102]. Later in the year Merlin was back in Geneva, and in theory he should have returned to the assignment to the regular 6 a.m.-7 a.m. service; he seems to have done this, but it is not clear that Colladon went back to the dawn schedule, since Maubué remained involved at that service and there are no baptisms by Colladon recorded for that hour later in the year.

1550 ST. GERVAIS SUNDAYS TOTAL 39 services, 43 babies

Dawn: 9 services, 12 babies. Regular rotation 4 a.m. or 5 a.m. **Fabri** (9 services, 12 babies; March 30 at 5 a.m.; May 4, June 1 & 8, Sept. 14[2] at 4 a.m.; Oct. 12 & 26, Nov. 2, Dec. 7[3] at 5 a.m. Apparently Fabri is responsible for this service every week.

Eight o'clock: 6 services, 7 babies. **Des Gallars** (4 services, 4 babies; Aug. 17 & 31, Oct. 19, Nov. "28" = 30: alternates weeks opposite Chauvet in early April and then again in early Oct., according to same pattern as weekday schedule). **Chauvet** (2 services, 3 babies; May 4, Nov. 23[2]).

Catechism: 10 services, 10 babies. **Fabri** (6 services, 6 babies; April "22" = 20, June 22, July 27, Oct. 12, Nov. 9, Dec. 7). **Chauvet** (4 services, 4 babies; Jan. 12, Aug. 31, Oct. 19, Nov. 16).

Afternoon: 3 services, 3 babies. **Calvin** (1 service, 1 baby; Dec. "26" = 28). **Des Gallars** (2 services, 2 babies; April "12" = 13, Sept. 7).

Other: 11 services, 11 babies, no times listed. **Fabri** (4 services, 4 babies; Jan. 5 & 26, March 2 & 16). **Chauvet** (6 services, 6 babies; Feb. 2, March 23 & 30, April 27, June 15, July 13; probably 8 a.m. or catechism). **Des Gallars** (1 service, 1 baby; March 9).

1550 ST. GERVAIS WEEKDAYS TOTAL 72 services, 85 babies

Mondays: 15 services, 16 babies. One service at 6 a.m. or 7 a.m. **Des Gallars** (8 services, 9 babies; Jan. 13, April "13" = 14 & 28, May 26, Aug. 4, Sept. 1, Oct. 6 & 20[2]; alternates weeks opposite Chauvet, changes weeks soon after April 2, changes again probably after Oct. 3). **Chauvet** (7 services, 7 babies; Jan. 20, March 3 & 17, April 21, May 19, Sept. 8, Nov. 10; alternates weeks opposite Des Gallars). This pattern of alternation is borne out by the rest of the week and will not be noted again under each day.

Tuesdays: 11 services, 14 babies. One service 6 a.m. or 7 a.m. **Des Gallars** (6 services, 7 babies; Feb. 11, April 29, May 27, Sept. 2 [2 = twins], Dec. 2 & 16; alternates weeks opposite Chauvet according to pattern listed for Monday). **Chauvet** (4 services, 5 babies; Feb. 18, June 17, Oct. 14, Nov. 11[2]; alternates weeks opposite Des Gallars). **Fabri** (1 service, 2 babies; Aug. 26 at 6 a.m.).

Wednesdays: 17 services, 22 babies. Two services, 4 a.m. or 5 a.m. and 7 a.m. or 8 a.m. Once two ministers baptized on the same day, probably different services: July 2 Fabri at 4 a.m. and Chauvet [6 a.m.]

Dawn: 4 services, 4 babies. **Fabri** (June 4, July 2, Oct. 8 at 4 a.m.; Dec. 17 at 5 a.m.)

Later service: 13 services, 18 babies. **Des Gallars** (6 services, 9 babies; July 9 at 7 a.m.; Dec. 3[2] at 8 a.m; Feb. 12, April 30, May 28, Oct. 22[3] no times given; alternates weeks opposite Chauvet according to pattern listed for Monday). **Chauvet** (7 services, 9 babies; July 2 probably at 7 a.m. [entry after Fabri at 4 a.m.]), Feb. 19, March 19, April 2 & 23[3], Sept. 10, Nov. 12 no times given; alternates weeks opposite Des Gallars).

Thursdays: 16 services, 17 babies. One service at 6 a.m. or 7 a.m. **Des Gallars** (8 services, 8 babies; Jan. 2 & 16, Feb. 13, May 29, Aug. 21, Sept. 4, Oct. 2; also May [day of week given but not date, possibly 8, probably 15?]; alternates weeks opposite Chauvet according to pattern listed for Monday). **Chauvet** (6 services, 6 babies; Jan. 23,

May 22, July 17, Sept. 25, Nov. 13 & 27; alternates weeks opposite Des Gallars). **Fabri** (2 services, 3 babies; July 31 at 8 a.m. [!] [33]; Feb. 27[2]).

Fridays: 7 services, 10 babies. One service at 6 a.m. or 7 a.m. **Des Gallars** (4 services, 5 babies; Jan. 17, May 2, Oct. 3 & 24[2]; alternates opposite Chauvet acording to pattern listed for Monday). **Chauvet** (3 services, 5 babies; March 7[2], Sept. 26[2], Dec. 26; alternates opposite Des Gallars).

Saturdays: 6 services, 6 babies. One service at 6 a.m. or 7 a.m. **Des Gallars** (2 services, 2 babies; Jan. 18, March 29; alternates opposite Chauvet according to pattern listed for Monday). **Chauvet** (4 services, 4 babies; May 24, June 21, Sept. 27, Oct. 4; alternates opposite Des Gallars).

1551 ST. GERVAIS SUNDAYS TOTAL 45 services, 58 babies

Dawn: 14 services, 18 babies. Regular rotation 4 a.m. or 5 a.m. **Fabri** (14 services, 18 babies, though one instance crossed out; Jan. 11 & 18, March 1 & 8 & 15 [crossed out] at 5 a.m.; April 5, May 31, June 7 & 28[3], Aug. 9 & 23 at 4 a.m.; Sept. 20, Dec. 6 & 13[3] at 5 a.m.) Apparently Fabri is responsible for this service every week.

Eight o'clock: 13 services, 18 babies. **Des Gallars** (6 services, 8 babies; Feb. 8, April 12, June 7, Sept. 27, Nov. 1[3] & 29; alternates weeks opposite Chauvet, changes in early April, then again in early Oct.; see weekday schedule). **Chauvet** (7 services, 10 babies; Jan. 18[2], Feb. 1, March 1, May 3[2] & 31[2], July 12, Sept. 20; alternates weeks opposite Des Gallars).

Catechism: 9 services, 11 babies. **Fabri** (6 services, 7 babies; Jan. 4 & 18, Feb. 1, Sept. 27, Nov. 8[2], Nov. "20" = 22; alternates weeks). **Chauvet** (3 services, 4 babies; March 1, July 12, Nov. 29[2]).

Afternoon: 5 services, 6 babies. **Calvin** (3 services, 3 babies; March 8, Oct. 4, Dec. 27 [34]). **Chauvet** (1 service, 2 babies; Sept. 6). **Fabri** (1 service, 1 baby; Nov. 1 at 3 p.m.).

Other: 4 services, 5 babies, no times listed. **Chauvet** (2 services, 3 babies; March 22[2], June 14). **Des Gallars** (2 services, 2 babies; May 17, June 14). Both Chauvet and Des Gallars on 14 June, which suggests that one may have been morning and one another time.

---

[33] On July 31, 1550 Fabri lists a service at 8 a.m.; there would not be any weekday service at St. Gervais at this hour in mid-summer, and there was a second service only on Wednesdays (which would be at 7 a.m. in summer). This entry is possibly a mistake of time; the most likely thing is that Fabri accidently wrote the time at which he performed a number of baptisms on Sundays at St. Pierre. Besides Cop, he is the minister in these early years who most often entered times, and perhaps for that reason he also makes the most mistakes.

[34] This was the Sunday the Lord's Supper was held and Calvin would be in St. Pierre in the morning, but he was probably preaching in St. Gervais in the afternoon. This could possibly have been at catechism, but that is unlikely for several reasons; usually Calvin marked that reference; all of his baptisms at St. Gervais for which times are given are Sunday afternoons; and he would not have crossed the city several hours before he was due to preach, especially after the heavy morning of the Supper service.

1551 ST. GERVAIS WEEKDAYS TOTAL 80 services, 102 babies

Mondays: 9 services, 11 babies. One service at 6 a.m. or 7 a.m. **Des Gallars** (3 services, 3 babies; Oct. 19, Nov. 30, Dec. 28; alternates weeks opposite Chauvet until early April [Chauvet has first and second weeks in a row, though there is one exception on April 17 when Chauvet baptized on a day that would have been Des Gallars' rotation], then in early Oct. they changed back for the rest of the year; this pattern holds for the rest of the weekdays and will not be repeated each day.). **Chauvet** (4 services, 6 babies; Jan. 19[2] & 26, May 4[2], Oct. 26; alternate weeks opposite Des Gallars except Jan. 26). **Fabri** (1 service, 1 baby; June 1 at 6 a.m.). **Cop** (1 service, 1 baby; Dec. 14 at 7 a.m.).

Tuesdays: 12 services, 14 babies. One service at 6 a.m. or 7 a.m. **Des Gallars** (5 services, 5 babies; March "23" = 24, April 28, May 26, July 7, Dec. 1; alternates weeks opposite Chauvet according to pattern listed for Monday). **Chauvet** (5 services, 6 babies; March 3, June 2[2], Aug. 25, Dec. 8 & 22; alternates weeks opposite Des Gallars). **Fabri** (2 services, 3 babies; June 30[2] at 6 a.m.; April 14 at 4 a.m. [!] There was no dawn service this day; Fabri evidently confused about writing time, since he normally served at the dawn services]).

Wednesdays: 29 services, 37 babies. Two services at 4 a.m. or 5 a.m. and 7 a.m. or 8 a.m. Aug. 26 at 8 a.m. is probably a mistake for 7 a.m.; this day there was also probably one at 4 a.m., since two baptisms are listed (Fabri at [dawn?] and Chauvet at 8 a.m.).

Dawn: 8 services, 11 babies. **Fabri** (Jan. 21, Feb. 25, March 11 at 5 a.m.; April 29, June 17, July 1 at 4 a.m.; Sept. 23 at 5 a.m.; Aug. 26[4; 1 illegit.] no time given but probably dawn).

Later service: 21 services, 26 babies. **Des Gallars** (8 services, 10 babies; July 22 at 7 a.m.; Oct. 21[3], Dec. 30 at 8 a.m.; Jan. 28, May 27, Sept. 16, Dec. 2 & "17" = 16 no times given; alternates weeks opposite Chauvet according to pattern listed for Monday). **Chauvet** (12 services, 15 babies; Jan. 21, Feb. 4 & 18, March 4[2], April 8 & 22, May 6, Aug. 12 & 26, Nov. 25, Dec. 9 & 23[3]; alternates weeks opposite Des Gallars). **Fabri** (1 service, 1 baby; Jan. 14 at 8 a.m.)

Thursdays: 13 services, 18 babies. One service at 6 a.m. or 7 a.m. **Des Gallars** (8 services, 11 babies; Jan. 1 & 15, May 14[2=twins], Aug. 20[2], Sept. 3, Oct. 22, Nov. 19[2], Dec. 3; alternates weeks opposite Chauvet according to pattern listed for Monday). **Chauvet** (5 services, 7 babies; Feb. 5, April 2, July 16, Sept. 10, Oct. 15[3]; alternates weeks opposite Des Gallars).

Fridays: 9 services, 12 babies. One service at 6 a.m. or 7 a.m. **Des Gallars** (4 services, 5 babies; Jan. 16, June 26[2], July 24, Oct. 23; alternates weeks opposite Chauvet according to pattern listed for Monday). **Chauvet** (6 services, 7 babies; Feb. 20, April 17, May 8[2] & 22, July 31, Dec. 25; alternate weeks opposite Des Gallars, except April 17).

Saturdays: 8 services, 10 babies. One service at 6 a.m. or 7 a.m. **Des Gallars** (3 services, 4 babies; Jan. 3, March 28[2], June 13; alternates weeks opposite Chauvet according to pattern listed for Monday). **Chauvet** (5 services, 6 babies; April 11[2=twins], July 25, Sept. 12, Oct. 31, Dec. 26; alternates weeks opposite Des Gallars).

COMMENT on 1550-51: Total services 111 + 125 = 236, total babies 128 + 160 = 288. There are four services on Sundays. Generally baptisms seem approximately evenly divided among dawn, morning, and catechism services, with the fewest in the afternoon, although that is the only time recorded for a baptism by Calvin, since he was probably preaching at St. Gervais on most Sunday afternoons from early 1546 until the spring of 1552. The number of baptisms increases by 32 from 1550 to 1551, a significant amount.

There are services and baptisms on all the weekdays at St. Gervais, with Wednesdays the most popular days. Apparently there was only one service on Mondays, Tuesdays, Thursdays, Fridays, and Saturdays, at 6 a.m. or 7 a.m., depending on the season. There were two services on Wednesday, one at dawn and one at 7 a.m. or 8 a.m., exactly the same pattern as for St. Pierre on Wednesdays, which suggests the importance of the day of prayer; two services meant that everyone could participate, even if a household had to come in relays.

The organization of ministerial rotation is fairly clear. It is evident that Des Gallars and Chauvet are the ministers assigned to the parish regularly. They preach at the Sunday morning 8 a.m. service on alternate weeks, and also do the regular daily services in alternate weeks, taking the later of the two Wednesday services. Sunday afternoons in these years Calvin is preaching at St. Gervais and occasionally he baptizes, but usually he does weddings, while other ministers stand by to perform baptisms when he preaches. Fabri is apparently responsible for all the dawn services, both Sundays and Wednesdays, and probably also for most of the Sunday catechism (a combination of services which the Company of Pastors tended to group together because they were out of the common alternation patterns. Chauvet does a few catechisms.

1553 ST. GERVAIS SUNDAYS TOTAL 40 services, 46 babies

Dawn: 12 services, 13 babies. Regular rotation 4 a.m. or 5 a.m. **St. André** (10 services, 11 babies; Feb. 26, March 5 at 5 a.m.; May 7, June 11, July 16, Aug. 13, Sept. 17 at 4 a.m.; Oct. 22[2], Nov. 12 & 19 at 5 a.m.; probably responsible for dawn regularly). **Chauvet** (1 service, 1 baby; June 18 at 4 a.m.). **Fabri** (1 service, 1 baby; April 16 at 4 a.m.).

Eight o'clock: 13 services, 14 babies. **Chauvet** (8 services, 9 babies; July 16, Sept. 17, [Sept. "25" = 24][35], Oct. 1 & 22 & 29, Dec. 10 & 31[2]). **Fabri** (4 services, 4 babies; Feb. 12, March 12, Nov. 19, Dec. 17). **Cop** (1 service, 1 baby; Oct. 15).

Catechism: 10 services, 14 babies. **Chauvet** (8 services, 10 babies; Feb. 12, March 12, May 14, Aug. 20 & 27, Nov. 5[3], Dec. 3 & 17; alternates weeks except May 14, Aug. 20). **Des Gallars** (1 service, 3 babies; May 7). **Fabri** (1 service, 1 baby; Sept. 17).

Afternoon: 1 service, 1 baby, **Chauvet** (Sept. 3).

Other: 4 services, 4 babies, no times listed. **Chauvet** (3 services, 3 babies; Jan. 8 & 22, Aug. 6). **Poupin** (1 service, 1 baby; July 23).

---

35 One service by Chauvet which is listed as Sept. 25 at 8 a.m. should actually have been Sept. 24, Sunday; he often baptized at the morning service on Sunday and there is no entry for Sept. 24. This entry "Sept. 25" is the only one between Sept. 21 and Sept. 28, and it does not name a day of the week. There is no service at 8 a.m. on Mondays at St. Gervais, and Chauvet does not usually give a time unless he is distinguishing one service from others on the same day, so either the date or the time is wrong. Here it is assumed that the date is wrong.

1553: ST. GERVAIS WEEKDAYS TOTAL 88 services, 105 babies

Mondays: 13 services, 18 babies. One service at 6 a.m. or 7 a.m. **Chauvet** (6 services, 8 babies; April 3[2], May 1, July 24[2], Oct. 2 & 16, Dec. 25; alternates weeks opposite Fabri and then Bourgoing; some overlap of all three from Aug. 28 until mid-Sept. when Bourgoing takes over). **Fabri** (3 services, 5 babies; Feb. 27[3] at 7 a.m.; July 3, Sept. 4 at 6 a.m.; probably alternates weeks opposite Chauvet except Sept. 4). **Bourgoing** (3 services, 4 babies; Aug. 28, Oct. 9[2] & 23; alternates weeks opposite Chauvet later in the year). **Poupin** (1 service, 1 baby; Nov. 27).

Tuesdays: 20 services, 25 babies. One service at 6 a.m. or 7 a.m. **Chauvet** (9 services, 10 babies; Jan. 24, Feb. 7, March 7, June 13 & 27, Aug. 22, Sept. 19[2], Oct. 31, Dec. 26; alternates weeks opposite Fabri, then Bourgoing). **Fabri** (9 services, 11 babies; Jan. 17, Feb. 14, March 14, March 28 at 7 a.m.; April 11[2], May 9 & 23, Aug. 1, Sept. 12[2] at 6 a.m.; alternates weeks opposite Chauvet except Jan. 24). **Bourgoing** (2 services, 4 babies; Oct. 10 & 24[3]; alternates weeks opposite Chauvet).

Wednesdays: 26 services, 30 babies. Two services at 4 a.m. or 5 a.m. and 7 a.m. or 8 a.m.

Dawn: 5 services, 5 babies. **St. André** (4 services, 4 babies; May 31, June 7, July 26 at 4 a.m.; Oct. 25 at 5 a.m.) **Chauvet** (1 service, 1 baby; July 19 at 4 a.m.)

Later service: 21 services, 25 babies. **Chauvet** (9 services, 11 babies; Jan. 11, March 8, May 17, June 14[2], Aug. 9 & 23, Oct. 18, Nov. 29, Dec. 27[2] no time given; alternates weeks opposite Fabri and Bourgoing). **Fabri** (7 services, 7 babies; Jan. 4, March 15 at 8 a.m.; April 26, May 10 & 24, June 7, Sept. 13 at 7 a.m.; alternates weeks opposite Chauvet). **Bourgoing** (4 services, 6 babies; Aug. 30, Oct. 11 & 25[3], Dec. 20 [no times given but Oct. 25 entry follows one by St. André for dawn]; alternates weeks opposite Chauvet). **St. André** (1 service, 1 baby; May 3 at 7 a.m.)

Thursdays: 13 services, 15 babies. One service at 6 a.m. or 7 a.m. **Chauvet** (9 services, 11 babies; Feb. 9 & 23, April 20, Aug. 10[2], Sept. 7 & 21 & 28, Nov. 2[2], Dec. 28; alternates weeks opposite Bourgoing except Sept. 28). **Bourgoing** (1 service, 1 baby; Oct. 26; alternates weeks opposite Chauvet). **Des Gallars** (2 services, 2 babies; Jan. 19, June 8; in sequence with [Fabri &] Bourgoing). **St. André** (1 service, 1 baby; May 4).

Fridays: 8 services, 8 babies. One service at 6 a.m. or 7 a.m. **Chauvet** (5 services, 5 babies; Jan. 13, Aug. 11, Sept. 29, Oct. 6, Dec. 29; alternates weeks opposite Fabri & Bourgoing except Sept. 29). **Fabri** (1 service, 1 baby; Sept. 1 at 6 a.m.; opposite Chauvet). **Bourgoing** (1 service, 1 baby; Dec. 22; opposite Chauvet). **Des Gallars** (1 service, 1 baby; March 3; in sequence with Fabri).

Saturdays: 8 services, 9 babies. One service at 6 a.m. or 7 a.m. **Chauvet** (3 services, 3 babies; Feb. 11, March 25, May 13; alternates weeks opposite Fabri except May 13). **Fabri** (2 services, 3 babies; Jan. 7 at 7 a.m., Sept. 2[2] at 6 a.m.; alternates weeks opposite Chauvet). **Des Gallars** (2 services, 2 babies; Feb. 18, July 22; in sequence with Fabri). **Colladon** (1 service, 1 baby; Sept. 16).

COMMENT on 1553: TOTAL: 128 services, 151 babies. Sundays continue the usual format of four services. Weekdays continue to have services all six days, though Wednesday has two. The "ordinary" times are 6 a.m. or 7 a.m. Mon.-Tues., Thurs.-Sat., while Wed. has a dawn service (4 a.m. or 5 a.m.) and a second service (7 a.m. or 8 a.m.). Now the

Sunday 8 a.m. service rivals the dawn and catechism service in numbers of baptisms, but the afternoon service is rarely used for baptisms. (This may be because it was one of the only two times on Sundays when marriages could be performed.) The number of babies is almost comparable with 1553, a drop of only 9.

Chauvet remained one of the ministers regularly assigned to the parish of St. Gervais. His alternate(s) apparently changed during the course of the year, being first Fabri and Des Gallars together, and then Bourgoing.

1555 ST. GERVAIS SUNDAYS TOTAL 65 services, 81 babies

Dawn: 12 services, 16 babies. Regular rotation at 4 a.m. or 5 a.m. **Fabri** (Jan. 13 & 20 [2] & 27, Feb. 10 & 17[2] at 5 a.m.; June 16, July 7 & 28 at 4 a.m.; Sept. 29, Oct. 6, Nov. 24, Dec. 15[3] at 5 a.m.) Clearly Fabri responsible for all dawn services.

Eight o'clock: 24 services, 33 babies. **Chauvet** (18 services, 23 babies; Jan. 13[2], Feb. 10, March 24[2], April 21, May 5, June 23, July 7, Aug. 4 & 18 & 25, Sept. 8 & 15[2] & 22, Oct. 6, Nov. 10[2] & 24, Dec. 1[2] & 8). **St. André** (2 services, 4 babies; Nov. 3[2] & 17[2]). During the first part of the year Chauvet alternates weeks with Poupin's entries for which no times are given; the two switch weeks in mid-June, but by mid-August Poupin disappears, Chauvet is left alone until St. André provides some support. **Poupin** (4 services, 6 babies; Jan. 20, Feb. 3[2], March 10, May 12[2], June 16).[36]

Catechism: 19 services, 21 babies. **Fabri** (10 services, 11 babies; Jan. 13 [called "sermon de mydi"], Feb. 10 & 17[2] & 24, May 5 & 19, June 9, July 7, Aug. 18, Nov. 10). **Chauvet** (8 services, 8 babies; Feb. 3, May 12, Aug. 4, Sept. 22, Oct. 6, Dec. 1 & 15 & 29). Apparently the two alternate weeks until mid-June, then switch, with the exception of Aug. 4; Chauvet's schedule is the opposite of his 8 a.m. one. **St. André** (1 service, 2 babies; March 10 recorded in marriage records).

Afternoon: 4 services, 4 babies. **Chauvet** (1 service, 1 baby; April 28). **Bourgoing** (2 services, 2 babies; Feb. 10, March 3). **Poupin** (1 service, 1 baby; Feb. 3)[37]

Other: 6 services, 7 babies, no times listed. **Poupin** (5 services, 5 babies; March 17 & 31, July 14 & 28, no clear way to distinguish times). **Chauvet** (1 service, 2 babies; Oct. 20).

1555 ST. GERVAIS WEEKDAYS TOTAL 85 services, 101 babies

Mondays: 8 (9) services, 8 (11) babies. One service at 6 a.m. or 7 a.m. **Poupin** (3 [4] services, 3 [6] babies; Jan. 7, July 15 & 29; also probably April 15[38][3]). **Chauvet** (4 services, 4 babies; March 25, June 3, Aug. 19, Dec. 23). **Fabri** (1 service, 1 baby; Dec. 16 at 7 a.m.).

Tuesdays: 16 services, 19 babies. One service at 6 a.m. or 7 a.m. **Poupin** (9 services, 12 babies; Jan. 8[2] & 22, Feb. 5 & 19, March 5[2] & 19[2], April 30, May 14, July 2).

---

36   Poupin gives no times, but these are entered before catechism records, so it is assumed that they are 8 a.m. The one on March 10 is recorded in the marriage records.

37   Poupin gives no time, but this is entered after Chauvet at catechism, on the same day that Poupin entered a baptism before catechism, so the two entries signify two services.

38   Poupin enters 3 baptisms between the entries for April 13 and April 18, but the date is not clear; it could be April 15.

Chauvet (4 services, 4 babies; April 23, Sept. 3 & 17, Oct. 15). **Cop** (1 service, 1 baby; July 2 at 6 a.m.). **Jean Perrier** (2 services, 2 babies; Aug. 27, Sept. 10).

Wednesdays: 29 services, 38 babies. Two services at 4 a.m. or 5 a.m. and 7 a.m. or 8 a.m. Oct. 23 Fabri at 5 a.m. and Cop at 8 a.m. (though entries listed in reverse order).

Dawn: 6 services, 8 babies. **Fabri** (April 24, May 1, Sept. 18[2] at 4 a.m.; Oct. 23[2], Nov. 20, Dec. 4 at 5 a.m.)

Later service: 23 services, 30 babies. **Poupin** (8 services, 13 babies; Feb. 6 & 20[2], March 6 & 13[2] & 20[2], April 10[2], July 3[2], Aug. 14; alternates weeks opposite Chauvet except March 13, changes @end March). **Chauvet** (11 services, 13 babies; Jan. 2[2] & 30, Feb. 13[2], May 8, June 12, July 31, Aug. 7 & 28, Oct. 2 & 30, Nov. 6). **Bourgoing** (1 service, 1 baby; April 3). **Cop** (2 services, 2 babies; Oct. 23, Dec. 18 at 8 a.m.) **Fabri** (1 service, 1 baby; Jan. 16 at 8 a.m.)

Thursdays: 13 services, 15 babies. One service at 6 a.m. or 7 a.m. **Poupin** (4 services, 5 babies; Feb. 21, March 7[2], April 18, June 20). **Chauvet** (5 services, 5 babies; June 13, Aug. 22, Sept. 5 & 19, Nov. 28). **Macar** (1 service, 2 babies; March 14 at 6 a.m.[should be 7]). **D'Airebaudouze** (1 service, 1 baby; Aug. 1 at 6 a.m.). **Colladon** (1 service, 1 baby; Sept. 12). **Mathieu Matisien** (1 service, 1 baby; Aug. 29).

Fridays: 11 services, 11 babies. One service at 6 a.m. or 7 a.m. **Poupin** (4 services, 4 babies; Jan. 25, Feb. 22, May 3 & 17). **Chauvet** (5 services, 5 babies; Feb. 1 & 15, Aug. 23, Sept. 20, Nov. 15). **Macar** (2 services, 2 babies; March 15, May 10).

Saturdays: 7 services, 7 babies. One service at 6 a.m. or 7 a.m. **Poupin** (1 service, 1 baby; May 4). **Chauvet** (4 services, 4 babies; April 13[39] & 20, Aug. 24, Sept. 7). **D'Airebaudouze** = D'Anduze (2 services, 2 babies; Sept. 14, Dec. 7).

COMMENT on 1555: TOTAL 150 services, 182 babies. Sundays continue to have the four services, with regular rotation for dawn. There is a preference for baptisms at the main morning service, followed closely by the numbers at catechism, and afternoon remains the least popular (probably because there were more weddings then). The weekday services continue, Mon.-Tues., Thurs.-Sat. at the "ordinary" hours of 6 a.m. or 7 a.m. according to the season. Wednesday continues to have two services, one at dawn and one later; dawn rotates, and apparently the later one also rotates between 7 a.m. and 8 a.m. (the same Wed. pattern as St. Pierre). The number of babies is significantly higher than in 1553, an increase of 31, and 22 higher than in 1551.

Chauvet continues as the mainstay of the St. Gervais pastoral corps, apparently taking half of the Sunday morning services and "ordinary" weekdays, with the second service on Wed. His alternate seems to have been Poupin, until the latter's health failed again sometime in late August (no baptisms by him are recorded after Aug. 14 here, or after Aug. 18 in La Magdeleine). Fabri continued to have responsibility for the dawn services, both Sundays and Wednesdays, and probably he either did the catechism or shared with this Chauvet.

---

[39] In this service the godfather is the baby's own father.

1557 ST. GERVAIS SUNDAYS TOTAL 67 services, 82 babies

Dawn: 6 services, 6 babies. Regular rotation at 4 a.m. or 5 a.m. **Macar** (1 service, 1 baby; Aug. 29). **Cop** (1 service, 1 baby; Aug. 22 at 4 a.m.). **Enoc** (1 service, 1 baby; May 9 at 5 a.m. [!]). **Dupont** (3 services, 3 babies; Sept. 19, Oct. 3, Nov. 14 at 5 a.m.).

Eight o'clock: 26 services, 32 babies. **Chauvet** (18 services, 21 babies; Jan. 10 & 24, Feb. 28, March 7, April 11[2], June 13 & 20 & 27, Aug. 1 & 15 & 29, Sept. 12 & 26, Oct. 10 & 24, Nov. 14 & 21[3], Dec. 19; alternates weeks except Feb. 28, March 11, June 20; changes mid-year, except Nov. 14). **Enoc** (3 services, 3 babies; Sept. 19, Oct. 3 & 17; alternates weeks opposite Chauvet). **St. André** (3 services, 6 babies; Jan. 3 & 17[3], Feb. 21[2]; alternates weeks opposite Chauvet except Feb. 21). **Macar** (1 service, 1 baby; May 2). **Cop** (1 service, 1 baby; April 25).

Catechism: 16 services, 19 babies. **Enoc** (10 services, 10 babies; Jan. 10 & 31, Feb. 7 & 21, March 7 & 28, April 4, May 30, June "8" = 6, July 11; alternates weeks except Jan. 31, March 28, June 6). **Macar** (2 services, 3 babies; April 25[2], June 20). **Dupont** (4 services, 6 babies; Sept. 26[2], Oct. 17 & 24[2], Nov. 14).

Afternoon: 8 services, 9 babies. **Chauvet** (5 services, 6 babies; March 7[2], May 30, June 27, Sept. 5, Oct. 31; alternates weeks). **Enoc** (2 services, 2 babies; May 2, Aug. 1). **Macar** (1 service, 1 baby; March 28).

Other: 11 services, 16 babies, no times listed. **Enoc** (7 services, 12 babies; Feb. 21[2], March 28 [probably dawn], May 30 [probably afternoon], Aug. 22[2], Oct. 31[2], Nov. 28 [2] [possibly 8 a.m.], Dec. 5[2]). **Chauvet** (1 service, 1 baby; May 30 probably 8 a.m.). **Dupont** (3 services, 3 babies; July 25, Aug. 1 & 8, probably dawn).

1557 ST. GERVAIS WEEKDAYS TOTAL 75 services, 93 babies

Mondays: 9 services, 9 babies. One service at 6 a.m. or 7 a.m. **Chauvet** (3 services, 3 babies; Aug. 2, Oct. 11, Nov. 8; alternates weeks opposite Enoc). **Enoc** (2 services, 2 babies; Sept. 20, Dec. 27; alternates weeks opposite Chauvet). **St. André** (2 services, 2 babies; Jan. 18, Feb. 8). **Cop** (1 service, 1 baby; July 12).

Tuesdays: 10 services, 12 babies. One service at 6 a.m. or 7 a.m. **Chauvet** (5 services, 7 babies; April 13, June 8 & 22, July 6[2], Aug. 17[2]; alternates weeks). **Enoc** (2 services, 2 babies; Sept. 7, Dec. 7). **Bourgoing** (1 service, 1 baby; April 27). **Colladon** (1 service, 1 baby; May 25). **Cop** (1 service, 1 baby; Aug. 24).

Wednesdays: 21 services (plus 1 crossed out), 30 babies (plus one). Two services at 4 a.m. or 5 a.m. and 7 a.m. or 8 a.m.

Dawn: 4 services, 4 babies. **Dupont** (1 service, 1 baby; Sept. 15 at 5 a.m. [Aug. 11 at 4 a.m. crossed out.]). **Chauvet** (1 service, 1 baby; Feb. 10 at 5 a.m.) **Enoc** (2 services, 2 babies; Jan. 13, March 10 at 5 a.m.)

Later service: 17 services, 26 babies. **Chauvet** (9 services, 15 babies; March 3 at 8 a.m.; Jan. 27, Feb. 3[2], March 17[2] & 31[2], April 14[2], Aug. 4, Sept. 1[3], Dec. 15 no time given, probably later). **Enoc** (5 services, 7 babies; Sept. "23" = 22 at 8 a.m.; July 28, Sept. 8, Nov. 3, Dec. 8[3] no time given, probably later). **Des Gallars** (2 services, 2 babies; April 21, July 14). **St. André** (1 service, 2 babies; Feb. 10 at 8 a.m.). Apparently for the first several months Chauvet and Enoc alternated weeks for the dawn service [which Dupont took over after July 23]; later they appear to alternate weeks for the second service (since most of the dates for which there are no times listed fall into this alternating pattern with the dates given for the later service).

Thursdays: 15 services, 20 babies. One service at 6 a.m. or 7 a.m. **Chauvet** (9 services, 11 babies; Feb. 4, March 18[2], May 27, July 8[2], Aug. 19, Sept. 16, Oct. 21 & 28, Dec. 16; alternates weeks with Enoc except Oct. 21, Dec. 16). **Enoc** (4 services, 5 babies; Jan. 28, Sept. 9, Nov. 4[2] & 11; alternates weeks with Chauvet except Nov. 11). **St. André** (1 service, 1 baby: Feb. 25). **Cop** (1 service, 3 babies; Aug. 26).

Fridays: 16 services, 18 babies. One service at 6 a.m. or 7 a.m. **Chauvet** (4 services, 4 babies; Jan. 29, March 5, April 16, July 9; alternates weeks except Jan. 29). **Enoc** (3 services, 3 babies; Aug. 20, Sept. "Friday 25" = 24, Dec. 24). **St. André** (2 services, 3 babies; Jan. 22, Feb. 26[2]). **D'Airebaudouze** (2 services, 2 babies; Jan. 8, March 26). Cop (1 service, 1 baby; Aug. 27). **Malaisie** (2 services, 3 babies; March 12, April 30[2]). **Dupont** (2 services, 2 babies; July 23, Oct. 22).

Saturdays: 4 services, 4 babies. One service at 6 a.m. or 7 a.m. **Chauvet** (3 services, 3 babies; Feb. 20, March 20, Nov. 13; alternates weeks). **Enoc** (1 service, 1 baby: Dec. 25).

COMMENT on 1557 Total services 142, total babies 175. The four Sunday services continue, with the 8 a.m. morning service now more popular than any of the other three (perhaps this reflects the preferences of the ministers as well as of the people). The number of babies is almost comparable to 1555, with a drop of only 7.

Weekday services are still held on all six days, with Wednesdays slightly more popular for baptisms than the other days, probably because there were two services from which to choose (dawn and 7 a.m. or 8 a.m.). For the other weekdays no times are listed, which suggests that there is still only one service each day (and no need to distinguish). This service almost certainly continued to be held at the time indicated in 1550-51, i.e., 6 a.m. or 7 a.m. (The fact that there is no other mention of a later time confirms that Fabri's single reference to an 8 a.m. in summer was an error.)

Apparently Chauvet continued to anchor the parish, with Enoc as his chief alternate. Chauvet appears to have had primary responsibility for Sunday morning and afternoon; Enoc may have had primary responsibility for dawn and catechism (until Dupont was appointed). Chauvet and Enoc shared the duty for the weekday services. On July 23 the Company assigned them this task and appointed Dupont to do the Sunday and Wednesday dawn services and the catechism.[40] From the records it is obvious that in alternate weeks Chauvet and Enoc were already covering the daily service at the "ordinary" hour (6 a.m. or 7 a.m. on all days except Wednesdays), and both services (dawn and the later one at 7 a.m. or 8 a.m.) on Wednesdays. Beginning July 23 they would apparently do only the later service on Wednesdays, leaving the dawn to Dupont.

1559 ST. GERVAIS SUNDAYS TOTAL 83 services, 120 babies.

Dawn: 11 services, 14 babies. Regular rotation 4 a.m. or 5 a.m. **Macar** (4 services, 5 babies; Jan. 8, Dec. 17 at 5 a.m.; May 7[2] "du matin"; March 19 no time given but entry before 8 a.m.). **Chauvet** (3 services, 5 babies; Jan. 29[2], March 12 at 5 a.m., June 18[2] at

────────────
40   RCP 2, pp. 77-78.

4 a.m.; alternate weeks). **Enoc** (3 services, 3 babies; Aug. 20 at 4 a.m., Oct. 1, Nov. 26, no time given but before entries for 8 a.m.). **Bourgoing** (1 service, 1 baby; Feb. 5 "l'aube du jour").

Eight o'clock: 16 services, 28 babies. **Chauvet** (11 services, 21 babies; Jan. 8, Feb. 5 [2], March 19, Aug. 27[2], Sept. 10 & 24[3], Oct. 1[2] & 8 & 22[4], Nov. 5[2] & 26[2]; alternates weeks except Oct. 1, Nov. 26; changes at mid-year). **Enoc** (3 services, 4 babies; Jan. 29[2], April 9, Oct. 15; alternates with Chauvet). **Bourgoing** (1 service, 2 babies; March 5). **Macar** (1 service, 1 baby; Jan. 22).

Catechism: 18 services, 28 babies. **Enoc** (8 services, 10 babies; March 12, April 9, Aug. "12" = 13, Sept. 17, Oct. 1 & 8[3], Nov. 19, Dec. 3; alternates weeks except Sept. 17, Oct. 1). **Macar** (4 services, 7 babies; Feb. 12[2], March 19[2] "au sermon de l'examen," May 21, Sept. 24[2]; alternates weeks except March 19). **Colladon** (1 service, 2 babies; Oct. 22). **Chauvet** (2 services, 3 babies; Oct. 29, Dec. 10[2]). **Dupont** (1 service, 2 babies; Jan. 22). **Cop** (1 service, 3 babies; Jan. 29). **Bourgoing** (1 service, 1 baby; May 28).

Afternoon: 8 services, 10 babies. **Chauvet** (5 services, 7 babies; Jan. 22 & 29 at 2 p.m.; Sept. 3[3], Oct. 1 & 29 at 3 p.m.). **Enoc** (1 service, 1 baby; May 28). **Beza** (2 services, 2 babies; May 21, Sept. 10).

Other: 30 services, 40 babies, no times listed. Some of these by Enoc may have been at dawn, some at other times; those by Beza may have been afternoon. **Enoc** (14 services, 16 babies; Jan. 1 & 15[2], April 2 & 23 & 30, May 7 & 21, June 11, July 2 & 16[2], Oct. 15 & 29, Nov. "20" = 19, Dec. 3). **Beza** (9 services, 15 babies; June 4 & 25, July 23[3], Aug. 20 [2], Sept. 17, Nov. 5 & 12, Dec. 10 & 31[4]; alternates weeks except June 4, Nov. 5, Dec. 31). **Macar** (2 services, 2 babies; April 23, Dec. 31). **Chauvet** (2 services, 4 babies; March 26[3], Dec. 3). **Bourgoing** (1 service, 1 baby; Aug. 27). **Morel** (1 service, 1 baby; Nov. 5). **Merlin** (1 service, 1 baby; Oct. 1).

NB on 1 Oct. Enoc and Chauvet alternate all day: Enoc dawn, Chauvet 8 a.m., Enoc catechism, Chauvet 3 p.m. NB earliest service by Beza is 21 May, since he was appointed minister at St. Gervais on March 17.[41]

1559 ST. GERVAIS WEEKDAYS TOTAL 119 services, 144 babies.

Mondays: 18 services, 19 babies. One service at 6 a.m. or 7 a.m. **Chauvet** (10 services, 10 babies; Jan. 16 & 23 & 30, Feb. 6, Aug. 14 & 28, Sept. 11, Nov. 6, Dec. 11 & 25. He alternates weeks opposite Enoc until end of June (except Jan. 16 & 30), then changes weeks by July 1, changes again end of Oct.; this pattern holds for the rest of the week and will not be repeated.). **Enoc** (3 services, 3 babies; June 19, Oct. 16 & 30; alternates weeks opposite Chauvet except June 19). **Macar** (1 service, 2 babies; Oct. 2). **Cop** (1 service, 1 baby; March 6). **Beza** (2 services, 2 babies; Sept. 4, Dec. 18). **Colladon** (1 service, 1 baby; May 8).

Tuesdays: 18 services, 22 babies. One service at 6 a.m. or 7 a.m. **Chauvet** (10 services, 11 babies; Jan. 10, March 21, May 2 & 30[2], June 6, Aug. 1 & 29, Sept. 26, Dec. 12 & 26; alternates weeks opposite Enoc (except June 6) according to pattern listed for Monday). **Enoc** (5 services, 8 babies; Jan 31[2], Feb. 14, March 28[2], Oct. 3[2] & 31; alternates weeks opposite Chauvet). **Beza** (3 services, 3 babies; June 27, July 25, Dec. 5).

Wednesdays: 29 services, 36 babies. Two services at 4 a.m. or 5 a.m. and 7 a.m. or 8 a.m. On 25 Oct. there are two services in sequence by Chauvet and Macar, neither gives time; Chauvet is entered first, then Macar, but Chauvet usually did the later service, so this may be a reversal of order in entering the baptisms.

Dawn: 1 service, 1 baby +? **Macar** (Oct. 25: probably dawn). Possibly others did baptisms at dawn but it is impossible to determine.

Later service: 28 services, 35 babies. **Chauvet** (12 services, 15 babies; Jan. 11, Feb. 8 at 8 a.m.; Oct. 4 at 7 a.m. No times given: Feb. 22, April 5, May 3 & 31, July 5, Aug. 2, Oct. 25, Nov. 29[3], Dec. 13[2]; alternates weeks opposite Enoc according to pattern listed for Monday). **Enoc** (8 services, 10 babies; Jan. 18[2], March 1 & 29[2], April 12, May 24, June 21, Oct. 18, Nov. 1; alternates weeks opposite Chauvet). **Beza** (7 services, 9 babies; June 7 & 28, July 26, Aug. 23, Sept. 20[2], Nov. 15, Dec. 6[2]; mostly alternates but seems to do certain weeks/month). **Merlin** (1 service, 1 baby; March 22 [called "lundy" which would have been 20th, but entry comes between Chauvet March 21 & 23]).[42]

Thursdays: 29 services, 36 babies. One service at 6 a.m. or 7 a.m. **Chauvet** (13 services, 14 babies; Jan. 12 & 26, Feb. 9 & 23, March 23, April 6, May 4 & 18, Aug. 31, Sept. 28, Oct. 12, Nov. 30[2], Dec. 28; alternates weeks opposite Enoc according to pattern listed for Monday). **Enoc** (6 services, 10 babies; Jan. 19, Feb. 2, March 2, May 11 & 25[4], Oct. 19[2]; alternates weeks opposite Chauvet). **Beza** (7 services, 8 babies; June 15 & 29 [2], July 27, Sept. 7, Nov. 16, Dec. 7 & 21; alternates weeks). **Colladon** (2 services, 3 babies; April 27[2], Aug. 10). **Des Gallars** (1 service, 1 baby; Oct. 5).

Fridays: 13 services, 16 babies. One service at 6 a.m. or 7 a.m. **Chauvet** (6 services, 9 babies; Feb. 10[2] & 24, Oct. 6[2] & 13[2] & 27, Nov. 10; alternates weeks opposite Enoc, except Oct. 6 & Nov. 10, according to pattern listed for Monday). **Enoc** (3 services, 3 babies; Feb. 3 & 17, March 3; alternates weeks opposite Chauvet). **Beza** (4 services, 4 babies; June 30, Nov. 17, Dec. 8 & 22).

Saturdays: 12 services, 15 babies. One service at 6 a.m. or 7 a.m. **Chauvet** (6 services, 7 babies; Jan. 14, Feb. 11, May 6, June 10, Aug. 5, Sept. 2[2]; alternates weeks except June 10 confusion). **Beza** (5 services, 6 babies; July 1[2], Sept. 9 & 23, Dec. 9 & 23; alternates weeks). 1 service, 2 babies no minister listed; Nov. 18.

Comment on 1559: Total services 202, total babies 264. On Sundays there continue to be four services; since so many services do not have times listed, it is not possible to say whether any one service was favored over the others as a time for baptisms. The weekdays continue to have services every day, apparently only one per day on most days; this rotated with the seasons, 6 a.m. or 7 a.m. The exception is Wednesday, which continued to have two services, at dawn and at 7 a.m. or 8 a.m. The number of babies is much much higher than 1557, an increase of 89 in raw figures, equally 50%. The influx of refugees which led to the opening of a fourth parish, St. Germain, is clearly evident here where the one parish had to expand its services greatly.

---

[42]   In general, the later service was probably more popular (as seen in numbers of babies baptized on other weekdays) so it is assumed that unmarked ones by ministers who regularly do the later services are later.

The ministers of the parish continue to have Chauvet as their long-standing anchor. Apparently he was still alternating with Enoc for the weekday services, and probably for the main Sunday morning and afternoon services. Beza seems to have taken an active part in both Sunday and weekday services, sometimes in alternation with Chauvet (following Enoc's schedule). It may be that Macar was called upon for the dawn services on Sundays and Wednesdays. It is not clear how responsibility for catechism was assigned.

1562 ST. GERVAIS SUNDAYS TOTAL 68 services, 93 babies

Dawn: 8 services, 8 babies. Regular rotation at 4 a.m. or 5 a.m. **Colladon** (1 service, 1 baby; Jan. 18 "l'aube du jour"). **Merlin** (2 services, 2 babies; March 15 at 5 a.m., May 10 at 4 a.m.). **D'Airebaudouze** (3 services, 3 babies; March 22 at 5 a.m.; April 19 at 4 a.m.; Nov. 15 at 5 a.m.). **Enoc** (1 service, 1 baby; Oct. 4 at 4 a.m. [!][43]. **Giles** ministre of Vandoeuvre (1 service, 1 baby; April 12 at 4 a.m.).

Eight o'clock: 19 services, 30 babies. **Enoc** (7 services, 10 babies; March 1 & 8, July 5 [2], Aug. 23[3], Oct. 4 & 18, Nov. 1; alternates weeks opposite Gaigneulx except March 1; same schedule as Chauvet, Merlin). **Chauvet** (2 services, 4 babies; Feb. 1[2], March 15[2]; alternates weeks, same schedule as Enoc). **Merlin** (3 services, 4 babies; May 10, July 19[2], Sept. 13; alternates weeks). **Gaigneulx** (6 sevices, 10 babies; Aug. 30 [3], Sept. 27, Nov. 8 & 22, Dec. 6 & 20[3]; alternates weeks opposite Enoc). **Cop** (1 service, 2 babies; April 19).

Catechism: 16 services, 17 babies. **Enoc** (4 services, 5 babies; April 12, June 28[2], Oct. 4 & 18; alternates weeks except April 12, same schedule as his own 8 a.m.). **Gaigneulx** (4 services, 4 babies; Aug. 2, Sept. 27, Nov. 22, Dec. 20; alternates weeks opposite Enoc, same schedule as his own 8 a.m.). **Merlin** (2 services, 2 babies; May 3, June 14; alternates weeks, same schedule as Enoc). **Cop** (2 services, 2 babies; March 1 & 15; alternates week, same schedule as Gaigneulx). **D'Airebaudouze** (1 service, 1 baby; July 5; same schedule as Gaigneulx and Cop). **Colladon** (3 services, 3 babies; Feb. 22, March 22, May 24; alternates weeks except. May 24, same schedule as Enoc & Merlin).

Afternoon 12 services, 12 babies. **Enoc** (7 services, 7 babies; March 1 & 15 & 29, June 7, July 5, Sept. 27, Nov. 8; alternates weeks opposite Gaigneulx & they exchange weeks after July 5; also opposite his own 8 a.m. baptisms). **Gaigneulx** (4 services, 4 babies; July 12 & 26, Sept. 6, Dec. 27; alternates weeks with Enoc, opposite of his own 8 a.m. baptisms). **Colladon** (1 service, 1 baby; Feb. 8; opposite week from Enoc).

ALSO 13 services, 26 babies, no times listed. **Enoc** (12 services, 23 babies; Jan. 4[2] & 11[2] & 18, Feb. 8[2] & 22[2], April 5[3], June 7 & 14[3] & 28[3], July 12, Nov. 29, Dec. 13 [2]; alternates weeks except Jan. 4 & 18, June 7; the other nine fit the rotation for 8 a.m. & catechism, but June 7 is probably 8 a.m. or catechism because there is another baptism by Enoc on June 7 in the afternoon). 1 service 1 baby (visiting minister – "le frere de la La Fandoge")

---

43   He writes Oct. 9 at 4 a.m. But the entry comes before Oct. 4 at 8 a.m. and he probably means 5 a.m.

1562 ST. GERVAIS WEEKDAYS TOTAL 54 services, 60 babies

Mondays: 11 services, 12 babies. One service at 6 a.m. or 7 a.m. **Enoc** (3 services, 3 babies; April 6, July 13, Oct. 5; alternates weeks opposite Gaigneulx). **Gaigneulx** (5 services, 6 babies; June 22, Aug. 3[2] at 6 a.m.; Aug. 31, Sept. 14, Nov. 9 no time given; alternates weeks opposite Enoc). **Le Duc** (1 service, 1 baby; March 2). **D'Aire-baudouze** (1 service, 1 baby; Dec. 28). **Boullier** (1 service, 1 baby; Jan. 5).

Tuesdays: 6 services, 6 babies. One service at 6 a.m. or 7 a.m. **Enoc** (3 services, 3 babies; June 30, July 28, Oct. 6; alternates weeks opposite Gaigneulx). **Gaigneulx** (3 services, 3 babies; Sept. 1, Oct. 27, Nov. 24; alternates weeks opposite Enoc).

Wednesdays: 15 services, 17 babies. Two services at 4 a.m. or 5 a.m. and at 8 a.m.

Dawn: 2 services, 2 babies +? **Gaigneulx** (May 20 at 4 a.m.). **Colladon** (Dec. 16 "dawn")

Later service: 14 services, 16 babies. **Enoc** (6 services, 7 babies; Jan. 14, Feb. 25, Sept. 23, Oct. 7, Nov. 4[2], Dec. 2; alternates weeks opposite Gaigneulx). **Gaigneulx** (7 services, 8 babies; Aug. 5, Sept. 2, Nov. 11[2] & 25, Dec. 9 & 23 at 8 a.m.; Sept. "31" = 30 [44] no time given; alternates weeks opposite Enoc except May 20). **Le Duc** (1 service, 1 baby; April 1).

Thursdays: 11 services, 11 babies. One service at 6 a.m. or 7 a.m. **Enoc** (6 services, 6 babies; Jan. 15, Feb. "14" = 12 [45], June 11, July 2, Sept. 24, Nov. 5; alternate weeks opposite Gaigneulx except June 11). **Gaigneulx** (3 services, 3 babies; Aug. 6, Sept. 30, Oct. 1; alternate weeks opposite Enoc). **Colladon** (2 services, 2 babies; Sept. 10, Nov. 19).

Fridays: 8 services, 11 babies. One service at 6 a.m. or 7 a.m. **Enoc** (6 services, 7 babies; Feb. "26" = 27, April 10, June 5, Aug. 14 & 28[2], Nov. 6; alternates weeks opposite Gaigneulx). **Gaigneulx** (1 service, 3 babies; Aug. 7; alternates weeks opposite Enoc). **Corneille** (?) (1 service, 1 baby; Nov. 20).

Saturdays: 2 services, 2 babies. One service at 6 a.m. or 7 a.m. **Enoc** (1 service, 1 baby; Jan. 3). **Gaigneulx** (1 service, 1 baby; Sept. 5).

COMMENT on 1562 Total 122 services, 153 babies. Baptisms continue at the four services on Sundays, with dawn apparently the least popular. The weekdays also continue as before, with one exception. As before, there is one service every day of the week except Wednesday, and these are at the same times as in 1557: Mondays, Tuesdays, Thursdays, Fridays, and Saturdays at 6 or 7 a.m. The first service on Wednesdays is still at dawn with times rotating for the seasons, but the second service now consistently at 8 a.m. This pattern follows the 1561 *Ordinances* instructions, except for the time for the second service on Wednesdays, which, like that at St. Pierre, is later than the "ordinary" sermon. The number of babies has dropped very significantly since 1559, a total of 111, more than 42%. Thus 1562 numbers are also below 1557 (22 fewer) and 1555 (29 fewer), virtually bringing the numbers back to 1553 (only 2 more in 1562 than 1553).

---

[44] One is labeled "31 et dernier Sept." (!). It is entered here, assuming that Sept. 30 is intended.

[45] Here as elsewhere when day of the week and date are not in accord, unless there is other evidence to clarify, it is assumed that the day of the week is correct, since numbers often appear to have caused more confusion than weekday names. Occasionally preference is given to the number, e.g., if it is situated between two other dates which make clear the sequence.

The two main ministers of the parish are now Enoc and Gaigneulx. Chauvet occasionally baptizes on Sundays, but he is no longer the central figure. Enoc and Gaigeulx apparently take the Sunday 8 a.m. and catechism on the same day, while the other has the afternoon service; the following week, the one who did the morning service and catechism has the daily service.

1564: ST. GERVAIS SUNDAYS TOTAL 67 services, 101 babies

Dawn: 10 services, 14 babies. Regular rotation at 4 a.m or 5 a.m. **Enoc** (2 services, 2 babies; Jan. 2, Nov. 19 at 5 a.m.). **Des Bordes** (2 services, 6 babies; Nov. 5 at 5 a.m.; Feb. 6[5] no specific time). **Gaignueulx** (1 service, 1 baby; April 16 at 4 a.m.). **Colladon** (2 services, 2 babies; May 7, Oct. 29 "l'aube du jour"). **Cop** (1 service, 1 baby; June 25 at 4 a.m.). **Maubué** (1 service, 1 baby; July 30 at 4 a.m.). **Trembley** (1 service, 1 baby; Aug. 20 at 4 a.m.) [NB Des Bordes baptizes 5 babies at once.]

Eight o'clock: 29 services, 50 babies. **Enoc** (11 services, 23 babies; Jan. 9[3], Feb. 6[2] & "2" = 20[2], March 19, April 30[3], June 11[3] & 25[2], July 23, Aug. 20[4], Sept. 17, Oct. 15; alternates weeks oppposite Gaigneulx). **Gaigneulx** (10 services, 12 babies; Jan. 16, Feb. 27[3], March 12 & 26, April 9 & 23, May 7, July 16 & 30, Aug. 27; alternates weeks opposite Enoc). **Des Bordes** (4 services, 8 babies; Oct. 8 & 29[2], Nov. 12[3], Dec. 10[2]; alternates weeks except Oct. 8, shares Enoc's schedule). **Cop** (3 services, 6 babies; Oct. 1, Dec. 17[3] & 31[2]; alternates weeks except Oct. 1, shares Gaigneulx's schedule). **Colladon** (1 service, 1 baby; Aug. 6; Enoc's schedule).

Catechism: 13 services, 19 babies. **Enoc** (8 services, 14 babies; Feb. 6, March 5 & 19 [2], April 16[3], May 14, July 9[2], Aug. 20[2], Sept. 17[2]; alternates weeks opposite Gaigneulx; same schedule as his own 8 a.m. service). **Gaigneulx** (4 services, 4 babies; Jan. 30, Feb. 13 & 27, May 7; alternates weeks opposite Enoc; same schedule as his own 8 a.m. service). **Maubué** (1 service, 1 baby; June 25; Enoc's schedule).

Afternoon: 8 services, 9 babies. **Enoc** (4 services, 5 babies; March 26, May 21[2], June 11, July 2; alternates weeks opposite Gaigneulx except June 11; also opposite his own 8 a.m. & catechism schedule). **Gaignueulx** (2 services, 2 babies; Jan. 9 at 2 p.m.; April 16 at 3 p.m.; alternates weeks opposite Enoc; also opposite his own 8 a.m. & catechism schedule). **Trembley** (1 service, 1 baby: Sept. 17, no time given but after catechism entries; Gaigneulx's schedule). **Cop** (1 service, 1 baby; Dec. 24 at 2 p.m.; Enoc's schedule).

Other: 7 services, 9 babies, no times listed. **Trembley** (6 services, 8 babies; "Sept. 30" = Oct. 1, Oct. 8, Nov. 5[3] & 12 & 26, Dec. 31, probably dawn or catechism). **Enoc** (1 service, 1 baby; Jan. 9, probably 8 a.m. or catechism).

1564: ST. GERVAIS WEEKDAYS TOTAL 57 services, 69 babies

Mondays: 9 services, 10 babies. One service at 6 a.m. or 7 a.m. **Enoc** (2 services, 2 babies; June 26, July 10; alternates weeks opposite Gaigneulx). **Gaigneulx** (4 services, 5 babies; Jan. 31, Feb. 28[2], June 5, July 31; alternates weeks opposite Enoc). **Des Bordes** (2 services, 2 babies; Nov. 27, Dec. 25; alternates weeks, follows Enoc's schedule). **Cop** (1 service, 1 baby; Dec. 18; follows Gaigneulx's schedule).

Tuesdays: 13 services, 15 babies. One service at 6 a.m. or 7 a.m. **Enoc** (2 services, 3 babies; Feb. 22, May 30[2]; alternates weeks opposite Gaigneulx). **Gaigneulx** (8 services, 9 babies; Jan. 4 & 18[2], Feb. 15, May 9, June 6, Aug. 15 & 29, Sept. 12; alternates weeks opposite Enoc). **Trembley** (2 services, 2 babies; Oct. "9" = 10 [assume day "mardy" more accurate than date], Nov. 21; alternates weeks, Enoc's schedule). **Des Bordes** (1 service, 1 baby; Dec. 26; Enoc's schedule).

Wednesdays: 18 services, 25 babies. (Two services? Dawn and 8 a.m.) There is evidence for the later service year-round at 8 a.m., but no baptisms are recorded for a dawn service [presuming there was one, as stipulated in 1561 and practiced in 1562]. **Enoc** (2 services, 4 babies; March 22[2] at 8 a.m., April 19[2]; alternates weeks opposite Gaigneulx). **Gaigneulx** (11 services, 14 babies; March 1 & 15 & 29, April 12[2] & 26[2], May 10 & 24[2], July 5, Aug. 9 & 30, Sept. 13 at 8 a.m.; alternates weeks opposite Enoc except Aug. 9.) **Des Bordes** (3 services, 3 babies; Oct. 18, Nov. 1, Dec. 27 at 8 a.m.; alternates weeks, follows Enoc's schedule). **Cop** (2 services, 4 babies; Dec. 6[2] & 20[2] at 8 a.m.; alternates weeks, follows Gaigneulx's schedule).

Thursdays: 8 services, 8 babies. One service at 6 a.m. or 7 a.m. **Enoc** (1 service, 1 baby; July 27; alternates weeks opposite Gaigneulx). **Gaigneulx** (5 services, 5 babies; March 30, April 27, May 11, Aug. 31, Sept. 14; alternates weeks opposite Enoc). **Des Bordes** (1 service, 1 baby; Dec. 14; Enoc's schedule). **Cop** (1 service, 1 baby; Dec. 21; Gaigneulx's schedule).

Fridays 5 services, 6 babies. One service at 6 a.m. or 7 a.m. **Gaigneulx** (3 services, 4 babies; Feb. 4, June 9, July 21[2]). **Trembley** (1 service, 1 baby; Oct. 20 [46]). **Des Bordes** (1 service, 2 babies, Dec. 1).

Saturdays: 4 services, 5 babies. One service at 6 a.m. or 7 a.m. **Gaigneulx** (1 service, 1 baby; March 4). **Des Bordes** (1 service, 2 babies; Nov. 18). **Trembley** (2 services, 2 babies; "Sat." Oct. 14 [written, 4 crossed out, 5 written, but "Sat." left untouched], Nov. 25).

COMMENT on 1564: Total 124 services, 170 babies. Sundays continue as usual to have four services. As with St. Pierre, there is a significant increase in the number of baptisms at the main morning service, though the other three are still used, and the afternoon perhaps has a few more than before. Weekdays there are services every day; Mon.-Tues. and Thurs.-Sat. these are probably at the "ordinary sermon" time of 6 a.m. or 7 a.m. if it follows the pattern of 1562 and the regulations of the revised *Ecclesiastical Ordinances*. Wednesday presents a bit of a question, since the only time listed is 8 a.m.; this would be the regular second service time, and presumably there was still the dawn service at its usual rotation times, as seen in the 1562 records and stipulated in the *Ordinances*, though this is not manifested by actual records of baptisms. The number of babies is significantly higher than in 1562 with 27 more babies, which is only 5 fewer than 1557 and 12 fewer than 1555.

There are still two principal ministers, the same as in 1562, Enoc and Gaigneuelx sharing the work in much the same fashion as two years before. The one who does Sunday morning at 8 a.m. also does catechism and the daily services the following week; the other does only the Sunday afternoon service that week. The next week the pattern is reversed. It is not clear whether a single minister is assigned to dawn services on Sunday, and

---

[46]   The date is not very legible, identified as "Friday Oct. 19" = probably Oct. 20 – the entry comes after Oct. 18 before Oct. 29.

although it is likely that dawn services continue on Wednesdays, the evidence for that is indirect: the fact that the ministers who record baptisms at 8 a.m. give the time. Usually, if there is only one service, ministers do not bother to identify the time; since the Wednesday baptisms are consistently identified as 8 a.m., it is almost certain that they are being distinguished from a service at another time. Then the question would be why parents did not bring their babies for dawn baptisms, and that can only be a matter of speculation. If the Sunday dawn baptism records are accurate, there was a rather frequent turn-over in the ministers who did dawn baptisms, and thus people may have chosen to come to the later service when they knew who was going to be preaching.

1550 La Magdeleine SUNDAYS TOTAL 32 services, 46 babies

Eight o'clock: 2 services, 3 babies, by **Poupin** (Jan. 12; Aug. 31[2], Oct. 5 no time but before catechism baptism).

Catechism: 17 services, 24 babies. **Cop** (8 services, 11 babies; Jan. 19, March 2 & 16, April 20[2], Aug. 10, Oct. 5, Nov. 2[3] & 16; alternates weeks with Bourgoing, except April 20, switching perhaps May?). **Bourgoing** (7 services, 10 babies; Jan. 12, Feb. 23, March 9[3], May 18[2], Aug. 31, Oct. 12, Nov. 23; alternates weeks with Cop, switching rhythm perhaps after May 18). **Poupin** (1 service, 2 babies; July 6). **Des Gallars** (1 service, 1 baby; June 15).

Afternoon: none.

Other: 13 services, 19 babies, no times listed. All by **Poupin** (Feb. 16[2], April 13, July 27, Aug. 3[2] & 24[3], Sept. 14 & 28, Oct. 5 & 19 & 26, Nov. 30[2], Dec. 14 & 21[2]; no clear pattern evident. Probably Poupin was doing all the 8 a.m. at La Magdeleine, parallel to Calvin doing all 8 a.m. at St. Pierre.)

1550 La Magdeleine WEEKDAYS TOTAL 94 services, 114 babies

Mondays: 18 services, 21 babies. One service at 6 a.m. or 7 a.m. **Poupin** (11 services, 12 babies; Jan. 13 at 7 a.m.; Feb. 24, March 24, June 30, Aug. 11[2] & 25, Sept. 22 & 29, Nov. 17, Dec. 22 & 29; alternates weeks opposite Calvin, except Sept. 29, Dec. 22). **Calvin** (2 services, 2 babies; March 3, Nov. 23=24[47]; alternates weeks opposite Poupin; all other ministers follow Calvin's schedule). **Bourgoing** (2 services, 2 babies; Feb. 3, Sept. 1). **Fabri** (1 service, 1 baby; April 14). **Chauvet** (1 service, 3 babies; May 26). 1 service, 1 baby, no minister named (April 28).

Tuesdays: 19 services, 28 babies. One service at 6 a.m. or 7 a.m. **Poupin** (10 services, 17 babies; Feb. 4[4] & 25[2], May 20, June 17[3], July 15[2], Aug. 26, Sept. 9, Nov. 4, Dec. 2 & 30; alternates weeks opposite Calvin, except Feb. 4). **Calvin** (2 services, 4 babies; April 1[3], Sept. 16; alternates weeks opposite Poupin; all other ministers follow Calvin's schedule). **Chauvet** (4 services, 4 babies; May 13, June 10 & 24, Sept. 2). **Bourgoing** (2 services, 2 babies; Jan. 7, Feb. 18). **Fabri** (1 service, 1 baby; Jan. 21).

Wednesdays: none.[48]

Thursdays: 23[25] services, 25[27] babies. One service at 6 a.m. or 7 a.m. **Poupin** (13[15] services, 14[16] babies; Jan. 2 & 16, Feb. 13 & 27, March 13, April 24[2], June 5 & 12, July 3, Aug. 28, Sept. 11, Dec. 4 & 18; alternates weeks [opposite Calvin] except June 12; all other ministers in alternate weeks, which was Calvin's schedule) [plus

---

[47] No time is given but it is listed after Bourgoing's catechism entry; there was no Sunday afternoon service in 1550, and when Calvin does baptisms he is usually preaching, which he would not be doing at catechism; so it may have been a mistake for Mon. 24; OC 21:471 reads it so.

[48] 2 services, 2 babies, by **Poupin** (March 26, Oct. 22 [these days are part of his scheduled weeks]). It seems probable that he entered them here by accident, and they should have been in the register for St. Pierre, because the weekly service was held there on Wednesday. Alternatively, they might have been wrongly dated; Poupin is the least careful about records. Since it would be easier to confuse the date than the parish book, these two are arbitrarily added to the counts for Thursday, which seems to have been a very popular day for baptisms.

March 26=27, Oct. 22=23]. **Bourgoing** (5 services, 6 babies; Jan. 9, March 6, June 26[2], July 24, Dec. 25). **Chauvet** (3 services, 3 babies; April 17, Sept. 4 & 18). **Cop** (1 service, 1 baby; May 1 at 6 a.m.). **Fabri** (1 service, 1 baby; Oct. 30 at 7 a.m.).

Fridays: 17 services, 20 babies. One service 6 a.m. or 7 a.m. **Poupin** (8 services, 8 babies; Jan. 17 & 31, April 11, June 6, Aug. 29, Sept. 26, Oct. 10, Dec. 5; alternates weeks; all other ministers, except one day by Des Gallars, are in opposite weeks, Calvin's schedule). **Bourgoing** (5 services, 5 babies; Feb. 21, March 21, May 30, Aug. 22, Oct. 31). **Fabri** (1 service, 3 babies; April 4 at 8 a.m. [!] [49]). **Des Gallars** (1 service, 2 babies; May 23). **Chauvet** (2 services, 2 babies; Sept. 5, Oct. 3).

Saturdays: 15 services, 18 babies. One service 6 a.m. or 7 a.m. [one entry at 8 a.m. probably Fabri's error]. **Poupin** (7 services, 8 babies; March 1, May 10, June 21[2], July 5, Aug. 16, Oct. 18, Dec. 20; alternates weeks opposite Calvin except Oct. 18). **Calvin** (1 service, 1 baby; Sept. 20; alternates weeks opposite Poupin, all other ministers follow Calvin's schedule except Fabri who gives same date as Poupin). **Bourgoing** (3 services, 4 babies; May 17, Aug. 9[2=twins], Dec. 27). **Chauvet** (3 services, 4 babies; May 31, Aug. 23, Oct. 11[2]). **Fabri** (1 service, 1 baby; Oct. 18 at 8 a.m.[!]).

Fabri's entry is followed immediately by Poupin's baptismal record for the same date, which seems to indicate two baptisms by different ministers the same day after the same service. This appears to have happened occasionally at La Magdeleine; cf. Sun. July 19, 1554, entry by Poupin followed by one by Fabri "audit sermon," and instance of Morel and Dupont of Nov. 18, 1557.

1551 La Magdeleine SUNDAYS TOTAL 29 services, 44 babies

Eight o'clock: 2 services, 3 babies by **Poupin** (June 21[2], Aug. 23 [times not given but entry made before catechism baptisms by Bourgoing and Cop]).

Catechism: 11 services, 16 babies. **Cop** (6 services, 9 babies; Feb. 8, June 14, July 12 [2] [50], Aug. 23, Oct. 18, Nov. 29[3, 1+ girl-boy twins]; alternates weeks opposite Bourgoing). **Bourgoing** (4 services, 5 babies; Feb. 1[2], June 21, Aug. 16, Aug. "31" = 30; alternates weeks opposite Cop). **Fabri** (1 service, 2 babies; March 1).

Other: 16 services, 25 babies, no times listed. **Poupin** (15 services, 22 babies; Feb. 8 & 15[2] [51], March 8, April 5 & 19[2], July 5[2], Sept. 20[2] & 27[3], Oct. 4 & 11 & 18 & 25,

---

49   There are two days in 1550, Fri. April 4 and Sat. Oct. 18, when Fabri enters the time as 8 a.m.; in 1551 this happens again on Tues. Jan. 20 and Thurs. Jan. 22; in 1552 on Thurs. Jan. 21 and Sat. Jan. 23; in 1553 on Mon. March 20 and Tues. April 4 and Thurs. May 25 and Fri. July 28; in 1554 on Mon. June 15 and Tues. June 26, Fri. April 6 and Fri. Nov. 2 and Sat. April 7 and Sat. July 14. These are probably errors, since there are no weekday services at 8 a.m. except the second Wednesday one. Fabri's error may be owed in part to the fact that baptisms were at the end of the sermon time, and the dates when he confuses the time would have begun at 7 a.m. and be concluding at 8 a.m. It is more likely, however, that he simply made a mistake, because in the rest of the entries he gives the time accurately. A further significant possibility is a copyist's error, because La Magdeleine records were recopied in the 18th century and the originals are no longer extant. Dupont does the same on Fri. Dec. 17, 1557.

50   In this instance the father was also the godfather!

51   In this instance an older brother was the godfather.

Nov. 1[2] & 8, Dec. 13; it is probable that all of these are 8 a.m.). **Bourgoing** (1 service, 3 babies; June 7; probably catechism).

1551 La Magdeleine WEEKDAYS TOTAL 100 services, 138 babies

Mondays: 20 services, 29 babies. One service at 6 a.m. or 7 a.m. **Poupin** (12 services, 16 babies; Jan. 19 & 26,[52] Feb. 23, March 9[3], June 1[2] & 15, Aug. 10[2], Sept. 7 & 21, Nov. 2 & 16, Dec. 28; alternates weeks opposite Calvin). **Calvin** (1 service, 1 baby; Nov. 23; alternates weeks opposite Poupin, all other ministers follow Calvin's schedule except Cop on July 13). **Fabri** (4 services, 6 babies; March 30[2] at 7 a.m.; May 11 at 6 a.m.; Oct. 26[2], Dec. 21 at 7 a.m.). **Bourging** (2 services, 3 babies; June 22, Aug. 17 [2]). **Cop** (1 service, 3 babies [1+ twin girls]; July 13 at 6 a.m.).

Tuesdays: 22 services, 30 babies. One service at 6 a.m. or 7 a.m. **Poupin** (8 services, 10 babies; Jan. 27[2], March 10, April 7, June 2 & 30, Oct. 6[2], Nov. 17, Dec. 1; alternates weeks opposite Calvin). **Calvin** (1 service, 1 baby; "mardy Dec. 9" = 8[53]; alternates weeks opposite Poupin, all other ministers follow Calvin's schedule). **Fabri** (9 services, 14 babies; Jan. 20[2] at 8 a.m. [!], Feb. 3, March 17 & 31 at 7 a.m.; April 14[2], July 21 [2], Aug. 4[3, 1+ girl-boy twins] at 6 a.m.; Sept. 15, Nov. 10 at 7 a.m.). **Chauvet** (2 services, 3 babies; June 9[2], Sept. 1). **Bourgoing** (2 services, 2 babies; April 28, Aug. 18).

Wednesdays: None

Thursdays: 26 services, 38 babies. One service at 6 a.m. or 7 a.m. **Poupin** (15 services, 22 babies; Jan. 1[2] & 29, Feb. 12, March 12[2] & 26, April 9, May 7[3], June 18[2], July 30, Oct. 8 & 22, Nov. 5[2] & 19, Dec. 3[2] & 31; alternates weeks opposite Calvin). **Calvin** (1 service, 1 baby; Dec. 10; alternates weeks opposite Poupin, all other ministers follow Calvin's schedule). **Fabri** (5 services, 9 babies; Jan. 8[3][54], Feb. 5 at 7 a.m.; Jan. 22[2] at 8 a.m. [!]; Oct. 29[2] at 7 a.m.; June 11 no time given). **Bourgoing** (3 services, 3 babies; April 16, May 28, June 25). **Chauvet** (2 services, 3 babies; July 23, Sept. 3[2]).

Fridays: 19 services, 24 babies. One service at 6 a.m. or 7 a.m. **Poupin** (7 services, 11 babies; Jan. 2, Feb. 13[4, 2= girl twins], March 13, June 19, Sept. 25, Oct. 9, Dec. 4[2]; alternates weeks opposite Calvin). **Calvin** (1 service, 1 baby; July 24; alternates weeks opposite Poupin, all other ministers follow Calvin's schedule). **Fabri** (5 services, 6 babies; Feb. 20[2], March 20 at 7 a.m.; April 3 at 6 a.m.; Nov. 13 at 7 a.m.; Oct. 30 no time given). **Bourgoing** (4 services, 4 babies; Jan. 9, June 26, July 10, Dec. 11). **Chauvet** (1 service, 1 baby; Sept. 18). **Des Gallars** (1 service, 1 baby; March 6).

Saturdays: 13 services, 17 babies. One service at 6 a.m or 7 a.m. **Poupin** (8 services, 10 babies; Feb. 14 & 28, April 11, Aug. 1, Sept. 12, Oct. 10[2], Dec. 5 & 19[2]; alternates weeks opposite Calvin). **Calvin** (1 service, 1 baby; July 25; alternates weeks opposite Poupin, all other ministers follow Calvin's schedule). **Fabri** (2 services, 3 babies; March 21

---

52 In this instance the father was also the godfather.

53 The record says "mardy 9" but Tuesday is the 8th. Most often in such cases it is the day, not the date, which is correct; and if it were Wed. this would be the only Wed. baptism in La Magdeleine in 1551, and Calvin's only other Wed. baptism this year is in St. Pierre, so it is probable that the date is wrong and the day of the week correct. Annales also says "Tues. 8"; OC 21:495.

54 An interesting note: on Jan. 8 Fabri says of the godfather "de retour au sermon de 7 heures du matin," as if he had brought the child, left during the sermon, and returned for the baptism.

[2 girl-boy twins] at 7 a.m.; Sept. 5 at 6 a.m.). **Chauvet** (1 service, 2 babies[2=twins]; May 16). **Bourgoing** (1 service, 1 baby; June 13).

COMMENT on 1550-51 Total services 126 + 129 = 255, total babies 160 + 182 = 342. There are no dawn services mandated in the 1541 *Ordinances*; of the three planned for Sundays, La Magdeleine is still missing the afternoon service in 1550-51. Most baptisms are celebrated at the catechism, with some at the morning service. Apparently there are services on five of the six weekdays, all except Wednesday; these services are at 6 a.m. or 7 a.m. according to the season, and there are a significant number of baptisms on every day. There are apparently no baptisms on Wednesdays, because the two listed by Poupin in 1550 are probably mistakes which should have been another day. The number of babies increases fairly significantly from 1550 to 1551, a total of 22.

The organization of the preaching responsibilities is fairly clear, though some points are not certain. Cop and Bourgoing appear to alternate doing the catechism – in fact, they appear to do La Magdeleine catechism on the same days that they preach at the dawn service at St. Pierre. Poupin may have done the Sunday morning service every week (while Calvin preached in St. Pierre). The weekday sermons were done by Calvin and Poupin in alternate weeks, as appears from the fact that Poupin's baptisms are almost all done in alternate weeks, though occasionally he (like other ministers) baptized after one of Calvin's sermons. Calvin rarely baptized, though there are examples on every day of the week except Wednesday; the other ministers all perform baptisms on the week when Calvin would be preaching, evidently to relieve him of some extra work. However, the fact that there are no baptisms on Wednesdays in this parish but there are in the corresponding records for St. Pierre at a time when no service was officially scheduled makes it all but certain that Calvin and Poupin were doing the second Wednesday service at St. Pierre.

1552 La Magdeleine SUNDAYS TOTAL 38 services, 51 babies

Eight o'clock: 8 services, 9 babies. **Cop** (1 service, 1 baby; Aug. 14). **Poupin** (7 services, 8 babies; probably most of his were at this hour; those for Feb. 21, March 20[2] & 27, April 3, June 12 & 19 & 26 are entered before catechism entries for those days).

Catechism: 14 services, 20 babies. **Cop** (7 services, 7 babies; Feb. 21, March 20, April 3, June 12 & 26, Nov. 20, Dec. 4). **Bourgoing** (3 services, 5 babies; Jan. 3 & 17, March 27[3]). **Des Gallars** (4 services, 8 babies; Aug. 14[3] & 28, Oct. 23[3], Nov. 27).

Other: 16 services, 22 babies, no times listed. **Poupin** (14 services, 20 babies; Jan. 24, Feb. 14, March 13, April 10, May 29, July 10[2] & 17[2], Sept. 11, Oct. 2 & 30, Nov. 6, Dec. 11 & 18[4] & 25[2]; these are probably at 8 a.m.). **Des Gallars** (1 service, 1 baby; June 19). **Vallier** ministre de Lausanne (1 service, 1 baby; July 31).

1552 La Magdeleine WEEKDAYS TOTAL 100 services, 136 babies

Mondays: 17 services, 23 babies. One service at 6 a.m. or 7 a.m. **Poupin** (8 services, 12 babies; Jan. 25, April 4[2] & 18, June 27, July 11, Aug. 22[2], Oct. 3[3], Nov. 28; alternates weeks with St. André et al.). **St. André** (7 services, 9 babies; Sept. 19 at 6 a.m.; June 6, Aug. 1 & 15[3], Nov. 7 & 14 & 21 no times; alternates with Poupin except Sept. 19,

Nov. 14. St. André and others do Calvin's schedule, opposite Poupin; this holds for the rest of the week). **Fabri** (2 services, 2 babies; Jan. 18 at 7 a.m.; April 11 at 6 a.m.; same schedule as St. André).

Tuesdays: 21 services, 27 babies. One service at 6 a.m. or 7 a.m. **Poupin** (7 services, 8 babies; Jan. 26, Feb. 23, March 8[2], May 3, June 28, Aug. 9, Nov. 29: alternates weeks with St. André et al.). **St. André** (5 services, 8 babies; July 5 & 19[3], Oct. 25, Nov. 15[2] & 22; alternates with Poupin except Nov. 15; Calvin's schedule). **Fabri** (5 services, 7 babies; Feb. 16[3], March 15, April 19 [!] at 7 a.m.; May 17 & 24 at 6 a.m.; same schedule as St. André except April 19, May 17). **Bourgoing** (1 service, 1 baby; Jan. 5). **Calvin** (1 service, 1 baby; Dec. 20). **Chauvet** (2 services, 2 babies; June 21, Sept. 13).

Wednesdays: none

Thursdays: 27[28] services, 34[35] babies. One service at 6 a.m. or 7 a.m. **Poupin** (12 [13] services, 16[17] babies; Jan. 14, Feb. 25[2], March 10, April 7, May 19, June 2 & 16, Aug. 25[2, Nov. 3[55][2] & 17[2], Dec. 1 & 15; alternates with St. André et al.) [**Poupin**. July 27, 1 service, 1 baby, July "27" = 26?][56] **St. André** (6 services, 7 babies; June 9, Aug. 4, Sept. 22, Nov. 10, Dec. 8[2] & 22; alternates with Poupin except Sept. 22; others follow St. André) **Bourgoing** (1 service, 1 baby; March 17). **Cop** (1 service, 1 baby; March 3 at 7 a.m.). **Fabri** (5 services, 6 babies; Jan. 21[2] at 8 a.m.[!]; March 31, April 14 at 7 a.m.; April 28, May 26 at 6 a.m.). **Chauvet** (2 services, 3 babies; June 23[2], Sept. 15).

Fridays: 21 services, 34 babies. One service at 6 a.m. or 7 a.m. **Poupin** (10 services, 13 babies; Jan. 15, Feb. 12, March 11, April 22, Oct. 7 & 21, Nov. 4[2] & 18[2], Dec. 16[57][2] & 30; alternates weeks except Dec. 16 & 30; alternates with St. André et al.). **St. André** (5 services, 12 babies; July 22[2], Aug. 19, Sept. 23[5], Oct. 28, Dec. 23[3]; alternates weeks except Sept. 23; alternates with Poupin). **Bourgoing** (2 services, 3 babies; Jan. 22[2], April 1). **Fabri** (2 services, 4 babies; Feb. 5[2], April 15[2] at 7 a.m.). **Chauvet** (2 services, 2 babies; July 8, Sept. 2). [NB St. André baptizes 5 babies at once.]

Saturdays: 13 services, 17 babies. One service at 6 a.m. or 7 a.m. **Poupin** (6 services, 6 babies; Jan. 16, May 7, June 4, July 23, Nov. 5, Dec. 31; alternates weeks except July 23; alternates with St. André et al.). **St. André** (3 services, 4 babies; Oct. 1, Nov. 26[2], Dec. 24; alternates with Poupin). **Fabri** (2 services, 3 babies; Jan. 23[2] at 8 a.m.[!]; May 28 at 6 a.m.). **Chauvet** (2 services, 4 babies; April 16[2], July 9[2]).

Comment on 1552: 138 services, 187 babies. For the Sundays there are two regular services, the 8 a.m. and catechism. It is probable that Poupin was doing almost all of the sermons at 8 a.m., but since he never gives a time it is difficult to be sure. There is no clear pattern for responsibility for catechism, but it is likely that Cop was the anchor, with Bourgoing and then Des Gallars as his usual alternates, though Poupin also does a fair

---

55   The number "13" is written at the beginning of the entries for Nov., before ones for Nov. 4 and 5.

56   The day of week is not named; July 27 is Wed. but this is probably an error for an entry on Tues. or Thurs.; is it arbitrarily included here on Thurs. Poupin was a very poor bookkeeper.

57   Actual date missing, but "vendredi" written, and it comes between Dec. 11 and 18.

number of baptisms at catechism. There continue to be services at 6 a.m. or 7 a.m. on Mon.-Tues., and Thurs.-Sat. Poupin and Calvin alternate preaching; Poupin does baptisms at his services but Calvin usually does not; his colleagues stand by to do the baptisms on the days when Calvin preaches (their records of baptisms alternate with Poupin's schedule and fit with Calvin's rare baptisms – and sermon dates). St. André is apparently the one most often on call for Calvin though many of the others take turns being available, probably on a weekly basis, e.g., Chauvet does baptisms on Tuesday and Thursday June 21 and 23 and Sept. 13 and 15, and Friday and Saturday July 8 and 9. Fabri does Monday, Thursday and Friday April 11 and 14 and 15. The number of babies has increased very slightly (by 5) since 1551.

1553 La Magdeleine SUNDAYS TOTAL 36 services, 50 babies

Eight o'clock: 5 services, 5 babies. **Fabri** (3 services, 3 babies: March 5 & 19, Oct. 1). **Bourgoing** (1 service, 1 baby; Dec. 17). **Des Gallars** (1 service, 1 baby; April 9, probably morning because entered before Cop's at catechism.)

Catechism: 16 services, 24 babies. **Fabri** (7 services, 8 babies: Jan. 29, March 5 & 12 & 19, May 14[2], June "15" = 11 ["sermon de midi"], Sept. 10; alternates weeks except Jan. 29, March 12, Sept. 10). **Cop** (5 services, 10 babies; March 26[3], April 9, July 30[3], Sept. 24, Dec. 3[2]; alternates weeks). **Bourgoing** (3 services, 5 babies; July 30, Oct. 22, Nov. 26[3, 1+ twin girls]). **Des Gallars** (1 service, 1 baby; June 25).

Other: 15 services, 21 babies, no time listed. **Poupin** (6 services, 9 babies; Feb. 5 & 19, May 28, Aug. 20 [follows St. André's entry], Oct. 29[4], Nov. 12; alternates weeks). **Des Gallars** (3 services, 3 babies; April "22" = 23, May 7, June 18). **Bourgoing** (5 services, 8 babies; Aug. 13 & 27, Oct. 15, Nov. 5[4], Dec. 10). **St. André** (1 service, 1 baby; Aug 20; precedes one by Poupin; it is possible St. André was in the morning and Poupin at catechism, but this is educated guessing based on the fact that Poupin was no longer able to preach.)

1553 La Magdeleine WEEKDAYS TOTAL 101 services, 144 babies

Mondays: 24 services, 33 babies. One service at 6 a.m. or 7 a.m. **Calvin** (1 service, 1 baby: Oct. 9; same schedule as St. André). **St. André** (11 services, 15 babies; Jan. 30, Feb. 13, March 27[2], April 24[2], June 5[2] & 26, July 24, Aug. 28, Oct. 30, Nov. 20, Dec. 4[2]; alternates weeks except June 26, July 24, Oct. 30; same schedule as Calvin). **Fabri** (10 services, 14 babies; Feb. 6, April 3[3] at 7 a.m.; April 17, May 1, Sept. 18 at 6 a.m.; Oct. 2[2], Nov. 27, Dec. 25[2] at 7 a.m.; March 20 at 8 a.m. [!]; May 15 no time; alternates weeks opposite Calvin & St. André). **Chauvet** (1 service, 2 babies: July 3). **Bourgoing** (1 service, 1 baby, Sept. 4; same schedule with Fabri).

Tuesdays: 22 services, 30 babies. One service at 6 a.m. or 7 a.m. **St. André** (10 services, 12 babies; Jan. 31, Feb. 28, March 28, April 25, May 9[3], Aug. 1 & 15, Sept. 26, Oct. 10, Nov. 14; alternates weeks except Nov. 14). **Fabri** (10 services, 14 babies; Feb. 7, March 7 at 7 a.m.; April 4[2] at 8 a.m. [!]; May 2[2, one illegit.] & 16, July 25[2], Aug. 8, Sept. 19 at 6 a.m.; Dec. 12 & 26[2] at 7 a.m.; alternates weeks with St. André). **Bourgoing** (2 services, 4 babies; Sept. 5 & 12[3]; alternates weeks opposite St. André, except Sept. 12).

Wednesdays: none. [58]

Thursdays: 23[24] services, 36[38] babies. One service at 6 a.m. or 7 a.m. **Calvin** (1 service, 2 babies; June 8). **St. André** (10 services, 12 babies; March 2, April 13 & 27, June 22[2], July 6 & 20, Sept. 28, Nov. 16, Dec. 7 & 21[2]; alternates weeks except Nov. 16, on Calvin's schedule). **Des Gallars** (6 services, 7 babies; March 23, April 6, May 18[2], June 1 & & 15 & 29; same schedule as Fabri, opposite Calvin and St. André). **Fabri** (4 services, 10 babies; May 25[2] at 8 a.m.[!]; Sept. 7[2] at 6 a.m.; Oct. 5[3], Dec. 28 [3] at 7 a.m.; alternates weeks except May 25; same schedule as Des Gallars, opposite Calvin and St. André). **Cop** (2 services, 5 babies; Oct. 19[3], Nov. 30[2] at 7 a.m.). **Chauvet** (1 service, 1 baby; March 30). [1 service, 2 babies, no minister named: Oct. 25 =26].

Fridays: 18 services, 25 babies. One service at 6 a.m. or 7 a.m. **St. André** (8 services, 14 babies; Jan. 20, March 17, Aug. 18[3], Sept. 1[2], Oct. 13 & 20[2], Nov. 3[2], Dec. 22[2]; alternates weeks except Oct. 20, Nov. 3; opposite Des Gallars, Fabri, Bourgoing). **Des Gallars** (2 services, 3 babies; March 24[2], May 5; alternates weeks, opposite St. André). **Fabri** (5 services, 5 babies; July 21 [11 written, but set between entries for July 20 and 22], July 28 at 8 a.m.[!]; July 21; same schedule with Des Gallars, opposite others.) **Bourgoing** (2 services, 2 babies; Aug. 11 & 25; alternates weeks opposite St. André). Unnamed minister (1 service, 1 baby; March 31).

Saturdays: 13 services, 18 babies. One service at 6 a.m. or 7 a.m. **St. André** (5 services, 8 babies; March 4[2], July 22[2], Sept. 2[2], Oct. 14, Nov. 4; alternates weeks except Nov. 4, opposite Des Gallars, Fabri, Bourgoing). **Des Gallars** (1 service, 1 baby; April 8; same schedule with Fabri). **Fabri** (4 services, 5 babies; Sept. 9 at 6 a.m.; Oct. 7[2], Dec. 9 & 30 at 7 a.m.; on Dec. 9 "catechisme" written and crossed out; alternates weeks except Dec. 9; opposite St. André). [59] **Bourgoing** (1 service, 1 baby; Aug. 12). **Chauvet** (1 service, 2 babies; Jan. 21). **Poupin** (1 service, 1 baby; Oct. 21).

COMMENT on 1553: TOTALS: 138 services, 194 babies. Sunday services are mid-morning and catechism; there are no dawn or afternoon services. Weekday services are held daily except Wednesdays, with the usual rotation of the "ordinary sermon" at 6 a.m. and 7 a.m., but there are some cases where Fabri appears to have given the wrong time: Mon. March 20 & Tues. April 4 & Thurs. May 25 & Fri. July 28 at 8 a.m. There is only one baptism recorded for Wednesday, by an unnamed person, so it is almost certainly a mistake; this is in keeping with the pattern of 1550-1552, when it appears that there was no service at La Magdeleine on Wednesdays until mid-1555. The number of babies is close to the previous year, only 7 more than in 1552.

On January 6 Poupin was relieved of his weekday services in La Magdeleine but apparently continued to do baptisms especially in St. Pierre though also a few in La Magdeleine. Des Gallars and Fabri took over for Poupin, with Calvin to do the day of prayer service every Wednesday and Fabri to do Calvin's Saturday in La Magdeleine. The outline of baptisms indicates that St. André seems to have done the

---

[58] On Oct. 25, which is a Wed., 1 service, 2 babies, entered, but no minister is named; probably a mistake for a different day so recorded here under Thurs.

[59] Dec. 9 might have been a replacement for Calvin's sermon.

baptisms during Calvin's week. Fabri and Des Gallars were also fairly busy on the days they preached, with Bourgoing taking Des Gallars' place for the second part of the year when the latter was ordered to move to the village of Jussy and Bourgoing to serve in the city. (Des Gallars objected to this change, but was forced to accept it; he was, however, given the month of August to go to France on family business.[60]) Some weeks the assigned substitutes for Poupin appear to have divided the week's work, at least the baptisms (and perhaps the sermons?). Fabri-Des Gallars-Bourgoing were at St. Gervais alternate weeks from those they were at La Magdeleine, thus in effect never having a week off; in St. Gervais they had the weeks beginning Jan. 2, 16, 30 and so forth, while at La Magdeleine they had the weeks beginning Jan. 9, 23, Feb. 6, 20 and so forth. Calvin was preaching the day of prayer service in St. Pierre and there was no Wednesday service at La Magdeleine. It appears that Cop did catechism atLa Magdeleine on the same schedule as his dawn services at St. Pierre, though now he seems to be working with Fabri most of the time, with Bourgoing only rarely present.

1554 La Magdeleine SUNDAYS TOTAL 43 services, 54 babies

Eight o'clock: 13 services, 14 babies. **St. André** (11 services, 12 babies; Jan. 7 & 14, March 11, July 15 (listed before his own catechism service), Aug. 12 & 26, Oct. 14 & 28, Nov. 4 & 25[2], Dec. 9). **Bourgoing** (2 services, 2 babies; Jan. 21; Dec. 16 [probably morning because listed before catechism]).

Catechism: 20 services, 25 babies. **St. André** (5 services, 6 babies; March 11[2], April 15, July 15 & 22, Dec. 2). **Bourgoing** (2 services, 2 babies; Jan. 7, Feb. 25). **Cop** (3 services, 3 babies; Jan. 28, Feb. 18, June 24). **Fabri** (9 services, 13 babies; Feb. 4[2] & 11, April 22, Aug. 5, Sept. 9 & 23, Oct. 21[4], Nov. 18, Dec. 16). 1 service, 1 baby, April 1, no minister named.

Other: 10 services, 15 babies, no times listed. **Poupin** (7 services, 12 babies; April 8, Sept. 30[2], Oct. 7[3] & 28, Nov. 25[2], Dec. 9 & 30[2]). **St. André** (2 services, 2 babies; July 8, Aug. 19[61]). **Fabri** (1 service, 1 baby; Aug. 19).

1554 La Magdeleine WEEKDAYS TOTAL 133 services, 192 babies

Mondays: 24 services, 36 babies. One service at 6 a.m. or 7 a.m. **St. André** (21 services, 31 babies; Jan. 8 & 22[3] & 29, March 5 & 19, May 7[2] & 14 & "22" = 21 ["lundi 22" written], June 4, July 2 & 9, Aug. 6[2] & 13 & 27, Sept. 3, Oct. 1 & 8 & 15[2], Nov. 5[2] & 26[3], Dec. 24[3]). **Fabri** (1 service, 1 baby; June 25 at 8 a.m.[!]). **Calvin** (2 services, 4 babies; Dec. 3 & 17[3]).

Tuesdays: 33 services, 56 babies. One service at 6 a.m. or 7 a.m. **St. André** (23 services, 37 babies; Jan. 9[2] & 16 & 23, Feb. 13[62][3], March 13 & 20[2] & 27, April 17, May 1[3] & 8

60 July 25, 1553. OC 21:547 .

61 Here it appears that two ministers performed baptisms at the same service. Fabri's entry comes after that of St. André and says "audit sermon," though neither gives a time; probably it would be catechism, since more babies were baptized then.

62 "mardi 23" is written, between Feb. 11 and Feb. 16.

& 15 & 22[2], June 5 & 12[2], July 17[2 – 1 illegit. [63]] & 24[2], Aug. 21[4], Sept. 4 & 18[2], Oct. 2 & 23 & 30[64], Dec. 4.) **Bourgoing** (2 services, 2 babies; July 3, Oct. 9). **Fabri** (1 service, 1 baby; June 26 at 8 a.m.[!]). **Calvin** (2 services, 2 babies; June 19, Dec. 18). **Chauvet** (4 services, 12 babies; April 10[2], July 31[3], Aug. 28[6], Sept. 11). **Cop** (1 service, 2 babies; Dec. 11). [NB Chauvet baptizes 6 babies at once!]

Wednesdays: none[65]

Thursdays: 32[33] services, 46[47] babies. One service at 6 a.m. or 7 a.m. **St. André** (22 services, 35 babies; Jan. 4 & 11 & 25, Feb. 22, March 1[3] & 8[2] & 29[2], April 5 & 19 [2], May 3 & 10[66] & 17, July 5[2], Sept. 20, Oct. 4[2] & 18 & 25, Nov. 1 & 29[4], Dec. 6 & 20[2] & 27[3]). **Fabri** (2 services, 2 babies; July 26 at 6 a.m.) [Nov. 14 = 15 at 8 a.m.]. **Calvin** (2 services, 2 babies; June 21, Dec. 13). **Chauvet** (5 services, 6 babies; Jan. 18, Feb. 1, Aug. 2, Oct. 11, Nov. 8[2]). **Cop** (1 service, 1 baby; Sept. 27 at 6 a.m.). 1 service, 1 baby, May 31 at 8 a.m. no name given.

Fridays: 23 services, 29 babies. One service at 6 a.m. or 7 a.m. **St. André** (10 services, 11 babies; Jan. 26 at 7 a.m.; Feb. 16, March 30, April 27[2], May 11,[67] Oct. 5 & 26, Nov. 23, Dec. 7 & 21). **Bourgoing** (1 service, 1 baby; June 22). **Fabri** (8 services, 10 babies; Feb. 23, March 23 at 7 a.m.; April 6 at 8 a.m.[!]; May 4[2], Sept. 7[2] & 21 & 28 at 6 a.m.; Nov. 2 at 8 a.m.[!]). **Chauvet** (4 services, 7 babies; Jan. 19[3], Feb. 2, Aug. 3[2], Oct. 12).

Saturdays: 20 services, 24 babies. One service at 6 a.m. or 7 a.m. **St. André** (9 services, 9 babies; Feb. 3, April 28, May 12 & 26, July 21, Sept. 1 & 15, Oct. 13, Nov. 24). **Bourgoing** (1 service, 1 baby; June 23). **Fabri** (9 services, 13 babies; Jan. 13[3] & 27, Feb. 24, March 10 at 7 a.m.; April 7[2] at 8 a.m.[!]; April 21 at 6 a.m.; May 19, July 14[2] at 8 a.m.[!]; Sept. 22 at 6 a.m.). 1 service, 1 baby, Aug. 25 at 6 a.m. no minister named.

Comment on 1554: 176 services, 246 babies. Sunday still has two services, morning and catechism. Weekdays Monday-Tuesday, Thursday-Saturday at 6 a.m./7 a.m. The number of babies has increased significantly in 1554, when there are 52 more or 26%.

For Sundays, a number of ministers are involved, with St. André as the probable anchor for 8 a.m. and Fabri most often at catechism, with Cop and Bourgoing often at catechism. Poupin may not have been preaching, but he does a number of baptisms, including on days when St. André also did baptisms at 8 a.m., so some of Poupin's may have been at catechism (Oct. 28, Nov. 25, Dec. 9). One day, Aug. 19, St. André and Fabri do baptisms at the same service (i.e., two liturgies? Or two ministers in the same liturgy?). For the weekdays it is probable that St. André was Calvin's main alternate, as well as doing

---

63   Jeanne daughter of Pierre De La Marts and Maurise daughter of Jean Michel, born outside of marriage, was presented by Jean Sabre.

64   "mardi 23" is written, but there is an earlier different entry for the 23rd, also by St. André, and this present entry comes after Oct. 28.

65   Fabri records a baptism on Nov. 14 at 7 a.m. He does not give the day of week, and this is probably a mistake for another day; it is recorded here under Thurs.

66   "jeudi 19" is written but it comes after May 8, in a series of misnumbered entries, before May 15 and 17.

67   "vendredi 20" is written, then 20 corrected to 10, but Friday is the 11[2]. This comes after the "jeudi 19" which should be jeudi 10.

baptisms when Calvin preached. (St. André seems to do most of the baptisms, but he could not have been preaching every week and Calvin certainly was preaching in alternate weeks if not every week, first on Ezekiel, then Job). Fabri has a large role; he was preaching on Saturday in Calvin's week, but also seems to have had responsibility later in the week. Other ministers also take services at different times; e.g., Chauvet seems to have the latter part of the week a number of times (Jan. 18-19, Feb. 1-2, Aug. 2-3, Oct. 11-12).

1555 La Magdeleine SUNDAYS TOTAL 55 services, 88 babies

Eight o'clock: 22 services, 32 babies. **St. André** (12 services, 15 babies; Jan. 6, Feb. 24, March 3[2] & 10 & "30" = 31[2], April 21, May 5 & 19[68], June 9 & 16 [no time but entered before catechism], Aug. 11, Nov. 24[2]). **Bourgoing** (5 services, 9 babies; Aug. 25[3], Sept. 8 & 22[3], Oct. 6, Dec. 15). **Fabri** (1 service, 1 baby; Sept. 15). **Cop** (2 services, 2 babies; Oct. 27, Dec. 8). **Des Gallars** (2 services, 5 babies; Dec. 1[4] & 29).

Catechism: 19 services, 33 babies. **Fabri** (16 services, 27 babies; Jan. "8" = 6[69][2], March 3[3] & 17[2], April 21 & 28, June 16, July 14[2], Aug. 4 & 11[2] & 25, Sept. 22, Oct. 6 & 20, Dec. 1[2] & 8[2] & 29[4]). **St. André** (3 services, 6 babies; Feb. 24[2], March 30[2], Nov. 24[2]).

Afternoon: Part way through the year a service is begun in on Sunday afternoon, finally completing the mandate of the 1541 *Ordinances*. 1 service, 2 babies. **Bourgoing** (Dec. 22 "vespres")

Other: 13 services, 21 babies, no times listed. **Poupin** (11 services, 16 babies; Jan. 27, Feb. 10[3] & 17[3], March 10 & 24[2], April 7, May 5 & 19, June 23, July 7, Aug. 18). **St. André** (1 service, 2 babies; June 30). **Des Gallars** (1 service, 3 babies; Nov. 3).

1555 La Magdeleine WEEKDAYS TOTAL 150 services, 208 babies

Mondays: 25 services, 35 babies. One service at 6 a.m. or 7 a.m. **St. André** (12 services, 21 babies; Jan. 7[2] & 14[2], Feb. 4 & 25, March 4[3], April 15[2], May 13 & 20[3] & 27, June 3[3], July 8, Aug. "lundi 13" = 12). **Calvin** (3 services, 4 babies; March 25, Oct. 21, Dec. 30[70][2]; alternates weeks). **Cop** (2 services, 2 babies; Sept. 2 & 30.) **Fabri** (1 service, 1 baby; March 11 at 6 a.m.[!]). **Chauvet** (3 services, 3 babies; Sept. 9, Dec. 2 & 16; same schedule as Calvin). **Bourgoing** (1 service, 1 baby; Oct. 7). **Des Gallars** (3 services, 3 babies; Oct. 28, Nov. 25, Dec. "lundi 22" = 23[71]; opposite Calvin).

Tuesdays: 32 services, 38 babies. One service at 6 a.m. or 7 a.m. **St. André** (16 services, 19 babies; Jan. 22 & 29, Feb. 5 & 12, March 19[2], May 14 & 21, June 11 & 18 & 25[3],

---

68 This one is listed as "sermon du matin" which usually means dawn, but there is no dawn service at La Magdeleine, and this designation can mean morning as distinguished from catechism or afternoon.

69 Fabri calls this "sermon du midy dit le catechisme" or on April 28 "sermon du midi" or on Sept. 22 "sermon du catechisme."

70 Calvin writes "lundi penultieme 29" but Monday and penultimate are both 30.

71 Throughout this week and also during the previous one, Des Gallars mixed up the date: "lundi 22" = Dec. 23, "mardi 23" = Dec. 24, "jeudi 24" = Thurs. Dec. 26?

July 2 & 9 & 23, Aug. 6 & 20, Nov. "mardi 27" = 26). **Calvin** (1 service, 1 baby; Aug. 27). **Cop** (2 services, 2 babies; April 9 "entre 6 et 7," Oct. 22). **Chauvet** (8 services, 9 babies; March 5, July 30, Sept. 10 & 24[2], Nov. 5, Dec. 3 & 17 & 31). **Bourgoing** (2 services, 2 babies; Sept. 3 & 17). **Des Gallars** (3 services, 5 babies; Oct. 1[3] & 15, Dec. "mardi 23" = 24).

Wednesdays: 9 services, 9 babies. Part way through the year a service is begun on Wednesdays (at 7 a.m. or 8 a.m.) **St. André** (1 service, 1 baby; Nov. 6 at 8 a.m.). **Calvin** (1 service, 1 baby; Sept. 18[72]). **Cop** (2 services, 2 babies; Sept. 11, Oct. 2). **Bourgoing** (2 services, 2 babies; Aug. 21, Nov. 13). **Des Gallars** (3 services, 3 babies; Oct. 16 & 30, Dec. "mardi 18" = Wed. 18).[73] Apparently this service was newly introduced in late summer, because almost all entries are explicitly marked "mercredy."

Thursdays: 40 services, 63 babies. One service at 6 a.m. or 7 a.m. **St. André** (20 services, 26 babies; Jan. 3 & 10 & 17[3], Feb. 14 & 28, March 7[2], April 4 & 18 & 25[2], May 2 & 16 & 23, June 6 & 13 & 27, July 4 & 11[3] & 18 & 25, Aug. 8). **Cop** (2 services, 3 babies; March 14 "entre 6 et 7," Sept. 19[2], no time). **Fabri** (4 services, 6 babies; Feb. 21, Sept. 5 at 6 a.m.; Oct. 10[3] at 7 a.m.; March 28, no time). **Chauvet** (10 services, 18 babies; May 30, Aug. 1 & 15 & 29[4], Sept. 12[2] & 26, Oct. 24[2], Nov. 21, Dec. 5[3] & 19[2]). **Des Gallars** (4 services, 10 babies; Oct. 31, Nov. 28, Dec. 12[2], Dec. "jeudi 24" = 26[74][4]).

Fridays: 23 services, 37 babies. One service at 6 a.m. or 7 a.m. **St. André** (9 services, 13 babies; Jan. 4, March 1[2] & 15[2], April 19[2], May 10[2] & 17 & 24, July 5 & 19). **Calvin** (1 service, 1 baby; Dec. 6[75]). **Cop** (1 service, 1 baby; March 29 "entre 6 et 7").

---

[72] This entry presents some problems. Calvin was preaching on this day, and usually he preached at St. Pierre on Wednesdays, for the second service of the day of prayer. He would not preach in one place and do a baptism in another; if the parents wanted Calvin to baptize the baby in their parish of La Magdeleine, they could come on another day that week, when Calvin would be preaching at La Magdeleine. The entries are clearly written: Bourgoing on "mardi 17," Calvin on "mercredi 18," and Cop on "jeudi 19." But this seems puzzling, if not mistaken; a Wednesday service at La Magdeleine was authorized in June 1555, and baptisms begin by Aug. 21, but considering all Calvin's other baptisms on Wed., e.g., the previous week on Sept. 11 at St. Pierre, it would be more than a little odd if he preached at La Magdeleine on this particular Wed. (and there is a sermon on Deut. recorded for Sept. 18). OC 21:614 actually calls this "mardi 18" but neither day nor date is correct. In this period Calvin was doing all the Wed. services in Greater Geneva; perhaps there was some local difficulty which made St. Pierre temporarily not practical? Maybe Calvin's presence at La Magdeleine on a Wed. was considered important as a way to affirm the recently added service?

[73] Usually it is assumed that the day is correct and the date inaccurate, here the reverse seems to be true, because there are entries for Dec. 16 and Dec. 17 by Chauvet, and normally if two ministers do baptisms at the same service the second one indicates that by saying "au mesme sermon" or something similar.

[74] This date presents a problem; it is assumed that the day of the week is correct and the date wrong. Des Gallars may have been preoccupied, for he made a considerable number of errors in December, though colleagues also made a number.

[75] A humorous example of the inaccuracies of the recopied registers is found here. The name of the godfather is clearly written as "Marthe Raymond Chauvet" instead of "Maistre."

Fabri (6 services, 10 babies; Jan. 11 at 7 a.m.; March 8[4], May 3 & 31[2], June 28, Aug. 9 at 6 a.m.). **Chauvet** (3 services, 5 babies; Oct. 25[3], Nov. 22, Dec. 20). **Des Gallars** (3 services, 7 babies; Oct. 4[2] & 18, Dec. 13[4]).

<u>Saturdays:</u> 21 services, 26 babies. One service at 6 a.m. or 7 a.m. **St. André** (7 services, 8 babies; Jan. 5 & 19, Feb. 2 & 16, April 13, June 15[2] & 22). **Fabri** (11 services, 15 babies; Jan. 12 & 26 at 7 a.m.; March 9[2], April 20[2], Aug. 24, Sept. 21 at 6 a.m.; Feb. 9 & 23, May 18, June 1[3], Aug. 10, no times). **Chauvet** (2 services, 2 babies; Oct. 12 & 26). **Des Gallars** (1 service, 1 baby; Nov. 23).

<u>COMMENT</u> on 1555: TOTAL 205 services, 296 babies. Until mid-year, Sundays continued to have two services, the main morning one and catechism. In June the council requested and the ministers agreed that there would be a service in the afternoon on Sundays and one on Wednesdays,[76] provided another minister was hired.[77] Thus by the latter part of 1555 there were three services on Sundays, and baptisms were beginning to be performed on Sunday afternoons (and the first weddings on Sundays). There are baptisms at all three services, with catechism the most popular time, the afternoon the least so. The first part of the year the weekdays had continued the usual pattern of services on Mon.-Tues., Thurs.- Sat., rotating between 6 a.m. and 7 a.m. according to the season. When the new Wed. service was added it was apparently set at 7 a.m. or 8 a.m., the time of the second (later) Wed. services in the other parishes and by Aug. 21 the first baptism on Wednesday is recorded, and others follow. The number of babies continues to rise at a significant rate; there are 50 more in 1555 than the previous year. These statistics demonstrate that the sharp rise in population which begins in the mid-1550s was first evident in this parish beginning several years before it became visible elsewhere (and contributing to the need for the new parish of St. Germain).

The organization of ministers continued to be linked with that of St. Pierre, though now with some differences. St. André was the anchor for Sunday mornings and probably Calvin's alternate on weekdays, although he also did baptisms when Calvin preached. Later in the year, apparently others like Chauvet became the ones to do the baptisms when Calvin preached. Calvin's one baptism on a Wed. is a week when he was not preaching but

---

76 Records of Sunday marriages at La Magdeleine begin on 22 Sept. 1555 and are labeled "afternoon" by 1556; since the dawn and afternoon services were the only Sunday times at which weddings were performed, it must indicate that the Sunday afternoon services were instituted following the council's order. A Wednesday service was added – in addition to the one which was supposed to be at La Magdeleine and was in fact at St. Pierre, so that now La Magdeleine had a service on Wed.

77 The Sunday service in question here is at dawn (the language indicates this and there already was one at 8 a.m.), but there does not appear to be any trace of such a thing actually being established. The question of Wednesday is less clear. Technically there was already one service on Wednesday but it was actually being preached at St. Pierre; the present instruction is a plan to add another Wednesday sermon in this part of the city, in addition to the two at St. Pierre (dawn and 7 a.m. or 8 a.m.). This would give La Magdeleine a service on every weekday, with the Wednesday one at a later hour in accord with the day of prayer practice. That time would fit with the instruction to Baduel on April 13, 1556, to give his trial sermon at La Magdeleine at 8 a.m. on the 15th (assuming the church would be occupied at 7 a.m.).

he was preaching that day (because he was doing every Wed. to cover day of prayer while Poupin ill). Fabri seems to have been responsible for catechism at La Magdeleine at times when he was not doing this at St. Gervais. (Apparently those were days when Chauvet did the St. Gervais catechism?)

1557 La Magdeleine SUNDAYS TOTAL 53 services, 81 babies

Eight o'clock: 19 services, 23 babies. **Bourgoing** (15 services, 18 babies; Jan. 10 & 24 & 31, Feb. 7, March 7[2] & 14, May 9 & 30[2], June 13 & 27, Aug. 8 & 22 [no time but before catechism entry], Sept. 19[2], Oct. 17, Nov. 28, Dec. 5; alternates weeks except Jan. 31, March 14, May 9, Dec. 5). **Chauvet** (1 service, 1 baby; Dec. 5). **Enoc** (3 services, 4 babies; Sept. 26, Nov. 14[2] & 28 [probably 8 because before catechism]). (Chauvet and Enoc on opposite schedule from Bourgoing)

Catechism: 23 services, 46 babies. **Bourgoing** (8 services, 17 babies; Jan. 10[3] & 17 [3] & 24[3] & 31[2], Feb. 21 & 28[3], May 16 & 23; Jan. almost same as 8 a.m.). **Cop** (7 services, 12 babies; April 4, Sept. 19, Oct. 17[4] & 31, Nov. 14 & 28, Dec. 12[3]; alternates weeks except April 4; same as Bourgoing's 8 a.m.). **Macar** (5 services, 9 babies; Aug. 15 & 22[2], Sept. 12[2] & 26[3], Nov. 21; alternates weeks except Aug. 22; opposite Bourgoing's 8 a.m. most of the time). **Des Gallars** (2 services, 4 babies; Jan. 3[2], Feb. 7 [2]). **Colladon** (1 service, 4 babies: Dec. 5).

Afternoon: 5 services, 5 babies. **Bourgoing** (4 services, 4 babies; July 11, Aug. 22, Sept. 5, Oct. 31; alternates weeks, same schedule as 8 a.m.). **Des Gallars** (1 service, 1 baby; Jan. 31 at 2 p.m.).

Other: 6 services, 7 babies, no times listed. **Des Gallars** (4 services, 4 babies; Feb. 14, March 21 & 28, July 4 – either catechism or 3 p.m.). **Cop** (1 service, 1 baby; Oct. 3). **Colladon** (1 service, 2 babies, Dec. 19).

1557 La Magdeleine WEEKDAYS TOTAL 169 services, 243 babies

Mondays: 25 services, 35 babies. One service at 6 a.m. or 7 a.m. **Calvin** (1 service, 1 baby; Sept. 6). **Des Gallars** (9 services, 12 babies; Feb. 1 & 15, March 1, April 12 & 26 [2], May 3[2], June 21, July 5 & 19[2=twins]; alternates weeks except May 3; same schedule as Bourgoing). **Bourgoing** (4 services, 4 babies; Oct. 11, Nov. 8, Dec. 6 & 20; alternates weeks, same schedule as Des Gallars). **Macar** (5 services, 8 babies; Jan. 25 [2], May 24[2], July 26, Nov. 15[2] & 29; alternates weeks except May 24; opposite from Des Gallars). **Enoc** (3 services, 6 babies; March 22, April 5[3] & 19[2]; alternates weeks, same schedule as Calvin/ Macar). **Dupont** (2 services, 3 babies; Sept. 20[2], Dec. 27; alternates weeks, same schedule as Calvin/Macar). **Chauvet** (1 service, 1 baby; June 14; same schedule as Calvin/ Macar).

Tuesdays: 31 services, 47 babies. One service at 6 a.m. or 7 a.m. **Des Gallars** (8 services, 13 babies; Jan. 5[3] & 19, Feb. 16, March 2[2] & 30, April 13[2] & 27[2], May 25; alternates weeks, opposite Enoc). **Bourgoing** (4 services, 6 babies; Oct. 12 & 26 [2], Dec. 7 & 21[2]; alternates weeks, same as Des Gallars, opposite Macar). **Macar** (4 services, 6 babies; June 1, Oct. 19, Nov. 2[3] & 30; alternates weeks, same as Enoc, opposite Bourgoing). **Enoc** (9 services, 14 babies; Jan. 26, Feb. 9[2] & 23[2], March 9[3], April 6[2] & 20, May 18, June 15[illegit] & 29; alternates weeks, same as Macar, opposite

Des Gallars). **Dupont** (4 services, 5 babies; Sept. 21, Oct. 5, Dec. 14 & 28[2]; alternates weeks, same as Macar, oppposite Bourgoing). **Chauvet** (1 service, 2 babies; Sept. 7; Macar's schedule). 1 service, 1 baby; Nov. 16, minister not named.

Wednesdays: 31 services, 37 babies. *One service probably at 6 a.m. or 7 a.m.* **Bourgoing** (12 services, 15 babies; Jan. 6[2] & 27, March 3 & 17 & 24[2] & 31, May 5, June 2, July 7[2] & 14 & 28, Sept. 1; no clear pattern.[78] **Des Gallars** (1 service, 1 baby; April 28). **Macar** (5 services, 7 babies; Feb. 10 & 17, May 19[2], June 23, Aug. 18 [2]). **Enoc** (2 services, 2 babies; Jan. 13, Oct. 27). **Colladon** (5 services, 6 babies; Sept. 15 & 29, Nov. 10, Dec. 8[2] & 22; alternates weeks opposite Cop and Morel). **Cop** (2 services, 2 babies; Aug. 25, Oct. 20; alternates weeks, same as Morel, opposite Colladon). **Morel** (3 services, 3 babies; Nov. 3 & 17, Dec. 1; alternates weeks, same as Cop, opposite Colladon). **Chauvet** (1 service, 1 baby; Sept. 8 at 7 a.m.).

Thursdays: 33 services, 58 babies. One service 6 a.m. or 7 a.m. **Des Gallars** (9 services, 19 babies; Jan. 7[2] & 21[3], Feb. 18[2], March 4[2] & 18, April 15, May 27, July 22[4], Aug. 5[3]; alternates weeks, same schedule as Bourgoing). **Bourgoing** (5 services, 7 babies; Aug. "29" = 19, Sept. 30[2], Oct. 14, Nov. 25[2=twins], Dec. 9; alternates weeks, follows Des Gallars' schedule). **Macar** (8 services, 12 babies; Jan. 28[2], March 25, April 22[2], June 3, June 18 ["jeudy"] = 17, July 15[2], Sept. 23[2], Dec. 2; alternates weeks, opposite Des Gallars & Bourgoing). **Enoc** (3 services, 6 babies; Jan. 14[2], Feb. 11 [2], March "10" = 11[2]; alternates weeks, follows Macar's schedule opposite Des Gallars). **Dupont** (6 services, 12 babies; Aug. 12[2], Sept. 9, Oct. 21[4], Nov. 4 & 18[79][2], Dec. 16[2]; alternates weeks, follows Macar & Enoc, opposite Bourgoing). **Colladon** (1 service, 1 baby; Dec. 30). **Morel** (1 service, 1 baby: Nov. 18).

Fridays: 31 services, 41 babies. One service 6 a.m. or 7 a.m. **Calvin** (1 service, 2 babies; Jan. 29). **Des Gallars** (9 services, 11 babies; Jan. 22, Feb. 19[3], March 5, April 2 & 16 & 30, May 28,[80] July 9 & 23; alternates weeks). **Bourgoing** (3 services, 4 babies; Aug. 20, Oct. 1 & 15[2]; alternates weeks, follows Des Gallars). **Macar** (4 services, 5 babies; Feb. 12, Oct. 8 & 22, Dec. 3[2]; alternates weeks, opposite Des Gallars & Bourgoing). **Enoc** (7 services, 11 babies; Jan. 1[5], March 12 & 26, May 7 & 21, June 4, July 2; alternates weeks, follows Macar, opposite Des Gallars). **Dupont** (6 services, 7 babies; Dec. 17 "at 8 a.m." [!]; Aug. 13, Sept. "19" = 10, Nov. 5 & 19[2], Dec. 31; alternates weeks, follows Macar, opposite Bourgoing). **Morel** (1 service, 1 baby; Nov. 13). [On 1 Jan. Enoc baptized five babies at once.]

---

[78] In July the Company of Pastors assigned Bourgoing to do the Wednesday services at La Magdeleine, probably a continuation of his earlier work during the year. However, this was soon to change, because when Des Gallars left for France on Aug. 16, Bourgoing replaced him. RCP 2, pp. 77-78.

[79] On Nov. 18 there is one entry by Morel followed by two by Dupont, another instance of two baptismal actions by different ministers in sequence after the same service. It seems very unlikely that there were two services, so one must wonder if two ministers participated in the same service?

[80] This baby was illegitimate, born to a woman staying at the hospital who had not yet named the father; the baby's godfather was the hospitalier, Jean Colondaz.

Saturdays: 18 services, 25 babies. One service at 6 a.m. or 7 a.m. **Des Gallars** (2 services, 3 babies; April 3, July 24[2]: alternates weeks, same schedule as Bourgoing). **Bourgoing** (4 services, 5 babies; March 20, Aug. 21, Nov. 27, Dec. 25[2]; alternates weeks, on Des Gallars' schedule, opposite Macar, Enoc, Dupont). **Macar** (1 service, 1 baby; July 31). **Enoc** (8 services, 12 babies; Jan. 2 & 16, Feb. 13 & 27[2], March 13[2], April 10[2], June 5, July 3[2]; alternates weeks, follows Macar, opposite Des Gallars/ Bourgoing). **Dupont** (2 services, 2 babies; Sept. 11 & 25; alternates weeks, follows Macar, opposite Des Gallars/ Bourgoing). **St. André** (1 service, 2 babies: Jan. 30).

COMMENT on 1557 Total services 222, total babies 324. Since mid-1555 there have been three services on Sundays. There are baptisms at all three, with catechism the most popular time, Sunday afternoon the least so. The number of babies is continuing to increase but not quite as much: 29 for this year; this is consistent with the fact that the new parish of St. Germain was opened this year, easing the load for both St. Pierre and La Magdeleine.

When making their preaching assignments on July 23, 1557, the ministers had agreed that Calvin and Des Gallars would be the regular weekday preachers at La Magdeleine in alternate weeks.[81] This schedule is borne out by the records of Des Gallars' baptisms, which occur in alternate weeks, different from the one when Calvin baptized (Calvin on Jan. 29 is off-rhythm with Des Gallars). In fact, this pattern was not new; it held true at least from the beginning of the year. However, it was soon to change, because on Aug. 16 Des Gallars left for France to serve the church in Paris. The baptismal records indicate that Bourgoing took up Des Gallars' work in the week opposite Calvin's preaching. Throughout the year, however, Calvin did very few baptisms; when he was preaching, other ministers stood by to do the baptisms: Macar and Enoc in the first half of the year, and Macar and Dupont later in the year. Evidently at times Enoc and Macar did the baptisms on alternate days in the same week, though Macar and Dupont apparently took the first half or the second half of the week. According to the Company's plan, Bourgoing was assigned to do the Sunday 8 a.m. service and catechism at La Magdeleine, and also the regular service on Wednesday when Calvin went across to St. Pierre for the day of prayer service, but evidently Bourgoing was considered the logical person to fill out Des Gallars' service opposite Calvin. As for Sunday catechism: it appears that Cop still does it on the same schedule as his dawn service at St. Pierre. The Sunday morning service is apparently covered by Bourgoing [all the time?] and [afternoon also?].

1559 La Magdeleine SUNDAYS TOTAL 61 services, 90 babies.

Eight o'clock: 15 services, 25 babies. **Des Gallars** (8 services, 12 babies; July 9, Aug. 13, Oct. 22[3] & 29, Nov. 5 & 26[3], Dec. 3 & 17 [several of these are not marked with times but are entered before catechism entries by Des Gallars himself]; alternates weeks except July 9, Oct. 26, Nov. 26). **Macar** (2 services, 2 babies; Feb. 5, July 23; alternates weeks). **Enoc** (1 service, 5 babies; Jan. 8). **Cop** (2 services, 3 babies; Jan. 29,

---

[81]   RCP II, pp. 77-78.

May 21[2]; alternates weeks). **Viret** (1 service, 2 babies; June 11). **Colladon** (1 service, 1 baby; June 25). [NB Enoc baptized 5 babies at once.]

Catechism: 25 services, 40 babies. **Des Gallars** (8 services, 18 babies; July 9, Aug. 13 [3], Oct. 29[2], Nov. "20" = 19[4] & 26[3], Dec. 3[3] & "11" = 10 & 31). **Bourgoing** (5 services, 6 babies; April 9 & 16, June 11 & 25, Oct. 22[2]). **Cop** (5 services, 7 babies; Jan. 22[2], Feb. 19, April 2[2], Aug. 6, Oct. 15). **Colladon** (4 services, 5 babies; Jan. 8 & 15 & 29[2], Feb. 12). **Macar** (1 service, 1 baby; March 12). **Enoc** (2 services, 3 babies; July 23, Nov. 5[2]).

Afternoon: 8 services, 9 babies. **Enoc** (1 service, 1 baby; Jan. 22). **Cop** (2 services, 3 babies; June 11, Oct. 29[2]). **Colladon** (3 services, 3 babies; April 2, Aug. 27, Sept. 10). **Morel** (2 services, 2 babies; Nov. "20" = 19, Dec. 31 [entry given after catechism by Des Gallars]).

Other: 13 services, 16 babies, no times listed. **Des Gallars** (6 services, 9 babies; Feb. 26, March 19, May 7[3], Aug. 20, Sept. 10[2] & 24). **Enoc** (1 service, 2 babies; Jan. 1). **Colladon** (2 services, 2 babies; July 2 & 16). **Beza** (1 service, 1 baby; May 28). **Bourgoing** (1 service, 2 babies; July 30). **Viret** (2 services, 2 babies; June 18 & 20). [82]

1559 La Magdeleine WEEKDAYS TOTAL 155 services, 232 babies.

Mondays: 21 services, 32 babies. One service at 6 a.m. or 7 a.m. **Des Gallars** (4 services, 7 babies; Jan. 30, Feb. 13[3], April 10[2] & 24; alternates weeks opposite Macar first half of year). **Bourgoing** (7 services, 7 babies; Jan. 16, July 24, Aug. 7, Sept. 4 & 18, Nov. 27, Dec. 25; alternates weeks opposite Macar, changes weeks mid-June). **Macar** (9 services, 16 babies; Feb. 6[3], March 20[2], May 15[3] & 29, July 17, Aug. 28[2], Nov. 6[2] & 20, Dec. 18; alternates weeks opposite Des Gallars & Bourgoing, changes weeks mid-June). 1 service, 2 babies; April 3, no minister named.

Tuesdays: 24 services, 36 babies. One service (6 a.m. or 7 a.m.) **Des Gallars** (2 services, 2 babies; March 14 & 28; alternates weeks opposite Macar). **Bourgoing** (7 services, 9 babies; July 25[2], Sept. 19, Oct. 3, Nov. 14 & 28[2], Dec. 12 & 26; alternates weeks opposite Macar). **Macar** (14 services, 23 babies; Jan. 24, Feb. 7[4] & 21, March 21, April 4, May 16 & 30[3], July 18, Aug. 15 & 29[4], Sept. 12[2] & 26, Nov. 21, Dec. 5; alternates weeks opposite Des Gallars & Bourgoing, changes mid-June). **Cop** (1 service, 2 babies; May 23).

Wednesdays: 33 services, 54 babies. One service (7 a.m. or 8 a.m.); beginning late in the year an additional service at dawn was added. On Dec. 20 Colladon does a service at 5 a.m. and Des Gallars at 8 a.m.

Dawn: 1 service, 1 baby +? **Colladon** (1 service, 1 baby; Dec. 20 at 5 a.m.) A second, dawn service on Wed. was introduced in later 1559 until September 1560 when the Wednesday schedule appears to have returned to the original plan (one service at 6 or 7 a.m. like all the other days). [83]

Later service: 32 services, 53 babies. **Cop** (5 services, 8 babies; Jan. 11[2], Feb. 8[2], March 15, April 5, May 17[2]; alternates weeks except March 15; opposite Colladon, same

---

82   These are recorded in marriage records ; on the 20th the father is the godfather.

83   It is possible that some of the other baptisms might have been at dawn, but for a newly instituted service the minister would probably have marked the time.

schedule as Macar). **Colladon** (2 services, 3 babies: Jan. 4[2] at 8 a.m.; Oct. 25 no time given). **Des Gallars** (4 services, 6 babies; Dec. 20 at 8 a.m.; March 8, April 19[2], Dec. 13 [2] no times given). **Bourgoing** (11 services, 19 babies; Feb. 15[2], March 1, May 24, June 7, Aug. 9, Sept. 6[2] & 20[2], Oct. 4[3] & 18[2], Nov. 1 & 29[3]; alternates weeks, changes weeks mid-June; opposite Macar). **Macar** (6 services, 10 babies; July 5[3], Aug. 2 & 30[2], Sept. 13[2], Nov. 8 & 15; alternates weeks except Nov. 15; same as Cop, opposite Bourgoing). **Beza** (1 service, 1 baby; Sept. 27). **Morel** (1 service, 1 baby; Dec. 27). **Enoc** (1 service, 3 babies; Feb. 22). **Chauvet** (1 service, 2 babies; Dec. 6).

Thursdays: 24 services, 44 babies. One service at 6 a.m. or 7 a.m. **Des Gallars** (2 services, 6 babies; Feb. 2[2], March 30[4]; alternates weeks, like Bourgoing, opposite Macar). **Bourgoing** (6 services, 13 babies; Aug. 24[2], Sept. 21[2], Oct. 5[2], Nov. 9[3] & 30, Dec. 14[3]; alternates weeks, changes weeks before June 30, opposite Macar). **Macar** (12 services, 19 babies; Jan. 12[3] & 26[2], Feb. 23, March 23, April 6 & 20[3], July 20, Sept. 14 & 28, Oct. 12[2], Nov. 23, Dec. 7[2]; alternates weeks, changes weeks mid-year, opposite Des Gallars and Bourgoing). **Colladon** (1 service, 1 baby; Jan. 19). **Cop** (1 service, 1 baby; Nov. 2). **Viret** (2 services, 4 babies; June 1[2] & 8[2]).

Fridays: 36 services, 46 babies. One service at 6 a.m. or 7 a.m. **Des Gallars** (4 services, 6 babies; Feb. 3[3] & 17, March 3, April 28). **Bourgoing** (10 services, 13 babies; June 30, July 28, Aug. 25, Sept. 22, Oct. 6[2] & 20[2], Nov. 3, Dec. 1 & 15[3] & 29; alternates weeks, changes mid-June, follows Des Gallars, opposite Macar). **Macar** (18 services, 22 babies; Jan. 27[3], Feb. 24, March 10 & 24, April 7, May 5 & 19, June 16[2] & 23, July 7, Aug. 4 & 18, Sept. 15 & 29[2], Oct. 13 & 27, Dec. 8 & 22; alternates weeks, changes by June 23, opposite Des Gallars & Bourgoing). **Viret** (1 service, 2 babies; June 9). **Le Court** (1 service, 1 baby; Jan. 6). **D'Airebaudouze** (1 service, 1 baby; Jan. 20). **Enoc** (1 service, 1 baby; Jan. 20). [D'Airebaudouze and Enoc at same service.]

Saturdays: 17 services, 20 babies. One service at 6 a.m. or 7 a.m. **Des Gallars** (1 service, 2 babies; March 18; with Bourgoing opposite Macar). **Bourgoing** (4 services, 4 babies; July 1 & 15, Sept. 9, Dec. 16; alternates weeks, changes mid-June, with Des Gallars opposite Macar). **Macar** (9 services, 11 babies; Feb. 25[2], April 8[2] & 22, May 6, June 3, Aug. 19, Sept. 2 & 30, Dec. 23; alternates weeks, changes mid-June, opposite Des Gallars & Bourgoing). **Le Court** (1 service, 1 baby; May 27). **Colladon** (1 service, 1 baby; June 24). **Merlin** (1 service, 1 baby; Nov. 4).

COMMENT on 1559: Total services 216, total babies 322. There continue to be only three services on Sundays; catechism may be the most popular time for baptisms, and afternoons the least, though it is not possible to be sure because too many services do not have times. There continues to be one service on each weekday, but starting late in the year there are two services on Wednesdays, and the times have been altered to match the other parishes: rotation for a dawn service, rotation for a later service at 7 a.m. or 8 a.m. The number of baptismal services and babies baptized continues to be higher than in the other parishes, even without a Sunday dawn service. The number of babies is actually almost exactly the same, only 2 fewer than 1557.

The new dawn service on Wednesday appears to be covered by Cop and Colladon, who are also doing some of the catechism services (on days when they have the dawn service and not catechism, at St. Pierre). The main Sunday services morning and afternoon seem to be in the hands of Viret at least from the beginning of March. Usually it appears that several ministers have the chief responsibility for weekday baptisms, in alternation: Macar and Des Gallars in the first part of the year, Macar and Bourgoing in the latter part after Des Gallars went back to France on family business (May 16 permission for leave) [84], but there are many services by many different colleagues. During the first half of the year, St. Pierre had only its three traditional dawn services (Mon.-Wed.-Fri.).

In the first part of the year Calvin was seriously ill and did not preach regularly on weekdays. Although his name does not figure in the baptismal records until June 1 at St. Pierre, Viret had rejoined the Genevan pastoral corps by the beginning of March 1559, when he took Calvin's place; when Calvin returned to preaching in June, the two were opposite each other. This led to larger crowds gathering for the daily service at La Magdeleine to hear the two popular preachers from the earliest days of the reformed church, and in the summer La Magdeleine became too warm because of the crowding. Thus on June 19 it was decreed that the weekday service should move to St. Pierre while it was so hot. In effect, however, this temporary change became permanent; by mid-year St. Pierre had begun to have services all six weekdays at the "ordinary" hour of 6 a.m. or 7 a.m., and that continued at least throughout Calvin's lifetime. When Calvin and Viret moved to preach daily at St. Pierre, it appears that Macar and Bourgoing became the regular weekday preachers at La Magdeleine.

1560-61: On 6 Sept. 1560, Calvin requested that dawn services at La Magdeleine and the weekday ones at St. Germain be temporarily suspended for lack of pastoral personnel, and the council agreed (the only dawn weddings/ baptisms at La Magdeleine are Nov. 1559 to July 1560). In mid-Oct. 1561 the decreasing numbers of people led to closing St. Germain.

1562 La Magdeleine SUNDAYS TOTAL 57 services, 90 babies

Eight o'clock: 13 services, 22 babies. **Chauvet** (6 services, 11 babies; April 5[2], July 26[2], Sept. 20[2], Oct. 18, Nov. 15[3], Dec. 13; alternates weeks opposite D'Airebaudouze). **D'Airebaudouze** (7 services, 11 babies; Feb. 15[2], March 1 & 15, April 12 [2], June 7, Aug. "29" = 30[3], Nov. 22; alternates weeks opposite Chauvet).

Catechism: 20 services, 32 babies. **Chauvet** (12 services, 18 babies; Jan. 25, March 1, April 19[2], May 31[2], July 12 & 26, Aug. 9 & 23, Sept. 20, Oct. 18, Nov. 29[5], Dec. 13; alternates weeks except March 1, opposite D'Airebaudouze, same schedule as his own 8 a.m. baptisms). **D'Airebaudouze** (7 services, 13 babies; Feb. 15[2], March 15[2], April 12[2], June 7[2], July 5[2], Aug. 30, Nov. 22[2=twins]; alternates weeks opposite Chauvet, same schedule as his own 8 a.m. baptisms). **Cop** (1 service, 1 baby; May 3). [NB Chauvet baptizes 5 babies at once.]

Afternoon: 13 services, 14 babies. **Chauvet** (5 services, 5 babies; Feb. 8, Sept. 13, Oct. 11 at 3 p.m., Nov. 22, Dec. 6 at 2 p.m.; alternates weeks opposite D'Airebaudouze except. Feb. 8, also opposite his own 8 a.m. and catechism baptisms). **D'Airebaudouze** (4 services, 4 babies; March 22, May 31, July 26 at 3 p.m., Dec. 13 at 2 p.m.; alternates

84   March 3 & May 16, 1559, OC 21:711 & 715.

weeks opposite Chauvet, also opposite his own 8 a.m. and catechism baptisms). **Cop** (2 services, 3 babies; June 28 at 3 p.m., Dec. 20[2] at 2 p.m.). **Pinault** (1 service, 1 baby; May 10). Colladon (1 service, 1 baby; July 12).

Other: 11 services, 22 babies, no times listed. **Chauvet** (2 services, 3 babies; May 24, June 28[2]). **D'Airebaudouze** (9 services, 19 babies; Jan. 18[2], Feb. 1[2] & 8[2], Aug. 2, Sept. 6[3], Oct. 11[2], Nov. 1[2], Dec. 6 & 20[4]).

1562 La Magdeleine WEEKDAYS TOTAL 112 services, 150 babies

Mondays: 14 services, 20 babies. One service at 6 a.m. or 7 a.m. **Chauvet** (9 services, 12 babies; Jan. 12, Feb. 9 & 23, March 23, July 13, Aug. 10[3], Oct. 5[2] & 19, Dec. 14; alternates weeks opposite D'Airebaudouze). **D'Airebaudouze** (5 services, 8 babies; March 2[2], Aug. 31, Sept. 28, Oct. 26[3], Dec. 21; alternates weeks opposite Chauvet). The minister who does the Sunday 8 a.m. and catechism does the following week's daily services.

Tuesdays: 14 services, 22 babies. One service at 6 a.m. or 7 a.m. **Chauvet** (6 services, 10 babies; April 21[2], June 2, July 28, Sept. 22, Nov. 3[3], Dec. 1[2]; alternates weeks opposite D'Airebaudouze). **D'Airebaudouze** (8 services, 12 babies; Jan. 6, March 17 & 31[2], July 7[2], Aug. 4, Nov. 10 & 24, Dec. 22[3]; alternates weeks opposite Chauvet).

Wednesdays: 35 services, 46 babies. One service probably 8 a.m. **Chauvet** (19 services, 27 babies; Jan. 14[2] & 28, Feb. 11[2], March 25, April 1 & 22, June 17[2], July 15 & 29[2], Aug. 12 & 26, Sept. 9 & 23, Oct. 7, Nov. 4 & 18[3], Dec. 2 & 16 & 30[3]; alternates weeks opposite D'Airebaudouze except April 1). **D'Airebaudouze** (14 services, 17 babies; Jan. 21, Feb. 4 & 18, March 4, April 15, July 22, Aug. 5[2], Sept. 2 & 16 & 30, Oct. 28, Nov. 11[3] & 25, Dec. 23; alternates weeks opposite Chauvet). **Pinault** (2 services, 2 babies; May 13, Dec. 9).

Thursdays: 19 services, 26 babies. One service at 6 a.m. or 7 a.m. **Chauvet** (13 services, 19 babies; Jan. 1[2] & 15[2], Feb. 26, May 21[2], June 4, July 16 & 23, Aug. 27[2], Sept. 10, Nov. 5[2] & 19, Dec. 17 & 24[2]; alternates weeks opposite D'Airebaudouze except July 23, Dec. 24). **D'Airebaudouze** (3 services, 4 babies; Feb. 19, Aug. 6, Nov. 26 [2]; alternates weeks opposite Chauvet). **Pinault** (1 service, 1 baby; May 14). **Duperril** (1 service, 1 baby; Aug. 13). 1 service, 1 baby; Oct. 29, no minister named.

Fridays: 19 services, 24 babies. One service at 6 a.m. or 7 a.m. **Chauvet** (9 services, 12 babies; Jan. 16[2], March 13, April 10 & 24, June 5[2], July 3, Oct. 23, Dec. 4[2] & 18; alternates weeks opposite D'Airebaudouze). **D'Airebaudouze** (7 services, 9 babies; Feb. 20, March 6 & 20, July 24, Aug. 21, Sept. 18[3], Dec. 25; alternates weeks opposite Chauvet). Pinault (1 service, 1 baby; Jay 15). **Maubué** (1 service, 1 baby; June 12). **Colladon** (1 service, 1 baby; Feb. 27).

Saturdays: 11 services, 12 babies. One service at 6 a.m. or 7 a.m. **Chauvet** (2 services, 2 babies; June 6, Oct. 10; alternates weeks opposite D'Airebaudouze). **D'Airebaudouze** (7 services, 8 babies; Jan. 3[2] & 24, Feb. 7, April 18, Aug. 22, Sept. 19, Dec. 26; alternates weeks opposite Chauvet except Jan. 3). **Pinault** (1 service, 1 baby; Feb. 28). 1 service, 1 baby, Aug. 8, no minister named.

COMMENT on 1562 Total 169 services, 240 babies. La Magdeleine has the three Sunday services, and baptisms are performed fairly equally at all, though catechism is probably the most popular (without times for all baptisms it is not possible to be definite). The weekday services continue every day, Monday through Saturday, but there appears to be definitely only one per day. This organization fits the regulations of the 1561 *Ordinances*. If the times followed the tradition and the regulations, they would alternate between 6 a.m. or 7 a.m., according to the season. There is no evidence for Wednesday, but it may have been fixed at 8 a.m. regularly, as in the other parishes and as seems to be the case at La Magdeleine in 1564. The number of babies is significantly lower than in 1557-59; in raw figures it is 84-82, about 25%.

Two ministers have regular responsibility for the whole work at La Magdeleine, in this case, Chauvet and D'Airebaudouze. One does Sunday 8 a.m. and catechism, plus the daily services that week; the other does only the Sunday afternoon service. The next week the responsibilities are reversed. Other ministers do baptisms, of course.

1564 La Magdeleine SUNDAYS 74 services, 114 babies

Eight o'clock: 37 services, 63 babies. **Chauvet** (18 services, 28 babies; Jan. 9, Feb. 6 & 20, March 5[3] & 19[3], April 30, June 11[4], July 9[85] & 23, Aug. 13 & 20[3], Sept. 17, Oct. 1 & 15 & 29, Nov. "16" = 12, Nov. 26, Dec. 10[2]; alternates weeks opposite Des Bordes & Colladon except Aug. 13). **Des Bordes** (10 services, 17 babies; Jan. 2 & 30, Feb. 13[5] & 27, March 12, April 9, May 7[2], June 4, July 16[2] & 30[2]; alternates weeks opposite Chauvet). **Colladon** (9 services, 18 babies; Aug. 27[3], Sept. 10[3] & 24[2], Oct. 8[2], Nov. 5 & 19[2], Dec. 3 & 17[2] & 31[2]; alternates weeks opposite Chauvet). [NB Des Bordes baptizes 5 babies at once.]

Catechism: 25 services, 36 babies. **Chauvet** (11 services, 14 babies; Jan. 23, April 30, May 28, June 11[2], July 23, Aug. 20, Sept. 17[2], Oct. 15[2] & 29, Nov. 12[86] & 26; alternates weeks opposite Des Bordes & Colladon; same schedule as his own 8 a.m.). **Des Bordes** (8 services, 12 babies; Jan. 2 & 16[2], March 12, April 9[2] & 23[3], May 7, July 2 & 30; alternates weeks opposite Chauvet, same schedule as his own 8 a.m.). **Colladon** (4 services, 4 babies; Sept. 24, Nov. 5 & 19, Dec. 3; alternates weeks opposite Chauvet, same schedule as his own 8 a.m.). **Enoc** (1 service, 5 babies; Dec. 10). **Maubué** (1 service, 1 baby; Dec. 31). [NB Enoc baptizes 5 babies at once.]

Afternoon: 10 services, 11 babies. **Chauvet** (3 services, 3 babies; May 21, Nov. 19, Dec. 17; alternates weeks opposite Des Bordes & Colladon, different schedule from his 8 a.m. and catechism). **Des Bordes** (4 services, 5 babies; April 2[2] & 30, May 14, July 9; alternates weeks opposite Chauvet, different schedule from his own 8 a.m. and catechism). **Colladon** (2 services, 2 babies; Oct. 1, Dec. 10; alternates weeks opposite Chauvet, different schedule from his own 8 a.m. and catechism). **Cop** (1 service, 1 baby; July 30).

Other: 2 services, 4 babies, no times listed. **Colladon** (Sept. 3[3], Dec. 24; the alternation schedule suggests these are afternoon services).

---

85   He writes "9 a.m." but all the other entries say 8 a.m.

86   He writes "ce mesme" on the "16" when he apparently means Nov. 12 because there would be no catechism on the 16th (a weekday), and Colladon does catechism on Nov. 5 and 19. The entry after Chauvet's is Colladon's clearly marked for Sun. Nov. 19.

1564: La Magdeleine WEEKDAYS 112 services, 146 babies

Mondays: 17 services, 20 babies. One service at 6 a.m. or 7 a.m. **Chauvet** (8 services, 11 babies; Jan. 24, Feb. 7, April 17, June 26, July 10[2], Aug. 7, Nov. 27, Dec. 25[3]; alternates weeks opposite Des Bordes & Colladon). **Des Bordes** (6 services, 6 babies; Jan. 31, March 13, April 10, June 19, July 3 & 31; alternates weeks opposite Chauvet). **Colladon** (3 services, 3 babies; Sept. 25, Nov. 6, Dec. 18; alternates week opposite Chauvet).

Tuesdays: 19 services, 27 babies. One service at 6 a.m. or 7 a.m. **Chauvet** (13 services, 18 babies; Jan. 11[2] & 25, Feb. 8[2] & 22, April 4 & 18[2], May 2[2] & 16, July 11, Aug. 8 & 22, Sept. 5, Oct. 31[2]; alternates weeks opposite Des Bordes & Colladon). **Des Bordes** (5 services, 6 babies; Feb. 1 & 15, June 6[2], July 4 & 18; alternates weeks opposite Chauvet). **Colladon** (1 service, 3 babies; Nov. 21; alternates weeks opposite Chauvet).

Wednesdays: 28 services, 40 babies. One service 8 a.m. **Chauvet** (12 services, 16 babies; Feb. 9, March 8, May 17[2] & 31, June 14, July 26[2], Aug. 9, Sept. 6[2] & 20[2], Oct. 18, Nov. 1; alternates weeks opposite Des Bordes & Colladon). **Des Bordes** (9 services, 12 babies; Jan. 19[3], Feb. 2 & 16[2], March 1 & 15, April 12, May 24, July 19, Aug. 16 at 8 a.m.; alternates weeks opposite Chauvet). **Colladon** (7 services, 12 babies; Aug. 30, Sept. 13[2] & 27[4], Oct. 11 & 25[2], Nov. 8, Dec. 20; alternates weeks opposite Chauvet).

Thursdays: 19 services, 23 babies. One service at 6 a.m. or 7 a.m. **Chauvet** (10 services, 11 babies; Jan. 13 & 27[2], April 6, May 4 & 18, June 1 & 29, July 27, Sept. 21, Nov. 16). **Des Bordes** (6 services, 8 babies; Feb. 17, March 16 & 30, June 8[3], July 6, Aug. 3; alternates weeks opposite Chauvet). **Colladon** (3 services, 4 babies; Feb. 10[2], Oct. 12 & 26; alternates weeks opposite Chauvet except Feb. 10 [before Colladon took Des Bordes' place]).

Fridays: 19 services, 26 babies. One service at 6 a.m. or 7 a.m. **Chauvet** (8 services, 12 babies; March 24, April 7 & 21[3], May 5[2], July 14, Sept. 8, Oct. 6, Dec. 29[2]; alternates weeks opposite Des Bordes & Colladon). **Des Bordes** (6 services, 7 babies; Jan. 7 & 21, Feb. 4[2] & 18 & 25, June 23; alternates weeks opposite Chauvet except Feb. 25). **Colladon** (5 services, 7 babies; Sept. 1[3, 1+ twins] & 29, Oct. 13, Nov. 10 & 24; alternates weeks opposite Chauvet).

Saturdays: 10 services, 10 babies. One service at 6 a.m. or 7 a.m. **Chauvet** (6 services, 6 babies; Jan. 29, May 20, June 17, Sept. 23, Oct. 7, Dec. 2; alternates weeks opposite Des Bordes & Colladon). **Des Bordes** (2 services, 2 babies; Jan. 8, April 29; alternates weeks opposite Chauvet). **Colladon** (1 service, 1 baby; Sept. 2; alternates weeks opposite Chauvet). **Pinault** (1 service, 1 baby; Jan. 15).

COMMENTS on 1564: Total: 186 services, 260 babies. There are three services on Sundays and one every weekday. It appears that, although there is only one Wednesday service and it is supposed to be at the same hour as the daily service (according to the revised *Ecclesiastical Ordinances* of 1561), it is now being scheduled at 8 a.m. year-round, as at St. Pierre and St. Gervais. The number of babies has increased somewhat in 1564, with 20 more than in 1562.

The two ministers assigned to the parish in the first half of the year, Chauvet and Des Bordes, alternate weeks in the same manner as Chauvet did with D'Airebaudouze in 1562, and from mid-August through the rest of the year Chauvet alternates opposite Colladon in the same pattern. On Sundays this means that the one who does the morning service does the catechism but not the afternoon service, so that apparently preaching at the morning and afternoon services was intended to alternate. On weekdays, each one had a week, alternately; the one who did the Sunday morning service and catechism also took the following week of daily services, while the one who did the Sunday afternoon service was free the following week.

Comments on Difficulties in the Baptismal Registres

All ministers occasionally confuse day of the week and date, and unless there is more evidence in the records which precede and follow the mistaken entry, one is left wondering which is intended.[87] In the early years Fabri and Cop are almost the only ministers who consistently give times of services, later Colladon, Des Bordes, and Gaigneulx are also likely to give the time. It is natural that in the course of their records there should be some errors. Cop is usually the more careful of the first two,[88] while Fabri often makes mistakes, as is evident in the records of all three parishes, but especially La Magdeleine. (Fewer records of Colladon, Gaigneulx, and Des Bordes have been examined, so the basis of comparison is not complete; Colladon appears to make some mistakes, the other two seem in general to be fairly accurate.)

---

[87]   Usually the ministers give only a date, very rarely only a day of the week (e.g., Des Gallars "jeudy" in mid May 1550, St. Gervais, when there are not enough entries on either side to tell whether it is 8 or 15 May). [Here dates are given in the order day-month because the ministers usually write the day of the week and then the date of the month.] Sometimes they give both date and day of the week; usually these are correct but occasionally the two do not agree. Examples: Bourgoing "mercredy 21" Jan. 1550 (St. Pierre, repeated twice for services at dawn and later, but Wed. is 22nd), "31" Aug. 1551 (catechism atLa Magdeleine, but Sun. is 30th), "29 Aug." 1557 (Magdeleine, but evident mistake for 19). Des Gallars "dimenche 28" Nov. 1550 (St. Gervais, but Sunday is 30th), "lundy 20" June 1557 (Magdeleine, but Mon. is 21st), "dimance 20" Nov. 1559 (Magdeleine, but Sun. is 19th), "dimance 11" Dec. 1559 (Magdeleine, but Sun. is 10th). Fabri "22" April 1550 (catechism St. Gervais but Sunday is 20th), "25" Nov. 1551 (catechism St.Gervais, but Sunday is the 22nd). Chauvet "mardy 23" March 1551 (St. Gervais, but Tues. is 24th). St. André "dimenche 5" Jan. 1557 (St. Gervais, but Sun. is 3rd). Macar "jeudy 18" June 1557 (Magdeleine, but Thurs. is 17th); "le dimance 28" Oct. 1559 (St. Pierre, but Sun. is 29). Enoc "mercredy 9" March 1557 (St. Pierre, but Wed. is 10th) and "jeudy 10" March 1557 (Magdeleine, but Thurs. is 11th), "mercredy 23" Sept. 1557 (St. Gervais, but Wed. is 22nd), "vendredi 25" Sept. 1557 (St. Gervais, but Fri. is 24th), "ce jeudy 19" Aug. 1559 (St. Pierre, but Thurs. is 20th), "dimanche 20" Nov. 1559 (St. Gervais, but Sun. is 19th – writes this twice, once without a time, once for catechism), "dimenche 9" Oct. 1562 (St. Gervais, but Sun. is 4th; here Enoc also gets the time wrong for the dawn service, writing 4 a.m. instead of 5 a.m.), "jeudy 14" Feb. 1562 (St. Gervais, but Thurs. is 11th), "mercredy 25" Feb. 1562 (St. Gervais, but Wed. is 24th), "jeudy 10" March 1557 (Magdeleine, but Thurs. is 11th). Gaigneux writes "31" (!) Sept. in 1562 (St. Gervais). D'Airebaudouze "29" Aug. 1562 (Magdeleine for Sunday morning service, but Sun. is 30th). Colladon "dimenche 4 Aug." 1559 (St. Pierre, Sun. is 6th and Cop is doing a baptism at dawn that day, at the time Colladon lists, so this has to be Fri. 4th.) Merlin "lundy 22" March 1559 (St. Gervais, but 22nd is Wed.). Morel "dimance 20" Nov. 1559 (Magdeleine, but Sun. is 19th). Occasionally someone will mark a correction, e.g., for Poupin's entry 5 March 1553 (St. Pierre), where "4" was written and corrected to "5." cf. Calvin's baptisms for "26" Dec. 1550 (where Sunday is 28th), "mercredy 9" 1555; marriages for "dimenche 28" May 1552 (when Sunday is 29th), le "penultiesme de Juilliet" 1552 (afternoon service, when Sunday is 31st), "mardy 6" April 1562 (when 6th is Monday).

[88]   The most significant example is giving 18 Oct. 1551 instead of 17 Oct., the Sunday; above at n.8.

<u>PROBLEM for services at La Magdeleine, 1550-57:</u> There is a peculiarity in the baptismal records at La Magdeleine in the early and mid 1550s, which does not seem easy to fit into any picture of Geneva's regular service times. Between 1550 and 1557, at irregular intervals, there are references to services held at 8 a.m. both in winter and in summer, but none of these are on Wednesdays. All except one entry are given by Jean Fabri. It would seem that this is some kind of error on Fabri's part, but before that can be concluded it is necessary to examine the evidence.

First there are the references to a weekday service at 8 a.m. on days which are not Wednesdays. In 1550-51 the time of a baptismal service is identified by Fabri as 8 a.m. four times for four different days of the week, none of them Wednesdays. Once is Fri. 4 April 1550 at 8 a.m.; a second is Sat. 18 Oct. 1550 at 8 a.m., a third is Tues. 20 Jan. 1551 at 8 a.m., a fourth is Thurs. 22 Jan. 1551 at a.m. This pattern continues – Fabri is one of the rare ministers who regularly gives the times of services, so it is possible to trace his activities fairly well. The examination of Fabri's entries from 1552 until his dismissal in 1556 reveals that there are thirteen entries for 8 a.m., with between three and six per year for 1552, 1553, and 1554, and instances for every day of the week except Wednesday. [89] In 1557 there is a single reference to a service at 8 a.m. by Dupont, on a Friday. This evidence would suggest that there is a second service at La Magdeleine, which in winter immediately follows the regular one, in summer is one hour later.

---

[89] FABRI at La Magdeleine on Weekdays, 1552-56

<u>Mondays</u> Most times are 6 or 7 a.m. (<u>1552</u> 18 Jan., 11 April; <u>1553</u> 6 Feb., 3 April, 17 April, 1 May, 18 Sept., 2 Oct., 27 Nov., 25 Dec.; <u>1555</u> 11 March; <u>1556</u> 18 May).
Two, however, are at 8 a.m. (<u>1553</u> 20 March, <u>1554</u> 25 June).
<u>Tuesdays</u> Most again are at 6 or 7 a.m. (<u>1552</u> 16 Feb., 15 March, 19 April, 17 May, 24 May; <u>1553</u> 7 Feb., 7 March, 2 May, 16 May, 25 July, 8 Aug., 19 Sept., 12 Dec., 26 Dec.).
Two again are at 8 a.m. (<u>1553</u> 4 March, <u>1554</u> 26 June).
<u>Wednesdays</u> Once, 14 Nov. 1554, at 7 a.m.
<u>Thursdays</u> Most again are at 6 or 7 a.m. (<u>1552</u> 31 March, 14 April, 26 May; <u>1553</u> 7 Sept., 5 Oct., 28 Dec.; <u>1554</u> 26 July; <u>1555</u> 5 Sept.).
Two again are at 8 a.m. (<u>1552</u> 21 Jan., <u>1553</u> 25 May).
<u>Fridays</u> Most again are at 6 or 7 a.m. (<u>1552</u> 5 Feb., 15 April, 28 April; <u>1553</u> 8 Sept., 6 Oct., 17 Nov.; <u>1554</u> 26 Jan., 23 Feb., 23 March, 4 May, 7 Sept., 21 Sept., 28 Sept.; <u>1555</u> 11 Jan., 21 Feb., 8 March, 3 May, 31 May, 28 June, 9 Aug., 10 Oct.).
Three again are at 8 a.m. (<u>1553</u> 28 July, <u>1554</u> 6 April, 2 Nov.).
<u>Saturdays</u> Most again are at 6 or 7 a.m. (<u>1553</u> 9 Sept., 7 Oct., 9 Dec., 30 Dec.; <u>1554</u> 13 Jan., 27 Jan., 24 Feb., 10 March, 21 April, 22 Sept.; <u>1555</u> 12 Jan., 26 Jan., 9 March, 20 April, 1 June, 24 Aug., 21 Sept.).
Four again are at 8 a.m. (<u>1552</u> 23 Jan., 28 May, <u>1554</u> 7 April, 14 July).
Totals: 21 and 23 Jan., 28 May <u>1552</u> = 3; 4 March and 20 March, 25 May, 28 July <u>1553</u> = 4; 6 and 7 April, 25 and 26 June, 14 July, 2 Nov. <u>1554</u> = 6. NB that in two cases it is two days in a row and a third time two days apart, as if the writer were not thinking but simply copying himself. NOTE BENE In these same years, there are some entries by Michel Cop. Along with Fabri Cop was one of the few to give times of services on most days when there were multiple services, though he performed fewer baptisms at La Magdeleine than did Fabri. Cop's records all give the times as 6 or 7 a.m. (<u>Tuesday</u> 9 Dec. 1555 "entre 6 et 7"; <u>Thursdays</u> 3 March 1552, 19 Oct. 1553, 30 Nov. 1553, all at 7 a.m.; 27 Sept. 1554 at 6; 14 March 1555 and 29 March "entre 6 et 7").

There is good reason to think that in fact there was no second service at La Magdeleine on any weekday other than Wednesdays, and that only for a brief period in late 1559-1560. Most of the "evidence" is circumstantial but it is quite significant. In 1555 when a service began to be held regularly on Wednesday (in place of the one belonging to La Magdeleine's cycle which was usually held at St. Pierre), the preacher for it had to be specifically assigned. Secondly, the service added @mid-1555 was for the day of prayers, and except for that day, which was special and which was accorded a distinctive place, there are no weekday services in Geneva which begin at 8 a.m. If La Magdeleine were to have two services each day, the second would hardly be at 8 a.m., since this would guarantee the loss of most of the workday morning for anyone who attended it. (When multiple services are held on weekdays at St. Pierre, beginning in 1559, the earlier one is at dawn and the second at 6 a.m. or 7 a.m., except on Wednesdays.) Thirdly, when the Company assigns weekday preachers to La Magdeleine in 1557, only two men are named, the same as for the other parishes which have only one regular service per day except on Wednesdays. For La Magdeleine to have two services every weekday, when no other parish did, is thus extremely unlikely; even with the addition of one or two pastors to the Company, this would require more personnel than appears available. Furthermore, even in 1562, when the full organization of the preaching services was complete, there were never two weekday services per day at La Magdeleine and at that point even the second Wednesday service had been dropped.

Several other pieces of evidence about the use of La Magdeleine suggest that it would have been impossible to have had a regular French service at 8 a.m. Beginning in November 1551, the Italian community was using La Magdeleine was for worship on weekdays at the hour immediately after the "ordinary" (French) service. [90] This "ordinary sermon" was at 6 a.m. or 7 a.m., so the Italian service had to be at 7 a.m. or 8 a.m., and this would make it impossible to have a second French service, at least in winter (the season from which ten of the eighteen entries come). How many weekdays the Italians held services is not clear, but by Nov. 1555 when they began to share a building with the English community, both refugee groups had services on three week days, the Italians on Thursdays-Saturdays, the English on Mondays-Wednesdays. [91] The fact that Fabri lists a service at 8 a.m. on every day of the week except Wednesday indicates that the Italians could have had only that one day, if there had been a second French service at 8 a.m. Another bit of data indicates that La Magdeleine was occasionally used for extraordinary sermons (by candidates for the ministry); on Monday April 13, 1556, Claude Baduel is instructed to preach at La Magdeleine the following Wednesday at 8 a.m., so that the pastors and council members can determine whether his voice is sufficiently strong to be heard in a city church. [92] Furthermore, although the time of the second Wednesday service is not certain, it is clear that after about mid-1555 there was one. However, if there had

---

[90] OC 21:493, 26 Nov. 1551 (RC f102): "Arreste... leur sera donne place au temple de la Magdalenne et l'heure asçavoir incontinent apres le sermon ordinaire que se y faict."

[91] OC 21:620, 25 Nov. 1555 (RC f46): Italians "a l'heure qu'ilz hont acoustume et lesdictz Anglois... à neufz heures..."

[92] OC 21:634, 13 April 1556 (RC f89v): "mecredy prochain en nostre eglise de La Magdeleine à huyct heures du matin..."

been two services on other days of the week before this, it is incomprehensible why there would have been only one on the most important weekday, the day of prayers, and why it would have been necessary to order the addition of one that day in 1555. These years, 1551-57, are exactly the years when Fabri and Dupont recorded baptisms at 8 a.m. for all weekdays except Wednesdays. Unless, then, people were scheduling services one on top of the other, the entries by Fabri and Dupont must either be mistakes or have some other meaning than verifying a second service at La Magdeleine at 8 a.m. on weekdays.

It seems then, that Fabri's times do not mean that La Magdeleine had a second service on regular weekdays in the 1550s. It is not insignificant that these peculiarities are found in the records of La Magdeleine, which were recopied in the 18th century and in which the copyists made a number of errors, including giving the year as 1577 instead of 1557 for a number of months. It is not beyond the bounds of possibility that numbers were mixed up. This is a risky hypothesis, but it seems to fit the overall situation better than the idea of two weekday services every day at a time when no other parish had that, when St. Pierre had weekday services on only three days (despite council demands for more), when La Magdeleine itself had only one on Wednesdays until mid- 1559, and when a second community was using the same building immediately after the "ordinary" sermon.

APPENDIX TWO: MARRIAGE RECORDS

Marriages in the Three Parishes of Geneva
St. Pierre & St. Gervais for Eight Years, 1550, 1551, 1553, 1555, 1557, 1559, 1562, 1564; Magdeleine for Fifteen, 1550-1564

1550 ST. PIERRE SUNDAYS TOTAL 42 services, 55 couples

Dawn: 20 services, 26 couples. Regular rotation 4 a.m. or 5 a.m. **Cop** (10 services, 14 couples; Jan 19[2], Feb. 2 & 16, March 2 & 16 at 5 a.m.; May 11[2], June 8, Aug. 24 at 4 a.m.; Nov. 2, Dec. 14[3][1] at 5 a.m.; alternates weeks opposite Bourgoing, switches weeks @mid-Aug.). **Bourgoing** (8 services, 10 couples; May 18, June 1 & 15[2] & 22, Aug. 17[2] at 4 a.m.; Nov. 9 & 23, Dec. 21 at 5 a.m.; alternates weeks opposite Cop, except June 22; switches weeks @mid-Aug.). **Calvin** (1 service, 1 couple; Sept. 14 "au matin"). 1 service, 1 couple (Jan. 12) minister not named, but it would be Bourgoing's rotation.

Afternoon: 21 services, 27 couples. **Cop** (6 services, 7 couples; Jan. 26 at 2 afternoon; Feb. 23, May 4 & 18, Dec. 7 at 3 afternoon; Dec. 21 at 2 afternoon; alternates weeks opposite Bourgoing, switches weeks @mid-August; same schedule as Calvin. This is opposite his dawn service schedule). **Bourgoing** (12 services, 14 couples; Jan. 5 at 2 afternoon, Feb. 16, March 30, April 27, June 8[3] & 15, July 6, Aug. 3 & 24, Sept. 21, Nov. "26" = 16 & 30; alternates weeks opposite Cop, except June 15, switches weeks @mid-Aug.). **Calvin** (3 services, 6 couples; Feb. 9, July 13[3], Sept. 14[2]).

Other: 1 service, 2 couples no time given, by **Bourgoing** (Aug. 31)[2]

1550 ST. PIERRE WEEKDAYS TOTAL 18 services, 23 couples

Mondays 16 services, 21 couples. All at dawn, regular rotation 4 or 5 a.m. **Cop** (6 services, 9 couples; Jan. 13[2] & 27[2] at 5 a.m.; June 30, Aug. 25[2] at 4 a.m.; Dec. 15 & 29 at 5 a.m.; alternates weeks opposite Bourgoing). **Bourgoing** (7 services, 8 couples; March 3 at 4 a.m.; April 14 & 28, May 26[2], June 9, Aug. 18, Sept. 1 at 4 a.m.; alternates weeks opposite Cop). **Fabri** (2 services, 2 couples; Feb. 24 at 5 a.m.; June 23 at 4 a.m.). **Ecclesia** (1 service, 2 couples; June 16 at 4 a.m.).

Fridays 2 services, 2 couples. **Cop** (Nov. 5 at 5 a.m.); **Bourgoing** (Oct. 31 at 5 a.m.)

---

1   Two couples were married; the third, Robert Estienne and Marguerite du Chemin, had their marriage (contracted in France) "confirmed."

2   A puzzle is the listing for Nov. 2 "du matin 9" by Cop; there were no weddings at the main service, so "9" cannot mean the mid-morning service at 8 a.m./9 a.m. There is already a wedding on Nov. 2 by Cop and one on Nov. 9 by Bourgoing, so this probably does not mean an additional service by Cop on Nov. 9. Given the conundrum, the wedding is noted here but not included in the table.

NOTE: At this time apparently the one who did the dawn service on Sunday also did the weekday dawn services. **COP**. Dawn Sun.-Mon. = Aug. 24 & 25, Dec. 14 & 15. Dawn Sun.-Fri. = Nov. 2 & 5. **BOURGOING**. Dawn Sun.-Mon. = Aug. 17 & 18

1551 ST. PIERRE SUNDAYS TOTAL 45 services, 52 couples.

Dawn: 26 services, 32 couples. Regular rotation 4 a.m. or 5 a.m. **Cop** (15 services, 19 couples; Jan. 11, Feb. 8, March 8 at 5 a.m.; May 31, June 14[2] & 28[2], July 12[2] & 26, Aug. 23, Sept. 13[2] & 20 at 4 a.m.; Nov. 1 & 15 & 29, Dec. 13 at 5 a.m.; alternates weeks opposite Bourgoing except Sept. 13). **Bourgoing** (10 services, 12 couples; Jan. 4, Feb. 15 at 5 a.m.; June 21, July 5, Aug. 16 at 4 a.m.; Oct. 25[3], Nov. 8 & 22, Dec. 6 & 20 at 5 a.m.; alternates weeks opposite Cop). **Des Gallars** (1 service, 1 couple; March 1 at 5 a.m.).

Afternoon: 16 services, 17 couples. **Cop** (9 services, 10 couples; March 15, April 26 [2], June 21, July 19, Aug. 2, Oct. 11 & 25 at 3 afternoon; Nov. 1, Dec. 20 at 2 afternoon; alternates weeks opposite Bourgoing except Nov. 1; these are also opposite his dawn services). **Bourgoing** (6 services, 6 couples; Jan. 25 at 2 afternoon; March 8, April 5, June 28, Sept. 20, Oct. 18 at 3 afternoon; alternates weeks opposite Cop; also opposite his own dawn services). **Calvin** (1 service, 1 couple; June 7).

Other: 3 services, 3 couples, no times listed. **Bourgoing** (April 12 & 19, May 3).

1551 ST. PIERRE WEEKDAYS TOTAL 21 services, 22 couples

Mondays: 14 services, 15 couples. Regular rotation 4 a.m. or 5 a.m. **Cop** (7 services, 7 couples; Feb. 9 at 5 a.m.; April 6, June 15, July 13 & 27, Aug. 10 at 4 a.m.; Oct. 19 at 5 a.m.; alternates weeks opposite Bourgoing). **Bourgoing** (7 services, 8 couples; Jan. 5[2], Feb. 16, March 16 at 5 a.m.; June 8, July 6, Aug. 31, Sept. 28 at 4 a.m.; altnerates weeks opposite Cop).

Wednesdays: 7 services, 7 couples. Regular rotation 4 a.m. or 5 a.m. **Cop** (3 services, 3 couples; Jan. 21 at 5 a.m.; July 1 & 29 at 4 a.m.; alternates weeks opposite Bourgoing except Jan. 21). **Bourgoing** (4 services, 4 couples; Sept. 2 at 4 a.m.; Dec. 9 at 5 a.m.; April 1, May 13 [no time given]; alternates weeks opposite Cop).

Fridays: none.

NOTE: Continues practice that the minister who does the dawn service Sunday also does the weekday dawn services. **COP**. Dawn Sun.-Mon. = Feb. 8 & 9; June 14 & 15; July 12 & 13. Dawn Sun.-Mon.-Wed. = July 26 & 27 & 29. **BOURGOING**. Dawn Sun.-Mon. = Jan. 4 & 5; Feb. 15 & 16.

1553 ST. PIERRE SUNDAYS TOTAL 62 [64] services, 92 [98] couples.

Dawn: 22 services, 37 couples. Regular rotation 4 a.m. or 5 a.m. **Cop** (18 services, 32 couples; Jan. 1[2] & 15[4], Feb. 12[2] & 26, March 26 at 5 a.m.; April 9 & 23, June 4, July 2[3] & 16 & 30, Aug. 27, Sept. 10[2] & 24[2] at 4 a.m.; Nov. 19[4], Dec. 3 & 17 & 31[3] at 5 a.m.; alternates weeks). **St. André** (2 services, 3 couples; April 16, May 14[2] at 4 a.m.; alternates weeks opposite Cop). **Des Gallars** (1 service, 1 couple; March 19 apparently at 5 a.m.). **Poupin** (1 service, 1 couple: June 11 "du matin").

Afternoon: 28 services, 40 couples. **Calvin** (24 services, 35 couples; Jan. 1[2] & 22 & 29[2], Feb. 5 & 12 & 26, March 5[2] & 26, April 9[2] & 30[2], May 7[2] & 14, June 11 & 18,

July 23[2], Aug. 6 & 20[2], Sept. 24[2], Nov. 5[2] & 12[2][3] & 19, Dec. 3 & 10 & 31). **Farel** (1 service, 1 couple; June 4). **St. André** (2 services, 2 couples; May 28, Dec. 17). **Cop** (1 service, 2 couples; Sept. 10).

Other: 12 [14] services, 15 [21] couples no time given. **Poupin** (10 [11] services, 13 [16] couples; Jan. 8[2], Feb. 19, Oct. 15 & 29; also Jan. 22, March 5[3], May 28, July 23, Aug. 20, which were possibly at dawn because these precede entries for afternoon marriages; Sept. 24 follows Calvin's afternoon entry. Also some confusion about two entries in Poupin's hand, one for Calvin on Oct. 22 for three couples, the other for himself the same day, also three couples.). **Calvin** (possibly 1 service, 3 couples; Oct. 22). **Des Gallars** (2 services, 2 couples; March 12, April 30, latter possibly dawn).

1553 ST. PIERRE WEEKDAYS TOTAL 37 services, 44 couples

Mondays: 25 services, 32 couples. Regular rotation 4 a.m. or 5 a.m. **Cop** (10 services, 12 couples; Jan. 9, April 3 at 5 a.m.; May 1 & 15, June 12, Sept. 18 at 4 a.m.; Oct. 2 & 30, Dec. 11 & 25[3] at 5 a.m.; alternates weeks). **Poupin** (13 services, 17 couples; Jan. 16 & 23, Feb. 13 & 27, March 13[2], May "21" = 22[2], June 5[2] & 19[2][4] & 26, July 3, Oct. 9 & 23, Dec. 18). **St. André** (1 service, 1 couple; May 8). **Des Gallars** (1 service, 2 couples; Jan. 2).

Wednesdays: 10 services, 10 couples. Regular rotation 4 a.m. or 5 a.m. **Cop** (4 services, 4 couples; April 5 at 5 a.m.; June 14, Sept. 6 at 4 a.m.; Nov. 1 at 5 a.m.). **Poupin** (5 services, 5 couples; April 26, June 29 = 28, Oct. 25, Nov. 9 = 8, Dec. 20)[5]. **Bourgoing** (1 service, 1 couple; Oct. 4 at 5 a.m.).

Fridays: 2 services, 2 couples. **Poupin** (30 June, 8 Dec.).

NOTE: Now apparently the minister who does the Sunday dawn service does the weekday services in the alternate week; see e.g., Cop for Dec. 3 & 17 & 31 on Sundays, but 11 & 25 on Mondays; Sept. 10 & 24 on Sundays, Sept. 18 on Monday. **COP**: Mon.-Wed. = April 3 & 5, June 12 & 14, Oct. 30 & Nov. 1.

1555 ST. PIERRE SUNDAYS TOTAL 55 services, 103 couples

Dawn: 33 services, 67 couples. Regular rotation 4 a.m. or 5 a.m. **Cop** (18 services, 32 couples; Feb. 10[2], March 10 & 24[6], April 7 at 5 a.m.; April 21[2], May 5 & 19[2], June 16 & 30, July 14, Aug. 11[2], Sept. 8[2] & 22[2] at 4 a.m.; Oct. 6 & 20, Dec. 1[3] & 15 & 29[2] at 5 a.m.; alternates weeks opposite Bourgoing). **Bourgoing** (15 services, 35 couples; Jan. 20[2], Feb. 3 & 17[4], March 3[3] & 17[5], April 28, May 12[3] & 26, June 9 & 23[4], July 7[3] & 21[2], Aug. 4, Oct. 27[2], Nov. 24[2] "du matin"; alternates weeks opposite Cop).

---

3   The entry for Nov. 12 is in Cop's hand, labeled "Calvin"; that for Nov. 19 is not labeled but it is Calvin's hand.

4   Here one couple was married, one (apparently pledged while in Roman lands) had the marriage "ratified."

5   Poupin almost never gives a time, but it is probable that these were dawn services, since weddings were not considered appropriate for the main day of prayer.

Afternoon: 19 services, 29 couples. **Calvin** (17 services, 27 couples; Jan. 6 & 20, Feb. 10[2][6] & 17[3] & 24, March 3, April 28[2], May 19, June 9[3] & 16[4] & 23 & 30[2], July 28, Aug. 4, Sept. 8 & 29, Oct. 14=13). **Cop** (2 services, 2 couples; March 10, April 7 at 3 afternoon).

Other: 3 services, 7 couples, times not listed. **Calvin** (2 services, 3 couples; Aug. 25[2], Nov. 3[7] – probably afternoon). **Des Gallars** (1 service, 4 couples; Aug. 18).

1555 ST. PIERRE WEEKDAYS TOTAL 38 services, 48 couples

Mondays: 29 services, 39 couples. Regular seasonal. **Cop** (11 services, 15 couples; Jan. 7[2], Feb. 4, April 15 [!] at 5 a.m.; May 13[2], June 10[2] & 24[2], July 8, Aug. 19, Sept. 16 at 4 a.m.; Dec. 23 at 5 a.m.; Nov. 11 no time given; alternates weeks opposite Bourgoing). **Bourgoing** (16 services, 22 couples; Jan. 14 & 28, March 11 & 25, April 8, May 6[2] & 20, June 3, July 1[3] & 15 & 29, Sept. 9[2] & 23[2], Nov. 4 & 18[2], Dec. 2 "du matin"; alternates weeks opposite Cop). **D'Airebaudouze** (2 services, 2 couples; Sept. 2 at 4 a.m.; Sept. 30 "matin").

Tuesdays: none

Wednesdays: 7 services, 7 couples. (Apparently) regular rotation 4 a.m. or 5 a.m. It is probable that no marriages were performed at the later service. **Cop** (1 service, 1 couple; May 15 at 4 a.m.). **Bourgoing** (5 services, 5 couples; June 5, July 17, Oct. 23, Dec. 18 "du matin"; Jan. 2 no time). **Colladon** (1 service, 1 couple; Sept. 4 at 4 a.m.).

Thursdays: none

Fridays: 2 services, 2 couples. **Bourgoing** (June 21, Aug. 2 "du matin").

Saturdays: none

NOTE: As in 1553, the minister who does the Sunday dawn does the three weekday dawn services in the alternate week. **COP**. Mon.-Wed. on May 13 & 15. **BOURGOING**. Mon.-Wed. on June 3 & 5, July 15 & 17.

1557 ST. PIERRE SUNDAYS TOTAL 68 services, 122 couples

Dawn: 40 services, 74 couples. Regular rotation 4 a.m. or 5 a.m. **Cop** (17 services, 26 couples; Jan. 10[5] & 24, Feb. 7, March 7 & 21 at 5 a.m.; May 2 & 30, June 13[2] & 27, July 11, Aug. 8[2] at 4 a.m.; Oct. 3 & 17 & 31[2], Nov. 14[2] & 28, Dec. 12[2] at 5 a.m.; alternates weeks opposite Macar). **Macar** (21 services, 45 couples; Jan. 17[5], Feb. 14 & 28, March 14 & 28, April 11[5] at 5 a.m.; April 25, May 9[5] & 23[4], June 20[2], July 4[2] & 18[3], Aug. 1 & 15, Sept. 12 at 4 a.m.; Sept. 26[2], Oct. 24[3], Nov. 7[2] & 21, Dec. 5 & 19 [2] at 5 a.m.; alternates weeks opposite Cop). **Bourgoing** (1 service, 1 couple; Aug. 29 "l'aube du jour"). **Chauvet** (1 service, 2 couples; Jan. 3 at 5 a.m.).

Afternoon: 25 services, 40 couples. **Calvin** (23 services, 37 couples; Jan. 10, Feb. 14[2] & 21, March 21, April 4 & 25[4], May 2[3] & 30, June 13 & 27[3], July 4[2] & 25, Aug. 1 & 8 [3] & 22, Sept. 12, Oct. 17 & 24 & 31[2], Nov. 21[2] & 28, Dec. 5 & 19[2]). **Farel** (1 service, 1 couple; March 14). **Cop** (1 service, 2 couples; Jan. 3 at 2 afternoon).

Other: 3 services, 8 couples, no times listed. All by **Calvin** (Jan. 24[2], May 9[3], Aug. 15[3]), almost certainly afternoon because entered after dawn services.

---

6   This marriage service is entered in the baptismal records, transferred here.

7   In Cop's hand but labeled "Calvin."

1557 ST. PIERRE WEEKDAYS TOTAL 41 services, 55 couples

Mondays: 33 services, 47 couples. Regular rotation 4 a.m. or 5 a.m. **Cop** (15 services, 20 couples; Jan. 4[2] & 18, Feb. 1[2] & 15, March 15 at 5 a.m.; April 26, May 10 & 24, June 7[4] & 21, July 5, Aug. 30 at 4 a.m.; Nov. 8, Dec. 6 & 20 at 5 a.m.; alternates weeks opposite Macar). **Macar** (17 services, 24 couples; Jan. 11 & 25, Feb. 22[3], March 8 & 22, April 5 & 19[2], May 17, June 28, July 12 & 26, Sept. 6[2] & 20[2], Oct. 18, Nov. 15[3] & 29, Dec. 13; alternates weeks opposite Cop). **Colladon** (1 service, 3 couples: July 19 at 4 a.m.).

Wednesdays: 6 services, 6 couples. All except one identified as dawn. **Cop** (2 services, 2 couples; March 31, Dec. 22 at 5 a.m.; alternates weeks opposite Macar). **Macar** (4 services, 4 couples; March 24 at 5 a.m., June 16, Aug. 11 at 4 a.m., Aug. 25 no time given; alternates weeks opposite Cop).

Fridays: 2 services, 2 couples. **Cop** (May 14, June 4 at 4 a.m.).

NOTE: Continues practice that the minister who does Sunday dawn does the weekday dawn services in the alternate week, e.g., compare Cop's records. **COP**: Mon.-Wed. = Dec. 20 & 22; Mon.-Fri. = May 10 & 14. **MACAR**. Mon.-Wed.= March 22 & 24.

1559 ST. PIERRE SUNDAYS TOTAL 58 services, 103 couples

Dawn: 33 services, 66 couples. Regular rotation 4 a.m. or 5 a.m. **Cop** (15 services, 31 couples; Jan. 22, Feb. 5[4] & 19 at 5 a.m.; April 2 & 16[4] & 30[3], May 28[3], June 11[2], July 9[4] & 23, Aug. 6 & 20, Sept. 17[2] at 4 a.m.; Nov. 12[2] & 26 at 5 a.m.; alternates weeks opposite Colladon). **Colladon** (17 services, 30 couples; Jan. 1 & 15 & 29, Feb. 12[3] & 26 at 5 a.m; April 23, May 7[2] & 21[3], June 4[3], July 2[2] & 30, Aug. 13[2] & 27, Sept. 24 at 4 a.m.; Nov. 5[3], Dec. 3[3][8] & 31 at 5 a.m; alternates weeks opposite Cop). **Bourgoing** (1 service, 5 couples; March 12 at l'aube du jour).

Afternoon: 21 services, 31 couples. **Viret** (17 services, 26 couples; March 12 & 19, April 9 & 30, May 7[2] & 28[2], July 9[3] & 30[2], Aug. 6 & 20 & 27, Oct. 1 & 8[3] & "28"=29, Nov. 26, Dec. 3[2] & 10[2] all listed at 3 afternoon, though probably should have been 2 afternoon in Nov.-Dec.). **Calvin** (1 service, 1 couple; Dec. 17[9]). **Cop** (1 service, 1 couple; Jan. 15 at 2 afternoon). **Des Gallars** (2 services, 3 couples; Feb. 12[2] "du soir"; March 5 at 3 afternoon)

Other: 4 services, 6 couples no time given. **Viret** (3 services, 4 couples; July 16[2] & 23, Nov. 5; these probably afternoon.) **Colladon** (1 service, 2 couples; July 16; probably dawn because before Viret).

1559 ST. PIERRE WEEKDAYS TOTAL 55 services, 89 couples

Mondays: 42 services, 74 couples. Regular rotation of seasons; one dawn service at 4 a.m. or 5 a.m. throughout year, but in the summer (by July 3) a second service at the "ordinary" time of 6 a.m. or 7 a.m. had been introduced. Some days there are marriages at both services: July 3 at 4 a.m. by Cop and 6 a.m. by Viret; July 31 at 4 a.m. by Colladon and

---

8   Married two couples, "confirmed conversation" which another couple had in "papauté."

9   Entry in Colladon's hand, but labeled "Calvin."

6 a.m. by Viret; Oct. 16 at 5 a.m. by Colladon and then by Calvin (almost certainly 7 a.m.); Oct. 23 at 5 a.m. by Cop and 7 a.m. by Viret, Nov. 13 at 5 a.m. by Colladon and 7 a.m. by Calvin.

Dawn: 36 services, 67 couples. **Cop** (16 services, 36 couples; Jan. 16 & 30, Feb. 27[2], March 13[3] & 27[7][10], May 8[4], June 19 no times given but evidently dawn; July 3[2] & 17, Aug. 21[2] & 28[3], Sept. 11[2] at 4 a.m.; Oct. 2 & 9[2] & 23[2], Nov. 6[2] at 5 a.m.; alternates weeks opposite Colladon except Aug. 21 & Oct. 2). **Colladon** (19 services, 29 couples; Jan. 23[2], Feb. 20, March 6[2] & 20 at 5 a.m.; April 17, May 1[2] & 15 & 22[2] & 29, June 26[2], July 24, Aug. 14, Sept. 4[3] & 18 at 4 a.m.; Oct. 16[2] & "29" = 30[11], Nov. 13, Dec. 25[3] at 5 a.m.; alternates weeks opposite Cop except May 22 & Aug. 14). **Chauvet** (1 service, 2 couples; July 31 at 4 a.m.)

Later service: 6 services, 7 couples. **Calvin** (2 services, 2 couples; Oct. 16 (probably 7 a.m.), Nov. 13[12] at 7 a.m.; alternates weeks opposite Viret). **Viret** (4 services, 5 couples; July 3 & 31 at 6 a.m.; Oct. 23[2], Nov. 20 at 7 a.m.; alternate weeks opposite Calvin).

Tuesdays: 2 services, 2 couples. No time given, but from other evidence in baptismal records, and the names of the ministers, this is "ordinary" service time, introduced in mid-summer. Each entry is designated by both "mardi" and date, since this was an innovation. **Calvin** (1 service, 1 couple; Dec. 12[13]). **Viret** (1 service, 1 couple; Oct. 24).

Wednesdays: 9 services, 11 couples. Regular rotation of seasons, only dawn service represented here because Calvin discouraged weddings at the main day of prayer service. **Cop** (5 services, 5 couples; Feb. 1 at 5 a.m.; June 7, Sept. 13 & 27 at 4 a.m.; Nov. 22 at 5 a.m.; alternates weeks opposite Colladon). **Colladon** (4 services, 6 couples; Jan. 25 at 5 a.m.; May 17[3], Aug. 9 at 4 a.m.; Dec. 27 at 5 a.m.; alternates weeks opposite Cop).

Thursdays: 1 service, 1 couple. Evidently, like Tuesdays, newly introduced in mid-summer at the "ordinary" time. **Calvin** (Nov. 2).

Fridays: 1 service, 1 couple. **Colladon** (Dec. 29 at 5 a.m.).

Saturdays: none.

NOTE: In mid-summer a second service at the "ordinary" hour is added to the three traditional dawn services. Here continues the practice that the minister who does the Sunday dawn does the alternate weekday dawn services.

1562 ST. PIERRE SUNDAYS TOTAL 36 services, 49 couples

Dawn: 11 services, 13 couples. Regular rotation 4 a.m. or 5 a.m. **Cop** (7 services, 9 couples; April 26, May 10[2], June 21[2], July 5, Aug. 2 at 4 a.m.; Nov. 22, Dec. 20 at 5 a.m.; alternates weeks opposite Colladon). **Colladon** (4 services, 4 couples; May 3, July 26, Sept. 13, Oct. 4 "l'aube du jour"; alternates weeks opposite Cop except Sept. 13).

Afternoon: 23 services, 33 couples. **Merlin** (21 services, 31 couples; Jan. 4[2] & 11[3] at 2 afternoon; Feb. 15, March 1 & 15 & 22[4], April 19 & 26[2], May 10 & 31[2], June 7 &

---

[10] This entry by Cop for 7 couples at one service may hold the record, though on some other occasions there are 6 couples at once.

[11] This entry and the one for Viret for this date are in Colladon's hand.

[12] Entry in Colladon's hand.

[13] Entry not in Calvin's hand..

14[2] & 28, July 5 & 12, Aug. 23 & 30, Oct. 18, Nov. 15 at 3 afternoon; Nov. 22, Dec. 20 [2] at 2 afternoon). **Beza** (2 services, 2 couples; Sept. 13 & 20 at 3 afternoon).

Other: 2 services, 3 couples by **Merlin** (Feb. 1[2] & 8) – probably afternoon.

1562 ST. PIERRE WEEKDAYS TOTAL 30 services, 34 couples

Mondays: 22 services, 26 couples. Regular rotation for two services, 4 a.m. or 5 a.m., 6 a.m. or 7 a.m. Several times services on same day: Feb. 2, Colladon at 5 a.m. and Calvin at 7 a.m.; May 18, Gaigneulx at 4 a.m., Calvin at 6 a.m.; Oct. 19, Cop at 5 a.m., Merlin at 7 a.m.

Dawn: 16 services, 20 couples. **Cop** (7 services, 10 couples; Feb. 9 at 5 a.m.; June 1 & 29, Aug. 10[2] at 4 a.m.; Oct. 5[2] & 19, Dec. 14[2] at 5 a.m.; alternates weeks opposite Colladon). **Colladon** (7 services, 8 couples; Jan. 19[2], April 13, May 25, Aug. 3, Sept. 14, Dec. 21 at "l'aube du jour"; Feb. 2 at 5 a.m.; alternates weeks opposite Cop). **Gaigneulx** (2 services, 2 couples; May 18 at 4 a.m.; June 8 at dawn).

Later service: 6 services, 6 couples. **Calvin** (2 services, 2 couples; Feb. 2 at 7 a.m.; May 18 at 6 a.m.). **Merlin** (4 services, 4 couples; Aug. 17 at 6 a.m.; Oct. 19, Dec. 28 at 7 a.m.; July 20 no time given).

Tuesdays: 3 services, 3 couples. **Cop** (1 service, 1 couple; Oct. 27). **Merlin** (1 service, 1 couple; July 7). **Calvin** (1 service, 1 couple; "ce mardi 6" = April 7 at 6 a.m.).

Wednesdays: [in principle 2 times of services] 1 service, 1 couple, by **Colladon** (July 8) at dawn.

Thursdays: 1 service, 1 couple, by **Cop** (Nov. 26).

Fridays: 3 services, 3 couples. Two times of services. **Cop** (1 service, 1 couple; Sept. 11 at 4 a.m.). **Colladon** (1 service, 1 couple; April 3 [14]). **Merlin** (1 service, 1 couple; Aug. 21 at 6 a.m.).

Saturdays: none.

NOTE: Continues practice of two services with seasonal rotation. Also continues practice that the minister who does the Sunday dawn service does the alternate weekday dawn services.

1564 ST. PIERRE SUNDAYS TOTAL 35 services, 46 couples.

Dawn: 9 services, 9 couples. Regular rotation 4 a.m or 5 a.m. **Cop** (5 services, 5 couples; Jan. 2, Feb. 27 at 5 a.m.; May 7, June 4 & 18 at 4 a.m.; alternate weeks opposite Colladon). **Colladon** (2 services, 2 couples; Feb. 20, April 30 "l'aube du jour"; alternates weeks opposite Cop). **Maubué** (1 service, 1 couple; July 16 "du matin"). **Enoc** (1 service, 1 couple; Nov. 26 at 5 a.m.).

Afternoon: 23 services, 32 couples. **Beza** (6 services, 12 couples; Jan. 2[3] & 9 & 30[2] at 2 a.m.; Feb. 20[2] "du soir" & 27, March 26[3] at 3 afternoon). **Cop** (3 services, 3 couples; April 9 & 30, May 7). **Colladon** (8 services, 10 couples; May 28[2], June 4[2] & 11 & 18 & 25, July 2 & 16, Aug. 13). **Merlin** (5 services, 6 couples; Aug. 27, Sept. 17, Oct. 1 & 8 & 29[2]). **Gaigneulx** (1 service, 1 couple; Dec. 17 at 2 afternoon).

Other: 3 services, 5 couples no time given. **Beza** (1 service, 2 couples; Jan. 23). **Merlin** (2 services, 3 couples; Sept. 24[2], Oct. 15).

---

14   Bride is a woman abandoned 16 years before.

1564 ST. PIERRE WEEKDAYS TOTAL 40 services, 44 couples

Mondays: 32 services, 36 couples. Two services, regular rotatation of seasons for each one. Some days marriages performed at both services: April 3 by Cop at 4 a.m. and Colladon at 6 a.m.; May 15 by Cop at 4 a.m. and Colladon at 6 a.m.; May 22 by Maubué at 4 a.m. and Colladon at 6 a.m.; June 5 by Maubué at 4 a.m. and Beza at 6 a.m.; Sept. 4 by Cop at 4 a.m. and Merlin at 6 a.m.

Dawn: 19 services, 21 couples. **Cop** (10 services, 10 couples; Feb. 21 at 5 a.m.; April 3, May 1 & 15, June 12, July 24, Aug. 7, Sept. 4 at 4 a.m.; Oct. 16 & 30 at 5 a.m.; alternates weeks opposite Colladon.) **Colladon** (3 services, 4 couples: Feb. 14[2], May 8, Nov. 13 "l'aube du jour"; alternate weeks opposite Cop except Nov. 13. **Enoc** (2 services, 2 couples; Dec. 4 & 18 at 5 a.m.). **Maubué** (2 services, 2 couples; May 22, June 5 at 4 a.m.). **Des Bordes** (1 service, 1 couple; Sept. 11 at 4 a.m.). **Jean Hellin** (1 service, 2 couples; May 1 at 4 a.m.).

Later service: 11 services, 13 couples. **Colladon**: (4 services, 6 couples; April 3 & 17, May 15[2] & 29[2] at 6 a.m.) Cop (2 services, 2 couples; Jan. 17, March 20 at 7 a.m.) **Beza** (5 services, 5 couples; March 6 at 7 a.m., June 5 at 6 a.m.; Jan. 24, July 17, Oct. 9 no time given). **Merlin** (2 services, 2 couples; Aug. 21, Sept. 4 at 6 a.m.).

Tuesdays: 4 services, 4 couples. Regular rotation 6 a.m. or 7 a.m. **Beza** (2 services, 2 couples; Jan. 4 at 7 a.m.; May 23 at 6 a.m.). **Colladon** (1 service, 1 couple; March 14). **Des Bordes** (1 service, 1 couples; April 18).

Wednesdays: 2 services, 2 couples. Regular rotation of times, only dawn service represented here. **Cop** (Feb. 23 at 5 a.m.; May 31 at 4 a.m.).

Thursdays: 1 service, 1 couple. **Gaigneulx** (April 6).

Fridays: 1 service, 1 couple. **Cop** (Feb. 25 at 5 a.m.).

Saturdays: none

NOTE: Continues practice that the minister who does Sunday dawn does the alternate weekday dawn services. **COP**. Mon.-Wed.-Fri.= Feb. 21 & 23 & 25.

1550 ST. GERVAIS SUNDAYS TOTAL 10 services, 14 couples

Dawn: 3 services, 3 couples. Regular rotation 4 a.m. or 5 a.m. **Fabri** (3 services, 3 couples; April 13, Sept. 28 at 4 a.m.; Nov. 16 at 5 a.m.).

Afternoon: 6 services, 10 couples. **Calvin** (5 services, 8 couples; April 13 & 20 & 27 [4], June 29, Oct. 5). **Viret** (1 service, 2 couples; Jan. 5).

Other: 1 service, 1 couple, no time listed; by **Calvin** (June 1, probably afternoon).

1550 ST. GERVAIS WEEKDAYS TOTAL 8 services, 9 couples

Mondays: 2 services, 2 couples. No times given, probably "ordinary" 6 a.m. or 7 a.m. **Des Gallars** (Feb. 24, June 9).

Tuesdays 1 service, 1 couple. **Des Gallars** ("mardy 27" = April 29).

Wednesdays: 3 services, 4 couples. Dawn service, probably rotation 4 a.m. or 5 a.m. **Fabri** (2 services, 3 couples; Sept. 10[2] & 17 at 4 a.m.). **Chauvet** (1 service, 1 couple; Dec. 24).

Thursdays: 1 service, 1 couple. **Des Gallars** (Nov. 20).

Fridays: 1 service, 1 couple. **Des Gallars** (Sept. 5).

Saturdays: none

NOTE: There seem to be dawn services only on Sundays and Wednesdays, served by one minister; the regular weekday services are maintained by Chauvet and Des Gallars.

1551 ST. GERVAIS SUNDAYS TOTAL 25 services, 26 couples

Dawn: 10 services, 10 couples. Regular rotation 4 a.m. or 5 a.m. **Fabri** (Jan. 11 & 18, Feb. 8, March 1 & 15 at 5 a.m.; May 3, July 19 at 4 a.m.; Sept. 13[15], Nov. 29, Dec. 20 at 5 a.m.)

Afternoon: 14 services, 15 couples. **Calvin** (12 services, 13 couples; Jan. 4 & 11[2], Feb. 1 & 8, March 15, April 19, May 10, June 21[16], July 5, Sept. 13, Nov. 1, Dec. 6). **Viret** (1 service, 1 couple; June 7). **Chauvet** (1 service, 1 couple; April 26).

Other: 1 service, 1 couple no time given. **Fabri** (May 31, probably dawn).

1551 ST. GERVAIS WEEKDAYS No marriages recorded.

1553 ST. GERVAIS SUNDAYS TOTAL 27 services, 28 couples

Dawn: 13 services, 14 couples. Regular rotation 4 a.m. or 5 a.m. **St. André** (11 services, 12 couples; Jan. 15, Feb. 19 & 26 at 5 a.m.; April 9[2], June 4, July 23 at 4 a.m.; Oct. 8 & 22, Nov. 19, Dec. 3 & 17 at 5 a.m.). **Cop** (1 service, 1 couple; May 14 at 4 a.m.). **Fabri** (1 service, 1 couple; April 16 at 4 a.m.).

Afternoon: 6 services, 6 couples. **Cop** (5 services, 5 couples; Feb. 5 & 19 at 2 afternoon; June 11, Oct. 29, Nov. 12 at 3 afternoon). **Des Gallars** (1 service, 1 couple; April 9).

Other: 8 services, 8 couples no time given. **Poupin** (7 services, 7 couples; Jan. "28" = 29, Feb. 12 & 26, July 16 & 23, Sept. 10, Oct. 8). **Chauvet** (1 service, 1 couple; Oct. 29).

1553 ST. GERVAIS WEEKDAYS TOTAL 9 services, 10 couples

Mondays: 3 services, 4 couples. Probably rotation for "ordinary" 6 a.m. or 7 a.m. **Fabri** (1 service, 1 couple; Sept. 4 at 6 a.m.). **Chauvet** (1 service, 1 couple; April 3). **Poupin** (1 service, 2 couples; Aug. 14).

Tuesdays: none

Wednesdays: 3 services, 3 couples. Regular rotation 4 a.m. or 5 a.m.; no instances of weddings at later service. **St. André** (3 services, 3 couples; Feb. 15, April 5 at 5 a.m.; Sept. 20 at 4 a.m.).

Thursdays: 2 services, 2 couples. **Des Gallars** (1 service, 1 couple; June 22). **Chauvet** (1 service, 1 couple; Nov. 30).

Fridays: 1 service, 1 couple. **Chauvet** (July 28).

Saturdays: none.

---

15 Ratification of a marriage contracted elsewhere ["under the papacy"].

16 No name given but it is Calvin's hand.

NOTE: The minister charged with Sunday dawn also does the Wednesday dawn service (the one weekday when there were two services).

1555 ST. GERVAIS SUNDAYS TOTAL 35 services, 42 couples

Dawn: 16 services, 19 couples. Regular rotation 4 a.m. or 5 a.m. **Fabri** (Feb. 24, March 10[2] [17], March 24 at 5 a.m.; May 5[2], June 9 & 23 & 30, July 14, Aug. 25[2] at 4 a.m.; Sept. 29, Oct. 20 [18], Nov. 17 & 24, Dec. 1 & 8 & 29 at 5 a.m.)

Afternoon: 16 services, 18 couples. **Bourgoing** (11 services, 13 couples; April 21[2], May 5 & 19, June 16, July 7[2], Aug. 4, Sept. 15 & 29, Oct. 27, Nov. 3, Dec. 8). **Cop** (4 services, 4 couples; Sept. 8 & 22, Oct. 30 at 3 afternoon, Nov. 17 at 2 afternoon). **Fabri** (1 service, 1 couple; March 31 at 3 afternoon).

Other: 3 services, 5 couples no time given. **Poupin** (1 service, 1 couple; Feb. 3). **Bourgoing** (2 services, 4 couples; Jan. 6, Feb. 17[3] probably afternoon).

1555 ST. GERVAIS WEEKDAYS TOTAL 11 services, 13 couples

Mondays: 5 services, 5 couples. **Chauvet** (Jan. 14). **Colladon** (Feb. 25). **Poupin** (July 1). **St. André** (Nov. 4). **Des Gallars** (Dec. 2).

Tuesdays: none.

Wednesdays: 4 services, 4 couples. Regular rotation 4 a.m. or 5 a.m. **Fabri** (March 13 at 5 a.m.; June 5, Sept. 11 at 4 a.m.; Nov. 27 at 5 a.m.).

Thursdays: 1 service, 1 couple. **Poupin** (Feb. 21).

Fridays: 1 service, 3 couples. **Chauvet** (March 1).

Saturdays: none

NOTE: All the dawn services on Sundays and Wednesdays are done by Fabri.

1557 ST. GERVAIS SUNDAYS TOTAL 31 services, 42 couples

Dawn 11 services, 16 couples. Regular rotation 4 a.m. or 5 a.m. **Enoc** (5 services, 9 couples; Jan. 10[2] & 17[2], April 11 at 5 a.m.; June 13[2], July 4[2] at 4 a.m.). **Dupont** (5 services, 6 couples: Sept. 19 & 26[2], Oct. 24, Dec. 5 & 19 at 5 a.m.). **Cop** (1 service, 1 couple; Aug. 22 at 4 a.m.).

Afternoons: 17 services, 21 couples. **Chauvet** (8 services, 9 couples; Jan. 10 & 17 at 2 afternoon; Feb. 7 & 21, June 13[2], July 11, Oct. 3, Nov. 7 at 3 afternoon). **St. André** (2 services, 3 couples; Jan. 31[2] at 2 afternoon; Feb. 14 at 3 afternoon). **Enoc** (5 services, 5 couples; April 25, May 2 & 9, Sept. "11" = 12, Oct. 10 at 3 afternoon). **Calvin** (1 service, 3 couples; July 18). **Dupont** (1 service, 1 couple; Nov. 21).

Other: 3 services, 5 couples no time given by **Enoc** (Feb. 14, March 14[3], April 4; one probably 5 a.m. because entry by St. André for 3 afternoon follows, one probably 3 afternoon).

---

[17]   There are two different entries labeled March 10, on different pages, with different names of the couples; the first is given as 5 a.m., the second as 4 a.m. Since it is assumed that Fabri repeated the date when he moved to the next page, this is counted as two couples but one service, and he made a mistake on the time in the second entry because the season is still winter schedule.

[18]   Fabri writes "huict h." but crosses it out and puts 5.

1557 ST. GERVAIS WEEKDAYS TOTAL 3 services, 3 couples
Mondays: 1 service, 1 couple. **Chauvet** (Feb. 15).
Wednesdays: 2 services, 2 couples. Dawn. **Enoc** (1 service, 1 couple; June 9 at 4 a.m.).
Dupont (1 service, 1 couple; Aug. 11 at 4 a.m.).

1559 ST. GERVAIS SUNDAYS TOTAL 44 services, 61 couples
Dawn: 18 services, 22 couples. Regular rotation 4 a.m. or 5 a.m. **Chauvet** (4 services, 5 couples; Jan. 29[2], Feb. 12, March 12 at 5 a.m.; June 18 at 4 a.m.; alternate weeks). **Enoc** (7 services, 9 couples; April 2 & 16, July 16, Aug. 20, Oct. 1 at 4 a.m.; Oct. 8, Dec. 3[3] at 5 a.m.). **Macar** (3 services, 3 couples; March 5 at 5 a.m.; May 7 & 28 at 4 a.m.). **Dupont** (1 service, 1 couple; Jan. 15 at 5 a.m.) **Bourgoing** (2 services, 3 couples; Feb. 5[2], June 4 "l'aube du jour"). **Morel** (1 service, 1 couple; Oct. 15 at 5 a.m.).
Afternoon: 19 services, 29 couples. **Chauvet** (13 services, 19 couples; Jan. 1 & 15[2] & 22 & 29 at 2 afternoon; Feb. 5[5], June 11, July 9, Aug. 20, Oct. 15 & 29 at 3 afternoon; Nov. 12, Dec. 3[2] & 31 at 2 afternoon). **Enoc** (3 services, 4 couples; March 12[2], April 2, May 28). **Beza** (2 services, 4 couples; July 16 & 30[3]). 1 service, 2 couples (no minister named, hand not distinctive; Nov. 26).
Other: 7 services, 10 couples no time given. **Chauvet** (1 service, 1 couple; May 21). **Enoc** (5 services, 8 couples; March 5 & 19, April 30[2], July 2[3] [19], Aug. 6). **Beza** (1 service, 1 couple; Dec. 10).

1559 ST. GERVAIS WEEKDAYS TOTAL 15 services, 16 couples
Mondays: 10 services, 11 couples. **Chauvet** (6 services, 7 couples; Feb. 20[2], May 15, July 17, Oct. 9 & 23, Dec. 18). **Enoc** (2 services, 2 couples; Feb. 27, March 27). **Beza** (2 services, 2 couples; June 12, Dec. 4).
Tuesdays: none.
Wednesdays: 4 services, 4 couples. [probably dawn, since weddings were not usually done at the main day of prayer service] **Chauvet** (1 service, 1 couple; 24 May). **Enoc** (1 service, 1 couple; Sept. 6). **Macar** (2 services, 2 couples; Feb. 15, June 7).
Thursdays: 1 service, 1 couple. **Enoc** (Jan. 19).
Fridays: none.
Saturdays: none.
NOTE: Apparently the one who does dawn Sun. also does the following week, the one who does afternoon Sun. is free for the rest of the week.

1562 ST. GERVAIS SUNDAYS TOTAL 29 services, 41 couples
Dawn: 5 service, 6 couples. Regular rotation 4 a.m. or 5 a.m. **Chauvet** (1 service, 1 couple; April 26 at 4 a.m.). **Merlin** (1 service, 1 couple; May 31 at 4 a.m.). **Gaigneulx** (1 service, 2 couples; July 12 at 4 a.m.). **D'Airebaudouze** (1 service, 1 couple; Feb. 22; "sinc heures"). **Cop** (1 service, 1 couple; Oct. 18 at 5 a.m.).
Afternoon: 17 services, 27 couples. **Chauvet** (1 service, 1 couple; May 3). **Enoc** (6 services, 10 couples; Feb. 22, May 10[2] & 24[4], June 14 & 21 at 3 afternoon, Dec. 20 at

---

[19] One couple was minister Chauvet marrying the daughter of a widow.

2 afternoon). **Gaigneulx** (3 services, 4 couples; July 19, Aug. 23 at 3 afternoon; Nov. 15 [2] at 2 afternoon). **Colladon** (6 services, 9 couples; Jan. 11 & 25, Feb. 8, April 5[3] & 19 "du soir"; Dec. 13[2] at 2 afternoon). **Cop** (1 service, 3 couples; April 26 at 3 afternoon).

Other: 7 services, 8 couples, no time given. **Enoc** (4 services, 5 couples; March 1 & 15, June 7, July 5[2]). **Gaigneulx** (1 service, 1 couple; June "27" = 28). **D'Airebaudouze** (1 service, 1 couple; April 5).

1562 ST. GERVAIS WEEKDAYS No marriages recorded.

1564 ST. GERVAIS SUNDAYS TOTAL 28 services, 46 couples
Dawn: 9 services, 12 couples. Regular rotation 4 a.m. or 5 a.m. **Chauvet** (2 services, 3 couples; March 12 at 5 a.m.; April 23[2] at 4 a.m.). **Gaigneulx** (2 services, 2 couples; Jan. 23 at 5 a.m.; May 26=28 at 4 a.m.). **Des Bordes** (2 services, 2 couples; March 19 at 5 a.m.; April 30 at 4 a.m.) **Colladon** (1 service, 1 couple; March 26 "l'aube du jour"). **Cop** (1 service, 3 couples; Feb. 20 at 5 a.m.). **Trembley** (1 service, 1 couple; Aug. 20 at 4 a.m.)

Afternoon: 17 services, 32 couples. **Enoc** (8 services, 15 couples; Jan. 2 & 16 at 2 afternoon; Feb. 13[2], April 9[2], June 4[2] & 11[2], July 2 & 30[4] [no time given but is 3 p. m]. **Gaignueulx** (8 services, 16 couples; Jan. 9[3] at 2 afternoon; March 5 & 19, April 16 [4], May 26=28[4], July 9, Aug. 6 & 20 at 3 afternoon) [**Des Bordes** 1 service, 1 couple; Dec. 31 at 2 afternoon, no name given but his hand].

Other: 2 services, 2 couples. **Beza** (1 service, 1 couple; Sept. 24). **Enoc** (1 service, 1 couple; June 25 gives time as "huit heures" but marriages were not allowed at the morning service, and no other instance has ever been found, so this must be an error).[20]

1564 ST. GERVAIS WEEKDAYS TOTAL 3 services, 3 couples
Mondays: 2 services, 2 couples. **Gaigneulx** (1 service, 1 couple; Sept. 11). **Des Bordes** (1 service, 1 couple; Oct. 30 with no name given but his hand.]
Tuesdays: 1 service, 1 couple. **Gaigneulx** (May 9).

1550 MAGDELEINE SUNDAYS
none: there were no dawn or afternoon services.

1550 MAGDELEINE WEEKDAYS TOTAL 2 services, 2 couples
Mondays: 1 service, 1 couple. **Calvin** (April 28).
Tuesdays: 1 service, 1 couple. **Poupin** (May 6).
Wednesdays: none.
Thursdays: none.
Fridays: none.
Saturdays: none.

---

[20]   Elsewhere, on May 10, 1562, Enoc begins to write "huit" and crosses it out to write "troys."

1551 MAGDELEINE SUNDAYS
none.

1551 MAGDELEINE WEEKDAYS TOTAL 2 services, 2 couples
Mondays: none.
Tuesdays: 1 service, 1 couple. **Poupin** (Dec. 29).
Wednesdays: none.
Thursdays: none.
Fridays: none.
Saturdays: 1 service, 1 couple. **Calvin** (June 13).

1552 MAGDELEINE SUNDAYS
none.

1552 MAGDELEINE WEEKDAYS TOTAL 1 service, 1 couple
Mondays: none.
Tuesdays: 1 service, 1 couple. **Jaques Valier** (July 19). [21]
Wednesdays: none.
Thursdays: none.
Fridays: none.
Saturdays: none.

1553 MAGDELEINE SUNDAYS
none.

1553 MAGDELEINE WEEKDAYS TOTAL 1 service, 1 couple
Mondays: 1 service, 1 couple. **Fabri** (Dec. 25 at 7 a.m.).
Tuesdays: none.
Wednesdays: none.
Thursdays: none.
Fridays: none.
Saturdays: none.

1554 MAGDELEINE SUNDAYS
none.

1554 MAGDELEINE WEEKDAYS TOTAL 5 services, 5 couples
Mondays: 4 services, 4 couples. **Calvin** (3 services, 3 couples; Feb. 19 at 7 a.m.;
Feb. 26 no time given; "lundi" June "19" = 18). **St. André** (1 service, 1 couple; Sept. 3).

---

21 The text says "dimanche 19 [July]" but this appears impossible. The 19th is actually a Tuesday, and there is no other evidence for any Sunday afternoon service at the Magdeleine before mid-1555. The minister, Jaques Vallier, was a visitor from Lausanne, and it is quite possible that he made an error in the original entry.

Tuesdays: none.
Wednesdays: none.
Thursdays: 1 service, 1 couple. **Calvin** (May 24).
Fridays: none.
Saturdays: none.

1555 MAGDELEINE SUNDAYS TOTAL 1 service, 1 couple
[afternoon] 1 service, 1 couple. **Bourgoing** (Sept. 22).[22]

1555 MAGDELINE WEEKDAYS TOTAL 8 services, 8 couples
Mondays: 6 services, 6 couples. **Calvin** (July 1). **St. André** (April 15, Aug. 19). **Viret** (July 15). **Farel** (Sept. 16). **Cop** (Sept. 2).
Tuesdays: 1 service, 1 couple. **Calvin** (May 7).
Wednesdays: none.
Thursdays: none.
Fridays: none.
Saturdays: 1 service, 1 couple. **Calvin** (July 20).

1556 MAGDELEINE SUNDAYS TOTAL 6 services, 6 couples
Afternoon: 2 services, 2 couples. **Farel** (1 service, 1 couple; March 22 "apres midi"). **Cop** (1 service, 1 couple; Aug. 30 at 3 afternoon).
Other: 4 services, 4 couples no time given, by **Des Gallars** (May 17 & 31, July 12, Nov. 8). These were almost certainly afternoon, because there were no dawn services and marriages were not allowed at the morning service.

1556 MAGDELEINE WEEKDAYS TOTAL 7 services, 7 couples
Mondays: 6 services, 6 couples. **Calvin** (2 services, 2 couples; June 1 & 29). **Farel** (1 service, 1 couple; April 27). **Des Gallars** (2 services, 2 couples; March 9, May 25). **Macar** (1 service, 1 couple; Nov. 30)
Tuesdays: none
Wednesdays: none
Thursdays: 1 service, 1 couple. **Calvin** (27 Feb. at 7 a.m.)
Fridays: none
Saturdays: none

[22] No time is given, but the afternoon service had just been begun, and there was no dawn service. **NB**: Baptismal records also begin to name the afternoon service; Sun. Dec. 22, 1555, Bourgoing baptizes two babies "au vespre." Although it is never as popular as 8 a.m. or catechism, there are more baptisms in the afternoon in 1556; Feb. 23 at 3 afternoon by Bourgoing, Sept. 6 at 3 afternoon by St. André, Oct. 11 at 3 afternoon by Des Gallars, Nov. 15 at 2 afternoon by Des Gallars.

1557 MAGDELEINE SUNDAYS[23] TOTAL 9 services, 9 couples
  Afternoon: 7 services, 7 couples. **Bourgoing** (7 services, 7 couples; Feb. 14, July 11, Sept. 19 & 26, Oct. 31, Dec. 12 & 19 at "vespre").
  Other: 2 services, 2 couples no time given, by **Des Gallars** (Jan. 10, June 13).

1557 MAGDELEINE WEEKDAYS TOTAL 8 services, 8 couples
  Mondays: 8 services, 8 couples. **Calvin** (4 services, 4 couples; March 8, June 7 & 14[24], Sept. 6). **Des Gallars** (3 services, 3 couples; Jan. 4, June 14, July 5). **Bourgoing** (1 service, 1 couple; Nov. 8).
    Tuesdays: none.
    Wednesdays: none.
    Thursdays: none.
    Fridays: none.
    Saturdays: none.

1558 MAGDELEINE SUNDAYS TOTAL 11 services, 13 couples
  Afternoons: 11 services, 13 couples. **Des Gallars** (6 services, 7 couples; April 17, May 15[2], Aug. 7 at 3 afternoon; Aug. 21 "soir"; June 19, Aug. 28 no time given). **Bourgoing** (3 services, 3 couples; July 3, Sept. "16" = 11 or 18, Nov. 20 at vespre). **Cop** (1 service, 1 couple; Jan. 23). **Enoc** (1 service, 2 couples; Dec. 18).

1558 MAGDELEINE WEEKDAYS TOTAL 12 services, 12 couples
  Mondays: 5 services, 5 couples. **Calvin** (1 service, 1 couple; Sept. 5). **Des Gallars** (3 services, 3 couples; Jan. 31, April 11, Sept. 26). **Macar** (1 service, 1 couple; Dec. 26).
    Tuesdays: 3 services, 3 couples. **Calvin** (1 service, 1 couple; April 19). **Des Gallars** (1 service, 1 couple; Jan. 4) **Macar** (1 service, 1 couple; "mardi" Dec. 14 = 13).
    Wednesdays: none
    Thursdays: 2 services, 2 couples. **Calvin** (1 service, 1 couple; May 5). **Des Gallars** (1 service, 1 couple; Feb. 3)
    Fridays: 1 service, 1 couple. **Calvin** (1 service, 1 couple; Jan. 28)
    Saturdays: 1 service, 1 couple. **Des Gallars** (Feb. 19)

---

23   The Magdeleine records were re-copied in the 18th c. and the copyist accidently labeled most of this year "1577" (beginning in February, continuing to the end of Sept.; Oct. is again marked 1557).

24   Here apparently both Des Gallars and Calvin perform marriages on June 14, entries in that order. This would suggest an earlier and later service, although usually when that is the case the two service times are given. There is no evidence of two services, and thus it must be supposed that here, as in several instances of baptisms, two ministers carried out the rite at the same preaching service. They probably spoke the liturgy only once, but each one addressed the questions to the respective couple he was marrying.

1559 MAGDELEINE SUNDAYS TOTAL 22 services, 26 couples

Dawn: 3 services, 4 couples (begun late in the year: see discussion below). **Morel** (3 services, 4 couples: Nov. 28, Dec. 17 & 31[2]).[25]

Afternoon: 18 services, 21 couples. **Macar** (3 services, 3 couples; Jan. 1 & 15 at 2 afternoon; June 18 no time given). **Colladon** (3 services, 3 couples; April 2, Aug. 20, Oct. 8 at 3 afternoon). **Enoc** (1 service, 1 couple; June 4 at 3 afternoon) **Cop** (4 services, 4 couples; June 11, Oct. 29 at 3 afternoon; July 23, Aug. 13 no time given). **Des Gallars** (4 services, 7 couples; Feb. 19[2] & 26, April 30[3], July 30; no time given). **Morel** (3 services, 4 couples: Nov. 28, Dec. 17 & 31[2]).

Morel (1 service, 1 couple; Dec. 2 = 3, no time given and no other marriages that day by which to deduce time; it would be his rotation for either time).

1559 MAGDELEINE WEEKDAYS TOTAL 7 services, 7 couples

Mondays: 4 services, 4 couples. **Macar** (2 services, 2 couples; July 17, Nov. 20). **Bourgoing** (2 services, 2 couples; Dec. 11 & 25).

Tuesdays: 1 service, 1 couple. **Macar** (July 4).

Wednesdays: none.

Thursdays: 1 service, 1 couple. **Macar** (Sept. jeudi 27 = 28).

Fridays: none.

Saturdays: 1 service, 1 couple. **Des Gallars** (Feb. 4).

1560 MAGDELEINE SUNDAYS TOTAL 20 services, 25 couples

Dawn: 2 services, 2 couples. **Colladon** (May 26 at 4 a.m.). **Morel** (July 21 "au sermon du matin") [service discontinued in Sept.].

Afternoon: 6 services, 7 couples. **Calvin** (May 26 at 3 afternoon "apres midi"; Oct. 27 "apres midi"). **Des Gallars** (May 5 at 3 afternoon). **Chauvet** (Nov. 10 at 3 afternoon). **Morel**: (2 services, 3 couples: Sept. 22, Dec. 29[2])

Other: 12 services, 16 couples no time given, though afternoon is more likely than dawn. **Morel** (11 services, 15 couples; Feb. 25, March 3[2] & 17, April 28[2], June 9[2], July 14 & 28, Aug. 11 & 25). **Macar** (2 services, 2 couples; Feb. 4, Aug. 18). **Colladon** (1 service, 2 couples; April 21).

1560 MAGDELEINE WEEKDAYS TOTAL 5 services, 7 couples

Mondays: 2 services, 2 couples. **Enoc** (1 service, 1 couple; July 29). **Bourgoing** (1 service, 1 couple. Sept. 2).

Tuesdays: 1 service, 1 couple. **Morel** (June 4).

Wednesdays: 1 service, 1 couple. **Morel** (Feb. 28).

Thursdays: none.

Fridays: none.

Saturdays: 1 service, 3 couples. **Morel** (Jan. 20).

---

[25] No times are given but these are before his own entries for marriages which are marked Nov. 28 "du soir le meme jour" and Dec. 17 "2 h. ledit jour" and Dec. 31 "ce dernier 31, le meme jour sermon du soir, item." In effect, Morel has introduced each couple after the first one with some formula.

1561 MAGDELEINE SUNDAYS TOTAL 22 services, 28 couples

Afternoon: 16 services, 22 couples. **Chauvet** (7 services, 9 couples; Jan. 5, April 13 [!] at 2 afternoon; Feb. 16[2], April 20, July 20, Aug. 10 at 3 afternoon; Nov. 30[2] at 2 afternoon). **Colladon** (3 services, 4 couples; Jan. 26 at 2 afternoon; May 18[2], Oct. 19 =20 at 3 afternoon). **Morel** (1 service, 1 couple; Feb. 23 "au soir"). **D'Airebaudouze** (3 services, 6 couples; April 27[3], June 15[2] at 3 afternoon; May 4 "du soir"). **Cop** (1 service, 1 couple; May 11 at 3 afternoon). **Bourgoing** (1 service, 1 couple; June 22 "vespre").

Other: 6 services, 6 couples no time given, but they must be afternoon because now that the dawn service has been discontinued that is the only service where weddings are celebrated. **D'Airebaudouze** (1 service, 1 couple; March 2). **Morel** (2 services, 2 couples; March 9 & 30). **Bourgoing** (1 service, 1 couple; June 1). **Chauvet** (1 service, 1 couple; Nov. 16). **Cop** (1 service, 1 couple; Dec. 21).

1561 MAGDELEINE WEEKDAYS TOTAL 5 services, 5 couples

Mondays: 3 services, 3 couples. **Bourgoing** (Jan. 6, May 12, Sept. 1).
Tuesdays: 2 services, 2 couples. **Chauvet** (March 25, April 8).
Wednesday: none.
Thursdays: none.
Fridays: none.
Saturdays: none.

1562 MAGDELEINE SUNDAYS TOTAL 15 services, 17 couples

Afternoon: 14 services, 16 couples. **Chauvet** (7 services, 8 couples; Jan. 4[2] at 2 afternoon; Feb. 15, May 10 & 24, June 21, Nov. 8 at 3 afternoon; Nov. 29 at 2 afternoon). **D'Airebaudouze** (4 services, 4 couples; April 5 & 12 & 19, July 26 at 3 afternoon/ "soir"). **Cop** (1 service, 2 couples; June 28 at 3 afternoon). **Colladon** (1 service, 1 couple; July 12 "du soir"). **Gaigneulx** (1 service, 1 couple; June 14 at 3 afternoon)

Other: 1 service, 1 couple by **Chauvet** (Feb. 1), no time given but certainly afternoon.

1562 MAGDELEINE WEEKDAYS TOTAL 11 services, 11 couples

Mondays: 8 services, 8 couples. **Chauvet** (5 services, 5 couples; Jan. 26, April 20, Sept. 7 & 21, Nov. 30). **D'Airebaudouze** (3 services, 3 couples; March 30, July 6, Oct. 5).
Tuesdays: 1 service, 1 couple, by **Chauvet** (Dec. 1).
Wednesdays: none.
Thursdays: 2 services, 2 couples, by **Chauvet** (May 7, Oct. 22).
Fridays: none.
Saturdays: none.

1563 MAGDELEINE SUNDAYS TOTAL 22 services, 24 couples

Afternoon: 16 services, 18 couples. **Chauvet** (10 services, 12 couples; Jan. 3 at 2 afternoon; March 14, June 20[2], Aug. 1 & 15, Oct. 10 & 31[2], Nov. 7 at 3 afternoon; Nov. 21, Dec. 19 at 2 afternoon) **Des Bordes** (5 services, 5 couples; March "22" = 21, April 4, Sept. 19, Nov. 14 at 3 afternoon; Nov. 28 at 2 afternoon) **Gaigneulx** (1 service, 1 couple; Oct. 24 at 3 afternoon)

Other: 6 services, 6 couples no time given but only afternoon possible. **Chauvet** (4 services, 4 couples; June 6, Sept. 12 & 26, Dec. 26). **Bourgoing** (1 service, 1 couple; July 4). **D'Airebaudouze** (1 service, 1 couple; March 7).

1563 MAGDELEINE WEEKDAYS TOTAL 4 services, 4 couples
Mondays: 2 services, 2 couples. **Chauvet** (April 19, Nov. 29).
Tuesdays: none.
Wednesdays: none.
Thursdays: 1 service, 1 couple. **Chauvet** (Jan. 28).
Fridays: 1 service, 1 couple. **Chauvet** (June 18).
Saturdays: none.

1564 MAGDELEINE SUNDAYS TOTAL 19 services, 23 couples
Afternoon: 18 services, 22 couples. **Chauvet** (8 services, 8 couples; Jan. 2 & 16 at 2 afternoon; Feb. 27, March 5 & 26, April 30, Aug. 13, Sept. 10 at 3 afternoon) **Des Bordes** (4 services, 6 couples; Feb. 20[2], June 25, July 9 & 23[2] at 3 afternoon/ "soir"). **Colladon** (5 services, 7 couples; Aug. 20[2], Sept. 17, Oct. 15, Nov. 12[2], Dec. 10 at 3 afternoon/ "soir"). **Maubué** (1 service, 1 couple; July 2 "soir").
Other: 1 service, 1 couple, no time given but must be afternoon, by **Chauvet** (March 12).

1564 MAGDELEINE WEEKDAYS TOTAL 1 service, 1 couple
Mondays: none.
Tuesdays: 1 service, 1 couple. **Des Bordes** (March 14).
Wednesdays: none.
Thursdays: none.
Fridays: none.
Saturdays: none.

SUMMARY: It is notable that of the two Sunday occasions for marriages, dawn and afternoon, the latter was when Calvin preached, and for some years he appears to have performed a majority of the weddings at that hour.

SUNDAYS
These were by far the most popular days for weddings.
St. Pierre
Clearly the great majority of couples were married at St. Pierre on Sundays. In the early years about half were married at the dawn service, the rest on Sunday afternoons.
    1550: 20 dawn services/26 couples, 21 afternoon. services/27 couples
Over time the proportions fluctuated between the two services with a shift toward dawn.
    1551: 26 dawn services /37 couples, 16 afternoon services/17 couples
Then a slight move back toward afternoon.
    1553: 22 dawn services/37 couples, 28 afternoon services/40 couples

Then back toward dawn.

1555: 33 dawn services/67 couples, 19 afternoon services/29 couples
1557: 40 dawn services/74 couples; 25 afternoon services/40 couples
1559: 33 dawn services /66 couples, 21 afternoon services/31 couples

Then a move back toward afternoon.

1562: 11 dawn services/13 couples, 23 afternoon services/33 couples
1564: 9 dawn services/9 couples, 23 afternoon services/32 couples.

St. Gervais

Dawn and afternoon services were also the two times for weddings at St. Gervais, and some of the same variation is visible as at St. Pierre.

Slight preference for afternoon (Calvin was preaching then in these years)

1550: 3 dawn services/3 couples, 5 afternoon services/9 couples
1551: 10 dawn services/10 couples, 14 afternoon services/15 couples

Then a move toward dawn

1553: 13 dawn services/14 couples, 6 afternoon services/6 couples

Toward a balance

1555: 16 dawn services/19 couples, 16 afternoon services/18 couples

Then back more and more toward afternoon

1557: 11 dawn services/16 couples, 17 afternoon services/21 couples
1559: 18 dawn services/22 couples, 19 afternoon services/29 couples
1562: 4 dawn services/5 couples, 17 afternoon services/27 couples
1564: 9 dawn services/12 couples, 17 afternoon services/32 couples

La Magdeleine

Until 1555, La Magdeleine did not have a Sunday afternoon service, and it never had been intended to have a dawn service, so there were very few Sunday marriages in this parish.

None: In the early years (1550-1554).

Only afternoon from mid-1555.

1555: 1 service/1 couple
1556: 6 services/6 couples
1557: 9 services /9 couples
1558: 11 services/13 couples

Briefly in 1559-60 there was a dawn service but it appears that afternoon was still preferred.

1559: 3 dawn services/4 couples, 18 afternoon services/21 couples
1560: 2 dawn services/2 couples, 6 afternoon services /7 couples
    [12 services/16 couples not identified; probably afternoon but they are in the time period when there was a dawn service]

Then it was again only afternoon.

1561: 22 services /28 couples
1562: 15 services/17 couples
1563: 22 services/24 couples
1564: 91 services/23 couples

WEEKDAYS

Weekdays were generally less popular times for weddings, but of the work days Mondays were the most common.

St. Pierre

There were only dawn services in the 1550s until mid-1559.

<u>1550:</u> 17 services/28 couples
<u>1551:</u> 21 services/22 couples
<u>1553:</u> 37 services/44 couples
<u>1555:</u> 38 services/48 couples
<u>1557:</u> 41 services/55 couples

Beginning mid-1559 there were two services on three days (Mon., Wed., and Fri.) and one each on the other three. Even then the dawn services remained the more frequent ones for marriages.

<u>1559:</u> Mon. 36 dawn services/67 couples; 6 later service/7 couples; Wed. 9 dawn services/9 couples; none later; Fri. 1 dawn service/1 couple; none later.

<u>1562:</u> Mon. 16 dawn services/20 couples; 6 later services/6 couples; Wed. 1 dawn service/1 couple; none later; Fri. 2 dawn services/2 couples; 1 later service/1 couple.

<u>1564:</u> Mon. 19 dawn services/21 couples; 11 later services/13 couples; Tues. 4 services/4 couples; Wed. 2 dawn services/2 couples; no later services; Thurs. 1 service/1 couple; Fri. 1 dawn service/1 couple; no later services.

St. Gervais

There were very few weekday marriages but these could take place on any day at the regular 6 or 7 a.m. service; those on Wednesday, the only day which had two services, were celebrated at the dawn service.

<u>1550:</u> 8 services/9 couples; Mon. 2 services/ 2 couples; Wed. dawn 3 services/ 4 couples; Tues./Thurs./Fri. each 1 service/1 couple

<u>1551:</u> none

<u>1553:</u> 9 services/10 couples; Mon. 3 services/4 couples; Wed. dawn 3 services/ 3 couples; Thurs. 2 services/ 2 couples; Fri. 1 service/1 couple.

<u>1555:</u> 11 services/13 couples: Mon. 5 services/ 5 couples; Wed. dawn 4 services/ 4 couples; Thurs. 1 service/ 1 couple; Fri. 1 service/3 couples.

<u>1557:</u> 3 services/3 couples: Mon. 1 service/ 1 couple; Wed. dawn 2 services/ 2 couples.

<u>1559:</u> 15 services/16 couples: Mon. 10 services/11 couples; Wed. dawn 4 services/ 4 couples; Thurs. 1 service/1 couple

<u>1562:</u> none

<u>1564:</u> 3 services/3 couples: Mon. 2 services/ 2 couples; Tues. 1 service/ 1 couple.

La Magdeleine

On weekdays Magdeleine had only one service per day, and Mondays were the most commonly chosen for weddings although there are instances of marriages on all the days of the week except Wednesdays. Most of these listed were by Calvin until 1559.

<u>1550:</u> 2 services/2 couples: Mon. 1 service/1 couple; Tues. 1 service/1 couple.

1551: 2 services/2 couples: Tues. 1 service/1 couple; Sat. 1 service/1 couple.

1552: 1 service/1 couple: Tues.

1553: 1 service/1 couple: Mon.

1554: 5 services/5 couples: Mon. 4 services/4 couples; Thurs. 1 service/1 couple

1555: 8 services/8 couples: Mon. 6 services/6 couples; Tues. 1 service/1 couple; Sat. 1 service/1 couple

1556: 7 services/7 couples: Mon. 6 services/6 couples; Thurs. 1 service/ 1 couple

1557: 8 services/8 couples: all Mon.

1558: 12 services/ 12 couples: Mon. 5 services/5 couples; Tues. 3 services/3 couples; Thurs. 2 services/ 2 couples; Fri. 1 service/1 couple; Sat. 1 service/1 couple

1559: 7 services/7 couples: Mon. 4 services/4 couples; Tues. 1 service/1 couple; Thurs. 1 service/1 couple; Sat. 1 service/1 couple

1560: 5 services/7 couples: Mon. 2 services/2 couples; Tues. 1 service/1 couple; Wed. 1 service/1 couple; Sat. 1 service/3 couples

1561: 5 services/5 couples: Mon. 3 services/3 couples; Tues. 2 services/2 couples

1562: 11 services/11 couples: Mon. 8 services/8 couples; Tues. 1 service/1 couple; Thurs. 2 services/2 couples

1563: 4 services/4 couples: Mon. 2 services/2 couples; Thurs. 1 service/1 couple; Fri. 1 service/1 couple

1564: 1 service/1 couple, Tues.

1559-1560 LA MAGDELEINE DAWN SERVICE?

However, there are some oddities about some of Morel's entries. For Nov. 28 there are two distinct entries, one labeled simply "dimanche" and the second one called "le meme jour" and given the time "du soir." On Dec. 17 there are again two entries, one labeled simply "dimanche", the other called "ledit jour" and marked with the exact time of 2 afternoon On Dec. 31 there are four entries, labeled "ce dernier 31," "le meme," "le meme jour sermon du soir," and "item." Usually "item" designates the same service by the same minister, but normally "ledit jour" or "le meme jour" indicates a different service on the same day, either by a different minister or by the same minister at a different time. Also, in the case of Dec. 31, it would be odd to give the time only for the third entry, if all were at the same hour; one would expect the time in the first entry, if it applied to all the couples.

A similar pattern continues for Morel in early 1560. On March 3 "dimanche 3" and "le meme jour"; on April 28 "dimanche 28" and "le meme jour"; June 8 has "le 9 dudit" and "le meme jour." From the entries by Colladon and Calvin for May 26, and Morel's for July 21, we know that there definitely was a dawn service. However, Morel's language must be used with caution. On Jan. 20, a Monday, there are three entries: "le 20," "item," and "le meme jour"; this indicates that Morel's way of entering data may not always have the significance of different services.

These apparently "double" entries mark the beginning of that short-lived experiment at the height of the population explosion owed in good measure to the French refugees. A dawn service was introduced on Sundays and Wednesdays sometime in late 1559, and then dropped along with the Wednesday one in Sept. 1560.

APPENDIX THREE: MINISTERIAL ROTATIONS

Pastoral Rotation among the Three Parishes of St. Pierre, St. Gervais, and Magdeleine as seen in the Records of Baptisms and Marriages

Introductory Notes: The ministers who performed baptisms and marriages are listed in alphabetical order by years. The baptisms and weddings recorded for each minister are identified by the parish but all of the services he does in that year are grouped under his name, regardless of parish. Under each minister's name, for each parish, the (more numerous) baptisms are listed chronologically through the year, according to the day and time of the service; then the weddings, in the same way.

For cases where ministers perform many services, especially where two are the regular alternates for a particular time and place, two kinds of additional data are provided. One is a list of services at which the minister performs both wedding and baptism. The other is a notice of the frequency of services which can indicate the weeks when that particular minister was responsible. Both of these serve to identify the rhythm of the regular alternation or rotation.

Most of the time when a minister performed either a baptism or a wedding, he was preaching and in charge of the whole service. The one exception to this rule seems to have been Calvin; he preached far more often than he performed weddings or baptisms. Frequently his colleagues stood by to do this task for him; so, in some instances a minister's "week" of baptismal or marriage liturgies may in fact coincide with Calvin's preaching. Underlined dates are those for which a sermon by Calvin exists (or was certainly preached); underlined dates in italics are those for which a sermon by Calvin exists but the specific dates are hypothetical. (For example, the 159 sermons on Job and 107 sermons on 1 Samuel have no dates as such, but hypothetical dates have been identified by processes described elsewhere.) Since so many of Calvin's sermons have been lost, the correlation between sermons and the dates of baptisms or weddings, including those by Calvin himself, is very much incomplete. That is, more baptisms or weddings were held on days when Calvin was preaching than is evident in this table. However, the table does provide evidence for two things: the correlation between days when Calvin was preaching and the days he performed most of his baptisms and weddings, and the fact that other ministers performed many baptisms [and probably some weddings] when Calvin was preaching.

1550

BOURGOING

BOURGOING – St. Pierre 1550 BAPTISMS

Sun. dawn: opposite Cop, Feb. 9 & 23, March 9, April 20, June 1 & 15 & 22 & 29, July 13 & 27, Aug. 17 & 31, Oct. 26

Sun. 8 a.m.: Oct. 12 & 26

Sun. afternoon: July 20, Sept. 7

Sun.? May 18, Oct. 12

* * * * * * * * * * * * * *

Mon. dawn: opposite Cop, Feb. 3, Dec. 22

Wed. dawn: opposite Cop, Jan. 22, March 19, April 2 & 30, May 14, June 4 & 25, July 23, Aug. 20, Sept. 17

Wed. 7 a.m/8 a.m.: opposite Poupin, Jan. 22, March 5, July 23, Sept. 3 & 10, Nov. 26, Dec. 24 [Calvin's schedule]

Fri. dawn: opposite Cop, Feb. 7 & 21, June 6, Sept. 19, Nov. 28, Dec. 26

WEDDINGS

Sun. dawn: [Jan. 12], May 18, June 1 & 15 & 22, Aug. 17, Nov. 9 & 23, Dec. 21

Sun. afternoon: Jan. 5, Feb. 16, March 30, April 27, June 8 & 15, July 6, Aug. 3 & 24, Sept. 21, Nov.16 & 30

Sun.??: Aug. 31

* * * * * * * * * * * * * *

Mon. dawn: March 3, April 14 & 28, May 26, June 9, Aug. 18, Sept. 1

Fri. dawn: Oct. 31

  Bourgoing both services: Sun. dawn: June 1 & 15 & 22, Aug. 17

Bourgoing weeks M-F Feb. 3 & 7; M-W April 28 & 30; S-W-F June 1 & 4 & 6; S-M-W Aug. 17 & 18 & 20; W-F Sept. 17 & 19; S-M-W-F Dec. 21 & 22 & 24 & 26

BOURGOING – Magdeleine 1550 BAPTISMS

Catechism: opposite Cop Jan. 12, Feb. 23, March 9, May 18, Aug. 31, Oct. 12, Nov. 23

* * * * * * * * * * * * * *

Mon. [6 a.m./ 7 a.m.]: Feb. 3, Sept. 1

Tues. [6 a.m./ 7 a.m.]: Jan. 7, Feb. 18

Thurs. [6 a.m./ 7 a.m.]: Jan. 9, March 6, June 26, July 24, Dec. 25

Fri. [6 a.m./ 7 a.m.]: Feb. 21, March 21, May 30, Aug. 22, Oct. 31

Sat. [6 a.m./7 a.m.]: May 17, Aug. 9, Dec. 27

  Bourgoing weeks T-Th Jan. 7 & 9; T-F Feb. 18 & 21; Th-S Dec. 25 & 27

CALVIN

CALVIN – St. Pierre 1550 WEDDINGS

Sun. dawn: Sept. 14

Sun. afternoon: Feb. 9, July 13, Sept. 14

Calvin preached on Wed. at 7 a.m./8 a.m. Other ministers do baptisms: Bourgoing Jan. 22, March 5, July 22, Sept. 3, Nov. 26, Dec. 24; Poupin Sept. 17; Chauvet Oct. 1.

CALVIN – St. Gervais 1550 BAPTISMS

Sun. afternoon: Dec. 28

WEDDINGS

Sun. afternoon: April 13 & 20 & 27, June 1 & June 29, Oct. 5

  Calvin preached on Sunday afternoons [probably most weeks]

CALVIN – Magdeleine 1550 BAPTISMS

Mon. [6 a.m./7 a.m.]: opposite Poupin, March 3, Nov. 24

Tues. [6 a.m./7 a.m.]: opposite Poupin, April 1, Sept. 16

Sat. [6 a.m./7 a.m.]: opposite Poupin, Sept. 20

WEDDINGS

Mon. [6 a.m./7 a.m.]: April 28

Baptisms by others in Calvin's week:

Multiple ministers in one week: Bourgoing-Poupin M-T Feb. 3 & 4; Calvin-Bourgoing M-Th March 3 & 6; Calvin-Fabri T-F April 1 & 4; Fabri-Chauvet M-Th April 14 & 17; Calvin-Cop M-Th April 28 & May 1; Chauvet-Bourgoing T-S May 13 & 17; Chauvet-Bourgoing-Chauvet M-F-S May 26 & 30 & 31; Chauvet-Poupin T-Th June 10 & 13; Chauvet-Bourgoing T-Th June 24 & 26; Bourgoing-Chauvet F-S Aug. 22 & 23; Bourgoing-Chauvet-Chauvet-Chauvet M-T-Th-F Sept. 1 & 2 & 4 & 5; Calvin-Chauvet-Calvin T-Th-S Sept. 16 & 18 & 20; Poupin-Chauvet M-F Sept. 29 & Oct. 3; Fabri-Bourgoing Th-F Oct. 30 & 31; Poupin-Bourgoing-Bourgoing M-Th-S Dec. 22 & 25 & 27.

One minister doing several in one week: Bourgoing T-Th Jan. 7 & 9, T-F Feb. 18 & 21

One baptism in week: Bourgoing F March 21, S Aug. 9; Calvin M Nov. 24; Fabri T Jan. 21; Poupin S Oct. 18

CHAUVET

CHAUVET – St. Pierre 1550 BAPTISMS

Sun. 8 a.m.: Sept. 28

* * * * * * * * * * * * * * *

Wed. 7 a.m. /8 a.m.: Oct. 1

Fri. dawn: Sept. 5

CHAUVET – St. Gervais 1550 BAPTISMS

Sun. 8 a.m.: opposite Des Gallars, May 4, Nov. 23

Catechism: Jan. 12, Aug. 31, Oct. 19, Nov. 16

Sun.? Feb. 2, March 23 & 30, April 27, June 15, July 13 [some catechism opposite Fabri, some 8 a.m.]

* * * * * * * * * * * * * * *

Mon. [6 a.m./7 a.m.]: opposite Des Gallars, Jan. 20, March 3 & 17, April 21, May 19, Sept. 8, Nov. 10

Tues. [6 a.m./7 a.m.]: opposite Des Gallars, Feb. 18, June 17, Oct. 14, Nov. 11

Wed. [7 a.m./8 a.m.]: opposite Des Gallars, Feb. 19, March 19, April 2 & 23, July 2, Sept. 10, Nov. 12

Thurs. [6 a.m./7 a.m.]: opposite Des Gallars, Jan. 23, May 22, July 17, Sept. 25, Nov. 13 & 27

Fri. [6 a.m./7 a.m.]: opposite Des Gallars, March 7, Sept. 26, Dec. 26

Sat. [6 a.m./7 a.m.]: opposite Des Gallars, May 24, June 21, Sept. 27, Oct. 4

WEDDINGS

Wed. [probably dawn]: Dec. 24

Chauvet weeks M-Th Jan. 20 & 23; T-W Feb. 18 & 19; M-F March 3 & 7; M-W March 17 & 19; April 21 & 23; M-Th-S May 19 & 22 & 24; T-S June 1 &21; M-W Sept. 8 & 10; Th-F-S Sept. 25 & 26 & 27; M-T-Th Nov. 10 & 11 &12 & 13

CHAUVET – Magdeleine 1550 BAPTISMS

Mon. [6 a.m./7 a.m.]: May 26

Tues. [6 a.m./7 a.m.]: May 13, June 10 & 24, Sept. 2

Thurs. [6 a.m./ 7 a.m.]: April 17, Sept. 4 & 18

Fri. [6 a.m./ 7 a.m.]: Sept. 5, Oct. 3

Sat. [6 a.m./ 7 a.m.]: May 31, Aug. 23, Oct. 11

Chauvet weeks: M-S May 26 & 31; T-Th-F Sept. 2 & 4 & 5

COP

COP – St. Pierre 1550 BAPTISMS

Sun. dawn: opposite Bourgoing, Jan. 5, Feb. 2 & 16, March 16 & 30, April 13, May 4 & 11, June 8, July 6, Aug. 10 & 24, Sept. 21, Oct. 5 & 19, Nov. 2 & 16 & 30

Catechism: May 11

Sun. afternoon: April 6

****

Mon. dawn: opposite Bourgoing, April 7, June 30, Aug. 11, Sept. 8 & 22, Dec. 29

Wed. dawn: opposite Bourgoing, Jan. 29, March 12, April 9, May 21, July 30, Sept. 3 & 24, Oct. 22, Dec. 17

Fri. dawn: opposite Bourgoing, Jan. 17, March 28, July 4, Dec. 5

WEDDINGS

Sun. dawn: Jan 19, Feb. 2 & 16, March 2 & 16, May 11, June 8, Aug. 24, Nov. 2, Dec. 14

Sun. afternoon: Jan. 26, Feb. 23, May 4 & 18, Dec. 7 & 21

****

Mon. dawn: Jan. 13 & 27, June 30, Aug. 25, Dec. 15 & 29

Fri. dawn: Dec. 5

Cop both services: Sun. dawn: Feb. 2 & 16, March 16, May 11, June 8, Aug. 24, Nov. 2. Mon.: June 30, Dec. 29. Fri. dawn: Dec. 5

Cop weeks M-F Jan. 13 & 17; M-W Jan. 27 & 29; M-W April 7 & 9; S-M Aug. 10 & 11; S-M-W Aug. 24 & 24 & Sept. 3; S-M-W Sept. 21 & 22 & 24; S-W Oct. 19 & 22; S-W Nov. 2 & 5; S-F Nov. 30 & Dec. 5; S-M-W Dec. 14 & 15 & 17

COP – Magdeleine 1550 BAPTISMS

Catechism: opposite Bourgoing, Jan. 19, March 2 & 16, April 20, Aug. 10, Oct. 5, Nov. 2 & 16

****

Thurs. 6 a.m./ 7 a.m.: May 1

DES GALLARS

DES GALLARS – St. Pierre 1550 BAPTISMS

Catechism: opposite Fabri, April 20, June 1 & 8 & 22, July 27, Aug. 24, Nov. 9, Dec. 7

DES GALLARS – St. Gervais 1550 BAPTISMS

Sun. 8 a.m.: Aug. 17 & 31, Oct. 19, Nov. 30

Sun. afternoon: April 13, Sept. 7

Sun.? March 9

****

Mon. [6 a.m./7 a.m.]: opposite Chauvet, Jan. 13, April 14 & 28, May 26, Aug. 4, Sept. 1, Oct. 6 & 20

Tues. [6 a.m./7 a.m.]: opposite Chauvet, Feb. 11, April 29, May 27, Sept. 2, Dec. 2 & 16

Wed. 7 a.m./8 a.m.: opposite Chauvet, Feb. 12, April 30, May 28, July 9, Oct. 22, Dec. 3

Thurs. [6 a.m./7 a.m.]: opposite Chauvet, Jan. 2 & 16, Feb. 13, May 29, Aug. 21, Sept. 4, Oct. 2

Fri. [6 a.m./7 a.m.]: opposite Chauvet, Jan. 17, May 2, Oct. 3 & 24

Sat. [6 a.m./7 a.m.]: opposite Chauvet, Jan. 18, March 29

WEDDINGS

Mon. [6 a.m./7 a.m.]: Feb. 24, June 9

Tues. [6 a.m./7 a.m.]: April 29

Thurs. [6 a.m.7 a.m.]: Nov. 20

Fri. [6 a.m.7 a.m.]: Sept. 5

Des Gallars both services: Tues. April 29

Des Gallars M-Th-F-S Jan. 13 & 16 & 17 & 18; T-W-Th Feb. 11 & 12 & 13; M-T-W-F April 28 & 29 & 30 & May 2; M-T-W-Th May 26 & 27 & 28 & 29; M-T-Th-F Sept. 1 & 2 & 4 & 5; Th-F Oct. 2 & 3; M-W-F Oct. 20 & 22 & 24; T-W Dec. 2 & 3

Changes: Chauvet Mar 29, Des Gallars April 14; Des Gallars Oct. 2 & 3, Chauvet Oct. 4

DES GALLARS – Magdeleine 1550 BAPTISMS
Catechism: June 15

* * * * * * * * * * * * * *

Fri. [6 a.m./ 7 a.m.]: May 23

ECCLESIA
ECCLESIA – St. Pierre 1550 WEDDINGS
Mon. dawn: June 16

FABRI
FABRI – St. Pierre 1550 BAPTISMS
Catechism: opposite Des Gallars, March 23, April 13 & 27, July 13, Sept. 28, Oct. 19, Nov. 16 & 30, Dec. 14

* * * * * * * * * * * * * *

Wed. 7 a.m. /8 a.m.: Jan. 1

Fri. dawn: June 20
   WEDDINGS
Mon. dawn: Feb. 24, June 23

FABRI – St. Gervais 1550 BAPTISMS
Sun. dawn: March 30, May 4, June 1 & 8, Sept. 14, Oct. 12 & 26, Nov. 2, Dec. 7

Catechism: April 20, June 22, July 27, Oct. 12, Nov. 9, Dec. 7

Sun.? Jan. 5 & 26, March 2 & 16 [either dawn or catechism]

* * * * * * * * * * * * * *

Tues. [6 a.m./7 a.m.]: Aug. 26

Wed. dawn: June 4, July 2, Oct. 8, Dec. 17

Thurs. [6 a.m./7 a.m.]: Feb. 27, July 31
   WEDDINGS
Sun. dawn: April 13, Sept. 28, Nov. 16

Wed. dawn: Sept. 10 & 17

FABRI – Magdeleine 1550 BAPTISMS
Mon. [6 a.m./ 7 a.m.]: April 14

Tues. [6 a.m./ 7 a.m.]: Jan. 21

Thurs. 6 a.m./ 7 a.m.: Oct. 30

Fri. [6 a.m./ 7 a.m.]: April 4

Sat. [6 a.m./ 7 a.m.]: Oct. 18

POUPIN
POUPIN – St. Pierre 1550 BAPTISMS
Sun. 8 a.m.: June 15 [probably Aug. 10]

Wed. 7 a.m./8 a.m.: opposite Calvin, Jan. 15 & 29, Feb. 26, May 7, June 18, July 30, Sept. 17, Oct. 22, Nov. 5, Dec. 3

POUPIN – Magdeleine 1550 BAPTISMS
Sun. 8 a.m.: Jan. 12 [probably Feb. 16, April 13, July 27, Aug. 3 & 24 & 31, Sept. 14 & 28, Oct. 5 & 19 & 26, Nov. 30, Dec. 14 & 21]

Catechism: July 6

* * * * * * * * * * * * * *

Mon. [6 a.m./7 a.m.]: opposite Calvin et al. Jan. 13, Feb. 24, March 24, June 30, Aug. 11 & 25, Sept. 22 & 29, Nov. 17, Dec. 22 & 29

Tues. [6 a.m./7 a.m.]: opposite Calvin et al. Feb. 4 & 25, May 20, June 17, July 15, Aug. 26, Sept. 9, Nov. 4, Dec. 2 & 30

Thurs. [6 a.m./7 a.m.]: opposite Calvin et al. Jan. 2 & 16, Feb. 13 & 27, March 13, April 24, June 5 & 12, July 3, Aug. 28, Sept. 11, Dec. 4 & 18

Fri. [6 a.m./7 a.m.]: opposite Calvin et al. Jan. 17 & 31, April 11, June 6, Aug. 29, Sept. 26, Oct. 10, Dec. 5

Sat. [6 a.m./7 a.m.]: opposite Calvin et al. March 1, May 10, June 21, July 5, Aug. 16, Oct. 18, Dec. 20
   WEDDINGS
Tues. [6 a.m./7 a.m.]: May 6

Poupin weeks M-Th-F Jan. 13 & 16 & 17; M-T-Th-S Feb. 24 & 25 & 27 &

March 1; T-S May 6 & 10; Th-F June 5 & 6; T-S June 17 & 21; M-Th-S June 30 & July3 & 5; Aug. 11 & 16; M-T-Th-F Aug. 25 & 26 & 28 & 29; T-Th Sept. 9 & 11; M-F Sept. 22 & 26; T-Th-F Dec. 2 & 4 & 5; Th-S Dec. 18 & 20; M-T Dec. 29 & 30

VIRET

VIRET – St. Gervais 1550 WEDDINGS

Sun. afternoon: Jan. 5

1551

BOURGOING

BOURGOING – St. Pierre 1551 BAP-TISMS

Sun. dawn: opposite Cop, Jan. 4 & 18, Feb. 15, June 21, Sept. 13, Oct. 11 & 25, Nov. 8 & 22, Dec. 6 & 20

Sun. 8 a.m.: May 24

Catechism: Sept. 27

Sun.? Feb. 1, March 15, April 12, May 10, June 7, July 5 – dawn or catechism?

* * * * * * * * * * * * * *

Mon. dawn: opposite Cop, Feb. 2, March 30, April 27, May 25, June 22, Nov. 9

Wed. dawn: opposite Cop, Jan. 7, Feb. 4, March 18, April 15, May 20 & 27, June 10, July 8, Aug. 19, Sept. 2, Nov. 25, Dec. 9

Fri. dawn: regularly; opposite Cop, April 3, June 12, Sept. 4, Oct. 2

WEDDINGS

Sun. dawn: Jan. 4, Feb. 15, June 21, July 5, Aug. 16, Oct. 25, Nov. 8 & 22, Dec. 6 & 20

Sun. afternoon: Jan. 25, March 8, April 5, June 28, Sept. 20, Oct. 18

Sun.??: April 12 & 19, May 3

* * * * * * * * * * * * * *

Mon. dawn: Jan. 5, Feb. 16, March 16, June 8, July 6, Aug. 31, Sept. 28

Wed. dawn: April 1, May 13, Sept. 2, Dec. 9

Bourgoing both services: Sun. dawn: Jan. 4, Feb. 15, June 21, Oct. 25, Nov. 8 & 22, Dec. 6 & 20

Bourgoing weeks S-M-W Jan. 4 & 5 & 7; M-W Feb. 2 & 4; S-M Feb. 15 & 16; M-W March 16 &18; M-W-F March 30 & April 1 & 3; May 25 & 27; M-W-F June 8 & 10 & 12; S-M June 21 & 22; S-M-W July 5 & 6 & 8; S-W Aug. 16 & 19; M-W-F Aug. 31 & Sept. 2 & 4; M-F Sept. 28 & Oct. 2; S-M Nov. 8 & 9; S-W Nov. 22 & 25; S-W Dec. 6 & 9.

BOURGOING – Magdeleine 1551 BAP-TISMS

Catechism: opposite Cop Feb. 1, June 21, Aug. 16, Aug. 30 [probably June 7]

* * * * * * * * * * * * * *

Mon. [6 a.m./7 a.m.]: June 22, Aug. 17

Tues. [6 a.m./7 a.m.]: April 28, Aug. 18

Thurs. [6 a.m./7 a.m.]: April 16, May 28, June 25

Fri. [6 a.m./7 a.m.]: Jan. 9, June 26, July 10, Dec. 11

Sat. [6 a.m./7 a.m.]: June 13

Bourgoing weeks: M-Th-F June 22 & 25 & 26; M-Th Aug. 17 & 18.

CALVIN

CALVIN – St. Pierre 1551 BAPTISMS

Wed. [7a.m./ 8 a.m.]: April 1

WEDDINGS

Sun. afternoon: June 7

Calvin preaching on Wed. at 7 a.m./8 a.m. Other ministers do baptisms: Fabri April 29, July 22, Aug. 5, Sept. 30, Dec. 9 & 23; Poupin March 4; Chauvet Sept. 2.

CALVIN – St. Gervais 1551 BAPTISMS

Sun. afternoon: March 8, Oct. 4 (probably Dec. 27)

WEDDINGS

Sun. afternoon: Jan. 4 & 11, Feb. 1 & Feb. 8, March 15, April 19, May 10, June 21, July 5, Sept. 13, Nov. 1, Dec. 6

CALVIN – Magdeleine 1551 BAPTISMS

Mon. [6 a.m./7 a.m.]: Nov. 23

Tues. [6 a.m./7 a.m.]: Dec. 8

Thurs. [6 a.m./7 a.m.]: Dec. 10

Fri. [6 a.m./7 a.m.]: July 24

Sat. [6 a.m./7 a.m.]: July 25

WEDDINGS

Sat. [6 a.m./7 a.m.]: June 13

    Calvin weeks: F-S July 24 & 25; T-Th Dec. 8 & 10

Baptisms by others in Calvin's weeks:

    Multiple ministers in one week: Fabri-Bourgoing Th-F Jan. 8 & 9; Chauvet-Fabri-Bourgoing T-Th-S June 9 & 11 & 13; Fabri-Chauvet M-S May 11 & 16; Fabri-Chauvet-Calvin-Calvin T-Th-F-S July 21 & 24 & 24 & 25; Chauvet-Chauvet-Fabri T-Th-S Sept. 1 & 3 & 5; Fabri-Poupin-Chauvet T-Th-F Sept. 15 & 17 & 18; Calvin-Calvin-Bourgoing T-Th-F Dec. 8 & 10 & 11.

    One minister doing several in one week: Bourgoing: M-Th-F June 22 & 25 & 26; M-Th Aug. 17 & 18. Fabri: T-Th Jan. 20 & 22; T-Th Feb. 3 & 5; F-S March 20 & 21; M-T-F March 30 & 31 & April 3; M-F-S Oct. 26 & 29 & 30; T-F Nov. 10 & 13. Chauvet T-Th Sept. 1 & 3

    One baptism in week: Bourgoing T April 28, Th May 28, F July 10; Calvin M Nov. 23; Fabri F Feb. 20, T Aug. 4, M Dec. 21; Des Gallars F March 6.

NB: On Sat. June 13 Calvin performs a marriage and Bourgoing performs a baptism at the same service.

CHAUVET

CHAUVET – St. Pierre 1551 BAPTISMS

Wed. 7 a.m./8 a.m.: Sept. 2

CHAUVET – St. Gervais 1551 BAPTISMS

Sun. 8 a.m.: opposite Des Gallars, Jan. 18, Feb. 1, March 1, May 3 & 31, July 12, Sept. 20

Catechism: March 1, July 12, Nov. 29

Sun. afternoon: Sept. 6

Sun.? March 22, June 14

* * * * * * * * * * * * * *

Mon. [6 a.m./7 a.m.]: opposite Des Gallars, Jan. 19 & 26, May 4, Oct. 26

Tues. [6 a.m./7 a.m.]: opposite Des Gallars, March 3, June 2, Aug. 25, Dec. 8 & 22

Wed. [7 a.m./8 a.m.]: opposite Des Gallars, Jan. 21, Feb. 4 & 18, March 4, April 8 & 22, May 6, Aug. 12 & 26, Nov. 25, Dec. 9 & 23

Thurs. [6 a.m./7 a.m.]: opposite Des Gallars, Feb. 5, April 2, July 16, Sept. 10, Oct. 15

Fri. [6 a.m./7 a.m.]: opposite Des Gallars, Feb. 20, April 17, May 8 & 22, July 31, Dec. 25

Sat. [6 a.m./7 a.m.]: opposite Des Gallars, April 11, July 25, Sept. 12, Oct. 31, Dec. 26

WEDDINGS

Sun. afternoon: April 26

Chauvet weeks [Sun. 8 a.m. with week] S-M-W Jan. 18 & 19 & 21; S-W-Th Feb. 1 & 4 & 5; W-F Feb. 18 & 20; S-T-W March 1 & 3 & 4; W-S April 8 & 11; S-M-W-F May 3 & 4 & 6 & 8; T-W Aug. 25 & 26; Th-S Sept. 10 & 12; M-S

Oct. 26 & 31; T-W Dec. 8 & 9; T-W-F-S Dec. 22 & 23 & 25 & 26.

CHAUVET – Magdeleine 1551 BAPTISMS

Tues. [6 a.m./7 a.m.]: June 9, Sept. 1

Thurs. [6 a.m./7 a.m.]: July 23, Sept. 3

Fri. [6 a.m./7 a.m.]: Sept. 18

Sat. [6 a.m./7 a.m.]: May 16

    Chauvet weeks T-Th Sept. 1 & 3

COP

COP – St. Pierre 1551 BAPTISMS

Sun. dawn: opposite Bourgoing, Feb. 8 & 22, March 8, April 5 & 19, May 31, June 28, July 12 & 26, Oct. 18, Nov. 15 & 29, Dec. 13

Sun. 8 a.m.: April 5

Sun. afternoon: Jan. 4, March 1 & 29, Oct. 25

* * * * * * * * * * * * * *

Mon. dawn: opposite Bourgoing, Jan. 26, March 9, May 18, Nov. 30, Dec. 28

Wed. dawn: opposite Bourgoing, Jan. 14 & 28, Feb. 11, March 11, April 22, July 1, Oct. 7, Nov. 4 & 18, Dec. 2

Fri. dawn: opposite Bourgoing, April 10, Nov. 6, Dec. 18

    WEDDINGS

Sun. dawn: Jan. 11, Feb. 8, March 8, May 31, June 14 & 28, July 12 & 26, Aug. 23, Sept. 13 & 20, Nov. 1 & 15 & 29, Dec. 13

Sun. afternoon: March 15, April 26, June 21, July 19, Aug. 2, Oct. 11 & 25, Nov. 1, Dec. 20

* * * * * * * * * * * * * *

Mon. dawn: Feb. 9, April 6, June 15, July 13 & 27, Aug. 10, Oct. 19

Wed. dawn: Jan. 21, July 1 & 29

Cop both services: Sun. dawn: Feb. 8, March 8, May 31, June 28, July 12 &

26, Nov. 15 & 29, Dec. 13. Wed. dawn: July 1

Cop weeks S-W Jan. 11 & 14; M-W Jan. 26 & 28; S-M-W Feb. 8 & 9 & 11; S-M-W March 8 & 9 & 11; S-M-F April 5 & 6 & 10; S-W April 19 & 22; S-M June 14 & 15; S-W June 28 & July 1; S-M-W July 26 & 27 & 29; S-W-F Nov. 1 & 4 & 6; S-W Nov. 15 & 18; S-M-W Nov. 29 & 30 & Dec. 2.

COP – St. Gervais 1551 BAPTISMS

Mon. 6 a.m./7 a.m.: Dec. 14

COP – Magdeleine 1551 BAPTISMS

Catechism: opposite Bourgoing Feb. 8, June 14, July 12, Aug. 23, Oct. 18, Nov. 29

* * * * * * * * * * * * * *

Mon. 6 a.m./7 a.m.: July 13

DES GALLARS

DES GALLARS – St. Pierre 1551 BAPTISMS

Catechism: opposite Fabri, Jan. 4 & 18, March 1, April 5 & 19, May 3, June 7 & 14, July 19, Aug. 9, Oct. 11, Dec. 6

* * * * * * * * * * * * * *

Mon. dawn: April 20

Wed. dawn: Sept. 23

Fri. dawn: Jan. 23

    WEDDINGS

Sun. dawn: March 1

    Des Gallars both services: Sun. dawn March 1

DES GALLARS – St. Gervais 1551 BAPTISMS

Sun. 8 a.m.: opposite Chauvet, Feb. 8, April 12, June 7, Sept. 27, Nov. 1 & 29

Sun.? May 17, June 14

* * * * * * * * * * * * * *

Mon. [6 a.m./7 a.m.]: opposite Chauvet, Oct. 19, Nov. 30, Dec. 28

Tues. [6 a.m./7 a.m.]: opposite Chauvet, March 24, April 28, May 26, July 7, Dec. 1

Wed. 7 a.m./8 a.m.: opposite Chauvet, Jan. 28, May 27, July 22, Sept. 16, Oct. 21, Dec. 2 & 16 & 30

Thurs. [6 a.m./7 a.m.]: opposite Chauvet, Jan. 1 & 15, May 14, Aug. 20, Sept. 3, Oct. 22, Nov. 19, Dec. 3

Fri. [6 a.m./7 a.m.]: opposite Chauvet, Jan. 16, June 26, July 24, Oct. 23

Sat. [6 a.m./7 a.m.]: opposite Chauvet, Jan. 3, March 28, June 13

Des Gallars weeks Th-S Jan. 1 & 3; Th-F Jan. 15 & 16; W-S March 24 & 28; T-W May 26 & 27; M-W-Th.-F Oct. 19 & 21 & 22 & 23

DES GALLARS – Magdeleine 1551 BAPTISMS

Fri. [6 a.m./7 a.m.]: March 6

FABRI

FABRI – St. Pierre 1551 BAPTISMS

Sun. 8 a.m.: April 12, May 3 & 10 & 31, July 19, Aug. 30, Oct. 25, Nov. 1, Dec. 20

Catechism: opposite Des Gallars, Jan. 11 & 25, May 24, July 5, Oct. 4, Dec. 13

* * * * * * * * * * * * * *

Mon. dawn: May 18

Wed. 7 a.m./8 a.m.: March 25, April 29, July 22, Aug. 5, Sept. 30, Dec. 9 & 23

Fri. dawn: April 24

FABRI – St. Gervais 1551 BAPTISMS

Sun. dawn: Jan. 11 & 18, March 1 & 8, April 5, May 31, June 7 & 28, Aug. 9 & 23, Sept. 20, Dec. 6 & 13

Catechism: Jan. 4 & 18, Feb. 1, Sept. 27, Nov. 8, Nov. 22

Sun. afternoon: Nov. 1

* * * * * * * * * * * * * *

Mon. 6 a.m./7 a.m.: June 1

Tues. 6 a.m./7 a.m.: April 14, June 30

Wed. dawn: Jan. 21, Feb. 25, March 11, April 29, June 17, July 1, Sept. 23

Wed. 7 a.m./8 a.m.: June 17

WEDDINGS

Sun. dawn: Jan. 11 & 18, Feb. 8, March 1 & 15, May 3 & 31, July 19, Sept. 13, Nov. 29, Dec. 20

Fabri both services: Sun. dawn: Jan. 11 & 18, March 1, May 31

FABRI – Magdeleine 1551 BAPTISMS

Catechism: March 1

* * * * * * * * * * * * * *

Mon. 6 a.m./7 a.m.: March 30, May 11, Oct. 26, Dec. 21

Tues. 6 a.m./7 a.m.: Jan. 20, Feb. 3, March 17 & 31, April 14, July 21, Aug. 4, Sept. 15, Nov. 10

Thurs. 6 a.m./ 7 a.m.: Jan. 8 & 22, Feb. 5, June 11, Oct. 29

Fri. 6 a.m./ 7 a.m.: Feb. 20, March 20, April 3, Oct. 30, Nov. 13

Sat. 6 a.m./ 7 a.m.: March 21, Sept. 5

Fabri weeks T-Th Jan. 20 & 22; T-Th Feb. 3 & 5; F-S March 20 & 21; M-T March 30 & 31; M-F-S Oct. 26 & 29 & 30; T-F Nov. 10 & 13

POUPIN

POUPIN – St. Pierre 1551 BAPTISMS

Sun. probably 8 a.m. April 26

* * * * * * * * * * * * * *

Mon. dawn: April 6

Wed. [7 a.m./8 a.m.]: opposite Calvin, Jan. 14 & 28, March 4 & 11, May 20, July 1 & 15 & 29, Aug. 12, Oct. 21, Nov. 4, Dec. 30

POUPIN – Magdeleine 1551 BAPTISMS

Sun. 8 a.m.: June 21, Aug. 23 [probably Feb. 8 & 15, March 8, April 5 & 19, July 5, Sept. 20 & 27, Oct. 4 & 11 & 18 & 25, Nov. 1 & 8, Dec. 13]

* * * * * * * * * * * * * *

Mon. [6 a.m./7 a.m.]: opposite Calvin et al., Jan. 19 & 26, Feb. 23, March 9, June 1 & 15, Aug. 10, Sept. 7 & 21, Nov. 2 & 16, Dec. 28

Tues. [6 a.m./7 a.m.]: opposite Calvin et al., Jan. 27, March 10, April 7, June 2 & 30, Oct. 6, Nov. 17, Dec. 1

Thurs. [6 a.m./7 a.m.]: opposite Calvin et al., Jan. 1 & 29, Feb. 12, March 12 & 26, April 9, May 7, June 18, July 30, Oct. 8 & 22, Nov. 5 & 19, Dec. 3 & 31

Fri. [6 a.m./7 a.m.]: opposite Calvin et al., Jan. 2, Feb. 13, March 13, June 19, Sept. 25, Oct. 9, Dec. 4

Sat. [6 a.m./7 a.m.]: opposite Calvin et al., Feb. 14 & 28, April 11, Aug. 1, Sept. 12, Oct. 10, Dec. 5 & 19

WEDDINGS

Tues. [6 a.m./7 a.m.]: Dec. 29

Poupin weeks Th-F Jan. 1 & 2; M-T-Th Jan. 26 & 27 & 29; Th-F-S Feb. 12 & 13 & 14; M-F Feb. 23 & 28; M-T-Th-F March 9 & 10 & 12 & 13; T-Th-S April 7 & 9 & 11; M-T June 1 & 2; M-Th-F June 15 & 18 &19; Th-S July 30 & Aug. 1; M-F Sept. 21 & 25; T-Th-F-S Oct. 6 & 8 & 9 & 10; M-Th Nov. 2 & 5; M-T-Th Nov. 16 & 17 & 19; T-Th-F-S Dec. 1 & 3 & 4 & 5; M-T-Th Dec. 28 & 29 & 31

VIRET

VIRET – St. Gervais 1551 WEDDINGS

Sun. afternoon: June 7

1552

Magdeleine only

BOURGOING – Magdeleine 1552 BAP-TISMS

Catechism: Jan. 3 & 17, March 27

* * * * * * * * * * * * * *

Tues. [6 a.m./7 a.m.]: Jan. 5

Thurs. [6 a.m./7 a.m.]: March 17

Fri. [6 a.m./7 a.m.]: Jan. 22, April 1

CALVIN – Magdeleine 1552 BAPTISMS

Tues. [6 a.m./7 a.m.] Dec. 20

Baptisms by other ministers in Calvin's week:

Multiple ministers: Fabri-Fabri-Bourgoing-Fabri M-Th-F-S Jan. 18 & 21 & 22 & 23; Fabri-Bourgoing T-Th March 15 & 17; Fabri-Bourgoing Th-F March 31 & April 1; Fabri-Fabri-Fabri-Chauvet M-Th-F-S April 11 & 14 & 15 & 16; St. André-Chauvet-Chauvet T-F-S July 5 & 8 & 9; St. André-St. André-Poupin T-F-S July 19 & 22 & 23; Calvin-St. André-St. André-St. André T-Th-F-S Dec. 20 & 22 & 23 & 24.

One minister several in one week: Fabri T-Th-S May 24 & 26 & 28; Chauvet T-Th June 21 & 23; T-Th Sept. 13 & 15; St. André M-Th Aug. 1 & 4; M-F Aug. 15 & 19; T-F Oct. 25 & 28; M-Th Nov. 7 & 10; M-T-S Nov. 21 & 22 & 26.

One baptism in a week: Bourgoing T Jan. 5; Chauvet F Sept. 2; Cop Th March 3; Fabri F Feb. 5, Th April 28; St. André S Oct. 1, Th Dec. 8.

CHAUVET – Magdeleine 1552 BAP-TISMS

Tues. [6 a.m./7 a.m.]: June 21, *Sept. 13*

Thurs. [6 a.m./7 a.m.]: June 23, *Sept. 15*

Fri. [6 a.m./7 a.m.]: July 8, *Sept. 2*

Sat. [6 a.m./7 a.m.]: April 16, July 9

    Chauvet weeks T-Th June 21 & 23; F-S July 8 & 9; T-Th Sept. 13 & 15.

COP – Magdeleine 1552 BAPTISMS

Sun. 8 a.m.: Aug. 14

Catechism: opposite Bourgoing/ Des Gallars Feb. 21, March 20, April 3, June 12 & 26, Nov. 20, Dec. 4

* * * * * * * * * * * * * *

Thurs. 6 a.m./7 a.m.: March 3

DES GALLARS – Magdeleine 1552 BAPTISMS

Catechism: opposite Cop Aug. 14 & 28, Oct. 23, Nov. 27

Sun.? June 19

FABRI – Magdeleine 1552 BAPTISMS

Mon. 6 a.m./7 a.m.: Jan. 18, April 11

Tues. 6 a.m./7 a.m.: Feb. 16, March 15, April 19, May 17 & 24

Thurs. 6 a.m./7 a.m.: Jan. 21, March 31, April 14 & 28, May 26

Fri. 6 a.m./7 a.m.: Feb. 5, April 15

Sat. 6 a.m./7 a.m.: Jan. 23, May 28

    Fabri weeks M-Th-S Jan. 18 & 21 & 23; M-Th-F April 11 & 14 & 15; T-Th-S May 24 & 26 & 28.

POUPIN – Magdeleine 1552 BAPTISMS

Sun. 8 a.m.: Feb. 21, March 20 & 27, April 3, June 12 & 19 & 26

Sun.? Jan. 24, Feb. 14, March 13, April 10, May 29, July 10 & 17, Sept. 11, Oct. 2 & 30, Nov. 6, Nov. 11 & 18 & 25 [probably 8 a.m.]

* * * * * * * * * * * * * *

Mon. [6 a.m./7 a.m.]: opposite Calvin et al. Jan. 25, April 4 & 18, June 27, July 11, Aug. 22, Oct. 3, Nov. 28

Tues. [6 a.m./7 a.m.]: opposite Calvin et al. Jan. 26, Feb. 23, March 8, May 3, June 28, Aug. 9, Nov. 29

Thurs. [6 a.m./7 a.m.]: opposite Calvin et al. Jan. 14, Feb. 25, March 10, April 7, May 19, June 2 & 16, Aug. 25, Nov. 3 & 17, Dec. 1

Fri. [6 a.m./7 a.m.]: opposite Calvin et al. Jan. 15, Feb. 12, March 11, April 22, Oct. 7 & 21, Nov. 4 & 18, Dec. 16 & 30

Sat. [6 a.m./7 a.m.]: opposite Calvin et al. Jan. 16, May 7, June 4, *July 23*, Nov. 5, Dec. 31

Poupin weeks Th-F-S Jan. 14 & 15 & 16; M-T Jan 25 & 26; T-Th Feb. 23 & 25; T-Th-F March 8 & 10 & 11; M-Th April 4 & 7; M-F April 18 & 22; Th-S June 2 & 4; M-T June 27 & 28 M-F Oct. 3 & 7; Th-F-S Nov. 3 & 4 & 5; Th-F Nov. 17 & 18; F-S Dec. 30 & 31.

ST. ANDRE – Magdeleine 1552 BAPTISMS

Mon. 6 a.m./7 a.m.: June 6, *Aug. 1 & 15*, Sept. 19, Nov. 7 & 14 & 21

Tues. [6 a.m./7 a.m.]: July 5 *& 19*, *Oct. 25*, Nov. 15 *& 22*

Thurs. [6 a.m./7 a.m.]: June 9, *Aug. 4*, Sept. 22, Nov. 10, Dec. 8 & 22

Fri. [6 a.m./7 a.m.]: *July 22*, *Aug. 19*, Sept. 23, *Oct. 28*, Dec. 23

Sat. [6 a.m./7 a.m.]: *Oct. 1*, Nov. 26, Dec. 24

St. André weeks M-Th June 6 & 9; T-F July 19 & 22; M-Th Aug. 1 & 4; M-F Aug. 15 & 19; M-Th-F Sept. 19 & 22 & 23; T-F Oct. 25 & 28; M-Th Nov. 7 & 10; M-T Nov. 14 & 15; M-T-S Nov. 21 & 22 & 26; Th-F-S Dec. 22 & 23 & 24.

JAQUES VALLIER of Lausanne BAP-TISMS

Sun.? July 31

WEDDINGS

Tues. [6 a.m./7 a.m.]: *July 19*

1553

BOURGOING

BOURGOING – St. Pierre 1553 BAP-TISMS

Sun. dawn: opposite Cop, Sept. 17, Oct. 1

Catechism: Sept. 10, Oct. 29, Dec. 3 & 10

Sun.? Sept. 10 [probably 8 a.m.]

* * * * * * * * * * * * * *

Wed. dawn: Oct. 4

BOURGOING – St. Gervais 1553 BAP-TISMS

Mon. 6 a.m./7 a.m.: opposite Chauvet, Aug. 28, Oct. 9 & 23

Tues. 6 a.m./7 a.m.: opposite Chauvet, Oct. 10 & 24

Wed. 7 a.m./8 a.m.: opposite Chauvet, Aug. 30, Oct. 11 & 25, Dec. 20

Thurs. [6 a.m./7 a.m.]: opposite Chauvet, Oct. 26

Fri. [6 a.m./7 a.m.]: opposite Chauvet, Dec. 22

Bourgoing weeks M-T-W Oct. 9 & 10 &11; M-T-W-Th Oct. 23 & 24 & 25 & 26; W-F Dec. 20 & 22

Week shared with Fabri: Bour-going M-W Aug. 28 & 29; Fabri F-S Sept. 1 & 2

BOURGOING – Magdeleine 1553 BAP-TISMS

Sun. 8 a.m.: Dec. 17

Catechism: Oct. 22, Nov. 26

Sun.? July 30, Aug. 13 & 27, Oct. 15, Nov. 5, Dec. 10

* * * * * * * * * * * * * *

Mon. [6 a.m./7 a.m.]: with Fabri, Sept. 4

Tues. [6 a.m./7 a.m.]: with Fabri, Sept. 5 & 12

Fri. [6 a.m./7 a.m.]: Aug. 11 & 25

Sat. [6 a.m./7 a.m.]: Aug. 12

Bourgoing weeks F-S Aug. 11 & 12; M-T Sept. 4 & 5.

Substituting for Poupin; see below.

CALVIN

CALVIN – St. Pierre 1553 BAPTISMS

Sun. 8 a.m.: Feb. 26, Aug. 20, Dec. 10

Sun. afternoon: *Feb. 12*

WEDDINGS

Sun. afternoon: Jan. 1 & 22 & 29, Feb. 5 & 12 & 26, March 5 & 26, April 9 & 30, May 7 & 14, June 11 & 18, July 23, Aug. 6 & 20, Sept. 24, Nov. 5 & 12 & 19 Dec. 3 & 10 & 31 [probably Oct. 22]

Calvin both services: Sun. afternoon: Feb. 12

Calvin preached on Wed. at 7 a.m./8 a.m. Other ministers do baptisms: St. André Jan. 11 & 18, Feb. 1 & 8 & 15, Sept. 27, Oct. 11 & 25, Nov. 8 & 29, Dec. 6 & 29. Des Gallars Jan. 4. Poupin Jan. 18, March 8. [probably also other Wed. these same three, but it is not possible to determine exactly which days Calvin was preaching]

CALVIN – Magdeleine 1553 BAPTISMS

Mon. [6 a.m./7 a.m.]: Oct. 9

Thurs. [6 a.m./7 a.m.]: June 8

Baptisms by other ministers in Calvin's week:

Multiple ministers: St. André-Chauvet F-S Jan. 20 & 21; St. André-St. André-Chauvet M-T-Th March 27 & 28 & 30; St. André-Calvin M-Th June 5 & 8; Chauvet-St. André M-Th July 3 & 6; St. André-Fabri-St. André

Th-F-S July 20 & 21 & 22; <u>Calvin-St. André-St. André-St. André</u> M-T-F-S Oct. 9 & 10 & 13 & 14; <u>St. André-St. André-Fabri</u> M-Th-S Dec. 5 & 7& 9;

One minister several in one week: <u>St. André</u> M-T Jan. 30 & 31; T-Th-S Feb. 28 & March 2 & 4; M-T-Th April 24 & 26 & 27; T-F Aug.15 & 18; M-F-S Aug. 28 & Sept. 1 & 2; T-Th Sept. 26 & 28; Th-F Dec. 21 & 22.

One baptism in a week: <u>St. André</u> M Feb. 13, Th April 13, T- May 9, Th June 22, T Aug. 1, M. Nov. 20; <u>Fabri</u> Th May 25; <u>Bourgoing</u> T Sept. 12.

CHAUVET

<u>CHAUVET – St. Pierre 1553 BAPTISMS</u>
Sun.? Dec. 24

<u>CHAUVET – St. Gervais 1553 BAP-TISMS</u>
Sun. dawn: June 18

Sun. 8 a.m.: July 16, Sept. 17 & 24, Oct. 1 & 22 & 29, Dec. 10 & 31

Catechism: Feb. 12, March 12, May 14, Aug. 20 & 27, Nov. 5, Dec. 3 & 17

Sun. afternoon: Sept. 3

Sun.? Jan. 8 & 22, Aug. 6 [probably 8 a.m.?]

* * * * * * * * * * * * * *

Mon. [6 a.m./7 a.m.]: opposite Fabri/Bourgoing, April 3, May 1, July 24, Oct. 2 & 16, Dec. 25

Tues. [6 a.m./7 a.m.]: opposite Fabri/Bourgoing, Jan. 24, Feb. 7, March 7, June 13 & 27, Aug. 22, Sept. 19, Oct. 31, Dec. 26

Wed. dawn: July 19

Wed. [7 a.m./8 a.m.]: opposite Fabri/Bourgoing, Jan. 11, March 8, May 17, June 14, Aug. 9 & 23, Oct. 18, Nov. 29, Dec. 27

Thurs. [6 a.m./7 a.m.]: opposite Fabri/Bourgoing, Feb. 9 & 23, April 20, Aug. 10, Sept. 7 & 21 & 28, Nov. 2, Dec. 28

Fri. [6 a.m./7 a.m.]: opposite Fabri/Bourgoing, Jan. 13, Aug. 11, Sept. 29, Oct. 6, Dec. 29

Sat. [6 a.m./7 a.m.]: opposite Fabri/Bourgoing, Feb. 11, March 25, May 13

WEDDINGS
Sun.?: Oct. 29 [probably afternoon]

* * * * * * * * * * * * * *

Thurs. 6 a.m./7 a.m.: Nov. 30

Fri. 6 a.m./7 a.m.: July 28

<u>Chauvet</u> weeks S-W-F Jan. 8 & 11 & 13; T-Th-S Feb. 7 & 9 & 11; T-W March 7 & 8; T-W June 13 & 14; M-F July 24 & 28; S-W-Th-F Aug. 6 & 9 & 10 & 11; T-W Aug. 22 & 23; S-T-Th Sept. 17 & 19 & 21; S-Th-F Sept. 24 & 28 & 29; S-M-F Oct. 1 & 2 & 6; M-W Oct. 16 & 18; T-Th Oct. 31 & Nov. 2; M-T-W-Th.-F Dec. 25 & 26 & 27 & 28 & 29.

<u>CHAUVET – Magdeleine 1553 BAP-TISMS</u>
Mon. [6 a.m./7 a.m.]: July 3

Thurs. [6 a.m./7 a.m.]: March 30

Sat. [6 a.m./7 a.m.]: Jan. 21

COLLADON

<u>COLLADON – St. Gervais 1553 BAP-TISMS</u>
Sat. [6 a.m./7 a.m.]: Sept. 16

COP

<u>COP – St. Pierre 1553 BAPTISMS</u>
Sun. dawn: opposite Bourgoing or St. Andre, Jan. 1, Feb. 12 & 26, March 26, May 7, June 25, July 2 & 16 & 30, Aug. 13, Sept. 24, Oct. 8, Nov. 5 & 19, Dec. 31

Catechism: March 12, April 23

＊＊＊＊＊＊＊＊＊＊＊＊＊＊＊

Mon. dawn: Feb. 20; Aug. 21, Sept. 4, Nov. 27, Dec. 25

Wed. dawn: Jan. 11, Feb. 8, May 10, July 12, Aug. 23, Oct. 18, Nov. 1 & 15 & 29, Dec. 13

Wed. 7 a.m./8 a.m.: July 19, Sept. 13

Fri. dawn: April 7, June 16, Dec. 29

WEDDINGS

Sun. dawn: Jan. 1 & 15, Feb. 12 & 26, March 26, April 9 & 23, June 4, July 2 & 16 & 30, Aug. 27, Sept. 10 & 24, Nov. 19, Dec. 3 & 17 & 31

Sun. afternoon: Sept. 10

＊＊＊＊＊＊＊＊＊＊＊＊＊＊＊

Mon. dawn: Jan. 9, April 3, May 1 & 15, June 12, Sept. 18, Oct. 2 & 30, Dec. 11 & 25

Wed. dawn: April 5, June 14, Sept. 6, Nov. 1

Cop both services: Sun. dawn: Jan. 1, Feb. 12 & 26, March 26, July 2 & 16 & 30, Sept. 24, Nov. 19, Dec. 31; Mon. dawn: Dec. 25; Wed. dawn: Nov. 1

Cop weeks M-W Jan. 9 & 11; M-W-F April 3 & 5 & 7; M-W-F June 12 & 14 & 16; M-W Aug. 21 & 23; M-W Sept. 4 & 6; M-W Nov. 27 & 29; M-W Dec. 11 & 13; M-F Dec. 25 & 29 [taken together clearly alternates weeks except May 10]

COP – St. Gervais 1553 BAPTISMS

Sun. 8 a.m.: Oct. 15

WEDDINGS

Sun. dawn: May 14

Sun. afternoon: Feb. 5 & 19, June 11, Oct. 29, Nov. 12

COP – Magdeleine 1553 BAPTISMS

Catechism: March 26, April 9, July 30, Sept. 24, Dec. 3

＊＊＊＊＊＊＊＊＊＊＊＊＊＊＊

Thurs. 6 a.m./7 a.m.: Oct. 19, Nov. 30

Weeks substituting for Poupin = Th-F-S Cop-St. André-Poupin Oct. 19 & 20 & 21; M-F Fabri-Cop Nov. 27 & 30

DES GALLARS

DES GALLARS – St. Pierre 1553 BAPTISMS

Sun.? March 19

＊＊＊＊＊＊＊＊＊＊＊＊＊＊＊

Mon. dawn: Jan. 2

Wed. dawn: Jan. 4

WEDDINGS

Sun. dawn: March 19

Sun.? March 12, April 30

＊＊＊＊＊＊＊＊＊＊＊＊＊＊＊

Mon. dawn: Jan. 2

Des Gallars both services: Mon. dawn Jan. 2

DES GALLARS – St. Gervais 1553 BAPTISMS

Catechism: May 7

＊＊＊＊＊＊＊＊＊＊＊＊＊＊＊

Thurs. 6 a.m./7 a.m.: opposite Chauvet, Jan. 19, June 8

Fri. [6 a.m./7 a.m.]: opposite Chauvet, March 3

Sat. [6 a.m./7 a.m.]: opposite Chauvet, Feb. 18, July 22

WEDDINGS

Thurs. 6 a.m./7 a.m.: June 22

DES GALLARS – Magdeleine 1553 BAPTISMS

Sun. 8 a.m.: April 9

Catechism: June 25

Sun.? April 23, May 7, June 18

* * * * * * * * * * * * * *
Thurs. [6 a.m./7 a.m.]: March 23, April 6, May 18, June 1 & & 15 & 29

Fri. [6 a.m./7 a.m.]: March 24, May 5

Sat. [6 a.m./7 a.m.] April 8

Des Gallars week Th-F March 23 & 24

Substituting for Poupin; see below.

FABRI

FABRI – St. Pierre 1553 BAPTISMS

Sun. afternoon: May 21, Sept. 3

* * * * * * * * * * * * * *
Wed. 7 a.m./8 a.m.: Feb. 22, May 3, May 31, June 14, July 26, Aug. 9, Sept. 20

FABRI – St. Gervais 1553 BAPTISMS

Sun. dawn: April 16

Sun. 8 a.m.: Feb. 12, March 12, Nov. 19, Dec. 17

Catechism: Sept. 17

* * * * * * * * * * * * * *
Mon. 6 a.m./7 a.m.: opposite Chauvet, Feb. 27, July 3, Sept. 4

Tues. 6 a.m./7 a.m.: opposite Chauvet, Jan. 17, Feb. 14, March 14 & 28, April 11, May 9 & 23, Aug. 1, Sept. 12

Wed. 7 a.m./8 a.m.: opposite Chauvet, Jan. 4, March 15, April 26, May 10 & 24, June 7, Sept. 13

Fri. 6 a.m./7 a.m.: opposite Chauvet, Sept. 1

Sat. 6 a.m./7 a.m.: opposite Chauvet, Jan. 7, Sept. 2

WEDDINGS

Sun. dawn: April 16

* * * * * * * * * * * * * *
Mon. [6 a.m./7 a.m.]: Sept. 4

Fabri both services: Sun. dawn: April 16, Mon. Sept. 4

Fabri weeks W-S Jan. 4 & 7; T-W March 14 & 15; T-W May 9 & 10; May 23 & 24; T-W Sept. 12 & 13

Week shared with Bourgoing: Bourgoing M-W Aug. 28 & 30 & Fabri F-S Sept. 1 & 2

FABRI – Magdeleine 1553 BAPTISMS

Sun. 8 a.m.: March 5 & 19, Oct. 1

Catechism: Jan. 29, March 5 & 12 & 19, May 14, June 11, Sept. 10

* * * * * * * * * * * * * *
Mon. 6 a.m./7 a.m.: opposite Calvin/ St. André, Feb. 6, March 20, April 3 & 17, May 1 & 15, Sept. 18, Oct. 2, Nov. 27, Dec. 25

Tues. 6 a.m./7 a.m: opposite Calvin/ St. André, Feb. 7, March 7, April 4, May 2 & 16, July 25, Aug. 8, Sept. 19, Dec. 12 & 26

Thurs. [6 a.m./7 a.m.]: May 25, Sept. 7, Oct. 5, Dec. 28

Fri. 6 a.m./7 a.m.: July 21 & 28

Sat. 6 a.m./7 a.m.: Sept. 9, Oct. 7, Dec. 9 & 30

WEDDINGS

Mon. 6 a.m./7 a.m.: Dec. 25

Fabri week M-T Feb. 6 & 7; April 3 & 4; May 1 & 2; May 15 & 16; T-F July 25 & 28; Th-S Sept. 7 & 9; M-T Sept. 18 & 19; M-Th-S Oct. 2 & 5 & 7; M-T-Th-S Dec. 25 & 26 & 28 & 30.

Substituting for Poupin; see below.

FAREL

FAREL – St. Pierre 1553 WEDDINGS

Sun. afternoon: June 4

POUPIN

POUPIN – St. Pierre 1553 BAPTISMS

Sun. dawn: July 23, Nov. 12, Dec. 10

Sun.? Jan. 8, March 5 & 19, Oct. 15, Oct. 22 probably Sun. 8 a.m.

* * * * * * * * * * * * * *
Wed. probably dawn: June 28

Wed. [7 a.m./8 a.m.]: Jan. 18, March 1, May 24, June 7 & 21

Fri. dawn: possibly opposite Cop, Feb. 17, March 17 & 31, May 26, June 9 & 30, Aug. 4 [alternates weeks except June 30]
    WEDDINGS

Sun. dawn: June 11 [probably dawn Jan. 22, March 5, May 28, July 23, Aug. 20]

Sun. [probably afternoon]: Jan. 8, Feb. 19, Oct. 15 & 29

* * * * * * * * * * * * * *

Mon. dawn: Jan. 16 & 23, Feb. 13 & 27, March 13, May 22, June 5 & 19 & 26, July 3, Oct. 9 & 23, Dec. 18

Wed. [probably dawn]: April 26, June 28, Oct. 25, Nov. 8, Dec. 20

Fri. dawn: 30 June, Dec 8

    Poupin both services: Sun. dawn: July 23; Wed. dawn: June 28

Poupin weeks M-F Feb. 13 & 17; M-F March 13 & 17; M-F June 5 & 9; M-F June 26 & 28 & 30; M-W Oct. 23 [&25]; M-W Dec. 18 [&20]

POUPIN – St. Gervais 1553 BAPTISMS

Sun.? July 23 [probably 8 a.m.]

* * * * * * * * * * * * * *

Mon. [6 a.m./7 a.m.]: Nov. 27
    WEDDINGS

Sun.?: Jan. 29, Feb. 12 & 26, July 16 & 23, Sept. 10, Oct. 8 [probably afternoon]

* * * * * * * * * * * * * *

Mon. [6 a.m./7 a.m.]: Aug. 14

POUPIN – Magdeleine 1553 BAPTISMS

Sun.? Feb. 5 & 19, May 28, Aug. 20, Oct. 29, Nov. 12

* * * * * * * * * * * * * *

Sat. [6 a.m./7 a.m.]: Oct. 21

ST. ANDRE

ST. ANDRE – St. Pierre 1553 BAPTISMS

Sun. dawn: opposite Cop, April 2, May 14

Sun. 8 a.m.: May 14, July 2 & 23, Aug. 27, Sept. 24, Oct. 1 & 8, Nov. 12 & 26

Catechism: Jan. 1 & 15 & 22, Feb. 5 & 12 & 26, March 26, April 30, May 14, June 25, July 9, Aug. 6 & 13 & 20, Sept. 24, Oct. 1 & 8, Nov. 5 & 12 & 26, Dec. 17 & 31

Sun. afternoon: Feb. 5 & 26, Aug. 20, Sept. 17

Sun.? March 5, April 16 & 30, July 16 [if April 16 is an afternoon, have a Calvin sermon]

* * * * * * * * * * * * * *

Wed. [probably dawn]: March 8, Sept. 27

Wed. 7 a.m./8 a.m.: Jan. 11 & 25, Feb. 1 & 8 & 15, April 26, May 10, May 17, June 28, July 5, Aug. 2 & 16, Oct. 11 & 25, Nov. 8 & 15 & 29, Dec. 6 & 27

Fri. dawn: May 12, Oct. 6
    WEDDINGS

Sun. dawn: April 16, May 14

Sun. afternoon: May 28, Dec. 17

* * * * * * * * * * * * * *

Mon. dawn: May 8

    St. André both services: Sun. dawn: May 14

ST. ANDRE – St. Gervais 1553 BAPTISMS

Sun. dawn: Feb. 26, March 5, May 7, June 11, July 16, Aug. 13, Sept. 17, Oct. 22, Nov. 12 & 19

* * * * * * * * * * * * * *

Wed. dawn: May 31, June 7, July 26, Oct. 25

Wed. 7 a.m./8 a.m.: May 3

Thurs. [6 a.m./7 a.m.]: May 4

WEDDINGS

Sun. dawn: Jan. 15, Feb. 19 & 26, April 9, June 4, July 23, Oct. 8 & 22, Nov. 19, Dec. 3 & 17

Sun. afternoon: April 9

* * * * * * * * * * * * * *

Wed. dawn: Feb. 15, April 5, Sept. 20

ST. ANDRE – Magdeleine 1553 BAP-TISMS

Sun.? Aug. 20

* * * * * * * * * * * * * *

Mon. [6 a.m./7 a.m.]: Jan. 30, Feb. 13, March 27, April 24, June 5 & 26, July 24, Aug. 28, Oct. 30, Nov. 20, Dec. 4

Tues. [6 a.m./7 a.m.]: Jan. 31, Feb. 28, March 28, April 25, May 9, Aug. 1 & 15, Sept. 26, Oct. 10, Nov. 14

Thurs. [6 a.m./7 a.m.]: March 2, April 13 & 27, June 22, July 6 & 20, Sept. 28, Nov. 16, Dec. 7 & 21

Fri. [6 a.m./7 a.m.]: Jan. 20, March 17, Aug. 18, Sept. 1, Oct. 13 & 20, Nov. 3, Dec. 22

Sat. [6 a.m./7 a.m.]: March 4, July 22, Sept. 2, Oct. 14, Nov. 4

St. André weeks M-T Jan. 30 & 31; Th-S March 2 & 4; M-T March 27 & 28; M-T-Th April 24 & 25 & 27; Th-S July 20 &22; M-F-S Aug. 28 & Sept. 1 & 2; T-F-S Oct. 10 & 13 & 14; M-F-S Oct. 30 & Nov. 3 & 4; T-F-S Oct. 10 & 13 & 14; Th-F Dec. 21 & 22.

Complicated system for covering Poupin's illness in 1553

Fabri-Des Gallars-Bourgoing were at St. Gervais alternate weeks from those they were at Magdeleine, thus in effect never having a week off; in St. Gervais they had the weeks beginning Jan. 2, 16, 30 and so forth, while at Magdeleine they had the weeks beginning Jan. 9, 23, Feb. 6, 20 and so forth.

Fabri and Des Gallars share weekdays at St. Gervais in first part of year.

Fabri-Des Gallars T-Th Jan. 17 & 19; Fabri-Des Gallars T-S Feb. 14 & 18; Fabri-Des Gallars M-F Feb. 27 & March 3; Fabri-Des Gallars W-Th June 7 & 8.

(Some weeks baptisms only by one but it is assumed that the other is also preaching; Fabri W-F Jan. 4 & 7, T-W March 14 & 15, T March 28, T April 11, W April 28, T-W May 9 & 10, T-W May 23 & 24, M July 3, T Aug. 1. Des Gallars Th June 22, S July 22.)

[At one point Chauvet fills in for Fabri-Des Gallars on Sat. May 13]

Meanwhile they are doing weekdays at Magdeleine:

Fabri-Des Gallars-Des Gallars M-Th-F March 20 & 23 & 24; Fabri-Fabri-Des Gallars-Des Gallars M-T-Th-S April 3 & 4 & 6 & 8; Fabri-Fabri-Des Gallars M-T-F May 1 & 2 & 5; Fabri-Fabri-Des Gallars M-T-Th May 15 & 16 & 18.

(Some weeks baptisms only by one but it is assumed that the other is also preaching; Fabri M-T Feb. 6 & 7, T March 7, M April 17, M July 3. Des Gallars Th June 1, Th June 15, S July 22.) One week St. André-Des Gallars M-Th June 26 & 29.

Fabri and Bourgoing share weekdays at St. Gervais in the later part of the year. At first they divide the week, then they each take a full week. Chauvet fills in last week of Sept. [3 in a row] plus last week of Nov.

Divide: Bourgoing-Bourgoing-Fabri-Fabri M-W Aug. 28 & 30 & Sept. 1 & 2.

Full week: <u>Fabri</u> T-W Sept. 12 & 13. <u>Bourgoing</u> M-T-W Oct. 9 & 10 & 11; M-T-W-Th Oct. 23 & 24 & 25 & 26; W-F Dec. 20 & 22.

<u>Meanwhile they are doing weekdays at Magdeleine.</u>

Divide: Fabri-Bourgoing-Bourgoing T-F-S Aug. 8 & 11 & 12; <u>Bourgoing-Bourgoing-Fabri-Fabri</u> M-T-Th-S Sept. 4 & 5 & 7 & 9;

Full week: <u>Bourgoing</u> F Aug. 25. <u>Fabri</u> M-T Sept. 18 & 19, M-Th-S Oct. 2 & 5 & 7, T Dec. 12, M-T-Th-S Dec. 25 & 25 & 28 & 30.

<u>St. André fills in at points opposite Fabri</u>

Divide: <u>St. André-Fabri-Fabri</u> M-T-F July 24 & 25 & 28.

Full week: <u>St. André</u> M-F-S Oct. 30 & Nov. 3 & 4; T-Th Nov. 14 & 16.

One week <u>Fabri-Cop</u>, M-Th Nov. 27 & 30.

1554

Magdeleine only

BOURGOING – Magdeleine 1554 BAPTISMS

Sun. 8 a.m.: Jan 21, Dec. 16

Catechism: Jan. 7, Feb. 25

* * * * * * * * * * * * * *

Tues. [6 a.m./7 a.m.]: *July 3*, *Oct. 9*

Fri. [6 a.m./7 a.m.]: *June 22*

Sat. [6 a.m./7 a.m.]: *June 23*

Bourgoing week F-S June 22 & 23

CALVIN – Magdeleine 1554 BAPTISMS

Mon. [6 a.m./7 a.m.]: *Dec. 3 & 17*

Tues. [6 a.m./7 a.m.]: *June 19, Dec. 18*

Thurs. [6 a.m./7 a.m.]: *June 21,* Dec. 13

WEDDINGS

Mon. [6 a.m./7 a.m.]: <u>Feb. 19 & 26</u>, *June 18*

Thurs. [6 a.m./7 a.m.]: *May 24*

<u>Calvin</u> weeks T-Th June 19 & 21; M-T Dec. 17 & 18

Baptisms by other ministers in Calvin's week [NB two weeks in Feb. & Dec. Calvin did extra]:

Multiple ministers: <u>St. André-Chauvet-Chauvet</u> T-Th-F Jan. 16 & 18 & 19; St. <u>André-Chauvet-Chauvet-St. André</u> M-Th-F-S Jan. 29 & Feb. 1 & 2 & 3; [Calvin-St. André-Fabri-Fabri M-Th-F-S Feb. 19 & 22 & 23 & 24]; <u>Calvin-St. André</u> M-Th Feb. 26 & March 1; <u>St. André-St. André-Calvin-St. André</u> M-T-Th-S May 21 & 22 & 24 & 26; <u>Calvin-Calvin-Calvin-Bourgoing-Bourgoing</u> M-T-Th-F-S June 18 & 19 & 21 & 22 & 23; <u>St. André-Bourgoing-St. André</u> M-T-Th July 2 & 3 & 5; <u>St. André-Chauvet-St. André</u> M-T-S Aug. 27 & 28 & Sept. 1; <u>Chauvet-St. André</u> T-S Sept. 11 & 15; <u>Cop-Fabri</u> Th-F Sept. 28 & 29; <u>St. André-Bourgoing-Chauvet-Chauvet-St. André</u> M-T-Th-F-S Oct. 8 & 9 & 11 & 12 & 13; <u>St. André-Chauvet</u> M-Th Nov. 5 & 8; <u>Calvin-St. André-St. André-St. André</u> M-T-Th-F Dec. 3 & 4 & 6 & 7; [Cop-Calvin T-Th Dec. 11 & 13]; <u>Calvin-Calvin-St. André-St. André</u> M-T-Th-F Dec. 17 & 18 & 20 & 21.

One minister several in one week: <u>St. André</u> T-F Feb. 13 & 16, T-Th-F March 27 & 29 & 30, F-S April 27 & 28, M-T-Th-F-S May 7 & 8 & 10 & 11 & 12, M-T June 4 & 5; T-S July 17 & 21, T-Th-F Oct. 23 & 25 & 26, F-S Nov. 23 & 24. <u>Chauvet</u> T-Th-F July 31 & Aug. 2 & 3.

One baptism in a week: <u>St. André</u> T March 13, M Aug. 13. <u>Chauvet</u> T April 10

CHAUVET – Magdeleine 1554 BAPTISMS

Tues. [6 a.m./7 a.m.]: April 10, *July 31*, *Aug. 28*, *Sept. 11*

Thurs. [6 a.m./7 a.m.]: Jan. 18, Feb. 1, *Aug. 2*, *Oct. 11*, *Nov. 8*

Fri. [6 a.m./7 a.m.]: Jan. 19, Feb. 2, *Aug. 3*, *Oct. 12*

Chauvet weeks Th-F Jan. 18 & 19; Feb. 1 & 2. T-Th-F July 31 & Aug. 2 & 3; Th-F Oct. 11 & 12

COP – Magdeleine 1554 BAPTISMS

Catechism: Jan. 28, Feb. 18, June 24

* * * * * * * * * * * * * *

Tues. [6 a.m./7 a.m.]: Dec. 11

Thurs. 6 a.m./7 a.m.: *Sept. 27*

FABRI – Magdeleine 1554 BAPTISMS

Catechism: Feb. 4 & 11, April 22, Aug. 5, Sept. 9 & 23, Oct. 21, Nov. 18, Dec. 16

Sun.? Aug. 19

* * * * * * * * * * * * * *

Mon. 6 a.m./7 a.m.: June 25

Tues. 6 a.m./7 a.m.: June 26

Thurs. 6 a.m./7 a.m.: July 26

Fri. 6 a.m./7 a.m.: Feb. 23, March 23, April 6, May 4, Sept. 7 & 21 *& 28*, Nov. 2

Sat. 6 a.m./7 a.m.: Jan. 13 & 27, Feb. 24, March 10, April 7 & 21, May 19, July 14, Sept. 22

Fabri weeks F-S Feb. 23 & 24; F-S April 6 & 7; M-T June 25 & 26; F-S Sept. 21 & 22.

POUPIN – Magdeleine 1554 BAPTISMS

Sun.? April 8, Sept. 30, Oct. 7 & 28, Nov. 25, Dec. 9 & 30

ST. ANDRE – Magdeleine 1554 BAPTISMS

Sun. 8 a.m.: Jan. 7 & 14, March 11, July 15, Aug. 12 & 26, Oct. 14 & 28, Nov. 4 & 25, Dec. 9

Catechism: March 11, April 15, July 15 & 22, Dec. 2

Sun.? July 8, Aug. 19

* * * * * * * * * * * * * *

Mon. [6 a.m./7 a.m.]: Jan. 8 & 22 *& 29*, March 5 & 19, *May 7* & 14 *& 21*, June 4, *July 2* & 9, Aug. 6 *& 13 & 27*, Sept. 3, Oct. 1 *& 8* & 15, *Nov. 5* & 26, Dec. 24

Tues. [6 a.m./7 a.m.]: Jan. 9 *& 16* & 23, *Feb. 13*, *March 13* & 20 *& 27*, April 17, May 1 *& 8* & 15 *& 22*, *June 5* & 12, *July 17* & 24, Aug. 21, Sept. 4 & 18, Oct. 2 *& 23* & 30, *Dec. 4*

Thurs. [6 a.m./7 a.m.]: Jan. 4 & 11 & 25, Feb. 22, *March 1* & 8 *& 29*, April 5 & 19, *May 3 & 10* & 17, *July 5*, Sept. 20, Oct. 4 & 18 *& 25*, Nov. 1 & 29, *Dec. 6 & 20* & 27.

Fri. [6 a.m./7 a.m.]: Jan. 26, Feb. 16, *March 30*, April 27, *May 11*, Oct. 5 & 26, *Nov. 23, Dec. 7 & 21*

Sat. [6 a.m./7 a.m.]: Feb. 3, April 28, May 12 *& 26*, *July 21*, *Sept. 1 & 15*, Oct. 13, Nov. 24

WEDDINGS

Mon. 6 a.m./7 a.m.: Sept. 3

St. André both services: Mon. Sept. 3

St. André weeks M-T-Th Jan. 8 & 9 &11; M-T-Th-F Jan. 22 & 23 & 25 & 26; T-F Feb. 13 & 6; M-Th March 5 & 8; M-T March 19 & 20; T-Th-F March 27 & 29 & 30; T-Th April 17 & 19; F-S April 27 & 28; T-Th May 1 & 3; M-T-Th-F May 7 & 8 & 10 & 11 &12; M-T-Th May 14 & 15 & 17; M-T-S May 21 & 22 & 26; M-T June 4 & 5; M-Th July 2 & 5; T-S July 17 & 21; M-S Aug. 28 & Sept. 1; M-T Sept. 3 & 4; T-Th Sept. 18 & 20; M-T-Th-F Oct. 1 & 2 & 4 & 5; M-Th Oct. 8 & 13; T-Th

Oct. 15 & 18; T-Th-F Oct. 23 & 25 & 26; T-Th Oct. 30 & Nov. 1; F-S Nov. 23 & 24; M-Th Oct. 26 & 29; T-Th-F Dec. 4 & 6 & 7; Th-F Dec. 20 & 21; M-Th Dec. 24 & 27.

St. Gervais ministers substituting at Magdeleine: For 1554 the system was somewhat less complicated. Apparently St. André became Calvin's alternate, as well as doing many baptisms when Calvin was preaching. Fabri continued to come from St. Gervais to Magdeleine for a few days; it appears that he mainly did Saturdays (usually not in Calvin's week) and occasional Fridays. When Bourgoing did baptisms they were in Calvin's week, so he was obviously no longer dividing the time with Fabri.

1555

BOURGOING

BOURGOING – St. Pierre 1555 BAPTISMS

Sun. dawn: opposite Cop, Feb. 17, March 3 & 31, April 28, May 12, June 9, July 7, Aug. 4, Sept. 15 & 29, Oct. 13 & 27, Dec. 8

Sun. 8 a.m.: March 10, July 14

Catechism: opposite his dawn schedule March 10, April 7, Nov. 17 & 24, Dec. 15

Sun. afternoon: March 31

Sun.? Jan. 6 & 20, Feb. 3, March 17 – probably dawn

* * * * * * * * * * * * * *

Mon. dawn: opposite Cop, Feb. 25, June 3, Sept. 23, Oct. 7 & 21, Nov. 18, Dec. 30

Wed. dawn: opposite Cop, Feb. 27, March 27, June 5, Sept. 11 & 25, Oct. 9

Wed. 7 a.m./8 a.m.: Sept. 25, possibly *Feb. 20*

Fri. dawn: opposite Cop, March 1 & 29, May 10, July 5, Aug. 2 & 16 & 30, Sept. 27, Oct. 25, Nov. 8

WEDDINGS

Sun. dawn: Jan. 20, Feb. 3 & 17, March 3 & 17, April 28, May 12 & 26, June 9 & 23, July 7 & 21, Aug. 4, Oct. 27, Nov. 24

* * * * * * * * * * * * * *

Mon. dawn: Jan. 14 & 28, March 11 & 25, April 8, May 6 & 20, June 3, July 1 & 15 & 29, Sept. 9 & 23, Nov. 4 & 18, Dec. 2

Wed. dawn: Jan. 2, June 5, July 17, Oct. 23, Dec. 18

Fri. dawn: June 21, Aug. 2

Bourgoing both services: Sun. dawn: Feb. 17, March 3, April 28, May 12, June 9, July 7, Aug. 4, Oct. 27, [probably Jan. 20, Feb. 3, March 17]; Mon. dawn: June 3, Sept. 23, Nov.18; Wed. dawn: June 5; Fri. dawn: Aug. 2

Bourgoing weeks M-W-F Feb. 25 & 27 & March 1; M-W-F March 25 & 27 & 29; M-F May 6 &10; M-W June 3 & 5; M-F July 1 & 5; M-W July 15 & 17; M-F July 29 & Aug. 2; M-W Sept. 9 & 11; M-W-F Sept. 23 & 25 & 27; M-W Oct. 7 & 9; M-W-F Oct. 21 & 23 & 25; M-F Nov. 4 & 8

BOURGOING – St. Gervais 1555 BAPTISMS

Sun. afternoon: Feb. 10, March 3

* * * * * * * * * * * * * *

Wed. [7 a.m./8 a.m.]: April 3

WEDDINGS

Sun. afternoon: Jan. 6, Feb. 17, April 21, May 5 & 19, June 16, July 7, Aug. 4, Sept. 15 & 29, Oct. 27, Nov. 3, Dec. 8

BOURGOING – Magdeleine 1555 BAPTISMS

Sun. 8 a.m.: frequently in second part of year Aug. 25, Sept. 8 & 22, Oct. 6, Dec. 15

Sun. afternoon: Dec. 22 [service new]

* * * * * * * * * * * * * * *
Mon. [6 a.m./7 a.m.]: Oct. 7

Tues. [6 a.m./7 a.m.]: Sept. 3 & 17

Wed. [7 a.m./8 a.m.]: Aug. 21, Nov. 13
  WEDDINGS
Sun. afternoon: Sept. 22

CALVIN

CALVIN – St. Pierre 1555 BAPTISMS
Catechism: Aug. 25, Sept. 22

* * * * * * * * * * * * * * *
Wed. [7 a.m./8 a.m.]: Sept. 11
  WEDDINGS
Sun. afternoon: *Jan. 6 & 20, Feb. 10 & 17 & 24, March 3, April 28, May 19, June 9 & 16 & 23 & 30, July 28, Aug. 4, Sept. 8 & 29, Oct. 13*

Sun. [probably afternoon] *Aug. 25*, Nov. 3

Calvin preaching on Wed. at 7 a.m./8 a.m.
  Other ministers do baptisms: St. André Jan. 2 & 9 & 16 & 30, March 27, April 17 & 24, May 1 & 8 & 15 & 22, June 19 & 26, July 24, Aug. 14 & 21, Oct. 30. Fabri July 21, Oct. 9 & 16 & 22, Nov. 20. Bourgoing Sept. 25.

CALVIN – Magdeleine 1555 BAPTISMS
Mon. [6 a.m./7 a.m.]: March 25, Oct. 21, Dec. 30

Tues. [6 a.m./7 a.m.]: Aug. 27

Wed. [6 a.m./7 a.m.]: Sept. 18 [this is an off-week]

Fri. [6 a.m./7 a.m.]: Dec. 6
  WEDDINGS
Mon. [6 a.m./7 a.m.]: July 1

Tues. [6 a.m./7 a.m.]: May 7

Sat. [6 a.m./7 a.m.]: July 20
    Baptisms by other ministers in Calvin's week:
    Multiple ministers: Fabri-Cop-St. André M-Th-F March 11 & 14 &

15; Calvin-Fabri-Cop M-Th-F March 25 & 28 & 29; Cop-St. André April 9 & 13; Calvin-St. André T-F May 7 & 10; Calvin-St. André-St. André-St. André M-T-Th-F July 1 & 2 & 4 & 5; St. André-St. André-Calvin Th-F-S July 18 & 19 & 20; Bourgoing-Fabri M-Th Oct. 7 & 10; Calvin-Cop M-T Oct. 21 & 22.

One minister several in one week: St. André Th-F-S Jan 3 & 4 & 5, M-Th-S Jan. 14 & 17 & 19, T-S Jan 29 & Feb. 2; T-Th-S Feb. 13 & 14 & 16; M-T-F Feb. 25 & 28 & March 1, M-T-Th-F May 20 & 21 & 23 & 24, M-Th June 3 & 6, T-S June 18 & 22.

One baptism in a week: St. André M Aug. 12, Des Gallars W Dec. 18.

CHAUVET

CHAUVET – St. Pierre 1555 BAPTISMS
Sun. 8 a.m.: *April 28, Aug. 11*, Nov. 3 & 17

Sun. afternoon: *Sept. 8*, Dec. 22

* * * * * * * * * * * * * * *
Wed. 7 a.m./8 a.m.: March 20, probably July 3

CHAUVET – St. Gervais 1555 BAPTISMS
Sun. 8 a.m.: opposite Poupin/ St. André, Jan. 13, Feb. 10, March 24, April 21, May 5, June 23, July 7, Aug. 4 & 18 & 25, Sept. 8 & 15 & 22, Oct. 6, Nov. 10 & 24, Dec. 1 & 8

Catechism: opposite Fabri, opposite his own 8 a.m. schedule

Sun. afternoon: April 28

Sun.? Oct. 20

* * * * * * * * * * * * * * *
Mon. [6 a.m./7 a.m.]: opposite Poupin, March 25, June 3, Aug. 19, Dec. 23

Tues. [6 a.m./7 a.m.]: opposite Poupin, April 23, Sept. 3 & 17, Oct. 15

Wed. [7 a.m./8 a.m.]: opposite Poupin, Jan. 2 & 30, Feb. 13, May 8, June 12, July 31, Aug. 7 & 28, Oct. 2 & 30, Nov. 6

Thurs. [6 a.m./7 a.m.]: opposite Poupin, June 13, Aug. 22, Sept. 5 & 19, Nov. 28

Fri. [6 a.m./7 a.m.]: opposite Poupin, Feb. 1 & 15, Aug. 23, Sept. 20, Nov. 15

Sat. [6 a.m./7 a.m.]: opposite Poupin, April 13 & 20, Aug. 24, Sept. 7

WEDDINGS

Mon. 6 a.m./7 a.m.: Jan. 14

Fri. 6 a.m./7 a.m.: March 1

Chauvet weeks W-F Jan. 30 & Feb. 1; W-F Feb. 13 & 15; W-Th June 12 & 13; M-Th-F-S Aug. 19 & 22 & 23 & 24; T-Th-S Sept. 3 & 5 & 7; T-Th-F Sept. 17 & 19 & 20.

CHAUVET – Magdeleine 1555 BAPTISMS

Mon. [6 a.m./7 a.m.]: Sept. 9, Dec. 2 & 16

Tues. [6 a.m./7 a.m.]: March 5, July 30, Sept. 10 & 24, Nov. 5, Dec. 3 & 17 & 31

Thurs. [6 a.m./7 a.m.]: May 30, Aug. 1 & 15 & 29, Sept. 12 & 26, Oct. 24, Nov. 21, Dec. 5 & 19

Fri. [6 a.m./7 a.m.]: Oct. 25, Nov. 22, Dec. 20

Chauvet weeks M-T-Th Sept. 9 & 10 & 12; Th-F Oct. 24 & 25; Th-F Nov. 21 & 22; M-T-Th Dec. 2 & 3 & 5; M-T-Th-F Dec. 16 & 17 & 19 & 20

COLLADON

COLLADON – St. Pierre 1555 BAPTISMS

Wed. dawn: Oct. 2

WEDDINGS

Wed. dawn: Sept. 4

COLLADON – St. Gervais 1555 BAPTISMS

Thurs. [6 a.m./7 a.m.]: Sept. 12

WEDDINGS

Mon. 6 a.m./7 a.m.: Feb. 25

COP

COP – St. Pierre 1555 BAPTISMS

Sun. dawn: opposite Bourgoing, Jan. 13, Feb. 10, March 10 & 24, April 7, May 5 & 19, June 16 & 30, July 14 & 28, Aug. 11 & 18 & 25, Sept. 8 & 22, Oct. 6 & 20, Nov. 3 & 17, Dec. 1 & 29

Sun. 8 a.m.: Sept. 15

Catechism: opposite his dawn schedule; possibly opposite Bourgoing though sometimes extra ones, Feb. 3 & 17 & 24, March 24 & 31, April 21 & 28, May 19 & 26, June 16, July 21 & 28, Aug. 11 & 18, Sept. 29, Oct. 27, Nov. 10, Dec. 1 & 8 & 29

Sun. afternoon: *Feb. 3*

* * * * * * * * * * * * * *

Mon. dawn: opposite Bourgoing, June 10, July 8 & 22, Dec. 23

Wed. dawn: opposite Bourgoing, March 6 & 20, June 26, Aug. 21, Sept. 18, Nov. 27, Dec. 25

Wed. 7 a.m./8 a.m.: March 13

Fri. dawn: opposite Bourgoing, March 22, April 19, June 28, Aug. 9 & 23, Nov. 1

WEDDINGS

Sun. dawn: Feb. 10, March 10 & 24, April 7 & 21, May 5 & 19, June 16 & 30, July 14, Aug. 11, Sept. 8 & 22, Oct. 6 & 20, Dec. 1 & 15 & 29

Sun. afternoon: March 10, April 7

* * * * * * * * * * * * * *

Mon. dawn: Jan. 7, Feb. 4, April 15, May 13, June 10 & 24, July 8, Aug. 19, Sept. 16, Dec. 23

Wed. dawn: May 15

Cop both services: Sun. dawn: Feb. 10, March 10 & 24, April 7, May 5 & 19,

June 16 & 30, July 14, Aug. 11, Sept. 8 & 22, Oct. 6 & 20, Dec. 1 & 29; Mon. dawn: June 10, July 8, Dec. 23

Cop weeks W-F March 20 & 22; M-F April 15 & 19; M-W May 13 & 15; M-W-F June 24 & 26 & 28; M-W-F Aug. 19 & 21 & 23; M-W Sept. 16 & 18; M-W Dec. 23 & 25

COP – St. Gervais 1555 BAPTISMS

Tues 6 a.m./7 a.m.: July 2

Wed. 7 a.m./8 a.m.: Oct. 23, Dec. 18

WEDDINGS

Sun. afternoon: Sept. 8 & 22, Oct. 30, Nov. 17

COP – Magdeleine 1555 BAPTISMS

Sun. 8 a.m.: Oct. 27, Dec. 8

* * * * * * * * * * * * * *

Mon. [6 a.m./7 a.m.]: Sept. 2 & 30

Tues. 6 a.m./7 a.m.: April 9, Oct. 22

Wed. [7 a.m./8 a.m.]: Sept. 11, Oct. 2

Thurs. 6 a.m./7 a.m.: March 14, Sept. 19

Fri. 6 a.m./7 a.m.: March 29

WEDDINGS

Mon. [6 a.m./7 a.m.]: Sept. 2
Cop both services: Mon. Sept. 2

D'AIREBAUDOUZE

D'AIREBAUDOUZE – St. Pierre WEDDINGS

Mon. dawn: Sept. 30

D'AIREBAUDOUZE – St. Gervais 1555 BAPTISMS

Thurs. 6 a.m./7 a.m.: Aug. 1

Sat. [6 a.m./7 a.m.]: Sept. 14, Dec. 7

DES GALLARS

DES GALLARS – St. Pierre BAPTISMS

Wed. 7 a.m./8 a.m.: Dec. 11

WEDDINGS

Sun.?: *Aug. 18 [afternoon]*

DES GALLARS – St. Gervais 1555 WEDDINGS

Mon. 6 a.m./7 a.m.: Dec. 2

DES GALLARS – Magdeleine 1555 BAPTISMS

Sun. 8 a.m.: Dec. 1 & 29

Sun.? Nov. 3

* * * * * * * * * * * * * *

Mon. [6 a.m./7 a.m.]: opposite Calvin, Oct. 28, Nov. 25, Dec. 23

Tues. [6 a.m./7 a.m.]: opposite Calvin, Oct. 1 & 15, Dec. 24.

Wed. [7 a.m./8 a.m.]: opposite Calvin, Oct. 16 & 30, Dec. 18

Thurs. [6 a.m./7 a.m.]: opposite Calvin, Oct. 31, Nov. 28, Dec. 12 & 26

Fri. [6 a.m./7 a.m.]: opposite Calvin, Oct. 4 & 18, Dec. 13

Sat. [6 a.m./7 a.m.]: opposite Calvin, Nov. 23

Des Gallars weeks T-F Oct. 1 & 4; T-W-F Oct. 15 & 16 & 18; M-W Oct. 28 & 30; M-Th Nov. 25 & 28; Th-F Dec. 12 & 13; M-T-Th. Dec. 23 & 24 & 26

FABRI

FABRI – St. Pierre 1555 BAPTISMS

Sun. 8 a.m.: *May 19, June 9, Aug. 18, Oct. 13* & 20 & 27, Dec. 8 & 29

Sun. afternoon: *Sept. 1*

* * * * * * * * * * * * * *

Wed. 7 a.m./8 a.m.: July 31, Oct. 9 & 16 & 23, Nov. 20

FABRI – St. Gervais 1555 BAPTISMS

Sun. dawn: Jan. 13 & 20 & 27, Feb. 10 & 17, June 16, July 7 & 28, Sept. 29, Oct. 6, Nov. 24, Dec. 15

Catechism: opposite Chauvet Jan. 13, Feb. 10 & 17 & 24, May 5 & 19, June 9, July 7, Aug. 18, Nov. 10

* * * * * * * * * * * * * *

Mon. 6 a.m./7 a.m.: Dec. 16

Wed. dawn: April 24, May 1, Sept. 18, Oct. 23, Nov. 20, Dec. 4

Wed. 7 a.m./8 a.m.: Jan. 16

WEDDINGS

Sun. dawn: Feb. 24, March 10 & 24, May 5, June 9 & 23 & 30, July 14, Aug. 25, Sept. 29, Oct. 20, Nov. 17 & 24, Dec. 1 & 8 & 29

Sun. afternoon: March 31

* * * * * * * * * * * * * *

Wed. dawn: March 13, June 5, Sept. 11, Nov. 27

Fabri both services: Sun. dawn: Sept. 29, Nov. 24.

FABRI – Magdeleine 1555 BAPTISMS

Sun. 8 a.m.: Sept. 15

Catechism: regularly Jan. 6, March 3 & 17, April 21 & 28, June 16, July 14, Aug. 4 & 11 & 25, Sept. 22, Oct. 6 & 20, Dec. 1 & 8 & 29

* * * * * * * * * * * * * *

Mon. 6 a.m./7 a.m.: March 11

Thurs. 6 a.m./7 a.m.: Feb. 21, March 28, Sept. 5, Oct. 10

Fri. 6 a.m./7 a.m.: Jan. 11, March 8, May 3 & 31, June 28, Aug. 9

Sat. 6 a.m./7 a.m.: Jan. 12 & 26, Feb. 9 & 23, March 9, April 20, May 18, June 1, Aug. 10 & 24, Sept. 21

Fabri weeks F-S Jan. 11 & 12; Th-S Feb. 21 & 23; F-S March 8 & 9; F-S Aug. 9 & 10.

FAREL

FAREL – Magdeleine 1555 WEDDINGS

Mon. [6 a.m./7 a.m.]: Sept. 16

MACAR

MACAR – St. Gervais 1555 BAPTISMS

Thurs. 6 a.m./7 a.m.: March 14

Fri. [6 a.m./7 a.m.]: March 15, May 10

MATHIEU MATISIEN

MATHIEU MATISIEN – St. Gervais 1555 BAPTISMS

Thurs. [6 a.m./7 a.m.]: Aug. 29

JEAN PERRIER

JEAN PERRIER – St. Gervais 1555 BAPTISMS

Tues. [6 a.m./7 a.m.]: Aug. 27, Sept. 10

POUPIN

POUPIN – St. Gervais 1555 BAPTISMS

Sun. 8 a.m.: opposite Chauvet, Jan. 20, Feb. 3, March 31, May 12, June 16

Sun. afternoon: Feb. 3, March 10

Sun.? March 17, July 14 & 28

* * * * * * * * * * * * * *

Mon. [6 a.m./7 a.m.]: opposite Chauvet, Jan. 7, April 15, July 15 & 29

Tues. [6 a.m./7 a.m.]: opposite Chauvet, Jan. 8 & 22, Feb. 5 & 19, March 5 & 19, April 30, May 14, July 2

Wed. [7 a.m./8 a.m.]: opposite Chauvet, Feb. 6 & 20, March 6 & 13 & 20, April 10, July 3, Aug. 14

Thurs. [6 a.m./7 a.m.]: opposite Chauvet, Feb. 21, March 7, April 18, June 20

Fri. [6 a.m./7 a.m.]: opposite Chauvet, Jan. 25, Feb. 22, May 3 & 17

Sat. [6 a.m./7 a.m.]: opposite Chauvet, May 4

WEDDINGS

Sun.?: Feb. 3 [probably afternoon]

* * * * * * * * * * * * * *

Mon. 6 a.m./7 a.m.: July 1

Thurs. 6 a.m./7 a.m.: Feb. 21 .

Poupin both services: Tues. Feb. 21 and probably Sun. afternoon Feb. 3

Poupin weeks M-T Jan. 7 & 8; T-F Jan. 22 & 25; T-W Feb. 5 & 6; T-W-Th-F Feb. 19 & 20 & 21 & 22; T-W-Th March 5 & 6 & 7; T-W March 19 & 20; M-Th April 15 & 18; T-F-S April 30 & May 3 & 4; T-F May 14 & 17; M-T July 1 & 2.

POUPIN – Magdeleine 1555 BAPTISMS

Sun.: Jan. 27, Feb. 10 & 17, March 10 & 24, April 7, May 5 & 19, June 23, July 7, Aug. 18 [could be morning or catechism; probably not afternoon even after Sun. afternoon services began late in the year] March 10 is probably morning.

ST. ANDRE

ST.ANDRE – St. Pierre 1555 BAPTISMS

Sun. afternoon: *April 14, June 2 & 9, July 7*

* * * * * * * * * * * * * * *

Wed. [7 a.m./8 a.m.]: *Jan. 2 & 9 & 16*, Feb. 27, March 6 & 27, April 3, May 8 & 15 & 22, June 19 & 26, July 10 & 24, Aug. 14 & 21, Oct. 30 [probably also *Jan. 30*, May 1]

ST. ANDRE – St. Gervais 1555 BAP-TISMS

Sun. 8 a.m.: Nov. 3 & 17

Catechism: March 10

ST. ANDRE – Magdeleine 1555 BAP-TISMS

Sun. 8 a.m.: regularly Jan. 6, Feb. 24, March 3 & 10 & 31, April 21, May 5 & 19, June 9 & 16, Aug. 11, Nov. 24

Catechism: Feb. 24, March 30, Nov. 24

Sun.? June 30 [probably 8 a.m.]

* * * * * * * * * * * * * * *

Mon. [6 a.m./7 a.m.]: Jan. 7 *& 14*, Feb. 4 & 25, March 4, April 15, May 13 & 20 & 27, June 3, July 8, Aug. 12

Tues. [6 a.m./7 a.m.]: Jan. 22 *& 29*, Feb. 5 *& 12*, March 19, May 14 & 21, June 11 & 18 & 25, July 2 & 9 & 23, Aug. 6 & 20, Nov. 26

Wed. 7 a.m./8 a.m.: Nov. 6

Thurs. [6 a.m./7 a.m.]: *Jan. 3* & 10 *& 17*, *Feb. 14* & 28, March 7, April 4 & 18 & 25, May 2 & 16 & 23, June 6 & 13 & 27, July 4 & 11 & 18 & 25, Aug. 8

Fri. [6 a.m./7 a.m.]: *Jan. 4*, March 1 & 15, April 19, May 10 & 17 & 24, July 5 & 19

Sat. [6 a.m./7 a.m.]: Jan. 5 & 19, Feb. 2 & 16, April 13, June 15 & 22

WEDDINGS

Mon. [6 a.m./7 a.m.]: April 15, Aug. 19

St. André both services: Mon. April 15

St. André weeks Th-F Jan. 3 & 4; M-Th Jan. 7 & 10; M-Th-S Jan. 14 & 17 & 19; T-S Jan. 29 & Feb. 2; M-T Feb. 4 & 5; T-W-S Feb. 12 & 14 & 16; M-Th-F Feb. 25 & 28 & March 1; M-Th March 4 & 7; M-Th-F April 15 & 18 & 19; M-T-Th-F May 13 & 14 & 16 & 17; M-T-Th-F May 20 & 21 & 23 & 24; M-Th June 3 & 6; T-Th-S June 11 & 13 & 15; T-S June 18 & 22; T-Th June 25 & 27; M-Th-F July 2 & 4 & 5; M-T-Th July 8 & 9 & 11; Th-F July 18 & 19; T-Th July 23 & 25; T-Th Aug. 6 & 8; M-T Aug. 19 & 20.

VIRET

VIRET – Magdeleine 1555 WEDDINGS

Mon. [6 a.m./7 a.m.]: July 15

1556

Magdeleine Weddings only

CALVIN – Magdeleine 1556 WED-DINGS

Mon. [6 a.m./7 a.m.]: June 1 & 29

Thurs. 6 a.m./7 a.m.: Feb. 27

COP – Magdeleine 1556 WEDDINGS

Sun. afternoon: Aug. 30

DES GALLARS – Magdeleine 1556 WEDDINGS

Sun. afternoon: May 17 & 31, July 12, Nov. 8

* * * * * * * * * * * * * *

Mon. [6 a.m./7 a.m.]: March 9, May 25

FAREL – Magdeleine 1556 WEDDINGS

Sun. afternoon: March 22

* * * * * * * * * * * * * *

Mon. [6 a.m./7 a.m.]: April 27

MACAR – Magdeleine 1556 WEDDINGS

Mon. [6 a.m./7 a.m.]: Nov. 30

1557

BOURGOING

BOURGOING – St. Pierre 1557 BAP-TISMS

Sun. dawn: Aug. 29

Sun. 8 a.m.: Aug. 29

Catechism: Aug. 29

* * * * * * * * * * * * * *

Wed. dawn: Feb. 10

Wed. 7 a.m./8 a.m.: Oct. 28

WEDDINGS

Sun. dawn: Aug. 29

Bourgoing both services: Aug. 29

BOURGOING – St. Gervais 1557 BAP-TISMS

Tues. 6 a.m./7 a.m.: April 27

BOURGOING – Magdeleine 1557 BAP-TISMS

Sun. 8 a.m.: Jan. 10 & 24 & 31, Feb. 7, March 7 & 14, May 9 & 30, June 13 & 27, Aug. 8 & 22, Sept. 19, Oct. 17, Nov. 28, Dec. 5

Catechism: Jan. 10 & 17 & 24 & 31, Feb. 21 & 28, May 16 & 23: same as 8 a.m.

Sun. afternoon: July 11, Aug. 22, Sept. 5, Oct. 31: same as 8 a.m.

* * * * * * * * * * * * * *

Mon. [6 a.m./7 a.m.]: Oct. 11, Nov. 8, Dec. 6 & 20

Tues. [6 a.m./7 a.m.]: Oct. 12 & 26, Dec. 7 & 21

Wed. [7 a.m./8 a.m.]: Jan. 6 & 27, March 3 & 17 & 24 & 31, May 5, June 2, July 7 & 14 & 28, Sept. 1

Thurs. [6 a.m./7 a.m.]: Aug. 19, Sept. 30, Oct. 14, Nov. 25, Dec. 9

Fri. [6 a.m./7 a.m.]: Aug. 20, Oct. 1 & 15

Sat. [6 a.m./7 a.m.]: March 20, Aug. 21, Nov. 27, Dec. 25

WEDDINGS

Sun. afternoon: Feb. 14, July 11, Sept. 19 & 26, Oct. 31, Dec. 12 & 19

* * * * * * * * * * * * * *

Mon. [6 a.m./7 a.m.]: Nov. 8

Bourgoing both services: Sun. afternoon: July 11, Oct. 31; Mon. Nov. 8.

Bourgoing weeks W-S March 17 & 20; Th-F-S Aug. 19 & 20 & 21; T-W-Th-F Oct. 11 & 12 & 14 & 15; Th-S Nov. 25 & 27; M-T-Th Dec. 6 & 7 & 9; M-T-S Dec. 20 & 21 & 25.

CALVIN

CALVIN – St. Pierre 1557 BAPTISMS

Catechism: Aug. 22

Sun. afternoon: Nov. 7, probably April 11

Sun.? May 23 [probably afternoon]

WEDDINGS

Sun. afternoon: Jan. 10 & 24, Feb. 14 & 21, March 21, April 4 & 25, May 2 & 9 & 30, June 13 & 27, July 4 & 25, Aug. 1 & 8 & 15 & 22, Sept. 12, Oct. 17 & 24 & 31, *Nov. 21 & 28, Dec. 5* & 19

Calvin preached on Wed. at 7 a.m./ 8 a.m. Other ministers do baptisms: Macar Feb. 24, March 24, May 5, July 28, Aug. 25, Sept. 8 & 22, Oct. 6 & 13, Nov. 3 & 17.

CALVIN – St. Gervaris 1557 WEDDINGS

Sun. afternoon: July 18

CALVIN – Magdeleine 1557 BAPTISMS

Mon. [6 a.m./7 a.m.]: Sept. 6

Fri. [6 a.m./7 a.m.]: Jan. 29

WEDDINGS

Mon. [6 a.m./7 a.m.]: March 8, June 7 & 14, Sept. 6

Calvin both services when preaching: Mon. Sept. 6

Baptisms by other ministers in Calvin's week: [Wed. excluded because Calvin at St. Pierre]

Multiple ministers: Macar-Enoc-Macar-Calvin-St. André M-T-Th-F-S Jan. 25 & 26 & 28 & 29 & 30; Enoc-Enoc-Macar-Enoc T-Th-F-S Feb. 9 & 11 & 12 & 13; Calvin-Enoc-Enoc-Enoc-Enoc M-T-Th-F-S March 8 & 9 & 11 & 12 & 13; Enoc-Macar-Enoc M-T-F March 22 & 25 & 26; Enoc-Enoc-Macar M-T-Th April 19 & 20 & 22; Des Gallars-Enoc M-F May 3 & 7; Macar-Macar-Enoc-Enoc T-Th-F-S June 1 & 3 & 4 & 5; Calvin/Chauvet/Des Gallars-Enoc-Macar M-T-Th June 14 & 15 & 17; Calvin-Chauvet-Dupont-Dupont-Dupont M-T-Th-F-S Sept. 6 & 7 & 9 & 10 & 11; Dupont-Dupont-Macar-Dupont M-T-Th-S Sept. 20 & 21 & 23 & 25; Dupont-Macar T-F Oct. 5 & 8; Macar-Dupont-Macar T-Th-F Oct. 19 & 21 & 22; Macar-Dupont-Dupont T-Th-F Nov. 2 & 4 & 5; Macar-Morel/Dupont-Dupont M-Th-F Nov. 15 & 18 & 19; Dupont-Dupont-Colladon-Dupont M-T-Th-F Dec. 27 & 28 & 30 & 31.

One minister several in one week: Enoc F-S Jan. 1 & 2; Th-S Jan 14 & 16; M-T-S April 3 & 4 & 10; T-F-S June 29 & July 1 & 2. Dupont Th-F Aug. 12 & 13; T-Th-F Dec. 14 & 16 & 17. Macar M-T-Th-F Nov. 29 & 30 & Dec. 2 & 3.

CHAUVET

CHAUVET – St. Pierre 1557 WEDDINGS

Sun. dawn: Jan. 3

CHAUVET – St. Gervais 1557 BAPTISMS

Sun. 8 a.m.: opposite Enoc/St.André, Jan. 10 & 24, Feb. 28, March 7, April 11, June 13 & 20 & 27, Aug. 1 & 15 & 29, Sept. 12 & 26, Oct. 10 & 24, Nov. 14 & 21, Dec. 19 [probably May 30]

Sun. afternoon: opposite Enoc, March 7, May 30, June 27, Sept. 5, Oct. 31

* * * * * * * * * * * * * *

Mon. [6 a.m./7 a.m.]: opposite Enoc, Aug. 2, Oct. 11, Nov. 8

Tues. [6 a.m./7 a.m.]: opposite Enoc, April 13, June 8 & 22, July 6, Aug. 17

Wed. dawn: Feb. 10

Wed. 7 a.m./8 a.m.: opposite Enoc, March 3 [probably Jan. 27, Feb. 3, March 17 & 31, April 14, Aug. 4, Sept. 1, Dec. 15]

Thurs. [6 a.m./7 a.m.]: opposite Enoc, Feb. 4, March 18, May 27, July 8, Aug. 19, Sept. 16, Oct. 21 & 28, Dec. 16

Fri. [6 a.m./7 a.m.]: opposite Enoc, Jan. 29, March 5, April 16, July 9

Sat. [6 a.m./7 a.m.]: opposite Enoc, Feb. 20, March 20, Nov. 13

WEDDINGS

Sun. afternoon: Jan. 10 & 17, Feb. 7 & 21, June 13, July 11, Oct. 3, Nov. 7

* * * * * * * * * * * * * *

Mon. 6 a.m./7 a.m.: Feb. 15

Chauvet weeks W-Th Feb. 3 & 4; M-S Feb. 15 & 21; W-F March 3 & 5; W-Th-S March 17 & 18 & 20; T-W-F April 13 & 14 &16; T-F July 6 & 9; M-W Aug. 2 & 4; T-Th Aug. 17 & 19; W-Th Dec. 15 & 16.

CHAUVET – Magdeleine 1557 BAP-TISMS

Sun. 8 a.m: Dec. 5

* * * * * * * * * * * * * *

Mon. [6 a.m./7 a.m.]: June 14

Tues. [6 a.m./7 a.m.]: Sept. 7

Wed. [7 a.m./8 a.m.]: Sept. 8

COLLADON

COLLADON – St. Pierre 1557 BAP-TISMS

Sun. 8 a.m.: *Dec. 12*

Sun. afternoon: Aug. 29

WEDDINGS

Mon. dawn: July 19

COLLADON – St. Gervais 1557 BAP-TISMS

Tues. 6 a.m./7 a.m.: May 25

COLLADON – Magdeleine 1557 BAP-TISMS

Catechism: Dec. 5

Sun.? Dec. 19

* * * * * * * * * * * * * *

Wed. [7 a.m./8 a.m.]: Sept. 15 & 29, Nov. 10, Dec. 8 & 22

Thurs. [6 a.m./7 a.m.]: Dec. 30

COP

COP – St. Pierre 1557 BAPTISMS

Sun. dawn: opposite Macar, Jan. 10 & 24, Feb. 7 & 21, March 7, May 2 & 9 & 16, June 13 & 27, July 25, Sept. 19, Oct. 3 & 31, Nov. 14

Catechism: opposite Macar and opposite own dawn schedule Jan. 17 & 31, Feb. 14, March 14 & 28, April 11 & 25, May 2 & 9 & 16, June 20, Aug. 15, Oct. 10, Nov. 7 & 21, Dec. 5

* * * * * * * * * * * * * *

Mon. dawn: opposite Macar, June 7

Wed. dawn: opposite Macar, Jan. 20, June 23, Sept. 1 &. 29, Nov. 10, Dec. 8 & 22

Fri. dawn: opposite Macar, Jan. 29, July 23, Aug. 6, Oct. 1

WEDDINGS

Sun. dawn: Jan. 10 & 24, Feb. 7, March 7 & 21, May 2 & 30, June 13 & 27, July 11, Aug. 8, Oct. 3 & 17 & 31, Nov. 14 & 28, Dec. 12

Sun. afternoon: Jan. 3

* * * * * * * * * * * * * *

Mon. dawn: Jan. 4 & 18, Feb. 1 & 15, March 15, April 26, May 10 & 24, June 7 & 21, July 5, Aug. 30, Nov. 8, Dec. 6 & 20

Wed. dawn: March 31, Dec. 22

Fri. dawn: June 14

Cop both services: Sun. dawn: Jan. 10 & 24, Feb. 7, March 7, May 2, June 13 & 27, Oct. 3 & 21, Nov. 14; Mon. dawn: June 7; Wed. dawn: Dec. 22.

Cop weeks M-W Jan. 18 & 20; M-W June 21 & 23; M-W Aug. 30 & Sept. 1; W-F Sept. 29 & Oct. 1; M-W Nov. 8 & 10; M-W Dec. 6 & 8; M-W Dec. 20 & 22

COP – St. Gervais 1557 BAPTISMS

Sun. dawn: Aug. 22

Sun. 8 a.m.: April 25

* * * * * * * * * * * * * *

Mon. 6 a.m./7 a.m.: July 12

Tues. 6 a.m./7 a.m.: Aug. 24

Thurs. 6 a.m./7 a.m.: Aug. 26

Fri. 6 a.m./7 a.m.: Aug. 27

WEDDINGS

Sun. dawn: Aug. 22

Cop both services: Aug. 22

Cop week T-Th-F Aug. 24 & 26 & 27

[+ Sun. Aug. 22]

COP – Magdeleine 1557 BAPTISMS

Catechism: April 4, Sept. 19, Oct. 17 & 31, Nov. 14 & 28, Dec. 12

Sun. [probably catechism] Oct. 3

* * * * * * * * * * * * * *

Wed. [7 a.m./8 a.m.]: Aug. 25, Oct. 20

D'AIREBAUDOUZE

D'AIREBAUDOUZE – St. Gervais 1557 BAPTISMS

Fri. [6 a.m./7 a.m.]: Jan. 8, March 26

DES GALLARS

DES GALLARS – St. Pierre 1557 BAPTISMS

Sun. dawn: April 4

Sun.? July 18

* * * * * * * * * * * * * *

Wed. 7 a.m./8 a.m.: opposite Macar/ Calvin, Jan. 20, Feb. 3 & 17, March 17 & 31, April 28, May 26, June 9, & 23, Aug. 4

DES GALLARS – St. Gervais 1557 BAPTISMS

Wed. [7 a.m./8 a.m.]: April 21, July 14

DES GALLARS – Magdeleine 1557 BAPTISMS

Catechism: Jan. 3, Feb. 7

Sun. afternoon: Jan. 31

Sun.? Feb. 14, March 21 & 28, July 4

* * * * * * * * * * * * * *

Mon. [6 a.m./7 a.m.]: Feb. 1 & 15, March 1, April 12 & 26, May 3, June 21, July 5 & 19

Tues. [6 a.m./7 a.m.]: Jan. 5 & 19, Feb. 16, March 2 & 30, April 13 & 27, May 25

Wed. [7 a.m./8 a.m.]: April 28

Thurs. [6 a.m./7 a.m.]: Jan. 7 & 21, Feb. 18, March 4 & 18, April 15, May 27, July 22, Aug. 5

Fri. [6 a.m./7 a.m.]: Jan. 22, Feb. 19, March 5, April 2 & 16 & 30, May 28, July 9 & 23

Sat. [6 a.m./7 a.m.]: April 3, July 24

WEDDINGS

Sun. afternoon: Jan. 10, June 13

* * * * * * * * * * * * * *

Mon. [6 a.m./7 a.m.]: Jan. 4, June 14, July 5

Des Gallars weeks M-T-Th. Jan. 4 & 5 & 7; T-Th-F Jan. 19 & 21 & 22; M-T-Th-F Feb. 15 & 16 & 18 & 19; M-T-Th-F March 1 & 2 & 4 & 5; T-F-S March 30 & April 2 & 3; April 12 & 13 & 15 & 16; M-T-W-F April 26 & 27 & 28 & 30; T-Th.-F May 25 & 27 & 28; M-F July 5 & 9; M-Th-F-S July 19 & 22 & 23 & 24.

DUPONT

DUPONT – St. Pierre 1557 BAPTISMS

Sun. 8 a.m.: Sept. 19

DUPONT – St. Gervais 1557 BAPTISMS

Sun. dawn: Sept. 19, Oct. 3, Nov. 14

Catechism: opposite Enoc, Sept. 26, Oct. 17 & 24, Nov. 14.

Sun.? July 25, Aug. 1 & 8

* * * * * * * * * * * * * *

Wed. dawn: Sept. 15

Fri. [6 a.m./7 a.m.]: July 23, Oct. 22

WEDDINGS

Sun. dawn: Sept. 19 & 26, Oct. 24, Dec. 5 & 19

Sun. afternoon: Nov. 21

* * * * * * * * * * * * * *

Wed. dawn: Aug. 11

Dupont both services: Sun. dawn: Sept. 19

DUPONT – Magdeleine 1557 BAPTISMS

Mon. [6 a.m./7 a.m.]: Sept. 20, Dec. 27

Tues. [6 a.m./7 a.m.]: Sept. 21, Oct. 5, Dec. 14 & 28

Thurs. [6 a.m./7 a.m.]: Aug. 12, Sept. 9, Oct. 21, Nov. 4 & 18, Dec. 16

Fri. [6 a.m./7 a.m.]: Aug. 13, Sept. 10, Nov. 5 & 19, Dec. 17 & 31*

Sat. [6 a.m./7 a.m.]: Sept. 11 & 25

Dupont weeks Th-F Aug. 12 & 13; Th-F-S Sept. 9 & 10 & 11; M-T-S Sept. 20 & 21 & 25; T-Th-F Dec. 14 & 16 & 17; M-T-F Dec. 27 & 28 & 31.

ENOC

ENOC – St. Pierre 1557 BAPTISMS

Sun. 8 a.m.: May 2

Sun. afternoon: Feb. 28, March 7

* * * * * * * * * * * * * *

Wed. [7 a.m./8 a.m.]: Feb. 10, March 10

ENOC – St. Gervais 1557 BAPTISMS

Sun. dawn: May 9 [probably March 28]

Sun. 8 a.m.: opposite Chauvet, Sept. 19, Oct. 3 & 17 [possibly Nov. 28]

Catechism: Jan. 10 & 31, Feb. 7 & 21, March 7 & 28, April 4, May 30, June 6, July 11

Sun. afternoon: opposite Chauvet, May 2, Aug. 1 [probably May 30]

Sun.? Feb. 21, Aug. 22, Oct. 31, Dec. 5

* * * * * * * * * * * * * *

Mon. [6 a.m./7 a.m.]: opposite Chauvet, Sept. 20, Dec. 27

Tues. [6 a.m./7 a.m.]: opposite Chauvet, Sept. 7, Dec. 7

Wed. dawn: opposite Chauvet, Jan. 13, March 10

Wed. [7 a.m./8 a.m.]: opposite Chauvet, Sept. 22 [probably July 28, Sept. 8, Nov. 3, Dec. 8]

Thurs. [6 a.m./7 a.m.]: opposite Chauvet, Jan. 28, Sept. 9, Nov. 4 & 11

Fri. [6 a.m./7 a.m.]: opposite Chauvet, Aug. 20, Sept. 24, Dec. 24

Sat. [6 a.m./7 a.m.]: opposite Chauvet, Dec. 25

WEDDINGS

Sun. dawn: Jan. 10 & 17, [Feb. 14], April 11, June 13, July 4

Sun. afternoon: April 25, May 2 & 9, Sept. 12, Oct. 10

Sun.?: March 14, April 4

* * * * * * * * * * * * * *

Wed. dawn: June 9

Enoc weeks T-W-Th Sept. 7 & 8 & 9; W-F Sept. 22 & 24; W-Th Nov. 3 & 4; F-S Dec. 24 & 25

ENOC – Magdeleine 1557 BAPTISMS

Sun. 8 a.m.: Sept. 26, Nov. 14 & 28

* * * * * * * * * * * * * *

Mon. [6 a.m./7 a.m.]: March 22, April 5 & 19

Tues. [6 a.m./7 a.m.]: Jan. 26, Feb. 9 & 23, March 9, April 6 & 20, May 18, June 15 & 29

Wed. [7 a.m./8 a.m.]: Jan. 13, Oct. 27

Thurs. [6 a.m./7 a.m.]: Jan. 14, Feb. 11, March 11

Fri. [6 a.m./7 a.m.]: Jan. 1, March 12 & 26, May 7 & 21, June 4, July 2

Sat. [6 a.m./7 a.m.]: Jan. 2 & 16, Feb. 13 & 27, March 13, April 10, June 5, July 3

Enoc weeks F-S Jan. 1 & 2; W-Th-S Jan. 13 & 14 & 16; T-Th-S Feb. 9 & 11 & 13; T-S Feb. 23 & 27; T-Th-F-S March 9 & 11 & 12 & 13; M-T-S April 5 & 6 & 10; M-T April 19 & 20; F-S June 4 & 5; F-S July 2 & 3.

Enoc and Macar share weeks M-T-Th Jan. 25 & 26 & 28; T-W-Th-F-S Feb. 9 & 10 & 11 & 12 & 13 alternating days all week! T-W-F May 18 & 19 & 21 alternating days; T-Th-F-S June 1 & 3 & 4 & 5.

FAREL

FAREL – St. Pierre 1557 WEDDINGS

Sun. afternoon: March 14

MACAR

MACAR – St. Pierre 1557 BAPTISMS

Sun. dawn: opposite Cop, Jan. 17, Feb. 14 & 28, April 11, May 23, June 20, July 4, Aug. 1 & 22, Sept. 12 & 26, Oct. 24

Sun. 8 a.m.: Jan. 24, Feb. 21 & 28, June 20, Oct. 3, *Dec. 5*

Catechism: opposite Cop and opposite own dawn schedule, Jan. 10 & 24, Feb. 21, March 7, April 4, June 13 & 27, Aug. 1, Sept. 19, Oct. 17, Nov. 14 & 28, Dec. 12

Sun. afternoon: Sept. 5 & 12, Oct. 10 & 24, Dec. 19

Sun.? May 2

* * * * * * * * * * * * * *

Mon. dawn: opposite Cop, April 19, Sept. 6

Wed. dawn: opposite Cop, Feb. 24, March 24, May 19, June 16, July 28, Sept. 8, Oct. 20, Nov. 3, Dec. 15 [possibly Dec. 1]

Wed. 7 a.m./8 a.m.: same schedule as dawn, same schedule as Calvin's sermons, opposite Des Gallars Jan 13, Feb. 24, March 24, May 5 & 19, July 28, Aug. 25, Sept. 8 & 22, Oct. 6 & 13, Nov. 3 & 17

Fri. dawn: opposite Cop, Jan. 15, Aug. 27

WEDDINGS

Sun. dawn: Jan. 17, Feb. 14 & 28, March 14 & 28, April 11 & 25, May 9 & 23, June 20, July 4 & 18, Aug. 1 & 15, Sept. 12 & 26, Oct. 24, Nov. 7 & 21, Dec. 5 & 19

* * * * * * * * * * * * * *

Mon. dawn: Jan. 11 & 25, Feb. 22, March 8 & 22, April 5 & 19, May 17, June 28, July 12 & 26, Sept. 6 & 20, Oct. 18, Nov. 15 & 29, Dec. 13

Wed. dawn: March 24, June 16, Aug. 11 & 25

Macar both services: Sun. dawn: Jan. 17, Feb. 14 & 28, April 11, May 23, June 20, July 4, Aug. 1, Sept. 12 & 26, Oct. 24; Mon. dawn: April 19, Sept. 6; Wed. dawn: March 24, June 16.

Macar week (dawn): M-F Jan. 11 & 15; M-W Feb. 22 & 24; M-W March 22 & 24; M-W May 17 & 19; M-W July 26 & 28; M-W Sept. 6 & 8; M-W Oct. 18 & 20; M-W Nov. 29 & Dec. 1; M-W Dec. 13 & 15.

MACAR – St. Gervais 1557 BAPTISMS

Sun. dawn: Aug. 29

Sun. 8 a.m.: May 2

Catechism: April 25, June 20

Sun. afternoon: March 28

MACAR – Magdeleine 1557 BAPTISMS

Catechism: Aug. 15 & 22, Sept. 12 & 26, Nov. 21

* * * * * * * * * * * * * *

Mon. [6 a.m./7 a.m.]: Jan. 25, May 24, July 26, Nov. 15 & 29

Tues. [6 a.m./7 a.m.]: June 1, Oct. 19, Nov. 2 & 30

Wed. [7 a.m./8 a.m.]: Feb. 10 & 17, May 19, June 23, Aug. 18

Thurs. [6 a.m./7 a.m.]: Jan. 28, March 25, April 22, June 3 & 17, July 15, Sept. 23, Dec. 2

Fri. [6 a.m./7 a.m.]: Feb. 12, Oct. 8 & 22, Dec. 3

Sat. [6 a.m./7 a.m.]: July 31

Macar weeks M-Th Jan. 25 & 28; W-F Feb. 10 & 12; M-S July 26 & 31; T-F Oct. 19 & 22; M-T-Th-F Nov. 29 & 30 & Dec. 2 & 3

Macar and Dupont share weeks T-F Oct. 5 & 8; T-Th Oct. 19 & 21;M-Th-F Nov. 15 & 18 & 19;

MALISIEN

MATHIEU MALISIEN – St. Gervais 1557 BAPTISMS

Fri. 6 a.m./7 a.m.: March 12, April 30

MOREL

MOREL – St. Pierre 1557 BAPTISMS

Catechism: July 25

* * * * * * * * * * * * * *

Wed. 7 a.m./8 a.m.: July 21

MOREL – Magdeleine 1557 BAPTISMS

Wed. [7 a.m./8 a.m.]: Nov. 3 & 17, Dec. 1

Thurs. [6 a.m./7 a.m.]: Nov. 18

Fri. [6 a.m./7 a.m.]: Nov.13

ST. ANDRE

ST. ANDRE – St. Pierre 1557 BAPTISMS

Catechism: Jan. 3

ST. ANDRE – St. Gervais 1557 BAPTISMS

Sun. 8 a.m.: opposite Chauvet Jan. 3 & 17, Feb. 21

* * * * * * * * * * * * * *

Mon. [6 a.m./7 a.m.]: Jan. 18, Feb. 8

Wed. 7 a.m./8 a.m.: Feb. 10

Thurs. [6 a.m./7 a.m.: Feb. 25

Fri. [6 a.m./7 a.m.: Jan. 22, Feb. 26

   WEDDINGS

Sun. afternoon: Jan. 31, Feb. 14

ST. ANDRE – Magdeleine 1557 BAPTISMS

Sat. [6 a.m./7 a.m.]: Jan. 30

1558

Magdeleine Weddings only

BOURGOING – Magdeleine 1558 WEDDINGS

Sun. afternoon: July 3, Nov. 20 [Sept. 11 or 18]

CALVIN – Magdeleine 1558 WEDDINGS

Mon. [6 a.m./7 a.m.]: Sept. 5

Tues. [6 a.m./7 a.m.]: April 19

Thurs. [6 a.m./7 a.m.]: May 5

Fri. [6 a.m./7 a.m.]: Jan. 28

COP – Magdeleine 1558 WEDDINGS

Sun. afternoon: Jan. 23

DES GALLARS – Magdeleine 1558 WEDDINGS

Sun. afternoon: April 17, May 15, June 19, Aug. 7 & 21 & 28

* * * * * * * * * * * * * *

Mon. [6 a.m./7 a.m.]: Jan. 31, April 11, Sept. 26

Tues. [6 a.m./7 a.m.]: Jan. 4

Thurs. [6 a.m./7 a.m.]: Feb. 3

Sat. [6 a.m./7 a.m.]: Feb. 19

ENOC – Magdeleine 1558 WEDDINGS
Sun. afternoon: Dec. 18

MACAR – Magdeleine 1558 WED-DINGS
Mon. [6 a.m./7 a.m.]: Dec. 26

Tues. [6 a.m./7 a.m.]: Dec. 13

1559

BEZA

BEZA – St. Gervais 1559 BAPTISMS

Sun. 8 a.m.: [probably Aug. 20, Nov. 12, Dec. 31 are 8 a.m. because Chauvet does weddings on those afternoons] [July 23 also because Beza preaching July 16 & 30 afternoon] [probably Sept. 17 because alternate week from Sept. 10 afternoon] [probably June 25 because he has week]

Sun. afternoon: May 21, Sept. 10 [probably Nov. 5 because Chauvet in morning]

Sun.? June 4, Dec. 10

* * * * * * * * * * * * * *

Mon. [6 a.m./7 a.m.]: opposite Chauvet, Sept. 4, Dec. 18

Tues. [6 a.m./7 a.m.]: opposite Chauvet, June 27, July 25, Dec. 5

Wed. [7 a.m./8 a.m.]: opposite Chauvet, June 7 & 28, July 26, Aug. 23, Sept. 20, Nov. 15, Dec. 6

Thurs. [6 a.m./7 a.m.]: opposite Chauvet, June 15 & 29, July 27, Sept. 7, Nov. 16, Dec. 7 & 21

Fri. [6 a.m./7 a.m.]: opposite Chauvet, June 30, Nov. 17, Dec. 8 & 22

Sat. [6 a.m./7 a.m.]: opposite Chauvet, July 1, Sept. 9 & 23, Dec. 9 & 23

WEDDINGS

Sun. afternoon: July 16 & 30 [Dec. 10 probably afternoon because he did not do dawn]

* * * * * * * * * * * * * *

Mon. 6 a.m./ 7 a.m.: June 12, Dec. 4

Beza both services: [Sun. afternoon] Dec. 10

Beza weeks M-Th June 12 & 15; T-W-Th-F-S June 27 & 28 & 29 & 30 & July 1; T-W-Th July 25 & 26 & 27; M-Th-S Sept. 4 & 7 & 9; W-S Sept. 20 & 23; W-Th-F Nov 15 & 16 & 17; M-T-W-Th-F-S Dec. 4 & 5 & 6 & 7 & 8 & 9; M-Th-F-S Dec. 18 & 21 & 22 & 23.

BEZA – Magdeleine 1559 BAPTISMS

Sun.? May 28

Wed. [7 a.m./8 a.m.]: Sept. 27

BOURGOING

BOURGOING – St. Pierre 1559 WED-DINGS

Sun. dawn: March 12

BOURGOING – St. Gervais 1559 BAP-TISMS

Sun. dawn: March 5

Sun. 8 a.m.: March 5

Catechism: May 28

Sun.? Aug. 27

WEDDINGS

Sun. dawn: Feb. 5, June 4

BOURGOING – Magdeleine 1559 BAP-TISMS

Catechism: April 9 & 16, June 11 & 25, Oct. 22

Sun.? July 30

* * * * * * * * * * * * * * *

Mon. [6 a.m./7 a.m.]: Jan. 16, July 24, Aug. 7, Sept. 4 & 18, Nov. 27, Dec. 25

Tues. [6 a.m./7 a.m.]: July 25, Sept. 19, Oct. 3, Nov. 14 & 28, Dec. 12 & 26

Wed. [7 a.m./8 a.m.]: Feb. 15, March 1, May 24, June 7, Aug. 9, Sept. 6 & 20, Oct. 4 & 18, Nov. 1 & 29

Thurs. [6 a.m./7 a.m.]: Aug. 24, Sept. 21, Oct. 5, Nov. 9 & 30, Dec. 14

Fri. [6 a.m./7 a.m.]: June 30, July 28, Aug. 25, Sept. 22, Oct. 6 & 20, Nov. 3, Dec. 1 & 15 & 29

Sat. [6 a.m./7 a.m.]: July 1 & 15, Sept. 9, Dec. 16

WEDDINGS

Mon. [6 a.m./7 a.m.]: Dec. 11 & 25

Bourgoing both services: Mon. Dec. 25

Bourgoing weeks F-S June 30 & July 1; M-T-F July 24 & 25 & 28; M-W Aug. 7 & 9; Th-F Aug. 24 & 25; M-W-S Sept. 4 & 6 & 9; M-T-W-Th-F Sept. 18 & 19 & 20 & 21 & 22; T-W-Th-F Oct. 3 & 4 & 5 & 6; W-F Oct. 18 & 20; M-T-W-Th-F Nov. 27 & 28 & 29 & 30 & Dec. 1; M-T-Th-F-S Dec. 11 & 12 & 14 & 15 & 16; M-T-F Dec. 25 & 26 & 29.

CALVIN

CALVIN – St. Pierre 1559 WEDDINGS

Sun. afternoon: Dec. 17

* * * * * * * * * * * * * * *

Mon. 6 a.m./7 a.m.: Oct. 16, Nov. 13

Tues. 6 a.m./7 a.m.: Dec. 12

Thurs. [6 a.m./7 a.m.]: Nov. 2

Baptisms by other ministers in Calvin's week:

At Magdeleine one baptism in a week: Macar S June 16

At St. Pierre:

Multiple ministers [beginning late June]: Macar-Colladon-Macar M-W-F June 26 & 28 & 30; Macar-Des Gallars W-S July 26 & 29; Enoc-Macar W-F Aug. 9 & 11; Macar-Enoc M-S Aug. 21 & 26; Enoc-Macar-Macar Sept. 20 & 21 & 23; Calvin-Macar M-W Oct. 16 & 18; Macar-Macar/Calvin-Macar T-Th-S Oct. 31 & Nov. 2 & 4; Calvin-Enoc-Colladon M-T-W Nov. 13 & 14 & 15; D'Airebaudouze-Morel T-Th Nov. 28 & 30; Colladon/Calvin-Macar T-Th Dec. 12 & 14; Colladon-Macar-Colladon-Des Gallars M-T-W-S Dec. 25 & 26 & 27 & 30.

One minister several in one week: Macar T-W July 11 & 12, W-Th Oct. 4 & 5; Enoc M-T-Th Sept. 4 & 5 & 7.

NB: Calvin does a wedding on Nov. 2 at the same service that Macar does a baptism; Calvin does a wedding on Dec. 18 at the same service Colladon does a baptism.

CHAUVET

CHAUVET – St. Pierre 1559 BAPTISMS

Wed. 7 a.m./8 a.m.: March 29

WEDDINGS

Mon. dawn: July 31

CHAUVET – St. Gervais 1559 BAPTISMS

Sun. dawn: Jan. 29, March 12, June 18

Sun. 8 a.m.: opposite Enoc/ Beza, Jan. 8, Feb. 5, March 19, Aug. 27, Sept. 10 & 24, Oct. 1 & 8 & 22, Nov. 5 & 26

Catechism: Oct. 29, Dec. 10

Sun. afternoon: Jan. 22 & 29, Sept. 3, Oct. 1 & 29

Sun.? March 26, Dec. 3

* * * * * * * * * * * * * * *

Mon. [6 a.m./7 a.m.]: opposite Enoc/ Beza, Jan. 16 & 23 & 30, Feb. 6, Aug. 14 & 28, Sept. 11, Nov. 6, Dec. 11 & 25

Tues. [6 a.m./7 a.m.]: opposite Enoc/ Beza, Jan. 10, March 21, May 2 & 30, June 6, Aug. 1 & 29, Sept. 26, Dec. 12 & 26

Wed. 7 a.m./8 a.m.: opposite Enoc/ Beza, Jan. 11, Feb. 8 & 22, April 5, May 3 & 31, July 5, Aug. 2, Oct. 4 & 25, Nov. 29, Dec. 13

Thurs. [6 a.m./7 a.m.]: opposite Enoc/ Beza, Jan. 12 & 26, Feb. 9 & 23, March 23, April 6, May 4 & 18, Aug. 31, Sept. 28, Oct. 12, Nov. 30, Dec. 28

Fri. [6 a.m./7 a.m.]: opposite Enoc/ Beza, Feb. 10 & 24, Oct. 6 & 13 & 27, Nov. 10

Sat. [6 a.m./7 a.m.]: opposite Enoc/ Beza, Jan. 14, Feb. 11, May 6, June 10, Aug. 5, Sept. 2

WEDDINGS

Sun. dawn: Jan. 29, Feb. 12, March 12, June 18

Sun. afternoon: Jan. 1 & 15 & 22 & 29, Feb. 5, June 11, July 9, Aug. 20, Oct. 15 & 29, Nov. 12, Dec. 3 & 31

Sun.?: May 21 [probably afternoon]

* * * * * * * * * * * * * * *

Mon. 6 a.m./7 a.m.: Feb. 20, May 15, July 17, Oct. 9 & 23, Dec. 18

Wed. [dawn?]: May 24

Chauvet both services: Sun. dawn: Jan. 29, March 12, June 18

Chauvet weeks T-W-Th-S Jan. 10 &11 &12 &14; M-Th Jan. 23 & 26; M-W-Th-F-S Feb. 6 & 8 & 9 & 10 & 11; M-W-Th-F Feb. 20 & 22 & 23 & 24; T-Th March21 & 23; W-Th April 5 & 6; T-W-Th-S May 2 & 3 & 4 & 6; M-Th May 15 & 18; T-W May 30 & 31; T-S June 6 & 10; T-W-S Aug. 1 & 2 & 5; M. T-Th-S Aug. 28 & 29 & 31 & Sept. 2; T-Th Sept. 26 & 28; W-F Oct. 4 & 6; M-Th-F Oct. 9 & 12 & 13; M-W-F Oct. 23 & 25 & 27; M-F Nov. 4 & 10; W-Th Nov. 29 & 30; M-T-W Dec. 11 & 12 & 13; M-T-Th Dec. 25 & 26 & 28.

Chauvet and his alternate switch weeks three times, in May-June, again in Oct., and again in Nov. The first time Chauvet does two weeks in a row at those points: T-W May 30 & 31, along with T-S June 6 & 10. The second time apparently several ministers take turns: because there are baptisms by Macar-Enoc-Chauvet-Des Gallars-Chauvet M-T-W-Th-F. Then Chauvet has the next week M-Th-F Oct. 9 & 12 & 13. The third time in Nov. is it not sure how it is divided because there are no baptisms or weddings in the weekdays of Nov. 20-25, but Chauvet has the next week and Beza the following one. Dec. 18 baptism by Beza, wedding by Chauvet

CHAUVET – Magdeleine 1559 BAP-TISMS

Wed. [7 a.m./8 a.m.]: Dec. 6

COLLADON

COLLADON – St. Pierre 1559 BAP-TISMS

Sun. dawn: opposite Cop, Jan. 1 & 15 & 29; April 9, May 7, June 4 & 18, July 16, Aug. 27, Sept. 10 & 24, Oct. 8 & 22, Dec. 31

Sun. 8 a.m.: March 19, *July 16, Sept. 10, Oct. 8 & 15*

Catechism: opposite Cop, opposite his own dawn schedule March 5 & 19, April 16 & 30, June 11 & 25, July 9 & 23, Aug. 6 & 13, Sept. 17 & 24, Nov. 26

Sun. afternoon: April 14, July 9 & 23

* * * * * * * * * * * * * *

Mon. dawn: opposite Cop, Oct. 16

Mon. 6 a.m./7 a.m.: Dec. 25 [probably Dec. 18]

Tues. 6 a.m./7 a.m.: Sept. 12, Dec. 12 & 19

Wed. dawn: opposite Cop, Feb. 8, March 8, June 28, Aug. 9, Sept. 6, Nov. 29 [probably June 21, Aug. 16]

Wed. 7 a.m./8 a.m.: May 3 & 31, June 28, July 5, Aug. 2 & 30, Sept. 27, Dec. 27 [probably Nov. 15 and Dec. 20]

Thurs. 6 a.m./7 a.m.: June 22

Fri. dawn: opposite Cop, Jan. 13, Feb. 24, March 24, Aug. 4 & 25, Oct. 6

Fri. 6 a.m./7 a.m.: Sept. 15

Sat. [6 a.m./7 a.m.]: Sept. 2 & 16

WEDDINGS

Sun. dawn: Jan. 1 & 15 & 29, Feb. 12 & 26, April 23, May 7 & 21, June 4, July 2 & 16 & 30, Aug. 13 & 27, Sept. 24, Nov. 5, Dec. 3 & 31

* * * * * * * * * * * * * *

Mon. dawn: Jan. 23, Feb. 20, March 6 & 20, April 17, May 1 & 15 & 22 & 29, June 26, July 24, Aug. 14, Sept. 4 & 18, Oct. 16 & 30, Nov. 13, Dec. 25

Wed. dawn: Jan. 25, May 17, Aug. 9, Dec. 27

Fri. dawn: Dec. 29

Colladon both services: Sun. dawn: Jan. 1 & 15 & 29, May 7, June 4, July 16, Aug. 27, Sept. 24, Dec. 31; Mon. dawn: Oct. 16; Wed. dawn: Aug. 9.

Colladon weeks dawn: M-W Jan. 23 & 25; M-F Feb. 20 & 24; M-W March 6 & 8; M-W May 15 & 17; M-W June 26 & 28; M-W Sept. 4 & 6; M-W Nov. 13 [&15]; M-W-F Dec. 25 & 27 & 29. Later service: T-F-S Sept. 12 & 15 & 16; M-T-W Dec. 18 & 19 & 20.

    NB: Dec. 25 dawn wedding, Dec. 25 7 a.m. baptism

COLLADON – St. Gervais 1559 BAPTISMS

Catechism: Oct. 22

* * * * * * * * * * * * * *

Mon. [6 a.m./7 a.m.]: May 8

Thurs. [6 a.m./7 a.m.]: April 27, Aug. 10

COLLADON – Magdeleine 1559 BAPTISMS

Sun. 8 a.m.: June 25

Catechism: Jan. 8 & 15 & 29, Feb. 12

Sun. afternoon: April 2, Aug. 27, Sept. 10

Sun.? July 2 & 16

* * * * * * * * * * * * * *

Wed. dawn: Dec. 20 [just begun dawn service]

Wed. [7 a.m./8 a.m.]: Jan. 4, Oct. 25

Thurs. [6 a.m./7 a.m.]: Jan. 19

Sat. [6 a.m./7 a.m.]: June 24

WEDDINGS

Sun. afternoon: April 2, Aug. 20, Oct. 8

Colladon both services: Sun. afternoon: April 2

COP

COP – St. Pierre 1559 BAPTISMS

Sun. dawn: opposite Colladon, Feb. 5, March 5 & 19, May 28, June 11 & 25, July 9, Aug. 6, Sept. 17, Oct. 15

Catechism: opposite Colladon, opposite his own dawn schedule Feb. 12 & 26, March 12, April 23, June 4 & 18, July 2 & 30, Aug. 20, Sept. 10, Oct. 1 & 8, Nov. 5 & 19, Dec. 3

* * * * * * * * * * * * * *

Mon. dawn: opposite Colladon, Jan. 30, Aug. 21, Oct. 9, Nov. 6

Mon. 6 a.m./7 a.m.: Aug. 28, Sept. 11

Tues. 6 a.m./7 a.m.: Sept. 26

Wed. dawn: opposite Colladon, Jan. 4, April 26, Aug. 2

Wed. 7 a.m./8 a.m.: Dec. 6

Fri. dawn: opposite Colladon, July 7, probably May 12

Sat. [6 a.m./7 a.m.]: Aug. 5, Oct. 14, Nov. 25, Dec. 9

WEDDINGS Sun. dawn: Jan. 22, Feb. 5 & 19, April 2 & 16 & 30, May 28, June 11, July 9 & 23, Aug. 6 & 20, Sept. 17, Nov. 12 & 26

Sun. afternoon: Jan. 15

* * * * * * * * * * * * * *

Mon. dawn: Jan. 16 & 30, Feb. 27, March 13 & 27, May 8, June 19, July 3 & 17, Aug. 21 & 28, Sept. 11, Oct. 2 & 9 & 23, Nov. 6

Wed. dawn: Feb. 1, June 7, Sept. 13 & 27, Nov. 22

Cop both services: Sun. dawn: Feb. 5, May 28, June 11, July 9, Aug. 6, Sept. 17; Mon. dawn: Jan. 30, Aug. 21, Oct. 9, Nov. 6

Cop weeks dawn: M-W Jan. 30 & Feb. 1; M-F July 3 & 7; M-W Sept. 11 & 13; later services W-S Dec. 6 & 9

COP – St. Gervais 1559 BAPTISMS

Catechism: Jan. 29

* * * * * * * * * * * * * *

Mon. [6 a.m./7 a.m.]: March 6

COP – Magdeleine 1559 BAPTISMS

Sun. 8 a.m.: Jan. 29, May 21

Catechism: Jan. 22, Feb. 19, April 2, Aug. 6, Oct. 15

Sun. afternoon: June 11, Oct. 29

* * * * * * * * * * * * * *

Tues. [6 a.m./7 a.m.]: May 23

Wed. [7 a.m./8 a.m.]: Jan. 11, Feb. 8, March 15, April 5, May 17

Thurs. [6 a.m./7 a.m.]: Nov. 2

WEDDINGS

Sun. afternoon: June 11, July 23, Aug. 13, Oct. 29

Cop both services: Sun. afternoon: June 11, Oct. 29

LE COURT

Le COURT – Magdeleine 1559 BAPTISMS

Fri. [6 a.m./7 a.m.]: Jan 6

Sat. [6 a.m./7 a.m.]: May 27

D'AIREBAUDOUZE

D'AIREBAUDOUZE – Magdeleine 1559 BAPTISMS

Fri. [6 a.m./7 a.m.]: Jan. 20

DES GALLARS

DES GALLARS – St. Pierre 1559 BAPTISMS

Tues. [6 a.m./7 a.m.]: Nov. 28

Sat. [6 a.m./7 a.m.]: July 29, Dec. 30

WEDDINGS

Sun. afternoon: Feb. 12, March 5

DES GALLARS – St. Gervais 1559 BAPTISMS

Thurs. [6 a.m./7 a.m.]: Oct. 5

DES GALLARS – Magdeleine 1559 BAPTISMS

Sun. 8 a.m.: regularly July 9, Aug. 13, Oct. 22 & 29, Nov. 5 & 26, Dec. 3 & 17

Catechism: July 9, Aug. 13, Oct. 29, Nov. "20" = 19, Nov. 26, Dec. 3 & 10 & 31

Sun.? Feb. 26, March 19, May 7, Aug. 20, Sept. 10 & 24

* * * * * * * * * * * * * *

Mon. [6 a.m./7 a.m.]: Jan. 30, Feb. 13, April 10 & 24

Tues. [6 a.m./7 a.m.]: March 14 & 28

Wed. [7 a.m./8 a.m.]: March 8, April 19, Dec. 13 & 20

Thurs. [6 a.m./7 a.m.]: Feb. 2, March 30

Fri. [6 a.m./7 a.m.]: Feb. 3 & 17, March 3, April 28

Sat. [6 a.m./7 a.m.]: March 18

WEDDINGS

Sun. afternoon: Feb. 19 & 26, April 30,
July 30

****

Sat. [6 a.m./7 a.m.]: Feb. 4

Des Gallars weeks M-Th-F-S Jan. 30 &
    Feb. 2 & 3 & 4; M-Th Feb. 13 & 17;
    T-S March 14 & 18; T-Th March 28 &
    30; M-F April 24 & 28

DUPONT

DUPONT – St. Gervais 1559 BAPTISMS

Catechism: Jan.22

WEDDINGS

Sun. dawn: Jan. 15

ENOC

ENOC – St. Pierre 1559 BAPTISMS

Sun. 8 a.m.: *Aug. 27???*

Sun. afternoon: Aug. 13

Sun.? April 30

****

Mon. [6 a.m./7 a.m.]: Aug. 14, Sept. 4

Tues. [6 a.m./7 a.m.]: Aug. 1, Sept. 5,
Oct. 24, Nov. 14

Wed. [7 a.m./8 a.m.]: July 19, Aug. 9,
Sept. 13 & 20, Nov. 8

Thurs. [6 a.m./7 a.m.]: July 20, Sept. 7 &
28, Nov. 9

Fri. [6 a.m./7 a.m.]: Nov. 24

Sat. [6 a.m./ 7 a.m.]: Aug. 26, Oct. 28

Enoc weeks W-Th July 19 & 20; M-T-Th
    Sept. 4 & 5 & 7; T-S Oct. 24 & 28;
    W-Th. Nov. 8 & 9

ENOC – St. Gervais 1559 BAPTISMS

Sun. dawn: Aug. 20, Oct. 1, Nov. 26 [pro-
bably July 16, Dec. 3]

Sun. 8 a.m.: opposite Chauvet, Jan. 29,
April 9, Oct. 15 [Nov. 19]

Catechism: March 12, April 9, Aug.13,
Sept. 17, Oct. 1 & 8, Nov. 19, Dec. 3

Sun. afternoon: May 28

Sun.? Jan. 1 & 15, April 2 & 23 & 30, May 7
& 21, June 11, July 2 & 16, Oct. 15 & 29,
Nov. 19, Dec. 3

****

Mon. [6 a.m./7 a.m.]: opposite Chauvet,
June 19, Oct. 16 & 30

Tues. [6 a.m./7 a.m.]: opposite Chauvet,
Jan 31, Feb. 14, March 28, Oct. 3 & 31

Wed. [7 a.m./8 a.m.]: opposite Chauvet,
Jan. 18, March 1 & 29, April 12, May 24,
June 21, Oct. 18, Nov. 1

Thurs. [6 a.m./7 a.m.]: opposite Chauvet,
Jan. 19, Feb. 2, March 2, May 11 & 25,
Oct. 19

Fri. [6 a.m./7 a.m.]: opposite Chauvet,
Feb. 3 & 17, March 3

WEDDINGS

Sun. dawn: April 2 & 16, July 16, Aug. 20,
Oct. 1 & 8, Dec. 3 [probably March 5 & 19,
April 30,

Sun. afternoon: March 12, April 2, May 28

Sun.?: March 5 & 19, April 30, July 2,
Aug. 6

****

Mon. 6 a.m./7 a.m.: Feb. 27, March 27

Wed. [dawn?]: Sept. 6

Thurs. 6 a.m./7 a.m.: Jan. 19

    Enoc both services: Sun. dawn:
Aug. 20, Oct. 1 [maybe Dec. 3]; Thurs.
Jan. 19

Enoc weeks W-Th Jan. 18 & 19; T-Th-F
    Jan. 31 & Feb. 2 & 3; T-F Feb. 14 & 17;
    T-W-Th-F Feb. 27 & March 1 & 2 & 3;
    T-W March 28 & 29; W-Th May 24 &
    25; M-W June 19 & 21; M-W-Th
    Oct. 16 & 18 & 19; M-T-W Oct. 30
    & 31 & Nov. 1.

ENOC – Magdeleine 1559 BAPTISMS

Sun. 8 a.m.: Jan. 8

Catechism: July 23, Nov. 5

Sun. afternoon: Jan. 22

Sun.? Jan. 1

* * * * * * * * * * * * * *

Wed. [7 a.m./8 a.m.]: Feb. 22

Fri. [6 a.m./7 a.m.]: Jan. 20

WEDDINGS

Sun. afternoon: June 4

MACAR

MACAR – St. Pierre 1559 BAPTISMS

Sun. 8 a.m.: July 9, Sept. 24

Catechism: April 2

Sun. afternoon: March 19, June 4

Sun.? Oct. 29

* * * * * * * * * * * * * *

Mon. [6 a.m./7 a.m.]: June 26, Aug. 21

Tues. [6 a.m./7 a.m.]: July 11, Oct. 31, Dec. 26

Wed. 7 a.m./8 a.m.: Feb. 8, March 22, April 12 [probably June 7, July 12 & 26, Oct. 4 & 18]

Thurs. [6 a.m./7 a.m.]: opposite Enoc & Colladon, Sept. 21, Oct. 5, Nov. 2, Dec. 14

Fri. [6 a.m./7 a.m.]: June 30, Aug. 11

Sat. [6 a.m./7 a.m.]: Sept. 23, Nov. 4

Macar weeks M-Th June 26 & 30; Th-S Sept. 21 & 23; T-W July 11 & 12; W-Th Oct. 4 & 5; T-Th-S Oct. 31 & Nov. 2 & 4

MACAR – St. Gervais 1559 BAPTISMS

Sun. dawn: Jan. 8, March 19, May 7, Dec. 17

Sun. 8 a.m.: Jan. 22

Catechism: Feb. 12, March 19, May 21, Sept. 24

Sun.? April 23, Dec. 31 [probably dawn]

* * * * * * * * * * * * * *

Mon. [6 a.m./7 a.m.]: Oct. 2

Wed. [dawn]: Oct. 25

WEDDINGS

Sun. dawn: March 5, May 7 & 28

* * * * * * * * * * * * * *

Wed. [dawn?]: Feb. 15, June 7

Macar both services: Sun. dawn: May 7.

MACAR – Magdeleine 1559 BAPTISMS

Sun. 8 a.m.: Feb. 5, July 23

Catechism: March 12

* * * * * * * * * * * * * *

Mon. [6 a.m./7 a.m.]: Feb. 6, March 20, May 15 & 29, July 17, Aug. 28, Nov. 6 & 20, Dec. 18

Tues. [6 a.m./7 a.m.]: Jan. 24, Feb. 7 & 21, March 21, April 4, May 16 & 30, July 18, Aug. 15 & 29, Sept. 12 & 26, Nov. 21, Dec. 5

Wed. [7 a.m./8 a.m.]: July 5, Aug. 2 & 30, Sept. 13, Nov. 8 & 15

Thurs. [6 a.m./7 a.m.]: Jan. 12 & 26, Feb. 23, March 23, April 6 & 20, July 20, Sept. 14 & 28, Oct. 12, Nov. 23, Dec. 7

Fri. [6 a.m./7 a.m.]: Jan. 27, Feb. 24, March 10 & 24, April 7, May 5 & 19, June 16 & 23, July 7, Aug. 4 & 18, Sept. 15 & 29, Oct. 13 & 27, Dec. 8 & 22

Sat. [6 a.m./7 a.m.]: Feb. 25, April 8 & 22, May 6, June 3, Aug. 19, Sept. 2 & 30, Dec. 23

WEDDINGS

Sun. afternoon: Jan. 1 & 15, June 18

* * * * * * * * * * * * * *

Mon. [6 a.m./7 a.m.]: July 17, Nov. 20

Tues. [6 a.m./7 a.m.]: July 4

Thurs. [6 a.m./7 a.m.]: Sept. 28

Macar both services: Mon. July 17, Nov. 20; Thurs. Sept. 28

Macar weeks: T-Th-F Jan. 24 & 26 & 27; M-T Feb. 6 & 7; T-Th-F-S Feb. 21 &

23 & 24 & 25; M-T-Th-F March 20 & 21 & 23 & 24; T-Th-F-S April 4 & 6 & 7 & 8; Th-S April 20 & 22; F-S May 5 & 6; M-T-F May 15 & 16 & 19; M-T-S May 29 & 30 & June 3; T-W-F July 4 & 5 & 7; M-T-Th July 17 & 18 & 20; W-F Aug. 2 & 4; T-F-S Aug. 15 & 18 &19; M-T-Th-S Aug. 28 & 29 & 30 & Sept. 2; T-W-Th-F Sept. 12 & 13 & 14 & 15; T-Th-F-S Sept. 26 & 28 & 29 & 30; Th-F Oct. 12 & 13; M-W Nov. 6 & 8; M-T-Th Nov. 20 & 21 & 23; T-Th.-F Dec. 5 & 7 & 8; M-F-S Dec. 18 & 22 & 23.

MERLIN

MERLIN – St. Gervais 1559 BAPTISMS
Sun.? Oct. 1

* * * * * * * * * * * * * * *
Wed. [?7a.m./8 a.m.]: March 22

MERLIN – Magdeleine 1559 BAPTISMS
Sat. [6 a.m./7 a.m.]: Nov. 4

MOREL

MOREL – St. Pierre 1559 BAPTISMS
Catechism: Oct. 22
Sun.? Oct. 15

* * * * * * * * * * * * * * *
Thurs. [6 a.m./7 a.m.]: Nov. 30

MOREL – St. Gervais 1559 BAPTISMS
Sun.? Nov. 5
WEDDINGS
Sun. dawn: Oct. 15
Tues. 6 a.m./7 a.m.: Oct. 24

MOREL – Magdeleine 1559 BAPTISMS
Sun. afternoon: Nov. 19, Dec. 31
* * * * * * * * * * * * * * *
Wed. [7 a.m./8 a.m.]: Dec. 27

WEDDINGS
Sun. dawn: Nov. 28, Dec. 17 & 31
Sun. afternoon: Nov. 28, Dec. 17 & 31
Sun.?: Dec. 3

VIRET

VIRET – St. Pierre 1559 BAPTISMS
Tues. [6 a.m./7 a.m.]: Nov. 7
WEDDINGS
Sun. afternoon: March 12 & 19, April 9 & 30, May 7 & 28, July 9 & 16 & 23 & 30, Aug. 6 & 20 & 27, Oct. 1 & 8 & 29, Nov. 5 & 26, Dec. 3 & 10

* * * * * * * * * * * * * * *
Mon. 6 a.m./7 a.m.: July 3 & 31, Oct. 23, Nov. 20

VIRET – Magdeleine 1559 BAPTISMS
Sun. a.m.: June 11

* * * * * * * * * * * * * * *
Thurs. [6 a.m./7 a.m.]: June 1 & 8
Fri. [6 a.m./7 a.m.]: June 9

1560

Magdeleine Weddings only

BOURGOING – Magdeleine 1560 WEDDINGS
Mon. [6 a.m./7 a.m.]: Sept. 2

CALVIN – Magdeleine 1560 WEDDINGS
Sun. afternoon: May 26, Oct. 27 [NB Ps. Text]

CHAUVET – Magdeleine 1560 WEDDINGS
Sun. afternoon: Nov. 10

COLLADON – Magdeleine 1560 WED-DINGS
Sun. dawn: May 26
Sun.?: April 21

DES GALLARS – Magdeleine 1560 WEDDINGS
Sun. afternoon: May 5

ENOC – Magdeleine 1560 WEDDINGS
Mon. [6 a.m./7 a.m.]: July 29

MACAR – Magdeleine 1560 WEDDINGS
Sun. [probably afternoon]?: Feb. 4, Aug. 18

MOREL – Magdeleine 1560 WEDDINGS
Sun. dawn: July 21
Sun. [probably afternoon]?: Feb. 25, March 3 & 17, April 28, June 9, July 14 & 28, Aug. 11 & 25, Sept. 22, Dec. 29
* * * * * * * * * * * * * *
Tues. [6 a.m./7 a.m.]: June 4
Wed. [dawn?]: Feb. 28
Sat. [6 a.m./7 a.m.]: Jan. 20

1561

Magdeleine Weddings only

BOURGOING – Magdeleine 1561 WEDDINGS
Sun. afternoon: June 1 & 22
Mon. [6 a.m./7 a.m.]: Jan. 6, May 12, Sept. 1

CHAUVET – Magdeleine 1561 WED-DINGS
Sun. afternoon: Jan. 5, Feb. 16, April 13 & 20, July 20, Aug. 10, Nov. 16 & 30

* * * * * * * * * * * * * *
Tues. [6 a.m./7 a.m.]: March 25, April 8

COLLADON – Magdeleine 1561 WED-DINGS
Sun. afternoon: Jan. 26, May 18, Oct. 20

COP – Magdeleine 1561 WEDDINGS
Sun. afternoon: May 11, Dec. 21

D'AIREBAUDOUZE – Magdeleine 1561 WEDDINGS
Sun. afternoon: March 2, April 27, May 4, June 15

MOREL – Magdeleine 1561 WED-DINGS
Sun. afternoon: Feb. 23, March 9 & 30

1562

BEZA
BEZA – St. Pierre 1562 WEDDINGS
Sun. afternoon: Sept. 13 & 20

BOULLIER
BOULLIER – St. Gervais 1562 BAP-TISMS
Mon. [6 a.m.7 a.m.]: Jan. 5

CALVIN
CALVIN – St. Pierre 1562 BAPTISMS
Tues. [6 a.m./7 a.m.]: *Feb. 17*
    WEDDINGS
Mon. 6 a.m./7 a.m.: *Feb. 2*, May 18
Tues. 6 a.m./7 a.m.: *April 7*
        Baptisms by other ministers in Calvin's week:
        Multiple ministers: Chauvet-Colladon T-W Jan. 6 & 7; Calvin-Colladon

M-S Feb. 2 & 7; Calvin-Chauvet-Chauvet-Chauvet T-W-Th-S Feb. 17 & 18 & 19 & 21; Calvin-D'Airebaudouze T-W April 7 & 8; D'Airebaudouze-Merlin April 21 & 25; Merlin-Colladon-Cop T-W-Th May 5 & 6 & 7; Merlin-Merlin-Cop M-W-Th June 15 & 17 & 18; Gaigneulx-Colladon-D'Airebaudouze W-Th-S Aug. 26 & 27 & 29; D'Airebaudouze-Gaigneulx-Gaigneulx T-W-Th Sept. 8 & 9 & 10; D'Airebaudouze-Gaigneulx W-Th Sept. 23 & 24; Cop-Enoc T-W Oct. 27 & 28; Chauvet-Chauvet-Colladon T-Th-S Dec. 8 & 10 & 12; Enoc-Chauvet T-W Dec. 23 & 23.

One minister several in one week: Chauvet M-T Nov. 9 & 10

One baptism in a week: Chauvet W Jan. 21. D'Airebaudouze S March 14, T Aug. 11. Colladon W March 25, S July 4, Th July 20. Cop T June 2, Th Nov. 26

CHAUVET

CHAUVET – St. Pierre 1562 BAPTISMS

Sun. 8 a.m.: June 7, Aug. 2, Sept. 27

* * * * * * * * * * * * * * *

Mon. [6 a.m./7 a.m.]: Nov. 9

Tues. [6 a.m./7 a.m.]: *Jan. 6*, Nov. 10, Dec. 8.

Wed. 7 a.m./8 a.m.: *Jan. 21*, probably *Feb. 18*, Dec. 23

Thurs. [6 a.m./7 a.m.]: *Feb. 19*, Dec. 10

Sat. [6 a.m./7 a.m.]: *Feb. 21*

Chauvet weeks W-Th-S Feb. 18 & 19 & 21; M-T Nov. 9 & 10; T-Th Dec. 8 & 10

CHAUVET – St. Gervais 1562 BAPTISMS

Sun. 8 a.m.: Feb. 1, March 15

WEDDINGS

Sun. dawn: April 26

Sun. afternoon: May 3

CHAUVET – Magdeleine 1562 BAPTISMS

Sun. 8 a.m.: Feb. 15, March 1 & 15, April 12, June 7, Aug. 30, Nov. 22

Catechism: Jan. 25, March 1, April 19, May 31, July 12 & 26, Aug. 9 & 23, Sept. 20, Oct. 18, Nov. 29, Dec. 13

Sun. afternoon: Feb. 8, Sept. 13, Oct. 11, Nov. 22, Dec. 6

Sun.?: May 24, June 28

* * * * * * * * * * * * * * *

Mon. [6 a.m./7 a.m.]: Jan. 12, Feb. 9 & 23, March 23, July 13, Aug. 10, Oct. 5 & 19, Dec. 14

Tues. [6 a.m./7 a.m.]: April 21, June 2, July 28, Sept. 22, Nov. 3, Dec. 1

Wed. [7 a.m./7 a.m.]: Jan. 14 & 28, Feb. 11, March 25, April 1 & 22, June 17, July 15 & 29, Aug. 12 & 26, Sept. 9 & 23, Oct. 7, Nov. 4 & 18, Dec. 2 & 16 & 30

Thurs. [6 a.m./7 a.m.]: Jan. 1 & 15, Feb. 26, May 21, June 4, July 16 & 23, Aug. 27, Sept. 10, Nov. 5 & 19, Dec. 17 & 24

Fri. [6 a.m./7 a.m.]: Jan. 16, March 13, April 10 & 24, June 5, July 3, Oct. 23, Dec. 4 & 18

Sat. [6 a.m./7 a.m.]: June 6, Oct. 10

WEDDINGS

Sun. afternoon: Jan. 4, Feb. 1 &15, May 10 & 24, June 21, Nov. 8 & 29

* * * * * * * * * * * * * * *

Mon. [6 a.m./7 a.m.]: Jan. 26, April 20, Sept. 7 & 21, Nov. 30

Tues. [6 a.m./7 a.m.]: Dec. 1

Thurs. [6 a.m./7 a.m.]: May 7, Oct. 22

Chauvet both services: Tues. Dec. 1

Chauvet weeks: M-W-Th-F Jan. 12 & 14 & 15 & 16; M-W Jan. 26 & 28; M-W Feb. 9 & 11; M-Th Feb. 23 & 26; M-W March 23 & 25; M-T-W-F April 20 & 21 & 22 & 24; T-Th-F-S

June 2 & 4 & 5 & 6; M-W-Th July 13 & 15 & 16; T-W July 28 & 29; M-W Aug. 10 & 12; W-Th Aug. 26 & 27; M-W-Th Sept. 7 & 9 & 10; M-T-W Sept. 21 & 22 & 23; M-W-S Oct. 5 & 7 & 10; M-Th-F Oct. 19 & 22 & 23; T-W-Th Nov. 3 & 4 & 5; W-Th Nov. 18 & 19; M-T-W-F Nov. 30 & Dec. 1 & 2 & 4; M-W-Th-F Dec. 14 & 16 & 17 & 18.

COLLADON

COLLADON – St. Pierre 1562 BAPTISMS

Sun. dawn: opposite Cop, March 8 & 22, April 5, May 3, June 14 & 28, July 26, Oct. 4, Nov. 15

Sun. 8 a.m.: Jan. 4, Feb. 15, March 8, Sept. 20, Dec. 6 & 13

Catechism: opposite Cop, opposite his own dawn schedule Jan. 18, Feb. 15, March 15, April 12, July 5, Aug. 2 & 30, Sept. 27, Oct. 11, Dec. 6

Sun.? May 10, Sept. 20

* * * * * * * * * * * * * * *

Wed. dawn: opposite Cop, Jan. 21, Feb. 4, March 4 & 18, June 24, Sept. 30, Nov. 11

Wed.? Aug. 12

Wed. [7 a.m./8 a.m.]: *Jan. 7*, March 25, *May 6*

Thurs. [6 a.m./7 a.m.]: July 30, Aug. 27

Fri. dawn: opposite Cop, Jan. 9, March 6, Aug. 21

Sat. [6 a.m./7 a.m.]: *Feb. 7*, *July 4*, Dec. 12

WEDDINGS

Sun. dawn: May 3, July 26, Sept. 13, Oct. 4

* * * * * * * * * * * * * * *

Mon. dawn: Jan. 19, April 13, May 25, Aug. 3, Sept. 14, Dec. 21

Wed. dawn: July 8

Fri [probably dawn]: April 3

Colladon both services: Sun. dawn: May 3, July 26, Oct. 4

Colladon weeks dawn: M-W Jan. 19 & 21; W-F March 4 & 6.

COLLADON – St. Gervais 1562 BAPTISMS

Sun. dawn: Jan. 18

Catechism: some Feb. 22, March 22, May 24

Sun. afternoon: Feb. 8

* * * * * * * * * * * * * * *

Wed. [4 a.m./5 a.m.]: Dec. 16

Thurs. [6 a.m./7 a.m.]: Sept. 10, Nov. 19

WEDDINGS

Sun. afternoon: Jan. 11 & 25, Feb. 8, April 5 & 19, Dec. 13

COLLADON – Magdeleine 1562 BAPTISMS

Sun. afternoon: July 12

* * * * * * * * * * * * * * *

Fri. [6 a.m./7 a.m.]: Feb. 27

WEDDINGS

Sun. afternoon: July 12

Colladon both services: Sun. afternoon: July 12

COP

COP – St. Pierre 1562 BAPTISMS

Sun. dawn: opposite Colladon, Jan. 11, Feb. 1, March 15, April 12, May 24, June 7 & 21, July 19, Aug. 2 & 30, Sept. 27, Oct. 11 & 25, Nov. 29, Dec. 6 & 13

Catechism: opposite Colladon; opposite his own dawn schedule, Jan. 25, Feb. 22, March 8, April 19, May 31, June 7, July 26, Aug. 9 & 23, Sept. 20, Oct. 4 & 18, Nov. 15 & 29, Dec. 13

* * * * * * * * * * * * * * *

Mon. dawn: opposite Merlin, April 6, Aug. 24, Sept. 21, Oct. 19, Nov. 2

Tues. [6 a.m./7 a.m.]: June 2

Wed. dawn: opposite Colladon, Jan. 28, April 8

Thurs. [6 a.m./7 a.m.]: <u>May 7</u>, <u>June 18</u>

Fri. dawn: opposite Colladon, June 19
    WEDDINGS

Sun. dawn: April 26, May 10, June 21, July 5, Aug. 2, Nov. 22, Dec. 20

* * * * * * * * * * * * * *

Mon. dawn: Feb. 9, June 1 & 29, Aug. 10, Oct. 5 & 19, Dec. 14

Tues. 6 a.m./7 a.m.: Oct. 27

Thurs. 6 a.m./7 a.m.: Nov. 26

Fri. dawn: Sept. 11

    Cop both services: Sun. dawn: June 21, Aug. 2; Mon. dawn: Oct. 19.

COP – St. Gervais 1562 BAPTISMS

Sun. 8 a.m.: April 19

Catechism: March 1 & 15
    WEDDINGS

Sun. dawn: Oct. 18

Sun. afternoon: April 26

COP – Magdeleine 1562 BAPTISMS

Catechism: May 3

Sun. afternoon: June 28, Dec. 20
    WEDDINGS

Sun. afternoon: June 28

    Cop both services; Sun. afternoon: June 28

CORNEILLE

CORNEILLE – St. Gervais 1562 BAPTISMS

Fri. [6 a.m./7 a.m.]: Nov. 20

D'AIREBAUDOUZE

D'AIREBAUDOUZE – St. Pierre 1562 BAPTISMS

Sun. dawn: Aug. 9

Sun. 8 a.m.: Aug. 9

Catechism: March 1

* * * * * * * * * * * * * *

Tues. [6 a.m./7 a.m.]: <u>*April 21*</u>, <u>Aug. 11</u>, <u>Sept. 8</u>

Wed. 7 a.m./8 a.m.: <u>*April 8*</u>, <u>Sept. 23</u>

Sat. [6 a.m./7 a.m.]: <u>*March 14*</u>, <u>Aug. 29</u>

D'AIREBAUDOUZE – St. Gervais 1562 BAPTISMS

Sun. dawn?: March 22, April 19, Nov. 15

Catechism: July 5

* * * * * * * * * * * * * *

Mon. [6 a.m.7 a.m.]: Dec. 28
    WEDDINGS

Sun. dawn: Feb. 22

Sun.?: April 5

D'AIREBAUDOUZE – Magdeleine 1562 BAPTISMS

Sun. 8 a.m.: April 5, July 26, Sept. 20, Oct. 18, Nov. 15, Dec. 13

Catechism: Feb. 15, March 15, April 12, June 7, July 5, Aug. 30, Nov. 22

Sun. afternoon: March 22, May 31, July 26 at 3 p.m., Dec. 13

Sun.? Jan. 18, Feb. 1 & 8, Aug. 2, Sept. 6, Oct. 11, Nov. 1, Dec. 6 & 20

* * * * * * * * * * * * * *

Mon. [6 a.m./7 a.m.]: March 2, Aug. 31, Sept. 28, Oct. 26, Dec. 21

Tues. [6 a.m./7 a.m.]: Jan. 6, March 17 & 31, July 7, Aug. 4, Nov. 10 & 24, Dec. 22

Wed. [7 a.m./7 a.m.]: Jan. 21, Feb. 4 & 18, March 4, April 15, July 22, Aug. 5, Sept. 2 & 16 & 30, Oct. 28, Nov. 11 & 25, Dec. 23

Thurs. [6 a.m./7 a.m.]: Feb. 19, Aug. 6, Nov. 26

Fri. [6 a.m./7 a.m.]: Feb. 20, March 6 & 20, July 24, Aug. 21, Sept. 18, Dec. 25

Sat. [6 a.m./7 a.m.]: Jan. 3 & 24, Feb. 7, April 18, Aug. 22, Sept. 19, Dec. 26

WEDDINGS

Sun. afternoon: April 5 & 12 & 19, July 26

****

Mon. [6 a.m./7 a.m.]: March 30, July 6, Oct. 5

D'Airebaudouze both services: Sun. afternoon: July 26

D'Airebaudouze weeks W-S Jan. 21 & 24; W-S Feb. 4 & 7; W-Th-F Feb. 18 & 19 & 20; M-W-F March 2 & 4 & 6; T-F Mach 17 & 20; M-T March 30 & 31; W-S April 15 & 18; M-T July 6 & 7; W-F July 22 & 24; T-W-Th Aug. 4 & 5 & 6; F-S Aug. 21 & 22; M-W Aug. 31 & Sept. 2; W-F-S Sept. 16 & 18 & 19; M-W Sept. 28 & 30; M-W Oct. 26 & 28; T-W Nov. 10 & 11; T-W-Th Nov. 24 & 25 & 26; M-T-W-F-S Dec. 21 & 22 & 23 & 25 & 26.

LE DUC

Le DUC – St. Gervais 1562 BAPTISMS

Mon. [6 a.m.7 a.m.]: March 2

Wed.?: April 1

DUPERRIL

DUPERRIL – Magdeleine 1562 BAPTISMS

Thurs. [6 a.m./7 a.m.]: Aug. 13

ENOC

ENOC – St. Pierre 1562 BAPTISMS

Sun.? Jan. 11, either catechism or afternoon

****

Tues. [6 a.m./7 a.m.]: Dec. 22

Wed. [7 a.m./8 a.m.]: Oct. 28

ENOC – St. Gervais 1562 BAPTISMS

Sun. dawn: Oct. 4

Sun. 8 a.m.: opposite Gaigneulx, March 1 & 8, July 5, Aug. 23, Oct. 4 & 18, Nov. 1

[probably Feb. 22, June 14 & 28 because before catechism]

Catechism: same schedule as his 8 a.m., April 12, June 28, Oct. 4 & 18

Sun. afternoon: opposite Gaigneulx, March 1 & 15 & 29, June 7, July 5, Sept. 27, Nov. 8 [probably Jan. 4 & 18]

Sun.?: Jan. 11, Feb. 8, April 5, June 7, July 12, Nov. 29, Dec. 13

****

Mon. [6 a.m./7 a.m.]: opposite Gaigneulx, April 6, July 13, Oct. 5

Tues. [6 a.m./7 a.m.]: opposite Gaigneulx, June 30, July 28, Oct. 6

Wed. 7 a.m./8 a.m.: opposite Gaigneulx, Jan. 14, Feb. 25, Sept. 23, Oct. 7, Nov. 4, Dec. 2

Thurs. [6 a.m./7 a.m.]: opposite Gaigneulx, Jan. 15, Feb. 12, June 11, July 2, Sept. 24, Nov. 5

Fri. [6 a.m./7 a.m.]: opposite Gaigneulx, Feb. 27, April 10, June 5, Aug. 14 & 28, Nov. 6

Sat. [6 a.m./7 a.m.]: opposite Gaigneulx, Jan. 3

WEDDINGS

Sun. afternoon: Feb. 22, May 10 & 24, June 14 & 21, Dec. 20 [probably March 1 & 15, June 7, July 5]

Enoc both services: Sun. afternoon [?] March 1 & 15, June 7, July 5.

Enoc weeks W-Th Jan. 14 & 15; W-F Feb. 25 & 27; M-F April 6 & 10; T-Th June 30 & July 2; W-Th Sept. 23 & 24; M-T-W Oct. 5 & 6 & 7; W-Th-F Nov. 4 & 5 & 6

GAIGNEULX

GAIGNEULX – St. Pierre 1562 BAPTISMS

Wed. dawn: Sept. 16

Wed. 7 a.m./8 a.m.: Aug. 26, Sept. 9

Thurs. [6 a.m./7 a.m.]: Sept. 10 & 24

WEDDINGS

Mon. dawn: May 18

GAIGNEULX – St. Gervais 1562 BAP-TISMS

Sun. 8 a.m.: opposite Enoc second part of year, Aug. 30, Sept. 27, Nov. 8 & 22, Dec. 6 & 20

Catechism: opposite Enoc second part of year, Aug. 2, Sept. 27, Nov. 22, Dec. 20

Sun. afternoon: July 12 & 26, Sept. 6, Dec. 27

* * * * * * * * * * * * * * *

Mon. [6 a.m.7 a.m.]: opposite Enoc, June 22, Aug. 3 & 31, Sept. 14, Nov. 9

Tues. [6 a.m.7 a.m.]: opposite Enoc, Sept. 1, Oct. 27, Nov. 24

Wed. dawn: May 20

Wed. 7 a.m./8 a.m.: opposite Enoc, Aug. 5, Sept. 2 & 30, Nov. 11 & 25, Dec. 9 & 23 [probably Sept. 30]

Thurs. [6 a.m./7 a.m.]: opposite Enoc, Aug. 6, Oct. 1

Fri. [6 a.m./7 a.m.]: opposite Enoc, Aug. 7

Sat. [6 a.m./7 a.m.]: opposite Enoc, Sept. 5

WEDDINGS

Sun. dawn: July 12

Sun. afternoon: July 19, Aug. 23, Nov. 15 [probably June 28]

Gaigneulx weeks [Sun Aug. 2] M-W-Th-F Aug. 3 & 5 & 6 &7 [Sun Aug. 30] M-T-W-S Aug. 31 & Sept. 1 & 2 & 5 [Sun p.m. Sept. 6] [Sun Nov. 8] M-W Nov. 9 & 11 [Sun Nov. 22] T-W Nov. 24 & 25 [Sun. Dec. 20] W Dec. 23 [Sun p.m. Dec. 27]

GAIGNEULX – Magdeleine 1562 WED-DINGS

Sun. afternoon: June 14

GILES

GILES of Vandoeuvre – St. Gervais 1562 BAPTISMS

Sun. dawn: April 12

MAUBUE

MAUBUE – Magdeleine 1562 BAP-TISMS

Fri. [6 a.m./7 a.m.]: June 12

MERLIN

MERLIN – St. Pierre 1562 BAPTISMS

Sun. 8 a.m.: Jan 11, Feb. 1, April 5, May 24, July 12, Aug. 30, Oct. 4, Nov. 1 & 8, Dec. 20

Sun. afternoon: Jan. 4, Feb. 1 & 15, May 17, Sept. 6, Nov. 15, Dec. 20

Sun.? April 26, Oct. 25, Dec. 27: probably 8 a.m. or afternoon

* * * * * * * * * * * * * * *

Mon. dawn: May 18

Mon.? Dec. 21

Mon. 6 a.m./7 a.m.: Aug. 3 & 31, Oct. 19, Dec. 28 [probably Nov. 16]

Tues. [6 a.m./7 a.m.]: Feb. 10, March 3, April 28, *May 5*, Aug. 18, Sept. 1, Oct. 6, Nov. 3 & 17; Dec. 29

Wed. 7 a.m./8 a.m.: March 4 & 18, April 1, May 13, June 17, Dec. 2 & 16 [probably April 15, Aug. 5 & 19, Nov. 4]

Thurs. [6 a.m./7 a.m.]: Jan. 1 & 15, March 19, April 16 & 30, May 14 & 28, July 9, Aug. 20, Nov. 5 & 19

Fri. [6 a.m./7 a.m.]: May 29

Sat. [6 a.m./7 a.m.]: Jan. 17, March 21, April 25, May 16, June 27, Sept. 5, Nov. 21, Dec. 5

WEDDINGS

Sun. afternoon: Jan. 4 & 11, Feb. 1 & 8 & 15, March 1 & 15 & 22, April 19 & 26, May 10 & 31, June 7 & 14 & 28, July 5 &

12, Aug. 23 & 30, Oct. 18, Nov. 15 & 22, Dec. 20

* * * * * * * * * * * * * * *

Mon. 6 a.m./7 a.m.: July 20, Aug. 17, Oct. 19, Dec. 28

Tues. 6 a.m./7 a.m.: July 7

Fri. 6 a.m./7 a.m.: Aug. 21

Merlin both services: Sun. afternoon: Jan. 4, Feb. 1, Nov. 15, Dec. 20; Mon. Oct. 19, Dec. 28.

Merlin weeks later daily service: Th-S Jan. 15 & 17; T-W March 3 & 4; W-Th-S March 18 & 19 & 21; W-Th April 15 & 16;T-Th April 28 & 30; W-Th-S May 13 & 14 & 16; T-Th July 7 & 9; T-W-Th-F Aug. 18 &19 & 20 & 21; M-T-S Aug. 31 & Sept. 1 & 5; T-W-Th Nov. 3 & 4 & 5; M-T-Th-S Nov. 16 & 17 & 19 & 21; M-T Dec. 28 & 29.

MERLIN – St. Gervais 1562BAPTISMS

Sun. dawn: March 15, May 10

Sun. 8 a.m.: May 10, July 19, Sept. 13

Catechism: May 3, June 14

   WEDDINGS

Sun. dawn: May 31

Minister of La Fandoge – St. Gervais 1562 BAPTISMS

Sun.?: July 5

PINAULT

PINAULT – Magdeleine 1562 BAPTISMS

Sun. afternoon: May 10

* * * * * * * * * * * * * * *

Wed. [7 a.m./7 a.m.]: May 10

Thurs. [6 a.m./7 a.m.]: May 14

Sat. [6 a.m./7 a.m.]: Feb. 28

1563

Magdeleine Weddings only

BOURGOING – Magdeleine 1563 WEDDINGS

Sun. afternoon: July 4

CHAUVET – Magdeleine 1563 WEDDINGS

Sun. afternoon: Jan. 3, March 14, June 6 & 20, Aug. 1 & 15, Sept. 12 & 26, Oct. 10 & 31, Nov. 7 & 21, Dec. 19 & 26

* * * * * * * * * * * * * * *

Mon. [6 a.m./7 a.m.]: April 19, Nov. 29

Thurs. [6 a.m./7 a.m.]: Jan. 28

Fri. [6 a.m./7 a.m.]: June 18

D'AIREBAUDOUZE – Magdeleine 1563 WEDDINGS

Sun. afternoon: March 7

DES BORDES – Magdeleine 1563 WEDDINGS

Sun. afternoon: March 21, April 4, Sept. 19, Nov. 14 & 28

GAIGNEULX – Magdeleine 1563 WEDDINGS

Sun. afternoon: Oct. 24

1564

BEZA

BEZA – St. Pierre 1564 BAPTISMS

Sun. 8 a.m.: March 12, April 30, May 7 & 14, June 18, July 2 & 16 & 23

Catechism: Nov. 26

Sun.? March 5, May 28, Aug. 27, Oct. 29, Nov. 12 & 26

* * * * * * * * * * * * * * *

Mon. 6 a.m./7 a.m.: March 6, April 24, May 22, Aug. 14 & 28, Nov. 6, Dec. 18

Tues. [6 a.m./7 a.m.]: Jan. 25, Feb. 8 & 22, April 25, May 23

Wed. 7 a.m./8 a.m.: Jan. 26, Feb. 16 & 23, March 8 & 29, May 24, June 7 & 21, July 5, Aug. 16

Thurs. [6 a.m./7 a.m.]: Jan. 13, Feb. 10 & 24, April 13, May 25, Aug. 3, Sept. 14, Oct. 12 & 26, Dec. 21

Sat. [6 a.m./7 a.m.]: Jan. 15, April 1 & 29, June 10, Aug. 19, Sept. 2 & 16

WEDDINGS

Sun. afternoon: Jan. 2 & 9 & 30, Feb. 20 & 27, March 26 [probably Jan. 23]

* * * * * * * * * * * * * * *

Mon. 6 a.m./7 a.m.: Jan. 24, March 6, June 5, July 17, Oct. 9

Tues. 6 a.m./7 a.m.: Jan. 4, May 23

Beza both services: Mon. March 6; Tues. May 23

Beza weeks: Th-S Jan. 13 & 15; T-W Jan. 25 & 26; T-Th Feb. 8 & 10; T-W-Th Feb. 22 & 23 & 24; M-W March 6 & 8; M-T-S April 24 & 25 & 29; M-T-W-Th May 22 & 23 & 24 & 25; W-S June 7 & 10; M-W-S Aug. 14 & 16 &19; Th-S Sept. 14 & 16; M-Th Dec. 18 & 21

BEZA – St. Gervais 1564 WEDDINGS

Sun. [probably afternoon]: Sept. 24

CHAUVET

CHAUVET – St. Pierre 1564 BAPTISMS

Sun. dawn: Nov. 5

Sun. 8 a.m.: Jan 30, Dec. 3

Sun.? April 9 before catechism, probably 8 a.m.

* * * * * * * * * * * * * * *

Mon. [6 a.m./7 a.m.]: Sept. 25

Wed. dawn: March 1 [probably Jan. 5 & 19, April 12, Nov. 8 & 22]

CHAUVET – St. Gervais 1564 WEDDINGS

Sun. dawn: March 12, April 23

CHAUVET – Magdeleine 1564 BAPTISMS

Sun. 8 a.m.: Jan. 9, Feb. 6 & 20, March 5 & 19, April 30, June 11, July 9 & 23, Aug. 13 & 20, Sept. 17, Oct. 1 & 15 & 29, Nov. 12 & 26, Dec. 10

Catechism: Jan. 23, April 30, May 28, June 11, July 23, Aug. 20, Sept. 17, Oct. 15 & 29, Nov. 12 & 26

Sun. afternoon: May 21, Nov. 19, Dec. 17

* * * * * * * * * * * * * * *

Mon. [6 a.m./7 a.m.]: Jan. 24, Feb. 7, April 17, June 26, July 10, Aug. 7, Nov. 27, Dec. 25

Tues. [6 a.m./7 a.m.]: Jan. 11 & 25, Feb. 8 & 22, April 4 & 18, May 2 & 16, July 11, Aug. 8 & 22, Sept. 5, Oct. 31

Wed. [8 a.m.]: Feb. 9, March 8, May 17 & 31, June 14, July 26, Aug. 9, Sept. 6 & 20, Oct. 18, Nov. 1

Thurs. [6 a.m./7 a.m.]: Jan. 13 & 27, April 6, May 4 & 18, June 1 & 29, July 27, Sept. 21, Nov. 16

Fri. [6 a.m./7 a.m.]: March 24, April 7 & 21, May 5, July 14, Sept. 8, Oct. 6, Dec. 29

Sat. [6 a.m./7 a.m.]: Jan. 29, May 20, June 17, Sept. 23, Oct. 7, Dec. 2

WEDDINGS

Sun. afternoon: Jan. 2 & 16, Feb. 27, March 5 & 12 & 26, April 30, Aug. 13, Sept. 10

Chauvet weeks: M-W-F Jan. 9 & 11 & 13; M-T-Th-S Jan. 24 & 25 & 27 & 29; M-T-W Feb. 7 & 8 & 9; T-Th-F April 4 & 6 & 7; T-W-F April 17 & 18 & 21; T-Th-F May 2 & 4 & 5; T-W-Th-S

May 16 & 17 & 18 & 20; W-Th May 31 & June 1; W-S June 14 & 17; M-Th June 26 & 29; M-T-F July 10 & 11 & 14; W-Th July 26 & 27; M-T-W Aug. 7 & 8 & 9; T-W-F Sept. 5 & 6 & 8; W-Th-S Sept. 20 & 21 & 23; F-S Oct. 6 & 7; T-W Oct. 31 & Nov. 1; M-F Nov. 27 & Dec. 2; M-F Dec. 25 & 29.

COLLADON

COLLADON – St. Pierre 1564 BAPTISMS

Sun. dawn: opposite Cop until May, Jan 9, Feb. 6 & 20, March 5 & 19, April 30

Sun. 8 a.m.: July 30

Catechism: opposite Cop, & opposite his own dawn schedule, Jan. 16, Feb. 13, March 12, April 9 & 23 & 30, May 7

Sun. afternoon: April 2, May 21

* * * * * * * * * * * * * *

Mon. 6 a.m./7 a.m.: opposite Beza, April 3, June 26

Tues. [6 a.m./7 a.m.]: opposite Beza, Feb. 29, June 13, Aug. 8

Wed. dawn: opposite Cop until May, Feb. 2 & 16

Wed. 7 a.m./8 a.m.: opposite Beza, June 28, July 26, Aug. 9

Thurs. [6 a.m./7 a.m.]: opposite Beza, Feb. 17, March 16, June 1, July 13, Aug. 10

Fri. dawn: opposite Cop until May, May 12

Sat. [6 a.m./7 a.m.]: opposite Beza, July 1 & 29, Aug. 12

WEDDINGS

Sun. dawn: Feb. 20, April 30

Sun. afternoon: May 28, June 4 & 11 & 18 & 25, July 2 & 16, Aug. 13

* * * * * * * * * * * * * *

Mon. dawn: Feb. 14, May 8, Nov. 13

Mon. 6 a.m./7 a.m.: April 3 & 17, May 15 & 29

Tues. 6 a.m./7 a.m.: March 14

Colladon both services: Sun. dawn: Feb. 20, April 30; Mon. 6 a.m.: April 3.

Colladon week dawn: M-W Feb. 14 & 16. later service T-Th March 14 & 16; M-Th May 29 & June 1; M-W-S June 26 & 28 & July 1; W-S July 26 & 29; T-W-S Aug. 8 & 9 & 12

COLLADON – St. Gervais 1564 BAPTISMS

Sun. dawn: May 7, Oct. 29

Sun. 8 a.m.: Aug. 6

WEDDINGS

Sun. dawn: March 26

COLLADON – Magdeleine 1564 BAPTISMS

Sun. 8 a.m.: Aug. 27, Sept. 10 & 24, Oct. 8, Nov. 5 & 19, Dec. 3 & 17 & 31

Catechism: Sept. 24, Nov. 5 & 19, Dec. 3

Sun. afternoon: Oct. 1, Dec. 10

Sun. [probably afternoon?]: Sept. 3, Dec. 24

* * * * * * * * * * * * * *

Mon. [6 a.m./7 a.m.]: Sept. 25, Nov. 6, Dec. 18

Tues. [6 a.m./7 a.m.]: Nov. 21

Wed. [8 a.m.]: Aug. 30, Sept. 13 & 27, Oct. 11 & 25, Nov. 8, Dec. 20

Thurs. [6 a.m./7 a.m.]: Feb. 10, Oct. 12 & 26

Fri. [6 a.m./7 a.m.]: Sept. 1 & 29, Oct. 13, Nov. 10 & 24

Sat. [6 a.m./7 a.m.]: Sept. 2

WEDDINGS

Sun. afternoon: Aug. 20, Sept. 17, Oct. 15, Nov. 12, Dec. 10

Colladon both services: Sun. afternoon: Dec. 10

Colladon weeks:W-F-S Aug. 30 & Sept. 1 & 2; T-Th-S Sept. 25 & 27 & 29; W-Th-F Oct. 11 & 12 & 13; W-Th

Oct. 25 & 26; M-W-F Nov. 6 & 8 & 10; T-F Nov. 21 & 24; M-W Dec. 18 & 20.

COP

COP – St. Pierre 1564 BAPTISMS

Sun. dawn: opposite Colladon, then Maubué, Jan. 16 & 30, March 12 & 26, May 7, June 4, July 2, Oct. 22

Sun. 8 a.m.: March 19

Catechism: opposite Colladon, & opposite his own dawn schedule, Feb. 20, June 25, July 2 & 9 & 23, Sept. 17

Sun. afternoon: May 7

* * * * * * * * * * * * * *

Mon. dawn: opposite Colladon/ Maubué, Feb. 21, Oct. 2

Wed. dawn: opposite Colladon/ Maubué, March 8, April 5, June 28, Aug. 23

Wed. 7 a.m./8 a.m.: Sept. 13

Fri. dawn: opposite Colladon/ Maubué, Feb. 25, Aug. 11

Sat. [6 a.m./7 a.m.]: Feb. 26, Sept. 30

WEDDINGS

Sun. dawn: Jan. 2, Feb. 27, May 7, June 4 & 18

Sun. afternoon: April 9 & 30, May 7

* * * * * * * * * * * * * *

Mon. dawn: Feb. 21, April 3, May 1 & 15, June 12, July 24, Aug. 7, Sept. 4, Oct. 16 & 30

Mon. 6 a.m./7 a.m.: Jan. 17, March 20

Wed. dawn: Feb. 23, May 31

Fri. dawn: Feb. 25

Cop both services: Sun. dawn: May 7, June 4; Sun. afternoon: May 7; Mon. dawn: Feb. 21; Fri. dawn: Feb. 25.

Cop weeks dawn: M-W-F Feb. 21 & 24 & 25; M-W April 3 & 5; M-F Aug. 7 &11

COP – St. Gervais 1564 BAPTISMS

Sun. dawn: June 25

Sun. 8 a.m.: Oct. 1, Dec. 17 & 31, Gaigneulx's schedule

Sun. afternoon: Dec. 24, Enoc's schedule

* * * * * * * * * * * * * *

Mon. [6 a.m./7 a.m.]: Dec. 18, Gaigneulx's schedule

Wed. 8 a.m.: Dec. 6 & 20, Gaigneulx's schedule

Thurs. [6 a.m./7 a.m.]: Dec. 21, Gaigneulx's schedule

WEDDINGS

Sun. dawn: Feb. 20

Cop week: [Sun Dec. 17] M-W-Th Dec. 18 & 20 & 21.

COP –Magdeleine 1564 BAPTISMS

Sun. afternoon: July 30

DES BORDES

DES BORDES – St. Pierre 1564 BAPTISMS

Sun. dawn: opposite Cop with Maubué Aug. 20, Oct. 1 & 15

Sun. 8 a.m.: Jan. 9

Catechism: opposite Cop with Maubué Sept. 10 & 24

Sun. afternoon: March 26

* * * * * * * * * * * * * *

Mon. dawn: opposite Cop with Maubué after May Sept. 11

Fri. dawn: opposite Cop with Maubué after May Sept. 1

WEDDINGS

Mon. dawn: Sept. 11

Tues. 6 a.m./7 a.m.: April 18

DES BORDES – St. Gervais 1564 BAPTISMS

Sun. dawn: Feb. 6, Nov. 5

Sun. 8 a.m.: Oct. 8 & 29, Nov. 12, Dec. 10, Enoc's schedule

* * * * * * * * * * * * * *

Mon. [6 a.m./7 a.m.]: Nov. 27, Dec. 25, Enoc's schedule

Tues. [6 a.m./7 a.m.]: Dec. 26, Enoc's schedule

Wed. 8 a.m.: Oct. 18, Nov. 1, Dec. 27, Enoc's schedule

Thurs. [6 a.m./7 a.m.]: Dec. 14, Enoc's schedule

Sat. [6 a.m./7 a.m.]: Nov. 18

  WEDDINGS

Sun. dawn: March 19, April 30

Sun. afternoon: Dec. 31

* * * * * * * * * * * * * *

Mon. 6 a.m./7 a.m.: Oct. 30

  Des Bordes weeks [Sun Oct. 29] M-W Oct. 30 & Nov. 1; [Sun Nov. 12] S Nov. 18; [Sun Dec. 10] Th Dec. 14; M-T-W Dec. 25 & 26 & 27

DES BORDES – Magdeleine 1564 BAPTISMS

Sun. 8 a.m.: Jan. 2 & 30, Feb. 13 & 27, March 12, April 9, May 7, June 4, July 16 & 30

Catechism: Jan. 2 & 16, March 12, April 9 & 23, May 7, July 2 & 30

Sun. afternoon: April 2 & 30, May 14, July 9

* * * * * * * * * * * * * *

Mon. [6 a.m./7 a.m.]: Jan. 31, March 13, April 10, June 19, July 3 & 31

Tues. [6 a.m./7 a.m.]: Feb. 1 & 15, June 6, July 4 & 18

Wed. [8 a.m.]: Jan. 19, Feb. 2 & 16, March 1 & 15, April 12, May 24, July 19, Aug. 16

Thurs. [6 a.m./7 a.m.]: Feb. 17, March 16 & 30, June 8, July 6, Aug. 3

Fri. [6 a.m./7 a.m.]: Jan. 7 & 21, Feb. 4 & 18 & 25, June 23

Sat. [6 a.m./7 a.m.]: Jan. 8, April 29

WEDDINGS

Sun. afternoon: Feb. 20, June 25, July 9 & 23

* * * * * * * * * * * * * *

Tues. [6 a.m./7 a.m.]: March 14

  Des Bordes both services: Sun. afternoon: July 9

Des Bordes weeks: F-S Jan. 7 & 8; W-F Jan. 19 & 21; M-T-W-F Jan. 31 & Feb. 1 & 2 & 4; T-W-Th-F Feb. 15 & 16 & 17 & 18; M-T-W-Th March 13 & 14 & 15 & 16; M-W April 10 & 12; T-Th June 6 & 8; M-F June 19 & 23; M-T-Th July 3 & 4 & 6; T-W July 18 & 19; M-Th July 31 & Aug. 3.

ENOC

ENOC – St. Pierre 1564 BAPTISMS

Sun. dawn: Oct. 29

Catechism: Nov. 19, Dec. 3

* * * * * * * * * * * * * *

Mon. [6 a.m./7 a.m.]: Dec. 4

Fri. dawn: Dec. 22

  WEDDINGS

Sun. dawn: Nov. 26

* * * * * * * * * * * * * *

Mon. dawn: Dec. 4 & 18

ENOC – St. Gervais 1564 BAPTISMS

Sun. dawn: Jan. 2, Nov. 19

Sun. 8 a.m.: opposite Gaigneulx, Jan. 9, Feb. 6 & 20, March 19, April 30, June 11 & 25, July 23, Aug. 20, Sept. 17, Oct. 15

Catechism: opposite Gaigneulx, same as his own 8 a.m. schedule Feb. 6, March 5 & 19, April 16, May 14, July 9, Aug. 20, Sept. 17

Sun. afternoon: opposite Gaigneulx, opposite his own 8 a.m./catechism schedule, March 26, May 21, June 11, July 2

Sun.? Jan. 9 [8 a.m. or catechism]

* * * * * * * * * * * * * * *

Mon. [6 a.m./7 a.m.]: opposite Gaigneulx, June 26, July 10

Tues. [6 a.m./7 a.m.]: opposite Gaigneulx, Feb. 22, May 30

Wed. 8 a.m.: opposite Gaigneulx, March 22, April 19

Thurs. [6 a.m./7 a.m.]: opposite Gaigneulx, July 27

   WEDDINGS

Sun. afternoon: Jan. 2 & 16, Feb. 13, April 9, June 4 & 11, July 2 & 30 [probably June 25]

   Enoc both services: Sun. afternoon: June 11, July 2

Enoc weeks [Sun Feb. 20] T Feb. 22; [Sun March 19] W March 22; [Sun June 25] M June 26; [Sun July 23] Th July 27

ENOC – Magdeleine 1564 BAPTISMS

Catechism: Dec. 10

GAIGNEULX

GAIGNEULX – St. Pierre 1564 BAPTISMS

Sun. 8 a.m.: Feb. 6, July 9

Sun. afternoon: Nov. 26, Dec. 24

* * * * * * * * * * * * * * *

Mon. 6 a.m./7 a.m.: Dec. 25

Tues. [6 a.m./7 a.m.]: Dec. 12 & 26

Thurs. [6 a.m./7 a.m.] April 20, Dec. 14

   WEDDINGS

Sun. afternoon: Dec. 17

* * * * * * * * * * * * * * *

Thurs. 6 a.m./7a.m.: April 6

   Gaigneulx week M-T Dec. 25 & 26

GAIGNEULX – St. Gervais 1564 BAPTISMS

Sun. dawn: April 16

Sun. 8 a.m.: opposite Enoc, Jan. 16, Feb. 27, March 12 & 26, April 9 & 23, May 7, July 16 & 30, Aug. 27

Catechism: opposite Enoc, same as his own 8 a.m. schedule, Jan. 30, Feb. 13 & 27, May 7

Sun. afternoon: opposite Enoc, opposite his own 8 a.m./catechism schedule, Jan. 9, April 16

* * * * * * * * * * * * * * *

Mon. [6 a.m./7 a.m.]: opposite Enoc, Jan. 31, Feb. 28, June 5, July 31

Tues. [6 a.m./7 a.m.]: opposite Enoc, Jan. 4 & 18, Feb. 15, May 9, June 6, Aug. 15 & 29, Sept. 12

Wed. 8 a.m.: opposite Enoc, March 1 & 15 & 29, April 12 & 26, May 10 & 24, July 5, Aug. 9 & 30, Sept. 13

Thurs. [6 a.m./7 a.m.]: opposite Enoc, March 30, April 27, May 11, Aug. 31, Sept. 14

Fri. [6 a.m./7 a.m.]: opposite Enoc, Feb. 4, June 9, July 21, Dec. 1

Sat. [6 a.m./7 a.m.]: March 4

WEDDINGS

Sun. dawn: Jan. 23, May 28

Sun. afternoon: Jan. 9, March 5 & 19, April 16, May 28, July 9, Aug. 6 & 20

* * * * * * * * * * * * * * *

Mon. 6 a.m./7 a.m.: Sept. 11

Tues. 6 a.m./7 a.m.: May 9

   Gaigneulx both services: Sun. afternoon: Jan. 9, April 16; Tues. May 9

Gaigneulx weeks [Sun Jan. 16] T Jan. 18; M-F Jan. 31 & Feb. 4; [Sun Feb. 27] M-W-S Feb. 18 & March 1 & 4; [Sun March 26] W-Th March 29 & 30; [Sun April 9] W April 12; [Sun April 23] W-Th April 26 & 27; [Sun May 7] T-W-Th May 9 & 10 & 11; M-Th-F June 5 & 6 & 9; [Sun July 16] F July 21; [Sun July 30] M July 31; [Sun Aug. 27] T-W-Th Aug. 29 & 30 & 31; M-T-W-Th Sept. 11 & 12 & 13 & 14.

JEAN HELLIN

JEAN HELLIN – St. Pierre 1564 WEDDINGS

Mon. dawn: May 1

MAUBUE

MAUBUE – St. Pierre 1564 BAPTISMS

Sun. dawn: opposite Cop with Des Bordes after May, May 28, July 9 & 23

Catechism: opposite Cop and his own dawn schedule, June 18, July 16 & 30, Dec. 10

* * * * * * * * * * * * * *

Mon. dawn: opposite Cop with Des Bordes after May, June 5

Wed. dawn: opposite Cop with Des Bordes after May, Aug. 2, Dec. 13

Fri. dawn: opposite Cop with Des Bordes after May, July 7, Dec. 1

WEDDINGS

Sun. dawn: July 16

* * * * * * * * * * * * * *

Mon. dawn: May 22, June 5

Maubué both services: Mon. dawn: June 5

MAUBUE – St. Gervais 1564 BAPTISMS

Sun. dawn: July 30

Catechism: June 25

MAUBUE – Magdeleine 1564 BAPTISMS

Catechism: Dec. 31

WEDDINGS

Sun. afternoon: July 2

MERLIN

MERLIN – St. Pierre 1564 BAPTISMS

Sun. 8 a.m.: Oct. 8

Sun. afternoon: [opposite Beza later in year] Aug. 20, Sept. 24

* * * * * * * * * * * * * *

Mon. 6 a.m./7 a.m.: [opposite Beza later in year] Aug. 21, Sept. 4

Wed. 7 a.m./8 a.m.: [opposite Beza later in year] Aug. 23

Thurs. [6 a.m./7 a.m.]: [opposite Beza later in year] Aug. 24, Sept. 28, Oct. 5

Sat. [6 a.m./7 a.m.]: [opposite Beza later in year] Oct. 21

WEDDINGS

Sun. afternoon: Aug. 27, Sept. 17, Oct. 1 & 8 & 29 [probably Sept. 24, Oct. 15]

* * * * * * * * * * * * * *

Mon. 6 a.m./7a.m.: Aug. 21, Sept. 4

Merlin both services: [probably Sun. afternoon Sept. 24]; Mon. Aug. 21, Sept. 4.

Merlin week M-W-Th Aug. 21 & 23 & 24

PERROT

PERROT – St. Pierre 1564 BAPTISMS

Sun. dawn: Dec. 17

PINAULT

PINAULT – St. Pierre 1564 BAPTISMS

Sat. [6 a.m./7 a.m.]: Nov. 11

PINAULT –Magdeleine 1564 BAPTISMS

Sat. [6 a.m./7 a.m.]: Jan. 15

TREMBLEY

TREMBLEY – St. Pierre 1564 BAPTISMS

Sat. [6 a.m./7 a.m.]: March 25

TREMBLEY – St. Gervais 1564 BAPTISMS

Sun. dawn: Aug. 20

Sun. afternoon: Sept. 17

Sun.? Oct. 1 & 8, Nov. 5 & 12 & 26, Dec. 31

* * * * * * * * * * * * * *

Tues. [6 a.m./7 a.m.]: Oct. 10, Nov. 21, Enoc's schedule

Fri. [6 a.m./7 a.m.]: Oct. 20, Enoc's schedule

Sat. [6 a.m./7 a.m.]: Oct. 14, Nov. 25

WEDDINGS

Sun. dawn: Aug. 20

Trembley both services: Sun. dawn: Aug. 20

Trembley weeks: T-S Oct. 10 & 14; T-S Nov. 21 & 25.

APPENDIX FOUR: BAPTISMS CELEBRATED BY CALVIN

Underlined dates are those for which a sermon by Calvin exists (or was certainly preached); underlined dates in italics are those for which a sermon by Calvin exists but the specific dates are hypothetical. For example, the 159 sermons on Job and 107 sermons on 1 Samuel have no dates as such, but hypothetical dates have been identified by processes described elsewhere. Dates in italics alone are those which is it virtually certain Calvin preached but for which the sermons are missing. For example, the two sermons on Lamentations on Sat. Sept. 5 and Mon. Sept. 15, 1550, would represent alternating weeks, the second corresponding to one with two baptisms at La Magdeleine on Tues. and Sat. Sept. 16 and 20.

1550[1]

Mon. March 3 (La Magdeleine)
Tues. April 1 (3 at La Magdeleine)
Tues. *Sept. 16* (La Magdeleine)
Sat. *Sept. 20* (La Magdeleine)
Mon. Nov. 24 (La Magdeleine)

Sun. Dec. 28 (St. Gervais) "au sermon dapres midy"

1551

Sun. March 8 (St. Gervais) "au sermon de vespres"
Wed. April 1 (St. Pierre)
Fri. July 24 (La Magdeleine)
Sat. July 25 (La Magdeleine)
Sun. Oct. 4 (St. Gervais) "au sermon du soir"
Mon. Nov. 23 (La Magdeleine)
Tues. Dec. 8 (La Magdeleine)
Thurs. Dec. 10 (La Magdeleine)
Sun. 27 Dec. (St. Gervais) [probably 3 p.m.]

1552

Tues. Dec. 20 (La Magdeleine)

1553

Sun. Feb. 12 (St. Pierre) "apres disne"
Sun. Feb. 26 (St. Pierre) [almost certainly 8 a.m.]

---

[1] Note: These lists are based on the work of the editors of the *Calvini Opera* in the *Annales*, OC 21, work for which we must all be very grateful! I have personally checked the years 1550-1551, 1553, 1555, 1557, 1559, 1562, 1564, in St. Pierre and St. Gervais for completeness, and these 8 years plus 1552 and 1554 for La Magdeleine. I have also checked every entry recorded in the *Annales* and found a number of entries omitted or mistakenly recorded by the editors; most omitted baptisms are on weekdays. It is probable that some entries are still missing, though I have briefly scanned the registers for St. Pierre and St. Gervais where the ministers' names are marked in the margins; La Magdeleine is harder to skim because the persons who recopied the registers placed the names of child and father in the margins and the ministers' names in the text.

Thurs. June 8 (2 at La Magdeleine)

Sun. Aug. 20 (2 at St. Pierre) "sermon de huict heures"

Mon. Oct. 9 (La Magdeleine)

Sun. Dec. 10 (St. Pierre) "sermon de huict heures"

1554

Sun. March 18 (St. Pierre) "apres disne"

Tues. June 19 (La Magdeleine)

Thurs. *June 21* (La Magdeleine)

Sun. June 24 (St. Pierre)[2]

Sun. Aug. 5 (St. Pierre) "apres midy"

Mon. Dec. 3 (La Magdeleine)

Thurs. Dec. 13 (La Magdeleine)

Sun. *Dec. 16* (St. Pierre) "apres disne"

Mon. Dec. 17 (3 at La Magdeleine)

Tues. Dec. 18 (La Magdeleine)

1555

Mon. March 25 (La Magdeleine)

Sun. Aug. 25 (2 at St. Pierre) "au catechisme"

Tues. Aug. 27 (La Magdeleine)

Wed. Sept. 11 (2 at St. Pierre)

Wed. Sept. 18 (La Magdeleine)

Sun Sept. 22 (St. Pierre) "au catechisme"

Mon. Oct. 21 (La Magdeleine)

Fri. Dec. 6 (La Magdeleine)

Mon. Dec. 30 (2 at La Magdeleine)

1556

Mon. April 6 (La Magdeleine)

1557

Fri. *Jan. 29* (2 at La Magdeleine)*

Sun. April 11 (St. Pierre) [3 p.m.]

Sun. May 23 (St. Pierre)

Sun. Aug. 22 (St. Pierre) "au catechisme"

Mon. Sept. 6 (La Magdeleine)

Sun. Nov. 7 (St. Pierre) "au sermon de vespres"

1558

Sat. Feb. 26 (2 at La Magdeleine)

Thurs. Sept. 22 (La Magdeleine)

Fri. Sept. 23 (La Magdeleine)

1560

Sun. May 12 (St. Gervais) 3 p.m.[3]

Sun. Sept. 1 (4 at St. Gervais) "apres midy"

Sun. Sept. 15 (2 at St. Pierre) "au catechisme"

Wed. Sept. 18 (2 at St. Pierre) "de huict heures"

1562

Tues. *Feb. 17* (St. Pierre)

SUMMARY: Calvin occasionally baptized at the main Sunday morning service at St. Pierre, where he was preaching. More often he baptized there on Sunday afternoons, probably when he was preaching there regularly in later years. There are three baptisms which are mornings, six afternoons, two which might be morning, catechism, or afternoon but probably are

---

[2]   This was probably at 8 a.m. but could also be at 3 p.m. The previous entry is for a baptism by Colladon at an earlier service on this same day, and the previous week Colladon had done one at the 4 a.m. service. However, these are the only two entries by Colladon in the St. Pierre register for months on either side of these dates; he was pastor at the country parish of Vandovre until elected to come to the city in July 1557 (cf. RCP 2, p. 76). Calvin seems to have been preaching both 8 a.m. and 3 p.m. in St. Pierre this year. Since Calvin normally did not baptize unless he was preaching, and he did not do catechism, it is unlikely to have been at that service.

[3]   This follows an entry for a baptism at 8 a.m. by Chauvet.

afternoons. Four times he also baptized at catechism services at St. Pierre, where he was almost certainly not preaching. Calvin also occasionally baptized at St. Gervais on Sunday afternoons, where he was preaching regularly from early 1546 to spring of 1552. There are a total of six baptisms, four definitely afternoons, two which may have been at catechism but probably were afternoons. The whole number of baptismal services recorded for Sundays from 1550 to 1560 is twenty-one, for twenty-eight babies.

More often Calvin performed baptisms on weekdays, a total of thirty-two services between 1550 and 1562 spread throughout the week, for forty-one babies. Most of these were at La Magdeleine where for many years he preached on most weekdays in alternate weeks, a few are at St. Pierre at the later Wednesday day of prayer service or (by mid-1559) when there were daily weekday services there and he was doing his regular weekday sermons there. The cumulative total is fifty-three services, sixty-nine babies.

APPENDIX FIVE: MARRIAGES PERFORMED BY CALVIN (ALL ARE SUNDAYS UNLESS OTHERWISE MARKED)

Underlined dates are those for which a sermon by Calvin exists (or was certainly preached); underlined dates in italics are those for which a sermon by Calvin exists but the specific dates are hypothetical. For example, the sermons on the Pastoral Epistles have no dates as such, but hypothetical dates have been identified by processes described elsewhere. Dates in italics alone are those which is it virtually certain Calvin preached but for which the sermons are missing. For example, the two sermons on Lamentations on Sat. Sept. 5 and Mon. Sept. 15, 1550, would represent alternating weeks, the second corresponding to one with two baptisms at La Magdeleine on Tues. and Sat. Sept. 16 and 20.

1550

Feb. 9 (St. Pierre) "dapres disner"

April 13 (St. Gervais) "de trois heures"

April 20 (St. Gervais) "apres disner"

April 27 (4 sets, St. Gervais) "de trois heures"

    Mon. April 28 (La Magdeleine)

June 1 (St. Gervais) [no time given]

June 29 (St. Gervais) "trois heures apres midy"

July 13 (3 sets, St. Pierre) "a trois heures apres midy"

Sept. 14 (St. Pierre) "au matin"[1]

Sept. 14 (2 sets, St. Pierre) "de trois heures"

Oct. 5 (St. Gervais) "apres disner"
    11 services, 17 couples

1551

Jan. 4 (2 sets, St. Gervais) "apres disnez"

Jan. 11 (St. Gervais) "apres disne"

Feb. 1 (St. Gervais) "apres disne"

Feb. 8 (St. Gervais) "apres disne"

March 15 (St. Gervais) "a trois heures"

April 19 (St. Gervais) "au soir"

May 10 (St. Gervais) "de trois heures"

June 7 (St. Pierre) " 3 heures apres midy"
    Sat. June 13 (La Magdeleine)

July 5 (St. Gervais) "apres midy"

Sept. 13 (St. Gervais) "apres disne"

Nov. 1 (St. Gervais) "au soir"

Dec. 6 (St. Gervais) "apres disne"
    13 services, 14 couples

---

1   Dawn service for Laurent de Normandie et Anne daughter of M. Leon Colladon; this is the only known dawn wedding by Calvin and he almost certainly was not preaching but simply doing the wedding.

<u>1552</u>
April 3 (2 sets, St. Gervais) "apres disne"
April 24 (3 sets, St. Pierre) "a trois heures apres midy"
May 1 (3 sets, St. Pierre) "a trois heures apres midy"
May 22 (St. Pierre) "a trois heures apres midy"
May 29 (2 sets, St. Pierre) "de trois heures"[2]
June 12 (3 sets, St. Pierre) "a trois heures apres midy"
June 19 (St. Pierre) "a trois heures apres midy"
June 26 (2 sets, St. Pierre, "de trois heures"
July 3 (St. Pierre) "d'apres midy"
July 10 (St. Pierre) "d'apres midy"
July 17 (St. Pierre) "de trois heures apres midy"
July 31 (St. Pierre) d'apres disner"[3]
Aug. 28 (3 sets, St. Pierre)[4]
Sept. 11 [St. Pierre) "au trois heures apres midy"
Oct. 9 (St. Pierre) "de 3 heures" [different hand]
Oct. 23 (St. Pierre) "apres midy"
Nov. 27 (St. Pierre) "apres midy"
Dec. 4 (2 sets, St. Pierre) "d'apres midy"
Dec. 11 (St. Pierre) "d'apres midy"
Dec. 18 (St. Pierre) "d'apres disne"
20 services, 32 couples

<u>1553</u>
Jan. 1 (2 sets, St. Pierre) "d'apres midy"

<u>Jan 22</u> (St. Pierre) "d'apres midy"
<u>Jan. 29</u> (2 sets, St. Pierre) "d'apres midy"
<u>Feb. 5</u> (St. Pierre) "d'apes midy"
<u>Feb. 12</u> (St. Pierre) "d'apres disne"
<u>Feb. 26</u> (St. Pierre) "d'apres disne"
<u>March 5</u> (2 sets, St. Pierre) "d'apres midy"[5]
<u>March 26</u> (St. Pierre) "d'apres disne"
<u>April 9</u> (2 sets, St. Pierre) "d'apres disne"
<u>April 30</u> (2 sets, St. Pierre) "d'apres disne"
<u>May 7</u> (2 sets, St. Pierre) "d'apres disne"
<u>May 14</u> (St. Pierre) "d'apres disne"
<u>June 11</u> (St. Pierre) "d'apres midy"
<u>June 18</u> (St. Pierre) "d'apres disne"
July 23 (2 sets, St. Pierre) "d'apres disne"
Aug. 6 (St. Pierre) "de trois heures apres midy"
Aug. 20 (2 sets, St. Pierre) "d'apres disne"
Sept. 24 (2 sets, St. Pierre) "d'apres disne"
Oct. 22 (3 sets, St. Pierre)[6]
Nov. 5 (2 sets, St. Pierre) "d'apres, disne"
Nov. 12 (2 sets, St. Pierre) "de 3 heures apres midy" [Cop's hand]
Dec. 3 (St. Pierre) "d'apres disner"
Dec. 10 (St. Pierre) "d'apres disner"
Dec. 31 (St. Pierre) "d'apres disne"
24 services, 37 couples

<u>1554</u>
Jan. 7 (St. Pierre) "d'apres disner"
Jan. 28 (2 sets, St. Pierre) "d'apres disne"
Feb. 4 (2 sets, St. Pierre)

---

2   Calvin writes "dimenche 28"
3   "penultiesme de Juilliet" but Sunday was the 31st and this had to be Sunday because of the hour.
4   No time is given; it follows entries for 4 a.m. so it is probably 3 p.m., since weddings were not allowed at 8 a.m.
5   This is preceded by three entries by Poupin who often baptized at the 8 a.m. service.
6   No time is given, and it is written in Poupin's hand; probably 3 p.m.

Mon. <u>Feb. 12</u> (La Magdeleine) "au sermon du matin a 7 heures"[7]

Feb 18 (3 sets, St. Pierre) "de 3 heures"

Mon. <u>Feb. 26</u> (La Magdeleine)

March 4 (St. Pierre) "de 3 heures" [different hand]

April 1 (3 sets, St. Pierre) "d'apres disne"

April 22 (St. Pierre) "d'apres disner"

April 29 (St. Pierre) "d'apres disner"

May 6 (St. Pierre) "d'apres disne"

Thurs. *May 24* (La Magdeleine)

May 27 (St. Pierre)

June 3 (St. Pierre) "apres disne"

Mon. *June 18* (La Magdeleine)[8]

July 15 (St. Pierre) "d'apres disne"

July 22 (2 sets, St. Pierre) "d'apres midy"

July 29 (St. Pierre) "a trois heures apres midy"

Aug. 5 (St. Pierre) "d'apres midy"

Sept. 9 (St. Pierre) "d'apres disne"

Oct. 7 (St. Pierre) "d'apres disne"

Oct. 21 (2 sets, St. Pierre) "d'apres disne"

Oct. 28 (St. Pierre) "d'apres disne"

Nov. 18 (St. Pierre) "apres disne"

Dec. 2 (St. Pierre) "apres disne"

Dec. 9 (St. Pierre)

26 services, 34 couples

1555

Jan. 6 (St. Pierre) "d'apres disne"

Jan. 20 (St. Pierre) "d'apres midy"

Feb. 10 (2 sets, St. Pierre) "après midi" [in baptismal records]

Feb. 17 (3 sets, St. Pierre) "apres disne"

Feb. 24 (St. Pierre) "d'apres midy"

March 3 (St. Pierre) "d'apres midy"

April 28 (2 sets, St. Pierre) "a trois heures"

Tues. <u>May 7</u> (La Magdeleine)

May 19 (St. Pierre) "d'apres disne"

June 9 (3 sets, St. Pierre) "apres midy"

June 16 (4 sets, St. Pierre) "apres midy"

June 23 (St. Pierre) "apres disne"

June 30 (2 sets, St. Pierre) "apres midy"

Mon <u>July 1</u> (La Magdeleine)

Sat. <u>July 20</u> (La Magdeleine)

July 28 (St. Pierre) "de trois heures apres midy"

Aug. 4 (St. Pierre) "a trois heures apres midy"

Aug. 25 (2 sets, St. Pierre) [probably 3 p.m.]

Sept. 8 (St. Pierre) "a tois heures apres midy"

Sept. 29 (St. Pierre) "d'apres midy"

Oct. 13 (St. Pierre) "d'apres midy"

Nov. 3 (St. Pierre) [Cop's hand, afternoon]

21 services, 31 couples

1556

Jan. 5 (St. Pierre) "après midy"

Jan 19 (St. Pierre) "apres midy"

Jan. 26 (St. Pierre) "d'apres midy"

Feb. 9 (2 sets, St. Pierre)

Feb. 16 (2 sets, St. Pierre) "apres midy"

Feb. 23 (St. Pierre) "apres disne"

Thurs. <u>Feb. 27</u> (La Magdeleine)

March 1 (2 sets, St. Pierre) "apres disne"

March 15 (3 sets, St. Pierre) "d'apres midy"

April 12 (4 sets, St. Pierre) "a'apres midy"

April 19 (St. Pierre) "d'apres midy"

April 26 (2 sets, St. Pierre) "d'apres midy"

May 3 (2 sets, St. Pierre) "d'apres disner"

---

7   Calvin's stepdaughter Judith, marrying Leonard Du Maser.

8   The register says Mon. June 19; OC 21:575 reads this as Mon. June 4; it seems probable that it is Mon. June 18, since the day of the week is usually correct and the date is often not, and OC editors apparently missed the "1" and read the 9 as "4."

May 31 (2 sets, St. Pierre) "de trois heures"
   Mon. June 1 (La Magdeleine)
   June 14 (St. Pierre) "apres disner"
   Mon. June 29 (La Magdeleine)
July 19 (St. Pierre) "de trois heures"
Aug. 2 (St. Pierre) "d'apres disne"
Aug. 9 (St. Pierre) "a trois heures"
Aug. 23 (St. Pierre) "d'apres disne"
Oct. 11 (St. Pierre) "a trois heures apres midy"
Oct. 18 (St. Pierre) "apres disne"
Oct. 25 (2 sets, St. Pierre) "apres disne"
Nov. 8 (St. Pierre) "apres disner"
Dec. 20 (St. Pierre) "apres midy"
   26 services, 38 couples

1557

Jan. 10 (St. Pierre) "apres midy"
Jan 24 (2 sets, St. Pierre)
Feb. 14 (2 sets, St. Pierre) "apres disne"
Feb. 21 (St. Pierre) "apres disner"
   Mon. March 8 (La Magdeleine)
March 21 (St. Pierre) "apres disne"
April 4 (St. Pierre) "apres disne"
April 25 (4 sets, St. Pierre) "apres midy"
May 2 (3 sets, St. Pierre) "3 heures" [Macar's hand]
May 9 (3 sets, St. Pierre)
May 30 (St. Pierre) "apres midy"
   Mon. June 7 (La Magdeleine)
June 13 (St. Pierre) "apres disne"
   Mon. June 14 (La Magdeleine) [9]
June 27 (3 sets, St. Pierre) "de trois heures"
July 4 (2 sets, St. Pierre) "apres midy"
July 18 (3 sets, St. Gervais) "a trois heures"
July 25 (St. Pierre) "de trois heures apres midy"
Aug. 1 (St. Pierre) "apres midy"

Aug. 8 (3 sets, St. Pierre) "apres disne"
Aug. 15 (3 sets, St. Pierre)
Aug. 22 (St. Pierre) "apres midy"
   Mon. Sept. 6 (La Magdeleine)
Sept. 12 (St. Pierre) "a trois heures"
Oct. 17 (St. Pierre) "apres disne"
Oct. 24 (St. Pierre) "apres midy"
Nov. 7 (2 sets, St. Pierre) "2 heures" [Macar's hand]
Nov. 21 (2 sets, St. Pierre) "2 heures" [different hand]
Nov. 28 (St. Pierre) "apres midy"
Dec. 5 (St. Pierre) "deux heures [different hand]
Dec. 19 (St. Pierre) "deux heures" [Macar's hand]
   31 services, 51 couples

1558

Jan. 2 (St. Pierre) "2 heures" [Cop's hand]
Jan. 16 (St. Pierre) "apres disner"
Jan. 23 (St. Pierre) "apres disne"
   Fri. Jan. 28 (La Magdeleine)
Feb. 13 (St. Pierre) "de trois heures"
Feb. 20 (St. Pierre) "apres midy"
March 20 (3 sets, St. Pierre) "au vespre"
   Tues. April 19 (La Magdeleine)
May 1 (3 sets, St. Pierre) "apres midy"
   Thurs, May 5 (La Magdeleine)
June 26 (St. Pierre) "de trois heures" [different hand]
July 24 (St. Pierre) "d'apres midy"
Aug 21 (2 sets, St. Pierre)
Aug. 28 (St. Pierre) "apres disne"
   Mon. Sept. 5 (La Magdeleine)
Sept. 11 (St. Pierre) "apres midy"
Sept. 25 (St. Pierre) "apres midy"
   17 services, 22 couples

---

[9]   This was probably at 6 a.m., since there is an entry by Des Gallars for the same day just before Calvin's and it is unlikely that they would both have done baptisms at the same service.

1559
Mon. Oct. 16 (St. Pierre)
Thurs. Nov. 2 (St. Pierre) [different hand]
Mon. Nov. 13 (St. Pierre) "de sept heures" [Colladon's hand]
Tues. Dec. 12 (St. Pierre) [Macar's hand]
Dec. 17 (St. Pierre) "de deux heures" [probably Colladon's hand]
5 services, 5 couples

1560
May 12 (St. Gervais) "a trois heures apres midy"[10]
May 26 (La Magdeleine) "de 3 heures apres midi"
June 9 (2 sets, St. Gervais) "de 3 heures" [different hand]
Tues. July 16 (St. Pierre) [Macar's hand]
Mon. Sept. 2 (St. Pierre) "de six heures"
Oct. 13 (St. Pierre) "de 3 heures" [probably Colladon's hand]
Mon. Oct. 14 (St. Pierre) "de 7 heures"
Oct. 27 (La Magdeleine) "d'apres midi"
8 services, 9 couples

1561
Mon. Jan. 13 (St. Pierre) [different hand]
Mon. Feb. 17 (St. Pierre) "de sept heures"
Thurs. June 12 (St. Pierre) [different hand]

Mon. June 23 (St. Pierre) "de six heures"
Aug. 31 (St. Pierre)
5 services, 5 couples

1562
Mon. Feb. 2 (St. Pierre) "de sept heures"[11]
Tues. April 7 (St. Pierre) "de six heures"[12]
Mon. May 18 (St. Pierre) "de six heures"[13]
3 services, 3 couples

1563
Thurs. Jan. 21 (St. Pierre) "de sept heures"
Mon. Aug. 2 (St. Pierre) "de six heures" [Colladon's hand][14]
2 services, 2 couples

Total, 1550-63 = 211 services, 299 couples.

SUMMARY: Calvin performed many marriages, far more marriages than baptisms. Almost always these were on Sunday afternoons; in 1550-51, up to April 1552, he was apparently preaching regularly at St. Gervais on Sunday afternoons and thus performed marriages there. After April 1552, he was evidently preaching regularly at St. Pierre on Sunday afternoons as well as mornings, and so he married couples at that service. There are only three other Sunday afternoons, one in

---

10 This May 12 and June 9, 1560, are Calvin's only marriages at St. Gervais after 3 April 3, 1552.

11 Follows entry by Colladon at 5 a.m.

12 Register says "mardy 6" and although Mondays were the most popular weekdays for marriage and marriages on Tuesdays were rare, usually the day of the week is more accurate than the date of the month.

13 Follows entry by Gaigneulx at 4 a.m.

14 Follows an entry by Colladon for a dawn marriage.

1557, two in 1560, when he performed marriages at St. Gervais. There are two Sunday afternoons in 1560 when he married couples at La Magdeleine. After his serious illness of 1558-59 Calvin apparently no longer regularly preached on Sunday afternoons so he could move about to do weddings elsewhere. Although not every single Sunday entry is marked with a time, there are none listed for any service except the afternoon, with the single exception of one dawn service for special friends in 1550.

Calvin occasionally married couples on weekdays, at La Magdeleine where he was preaching regularly during the week until about mid-1559. After that, Calvin's weekday marriages were always at St. Pierre. The days of the week include all work days except Wednesdays. Evidently Calvin did not consider it appropriate to perform marriages at the day of prayer any more than at the main Sunday service. Although one reason may partly have been the length of the service, it is probable that he also thought that a wedding did not accord with the intercessory and especially the penitential orientation of the prayer day.

At La Magdeleine no times are listed, probably because on Sundays weddings were only allowed at the dawn or afternoon services, which for years this parish did not have. In the first half of the 1550s there was only one Sunday morning service; the Sunday afternoon service was added in 1555, when Sunday weddings at La Magdeleine begin. For weekdays, La Magdeleine had one service, Mon.-Tues. and Thurs.-Sat. until 1555, when a Wednesday service was added. When a second dawn service was added temporarily (for one year) on Wednesdays in 1559, Calvin had moved to preaching daily at St. Pierre. At St. Pierre in the 1560s times are usually listed when Calvin himself filled out the register (in later years his colleagues often did that for him). Then it appears that Calvin was preaching at the second service, at 6 or 7 a.m. depending on the season, and a colleague at the dawn service.

APPENDIX SIX: SOME OF CALVIN'S RECORDED ACTS AS GODFATHER

Sun. Sept. 28, 1550 (St. Pierre), Jaqueline daughter of Adrian de St. Aman & Antoynete (at catechism, by Fabri)

Sun. Oct. 19, 1550 (St. Pierre), Anne daughter of Guillaume de Trie & Marguerite Budee (at catechism, by Fabri)

Sat. Feb. 14, 1551 (La Magdeleine), Anne daughter of Jean DeColigny & Francoise ([7 a.m.], by Poupin)

Tues. March 17, 1551 (La Magdeleine), Anne daughter of Antoine Foulon & Jeanne (at 7 a.m., by Fabri)

Sun. May 10, 1551 (St. Pierre), Jehan son of Esplin Guivade (?) & Pernette (at 8 a.m., by Fabri)[1]

Fri. June 19, 1551 (La Magdeleine), Jean son of Michel Cop & Aymé ([probably 6 a.m.], by Poupin)

Thurs. May 28, 1551 (La Magdeleine), Jean son of Corneille de Villette & Jeanne (6 a.m., by Bourgoing)

Sun. Sept. 27, 1551 (St. Pierre), Jehan son of André Le Court & Marquet (?) (at catechism, by Bourgoing)

Mon. June 6, 1552 (La Magdeleine), Jeanne daughter of Laurens Meigret & Marguerite ([6 a.m.], by St. André)

Mon. Aug. 15, 1552 (La Magdeleine), Anne daughter of Conrad Badius & Roberte ([6 a.m.], by St. André)

Fri. Sept. 23, 1552 (La Magdeleine), Jean son of Guy de Serignac dit du Tillac & Barbe ([6 a.m.], by St. André)

Fri. Nov. 18, 1552 (La Magdeleine), Jeanne daughter of Loys De CumaFoys & wife ([7 a.m.], by Poupin)

Sun. Feb. 5, 1553 (St. Pierre), Jeanne daughter of Philibert de Quarren (?) & Marguerite (at 2 p.m. service by St. André)

Thurs. June 1, 1553 (La Magdeleine), Jean son of Guillaume Prevost & Françoise ([6 a.m.], by Des Gallars)

Sun. June 15, 1553 (La Magdeleine), Jean son of Pierre DePer & Homberte (at catechism, by Fabri)

Fri. Oct. 20, 1553 (La Magdeleine), Anne daughter of Antoine Laboire & Anne ([7 a.m.], by St. André)

---

1 Register says May 18, but in fact this is an error for May 10; the baptism was recorded in the Marriage records on that date, but evidently when it was transferred to the baptismal records the date was confused.

Sun. Oct. 29, 1553 (La Magdeleine), Anne daughter of Jean Mallet & Francoise [2] (by Poupin)

[Wed.] [3] Nov. 15, 1553 (St. Pierre), Jean son of Larridan (?) Mergrit & Marguerite (at 8 a.m., by St. André)

Mon. Nov. 20, 1553 (La Magdeleine), Anne daughter of Antoine De Popillon & Isabeau ([7 a.m.], by St. André)

Wed. Dec. 27, 1553 (St. Pierre), Anne daughter of Jacques de Plenx (?) & Marguerite (at 8 a.m., by St. André)

Thurs. Dec. 6, 1554 (La Magdeleine), Jean son of Jean Jacqueme & Marguerite ([7 a.m.], by St. André)

Wed. Jan. 30, 1555 (St. Pierre), Jeanne daughter of Francois Brynect (?) & Jaquette ([probably 8 a.m.?], by St. André)

Sun. April 21, 1555 (St. Pierre), Semuel son of Jehan Morely & Magdelaine (at catechism, by Cop)

Sat. June 15, 1555 (La Magdeleine), Jaques son of Ines Camiaille & Antoinette ([6 a.m., by St. André)

Wed. July 24, 1555 (St. Pierre), Anne daughter of Francois du Pont & Estiennette (at 8 a.m., by St. André)

Sun. Aug. 18, 1555 (St. Pierre), Jehan son of Francoys Eschalart & Jehanne (at catechism, by Cop)

Sun. Sept. 29, 1555 (St. Pierre), Jehanne daughter of Jaques de Landes & Magdelaine (at catechism, by Cop)

Wed. Oct. 16, 1555 (St. Pierre), Jehan son of Jehan du Plilus (?) dit Despoye & Margarete (at 8 a.m., by Fabri)

Wed. Nov. 20, 1555 (St. Pierre), Jehanne daughter of Philibert Sarazin & Loyse (at 8 a.m., by Fabri)

Mon. Dec. 16, 1555 (La Magdeleine), Jeanne daughter of Loys Enoc & Francoise ([7 a.m.], by Chauvet)

Sat. Jan. 4, 1556, John son of William Stafford & Dorothy [4]

Sun. Jan. 19, 1556 (St. Pierre), David son of Laurent de Normandie & Anne (at catechism, by Bourgoing)

---

2   As usual Poupin gives no time, but it seems probable that it was catechism since Calvin would be preaching at St. Pierre in the morning – unless this entry belongs in the St. Pierre register?

3   The entry is dated "le 13" but it comes after one by Cop on "mercredi 15" at 5 a.m. The 13th would have been Monday, but there was no service at 8 a.m. on Mondays, and it is probable that Calvin was preaching at St. Pierre on Wednesdays at 8 a.m., usually in alternate weeks, but at this time (and for several years after) he had almost every Wednesday service.

4   Listed in Church of England Parish, the first of the baptismal records, "A. 1556": "the 4 of January. John Stafford the sonne of William Stafford Knight, John Calvin being the godfather." It is not absolutely sure where this baptism was held; it probably was done in Notre Dame la Neuve where the English congregation met. Each of the baptismal entries gives the date, child's name, father's name, and godfather's name. In mid-1558, the wording for "godfather " changes; the May entry still has "godfather" but beginning in July the word is "witness." These records name all the children baptized and couples married in the English church community, 1556-1558.

Wed. Feb. 19, 1556 (St. Pierre), David son of Germain Colladon & Claude (at 8 a.m., by Fabri)

Fri. Oct. 23, 1556 (La Magdeleine), Paula, daughter of Claude de Rouhault & Claude ([7 a.m., by Enoc)

Tues. Jan. 26, 1557 (La Magdeleine), Jean son of Jean Rousset de Truas (?) & Anne ([7 a.m., by Enoc)

Sat. March 13, 1557 (La Magdeleine), Jeanne daughter of Jean de Saint Martin & Loyse ([7 a.m.], by Enoc)

Sun. Oct. 10, 1557 (St. Pierre), Jean son of Louys Franc & Michee (au vespres, by Macar)[5]

Mon. Nov. 29, 1557 (La Magdeleine), Jean son of Leonard du Mazer & Judith ([7 a.m.], by Macar)[6]

Sat. May 7, 1558 (St. Gervais), Jehan son of Raymond Chauvet & Santamie ([6 a.m.], by Chauvet?![7])

Sun. Oct. 1, 1559 (St. Gervais), Marie daughter of Anselme Caille & Marie (at 3 p.m., by Chauvet).

Sun. Oct. 22, 1559 (St. Pierre), Sara daughter of Michel Jaquemin & Jaquete (at catechism, by Morel).

Thurs. Nov. 2, 1559 (St. Pierre), Judith daughter of Michel Roset & Claudine ([7 a.m.], by Macar).

Sun. Jan. 7, 1560 (St. Pierre), Jeanne daughter of Jean Girard & Guiluime ([no time given], by Macar)

Sun. Jan. 11, 1562 (St. Pierre), Jehan son of Francois Des Plans & Amie (at catechism or 3 p.m. by Enoc)

Thurs. May 14, 1562 (St. Pierre), Elizabeth daughter of Rene Besson & Anise ([6 a.m.], by Merlin)

Sun. Nov. 1, 1562 (St. Pierre), Jehan son of Louis Portire (?) and Claude (at 8 a.m., by Merlin)

Sun. Nov. 22, 1562 (La Magdeleine), David son of Francois De Beaumont & Claude (at catechism, by D'Airebaudouze – boy child of twins)

Sun. Dec. 6, 1562 (St. Pierre), Pierre son of Jehan Le Maistre and Anne Colladon (at catechism, by Colladon).

Sat. Dec. 13, 1562 (St. Pierre), Jehan son of Charles Maubué & and wife ([7 a.m.], by Colladon)

---

5   Macar may have been preaching, or he may have stepped forward after Calvin's sermon to do baptisms, because there are a considerable number of baptisms by him at the 3 p.m. service in 1557.

6   This was Calvin's stepdaughter's son.

7   No minister's name is given, but the entry is made in Chauvet's hand. However, it would be very surprising if he baptized his own child, so there may be some mistake.

SUMMARY: The list is not exhaustive (being complete only for the years 1550-51, 1553, 1555, 1557, 1559, and 1562, with the other entries found somewhat by chance), but the picture which emerges is interesting. Calvin most often gave a name similar to his own baptismal name, Jean or Jeanne or Anne, but he also gave other names such as Jacqueline or Paula or Sara or Judith or Marie or Elizabeth or David or Pierre or Semuel (David seems to have been the favorite of these). As the Stafford case illustrates, he refused to give his more distinctive surname, not probably because it was unacceptable in the way "Claude" was but because it would honor him personally in a way he felt was inappropriate. All but one of the Sunday baptisms examined here are identified as to times; most occurred at catechisms, two at the afternoon service, one at either catechism or afternoon, two at the morning service. At least on Sundays, Calvin evidently preferred to keep his role as godfather separate from his own preaching services, even if another minister could have performed the sacrament at the end of his service. The weekday services are spread through the days.

APPENDIX SEVEN: DATING CALVIN'S SERMONS
IN BIBLICAL ORDER
BY INTERCESSORY PRAYERS

Note: The sermon numbers correspond to the printed texts listed for each book. Thus, they are not always in chronological order but that is the order used here.

OLD TESTAMENT		
Genesis[1]		
1. M. Sep 4, '59	QNS[2]	
2. Tu Sep 5, '59	QNS	desja exposé
3. Wd Sep 6, '59	DTP[3]	hier nous traictasmes
4. Th Sep 7, '59	QNS	avons desja allegué
5. Fr Sep 8, '59	QNS	desja esté touché
6. S. Sep 9, '59	QNS	
7. M. Sep 18, '59	QNS	avons monstré par ci devant[4]
8. Tu Sep 19, '59	QNS	
9. Wd Sep 20, '59	DTP	
Th Sep 21, '59 none		

10. Fr Sep 22, '59	QNS	vismes mercredi dernier
11. S. Sep 23, '59	QNS	
12. M. Oct 2, '59	QNS	
13. Tu Oct 3, '59	QNS	
14. Wd Oct 4, '59	DTP	touchasmes desja hier
15. Th Oct 5, '59	QNS	
16. Fr Oct 6, '59	QNS	vismes hier
17. S. Oct 7, '59	QNS	
18. M. Oct 16, '59	QNS	avons veu par ci devant
19. Tu Oct 17, '59	QNS	fut hier traictée
20. Wd Oct 18, '59	DTP	desja exposé cy desssus [es[5]]

---

1 *Sermons sur la Genèse Chapitres 1,1-11,4 ; Sermons sur la Genèse Chapitres 11,5-20,7*, edit. Max Engammare. *Supplementa Calviniana XI/1 & XI/2* Neukirchen-Vluyn , 2000.

2 QNS = Que non seulement

3 DTP = Dieu tout puissant

4 The most common connotation for "ci devant" or "ci dessus" is the previous sermon when there has been a time lapse between it and the present sermon.

5 [es] signifies "earlier sermon(s)" meaning not the day before; it often means earlier in the same week (as here it probably refers particularly to sermon 18 on Monday), though it can also mean earlier in the exposition of the book in question.

21. Th Oct 19, '59	QNS	
22. Fr Oct 20, '59	QNS	
23. S. Oct 21, '59	QNS	
24. M. Oct 30, '59	QNS	veu par ci devant
25. Tu Oct 31, '59	QNS	vismes hier
26. Wd Nov 1, '59	DTP	
27. Th Nov 2, '59 sermon missing		
28. Fr Nov 3, '59	QNS	vismes hier
29. S. Nov 4, '59	QNS	
30. M. Nov 13, '59	QNS	
31. Tu Nov 14, '59	QNS	
32. Wd Nov 15, '59	DTP	vismes hier
Th Nov 16, '59 none		
33. Fr Nov 17, '59	QNS	
34. S. Nov 18, '59	QNS	veu par ci devant [es]
35. M. Dec 11, '59	QNS	
36. Tu Dec 12, '59	QNS	
37. Wd Dec 13, '59	DTP	
38. Th Dec 14, '59	QNS	
39. Fr Dec 15, '59	QNS	

40. S. Dec 16, '59	QNS	desja remonstré cy dessus [es]
41. M. Dec 25, '60 = '59	QNS	
42. M. Jan 8, '60	QNS	veu par cy devant
43. Tu Jan 9, '60	QNS	vismes hier
44. Wd Jan 10, '60	DTP	traitasmes hier
45. Th Jan 11, '60	QNS	
46. Fr Jan 12, '60	QNS	vismes hier
47. S. Jan 13, '60	QNS	vismes hier
48. M. Jan 22, '60	QNS	
49. Tu Jan 23, '60	QNS	avons veu [es]
50. Wd Jan 24, '60	DTP	traismes desja hier
51. Th Jan 25, '60	QNS	vismes hier
52. Fr Jan 26, '60	QNS	
53. S. Jan 27, '60	QNS	vismes hier
54. M. Feb 5, '60	QNS	veu [#53]
55. Tu Feb 6, '60	QNS	vismes hier
56. Wd Feb 7, '60	DTP[6]	vismes hier
57. Th Feb 8, '60	QNS	vismes hier
58. Fr Feb 9, '60	QNS	
59. S. Feb 10, '60	QNS	

---

6   On Feb 7, '60, the opening words of the Wednesday prayer are extended beyond the first phrase, and correspond to the day of prayer text. (The first phrase is the same for Sunday and day of prayer, but the following words differ, so this recorded sermon confirms the practice of the day of prayer text.) cf. S. XI/2, p. 631.

60. M. Feb 19, '60	QNS			15/76. S. Mar 23, '60	QNS	commençasmes hier
61. Tu Feb 20, '60	QNS			16/77. M. Apr 1, '60	QNS	
1/62. Wd Feb 21, '60	QNS[7]			17/78. Tu Apr 2, '60	QNS	
2/63. Th Feb 22, '60	QNS	fut hier commencée		18/79. Wd Apr 3, '60	QNS[8]	vismes hier
3/64. Fr Feb 23, '60	QNS			19/80. Th Apr 4, '60	QNS	vismes hier
4/65. S. Feb 24, '60	QNS	fut hier exposé		20/81. Fr Apr 5, '60	QNS	traictasmes hier
				21/82. S. Apr 6, '60	QNS	commençasmes hier
5/66. M. Mar 4, '60	QNS					
6/67. Tu Mar 5, '60	QNS	vismes hier		22/83. M. Apr 15, '60	QNS	commencé a declarer
7/68. Wd Mar 6, '60	DTP	commençasmes hier		23/84. Tu Apr 16, '60		QNS
8/69. Th Mar 7, '60	QNS	vismes hier		24/85. Wd Apr 17, '60		DTP
9/70. Fr Mar 8, '60	QNS	dismes hier		25/86. Th Apr 18, '60		QNS
S. Mar 9, '60 none				26/87. Fr Apr 19, '60	QNS	vismes hier
				27/88. S. Apr 20, '60	QNS	vismes hier
10/71. M. Mar 18, '60	QNS	dit ci-dessus [#70]				
11/72. Tu Mar 19, '60	QNS	veismes hier		28/89. M. Apr 29, '60	QNS	
12/73. Wd Mar 20, '60	DTP	vismes hier		29/90. Tu Apr 30, '60	QNS	commençasmes hier
13/74. Th Mar 21, '60	QNS	veismes hier				
14/75. Fr Mar 22, '60	QNS					

---

7   Here there seems to be a mistake of some sort; the weekday prayer is used, not the day of prayer; this is the first sermon of the second volume, according to Raguenier's catalogue (cf. S. II, p. xvii).

8   Again, there appears to be a mistake, perhaps by the scribe or even Raguenier, since this gives the weekday prayer phrase and not the day of prayer text.

30/91. Wd May 1, '60	DTP	veu par cy devant [#89]
31/92. Th May 2, '60	QNS	
32/93. Fr May 3, '60	QNS	vismes hier
33/94. S. May 4, '60	QNS	
34/95. M. May 13, '60	QNS	
35/96. Tu May 14, '60	QNS	
36/97. Wd May 15, '60	DTP	vismes hier
About 8 sermons missing between #97 & next 3		
1.S. Jun 1, '60[9]	QNS	vismes hier
2. M. Jun 10, '60	QNS	avons veu
3. Tu Jun 11, '60	QNS	commençasmes hier
About16 sermons missing between 3 on Abe &13 on Gen. 25-27		

1. [M. Jul 22, '60][10]	QNS	avons veu
2. [Tu Jul 23, '60]	QNS	Hier
3. [Wd Jul 24, '60]	DTP	[hier 58:51][11]
4. [Th Jul 25, '60]	QNS	[hier 58:60]
5. [Fr Jul 26, '60]	QNS	Hier
6. [S. Jul 27, '60]	QNS	Hier
7. [Tu Jul 31, '60]	QNS	avons veu
8. [M. Aug 5, '60]	QNS	avons veu
9. [Tu Aug 6, '60]	QNS	Hier
10. [Wd Aug 7, '60]	DTP	[hier 58:154]
11. [Th Aug 8, '60]	QNS	Hier
12. [Fr Aug 9, '60]	QNS	hier [+58:171, 176]
13. [S. Aug 10, '60]	QNS	hier [+58:190]
Deuteronomy[12]		
1.Wd Mar 21=20, '55	DTP[13]	

---

9   *Trois sermons sur le sacrifice d'Abraham* Geneve : Jacques Bourgeois, '61.

10   Richard Stauffer dates these sermons M. Jul 8 to S. Jul 27, '60, but he does not give his source for this dating; "Les sermons inédits de Calvin sur le livre de la Genèse," p. 36 n.4. The original printing does not include dates. In addition, there is one sermon more than would fit in two weeks, i.e., there are thirteen and only twelve would make up the regular M.-S. sequence for two weeks. Given the patterns of prayers and references to "hier," the extra sermon must be in a separate week. It is possible that Calvin filled in for one of his colleagues in his "off" week.

11   References to the *Opera Calvini*/ OC are given simply in numbers: volumn and column.

12   *Sermons sur le V livre de Moyse nomme Deuteronome.* Geneve : Thomas Courteau, 1567.

13   Calvin was doing all the Wed. day of prayer sermons, at the request of the Company of Pastors, and a colleague was doing the Sat. sermon in his week. RCP II, p. 150.

2. M. Mar 25, '55	QNS	desja dit
Tu Mar 26, '55 none		
3. Wd Mar 27, '55	DTP	
Absent in Bern[14]		
4. Th Apr 11, '55	QNS	veu par ci devant
5. Fr Apr 12, '55	QNS	
6. S. Apr 13, '55	QNS	
7. Wd Apr 16=17, '55	DTP	
8. M. Apr 22, '55	QNS	
9. Tu Apr 23, '55	QNS	commenceasmes hier
10 Wd Apr 24, '55	DTP	vismes hier
11. Th Apr 25, '55	QNS	
12. Fr Apr 26, '55	QNS	
S. Apr 27, '55 none		
13. Wd May 1, '55	DTP	traitté par ci devant
14. M. May 6, '55	QNS	veu par ci devant
15. Tu May 7, '55	QNS	

16. Wd May 8, '55	DTP	desja declairé ci-dessus?
17. Th May 9, '55	QNS	dit par ci devant [dif.text]
18. Fr May 10, '55	QNS	dismes hier
S. May 11, '55 none		
19.Wd May 15, '55	DTP	exposé par ci devant
20. M. May 20, '55	QNS	
21. Tu May 21, '55	QNS	hier exposé
22. Wd May 22, '55	DTP	Hier
23. Th May 23, '55	[QNS][15]	
24. Fr May 24, '55	QNS	commenceasmes hier
S. May 25, '55 none		
25. Wd May 29, '55	DTP	veu ci dessus
26. M. Jun 3, '55	QNS	avons di par ci devant
27. Tu Jun 4, '55	QNS	
28. Wd Jun 5, '55	DTP	par ci devant [saw miracles]
29. Th Jun 6, '55	QNS[16]	hier declairé

---

14 Travel to Bern Mar. 28 – Apr. 10, 1555; RCP 2,pp. 61-62; OC 21:609.

15 The bracketed [QNS] indicates that Calvin skipped the opening phrase "Que non seulement" of the weekday prayer and began with what is normally the second phrase, "vrais et fidelles ministers." Except for the opening line, it is the same prayer.

16 This sermon is labeled "M. Jun 16" but in fact the Biblical text fits in the sequence between Jun 5 and Jun 7, and Jun 16 is actually a Sat. when Calvin would not be preaching.

30. Fr Jun 7, '55	QNS	
S. Jun 8, '55 none		
31. Wd Jun 12, '55	DTP	veu par ci devant
32. M. Jun 17, '55	QNS	avons touché
Tu Jun 18, '55 none		
33. Wd Jun 19, '55	DTP	
34. Th Jun 20, '55	QNS	
35. Fr Jun 21, '55	QNS	traittasmes hier
S. Jun 22, '55 none		
36. Wd Jun 26, '55	DTP	
37. M. Jul 1, '55	QNS	avons desja veu
38. Tu Jul 2, '55	QNS	
39. Wd Jul 3, '55	DTP	
40. Th Jul 4, '55	QNS	veu par ci devant [es]
41. Fr Jul 5, '55	QNS	
S. Jul 6, '55 none		
M. Jul 15, '55 none		
42. Tu Jul 16, '55	QNS	
43. Wd Jul 17, '55	DTP	
44. Th Jul 18, '55	QNS	hier declairé
45. Fr Jul 19, '55	QNS	veu par ci devant
46. S. Jul 20, '55	QNS	commenceasmes hier

47. Wd Jul 24, '55	DTP	avons veu
48. M. Jul 29, '55	QNS	veu par ci devant
49. Tu Jul 30, '55	QNS	vismes hier
50. Wd Jul 31, '55	DTP	
51. Th Aug 1, '55	QNS	
52. Fr Aug 2, '55	QNS	vismes hier
53. S. Aug 3, '55	QNS	vismes hier
54. Wd Aug 7, '55	DTP	traitté par ci devant
55. M. Aug 12, '55	QNS	
56. Tu Aug 13, '55	QNS	vismes hier
57. Wd Aug 14, '55	DTP	commenceasmes hier
58. Th Aug 15, '55	QNS	
59. Fr Aug 16, '55	QNS	vismes hier
S. Aug 17, '55 none		
60. Wd Aug 21, '55	DTP	
61. M. Aug 26, '55	QNS[	
62. Tu Aug 27, '55	QNS	
63. Wd Aug 28, '55	DTP	vismes desja hier
64. Th Aug 29, '55	QNS	vismes hier
65. Fr Aug 30, '55	[QNS]	commenceasmes hier
66. S. Aug 31, '55	QNS	

67. Wd Sep 4, '55	DTP			88. Wd Oct 16, '55	DTP	
68. M. Sep 9, '55	QNS			89. M. Oct 21, '55	QNS	par ci devant nous avons veu
69. Tu Sep 10, '55	QNS	par ci devant [es]		90. Tu Oct 22, '55	QNS	
70. Wd Sep 11, '55	DTP	vismes hier		91. Wd Oct 23, '55	DTP	exposasmes hier
71. Th Sep 12, '55	QNS	ces jours passez		92. Th Oct 24, '55	QNS	
72. Fr Sep 13, '55	QNS	commencé hier		93. Fr Oct 25, '55	QNS	
73. S. Sep 14, '55	QNS	vismes hier		94. S. Oct 26, '55	QNS	fut hier entamé
74. Wd Sep 18, '55	DTP	declairé ci dessus		95. Wd Oct 30, '55	DTP	
75. M. Sep 23, '55	QNS	veu par ci devant		96. M. Nov 4, '55	QNS	veu par ci devant
76. Tu Sep 24, '55	QNS			97. Tu Nov 5, '55	QNS	
77. Wd Sep 25, '55	QNS[17]			98. Wd Nov 6, '55	DTP	fut hier declairé
78. Th Sep 26, '55	QNS			99. Th Nov 7, '55	[QNS]	
79. Fr Sep 27, '55	QNS			100. Fr Nov 8, '55	QNS	
80. S. Sep 28, '55	QNS			101. S. Nov 9, '55	[QNS]	
81. Wd Oct 2, '55	DTP			102. Wd Nov 13, '55	DTP	
82. M. Oct 7, '55	QNS			103. M. Nov 18, '55	QNS	avons veu par ci devant
83. Tu Oct 8, '55	QNS			104. Tu Nov 19, '55	[QNS]	
84. Wd Oct 9, '55	DTP	vismes hier		105. Wd Nov 20, '55	DTP	
85. Th Oct 10, '55	QNS			106. Th Nov 21, '55	[QNS]	vismes hier
86. Fr Oct 11, '55	QNS					
87. S. Oct 12, '55	QNS	vismes hier				

17   Here there seems to be a mistake, as the first phrase of the weekday prayer is given instead of the day of prayer text.

107. Fr Nov 22, '55	[QNS]	
S. Nov 23, '55 none		
108. Wd Nov 27, '55	DTP	
109. M. Dec 2, '55	QNS	
110. Tu Dec 3, '55	QNS	
111. Wd Dec 4, '55	DTP	hier fut remonstré
112. Th Dec 5, '55	QNS	
113. Fr Dec 6, '55	QNS	vismes hier
114. S. Dec 7, '55	QNS	
115. M. Dec 16, '55	QNS	veu par ci devant
116. Tu Dec 17, '55	QNS	vismes hier
117. Wd Dec 18, '55	DTP	vismes hier
118. Th Dec 19, '55	[QNS]	
119. Fr Dec 20, '55	[QNS]	fut hier monstré
120. S. Dec 21, '55	QNS	
121. Wd Dec 25, '56 = '55	DTP	
122. M. Dec 30, '56 = '55	QNS	
123. Tu Dec 31, '56= '55	QNS	
124. Wd Jan 1, '56	DTP	
125. Th Jan 2, '56	QNS	
126. Fr Jan 3, '56	[QNS]	

S. Jan 4, '56 none		
127. Wd Jan 8, '56	DTP	
M. Jan 13, '56 none		
128. Tu Jan 14, '56	QNS	
129. Wd Jan 15, '56	DTP	hier fut demené
130. Th Jan 16, '56	QNS	
131. Fr Jan 17, '56	QNS	
S. Jan 18, '56 none		
132. Wd Jan 22, '56	DTP	
133. M. Jan 27, '56	QNS	desja veu par ci devant
134. Tu Jan 28, '56	QNS	
135. Wd Jan 29, '56	DTP	hier fut touché
136. Th Jan 30, '56	QNS	
137. Fr Jan 31, '56	QNS	
138. S. Feb 1, '56	QNS	
139. Wd Feb 5, '56	DTP	
140. M. Feb 10, '56	QNS	
141. Tu Feb 11, '56	QNS	veu par ci devant [es]
142. Wd Feb 12, '56	DTP	
143. Th Feb 13, '56	[QNS]	
144. Fr Feb 14, '56	[QNS]	
S. Feb 15, '56 none		

145. Wd Feb 19, '56	DTP	
146. M. Feb 24, '56	QNS	exposé ci dessus
147. Tu Feb 25, '56	QNS	
148. Wd Feb 26, '56	DTP	fut desja entamé hier
149. Th Feb 27, '56	QNS	lecture d'hier
150. Fr Feb 28, '56	QNS	vismes hier
S. Feb 29, '56 none		
151. Wd Mar 4, '56	DTP	veu par ci devant
152. M. Mar 9, '56	QNS	
153. Tu Mar 19, '56	QNS	veu par ci devant??
154. Wd Mar 11, '56	DTP	
155. Th Mar 12, '56	QNS	fut hier desja entamé
156. Fr Mar 13, '56	QNS	veu ces jours passez
S. Mar 14, '56 none		
157. Wd Mar 18, '56	DTP	
158. M. Mar 23, '56	QNS	

159. Tu Mar 24, '56	QNS	
160. Wd Mar 25, '56	DTP	
161. Th Mar 26, '56	DTP[18]	fut hier desja touché
162. Fr Mar 27, '56	QNS	declairé par ci devant [es]
163. S. Mar 28, '56	QNS	
164. M. Apr 6, '56	QNS	
165. Tu Apr 7, '56	QNS	fut hier deduit
166. Wd Apr 8, '56	DTP	declaré ci devant
167. Th Apr 9, '56	QNS	commençasmes hier
168. Fr Apr 10, '56	QNS	commençasmes hier
169. S. Apr 11, '56	QNS	fut hier traitté
170. M. Apr 20, '56	QNS	
171. Tu Apr 21, '56	QNS	
172. Wd Apr 22, '56	DTP	vismes hier
173. Th Apr 23, '56	QNS	
174. Fr Apr 24, '56	QNS	
S. Apr 25, '56 none		
175. M. May 4, '56	QNS	
176. Tu[19] May 5, '56	QNS	

18 Here there is a mistake, with the first phrase of the day of prayer text instead of the weekday prayer. This is more rare than the reverse, since the scribe was accustomed to using the weekday one more often.

19 "Wed." written in error for "Tues." but the date May 5 is correct.

177. Wd May 6, '56	DTP	veu par ci devant [es]	189. Th Jun 18, '56	QNS	avons traitté par ci devant
178. Th May 7, '56	QNS		190. Fr Jun 19, '56	QNS	desja touché par ci dessus
179. Fr May 8, '56	QNS	vismes hier	191. S. Jun 20, '56	QNS	
S. May 9, '56 none					
			192. M. Jun 29, '56	QNS	
Calvin collapses in pulpit Sun, May 10 [21:80-81]			193. Tu Jun 30, '56	QNS	monstrasmes hier
			194. Wd Jul 1, '56	DTP	commençasmes hier
180. M. Jun 1, '56	QNS	desja veu par ci devant	195. Th Jul 2, '56	QNS	vismes hier
			196. Fr Jul 3, '56	QNS	vismes hier
181. Tu Jun 2, '56	QNS	vismes hier	197. S. Jul 4, '56	QNS	
182. Wd Jun 3, '56	DTP				
183. Th Jun 4, '56	QNS	vismes hier	198. M. Jul 13, '56	QNS	
184. Fr Jun 5, '56	QNS	vismes hier	199. Tu Jul 14, '56	QNS	furent hier exposez
185. S. Jun 6, '56	QNS	vismes hier	200. Wd Jul 15, '56	DTP	
186. M. Jun 15, '56	QNS		**First Samuel** [20]		
187. Tu Jun 16, '56	QNS		1. Fr Aug 8, '61	none [21]	
188. Wd Jun 17, '56	DTP	vismes hier	2. S. Aug 9, '61	QNS [22]	Hesterna

[20] *Iohannis Calvini Operum Omnium Theologicorum. Tomus Secundus: continens Homilias in 1. Librum Samuelis & conciones in Librum Iobi.* Genevae. Apud Iohannem Vignon, Petrum & Iacobum Chouet. MDCXVII

[21] "none" indicates that there may have been a prayer, but not one of the fixed prayers useful for dating.

[22] Varied initial words are used to begin the fixed prayer on the limited occasions when it is noted; for this reason, the French original is used to identify the prayer. Here "Neque vero nobis solis gratiam hanc, sed omnibus populi ac Gentibus de precemur" p. 11; "Atque non nobis solis" p. 37; "Neque nobis tantum hanc gratiam, sed omnibus etiam" p. 71; "Neque nobis tantum hanc gratiam, sed omnibus" p. 76; "Neque vero nobis solis istam gratiam, sed omnibus etiam deprecabimur" p. 82. See pp. 99, 110, 116, 127, 138; " & omnibus etiam populis" p. 143; pp. 151, 163, 175, 192, 203, 209, 219, 225, 267, 272, 290, 301, 313, 344, 373, 379, 384, 396, 402, 408, 413, 420, 425, 444, 450, 456, 467, 473, 518, 524, 566, 571, 587, 596, 602.

3. [M. Aug 18, '61]	none[23]	
4. [Tu Aug 19, '61]	none	
5. [Wd Aug 20, '61]	none	
6. [Th Aug 21, '61]	none	
7. [Fr Aug 22, '61]	QNS	Hesterna
8. [S. Aug 23, '61]	none	
9. [M. Sep 1, '61]	none	
10. [Tu Sep 2, '61]	none	
11. [Wd Sep 3, '61]	none	Hesterna
12. [Th Sep 4, '61]	none	Hesterna
13. [Fr Sep 5, '61]	QNS	
14. [S. Sep 6, '61]	QNS	Hesterna
15. [M. Sep 15, '61]	QNS	
16. [Tu Sep 16, '61]	none	Hesterna
17. [Wd Sep 17, '61]	none	Hesterna
18. [Th Sep 18, '61]	QNS	
19. [Fr Sep 19, '61]	none	
20. [S. Sep 20, '61]	QNS	
21. [M. Sep 29, '61]	QNS	
22. [Tu Sep 30, '61]	none	Hesterna

23. [Wd Oct 1, '61]	QNS	
24. [Th Oct 2, '61]	none	Hesterna
25. [Fr Oct 3, '61]	QNS	
26. [S. Oct 4, '61]	QNS	Hesterna
Absent from consistory Oct 9 & 16 [21:762]		
27. [M. Oct 13, '61]	none	
28. [Tu Oct 14, '61]	QNS	Hesterna
29. [M. Oct 27, '61]	none	Explicanda nobis iam superesset
30. [Tu Oct 28, '61]	QNS	Hesterna
Absent from consistory Oct 30 & Nov 6 [21:764]		
31. [M. Nov 10, '61]	none	
32. [Tu Nov 11, '61]	QNS	Hesterna
33. [Wd Nov 12, '61]	none	[Hesterna 29:603]
34. [Th Nov 13, '61]	none	
35. [Fr Nov 14, '61]	QNS	
36. [S. Nov 15, '61]	none	
37. [M. Nov 24, '61]	QNS	

---

23 From here to the end is reconstruction, with the assumption that there are a number of days – at least 8 – when Calvin does not preach. Fitting these 1 Samuel sermons right before the 2 Samuel ones means the last 1 Samuel could well have been Friday, May 22, '62, followed by the first on 2 Samuel the next day. Given the fact that Calvin was preaching during Passion Week (sermons published in S. VII), that would have been his week to preach and thus the 1 Samuel sermons would have been interrupted for three weeks (one his week off, then Passion Week, then his week off). There was also an exchange of rotation weeks with his alternate Merlin; see chap. 6 at n.177.

38. [Tu Nov 25, '61]	QNS	Hesterna
39. [Wd Nov 26, '61]	none	
40. [Th Nov 27, '61]	QNS	
41. [Fr Nov 28, '61]	QNS	superiore concione
42. [S. Nov 29, '61]	none	
43. [M. Dec 8, '61]	none	
44. [Tu Dec 9, '61]	none	Hesterna
45. [Wd Dec 10, '61]	none	
46. [Th Dec 11, '61]	none	Hesterna
47. [Fr Dec 12, '61]	none	
48. [S. Dec 13, '61]	QNS	Hesterna
49. [M. Dec 22, '61]	QNS	
50. [Tu Dec 23, '61]	none	
51. [Wd Dec 24, '61]	none	
52. [Thurs. Dec 25, '61]	QNS	superiore concione
53. [Fr Dec 26, '61]	none	Hesterna
54. [S. Dec 27, '61]	QNS	Hesterna
55. [M. Jan 5, '62]	none	
56. [Tu Jan 6, '62]	QNS	
57. [Wd Jan7, '62]	none	
58. [Th Jan 8, '62]	none	Hesterna

59. [Fr Jan 9, '62]	none	
60. [S. Jan 10, '62]	none	Hesterna
61. [M. Jan 19, '62]	QNS	
62. [Tu Jan 20, '62]	none	
63. [Wd Jan 21, '62]	none	Hesterna
64. [Th Jan 22, '62]	none	Hesterna
65. [Fr Jan 23, '62]	none	
66. [S. Jan 24, '62]	QNS	
67. [M. Feb 2, '62]	QNS	
68. [Tu Feb 3, '62]	QNS	
69. [Wd Feb 4, '62]	none	Hesterna
70. [Th Feb 5, '62]	QNS	
71. [Fr Feb 6, '62]	QNS	
72. [S. Feb 7, '62]	QNS	Hesterna
73. [M. Feb 16, '62]	QNS	
74. [Tu Feb 17, '62]	QNS	
75. [Wd Feb 18, '62]	QNS	Hesterna
76. [Th Feb 19, '62]	none	
77. [Fr Feb 20, '62]	QNS	
78. [S. Feb 21, '62]	QNS	
Exchange rotation with Merlin (alternate) [24]		

[24] Merlin's multiple baptisms and marriages provide a fairly clear idea of what weeks he was on duty as preacher, and these change rhythm in late February; his schedule had been weeks beginning M. Dec 29, 1552, Jan 12, Jan 26, Feb 9, Feb 23, 1553, but it is obvious from the baptisms that he continued the following week, Mar 2 and then skipped a week, to be on a different rhythm, Mar 2, Mar 16, Mar 30, Apr 13, Apr 27, May 4…

79. [M. Mar 9, '62]	QNS	vidimus hactenus
80. [Tu Mar 10, '62]	QNS	
81. [Wd Mar 11, '62]	DTP[25]	
82. [Th Mar 12, '62]	QNS	Hesterna
83. [Fr Mar 13, '62]	QNS	superiore concione
84. [S. Mar 14, '62]	none	
85. [M. Apr 6, '62]	none	
86. [Tu Apr 7, '62]	none	Hesterna
87. [Wd Apr 8, '62]	none	Hesterna
88. [Th Apr 9, '62]	almost none	
89. [Fr Apr 10, '62]	none	
90. [S. Apr 11, '62]	none	
91. [M. Apr 20, '62]	QNS	
92. [Tu Apr 21, '62]	QNS	
93. [Wd Apr 22, '62]	none	
94. [Th Apr 23, '62]	none	
95. [Fr Apr 24, '62]	none	Hesterna
96. [S. Apr 25, '62]	none	Hesterna
97. [M. May 4, '62]	none	
98. [Tu May 5, '62]	none	
99. [Wd May 6, '62]	none	Hesterna

100. [Th May 7, '62]	QNS	
101. [Fr May 8, '62]	QNS	Hesterna
102. [S. May 9, '62]	none	
103. [M. May 18, '62]	none	
104. [Tu May 19, '62]	QNS	
105. [Wd May 20, '62]	none	
106. [Th May 21, '62]	QNS	
107. [Fr May 22, '62]	QNS	
Second Samuel[26]		
1. S. May 23, '62	QNS	
2. M. Jun 1, '62	QNS	desja veu en partie
3. Tu Jun 2, '62	QNS	fut desia hier declaré
4. Wd Jun 3, '62	DTP	
5. Th Jun 4, '62	QNS	
6. Fr Jun 5, '62	QNS	
7. S. Jun 6, '62	QNS	fut hier traictée
8. M. Jun 15, '62	QNS	
9. Tu Jun 16, '62	QNS	veismes hier
10. Wd Jun 17, '62	DTP	veismes hier

---

25 "Hanc igitur ob causam sequentibus, verbis eius gratiam & favorem invocabimus, Domine Deus, &c. " p. 461.

26 *Predigten über das 2. Buch Samuelis*, hg. Hanns Rückert. *Supplementa Calviniana I* Neukirchen-Vluyn, 1961.

11. Th Jun 18, '62	QNS	fut hier traictté		32. Wd Aug 12, '62	DTP	
Fr-S. Jun 19-20 none				33. Th Aug 13, '62	QNS	vismes hier
				34. Fr Aug 14, '62	QNS	fut hier declaré
				35. S. Aug 15, '62	QNS	
12. M. Jun 29, '62	QNS	veu par cy devant				
13. Tu Jun 30, '62	QNS			36. M. Aug 24, '62	QNS	desja veu [#35]
14. Wd Jul 1, '62	DTP	commençasmes hier		37. Tu Aug 25, '62	QNS	vismes hier
15. Th Jul 2, '62	QNS	veismes hier		38. Wd Aug 26, '62	DTP	
16. Fr Jul 3, '62	QNS			39. Th Aug 27, '62	QNS	
17. S. Jul 4, '62	QNS			40. Fr Aug 28, '62	QNS	
				41. S. Aug 29, '62	QNS	
18. M. Jul 13, '62	QNS	veu… avons monstré				
19. Tu Jul 14, '62	QNS	commençasmes hier		42. M. Sep 7, '62	QNS	desja veu [#41]
				43. Tu Sep 8, '62	QNS	
20. Wd Jul 15, '62	DTP			44. Wd Sep 9, '62	DTP	
21. Th Jul 16, '62	QNS	vismes hier		45. Th Sep 10, '62	QNS	fut hier dit
22. Fr Jul 17, '62	QNS	vismes hier		46. Fr Sep 11, '62	QNS	
23. S. Jul 18, '62	QNS	vismes desja hier		47. S. Sep 12, '62	QNS	
		.				
24. M. Jul 27, '62	QNS			48. M. Sep 21, '62	QNS	
25. Tu Jul 28, '62	QNS	traictasmes hier		49. Tu Sep 22, '62	QNS	vismes hier
26. Wd Jul 29, '62	DTP			50. Wd Sep 23, '62	DTP	commençasmes hier
27. Th Jul 30, '62	QNS			51. Th Sep 24, '62	QNS	commençasmes hier
28. Fr Jul 31, '62	QNS	vismes hier		52. Fr Sep 25, '62	QNS	
29. S. Aug 1, '62	QNS			53. S. Sep 26, '62	QNS	
30. M. Aug 10, '62	QNS					
31. Tu Aug 11, '62	QNS	commençasmes hier		54. M. Oct 5, '62	QNS	desja commencé à voir

Tu-Sa none		
55. M. Oct 12, '62	QNS	
56. Tu Oct 13, '62	QNS	
57. Wd Oct 14, '62	DTP	vismes hier
58. Th Oct 15, '62	QNS	fut hier veu
Fr-Sa none		
59. M. Nov 9, '62	QNS	
60. Tu Nov 10, '62	QNS	
61. Wd Nov 11, '62	DTP	veismes hier
62. Th Nov 12, '62	QNS	vismes hier
63. Fr Nov 13, '62	QNS	vismes hier
64. S. Nov 14, '62	QNS	vismes hier
65. M. Nov 23, '62	QNS	
66. Tu Nov 24, '62	QNS	vismes hier
Wd-Sa none		
67. M. Dec 7, '62	QNS	commencé a monstrer
68. Tu Dec 8, '62	QNS	
69. Wd Dec 9, '62	DTP	vismes hier
70. Th Dec 10, '62	QNS	vismes hier
71. Fr Dec 11, '62	QNS	
72. S. Dec 12, '62	QNS	veu ci-dessus [es]
73. M. Jan 4, '63	QNS	
74. Tu Jan 5, '63	QNS	vismes hier
75. Wd Jan 6, '63	DTP	avons commencé a monstrer
76. Th Jan 7, '63	QNS	vismes hier
77. Fr Jan 8, '63	QNS	commençasmes hier
78. S. Jan 9, '63	QNS	vismes hier
79. M. Jan 18, '63	QNS	
80. Tu Jan 19, '63	QNS	
81. Wd Jan 20, '63	DTP	vismes hier
82. Th Jan 21, '63	QNS	
83. Fr Jan 22, '63	QNS	
84. S. Jan 23, '63	QNS	fut hier monstré
85. M. Feb 1, '63	QNS	veu comment David [es]
86. Tu Feb 2, '63	QNS	vismes hier
87. Wd Feb 3, '63	DTP	vismes hier
Job[27]		
1. M. Feb 26, '54	QNS	
2. Tu Feb 27, '54	QNS	hier
3. Wd Feb 28, '54	DTP	hier
4. [Th Mar 1, '54]	QNS	cy devant [es]
5. [Fr Mar 2, '54]	QNS	

---

[27] *Sermons de M. Iean Calvin sur le livre de Iob.* Geneve: Iean Bonnefoy, 1563

6. [M. Mar 12, '54]	QNS	
7. [Tu Mar 13, '54]	QNS	
1[=8 Wd Mar 14, '54]	DTP	cy devant [es]
2[=9 Th Mar 15, '54]	QNS	
10. [Fr Mar 16, '54]	QNS	hier [+ 33:131]
11. [S. Mar 17, '54]	QNS	
12. [M. Mar 26, '54]	QNS	cy devant
13. [Tu Mar 27, '54]	QNS	
14. [Wd Mar 28, '54]	DTP	
15. [Th Mar 29, '54]	QNS	hier
16. [Fr Mar 30, '54]	QNS	
Absent from consistory Apr 5 & 12[21:572]		
17. [Wd Apr 25, '54] [28]	DTP	
18. [Wd May 3, '54]	DTP	cy devant

19. [M. May 7, '54]	QNS	
20. [Tu May 8, '54]	QNS	
21. [Wd May 9, '54]	DTP	
22. [Th May 10, '54]	QNS	Hier
23. [Fr May 11, '54]	QNS	
24. [M. May 21, '54]	QNS	
25. [Tu May 22, '54]	QNS	
26. [Wd May 23, '54]	DTP	
27. [Th May 24, '54]	QNS	
28. [Fr May 25, '54]	QNS	
29. [S. May 26, '54]	QNS	Hier
30. [Wd May 30, '54]	DTP	
31. [M. Jun 4, '54]	QNS	
32. [Tu Jun 5, '54]	QNS	cy devant [es]
33. [Wd Jun 6, '54]	DTP	
34. [Th Jun 7, '54]	QNS	[hier 33:418, 427]
35. [Fr Jun 8, '54]	QNS	Hier

---

[28] While it is known that Calvin was back in Geneva by Apr 19 (according to the Consistory minutes, vol. IX:2 for Apr 19, 1554; p. IX,48), it is not clear that he was preaching even the Wed service (the 18th) that week. This seems to be a case in which his absence in Bern was combined with some other reason which prevented him from doing his regular week of preaching. Apr 25 would be the Wed of that regular rotation, but it appears that he did only the one day of his week. The next full week of his rotation began on May 7. The fact that he and his alternate continued their usual rotation is clear from the dates of the weddings Calvin does on May 24 and Jun 18. Except in very rare circumstances, e.g., for a special friend like Laurent de Normandie for whom he did a wedding at the dawn service when he was certainly not preaching, Calvin apparently did weddings only when he was already doing the service and preaching. Two weekday weddings at the ordinary service time (6 a.m.) were extremely unlikely unless these were couples who just happened to come when Calvin was preaching.

				57. [M. Jul 30, '54]	QNS	
36. [M. Jun 18, '54]	QNS	cy devant		58. [Tu Jul 31, '54]	QNS	Hier
37. [Tu Jun 19, '54]	QNS			59. [Wd Aug 1, '54]	DTP	Hier
38. [Wd Jun 20, '54]	DTP	[hier 33:471]		60. [Th Aug 2, '54]	QNS	Hier
39. [Th Jun 21, '54]	QNS	hier [+33:481]		61. [Fr Aug 3, '54]	QNS	Hier
40. [Fr Jun 22, '54]	QNS	Hier		62. [S. Aug 4, '54]	QNS	
41. [S. Jun 23, '54]	QNS	Hier				
				63. [Wd Aug 8, '54]	DTP	
42. [Wd Jun 27, '54]	DTP	cy devant				
43. [Th Jun 28, '54]	QNS	Hier		64. [M. Aug 13, '54]	QNS	
44. [Fr Jun 29, '54]	QNS	cy devant [es]		65. [Tu Aug 14, '54]	QNS	hier [+34:42, 43]
				66. [Wd Aug 15, '54]	DTP	
45. [M. Jul 2, '54]	QNS			67. [Th Aug 16, '54]	QNS	cy devant [es]
46. [Tu Jul 3, '54]	QNS			68. [Fr Aug 17, '54]	QNS	Hier
47. [Wd Jul 4, '54]	DTP					
48. [Th Jul 5, '54]	QNS	Hier		69. [Wd Aug 22, '54]	DTP	
49. [Fr Jul 6, '54]	QNS					
50. [S. Jul 7, '54]	QNS	Hier		70. [M. Aug 27, '54]	QNS	au dernier sermon
				71. [Tu Aug 28, '54]	QNS	[hier 34:71]
51. [M. Jul 16, '54]	QNS	cy devant		72. [Wd Aug 29, '54]	DTP	Hier
52. [Tu Jul 17, '54]	QNS	Hier		73. [Th Aug 30, '54]	QNS[29]	cy devant [es]
53. [Wd Jul 18, '54]	DTP	Hier		74. [Fr Aug 31, '54]	QNS	Hier
54. [Th Jul 19, '54]	QNS	hier [+33:669]				
55. [Fr Jul 20, '54]	QNS			75. [M. Sep 10, '54]	QNS	
56. [S. Jul 21, '54]	QNS	Hier		76. [Tu Sep 11, '54]	QNS	Hier

[29] Sermon 73 refers to an incident Calvin saw "hier" with his own eyes of a woman in prison for paillardise being given cakes (not bread and water). OC 34:144

77. [Wd Sep 12, '54]	DTP	Hier
78. [Th Sep 13, '54]	QNS[30]	
79. [Fr Sep 14, '54]	QNS	Hier
80. [S. Sep 15, '54]	QNS	Hier
81. [M. Sep 24, '54]	QNS	cy devant
82. [Tu Sep 25, '54]	QNS	hier [+34:262]
83. [Wd Sep 26, '54]	DTP	
84. [Th Sep 27, '54]	QNS	
85. [Fr Sep 28, '54]	QNS	cy devant
86. [S. Sep 29, '54]	QNS	hier
87. [Wd Oct 3, '54]	DTP	
88. [M. Oct 8, '54]	QNS	
89. [Tu Oct 9, '54]	QNS	hier
90. [Wd Oct 10, '54]	DTP	hier [+34:361]
91. [Th Oct 11, '54]	QNS	
92. [Fr Oct 12, '54]	QNS	
93. [Wd Oct 17, '54]	DTP	

94. [Th Oct 18, '54]	QNS	
95. [Fr Oct 19, '54]	QNS	
96. [S. Oct 20, '54]	[QNS]	Hier
97. [M. Oct 22, '54]	QNS	cy dessus
98. [Tu Oct 23, '54]	QNS	
99. [Wd Oct 24, '54]	DTP	hier
100. [Th Oct 25, '54]	QNS	[hier 34:488]
101. [Fr Oct 26, '54]	QNS	Hier
102. [S. Oct 27, '54]	QNS	
103. [Wd Oct 31, '54]	DTP	ci devant
104. [M. Nov 5, '54]	QNS	
105. [Tu Nov 6, '54]	[QNS]	[hier 34:550]
106. [Wd Nov 7, '54]	DTP	Hier
107. [Th Nov 8, '54]	QNS	
108. [Fr Nov 9, '54]	QNS	[hier 34:588]
109. [S. Nov 10, '54]	[QNS]	[hier 34:599]

---

[30] Calvin refers to a rebuke in the context of preparing people for the Lord's Supper, possibly the Sunday before it was held but probably the actual day. "Quand je parlay dimanche dernier de ceste insolence qui avoit esté faite si vilaine ici aupres à Cologny, ce sera à se justifier, et à conspirer à l'encontre de Dieu, et regarder comme on pourra couvrir une chose qui est toute notoire. …[rebuke]… Et povres gens, il estoit question de vous preparer à la Cene: je vous remonstroye ceste dissolution si vilaine pour vous y desplaire : c'estoit pour le moins (si vous n'estiez endiablez) que vous fussiez aucunement touchez pour vous renger: et vous venez au contraire comme enragez pour machiner tout mal. … En quelle conscience viendrez vous recevoir la cene de ma main?..." OC 34:202-203 (reference thanks to Naphy, *Calvin and the Consolidation*, p. 158 n.103.) This Sept. Supper appears to have been delayed one week, occurring on Sep 9 instead of the first Sunday.

110. [Wd Nov 14, '54]				126. [Wd Dec 19, '54]	DTP	hier
				127. [Th Dec 20, '54]	[QNS]	hier [+ 35:105]
111. [M. Nov 19, '54]	DTP	ci-dessus		128. [Fr Dec 21, '54]	QNS	[hier 35:117]
112. [Tu Nov 20, '54]						
113. [Wd Nov 21, '54]	QNS	cy devant [hier 34:650]		129. [Wd Dec 26, '54]	DTP	
114. [Th Nov 22, '54]	QNS			130. [M. Dec 31, '54]	QNS	
115. [Fr Nov 23, '54]	QNS	Hier		131. [Tu Jan 1, '55]	QNS	cy dessus [es]
				132. [Wd Jan 2, '55]	DTP	Hier
116. [Wd Nov 28, '54]	DTP			133. [Th Jan 3, '55]	QNS	Hier
				134. [Fr Jan 4, '55]	QNS	Hier
117. [M. Dec 3, '54]	QNS			135. [Wd Jan 9, '55]	DTP	cy dessus
118. [Tu Dec 4, '54]	[QNS]	[hier 34:716] [31]				
119. [Wd Dec 5, '54]	DTP			136. [M. Jan 14, '55]	QNS	
120. [Th Dec 6, '54]	QNS	hier		137. [Tu Jan 15, '55]	QNS	Hier
121. [Fr Dec 7, '54]	QNS	hier		138. [Wd Jan 16, '55]	DTP	Hier
				139. [Th Jan 17, '55]	QNS	
122. [Wd Dec 12, '54]	DTP			140. [Fr Jan 18, '55]	QNS	[hier 35:267]
123. [Th Dec 13, '54]	QNS	hier				
				141. [Wd Jan 23, '55]	DTP	cy devant
124. [M. Dec 17, '54]	QNS	au sermon prochain [last]		142. [M. Jan 28, '55]	[QNS]	
125. [Tu Dec 18, '54]	QNS	hier		143. [Tu Jan 29, '55]	QNS	Hier

---

31 Here in #118 see "cy devant" used at the beginning referring to earlier sermons: "Nous avons veu par cy devant, que Job se plaignoit de n'estre point escouté de Dieu pour obtenir raison"; OC 34:713; a bit later he refers to "hier." And in #128, "Nous avons veu par ci devant comme Dieu prouvoit à nostre salut"; OC 35:116

144. [Wd Jan 30, '55]	DTP	[hier 35:316]		156. [Wd Feb 27, '55]	DTP	hier [+35:466]
145. [Th Jan 31, '55]	QNS	hier [+ 35:344, 335]		157. [Th Feb 28, '55]	[QNS]	cy devant [es]
146. [Fr Feb 1, '55]	QNS			158. [Fr Mar 1, '55]	[QNS]	hier
147. [Wd Feb 6, '55]	DTP	cy devant		159. [Wd Mar 6, '55]	DTP	
148. [M. Feb 11, '55]	[QNS]			Travel to Bern [32]:		
149. [Tu Feb 12, '55]	QNS	[hier 35:376]				
150. [Wd Feb 13, '55]	DTP	[hier 35:391]		**Psalms** [33]		
151. [Th Feb 14, '55]	[QNS]			1. Wd Nov 4, 1545 [34]	None	Ps. 115
152. [Fr Feb 15, '55]	QNS			2. Wd Nov 11, 1545	DTP	Ps. 124
153. [Wd Feb 20, '55]	DTP			1. before Sep 20/ 29, '49 [35]	None	Ps. 16:3[4]
				2. before Sep 20/ 29, '49	none	Ps. 27:4
154. [M. Feb 25, '55]	QNS	cy devant		3. before Sep 20/ 29, '49	none	Ps. 27:8
155. [Tu Feb 26, '55]	QNS	hier [+ 35:453]				

---

[32]   Wd Mar 6, 1555, Calvin, Chauvet, and council members leave for Bern for a short trip ; on Mar 13 Bern sets the date for a conference on last Sun of month. Calvin et al. report back to council on M. Mar 18; leave again for Bern on Th Mar 28. See RCP 2, pp. 60, 61; OC 21:597-598.

[33]   Psalms were published in several small collections; here these are presented by collection, in chronological order: 1546 (2); 1552 (4); 1554 (22), 1981 (10). The metrical forms of the Psalms published in the16th c. appeared in the following years: Ps. 115 & 46 in 1542. Ps. 124, 16, 17, 27, 87 & 119 in 1551. Ps. 80, 89, 147, 148, 65 & 48 in 1562.

[34]   *Deux sermons faitz en la ville de Geneve, l'un le 4 Nov 1545, le second le mercredy suyvant*, [transcribed by Jean Cousin] Geneva: Jean Girard, 1546.

[35]   *Quatre sermons fort utiles pour nostre temps avec exposition du Pseaume 87.* Geneva: Robert Estienne, 1552 = [Ps. 16, Heb. 13, Ps. 27 (two sermons)]. Mülhaupt, "Einleitung," in *Psalmpredigten*, p. xxxviii, discusses dating, which he gives as before Sept. 20, 1549 (date of Calvin's preface), and adds that these three sermons could have been "an die erste Hälfte des Jahres 1549 oder noch früher." Peter & Gilmont, *Bibliotheca Calviniana* 1, p. 468, date these sermons before Sept. 29 because Calvin says the basis was notes [not full transcripts]; they place this before Raguenier began work officially on Sept. 29.

4. [after 1549] before Jul 4, 1552[36]	none	Ps. 87
1. Sun[pm] Jan 8, '53[37]	QNS	
2. Sun [pm] Jan 15, '53	QNS	dimanche passé [+32:502]
3. Sun [pm] Jan 22, '53	QNS	
4. Sun [pm] Jan 26 = 29, '53	QNS	
5. Sun [pm] Feb 5, '53	QNS	
6. Sun [pm] Feb 12, '53	QNS	
7. Sun [pm] Feb 19, '53	QNS	
8. Sun [pm] Feb 26, '53	QNS	
9. Sun [pm] Mar 5, '53	QNS	
Absent from consistory Mar16, '53 [21:538]		
10. Sun [pm] Mar 26, '53	QNS	

11. Sun [pm] Apr 2, '53	QNS	Easter p.m.
12. Sun [pm] Apr 9, '53	QNS	
13. Sun [pm] Apr 16,'53	QNS	
14. Sun [pm Apr 23, '53	QNS	
15. Sun [pm] Apr 30,'53	QNS	
16. Sun [pm] May 7, '53	QNS	
17. Sun [pm] May 14, '53	QNS	
18. Sun [pm] May 21,'53	QNS	Pentecost p.m.
19. Sun [pm] Jun 11, '53	QNS	
20. Sun [pm] Jun 18, '53	QNS	
21. Sun [pm] Jun 25, '53	QNS	
22. Sun [pm] Jul 2, '53	QNS[38]	
1. Sun pm, Feb 8, '51- partial sermon[39]		Ps. 80:9-20

---

36 Mülhaupt dates this between 1547 (beginning of Edward VI's reign) and Jul 4, 1552 (the date assigned to a fragment of a sermon on Ps. 87:1-7 by OC editors); "Einleitung," *Psalmpredigten*, pp. xxxvii-xxxviii. Peter & Gilmont, *Bibliotheca Calviniana* 1, p. 468, identify the date as later than the 1549 sermons in the same collection.

37 *Vingt deux sermons de M.Jean Calvin sur le Pseaume 119.* Geneva: François Estienne, 1562[printing used here].

38 "Ce dernier Huictain, qui est la conclusion de tout le Pseaume, monstre ce que nous avons desja souvent veu par cy devant…" OC 32: 737.

39 The following sermons come from *Psalmpredigten. Passions-, Oster-, und Pfingstpredigten*, hg. Erwin Mülhaupt. *Supplementa Calviniana VII* Neukirchen-Vluyn , 1981.

9. [before '54, probably @'51]	QNS	Ps. 89:31-39		8/74. Tu Mar 9, '57	QNS	
2. Sun Nov 12, '53	DTP	Ps. 147:12-20		Wd Mar 10, '57 none		
3. Sun Sep 30, '54	DTP	Ps. 148:1-14		9/75. Th Mar 11, '57	QNS	
4. Sun Jul 14, '55	DTP	Ps. 149:4-9		10/76. Fr Mar 12, '57	QNS	vismes hier
5. Sun May 30, '57	DTP	Ps. 65:6-14		S. Mar 13, '57 none		
10. Sun pm, May 12, '61=1560[40]	None	Ps. 46:2-6		11/77. M. Mar 22, '57	QNS	declaré par cy devant
6. Sun pm, May 19, '60	QNS	Ps. 46:7-12		12/78. Tu Mar 23, '57	QNS	
7. Sun pm, May 26, '60	QNS	Ps. 48:2-8		13/79. Wd Mar 24, '57	DTP	Desja... touché [#11-12]
8. Sun pm, Jun 9, '60	QNS	Ps. 48:9-15		14/80. Th Mar 25, '57	QNS	parlé hier
				15/81. Fr Mar 26, '57	QNS	
Isaiah[41]				16/82. S. Mar 27, '57	[QNS]	monstrasmes hier
1/67. M. Feb 22, '57	QNS			17/83. M. Apr 5, '57	QNS	
2/68. Tu Feb 23, 155	QNS			18/84. Tu Apr 6, '57	QNS	vismes hier
3/69. Wd Feb 24, '57	DTP	desja veu par cy devant [#1]		19/85. Wd Apr 7, '57	DTP	
4/70. Th Feb 25, '57	QNS			20/86. Th Apr 8, '57	QNS	traictasmes hier
5/71. Fr Feb 26, '57	QNS					
6/72. S. Feb 27, '57	QNS	vismes hier				
7/73. M. Mar 8, '57	[QNS]	veu par cy devant				

[40] The English translation which is the only one extant gives the date as May 12, 1561 "at after noone," S. VII, p. 73. However, May 12 is a Sunday in 1560, not 1561, and the context makes it clear that this is the first half of the exposition which is continued on May 19, 1560; cf. S. VII, p. 40.

[41] Three of the six original volumes are published in *Supplementa Calviniana*, plus one volume of extant sermons in Ms.Fr.19. Here each published volume will be noted in its place beginning with *Sermons sur le Livre d'Esaïe, chapitres 13-29*, pub. Georges Barrois. *Supplementa Calviniana II.* Neukirchen-Vluyn, 1961.

21/87. Fr Apr 9, '57	QNS			35/101. S. May 22, '57	QNS	declaré par cy devant
22/88. S. Apr 10, '57	QNS	monstrasmes hier				
				36/102. M. May 30, '57	QNS	veu cy dessus
23/89. M. Apr 19, '57	QNS			37/103. Tu Jun 1, '57	QNS	fut hier traicté
24/90. Tu Apr 20, '57	QNS			38/104. Wd Jun 2, '57	DTP	vismes hier
25/91. Wd Apr 21, '57	DTP			39/105. Th Jun 3, '57	QNS	vismes hier
26/92. Th Apr 22, '57	QNS			40/106. Fr Jun 4, '57	QNS	hier exposé
27/93. Fr Apr 23, '57	QNS			41/107. S. Jun 5, '57	QNS	vismes hier
28/94. S. Apr 24, '57	[QNS]	hier nous commenseasmes				
				42/108. M. Jun 7, '57		QNS
Mn-Tu May 3-4, none		.		43/109. M. Jun 14, '57	QNS	veu par cy devant
29/95. Wd May 5, '57	DTP			44/110. Tu Jun 15, '57	QNS	
30/96. Th May 6, '57	QNS			45/111. Wd Jun 16, '57	DTP	
31/97. Fr May 7, '57	[QNS]	commenceasmes hier		46/112. Th Jun 17, '57	QNS	commençasmes hier
32/98. S. May 8, '57	QNS			47/113. Fr Jun 18, '57	QNS	
				48/114. S. Jun 19, '57	QNS	
M. May 17, '57 none						
33/99. Tu May 18, '57	QNS	veu par cy devant		49/115. M. Jun 28, '57	[QNS]	
Wd May 19, '57 none				50/116. Tu Jun 29, '57	QNS	veu cy dessus [es]
34/100. Th May 20, '57	QNS			51/117. Wd Jun 30, '57	DTP	veu par cy devant [es]
Fr May 21, '57 none						

52/118. Th Jul 1, '57	QNS	vismes hyer
53/119. Fr Jul 2, '57	QNS	
54/120. S. Jul 3, '57	QNS	veismes hier
55/121. M. Jul 12, '57	QNS	veu par cy devant
56/122. Tu Jul 13, '57	QNS	veu par cy devant [es]
57/123. Wd Jul 14, '57	QNS[42]	veismes hyer
58/124. Th Jul 15, '57	QNS	veu par cy devant [es]
59/125. Fr Jul 16, '57	QNS	
60/126. S. Jul 17, '57	QNS	
61/127. M. Jul 26, '57	QNS	
62/128. Tu Jul 27, '57	QNS	commençasmes hier
63/129. Wd Jul 28, '57	DTP	veismes hier
64/130. Th Jul 29, '57	QNS	veismes hier
65/131. Fr Jul 30, '57	QNS	veismes hier
66/132. S. Jul 31, '57	QNS	veismes hier

1/133. Wd Aug 4, '57[43]	DTP	
2/134. M. Aug 9, '57	QNS	desja monstré cy dessus [es]
3/135. Tu Aug 10, '57	QNS	commençasmes hier
4/136. Wd Aug 11, '57	DTP	
5/137. Th Aug 12, '57	QNS	
6/138. Fr Aug 13, '57	QNS	veismes hier
7/139. S. Aug 14, '57	QNS	
8/140. M. Aug 23, '57	QNS	commencé d'exposer parcy devant
9/141. Tu Aug 24, '57	QNS	commençasmes hier
10/142. Wd Aug 25, '57	DTP	veismes hier
11/143. Th Aug 26, '57	QNS	
12/144. Fr Aug 27, '57	QNS	
13/145. S. Aug 28, '57	[QNS]	veïsmes hier
14/146. Wd Sep 1, '57	DTP	

---

[42] Here there is a mistake, as the first phrase of the weekday prayer is given instead of the day of prayer text.

[43] *Sermons sur le Livre d'Esaïe, Chapitres 30-41*, pub. Francis Higman, T. H. L. Parker, L. Thorpe. *Supplementa Calviniana III*. Neukirchen-Vluyn, 1995.

15/147. M. Sep 6, '57	QNS	declaré par cy devant		33/165. Wd Oct 13, '57	DTP	
16/148. Tu Sep 7, '57	QNS					
17/149. Wd Sep 8, '57	DTP			34/166. M. Oct 18, '57	QNS	avons desja veu
18/150. Th Sep 9, '57	QNS	commeneasmes hier		35/167. Tu Oct 19, '57	QNS	
19/151. Fr Sep 10, '57	QNS	veismes hier		36/168. Wd Oct 20, '57	DTP	vismes hier
20/152. S. Sep 11, '57	QNS	veismes hier		37/169. Th Oct 21, '57	QNS	
				38/170. Fr Oct 22, '57	QNS	commençames hier
21/153. M. Sep 20, '57	QNS			39/171. S. Oct 23, '57	QNS	vismes hier
22/154. Tu Sep 21, '57	QNS	vismes hier				
23/155. Wd Sep 22, '57	DTP	desja exposé		40/172. M. Nov 1, '57	QNS	
24/156. Th Sep 23, '57	QNS	commencé par cy devant [es]		41/173. Tu Nov 2, '57	QNS	veismes hier
25/157. Fr Sep 24, '57	QNS			42/174. Wd Nov 3, '57	DTP	
26/158. S. Sep 25, '57	QNS	vismes hier		43/175. Th Nov 4, '57	QNS	vismes hier
				44/176. Fr Nov 5, '57	QNS	
27/159. M. Oct 4, '57	QNS	commencé à voir		45/177. S. Nov 6, '57	QNS	fut hier traité
28/160. Tu Oct 5, '57	QNS	dismes hier				
29/161. Wd Oct 6, '57	DTP			46/178. M. Nov 15, '57	QNS	desja par ci devant
30/162. Th Oct 7, '57	QNS			47/179. Tu Nov 16, '57	QNS	
31/163. Fr Oct 8, '57	QNS	veismes hier		48/180. Wd Nov 17, '57	DTP	
32/164. S. Oct 9, '57	QNS	veismer hier		49/181. Th Nov 18, '57	QNS	veismes hier

50/182. Fr Nov 19, '57	QNS	veismes hier
51/183. S. Nov 20, '57	QNS	
52/184. M. Nov 29, '57	QNS	veu par ci devant
53/185. Tu Nov 30, '57	QNS	hier nous veismes
54/186. Wd Dec 1, '57	DTP	veismes hier
55/187. Th Dec 2, '57	QNS	monstrsmes hier
56/188. Fr Dec 3, '57	QNS	touchasmes desja hier
57/189. S. Dec 4, '57	QNS	
58/190. M. Dec 13, '57	QNS	
59/191. Tu Dec 14, '57	QNS	veu ci-dessus [es]
60/192. Wd Dec 15, '57	DTP	veismes hier
61/193. Th Dec 16, '57	QNS	hier nous dismes
62/194. Fr Dec 17, '57	QNS	dismes hier
63/195. S. Dec 18, '57	QNS	veismes hier
64/196. M. Dec 27, '58='57	QNS	veu par ci devant
65/197. Tu Dec 28, '58='57	QNS	veismes hier

66/198. Wd Dec 29, '58= '57	DTP	veismes hier
67/199. Th Dec 30, '57	QNS	
1/200.Fr Dec 31, '57 [44]	QNS	
2/201. Sa, Jan 1, '58	QNS	
3/202.Mn, Jan 10, '58	QNS	
4/203. Tu, Jan 11, '58	[QNS]	
5/204. Wd, Jan 12, '58	DTP	
6/205. Th, Jan 13, '58	QNS	
7/206. Fr, Jan 14, '58	QNS	
8/207. Sa, Jan 15, '58	QNS	
9/208. Wd, Jan 19, '58	DTP	
10/209. Mn, Jan 24, '58	QNS	
11/210. Tu, Jan 25, '58	QNS	
12/211. Wd, Jan 26, '58	DTP	
13/212. Th, Jan 27, '58	QNS	

[44] Ms.fr. 19 Genève, BGE from *l'Eglise française de Londres VIII f2* My special thanks to Dr. Max Engammare for his generous help in transcribing the initial words of the prayers.

14/213. Fr, Jan 28, '58	QNS		30/229. Wd, Mar 23, '58	DTP	
15/214. Sa, Jan 29, '58	QNS		31/230. Th, Mar 24, '58	QNS	
			32/231. Fr, Mar 25, '58	QNS	
16/215. Mn, Feb 7, '58	QNS		33/232. Sa, Mar 26, '58	QNS	
17/216. Tu, Feb 8, '58	QNS				
18/217. Wd, Feb 9, '58	DTP		Three week gap		
19/218. Th, Feb 10, '58	[QNS]				
20/219. Fr, Feb 11, '58	QNS		34/233. Mn, Apr 18, '58	QNS	
21/220. Sa, Feb 12, '58	QNS		35/234. Tu, Apr 19, '58	QNS	
			36/235. Wd, Apr 20, '58	DTP	
22/221. Mn, Feb 21, '58	QNS		37/236. Th, Apr 21, '58	QNS	
23/222. Tu, Feb 22, '58	QNS		38/237. Fr, Apr 22, '58	QNS	
24/223. Wd, Feb 23, '58	DTP		39/238. Sa, Apr 23, '58	QNS	
25/224. Th, Feb 24, '58	QNS				
26/225. Fr, Feb 25, '58	QNS		40/239. Mn, May 2, '58	QNS	
27/226. Sa, Feb 26, '58	[QNS]		41/240. Tu, May 3, '58	QNS	
			42/241. Wd, May 4, '58	DTP	
Three week gap			43/242. Th, May 5, '58	QNS	
			44/243. Fr, May 6, '58	QNS	
28/227. Mn, Mar 21, '58	QNS				
29/228. Tu, Mar 22, '58	QNS		45/244. Mn, May 16, '58	[QNS]	

46/245. Tu, May 17, '58	QNS		5/261. S. Jun 18, '58	QNS	
47/246. Wd, May 18, '58	DTP				
48/247. Th, May 19, '58	QNS		6/262. M. Jun 27, '58	QNS	commencé à traiter
49/248. Fr, May 20, '58	QNS		7/263. Tu Jun 28, '58	QNS	
50/249. Sa, May 21, '58	QNS		8/264. Wd Jun 29, '58	DTP	
			9/265. Th Jun 30, '58	QNS	
51/250. Mn, May 30, '58	QNS		10/266. Fr Jul 1, '58	QNS	
52/251. Tu, May 31, '58	QNS		11/267. S. Jul 2, '58	QNS	
53/252. Wd, Jun 1, '58	DTP				
54/253. Th, Jun 2, '58	QNS		12/268. M. Jul 11, '58	QNS	
55/254. Fr, Jun 3, '58	QNS		13/269. Tu Jul 12, '58	QNS	vismes hier
56/255. Sa, Jun 4, '58	QNS		14/270. Wd Jul 13, '58	DTP	desja veu par ci devant [es]
			15/271. Th Jul 14, '58	QNS	vismes hier
57/256. Mn, Jun 13, '58	QNS		16/272. Fr Jul 15, '58	QNS	vismes hier
			17/273. S. Jul 16, '58	QNS	vismes hier
1/257. Tu Jun 14, '58[45]	QNS				
2/258. Wd Jun15, '58	DTP	commençasmes hier	18/274. M. Jul 25, '58	QNS	
3/259. Th Jun 16, '58	QNS		19/275. Tu Jul 26, '58	QNS	vismes hier
4/260. Fr Jun 17, '58	QNS	declaré ci-dessus [es]	20/276. Wd Jul 27, '58	DTP	vismes hier

---

[45] *Sermons sur le Livre d'Esaïe, Chapitres 52,1-66,24*, 2 volumes, edit. Max Engammare. *Supplementa Calviniana IV/I & IV/II*. Neukirchen-Vluyn, 2012.

21/277. Th Jul 28, '58	QNS			38/294. Wd Sep 7, '58	DTP	
22/278. Fr Jul 29, '58	[QNS]			39/295. Th Sep 8, '58	QNS	le propos qui fut hier tenu
23/279. S. Jul 30, '58	QNS	vismes hier		40/296. Fr Sep 9, '58	QNS	fusmes hier admonestez
				41/297. S. Sep 10, '58	QNS	
24/280. M. Aug 8, '58	QNS	veu ci-dessus				
25/281. Tu Aug 9, '58	QNS			42/298. M. Sep 19, '58	QNS	au propos que desja... traicté
26/282. Wd Aug 10, '58	DTP	vismes hier		43/299. Tu Sep 20, '58	QNS	veismes hier
27/283. Th Aug 11, '58	QNS	vismes hier		44/300. Wd Sep 21, '58	DTP	vismes hier
28/284. Fr Aug 12, '58	QNS	commençasmes hier		1/301. Th Sep 22, '58	QNS	vismes hier
29/285. S. Aug 13, '58	QNS			2/302. Fr Sep 23, '58	QNS	par ci devant [es]
				3/303. S. Sep 24, '58	QNS	
30/286. M. Aug 22, '58	QNS	avons veu				
31/287. Tu Aug 23, '58	QNS	vismes hier		4/304. M. Oct 3, '58	QNS	avons desja veu
32/288. Wd Aug 24, '58	DTP	vismes hier		5/305. Tu Oct 4, '58 ms imcomplete		
33/289. Th Aug 25, '58	QNS	veu par cy devant [es]		6/306. Wd Oct 5, '58	DTP	
34/290. Fr Aug 26, '58	QNS	vismes hier		7/307. Th Oct 6, '58	QNS	
35/291. S. Aug 27, '58	QNS	vismes hier		8/308. Fr Oct 7, '58	QNS	vismes hier
				9/309. S. Oct 8, '58	QNS	commençasmes hier
36/292. M. Sep 5, '58	QNS			Calvin ill many months [21:87, 89]		
37/293. Tu Sep 6, '58	QNS					

10/310. M. Jun 12, '59	QNS	le prophete avait dit ci desssus
11/311. Tu Jun 13, '59	QNS	
12/312. Wd Jun 14, '59	DTP	vismes hier
13/313. Th Jun 15, '59	QNS	fut hier dit
14/314. Fr Jun 16, '59	QNS	vismes le serment [#57]
15/315. S. Jun 17, '59	QNS	vismes hier
16/316. M. Jun 26, '59	QNS	
17/317. Tu Jun 27, '59	QNS	vismes hier
18/318. Wd Jun 28, '59	DTP	vismes hier
19/319. Th Jun 29, '59	QNS	
20/320. Fr Jun 30, '59	QNS	
21/321. S. Jul 1, '59	QNS	
22/322. M. Jul 10, '59	QNS	veu ci-dessus
23/323. Tu Jul 11, '59	QNS	
24/324. Wd Jul 12, '59	DTP	le propos qui fut hier exposé
25/325. Th Jul 13, '59	QNS	vismes hier
26/326. Fr Jul 14, '59	QNS	
27/327. S. Jul 15, '59	QNS	Hier

28/328. M. Jul 24, '59	QNS	ouy par cy devant
29/329. Tu Jul 25, '59	QNS	vismes hier
30/330. Wd Jul 26, '59	DTP	
31/331. Th Jul 27, '59	QNS	Hier
Fr-S. Jul 28-29, '59 none		
32/332. M. Aug 7, '59	QNS	
33/333. Tu Aug 8, '59	QNS	vismes hier
34/334. Wd Aug 9, '59	DTP	
35/335. Th Aug 10, '59	QNS	ce qui fust hier traicté
36/336. Fr Aug 11, '59	QNS	
37/337. S. Aug 12, '59	QNS	
38/338. M. Aug 21, '59	QNS	veu par cy devant
39/339. Tu Aug 22, '59	QNS	ouismes hier
40/340. Wd Aug 23, '59	DTP	hier
41/341. Th Aug 24, '59	[QNS]	vismes hier
42/342. Fr Aug 25, '59	QNS	
43/343. S. Aug 26, '59	QNS	vismes hier

Jeremiah and Lamentations [46]			16. Wd Jul 24, '49	[DTP]	veu par cy devant
1.Fr Jun 14, '49	QNS[47]		17. Th Jul 25, '49	QNS	
2. S. Jun 15, '49	QNS	traictasmes hier	18. Fr Jul 26, '49	QNS	
			19. S. Jul 27, '49	QNS	vismes hyer
3. M. Jun 24, '49	QNS				
4. Tu Jun 25, '49	QNS		20. M. Aug 5, '49	QNS	declaré par cy devant
5. Wd Jun 26, '49	[DTP][48]		Tu Aug 6, '49 none		
6. Th Jun 27, '49	QNS	vismes hier	21. Wd Aug 7, '49	[DTP]	
7. Fr Jun 28, '49	QNS	demourasmes hyer	22. Th Aug 8, '49	QNS	
8. S. Jun 29, '49	QNS	monstrasmes hyer	23. Fr Aug 9, '49	QNS	commençasmes hier
9. M. Jul 8, '49	QNS		24. S. Aug 10, '49	QNS	vismes hyer
10. Tu Jul 9, '49	QNS	vismes hyer			
11. Wd Jul 10, '49	[DTP]	vismes hyer	M. Th Aug 12-15 none		
12. Th Jul 11, '49	QNS		25. Fr Aug 16, '49[49]	[QNS]	monstré par cy devant
13. Fr Jul 12, '49	QNS	commençasmes hier			
14. S. Jul 13, '49	QNS		1.S. Sep 6, '50	QNS	
			2. M. Sep 15, '50	QNS	veu cy dessus
15. M. Jul 22, '49	QNS				
Tu Jul 23, '49 none			**Ezekiel** [50]		

---

46   *Sermons sur les Livres de Jérémie et des Lamentations*, pub. Rodolphe Peter. *Supplementa Calviniana VI* Neukirchen-Vluyn , 1971.

47   Peter, S. VI, p. 6, gives a note on lines 20-29 regarding the final prayer, "la partie fixe prévue pour les jours de semaine, hormis le mercredi : *Et QNS…*" Instead of completing this sermon, he inserts the prayer from the commentary (lectures) on Jeremiah.

48   [DTP] indicates that Calvin skipped to the second phrase of the prayer, beginning with "Père celeste." The prayer is otherwise identical to the usual DTP prayer.

49   This was not Calvin's regular week to preach.

50   Transcription from Ms. fr. 21 & 22; see table of all sermons in S. X/III, pp. xiv-xvii. *Sermons sur le Livre des Revelations du prophete Ezechiel Chapitres 36-48.*

Ms. Fr. 21				23. Fr Jan 6, '53	QNS	
1. M. Nov 21, '52	[QNS]			24. S. Jan 7, '53	QNS	
2. Tu Nov 22, '52	QNS					
3. Wd Nov 23, '52	DTP			[Wd Jan 11, '53] [51]		
4. Th Nov 24, '52	QNS					
5. Fr Nov 25, '52	[QNS]			25. M. Jan 16, '53	QNS	cy devant
6. S. Nov 26, '52	QNS			26. Tu Jan 17, '53	QNS	
				27. Wd Jan 18, '53	DTP	
7. M. Dec 5, '52	QNS			28. Th Jan 19, '53	QNS	
8. Tu Dec 6, '52	QNS			29. Fr Jan 20, '53	QNS	
9. Wd Dec 7, '52	DTP			S. Jan 21, '53 none		
10. Th Dec 8, '52	[QNS]					
11. Fr Dec 9, '52	QNS			30. Wd Jan 25, '53	DTP	cy devant
12. S. Dec 10, '52	QNS					
				31. M. Jan 30, '53	QNS	cy devant
13. M. Dec 19, '52	QNS	cy devant		32. Tu Jan 31, '53	[QNS]	
14. Tu Dec 2=20, '52	QNS			33. Wd Feb 1, '53	DTP	hier
15. Wd Dec 21, '52	DTP			34. Th Feb 2, '53	QNS	hier
16. Th Dec 22, '52	QNS			35. Fr Feb 3, '53	QNS	veu... la lecture prochaine
17. Fr Dec 23, '52	QNS			S. Feb 4, '53 none		
18. S. Dec 24, '52	[QNS]					
19. M. Jan 2, '53	QNS	au sermon prochain		36. Wd Feb 8, '53	DTP	ci devant
20. Tu Jan 3, '53	QNS			37. M. Feb 13, '53	QNS	
21. Wd Jan 4, '53	DTP			38. Tu Feb 14, '53	QNS	
22. Th Jan 5, '53	QNS			39. Wd Feb 15, '53	DTP	

[51] Probable date of missing sermon (not transcribed by Raguenier); cf. "Introduction" by Erik de Boer, S. X/III, p. xiv.

40. Th Feb 16, '53	QNS		3/108. M. Sep 25, '53	QNS	cy devant
41. Fr Feb 17, '53	QNS		4/109. Tu Sep 26, '53	QNS	
S. Feb 18, '53 none			5/111. Wd Sep 27, '53	DTP	
			6/112. Th Sep 28, '53	[QNS]	
42. M. Feb 27, '53	QNS		7/113. Fr Sep 29, '53	QNS	hier
43. Tu Feb 28, '53	QNS		8/114. S. Sep 30, '53	[QNS]	
44. Wd Mar 1, '53	DTP	cy devant			
45. Th Mar 2, '53	QNS		9/115. M. Oct 9, '53	QNS	
46. Fr Mar 3, '53	QNS	Hier	10/116. Tu Oct 10, '53	QNS	
47. S. Mar 4, '53	QNS		11/117. Wd Oct 11, '53	DTP	
			12/118. Th Oct 12, '53	QNS	
48. Wd Mar 8, '53	DTP		13/119. Fr Oct 13, '53	[QNS]	
Absent from consistory Mar.16, 1553 [OC 21:538]			14/120. S. Oct 14, '53	QNS	
49. Wd Mar 22, '53	DTP				
Passion week			15/121. Wd Oct 18, '53	DTP	cy devant
50. Wd Apr 5, '53	DTP		None Oct 19: it was not Calvin's week to preach		
51. Th= M. Apr 10, '53	QNS	cy devant	16/122. Fr Oct 20, '53	QNS	
52. Tu Apr 11, '53	QNS	Hier			
53. Wd Apr 12, '53	DTP		17/123. M. Oct 23, '53	QNS	
54. Th Apr 13, '53	QNS		18/124. Tu Oct 24, '53	QNS	
55. Fr Apr 14, '53	QNS				
Ms. fr. 22					
1/106.Fr Sep 1, '53	QNS				
2/107. S. Sep 2, '53	QNS	Hier			

19/125. Wd Oct 25, '53	DTP			35/141. Wd Dec 6, '53	DTP	
20/126. Th Oct 26, '53	QNS			36/142. Th Dec 7, '53	QNS	cy devant
21/127. Fr Oct 27, '53	QNS			37/143. Fr Dec 8, '53	QNS	Hier
22/128. S. Oct 28, '53	QNS					
				38/144. M. Dec 18, '53	QNS	
23/129. M. Nov 6, '53	QNS			39/145. Tu Dec 19, '53	QNS	
24/130. Tu Nov 7, '53	QNS			40/146. Wd Dec 20, '53	DTP	
25/131. Wd Nov 8, '53	DTP			41/147. Th Dec 21, '53	QNS	
Th-S. Nov 9-11 none				42/148. Fr Dec 22, '53	QNS	
				43/149. S. Dec 23, '53	QNS	
26/132. M. Nov 20, '53	QNS	cy dessus				
27/133. Tu Nov 21, '53	QNS			44/150. Wd Dec 27, '54= '53	DTP	
28/134. Wd Nov 22, '53	DTP					
29/135. Th Nov 23, '53	QNS			45/151. M. Jan 1, '54	QNS	cy devant
30/136. Fr Nov 24, '53	QNS			46/152. Tu Jan 2, '54	QNS	
31/137. S. Nov 25, '53	QNS			47/153. Wd Jan 3, '54	DTP	
				48/154. Th Jan 4, '54	QNS	
32/138. Wd Nov 29, '53	DTP	cy devant		49/155. Fr Jan 5, '54	QNS	cy dessus
33/139. M. Dec 4, '53	QNS			50/156. Wd Jan 10, '54	DTP	
34/140. Tu Dec 5, '53	QNS					

51/157. M. Jan 15, '54	QNS	cy dessus		12/65/171. Wd Feb 14, '54	DTP	fut hier entamé
52/158. Tu Jan 16, '54	[QNS]			13/66/172. Th Feb 15, '54	QNS	desja monstré cy dessus [63]
53/159. Wd Jan 17, '54	DTP			14/67/173. Fr Feb 16, '54	[QNS]	
1/54/160. Th Jan 18, '54[52]	QNS			15/68/174. M. Feb 19, '54	[QNS]	
2/55/161. Fr Jan 19, '54	QNS	ouysmes hier		Tu Feb 20, '54 none [this was not Calvin's regular week to preach]		
				16/69/175. Wd Feb 21, '54	DTP	
3/56/162. Wd Jan 24, '54	DTP					
				Daniel[53]		
4/57/163. M. Jan 29, '54	QNS	traicté par cy devant		1. M. Jul 18, '52	QNS	par cy devant
5/58/164. Tu Jan 30, '54	QNS	tractasmes hier		2. Tu Jul 19, '52	QNS	commençames hier [+ 41:335]
6/59/165. Wd Jan 31, '54	DTP	declaré cy dessus [es]		3. Wd Jul 20, '52	DTP	mostrames hier
7/60/166. Th Feb 1, '54	QNS	vismes hier		4. Th Jul 21, '52	QNS	traittames hier
8/61/167. Fr Feb 2, '54	QNS	veu par cy devant [es]		5. Fr Jul 22, '52	QNS	vismes hier
				6. S. Jul 23, '52	QNS	monstrames hier [+41:380]
9/62/168. Wd Feb 7, '54	DTP					
				7. [M. Aug 1, '52]	QNS	avons ici à traitter
10/63/169. M. Feb 12, '54	QNS			8. [Tu Aug 2, '52]	QNS	touchames hier
				9. [Wd Aug 3, '52]	DTP	veu ci dessus…
11/64/170. Tu Feb 13, '54	QNS	monstra hier		10. [Th Aug 4, '52]	QNS	vismes hier
				11. [Fr Aug 5, '52]	QNS	veu par ci devant

---

52 *Sermons sur le Livre des Revelations du prophete Ezechiel Chapitres 36-48*, edit. Erik A. de Boer & B. Nagy. *Supplementa Calviniana X/3*. Neukirchen-Vluyn, 2006.

53 *Quarante sept sermons sur les huict derniers chapitres des propheties de Daniel*. La Rochelle, Barthelemy Berton, 1565.

12. [S. Aug 6, '52]	QNS	declarasmes hier [+ 41:443]		30. [M. Sep 26, '52]	QNS	par ci devant enseigné
				31. [Tu Sep 27, '52]	QNS	fut desja hier declaré
13. [M. Aug 15, '52]	QNS	declaré par ci devant		32. [Wd Sep 28, '52]	DTP	[hier 41:671]
14. [Tu Aug 16, '52]	QNS	vismes hier		33. [Th Sep 29, '52]	QNS	demourames hier [+ 41:678]
15. [Wd Aug 17, '52]	DTP			34. [Fr Sep 30, '52]	QNS	
16. [Th Aug 18, '52]	QNS	parlames hier		35. [S. Oct 1, '52]	QNS	[hier 42:14]
18=17. [Fr Aug 19, '52]	QNS	le propos qui fust hier touché				
18. [S. Aug 20, '52]	QNS	cy devant & [hier 41:504, 505]		36. [M. Oct 10, '52]	QNS	desja...parlé... il nous en faut refreschir
19. [M. Aug 29, '52]	QNS			37. [Tu Oct 11, '52]	QNS	
20. [Tu Aug 30, '52]	QNS	monstrames hier		38. [Wd Oct 12, '52]	DTP	
21. [Wd Aug 31, '52]	QNS(!)	vismes hier		39. [Th Oct 13, '52]	QNS	
22. [Th Sep 1, '52]	QNS	fut hier traitté [54]		40. [Fr Oct 14, '52]	QNS	vismes hier
23. [Fr Sep 2, '52]	QNS	fut hier touché		41. [S. Oct 15, '52]	QNS	par ci devant [es]
24. [S. Sep 3, '52]	QNS	[hier 41:556]				
25. [M. Sep 12, '52]	QNS	desja dit... a esté touché		42. [M. Oct 24, '52]	QNS	declaré par ci devant
26. [Tu Sep 13, '52]	QNS	laissames hier [+41:591, 601]		43. [Tu Oct 25, '52]	QNS	traitté par ci devant [es]
27. [Wd Sep 14, '52]	DTP	touchasmes hier [+41:606]		44. [Wd Oct 26, '52]	DTP	traittasmes hier [+ 42:134]
28. [Th Sep 15, '52]	QNS	ci-dessus & [hier 41:625]		45. [Th Oct 27, '52]	QNS	le propos... hier commencé
29. [Fr Sep 16, '52]	QNS	ces jours passés		46. [Fr Oct 28, '52]	QNS	
				47. [S. Oct 29, '52]	QNS	traittames hier [+ 42:162]

[54] "cy devant" may appear at the beginning because it refers to earlier sermons/ commonly repeated ideas, but "hier" added soon indicates that this sermon immediately follows the previous one. In #22 both words appear near the beginning: "Comme par ci-devant le prophete a condemné les roys, les gouverneurs... ce qui fust hier traitté," OC 41:544.

Micah[55]		
1.Wd Nov 12, '50	QNS[56]	
2. Th Nov 13, '50	QNS	vismes hier
3. Fr Nov 14, '50	QNS	commencé à exposer
4. S. Nov 15, '50	QNS	
5. M. Nov 24, '50	QNS	
6. Tu Nov 25, '50	QNS	
7. Wd Nov 26, '50	DTP	traictasmes hier
8. Th Nov 27, '50	[QNS]	
9. Fr Nov 28, '50	QNS	
10. S. Nov 29, '50	QNS	commenceasmes hier
11. M. Dec 8, '50	QNS	desja monstré
12. Tu Dec 9, '50	QNS	vismes hier
13. Wd Dec 10, '50	DTP	traictasmes hier
14. Th Dec 11, '50	QNS	tractasmes hier
15. Fr Dec 12, '50	QNS	monstrasmes hier
16. S. Dec 13, '50	QNS	vismes hier

17. M. Dec 22, '50	QNS	le propos qui a desja esté tenu
18. Tu Dec 23, '50	QNS	commenceasmes hier
19. Wd Dec 24, '50	DTP	commenceasmes hier
20. Th Dec 25, '51='50	QNS	vismes hier
21. Fr Dec 26, '51='50	QNS	monstrasmes hier
22. S. Dec 27, '51='50	QNS	monstrasmes hier
23. M. Jan 5, '51	QNS	
24. Tu Jan 6, '51	QNS	commenceasmes hier
25. Wd Jan 7, '51	DTP	
26. Th Jan 8, '51	QNS	
27. Fr Jan 9, '51	QNS	traictasmes hier
28. S. Jan 10, '51	QNS	
NEW TESTAMENT[57]		

---

55 *Sermons sur le Livre de Michée*, pub. Jean Daniel Benoit. *Supplementa Calviniana V*. Neukirchen-Vluyn, 1964.

56 Here there appears to be a mistake, since the first phrase of the weekday prayer is given instead of the day of prayer text.

57 The sermons here listed continue the Biblical order but with certain constraints because the gospels and Acts, which furnished the texts for the special Christological occasions, appear in two forms. One is the *lectio continua* exposition of the synoptics (no Johannine sermons survive) and Acts; these consecutive sermons are presented first in each category. Secondly, there are the anthologies of special Christological sermons which include texts from the gospel (synoptics) and Acts. Some of these sermons are no longer extant but known from a surviving *table of contents* of sermons actually preached on the Christological observances. Some of the sermons in the extant anthologies (one published 1558, the other 1981) were preached on the days that the Nativity, Passion-Resurrection, Pentecost were observed, while others are excerpts from the

GOSPEL HARMONY[58]				15. Sun [Nov 5, '59]	DTP	declaré par ci devant
1. Sun [Jul 16, '59]	DTP			16. Sun [Nov 12, '59]	DTP	veu par ci devant
2. Sun [Jul 23, '59]	DTP			17. Sun [Nov 19, '59]	DTP	desja exposé par ci devant
3. Sun [Jul 30, '59]	DTP			18. Sun [Nov 26, '59]	DTP	avons veu
4. Sun [Aug 6, '59]	DTP	commencé à veoir		19. Sun [Dec 3, '59]	DTP	
5. Sun [Aug 13, '59]	DTP	desja il en este traitté en partie … avons ouy ci dessus		20. Sun [Dec 10, '59]	DTP	declaré par ci devant
6. Sun [Aug 20, '59]	DTP			21. Sun [Dec 17, '59]	DTP	enseignez par ci devant [1 Tim] … dimanche prochain…à recevoir la saincte Cene [46:258]
7. Sun [Aug 27, '59]	DTP	veu comme la vierge Marie avoit		22. Sun [p.m. Dec 17, '59]	QNS	ce matin [46:269]
8. Sun Sep 3, '59	DTP	aujourdhuy… recevoir la saincte Cene[59]		23. Sun [Dec 24, '59] hemorrhages during the service [21:725]	DTP	a este touché ci-dessus… saincte Cene..maintenant à recevoir [46:282, 283]
9. Sun [Sep 10, '59]	DTP					
10. Sun [Sep 17, '59][60]	DTP	desja monstré.. desja veu [#9]		24. Sun [Jan 7, '60]	DTP	declairé ci-dessus
11. Sun [Sep 24, '59]	DTP			25. Sun [Jan 14, '60]	DTP	
12. Sun [Oct 1, '59]	DTP	avons monstré		26. Sun [Jan 21, '60]	DTP	veu par cy devant
13. Sun [Oct 8, '59]	DTP	veu par ci devant		27. Sun [Jan 28, '60]	DTP	avons veu
14. Sun [Oct 15, '59]	DTP			28. Sun Feb 4, '60	DTP	declairé par ci devant[61]
Between Sep 10 & Dec 17 two Sun are missing a sermon						

Acts series. The anthologies are presented after the *lectio continua* series for gospels and then for Acts; this means that some of the sermons will not be in chronological order.

58 *Soixante cinq sermons sur l'Harmonie ou Concordance des trois Evangelistes.* Geneve : Conrad Badius, 1562.

59 Consistory met Tu Aug. 30 as well as Th Sept. 1, in preparation for Supper; OC 21:701.

60 The dates in italics are very tentative. They should perhaps be marked as "between Sept. 10 and Dec.17," but it seems useful to give some suggestions.

61 On this day syndics were elected and the date is given, and on the next Sunday elders were elected.

29. Sun [Feb 11, '60]	DTP	veu par ci devant		41. *Sun [May 19, '60]*	DTP	avons veu ci-dessus
Feb 17 Calvin very ill [21:729 Sulzer letter to Bullinger]				Sun p.m., May 19, '60	QNS	Ps. 46:7-12
30. Sun [Feb 18, '60]	DTP	veu par ci devant		42. Sun [May 26, '60]	DTP	desja veu …. la saincte Cene … dimanche prochain [46:526]
31. Sun [Feb 25, '60]	DTP	commencé à exposer… aujourd'hui…				
30=32. Sun [Mar 3, '60]	DTP			**Pentecost Jun 2**	DTP	
33. Sun [Mar 10, '60]	DTP	desja dit [62]		42=43. Sun [Jun 9, '60]	DTP	
34. Sun [Mar 17, '60]	DTP	n'avons pas veu		Sun p.m., Jun 9, '60 [64]	QNS	Ps. 48:9-15
35. Sun [Mar 24, '60]	DTP	avons veu		44. *Sun [Jun 16, '60]*	DTP	desja monstré
36. Sun [Mar 31, '60]	DTP			45. *Sun [Jun 23, '60]*	DTP	
37. Sun [Apr 7, '60]	DTP	monstré par ci devant….. la saincte Cene … dimanche prochain [46:462]		46. *Sun [Jun 30, '60]*	DTP	avons veu
				47. *Sun [Jul 7, '60]*	DTP	traitté ci-dessus
				48. *Sun [Jul 14, '60]*	DTP	veu par ci devant
Easter Apr 14				49. *Sun [Jul 21, '60]*	DTP	desja veu
38. *Sun [Apr 21, '60]*	DTP			50. *Sun [Jul 28, '60]*	DTP	veismes dimanche passé
39. *Sun [Apr 28, '60]*	DTP	desja declaré		51. *Sun [Aug3, '60]*	DTP [65]	
between Apr 21 & May 26 1 Sun has no sermon				*Between Jun 9 & Aug 18 1 Sun has no sermon*		
41=40. Sun [May 12, '60]	DTP	declaré par ci devant		52. *Sun [Aug 18, '60]*	DTP	veu … desja… avons touché
Sun p.m., May 12, '60 [63]	None	Ps. 46:2-6				

---

62 After returning to papal territory and participating in Roman worship, two men had repented and confessed; they now were reconciled publicly.

63 Mülhaupt identifies this as 1560 because it was taken back to England by the refugees; the text itself says Sun. May 12, 1561, but May 12 was a Sunday in 1560 and Monday in 1561; also this is the first half of the exposition and the second half is dated May 19, 1560. Calvin was probably preaching at St. Gervais because he does a wedding there.

64 Calvin preaching at St. Gervais because he does a wedding for two couples.

65 "Nous avons ouy au pseaume qui a este chanté n'a guere…. [Ps. 33], OC 46:629.

53. Sun [Aug 25, '60]	DTP	desja veu ... la saincte Cene ... dimanche prochaine [46:668]
54. Sun Sep 1, '60	DTP	desja exposé ... la saincte Cene qui nous est apprestee [46:678,679-80]
55. Sun [Sep 8, '60]	DTP	avons veu
56. Sun [Sep 15, '60]	DTP	veismes dimanche passé
57. Sun [Sep 22, '60]	DTP	
58. Sun [Sep 29, '60]	DTP	
59. Sun [Oct 6, '60]	DTP[66]	[Merlin called, will present him next week]
60. Sun [Oct 13, '60]	DTP	
61. Sun [p.m. Oct 13, '60][67]	DTP[68]	ce matin [46:764]
61=62. Sun [Oct 20, '60]	DTP	
63. Sun [Oct 27, '60]	DTP	[will present minister next week][69]

64. Sun [Nov 3, '60]	DTP	
65. Sun [Nov 10, '60]	DTP	veismes dimanche passé [#64]
ANTHOLOGY 1558[70]		
Nativity		
1.Sun Dec 25, '52	DTP	
Passion Week-Easter ['58]		
2. Sun [Apr 3, '58]	DTP	dimanche prochain ...la saincte Cene 46:845/ p. 38
3. Sun [p.m. Apr 3, '58]	QNS	ce matin
4. Mn [Apr 4, '58]	QNS	
5. Tu [Apr 5, '58]	QNS	desja veu par ci devant [#3]
6. Wd [Apr 6, '58]	DTP	desja veu par ci devant [#5]

[66] Merlin elected as minister to come to the city from a village parish. (He was elected to the ministry 1559, departed to serve Admiral Coligny in 1561. RPC 2, pp. 86, 95, 101f.)

[67] Calvin preaching at St. Pierre where he does a wedding at this service.

[68] Here the scribe mistakenly gives the morning prayer formula, possibly because almost all the sermons on the Gospel Harmony are preached in the morning; this day Calvin preached morning and afternoon.

[69] On Oct. 14, 1560, Calvin proposes Pierre D'Airebaudouze (D'Anduze) to be called from the village of Jussy to the city; on Oct. 24 he asks the Senate to receive the report about the minister Pinaud who will replace D'Airebaudouze at Jussy, Oct. 14 & 24, OC 21:738 (RC 56 f87, 90v).

[70] *Plusieurs sermons de Jean Calvin*, edit. Wilhelmus H. Th. Moehn. *Ioannis Calvini Sermons*. Volume VIII. Geneve: Droz, 2011. Dating identified by Moehn, p. xxxv. Moehn, "Introduction," *Sermones*, p. xxxv, indicates that this series could be either 1557 or 1558. I believe it can be assigned to 1558 because in 1558 the week before Easter was Calvin's regular week to preach (see the three week gap in the Isaiah sermons 33 & 34 between Mar 26 & Apr 18), whereas in 1557 it was not his week to preach (see the Isaiah sermons 16 & 17 which go up to Passion Week, ending S. Mar 27, and begin again immediately after Easter, Apr 5).

7. Th [Apr 7, '58]	QNS	
8. Fr [Apr 8, '58]	QNS	veismes hier
9. Sa [Apr 9, '58]	QNS	veu ci-dessus [#6]
10.Sun Easter [Apr 10, '58]	DTP	aujourd'huy... saincte Cene OC 46:954/ p. 196
ANTHOLOGY *Table of Contents* "Feast Day" sermons; text lost[71]		
Sun Apr 14, '49 to Easter Sun Apr 21, '49	7 on pas-sion-resurr.	Matthew/ synoptics [not consecutive]
Christmas, Dec 25, '50='49[72]	1 on Luke[2]	
Sun Mar 30, '50 to Easter Sun Apr 6, '50	8 on pas-sion-resurr.	John 18-19 [consecutive sermons]
Wed, Mar 25, '51	1 on passion	John 18-19
Sun Mar 26, '53 to Easter Apr 2, '53	8 on pas-sion-resurr.	gospel not named [sermons consecutive]
Sun Dec 24, '54='53	1 on Luke[2]	

Sun Mar 18, '54 [Wed Mar 21, '54] Easter Mar 25, '54	3 on passion-resurr.	no gospel named
Sun, Dec 23, '55='54	1 on Luke[2]	
Sun Easter Apr 14, '55	1 on resurr.	Matthew/ synoptics
ANTHOLOGY 1981[73]		
Easter-Pentecost		
11. Sun Mar 26, '59 Easter	DTP	
12. Sun April 14, '60 Easter	DTP	
Passion Week '62		
15. M. Mar 23, '62	QNS	Hier[74]
16. Tu Mar 24, '62	QNS	
14. Wd Mar 25, '62	DTP	Hier
17. Th Mar 26, '62	QNS	
18. Fr Mar 27, '62	QNS	Hier
19. S. Mar 28, '62	QNS	Hier

---

71   Table printed in several S volumes, e.g., S. II, p. xv-xvii; S. VII, pp. xlvii-xlviii.

72   Mühlhaupt notes the tradition of beginning the new year on Dec 25; "Einleitung," S. VII, p. xlix; for discussion and examples of Geneva's mixed practice, see chap. 4 n.63.

73   *Psalmpredigten. Passions-, Oster-, und Pfingstpredigten*, hg. Erwin Mülhaupt. *Supplementa Calviniana VII* Neukirchen-Vluyn, 1981. These are sermons actually preached on the Christological observances.

74   Evidently the Passion sermons had begun on Sunday Mar. 22, 1562, but that one was not preserved in this set.

ACTS						
Acts of the Apostles [75]				7. Sun Feb 23, '50	DTP	veu par cy devant
				8. Sun [?] Mar 9, '50	QNS [79]	
1. Sun Aug 25, '49	[DTP]	dimanche prochain...la saincte cene p. 8		9. Sun Apr 13, '50	DTP	
				10. Sun Apr 20, '50	DTP [80]	
2. Sun Dec 22, '49	DTP	mercredi prochain... la cene p. 16		11. Sun May 11, '50	DTP [81]	veu par cy devant
				12. Sun May 18, '50	DTP	
3. Sun Dec 29, '49	DTP	par cy devant		13. Sun May 25, '50 Pentecost	DTP	
4. Sun Jan 19, '50	DTP [76]	traictasmes dimanche derrnier		14. Sun Jun 1, '50	DTP	
5. Sun [?] Jan 26, '50	QNS [77]	veu par cy devant		15. Sun Jun 8, '50	DTP [82]	traicté dimanche prochain [last]
6. Sun [?] Feb 2, '50	QNS [78]	traictasmes dimanche dernier		16. Sun Jun 22, '50	DTP	exposé par cy devant

---

[75] *Sermons on the Acts of the Apostles*, edit. By Willem Balke & Wilhelmus H. Th. Moehn. *Supplementa Calviniana VIII*. Neukirchen-Vluyn, 1994.

[76] This Sermon 3 begins with a reference to discussion of baptism on the previous Sunday, a missing sermon, S. X/3, p. 28 "Nous traictasmes dimanche derrenier que le baptesme n'est jamais sans son effect..." It concludes with an indication that the exposition of a point is not complete and will be continued the next week. S. X/3, p. 36 "... nous reserverons le rest à une aultre foys..."

[77] This may be a morning, with the wrong incipit of the prayer (the afternoon one), and the final statement before the concluding prayer makes it clear that this is the last (if not only) sermon on Acts on this Sunday. Sermon 4, S. X/3, p. 45 "Or il y a encores quelque chose à dire sur ce passage que nous reserverons à dimanche prochain." It is possible though very unlikely that there was only one sermon, in the afternoon on this day.

[78] Again this uses the first words of the afternoon prayer; the sermon also begins with a reference to the previous Sunday, which suggests that Calvin was preaching only one sermon per Sunday. Sermon 6, S. X/3, p. 46: "Nous traictasmes dimanche dernier les marques qui doibvent estre en l'Eglise de Dieu." This clearly refers to Acts 2:42 in the previous sermon. Again, probably a mistake on the prayer incipit.

[79] Same point as previous note.

[80] Here there is a reference to completing the exposition of a point the next time, Sermon 10, S. X/3, p. 88 "... nous le reserverons à dymanche prochain..."

[81] Here there is a reference to completing the exposition of a point the next time, which is probably the next Sunday because it begins "cy devant." Sermon 11, S. X/3, p. 89 : "Nous avons veu par cy devant..."

[82] Here the word "prochain" refers back to the previous Sunday which treated mutual love. Sermon 15, S. X/3, p. 121: "Il nous doibt bien souvenir de ce qui fut traicté dimanche prochain quant à la charité..."

17. Sun [?] Jun 29, '50	QNS[83]	commeneasmes dymanche[84]
18. Sun [?] Jul 6, '50	QNS[85]	veu par cy devant
19. Sun Jul 13, '50	DTP	
20. Sun p.m. Jul 13, '50	QNS	
21. Sun Jul 20, '50	DTP	dymanche passé
22. Sun Aug 3, '50	DTP	veu par cy devant
23. Sun [?] Aug 10, '50	QNS[86]	veu par cy devant
24. Sun Aug 17, '50	DTP[87]	commenceasmes dimanche dernier
25. Sun Aug 24, '50	DTP	
26. Sun Aug 31, '50	DTP	esté traicté cy dessus ... celebrer la saincte cene... dimanche prochain p. 232
27. Sun Sep 7, '50	DTP	la saincte cene... nous communicquons aujourd'huy p. 243
28. Sun [?] Sep 14, '50	QNS[88]	dimanche dernier

29. Sun Sep 21, '50	DTP	desja deduict cy dessus
30. Sun Sep 28, '50	DTP	dimanche dernier traictasmes
31. Sun Oct 5, '50	DTP	
32. Sun Oct 12, '50	DTP	
33. Sun Oct 19, '50	DTP	monstrasmes dimanche dernier
34. Sun Oct 26, '50	DTP	desja declaré
35. Sun Nov 2, '50	DTP	
36. Sun Nov 9, '50	DTP	desja exposé
37. Sun Nov 16, '50	DTP	
38. Sun Nov 23, '50	DTP	monstré par cy devant
39. Sun Nov 30, '50	DTP	veu par cy devant
40. Sun Dec 7, '50	DTP	desja touché cy dessus
41. Sun Dec 14, '50	DTP	
42. Sun Dec 21, '50	DTP	monstrasmes dimanche dernier
43. Sun Jan 4, '51	DTP	

83 Again this uses the incipit of the afternoon prayer; here the sermon refers back to the previous Sunday's discussion of miracles near the end of the sermon (16). Sermon 17, S. X/3, p. 140 "Nous commanceasmes dymenche à traicter, comment il nous fault faire nostre proffict des myracles..." Clearly the sequence is from Sermon 16 to Sermon 17, yet the words of the prayers indicate that 16 was preached in the morning and 17 in the afternoon.

84 This refers to the previous Sunday; if he meant the morning of the same day, he would say "ce matin."

85 Again this uses the first words of the afternoon prayer and this Sermon 18 seems to follow directly on Sermon 17, which is one Sunday to the next.

86 Again the afternoon prayer incipit confuses the timing.

87 This Sermon 24 begins with a reference to the previous week. S. X/3, p. 206 "Nous commenceasmes dimanche dernier à exposer le texte present..."

88 Again this Sermon 28 uses the first words of the afternoon prayer, yet it begins with a reference to the previous week's Sermon 27 discussion of Abraham (p. 242), and this Sermon 28 begins "Dimanche dernier nous traictasmes ce que recite icy sainct Estienne touchant de l'approbation qu'Abraham a donné de sa foy..." S. X/3, p. 246.

44. Sun Jan 11, '51	DTP	traicté cy dessus
ANTHOLOGY 1558		
Ascension		
11. Sun Sep 1, '49[89]	DTP	la Cene ...nous seront presentez p. 211
12. Sun Sep 8, '49	DTP	
13. Sun between Sep 15/Dec 8, '49	DTP	
14. Sun between Sep 15/Dec 8, '49	DTP	
Pentecost		
16. Sun between Sep 15/Dec 8, '49[90]	DTP	
17. Sun between Sep 15/Dec 8, '49	DTP	
18. Sun between Sep 15/Dec 8, '49	DTP	
15. Sun May 29, '58 Pentecost Day	DTP	

ANTHOLOGY *Table of Contents* "Feast Day" sermons; text lost[91]		
Sun Pentecost Jun 9, '49	1 on Acts [2]	
Sun Pentecost May 13, '54	1 on Acts [2]	
Sun Pentecost Jun 2, '55	1 on Acts 2	
ANTHOLOGY 1981[92]		
Pentecost		
13. Sun Jun 2, '60 Pentecost	DTP	
First Corinthians		
1. Sun Oct 20, '55[93]	DTP	
2. Sun p.m. Oct 20, '55	[QNS]	ce matin
3. Sun Oct 27, '55	DTP	
4. Sun p.m. Oct 27, '55	[QNS]	
5. Sun Nov 3, '55	DTP	veu par cy devant

---

89 *Plusieurs sermons*, now edited for *Ioannis Calvini Sermones VIII*, page references given. These four "Ascension" sermons were not preached on Ascension but were part of the *lectio continua* series on Acts; when *Plusieurs sermons* was put together in 1558, these were included to fill out the theme.

90 This is the *Plusieurs sermons* numbering. NB #15 is out of numerical order in order to place it in chronological order. Only the fourth of these "Pentecost" sermons was preached on the day of Pentecost in 1558. See Moehn, "Introduction," *Plusieurs sermons*, p. xxxv.

91 Table printed in several S volumes, e.g., S. II, p. xv-xvii; S. VII, pp. xlvii-xlviii.

92 *Psalmpredigten. Passions-, Oster-, und Pfingstpredigten*, hg. Erwin Mülhaupt. *Supplementa Calviniana VII* Neukirchen-Vluyn , 1981. These are sermons actually preached on the Christological observances.

93 Ms. fr. 26, chapters 1-9; my on-going transcription for *Supplementa Calviniana*.

6. Sun p.m. Nov 3, '55	QNS		23. Sun p.m. Jan 5, '56	QNS	ce matin
7. Sun Nov 10, '55	DTP		24. Sun Jan 12, '56	DTP	desja veu
8. Sun p.m. Nov 10, '55	QNS		No p.m. sermon		
9. Sun Nov 17, '55	DTP		25. Sun Jan 19, '56	DTP	
10. Sun p.m. Nov 17, '55	DTP[94]	ce matin	26. Sun p.m. Jan 19, '56	QNS	ce matin
11. Sun Nov 24, '55	DTP		27. Sun Jan 26, '56	DTP	desja monstré
12. Sun p.m. Nov 24, '55	QNS	ce matin	28. Sun p.m. Jan 26, '56	QNS	ce matin
13. Sun Dec 1, '55	DTP	traitté par cy devant	29. Sun Feb 2, '56	DTP	veu par cy devant
14. Sun p.m. Dec 1, '55	QNS	ce matin	30. Sun p.m. Feb 2, '56	QNS	
15. Sun Dec 8, '55	DTP[95]		31. Sun Feb 9, '56	DTP	veu cy devant
16. Sun p.m. Dec 8, '55	QNS		32. Sun p.m. Feb 9, '56	QNS	ce matin
17. Sun Dec 15, '55	DTP	declaré cy dessus …dimanche prochain la saincte cene f141b	33. Sun Feb 16, '56	DTP	veu par cy devant
18. Sun p.m. Dec 15, '55	QNS	ce matin	34. Sun p.m. Feb 16, '56	QNS	
			35. Sun Feb 23, '56	DTP	desja commencé à voir
19. Sun [p.m.] Dec 22, '55	QNS	dimanche prochain la saincte cene, f141b	36. Sun p.m. Feb 23, '56	QNS	ce matin
20. Sun Dec 29, '56='55	DTP	veu par cy devant	37. Sun Mar 1, '56	DTP	
21. Sun p.m. Dec 29, '56='55	QNS		38. Sun p.m. Mar 1, '56	QNS	ce matin
			39. Sun Mar 8, '56	DTP	par cy devant traicté
22. Sun Jan 5, '56	DTP	dimanche passé	40. Sun p.m. Mar 8, '56	QNS	
			41. Sun Mar 15, '56	DTP	

94   Here the incipit of the Sunday morning prayer text is used at an afternoon sermon.

95   « Par cy devant S[ainct] Paul avoit dict que la sagesse de Dieu n'est point cogneue sinon de ceulx qui sont bien disposez à la recepvoir ….» refers back to earlier verses of 1 Cor. 2, probably those found in sermons 14-15.

42. Sun p.m. Mar 15, '56	QNS	ce matin
No morning sermon		
43. Sun p.m. Mar 22, '56	QNS	veu par cy devant
No morning sermon: probably beginning Passion Week text		
44. Sun p.m. Mar 29, '56	QNS	
Easter		
45. Sun p.m. Apr 5, '56	QNS	
46. Sun Apr 12, '56	DTP	
47. Sun p.m. Apr 12, '56	QNS	veu par cy devant [es]
48. Sun Apr 19, '56	DTP	dimanche passé ... traictasmes
49. Sun p.m. Apr 19, '56	QNS	ce matin
No morning sermon		
50. Sun p.m. Apr 26, '56	QNS	
51. Sun May 3, '56	DTP	desja traicté par cy devant
52. Sun p.m. May 3, '56	QNS	
Calvin collapses in pulpit May 10 [21:81, 637]		
Pentecost		
53. Sun May 31, '56	DTP	
54. Sun p.m. May 31, '56	QNS	ce matin
55. Sun Jun 7, '56	DTP	
56. Sun p.m. Jun 7, '56	QNS	
57. Sun Jun 14, '56	DTP	
58. Sun p.m. Jun 14, '56	QNS	
1.Sun [Jun 21, '56] [96]	DTP	
2. Sun [p.m. Jun 21, '56]	QNS	
3. Sun [Jun 28, '56]	DTP	au sermon precedent
4. Sun [p.m. Jun 28, '56]	QNS	
5. Sun [Jul 5, '56]	DTP	
6. Sun [p.m. Jul 5, '56]	QNS	
7. Sun [Jul 12, '56]	DTP	veu dernierement
8. Sun [p.m. Jul 12, '56]	QNS	
9. Sun [Jul 19, '56]	DTP	traitte ci dessus
10. Sun [p.m. Jul 19, '56]	QNS	
11. Sun [Jul 26, '56]	DTP	vismes dimanche passe
12. Sun [p.m. Jul 26, '56]	QNS	declaré au sermon precedent
13. Sun [Aug 2, '56]	DTP	
14. Sun [p.m. Aug 2, '56]	QNS	dimanche prochain [49:764]

96   *Sermons sur le 10ᵉ et 11ᵉ chap. de la premier Epistre aux Corinthiens.* Geneve : Michel Blanchier, 1563.

15. Sun [Aug 9, '56]	DTP	ci devant ... [dimanche passé 49:775]
16. Sun [p.m. Aug 9, '56]	QNS	commencé ce matin [+49:780, 789]
17. Sun [Aug 16, '56]	DTP	esté declare par ci devant*
18. Sun [p.m. Aug 16, '56]	QNS	[ce matin 49:804]
No morning sermon		
19. Sun [p.m. Aug 23, '56]	QNS	
Travels to Frankfurt Aug 26, '56 – @ Oct 12? [21:647, 650]		
Galatians 97		
1. Sun p.m. Nov 14, '57	QNS	
2. Sun [Nov 21, '57]	DTP	
3. Sun [p.m. Nov 21, '57]	QNS	Ce matin
4. Sun [Nov 28, '57]	DTP	veu par ci devant
5. Sun [p.m. Nov 28, '57]	[QNS]	ce matin [+50:327]
6. Sun [Dec 5, '57]	DTP	
7. Sun [p.m. Dec 5, '57]	QNS	[ce matin 50:360]
8. Sun [Dec 12, '57]	DTP	
9. Sun [p.m. Dec 12, '57]	QNS	ce matin[+50:378]
10. Sun Dec 19, '57	DTP	veu par ci devant
11. Sun p.m. Dec 19, '57	QNS	[ce matin 50:403, 405] ... dimanche prochaine la Cene [50:413]
12. Sun p.m. Dec 26, '57	QNS	exposé par ci devant
13. Sun [Jan 2, '58]	DTP	veu par ci devant
14. Sun [p.m. Jan 2, '58]	QNS	ce matin
15. Sun [Jan 9, '58]	DTP	
16. Sun [p.m. Jan 9, '58]	QNS	[ce matin 50:476]
17. Sun [Jan 16, '58]	DTP	
18. Sun [p.m. Jan 16, '58]	QNS	[ce matin 50:497]
19. Sun [Jan 23, '58]	DTP	
20. Sun [p.m. Jan 23, '58]	QNS	[ce matin 50:525, 527]
21. Sun [Jan 30, '58]	DTP	veu par ci devant
22. Sun [p.m. Jan 30, '58]	QNS	ce matin
23. Sun [Feb 6, '58]	DTP	veu ci dessus
24. Sun [p.m. Feb 6, '58]	QNS	
25. Sun [Feb 13, '58]	DTP	desja exposé
26. Sun [p.m. Feb 13, '58]	QNS	veu par ci devant [es]
27. Sun [Feb 20, '58]	DTP	traitté cidevant
28. Sun [p.m. Feb 20, '58]	QNS	
29. Sun [Feb 27, '58]	DTP	
30. Sun [p.m. Feb 27, '58]	QNS	ce matin [+50:645, 650]

---

97 *Opera Calvini*, vol. 50: rare instance of providing all prayers.

31. Sun [Mar 6, '58]	DTP	veu ci dessus		3. Sun p.m. [May 22, '58]	QNS	ce matin [+51:274, 277]
No p.m. sermon				Pentecost		
32. Sun [Mar 13, '58]	DTP	veu par ci devant		4. Sun p.m. May 29, '58	QNS	ci devant
No p.m. sermon				5. Sun [Jun 5, '58]	DTP	ci devant
33. Sun [Mar 20, '58]	DTP			6. Sun [p.m. Jun 12, '58]	QNS	ci devant
34. Sun [p.m. Mar 20, '58]	QNS	[ce matin 51:16]		7. Sun [Jun 19, '58]	DTP	
35. Sun [Mar 27, '58]	DTP			8. Sun [p.m. Jun 19, '58]	QNS	ce matin [+51:339]
36. Sun [p.m. Mar 27, '58]	QNS	ce matin [+51:33, 39, 42]		9. Sun [Jun 26, '58]	DTP	ci devant
				10. Sun [p.m. Jun 26, '58]	QNS	ce matin [+51:365, 368, 369, 371]
Sunday & Passion Week				11. Sun [Jul 3, '58]	DTP	
37. Sun [p.m. Apr 10, '58]	QNS			12. Sun [p.m. Jul 3, '58]	QNS	ce matin [+OC 51:389]
38. Sun [Apr 17, '58]	DTP			A Sun missing between May 29 & Aug 28		
39. Sun [p.m. Apr 17, '58]	QNS	ce matin [+51:83]		13. Sun [Jul 17, '58]	DTP	ci devant
40. Sun [Apr 24, '58]	DTP			14. Sun [p.m. Jul 17, '58]	QNS	ce matin [+51:420]
No p.m. sermon				15. Sun [Jul 24, '58]	DTP	desja veu
41. Sun [May 1, '58]	DTP			16. Sun [p.m. Jul 24, '58]	QNS	
42. Sun [p.m. May 1, '58]	QNS			17. Sun [Jul 31, '58]	DTP	ci devant
43. Sun [May 8, '58]	DTP			18. Sun [p.m. Jul 31, '58]	QNS	ce matin [+51:472]
				19. Sun [Aug 7, '58]	DTP	
Ephesians [98]				20. Sun [p.m. Aug 7, '58]	QNS	ce matin [+51:488, 492]
1. Sun p.m. May 15, '58	QNS					
2. Sun [May 22, '58]	DTP	cy devant; preparer à recevoir … la sainct Cene 51:270				

---

[98] *Sermons de Jean Calvin sur l'epistre S. Paul apostre aux Ephesiens.* Geneve : Jean Baptiste Pinereul, 1562.

21. Sun [Aug 14, '58]	DTP			35. Sun [Oct 2, '58]	DTP	
22. Sun [p.m. Aug 14, '58]	QNS	ce matin		36. Sun [p.m. Oct 2, '58]	QNS	ce matin
23. Sun [Aug 21, '58]	DTP	ci devant		37. Sun [Oct 9, '58]	DTP	
24. Sun [p.m. Aug 21, '58]	QNS	ce matin		38. Sun [p.m. Oct 9, '58]	QNS	ce matin
25. Sun [Aug 28, '58]	QNS[99]	ci devant		39. Sun [Oct 16, '58]	DTP	ci-dessus
26. Sun [p.m. Aug 28, '58]	QNS	ce matin [+51:569]; la saincte Cene dimanche prochain [51:578]		40. Sun [p.m. Oct 16, '58]	QNS	ce matin
				41. Sun [Oct 23, '58]	DTP	
27. Sun Sep 4, '58	DTP	ci devant … venir à cette saincte table [51:591]		Calvin ill many months[101]		
28. Sun [p.m. Sep 4, '58]	QNS					
29. Sun [Sep 11, '58]	DTP			42. Sun Jun 11, '59	DTP	
30. Sun [p.m. Sep 11, '58]	QNS	[ce matin 51:621, 622][100]		43. Sun [Jun 18, '59]	DTP	
31. Sun [Sep 18, '58]	DTP	dimanche passé		44. Sun [Jun 25, '59]	DTP	
32. Sun [p.m. Sep 18, '58]	QNS			45. Sun [Jul 2, '59]	DTP	
33. Sun [Sep 25, '58]	DTP			46. Sun [p.m. Jul 2, '59]	QNS	ce matin [51:825]
34. Sun [p.m. Sep 25, '58]	QNS			47. Sun [Jul 9, '59]	DTP	
				48. Sun [p.m. Jul 9, '59]	QNS	ce matin
				ANTHOLOGY 1558[102]		

99 Here the first words of the afternoon prayer are used, instead of the morning text, but this seems to be a morning sermon because the following one speaks of "this morning."

100 In a number of sermons "ce matin" is found later in the text, as in this case Eph. #30, even if it is not at the beginning, though also often when it is at the beginning; e.g., Eph. #3, 8, 10, 12, 14, 18, 20, 26, 36, 46.

101 Calvin absent from Consistory from Oct 20, '58 to Feb 2, '59 [OC 21:707] Calvin sick with quartan fever, before Oct 27, '58; writes from bed Nov 24, '58 [OC 21:707, 708] Calvin does not preach on weekdays after S. Oct 8, '58, until Jun 12, '59 [Isaiah]

102 *Plusieurs sermons de Jean Calvin*, edit. Wilhelmus H. Th. Moehn. *Ioannis Calvini Sermons*. Volume VIII. Geneve: Droz, 2011. Dating identified by Moehn, p. xxxv.

Last Coming		
19. Sun summer '54	DTP	
Timothy and Titus [103]		
First Timothy		
1. Sun Sep 16, '54	DTP	
2. Sun p.m. Sep 16, '54	QNS	[ce matin 53:17, 21]
3. Sun [Sep 23, '54]	DTP	
4. Sun p.m. [Sep 23, '54]	QNS	ce matin [+53:47]
5. Sun p.m. [Sep 30, '54]	QNS	dimanche passé
6. Sun [Oct 7, '54]	DTP	
7. Sun p.m. [Oct 7, '54]	QNS	[ce matin 53:84, 86]
8. Sun [Oct 14, '54]	DTP	
9. Sun p.m. [Oct 14, '54]	QNS	ce matin [53:101]
10. Sun [Oct 21, '54]	DTP	
11. Sun p.m. [Oct 21, '54]	QNS	
12. Sun [Oct 28, '54]	DTP	
13. Sun p.m. [Oct 28, '54]	QNS	
14. Sun Nov 4, '54 [104]	DTP	
15. Sun p.m., Nov 4, '54	QNS	ce matin
16. Sun [Nov 11, '54]	DTP	
17. Sun p.m. [Nov 11, '54]	QNS	ce matin
18. Sun [Nov 18, '54]	DTP	
19. Sun p.m. [Nov 18, '54]	QNS	
20. Sun [Nov 25, '54]	DTP	
21. Sun p.m. [Nov 25, '54]	QNS	ce matin
22. Sun [Dec 2, '54]	DTP	
23. Sun p.m. [Dec 2, '54]	[QNS]	[ce matin 53:274]
24. Sun [Dec 9, '54]	DTP	
25. Sun p.m. [Dec 9, '54]	QNS	ce matin
26. Sun [Dec 16, '54]	DTP	la Cene. dimanche prochain 50:314
27. Sun p.m. [Dec 16, '54]	QNS	ce matin
28. Sun p.m. [Dec 23, '54]	QNS	
29. Sun [Dec 30, '54]	DTP	
30. Sun p.m. [Dec 30, '54]	QNS	ce matin
31. Sun [Jan 6, '55]	DTP	
32. Sun p.m. [Jan 6, '55]	QNS	ce matin [+53:389]
33. Sun [Jan 13, '55]	DTP	
34. Sun p.m. [Jan 13, '55]	QNS	ce matin
35. Sun [Jan 20, '55]	DTP	

---

[103] *Sermons sur les deux Epistres à Timothée et sur l'Epistre à Tite.* Geneva: Conrad Badius, 1561.

[104] The date is given in the publication of sermons 14 & 15 by Jean Girard in 1555; see Peter & Gilmont, *Bibliotheca* II, p. 585.

36. Sun p.m. [Jan 20, '55]	[QNS]	
37. Sun [Jan 27, '55]	DTP	
38. Sun p.m. [Jan 27, '55]	QNS	[ce matin 53:458]
39. Sun [Feb 3, '55]	DTP	
40. Sun p.m. [Feb 3, '55]	[QNS]	
41. Sun [Feb 10, '55]	DTP	
42. Sun p.m. [Feb 10, '55]	QNS	
43. Sun [Feb 17, '55]	DTP	
44. Sun p.m. [Feb 17, '55]	QNS	
45. Sun [Feb 24, '55]	DTP	
46. Sun p.m. [Feb 24, '55]	QNS	ce matin
47. Sun [Mar 3, '55]	DTP	
48. Sun p.m. [Mar 3, '55]	QNS	
Absent in Bern[105]		
49. Sun [Mar 17, '55]	DTP	
50. Sun p.m. [Mar 17, '55]	QNS	ce matin
51. Sun [Mar 24, '55]	DTP	
52. Sun p.m. [Mar 24, '55]	QNS	ce matin [+53:630]
Absent in Bern[106]		
53. Sun p.m. [Apr 14, '55]	QNS	

54. Sun [Apr 21, '55]	DTP	
Second Timothy		
1. Sun p.m.[107] [Apr 21, '55]	QNS	
2. Sun [Apr 28, '55]	DTP	
3. Sun p.m. [Apr 28, '55]	QNS	[ce matin 54:31]
4. Sun [May 5, '55]	DTP	
5. Sun p.m. [May 5, '55]	QNS	ce matin
6. Sun [May 12, '55]	DTP	
7. Sun p.m. [May 12, '55]	QNS	ce matin
8. Sun [May 19, '55]	DTP	ci devant
9. Sun p.m. [May 19, '55]	QNS	ce matin
10. Sun May 26, '55	DTP	ci devant ... dimanche prochain ...la saincte Cene 54:125
11. Sun p.m. May 26, '55	QNS	
12. Sun p.m. Jun 2, '55	QNS	ci devant ... [ce matin 54:145]; au matin nous avons eu la Cene [54:152]
13. Sun [Jun 9, '55]	DTP	ci devant
14. Sun p.m. [Jun 9, '55]	QNS	ce matin
No morning sermon		

105 Calvin travels to Bern, Mar 6-16, '55, RCP II, p.60, OC 21: 597-98.

106 Calvin travels to Bern, Mar 28-Apr 10/11, '55, RCP II, p. 61, OC 21:600-02

107 Raguenier's catalog says Apr 21, '55, morning, but this seems to be an error; it is not the only one in his list.

15. Sun p.m. [Jun 16, '55]	QNS	
16. Sun [Jun 23, '55]	DTP	
17. Sun p.m. [Jun 23, '55]	QNS	ce matin [+ 54:200]
18. Sun [Jun 30, '55]	DTP	ci devant
19. Sun p.m. [Jun 30, '55]	QNS	
20. Sun [Jul 7, '55]	DTP	
21. Sun p.m. [Jul 7, '55]	QNS	[ce matin 54:247, 256]
22. Sun p.m. [Jul 14, '55]	QNS	
23. Sun [Jul 21, '55]	DTP	
24. Sun p.m. [Jul 21, '55]	QNS	[ce matin 54:285, 288]
25. Sun [Jul 28, '55]	DTP	au dernier sermon
26. Sun p.m. [Jul 28, '55]	QNS	ce matin
27. Sun [Aug 4, '55]	DTP	
28. Sun p.m. [Aug 4, '55]	QNS	
29. Sun [Aug 11, '55]	DTP	ci devant
30. Sun p.m. [Aug 11, '55]	QNS	
Titus		
1. Sun [Aug 18, '55]	DTP	
2. Sun p.m. [Aug 18, '55]	QNS	ce matin

3. Sun Aug 25, '55	DTP	la saincte Cene dimanche prochain [54:415]
4. Sun p.m. Aug 25, '55	[QNS]	ce matin [+ 54:420]
5. Sun Sep 1, '55	DTP	la saincte Cene qui nous est mise devant [54:443]
6. Sun p.m. [Sep 1, '55]	QNS	
7. Sun [Sep 8, '55]	DTP	ci devant
8. Sun p.m. [Sep 8, '55]	QNS	ce matin [+ 54:475]
No morning sermon		
9. Sun p.m. [Sep 15, '55]	QNS	sermon prochain [last]
10. Sun [Sep 22, '55]	DTP	ci devant
11. Sun p.m. [Sep 22, '55]	QNS	ce matin
12. Sun [Sep 29, '55]	DTP	dimanche dernier
13. Sun p.m. [Sep 29, '55]	QNS	ce matin
14. Sun [Oct 6, '55]	DTP	
15. Sun p.m. [Oct 6, '55]	QNS	ce matin
16. Sun [Oct 13, '55]	DTP	ci devant
17. Sun p.m. [Oct 13, '55]	QNS	ce matin
Hebrews		
Summer '49 [108]		

---

108 *Quatre sermons fort utiles pour nostre temps avec exposition du Pseaume 87.* Geneva: Robert Estienne, '52 [Ps. 16, Heb. 13, Ps. 27 ; Ps. 87] In his "Einleitung," for S. VII, Mühlhaupt locates this sermon on a Sunday in July or August 1549, because Calvin began his Acts sermons on Aug 25, 1549, after completing Hebrews, and he figures that this text near the end of Hebrews must have been close to the end of the series on that book; S. VII, p. xxxix.

APPENDIX EIGHT PART ONE
RECORDED/EXTANT SERMONS ON THE OLD TESTAMENT PREACHED ON WEEKDAYS (EXCLUDES PSALMS PREACHED ON SUNDAYS) BY CALVIN

Unlike some of the New Testament sermons, all those on the Old Testament (except Psalms) were preached in *lectio continua* form, and so the sequence is clear.

Date	Biblical Text	Source
1549		
Jeremiah		
1.Fr Jun 14, '49	Jer 14:19-21	S. VI
2. S. Jun 15, '49	Jer 14:20–15:1	S. VI
3. M. Jun 24, '49	Jer 15:1-6	S. VI
4. Tu Jun 25, '49	Jer 15:7-10	S. VI
5. Wd Jun 26, '49	Jer 15:10-11, 14-15	S. VI
6. Th Jun 27, '49	Jer 15:12-13, 15-17	S. VI
7. Fr Jun 28, '49	Jer 15:18-19	S. VI
8. S. Jun 29, '49	Jer 15:19-21	S. VI
9. M. Jul 8, '49	Jer 16:1-7	S. VI
10. Tu Jul 9, '49	Jer 16:8-12	S. VI
11. Wd Jul 10, '49	Jer 16:12-15	S. VI
12. Th Jul 11, '49	Jer 16:14-19	S. VI
13. Fr Jul 12, '49	Jer 16:19-21	S. VI
14. S. Jul 13, '49	Jer 17:1-4	S. VI
15. M. Jul 22, '49	Jer 17:5-8	S. VI
Tu Jul 23, '49 none		
16. Wd Jul 24, '49	Jer 17:9-11	S. VI
17. Th Jul 25, '49	Jer 17:11-14	S. VI
18. Fr Jul 26, '49	Jer 17:13-16	S. VI
19. S. Jul 27, '49	Jer 17:17-23	S. VI
20. M. Aug 5, '49	Jer 17:24-27	S. VI
Tu Aug 6, '49 none		
21. Wd Aug 7, '49	Jer 18:1-10	S. VI
22. Th Aug 8, '49	Jer 18:11-14	S. VI
23. Fr Aug 9, '49	Jer 18:13-16	S. VI
24. S. Aug 10, '49	Jer 18:17-18	S. VI
M. Th Aug 12-15 none		
25. Fr Aug 16, '49	Jer 18:18-23	S. VI

1550				18. Tu Dec 23, '50	Mic 5:1-2	S. V
Lamentations 1:1-5				19. Wd Dec 24, '50	Mic 5:3-6	S. V
				20. Th Dec 25, '50	Mic 5:7-14	S. V
1.S. Sep 6, '50	Lam 1:1	S. VI		21. Fr Dec 26, '50	Mic 6:1-5	S. V
				22. S. Dec 27, '50	Mic 6:6-8	S. V
2. M. Sep 15, '50	Lam 1:1-5	S. VI				
				1551		
				23. M. Jan 5, '51	Mic 6:9-11	S. V
Micah				24. Tu Jan 6, '51	Mic 6:12-16	S. V
1.Wd Nov 12, '50	Mic 1:1-2	S. V		25. Wd Jan 7, '51	Mic 7:1-3	S. V
2. Th Nov 13, '50	Mic 1:3-5a	S. V		26. Th Jan 8, '51	Mic 7:4-7	S. V
3. Fr Nov 14, '50	Mic 1:5b-10	S. V		27. Fr Jan 9, '51	Mic 7:8-9	S. V
4. S. Nov 15, '50	Mic 1:11-16	S. V		28. S. Jan 10, '51	Mic 7:10-12	S. V
5. M. Nov 24, '50	Mic 2:1-3	S. V		**1552**		
6. Tu Nov 25, '50	Mic 2:4-5	S. V		**Daniel**		
7. Wd Nov 26, '50	Mic 2:6-7	S. V		1.M. Jul 18, '52	Dan 5:1-4	OC 41
8. Th Nov 27, '50	Mic 2:8-11	S. V		2. Tu Jul 19, '52	Dan 5:5-17	OC 41
9. Fr Nov 28, '50	Mic 2:12-13	S. V		3. Wd Jul 20, '52	Dan 5:17-21	OC 41
10. S. Nov 29, '50	Mic 3:1-4	S. V		4. Th Jul 21, '52	Dan 5:22-30	OC 41
				5. Fr Jul 22, '52	Dan 6:1-14	OC 41
11. M. Dec 8, '50	Mic 3:5-8	S. V		6. S. Jul 23, '52	Dan 6:5-10	OC 41
12. Tu Dec 9, '50	Mic 3:9-10	S. V				
13. Wd Dec 10, '50	Mic 3:11-12	S. V		7. [M. Aug 1, '52]	Dan 6:11-15	OC 41
14. Th Dec 11, '50	Mic 4:1-3	S. V		8. [Tu Aug 2, '52]	Dan 6:16-21	OC 41
15. Fr Dec 12, '50	Mic 4:4-7	S. V		9. [Wd Aug 3, '52]	Dan 6:22-24	OC 41
16. S. Dec 13, '50	Mic 4:8-10a	S. V		10. [Th Aug 4, '52]	Dan 6:25-29	OC 41
				11. [Fr Aug 5, '52]	Dan 7:1-6	OC 41
17. M. Dec 22, '50	Mic 4:10b-13	S. V		12. [S. Aug 6, '52]	Dan 7:7-8	OC 41

13. [M. Aug 15, '52]	Dan 7:9-14	OC 41	36. [M. Oct 10, '52]	Dan 11:14-19	OC 42
14. [Tu Aug 16, '52]	Dan 7:15-28	OC 41	37. [Tu Oct 11, '52]	Dan 11:20-30	OC 42
15. [Wd Aug 17, '52]	Dan 8:1-7	OC 41	38. [Wd Oct 12, '52]	Dan 11:30-32	OC 42
16. [Th Aug 18, '52]	Dan 8:8-9	OC 41	39. [Th Oct 13, '52]	Dan 11:33-34	OC 42
17. [Fr Aug 19, '52]	Dan 8:10-15	OC 41	40. [Fr Oct 14, '52]	Dan 11:34-35	OC 42
18=17 [S. Aug 20, 52]	Dan 8:16-27	OC 41	41. [S. Oct 15, '52]	Dan 11:36-38	OC 42
19. [M. Aug 29, '52]	Dan 9:1-2	OC 41	42. [M. Oct 24, '52]	Dan 11:39-45	OC 42
20. [Tu Aug 30, '52]	Dan 9:3-6	OC 41	43. [Tu Oct 25, '52]	Dan 12:1	OC 42
21. [Wd Aug 31, '52]	Dan 9:7-10	OC 41	44. [Wd Oct 26, '52]	Dan 12:1-2	OC 42
22. [Th Sep 1, '52]	Dan 9:11-16	OC 41	45. [Th Oct 27, '52]	Dan 12:2-4	OC 42
23. [Fr Sep 2, '52]	Dan 9:17-18	OC 41	46. [Fr Oct 28, '52]	Dan 12:5-7	OC 42
24. [S. Sep 3, '52]	Dan 9:19-22	OC 41	47. [S. Oct 29, '52]	Dan 12:8-13	OC 42
25. [M. Sep 12, '52]	Dan 9:23	OC 41	Several weeks between Daniel and Ezekiel.		
26. [Tu Sep 13, '52]	Dan 9:24	OC 41			
27. [Wd Sep 14, '52]	Dan 9:25-26	OC 41	**Ezekiel**		
28. [Th Sep 15, '52]	Dan 9:27	OC 41	1.M. Nov 21, '52	Ezk 1:1-2	Ms.fr.21
29. [Fr Sep 16, '52]	Dan 10:1	OC 41	2. Tu Nov 22, '52	Ezk 1:4-26	Ms.fr.21
			3. Wd Nov 23, '52	Ezk 1:4f	Ms.fr.21
30. [M. Sep 26, '52]	Dan 10:2-10	OC 41	4. Th Nov 24, '5	Ezk 1:26-2:4	Ms.fr.21
31. [Tu Sep 27, '52]	Dan 10:11-13	OC 41	5. Fr Nov 25, '52	Ezk 2:1-3	Ms.fr.21
32. [Wd Sep 28, '52]	Dan 10:14-20	OC 41	6. S. Nov 26, '52	Ezk 2:4-6	Ms.fr.21
33. [Th Sep 29, '52]	Dan 10:21-11:2	OC 41			
34. [Fr Sep 30, '52]	Dan 11:3-5	OC 42	7. M. Dec 5, '52	Ezk 2:7-10	Ms.fr.21
35. [S. Oct 1, '52]	Dan 11:6-13	OC 42	8. Tu Dec 6, '52	Ezk 3:1-3	Ms.fr.21
			9. Wd Dec 7, '52	Ezk 3:4-9	Ms.fr.21

10. Th Dec 8, '52	Ezk 3:10-13	Ms.fr.21	S. Jan 21, '53 none		
11. Fr Dec 9, '52	Ezk 3:14-16	Ms.fr.21			
12. S. Dec 10, '52	Ezk 3:17-19	Ms.fr.21	31. Wd Jan 25, '53	Ezk 8:5-12	Ms.fr.21
13. M. Dec 19, '52	Ezk 3:18-21	Ms.fr.21	32. M. Jan 30, '53	Ezk 8:13-18	Ms.fr.21
14. Tu Dec 20, '52	Ezk 3:22-26	Ms.fr.21	33. Tu Jan 31, '53	Ezk 9:1-2	Ms.fr.21
15. Wd Dec 21, '52	Ezk 3:25-4:3	Ms.fr.21	34. Wd Feb 1, '53	Ezk 9:3-6	Ms.fr.21
16. Th Dec 22, '52	Ezk 4:4-8	Ms.fr.21	35. Th Feb 2, '53	Ezk 9:7-11	Ms.fr.21
17. Fr Dec 23, '52	Ezk 4:9-17	Ms.fr.21	36. Fr Feb 3, '53	Ezk 10:1-12	Ms.fr.21
18. S. Dec 24, '52	Ezk 5:1-6	Ms.fr.21	S. Feb 4, '53 none		
1553			37. Wd Feb 8, '53	Ezk 10:13-22	Ms.fr.21
19. M. Jan 2, '53	Ezk 5:7-10	Ms.fr.21			
20. Tu Jan 3, '53	Ezk 5:11-12	Ms.fr.21	38. M. Feb 13, '53	Ezk 11:1-3	Ms.fr.21
21. Wd Jan 4, '53	Ezk 5:13-17	Ms.fr.21	39. Tu Feb 14, '53	Ezk 11:4-12	Ms.fr.21
22. Th Jan 5, '53	Ezk 6:1-3	Ms.fr.21	40. Wd Feb 15, '53	Ezk 11:13-15	Ms.fr.21
23. Fr Jan 6, '53	Ezk 6:3b-5	Ms.fr.21	41. Th Feb 16, '53	Ezk 11:16-18	Ms.fr.21
24. S. Jan 7, '53	Ezk 6:11-14	Ms.fr.21	42. Fr Feb 17, '53	Ezk 11:19-25	Ms.fr.21
			S. Feb 18, '53 none		
25.[Wd Jan 11, '53]	Ezk 7:1-4	Missed[1]			
			43. M. Feb 27, '53	Ezk 12:1-10	Ms.fr.21
26. M. Jan 16, '53	Ezk 7:5-11	Ms.fr.21	44. Tu Feb 28, '53	Ezk 12:11-16	Ms.fr.21
27. Tu Jan 17, '53	Ezk 7:12-15	Ms.fr.21	45. Wd Mar 1, '53	Ezk 12:17-28	Ms.fr.21
28. Wd Jan 18, '53	Ezk 7:16-22	Ms.fr.21	46. Th Mar 2, '53	Ezk 13:1-3	Ms.fr.21
29. Th Jan 19, '53	Ezk 7:23-27	Ms.fr.21	47. Fr Mar 3, '53	Ezk 13:3-9	Ms.fr.21
30. Fr Jan 20, '53	Ezk 8:1-4	Ms.fr.21	48. S. Mar 4, '53	Ezk 13:10-16	Ms.fr.21

---

[1]   This was preached; there is a gap in the exposition of the text according to Raguenier's records. It is probable that Rguenier did not know of the change in Calvin's schedule, so that he would be preaching on the Wed of his alternate's week; see chap. 2, at n. 69.

			10/116. Tu Oct 10, '53	Ezk 24:12-14	Ms.fr.22
49. Wd Mar 8, '53	Ezk 13:17-18a	Ms.fr.21		11/117. Wd Oct 11, '53	Ezk 24:15-18	Ms.fr.22
				12/118. Th Oct 12, '53	Ezk 24:19-27	Ms.fr.22
50. Wd Mar 22, '53	Ezk 14:18b-23	Ms.fr.21		13/119. Fr Oct 13, '53	Ezk 25:1-7	Ms.fr.22
				14/120. S. Oct 14, '53	Ezk 25:8-17	Ms.fr.22
51. Wd Apr 5, '53	Ezk 14:1-5	Ms.fr.21				
				15/121. Wd Oct 18, '53	Ezk 26:1-12	Ms.fr.22
52. M. Apr 10, '53	Ezk 14:6-8	Ms.fr.21				
53. Tu Apr 11, '53	Ezk 14:9-11	Ms.fr.21		Th Oct 19 none; not Calvin's week to preach		
54. Wd Apr 12, '53	Ezk 14:12-13	Ms.fr.21				
55. Th Apr 13, '53	Ezk 14:13-23	Ms.fr.21		16/122. Fr Oct 20, '53	Ezk 26:13-21	Ms.fr.22
56. Fr Apr 14, '53	Ezk 15:1-8	Ms.fr.21				
				17/123. M. Oct 23, 53	Ezk 27:1-24	Ms.fr.22
1/106.Fr Sep 1, '53	Ezk 23:1-6	Ms.fr.22		18/124. Tu Oct 24, '53	Ezk 27:25-36	Ms.fr.22
2/107. S. Sep 2, '53	Ezk 23:7-13	Ms.fr.22		19/125. Wd Oct 25, '53	Ezk 28:1-2	Ms.fr.22
				20/126. Th Oct 26, '53	Ezk 28:3-10	Ms.fr.22
3/108. M. Sep 25, 53	Ezk 23:14-22	Ms.fr.22		21/127. Fr Oct 27, '53	Ezk 28:11-19	Ms.fr.22
4/109. Tu Sep 26, 53	Ezk 23:22-34	Ms.fr.22		22/128. S. Oct 28, '53	Ezk 28:20-26	Ms.fr.22
5/111. Wd Sep 27, '53	Ezk 23:35-39	Ms.fr.22				
6/112. Th Sep 28, '53	Ezk 23:37-40	Ms.fr.22		23/129. M. Nov 6, '53	Ezk 29:1-3	Ms.fr.22
7/113. Fr Sep 29, '53	Ezk 23:42-49	Ms.fr.22		24/130. Tu Nov 7, 53	Ezk 29:4-9	Ms.fr.22
8/114. S. Sep 30, '53	Ezk 24:1-6	Ms.fr.22		25/131. Wd Nov 8, '53	Ezk 29:8-16	Ms.fr.22
9/115. M. Oct 9, '53	Ezk 24:6-11	Ms.fr.22				

Th-S. Nov 9-11 none				42/148. Fr Dec 22, '53	Ezk 33:21-24	Ms.fr.22
				43/149. S. Dec 23, '53	Ezk 33:24-29	Ms.fr.22
26/132. M. Nov20, '53	Ezk 29:17-21	Ms.fr.22				
27/133. Tu Nov 21, '53	Ezk 30:1-11	Ms.fr.22		44/150. Wd Dec 27, '53	Ezk 33:30-33	Ms.fr.22
28/134. Wd Nov 22,'53	Ezk 30:12-19	Ms.fr.22				
29/135. Th Nov 23, '53	Ezk 30:20-26	Ms.fr.22		**1554**		
30/136. Fr Nov 24, '53	Ezk 31:1-12	Ms.fr.22		45/151. M. Jan 1, '54	Ezk 34:1-2	Ms.fr.22
31/137. S. Nov 25, '53	Ezk 31:14-18	Ms.fr.22		46/152. Tu Jan 2, '54	Ezk 34:2-6	Ms.fr.22
				47/153. Wd Jan 3, '54	Ezk 34:7-13	Ms.fr.22
32/138. Wd Nov 29,'53	Ezk 32:1-8	Ms.fr.22		48/154. Th Jan 4, '54	Ezk 34:14-19	Ms.fr.22
				49/155. Fr Jan 5, '54	Ezk 34:20-25	Ms.fr.22
33/139. M. Dec 4, '53	Ezk 32:9-16	Ms.fr.22				
34/140. Tu Dec 5, '53	Ezk 32:17-26	Ms.fr.22		50/156. Wd Jan 10, '54	Ezk 34:26-31	Ms.fr.22
35/141. Wd Dec 6, '53	Ezk 32:27-32	Ms.fr.22				
36/142. Th Dec 7, '53	Ezk 33:1-6	Ms.fr.22		51/157. M. Jan 15, '54	Ezk 34:29-31	Ms.fr.22
37/143. Fr Dec 8, '53	Ezk 33:7-8	Ms.fr.22		52/158. Tu Jan 16, '54	Ezk 35:1-8	Ms.fr.22
				53/159. Wd Jan 17, '54	Ezk 35:9-15	Ms.fr.22
38/144. M. Dec 18, '53	Ezk 33:8-11	Ms.fr.22		1/54/160. Th Jan18, '54	Ezk 36:1-7	S. X/3
39/145. Tu Dec 19, '53	Ezk 33:11-14	Ms.fr.22		2/55/161. Fr Jan 19, '54	Ezk 36:8-15	S. X/3
40/146. Wd Dec 20, '53	Ezk 33:13-15	Ms.fr.22				
41/147. Th Dec 21, '53	Ezk 33:13-20	Ms.fr.22		3/56/162. Wd Jan24,'54	Ezk 36:16-19	S. X/3

4/57/163. M. Jan29,'54	Ezk 36:20-25	S. X/3	**Job**		
			1. M. Feb 26, '54	Job 1:1	OC 33
5/58/164. Tu Jan30,'54	Ezk 36:26-28	S. X/3	2. Tu Feb 27, '54	Job 1:2-5	OC 33
			3. Wd Feb 28, '54	Job 1:5	OC 33
6/59/165. Wd Jan31,'54	Ezk 36:29-32	S. X/3	4. [Th Mar 1, '54]	Job 1:6-8	OC 33
			5. [Fr Mar 2, '54]	Job 1:9-12	OC 33
7/60/166. Th Feb 1, 54	Ezk 36:33-38	S. X/3			
8/61/167. Fr Feb 2, '54	Ezk 37:1-8	S. X/3	6. [M. Mar 12, '54]	Job 1:13-19	OC 33
			7. [Tu Mar 13, '54]	Job 1:20-22	OC 33
			8. [Wd Mar 14, '54]	Job 2:1-6	OC 33
9/62/168. Wd Feb 7, 54	Ezk 37:9-14	S. X/3	9. [Th Mar 15, '54]	Job 2:7-10	OC 33
			10. [Fr Mar 16, '54]	Job 2:11-13	OC 33
			11. [S. Mar 17, '54]	Job 3:1-10	OC 33
10/63/169. M. Feb 12,'54	Ezk 37:15-22	S. X/3			
11/64/170. Tu Feb 13, '54	Ezk 37:23-28	S. X/3	12. [M. Mar 26, '54]	Job 3:11-19	OC 33
12/65/171. Wd Feb 14, '54	Ezk 38:1-13	S. X/3	13. [Tu Mar 27, '54]	Job 3:20-26	OC 33
13/66/172. Th Feb 15, '54	Ezk 38:14-23	S. X/3	14. [Wd Mar 28, '54]	Job 4:1-6	OC 33
14/67/173. Fr Feb 16, '54	Ezk 39:1-16	S. X/3	15. [Th Mar 29, '54]	Job 4:7-11	OC 33
			16. [Fr Mar 30, '54]	Job 4:12-19	OC 33
15/68/174. MnFeb19,'54	Ezk 39:17-29	S. X/3	Absent from consistory Apr 5 & 12 [21:572]		
Tu Feb 20, '54 none			17. [Wd Apr 25, '54]	Job 4:20-5:2	OC 33
16/69/175. WdFeb21,'54	Ezk 40-48	S. X/3	18. [Wd May 3, '54]	Job 5:3-7	OC 33
Last 3 Ezekiel not Calvin's week; Job in rotation.			19. [M. May 7, '54]	Job 5:8-10	OC 33
			20. [Tu May 8, '54]	Job 5:11-16	OC 33

21. [Wd May 9, '54]	Job 5:17-18	OC 33		44. [Fr Jun 29, '54]	Job 11:13-20	OC 33
22. [Th May 10, '54]	Job 5:19-27	OC 33				
23. [Fr May 11, '54]	Job 6:1-9	OC 33		45. [M. Jul 2, '54]	Job 12:1-6	OC 33
				46. [Tu Jul 3, '54]	Job 12:7-16	OC 33
24. [M. May 21, '54]	Job 6:8-14	OC 33		47. [Wd Jul 4, '54]	Job 12:14-16	OC 33
25. [Tu May 22, '54]	Job 6:15-23	OC 33		48. [Th Jul 5, '54]	Job 12:17-25	OC 33
26. [Wd May 23, '54]	Job 6:24-30	OC 33		49. [Fr Jul 6, '54]	Job 13:1-10	OC 33
27. [Th May 24, '54]	Job 7:1-6	OC 33		50. [S. Jul 7, '54]	Job 13:7-15	OC 33
28. [Fr May 25, '54]	Job 7:7-15	OC 33				
29. [S. May 26, '54]	Job 7:16-21	OC 33		51. [M. Jul 16, '54]	Job 13:16-22	OC 33
				52. [Tu Jul 17, '54]	Job 13:23-28	OC 33
30. [Wd May 30, '54]	Job 8:1-6	OC 33		53. [Wd Jul 18, '54]	Job 14:1-4	OC 33
				54. [Th Jul 19, '54]	Job 14:5-12	OC 33
31. [M. Jun 4, '54]	Job 8:7-13	OC 33		55. [Fr Jul 20, '54]	Job 14:13-15	OC 33
32. [Tu Jun 5, '54]	Job 8:13-22	OC 33		56. [S. Jul 21, '54]	Job 14:16-22	OC 33
33. [Wd Jun 6, '54]	Job 9:1-6	OC 33				
34. [Th Jun 7, '54]	Job 9:7-15	OC 33		57. [M. Jul 30, '54]	Job 15:1-10	OC 33
35. [Fr Jun 8, '54]	Job 9:16-22	OC 33		58. [Tu Jul 31, '54]	Job 15:8-16	OC 33
				59. [Wd Aug 1, '54]	Job 15:17-22	OC 33
36. [M. Jun 18, '54]	Job 9:23-28	OC 33		60. [Th Aug 2, '54]	Job 15:23-29	OC 33
37. [Tu Jun 19, '54]	Job 9:29-35	OC 33		61. [Fr Aug 3, '54]	Job 15:30-35	OC 33
38. [Wd Jun 20, '54]	Job 10:1-6	OC 33		62. [S. Aug 4, '54]	Job 16:1-9	OC 34
39. [Th Jun 21, '54]	Job 10:7-15	OC 33				
40. [Fr Jun 22, '54]	Job 10:16-17	OC 33		63. [Wd Aug 8, '54]	Job 16:10-17	OC 34
41. [S. Jun 23, '54]	Job 10:18-22	OC 33				
				64. [M. Aug 13, '54]	Job 16:18-22	OC 34
42. [Wd Jun 27, '54]	Job 11:1-6	OC 33		65. [Tu Aug 14, '54]	Job 17:1-5	OC 34
43. [Th Jun 28, '54]	Job 11:7-12	OC 33		66. [Wd Aug15, '54]	Job 17:6-16	OC 34

67. [Th Aug 16, '54]	Job 18:1-11	OC 34		89. [Tu Oct 9, '54]	Job 23:8-12	OC 34
68. [Fr Aug 17, '54]	Job 18:12-21	OC 34		90. [Wd Oct 10, '54]	Job 23:13-17	OC 34
				91. [Th Oct 11, '54]	Job 24:1-9	OC 34
69. [Wd Aug 22, '54]	Job 19:1-12	OC 34		92. [Fr Oct 12, '54]	Job 24:10-18	OC 34
70. [M. Aug 27, '54]	Job 19:13-16	OC 34		93. [Wd Oct 17, '54]	Job 24:19-25	OC 34
71. [Tu Aug 28, '54]	Job 19:17-25	OC 34		94. [Th Oct 18, '54]	Job 25:1-6	OC 34
72. [Wd Aug 29, '54]	Job 19:26-29	OC 34		95. [Fr Oct 19 '54]	Job 26:1-7	OC 34
73. [Th Aug 30, '54]	Job 20:1-7	OC 34		96. [S. Oct 20, '54]	Job 26:8-14	OC 34
74. [Fr Aug 31, '54]	Job 20:8-15	OC 34				
				97. [M. Oct 22, '54]	Job 27:1-4	OC 34
75. [M. Sep 10, '54]	Job 20:16-20	OC 34		98. [Tu Oct 23, '54]	Job 27:5-8	OC 34
76. [Tu Sep 11, '54]	Job 20:20-25	OC 34		99. [Wd Oct 24, '54]	Job 27:8-12	OC 34
77. [Wd Sep 12, '54]	Job 20:26-29	OC 34		100. [Th Oct 25, '54]	Job 27:13-19	OC 34
78. [Th Sep 13, '54]	Job 21:1-6	OC 34		101. [Fr Oct 26, '54]	Job 27:19-28:9	OC 34
79. [Fr Sep 14, '54]	Job 21:7-12	OC 34		102. [S. Oct 27, '54]	Job 28:10-28	OC 34
80. [S. Sep 15, '54]	Job 21:13-15	OC 34				
				103. [Wd Oct 31, '54]	Job 28:10-28	OC 34
81. [M. Sep 24, '54]	Job 21:16-21	OC 34				
82. [Tu Sep 25, '54]	Job 21:22-34	OC 34		104. [M. Nov 5, '54]	Job 29:1-7	OC 34
83. [Wd Sep 26, '54]	Job 22:1-8	OC 34		105. [Tu Nov 6, '54]	Job 29:8-13	OC 34
84. [Th Sep 27, '54]	Job 22:9-11	OC 34		106. [Wd Nov 7, '54]	Job 29:13-17	OC 34
85. [Fr Sep 28, '54]	Job 22:12-17	OC 34		107. [Th Nov 8, '54]	Job 29:18-25	OC 34
86. [S. Sep 29, '54]	Job 22:18-22	OC 34		108. [Fr Nov 9, '54]	Job 30:1-10	OC 34
				109. [S. Nov 10, '54]	Job 30:11-21	OC 34
87. [Wd Oct 3, '54]	Job 22:23-30	OC 34				
				110. [Wd Nov 14, '54]	Job 30:21-31	OC 34
88. [M. Oct 8, '54]	Job 23:1-7	OC 34				

				127. Th Dec 20, '54	Job 33:26-28	OC 35

111. [M. Nov 19, '54]	Job 31:1-4	OC 34
112. [Tu Nov 20, '54]	Job 31:5-8	OC 34
113. [Wd Nov 21, '54]	Job 31:9-15	OC 34
114. [Th Nov 22, '54]	Job 31:16-23	OC 34
115. [Fr Nov 23, '54]	Job 31:24-28	OC 34
116. [Wd Nov 28, '54]	Job 31:29-32	OC 34
117. [M. Dec 3, '54]	Job 31:33	OC 34
118. [Tu Dec 4, '54]	Job 31:36-40	OC 34
119. [Wd Dec 5, '54]	Job 32:1-3	OC 35
120. [Th Dec 6, '54]	Job 32:4-10	OC 35
121. [Fr Dec 7, '54]	Job 32:11-22	OC 35
122. [Wd Dec12, '54]	Job 33:1-7	OC 35
123. [Th Dec 13, '54]	Job 33:8-14	OC 35
124. M. Dec 17, '54	Job 33:14-17	OC 35
125. Tu Dec 18, '54[2]	Job 33:18-25	OC 35
126. Wd Dec 19, '54	Job 33:26	OC 35

127. Th Dec 20, '54	Job 33:26-28	OC 35
128. Fr Dec 21, '54	Job 33:29-34:3	OC 35
129. [Wd Dec 26, '54]	Job 34:4-10	OC 35
130. [M. Dec 31, '54]	Job 34:10-15	OC 35
1555		
131. [Tu Jan 1, '55]	Job 34:16-20	OC 35
132. [Wd Jan 2, '55]	Job 34:21-26	OC 35
133. [Th Jan 3, '55]	Job 34:26-29	OC 35
134. [Fr Jan 4, '55]	Job 34:29-32	OC 35
135. [Wd Jan 9, '55]	Job 34:33-37	OC 35
136. [M. Jan 14, '55]	Job 35:1-7	OC 35
137. [Tu Jan 15, '55]	Job 35:8-11	OC 35
138. [Wd Jan 16, '55]	Job 35:12-16	OC 35
139. [Th Jan17, '55]	Job 36:1-7	OC 35
140. [Fr Jan 18, '55]	Job 36:6-14	OC 35
141. [Wd Jan 23, '55]	Job 36:15-19	OC 35

---

2   Sermons #125 & #128, exist in Ms.Fr.40a, where they have dates. #125 is Dec. 18 & #128 is Dec. 21, 1554. See Parker, *Calvin's Preaching*, p.170. The organization here was calculated independently on the basis of the incipits; it not only verifies the distribution of the sermons for this week but also confirms the usefulness of the incipit pattern.

142. [M. Jan 28, '55]	Job 36:20-24	OC 35				
143. [Tu Jan 29, '55]	Job 36:25-33	OC 35		159. [Wd Mar 6, '55]	Job 42:9-17	OC 35
144. [Wd Jan 30, '55]	Job 37:1-6	OC 35		Absent in Bern[3]		
145. [Th Jan 31, '55]	Job 37:7-13	OC 35				
146. [Fr Feb 1, '55]	Job 37:14-24	OC 35		**Deuteronomy**		
				1.Wd Mar 20, '55	Deut 1:1-3	OC 25
147. [Wd Feb 6, '55]	Job 38:1-4	OC 35				
				2. M. Mar 25, '55	Deut 1:3-8	OC 25
148. [M. Feb 1, '55]	Job 38:4-11	OC 35		Tu Mar 26, '55 none		
149. [Tu Feb 12, '55]	Job 38:12-17	OC 35		3. Wd Mar 27, '55	Deut 1:9-15	OC 25
150. [Wd Feb 13, '55]	Job 38:18-32	OC 35		Absent in Bern		
151. [Th Feb 14, '55]	Job 38:33-39:7	OC 35				
152. [Fr Feb 15, '55]	Job 39:8-21	OC 35		4. Th Apr 11, '55	Deut 1:16-18	OC 25
				5. Fr Apr 12, '55	Deut 1:19-21	OC 25
153. [Wd Feb 20, '55]	Job 39:22-35	OC 35		6. S. Apr 13, '55	Deut 1:22-28	OC 25
154. [M. Feb 25, '55]	Job 39:36-40:6	OC 35		7. Wd Apr 17, '55	Deut 1:29-33	OC 25
155. [Tu Feb 26, '55]	Job 40:7-19	OC 35		8. M. Apr 22, '55	Deut 1:34-40	OC 25
156. [Wd Feb 27, '55]	Job 40:20-41:25	OC 35		9. Tu Apr 23, '55	Deut 1:37-42	OC 25
				10 Wd Apr 24, '55	Deut 1:42-46	OC 25
157. [Th Feb 28, '55]	Job 42:1-5	OC 35		11. Th Apr 25, '55	Deut 2:1-7	OC 26
158. [Fr Mar 1, '55]	Job 42:6-8	OC 35		12. Fr Apr 26, '55	Deut 2:8-23	OC 26
				S. Apr 27, '55 none		
				13. Wd May 1, '55	Deut 2:24-29	OC 26

---

3   Wd Mar 6, '55, Calvin, Chauvet, and council members leave for Bern for a short trip; on Mar 13 Bern sets the date for a conference on last Sunday of month. Calvin et al. report back to council on Mon Mar 18. See RCP 2, pp. 60, 61; OC 21:597-598.

			32. M. Jun 17, '55	Deut 5:8-10	OC 26
14. M. May 6, '55	Deut 2:26-37	OC 26	Tu Jun 18, '55 none		
15. Tu May 7, '55	Deut 3:1-11	OC 26	33. Wd Jun 19, '55	Deut 5:11	OC 26
16. Wd May 8, '55	Deut 3:12-22	OC 26	34. Th Jun 20, '55	Deut 5:12-14	OC 26
17. Th May 9, '55	Deut 3:23-25	OC 26	35. Fr Jun 21, '55	Deut 5:13-15	OC 26
18. Fr May 10, '55	Deut 3:26-29	OC 26	S. Jun 22, '55 none		
S. May 11, '55 none					
			36. Wd Jun 26, '55	Deut 5:16	OC 26
19.Wd May 15, '55	Deut 4:1-2	OC 26			
			37. M. Jul 1, '55	Deut 5:17	OC 26
20. M. May 20, '55	Deut 4:3-6	OC 26	38. Tu Jul 2, '55	Deut 5:18	OC 26
21. Tu May 21, '55	Deut 4:6-10	OC 26	39. Wd Jul 3, '55	Deut 5:19	OC 26
22. Wd May 22, '55	Deut 4:11-14	OC 26	40. Th Jul 4, '55	Deut 5:20	OC 26
23. Th May 23, '55	Deut 4:15-20	OC 26	41. Fr Jul 5, '55	Deut 5:21	OC 26
24. Fr May 24, '55	Deut 4:19-24	OC 26	S. Jul 6, '55 none		
S. May 25, '55 none					
			M. Jul 15, '55 none		
25. Wd May 29, '55	Deut 4:23-26	OC 26	42. Tu Jul 16, '55	Deut 5:22	OC 26
			43. Wd Jul 17, '55	Deut 5:23-27	OC 26
26. M. Jun 3, '55	Deut 4:27-31	OC 26	44. Th Jul 18, '55	Deut 5:28-33	OC 26
27. Tu Jun 4, '55	Deut 4:32-35	OC 26	45. Fr Jul 19, '55	Deut 6:1-4	OC 26
28. Wd Jun 5, '55	Deut 4:36-38	OC 26	46. S. Jul 20, '55	Deut 6:4-9	OC 26
29. Th Jun 6, '55	Deut 4:39-43	OC 26			
30. Fr Jun 7, '55	Deut 4:44-5:3	OC 26	47. Wd Jul 24, '55	Deut 6:10-13	OC 26
S. Jun 8, '55 none					
			48. M. Jul 29, '55	Deut 6:13-15	OC 26
31. Wd Jun 12, '55	Deut 5:4-7	OC 26	49. Tu Jul 30, '55	Deut 6:15-19	OC 26
			50. Wd Jul 31, '55	Deut 6:20-25	OC 26

51. Th Aug 1, '55	Deut 7:1-4	OC 26		72. Fr Sep 13, '55	Deut 10:15-17	OC 27
52. Fr Aug 2, '55	Deut 7:5-8	OC 26		73. S. Sep 14, '55	Deut 10:17-21	OC 27
53. S. Aug 3, '55	Deut 7:7-10	OC 26				
				74. Wd Sep 18, '55	Deut 11:1-4	OC 27
54. Wd Aug 7, '55	Deut 7:11-15	OC 26				
				75. M. Sep 23, '55	Deut 11:5-8	OC 27
55. M. Aug 12, '55	Deut 7:16-19	OC 26		76. Tu Sep 24, '55	Deut 11:8-15	OC 27
56. Tu Aug 13, '55	Deut 7:19-24	OC 26		77. Wd Sep 25, '55	Deut 11:16-21	OC 27
57. Wd Aug 14, '55	Deut 7:22-26	OC 26		78. Th Sep 26, '55	Deut 11:22-25	OC 27
58. Th Aug 15, '55	Deut 8:1-4	OC 26		79. Fr Sep 27, '55	Deut 11:26-32	OC 27
59. Fr Aug 16, '55	Deut 8:3-9	OC 26		80. S. Sep 28, '55	Deut 12:1-5	OC 27
S. Aug 17, '55 none						
				81. Wd Oct 2, '55	Deut 12:3-7	OC 27
60. Wd Aug 21, '55	Deut 8:10-14	OC 26				
				82. M. Oct 7, '55	Deut 12:8-14	OC 27
61. M. Aug 26, '55	Deut 8:14-20	OC 26		83. Tu Oct 8, '55	Deut 12:12-18	OC 27
62. Tu Aug 27, '55	Deut 9:1-6	OC 26		84. Wd Oct 9, '55	Deut 12:19-28	OC 27
63. Wd Aug 28, '55	Deut 9:6-7	OC 26		85. Th Oct 10, '55	Deut 12:29-32	OC 27
64. Th Aug 29, '55	Deut 9:8-12	OC 26		86. Fr Oct 11, '55	Deut 13:1-3	OC 27
65. Fr Aug 30, '55	Deut 9:13-14	OC 26		87. S. Oct 12, '55	Deut 13:2-5	OC 27
66. S. Aug 31, '55	Deut 9:15-21	OC 26				
				88. Wd Oct 16, '55	Deut 13:6-11	OC 27
67. Wd Sep 4, '55	Deut 9:20-24	OC 26				
				89. M. Oct 21, '55	Deut 13:12-18	OC 27
68. M. Sep 9, '55	Deut 9:25-29	OC 26		90. Tu Oct 22, '55	Deut 14:1-20	OC 27
69. Tu Sep 10, '55	Deut 10:1-8	OC 27		91. Wd Oct 23, '55	Deut 14:21-23	OC 27
70. Wd Sep 11, '55	Deut 10:8-11	OC 27		92. Th Oct 24, '55	Deut 14:24-29	OC 27
71. Th Sep 12, '55	Deut 10:12-14	OC 27		93. Fr Oct 25, '55	Deut 15:1-6	OC 27

94. S. Oct 26, '55	Deut 15:7-10	OC 27	114. S. Dec 7, '55	Deut 19:14-15	OC 27
95. Wd Oct 30, '55	Deut 15:11-15	OC 27	115. M. Dec 16, '55	Deut 19:16-21	OC 27
			116. Tu Dec 17, '55	Deut 19:19-20:4	OC 27
96. M. Nov 4, '55	Deut 15:16-23	OC 27	117. Wd Dec 18, '55	Deut 20:2-9	OC 27
97. Tu Nov 5, '55	Deut 16:1-4	OC 27	118. Th Dec 19, '55	Deut 20:10-18	OC 27
98. Wd Nov 6, '55	Deut 16:2-8	OC 27	119. Fr Dec 20, '55	Deut 20:16-20	OC 27
99. Th Nov 7, '55	Deut 16:9-12	OC 27	120. S. Dec 21, '55	Deut 21:1-9	OC 27
100. Fr Nov 8, '55	Deut 16:13-17	OC 27			
101. S. Nov 9, '55	Deut 16:18-19	OC 27	121. Wd Dec 25, '55	Deut 21:10-14	OC 27
102. Wd Nov 13, '55	Deut 16:20-22	OC 27	122. M. Dec 30, '55	Deut 21:15-17	OC 27
			123. Tu Dec 31, '55	Deut 21:18-21	OC 27
103. M. Nov 18, '55	Deut 17:2-7	OC 27			
104. Tu Nov 19, '55	Deut 17:8-13	OC 27	**1556**		
105. Wd Nov 20, '55	Deut 17:14-18	OC 27	124. Wd Jan 1, '56	Deut 21:22-23	OC 27
106. Th Nov 21, '55	Deut 17:16-20	OC 27	125. Th Jan 2, '56	Deut 22:1-4	OC 28
107. Fr Nov 22, '55	Deut 18:1-8	OC 27	126. Fr Jan 3, '56	Deut 22:5-8	OC 28
S. Nov 23, '55 none			S. Jan 4, '56 none		
108. Wd Nov 27, '55	Deut 18:9-15	OC 27	127. Wd Jan 8, '56	Deut 22:9-12	OC 28
109. M. Dec 2, '55	Deut 18:10-15	OC 27	M. Jan 13, '56 none		
			128. Tu Jan 14, '56	Deut 22:13-24	OC 28
110. Tu Dec 3, '55	Deut 18:16-20	OC 27	129. Wd Jan 15, '56	Deut 22:25-30	OC 28
111. Wd Dec 4, '55	Deut 18:21-22	OC 27	130. Th Jan 16, '56	Deut 23:1-3	OC 28
112. Th Dec 5, '55	Deut 19:1-7	OC 27	131. Fr Jan 17, '56	Deut 23:3-6	OC 28
113. Fr Dec 6, '55	Deut 19:8-13	OC 27	S. Jan 18, '56 none		

132. Wd Jan 22, '56	Deut 23:7-11	OC 28			
			152. M. Mar 9, '56	Deut 27:24-26	OC 28
133. M. Jan 27, '56	Deut 23:12-17	OC 28	153. Tu Mar 19, '56	Deut 28:1-2	OC 28
134. Tu Jan 28, '56	Deut 23:18-20	OC 28	154. Wd Mar 11, '56	Deut 28:2-8	OC 28
135. Wd Jan 29, '56	Deut 23:20-23	OC 28	155. Th Mar 12, '56	Deut 28:9-14	OC 28
136. Th Jan 30, '56	Deut 23:24-24:4	OC 28	156. Fr Mar 13, '56	Deut 28:15-24	OC 28
137. Fr Jan 31, '56	Deut 24:1-6	OC 28	S. Mar 14, '56 none		
138. S. Feb 1, '56	Deut 24:7-9	OC 28			
			157. Wd Mar 18, '56	Deut 28:25-29	OC 28
139. Wd Feb 5, '56	Deut 24:10-13	OC 28			
			158. M. Mar 23, '56	Deut 28:29-35	OC 28
140. M. Feb 10, '56	Deut 24:14-18	OC 28	159. Tu Mar 24, '56	Deut 28:36-45	OC 28
141. Tu Feb 11, '56	Deut 24:19-22	OC 28	160. Wd Mar 25, '56	Deut 28:46-50	OC 28
142. Wd Feb 12, '56	Deut 25:1-4	OC 28	161. Th Mar 26, '56	Deut 28:49-58	OC 28
143. Th Feb 13, '56	Deut 25:5-12	OC 28	162. Fr Mar 27, '56	Deut 28:59-64	OC 28
144. Fr Feb 14, '56	Deut 25:13-19	OC 28	163. S. Mar 28, '56	Deut 28:65-68	OC 28
S. Feb 15, '56 none					
			164. M. Apr 6, '56	Deut 29:1-4	OC 28
145. Wd Feb 19, '56	Deut 26:1-6	OC 28	165. Tu Apr 7, '56	Deut 29:5-8	OC 28
			166. Wd Apr 8, '56	Deut 29:9-18	OC 28
146. M. Feb 24, '56	Deut 26:5-12	OC 28	167. Th Apr 9, '56	Deut 29:18-21	OC 28
147. Tu Feb 25, '56	Deut 26:13-15	OC 28	168. Fr Apr 10, '56	Deut 29:22-29	OC 28
148. Wd Feb 26, '56	Deut 26:16-19	OC 28	169. S. Apr 11, '56	Deut 30:1-5	OC 28
149. Th Feb 27, '56	Deut 27:1-10	OC 28			
150. Fr Feb 28, '56	Deut 27:11-15	OC 28	170. M. Apr 20, '56	Deut 30:6-10	OC 28
S. Feb 29, '56 none			171. Tu Apr 21, '56	Deut 30:11-14	OC 28
			172. Wd Apr 22, '56	Deut 30:15-20	OC 28
151. Wd Mar 4, '56	Deut 27:16-23	OC 28	173. Th Apr 23, '56	Deut 31:1-8	OC 28

174. Fr Apr 24, '56	Deut 31:9-14	OC 28		193. Tu Jun 30, '56	Deut 33:7-8	OC 29
S. Apr 25, '56 none				194. Wd Jul 1, '56	Deut 33:9-11	OC 29
				195. Th Jul 2, '56	Deut 33:12-17	OC 29
175. M. May 4, '56	Deut 31:14-17	OC 28		196. Fr Jul 3, '56	Deut 33:18-19	OC 29
176. Tu May 5, '56	Deut 31:17-21	OC 28		197. S. Jul 4, '56	Deut 33:20-25	OC 29
177. Wd May 6, '56	Deut 31:22-30	OC 28				
178. Th May 7, '56	Deut 32:1-4	OC 28		198. M. Jul 13, '56	Deut 33:26-28	OC 29
179. Fr May 8, '56	Deut 32:5-7	OC 28		199. Tu Jul 14, '56	Deut 33:29-34:1-6	OC 29
S. May 9, '56 none				200. Wd Jul 15, '56	Deut 34:7-11	OC 29
Calvin collapses in pulpit Sun., May 10 [21:80-81]				**1557**		
				Isaiah		
				1/67. M. Feb 22, '57	Isa. 13:1-5	S. I I
180. M. Jun 1, '56	Deut 32:8-11	OC 28		2/68. Tu Feb 23, '57	Isa. 13:4-9	S. I I
181. Tu Jun 2, '56	Deut 32:11-15	OC 28		3/69. Wd Feb 24, '57	Isa. 13:10-22	S. I I
182. Wd Jun 3, '56	Deut 32:16-19	OC 28		4/70. Th Feb 25, '57	Isa. 14:1-2	S. I I
183. Th Jun 4, '56	Deut 32:20-22	OC 29		5/71. Fr Feb 26, '57	Isa. 14:3-8	S. I I
184. Fr Jun 5, '56	Deut 32:23-27	OC 29		6/72. S. Feb 27, '57	Isa. 14:9-15	S. I I
185. S. Jun 6, '56	Deut 32:28-31	OC 29				
				7/73. M. Mar 8, '57	Isa. 14:14-23	S. I I
186. M. Jun 15, '56	Deut 32:32-35	OC 29		8/74. Tu Mar 9, '57	Isa. 14:24-27	S. I I
187. Tu Jun 16, '56	Deut 32:36-39	OC 29		Wd Mar 10, '57 none		
188. Wd Jun 17, '56	Deut 32:39-43	OC 29		9/75. Th Mar 11, '57	Isa. 14:28-30	S. I I
189. Th Jun 18, '56	Deut 32:44-47	OC 29		10/76. Fr Mar 12, '57	Isa. 14:30-32	S. I I
190. Fr Jun 19, '56	Deut 32:48-52	OC 29		S. Mar 13, '57 none		
191. S. Jun 20, '56	Deut 33:1-3	OC 29				
192. M. Jun 29, '56	Deut 33:3-7	OC 29				

			28/94. S. Apr 24, '57	Isa. 22:4-11	S. I I	
11/77. M. Mar 22, '57	Isa. 15:1-9	S. I I				
12/78. Tu Mar 23, '57	Isa. 16:1-4	S. I I	Mon-Tues May 3-4, none			
13/79. Wd Mar 24, '57	Isa. 16:5-6	S. I I	29/95. Wd May 5, '57	Isa. 22:12-14	S. I I	
14/80. Th Mar 25, '57	Isa. 16:7-14	S. I I	30/96. Th May 6, '57	Isa. 22:15-18	S. I I	
15/81. Fr Mar 26, '57	Isa. 17:1-8	S. I I	31/97. Fr May 7, '57	Isa. 22:20-25	S. I I	
16/82. S. Mar 27, '57	Isa. 17:9-14	S. I I	32/98. S. May 8, '57	Isa. 23:1-9	S. I I	
17/83. M. Apr 5, '57	Isa. 18:1-4	S. I I	M. May 17, '57 none			
18/84. Tu Apr 6, '57	Isa. 18:5-7	S. I I	33/99. Tu May 18, '57	Isa. 23:10-14	S. I I	
19/85. Wd Apr 7, '57	Isa. 19:1-5	S. I I	Wd May 19, '57 none			
20/86. Th Apr 8, '57	Isa. 19:6-12	S. I I	34/100. Th May 20, '57	Isa. 23:15-18	S. I I	
21/87. Fr Apr 9, '57	Isa. 19:13-18	S. I I	Fr May 21, '57 none			
22/88. S. Apr 10, '57	Isa. 19:19-21	S. I I	35/101. S. May 22, '57	Isa. 23:17-18	S. I I	
23/89. M. Apr 19, '57	Isa. 19:23-25	S. I I	36/102. M. May 31, '57	Isa. 24:1-5	S. I I	
24/90. Tu Apr 20, '57	Isa. 20:1-6	S. I I	37/103. Tu Jun 1, '57	Isa. 24:6-13	S. I I	
25/91. Wd Apr 21, '57	Isa. 21:1-8	S. I I	38/104. Wd Jun 2, '57	Isa. 24:14-16	S. I I	
26/92. Th Apr 22, '57	Isa. 21:9-17	S. I I	39/105. Th Jun 3, '57	Isa. 24:17-22	S. I I	
27/93. Fr Apr 23, '57	Isa. 22:1-4	S. I I	40/106. Fr Jun 4, '57	Isa. 24:23-25:2	S. I I	
			41/107. S. Jun 5, '57	Isa. 25:2-6	S. I I	

42/108. M. Jun 7, '57	Isa. 25:7-10	S. I I
43/109. M. Jun 14, '57	Isa. 25:9-26:2	S. I I
44/110. Tu Jun 15, '57	Isa. 26:3-7	S. I I
45/111. Wd Jun 16, '57	Isa. 26:8-9	S. I I
46/112. Th Jun 17, '57	Isa. 26:10-13	S. I I
47/113. Fr Jun 18, '57	Isa. 26:13-19	S. I I
48/114. S. Jun 19, '57	Isa. 26:17-21	S. I I
49/115. M. Jun 28, '57	Isa. 26:20-21	S. I I
50/116. Tu Jun 29, '57	Isa. 27:1-5	S. I I
51/117. Wd Jun 30, '57	Isa. 27:6-9	S. I I
52/118. Th Jul 1, '57	Isa. 27:10-13	S. I I
53/119. Fr Jul 2, '57	Isa. 28:1-4	S. I I
54/120. S. Jul 3, '57	Isa. 28:5-10	S. I I
55/121. M. Jul 12, '57	Isa. 28:11-13	S. I I
56/122. Tu Jul 13, '57	Isa. 28:14-15	S. I I
57/123. Wd Jul 14, '57	Isa. 28:16-20	S. I I
58/124. Th Jul 15, '57	Isa. 28:19-22	S. I I
59/125. Fr Jul 16, '57	Isa. 28:23-29	S. I I
60/126. S. Jul 17, '57	Isa. 29:1-7	S. I I
61/127. M. Jul 26, '57	Isa. 29:8-10	S. I I
62/128. Tu Jul 27, '57	Isa. 29:11-14	S. I I
63/129. Wd Jul 28, '57	Isa. 29:15-16	S. I I
64/130. Th Jul 29, '57	Isa. 29:17-20	S. I I
65/131. Fr Jul 30, '57	Isa. 29:20-21	S. I I
66/132. S. Jul 31, '57	Isa. 29:22-24	S. I I
1/133. Wd Aug 4, '57	Isa. 30:1-3	S. III
2/134. M. Aug 9, '57	Isa. 30:4-9	S. III
3/135. Tu Aug 10, '57	Isa. 30:9-11	S. III
4/136. Wd Aug 11, '57	Isa. 30:12-16	S. III
5/137. Th Aug 12, '57	Isa. 30:17-19	S. III
6/138. Fr Aug 13, '57	Isa. 30:20-24	S. III
7/139. S. Aug 14, '57	Isa. 30:25-28	S. III
8/140. M. Aug 23, '57	Isa. 30:28-33	S. III
9/141. Tu Aug 24, '57	Isa. 31:1-3	S. III

10/142. Wd Aug 25, '57	Isa. 31:1b-5	S. III
11/143. Th Aug 26, '57	Isa. 31:6-9	S. III
12/144. Fr Aug 27, '57	Isa. 32:1-5	S. III
13/145. S. Aug 28, '57	Isa. 32:5-8	S. III
14/146. Wd Sep 1, '57	Isa. 32:11-16	S. III
15/147. M. Sep 6, '57	Isa. 32:17-20	S. III
16/148. Tu Sep 7, '57	Isa. 33:1-4	S. III
17/149. Wd Sep 8, '57	Isa. 33:5-10	S. III
18/150. Th Sep 9, '57	Isa. 33:9-14a	S. III
19/151. Fr Sep 10, '57	Isa. 33:14b-16	S. III
20/152. S. Sep 11, '57	Isa. 33:17-24	S. III
21/153. M. Sep 20, '57	Isa. 33:21-24	S. III
22/154. Tu Sep 21, '57	Isa. 34:1-3	S. III
23/155. Wd Sep 22, '57	Isa. 34:4-8	S. III
24/156. Th Sep 23, '57	Isa. 34:9-13	S. III
25/157. Fr Sep 24, '57	Isa. 34:14-35:2	S. III
26/158. S. Sep 25, '57	Isa. 35:3-6a	S. III

27/159. M. Oct 4, '57	Isa. 35:5-7	S. III
28/160. Tu Oct 5, '57	Isa. 35:8-10	S. III
29/161. Wd Oct 6, '57	Isa. 36:1-5	S. III
30/162. Th Oct 7, '57	Isa. 36:4-8	S. III
31/163. Fr Oct 8, '57	Isa. 36:9-17	S. III
32/164. S. Oct 9, '57	Isa. 36:18-22	S. III
33/165. Wd Oct 13, '57	Isa. 37:1-4	S. III
34/166. M. Oct 18, '57	Isa. 37:5-7	S. III
35/167. Tu Oct 19, '57	Isa. 37:8-13	S. III
36/168. Wd Oct 20, '57	Isa. 37:14-17	S. III
37/169. Th Oct 21, '57	Isa. 37:18-22	S. III
38/170. Fr Oct 22, '57	Isa. 37:23-27	S. III
39/171. S. Oct 23, '57	Isa. 37:28-30	S. III
40/172. M. Nov 1, '57	Isa. 37:31-35	S. III
41/173. Tu Nov 2, '57	Isa. 37:36-38	S. III
42/174. Wd Nov 3, '57	Isa. 38:1-3	S. III
43/175. Th Nov 4, '57	Isa. 38:4-8	S. III

44/176. Fr Nov 5, '57	Isa. 38:9-12a	S. III		61/193. Th Dec 16, '57	Isa. 41:2-6	S. III
45/177. S. Nov 6, '57	Isa. 38:12-15a	S. III		62/194. Fr Dec 17, '57	Isa. 41:5-9a	S. III
				63/195. S. Dec 18, '57	Isa. 41:9b-14	S. III
46/178. M. Nov 15, '57	Isa. 38:15-17	S. III				
47/179. Tu Nov 16, '57	Isa. 38:18-22	S. III		64/196. M. Dec 27, '57	Isa. 41:15-20	S. III
48/180. Wd Nov 17, '57	Isa. 39:1-2	S. III		65/197. Tu Dec 28, '57	Isa. 41:21-24	S. III
49/181. Th Nov 18, '57	Isa. 39:3-7	S. III		66/198. Wd Dec 29, '57	Isa. 41:23-25	S. III
50/182. Fr Nov 19, '57	Isa. 39:8	S. III		67/199. Th Dec 30, '57	Isa. 41:26-29	S. III
51/183. S. Nov 20, '57	Isa. 40:1-2	S. III				
				1/200.Fr Dec 31, '57	Isa. 42:1	Ms. fr.19
52/184. M. Nov 29, '57	Isa. 40:2-5	S. III				
53/185. Tu Nov 30, '57	Isa. 40:6-8	S. III		**1558**		
54/186. Wd Dec 1, '57	Isa. 40:6-10	S. III		2/201. Sa, Jan 1, '58	Isa. 42:3-5	Ms. Fr.19
55/187. Th Dec 2, '57	Isa. 40:9-11	S. III				
56/188. Fr Dec 3, '57	Isa. 40:12-14	S. III		3/202.Mn, Jan 10, '58	Isa. 42:6-9	Ms. Fr.19
57/189. S. Dec 4, '57	Isa. 40:15-22	S. III		4/203. Tu, Jan 11, '58	Isa. 42:10-14	Ms. Fr.19
				5/204. Wd, Jan 12, '58	Isa. 42:15-20	Ms. Fr.19
58/190. M. Dec 13, '57	Isa. 40:22-25	S. III		6/205. Th, Jan 13, '58	Isa. 42:21-25	Ms. Fr.19
59/191. Tu Dec 14, '57	Isa. 40:26-29	S. III		7/206. Fr, Jan 14, '58	Isa. 43:1-4	Ms. Fr.19
60/192. Wd Dec 15, '57	Isa. 40:30-41:1	S. III		8/207. Sa, Jan 15, '58	Isa. 43:5-8	Ms. Fr.19

9/208. Wd, Jan 19, '58	Isa. 43:9-12	Ms. Fr.19
10/209. Mn, Jan 24, '58	Isa. 43:10-13	Ms. Fr.19
11/210. Tu, Jan 25, '58	Isa. 43:14-20	Ms. Fr.19
12/211. Wd, Jan 26, '58	Isa. 43:20-25	Ms. Fr.19
13/212. Th, Jan 27, '58	Isa. 43:23-28	Ms. Fr.19
14/213. Fr, Jan 28, '58	Isa. 44:1-4	Ms. Fr.19
15/214. Sa, Jan 29, '58	Isa. 44:5-8	Ms. Fr.19
16/215. Mn, Feb 7, '58	Isa. 44:9-12	Ms. Fr.19
17/216. Tu, Feb 8, '58	Isa. 44:12-17	Ms. Fr.19
18/217. Wd, Feb 9, '58	Isa. 44:18-21	Ms. Fr.19
19/218. Th, Feb 10, '58	Isa. 44:20-23	Ms. Fr.19
20/219. Fr, Feb 11, '58	Isa. 44:24-28	Ms. Fr.19
21/220. Sa, Feb 12, '58	Isa. 45:1-4	Ms. Fr.19
22/221. Mn, Feb 21, '58	Isa. 45:5-8	Ms. Fr.19
23/222. Tu, Feb 22, '58	Isa. 45:9-11	Ms. Fr.19
24/223. Wd, Feb 23, '58	Isa. 45:13-15	Ms. Fr.19
25/224. Th, Feb 24, '58	Isa. 45:16-18	Ms. Fr.19
26/225. Fr, Feb 25, '58	Isa. 45:19-22	Ms. Fr.19
27/226. Sa, Feb 26, '58	Isa. 45:23-25	Ms. Fr.19
Three week gap		
28/227. Mn, Mar 21, '58	Isa. 46:1-4	Ms. Fr.19
29/228. Tu, Mar 22, '58	Isa. 46:5-8	Ms. Fr.19
30/229. Wd, Mar 23, '58	Isa. 46:9-13	Ms. Fr.19
31/230. Th, Mar 24, '58	Isa. 47:1-5	Ms. Fr.19
32/231. Fr, Mar 25, '58	Isa. 47:6-9	Ms. Fr.19
33/232. Sa, Mar 26, '58	Isa. 47:10-15	Ms. Fr.19
Three week gap		
34/233. Mn, Apr 18, '58	Isa. 48:1-2	Ms. Fr.19
35/234. Tu, Apr 19, '58	Isa. 48:3-8	Ms. Fr.19
36/235. Wd, Apr 20, '58	Isa. 48:9-11	Ms. Fr.19
37/236. Th, Apr 21, '58	Isa. 48:12-14	Ms. Fr.19
38/237. Fr, Apr 22, '58	Isa. 48:14b-17	Ms. Fr.19
39/238. Sa, Apr 23, '58	Isa. 48:18-22	Ms. Fr.19

40/239. Mn, May 2, '58	Isa. 49:1-3	Ms. Fr.19		57/256. Mn, Jun 13, '58	Isa. 51:19-23	Ms. Fr.19
41/240. Tu, May 3, '58	Isa. 49:4-5	Ms. Fr.19				
42/241. Wd, May 4, '58	Isa. 49:6-7	Ms. Fr.19		1/257.Tu Jun 14, '58	Isa. 52:1-4	S. IV
43/242. Th, May 5, '58	Isa. 49:8-9a	Ms. Fr.19		2/258. Wd Jun15, '58	Isa. 52:5-7	S. IV
44/243. Fr, May 6, '58	Isa. 49:9b-15	Ms. Fr.19		3/259. Th Jun 16, '58	Isa. 52:8-10	S. IV
				4/260. Fr Jun 17, '58	Isa. 52:11-12	S. IV
45/244. Mn, May 16, '58	Isa. 49:16-18a	Ms. Fr.19		5/261. S. Jun 18, '58	Isa. 52:13-53:1	S. IV
46/245. Tu, May 17, '58	Isa. 49:18b-23	Ms. Fr.19				
47/246. Wd, May 18, '58	Isa 49:23-25	Ms. Fr.19		6/262. M. Jun 27, '58	Isa. 53:1-4	S. IV
48/247. Th, May 19, '58	Isa. 50:1-3	Ms. Fr.19		7/263. Tu Jun 28, '58	Isa. 53:4-7	S. IV
49/248. Fr, May 20, '58	Isa. 50:4-7	Ms. Fr.19		8/264. Wd Jun 29, '58	Isa. 53:7-8	S. IV
50/249. Sa, May 21, '58	Isa. 50:8-11	Ms. Fr.19		9/265. Th Jun 30, '58	Isa. 53:9-10	S. IV
				10/266. Fr Jul 1, '58	Isa. 53:11	S. IV
51/250. Mn, May 30, '58	Isa. 51:1-3	Ms. Fr.19		11/267. S. Jul 2, '58	Isa. 53:12	S. IV
52/251. Tu, May 31, '58	Isa. 51:4-6	Ms. Fr.19				
53/252. Wd, Jun 1, '58	Isa. 51:7-8	Ms. Fr.19		12/268. M. Jul 11, '58	Isa. 54:1-4	S. IV
54/253. Th, Jun 2, '58	Isa. 51:9-11	Ms. Fr.19		13/269. Tu Jul 12, '58	Isa. 54:5-8	S. IV
55/254. Fr, Jun 3, '58	Isa. 51:12-16	Ms. Fr.19		14/270. Wd Jul 13, '58	Isa. 54:9-11	S. IV
56/255. Sa, Jun 4, '58	Isa. 51:17-22	Ms. Fr.19		15/271. Th Jul 14, '58	Isa. 54:11-14	S. IV
				16/272. Fr Jul 15, '58	Isa. 54:14-16	S. IV

17/273. S. Jul 16, '58	Isa. 54:17	S. IV	34/290. Fr Aug 26, '58	Isa. 58:3-5	S. IV
			35/291. S. Aug 27, '58	Isa. 58:6-9	S. IV
18/274. M. Jul 25, '58	Isa. 55:1-2	S. IV			
19/275. Tu Jul 26, '58	Isa. 55:2-4	S. IV	36/292. M. Sep 5, '58	Isa. 58:9-11	S. IV
20/276. Wd Jul 27, '58	Isa. 55:5-8	S. IV	37/293. Tu Sep 6, '58	Isa. 58:12-14	S. IV
21/277. Th Jul 28, '58	Isa. 55:8-13	S. IV	38/294. Wd Sep 7, '58	Isa. 59:1-2	S. IV
22/278. Fr Jul 29, '58	Isa. 56:1-2	S. IV	39/295. Th Sep 8, '58	Isa. 59:3-6	S. IV
23/279. S. Jul 30, '58	Isa. 56:3-5	S. IV	40/296. Fr Sep 9, '58	Isa. 59:7-9	S. IV
			41/297. S. Sep 10, '58	Isa. 59:10-13	S. IV
24/280. M. Aug 8, '58	Isa. 56:7-8	S. IV			
25/281. Tu Aug 9, '58	Isa. 56:9-12	S. IV	42/298. M. Sep 19, '58	Isa. 59:14-16	S. IV
26/282. Wd Aug 10, '58	Isa. 57:1-2	S. IV	43/299. Tu Sep 20, '58	Isa. 59:17-19	S. IV
27/283. Th Aug 11, '58	Isa. 57:3-4	S. IV	44/300. Wd Sep 21, '58	Isa. 59:20-21	S. IV
28/284. Fr Aug 12, '58	Isa. 57:5-9	S. IV	1/301. Th Sep 22, '58	Isa. 60:1-3	S. IV
29/285. S. Aug 13, '58	Isa. 57:9-11	S. IV	2/302. Fr Sep 23, '58	Isa. 60:3-7	S. IV
			3/303. S. Sep 24, '58	Isa. 60:7-12	S. IV
30/286. M. Aug 22, '58	Isa. 57:12-14	S. IV			
31/287. Tu Aug 23, '58	Isa. 57:15-18	S. IV	4/304. M. Oct 3, '58	Isa. 60:13-16	S. IV
32/288. Wd Aug 24, '58	Isa. 57:18-21	S. IV	5/305. Tu Oct 4, '58	Isa. 60:17-20	S. IV
33/289. Th Aug 25, '58	Isa. 58:1-3	S. IV	6/306. Wd Oct 5, '58	Isa. 60:20-22	S. IV

7/307. Th Oct 6, '58	Isa. 61:1	S. IV	23/323. Tu Jul 11, '59	Isa. 64:4-5	S. IV
8/308. Fr Oct 7, '58	Isa. 61:1-5	S. IV	24/324. Wd Jul 12, '59	Isa. 64:6-7	S. IV
9/309. S. Oct 8, '58	Isa. 61:6-8	S. IV	25/325. Th Jul 13, '59	Isa. 64:8-11	S. IV
Calvin ill for Many months [21:87, 89]			26/326. Fr Jul 14, '59	Isa. 65:1-3	S. IV
			27/327. S. Jul 15, '59	Isa. 65:4-7	S. IV
1559					
10/310. M. Jun 12, '59	Isa. 61:10-11	S. IV	28/328. M. Jul 24, '59	Isa. 65:7-9	S. IV
11/311. Tu Jun 13, '59	Isa. 62:1-2	S. IV	29/329. Tu Jul 25, '59	Isa. 65:10-12	S. IV
12/312. Wd Jun 14, '59	Isa. 62:3-7	S. IV	30/330. Wd Jul 26, '59	Isa. 65:13-15	S. IV
13/313. Th Jun 15, '59	Isa. 62:6-8	S. IV	31/331. Th Jul 27, '59	Isa. 65:16-18	S. IV
14/314. Fr Jun 16, '59	Isa. 62:8-10	S. IV	Fr-S. Jul 28-29 none		
15/315. S. Jun 17, '59	Isa. 62:11-12	S. IV			
			32/332. M. Aug 7, '59	Isa. 65:18-21	S. IV
16/316. M. Jun 26, '59	Isa. 63:1-4	S. IV	33/333. Tu Aug 8, '59	Isa. 66:18-21	S. IV
17/317. Tu Jun 27, '59	Isa. 63:3-7	S. IV	34/334. Wd Aug 9, '59	Isa. 66:1-2	S. IV
18/318. Wd Jun 28, '59	Isa. 63:8-9	S. IV	35/335. Th Aug 10, '59	Isa. 66:3-4	S. IV
19/319. Th Jun 29, '59	Isa. 63:10-14	S. IV	36/336. Fr Aug 11, '59	Isa. 66:5-6	S. IV
20/320. Fr Jun 30, '59	Isa. 63:15-16	S. IV	37/337. S. Aug 12, '59	Isa. 66:7-11	S. IV
21/321. S. Jul1, '59	Isa. 63:17-19	S. IV			
			38/338. M. Aug 21, '59	Isa. 66:12-14	S. IV
22/322. M. Jul 10, '59	Isa. 63:19-64:3	S. IV			

39/339. Tu Aug 22, '59	Isa. 66:15-18	S. IV
40/340. Wd Aug 23, '59	Isa. 66:18-19	S. IV
41/341. Th Aug 24, '59	Isa. 66:20-21	S. IV
42/342. Fr Aug 25, '59	Isa. 66:22-23	S. IV
43/343. S. Aug 26, '59	Isa. 66:24	S. IV
Genesis		
1. M. Sep 4, '59	Gen 1:1-2	S. XI
2. Tu Sep 5, '59	Gen 1:3-5	S. XI
3. Wd Sep 6, '59	Gen 1:6-13	S. XI
4. Th Sep 7, '59	Gen 1:14-19	S. XI
5. Fr Sep 8, '59	Gen 1:20-25	S. XI
6. S. Sep 9, '59	Gen 1:26-28	S. XI
7. M. Sep 18, '59	Gen 1:29-31	S. XI
8. Tu Sep 19, '59	Gen 2:1-6	S. XI
9. Wd Sep 20, '59	Gen 2:7-15	S. XI
Th Sep 21, '59 none		
10. Fr Sep 22, '59	Gen 2:15-17	S. XI
11. S. Sep 23, '59	Gen 2:18-21	S. XI
12. M. Oct 2, '59	Gen 2:22-24	S. XI
13. Tu Oct 3, '59	Gen 3:1-3	S. XI
14. Wd Oct 4, '59	Gen 3:4-6	S. XI
15. Th Oct 5, '59	Gen 3:7-10	S. XI
16. Fr Oct 6, '59	Gen 3:11-13	S. XI

17. S. Oct 7, '59	Gen 3:14-16	S. XI
18. M. Oct 16, '59	Gen 3:17-18	S. XI
19. Tu Oct 17, '59	Gen 3:19-22a	S. XI
20. Wd Oct 18, '59	Gen 3:22-24	S. XI
21. Th Oct 19, '59	Gen 4:1-5	S. XI
22. Fr Oct 20, '59	Gen 4:5-7	S. XI
23. S. Oct 21, '59	Gen 4:8-10	S. XI
24. M. Oct 30, '59	Gen 4:10-12	S. XI
25. Tu Oct 31, '59	Gen 4:12-14	S. XI
26. Wd Nov 1, '59	Gen 4:15-18	S. XI
27. Th Nov 2, '59	[Gen 4:19-22]	missing
28. Fr Nov 3, '59	Gen 4:23-26	S. XI
29. S. Nov 4, '59	Gen 5:1-25	S. XI
30. M. Nov 13, '59	Gen 5:21-32	S. XI
31. Tu Nov 14, '59	Gen 6:1-3	S. XI
32. Wd Nov 15, '59	Gen 6:1-4	S. XI
Th Nov 16, '59 none		
33. Fr Nov 17, '59	Gen 6:5-8	S. XI
34. S. Nov 18, '59	Gen 6:9-13	S. XI
35. M. Dec 11, '59	Gen 6:13-22	S. XI
36. Tu Dec 12, '59	Gen 7:1-5	S. XI
37. Wd Dec 13, '59	Gen 7:6-10	S. XI
38. Th Dec 14, '59	Gen 7:11-24	S. XI
39. Fr Dec 15, '59	Gen 8:1-4	S. XI

40. S. Dec 16, '59	Gen 8:6-19	S. XI		62/1. Wd Feb 21, '60	Gen 14:1-13	S. XI
				63. Th Feb 22, '60	Gen 14:13-17	S. XI
41. M. Dec 25, '59	Gen 8:20-22	S. XI		64. Fr Feb 23, '60	Gen 14:18-20	S. XI
				65. S. Feb 24, '60	Gen 14:20-24	S. XI
1560						
42. M. Jan 8, '60	Gen 9:1-3	S. XI		66/5. M. Mar 4, '60	Gen 15:1-4	S. XI
43. Tu Jan 9, '60	Gen 9:3-7	S. XI		67. Tu Mar 5, '60	Gen 15:4-6	S. XI
44. Wd Jan 10, '60	Gen 9:8-17	S. XI		68. Wd Mar 6, '60	Gen 15:6	S. XI
45. Th Jan 11, '60	Gen 9:18-21	S. XI		69. Th Mar 7, '60	Gen 15:6	S. XI
46. Fr Jan 12, '60	Gen 9:22-29	S. XI		70. Fr Mar 8, '60	Gen 15:6-7	S. XI
47. S. Jan 13, '60	Gen 9:24-29	S. XI		S. Mar 9, '60 none		
48. M. Jan 22, '60	Gen 10:1-32	S. XI		71/10. M. Mar 18, '60	Gen 15:8-10	S. XI
49. Tu Jan 23, '60	Gen 11:1-4	S. XI		72/11. Tu Mar 19, '60	Gen 15:11-14	S. XI
50. Wd Jan 24, '60	Gen 11:5-9	S. XI		73/12. Wd Mar 20, '60	Gen 15:15-16	S. XI
51. Th Jan 25, '60	Gen 11:10-31	S. XI		74/13. Th Mar 21, '60	Gen 15:17-21	S. XI
52. Fr Jan 26, '60	Gen 11:31–12:1	S. XI		75/14. Fr Mar 22, '60	Gen 16:1-4	S. XI
53. S. Jan 27, '60	Gen 12:1-3	S. XI		76/15. S. Mar 23, '60	Gen 16:5-9	S. XI
54. M. Feb 5, '60	Gen 12:4-7	S. XI		77/16. M. Apr 1, '60	Gen 16:11-16	S. XI
55. Tu Feb 6, '60	Gen 12:5-9	S. XI		78/17. Tu Apr 2, '60	Gen 17:1-3	S. XI
56. Wd Feb 7, '60	Gen 12:10-13	S. XI		79/18. Wd Apr 3, '60	Gen 17:4-8	S. XI
57. Th Feb 8, '60	Gen 12:11-16	S. XI		80/19. Th Apr 4, '60	Gen 17:9-13	S. XI
58. Fr Feb 9, '60	Gen 12:16-20	S. XI				
59. S. Feb 10, '60	Gen 13:1-7	S. XI				
60. M. Feb 19, '60	Gen 13:8-13	S. XI				
61. Tu Feb 20, '60	Gen 13:14-18	S. XI				

81/20. Fr Apr 5, '60	Gen 17:10-16	S. XI
82/21. S. Apr 6, '60	Gen 17:17-22	S. XI
83/22. M. Apr 15, '60	Gen 17:22-26	S. XI
84/23. Tu Apr 16, '60	Gen 18:1-8	S. XI
85/24. Wd Apr 17, '60	Gen 18:9-15	S. XI
86/25. Th Apr 18, '60	Gen 18:16-21	S. XI
87/26. Fr Apr 19, '60	Gen 18:22-26	S. XI
88/27. S. Apr 20, '60	Gen 18:24-33	S. XI
89/28. M. Apr 29, '60	Gen 19:1-5	S. XI
90/29. Tu Apr 30, '60	Gen 19:6-9	S. XI
91/30. Wd May 1, '60	Gen 19:10-14	S. XI
92/31. Th May 2, '60	Gen 19:15-17	S. XI
93/32. Fr May 3, '60	Gen 19:17-24	S. XI
94/33. S. May 4, '60	Gen 19:24-30	S. XI
95/34. M. May 13, '60	Gen 19:31-38	S. XI
96/35. Tu May 14, '60	Gen 20:1-4	S. XI
97/36. Wd May 15, '60	Gen 20:4-7	S. XI

1.S. Jun 1, '60	Gen 21:33–22:2	OC 23
2. M. Jun 10, '60	Gen 22:3-8	OC 23
3. Tu Jun 11, '60	Gen 22:9-14	OC 23
[June 12-July13, '60]		
1. [M. Jul 22, '60]	Gen 25:11-21	OC 58
2. [Tu Jul 23, '60]	Gen 25:20-22	OC 58
3. [Wd Jul 24, '60]	Gen 25:20-22	OC 58
4. [Th Jul 25, '60]	Gen 25:23-27	OC 58
5. [Fr Jul 26, '60]	Gen 25:28-33	OC 58
6. [S. Jul 27, '60]	Gen 26:1-5	OC 58
7. [Tu Jul 31, '60]	Gen 26:6-10	OC 58
8. [M. Aug 5, '60]	Gen 26:11-21	OC 58
9. [Tu Aug 6, '60]	Gen 26:23-25	OC 58
10. [Wd Aug 7, '60]	Gen 26:26-35	OC 58
11. [Th Aug 8, '60]	Gen 27:1-7	OC 58
12. [Fr Aug 9, '60]	Gen 27:11-19	OC 58
13. [S. Aug 10, '60]	Gen 27:29-36	OC 58
1561		
First Samuel		
1. Fr Aug 8, '61	1 Sam 1:1-5	OC 29
2. S. Aug 9, '61	1 Sam 1:6-8	OC 29
3. [M. Aug 18, '61]	1 Sam 1:11-18	OC 29
4. [Tu Aug 19, '61]	1 Sam 1:18-28	OC 29

5. [Wd Aug 20, '61]	1 Sam 2:1-3	OC 29		24. [Th Oct 2, '61]	1 Sam 7:1-3	OC 29
6. [Th Aug 21, '61]	1 Sam 2:4-8	OC 29		25. [Fr Oct 3, '61]	1 Sam 7:5-10	OC 29
7. [Fr Aug 22, '61]	1 Sam 2:8-11	OC 29		26. [S. Oct 4, '61]	1 Sam 7:12-17	OC 29
8. [S. Aug 23, '61]	1 Sam 2:11-17	OC 29		Absent from consistory Oct 9 [21:762]		
9. [M. Sep 1, '61]	1 Sam 2:18-25	OC 29				
10. [Tu Sep 2, '61]	1 Sam 2:25-30	OC 29		27. [M. Oct 13, '61]	1 Sam 8:1-6	OC 29[4]
11. [Wd Sep 3, '61]	1 Sam 2:27-30	OC 29		28. [Tu Oct 14, '61]	1 Sam 8:7-10	OC 29
12. [Th Sep 4, '61]	1 Sam 2:31-36	OC 29		Absent from consistory Oct 16 [21:762]		
13. [Fr Sep 5, '61]	1 Sam 3:1-10	OC 29				
14. [S. Sep 6, '61]	1 Sam 3:11-17	OC 29				
				29. [M. Oct 27, '61]	1 Sam 8:11-22	OC 29
15. [M. Sep 15, '61]	1 Sam 3:18-21	OC 29		30. [Tu Oct 28, '61]	1 Sam 9:1-16	OC 29
16. [Tu Sep 16, '61]	1 Sam 4:1-4	OC 29		Absent from consistory Oct 30 & Nov 6 [21:764]		
17. [Wd Sep 17, '61]	1 Sam 4:5-12	OC 29				
18. [Th Sep 18, '61]	1 Sam 4:13-22	OC 29				
19. [Fr Sep 19, '61]	1 Sam 5:1-6	OC 29		31. [M. Nov 10, '61]	1 Sam 9:17-25	OC 29
20. [S. Sep 20, '61]	1 Sam 5:7-12	OC 29		32. [Tu Nov 11, '61]	1 Sam 9:26–10:4	OC 29
				33. [Wd Nov 12, '61]	1 Sam 10:5-7	OC 29
21. [M. Sep 29, '61]	1 Sam 6:1-5	OC 29		34. [Th Nov 13, '60]	1 Sam 10:8-13	OC 29
22. [Tu Sep 30, '61]	1 Sam 6:6-12	OC 29		35. [Fr Nov 14, '60]	1 Sam 10:14-21	OC 29
23. [Wd Oct 1, '61]	1 Sam 6:13-21	OC 29		36. [S. Nov 15, '60]	1 Sam 10:22-27	OC 29

4   This distribution of the sermons for October and early November is hypothetical, but it fits with other patterns of Calvin's work, e.g., see 2 Sam sermons in Oct '62, where Merlin takes over Calvin's week on Tu and Calvin then does the next week. In this case, to fit the number of sermons to the time, it is hypothesized that Calvin tried to keep to his regular rotation but had to break off during the week. He was perhaps ill during his off week (Oct 6-11) but tried to do his regular preaching the next week, and had to break off again. He was able to attend consistory during the off week (Oct. 20-25) so he resumed work on the following Mn, but was again unable to complete the week and was still unwell the following week. Then, when he was able to return to preaching, he took up work again on his regular schedule.

37. [M. Nov 24, '61]	1 Sam 11:1-5	OC 29	60. [S. Jan 1-0, '62]	1 Sam 17:1-11	OC 30
38. [Tu Nov 25, '61]	1 Sam 11:6-10	OC 29			
39. [Wd Nov 26, '61]	1 Sam 11:11-15	OC 29	61. [M. Jan19, '62]	1 Sam 17:12-27	OC 30
40. [Th Nov 27, '61]	1 Sam 12:1-5	OC 29	62. [Tu Jan 20, '62]	1 Sam 17:28-37	OC 30
41. [Fr Nov 28, '61]	1 Sam 12:6-10	OC 29	63. [Wd Jan 21, '62]	1 Sam 17:38-45	OC 30
42. [S. Nov 29, '61]	1 Sam 12:12-18	OC 29	64. [Th Jan 22, '62]	1 Sam 17:46-47	OC 30
			65. [Fr Jan 23, '62]	1 Sam 17:48-58	OC 30
43. [M. Dec 8, '61]	1 Sam 12:19-22	OC 29	66. [S. Jan 24, '62]	1 Sam 18:1-9	OC 30
44. [Tu Dec 9, '61]	1 Sam 12:21-25	OC 29			
45. [Wd Dec 10, '61]	1 Sam 13:1-7	OC 30	67. [M. Feb 2, '62]	1 Sam 18:10-16	OC 30
46. [Th Dec 11, '61]	1 Sam 13:8-14	OC 30	68. [Tu Feb 3, '62]	1 Sam 18:17-21	OC 30
47. [Fr Dec 12, '61]	1 Sam 13:15–14:17	OC 30	69. [Wd Feb 4, '62]	1 Sam 18:22-30	OC 30
48. [S. Dec 13, '61]	1 Sam 14:18-34	OC 30	70. [Th Feb 5, '62]	1 Sam 19:1-7	OC 30
			71. [Fr Feb 6, '62]	1 Sam 19:8-16	OC30
49. [M. Dec 22, '61]	1 Sam 14:35-40	OC 30	72. [S. Feb 7, '62]	1 Sam 19:17-21	OC 30
50. [Tu Dec 23, '61]	1 Sam 14:41-52	OC 30			
51. [Wd Dec 24, '61]	1 Sam 15:1-7	OC 30	73. [M. Feb 16, '62]	1 Sam 19:22–20:3	OC 30
52. [Th Dec 25, '61]	1 Sam 15:8-11	OC 30	74. [Tu Feb 17, '62]	1 Sam 20:4-11	OC 30
53. [Fr Dec 26, '61]	1 Sam 15:12-19	OC 30	75. [Wd Feb 18, '62]	1 Sam 20:12-23	OC 30
54. [S. Dec 27, '61]	1 Sam 15:20-23	OC 30	76. [Th Feb 19, '62]	1 Sam 20:24-42	OC 30
			77. [Fr Feb 20, '62]	1 Sam 21:1-5	OC 30
1562			78. [S. Feb 21, '62]	1 Sam 21:7-15	OC 30
55. [M. Jan 5, '62]	1 Sam 15:24-29	OC 30	Calvin & Merlin (alternate) change rotation.		
56. [Tu Jan 6, '62]	1 Sam 15:30-35	OC 30	79. [M. Mar 9, '62]	1 Sam 22:1-5	OC 30
57. [Wd Jan7, '62]	1 Sam 16:1-2	OC 30	80. [Tu Mar 10, '62]	1 Sam 22:6-10	OC 30
58. [Th Jan 8, '62]	1 Sam 16:3-12	OC 30	81. [Wd Mar 11, '62]	1 Sam 22:11-23	OC 30
59. [Fr Jan 9, '62]	1 Sam 16:13-23	OC 30	82. [Th Mar 12, '62]	1 Sam 23:1-6	OC 30

83. [Fr Mar 13, '62]	1 Sam 23:7-18	OC 30
84. [S. Mar 14, '62]	1 Sam 23:19-28	OC 30
85. [M. Apr 6, '62]	1 Sam 24:1-8	OC 30
86. [Tu Apr 7, '62]	1 Sam 24:8-13	OC 30
87. [Wd Apr 8, '62]	1 Sam 24:14-20	OC 30
88. [Th Apr 9, '62]	1 Sam 24:21–25:1	OC 30
89. [Fr Apr 10, '62]	1 Sam 25:2-13	OC 30
90. [S. Apr 11, '62]	1 Sam 25:14-28	OC 30
91. [M. Apr 20, '62]	1 Sam 25:28-35	OC 30
92. [Tu Apr 21, '62]	1 Sam 25:36-43	OC 30
93. [Wd Apr 22, '62]	1 Sam 26:1-6	OC 30
94. [Th Apr 23, '62]	1 Sam 26:7-18	OC 30
95. [Fr Apr 24, '62]	1 Sam 26:19-25	OC 30
96. [S. Apr 25, '62]	1 Sam 26:22-25	OC 30
97. [M. May 4, '62]	1 Sam 27:1-12	OC 30
98. [Tu May 5, '62]	1 Sam 28:1-7	OC 30
99. [Wd May 6, '62]	1 Sam 28:7-14	OC 30
100. [Th May 7, '62]	1 Sam 28:13-18	OC 30
101. [Fr May 8, '62]	1 Sam 28:19-25	OC 30
102. [S. May 9, '62]	1 Sam 29:1-11	OC 30
103. [M. May 18, '62]	1 Sam 30:1-8	OC 30
104. [Tu May 19, '62]	1 Sam 30:9-20	OC 30
105. [Wd May 20, '62]	1 Sam 30:21-31	OC 30

106. [Th May 21, '62]	1 Sam 31:1-6	OC 30
107. [Fr May 22, '62]	1 Sam 31:7-13	OC 30
Second Samuel		
1.S. May 23, '62	2 Sam 1:1-16	S. I
2. M. Jun 1, '62	2 Sam 1:17-20	S. I
3. Tu Jun 2, '62	2 Sam 1:21-27	S. I
4. Wd Jun 3, '62	2 Sam 2:1-7	S. I
5. Th Jun 4, '62	2 Sam 2:8-17	S. I
6. Fr Jun 5, '62	2 Sam 2:18-32	S. I
7. S. Jun 6, '62	2 Sam 3:1-11	S. I
8. M. Jun 15, '62	2 Sam 3:12-25	S. I
9. Tu Jun 16, '62	2 Sam 3:26-39	S. I
10. Wd Jun 17, '62	2 Sam 4:1-7	S. I
11. Th Jun 18, '62	2 Sam 4:8-12	S. I
Fr S. Jun 19-20 none		
12. M. Jun 29, '62	2 Sam 5:1-5	S. I
13. Tu Jun 30, '62	2 Sam 5:6-12	S. I
14. Wd Jul 1, '62	2 Sam 5:13-17	S. I
15. Th Jul 2, '62	2 Sam 5:17-25	S. I
16. Fr Jul 3, '62	2 Sam 6:1-7	S. I
17. S. Jul 4, '62	2 Sam 6:6-12	S. I
18. M. Jul 13, '62	2 Sam 6:12-19	S. I
19. Tu Jul 14, '62	2 Sam 6:20-23	S. I

20. Wd Jul 15, '62	2 Sam 7:1-7	S. I		44. Wd Sep 9, '62	2 Sam 14:1-12	S. I
21. Th Jul 16, '62	2 Sam 7:6-13	S. I		45. Th Sep 10, '62	2 Sam 14:13-18	S. I
22. Fr Jul 17, '62	2 Sam 7:13-15	S. I		46. Fr Sep 11, '62	2 Sam 14:19-27	S. I
23. S. Jul 18, '62	2 Sam 7:14-17	S. I		47. S. Sep 12, '62	2 Sam 14:28-33	S. I
24. M. Jul 27, '62	2 Sam 7:18-21	S. I		48. M. Sep 21, '62	2 Sam 15:1-7	S. I
25. Tu Jul 28, '62	2 Sam 7:22-24	S. I		49. Tu Sep 22, '62	2 Sam 15:7-15	S. I
26. Wd Jul 29, '62	2 Sam 7:25-29	S. I		50. Wd Sep 23, '62	2 Sam 15:16-26	S. I
27. Th Jul 30, '62	2 Sam 8:1-12	S. I		51. Th Sep 24, '62	2 Sam 15:25-32	S. I
28. Fr Jul 31, '62	2 Sam 8:9-18	S. I		52. Fr Sep 25, '62	2 Sam 15:32-37	S. I
29. S. Aug 1, '62	2 Sam 9:1-13	S. I		53. S. Sep 26, '62	2 Sam 16:1-6	S. I
30. M. Aug 10, '62	2 Sam 10:1-12	S. I		54. M. Oct 5, '62	2 Sam 16:5-10	S. I
31. Tu Aug 11, '62	2 Sam 10:12-19	S. I		Tu-Sa none		
32. Wd Aug 12, '62	2 Sam 11:1-4	S. I				
33. Th Aug 13, '62	2 Sam 11:5-15	S. I		55. M. Oct 12, '62	2 Sam 16:9-15	S. I
34. Fr Aug 14, '62	2 Sam 11:14-27	S. I		56. Tu Oct 13, '62	2 Sam 16:16-23	S. I
35. S. Aug 15, '62	2 Sam 12:1-10	S. I		57. Wd Oct 14, '62	2 Sam 17:1-14	S. I
				58. Th Oct 15, '62	2 Sam 17:14-29	S. I
36. M. Aug 24, '62	2 Sam 12:7-12	S. I		Fr-Sa none		
37. Tu Aug 25, '62	2 Sam 12:13	S. I				
38. Wd Aug 26, '62	2 Sam 12:13-14	S. I		59. M. Nov 9, '62	2 Sam 17:23	S. I
39. Th Aug 27, '62	2 Sam 12:15-23	S. I		60. Tu Nov 10, '62	2 Sam 18:1-8	S. I
40. Fr Aug 28, '62	2 Sam 12:24-31	S. I		61. Wd Nov 11, '62	2 Sam 18:9-18	S. I
41. S. Aug 29, '62	2 Sam 13:1-14	S. I		62. Th Nov 12, '62	2 Sam 18:19–19:1	S. I
				63. Fr Nov 13, '62	2 Sam 19:2-11	S. I
42. M. Sep 7, '62	2 Sam 13:15-22	S. I		64. S. Nov 14, '62	2 Sam 19:12-24	S. I
43. Tu Sep 8, '62	2 Sam 13:24-39	S. I				

65. M. Nov 23, '62	2 Sam 19:25-40	S. I	76. Th Jan 7, '63	2 Sam 22:28-32	S. I
66. Tu Nov 24, '62	2 Sam 19:41–20:1	S. I	77. Fr Jan 8, '63	2 Sam 22:32-42	S. I
Wd-Sa none			78. S. Jan 9, '63	2 Sam 22:43-47	S. I
67. M. Dec 7, '62	2 Sam 20:1-10	S. I	79. M. Jan 18, '63	2 Sam 22:48-51	S. I
68. Tu Dec 8, '62	2 Sam 20:8-22	S. I	80. Tu Jan 19, '63	2 Sam 23:1-4	S. I
69. Wd Dec 9, '62	2 Sam 20:16–21:1	S. I	81. Wd Jan 20, '63	2 Sam 23:4-7	S. I
70. Th Dec 10, '62	2 Sam 21:1-9	S. I	82. Th Jan 21, '63	2 Sam 23:8-39	S. I
71. Fr Dec 11, '62	2 Sam 21:10-22	S. I	83. Fr Jan 22, '63	2 Sam 24:1-4	S. I
72. S. Dec 12, '62	2 Sam 22:1-4	S. I	84. S. Jan 23, '63	2 Sam 24:3-10	S. I
73. M. Jan 4, '63	2 Sam 22:5-13	S. I	85. M. Feb 1, '63	2 Sam 24:11-14	S. I
74. Tu Jan 5, '63	2 Sam 22:12-22	S. I	86. Tu Feb 2, '63	2 Sam 24:15-18	S. I
75. Wd Jan 6, '63	2 Sam 22:22-27	S. I	87. Wd Feb 3, '63	2 Sam 24:18-25	S. I

APPENDIX EIGHT PART TWO
RECORDED/ EXTANT SERMONS ON THE NEW
TESTAMENT/ PSALMS PREACHED ON SUNDAYS
BY CALVIN

The greatest number of texts come from *lectio continua* series. Sixteenth-century printings are found in *Opera Calvini* (OC) and some are beginning to be reprinted in modern critical editions *Ioannis Calvini Sermones* (Droz). Other series have been published in the *Supplementa Calviniana* (S), while a few remain in manuscript form awaiting critical editions in SC. There are also three anthologies of special Christological observances: *Plusieurs Sermons* (1558); the *table of contents* of a lost anthology; and the collection of Psalm and feast-day texts published in the SC 7 in 1981. The first two anthologies have been described in chap. 6. Some other individual sermons were preserved in varied ways, e.g., on Heb. 13:13 which is one of the four Calvin published himself along with four Psalm texts (1552). Other sermons are hypothetical: i.e., it is known that Calvin preached on the Nativity, Easter, and Pentecost but in many cases these are not named in any extant documents. The object here is to provide as complete a chronological listing of the New Testament and Psalms texts as possible. Almost all of these were preached on Sundays.

Date	Biblical Text	Source
1545		
Before Jul 20, 1545	Ps 43	mentioned OC 12:110
1. Wd Nov 4, 1545	Ps 115:1-3	OC 32
2. Wd Nov 11, 1545	Ps 124:1-8	OC 32
1549		
Sun Apr 14, '49 **passion week** to **Easter**. Apr 21, '49	7 on Mt. [26-28]	*Table*
Pentecost. Jun 9, '49	1 on Acts 2	*Table*
Hebrews		
2. Sun morn Summer '49	Heb. 13:13	OC 8:393-408

Psalms		
1. Sun p.m. summer '49	Ps 16:4	OC 8:377-392[1]
3. Sun p.m. summer '49	Ps 27:4	OC 8:409-424
4. Sun p.m. summer '49	Ps 27:8	OC 8:425-440
@Nov 17, '49	Ps 40	mentioned OC 21:71
Acts		
1. Sun Aug 25, '49[2]	Ac 1:1-2	S. VIII
11. Sun Sep 1, '49	Ac 1:1-4	OC 48 & Plusieurs
12. Sun Sep 8, '49	Ac 1:4-5	OC 48 & Plusieurs
13. Sun Sep 15-Dec 8, '49 @Sep 15	Ac 1:6-8	OC 48 & Plusieurs
14. Sun Sep 15-Dec 8, '49 @Sep 22	Ac 1:9-11	OC 48 & Plusieurs
Sep 29-Oct 20	[Ac 1:12-2:12]	@4 lost
16. Sun Sep 15-Dec 8, '49 @Oct 27	Ac 2:13-17	OC 48 & Plusieurs

17. Sun Sep 15-Dec 8, '49 @Nov 3	Ac 2:18-21	OC 48 & Plusieurs
18. Sun Sep 15-Dec 8, '49 @Nov 10	Ac 2:22-24	OC 48 & Plusieurs
Nov 17-Dec 15	[Ac 2:25-35]	@3 lost
2. Sun Dec 22, '49	Ac 2:36-38	S. VIII
Wed Dec 25, '49 Nativity	1 on Lk. [2]	table
3. Sun Dec 29, '49	Ac 2:38	S. VIII
1550		
4. Sun Jan 19, '50	Ac 2:39-40	S. VIII
5. Sun [?] Jan 26, '50[3]	Ac 2:41-42	S. VIII
6. Sun [?] Feb 2, '50	Ac 2:43-44	S. VIII
7. Sun Feb 23, '50	Ac 3:6-13	S. VIII
8. Sun [?] Mar 9, '50	Ac 3:17-19	S. VIII
Sun Mar 30,'50 full passion week, then Easter. Apr 6, '50	8 on passion/resurrection Jn. [18-20]	table
9. Sun Apr 13, '50	Ac 4:1-4	S. VIII
10. Sun Apr 20, '50	Ac 4:5-12	S. VIII
11. Sun May 11, '50	Ac 4:16, 18-19	S. VIII

[1]   Dates for Ps 16 & Ps 27 as found in Peter & Gilmont, *Bibliotheca Calviniana* I, p.465

[2]   The numbering may be a bit confusing; it should be correlated with the source. Here most of the Acts sermons are edited in S. VIII, but a few published in anthologies are inserted, e.g., *Plusieurs sermons*.

[3]   It is unclear whether these are morning or afternoon sermons; in principle Calvin was preaching on Acts in the morning at St. Pierre and Psalms in the afternoon at St. Gervais, but a number of these (marked [?])have the Sunday afternoon prayer instead of the morning one. As is apparent on July 13, 1550, & Sept. 14, 1551, there are occasional afternoon sermons on Acts.

12. Sun May 18, '50	Ac 4:41-26	S. VIII
13. **Pentecost**.May25, '50	Ac 4:24b-31	S. VIII
14. Sun Jun 1, '50	Ac 4:32-37	S. VIII
15. Sun Jun 8, '50	Ac 5:1-6	S. VIII
Sun Jun 15 visitation in villages of Cologny & Vandoeuvre⁴		
16. Sun Jun 22, '50	Ac 5:7-15	S. VIII
17. Sun [?] Jun 29, '50	Ac 5:13-16	S. VIII
18. Sun [?] Jul 6, '50	Ac 5:17-21a	S. VIII
19. Sun Jul 13, '50	Ac 5:25-32	S. VIII
20. Sun p.m. Jul 13, '50	Ac 5:30-32	S. VIII
21. Sun Jul 20, '50	Ac 5:33-35, 38-39	S. VIII
Sun Jul 27 visit to village; Viret preached in Geneva		
22. Sun Aug 3, '50	Ac 5:40-42	S. VIII
23. Sun [?] Aug 10, '50	Ac 6:1-3	S. VIII
24. Sun Aug 17, '50	Ac 6:1-6	S. VIII
25. Sun Aug 24, '50	Ac 6:7-9	S. VIII
26. Sun Aug 31, '50	Ac 6:11-15	S. VIII
27. Sun Sep 7, '50	Ac 7:1-4a	S. VIII
28. Sun p.m. Sep 14, '50	Ac 7:4b-6	S. VIII
29. Sun Sep 21, '50	Ac 7:8-9	S. VIII
30. Sun Sep 28, '50	Ac 7:9b-16a	S. VIII

31. Sun Oct 5, '50	Ac7:15-19	S. VIII
32. Sun Oct 12, '50	Ac7:20-22	S. VIII
33. Sun Oct 19, '50	Ac 7:23-31	S. VIII
34. Sun Oct 26, '50	Ac 7:31b-35	S. VIII
35. Sun Nov 2, '50	Ac7:35-37	S. VIII
36. Sun Nov 9, '50	Ac 7:37-38	S. VIII
37. Sun Nov 16, '50	Ac 7:38b-42	S. VIII
38. Sun Nov 23, '50	Ac 7:42-43	S. VIII
39. Sun Nov 30, '50	Ac 7:42-44	S. VIII
40. Sun Dec 7, '50	Ac 7:45-50	S. VIII
41. Sun Dec 14, '50	Ac 7:51	S. VIII
42. Sun Dec 21, '50	Ac 7:52-56	S. VIII
[Dec 28 **Nativity**	Luke 2]	
1551		
43. Sun Jan 4, '51	Ac 7:55-58	S. VIII
44. Sun Jan 11, '51	Ac 7:58-60	S. VIII
1.Sun p.m., Feb 8, '51	Ps 80:9-20	S. VII
Wed. Mar 25, '51 **passion**	1 on Jn. 18-19	*Table*
9. Sun[p.m., probably @'51]	Ps 89:31-39	S. VII
Sun [probably @'51]	Ps 87:1-7	OC 8:441-452

---

4   See Balke & Moehn, "Introduction," S. VIII, p. xviii, n.66-67, citing RCP 1, p. 73 for this, and letter to Viret (OC 13:603) for visit to village of Jussy on July 27.

1552		
1.Dec 25, '52 **Nativity**	Luke 2	OC 46 & *Plusieurs*
1553		
1.Sun [p.m.] Jan 8, '53	Ps 119:1-8	OC 32
2.Sun [p.m.] Jan 15, '53	Ps 119:9-16	OC 32
3. Sun [p.m.] Jan 22, '53	Ps 119:17-24	OC 32
4. Sun [p.m.] Jan 29, '53	Ps 119:25-32	OC 32
5. Sun [p.m.] Feb 5, '53	Ps 119:33-40	OC 32
6. Sun [p.m.] Feb 12, '53	Ps 119:41-48	OC 32
7. Sun [p.m.] Feb 19, '53	Ps 119:49-56	OC 32
8. Sun [p.m.] Feb 26, '53	Ps 119:57-64	OC 32
9. Sun [p.m.] Mar 5, '53	Ps 119:65-72	OC 32
Absent from consistory Mar 16 [OC 21:538]		
Sun Mar 26, '53 **passion**	8 total sermons; 1st of 7 passion	*table*
10. Sun [p.m.] Mar 26, '53	Ps 119:73-80	OC 32
Mon. Mar 27- **passion week**. Sat. Apr 1, '53,	2 through 7 on passion	*table*
Easter. Apr 2, '53	1 resurrection= last of 8	*table*

11. Sun [p.m.] Apr 2, '53	Ps 119:81-88	OC 32
12. Sun [p.m.] Apr 9, '53	Ps 119:89-96	OC 32
13. Sun [p.m.] Apr 16, '53	Ps 119:97-104	OC 32
14. Sun [p.m.] Apr 23, '53	Ps 119:105-112	OC 32
15. Sun [p.m.] Apr 30, '53	Ps 119:113-120	OC 32
16. Sun [p.m.] May 7, '53	Ps 119:121-128	OC 32
17. Sun [p.m.] May 14, '53	Ps 119:129-136	OC 32
18. Sun [p.m.] May 21, '53	Ps 119:137-144	OC 32
19. Sun [p.m.] Jun 11, '53	Ps 119:145-152	OC 32
20. Sun [p.m.] Jun 18, '53	Ps 119:153-160	OC 32
21. Sun [p.m.] Jun 25, '53	Ps 119:161-168	OC 32
22. Sun [p.m.] Jul 2, '53	Ps 119:169-176	OC 32
2. Sun Nov 12, '53	Ps. 147:12-20	S. VII
Dec 24, '53 **Nativity**	1 on Lk. [2]	*table*
1554		
Sun Mar 18, & Wed. Mar 21, '54, **passion**	2 on passion, no gospel cited	*table*
Easter. Mar 25, '54	1 on resurrection no gospel cited	*table*

Pentecost. May13, '54	1 on Acts 2	*table*		14. Sun Nov 4, '54[5]	1 Tim 2:5-6	OC 53
				15. Sun p.m. Nov 4, '54	1 Tim 2:5-6	OC 53
Thessalonians				16. Sun [Nov 11, '54]	1 Tim 2:8	OC 53
19. Sun summer '54	2 Thess. 1:6-10	OC 52 & *Plusieurs*		17. Sun p.m. [Nov 11, '54]	1 Tim 2:9-11	OC 53
				18. Sun [Nov 18, '54]	1 Tim 2:12-14	OC 53
First Timothy				19. Sun p.m. [Nov 18, '54]	1 Tim 2:13-15	OC 53
1.Sun Sep 16, '54	I Tim 1:1	OC 53		20. Sun [Nov 25, '54]	1 Tim 3:1-4	OC 53
2. Sun p.m. [Sep 16, '54]	I Tim 1:1-2	OC 53		21. Sun p.m. [Nov 25, '54]	1 Tim 3:1-4	OC 53
3. Sun [Sep 23, '54]	I Tim 1:3-4	OC 53		22. Sun [Dec 2, '54]	1 Tim 3:1-4	OC 53
4. Sun p.m. [Sep 23, '54]	I Tim 1:5-7	OC 53		23. Sun p.m. [Dec 2, '54]	1 Tim 3:3-5	OC 53
3.Sun [morn] Sep 30, '54	Ps 148:1-14	S. VII		24. Sun [Dec 9, '54]	1 Tim 3:6-7	OC 53
5. Sun p.m. [Sep 30, '54]	1 Tim 1:8-11	OC 53		25. Sun p.m. [Dec 9, '54]	1 Tim 3:8-10	OC 53
6. Sun [Oct 7, '54]	1 Tim 1:12-13	OC 53		26. Sun [Dec 16, '54]	1 Tim 3:14-15	OC 53
7. Sun p.m. [Oct 7, '54]	1 Tim 1:14-15	OC 53		27. Sun p.m. [Dec 16, '54]	1 Tim 3:16	OC 53
8. Sun [Oct 14, '54]	1 Tim 1:17-19	OC 53				
9. Sun p.m. [Oct 14, '54]	1 Tim 1:18-19	OC 53		Dec 23, '54 **Nativity**	1 on Lk. [2]	*Table*
10. Sun [Oct 21, '54]	1 Tim 1:19-20	OC 53				
11. Sun p.m. [Oct 21, '54]	1 Tim 2:1-2	OC 53		28. Sun p.m. [Dec 23, '54]	1 Tim 4:1-2	OC 53
12. Sun [Oct 28, '54]	1 Tim 2:1-2	OC 53		29. Sun [Dec 30, '54]	1 Tim 4:1-3	OC 53
13. Sun p.m. [Oct 28, '54]	1 Tim 2:3-5	OC 53				

---

5   The date is given in the publication of sermons 14 & 15 by Jean Girard in 1555; see Peter & Gilmont, *Bibliotheca* II, p. 585.

30. Sun p.m. [Dec 30, '54]	1 Tim 4:1-5	OC 53
1555		
31. Sun [Jan 6, '55]	1 Tim 4:6-7	OC 53
32. Sun p.m. [Jan 6, '55]	1 Tim 4:8	OC 53
33. Sun [Jan 13, '55]	1 Tim 4:9-11	OC 53
34. Sun p.m. [Jan 13, '55]	1 Tim 4:12-13	OC 53
35. Sun [Jan 20, '55]	1 Tim 4:14-15	OC 53
36. Sun p.m. [Jan 20, '55]	1 Tim 4:16	OC 53
37. Sun [Jan 27, '55]	1 Tim 5:1-2	OC 53
38. Sun p.m. [Jan 27, '55]	1 Tim 5:4-5	OC 53
39. Sun [Feb 3, '55]	1 Tim 5:7-12	OC 53
40. Sun p.m. [Feb 3, '55]	1 Tim 5:9-10	OC 53
41. Sun [Feb 10, '55]	1 Tim 5:11-15	OC 53
42. Sun p.m. [Feb 10, '55]	1 Tim 5:16-18	OC 53
43. Sun [Feb 17, '55]	1 Tim 5:17-20	OC 53
44. Sun p.m. [Feb 17, '55]	1 Tim 5:21-22	OC 53
45. Sun [Feb 24, '55]	1 Tim 5:23-25	OC 53
46. Sun p.m. [Feb 24, '55]	1 Tim 6:1-2	OC 53
47. Sun [Mar 3, '55]	1 Tim 6:3-5	OC 53

48. Sun p.m. [Mar 3, '55]	1 Tim 6:3-7	OC 53
Trip to Bern[6], Mar 6-16, '55		
49. Sun [Mar 17, '55]	1 Tim 6:9-11	OC 53
50. Sun p.m. [Mar 17, '55]	1 Tim 6:12-14	OC 53
51. Sun [Mar 24, '55]	1 Tim 6:13-16	OC 53
52. Sun p.m. [Mar 24, '55]	1 Tim 6:15-16	OC 53
Trip to Bern, Mar 28-Apr 10		
Easter. Apr 14, '55	1 on Mt. [28]	*table*
53. Sun p.m. [Apr 14, '55]	1 Tim 6:17-19	OC 53
54. Sun [Apr 21, '55][7]	1 Tim 6:20-21	OC 53
Second Timothy		
1. Sun p.m. [Apr 21, '55]	2 Tim 1:1-2	OC 54
2. Sun [Apr 28, '55]	2 Tim 1:3-5	OC 54
3. Sun p.m. [Apr 28, '55]	2 Tim 1:6-8	OC 54
4. Sun May 5, '55[8]	2 Tim 1:8-9	OC 54
5. Sun p.m. May 5, '55	2 Tim 1:9-10	OC 54

---

6   For this trip to Bern and the one later in the month, see RCP II, p.60, OC 21: 597-98.

7   Raguenier says 55 sermons on 1 Tim. but there are only 54; he says 31 sermons on 2 Tim. but there are only 30; see Appendix Eight Part Three.

8   The 2 sermons for May 5, 1555, appeared, marked with dates & morning & afternoon, as *Two godly sermons* (1576); see Parker, *Calvin's Preaching*, p. 167. The allocation here was made independently by the incipit pattern.

6. Sun [May 12, '55]	2 Tim 1:13-14	OC 54		24. Sun p.m. [Jul 21, '55]	2 Tim 3:16-17	OC 54
7. Sun p.m. [May 12, '55]	2 Tim 1:15-18	OC 54		25. Sun [Jul 28, '55]	2 Tim 4:1-2	OC 54
8. Sun [May 19, '55]	2 Tim 2:1-3	OC 54		26. Sun p.m. [Jul 28, '55]	2 Tim 4:2-5	OC 54
9. Sun p.m. [May 19, '55]	2 Tim 2:3-6	OC 54		27. Sun [Aug 4, '55]	2 Tim 4:5-6	OC 54
10. Sun May 26, '55	2 Tim 2:8-10	OC 54		28. Sun p.m. [Aug 4, '55]	2 Tim 4:7-8	OC 54
11. Sun p.m. May 26, '55	2 Tim 2:8-13	OC 54		29. Sun [Aug 11, '55]	2 Tim 4:8-13	OC 54
				30. Sun p.m. [Aug 11, '55]	2 Tim 4:14-22	OC 54
Pentecost. Jun 2, '55	1 on Acts 2	*table*				
12. Sun p.m. Jun 2, '55	2 Tim 2:14-15	OC 54		**Titus**		
13. Sun [Jun 9, '55]	2 Tim 2:16-18	OC 54		1. Sun [Aug 18, '55]	Tit 1:1-4	OC 54
14. Sun p.m. [Jun 9, '55]	2 Tim 2:19	OC 54		2. Sun p.m. [Aug 18, '55]	Tit 1:1-4	OC 54
15. Sun p.m. [Jun 16, '55]	2 Tim 2:20-21	OC 54		3. Sun Aug 25, '55	Tit 1:1-5	OC 54
16. Sun [Jun 23, '55]	2 Tim 2:22-26	OC 54		4. Sun p.m. Aug 25, '55	Tit 1:5-6	OC 54
17. Sun p.m. [Jun 23, '55]	2 Tim 2:23-26	OC 54		5. Sun Sep 1, '55	Tit 1:7-9	OC 54
18. Sun [Jun 30, '55]	2 Tim 2:25-26	OC 54		6. Sun p.m. [Sep 1, '55]	Tit 1:7-9	OC 54
19. Sun p.m. [Jun 30, '55]	2 Tim 3:1-5	OC 54		7. Sun [Sep 8, '55]	Tit 1:10-13	OC 54
20. Sun [Jul 7, '55]	2 Tim 3:6-7	OC 54		8. Sun p.m. [Sep 8, '55]	Tit 1:12-15	OC 54
21. Sun p.m. [Jul 7, '55]	2 Tim 3:8-9	OC 54		9. Sun p.m. [Sep 15, '55]	Tit 1:15-16	OC 54
				10. Sun [Sep 22, '55]	Tit 2:1-5	OC 54
4.Sun [morn] Jul 14, '55	Ps 149:4-9	S. VII		11. Sun p.m. [Sep 22, '55]	Tit 2:3-5	OC 54
22. Sun p.m. [Jul 14, '55]	2 Tim 3:10-13	OC 54		12. Sun [Sep 29, '55]	Tit 2:6-14	OC 54
23. Sun [Jul 21, '55]	2 Tim 3:14-15	OC 54		13. Sun p.m. [Sep 29, '55]	Tit 2:11-14	OC 54

14. Sun [Oct 6, '55]	Tit 2:15-3:2	OC 54
15. Sun p.m. [Oct 6, '55]	Tit 3:3-5	OC 54
16. Sun [Oct 13, '55]	Tit 3:4-7	OC 54
17. Sun p.m. [Oct 13, '55]	Tit 3:8-15	OC 54
First Corinthians		
1.Sun Oct 20, '55	1 Cor 1:1-5	Ms. fr.26
2. Sun p.m. Oct 20, '55	1 Cor 1:1-5	Ms. fr.26
3. Sun Oct 27, '55	1 Cor 1:4-7	Ms. fr.26
4. Sun p.m. Oct 27, '55	1 Cor 1:10-11	Ms. fr.26
5. Sun Nov 3, '55	1 Cor 1: 13-17	Ms. fr.26
6. Sun p.m. Nov 3, '55	1 Cor 1:18-20	Ms. fr.26
7. Sun Nov 10, '55	1 Cor1:20b-21	Ms. fr.26
8. Sun p.m. Nov 10, '55	1 Cor 1:22-25	Ms. fr.26
9. Sun Nov 17, '55	1 Cor 1:26-28	Ms. fr.26
10. Sun p.m. Nov 17, '55	1 Cor 1:30-31	Ms. fr.26
11. Sun Nov 24, '55	1 Cor 2:1-5	Ms. fr.26
12. Sun p.m. Nov 24, '55	1 Cor 2:3-5	Ms. fr.26
13. Sun Dec 1, '55	1 Cor 2:6-8	Ms. fr.26
14. Sun p.m. Dec 1, '55	1 Cor 2:11-13	Ms. fr.26
15. Sun Dec 8, '55	1 Cor 2:11b-16	Ms. fr.26
16. Sun p.m. Dec 8, '55	1 Cor 3:1-3	Ms. fr.26
17. Sun Dec 15, '55	1 Cor 3:3-7	Ms. fr.26
18. Sun p.m. Dec 15, '55	1 Cor 3:8-10	Ms. fr.26
[Dec 22, '55 **Nativity**	Luke 2]	
19. Sun [p.m.] Dec 22, '55	1 Cor 3:10-13	Ms. fr.26
20. Sun Dec 29, '55	1 Cor 3:12-15	Ms. fr.26
21. Sun p.m. Dec 29, '55	1 Cor 3:16-19	Ms. fr.26
1556		
22. Sun Jan 5, '56	1 Cor 3:19-23	Ms. fr.26
23. Sun p.m. Jan 5, '56	1 Cor 4:1-4	Ms. fr.26
24. Sun Jan 12, '56	1 Cor 4:4-5	Ms. fr.26
25. Sun Jan 19, '56	1 Cor 4:5-9	Ms. fr.26
26. Sun p.m. Jan 19, '56	1 Cor 4:8-10	Ms. fr.26
27. Sun Jan 26, '56	1 Cor 4:11-13	Ms. fr.26
28. Sun p.m. Jan 26, '56	1 Cor 4:14-15	Ms. fr.26
29. Sun Feb 2, '56	1 Cor 4:16-20	Ms. fr.26
30. Sun p.m. Feb 2, '56	1 Cor 4:21-5:2	Ms. fr.26

31. Sun Feb 9, '56	1 Cor 5:2-4	Ms. fr.26		47. Sun p.m. Apr 12, '56	1 Cor 7:25-28	Ms. fr.26
32. Sun p.m. Feb 9, '56	1 Cor 5:3-6	Ms. fr.26		48. Sun Apr 19, '56	1 Cor 7:29-35	Ms. fr.26
33. Sun Feb 16, '56	1 Cor 5:7-8	Ms. fr.26		49. Sun p.m. Apr 19, '56	1 Cor 7:36-40	Ms. fr.26
34. Sun p.m. Feb 16, '56	1 Cor 5:9-13	Ms. fr.26		50. Sun p.m. Apr 26, '56	1 Cor 8:1-3	Ms. fr.26
35. Sun Feb 23, '56	1 Cor 6:1-6	Ms. fr.26		51. Sun May 3, '56	1 Cor 8:4-7	Ms. fr.26
36. Sun p.m. Feb 23, '56	1 Cor 6:7-9	Ms. fr.26		52. Sun p.m. May 3, '56	1 Cor 8:8-13	Ms. fr.26
37. Sun Mar1, '56	1 Cor 6:9b-10	Ms. fr.26		Calvin ill May 10[9] but probably back for Pentecost		
38. Sun p.m. Mar 1, '56	1 Cor 6:11-12	Ms. fr.26		[**Pentecost**. May 24, '56	Acts 2]	
39. Sun Mar 8, '56	1 Cor 6:13-17	Ms. fr.26		53. Sun May 31, '56	1 Cor 9:1-3	Ms. fr.26
40. Sun p.m. Mar 8, '56	1 Cor 6:18-20	Ms. fr.26		54. Sun p.m. May 31, '56	1 Cor 9:1-6	Ms. fr.26
41. Sun Mar 15, '56	1 Cor 7:1-2	Ms. fr.26		55. Sun Jun 7, '56	1 Cor 9:7-14	Ms. fr.26
42. Sun p.m. Mar 15, '56	1 Cor 7:3-5	Ms. fr.26		56. Sun p.m. Jun 7, '56	1 Cor 9:15-18	Ms. fr.26
43. Sun p.m. Mar 22, '56	1 Cor 7:6-9	Ms. fr.26		57. Sun Jun 14, '56	1 Cor 9:19-22	Ms. fr.26
44. Sun p.m. Mar 29, '56	1 Cor 7:10-14	Ms. fr.26		58. Sun p.m. Jun 14, '56	1 Cor 9:23-27	Ms. fr.26
[**Easter**. Apr 5, '56	Mt. 28/Jn 20?]			1/59.Sun [Jun 21, '56]	1 Cor 10:1-5	OC 49
45. Sun p.m. Apr 5, '56	1 Cor 7:15-20	Ms. fr.26		2/60. Sun [p.m. Jun 21, '56]	1 Cor 10:3-6	OC 49
46. Sun Apr 12, '56	1 Cor 7:21-24	Ms. fr.26		3/61. Sun [Jun 28, '56]	1 Cor 10:7	OC 49

---

9   Calvin collapses in the pulpit on May 10, Des Gallars takes over his sermon; Calvin absent from consistory because not well May 19, '56, OC 21:637.

4/62. Sun [p.m. Jun 28, '56]	1 Cor 10:8-9	OC 49
5/63. Sun [Jul 5, '56]	1 Cor 10:10-11	OC 49
6/64. Sun [p.m. Jul 5, '56]	1 Cor 10:12-14	OC 49
7/65. Sun [Jul 12, '56]	1 Cor 10:15-18	OC 49
8/66. Sun [p.m. Jul 12, '56]	1 Cor 10:19-24	OC 49
9/67. Sun [Jul 19, '56]	1 Cor 10:25-30	OC 49
10/68. Sun [p.m. Jul 19, '56]	1 Cor 10:31-11:1	OC 49
11/69. Sun [Jul 26, '56]	1 Cor 11:2-3	OC 49
12/70. Sun [p.m. Jul 26, '56]	1 Cor 11:4-10	OC 49
13/71. Sun [Aug 2, '56]	1 Cor 11:11-16	OC 49
14/72. Sun [p.m. Aug 2, '56]	1 Cor 11:17-19	OC 49
15/73. Sun [Aug 9, '56]	1 Cor 22:20-23	OC 49
16/74. Sun [p.m. Aug 9, '56]	1 Cor 11:23-25	OC 49
17/75. Sun [Aug 16, '56]	1 Cor 11:23-26	OC 49
18/76. Sun [p.m. Aug 16, '56]	1 Cor 11:26-29	OC 49
19/77. Sun p.m. [Aug 23, '56]	1 Cor 11:30-32	OC 49
Trip to Frankfurt Aug 26, '56, returns about Oct 10[10]		

1557		
Psalms		
5. Sun May 30, '57	Ps 65:1-13	S. VII
Galatians		
1. Sun p.m. Nov 14, '57	Gal 1:1-5	OC 50
2. Sun [Nov 21, '57]	Gal 1:3-5	OC 50
3. Sun [p.m. Nov 21, '57]	Gal 1:6-8	OC 50
4. Sun [Nov 28, '57]	Gal 1:8-9	OC 50
5. Sun [p.m. Nov 28, '57]	Gal 1:11-12	OC 50
6. Sun [Dec 5, '57]	Gal 1:15-18	OC 50
7. Sun [p.m. Dec 5, '57]	Gal 1:22-2:2	OC 50
8. Sun [Dec 12, '57]	Gal 2:3-5	OC 50
9. Sun [p.m. Dec 12, '57]	Gal 2:6-8	OC 50
10. Sun Dec 19, '57	Gal 2:11-13	OC 50
11. Sun p.m. Dec 19, '57	Gal 2:14-16	OC 50
[Dec 26, '57 **Nativity**	Luke 2]	
12. Sun p.m. Dec 26, '57	Gal 2:15-16	OC 50
1558		
13. Sun [Jan 2, '58]	Gal 2:17-18	OC 50
14. Sun [p.m. Jan 2, '58]	Gal 2:20-21	OC 50
15. Sun [Jan 9, '58]	Gal 3:1-3	OC 50

---

10   See OC 21:647, 650; he does a wedding on Oct 11 so he must be back by Oct. 10.

16. Sun [p.m. Jan 9, '58]	Gal 3:3-5	OC 50		1.Sun [Apr 3, '58] full **passion week**	Mt 26:36-39	OC 46 & *Plusieurs*
17. Sun [Jan 16, '58]	Gal 3:7-9	OC 50		2. Sun [p.m. Apr 3, '58]	Mt 26:40-50	OC 46 & *Plusieurs*
18. Sun [p.m. Jan 16, '58]	Gal 3:11-14	OC 50		3. Mn [Apr 4, '58	Mt 26:51-66	OC 46 & *Plusieurs*
19. Sun [Jan 23, '58]	Gal 3:13-14	OC 50		4. Tu [Apr 5, '58]	Mt 26:67-27:11	OC 46 & *Plusieurs*
20. Sun [p.m. Jan 23, '58]	Gal 3:15-18	OC 50		5. Wd [Apr 6, '58]	Mt 27:11-26	OC 46 & *Plusieurs*
21. Sun [Jan 30, '58]	Gal 3:19-20	OC 50		6. Th [Apr 7, '58]	Mt 27:27-44	OC 46 & *Plusieurs*
22. Sun [p.m. Jan 30, '58]	Gal 3:21-25	OC 50		7. Fr [Apr 8, '58	Mt 27:45-54	OC 46 & *Plusieurs*
23. Sun [Feb 6, '58]	Gal 3:26-29	OC 50		8. Sa [Apr 9, '58	Mt 27:55-60	OC 46 & *Plusieurs*
24. Sun [p.m. Feb 6, '58]	Gal 4:1-4	OC 50		9. **Easter** [Apr 10, '58]	Mt 28:1-10	OC 46 & *Plusieurs*
25. Sun [Feb 13, '58]	Gal 4:4-7	OC 50				
26. Sun [p.m. Feb 13, '58]	Gal 4:8-11	OC 50		37. Sun [p.m. Apr 10, '58]	Gal 5:22-26	OC 51
27. Sun [Feb 20, '58]	Gal 4:11-14	OC 50		38. Sun [Apr 17, '58]	Gal 6:1-2	OC 51
28. Sun [p.m. Feb 20, '58]	Gal 4:15-20	OC 50		39. Sun [p.m. Apr 17, '58]	Gal 6:2-5	OC 51
29. Sun [Feb 27, '58]	Gal 4:21-25	OC 50		40. Sun [Apr 24, '58]	Gal 6:6-8	OC 51
30. Sun [p.m. Feb 27, '58]	Gal 4:26-31	OC 50		41. Sun [May 1, '58]	Gal 6:9-11	OC 51
31. Sun [Mar 6, '58]	Gal 5:1-3	OC 50		42. Sun [p.m. May 1, '58]	Gal 6:12-13	OC 51
32. Sun [Mar 13, '58]	Gal 5:4-6	OC 50		43. Sun [May 8, '58]	Gal 6:14-18	OC 51
33. Sun [Mar 20, '58]	Gal 5:7-10	OC 50				
34. Sun [p.m. Mar 20, '58]	Gal 5:11-14	OC 51				
35. Sun [Mar 27, '58]	Gal 5:14-18	OC 51				
36. Sun [p.m. Mar 27, '58]	Gal 5:19-23	OC 51				

Ephesians		
1.Sun p.m., May 15, '58	Eph 1:1-3	OC 51
2. Sun May 22, '58	Eph 1:3-4	OC 51
3. Sun p.m. May 22, '58	Eph 1:4-6	OC 51
15. **Pentecost**.	Ac 2:1-4	OC 48 & *Plusieurs*
4. Sun p.m. May 29, '58	Eph 1:7-10	OC 51
5. Sun [Jun 5, '58]	Eph 1:13-14	OC 51
6. Sun [p.m. Jun 12, '58]	Eph 1:15-18	OC 51
7. Sun [Jun 19, '58]	Eph 1:17-18	OC 51
8. Sun [p.m. Jun 19, '58]	Eph 1:19-23	OC 51
9. Sun [Jun 26, '58]	Eph 2:1-5	OC 51
10. Sun [p.m. Jun 26, '58]	Eph 2:3-6	OC 51
11. Sun [Jul 3, '58]	Eph 2:8-10	OC 51
12. Sun [p.m. Jul 3, '58]	Eph 2:11-13	OC 51
13. Sun [Jul 10, '58]	Eph 2:13-15	OC 51
14. Sun [p.m. Jul 10, '58]	Eph 2:16-19	OC 51
15. Sun [Jul 17, '58]	Eph 2:19-22	OC 51
16. Sun [p.m. Jul 17, '58]	Eph 3:1-6	OC 51
Absent from consistory Jul 21 [OC 21:699]		
17. Sun [Jul 31, '58]	Eph 3:7-9	OC 51
18. Sun [p.m. Jul 31, '58]	Eph 3:9-12	OC 51
19. Sun [Aug 7, '58]	Eph 3:13-16	OC 51
20. Sun [p.m. Aug 7, '58]	Eph 3:14-19	OC 51
21. Sun [Aug 14, '58]	Eph 3:20-4:2	OC 51
22. Sun [p.m. Aug 14, '58]	Eph 4:1-5	OC 51
23. Sun [Aug 21, '58]	Eph 4:6-8	OC 51
24. Sun [p.m. Aug 21, '58]	Eph 4:7-10	OC 51
25. Sun [Aug 28, '58]	Eph 4:11-12	OC 51
26. Sun [p.m. Aug 28, '58]	Eph 4:11-14	OC 51
27. Sun Sep 4, '58	Eph 4:15-16	OC 51
28. Sun [p.m. Sep 4, '58]	Eph 4:17-19	OC 51
29. Sun [Sep 11, '58]	Eph 4:20-24	OC 51
30. Sun [p.m. Sep 11, '58]	Eph 4:23-26	OC 51
31. Sun [Sep 18, '58]	Eph 4:26-28	OC 51
32. Sun [p.m. Sep 18, '58]	Eph 4:29-30	OC 51
33. Sun [Sep 25, '58]	Eph 4:31-5:2	OC 51
34. Sun [p.m. Sep 25, '58]	Eph 5:3-5	OC 51
35. Sun [Oct 2, '58]	Eph 5:8-11	OC 51
36. Sun [p.m. Oct 2, '58]	Eph 5:11-14	OC 51
37. Sun [Oct 9, '58]	Eph 5:15-18	OC 51
38. Sun [p.m. Oct 9, '58]	Eph 5:18-21	OC 51

39. Sun [Oct 16, '58]	Eph 5:22-26	OC 51	5. Sun [Aug 13, '59]	Lk 1:18-25	OC 46
40. Sun [p.m. Oct 16, '58]	Eph 5:25-27	OC 51	6. Sun [Aug 20, '59]	Lk 1:26-30	OC 46
41. Sun [Oct 23, '58]	Eph 5:28-30	OC 51	7. Sun [Aug 27, '59]	Lk 1:31-35	OC 46
Calvin ill many months. [11]			8. Sun Sep 3, '59	Lk 1:36-38	OC 46
			9. Sun [Sep 10, '59]	Lk 1:39-44	OC 46
			10. Sun [Sep 17, '59]	Lk 1:45-48	OC 46
1559			*11. Sun [Sep 24, '59]*	Lk 1:50-52	OC 46
11. **Easter.** Mar 26, '59	Mt 28:1-10	S. VII	*12. Sun [Oct 1, '59]*	Lk 1:52-55	OC 46
			13. Sun [Oct 8, '59]	Lk 1:56-64	OC 46
			14. Sun [Oct 15, '59]	Lk 1:65-68	OC 46
42. Sun [Jun 11, '59]	Eph 5:31-33	OC 51	*Between Sep 10 & Dec 17 3 Sun have no sermons*		
43. Sun [Jun 18, '59]	Eph 6:1-4	OC 51	*15. Sun [Nov 5, '59]*	Lk 1:69-72	OC 46
44. Sun [Jun 25, '59]	Eph 6:5-9	OC 51	*16. Sun [Nov 12, '59]*	Lk 1:73-78	OC 46
45. Sun [Jul 2, '59]	Eph 6:10-12	OC 51	*17. Sun [Nov 19, '59]*	Lk 1:73-78	OC 46
46. Sun [p.m. Jul 2, '59]	Eph 6:11-17	OC 51	*18. Sun [Nov 26, '59]*	Lk 1:78-80	OC 46
47. Sun [Jul 9, '59]	Eph 6:18-19	OC 51	*19. Sun [Dec 3, '59]*	Mt 1:1-16, Lk 3:23-38	OC 46
48. Sun [p.m. Jul 9, '59]	Eph 6:19-24	OC 51	*20. Sun [Dec 10, '59]*	Mt 1:1-16, Lk 3:23-38	OC 46
			21. Sun Dec 17, '59	Mt 1:18-21	OC 46
Gospel Harmony =Matthew = Mt, Mark =Mk, Luke = Lk			22. Sun [p.m. Dec 17, '59]	Mt 1:22-25	OC 46
1. Sun [Jul 16, '59]	Lk 1:1-4	OC 46			
2. Sun [Jul 23, '59]	Lk 1:5-10	OC 46	23. Dec 24, '59 **Nativity**. Calvin hemorrhages during the service [OC 21:725]	Lk 2:1-8	OC 46
3. Sun [Jul 30, '59]	Lk 1:11-15	OC 46			
4. Sun [Aug 6, '59]	Lk 1:16-18	OC 46			

11   Calvin is absent from Consistory from Oct 20, 1558 to Feb 2, 1559 [OC 21:707]. He was sick with quartan fever, before Oct 27, 1558; writes from bed Nov 24, 1558 [OC 21:707, 708]. He does not preach on weekdays after Sat. Oct 8, 1558, until Jun 12, 1559. He does occasional Sunday preaching for special observances by Easter Mar 1559.

24. Sun [Dec 31, '59]	Lk 2:9-14	OC 46	7. Sun p.m., May 12, '60	Ps 46:2-6 S. VII	
			42. Sun [May 19, '60]	Mt 3:4-6, Mk 1:4-6, Lk 3:3-6	OC 46
1560			6. Sun p.m., May 19, '60	Ps 46:7-12	S. VII
25. Sun [Jan 7, '60]	Lk 2:15-19	OC 46	43. Sun [May 26, '60]	Mt 3:7-9, Lk 3:7-8	OC 46
26. Sun [Jan 14, '60]	Lk 2:20-21	OC 46	7. Sun p.m., May 26, '60	Ps 48:2-8	S. VII
27. Sun [Jan 21, '60]	Mt 2:1-3	OC 46			
28. Sun [Jan 28, '60]	Mt 2:3-8	OC 46	13. **Pentecost**. Jun 2, '60	Ac 2:1-11	S. VII
29. Sun [Feb 4, '60]	Mt 2:9-11, Lk 2:22-24	OC 46			
30. Sun [Feb 11, '60]	Lk 2:25-28	OC 46	44. Sun [Jun 9, '60]	Mt 3:9-10, Lk 3:8-11	OC 46
31. Sun [Feb 18, '60]	Lk 2:28-33	OC 46	8. Sun p.m., Jun 9, '60	Ps 48:9-15	S. VII
32. Sun [Feb 25, '60]	Lk 2:34	OC 46	*45. Sun [Jun 16, '60]*	Mt. 3:11-12, Mk 1:7-8, Lk 3:12-18	OC 46
33. Sun [Mar 3, '60]	Lk 2:34-35	OC 46	*46. Sun [Jun 23, '60]*	Mt. 3:11-12, Mk 1:7-8, Lk 3:12-18	OC 46
34. Sun [Mar 10, '60]	Lk 2:36-39	OC 46	*47. Sun [Jun 30, '60]*	Mt 3:13-17, Mk 1:9-11, Lk 3:21-23	OC 46
Mar 17 Calvin very ill[12]			*48. Sun [Jul 7, '60]*	Mt 3:13-4:1, Mk 1:9-13, Lk 3:21-4:2	OC 46
35. Sun [Mar 24, '60]	Mt 2:13-15	OC 46	*49. Sun [Jul 14, '60]*	Mt 4:2-4, Lk 4:2-4	OC 46
36. Sun [Mar 31, '60]	Mt 2:16-22	OC 46	*50. Sun [Jul 21, '60]*	Mt 4:5-7, Lk 4:9-12	OC 46
37. Sun [Apr 7, '60]	Mt 2:23, Lk 2:40	OC 46	*51. Sun [Jul 28, '60]*	Mt 4:8-11, Mk 1:13, Lk 4:5-13	OC 46
			Between Jun 9 & Aug 18 3 Sun have no sermons		
12. **Easter**. April 14, '60	Mt. 28:1-10	S. VII			
38. Sun [Apr 21, '60]	Lk 2:41-49	OC 46			
39. Sun [Apr 28, '60]	Lk 2:50-52	OC 46			
40. Sun [May 5, '60]	Mt 3:1-3, Mk 1:1-3, Lk 3:1-2	OC 46			
41. Sun [May 12, '60]	Mt 3:1-3, Mk 1:1-3, Lk 3:1-2	OC 46			

---

12   OC 21:729; letter from Sulzer to Bullinger.

52. Sun [Aug 18, '60]	Mt 4:12, 17, Mk 1:14-15, Lk 3:19-20, 4:14-15	OC 46		62. Sun [Oct 27, '60]	Mt 5:1-4, Lk 6:20-21	OC 46
53. Sun Aug 25, '60	Lk 4:16-19	OC 46		63. Sun [Nov 3, '60]	Mt 5:5-6, Lk 6:20	OC 46
54. Sun Sep 1, '60	Lk 4:16-22	OC 46		64. Sun [Nov 10, '60]	Mt 5:8-10, Lk 6:22-23	OC 46
55. Sun [Sep 8, '60]	Lk 4:23-27	OC 46		65. Sun [Nov 17, '60]	Mt 5:8-12, Lk 6: 22-26	OC 46
56. Sun [Sep 15, '60]	Mt 4:13-16, Lk4:28-30	OC 46				
57. Sun [Sep 22, '60]	Mt 4:18-22, Mk 1:16-20, Lk 5:1-11	OC 46		**1562**		
58. Sun [Sep 29, '60]	Mt 4:23-25, Mk 1:21-22, Lk 4:31-32	OC 46		**Passion Week,** Mn-Sa		
59. Sun [Oct 6, '60]	Mk 1:23-27, Lk 4:33-36	OC 46		15. M. Mar 23, '62	Mt. 26:40-54	S. VII
60. Sun [Oct 13, '60]	Mt 8:14-18, Mk 1:29-39, Lk 4:38-43	OC 46		16. Tu Mar 24, '62	Mt. 26:55-75	S. VII
				14. Wd Mar 25, '62	Mt. 26:71–27:14	S. VII
61. Sun [Oct 20, '60]	Mk 3:13-19, Lk 6:12-19	OC 46		17. Th Mar 26, '62	Mt. 27:15-44	S. VII
				18. Fr Mar 27, '62	Mt. 27:45-56	S. VII
				19. S. Mar 28, '62	Mt. 27:57-66	S. VII

APPENDIX NINE: SERMONS PUBLISHED IN THE EARLY MODERN PERIOD

Records for 1546-1600 from *Bibliotheca Calvinina*, 1-3

The intent is to indicate the first time any sermons appeared in print. Items in **bold italics** indicate the first publication. Items in *underlined italics* indicate the first translation into whatever language is being presented. Items underlined are reprintings of sermons which had already appeared.

1546

Deux sermons faitz en la ville de Geneve, l'un le 4 nov. 1545, le second le mercredy suyvant, [transcribed by Jean Cousin] Geneva: Jean Girard, 1546

1552

Quatre sermons fort utiles pour nostre temps avec exposition du Pseaume 87. Geneva: Robert Estienne, 1552 [Ps. 16, Heb. 13, Ps. 27 (two sermons), plus Ps. 87]

1553

Certaine homilies conteining admonition for this time, with an Apologie [trans by Robert Horne] "Rome" [Wesel?], 1553. [trans. of 2 sermons, on Ps. 16 and Heb. 13]

Del fuggir le superstitioni che regugnano a la vera e sincera confession della fede. [Geneva: Jean Crespin], 1553. [second part is translation of Quatre sermons]

Homiliae quatuor et explanatio Ps. 87, trans. by Claude Baduel. Geneva: Jean Crespin, 1553.

1554

Vingtdeux sermons auxquels est exposé le Pseaume 119. Geneva: Jean Girard, 1554

Vingt-deux sermons sur le Pseaume 119. Geneva: [Zacharie Durant], 1554.

1555

Deux sermons prins de la premiere Epistre à Timothée au second chapitre. [signed D.R. = Denis Raguenier] [Geneva] Jean Girard, 1555. [two sermons preached Nov. 4, 1554, part of series]

<u>Six sermons à sçavoir quatre exhortatifs et deux òu il est traité du seul moyenneur.</u> [Geneva] Pierre-Jacques Poullain & René Houdouyn, 1555. [*Quatre sermons* & *Deux sermons*]

1556

<u>*Homiliae sive Conciones VII*</u>, trans. Claude Baduel. [Geneva] Jean Crespin, 1556. [*Quatre sermons* with first three from *Vingtdeux*]

1557

Sermons sur les dix commandemens. Geneva: Conrad Badius, 1557. [16 sermons]

1558

Plusieurs sermons touchant la divinité, humanité et nativité de N.S. Jesus Christ. [Geneva] Conrad Badius, 1558. [1 Bible study, 26 sermons]
Sermons sur le 10e et le 11e chapitre de la premiere Epistre aux Corinthians. [Geneva] Conrad Badius, 1558. [19 sermons]
<u>*Sermons sur les dix commandemens*.</u> Geneva: Conrad Badius, 1558 [original 16 plus 2 more on Deut. 4:15-24]

1559

<u>Sermons sur les dix commendemens.</u> Geneva: Etienne Anastaise, 1559
<u>Plusieurs sermons touchant la divinité, humanité et nativité de N.S. Jesus Christ.</u> [Geneva] Conrad Badius, 1559. [1 Bible study, 26 sermons] [1]

1560

Dixhuict sermons ausquels l'histoire de Melchisedec et la matiere de la justification sont deduites. [Geneva] Etienne Anastaise, 1560; [Geneva] Jean Bonnefoy, 1560. [7 on Gen. 14-15, 11 on Luke 1-2]
<u>*Sermons upon the songe that Ezechias made after he had bene sicke,*</u> trans. A.L. (Anne Locke). London: John Day, 1560. [4 on Isa. 38]
Traité de la predestination eternelle. Treze sermons de l'election gratuite de Dieu. [Geneva] Antoine Cercia, 1560. [Geneva] Jean Durant, 1560. [13 on Gen. 25-27]
<u>*Two godly and notable sermons preached in 1555*.</u> London: William Seres, [1560?] [text is 2 Tim. 1:8-10; translator not known]

1561

<u>*Four godlye sermons agaynst the polution of idolatries*.</u> London: Rowland Hall, 1561. [first translation for sermons three and four and exposition of Ps. 87]
Sermon où il est montré quelle doit estre la modestie des femmes en leur habillements. [Caen: Pierre Philippe?], 1561.

---

[1] This second edition noted by W. Moehn, *Sermones*, p. xiv, is not found in Peter & Gilmont.

Sermon de la modestie des femmes [second part of composite book beginning with Beza's *Conditions et vertus requises en la femme fidele...*] [Paris: Michel Fezandat], 1561.

Sermons sur les deux Epistres à Timothée et sur l'Epistre à Tite. Geneva: Conrad Badius, 1561. [54 on I Timothy, 30 on 2 Timothy, 17 on Titus]

Trois sermons sur le sacrifice d'Abraham. [Geneva: Jacques Bourgeois], 1561.

1562

Sermons sur les dix commandemens. Geneva: François Estienne, 1562.

Sermons sur les dix commandemens. [Lyon: Symphorien Barbier], 1562.

Sermons sur l'Epistre aux Ephesiens. Geneva: Jean-Baptiste Pinereul, 1562. [Some printed without place name] [48 sermons]

Sermons sur l'Epistre aux Ephesiens. [Lyon: Symphorien Barbier], 1562.

Sermons sur le cantique que feit le bon roy Ezechias. Geneva: François Estienne, 1562. [4 sermons]

Soixante cinq sermons sur l'Harmonie ou Concordance des trois Evangelistes. Geneva: Conrad Badius, 1562. [these were the only ones completed before Raguenier's death]

Soixante cinq sermons sur l'Harmonie ou Concordance des trois Evangelistes. Lyon: Symphorien Barbier, 1562. [also some without place or publisher named]

Three notable sermones upon the Psalm 46 [and 48], trans. William Warde. London: Rowland Hall, 1562. [Ps. 46:2-6 preserved only in English]

Treze sermons traitans de l'election gratuite de Dieu en Jacob et de la rejection en Esau. and Response à certaines calomnies et blasphemes. [no place, no name] 1562.

Vingtdeux sermons sur le Pseaume 119. Geneva: François Estienne, 1562.

1563

Plusieurs sermons touchant la divinité, humanité et nativité de N.S. Jesus Christ. Geneva: Michel Blanchier, 1563.

Sermons sur le 10e et 11e de la premiere Epistre aux Corinthiens. Geneva: Michel Blanchier, 1563.

Sermons sur l'Epistre aux Galatiens [Galates]. Geneva: François Perrin, 1563. [43 sermons]

Sermons sur le livre de Job. Geneva: Jean de Laon, 1563. [159 sermons]

Sermons sur les deux Epistres à Timothée et sur l'Epistre à Tite. Geneva: Jean Bonnefoy, 1563.

1565

Quarante sept sermons sur les huict derniers chapitres des propheties de Daniel. La Rochelle: Barthélemy Berton, 1565.

Sermons ausquels l'histoire de Melchisedec et la matiere de la justification sont deduites, avec l'exposition du sacrifice d'Abraham. Geneva: [Jean Bonnefoy for] Jean Durant, 1565.

1566

Deux sermons, l'un auquel tous chrestiens sont exhortez de fuir l'idolatrie exterieure, l'autre à souffrir persecution. [Orléans: Eloi Gibier], 1566. [first 2 of *Quatre sermons*]

1567

Sermons sur le V. livre de Moyse nommé Deutéronome. Geneva: Thomas Courteau, 1567. [200 sermons, including previously published ones on 10 commandments]

1569

Sermons sur le livre de Job. Geneva: François Perrin, 1569.

1574

Four sermons upon the songe that Ezechias made, trans. A.L. (Anne Locke). London: John Day, 1574.

Sermons upon the books of Job, trans. Arthur Golding. London: Henry Bynneman, 1574.

Sermons upon the books of Job, trans. Arthur Golding. London: Henry Bynneman, 1574. [different format]

Sermons upon the Epistle to the Galathians, trans. Arthur Golding. London: Henry Bynneman, 1574.

1577

The Sermons upon the Epistle to the Ephesians, trans. Arthur Golding. London: [Thomas Dawson & Thomas Gardiner]

1579

Foure sermons of matters very profitable for our time, With a brief exposition of the 87. psalme, trans. John Field. London: Thomas Dawson, 1579. [new trans.?; from French]

Sermons on the Epistles to Timothie and Titus, trans. L.T. (Lawrence Tomson]. London [Henry Middleton], 1579.

Sermons upon the booke of Job, trans. Arthur Golding. London: Thomas Dawson, 1579 (=1580).

Sermons upon the X. commandementes of the Lawe, trans. J. H. (John Harmar). London: Thomas Dawson, 1579.

Thirteen sermons, entreating of the free election of God in Jacob, trans. John Field. London: Thomas Dawson, 1579.

1580

Sermons upon the booke of Job, trans. Arthur Golding. London: Thomas Dawson, 1580.

Two and twentie sermons upon the 119th Psalme, trans. Thomas Stocker. London: Thomas Dawson, 1580.

1581

Divers sermons concerning the divinity, humanitie and nativitie of Jesus Christ, trans. Thomas Stocker. London: Thomas Dawson, 1581.

Predicatien over den Lofsanck des Coninckx Ezechie, trans. Th.O. Anvers: Jasper Troyens, 1581.

Sermon conteining an exhortation to suffer persecution, upon Heb. 13.13 (trans. John Field). London: Robert Waldegrave, 1581.

Sermons upon the X. commandementes of the Lawe, trans. J. H. (John Harmar). London: Thomas Dawson, 1581.

1583

The Sermons upon the fifth booke of Moses called Deuteronomie, trans. Arthur Golding. London: Henry Middleton, 1583.

1584

Sermons upon the booke of Job, trans. Arthur Golding. London: Thomas Dawson, 1584

Two godly and learned sermons, trans. Robert Horne [see *Certaine Homilies*], edited Anthony Munday. London: [John Charlewood], 1584.

1586

Vier Predigten, drey uber den englischen Gruss, die vierde uber das fünffte Gebott, trans. under direction of Kaspar Olevianus. Herborn: Christoph Rab, 1586.

1587-88

Predigten über das Buch Job, trans. from French under direction of Kaspar Olevianus. Herborn: Christoph Rab, 1587-88. [4 volumes, 2 in 1587, 2 in 1588].

1590

Soixante cinq sermons sur l'Harmonie ou Concordance des trois Evangelistes. Geneva: Jacob Stoer, 1590.

1592

Sermons on the historie of Mechisedech, trans. by Thomas Stocker. London: John Windet, 1592. [group of ten sermons collected in 1565 book].

1593

In librum Jobi Conciones, preface T. Beza. Geneva: Heritiers de Eustace Vignon, 1593.

1598

Vergaderinghe ofte proef-predicke, op het beginsel van den Evangelio des Joannis. Een predicatie vander geboorten Jesu Christi. Noch negen predicatien, trans. Jan Martini. Delft: Jan Andriesz [Cloeting], 1598. [congrégation and first 10 sermons of *Plusieurs sermons*]

1602

<u>*XL Predicaten I.C. gethogen uyt alle zyne Sermonen die hz ghedaen heeft over het Boeck Iob.*</u>
   Amsterdam: Laurens Jacobus, 1602.

1604

Ioannis Calvini homiliae in I. Librum Samuelis. Geneva: Gabriel Carterius, 1604.

<u>*Thien Predicatien I.C. In Welchke onder andere de gheschiedenisse Melchisedechs' end den handel des rechtveerdighmakinghe met de verclaringhe van Abrahmas offerhande verhaelt worden.*</u> Delf: I.
   Martin, Ian Andriess. 1604.

1615

<u>*Der 119. Psalm des Königes und Propheten Davis erklärt und augelegt in zwo und zwanzig Predigten.*</u>
   Cassel, Wessel. [1615]

APPENDIX TEN: TABLE FOR GUESTIMATING THE NUMBER OF CALVIN'S UNRECORDED SERMONS

PART ONE: NEW TESTAMENT IN CHRONOLOGICAL ORDER

Sermon Series, (almost) only on Sunday mornings

Book or Status	Texts	Dates	Verses & Sermons	Vss per Serm
Acts	28 chap. 880 vss		189 serm recorded[1]	
Extant	Acts 1:1-2	Aug 25, '49	2 vss, 1 serm	2
	Acts 2:36-7:60	Dec 22, '49 – Jan 11, '51	192 vss, 43 serm	4.409
Plusieurs sermons	Acts 1:1-11, 2:13-24	Sept 1- c.Dec 8, '49	23 vss, 7 serm	3.285

Lost	Acts 1:12-2:12	Sept 1- Dec 15, '49	15 vss, c.4 serm	c.4
	2:25-35	Sept 1- Dec 15, '49	11 vss, c.3 serm	c.4
	Acts 8:1-15:41	c.Jan 18, '51 –Nov '52	241 vss, 51+ serm[2]	c.4.725
	Acts 16:1-20:35[3]	Nov 16, '52- Sept 3, '53	178 vss, c.40 serm	c.4.45
	26 Sun.[4] 20:36-28:30	c. Sept 10, '53- Mar 18, '54	269 vss, c.54 serm	c.4.98

---

1   In the first part of Acts, some sermons were not recorded.

2   During this period Raguenier missed some sermons, and Calvin was probably absent occasionally (as was the case in 1549, when Acts 1:3-2:35 would have been preached).

3   Sept 3, '53 = Acts 20:31-32+ cf. Colladon, OC 21:71.

4   There are 27 Sundays between Sept 3,'53, and Mar. 25, '54, but one of these would be celebrated as the Nativity with the sermon on Luke 2. If Calvin began two sermons/ day, this would work out almost exactly.

Extant Sermon Series, Sun. morning-&-afternoon Chronological Order

One year: 54 + 30 + 8 [Sept 16, '54-Sept 8, '55] = 92 serm

Book or Status	Texts	Dates	Verses & Sermons	Vss per Serm
1 Tim.	6 chap. 113 vss		54 serm recorded[5]	
Extant	All 54 serm	Sept 16, '54- Apr 21, '55 a.m.	113 vss, 54 serm	2.092
2 Tim.	4 chap. 83 vss		30 serm recorded	
Extant	All 30 serm	Apr 21, '55 [p.m.]-c. Aug 11, '55 p.m.	83 vss, 30 serm	2.766
Titus	3 chap. 46 vss		17 serm recorded	
Extant	All 17 serm	c.Aug 18, '55 a.m.- c.Oct 13, '55 p.m.	46 vss, 17 serm	2.705

Book or Status	Texts	Dates	Verses & Sermons	Vss per Serm
1 Cor.	16 chap. 437 vss		110 recorded	
Extant	1 Cor. 1-11	Oct 20, '55-c. Aug 23, '56 p.-m.[6]	271 vss, 77 serm	3.519
Lost	1 Cor. 12-16	c.Oct 11, '56- c.Feb 21, '57[7]	166 vss, 23 serm	7.217

One year: 77 serm [plus c.6-7 week interruption for trip to Frankfurt]

Book or Status	Texts	Dates	Verses & Sermons	Vss per Serm
Gal.	6 chap. 149 vss		43 serm recorded	
Extant	All 43 serm	Nov. 14, '57, p.-m.-c. May 8, '58 a.m.[8]	149 vss, 43 serm	3.456

---

5 Raguenier's catalogue lists 55 sermons on 1 Tim. and 31 on 2 Tim. but in fact there are only 54 and 30 respectively. This means also that Raguenier's note that 2 Tim. began on Apr 21, '55, in the morning is not accurate; see Gagnebin, "L'histoire des manuscrits des sermons de Calvin," SC 2, p. xv.

6 This period includes Nativity, Easter, & Pentecost, plus illness for about two weeks = c.8 preaching times missed, plus two weeks there is only one sermon, so 10 possible 1 Cor. sermon times missed.

7 Calvin ill in Nov., a sermon missing for Nativity, so c.3 preaching times missed.

8 This period includes Nativity, Passion Sunday, & Easter, starts on an afternoon and ends on a morning, plus in two weeks there is only one sermon = c.8 preaching times missed.

Eph.	6 chap. 139 vss		48 serm recorded	
<u>Extant</u>	All 48 serm	May 15, '58, p.-m.- c. Oct 23, '58	139 vss, 48 serm [41 May-Oct.]	2.895
Calvin ill Oct '58- June '59		June 11, '59-c. July 9, '59 p.m.		

Phlm	1 chap. 25 vss	guess 2.5 vss/ serm	10 serm
Jas.	5 chap. 107 vss	guess 2.8 vss/ serm	38.21 serm
1 Pet.	5 chap. 105 vss	guess 3 vss/ serm	35 serm
2 Pet.	3 chap. 61 vss	guess 3.5 vss/ serm	17.42 serm
1 John	5 chap. 105 vss	guess 2.5 vss/ serm	42 serm

Total = 720 serm

One year: 43 + 41 = 84 serm [plus 3-4 weeks illness]

Conclusion: In an average year when Calvin is working through the same book morning-and-afternoon there are about 90+ Sunday sermons/ year in a *lectio continua* series.

Hypothetical Sermon Series, Projected for (1536-38) 1542-49

Book	Text	Vss per Serm	Sermons
Gospel of John	21 chap 878 vss	guess 2.5 vss/ serm	351.2 serm
Rom.	16 chap. 413 vss	guess 2.5 vss/ serm	165.2 serm
Phil.	4 chap. 104 vss	guess 3 vss/ serm	34.666 serm
Col.	4 chap. 95 vss	guess 3.5 vss/ serm	27.14 serm

Preached but not recorded, (mostly) only in the mornings on Sundays

Book	Text	Dates	Vss per Serm	No. of Serm
Heb.	13 chap 260 vss	c.Aug. '47-c. Aug 18, '49	guess 3	86.66 = 87
			guess 24 months	[3.66 serm/ month]

There are about 720 NT serm probably preached before 1548 which are not mentioned anywhere. At the rate of 90/ year, this would mean Sundays for about c.8 years. Since only c.4.1 years (late 1541-45) were probably morning and afternoon, this would leave c.3.9 years' worth to be divided between Oct 1536-Apr 1538 (about 18 months) and Jan 1546 through mid-1547. Since in 1546-47 Calvin was at St. Pierre only in the mornings, he might have averaged 45 sermons/ year (allowing for interruptions for the Nativity, Passion Week, Easter, and Pentecost, as with Acts), or 90 for two years. If Romans occupied him for Sundays in 1536-38, with some left over, there would still have been more sermons than would fit in these years. Some of these books might have been preached in Strasbourg (1538-41), and/or on weekdays in the first Genevan period.

PART TWO: DATED OLD TESTAMENT SERMONS

<u>Extant (or Partially) Sermon Series, delivered daily, Chronological order</u>

Law and History

Book or Status	Text	Dates	Verses & Sermons	Verses per Sermon	No. of Months	Serm per month
Deut.	34 chap 939 vss	200 serm recorded				
<u>Extant</u>	all 34 chap.	Mar 20, '55-July 15, '56	939 vss, 200 serm	4.695	c.15.75	12.698

Book or Status	Text	Dates	Verses & Sermons	Verses per Sermon	No. of Months	Serm per month
Gen.	50 chap. 1499 vss.	123 serm recorded[1]				
<u>Extant</u>	Gen. 1:1-20:7	Sept 4, '59-May 15, '60	471 vss, 97 serm	4.855	c.8.5	c.11.4
	Gen. 21:33-22:14	June 1, 10-11, '60	16 vss, 3 serm	5.333		
	Gen. 25:11-27:36	c.Jul 22 – Aug 10, '60	95 vss, 13 serm	7.307	c.1	
<u>Lost</u>	Gen. 20:8-21:32	c.May 16, '60-May 30, '60	43 vss, 7 serm	c.6.142	c..5	
	Gen. 22:15-25:10	c.June 12-29, '60	106 vss, 16 serm	c.6.625	c.1.3	
	Gen. 28:1-50:26	c.Aug 5, '60-Aug 7, '61?	874 vss, 126.66 serm???	c.6.9	c.12	c.12.3

---

1   Raguenier's catalogue records two volumes, 66 & 67 sermons respectively. The 97 sermons on Gen. 1:1-20:4 at 4.855 vss/ serm are published in S. XI. The remaining extant srmons are 3 on Gen 21:33-22:2 and 13 on Gen 25:11-27:36, averaging 6.9 vss/ serm. About 7 on Gen. 20:8-21:32 and about 16 on Gen 22:15-25:10 would fit between these, making 136, which would include Raguenier's 123 bound in 2 volumes and 13 as yet unbound. At this pace, Calvin would produce about 126 serm for the rest of the book, a total of 262.

2 Sam.	24 chap. 656 vss	87 serm recorded				
<u>Extant</u>	May 23, '62-Feb 3, '63	all 87 serm	656 vss, 87 serm	7.540	c.8.5	10.235

Prophets

Jer.	52 chap 1337vss	25 + 91 serm recorded[2]				
<u>Extant</u>	Jer 14:19-18:23	June 14, '49-Aug 16, '49	96 vss., 25 serm	3.84	c.2	c.12.5
<u>Not recorded</u>	Jer 1:1-14:18	c.Oct. '48-June 13, '49	365 vss, 95 serm	c.3.84	c.7.7[3]	c.12.5
	Jer 19:1-25:24	c.Aug 19, '49-Nov. 11, '49	142 vss, 37 serm	c.3.84	c.2.96	c.12.5
<u>Lost</u>	Jer 25:24-52:34	Nov. 12, '49-Sept 5, '50	724 vss, 91+ [13?] serm.[4]		c.8.3[5]	
Micah	7 chap. 105 vss	28 serm recorded				
<u>Extant</u>	all 7 chap	Nov. 12, '50-Jan 10, '51	105 vss, 28 serm	3.75	c.2	c.14
Daniel	12 chap. 356 vss	47 serm recorded				

---

2   There are 25 extant sermons recorded by Raguenier before he officially began work; these are not listed in his catalogue. His catalogue lists 91 beginning Nov. 12, '49, but these are no longer extant. For present purposes, based on the number of preaching days in Calvin's weeks between the last extant sermon on Aug 17 (not his week to preach) and Nov. 12, it is probable that Calvin preached about 37 sermons (c. 4 vss/ serm = close to what he was averaging).

3   In April '49 Calvin preached on the gospel for Passion Week. What would otherwise be c. 7.7 months is c. 8.1.

4   Raguenier affirms that he did not get all the sermons in sequence, so 91 is a partial number for the remaining ones. If the c.4 vss/ serm held true, this would add 90 more sermons, for a total of 181. It is almost impossible that Raguenier missed half of the sermons preached; since Lam. began on Sept 6, 1550, Calvin must have increased the number of vss/ serm.

5   In Mar-Apr '50 Calvin preached on the gospel for Passion Week. What would otherwise be c. 8.8 months between Nov. 12, '49 & Sept 5, '50, comes to c.8.3.

Extant	Dan. 5:1-12:13	July 18, '52-c.Oct 29, '52	219 vss, 47 serm	4.695	c.3.5	c.13.4
Not recorded	Dan. 1:1-4:37	Early May–Jul 9, '52	137 vss, c.29.14 serm	[4.7]	c.2.2	
Ezek.	48 chap. 1272 vss	175 serm recorded[6]				
Extant	Ezek. 1:1-15:8	Nov 21, '52-Apr 14, '53	298 vss, 56 serm	5.32	c.5	c.11.2
	Ezek. 23:1-39:29	Sept 1, '53-Feb 21, '54	470 vss, 68 serm	6.91	c.6	c.11.5
Lost	Ezek. 16:1-22:31	Apr 23, '53-Aug 31, '53	245 vss, 50 serm	4.9	c.4.3	c.11.68
Isaiah	66 chap., 1192 vss	343serm recorded				
Extant	Isa. 13:1-61:8	Feb 22, '57-Oct 8, '58	813 vss, 243 serm	3.345	c.19.5	12.46
	Isa. 61:10-66:24	June 12-Aug 26, '59	137 vss, 34 serm	4.029	c.2.7	12.59
Lost	Isa. 1:1-12:6	Jul 15, '56-Feb12,'57	242 vss, 66 serm	3.66	c.7	9.42

Projected for 1542-49

Genesis. FIRST time: c.262 serm, average
13/month = 20+ months.
So if begin c. Jan 1, 1542, then conclude c.Aug 1543 or a little later.

Isaiah. FIRST time: c.343 serm, average
13/month = 26.4 months + 1.5 months for three
Passion Weeks (1546, 47, 48) = 27.9 months. It
began Jan 27, 1546, so it might have concluded
c.June 1, 1548. There would be space for several
of the minor prophets before beginning Jeremiah
in October 1548.

---

6   The last sermon covers chap. 40-48 so the calculation here is made on the basis of 39 chap. 1012
vss.

APPENDIX TEN: PART THREE: PSALMS

Extant = Nov. 4 & 11, 1545 [Wed.] = Ps. 115:1-3 & 124:1-8 = 2 serm
   = c.'49 = Ps. 16:4, Ps. 27:4, Ps. 27:8 = 3 serm (?) [*Quatre Sermons*]
   = c.'51 [Sun. afternoons] = Ps. 80:9-20, Ps. 89:31-39, Ps. 87:1-7 = 3 serm
   = Jan 8 –July 2, '53 [afternoons] = Ps. 119, 176 vss. = 22 serm (8 vss/ serm)
   = Sept 30, '54 [morning] = Ps. 148:1-14 = 1 serm
   = July 14, '55 [morning] = Ps. 149:4-9 = 1 serm
   = May 30, '57 [?] = Ps 65:6-14 = 1 serm
   = May 12 & 19, '60 [afternoons] = Ps. 46:2-6 & 7-12 = 2 serm
   = May 26, June 9, '60 [afternoons] = Ps. 48:2-8 & 9-15 = 2 serm

Most of the extant sermons average from 5 or 6 to 8 or 9 verses (with occasional sermons, e.g., on Ps. 115 or Ps. 148 in which although the whole text was probably read, only a relatively few verses were actually expounded).

Sermons Preached by Mid-Summer 1549[1]
36 Metrical Psalms in 1542 = Ps. 1-15, 19, 22, 24-25, 32, 36-38, 46, 51, 91, 103-104, 113-115, 130, 137-138, 143 = 36 Ps., 490 vss. = c.70 serm [assuming 7 vss/ serm]

15 more of Marot's metrical Psalms 1543 = 18, 23, 33, 35, 43, 45, 50, 72, 79, 86, 101, 107, 110, 118, 128 = 15 Ps., 294 vss. = c.42+ serm [assuming 7 vss/ serm]

By 1543 metrical = Ps. 1-15, 18-19, 22-25, 32-33, 35-38, 46, 50-51, 72, 79, 86, 91, 101, 103-104, 107, 110, 113-115, 118, 128, 130, 137-138, 143.

By mid-summer 1549 Calvin had preached on all of these plus the 13 Psalms missing between Ps. 1 & Ps. 40 = 16-17, 20-21, 26-31, 34, 39-40 = 13 Ps., 182 vss = 26 serm [assuming 7 vss/serm] These include the sermons on Ps. 16 & 27 which were the basis of Calvin's *Quatre Sermons*.

(To this might be added Ps. 90, which Calvin was apparently explaining on March 28, 1546, when Alliod caused the disturbance. He might have chosen that text for this special occasion, as he did Ps. 115 & 124 for the day of prayer in Nov. 1545.)

---

1   For the divisions listed here, chap. 6 at nn.63ff.

Calvin had probably preached at least 138 sermons [perhaps 141, if Ps. 90 & 124 are included] on about 64 [66] Psalms by summer 1549. He had been at St. Gervais on Sunday afternoons since about Feb 1546, although he was not there every week. In 1550 there were at least 3 Sunday afternoons when he did weddings at St. Pierre, and two other Sundays when he was absent on visitation.[2] Assuming that this was normal, over the course of 3.5 years at St. Gervais (c.Feb. 1546-mid-summer 1549), he would have missed 15-18 Sundays at St. Gervais. Estimate that Calvin preached at St. Gervais about 10.5 months/ year (counting 4.5 Sundays/ month) for 3.5 years by summer 1549, this would be 141.5 Sundays. All of these estimates are very hypothetical, it is probably safe to say that Calvin was preaching on Psalms every Sunday afternoon that he was at St. Gervais.

Sermons Preached after Mid-Summer 1549

On Nov. 17, 1549, Raguenier began recording Psalms sermons; his catalogue gives the number as 72, which he indicates did not include the whole because he missed transcribing some when he was ill for about thirteen or fourteen weeks, April-July '52. This does not include those between mid-summer and Nov. 10; and he may also have missed others during this time. These 72 sermons were among those hypothetically enumerated as follows.

By 1551 metrical = Ps. 1-15, 18-19, 22-25, 32-33, 35-38, 46, 50-51, 72, 79, 86, 90-91, 101, 103-104, 107, 110, 113-115, 118-134, 137-138, 143.

From mid-summer 1549 to about the end of August 1553, Calvin probably continued his sequence of Psalms not yet put into metrical form and added to them the ones which were translated into meter for the 1551 Psalter. The latter were Ps. 90, 120-127, 131-134, but he had already preached on Ps. 90 and 124 (March 1546 and Nov. 1545) so this makes Ps. 120-123, 125-127, 131-134, a total of 69 vss or about 10 sermons plus 176 vss for Ps. 119 in 22 sermons. The unversified Psalms after Ps. 40 were Ps. 41-45, 47-49, 52-71, 73-78, 80-85, 87-89, 92-100, 102, 105-106, 108-109, 111, 116-117, 135-136, 139-142, 144-150; this is 1269 vss or about 181 sermons [assuming 7 vss/ sermon]. It is assumed that Calvin continued to preach on Psalms on Sunday afternoons between mid-summer 1549 and Sept. 3, 1553 (when he may have begun to preach on Acts morning and afternoon, in order to complete the more than eight chapters by Mar. 26, 1554 when he began 1 Thessalonians). This makes 213 sermons, more than can fit in the time of about 212 Sundays (July 1549-through Aug. 1553), given the fact that he usually missed some Sundays during the years when he was at St. Gervais. However, once he moved back to St. Pierre on Sunday afternoons, around April 1552, Calvin may have managed every Sunday, and thus he could have come close to finishing the Psalms by Sept. 3, 1553. Thereafter he might have continued some more Sunday afternoons of Psalms in this autumn, or he might have left some of the final praise Psalms for Sunday mornings, since there are several extant for the next years, e.g., Ps. 148:1-14 on Sept 30, 1554, and Ps. 149:4-9 on July 14, 1555.

---

[2] See Appendix Eight Part Two for absences on June 15 & July 27, 1550. Appendix Five for Calvin's Weddings.

APPENDIX ELEVEN: SOME PRAYER TEXTS FOR THE HOUSEHOLD AND VISITING THE SICK

Part One: Household Devotions

Here are presented two versions of the household prayers, one published in Geneva the other in France. [1] The text in italics is only in the Genevan publication, the underlined text is only in the French ones, the rest of the text is common to both. Orthographic differences are not marked, nor are inversions of words. The page divisions are given only for the text being copied.

Genevan printings:

Catechism section of *Les pseaumes mis en rime françoise*... de l'imprimerie de Françoys Jaquy pour Antoine Vincent, 1562 Avec privilege du roy [reissued with the New Testament by Jaquy in 1563 = MHR O4e (563)], pp. 96-100.

Liturgy section of *Les pseaumes mis en rime françoise*.. par Jean Baptiste Pinereul pour Antoine Vincent, 1563 Avec privilege du roy1563 [Su 4939 Res] pp. cc7v-dd1v.

French printings:

Catechism section of *Cent cinquante pseaumes de David... La forme des prieres ecclesiastiques... Le catechisme...* à Caen, par Pierre le Chandelier, 1563 [MHR O4e (563)a] pp. I3v-I5v.

Catechism section of *Les pseaumes mis en rime françoise...* à Caen, chez Simon Mangeant, 1565. [MHR O6e (565)] pp. M3v-M4v.

[96] [p. cc7v] Priere pour dire du soir

[p. I3v] Exercice d'oraison pour toutes familles Chrestiennes.
On fait ceste priere devant celle du matin & devant celle du soir.

Exhortation.

---

1   Transcription rules : "i" and "j", "u" and "v" are distinguished ; punctuation and capitalization are unchanged, but in the long prayer for the sick paragraphs have been introduced.

Mes freres, que chacun de se prosterne Prosternons nous tous bien humblement devant la haute & souveraine majesté de nostre bon Dieu & Pere, nous recognoissans tels que nous sommes, assavoir, povres & miserables pecheurs: le prians de bon coeur, comme il s'ensuit.

Seigneur Dieu Pere Eternel, nous te supplions qu'il te plaise jetter l'oeil de ta clemence paternelle sur nous tes povres serviteurs: ne nous imputant point tant de fautes & offenses, par lesquelles nous sommes redevables à ton jugement, & par lesquelles nous ne cessons de provoquer ton ire à l'encontre de nous. Et d'autant que nous sommes trop indignes pour comparoir devant ta sainte majesté, qu'il te plaise de nous recevoir au Nom de ton fils bien aimé, nostre Seigneur Jesus Christ, acceptant le merite de sa mort & Passion pour recompense de toutes noz fautes, regardant plustost à l'obeissance qu'il t'a rendue *et* que non pas à tant de *iniquitez* fautes que nous commettons journellement contre ta *saincte* majesté.[2]

Seigneur Dieu, puis qu'il t'a pleu creer la nuict pour le repos de l'homme, comme tu luy as ordonné le jour pour travailler, vueille-nous faire la grace de tellement reposer ceste nuict selon le corps, que nos ames veillent tousjours à toy, & que nos coeurs soyent eslevez en ton amour, & qeue tellement nous-nous demettions de toutes solicitudes terriennes, pour nous soulager selon que nostre infirmité le requiert, que jamais n ous ne toublions: mais que la souvenance de ta bonté & grace demeure tousjours imprimee en nostre memoire, & que par ce moyen nos consciences ayent aussi bien l eur repos spirituel, comme les corps prennent le leur.

D'avantage, que nostre dormir ne soit point excessif pour compaire outre mesure à l'aise de nostre chair *[97]* mais seulement pour satisfaire à la fragilité de nostre nature, à fin de nous disposer à ton service. Aussi qu'il te plaise nous conserver impollus, tant en nos corps qu'en nos esprits, & nous conserver contre tous dangers, à ce que nostre dormir mesme soit à la gloire de ton Nom.

Et pource que le jour ne s'est point passé que nous ne t'ayons offensé en plusieurs sortes, selon que nous sommes povres pecheurs: ainsi que tout est maintenant caché par les tenebres que tu envoyes sur la terre: vueille aussi ensevelir toutes nos fautes par ta misericorde, à fin que par icelles nous ne soyons reculez de ga face.[3]

Qu'il te plaise aussi, *O Seigneur Dieu*, nous illuminer par ton saint Esprit en la vraye intelligence de ta *saincte* volonté, laquelle nous as revelée en ta Parole. *[I4r]* Et fay aussi que nous te rendions l'amour & la crainte que doivent vrays & fideles serviteurs à leurs maistres, & enfans à leurs peres: puis qu'il t'a *[c8v]* pleu nous faire ceste grace de nous recevoir au nombre de tes serviteurs & enfans.[4]

[97] [c8v] Priere generale pour la necessité de l'Eglise, qui se peut adjouster apres la priere du matin & du soir.

---

2   This is a variant of Calvin's prayer for illumination-and-sealing on regular weekdays, extempore #1 as recorded by Bourgeois in the Abraham sermons 1561, OC 23:741.

3   This is Calvin's evening prayer from the catechism, voiced in the plural.

4   These two sentences come from Calvin's prayer for illumination-and-sealing used on Sunday morning and the day of prayer, as recorded by Bourgeois in the Abraham sermons 1561, extempore #3; OC 23:742.

[I4r] Ce qui s'ensuit se doit dire tant apres la priere du matin, que celle du soir.

Et combien que nous ne soyons pas dignes d'ouvrir la bouche pour nous-mesmes, & pour te requerir en nostre necessité: neantmoins, puis qu'il t'a pleu nous commander de prier les uns pour les autres, nous te prions pour tous nos povres freres & membres, lesquels tu visites par diverses manieres de tribulations. Pour les peuples que tu affliges, par guerre, peste, famine, ou par tes autres verges: pour les personnes qui sont battues de povreté, prison, maladie, ou bannissement, ou autre calamité de corps ou affliction d'esprit: *qu'il te plaise leur donner* que tu leur donnes à tous bonne patience, jusques à ce que tu leur envoyes plein allegement de leurs maux.[5]

Singulierement, Seigneur, nous te recommandons *[98]* tous les povres malades qui sont du corps de *ton* ceste Eglise, & qui se recommandent & attendent *aux prieres de tes fideles* à noz prieres, qu'il te plaise leur envoyer ce que tu cognois leur estre necessaire, tant pour le salut de leur ame, que pour la santé de leur corps, leur *faisant sentir & gouster au vif* monstrant ton affection paternelle, qui est, de les chastier pour leur amendement, afin que de tout leur coeur ils se convertissent à toy, & estans convertis reçoivent entiere consolation, & soyent delivrez de leurs maux.[6]

[I4v] Aussi nous te prions pour tous noz povres freres tes fideles, qui sont aujourd'huy dispersez en ceste captivité de Babylone souz l'Antechrist Romain, ou qui sont esgarez & espars en quelque autre lieu que se soit, comme povres brebis entre la gueule des loups, qui sont privez de ceste pasture celeste de ta Parole qui nous est journellement administrée par ta grace: qui n'ont pas la liberté de pouvoir invoquer ton sainct Nom *[dd1r]* publicquement comme nous avons. Et ceux aussi qui pour leurs affaires & negoces sont maintenant *voyagers* en voyage entre les ennemis de ta verité, *en* au peril & danger de leur vie, sinon qu'ils soyent soustenus & preservez par ta vertu, qu'il te plaise, Seigneur, les ramener à ton troupeau *& en ton Eglise*, à fin qu'en la congregation de tes fideles, *c'est à dire en ton Eglise*, ils te puissent encores louer & magnifier, & benir ton saint Nom, de se voir ainsi delivrez par ta main.[7]

Et sur tout, Seigneur, nous te prions pour tous nos freres qui sont detenus prisonniers, ou persecutez, comment que ce soit, pour le tesmoignage de ta verité, que tu les fortifies en vraye constance & invincible, que tu les consoles & *que tu* leur assistes, *ne permettant* que tu ne permettes point aux meschans & loups ravissant d'executer leur rage à l'encontre d'eux: toutes-fois, s'il te plaist *les employer* t'en servir pour rendre tesmoignage à ta verité par leur sang & par leur mort, *qu'il te plaise te monstrer* que tu te monstres tellement victorieux en eux, que pour menaces qu'on leur *face* sache faire, ne pour tourmens qu'on leur *presente* puisse presenter, ils ne declinent jamais, *[99]* ne varient de ta saincte vocation, estans fortifiez par ton saint Esprit, *auquel* duquel les ennemis de ta verité ne puissent point resister.[8]

---

5   The first part comes from the day of prayer intercessions (OS 2, p. 29), the rest from Calvin's weekday intercessions, extempore #3; OC 23:756.

6   Here are elements of the Sunday and day of prayer intercessions, OS 2, pp. 22, 29-30.

7   This is a variant of the 1552 addition to the Sunday intercession, OS 2, p. 22. The language seems to be shaped by someone like Conrad Badius, because it echoes words in his preface to the sermons on the Ten Commandments, published in 1557; see chap. 6 at n.266f.

8   This is a variant of Calvin's weekday intercession, OC 23:756. There are echoes of the 1552 addtions to the Sunday and day of prayer intercessions, OS 2, pp. 22, 29-30.

[I5r] En general, *qu'il te plaise, Seigneur, te monstrer* Seigneur, monstre toy protecteur de ta povre & desolée Eglise, & renverser toutes les pratiques & *entreprises que* machinations qui se font par l'Antechrist de Rome *avec* par tous ses suppostz & adherans, & *autres* par tous les adversaires de ta verité, tant manifestes que domestiques *font contre icelle*: à ce que le regne ne nostre Seigneur Jesus Christ ton fils bien aimé ne soit point empesché ne retardé par tout ce qu'ils complotent & machinent par ensemble, mais qu'il s'avance & florisse tousjours de plus en plus jusqu'à ce qu'il soit venu en sa plenitude & perfection.[9]

Qu'il te plaise aussi gouverner & conduire Et que pour ce faire tu gouvernes & conduises par ton sainct Esprit, tous roys, princes & suppperieurs qui ont le gouvernement de ton glaive, à ce qu'ils *l'employent à* ne demandent sinon l'exaltation de ton sainct Nom, & que eux & leurs sujets s'assujettissent *du tout* à toy & à ta saincte Parole: *pour* de laquelle *publier* aussi il te plaise susciter vrais & fideles Ministres *& annonciateurs [dd1v] d'icelle,* qui executent si bien & si fidelement leur *charge* offices*:* & que par *leur ministere (qui est* la predication de ton sainct Evangile) *nous soyons instruits,* lequel il nous annoncent, & par la vertu de ton sainct Esprit nous soyons si vivement touchez en noz coeurs, *pour renoncer* que renonçons à nous-mesmes & à noz propres affections *& desires, pour ne desirer* nous ne demandions sinon de nous renger paisiblement à ta saincte volonté, pour resister à toutes les tentations de Satan, & à tous les assaux qu'il dresse *assiduellement* journellement & à chacune minutte contre nous. Et ce pendant *aussi,* que tes *loyaux* bons serviteurs & ministres *desirent & taschent* ne demandent sinon d'amener au troupeau de ce grand Pasteur Jesus Christ, les povres brebis qui en sont esgarées, & y entretenir & maintenir celles qui y sont desja introduites, à fin que tous ensemble, vivans en bonne paix & concorde [I 5v] fraternelle les uns avec les autres (comme tu le commandes) nous t'adorions comme nostre seul Dieu, & donnions honneur & hommage à nostre Seigneur Jesus Christ comme à nostre Maistre, Roy & Legislateur. *Amen* Ainsi soit-il*.[10]

[100] De toutes ces choses *donc,* Seigneur, & *de toutes les* des autres lesquelles tu cognois mieux que nous-mesmes nous estre necessaires, nous te requerons & prions *humblement* ainsi que ce bon Sauveur Jesus Christ nous à enseigné de prier, en disant:

Nostre pere qui es à cieux, & c.

Nous te prions aussi, Seigneur, *qu'il te plaise* avoir pitié de l'infirmité qui est en nous, pour & subvenir à nostre incredulité, & nous augmenter la foy que nous avons receue par ton sainct Evangile: de laquelle nous te ferons confession *de coeur & de bouche,* disant:

Je croy en Dieu le pere tout-puissant & c.

La benediction de Dieu nostre Pere, & la paix de nostre Seigneur Jesus Christ nous soit donnée, & multipliée à tout jamais par la communication du sainct Esprit. *Amen* Ainsi soit-il

Here Simon Mangeant adds another paragraph and the recitation of the Decalogue.

p. M4r: "Finalement, qu'il te plaise, Seigneur, que la foy de laquelle nous venons faire confession ne soit morte, mais vive, & sans feintise produise en nous les fruits de justice &

---

[9]   This is a variant combining various intercessions (e.g., the 1552 additions to the day of prayer and Calvin's weekday prayer). For example "ennemis" (OS 2, p. 30), "Antechrist de Rome" (OC 23:756).

[10] This combines elements of the Sunday and day of prayer intercessions, OS 2, pp. 20, 21, 22. There are echoes of Calvin's weekday intercession (OC 23:756).

sainteté, suivant ta sainte loy, laquelle nous a esté baillee par ton fidele serviteur Moyse, ainsi qui'il s'ensuit, Escoute, Israel, Je suis le Seigneur ton Dieu..."

* * * * * * * * * * * * * *

Part Two: Prayers for the Sick

Les pseaumes mis en rime françoise... par Jean Baptiste Pinereul pour Antoine Vincent, 1563 Avec privilege du roy [Su 4939 Res], in the catechism section, pp. dd2r-dd3r.
The identical text is found in S. Honorati's "Lyon" [Genevan] text, pp. cc8v-dd1v.

Liturgy section of, *Cent cinquante pseaumes de David... La forme des prieres ecclesiastiques... Le catechisme...* à Caen, par Pierre le Chandelier, 1563 [MHR O4e (563)a] pp. C3v-C5r.

The base text is the 1563 "Genevan" one which is reprinted in 1570; the variants or additions are from the Caen version and are underlined. The paragraphs have been added.

[dd2r] Oraison pour dire en la visitation d'un povre malade

O Seigneur Dieu tout-puissant, eternel & plein de grande benignité, entre plusieurs & divers chastimens par lesquels tu nous appeles à toy, tu as accoustumé de dompter nostre chair par beaucoup & diverses maladies, luy ostant sa nonchalance, & luy resueillant sa stupidité par infirmitez dangereuses: & lors tu bailles advertissement de la vie mal-heureusement passée, & de la fin d'icelle, voire de la mort bien prochaine par tourmens & angoisses bien pressantes, qui sont comme les avant-coureurs d'icelle: & aussi du grand & dernier jour de ton jugement, & de la vie eternelle qui s'en ensuyvra, laquelle sera continuee aux bons en gloire & beatitude, & aux meschans en ignominie & damnation de la gehenne. Desquelles choses la chair ayant la bride laschée, ne veut ouir nullement parler.
Or maintenant, Seigneur, nous avons trouvé c'est [cest!] homme abbattu de maladie detenu au lict, & soustenant la rigueur de ton fleau & la severité de ta verge, envers lequel le sentiment du peché est resueillé, & l'image de la mort se presente maintenant devant ses les yeux. Et pourtant nous povres pecheurs, qui attendons ceste mesme heure d'adversité, selon la condition de nostre nature, nous te prions humblement avec ce povre malade, que tu n'exerces point rigoreux jugement à l'encontre de luy selon qu'il a merité. & luy fay ceste grace pour l'amour de Jesus Christ nostre Seigneur ton Fils bien-aimé, qui a soustenu la coulpe de ce povre malade & de nous tous au gibet de la croix. Mais plustost, Seigneur debonnaire, jette les yeux de ta misericorde sur luy: & le regardant comme racheté, donne luy grace & constance de courage, par laquelle il reçoive paisiblement ceste gracieuse correction & visitation paternelle: qu'il l'endure patiemment en obeissance volontaire, se submettant de tout son coeur & gré à la benevolence de toy qui le frappes. Assiste-luy en toutes ses adversitez & fascheries, & sois sa [dd2v] protection & defense contre le danger qui est bien prochain de luy: & principalement si sa conscience descou-verte luy fait accusation de ses pechez interieurs, alors, Seigneur plein de bonté, mets à l'opposite les durs tormens & le Sacrifice volontaire de ton Fils bien-aimé Jesus Christ

Fils Jesus Christ: ton Fils bien-aimé: lequel a porté noz infirmitez, & a enduré la peine que nous-mesmes avons merité, estant fait peché pour nous, quand pour noz pechez & offenses il a souffert la mort, lesquels il a lavez par son sang, & ressusitant des morts a esté fait nostre justice & parfaire redemption. Fay que ce povre malade sente le fruit & la vertu de ces benefices par foy, & estans pressé de ceste angoisse qu'il experimente ta bonté & aide, & qu'en la fin de ses jours il ait quelque goust de tes benefices, & dons du Seigneur Jesus. Donne luy grace que d'un bon coeur & en certitude de foy il reçoive pour sa consolation un si grand thresor de felicité, cest à dire, la remission de ses des pechez à cause de ton Fils Jesus Christ lequel mesme maintenant luy est en ce lieu offert par le ministere de la Parole preschée, & l'usage des Sacramens, qu'il a frequentez avec nous en la congregation & Eglise de tes esleuz & fideles: que cela luy soit pour une defense invincible contre les bruits de sa conscience qui l'accuse si fort, & contre les ruses & finesses du diable. Et d'avantage que ceste foy luy soit comme un bouclier, par lequel il repousse les estonnemens de la mort, & qui le face hardiment cheminer pour parvenir à la vie eternelle & bien-heureuse, que quand il l'aura apprehendee, il en jouisse eternellement. O Pere celeste, ay le donc pour entierement recommendé.

O nostre bon Dieu, en ceste sorte, pource qu'il est malade, tu le gueriras: il est gisant, tu le releveras: il est couché, tu le redresseras: il est foible, tu le fortifieras: il recognoist son impureté & ses macules & ordures, tu le laveras: il est navré, tu luy appliqueras santé saincte & bonne medecine: il est saisi de crainte & tremblement, tu luy donneras bon courage. Et pour ce que tu cognoit toutes choses, & peux selon ton bon plaisir conferer tout ce qui est necessaire & expedient, tu le rassasieras, car il est grandement tormenté de faim & de soif. O Seigneur, reçoy-le à toy: car il a son recours droit à toy: & le ren constant & ferme à obeir à tes commandemens & saintes ordonnances: bref, pardonne luy tous ses pechez, toutes ses fautes & offenses, par lesquelles il a grievement provoqué ton ire & la rigueur de ton jugement contre soy. En lieu de la mort, Seigneur, ottroye luy la vie avec toy en gloire: & si tu cognois qu'il puisse encore faire quelque profit à cultiver ta vigne en ceste mortalité, & de plus grande diligence [dd3r] & sollicitude se conformer à l'exemple de ton Fils Jesus Christ, conserve-le: mais que ce soit en luy augmentant tes graces, toutesfois que ta volonté soit faite en tout & par tout, qui est bonne à tout jamais.

Donne-nous, Seigneur, toutes ces choses aussi bien qu'à ce povre homme abbatu de maladie, par le seul Seigneur Jesus Redempteur, medecin & Sauveur des povres pecheurs, nostre seul bouclier & defense asseuree: & lequel pour donner exemple & grand consolation aux povres pecheurs, a mené avec soy en paradis le brigand qui estoit crucifié aupres de luy: lequel Seigneur Jesus vit & regne avec toy en unité du saint Esprit vray Dieu à perpetuité. Ainsi soit-il.

INDICES

Index of Propers Names

Index of Biblical Texts

BIBLICAL REFERENCES (DOES NOT INCLUDE APPENDICES)

NEW TESTAMENT

LIST OF ILLUSTRATIONS

TABLE OF CONTENTS

RÉALISATION : IGS-CP À L'ISLE-D'ESPAGNAC

IMPRIMERIE F. PAILLART, B.P. 30324, 80103 ABBEVILLE − (15285)
DÉPÔT LÉGAL : 4ᵉ TRIMESTRE 2015